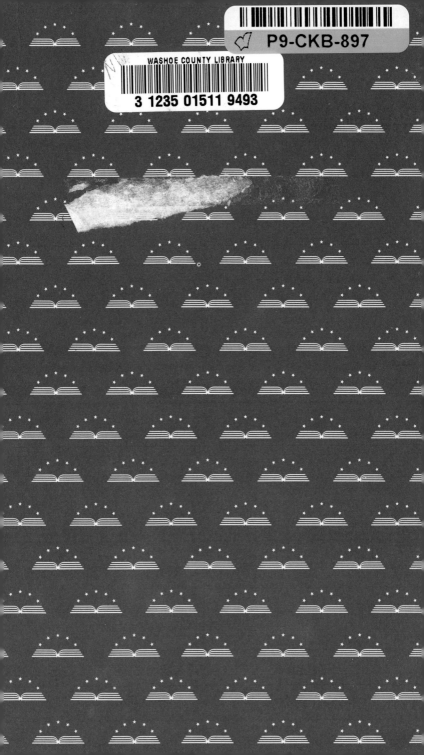

HENRY DAVID THOREAU

A Week on the Concord and Merrimack Rivers
Walden; or, Life in the Woods
The Maine Woods
Cape Cod

THE LIBRARY OF AMERICA

The paper used in this publication meets the minimum
requirements of the American National Standard
for Information Sciences—Permanence of Paper for
Printed Library Materials, ANSI Z39.48-1984

Distributed to the trade in the United States
by Penguin Books USA Inc
and in Canada by Penguin Books Canada Ltd.

Library of Congress Catalog Card Number: 85–5175
For cataloging information, see end of volume.
ISBN 0–940450–27–5

Tenth Printing
The Library of America—28

Manufactured in the United States of America

ROBERT F. SAYRE
WROTE THE NOTES FOR THIS VOLUME

Contents

A WEEK ON THE CONCORD AND MERRIMACK RIVERS

Where'er thou sail'st who sailed with me,
Though now thou climbest loftier mounts,
And fairer rivers dost ascend,
Be thou my Muse, my Brother—.

I am bound, I am bound, for a distant shore,
By a lonely isle, by a far Azore,
There it is, there it is, the treasure I seek,
On the barren sands of a desolate creek.

I sailed up a river with a pleasant wind,
New lands, new people, and new thoughts to find;
Many fair reaches and headlands appeared,
And many dangers were there to be feared;
But when I remember where I have been,
And the fair landscapes that I have seen,
THOU seemest the only permanent shore,
The cape never rounded, nor wandered o'er.

Fluminaque obliquis cinxit declivia ripis;
Quæ, diversa locis, partim sorbentur ab ipsa;
In mare perveniunt partim, campoque recepta
Liberioris aquæ, pro ripis litora pulsant.

OVID, Met. I. 39.

He confined the rivers within their sloping banks,
Which in different places are part absorbed by the earth,
Part reach the sea, and being received within the plain
Of its freer waters, beat the shore for banks.

Concord River

"Beneath low hills, in the broad interval
 Through which at will our Indian rivulet
 Winds mindful still of sannup and of squaw,
 Whose pipe and arrow oft the plough unburies,
 Here, in pine houses, built of new-fallen trees,
 Supplanters of the tribe, the farmers dwell."

EMERSON.

THE MUSKETAQUID, or Grass-ground River, though probably as old as the Nile or Euphrates, did not begin to
have a place in civilized history, until the fame of its grassy
meadows and its fish attracted settlers out of England in
1635, when it received the other but kindred name of CON-
CORD from the first plantation on its banks, which appears
to have been commenced in a spirit of peace and harmony.
It will be Grass-ground River as long as grass grows and
water runs here; it will be Concord River only while men
lead peaceable lives on its banks. To an extinct race it was
grass-ground, where they hunted and fished, and it is still
perennial grass-ground to Concord farmers, who own the
Great Meadows, and get the hay from year to year. "One
branch of it," according to the historian of Concord, for I
love to quote so good authority, "rises in the south part of
Hopkinton, and another from a pond and a large cedar-
swamp in Westborough," and flowing between Hopkinton
and Southborough, through Framingham, and between Sudbury and Wayland, where it is sometimes called Sudbury
River, it enters Concord at the south part of the town, and
after receiving the North or Assabeth River, which has its
source a little farther to the north and west, goes out at the
northeast angle, and flowing between Bedford and Carlisle,
and through Billerica, empties into the Merrimack at Lowell.
In Concord it is, in summer, from four to fifteen feet deep,
and from one hundred to three hundred feet wide, but in
the spring freshets, when it overflows its banks, it is in some
places nearly a mile wide. Between Sudbury and Wayland
the meadows acquire their greatest breadth, and when covered with water, they form a handsome chain of shallow

vernal lakes, resorted to by numerous gulls and ducks. Just
above Sherman's Bridge, between these towns, is the largest
expanse, and when the wind blows freshly in a raw March
day, heaving up the surface into dark and sober billows or
regular swells, skirted as it is in the distance with alder-
swamps and smoke-like maples, it looks like a smaller Lake
Huron, and is very pleasant and exciting for a landsman to
row or sail over. The farm-houses along the Sudbury shore,
which rises gently to a considerable height, command fine
water prospects at this season. The shore is more flat on the
Wayland side, and this town is the greatest loser by the
flood. Its farmers tell me that thousands of acres are flooded
now, since the dams have been erected, where they remember to have seen the white honeysuckle or clover growing
once, and they could go dry with shoes only in summer.
Now there is nothing but blue-joint and sedge and cut-grass
there, standing in water all the year round. For a long time,
they made the most of the driest season to get their hay,
working sometimes till nine o'clock at night, sedulously paring with their scythes in the twilight round the hummocks
left by the ice; but now it is not worth the getting when
they can come at it, and they look sadly round to their
wood-lots and upland as a last resource.

It is worth the while to make a voyage up this stream, if
you go no farther than Sudbury, only to see how much
country there is in the rear of us; great hills, and a hundred
brooks, and farm-houses, and barns, and haystacks, you
never saw before, and men everywhere, Sudbury, that is
Southborough men, and Wayland, and Nine-Acre-Corner
men, and Bound Rock, where four towns bound on a rock
in the river, Lincoln, Wayland, Sudbury, Concord. Many
waves are there agitated by the wind, keeping nature fresh,
the spray blowing in your face, reeds and rushes waving;
ducks by the hundred, all uneasy in the surf, in the raw
wind, just ready to rise, and now going off with a clatter
and a whistling like riggers straight for Labrador, flying
against the stiff gale with reefed wings, or else circling round
first, with all their paddles briskly moving, just over the surf,
to reconnoitre you before they leave these parts; gulls wheeling overhead, muskrats swimming for dear life, wet and

cold, with no fire to warm them by that you know of; their labored homes rising here and there like haystacks; and countless mice and moles and winged titmice along the sunny windy shore; cranberries tossed on the waves and heaving up on the beach, their little red skiffs beating about among the alders;—such healthy natural tumult as proves the last day is not yet at hand. And there stand all around the alders, and birches, and oaks, and maples full of glee and sap, holding in their buds until the waters subside. You shall perhaps run aground on Cranberry Island, only some spires of last year's pipe-grass above water, to show where the danger is, and get as good a freezing there as anywhere on the Northwest Coast. I never voyaged so far in all my life. You shall see men you never heard of before, whose names you don't know, going away down through the meadows with long ducking-guns, with water-tight boots wading through the fowl-meadow grass, on bleak, wintry, distant shores, with guns at half-cock, and they shall see teal, blue-winged, green-winged, shelldrakes, whistlers, black ducks, ospreys, and many other wild and noble sights before night, such as they who sit in parlors never dream of. You shall see rude and sturdy, experienced and wise men, keeping their castles, or teaming up their summer's wood, or chopping alone in the woods, men fuller of talk and rare adventure in the sun and wind and rain, than a chestnut is of meat; who were out not only in '75 and 1812, but have been out every day of their lives; greater men than Homer, or Chaucer, or Shakespeare, only they never got time to say so; they never took to the way of writing. Look at their fields, and imagine what they might write, if ever they should put pen to paper. Or what have they not written on the face of the earth already, clearing, and burning, and scratching, and harrowing, and ploughing, and subsoiling, in and in, and out and out, and over and over, again and again, erasing what they had already written for want of parchment.

As yesterday and the historical ages are past, as the work of to-day is present, so some flitting perspectives, and demi-experiences of the life that is in nature are in time veritably future, or rather outside to time, perennial, young, divine, in the wind and rain which never die.

> The respectable folks,—
> Where dwell they?
> They whisper in the oaks,
> And they sigh in the hay;
> Summer and winter, night and day,
> Out on the meadow, there dwell they.
> They never die,
> Nor snivel, nor cry,
> Nor ask our pity
> With a wet eye.
> A sound estate they ever mend,
> To every asker readily lend;
> To the ocean wealth,
> To the meadow health,
> To Time his length,
> To the rocks strength,
> To the stars light,
> To the weary night,
> To the busy day,
> To the idle play;
> And so their good cheer never ends,
> For all are their debtors, and all their friends.

Concord River is remarkable for the gentleness of its current, which is scarcely perceptible, and some have referred to its influence the proverbial moderation of the inhabitants of Concord, as exhibited in the Revolution, and on later occasions. It has been proposed, that the town should adopt for its coat of arms a field verdant, with the Concord circling nine times round. I have read that a descent of an eighth of an inch in a mile is sufficient to produce a flow. Our river has, probably, very near the smallest allowance. The story is current, at any rate, though I believe that strict history will not bear it out, that the only bridge ever carried away on the main branch, within the limits of the town, was driven up stream by the wind. But wherever it makes a sudden bend it is shallower and swifter, and asserts its title to be called a river. Compared with the other tributaries of the Merrimack, it appears to have been properly named Musketaquid, or Meadow River, by the Indians. For the most part, it creeps through broad meadows, adorned with scattered oaks, where the cranberry is found in abundance, covering the ground like a moss-bed. A row of sunken dwarf willows borders the stream on one or both sides, while at a greater distance the meadow is skirted with maples, alders, and other fluviatile trees, overrun with the grape-vine, which bears fruit in its season, purple, red, white, and other grapes. Still farther from the stream, on the edge of the firm land, are seen the gray and white dwellings of the inhabitants. According to the valuation of 1831, there were in Concord two thousand one hundred and eleven acres, or about one seventh of the whole territory in meadow; this standing next in the list after pasturage and unimproved lands, and, judging from the returns of previous years, the meadow is not reclaimed so fast as the woods are cleared.

Let us here read what old Johnson says of these meadows in his "Wonder-working Providence," which gives the account of New England from 1628 to 1652, and see how matters looked to him. He says of the Twelfth Church of Christ gathered at Concord: "This town is seated upon a fair fresh river, whose rivulets are filled with fresh marsh, and her streams with fish, it being a branch of that large river of Merrimack. Allwifes and shad in their season come up to this town, but salmon and dace cannot come up, by reason of the rocky falls, which causeth their meadows to lie much covered with water, the which these people, together with their neighbor town, have several times essayed to cut through but cannot, yet it may be turned another way with an hundred pound charge as it appeared." As to their farming he says: "Having laid out their estate upon cattle at 5 to 20 pound a cow, when they came to winter them with inland hay, and feed upon such wild fother as was never cut before, they could not hold out the winter, but, ordinarily the first or second year after their coming up to a new plantation, many of their cattle died." And this from the same author "Of the Planting of the 19th Church in the Mattachusets' Government, called Sudbury": "This year [does he mean 1654] the town and church of Christ at Sudbury began to have the first foundation stones laid, taking up her station in the inland country, as her elder sister Concord had formerly done, lying further up the same river, being furnished with great plenty of fresh marsh, but, it lying

very low is much indamaged with land floods, insomuch that
when the summer proves wet they lose part of their hay; yet
are they so sufficiently provided that they take in cattle of
other towns to winter."

The sluggish artery of the Concord meadows steals thus
unobserved through the town, without a murmur or a pulse-
beat, its general course from southwest to northeast, and its
length about fifty miles; a huge volume of matter, ceaselessly
rolling through the plains and valleys of the substantial earth
with the moccasoned tread of an Indian warrior, making
haste from the high places of the earth to its ancient reservoir.
The murmurs of many a famous river on the other side of the
globe reach even to us here, as to more distant dwellers on its
banks; many a poet's stream floating the helms and shields of
heroes on its bosom. The Xanthus or Scamander is not a mere
dry channel and bed of a mountain torrent, but fed by the
everflowing springs of fame; —

> "And thou Simois, that as an arrowe, clere
> Through Troy rennest, aie downward to the sea"; —

and I trust that I may be allowed to associate our muddy but
much abused Concord River with the most famous in history.

> "Sure there are poets which did never dream
> Upon Parnassus, nor did taste the stream
> Of Helicon; we therefore may suppose
> Those made not poets, but the poets those."

The Mississippi, the Ganges, and the Nile, those journeying atoms from the Rocky Mountains, the Himmaleh, and
Mountains of the Moon, have a kind of personal importance
in the annals of the world. The heavens are not yet drained
over their sources, but the Mountains of the Moon still send
their annual tribute to the Pasha without fail, as they did to
the Pharaohs, though he must collect the rest of his revenue
at the point of the sword. Rivers must have been the guides
which conducted the footsteps of the first travellers. They are
the constant lure, when they flow by our doors, to distant
enterprise and adventure, and, by a natural impulse, the
dwellers on their banks will at length accompany their currents to the lowlands of the globe, or explore at their invita-

tion the interior of continents. They are the natural highways of all nations, not only levelling the ground and removing obstacles from the path of the traveller, quenching his thirst and bearing him on their bosoms, but conducting him through the most interesting scenery, the most populous portions of the globe, and where the animal and vegetable kingdoms attain their greatest perfection.

I had often stood on the banks of the Concord, watching the lapse of the current, an emblem of all progress, following the same law with the system, with time, and all that is made; the weeds at the bottom gently bending down the stream, shaken by the watery wind, still planted where their seeds had sunk, but erelong to die and go down likewise; the shining pebbles, not yet anxious to better their condition, the chips and weeds, and occasional logs and stems of trees that floated past, fulfilling their fate, were objects of singular interest to me, and at last I resolved to launch myself on its bosom and float whither it would bear me.

Saturday

"Come, come, my lovely fair, and let us try
These rural delicates."
Christ's Invitation to the Soul. QUARLES.

AT LENGTH, on Saturday, the last day of August, 1839, we two, brothers, and natives of Concord, weighed anchor in this river port; for Concord, too, lies under the sun, a port of entry and departure for the bodies as well as the souls of men; one shore at least exempted from all duties but such as an honest man will gladly discharge. A warm drizzling rain had obscured the morning, and threatened to delay our voyage, but at length the leaves and grass were dried, and it came out a mild afternoon, as serene and fresh as if Nature were maturing some greater scheme of her own. After this long dripping and oozing from every pore, she began to respire again more healthily than ever. So with a vigorous shove we launched our boat from the bank, while the flags and bulrushes courtesied a God-speed, and dropped silently down the stream.

Our boat, which had cost us a week's labor in the spring, was in form like a fisherman's dory, fifteen feet long by three and a half in breadth at the widest part, painted green below, with a border of blue, with reference to the two elements in which it was to spend its existence. It had been loaded the evening before at our door, half a mile from the river, with potatoes and melons from a patch which we had cultivated, and a few utensils, and was provided with wheels in order to be rolled around falls, as well as with two sets of oars, and several slender poles for shoving in shallow places, and also two masts, one of which served for a tent-pole at night; for a buffalo-skin was to be our bed, and a tent of cotton cloth our roof. It was strongly built, but heavy, and hardly of better model than usual. If rightly made, a boat would be a sort of amphibious animal, a creature of two elements, related by one half its structure to some swift and shapely fish, and by the other to some strong-winged and graceful bird. The fish shows where there should be the greatest breadth of beam and depth in the hold; its fins direct where to set the oars, and the tail gives some hint for the form and position of the rudder. The bird shows how to rig and trim the sails, and what form to give to the prow that it may balance the boat, and divide the air and water best. These hints we had but partially obeyed. But the eyes, though they are no sailors, will never be satisfied with any model, however fashionable, which does not answer all the requisitions of art. However, as art is all of a ship but the wood, and yet the wood alone will rudely serve the purpose of a ship, so our boat, being of wood, gladly availed itself of the old law that the heavier shall float the lighter, and though a dull water-fowl, proved a sufficient buoy for our purpose.

> "Were it the will of Heaven, an osier bough
> Were vessel safe enough the seas to plough."

Some village friends stood upon a promontory lower down the stream to wave us a last farewell; but we, having already performed these shore rites, with excusable reserve, as befits those who are embarked on unusual enterprises, who behold but speak not, silently glided past the firm lands of Concord, both peopled cape and lonely summer meadow, with steady sweeps. And yet we did unbend so far as to let our guns speak for us, when at length we had swept out of sight, and thus left the woods to ring again with their echoes; and it may be many russet-clad children, lurking in those broad meadows, with the bittern and the woodcock and the rail, though wholly concealed by brakes and hardhack and meadow-sweet, heard our salute that afternoon.

We were soon floating past the first regular battle-ground of the Revolution, resting on our oars between the still visible abutments of that "North Bridge," over which in April, 1775, rolled the first faint tide of that war, which ceased not, till, as we read on the stone on our right, it "gave peace to these United States." As a Concord poet has sung:—

> "By the rude bridge that arched the flood,
>   Their flag to April's breeze unfurled,
> Here once the embattled farmers stood,
>   And fired the shot heard round the world.

> "The foe long since in silence slept;
>   Alike the conqueror silent sleeps;
> And Time the ruined bridge has swept
>   Down the dark stream which seaward creeps."

Our reflections had already acquired a historical remoteness from the scenes we had left, and we ourselves essayed to sing.

> Ah, 't is in vain the peaceful din
>   That wakes the ignoble town,
> Not thus did braver spirits win
>   A patriot's renown.
>
> There is one field beside this stream,
>   Wherein no foot does fall,
> But yet it beareth in my dream
>   A richer crop than all.
>
> Let me believe a dream so dear,
>   Some heart beat high that day,
> Above the petty Province here,
>   And Britain far away;
>
> Some hero of the ancient mould,
>   Some arm of knightly worth,
> Of strength unbought, and faith unsold,
>   Honored this spot of earth;
>
> Who sought the prize his heart described,
>   And did not ask release,
> Whose free-born valor was not bribed
>   By prospect of a peace.
>
> The men who stood on yonder height
>   That day are long since gone;
> Not the same hand directs the fight
>   And monumental stone.
>
> Ye were the Grecian cities then,
>   The Romes of modern birth,
> Where the New England husbandmen
>   Have shown a Roman worth.

In vain I search a foreign land
   To find our Bunker Hill,
And Lexington and Concord stand
   By no Laconian rill.

With such thoughts we swept gently by this now peaceful pasture-ground, on waves of Concord, in which was long since drowned the din of war.

But since we sailed
Some things have failed,
And many a dream
Gone down the stream.

Here then an aged shepherd dwelt,
Who to his flock his substance dealt,
And ruled them with a vigorous crook,
By precept of the sacred Book;
But he the pierless bridge passed o'er,
And solitary left the shore.

Anon a youthful pastor came,
Whose crook was not unknown to fame,
His lambs he viewed with gentle glance,
Spread o'er the country's wide expanse,
And fed with "Mosses from the Manse."
Here was our Hawthorne in the dale,
And here the shepherd told his tale.

That slight shaft had now sunk behind the hills, and we had floated round the neighboring bend, and under the new North Bridge between Ponkawtasset and the Poplar Hill, into the Great Meadows, which, like a broad moccason print, have levelled a fertile and juicy place in nature.

On Ponkawtasset, since, we took our way,
Down this still stream to far Billericay,
A poet wise has settled, whose fine ray
Doth often shine on Concord's twilight day.

Like those first stars, whose silver beams on high,
Shining more brightly as the day goes by,

Most travellers cannot at first descry,
But eyes that wont to range the evening sky,

And know celestial lights, do plainly see,
And gladly hail them, numbering two or three;
For lore that 's deep must deeply studied be,
As from deep wells men read star-poetry.

These stars are never paled, though out of sight,
But like the sun they shine forever bright;
Ay, *they* are suns, though earth must in its flight
Put out its eyes that it may see their light.

Who would neglect the least celestial sound,
Or faintest light that falls on earthly ground,
If he could know it one day would be found
That star in Cygnus whither we are bound,
And pale our sun with heavenly radiance round?

Gradually the village murmur subsided, and we seemed to be embarked on the placid current of our dreams, floating from past to future as silently as one awakes to fresh morning or evening thoughts. We glided noiselessly down the stream, occasionally driving a pickerel or a bream from the covert of the pads, and the smaller bittern now and then sailed away on sluggish wings from some recess in the shore, or the larger lifted itself out of the long grass at our approach, and carried its precious legs away to deposit them in a place of safety. The tortoises also rapidly dropped into the water, as our boat ruffled the surface amid the willows, breaking the reflections of the trees. The banks had passed the height of their beauty, and some of the brighter flowers showed by their faded tints that the season was verging towards the afternoon of the year; but this sombre tinge enhanced their sincerity, and in the still unabated heats they seemed like the mossy brink of some cool well. The narrow-leaved willow (*Salix Purshiana*) lay along the surface of the water in masses of light green foliage, interspersed with the large balls of the button-bush. The small rose-colored polygonum raised its head proudly above the water on either hand, and flowering at this season and in these localities, in front of dense fields of the white species which skirted the sides of the stream, its little streak of red looked very rare and precious. The pure white blossoms of the arrow-head stood in the shallower parts, and a few cardinals on the margin still proudly surveyed themselves reflected in the water, though the latter, as well as the pickerel-weed, was now nearly out of blossom. The snakehead, *Chelone glabra*, grew close to the shore, while a kind of coreopsis, turning its brazen face to the sun, full and rank, and a tall dull red flower, *Eupatorium purpureum*, or trumpet-weed, formed the rear rank of the fluvial array. The bright blue flowers of the soap-wort gentian were sprinkled here and there in the adjacent meadows, like flowers which Proserpine had dropped, and still farther in the fields or higher on the bank were seen the purple Gerardia, the Virginian rhexia, and drooping neottia or ladies'-tresses; while from the more distant waysides which we occasionally passed, and banks where the sun had lodged, was reflected still a dull yellow beam from the ranks of tansy, now past its prime. In short, Nature seemed to have adorned herself for our departure with a profusion of fringes and curls, mingled with the bright tints of flowers, reflected in the water. But we missed the white water-lily, which is the queen of river flowers, its reign being over for this season. He makes his voyage too late, perhaps, by a true water clock who delays so long. Many of this species inhabit our Concord water. I have passed down the river before sunrise on a summer morning between fields of lilies still shut in sleep; and when, at length, the flakes of sunlight from over the bank fell on the surface of the water, whole fields of white blossoms seemed to flash open before me, as I floated along, like the unfolding of a banner, so sensible is this flower to the influence of the sun's rays.

As we were floating through the last of these familiar meadows, we observed the large and conspicuous flowers of the hibiscus, covering the dwarf willows, and mingled with the leaves of the grape, and wished that we could inform one of our friends behind of the locality of this somewhat rare and inaccessible flower before it was too late to pluck it; but we were just gliding out of sight of the village spire before it occurred to us that the farmer in the adjacent meadow would go to church on the morrow, and would carry this news for us; and so by the Monday, while we should be floating on the Merrimack, our friend would be reaching to pluck this blossom on the bank of the Concord.

After a pause at Ball's Hill, the St. Ann's of Concord voyageurs, not to say any prayer for the success of our voyage, but to gather the few berries which were still left on the hills, hanging by very slender threads, we weighed anchor again, and were soon out of sight of our native village. The land seemed to grow fairer as we withdrew from it. Far away to the southwest lay the quiet village, left alone under its elms and buttonwoods in mid afternoon; and the hills, notwithstanding their blue, ethereal faces, seemed to cast a saddened eye on their old playfellows; but, turning short to the north, we bade adieu to their familiar outlines, and addressed ourselves to new scenes and adventures. Naught was familiar but the heavens, from under whose roof the voyageur never passes; but with their countenance, and the acquaintance we had with river and wood, we trusted to fare well under any circumstances.

From this point, the river runs perfectly straight for a mile or more to Carlisle Bridge, which consists of twenty wooden piers, and when we looked back over it, its surface was reduced to a line's breadth, and appeared like a cobweb gleaming in the sun. Here and there might be seen a pole sticking up, to mark the place where some fisherman had enjoyed unusual luck, and in return had consecrated his rod to the deities who preside over these shallows. It was full twice as broad as before, deep and tranquil, with a muddy bottom, and bordered with willows, beyond which spread broad lagoons covered with pads, bulrushes, and flags.

Late in the afternoon we passed a man on the shore fishing with a long birch pole, its silvery bark left on, and a dog at his side, rowing so near as to agitate his cork with our oars, and drive away luck for a season; and when we had rowed a mile as straight as an arrow, with our faces turned towards him, and the bubbles in our wake still visible on the tranquil surface, there stood the fisher still with his dog, like statues under the other side of the heavens, the only objects to relieve the eye in the extended meadow; and there would he stand abiding his luck, till he took his way home through the fields at evening with his fish. Thus, by one bait or another, Nature allures inhabitants into all her recesses. This man was the last of our townsmen whom we saw, and we silently through him bade adieu to our friends.

The characteristics and pursuits of various ages and races of men are always existing in epitome in every neighborhood. The pleasures of my earliest youth have become the inheritance of other men. This man is still a fisher, and belongs to an era in which I myself have lived. Perchance he is not confounded by many knowledges, and has not sought out many inventions, but how to take many fishes before the sun sets, with his slender birchen pole and flaxen line, that is invention enough for him. It is good even to be a fisherman in summer and in winter. Some men are judges these August days, sitting on benches, even till the court rises; they sit judging there honorably, between the seasons and between meals, leading a civil politic life, arbitrating in the case of Spaulding *versus* Cummings, it may be, from highest noon till the red vesper sinks into the west. The fisherman, meanwhile, stands in three feet of water, under the same summer's sun, arbitrating in other cases between muckworm and shiner, amid the fragrance of water-lilies, mint, and pontederia, leading his life many rods from the dry land, within a pole's length of where the larger fishes swim. Human life is to him very much like a river,

"renning aie downward to the sea."

This was his observation. His honor made a great discovery in bailments.

I can just remember an old brown-coated man who was the Walton of this stream, who had come over from Newcastle, England, with his son,—the latter a stout and hearty man who had lifted an anchor in his day. A straight old man he was who took his way in silence through the meadows, having passed the period of communication with his fellows; his old experienced coat, hanging long and straight and brown as the yellow-pine bark, glittering with so much smothered sun-

light, if you stood near enough, no work of art but naturalized at length. I often discovered him unexpectedly amid the
pads and the gray willows when he moved, fishing in some
old country method,—for youth and age then went a fishing
together,—full of incommunicable thoughts, perchance
about his own Tyne and Northumberland. He was always to
be seen in serene afternoons haunting the river, and almost
rustling with the sedge; so many sunny hours in an old man's
life, entrapping silly fish; almost grown to be the sun's familiar; what need had he of hat or raiment any, having served
out his time, and seen through such thin disguises? I have
seen how his coeval fates rewarded him with the yellow
perch, and yet I thought his luck was not in proportion to his
years; and I have seen when, with slow steps and weighed
down with aged thoughts, he disappeared with his fish under
his low-roofed house on the skirts of the village. I think nobody else saw him; nobody else remembers him now, for he
soon after died, and migrated to new Tyne streams. His fishing was not a sport, nor solely a means of subsistence, but a
sort of solemn sacrament and withdrawal from the world, just
as the aged read their Bibles.

Whether we live by the seaside, or by the lakes and rivers,
or on the prairie, it concerns us to attend to the nature of
fishes, since they are not phenomena confined to certain localities only, but forms and phases of the life in nature universally dispersed. The countless shoals which annually coast
the shores of Europe and America are not so interesting to
the student of nature, as the more fertile law itself, which
deposits their spawn on the tops of mountains, and on the
interior plains; the fish principle in nature, from which it results that they may be found in water in so many places, in
greater or less numbers. The natural historian is not a fisherman, who prays for cloudy days and good luck merely, but as
fishing has been styled, "a contemplative man's recreation,"
introducing him profitably to woods and water, so the fruit
of the naturalist's observations is not in new genera or species, but in new contemplations still, and science is only a
more contemplative man's recreation. The seeds of the life of
fishes are everywhere disseminated, whether the winds waft

them, or the waters float them, or the deep earth holds them; wherever a pond is dug, straightway it is stocked with this vivacious race. They have a lease of nature, and it is not yet out. The Chinese are bribed to carry their ova from province to province in jars or in hollow reeds, or the water-birds to transport them to the mountain tarns and interior lakes. There are fishes wherever there is a fluid medium, and even in clouds and in melted metals we detect their semblance. Think how in winter you can sink a line down straight in a pasture through snow and through ice, and pull up a bright, slippery, dumb, subterranean silver or golden fish! It is curious, also, to reflect how they make one family, from the largest to the smallest. The least minnow that lies on the ice as bait for pickerel, looks like a huge sea-fish cast up on the shore. In the waters of this town there are about a dozen distinct species, though the inexperienced would expect many more.

It enhances our sense of the grand security and serenity of nature, to observe the still undisturbed economy and content of the fishes of this century, their happiness a regular fruit of the summer. The Fresh-Water Sun-Fish, Bream, or Ruff, *Pomotis vulgaris*, as it were, without ancestry, without posterity, still represents the Fresh-Water Sun-Fish in nature. It is the most common of all, and seen on every urchin's string; a simple and inoffensive fish, whose nests are visible all along the shore, hollowed in the sand, over which it is steadily poised through the summer hours on waving fin. Sometimes there are twenty or thirty nests in the space of a few rods, two feet wide by half a foot in depth, and made with no little labor, the weeds being removed, and the sand shoved up on the sides, like a bowl. Here it may be seen early in summer assiduously brooding, and driving away minnows and larger fishes, even its own species, which would disturb its ova, pursuing them a few feet, and circling round swiftly to its nest again: the minnows, like young sharks, instantly entering the empty nests, meanwhile, and swallowing the spawn, which is attached to the weeds and to the bottom, on the sunny side. The spawn is exposed to so many dangers, that a very small proportion can ever become fishes, for beside being the con-

stant prey of birds and fishes, a great many nests are made
so near the shore, in shallow water, that they are left dry in
a few days, as the river goes down. These and the lamprey's
are the only fishes' nests that I have observed, though the
ova of some species may be seen floating on the surface. The
breams are so careful of their charge that you may stand
close by in the water and examine them at your leisure. I
have thus stood over them half an hour at a time, and
stroked them familiarly without frightening them, suffering
them to nibble my fingers harmlessly, and seen them erect
their dorsal fins in anger when my hand approached their
ova, and have even taken them gently out of the water with
my hand; though this cannot be accomplished by a sudden
movement, however dexterous, for instant warning is conveyed to them through their denser element, but only by letting the fingers gradually close about them as they are
poised over the palm, and with the utmost gentleness raising
them slowly to the surface. Though stationary, they keep up
a constant sculling or waving motion with their fins, which
is exceedingly graceful, and expressive of their humble happiness; for unlike ours, the element in which they live is a
stream which must be constantly resisted. From time to time
they nibble the weeds at the bottom or overhanging their
nests, or dart after a fly or a worm. The dorsal fin, besides
answering the purpose of a keel, with the anal, serves to
keep the fish upright, for in shallow water, where this is not
covered, they fall on their sides. As you stand thus stooping
over the bream in its nest, the edges of the dorsal and caudal
fins have a singular dusty golden reflection, and its eyes,
which stand out from the head, are transparent and colorless. Seen in its native element, it is a very beautiful and
compact fish, perfect in all its parts, and looks like a brilliant
coin fresh from the mint. It is a perfect jewel of the river,
the green, red, coppery, and golden reflections of its mottled
sides being the concentration of such rays as struggle
through the floating pads and flowers to the sandy bottom,
and in harmony with the sunlit brown and yellow pebbles.
Behind its watery shield it dwells far from many accidents
inevitable to human life.

There is also another species of bream found in our river,

without the red spot on the operculum, which, according to M. Agassiz, is undescribed.

The Common Perch, *Perca flavescens*, which name describes well the gleaming, golden reflections of its scales as it is drawn out of the water, its red gills standing out in vain in the thin element, is one of the handsomest and most regularly formed of our fishes, and at such a moment as this reminds us of the fish in the picture which wished to be restored to its native element until it had grown larger; and indeed most of this species that are caught are not half grown. In the ponds there is a light-colored and slender kind, which swim in shoals of many hundreds in the sunny water, in company with the shiner, averaging not more than six or seven inches in length, while only a few larger specimens are found in the deepest water, which prey upon their weaker brethren. I have often attracted these small perch to the shore at evening, by rippling the water with my fingers, and they may sometimes be caught while attempting to pass inside your hands. It is a tough and heedless fish, biting from impulse, without nibbling, and from impulse refraining to bite, and sculling indifferently past. It rather prefers the clear water and sandy bottoms, though here it has not much choice. It is a true fish, such as the angler loves to put into his basket or hang at the top of his willow twig, in shady afternoons along the banks of the stream. So many unquestionable fishes he counts, and so many shiners, which he counts and then throws away. Old Josselyn in his "New England's Rarities," published in 1672, mentions the Perch or River Partridge.

The Chivin, Dace, Roach, Cousin Trout, or whatever else it is called, *Leuciscus pulchellus*, white and red, always an unexpected prize, which, however, any angler is glad to hook for its rarity. A name that reminds us of many an unsuccessful ramble by swift streams, when the wind rose to disappoint the fisher. It is commonly a silvery soft-scaled fish, of graceful, scholarlike, and classical look, like many a picture in an English book. It loves a swift current and a sandy bottom, and bites inadvertently, yet not without appetite for the bait. The minnows are used as bait for pickerel in the winter. The red chivin, according to some, is still the same fish, only older, or with its tints deepened as they think by the darker water it inhabits, as the red clouds swim in the twilight atmosphere. He who has not hooked the red chivin is not yet a complete angler. Other fishes, methinks, are slightly amphibious, but this is a denizen of the water wholly. The cork goes dancing down the swift-rushing stream, amid the weeds and sands, when suddenly, by a coincidence never to be remembered, emerges this fabulous inhabitant of another element, a thing heard of but not seen, as if it were the instant creation of an eddy, a true product of the running stream. And this bright cupreous dolphin was spawned and has passed its life beneath the level of your feet in your native fields. Fishes too, as well as birds and clouds, derive their armor from the mine. I have heard of mackerel visiting the copper banks at a particular season; this fish, perchance, has its habitat in the Coppermine River. I have caught white chivin of great size in the Abol-jacknagesic, where it empties into the Penobscot, at the base of Mount Ktaadn, but no red ones there. The latter variety seems not to have been sufficiently observed.

The Dace, *Leuciscus argenteus*, is a slight silvery minnow, found generally in the middle of the stream, where the current is most rapid, and frequently confounded with the last named.

The Shiner, *Leuciscus crysoleucas*, is a soft-scaled and tender fish, the victim of its stronger neighbors, found in all places, deep and shallow, clear and turbid; generally the first nibbler at the bait, but, with its small mouth and nibbling propensities, not easily caught. It is a gold or silver bit that passes current in the river, its limber tail dimpling the surface in sport or flight. I have seen the fry, when frightened by something thrown into the water, leap out by dozens, together with the dace, and wreck themselves upon a floating plank. It is the little light-infant of the river, with body armor of gold or silver spangles, slipping, gliding its life through with a quirk of the tail, half in the water, half in the air, upward and ever upward with flitting fin to more crystalline tides, yet still abreast of us dwellers on the bank. It is almost dissolved by the summer heats. A slighter and lighter colored shiner is found in one of our ponds.

The Pickerel, *Esox reticulatus*, the swiftest, wariest, and most ravenous of fishes, which Josselyn calls the Fresh-Water or River Wolf, is very common in the shallow and weedy lagoons along the sides of the stream. It is a solemn, stately, ruminant fish, lurking under the shadow of a pad at noon, with still, circumspect, voracious eye, motionless as a jewel set in water, or moving slowly along to take up its position, darting from time to time at such unlucky fish or frog or insect as comes within its range, and swallowing it at a gulp. I have caught one which had swallowed a brother pickerel half as large as itself, with the tail still visible in its mouth, while the head was already digested in its stomach. Sometimes a striped snake, bound to greener meadows across the stream, ends its undulatory progress in the same receptacle. They are so greedy and impetuous that they are frequently caught by being entangled in the line the moment it is cast. Fishermen also distinguish the brook pickerel, a shorter and thicker fish than the former.

The Horned Pout, *Pimelodus nebulosus*, sometimes called Minister, from the peculiar squeaking noise it makes when drawn out of the water, is a dull and blundering fellow, and like the eel vespertinal in his habits, and fond of the mud. It bites deliberately as if about its business. They are taken at night with a mass of worms strung on a thread, which catches in their teeth, sometimes three or four, with an eel, at one pull. They are extremely tenacious of life, opening and shutting their mouths for half an hour after their heads have been cut off. A bloodthirsty and bullying race of rangers, inhabiting the fertile river bottoms, with ever a lance in rest, and ready to do battle with their nearest neighbor. I have observed them in summer, when every other one had a long and bloody scar upon his back, where the skin was gone, the mark, perhaps, of some fierce encounter. Sometimes the fry, not an inch long, are seen darkening the shore with their myriads.

The Suckers, *Catostomi Bostonienses* and *tuberculati*, Common and Horned, perhaps on an average the largest of our fishes, may be seen in shoals of a hundred or more, stemming the current in the sun, on their mysterious migrations, and sometimes sucking in the bait which the fisherman suffers to float toward them. The former, which sometimes grow to a large size, are frequently caught by the hand in the brooks, or

like the red chivin, are jerked out by a hook fastened firmly
to the end of a stick, and placed under their jaws. They are
hardly known to the mere angler, however, not often biting
at his baits, though the spearer carries home many a mess in
the spring. To our village eyes, these shoals have a foreign and
imposing aspect, realizing the fertility of the seas.

The Common Eel, too, *Muræna Bostoniensis*, the only species of eel known in the State, a slimy, squirming creature,
informed of mud, still squirming in the pan, is speared and
hooked up with various success. Methinks it too occurs in
picture, left after the deluge, in many a meadow high and dry.

In the shallow parts of the river, where the current is rapid,
and the bottom pebbly, you may sometimes see the curious
circular nests of the Lamprey Eel, *Petromyzon Americanus*, the
American Stone-Sucker, as large as a cart-wheel, a foot or two
in height, and sometimes rising half a foot above the surface
of the water. They collect these stones, of the size of a hen's
egg, with their mouths, as their name implies, and are said to
fashion them into circles with their tails. They ascend falls by
clinging to the stones, which may sometimes be raised, by
lifting the fish by the tail. As they are not seen on their way
down the streams, it is thought by fishermen that they never
return, but waste away and die, clinging to rocks and stumps
of trees for an indefinite period; a tragic feature in the scenery
of the river bottoms worthy to be remembered with Shakespeare's description of the sea-floor. They are rarely seen in
our waters at present, on account of the dams, though they
are taken in great quantities at the mouth of the river in Lowell. Their nests, which are very conspicuous, look more like
art than anything in the river.

If we had leisure this afternoon, we might turn our prow
up the brooks in quest of the classical trout and the minnows.
Of the last alone, according to M. Agassiz, several of the species found in this town are yet undescribed. These would,
perhaps, complete the list of our finny contemporaries in the
Concord waters.

Salmon, Shad, and Alewives were formerly abundant here,
and taken in weirs by the Indians, who taught this method to
the whites, by whom they were used as food and as manure,
until the dam, and afterward the canal at Billerica, and the

factories at Lowell, put an end to their migrations hither-
ward; though it is thought that a few more enterprising shad
may still occasionally be seen in this part of the river. It is
said, to account for the destruction of the fishery, that those
who at that time represented the interests of the fishermen
and the fishes, remembering between what dates they were
accustomed to take the grown shad, stipulated, that the dams
should be left open for that season only, and the fry, which
go down a month later, were consequently stopped and destroyed by myriads. Others say that the fish-ways were not
properly constructed. Perchance, after a few thousands of
years, if the fishes will be patient, and pass their summers
elsewhere, meanwhile, nature will have levelled the Billerica
dam, and the Lowell factories, and the Grass-ground River
run clear again, to be explored by new migratory shoals, even
as far as the Hopkinton pond and Westborough swamp.

One would like to know more of that race, now extinct,
whose seines lie rotting in the garrets of their children, who
openly professed the trade of fishermen, and even fed their
townsmen creditably, not skulking through the meadows to a
rainy afternoon sport. Dim visions we still get of miraculous
draughts of fishes, and heaps uncountable by the river-side,
from the tales of our seniors sent on horseback in their childhood from the neighboring towns, perched on saddle-bags,
with instructions to get the one bag filled with shad, the other
with alewives. At least one memento of those days may still
exist in the memory of this generation, in the familiar appel-
lation of a celebrated train-band of this town, whose un-
trained ancestors stood creditably at Concord North Bridge.
Their captain, a man of piscatory tastes, having duly warned
his company to turn out on a certain day, they, like obedient
soldiers, appeared promptly on parade at the appointed time,
but, unfortunately, they went undrilled, except in the ma-
neuvres of a soldier's wit and unlicensed jesting, that May
day; for their captain, forgetting his own appointment, and
warned only by the favorable aspect of the heavens, as he had
often done before, went a-fishing that afternoon, and his
company thenceforth was known to old and young, grave and
gay, as "The Shad," and by the youths of this vicinity this
was long regarded as the proper name of all the irregular

militia in Christendom. But, alas! no record of these fishers' lives remains that we know, unless it be one brief page of hard but unquestionable history, which occurs in Day Book No. 4, of an old trader of this town, long since dead, which shows pretty plainly what constituted a fisherman's stock in trade in those days. It purports to be a Fisherman's Account Current, probably for the fishing season of the year 1805, during which months he purchased daily rum and sugar, sugar and rum, N. E. and W. I., "one cod line," "one brown mug," and "a line for the seine"; rum and sugar, sugar and rum, "good loaf sugar," and "good brown," W. I. and N. E., in short and uniform entries to the bottom of the page, all carried out in pounds, shillings, and pence, from March 25th to June 5th, and promptly settled by receiving "cash in full" at the last date. But perhaps not so settled altogether. These were the necessaries of life in those days; with salmon, shad, and alewives, fresh and pickled, he was thereafter independent on the groceries. Rather a preponderance of the fluid elements; but such is the fisherman's nature. I can faintly remember to have seen this same fisher in my earliest youth, still as near the river as he could get, with uncertain undulatory step, after so many things had gone down stream, swinging a scythe in the meadow, his bottle like a serpent hid in the grass; himself as yet not cut down by the Great Mower.

Surely the fates are forever kind, though Nature's laws are more immutable than any despot's, yet to man's daily life they rarely seem rigid, but permit him to relax with license in summer weather. He is not harshly reminded of the things he may not do. She is very kind and liberal to all men of vicious habits, and certainly does not deny them quarter; they do not die without priest. Still they maintain life along the way, keeping this side the Styx, still hearty, still resolute, "never better in their lives"; and again, after a dozen years have elapsed, they start up from behind a hedge, asking for work and wages for able-bodied men. Who has not met such

> "a beggar on the way,
> Who sturdily could gang? . . . .
> Who cared neither for wind nor wet,
> In lands where'er he past?"

"That bold adopts each house he views, his own;
  Makes every pulse his checquer, and, at pleasure,
  Walks forth, and taxes all the world, like Cæsar";—

as if consistency were the secret of health, while the poor inconsistent aspirant man, seeking to live a pure life, feeding on air, divided against himself, cannot stand, but pines and dies after a life of sickness, on beds of down.

The unwise are accustomed to speak as if some were not sick; but methinks the difference between men in respect to health is not great enough to lay much stress upon. Some are reputed sick and some are not. It often happens that the sicker man is the nurse to the sounder.

Shad are still taken in the basin of Concord River at Lowell, where they are said to be a month earlier than the Merrimack shad, on account of the warmth of the water. Still patiently, almost pathetically, with instinct not to be discouraged, not to be *reasoned* with, revisiting their old haunts, as if their stern fates would relent, and still met by the Corporation with its dam. Poor shad! where is thy redress? When Nature gave thee instinct, gave she thee the heart to bear thy fate? Still wandering the sea in thy scaly armor to inquire humbly at the mouths of rivers if man has perchance left them free for thee to enter. By countless shoals loitering uncertain meanwhile, merely stemming the tide there, in danger from sea foes in spite of thy bright armor, awaiting new instructions, until the sands, until the water itself, tell thee if it be so or not. Thus by whole migrating nations, full of instinct, which is thy faith, in this backward spring, turned adrift, and perchance knowest not where men do *not* dwell, where there are *not* factories, in these days. Armed with no sword, no electric shock, but mere Shad, armed only with innocence and a just cause, with tender dumb mouth only forward, and scales easy to be detached. I for one am with thee, and who knows what may avail a crow-bar against that Billerica dam?—Not despairing when whole myriads have gone to feed those sea monsters during thy suspense, but still brave, indifferent, on easy fin there, like shad reserved for higher destinies. Willing to be decimated for man's behoof after the spawning season. Away with the superficial and selfish phil-*anthropy* of men,—who knows what admirable virtue of fishes may be below low-water-mark, bearing up against a hard destiny, not admired by that fellow-creature who alone can appreciate it! Who hears the fishes when they cry? It will not be forgotten by some memory that we were contemporaries. Thou shalt erelong have thy way up the rivers, up all the rivers of the globe, if I am not mistaken. Yea, even thy dull watery dream shall be more than realized. If it were not so, but thou wert to be overlooked at first and at last, then would not I take their heaven. Yes, I say so, who think I know better than thou canst. Keep a stiff fin then, and stem all the tides thou mayst meet.

At length it would seem that the interests, not of the fishes only, but of the men of Wayland, of Sudbury, of Concord, demand the levelling of that dam. Innumerable acres of meadow are waiting to be made dry land, wild native grass to give place to English. The farmers stand with scythes whet, waiting the subsiding of the waters, by gravitation, by evaporation or otherwise, but sometimes their eyes do not rest, their wheels do not roll, on the quaking meadow ground during the haying season at all. So many sources of wealth inaccessible. They rate the loss hereby incurred in the single town of Wayland alone as equal to the expense of keeping a hundred yoke of oxen the year round. One year, as I learn, not long ago, the farmers standing ready to drive their teams afield as usual, the water gave no signs of falling; without new attraction in the heavens, without freshet or visible cause, still standing stagnant at an unprecedented height. All hydrometers were at fault; some trembled for their English even. But speedy emissaries revealed the unnatural secret, in the new float-board, wholly a foot in width, added to their already too high privileges by the dam proprietors. The hundred yoke of oxen, meanwhile, standing patient, gazing wishfully meadow-ward, at that inaccessible waving native grass, uncut but by the great mower Time, who cuts so broad a swathe, without so much as a wisp to wind about their horns.

That was a long pull from Ball's Hill to Carlisle Bridge, sitting with our faces to the south, a slight breeze rising from the north, but nevertheless water still runs and grass grows,

for now, having passed the bridge between Carlisle and Bedford, we see men haying far off in the meadow, their heads
waving like the grass which they cut. In the distance the wind
seemed to bend all alike. As the night stole over, such a freshness was wafted across the meadow that every blade of cut-
grass seemed to teem with life. Faint purple clouds began to
be reflected in the water, and the cow-bells tinkled louder
along the banks, while, like sly water-rats, we stole along
nearer the shore, looking for a place to pitch our camp.

At length, when we had made about seven miles, as far as
Billerica, we moored our boat on the west side of a little rising ground which in the spring forms an island in the river.
Here we found huckleberries still hanging upon the bushes,
where they seemed to have slowly ripened for our especial
use. Bread and sugar, and cocoa boiled in river water, made
our repast, and as we had drank in the fluvial prospect all day,
so now we took a draft of the water with our evening meal
to propitiate the river gods, and whet our vision for the sights
it was to behold. The sun was setting on the one hand, while
our eminence was contributing its shadow to the night, on
the other. It seemed insensibly to grow lighter as the night
shut in, and a distant and solitary farm-house was revealed,
which before lurked in the shadows of the noon. There was
no other house in sight, nor any cultivated field. To the right
and left, as far as the horizon, were straggling pine woods
with their plumes against the sky, and across the river were
rugged hills, covered with shrub oaks, tangled with grape-
vines and ivy, with here and there a gray rock jutting out
from the maze. The sides of these cliffs, though a quarter of
a mile distant, were almost heard to rustle while we looked at
them, it was such a leafy wilderness; a place for fauns and
satyrs, and where bats hung all day to the rocks, and at evening flitted over the water, and fire-flies husbanded their light
under the grass and leaves against the night. When we had
pitched our tent on the hillside, a few rods from the shore,
we sat looking through its triangular door in the twilight at
our lonely mast on the shore, just seen above the alders, and
hardly yet come to a stand-still from the swaying of the
stream; the first encroachment of commerce on this land.
There was our port, our Ostia. That straight geometrical line

against the water and the sky stood for the last refinements of
civilized life, and what of sublimity there is in history was
there symbolized.

For the most part, there was no recognition of human life
in the night, no human breathing was heard, only the breathing of the wind. As we sat up, kept awake by the novelty of
our situation, we heard at intervals foxes stepping about over
the dead leaves, and brushing the dewy grass close to our
tent, and once a musquash fumbling among the potatoes and
melons in our boat, but when we hastened to the shore we
could detect only a ripple in the water ruffling the disk of a
star. At intervals we were serenaded by the song of a dreaming sparrow or the throttled cry of an owl, but after each
sound which near at hand broke the stillness of the night,
each crackling of the twigs, or rustling among the leaves,
there was a sudden pause, and deeper and more conscious
silence, as if the intruder were aware that no life was rightfully
abroad at that hour. There was a fire in Lowell, as we judged,
this night, and we saw the horizon blazing, and heard the
distant alarm-bells, as it were a faint tinkling music borne to
these woods. But the most constant and memorable sound of
a summer's night, which we did not fail to hear every night
afterward, though at no time so incessantly and so favorably
as now, was the barking of the house-dogs, from the loudest
and hoarsest bark to the faintest aerial palpitation under the
eaves of heaven, from the patient but anxious mastiff to the
timid and wakeful terrier, at first loud and rapid, then faint
and slow, to be imitated only in a whisper; wow-wow-wow-
wow—wo—wo—w—w. Even in a retired and uninhabited
district like this, it was a sufficiency of sound for the ear of
night, and more impressive than any music. I have heard the
voice of a hound, just before daylight, while the stars were
shining, from over the woods and river, far in the horizon,
when it sounded as sweet and melodious as an instrument.
The hounding of a dog pursuing a fox or other animal in the
horizon, may have first suggested the notes of the hunting-
horn to alternate with and relieve the lungs of the dog. This
natural bugle long resounded in the woods of the ancient
world before the horn was invented. The very dogs that sul-
lenly bay the moon from farm-yards in these nights excite

more heroism in our breasts than all the civil exhortations or war sermons of the age. "I would rather be a dog, and bay the moon," than many a Roman that I know. The night is equally indebted to the clarion of the cock, with wakeful hope, from the very setting of the sun, prematurely ushering in the dawn. All these sounds, the crowing of cocks, the baying of dogs, and the hum of insects at noon, are the evidence of nature's health or *sound* state. Such is the never-failing beauty and accuracy of language, the most perfect art in the world; the chisel of a thousand years retouches it.

At length the antepenultimate and drowsy hours drew on, and all sounds were denied entrance to our ears.

> Who sleeps by day and walks by night,
> Will meet no spirit but some sprite.

Sunday

"The river calmly flows,
  Through shining banks, through lonely glen,
Where the owl shrieks, though ne'er the cheer of men
    Has stirred its mute repose,
Still if you should walk there, you would go there again."
                                        CHANNING.

"The Indians tell us of a beautiful River lying far to the
south, which they call Merrimack."
              SIEUR DE MONTS, *Relations of the Jesuits*, 1604.

IN THE MORNING the river and adjacent country were covered with a dense fog, through which the smoke of our
fire curled up like a still subtiler mist; but before we had
rowed many rods, the sun arose and the fog rapidly dispersed,
leaving a slight steam only to curl along the surface of the
water. It was a quiet Sunday morning, with more of the auroral rosy and white than of the yellow light in it, as if it
dated from earlier than the fall of man, and still preserved a
heathenish integrity: —

> An early unconverted Saint,
> Free from noontide or evening taint,
> Heathen without reproach,
> That did upon the civil day encroach,
> And ever since its birth
> Had trod the outskirts of the earth.

But the impressions which the morning makes vanish with
its dews, and not even the most "persevering mortal" can preserve the memory of its freshness to mid-day. As we passed
the various islands, or what were islands in the spring, rowing
with our backs down stream, we gave names to them. The
one on which we had camped we called Fox Island, and one
fine densely wooded island surrounded by deep water and
overrun by grape-vines, which looked like a mass of verdure
and of flowers cast upon the waves, we named Grape Island.
From Ball's Hill to Billerica meeting-house, the river was still
twice as broad as in Concord, a deep, dark, and dead stream,

flowing between gentle hills and sometimes cliffs, and well wooded all the way. It was a long woodland lake bordered with willows. For long reaches we could see neither house nor cultivated field, nor any sign of the vicinity of man. Now we coasted along some shallow shore by the edge of a dense palisade of bulrushes, which straightly bounded the water as if clipt by art, reminding us of the reed forts of the East-Indians, of which we had read; and now the bank slightly raised was overhung with graceful grasses and various species of brake, whose downy stems stood closely grouped and naked as in a vase, while their heads spread several feet on either side. The dead limbs of the willow were rounded and adorned by the climbing mikania, *Mikania scandens*, which filled every crevice in the leafy bank, contrasting agreeably with the gray bark of its supporter and the balls of the button-bush. The water willow, *Salix Purshiana*, when it is of large size and entire, is the most graceful and ethereal of our trees. Its masses of light green foliage, piled one upon another to the height of twenty or thirty feet, seemed to float on the surface of the water, while the slight gray stems and the shore were hardly visible between them. No tree is so wedded to the water, and harmonizes so well with still streams. It is even more graceful than the weeping willow, or any pendulous trees, which dip their branches in the stream instead of being buoyed up by it. Its limbs curved outward over the surface as if attracted by it. It had not a New England but an Oriental character, reminding us of trim Persian gardens, of Haroun Alraschid, and the artificial lakes of the East.

As we thus dipped our way along between fresh masses of foliage overrun with the grape and smaller flowering vines, the surface was so calm, and both air and water so transparent, that the flight of a kingfisher or robin over the river was as distinctly seen reflected in the water below as in the air above. The birds seemed to flit through submerged groves, alighting on the yielding sprays, and their clear notes to come up from below. We were uncertain whether the water floated the land, or the land held the water in its bosom. It was such a season, in short, as that in which one of our Concord poets sailed on its stream, and sung its quiet glories.

"There is an inward voice, that in the stream
Sends forth its spirit to the listening ear,
And in a calm content it floweth on,
Like wisdom, welcome with its own respect.
Clear in its breast lie all these beauteous thoughts,
It doth receive the green and graceful trees,
And the gray rocks smile in its peaceful arms."

And more he sung, but too serious for our page. For every oak and birch too growing on the hill-top, as well as for these elms and willows, we knew that there was a graceful ethereal and ideal tree making down from the roots, and sometimes Nature in high tides brings her mirror to its foot and makes it visible. The stillness was intense and almost conscious, as if it were a natural Sabbath, and we fancied that the morning was the evening of a celestial day. The air was so elastic and crystalline that it had the same effect on the landscape that a glass has on a picture, to give it an ideal remoteness and perfection. The landscape was clothed in a mild and quiet light, in which the woods and fences checkered and partitioned it with new regularity, and rough and uneven fields stretched away with lawn-like smoothness to the horizon, and the clouds, finely distinct and picturesque, seemed a fit drapery to hang over fairy-land. The world seemed decked for some holiday or prouder pageantry, with silken streamers flying, and the course of our lives to wind on before us like a green lane into a country maze, at the season when fruit-trees are in blossom.

Why should not our whole life and its scenery be actually thus fair and distinct? All our lives want a suitable background. They should at least, like the life of the anchorite, be as impressive to behold as objects in the desert, a broken shaft or crumbling mound against a limitless horizon. Character always secures for itself this advantage, and is thus distinct and unrelated to near or trivial objects, whether things or persons. On this same stream a maiden once sailed in my boat, thus unattended but by invisible guardians, and as she sat in the prow there was nothing but herself between the steersman and the sky. I could then say with the poet,—

"Sweet falls the summer air
Over her frame who sails with me;
Her way like that is beautifully free,
Her nature far more rare,
And is her constant heart of virgin purity."

At evening still the very stars seem but this maiden's emissaries and reporters of her progress.

Low in the eastern sky
Is set thy glancing eye;
And though its gracious light
Ne'er riseth to my sight,
Yet every star that climbs
Above the gnarled limbs
 Of yonder hill,
Conveys thy gentle will.

Believe I knew thy thought,
And that the zephyrs brought
Thy kindest wishes through,
As mine they bear to you,
That some attentive cloud
Did pause amid the crowd
 Over my head,
While gentle things were said.

Believe the thrushes sung,
And that the flower-bells rung,
That herbs exhaled their scent,
And beasts knew what was meant,
The trees a welcome waved,
And lakes their margins laved,
 When thy free mind
To my retreat did wind.

It was a summer eve,
The air did gently heave
While yet a low-hung cloud
Thy eastern skies did shroud;

The lightning's silent gleam,
Startling my drowsy dream,
    Seemed like the flash
Under thy dark eyelash.

Still will I strive to be
As if thou wert with me;
Whatever path I take,
It shall be for thy sake,
Of gentle slope and wide,
As thou wert by my side,
    Without a root
To trip thy gentle foot.

I'll walk with gentle pace,
And choose the smoothest place,
And careful dip the oar,
And shun the winding shore,
And gently steer my boat
Where water-lilies float,
    And cardinal flowers
Stand in their sylvan bowers.

It required some rudeness to disturb with our boat the mirror-like surface of the water, in which every twig and blade of grass was so faithfully reflected; too faithfully indeed for art to imitate, for only Nature may exaggerate herself. The shallowest still water is unfathomable. Wherever the trees and skies are reflected, there is more than Atlantic depth, and no danger of fancy running aground. We notice that it required a separate intention of the eye, a more free and abstracted vision, to see the reflected trees and the sky, than to see the river bottom merely; and so are there manifold visions in the direction of every object, and even the most opaque reflect the heavens from their surface. Some men have their eyes naturally intended to the one and some to the other object.

"A man that looks on glass,
    On it may stay his eye,
Or, if he pleaseth, through it pass,
    And the heavens espy."

Two men in a skiff, whom we passed hereabouts, floating buoyantly amid the reflections of the trees, like a feather in mid-air, or a leaf which is wafted gently from its twig to the water without turning over, seemed still in their element, and to have very delicately availed themselves of the natural laws. Their floating there was a beautiful and successful experiment in natural philosophy, and it served to ennoble in our eyes the art of navigation; for as birds fly and fishes swim, so these men sailed. It reminded us how much fairer and nobler all the actions of man might be, and that our life in its whole economy might be as beautiful as the fairest works of art or nature.

The sun lodged on the old gray cliffs, and glanced from every pad; the bulrushes and flags seemed to rejoice in the delicious light and air; the meadows were a-drinking at their leisure; the frogs sat meditating, all sabbath thoughts, summing up their week, with one eye out on the golden sun, and one toe upon a reed, eying the wondrous universe in which they act their part; the fishes swam more staid and soberly, as maidens go to church; shoals of golden and silver minnows rose to the surface to behold the heavens, and then sheered off into more sombre aisles; they swept by as if moved by one mind, continually gliding past each other, and yet preserving the form of their battalion unchanged, as if they were still embraced by the transparent membrane which held the spawn; a young band of brethren and sisters trying their new fins; now they wheeled, now shot ahead, and when we drove them to the shore and cut them off, they dexterously tacked and passed underneath the boat. Over the old wooden bridges no traveller crossed, and neither the river nor the fishes avoided to glide between the abutments.

Here was a village not far off behind the woods, Billerica, settled not long ago, and the children still bear the names of the first settlers in this late "howling wilderness"; yet to all intents and purposes it is as old as Fernay or as Mantua, an old gray town where men grow old and sleep already under moss-grown monuments,—outgrow their usefulness. This is ancient Billerica, (Villa-rica?) now in its dotage, named from the English Billericay, and whose Indian name was Shawshine. I never heard that it was young. See, is not nature

here gone to decay, farms all run out, meeting-house grown
gray and racked with age? If you would know of its early
youth, ask those old gray rocks in the pasture. It has a bell
that sounds sometimes as far as Concord woods; I have
heard that,—ay, hear it now. No wonder that such a sound
startled the dreaming Indian, and frightened his game, when
the first bells were swung on trees, and sounded through the
forest beyond the plantations of the white man. But to-day I
like best the echo amid these cliffs and woods. It is no feeble
imitation, but rather its original, or as if some rural Orpheus
played over the strain again to show how it should sound.

> Dong, sounds the brass in the east,
> As if to a funeral feast,
> But I like that sound the best
> Out of the fluttering west.
>
> The steeple ringeth a knell,
> But the fairies' silvery bell
> Is the voice of that gentle folk,
> Or else the horizon that spoke.
>
> Its metal is not of brass,
> But air, and water, and glass,
> And under a cloud it is swung,
> And by the wind it is rung.
>
> When the steeple tolleth the noon,
> It soundeth not so soon,
> Yet it rings a far earlier hour,
> And the sun has not reached its tower.

On the other hand, the road runs up to Carlisle, city of the
woods, which, if it is less civil, is the more natural. It does
well hold the earth together. It gets laughed at because it is a
small town, I know, but nevertheless it is a place where great
men may be born any day, for fair winds and foul blow right
on over it without distinction. It has a meeting-house and
horse-sheds, a tavern and a blacksmith's shop, for centre, and
a good deal of wood to cut and cord yet. And

"Bedford, most noble Bedford,
I shall not thee forget."

History has remembered thee; especially that meek and humble petition of thy old planters, like the wailing of the Lord's own people, "To the gentlemen, the selectmen" of Concord, praying to be erected into a separate parish. We can hardly credit that so plaintive a psalm resounded but little more than a century ago along these Babylonish waters. "In the extreme difficult seasons of heat and cold," said they, " we were ready to say of the Sabbath, Behold what a weariness is it."—"Gentlemen, if our seeking to draw off proceed from any disaffection to our present Reverend Pastor, or the Christian Society with whom we have taken such sweet counsel together, and walked unto the house of God in company, then hear us not this day, but we greatly desire, if God please, to be eased of our burden on the Sabbath, the travel and fatigue thereof, that the word of God may be nigh to us, near to our houses and in our hearts, that we and our little ones may serve the Lord. We hope that God, who stirred up the spirit of Cyrus to set forward temple work, has stirred us up to ask, and will stir you up to grant, the prayer of our petition; so shall your humble petitioners ever pray, as in duty bound—" And so the temple work went forward here to a happy conclusion. Yonder in Carlisle the building of the temple was many wearisome years delayed, not that there was wanting of Shittim wood, or the gold of Ophir, but a site therefor convenient to all the worshippers; whether on "Buttrick's Plain," or rather on "Poplar Hill."—It was a tedious question.

In this Billerica solid men must have lived, select from year to year; a series of town clerks, at least; and there are old records that you may search. Some spring the white man came, built him a house, and made a clearing here, letting in the sun, dried up a farm, piled up the old gray stones in fences, cut down the pines around his dwelling, planted orchard seeds brought from the old country, and persuaded the civil apple-tree to blossom next to the wild pine and the juniper, shedding its perfume in the wilderness. Their old stocks still remain. He culled the graceful elm from out the woods and from the river-side, and so refined and smoothed his village plot. He rudely bridged the stream, and drove his team

afield into the river meadows, cut the wild grass, and laid bare
the homes of beaver, otter, muskrat, and with the whetting
of his scythe scared off the deer and bear. He set up a mill,
and fields of English grain sprang in the virgin soil. And with
his grain he scattered the seeds of the dandelion and the wild
trefoil over the meadows, mingling his English flowers with
the wild native ones. The bristling burdock, the sweet-scented
catnip, and the humble yarrow planted themselves along his
woodland road, they too seeking "freedom to worship God"
in their way. And thus he plants a town. The white man's
mullein soon reigned in Indian cornfields, and sweet-scented
English grasses clothed the new soil. Where, then, could
the Red Man set his foot? The honey-bee hummed through the
Massachusetts woods, and sipped the wild-flowers round the
Indian's wigwam, perchance unnoticed, when, with prophetic
warning, it stung the Red child's hand, forerunner of that
industrious tribe that was to come and pluck the wild-flower
of his race up by the root.

The white man comes, pale as the dawn, with a load of
thought, with a slumbering intelligence as a fire raked up,
knowing well what he knows, not guessing but calculating;
strong in community, yielding obedience to authority; of experienced race; of wonderful, wonderful common sense; dull
but capable, slow but persevering, severe but just, of little
humor but genuine; a laboring man, despising game and
sport; building a house that endures, a framed house. He
buys the Indian's moccasins and baskets, then buys his hunting-grounds, and at length forgets where he is buried and
ploughs up his bones. And here town records, old, tattered,
time-worn, weather-stained chronicles, contain the Indian
sachem's mark perchance, an arrow or a beaver, and the few
fatal words by which he deeded his hunting-grounds away.
He comes with a list of ancient Saxon, Norman, and Celtic
names, and strews them up and down this river,—Framingham, Sudbury, Bedford, Carlisle, Billerica, Chelmsford,—and this is New Angle-land, and these are the New
West Saxons whom the Red Men call, not Angle-ish or English, but Yengeese, and so at last they are known for Yankees.

When we were opposite to the middle of Billerica, the
fields on either hand had a soft and cultivated English aspect,

the village spire being seen over the copses which skirt the
river, and sometimes an orchard straggled down to the water-
side, though, generally, our course this forenoon was the
wildest part of our voyage. It seemed that men led a quiet
and very civil life there. The inhabitants were plainly cultivators of the earth, and lived under an organized political government. The school-house stood with a meek aspect,
entreating a long truce to war and savage life. Every one finds
by his own experience, as well as in history, that the era in
which men cultivate the apple, and the amenities of the garden, is essentially different from that of the hunter and forest
life, and neither can displace the other without loss. We have
all had our day-dreams, as well as more prophetic nocturnal
vision; but as for farming, I am convinced that my genius
dates from an older era than the agricultural. I would at least
strike my spade into the earth with such careless freedom but
accuracy as the woodpecker his bill into a tree. There is in my
nature, methinks, a singular yearning toward all wildness. I
know of no redeeming qualities in myself but a sincere love
for some things, and when I am reproved I fall back on to
this ground. What have I to do with ploughs? I cut another
furrow than you see. Where the off ox treads, there is it not,
it is farther off; where the nigh ox walks, it will not be, it is
nigher still. If corn fails, my crop fails not, and what are
drought and rain to me? The rude Saxon pioneer will sometimes pine for that refinement and artificial beauty which are
English, and love to hear the sound of such sweet and classical names as the Pentland and Malvern Hills, the Cliffs of
Dover and the Trosachs, Richmond, Derwent, and Winan-
dermere, which are to him now instead of the Acropolis and
Parthenon, of Baiæ, and Athens with its sea-walls, and Arcadia and Tempe.

> Greece, who am I that should remember thee,
> Thy Marathon and thy Thermopylæ?
> Is my life vulgar, my fate mean,
> Which on these golden memories can lean?

We are apt enough to be pleased with such books as Evelyn's
Sylva, Acetarium, and Kalendarium Hortense, but they imply
a relaxed nerve in the reader. Gardening is civil and social,

but it wants the vigor and freedom of the forest and the out-law. There may be an excess of cultivation as well as of any-thing else, until civilization becomes pathetic. A highly cultivated man,—all whose bones can be bent! whose heaven-born virtues are but good manners! The young pines spring-ing up in the cornfields from year to year are to me a refresh-ing fact. We talk of civilizing the Indian, but that is not the name for his improvement. By the wary independence and aloofness of his dim forest life he preserves his intercourse with his native gods, and is admitted from time to time to a rare and peculiar society with Nature. He has glances of starry recognition to which our saloons are strangers. The steady illumination of his genius, dim only because distant, is like the faint but satisfying light of the stars compared with the dazzling but ineffectual and short-lived blaze of candles. The Society-Islanders had their day-born gods, but they were not supposed to be "of equal antiquity with the *atua fauau po*, or night-born gods." It is true, there are the innocent pleasures of country life, and it is sometimes pleasant to make the earth yield her increase, and gather the fruits in their season, but the heroic spirit will not fail to dream of remoter retirements and more rugged paths. It will have its garden-plots and its *parterres* elsewhere than on the earth, and gather nuts and berries by the way for its subsistence, or orchard fruits with such heedlessness as berries. We would not always be sooth-ing and taming nature, breaking the horse and the ox, but sometimes ride the horse wild and chase the buffalo. The In-dian's intercourse with Nature is at least such as admits of the greatest independence of each. If he is somewhat of a stranger in her midst, the gardener is too much of a familiar. There is something vulgar and foul in the latter's closeness to his mis-tress, something noble and cleanly in the former's distance. In civilization, as in a southern latitude, man degenerates at length, and yields to the incursion of more northern tribes,

> "Some nation yet shut in
> With hills of ice."

There are other, savager, and more primeval aspects of nature than our poets have sung. It is only white man's poetry. Homer and Ossian even can never revive in London or

Boston. And yet behold how these cities are refreshed by the mere tradition, or the imperfectly transmitted fragrance and flavor of these wild fruits. If we could listen but for an instant to the chant of the Indian muse, we should understand why he will not exchange his savageness for civilization. Nations are not whimsical. Steel and blankets are strong temptations; but the Indian does well to continue Indian.

After sitting in my chamber many days, reading the poets, I have been out early on a foggy morning, and heard the cry of an owl in a neighboring wood as from a nature behind the common, unexplored by science or by literature. None of the feathered race has yet realized my youthful conceptions of the woodland depths. I had seen the red Election-bird brought from their recesses on my comrades' string, and fancied that their plumage would assume stranger and more dazzling colors, like the tints of evening, in proportion as I advanced farther into the darkness and solitude of the forest. Still less have I seen such strong and wilderness tints on any poet's string.

These modern ingenious sciences and arts do not affect me as those more venerable arts of hunting and fishing, and even of husbandry in its primitive and simple form; as ancient and honorable trades as the sun and moon and winds pursue, coeval with the faculties of man, and invented when these were invented. We do not know their John Gutenberg, or Richard Arkwright, though the poets would fain make them to have been gradually learned and taught. According to Gower,—

> "And Iadahel, as saith the boke,
>   Firste made nette, and fishes toke.
> Of huntyng eke he fond the chace,
> Whiche nowe is knowe in many place;
> A tent of clothe, with corde and stake,
> He sette up first, and did it make."

Also, Lydgate says:—

> "Jason first sayled, in story it is tolde,
> Toward Colchos, to wynne the flees of golde.
> Ceres the Goddess fond first the tilthe of londe;

*   *   *   *   *

> Also, Aristeus fonde first the usage
> Of mylke, and cruddis, and of honey swote;
> Peryodes, for grete avauntage,
> From flyntes smote fuyre, daryng in the roote."

We read that Aristeus "obtained of Jupiter and Neptune, that the pestilential heat of the dog-days, wherein was great mortality, should be mitigated with wind." This is one of those dateless benefits conferred on man, which have no record in our vulgar day, though we still find some similitude to them in our dreams, in which we have a more liberal and juster apprehension of things, unconstrained by habit, which is then in some measure put off, and divested of memory, which we call history.

According to fable, when the island of Ægina was depopulated by sickness, at the instance of Æacus, Jupiter turned the ants into men, that is, as some think, he made men of the inhabitants who lived meanly like ants. This is perhaps the fullest history of those early days extant.

The fable which is naturally and truly composed, so as to satisfy the imagination, ere it addresses the understanding, beautiful though strange as a wild-flower, is to the wise man an apothegm, and admits of his most generous interpretation. When we read that Bacchus made the Tyrrhenian mariners mad, so that they leapt into the sea, mistaking it for a meadow full of flowers, and so became dolphins, we are not concerned about the historical truth of this, but rather a higher poetical truth. We seem to hear the music of a thought, and care not if the understanding be not gratified. For their beauty, consider the fables of Narcissus, of Endymion, of Memnon son of Morning, the representative of all promising youths who have died a premature death, and whose memory is melodiously prolonged to the latest morning; the beautiful stories of Phaeton, and of the Sirens whose isle shone afar off white with the bones of unburied men; and the pregnant ones of Pan, Prometheus, and the Sphinx; and that long list of names which have already become part of the universal language of civilized men, and from proper are becoming common names or nouns,—the Sibyls, the Eumenides, the Parcæ, the Graces, the Muses, Nemesis, &c.

It is interesting to observe with what singular unanimity the farthest sundered nations and generations consent to give completeness and roundness to an ancient fable, of which they indistinctly appreciate the beauty or the truth. By a faint and dream-like effort, though it be only by the vote of a scientific body, the dullest posterity slowly add some trait to the mythus. As when astronomers call the lately discovered planet Neptune; or the asteroid Astræa, that the Virgin who was driven from earth to heaven at the end of the golden age, may have her local habitation in the heavens more distinctly assigned her,—for the slightest recognition of poetic worth is significant. By such slow aggregation has mythology grown from the first. The very nursery tales of this generation, were the nursery tales of primeval races. They migrate from east to west, and again from west to east; now expanded into the "tale divine" of bards, now shrunk into a popular rhyme. This is an approach to that universal language which men have sought in vain. This fond reiteration of the oldest expressions of truth by the latest posterity, content with slightly and religiously retouching the old material, is the most impressive proof of a common humanity.

All nations love the same jests and tales, Jews, Christians, and Mahometans, and the same translated suffice for all. All men are children, and of one family. The same tale sends them all to bed, and wakes them in the morning. Joseph Wolff, the missionary, distributed copies of Robinson Crusoe, translated into Arabic, among the Arabs, and they made a great sensation. "Robinson Crusoe's adventures and wisdom," says he, "were read by Muhammedans in the market-places of Sanaa, Hodyeda, and Loheya, and admired and believed!" On reading the book, the Arabians exclaimed, "O, that Robinson Crusoe must have been a great prophet!"

To some extent, mythology is only the most ancient history and biography. So far from being false or fabulous in the common sense, it contains only enduring and essential truth, the I and you, the here and there, the now and then, being omitted. Either time or rare wisdom writes it. Before printing was discovered, a century was equal to a thousand years. The poet is he who can write some pure mythology to-day without the aid of posterity. In how few words, for instance, the

Greeks would have told the story of Abelard and Heloise, making but a sentence for our classical dictionary,—and then, perchance, have stuck up their names to shine in some corner of the firmament. We moderns, on the other hand, collect only the raw materials of biography and history, "memoirs to serve for a history," which itself is but materials to serve for a mythology. How many volumes folio would the Life and Labors of Prometheus have filled, if perchance it had fallen, as perchance it did first, in days of cheap printing! Who knows what shape the fable of Columbus will at length assume, to be confounded with that of Jason and the expedition of the Argonauts. And Franklin,—there may be a line for him in the future classical dictionary, recording what that demigod did, and referring him to some new genealogy. "Son of —— and ——. He aided the Americans to gain their independence, instructed mankind in economy, and drew down lightning from the clouds."

The hidden significance of these fables which is sometimes thought to have been detected, the ethics running parallel to the poetry and history, are not so remarkable as the readiness with which they may be made to express a variety of truths. As if they were the skeletons of still older and more universal truths than any whose flesh and blood they are for the time made to wear. It is like striving to make the sun, or the wind, or the sea symbols to signify exclusively the particular thoughts of our day. But what signifies it? In the mythus a superhuman intelligence uses the unconscious thoughts and dreams of men as its hieroglyphics to address men unborn. In the history of the human mind, these glowing and ruddy fables precede the noonday thoughts of men, as Aurora the sun's rays. The matutine intellect of the poet, keeping in advance of the glare of philosophy, always dwells in this auroral atmosphere.

As we said before, the Concord is a dead stream, but its scenery is the more suggestive to the contemplative voyager, and this day its water was fuller of reflections than our pages even. Just before it reaches the falls in Billerica, it is contracted, and becomes swifter and shallower, with a yellow pebbly bottom, hardly passable for a canal-boat, leaving the broader and more stagnant portion above like a lake among the hills. All through the Concord, Bedford, and Billerica meadows we had heard no murmur from its stream, except where some tributary runnel tumbled in,—

Some tumultuous little rill,
  Purling round its storied pebble,
Tinkling to the selfsame tune,
From September until June,
  Which no drought doth e'er enfeeble.

Silent flows the parent stream,
  And if rocks do lie below,
Smothers with her waves the din,
As it were a youthful sin,
  Just as still, and just as slow.

But now at length we heard this staid and primitive river rushing to her fall, like any rill. We here left its channel, just above the Billerica Falls, and entered the canal, which runs, or rather is conducted, six miles through the woods to the Merrimack, at Middlesex, and as we did not care to loiter in this part of our voyage, while one ran along the tow-path drawing the boat by a cord, the other kept it off the shore with a pole, so that we accomplished the whole distance in little more than an hour. This canal, which is the oldest in the country, and has even an antique look beside the more modern railroads, is fed by the Concord, so that we were still floating on its familiar waters. It is so much water which the river *lets* for the advantage of commerce. There appeared some want of harmony in its scenery, since it was not of equal date with the woods and meadows through which it is led, and we missed the conciliatory influence of time on land and water; but in the lapse of ages, Nature will recover and indemnify herself, and gradually plant fit shrubs and flowers along its borders. Already the kingfisher sat upon a pine over the water, and the bream and pickerel swam below. Thus all works pass directly out of the hands of the architect into the hands of Nature, to be perfected.

It was a retired and pleasant route, without houses or travellers, except some young men who were lounging upon a bridge in Chelmsford, who leaned impudently over the rails to pry into our concerns, but we caught the eye of the most forward, and looked at him till he was visibly discomfited. Not that there was any peculiar efficacy in our look, but rather a sense of shame left in him which disarmed him.

It is a very true and expressive phrase, "He looked daggers at me," for the first pattern and prototype of all daggers must have been a glance of the eye. First, there was the glance of Jove's eye, then his fiery bolt, then, the material gradually hardening, tridents, spears, javelins, and finally, for the convenience of private men, daggers, krisses, and so forth, were invented. It is wonderful how we get about the streets without being wounded by these delicate and glancing weapons, a man can so nimbly whip out his rapier, or without being noticed carry it unsheathed. Yet it is rare that one gets seriously looked at.

As we passed under the last bridge over the canal, just before reaching the Merrimack, the people coming out of church paused to look at us from above, and apparently, so strong is custom, indulged in some heathenish comparisons; but we were the truest observers of this sunny day. According to Hesiod,

> "The seventh is a holy day,
> For then Latona brought forth golden-rayed Apollo,"

and by our reckoning this was the seventh day of the week, and not the first. I find among the papers of an old Justice of the Peace and Deacon of the town of Concord, this singular memorandum, which is worth preserving as a relic of an ancient custom. After reforming the spelling and grammar, it runs as follows: "Men that travelled with teams on the Sabbath, Dec. 18th, 1803, were Jeremiah Richardson and Jonas Parker, both of Shirley. They had teams with rigging such as is used to carry barrels, and they were travelling westward. Richardson was questioned by the Hon. Ephraim Wood, Esq., and he said that Jonas Parker was his fellow-traveller, and he further said that a Mr. Longley was his employer, who promised to bear him out." We were the men that were gliding northward, this Sept. 1st, 1839, with still team, and rigging not the most convenient to carry barrels, unquestioned by any

Squire or Church Deacon and ready to bear ourselves out if need were. In the latter part of the seventeenth century, according to the historian of Dunstable, "Towns were directed to erect '*a cage*' near the meeting-house, and in this all offenders against the sanctity of the Sabbath were confined." Society has relaxed a little from its strictness, one would say, but I presume that there is not less *religion* than formerly. If the *ligature* is found to be loosened in one part, it is only drawn the tighter in another.

You can hardly convince a man of an error in a lifetime, but must content yourself with the reflection that the progress of science is slow. If he is not convinced, his grandchildren may be. The geologists tell us that it took one hundred years to prove that fossils are organic, and one hundred and fifty more, to prove that they are not to be referred to the Noachian deluge. I am not sure but I should betake myself in extremities to the liberal divinities of Greece, rather than to my country's God. Jehovah, though with us he has acquired new attributes, is more absolute and unapproachable, but hardly more divine, than Jove. He is not so much of a gentleman, not so gracious and catholic, he does not exert so intimate and genial an influence on nature, as many a god of the Greeks. I should fear the infinite power and inflexible justice of the almighty mortal, hardly as yet apotheosized, so wholly masculine, with no sister Juno, no Apollo, no Venus, nor Minerva, to intercede for me, θυμῷ φιλέουσά τε, κηδομένη τε. The Grecian are youthful and erring and fallen gods, with the vices of men, but in many important respects essentially of the divine race. In my Pantheon, Pan still reigns in his pristine glory, with his ruddy face, his flowing beard, and his shaggy body, his pipe and his crook, his nymph Echo, and his chosen daughter Iambe; for the great god Pan is not dead, as was rumored. No god ever dies. Perhaps of all the gods of New England and of ancient Greece, I am most constant at his shrine.

It seems to me that the god that is commonly worshipped in civilized countries is not at all divine, though he bears a divine name, but is the overwhelming authority and respectability of mankind combined. Men reverence one another, not yet God. If I thought that I could speak with discrimination and impartiality of the nations of Christendom, I should praise them, but it tasks me too much. They seem to be the most civil and humane, but I may be mistaken. Every people have gods to suit their circumstances; the Society Islanders had a god called Toahitu, "in shape like a dog; he saved such as were in danger of falling from rocks and trees." I think that we can do without him, as we have not much climbing to do. Among them a man could make himself a god out of a piece of wood in a few minutes, which would frighten him out of his wits.

I fancy that some indefatigable spinster of the old school, who had the supreme felicity to be born in "days that tried men's souls," hearing this, may say with Nestor, another of the old school, "But you are younger than I. For time was when I conversed with greater men than you. For not at any time have I seen such men, nor shall see them, as Perithous, and Dryas, and ποιμενα λαων," that is probably Washington, sole "Shepherd of the People." And when Apollo has now six times rolled westward, or seemed to roll, and now for the seventh time shows his face in the east, eyes wellnigh glazed, long glassed, which have fluctuated only between lamb's wool and worsted, explore ceaselessly some good sermon book. For six days shalt thou labor and do all thy knitting, but on the seventh, forsooth, thy reading. Happy we who can bask in this warm September sun, which illumines all creatures, as well when they rest as when they toil, not without a feeling of gratitude; whose life is as blameless, how blameworthy soever it may be, on the Lord's Mona-day as on his Suna-day.

There are various, nay, incredible faiths; why should we be alarmed at any of them? What man believes, God believes. Long as I have lived, and many blasphemers as I have heard and seen, I have never yet heard or witnessed any direct and conscious blasphemy or irreverence; but of indirect and habitual, enough. Where is the man who is guilty of direct and personal insolence to Him that made him?

One memorable addition to the old mythology is due to this era,—the Christian fable. With what pains, and tears, and blood these centuries have woven this and added it to the mythology of mankind. The new Prometheus. With what miraculous consent, and patience, and persistency has this mythus been stamped on the memory of the race! It would seem as if it were in the progress of our mythology to dethrone Jehovah, and crown Christ in his stead.

If it is not a tragical life we live, then I know not what to call it. Such a story as that of Jesus Christ,—the history of Jerusalem, say, being a part of the Universal History. The naked, the embalmed, unburied death of Jerusalem amid its desolate hills,—think of it. In Tasso's poem I trust some things are sweetly buried. Consider the snappish tenacity with which they preach Christianity still. What are time and space to Christianity, eighteen hundred years, and a new world?—that the humble life of a Jewish peasant should have force to make a New York bishop so bigoted. Forty-four lamps, the gift of kings, now burning in a place called the Holy Sepulchre;—a church-bell ringing;—some unaffected tears shed by a pilgrim on Mount Calvary within the week.—

"Jerusalem, Jerusalem, when I forget thee, may my right hand forget her cunning."

"By the waters of Babylon there we sat down, and we wept when we remembered Zion."

I trust that some may be as near and dear to Buddha, or Christ, or Swedenborg, who are without the pale of their churches. It is necessary not to be Christian to appreciate the beauty and significance of the life of Christ. I know that some will have hard thoughts of me, when they hear their Christ named beside my Buddha, yet I am sure that I am willing they should love their Christ more than my Buddha, for the love is the main thing, and I like him too. "God is the letter Ku, as well as Khu." Why need Christians be still intolerant and superstitious? The simple-minded sailors were unwilling to cast overboard Jonah at his own request.—

> "Where is this love become in later age?
> Alas! 't is gone in endless pilgrimage
> From hence, and never to return, I doubt,
> Till revolution wheel those times about."

One man says,—

> "The world's a popular disease, that reigns
> Within the froward heart and frantic brains
> Of poor distempered mortals."

Another, that

> "all the world's a stage,
> And all the men and women merely players."

The world is a strange place for a playhouse to stand within it. Old Drayton thought that a man that lived here, and would be a poet, for instance, should have in him certain "brave, translunary things," and a "fine madness" should possess his brain. Certainly it were as well, that he might be up to the occasion. That is a superfluous wonder, which Dr. Johnson expresses at the assertion of Sir Thomas Browne that "his life has been a miracle of thirty years, which to relate, were not history but a piece of poetry, and would sound like a fable." The wonder is, rather, that all men do not assert as much. That would be a rare praise, if it were true, which was addressed to Francis Beaumont,—"Spectators sate part in your tragedies."

Think what a mean and wretched place this world is; that half the time we have to light a lamp that we may see to live in it. This is half our life. Who would undertake the enterprise if it were all? And, pray, what more has day to offer? A lamp that burns more clear, a purer oil, say winter-strained, that so we may pursue our idleness with less obstruction. Bribed with a little sunlight and a few prismatic tints, we bless our Maker, and stave off his wrath with hymns.

> I make ye an offer,
> Ye gods, hear the scoffer,
> The scheme will not hurt you,
> If ye will find goodness, I will find virtue.
> Though I am your creature,
> And child of your nature,
> I have pride still unbended,
> And blood undescended,
> Some free independence,
> And my own descendants.
> I cannot toil blindly,

Though ye behave kindly,
And I swear by the rood,
I'll be slave to no God.
If ye will deal plainly,
I will strive mainly,
If ye will discover,
Great plans to your lover,
And give him a sphere
Somewhat larger than here.

"Verily, my angels! I was abashed on account of my servant, who had no Providence but me; therefore did I pardon him." — *The Gulistan of Sadi.*

Most people with whom I talk, men and women even of some originality and genius, have their scheme of the universe all cut and dried,—very *dry*, I assure you, to hear, dry enough to burn, dry-rotted and powder-post, methinks,—which they set up between you and them in the shortest intercourse; an ancient and tottering frame with all its boards blown off. They do not walk without their bed. Some, to me, seemingly very unimportant and unsubstantial things and relations, are for them everlastingly settled,—as Father, Son, and Holy Ghost, and the like. These are like the everlasting hills to them. But in all my wanderings I never came across the least vestige of authority for these things. They have not left so distinct a trace as the delicate flower of a remote geological period on the coal in my grate. The wisest man preaches no doctrines; he has no scheme; he sees no rafter, not even a cobweb, against the heavens. It is clear sky. If I ever see more clearly at one time than at another, the medium through which I see is clearer. To see from earth to heaven, and see there standing, still a fixture, that old Jewish scheme! What right have you to hold up this obstacle to my understanding you, to your understanding me! You did not invent it; it was imposed on you. Examine your authority. Even Christ, we fear, had his scheme, his conformity to tradition, which slightly vitiates his teaching. He had not swallowed all formulas. He preached some mere doctrines. As for me, Abraham, Isaac, and Jacob are now only the subtilest imaginable essences, which would not stain the morning sky. Your scheme must be the framework of the universe; all other schemes will soon be ruins. The perfect God in his revelations of himself has never got to the length of one such proposition as you, his prophets, state. Have you learned the alphabet of heaven and can count three? Do you know the number of God's family? Can you put mysteries into words? Do you presume to fable of the ineffable? Pray, what geographer are you, that speak of heaven's topography? Whose friend are you that speak of God's personality? Do you, Miles Howard, think that he has made you his confidant? Tell me of the height of the mountains of the moon, or of the diameter of space, and I may believe you, but of the secret history of the Almighty, and I shall pronounce thee mad. Yet we have a sort of family history of our God,—so have the Tahitians of theirs,—and some old poet's grand imagination is imposed on us as adamantine everlasting truth, and God's own word! Pythagoras says, truly enough, "A true assertion respecting God, is an assertion of God"; but we may well doubt if there is any example of this in literature.

The New Testament is an invaluable book, though I confess to having been slightly prejudiced against it in my very early days by the church and the Sabbath school, so that it seemed, before I read it, to be the yellowest book in the catalogue. Yet I early escaped from their meshes. It was hard to get the commentaries out of one's head and taste its true flavor.—I think that Pilgrim's Progress is the best sermon which has been preached from this text; almost all other sermons that I have heard, or heard of, have been but poor imitations of this.—It would be a poor story to be prejudiced against the Life of Christ because the book has been edited by Christians. In fact, I love this book rarely, though it is a sort of castle in the air to me, which I am permitted to dream. Having come to it so recently and freshly, it has the greater charm, so that I cannot find any to talk with about it. I never read a novel, they have so little real life and thought in them. The reading which I love best is the scriptures of the several nations, though it happens that I am better acquainted with those of the Hindoos, the Chinese, and the Persians, than of the Hebrews, which I have come to last. Give me one of these Bibles and you have silenced me for a while. When I recover the use of my tongue, I am wont to worry my neighbors with the new sentences; but commonly they cannot see that there is any wit in them. Such has been my experience with the New Testament. I have not yet got to the crucifixion, I have read it over so many times. I should love dearly to read it aloud to my friends, some of whom are seriously inclined; it is so good, and I am sure that they have never heard it, it fits their case exactly, and we should enjoy it so much together,— but I instinctively despair of getting their ears. They soon show, by signs not to be mistaken, that it is inexpressibly wearisome to them. I do not mean to imply that I am any better than my neighbors; for, alas! I know that I am only as good, though I love better books than they.

It is remarkable that, notwithstanding the universal favor with which the New Testament is outwardly received, and even the bigotry with which it is defended, there is no hospitality shown to, there is no appreciation of, the order of truth with which it deals. I know of no book that has so few readers. There is none so truly strange, and heretical, and un-popular. To Christians, no less than Greeks and Jews, it is foolishness and a stumbling-block. There are, indeed, severe things in it which no man should read aloud more than once.—"Seek first the kingdom of heaven."—"Lay not up for yourselves treasures on earth."—"If thou wilt be perfect, go and sell that thou hast, and give to the poor, and thou shalt have treasure in heaven."—"For what is a man profited, if he shall gain the whole world, and lose his own soul? or what shall a man give in exchange for his soul?"—Think of this, Yankees!—"Verily, I say unto you, if ye have faith as a grain of mustard seed, ye shall say unto this mountain, Re-move hence to yonder place; and it shall remove; and nothing shall be impossible unto you."—Think of repeating these things to a New England audience! thirdly, fourthly, fif-teenthly, till there are three barrels of sermons! Who, without cant, can read them aloud? Who, without cant, can hear them, and not go out of the meeting-house? They never *were* read, they never *were* heard. Let but one of these sentences be rightly read, from any pulpit in the land, and there would not be left one stone of that meeting-house upon another.

Yet the New Testament treats of man and man's so-called spiritual affairs too exclusively, and is too constantly moral and personal, to alone content me, who am not interested solely in man's religious or moral nature, or in man even. I have not the most definite designs on the future. Absolutely speaking, Do unto others as you would that they should do unto you, is by no means a golden rule, but the best of current silver. An honest man would have but little occasion for it. It is golden not to have any rule at all in such a case. The book has never been written which is to be accepted without any allowance. Christ was a sublime actor on the stage of the world. He knew what he was thinking of when he said, "Heaven and earth shall pass away, but my words shall not pass away." I draw near to him at such a time. Yet he taught mankind but imperfectly how to live; his thoughts were all directed toward another world. There is another kind of success than his. Even here we have a sort of living to get, and must buffet it somewhat longer. There are various tough problems yet to solve, and we must make shift to live, betwixt spirit and matter, such a human life as we can.

A healthy man, with steady employment, as wood-chopping at fifty cents a cord, and a camp in the woods, will not be a good subject for Christianity. The New Testament may be a choice book to him on some, but not on all or most of his days. He will rather go a-fishing in his leisure hours. The Apostles, though they were fishers too, were of the solemn race of sea-fishers, and never trolled for pickerel on inland streams.

Men have a singular desire to be good without being good for anything, because, perchance, they think vaguely that so it will be good for them in the end. The sort of morality which the priests inculcate is a very subtle policy, far finer than the politicians, and the world is very successfully ruled by them as the policemen. It is not worth the while to let our imperfections disturb us always. The conscience really does not, and ought not to monopolize the whole of our lives, any more than the heart or the head. It is as liable to disease as any other part. I

have seen some whose consciences, owing undoubtedly to former indulgence, had grown to be as irritable as spoilt children,
and at length gave them no peace. They did not know when
to swallow their cud, and their lives of course yielded no milk.

> Conscience is instinct bred in the house,
> Feeling and Thinking propagate the sin
> By an unnatural breeding in and in.
> I say, Turn it out doors,
> Into the moors.
> I love a life whose plot is simple,
> And does not thicken with every pimple,
> A soul so sound no sickly conscience binds it,
> That makes the universe no worse than 't finds it.
> I love an earnest soul,
> Whose mighty joy and sorrow
> Are not drowned in a bowl,
> And brought to life to-morrow;
> That lives one tragedy,
> And not seventy;
> A conscience worth keeping,
> Laughing not weeping;
> A conscience wise and steady,
> And forever ready;
> Not changing with events,
> Dealing in compliments;
> A conscience exercised about
> Large things, where one *may* doubt.
> I love a soul not all of wood,
> Predestinated to be good,
> But true to the backbone
> Unto itself alone,
> And false to none;
> Born to its own affairs,
> Its own joys and own cares;
> By whom the work which God begun
> Is finished, and not undone;
> Taken up where he left off,
> Whether to worship or to scoff;
> If not good, why then evil,

If not good god, good devil.
Goodness!—yon hypocrite, come out of that,
Live your life, do your work, then take your hat.
I have no patience towards
Such conscientious cowards.
Give me simple laboring folk,
Who love their work,
Whose virtue is a song
To cheer God along.

I was once reproved by a minister who was driving a poor beast to some meeting-house horse-sheds among the hills of New Hampshire, because I was bending my steps to a mountain-top on the Sabbath, instead of a church, when I would have gone farther than he to hear a true word spoken on that or any day. He declared that I was "breaking the Lord's fourth commandment," and proceeded to enumerate, in a sepulchral tone, the disasters which had befallen him whenever he had done any ordinary work on the Sabbath. He really thought that a god was on the watch to trip up those men who followed any secular work on this day, and did not see that it was the evil conscience of the workers that did it. The country is full of this superstition, so that when one enters a village, the church, not only really but from association, is the ugliest looking building in it, because it is the one in which human nature stoops the lowest and is most disgraced. Certainly, such temples as these shall erelong cease to deform the landscape. There are few things more disheartening and disgusting than when you are walking the streets of a strange village on the Sabbath, to hear a preacher shouting like a boatswain in a gale of wind, and thus harshly profaning the quiet atmosphere of the day. You fancy him to have taken off his coat, as when men are about to do hot and dirty work.

If I should ask the minister of Middlesex to let me speak in his pulpit on a Sunday, he would object, because I do not *pray* as he does, or because I am not *ordained*. What under the sun are these things?

Really, there is no infidelity, now-a-days, so great as that which prays, and keeps the Sabbath, and rebuilds the churches. The sealer of the South Pacific preaches a truer doctrine. The church is a sort of hospital for men's souls, and as full of quackery as the hospital for their bodies. Those who are taken into it live like pensioners in their Retreat or Sailor's Snug Harbor, where you may see a row of religious cripples sitting outside in sunny weather. Let not the apprehension that he may one day have to occupy a ward therein, discourage the cheerful labors of the able-souled man. While he remembers the sick in their extremities, let him not look thither as to his goal. One is sick at heart of this pagoda worship. It is like the beating of gongs in a Hindoo subterranean temple. In dark places and dungeons the preacher's words might perhaps strike root and grow, but not in broad daylight in any part of the world that I know. The sound of the Sabbath bell far away, now breaking on these shores, does not awaken pleasing associations, but melancholy and sombre ones rather. One involuntarily rests on his oar, to humor his unusually meditative mood. It is as the sound of many catechisms and religious books twanging a canting peal round the earth, seeming to issue from some Egyptian temple and echo along the shore of the Nile, right opposite to Pharaoh's palace and Moses in the bulrushes, startling a multitude of storks and alligators basking in the sun.

Everywhere "good men" sound a retreat, and the word has gone forth to fall back on innocence. Fall forward rather on to whatever there is there. Christianity only hopes. It has hung its harp on the willows, and cannot sing a song in a strange land. It has dreamed a sad dream, and does not yet welcome the morning with joy. The mother tells her falsehoods to her child, but, thank Heaven, the child does not grow up in its parent's shadow. Our mother's faith has not grown with her experience. Her experience has been too much for her. The lesson of life was too hard for her to learn.

It is remarkable, that almost all speakers and writers feel it to be incumbent on them, sooner or later, to prove or to acknowledge the personality of God. Some Earl of Bridgewater, thinking it better late than never, has provided for it in his will. It is a sad mistake. In reading a work on agriculture, we have to skip the author's moral reflections, and the words "Providence" and "He" scattered along the page, to come at the profitable level of what he has to say. What he calls his religion is for the most part offensive to the nostrils. He should know better than expose himself, and keep his foul sores covered till they are quite healed. There is more religion in men's science than there is science in their religion. Let us make haste to the report of the committee on swine.

A man's real faith is never contained in his creed, nor is his creed an article of his faith. The last is never adopted. This it is that permits him to smile ever, and to live even as bravely as he does. And yet he clings anxiously to his creed, as to a straw, thinking that that does him good service because his sheet anchor does not drag.

In most men's religion, the ligature, which should be its umbilical cord connecting them with divinity, is rather like that thread which the accomplices of Cylon held in their hands when they went abroad from the temple of Minerva, the other end being attached to the statue of the goddess. But frequently, as in their case, the thread breaks, being stretched, and they are left without an asylum.

"A good and pious man reclined his head on the bosom of contemplation, and was absorbed in the ocean of a revery. At the instant when he awaked from his vision, one of his friends, by way of pleasantry, said, What rare gift have you brought us from that garden, where you have been recreating? He replied, I fancied to myself and said, when I can reach the rose-bower, I will fill my lap with the flowers, and bring them as a present to my friends; but when I got there, the fragrance of the roses so intoxicated me, that the skirt dropped from my hands.——'O bird of dawn! learn the warmth of affection from the moth; for that scorched creature gave up the ghost, and uttered not a groan: These vain pretenders are ignorant of him they seek after; for of him that knew him we never heard again:—O thou! who towerest above the flights of conjecture, opinion, and comprehension; whatever has been reported of thee we have heard and read; the congregation is dismissed, and life drawn to a close; and we still rest at our first encomium of thee!' "—*Sadi*.

By noon we were let down into the Merrimack through the locks at Middlesex, just above Pawtucket Falls, by a serene and liberal-minded man, who came quietly from his book, though his duties, we supposed, did not require him to open the locks on Sundays. With him we had a just and equal encounter of the eyes, as between two honest men.

The movements of the eyes express the perpetual and unconscious courtesy of the parties. It is said, that a rogue does not look you in the face, neither does an honest man look at you as if he had his reputation to establish. I have seen some who did not know when to turn aside their eyes in meeting yours. A truly confident and magnanimous spirit is wiser than to contend for the mastery in such encounters. Serpents alone conquer by the steadiness of their gaze. My friend looks me in the face and sees me, that is all.

The best relations were at once established between us and this man, and though few words were spoken, he could not conceal a visible interest in us and our excursion. He was a lover of the higher mathematics, as we found, and in the midst of some vast sunny problem, when we overtook him and whispered our conjectures. By this man we were presented with the freedom of the Merrimack. We now felt as if we were fairly launched on the ocean-stream of our voyage, and were pleased to find that our boat would float on Merrimack water. We began again busily to put in practice those old arts of rowing, steering, and paddling. It seemed a strange phenomenon to us that the two rivers should mingle their waters so readily, since we had never associated them in our thoughts.

As we glided over the broad bosom of the Merrimack, between Chelmsford and Dracut, at noon, here a quarter of a mile wide, the rattling of our oars was echoed over the water to those villages, and their slight sounds to us. Their harbors lay as smooth and fairy-like as the Lido, or Syracuse, or Rhodes, in our imagination, while, like some strange roving craft, we flitted past what seemed the dwellings of noble home-staying men, seemingly as conspicuous as if on an eminence, or floating upon a tide which came up to those villagers' breasts. At a third of a mile over the water we heard distinctly some children repeating their catechism in a cottage near the shore, while in the broad shallows between, a herd of cows stood lashing their sides, and waging war with the flies.

Two hundred years ago other catechizing than this was going on here; for here came the Sachem Wannalancet, and his people, and sometimes Tahatawan, our Concord Sachem, who afterwards had a church at home, to catch fish at the falls; and here also came John Eliot, with the Bible and Catechism, and Baxter's Call to the Unconverted, and other tracts, done into the Massachusetts tongue, and taught them Christianity meanwhile. "This place," says Gookin, referring to Wamesit,

"being an ancient and capital seat of Indians, they come to fish; and this good man takes this opportunity to spread the net of the gospel, to fish for their souls."—"May 5th, 1674," he continues, "according to our usual custom, Mr. Eliot and myself took our journey to Wamesit, or Pawtuckett; and arriving there that evening, Mr. Eliot preached to as many of them as could be got together, out of Matt. xxii. 1–14, the parable of the marriage of the king's son. We met at the wigwam of one called Wannalancet, about two miles from the town, near Pawtuckett falls, and bordering upon Merrimak river. This person, Wannalancet, is the eldest son of old Pasaconaway, the chiefest sachem of Pawtuckett. He is a sober and grave person, and of years, between fifty and sixty. He hath been always loving and friendly to the English." As yet, however, they had not prevailed on him to embrace the Christian religion. "But at this time," says Gookin, "May 6, 1674,"—"after some deliberation and serious pause, he stood up, and made a speech to this effect:—'I must acknowledge I have, all my days, used to pass in an old canoe, (alluding to his frequent custom to pass in a canoe upon the river,) and now you exhort me to change and leave my old canoe, and embark in a new canoe, to which I have hitherto been unwilling; but now I yield up myself to your advice, and enter into a new canoe, and do engage to pray to God hereafter.' " One "Mr. Richard Daniel, a gentleman that lived in Billerica," who with other "persons of quality" was present, "desired brother Eliot to tell the sachem from him, that it may be, while he went in his old canoe, he passed in a quiet stream; but the end thereof was death and destruction to soul and body. But now he went into a new canoe, perhaps he would meet with storms and trials, but yet he should be encouraged to persevere, for the end of his voyage would be everlasting rest."—"Since that time, I hear this sachem doth persevere, and is a constant and diligent hearer of God's word, and sanctifieth the Sabbath, though he doth travel to Wamesit meeting every Sabbath, which is above two miles; and though sundry of his people have deserted him, since he subjected to the gospel, yet he continues and persists."— *Gookin's Hist. Coll. of the Indians in New England,* 1674.

Already, as appears from the records, "At a General Court held at Boston in New England, the 7th of the first month, 1643–4."—"Wassamequin, Nashoonon, Kutchamaquin, Massaconomet, and Squaw Sachem, did voluntarily submit themselves" to the English; and among other things did "promise to be willing from time to time to be instructed in the knowledge of God." Being asked "Not to do any unnecessary work on the Sabbath day, especially within the gates of Christian towns," they answered, "It is easy to them; they have not much to do on any day, and they can well take their rest on that day."—"So," says Winthrop, in his Journal, " we causing them to understand the articles, and all the ten commandments of God, and they freely assenting to all, they were solemnly received, and then presented the Court with twenty-six fathom more of wampom; and the Court gave each of them a coat of two yards of cloth, and their dinner; and to them and their men, every of them, a cup of sack at their departure; so they took leave and went away."

What journeyings on foot and on horseback through the wilderness, to preach the Gospel to these minks and muskrats! who first, no doubt, listened with their red ears out of a natural hospitality and courtesy, and afterward from curiosity or even interest, till at length there were "praying Indians," and, as the General Court wrote to Cromwell, the " work is brought to this perfection, that some of the Indians themselves can pray and prophesy in a comfortable manner."

It was in fact an old battle and hunting ground through

which we had been floating, the ancient dwelling-place of a race of hunters and warriors. Their weirs of stone, their arrowheads and hatchets, their pestles, and the mortars in which they pounded Indian corn before the white man had tasted it, lay concealed in the mud of the river bottom. Tradition still points out the spots where they took fish in the greatest numbers, by such arts as they possessed. It is a rapid story the historian will have to put together. Miantonimo, —Winthrop,—Webster. Soon he comes from Montaup to Bunker Hill, from bear-skins, parched corn, bows and arrows, to tiled roofs, wheat-fields, guns and swords. Pawtucket and Wamesit, where the Indians resorted in the fishing season, are now Lowell, the city of spindles and Manchester of America, which sends its cotton cloth round the globe. Even we youthful voyagers had spent a part of our lives in the village of Chelmsford, when the present city, whose bells we heard, was its obscure north district only, and the giant weaver was not yet fairly born. So old are we; so young is it.

We were thus entering the State of New Hampshire on the bosom of the flood formed by the tribute of its innumerable valleys. The river was the only key which could unlock its maze, presenting its hills and valleys, its lakes and streams, in their natural order and position. The MERRIMACK, or Sturgeon River, is formed by the confluence of the Pemigewasset, which rises near the Notch of the White Mountains, and the Winnipiseogee, which drains the lake of the same name, signifying "The Smile of the Great Spirit." From their junction it runs south seventy-eight miles to Massachusetts, and thence east thirty-five miles to the sea. I have traced its stream from where it bubbles out of the rocks of the White Mountains above the clouds, to where it is lost amid the salt billows of the ocean on Plum Island beach. At first it comes on murmuring to itself by the base of stately and retired mountains, through moist primitive woods whose juices it receives, where the bear still drinks it, and the cabins of settlers are far between, and there are few to cross its stream; enjoying in solitude its cascades still unknown to fame; by long ranges of mountains of Sandwich and of Squam, slumbering like tumuli of Titans, with the peaks of Moosehillock, the Haystack, and Kearsarge reflected in its waters; where the maple and the raspberry, those lovers of the hills, flourish amid temperate dews;—flowing long and full of meaning, but untranslatable as its name Pemigewasset, by many a pastured Pelion and Ossa, where unnamed muses haunt, tended by Oreads, Dryads, Naiads, and receiving the tribute of many an untasted Hippocrene. There are earth, air, fire, and water,—very well, this is water, and down it comes.

> Such water do the gods distil,
> And pour down every hill
>   For their New England men;
> A draught of this wild nectar bring,
> And I'll not taste the spring
>   Of Helicon again.

Falling all the way, and yet not discouraged by the lowest fall. By the law of its birth never to become stagnant, for it has come out of the clouds, and down the sides of precipices worn in the flood, through beaver-dams broke loose, not splitting but splicing and mending itself, until it found a breathing-place in this low land. There is no danger now that the sun will steal it back to heaven again before it reach the sea, for it has a warrant even to recover its own dews into its bosom again with interest at every eve.

It was already the water of Squam and Newfound Lake and Winnipiseogee, and White Mountain snow dissolved, on which we were floating, and Smith's and Baker's and Mad Rivers, and Nashua and Souhegan and Piscataquoag, and Suncook and Soucook and Contoocook, mingled in incalculable proportions, still fluid, yellowish, restless all, with an ancient, ineradicable inclination to the sea.

So it flows on down by Lowell and Haverhill, at which last place it first suffers a sea change, and a few masts betray the vicinity of the ocean. Between the towns of Amesbury and Newbury it is a broad commercial river, from a third to half a mile in width, no longer skirted with yellow and crumbling banks, but backed by high green hills and pastures, with frequent white beaches on which the fishermen draw up their nets. I have passed down this portion of the river in a steamboat, and it was a pleasant sight to watch from its deck the

fishermen dragging their seines on the distant shore, as in
pictures of a foreign strand. At intervals you may meet with
a schooner laden with lumber, standing up to Haverhill, or
else lying at anchor or aground, waiting for wind or tide;
until, at last, you glide under the famous Chain Bridge, and
are landed at Newburyport. Thus she who at first was "poore
of waters, naked of renowne," having received so many fair
tributaries, as was said of the Forth,

> "Doth grow the greater still, the further downe;
>   Till that abounding both in power and fame,
>   She long doth strive to give the sea her name";

or if not her name, in this case, at least the impulse of her
stream. From the steeples of Newburyport you may review
this river stretching far up into the country, with many a
white sail glancing over it like an inland sea, and behold, as
one wrote who was born on its head-waters, "Down out at
its mouth, the dark inky main blending with the blue above.
Plum Island, its sand ridges scolloping along the horizon like
the sea-serpent, and the distant outline broken by many a tall
ship, leaning, *still*, against the sky."

Rising at an equal height with the Connecticut, the Merrimack reaches the sea by a course only half as long, and hence
has no leisure to form broad and fertile meadows, like the
former, but is hurried along rapids, and down numerous falls,
without long delay. The banks are generally steep and high,
with a narrow interval reaching back to the hills, which is
only rarely or partially overflown at present, and is much valued by the farmers. Between Chelmsford and Concord, in
New Hampshire, it varies from twenty to seventy-five rods in
width. It is probably wider than it was formerly, in many
places, owing to the trees having been cut down, and the
consequent wasting away of its banks. The influence of the
Pawtucket Dam is felt as far up as Cromwell's Falls, and many
think that the banks are being abraded and the river filled up
again by this cause. Like all our rivers, it is liable to freshets,
and the Pemigewasset has been known to rise twenty-five feet
in a few hours. It is navigable for vessels of burden about
twenty miles; for canal-boats, by means of locks, as far as
Concord in New Hampshire, about seventy-five miles from

its mouth; and for smaller boats to Plymouth, one hundred and thirteen miles. A small steamboat once plied between Lowell and Nashua, before the railroad was built, and one now runs from Newburyport to Haverhill.

Unfitted to some extent for the purposes of commerce by the sand-bar at its mouth, see how this river was devoted from the first to the service of manufactures. Issuing from the iron region of Franconia, and flowing through still uncut forests, by inexhaustible ledges of granite, with Squam, and Winnipiseogee, and Newfound, and Massabesic Lakes for its mill-ponds, it falls over a succession of natural dams, where it has been offering its *privileges* in vain for ages, until at last the Yankee race came to *improve* them. Standing at its mouth, look up its sparkling stream to its source,—a silver cascade which falls all the way from the White Mountains to the sea,—and behold a city on each successive plateau, a busy colony of human beaver around every fall. Not to mention Newburyport and Haverhill, see Lawrence, and Lowell, and Nashua, and Manchester, and Concord, gleaming one above the other. When at length it has escaped from under the last of the factories, it has a level and unmolested passage to the sea, a mere *waste water*, as it were, bearing little with it but its fame; its pleasant course revealed by the morning fog which hangs over it, and the sails of the few small vessels which transact the commerce of Haverhill and Newburyport. But its real vessels are railroad cars, and its true and main stream, flowing by an iron channel farther south, may be traced by a long line of vapor amid the hills, which no morning wind ever disperses, to where it empties into the sea at Boston. This side is the louder murmur now. Instead of the scream of a fish-hawk scaring the fishes, is heard the whistle of the steam-engine, arousing a country to its progress.

This river too was at length discovered by the white man, "trending up into the land," he knew not how far, possibly an inlet to the South Sea. Its valley, as far as the Winnipiseogee, was first surveyed in 1652. The first settlers of Massachusetts supposed that the Connecticut, in one part of its course, ran northwest, "so near the great lake as the Indians do pass their canoes into it over land." From which lake and the "hideous swamps" about it, as they supposed, came all the beaver that was traded between Virginia and Canada,—and the Potomac was thought to come out of or from very near it. Afterward the Connecticut came so near the course of the Merrimack that, with a little pains, they expected to divert the current of the trade into the latter river, and its profits from their Dutch neighbors into their own pockets.

Unlike the Concord, the Merrimack is not a dead but a living stream, though it has less life within its waters and on its banks. It has a swift current, and, in this part of its course, a clayey bottom, almost no weeds, and comparatively few fishes. We looked down into its yellow water with the more curiosity, who were accustomed to the Nile-like blackness of the former river. Shad and alewives are taken here in their season, but salmon, though at one time more numerous than shad, are now more rare. Bass, also, are taken occasionally; but locks and dams have proved more or less destructive to the fisheries. The shad make their appearance early in May, at the same time with the blossoms of the pyrus, one of the most conspicuous early flowers, which is for this reason called the shad-blossom. An insect called the shad-fly also appears at the same time, covering the houses and fences. We are told that "their greatest run is when the apple-trees are in full blossom. The old shad return in August; the young, three or four inches long, in September. These are very fond of flies." A rather picturesque and luxurious mode of fishing was formerly practised on the Connecticut, at Bellows Falls, where a large rock divides the stream. "On the steep sides of the island rock," says Belknap, "hang several arm-chairs, fastened to ladders, and secured by a counterpoise, in which fishermen sit to catch salmon and shad with dipping nets." The remains of Indian weirs, made of large stones, are still to be seen in the Winnipiseogee, one of the head-waters of this river.

It cannot but affect our philosophy favorably to be reminded of these shoals of migratory fishes, of salmon, shad, alewives, marsh-bankers, and others, which penetrate up the innumerable rivers of our coast in the spring, even to the interior lakes, their scales gleaming in the sun; and again, of the fry which in still greater numbers wend their way downward to the sea. "And is it not pretty sport," wrote Captain John

Smith, who was on this coast as early as 1614, "to pull up twopence, sixpence, and twelvepence, as fast as you can haul and veer a line?"—"And what sport doth yield a more pleasing content, and less hurt or charge, than angling with a hook, and crossing the sweet air from isle to isle, over the silent streams of a calm sea."

On the sandy shore, opposite the Glass-house village in Chelmsford, at the Great Bend where we landed to rest us and gather a few wild plums, we discovered the *Campanula rotundifolia*, a new flower to us, the harebell of the poets, which is common to both hemispheres, growing close to the water. Here, in the shady branches of an apple-tree on the sand, we took our nooning, where there was not a zephyr to disturb the repose of this glorious Sabbath day, and we reflected serenely on the long past and successful labors of Latona.

> "So silent is the cessile air,
>   That every cry and call,
> The hills, and dales, and forest fair
>   Again repeats them all.
>
> "The herds beneath some leafy trees,
>   Amidst the flowers they lie,
> The stable ships upon the seas
>   Tend up their sails to dry."

As we thus rested in the shade, or rowed leisurely along, we had recourse, from time to time, to the Gazetteer, which was our Navigator, and from its bald natural facts extracted the pleasure of poetry. Beaver River comes in a little lower down, draining the meadows of Pelham, Windham, and Londonderry. The Scotch-Irish settlers of the latter town, according to this authority, were the first to introduce the potato into New England, as well as the manufacture of linen cloth.

Everything that is printed and bound in a book contains some echo at least of the best that is in literature. Indeed, the best books have a use, like sticks and stones, which is above or beside their design, not anticipated in the preface, nor concluded in the appendix. Even Virgil's poetry serves a very different use to me to-day from what it did to his contemporaries. It has often an acquired and accidental value merely, proving that man is still man in the world. It is pleasant to meet with such still lines as,

> "Jam læto turgent in palmite gemmæ";
> Now the buds swell on the joyful stem.

"Strata jacent passim sua quæque sub arbore poma";
The apples lie scattered everywhere, each under its tree.

In an ancient and dead language, any recognition of living nature attracts us. These are such sentences as were written while grass grew and water ran. It is no small recommendation when a book will stand the test of mere unobstructed sunshine and daylight.

What would we not give for some great poem to read now, which would be in harmony with the scenery,—for if men read aright, methinks they would never read anything but poems. No history nor philosophy can supply their place.

The wisest definition of poetry the poet will instantly prove false by setting aside its requisitions. We can, therefore, publish only our advertisement of it.

There is no doubt that the loftiest written wisdom is either rhymed, or in some way musically measured,—is, in form as well as substance, poetry; and a volume which should contain the condensed wisdom of mankind need not have one rhythmless line.

Yet poetry, though the last and finest result, is a natural fruit. As naturally as the oak bears an acorn, and the vine a gourd, man bears a poem, either spoken or done. It is the chief and most memorable success, for history is but a prose narrative of poetic deeds. What else have the Hindoos, the Persians, the Babylonians, the Egyptians done, that can be told? It is the simplest relation of phenomena, and describes the commonest sensations with more truth than science does, and the latter at a distance slowly mimics its style and methods. The poet sings how the blood flows in his veins. He performs his functions, and is so well that he needs such stimulus to sing only as plants to put forth leaves and blossoms. He would strive in vain to modulate the remote and transient music which he sometimes hears, since his song is a vital func-

tion like breathing, and an integral result like weight. It is not
the overflowing of life but its subsidence rather, and is drawn
from under the feet of the poet. It is enough if Homer but
say the sun sets. He is as serene as nature, and we can hardly
detect the enthusiasm of the bard. It is as if nature spoke. He
presents to us the simplest pictures of human life, so the child
itself can understand them, and the man must not think twice
to appreciate his naturalness. Each reader discovers for himself that, with respect to the simpler features of nature, succeeding poets have done little else than copy his similes. His
more memorable passages are as naturally bright as gleams of
sunshine in misty weather. Nature furnishes him not only
with words, but with stereotyped lines and sentences from
her mint.

"As from the clouds appears the full moon,
　All shining, and then again it goes behind the shadowy
　　clouds,
　So Hector, at one time appeared among the foremost,
　And at another in the rear, commanding; and all with brass
　He shone, like to the lightning of ægis-bearing Zeus."

　He conveys the least information, even the hour of the day,
with such magnificence and vast expense of natural imagery,
as if it were a message from the gods.

　"While it was dawn, and sacred day was advancing,
　　For that space the weapons of both flew fast, and the
　　　people fell;
　　But when now the woodcutter was preparing his
　　　morning meal,
　　In the recesses of the mountain, and had wearied his
　　　hands
　　With cutting lofty trees, and satiety came to his mind,
　　And the desire of sweet food took possession of his
　　　thoughts;
　　Then the Danaans, by their valor, broke the phalanxes,
　　Shouting to their companions from rank to rank."

　When the army of the Trojans passed the night under arms,
keeping watch lest the enemy should re-embark under cover
of the dark,

"They, thinking great things, upon the neutral ground of
    war
Sat all the night; and many fires burned for them.
As when in the heavens the stars round the bright moon
Appear beautiful, and the air is without wind;
And all the heights, and the extreme summits,
And the wooded sides of the mountains appear; and
    from the heavens an infinite ether is diffused,
And all the stars are seen; and the shepherd rejoices in
    his heart;
So between the ships and the streams of Xanthus
Appeared the fires of the Trojans before Ilium.
A thousand fires burned on the plain; and by each
Sat fifty, in the light of the blazing fire;
And horses eating white barley and corn,
Standing by the chariots, awaited fair-throned Aurora."

The "white-armed goddess Juno," sent by the Father of
gods and men for Iris and Apollo,

"Went down the Idæan mountains to far Olympus,
    As when the mind of a man, who has come over much
    earth,
Sallies forth, and he reflects with rapid thoughts,
There was I, and there, and remembers many things;
So swiftly the august Juno hastening flew through the
    air,
And came to high Olympus."

His scenery is always true, and not invented. He does not
leap in imagination from Asia to Greece, through mid air,

ἐπειὴ μάλα πολλὰ μεταξύ
Ὄυρεά τε σκιοέντα, θαλάσσα τε ἠχήεσσα.

for there are very many
Shady mountains and resounding seas between.

If his messengers repair but to the tent of Achilles, we do not
wonder how they got there, but accompany them step by step
along the shore of the resounding sea. Nestor's account of

the march of the Pylians against the Epeians is extremely life-like:—

> "Then rose up to them sweet-worded Nestor, the shrill
>   orator of the Pylians,
> And words sweeter than honey flowed from his tongue."

This time, however, he addresses Patroclus alone: "A certain river, Minyas by name, leaps seaward near to Arene, where we Pylians wait the dawn, both horse and foot. Thence with all haste we sped us on the morrow ere 't was noonday, accoutred for the fight, even to Alpheus's sacred source," &c. We fancy that we hear the subdued murmuring of the Minyas discharging its waters into the main the livelong night, and the hollow sound of the waves breaking on the shore,—until at length we are cheered at the close of a toilsome march by the gurgling fountains of Alpheus.

There are few books which are fit to be remembered in our wisest hours, but the Iliad is brightest in the serenest days, and embodies still all the sunlight that fell on Asia Minor. No modern joy or ecstasy of ours can lower its height or dim its lustre, but there it lies in the east of literature, as it were the earliest and latest production of the mind. The ruins of Egypt oppress and stifle us with their dust, foulness preserved in cassia and pitch, and swathed in linen; the death of that which never lived. But the rays of Greek poetry struggle down to us, and mingle with the sunbeams of the recent day. The statue of Memnon is cast down, but the shaft of the Iliad still meets the sun in his rising.

> "Homer is gone; and where is Jove? and where
> The rival cities seven? His song outlives
> Time, tower, and god,—all that then was, save Heaven."

So too, no doubt, Homer had his Homer, and Orpheus his Orpheus, in the dim antiquity which preceded them. The mythological system of the ancients, and it is still the mythology of the moderns, the poem of mankind, interwoven so wonderfully with their astronomy, and matching in grandeur and harmony the architecture of the heavens themselves, seems to point to a time when a mightier genius inhabited the earth. But, after all, man is the great poet, and not Homer nor Shakespeare; and our language itself, and the common arts of life, are his work. Poetry is so universally true and independent of experience, that it does not need any particular biography to illustrate it, but we refer it sooner or later to some Orpheus or Linus, and after ages to the genius of humanity and the gods themselves.

It would be worth the while to select our reading, for books are the society we keep; to read only the serenely true; never statistics, nor fiction, nor news, nor reports, nor periodicals, but only great poems, and when they failed, read them again, or perchance write more. Instead of other sacrifice, we might offer up our perfect (τελεία) thoughts to the gods daily, in hymns or psalms. For we should be at the helm at least once a day. The whole of the day should not be daytime; there should be one hour, if no more, which the day did not bring forth. Scholars are wont to sell their birthright for a mess of learning. But is it necessary to know what the speculator prints, or the thoughtless study, or the idle read, the literature of the Russians and the Chinese, or even French philosophy and much of German criticism. Read the best books first, or you may not have a chance to read them at all. "There are the worshippers with offerings, and the worshippers with mortifications; and again the worshippers with enthusiastic devotion; so there are those the wisdom of whose reading is their worship, men of subdued passions and severe manners;—This world is not for him who doth not worship; and where, O Arjoon, is there another?" Certainly, we do not need to be soothed and entertained always like children. He who resorts to the easy novel, because he is languid, does no better than if he took a nap. The front aspect of great thoughts can only be enjoyed by those who stand on the side whence they arrive. Books, not which afford us a cowering enjoyment, but in which each thought is of unusual daring; such as an idle man cannot read, and a timid one would not be entertained by, which even make us dangerous to existing institutions,—such call I good books.

All that are printed and bound are not books; they do not necessarily belong to letters, but are oftener to be ranked with the other luxuries and appendages of civilized life. Base wares are palmed off under a thousand disguises. "The way to trade," as a pedler once told me, "is to *put it right through*," no matter what it is, anything that is agreed on.

> "You grov'ling worldlings, you whose wisdom trades
>   Where light ne'er shot his golden ray."

By dint of able writing and pen-craft, books are cunningly compiled, and have their run and success even among the learned, as if they were the result of a new man's thinking, and their birth were attended with some natural throes. But in a little while their covers fall off, for no binding will avail, and it appears that they are not Books or Bibles at all. There are new and patented inventions in this shape, purporting to be for the elevation of the race, which many a pure scholar and genius who has learned to read is for a moment deceived by, and finds himself reading a horse-rake, or spinning-jenny, or wooden nutmeg, or oak-leaf cigar, or steam-power press, or kitchen range, perchance, when he was seeking serene and biblical truths.

> "Merchants, arise,
> And mingle conscience with your merchandise."

Paper is cheap, and authors need not now erase one book before they write another. Instead of cultivating the earth for wheat and potatoes, they cultivate literature, and fill a place in the Republic of Letters. Or they would fain write for fame merely, as others actually raise crops of grain to be distilled into brandy. Books are for the most part wilfully and hastily written, as parts of a system, to supply a want real or imagined. Books of natural history aim commonly to be hasty schedules, or inventories of God's property, by some clerk. They do not in the least teach the divine view of nature, but the popular view, or rather the popular method of studying nature, and make haste to conduct the persevering pupil only into that dilemma where the professors always dwell.

> "To Athens gowned he goes, and from that school
>   Returns unsped, a more instructed fool."

They teach the elements really of ignorance, not of knowledge, for, to speak deliberately and in view of the highest truths, it is not easy to distinguish elementary knowledge. There is a chasm between knowledge and ignorance which the arches of science can never span. A book should contain pure discoveries, glimpses of *terra firma*, though by ship-wrecked mariners, and not the art of navigation by those who have never been out of sight of land. *They* must not yield wheat and potatoes, but must themselves be the unconstrained and natural harvest of their author's lives.

> "What I have learned is mine; I've had my thought,
> And me the Muses noble truths have taught."

We do not learn much from learned books, but from true, sincere, human books, from frank and honest biographies. The life of a good man will hardly improve us more than the life of a freebooter, for the inevitable laws appear as plainly in the infringement as in the observance, and our lives are sustained by a nearly equal expense of virtue of some kind. The decaying tree, while yet it lives, demands sun, wind, and rain no less than the green one. It secretes sap and performs the functions of health. If we choose, we may study the alburnum only. The gnarled stump has as tender a bud as the sapling.

At least let us have healthy books, a stout horse-rake or a kitchen range which is not cracked. Let not the poet shed tears only for the public weal. He should be as vigorous as a sugar-maple, with sap enough to maintain his own verdure, beside what runs into the troughs, and not like a vine, which being cut in the spring bears no fruit, but bleeds to death in the endeavor to heal its wounds. The poet is he that hath fat enough, like bears and marmots, to suck his claws all winter. He hibernates in this world, and feeds on his own marrow. We love to think in winter, as we walk over the snowy pastures, of those happy dreamers that lie under the sod, of dormice and all that race of dormant creatures, which have such a superfluity of life enveloped in thick folds of fur, impervious to cold. Alas, the poet too is, in one sense, a sort of dormouse gone into winter quarters of deep and serene thoughts, insensible to surrounding circumstances; his words are the relation of his oldest and finest memory, a wisdom drawn from the remotest experience. Other men lead a starved existence, meanwhile, like hawks, that would fain keep on the wing, and trust to pick up a sparrow now and then.

There are already essays and poems, the growth of this land, which are not in vain, all which, however, we could conveniently have stowed in the till of our chest. If the gods permitted their own inspiration to be breathed in vain, these might be overlooked in the crowd, but the accents of truth are as sure to be heard at last on earth as in heaven. They already seem ancient, and in some measure have lost the traces of their modern birth. Here are they who

> "ask for that which is our whole life's light,
> For the perpetual, true, and clear insight."

I remember a few sentences which spring like the sward in its native pasture, where its roots were never disturbed, and not as if spread over a sandy embankment; answering to the poet's prayer,

> "Let us set so just
> A rate on knowledge, that the world may trust
> The poet's sentence, and not still aver
> Each art is to itself a flatterer."

But, above all, in our native port, did we not frequent the peaceful games of the Lyceum, from which a new era will be dated to New England, as from the games of Greece. For if Herodotus carried his history to Olympia to read, after the cestus and the race, have we not heard such histories recited there, which since our countrymen have read, as made Greece sometimes to be forgotten?—Philosophy, too, has there her grove and portico, not wholly unfrequented in these days.

Lately the victor, whom all Pindars praised, has won another palm, contending with

> "Olympian bards who sung
> Divine ideas below,
> Which always find us young,
> And always keep us so."

What earth or sea, mountain or stream, or Muses' spring or grove, is safe from his all-searching ardent eye, who drives off

Phœbus' beaten track, visits unwonted zones, makes the gelid Hyperboreans glow, and the old polar serpent writhe, and many a Nile flow back and hide his head!

> That Phaeton of our day,
> Who'd make another milky way,
> And burn the world up with his ray;
>
> By us an undisputed seer,—
> Who'd drive his flaming car so near
> Unto our shuddering mortal sphere,
>
> Disgracing all our slender worth,
> And scorching up the living earth,
> To prove his heavenly birth.
>
> The silver spokes, the golden tire,
> Are glowing with unwonted fire,
> And ever nigher roll and nigher;
>
> The pins and axle melted are,
> The silver radii fly afar,
> Ah, he will spoil his Father's car!
>
> Who let him have the steeds he cannot steer?
> Henceforth the sun will not shine for a year;
> And we shall Ethiops all appear.

From *his*

> "lips of cunning fell
> The thrilling Delphic oracle."

And yet, sometimes,

> We should not mind if on our ear there fell
> Some less of cunning, more of oracle.

It is Apollo shining in your face. O rare Contemporary, let us have far-off heats. Give us the subtler, the heavenlier though fleeting beauty, which passes through and through, and dwells not in the verse; even pure water, which but reflects those tints which wine wears in its grain. Let epic trade-winds blow, and cease this waltz of inspirations. Let us oftener feel even the gentle southwest wind upon our cheeks blowing from the Indian's heaven. What though we lose a thousand meteors from the sky, if skyey depths, if star-dust and undissolvable nebulæ remain? What though we lose a thousand wise responses of the oracle, if we may have instead some natural acres of Ionian earth?

Though we know well,

"That 't is not in the power of kings [or presidents] to raise
   A spirit for verse that is not born thereto,
   Nor are they born in every prince's days";

yet spite of all they sang in praise of their "Eliza's reign," we have evidence that poets may be born and sing in *our* day, in the presidency of James K. Polk,

   "And that the utmost powers of English rhyme,"
   Were not " within *her* peaceful reign confined."

The prophecy of the poet Daniel is already how much more than fulfilled!

   "And who in time knows whither we may vent
   The treasure of our tongue? To what strange shores
   This gain of our best glory shall be sent,
   T' enrich unknowing nations with our stores?
   What worlds in th' yet unformed occident,
   May come refined with the accents that are ours."

Enough has been said in these days of the charm of fluent writing. We hear it complained of some works of genius, that they have fine thoughts, but are irregular and have no flow. But even the mountain peaks in the horizon are, to the eye of science, parts of one range. We should consider that the flow of thought is more like a tidal wave than a prone river, and is the result of a celestial influence, not of any declivity in its channel. The river flows because it runs down hill, and flows the faster the faster it descends. The reader who expects to float down stream for the whole voyage, may well complain of nauseating swells and choppings of the sea when his frail shore-craft gets amidst the billows of the ocean stream, which flows as much to sun and moon as lesser streams to it. But if we would appreciate the flow that is in these books, we must expect to feel it rise from the page like an exhalation, and wash away our critical brains like burr millstones, flowing to higher levels above and behind ourselves. There is many a book which ripples on like a freshet, and flows as glibly as a mill-stream sucking under a causeway; and when their authors are in the full tide of their discourse, Pythagoras and Plato and Jamblichus halt beside them. Their long, stringy, slimy sentences are of that consistency that they naturally flow and run together. They read as if written for military men, for men of business, there is such a despatch in them. Compared with these, the grave thinkers and philosophers seem not to have got their swaddling-clothes off; they are slower than a Roman army in its march, the rear camping to-night where the van camped last night. The wise Jamblichus eddies and gleams like a watery slough.

> "How many thousands never heard the name
>   Of Sidney, or of Spenser, or their books?
> And yet brave fellows, and presume of fame,
>   And seem to bear down all the world with looks."

The ready writer seizes the pen, and shouts, Forward! Alamo and Fanning! and after rolls the tide of war. The very walls and fences seem to travel. But the most rapid trot is no flow after all; and thither, reader, you and I, at least, will not follow.

A perfectly healthy sentence, it is true, is extremely rare. For the most part we miss the hue and fragrance of the thought; as if we could be satisfied with the dews of the morning or evening without their colors, or the heavens without their azure. The most attractive sentences are, perhaps, not the wisest, but the surest and roundest. They are spoken firmly and conclusively, as if the speaker had a right to know what he says, and if not wise, they have at least been well learned. Sir Walter Raleigh might well be studied if only for the excellence of his style, for he is remarkable in the midst of so many masters. There is a natural emphasis in his style, like a man's tread, and a breathing space between the sentences, which the best of modern writing does not furnish. His chapters are like English parks, or say rather like a Western forest, where the larger growth keeps down the underwood, and one may ride on horseback through the openings. All the distinguished writers of that period possess a greater vigor and naturalness than the more modern,—for it is allowed to slander our own time,—and when we read a quotation from one of them in the midst of a modern author, we seem to have come suddenly upon a greener ground, a greater depth and strength of soil. It is as if a green bough were laid across the page, and we are refreshed as by the sight of fresh grass in midwinter or early spring. You have constantly the warrant of life and experience in what you read. The little that is said is eked out by implication of the much that was done. The sentences are verdurous and blooming as evergreen and flowers, because they are rooted in fact and experience, but our false and florid sentences have only the tints of flowers without their sap or roots. All men are really most attracted by the beauty of plain speech, and they even write in a florid style in imitation of this. They prefer to be misunderstood rather than to come short of its exuberance. Hussein Effendi praised the epistolary style of Ibrahim Pasha to the French traveller Botta, because of "the difficulty of understanding it; there was," he said, "but one person at Jidda, who was capable of understanding and explaining the Pasha's correspondence." A man's whole life is taxed for the least thing well done. It is its net result. Every sentence is the result of a long probation. Where shall we look for standard English, but to the words of a standard man? The word which is best said came nearest to not being spoken at all, for it is cousin to a deed which the speaker could have better done. Nay, almost it must have taken the place of a deed by some urgent necessity, even by some misfortune, so that the truest writer will be some captive knight, after all. And perhaps the fates had such a design, when, having stored Raleigh so richly with the substance of life and experience, they made him a fast prisoner, and compelled him to make his words his deeds, and transfer to his expression the emphasis and sincerity of his action.

Men have a respect for scholarship and learning greatly out of proportion to the use they commonly serve. We are amused to read how Ben Jonson engaged, that the dull masks with which the royal family and nobility were to be enter-

tained should be "grounded upon antiquity and solid learning." Can there be any greater reproach than an idle learning?
Learn to split wood, at least. The necessity of labor and conversation with many men and things, to the scholar is rarely
well remembered; steady labor with the hands, which en-
grosses the attention also, is unquestionably the best method
of removing palaver and sentimentality out of one's style,
both of speaking and writing. If he has worked hard from
morning till night, though he may have grieved that he could
not be watching the train of his thoughts during that time,
yet the few hasty lines which at evening record his day's experience will be more musical and true than his freest but idle
fancy could have furnished. Surely the writer is to address a
world of laborers, and such therefore must be his own discipline. He will not idly dance at his work who has wood to
cut and cord before nightfall in the short days of winter; but
every stroke will be husbanded, and ring soberly through the
wood; and so will the strokes of that scholar's pen, which at
evening record the story of the day, ring soberly, yet cheerily,
on the ear of the reader, long after the echoes of his axe have
died away. The scholar may be sure that he writes the tougher
truth for the calluses on his palms. They give firmness to the
sentence. Indeed, the mind never makes a great and successful
effort, without a corresponding energy of the body. We are
often struck by the force and precision of style to which hard-
working men, unpractised in writing, easily attain when required to make the effort. As if plainness, and vigor, and sincerity, the ornaments of style, were better learned on the farm
and in the workshop, than in the schools. The sentences written by such rude hands are nervous and tough, like hardened
thongs, the sinews of the deer, or the roots of the pine. As
for the graces of expression, a great thought is never found in
a mean dress; but though it proceed from the lips of the Wol-
offs, the nine Muses and the three Graces will have conspired
to clothe it in fit phrase. Its education has always been liberal,
and its implied wit can endow a college. The world, which
the Greeks called Beauty, has been made such by being gradually divested of every ornament which was not fitted to endure. The Sibyl, "speaking with inspired mouth, smileless,
inornate, and unperfumed, pierces through centuries by the

power of the god." The scholar might frequently emulate the propriety and emphasis of the farmer's call to his team, and confess that if that were written it would surpass his labored sentences. Whose are the truly *labored* sentences? From the weak and flimsy periods of the politician and literary man, we are glad to turn even to the description of work, the simple record of the month's labor in the farmer's almanac, to restore our tone and spirits. A sentence should read as if its author, had he held a plough instead of a pen, could have drawn a furrow deep and straight to the end. The scholar requires hard and serious labor to give an impetus to his thought. He will learn to grasp the pen firmly so, and wield it gracefully and effectively, as an axe or a sword. When we consider the weak and nerveless periods of some literary men, who perchance in feet and inches come up to the standard of their race, and are not deficient in girth also, we are amazed at the immense sacrifice of thews and sinews. What! these proportions,—these bones,—and this their work! Hands which could have felled an ox have hewed this fragile matter which would not have tasked a lady's fingers! Can this be a stalwart man's work, who has a marrow in his back and a tendon Achilles in his heel? They who set up the blocks of Stonehenge did somewhat, if they only laid out their strength for once, and stretched themselves.

Yet, after all, the truly efficient laborer will not crowd his day with work, but will saunter to his task surrounded by a wide halo of ease and leisure, and then do but what he loves best. He is anxious only about the fruitful kernels of time. Though the hen should sit all day, she could lay only one egg, and, besides, would not have picked up materials for another. Let a man take time enough for the most trivial deed, though it be but the paring of his nails. The buds swell imperceptibly, without hurry or confusion, as if the short spring days were an eternity.

> Then spend an age in whetting thy desire,
> Thou needs't not *hasten* if thou dost *stand fast*.

Some hours seem not to be occasion for any deed, but for resolves to draw breath in. We do not directly go about the execution of the purpose that thrills us, but shut our doors behind us and ramble with prepared mind, as if the half were already done. Our resolution is taking root or hold on the earth then, as seeds first send a shoot downward which is fed by their own albumen, ere they send one upward to the light.

There is a sort of homely truth and naturalness in some books which is very rare to find, and yet looks cheap enough. There may be nothing lofty in the sentiment, or fine in the expression, but it is careless country talk. Homeliness is almost as great a merit in a book as in a house, if the reader would abide there. It is next to beauty, and a very high art. Some have this merit only. The scholar is not apt to make his most familiar experience come gracefully to the aid of his expression. Very few men can speak of Nature, for instance, with any truth. They overstep her modesty, somehow or other, and confer no favor. They do not speak a good word for her. Most cry better than they speak, and you can get more nature out of them by pinching than by addressing them. The surliness with which the woodchopper speaks of his woods, handling them as indifferently as his axe, is better than the mealy-mouthed enthusiasm of the lover of nature. Better that the primrose by the river's brim be a yellow primrose, and nothing more, than that it be something less. Aubrey relates of Thomas Fuller that his was "a very working head, insomuch that, walking and meditating before dinner, he would eat up a penny loaf, not knowing that he did it. His natural memory was very great, to which he added the art of memory. He would repeat to you forwards and backwards all the signs from Ludgate to Charing Cross." He says of Mr. John Hales, that, "He loved Canarie," and was buried "under an altar monument of black marble —— —— with a too long epitaph"; of Edmund Halley, that he "at sixteen could make a dial, and then, he said, he thought himself a brave fellow"; of William Holder, who wrote a book upon his curing one Popham who was deaf and dumb, "he was beholding to no author; did only consult with nature." For the most part, an author consults only with all who have written before him upon a subject, and his book is but the advice of so many. But a good book will never have been forestalled, but the topic itself will in one sense be new, and its author, by consulting with nature, will consult not only with those who have gone before, but with those who may come after. There is always room and occasion enough for a true book on any subject; as there is room for more light the brightest day and more rays will not interfere with the first.

We thus worked our way up this river, gradually adjusting our thoughts to novelties, beholding from its placid bosom a new nature and new works of men, and, as it were with increasing confidence, finding nature still habitable, genial, and propitious to us; not following any beaten path, but the windings of the river, as ever the nearest way for us. Fortunately we had no business in this country. The Concord had rarely been a river, or *rivus*, but barely *fluvius*, or between *fluvius* and *lacus*. This Merrimack was neither *rivus* nor *fluvius* nor *lacus*, but rather *amnis* here, a gently swelling and stately rolling flood approaching the sea. We could even sympathize with its buoyant tide, going to seek its fortune in the ocean, and, anticipating the time when "being received within the plain of its freer water," it should "beat the shores for banks,"—

"campoque recepta
Liberioris aquæ, pro ripis litora pulsant."

At length we doubled a low shrubby islet, called Rabbit Island, subjected alternately to the sun and to the waves, as desolate as if it lay some leagues within the icy sea, and found ourselves in a narrower part of the river, near the sheds and yards for picking the stone known as the Chelmsford granite, which is quarried in Westford and the neighboring towns. We passed Wicasuck Island, which contains seventy acres or more, on our right, between Chelmsford and Tyngsborough. This was a favorite residence of the Indians. According to the History of Dunstable, "About 1663, the eldest son of Passaconaway [Chief of the Penacooks] was thrown into jail for a debt of £45, due to John Tinker, by one of his tribe, and which he had promised verbally should be paid. To relieve him from his imprisonment, his brother Wannalancet and others, who owned Wicasuck Island, sold it and paid the debt." It was, however, restored to the Indians by the General

Court in 1665. After the departure of the Indians in 1683, it was granted to Jonathan Tyng in payment for his services to the colony, in maintaining a garrison at his house. Tyng's house stood not far from Wicasuck Falls. Gookin, who, in his Epistle Dedicatory to Robert Boyle, apologizes for presenting his "matter clothed in a wilderness dress," says that on the breaking out of Philip's war in 1675, there were taken up by the Christian Indians and the English in Marlborough, and sent to Cambridge, seven "Indians belonging to Narragansett, Long Island, and Pequod, who had all been at work about seven weeks with one Mr. Jonathan Tyng, of Dunstable, upon Merrimack River; and, hearing of the war, they reckoned with their master, and getting their wages, conveyed themselves away without his privity, and, being afraid, marched secretly through the woods, designing to go to their own country." However, they were released soon after. Such were the hired men in those days. Tyng was the first permanent settler of Dunstable, which then embraced what is now Tyngsborough and many other towns. In the winter of 1675, in Philip's war, every other settler left the town, but "he," says the historian of Dunstable, "fortified his house; and, although 'obliged to send to Boston for his food,' sat himself down in the midst of his savage enemies, alone, in the wilderness, to defend his home. Deeming his position an important one for the defence of the frontiers, in February, 1676, he petitioned the Colony for aid," humbly showing, as his petition runs, that, as he lived "in the uppermost house on Merrimac river, lying open to yᵉ enemy, yet being so seated that it is, as it were, a watch-house to the neighboring towns," he could render important service to his country if only he had some assistance, "there being," he said, "never an inhabitant left in the town but myself." Wherefore he requests that their "Honors would be pleased to order him *three or four men* to help garrison his said house," which they did. But methinks that such a garrison would be weakened by the addition of a man.

> "Make bandog thy scout watch to bark at a thief,
> Make courage for life, to be captain chief;
> Make trap-door thy bulwark, make bell to begin,
> Make gunstone and arrow show who is within."

Thus he earned the title of first permanent settler. In 1694 a law was passed "that every settler who deserted a town for fear of the Indians should forfeit all his rights therein." But now, at any rate, as I have frequently observed, a man may desert the fertile frontier territories of truth and justice, which are the State's best lands, for fear of far more insignificant foes, without forfeiting any of his civil rights therein. Nay, townships are granted to deserters, and the General Court, as I am sometimes inclined to regard it, is but a deserters' camp itself.

As we rowed along near the shore of Wicasuck Island, which was then covered with wood, in order to avoid the current, two men, who looked as if they had just run out of Lowell, where they had been waylaid by the Sabbath, meaning to go to Nashua, and who now found themselves in the strange, natural, uncultivated, and unsettled part of the globe which intervenes, full of walls and barriers, a rough and un-civil place to them, seeing our boat moving so smoothly up the stream, called out from the high bank above our heads to know if we would take them as passengers, as if this were the street they had missed; that they might sit and chat and drive away the time, and so at last find themselves in Nashua. This smooth way they much preferred. But our boat was crowded with necessary furniture, and sunk low in the water, and moreover required to be worked, for even *it* did not progress against the stream without effort; so we were obliged to deny them passage. As we glided away with even sweeps, while the fates scattered oil in our course, the sun now sinking behind the alders on the distant shore, we could still see them far off over the water, running along the shore and climbing over the rocks and fallen trees like insects,—for they did not know any better than we that they were on an island,—the unsym-pathizing river ever flowing in an opposite direction; until, having reached the entrance of the island brook, which they had probably crossed upon the locks below, they found a more effectual barrier to their progress. They seemed to be learning much in a little time. They ran about like ants on a burning brand, and once more they tried the river here, and once more there, to see if water still indeed was not to be walked on, as if a new thought inspired them, and by some peculiar disposition of the limbs they could accomplish it. At length sober common sense seemed to have resumed its sway, and they concluded that what they had so long heard must be true, and resolved to ford the shallower stream. When nearly a mile distant we could see them stripping off their clothes and preparing for this experiment; yet it seemed likely that a new dilemma would arise, they were so thoughtlessly throwing away their clothes on the wrong side of the stream, as in the case of the countryman with his corn, his fox, and his goose, which had to be transported one at a time. Whether they got safely through, or went round by the locks, we never learned. We could not help being struck by the seeming, though innocent indifference of Nature to these men's necessities, while elsewhere she was equally serving others. Like a true benefactress, the secret of her service is unchangeableness. Thus is the busiest merchant, though within sight of his Lowell, put to pilgrim's shifts, and soon comes to staff and scrip and scallop shell.

We, too, who held the middle of the stream, came near experiencing a pilgrim's fate, being tempted to pursue what seemed a sturgeon or larger fish, for we remembered that this was the Sturgeon River, its dark and monstrous back alternately rising and sinking in mid-stream. We kept falling behind, but the fish kept his back well out, and did not dive, and seemed to prefer to swim against the stream, so, at any rate, he would not escape us by going out to sea. At length, having got as near as was convenient, and looking out not to get a blow from his tail, now the bow-gunner delivered his charge, while the stern-man held his ground. But the halibut-skinned monster, in one of these swift-gliding pregnant moments, without ever ceasing his bobbing up and down, saw fit, without a chuckle or other prelude, to proclaim himself a huge imprisoned spar, placed there as a buoy, to warn sailors of sunken rocks. So, each casting some blame upon the other, we withdrew quickly to safer waters.

The Scene-shifter saw fit here to close the drama, of this day, without regard to any unities which we mortals prize. Whether it might have proved tragedy, or comedy, or tragi-comedy, or pastoral, we cannot tell. This Sunday ended by the going down of the sun, leaving us still on the waves. But

they who are on the water enjoy a longer and brighter twilight than they who are on the land, for here the water, as
well as the atmosphere, absorbs and reflects the light, and
some of the day seems to have sunk down into the waves.
The light gradually forsook the deep water, as well as the
deeper air, and the gloaming came to the fishes as well as to
us, and more dim and gloomy to them, whose day is a perpetual twilight, though sufficiently bright for their weak and
watery eyes. Vespers had already rung in many a dim and
watery chapel down below, where the shadows of the weeds
were extended in length over the sandy floor. The vespertinal
pout had already begun to flit on leathern fin, and the finny
gossips withdrew from the fluvial street to creeks and coves,
and other private haunts, excepting a few of stronger fin,
which anchored in the stream, stemming the tide even in their
dreams. Meanwhile, like a dark evening cloud, we were
wafted over the cope of their sky, deepening the shadows on
their deluged fields.

Having reached a retired part of the river where it spread
out to sixty rods in width, we pitched our tent on the east
side, in Tyngsborough, just above some patches of the beach
plum, which was now nearly ripe, where the sloping bank
was a sufficient pillow, and with the bustle of sailors making
the land, we transferred such stores as were required from
boat to tent, and hung a lantern to the tent-pole, and so our
house was ready. With a buffalo spread on the grass, and a
blanket for our covering our bed was soon made. A fire crack-
led merrily before the entrance, so near that we could tend it
without stepping abroad, and when we had supped, we put
out the blaze, and closed the door, and with the semblance of
domestic comfort, sat up to read the Gazetteer, to learn our
latitude and longitude, and write the journal of the voyage,
or listened to the wind and the rippling of the river till sleep
overtook us. There we lay under an oak on the bank of the
stream, near to some farmer's cornfield, getting sleep, and
forgetting where we were; a great blessing, that we are
obliged to forget our enterprises every twelve hours. Minks,
muskrats, meadow-mice, woodchucks, squirrels, skunks, rabbits, foxes, and weasels, all inhabit near, but keep very close
while you are there. The river sucking and eddying away all

night down toward the marts and the seaboard, a great wash and freshet, and no small enterprise to reflect on. Instead of the Scythian vastness of the Billerica night, and its wild musical sounds, we were kept awake by the boisterous sport of some Irish laborers on the railroad, wafted to us over the water, still unwearied and unresting on this seventh day, who would not have done with whirling up and down the track with ever increasing velocity and still reviving shouts, till late in the night.

One sailor was visited in his dreams this night by the Evil Destinies, and all those powers that are hostile to human life, which constrain and oppress the minds of men, and make their path seem difficult and narrow, and beset with dangers, so that the most innocent and worthy enterprises appear insolent and a tempting of fate, and the gods go not with us. But the other happily passed a serene and even ambrosial or immortal night, and his sleep was dreamless, or only the atmosphere of pleasant dreams remained, a happy natural sleep until the morning; and his cheerful spirit soothed and reassured his brother, for whenever they meet, the Good Genius is sure to prevail.

Monday

"I thynke for to touche also
The worlde whiche neweth everie daie,
So as I can, so as I maie."

GOWER.

"The hye sheryfe of Notynghame,
Hym holde in your mynde."

Robin Hood Ballads.

"His shoote it was but loosely shott,
Yet flewe not the arrowe in vaine,
For it mett one of the sheriffe's men,
And William a Trent was slaine."

Robin Hood Ballads.

"Gazed on the Heavens for what he missed on Earth."

Britania's Pastorals.

WHEN THE FIRST light dawned on the earth, and the birds awoke, and the brave river was heard rippling confidently seaward, and the nimble early rising wind rustled the oak leaves about our tent, all men, having reinforced their bodies and their souls with sleep, and cast aside doubt and fear, were invited to unattempted adventures.

"All courageous knichtis
Agains the day dichtis
The breest-plate that bricht is,
    To feght with their foue.
The stoned steed stampis
Throw curage and crampis,
Syne on the land lampis;
    The night is neir gone."

One of us took the boat over to the opposite shore, which was flat and accessible, a quarter of a mile distant, to empty it of water and wash out the clay, while the other kindled a fire and got breakfast ready. At an early hour we were again on our way, rowing through the fog as before, the river already awake, and a million crisped waves come forth to meet the sun when he should show himself. The countrymen, re-

cruited by their day of rest, were already stirring, and had
begun to cross the ferry on the business of the week. This
ferry was as busy as a beaver dam, and all the world seemed
anxious to get across the Merrimack River at this particular
point, waiting to get set over,—children with their two cents
done up in paper, jail-birds broke loose and constable with
warrant, travellers from distant lands to distant lands, men
and women to whom the Merrimack River was a bar. There
stands a gig in the gray morning, in the mist, the impatient
traveller pacing the wet shore with whip in hand, and shouting through the fog after the regardless Charon and his retreating ark, as if he might throw that passenger overboard
and return forthwith for himself; he will compensate him. He
is to break his fast at some unseen place on the opposite side.
It may be Ledyard or the Wandering Jew. Whence, pray, did
he come out of the foggy night? and whither through the
sunny day will he go? We observe only his transit; important
to us, forgotten by him, transiting all day. There are two of
them. May be, they are Virgil and Dante. But when they
crossed the Styx, none were seen bound up or down the
stream, that I remember. It is only a *transjectus*, a transitory
voyage, like life itself, none but the long-lived gods bound up
or down the stream. Many of these Monday men are ministers, no doubt, reseeking their parishes with hired horses,
with sermons in their valises all read and gutted, the day after
never with them. They cross each other's routes all the country over like woof and warp, making a garment of loose texture; vacation now for six days. They stop to pick nuts and
berries, and gather apples by the wayside at their leisure.
Good religious men, with the love of men in their hearts, and
the means to pay their toll in their pockets. We got over this
ferry chain without scraping, rowing athwart the tide of
travel,—no toll for us that day.

The fog dispersed and we rowed leisurely along through
Tyngsborough, with a clear sky and a mild atmosphere, leaving the habitations of men behind and penetrating yet farther
into the territory of ancient Dunstable. It was from Dunstable, then a frontier town, that the famous Captain Lovewell,
with his company, marched in quest of the Indians on the
18th of April, 1725. He was the son of "an ensign in the army

of Oliver Cromwell, who came to this country, and settled at Dunstable, where he died at the great age of one hundred and twenty years." In the words of the old nursery tale, sung about a hundred years ago, —

"He and his valiant soldiers did range the woods full wide,
    And hardships they endured to quell the Indian's pride."

In the shaggy pine forest of Pequawket they met the "rebel Indians," and prevailed, after a bloody fight, and a remnant returned home to enjoy the fame of their victory. A township called Lovewell's Town, but now, for some reason, or perhaps without reason, Pembroke, was granted them by the State.

"Of all our valiant English, there were but thirty-four,
  And of the rebel Indians, there were about four-score;
  And sixteen of our English did safely home return,
  The rest were killed and wounded, for which we all must
      mourn.

"Our worthy Capt. Lovewell among them there did die,
  They killed Lieut. Robbins, and wounded good young Frye,
  Who was our English Chaplin; he many Indians slew,
  And some of them he scalped while bullets round him flew."

Our brave forefathers have exterminated all the Indians, and their degenerate children no longer dwell in garrisoned houses nor hear any war-whoop in their path. It would be well, perchance, if many an "English Chaplin" in these days could exhibit as unquestionable trophies of his valor as did "good young Frye." We have need to be as sturdy pioneers still as Miles Standish, or Church, or Lovewell. We are to follow on another trail, it is true, but one as convenient for ambushes. What if the Indians are exterminated, are not savages as grim prowling about the clearings to-day? —

"And braving many dangers and hardships in the way,
    They safe arrived at Dunstable the thirteenth (?) day of
    May."

But they did not all "safe arrive in Dunstable the thirteenth," or the fifteenth, or the thirtieth "day of May." Eleazer Davis and Josiah Jones, both of Concord, for our native

town had seven men in this fight, Lieutenant Farwell, of
Dunstable, and Jonathan Frye, of Andover, who were all
wounded, were left behind, creeping toward the settlements.
"After travelling several miles, Frye was left and lost," though
a more recent poet has assigned him company in his last
hours.

> "A man he was of comely form,
> > Polished and brave, well learned and kind;
> Old Harvard's learned halls he left
> > Far in the wilds a grave to find.

> "Ah! now his blood-red arm he lifts;
> > His closing lids he tries to raise;
> And speak once more before he dies,
> > In supplication and in praise.

> "He prays kind Heaven to grant success,
> > Brave Lovewell's men to guide and bless,
> And when they 've shed their heart-blood true,
> > To raise them all to happiness."

>   *   *   *   *   *

> "Lieutenant Farwell took his hand,
> > His arm around his neck he threw,
> And said, 'Brave Chaplain, I could wish
> > That Heaven had made me die for you.' "

>   *   *   *   *   *

    Farwell held out eleven days. "A tradition says," as we learn
from the History of Concord, "that arriving at a pond with
Lieut. Farwell, Davis pulled off one of his moccasins, cut it
in strings, on which he fastened a hook, caught some fish,
fried and ate them. They refreshed him, but were injurious to
Farwell, who died soon after." Davis had a ball lodged in his
body, and his right hand shot off; but on the whole, he seems
to have been less damaged than his companion. He came into
Berwick after being out fourteen days. Jones also had a ball
lodged in his body, but he likewise got into Saco after fourteen days, though not in the best condition imaginable. "He

had subsisted," says an old journal, "on the spontaneous vegetables of the forest; and cranberries which he had eaten came
out of wounds he had received in his body." This was also
the case with Davis. The last two reached home at length, safe
if not sound, and lived many years in a crippled state to enjoy
their pension.

But alas! of the crippled Indians, and their adventures in
the woods,—

> "For as we are informed, so thick and fast they fell,
>   Scarce twenty of their number at night did get home
>   well,"—

how many balls lodged with them, how fared their cranberries, what Berwick or Saco they got into, and finally what
pension or township was granted them, there is no journal to
tell.

It is stated in the History of Dunstable, that just before his
last march, Lovewell was warned to beware of the ambus-
cades of the enemy, but "he replied, 'that he did not care for
them,' and bending down a small elm beside which he was
standing into a bow, declared 'that he would treat the Indians
in the same way.' This elm is still standing [in Nashua], a
venerable and magnificent tree."

Meanwhile, having passed the Horseshoe Interval in
Tyngsborough, where the river makes a sudden bend to the
northwest,—for our reflections have anticipated our progress
somewhat,—we were advancing farther into the country and
into the day, which last proved almost as golden as the preceding, though the slight bustle and activity of the Monday
seemed to penetrate even to this scenery. Now and then we
had to muster all our energy to get round a point, where the
river broke rippling over rocks, and the maples trailed their
branches in the stream, but there was generally a backwater
or eddy on the side, of which we took advantage. The river
was here about forty rods wide and fifteen feet deep. Occasionally one ran along the shore, examining the country, and
visiting the nearest farm-houses, while the other followed the
windings of the stream alone, to meet his companion at some
distant point, and hear the report of his adventures; how the

farmer praised the coolness of his well, and his wife offered the stranger a draught of milk, or the children quarrelled for the only transparency in the window that they might get sight of the man at the well. For though the country seemed so new, and no house was observed by us, shut in between the banks that sunny day, we did not have to travel far to find where men inhabited, like wild bees, and had sunk wells in the loose sand and loam of the Merrimack. There dwelt the subject of the Hebrew scriptures, and the Esprit des Lois, where a thin vaporous smoke curled up through the noon. All that is told of mankind, of the inhabitants of the Upper Nile, and the Sunderbunds, and Timbuctoo, and the Orinoko, was experience here. Every race and class of men was represented. According to Belknap, the historian of New Hampshire, who wrote sixty years ago, here too, perchance, dwelt "new lights," and free thinking men even then. "The people in general throughout the State," it is written, "are professors of the Christian religion in some form or other. There is, however, a sort of *wise men* who pretend to reject it; but they have not yet been able to substitute a better in its place."

The other voyageur, perhaps, would in the mean while have seen a brown hawk, or a woodchuck, or a musquash creeping under the alders.

We occasionally rested in the shade of a maple or a willow, and drew forth a melon for our refreshment, while we contemplated at our leisure the lapse of the river and of human life; and as that current, with its floating twigs and leaves, so did all things pass in review before us, while far away in cities and marts on this very stream, the old routine was proceeding still. There is, indeed, a tide in the affairs of men, as the poet says, and yet as things flow they circulate, and the ebb always balances the flow. All streams are but tributary to the ocean, which itself does not stream, and the shores are unchanged, but in longer periods than man can measure. Go where we will, we discover infinite change in particulars only, not in generals. When I go into a museum and see the mummies wrapped in their linen bandages, I see that the lives of men began to need reform as long ago as when they walked the earth. I come out into the streets, and meet men who declare that the time is near at hand for the redemption of the race. But as men lived in Thebes, so do they live in Dunstable to-day. "Time drinketh up the essence of every great and noble action which ought to be performed, and is delayed in the execution." So says Veeshnoo Sarma; and we perceive that the schemers return again and again to common sense and labor. Such is the evidence of history.

"Yet I doubt not through the ages one increasing purpose runs,
And the thoughts of men are widened with the process of the Suns."

There are secret articles in our treaties with the gods, of more importance than all the rest, which the historian can never know.

There are many skilful apprentices, but few master work-men. On every hand we observe a truly wise practice, in education, in morals, and in the arts of life, the embodied wisdom of many an ancient philosopher. Who does not see that heresies have some time prevailed, that reforms have al-ready taken place? All this worldly wisdom might be regarded as the once unamiable heresy of some wise man. Some inter-ests have got a footing on the earth which we have not made sufficient allowance for. Even they who first built these barns and cleared the land thus, had some valor. The abrupt epochs and chasms are smoothed down in history as the inequalities of the plain are concealed by distance. But unless we do more than simply learn the trade of our time, we are but appren-tices, and not yet masters of the art of life.

Now that we are casting away these melon seeds, how can we help feeling reproach? He who eats the fruit, should at least plant the seed; aye, if possible, a better seed than that whose fruit he has enjoyed. Seeds! there are seeds enough which need only to be stirred in with the soil where they lie, by an inspired voice or pen, to bear fruit of a divine flavor. O thou spendthrift! Defray thy debt to the world; eat not the seed of institutions, as the luxurious do, but plant it rather, while thou devourest the pulp and tuber for thy subsistence; that so, perchance, one variety may at last be found worthy of preservation.

There are moments when all anxiety and stated toil are becalmed in the infinite leisure and repose of nature. All laborers
must have their nooning, and at this season of the day, we
are all, more or less, Asiatics, and give over all work and reform. While lying thus on our oars by the side of the stream,
in the heat of the day, our boat held by an osier put through
the staple in its prow, and slicing the melons, which are a
fruit of the East, our thoughts reverted to Arabia, Persia, and
Hindostan, the lands of contemplation and dwelling-places of
the ruminant nations. In the experience of this noontide we
could find some apology even for the instinct of the opium,
betel, and tobacco chewers. Mount Sabér, according to the
French traveller and naturalist, Botta, is celebrated for producing the Kát-tree, of which "the soft tops of the twigs and
tender leaves are eaten," says his reviewer, "and produce an
agreeable soothing excitement, restoring from fatigue, banishing sleep, and disposing to the enjoyment of conversation."
We thought that we might lead a dignified Oriental life along
this stream as well, and the maple and alders would be our
Kát-trees.

It is a great pleasure to escape sometimes from the restless
class of Reformers. What if these grievances exist? So do you
and I. Think you that sitting hens are troubled with ennui
these long summer days, sitting on and on in the crevice of
a hay-loft, without active employment? By the faint cackling
in distant barns, I judge that dame Nature is interested still
to know how many eggs her hens lay. The Universal Soul,
as it is called, has an interest in the stacking of hay, the foddering of cattle, and the draining of peat-meadows. Away in
Scythia, away in India, it makes butter and cheese. Suppose
that all farms *are* run out, and we youths must buy old land
and bring it to, still everywhere the relentless opponents of
reform bear a strange resemblance to ourselves; or, perchance, they are a few old maids and bachelors, who sit
round the kitchen hearth and listen to the singing of the kettle. "The oracles often give victory to our choice, and not to
the order alone of the mundane periods. As, for instance,
when they say that our voluntary sorrows germinate in us as
the growth of the particular life we lead." The reform which
you talk about can be undertaken any morning before un-

barring our doors. We need not call any convention. When two neighbors begin to eat corn bread, who before ate wheat, then the gods smile from ear to ear, for it is very pleasant to them. Why do you not try it? Don't let me hinder you.

There are theoretical reformers at all times, and all the world over, living on anticipation. Wolff, travelling in the deserts of Bokhara, says, "Another party of derveeshes came to me and observed, 'The time will come when there shall be no difference between rich and poor, between high and low, when property will be in common, even wives and children.'" But forever I ask of such, What then? The derveeshes in the deserts of Bokhara and the reformers in Marlboro' Chapel sing the same song. "There's a good time coming, boys," but, asked one of the audience, in good faith, "Can you fix the date?" Said I, "Will you help it along?"

The nonchalance and *dolce-far-niente* air of nature and society hint at infinite periods in the progress of mankind. The States have leisure to laugh from Maine to Texas at some newspaper joke, and New England shakes at the double-entendres of Australian circles, while the poor reformer cannot get a hearing.

Men do not fail commonly for want of knowledge, but for want of prudence to give wisdom the preference. What we need to know in any case is very simple. It is but too easy to establish another durable and harmonious routine. Immediately all parts of nature consent to it. Only make something to take the place of something, and men will behave as if it was the very thing they wanted. They *must* behave, at any rate, and will work up any material. There is always a present and extant life, be it better or worse, which all combine to uphold. We should be slow to mend, my friends, as slow to require mending, "Not hurling, according to the oracle, a transcendent foot towards piety." The language of excitement is at best picturesque merely. You must be calm before you can utter oracles. What was the excitement of the Delphic priestess compared with the calm wisdom of Socrates?—or whoever it was that was wise.—Enthusiasm is a supernatural serenity.

> "Men find that action is another thing
> 　　Than what they in discoursing papers read;
> 　The world's affairs require in managing
> 　　More arts than those wherein you clerks proceed."

As in geology, so in social institutions, we may discover the causes of all past change in the present invariable order of society. The greatest appreciable physical revolutions are the work of the light-footed air, the stealthy-paced water, and the subterranean fire. Aristotle said, "As time never fails, and the universe is eternal, neither the Tanais nor the Nile can have flowed forever." We are independent of the change we detect. The longer the lever the less perceptible its motion. It is the slowest pulsation which is the most vital. The hero then will know how to wait, as well as to make haste. All good abides with him who waiteth *wisely*; we shall sooner overtake the dawn by remaining here than by hurrying over the hills of the west. Be assured that every man's success is in proportion to his *average* ability. The meadow flowers spring and bloom where the waters annually deposit their slime, not where they reach in some freshet only. A man is not his hope, nor his despair, nor yet his past deed. We know not yet what we have done, still less what we are doing. Wait till evening, and other parts of our day's work will shine than we had thought at noon, and we shall discover the real purport of our toil. As when the farmer has reached the end of the furrow and looks back, he can tell best where the pressed earth shines most.

To one who habitually endeavors to contemplate the true state of things, the political state can hardly be said to have any existence whatever. It is unreal, incredible, and insignificant to him, and for him to endeavor to extract the truth from such lean material is like making sugar from linen rags, when sugar-cane may be had. Generally speaking, the political news, whether domestic or foreign, might be written to-day for the next ten years, with sufficient accuracy. Most revolutions in society have not power to interest, still less alarm us; but tell me that our rivers are drying up, or the genus pine dying out in the country, and I might attend. Most events recorded in history are more remarkable than important, like eclipses of the sun and moon, by which all are attracted, but whose effects no one takes the trouble to calculate.

But will the government never be so well administered, inquired one, that we private men shall hear nothing about it? "The king answered: At all events, I require a prudent and able man, who is capable of managing the state affairs of my kingdom. The ex-minister said: The criterion, O Sire! of a wise and competent man is, that he will not meddle with such like matters." Alas that the ex-minister should have been so nearly right!

In my short experience of human life, the *outward* obstacles, if there were any such, have not been living men, but the institutions of the dead. It is grateful to make one's way through this latest generation as through dewy grass. Men are as innocent as the morning to the unsuspicious.

> "And round about good morrows fly,
> As if day taught humanity."

Not being Reve of this Shire,

> "The early pilgrim blithe he hailed,
> That o'er the hills did stray,
> And many an early husbandman,
> That he met on the way";—

thieves and robbers all, nevertheless. I have not so surely foreseen that any Cossack or Chippeway would come to disturb the honest and simple commonwealth, as that some monster institution would at length embrace and crush its free members in its scaly folds; for it is not to be forgotten, that while the law holds fast the thief and murderer, it lets itself go loose. When I have not paid the tax which the State demanded for that protection which I did not want, itself has robbed me; when I have asserted the liberty it presumed to declare, itself has imprisoned me. Poor creature! if it knows no better I will not blame it. If it cannot live but by these means, I can. I do not wish, it happens, to be associated with Massachusetts, either in holding slaves or in conquering Mexico. I am a little better than herself in these respects.—As for Massachusetts, that huge she Briareus, Argus and Colchian

Dragon conjoined, set to watch the Heifer of the Constitution and the Golden Fleece, we would not warrant our respect for her, like some compositions, to preserve its qualities
through all weathers.—Thus it has happened, that not the
Arch Fiend himself has been in my way, but these toils which
tradition says were originally spun to obstruct him. They are
cobwebs and trifling obstacles in an earnest man's path, it is
true, and at length one even becomes attached to his unswept
and undusted garret. I love man—kind, but I hate the institutions of the dead un-kind. Men execute nothing so faithfully as the wills of the dead, to the last codicil and letter.
They rule this world, and the living are but their executors.
Such foundation too have our lectures and our sermons, commonly. They are all *Dudleian*; and piety derives its origin still
from that exploit of *pius Æneas*, who bore his father, An-
chises, on his shoulders from the ruins of Troy. Or rather,
like some Indian tribes, we bear about with us the mouldering relics of our ancestors on our shoulders. If, for instance,
a man asserts the value of individual liberty over the merely
political commonweal, his neighbor still tolerates him, that is
he who is *living near* him, sometimes even sustains him, but
never the State. Its officer, as a living man, may have human
virtues and a thought in his brain, but as the tool of an institution, a jailer or constable it may be, he is not a whit superior to his prison key or his staff. Herein is the tragedy; that
men doing outrage to their proper natures, even those called
wise and good, lend themselves to perform the office of inferior and brutal ones. Hence come war and slavery in; and
what else may not come in by this opening? But certainly
there are modes by which a man may put bread into his
mouth which will not prejudice him as a companion and
neighbor.

> "Now turn again, turn again, said the pindèr,
>   For a wrong way you have gone,
> For you have forsaken the king's highway,
>   And made a path over the corn."

Undoubtedly, countless reforms are called for, because society is not animated, or instinct enough with life, but in the
condition of some snakes which I have seen in early spring,

with alternate portions of their bodies torpid and flexible, so that they could wriggle neither way. All men are partially buried in the grave of custom, and of some we see only the crown of the head above ground. Better are the physically dead, for they more lively rot. Even virtue is no longer such if it be stagnant. A man's life should be constantly as fresh as this river. It should be the same channel, but a new water every instant.

> "Virtues as rivers pass,
> But still remains that virtuous man there was."

Most men have no inclination, no rapids, no cascades, but marshes, and alligators, and miasma instead. We read that when in the expedition of Alexander, Onesicritus was sent forward to meet certain of the Indian sect of Gymnosophists, and he had told them of those new philosophers of the West, Pythagoras, Socrates, and Diogenes, and their doctrines, one of them named Dandamis answered, that "They appeared to him to have been men of genius, but to have lived with too passive a regard for the laws." The philosophers of the West are liable to this rebuke still. "They say that Lieou-hia-hoei, and Chao-lien did not sustain to the end their resolutions, and that they dishonored their character. Their language was in harmony with reason and justice; while their acts were in harmony with the sentiments of men."

Chateaubriand said: "There are two things which grow stronger in the breast of man, in proportion as he advances in years: the love of country and religion. Let them be never so much forgotten in youth, they sooner or later present themselves to us arrayed in all their charms, and excite in the recesses of our hearts an attachment justly due to their beauty." It may be so. But even this infirmity of noble minds marks the gradual decay of youthful hope and faith. It is the allowed infidelity of age. There is a saying of the Yoloffs, "He who was born first has the greatest number of old clothes," consequently M. Chateaubriand has more old clothes than I have. It is comparatively a faint and reflected beauty that is admired, not an essential and intrinsic one. It is because the old are weak, feel their mortality, and think that they have measured the strength of man. They will not boast; they will

be frank and humble. Well, let them have the few poor comforts they can keep. Humility is still a very human virtue.
They look back on life, and so see not into the future. The
prospect of the young is forward and unbounded, mingling
the future with the present. In the declining day the thoughts
make haste to rest in darkness, and hardly look forward to the
ensuing morning. The thoughts of the old prepare for night
and slumber. The same hopes and prospects are not for him
who stands upon the rosy mountain-tops of life, and him
who expects the setting of his earthly day.

I must conclude that Conscience, if that be the name of it,
was not given us for no purpose, or for a hinderance. However flattering order and expediency may look, it is but the
repose of a lethargy, and we will choose rather to be awake,
though it be stormy, and maintain ourselves on this earth and
in this life, as we may, without signing our death-warrant.
Let us see if we cannot stay here, where He has put us, on
his own conditions. Does not his law reach as far as his light?
The expedients of the nations clash with one another, only
the absolutely right is expedient for all.

There are some passages in the Antigone of Sophocles, well
known to scholars, of which I am reminded in this connection. Antigone has resolved to sprinkle sand on the dead body
of her brother Polynices, notwithstanding the edict of King
Creon condemning to death that one who should perform
this service, which the Greeks deemed so important, for the
enemy of his country; but Ismene, who is of a less resolute
and noble spirit, declines taking part with her sister in this
work, and says, —

> "I, therefore, asking those under the earth to consider
> me, that I am compelled to do thus, will obey those who
> are placed in office; for to do extreme things is not wise."

ANTIGONE.

> "I would not ask you, nor would you, if you still wished,
> do it joyfully with me. Be such as seems good to you. But
> I will bury him. It is glorious for me doing this to die. I
> beloved will lie with him beloved, having, like a criminal,
> done what is holy; since the time is longer which it is nec-
> essary for me to please those below, than those here, for

there I shall always lie. But if it seems good to you, hold in dishonor things which are honored by the gods."

ISMENE.

"I indeed do not hold them in dishonor; but to act in opposition to the citizens I am by nature unable."

Antigone being at length brought before King Creon, he asks,—

"Did you then dare to transgress these laws?"

ANTIGONE.

"For it was not Zeus who proclaimed these to me, nor Justice who dwells with the gods below; it was not they who established these laws among men. Nor did I think that your proclamations were so strong, as, being a mortal, to be able to transcend the unwritten and immovable laws of the gods. For not something now and yesterday, but forever these live, and no one knows from what time they appeared. I was not about to pay the penalty of violating these to the gods, fearing the presumption of any man. For I well knew that I should die, and why not? even if you had not proclaimed it."

This was concerning the burial of a dead body.

The wisest conservatism is that of the Hindoos. "Immemorial custom is transcendent law," says Menu. That is, it was the custom of the gods before men used it. The fault of our New England custom is that it is memorial. What is morality but immemorial custom? Conscience is the chief of conservatives. "Perform the settled functions," says Kreeshna in the Bhagvat-Geeta; "action is preferable to inaction. The journey of thy mortal frame may not succeed from inaction."—"A man's own calling with all its faults, ought not to be forsaken. Every undertaking is involved in its faults as the fire in its smoke."—"The man who is acquainted with the whole, should not drive those from their works who are slow of comprehension, and less experienced than himself."—"Wherefore, O Arjoon, resolve to fight," is the advice of the God to the irresolute soldier who fears to slay his best friends. It is a sublime conservatism; as wide as the world, and as unwearied as time; preserving the universe with Asiatic anxiety, in that state in which it appeared to their minds. These philosophers dwell on the inevitability and unchangeableness of laws, on the power of temperament and constitution, the three *goon* or qualities, and the circumstances of birth and affinity. The end is an immense consolation; eternal absorption in Brahma. Their speculations never venture beyond their own table-lands, though they are high and vast as they. Buoyancy, freedom, flexibility, variety, possibility, which also are qualities of the Unnamed, they deal not with. The undeserved reward is to be earned by an everlasting moral drudgery; the incalculable promise of the morrow is, as it were, weighed. And who will say that their conservatism has not been effectual? "Assuredly," says a French translator, speaking of the antiquity and durability of the Chinese and Indian nations, and of the wisdom of their legislators, "there are there some vestiges of the eternal laws which govern the world."

Christianity, on the other hand, is humane, practical, and, in a large sense, radical. So many years and ages of the gods those Eastern sages sat contemplating Brahm, uttering in silence the mystic "Om," being absorbed into the essence of the Supreme Being, never going out of themselves, but subsiding farther and deeper within; so infinitely wise, yet infinitely stagnant; until, at last, in that same Asia, but in the western part of it, appeared a youth, wholly unforetold by them,—not being absorbed into Brahm, but bringing Brahm down to earth and to mankind; in whom Brahm had awaked from his long sleep, and exerted himself, and the day began,—a new avatar. The Brahman had never thought to be a brother of mankind as well as a child of God. Christ is the prince of Reformers and Radicals. Many expressions in the New Testament come naturally to the lips of all Protestants, and it furnishes the most pregnant and practical texts. There is no harmless dreaming, no wise speculation in it, but everywhere a substratum of good sense. It never *reflects*, but it *repents*. There is no poetry in it, we may say, nothing regarded in the light of beauty merely, but moral truth is its object. All mortals are convicted by its conscience.

The New Testament is remarkable for its pure morality; the best of the Hindo Scripture, for its pure intellectuality. The reader is nowhere raised into and sustained in a higher, purer, or *rarer* region of thought than in the Bhagvat-Geeta. Warren Hastings, in his sensible letter recommending the translation of this book to the Chairman of the East India Company, declares the original to be "of a sublimity of conception, reasoning, and diction almost unequalled," and that the writings of the Indian philosophers " will survive when the British dominion in India shall have long ceased to exist, and when the sources which it once yielded of wealth and power are lost to remembrance." It is unquestionably one of the noblest and most sacred scriptures which have come down to us. Books are to be distinguished by the grandeur of their topics, even more than by the manner in which they are treated. The Oriental philosophy approaches, easily, loftier themes than the modern aspires to; and no wonder if it sometimes prattle about them. *It* only assigns their due rank respectively to Action and Contemplation, or rather does full justice to the latter. Western philosophers have not conceived of the significance of Contemplation in their sense. Speaking of the spiritual discipline to which the Brahmans subjected themselves, and the wonderful power of abstraction to which they attained, instances of which had come under his notice, Hastings says: —

"To those who have never been accustomed to the separation of the mind from the notices of the senses, it may not be easy to conceive by what means such a power is to be attained; since even the most studious men of our hemisphere will find it difficult so to restrain their attention, but that it will wander to some object of present sense or recollection; and even the buzzing of a fly will sometimes have the power to disturb it. But if we are told that there have been men who were successively, for ages past, in the daily habit of abstracted contemplation, begun in the earliest period of youth, and continued in many to the maturity of age, each adding some portion of knowledge to the store accumulated by his predecessors; it is not assuming too much to conclude, that as the mind ever gathers strength, like the body, by exercise, so in such an exercise it may in each have acquired the faculty to which they aspired, and that their collective studies may have led them to the discovery of new tracks and combinations of sentiment, totally different from the doctrines with which the learned of other nations are acquainted; doctrines which, however speculative and subtle, still as they possess the advantage of being derived from a source so free from every adventitious mixture, may be equally founded in truth with the most simple of our own."

"The forsaking of works" was taught by Kreeshna to the most ancient of men, and handed down from age to age,

"until at length, in the course of time, the mighty art was lost.

"In wisdom is to be found every work without exception," says Kreeshna.

"Although thou wert the greatest of all offenders, thou shalt be able to cross the gulf of sin with the bark of wisdom."

"There is not anything in this world to be compared with wisdom for purity."

"The action stands at a distance inferior to the application of wisdom."

The wisdom of a Moonee "is confirmed, when, like the tortoise, he can draw in all his members, and restrain them from their wonted purposes."

"Children only, and not the learned, speak of the speculative and the practical doctrines as two. They are but one. For both obtain the selfsame end, and the place which is gained by the followers of the one is gained by the followers of the other."

"The man enjoyeth not freedom from action, from the non-commencement of that which he hath to do; nor doth he obtain happiness from a total inactivity. No one ever resteth a moment inactive. Every man is involuntarily urged to act by those principles which are inherent in his nature. The man who restraineth his active faculties, and sitteth down with his mind attentive to the objects of his senses, is called one of an astrayed soul, and the practiser of deceit. So the man is praised, who, having subdued all his passions, performeth with his active faculties all the functions of life, unconcerned about the event."

"Let the motive be in the deed and not in the event. Be not one whose motive for action is the hope of reward. Let not thy life be spent in inaction."

"For the man who doeth that which he hath to do, without affection, obtaineth the Supreme."

"He who may behold, as it were inaction in action, and action in inaction, is wise amongst mankind. He is a perfect performer of all duty."

"Wise men call him a *Pandeet*, whose every undertaking is free from the idea of desire, and whose actions are consumed by the fire of wisdom. He abandoneth the desire of a reward of his actions; he is always contented and independent; and although he may be engaged in a work, he, as it were, doeth nothing."

"He is both a Yogee and a Sannyasee who performeth that which he hath to do independent of the fruit thereof; not he who liveth without the sacrificial fire and without action."

"He who enjoyeth but the Amreeta which is left of his offerings, obtaineth the eternal spirit of Brahm, the Supreme."

What, after all, does the practicalness of life amount to? The things immediate to be done are very trivial. I could postpone them all to hear this locust sing. The most glorious fact in my experience is not anything that I have done or may hope to do, but a transient thought, or vision, or dream, which I have had. I would give all the wealth of the world, and all the deeds of all the heroes, for one true vision. But how can I communicate with the gods who am a pencil-maker on the earth, and not be insane?

"I am the same to all mankind," says Kreeshna; "there is not one who is worthy of my love or hatred."

This teaching is not practical in the sense in which the New Testament is. It is not always sound sense in practice. The Brahman never proposes courageously to assault evil, but patiently to starve it out. His active faculties are paralyzed by the idea of cast, of impassable limits, of destiny and the tyranny of time. Kreeshna's argument, it must be allowed, is

defective. No sufficient reason is given why Arjoon should
fight. Arjoon may be convinced, but the reader is not, for his
judgment is *not* "formed upon the speculative doctrines of the
Sankhya Sastra." "Seek an asylum in wisdom alone"; but what
is wisdom to a Western mind? The duty of which he speaks
is an arbitrary one. When was it established? The Brahman's
virtue consists in doing, not right, but arbitrary things. What
is that which a man "hath to do"? What is "action"? What
are the "settled functions"? What is "a man's own religion,"
which is so much better than another's? What is "a man's
own particular calling"? What are the duties which are appointed by one's birth? It is a defence of the institution of
casts, of what is called the "natural duty" of the Kshetree, or
soldier, "to attach himself to the discipline," "not to flee from
the field," and the like. But they who are unconcerned about
the consequences of their actions are not therefore unconcerned about their actions.

Behold the difference between the Oriental and the Occidental. The former has nothing to do in this world; the latter is full of activity. The one looks in the sun till his eyes
are put out; the other follows him prone in his westward
course. There is such a thing as caste, even in the West; but
it is comparatively faint; it is conservatism here. It says, forsake not your calling, outrage no institution, use no violence, rend no bonds; the State is thy parent. Its virtue or
manhood is wholly filial. There is a struggle between the
Oriental and Occidental in every nation; some who would
be forever contemplating the sun, and some who are hastening toward the sunset. The former class says to the latter,
When you have reached the sunset, you will be no nearer to
the sun. To which the latter replies, But we so prolong the
day. The former " walketh but in that night, when all things
go to rest the night of *time*. The contemplative Moonee
sleepeth but in the day of *time*, when all things wake."

To conclude these extracts, I can say, in the words of San-
jay, "As, O mighty Prince! I recollect again and again this
holy and wonderful dialogue of Kreeshna and Arjoon, I continue more and more to rejoice; and as I recall to my memory
the more than miraculous form of Haree, my astonishment is
great, and I marvel and rejoice again and again! Wherever

Kreeshna the God of devotion may be, wherever Arjoon the mighty bowman may be, there too, without doubt, are fortune, riches, victory, and good conduct. This is my firm belief."

I would say to the readers of Scriptures, if they wish for a good book, read the Bhagvat-Geeta, an episode to the Mahabharat, said to have been written by Kreeshna Dwypayen Veias,—known to have been written by ——, more than four thousand years ago,—it matters not whether three or four, or when,—translated by Charles Wilkins. It deserves to be read with reverence even by Yankees, as a part of the sacred writings of a devout people; and the intelligent Hebrew will rejoice to find in it a moral grandeur and sublimity akin to those of his own Scriptures.

To an American reader, who, by the advantage of his position, can see over that strip of Atlantic coast to Asia and the Pacific, who, as it were, sees the shore slope upward over the Alps to the Himmaleh Mountains, the comparatively recent literature of Europe often appears partial and clannish, and, notwithstanding the limited range of his own sympathies and studies, the European writer who presumes that he is speaking for the world, is perceived by him to speak only for that corner of it which he inhabits. One of the rarest of England's scholars and critics, in his classification of the worthies of the world, betrays the narrowness of his European culture and the exclusiveness of his reading. None of her children has done justice to the poets and philosophers of Persia or of India. They have even been better known to her merchant scholars than to her poets and thinkers by profession. You may look in vain through English poetry for a single memorable verse inspired by these themes. Nor is Germany to be excepted, though her philological industry is indirectly serving the cause of philosophy and poetry. Even Goethe wanted that universality of genius which could have appreciated the philosophy of India, if he had more nearly approached it. His genius was more practical, dwelling much more in the regions of the understanding, and was less native to contemplation than the genius of those sages. It is remarkable that Homer and a few Hebrews are the most Oriental names which modern Europe, whose literature has taken its rise since the decline of the Persian, has admitted into her list of Worthies, and perhaps the *worthiest* of mankind, and the fathers of modern thinking,—for the contemplations of those Indian sages have influenced, and still influence, the intellectual development of mankind,—whose works even yet survive in wonderful completeness, are, for the most part, not recognized as ever having existed. If the lions had been the painters it would have been otherwise. In every one's youthful dreams philosophy is still vaguely but inseparably, and with singular truth, associated with the East, nor do after years discover its local habitation in the Western world. In comparison with the philosophers of the East, we may say that modern Europe has yet given birth to none. Beside the vast and cosmogonal philosophy of the Bhagvat-Geeta, even our Shakespeare seems sometimes youthfully green and practical merely. Some of these sublime sentences, as the Chaldæan oracles of Zoroaster, still surviving after a thousand revolutions and translations, alone make us doubt if the poetic form and dress are not transitory, and not essential to the most effective and enduring expression of thought. *Ex oriente lux* may still be the motto of scholars, for the Western world has not yet derived from the East all the light which it is destined to receive thence.

It would be worthy of the age to print together the collected Scriptures or Sacred Writings of the several nations, the Chinese, the Hindoos, the Persians, the Hebrews, and others, as the Scripture of mankind. The New Testament is still, perhaps, too much on the lips and in the hearts of men to be called a Scripture in this sense. Such a juxtaposition and comparison might help to liberalize the faith of men. This is a work which Time will surely edit, reserved to crown the labors of the printing-press. This would be the Bible, or Book of Books, which let the missionaries carry to the uttermost parts of the earth.

While engaged in these reflections, thinking ourselves the only navigators of these waters, suddenly a canal-boat, with its sail set, glided round a point before us, like some huge river beast, and changed the scene in an instant; and then another and another glided into sight, and we found ourselves in the current of commerce once more. So we threw our rinds in the water for the fishes to nibble, and added our breath to the life of living men. Little did we think, in the distant garden in which we had planted the seed and reared this fruit, where it would be eaten. Our melons lay at home on the sandy bottom of the Merrimack, and our potatoes in the sun and water at the bottom of the boat looked like a fruit of the country. Soon, however, we were delivered from this fleet of junks, and possessed the river in solitude, once more rowing steadily upward through the noon, between the territories of Nashua on the one hand, and Hudson, once Nottingham, on the other. From time to time we scared up a kingfisher or a summer duck, the former flying rather by vigorous impulses than by steady and patient steering with that short rudder of his, sounding his rattle along the fluvial street.

Erelong another scow hove in sight, creeping down the river; and hailing it, we attached ourselves to its side, and floated back in company, chatting with the boatmen, and obtaining a draught of cooler water from their jug. They appeared to be green hands from far among the hills, who had taken this means to get to the seaboard, and see the world; and would possibly visit the Falkland Isles, and the China seas, before they again saw the waters of the Merrimack, or, perchance, they would not return this way forever. They had already embarked the private interests of the landsman in the larger venture of the race, and were ready to mess with mankind, reserving only the till of a chest to themselves. But they too were soon lost behind a point, and we went croaking on our way alone. What grievance has its root among the New Hampshire hills? we asked; what is wanting to human life here, that these men should make such haste to the antipodes? We prayed that their bright anticipations might not be rudely disappointed.

> Though all the fates should prove unkind,
> Leave not your native land behind.
> The ship, becalmed, at length stands still;
> The steed must rest beneath the hill;
> But swiftly still our fortunes pace
> To find us out in every place.

The vessel, though her masts be firm,
Beneath her copper bears a worm;
Around the cape, across the line,
Till fields of ice her course confine;
It matters not how smooth the breeze,
How shallow or how deep the seas,
Whether she bears Manilla twine,
Or in her hold Madeira wine,
Or China teas, or Spanish hides,
In port or quarantine she rides;
Far from New England's blustering shore,
New England's worm her hulk shall bore,
And sink her in the Indian seas,
Twine, wine, and hides, and China teas.

We passed a small desert here on the east bank, between Tyngsborough and Hudson, which was interesting and even refreshing to our eyes in the midst of the almost universal greenness. This sand was indeed somewhat impressive and beautiful to us. A very old inhabitant, who was at work in a field on the Nashua side, told us that he remembered when corn and grain grew there, and it was a cultivated field. But at length the fishermen, for this was a fishing place, pulled up the bushes on the shore, for greater convenience in hauling their seines, and when the bank was thus broken, the wind began to blow up the sand from the shore, until at length it had covered about fifteen acres several feet deep. We saw near the river, where the sand was blown off down to some ancient surface, the foundation of an Indian wigwam exposed, a perfect circle of burnt stones, four or five feet in diameter, mingled with fine charcoal, and the bones of small animals which had been preserved in the sand. The surrounding sand was sprinkled with other burnt stones on which their fires had been built, as well as with flakes of arrow-head stone, and we found one perfect arrow-head. In one place we noticed where an Indian had sat to manufacture arrow-heads out of quartz, and the sand was sprinkled with a quart of small glass-like chips about as big as a fourpence, which he had broken off in his work. Here, then, the Indians must have fished before the whites arrived. There was another similar sandy tract about half a mile above this.

Still the noon prevailed, and we turned the prow aside to bathe, and recline ourselves under some buttonwoods, by a ledge of rocks, in a retired pasture sloping to the water's edge, and skirted with pines and hazels, in the town of Hudson. Still had India, and that old noontide philosophy, the better part of our thoughts.

It is always singular, but encouraging, to meet with common sense in very old books, as the Heetopades of Veeshnoo Sarma; a playful wisdom which has eyes behind as well as before, and oversees itself. It asserts their health and independence of the experience of later times. This pledge of sanity cannot be spared in a book, that it sometimes pleasantly reflect upon itself. The story and fabulous portion of this book winds loosely from sentence to sentence as so many oases in a desert, and is as indistinct as a camel's track between Mourzouk and Darfour. It is a comment on the flow and freshet of modern books. The reader leaps from sentence to sentence, as from one stepping-stone to another, while the stream of the story rushes past unregarded. The Bhagvat-Geeta is less sententious and poetic, perhaps, but still more wonderfully sustained and developed. Its sanity and sublimity have impressed the minds even of soldiers and merchants. It is the characteristic of great poems that they will yield of their sense in due proportion to the hasty and the deliberate reader. To the practical they will be common sense, and to the wise wisdom; as either the traveller may wet his lips, or an army may fill its water-casks at a full stream.

One of the most attractive of those ancient books that I have met with is the Laws of Menu. According to Sir William Jones, "Vyasa, the son of Parasara, has decided that the Veda, with its Angas, or the six compositions deduced from it, the revealed system of medicine, the Puranas or sacred histories, and the code of Menu, were four works of supreme authority, which ought never to be shaken by arguments merely human." The last is believed by the Hindoos "to have been promulged in the beginning of time, by Menu,

son or grandson of Brahma," and "first of created beings";
and Brahma is said to have "taught his laws to Menu in a
hundred thousand verses, which Menu explained to the
primitive world in the very words of the book now translated." Others affirm that they have undergone successive
abridgments for the convenience of mortals, " while the gods
of the lower heaven and the band of celestial musicians are
engaged in studying the primary code."—"A number of
glosses or comments on Menu were composed by the
Munis, or old philosophers, whose treatises, together with
that before us, constitute the Dherma Sastra, in a collective
sense, or Body of Law." Culluca Bhatta was one of the more
modern of these.

Every sacred book, successively, has been accepted in the
faith that it was to be the final resting-place of the sojourning
soul; but after all, it was but a caravansary which supplied
refreshment to the traveller, and directed him farther on his
way to Isphahan or Bagdat. Thank God, no Hindoo tyranny
prevailed at the framing of the world, but we are freemen of
the universe, and not sentenced to any caste.

I know of no book which has come down to us with
grander pretensions than this, and it is so impersonal and sincere that it is never offensive nor ridiculous. Compare the
modes in which modern literature is advertised with the prospectus of this book, and think what a reading public it addresses, what criticism it expects. It seems to have been
uttered from some eastern summit, with a sober morning
prescience in the dawn of time, and you cannot read a sentence without being elevated as upon the table-land of the
Ghauts. It has such a rhythm as the winds of the desert, such
a tide as the Ganges, and is as superior to criticism as the
Himmaleh Mountains. Its tone is of such unrelaxed fibre, that
even at this late day, unworn by time, it wears the English
and the Sanscrit dress indifferently; and its fixed sentences
keep up their distant fires still, like the stars, by whose dissipated rays this lower world is illumined. The whole book by
noble gestures and inclinations renders many words unnecessary. English sense has toiled, but Hindoo wisdom never per-
spired. Though the sentences open as we read them,
unexpensively, and at first almost unmeaningly, as the petals

of a flower, they sometimes startle us with that rare kind of wisdom which could only have been learned from the most trivial experience; but it comes to us as refined as the porcelain earth which subsides to the bottom of the ocean. They are clean and dry as fossil truths, which have been exposed to the elements for thousands of years, so impersonally and scientifically true that they are the ornament of the parlor and the cabinet. Any *moral* philosophy is exceedingly rare. This of Menu addresses our privacy more than most. It is a more private and familiar, and, at the same time, a more public and universal word, than is spoken in parlor or pulpit now-a-days. As our domestic fowls are said to have their original in the wild pheasant of India, so our domestic thoughts have their prototypes in the thoughts of her philosophers. We are dabbling in the very elements of our present conventional and actual life; as if it were the primeval conventicle where how to eat, and to drink, and to sleep, and maintain life with adequate dignity and sincerity, were the questions to be decided. It is later and more intimate with us even than the advice of our nearest friends. And yet it is true for the widest horizon, and read out of doors has relation to the dim mountain line, and is native and aboriginal there. Most books belong to the house and street only, and in the fields their leaves feel very thin. They are bare and obvious, and have no halo nor haze about them. Nature lies far and fair behind them all. But this, as it proceeds from, so it addresses, what is deepest and most abiding in man. It belongs to the noontide of the day, the midsummer of the year, and after the snows have melted, and the waters evaporated in the spring, still its truth speaks freshly to our experience. It helps the sun to shine, and his rays fall on its page to illustrate it. It spends the mornings and the evenings, and makes such an impression on us overnight as to awaken us before dawn, and its influence lingers around us like a fragrance late into the day. It conveys a new gloss to the meadows and the depths of the wood, and its spirit, like a more subtile ether, sweeps along with the prevailing winds of a country. The very locusts and crickets of a summer day are but later or earlier glosses on the Dherma Sastra of the Hindoos, a continuation of the sacred code. As we have said, there is an orientalism in the most restless pioneer, and the farthest west is but the farthest east. While we are reading these sentences, this fair modern world seems only a reprint of the Laws of Menu with the gloss of Culluca. Tried by a New England eye, or the mere practical wisdom of modern times, they are the oracles of a race already in its dotage, but held up to the sky, which is the only impartial and incorruptible ordeal, they are of a piece with its depth and serenity, and I am assured that they will have a place and significance as long as there is a sky to test them by.

Give me a sentence which no intelligence can understand. There must be a kind of life and palpitation to it, and under its words a kind of blood must circulate forever. It is wonderful that this sound should have come down to us from so far, when the voice of man can be heard so little way, and we are not now within ear-shot of any contemporary. The wood-cutters have here felled an ancient pine forest, and brought to light to these distant hills a fair lake in the southwest; and now in an instant it is distinctly shown to these woods as if its image had travelled hither from eternity. Perhaps these old stumps upon the knoll remember when anciently this lake gleamed in the horizon. One wonders if the bare earth itself did not experience emotion at beholding again so fair a prospect. That fair water lies there in the sun thus revealed, so much the prouder and fairer because its beauty needed not to be seen. It seems yet lonely, sufficient to itself, and superior to observation.—So are these old sentences like serene lakes in the southwest, at length revealed to us, which have so long been reflecting our own sky in their bosom.

The great plain of India lies as in a cup between the Himmaleh and the ocean on the north and south, and the Brahmapootra and Indus, on the east and west, wherein the primeval race was received. We will not dispute the story. We are pleased to read in the natural history of the country, of the "pine, larch, spruce, and silver fir," which cover the southern face of the Himmaleh range; of the "gooseberry, raspberry, strawberry," which from an imminent temperate zone overlook the torrid plains. So did this active modern life have even then a foothold and lurking-place in the midst of the stateliness and contemplativeness of those Eastern plains. In another era the "lily of the valley, cowslip, dandelion," were to work their way down into the plain, and bloom in a level zone of their own reaching round the earth. Already has the era of the temperate zone arrived, the era of the pine and the oak, for the palm and the banian do not supply the wants of this age. The lichens on the summits of the rocks will perchance find their level erelong.

As for the tenets of the Brahmans, we are not so much concerned to know what doctrines they held, as that they were held by any. We can tolerate all philosophies, Atomists, Pneumatologists, Atheists, Theists,—Plato, Aristotle, Leucippus, Democritus, Pythagoras, Zoroaster, and Confucius. It is the attitude of these men, more than any communication which they make, that attracts us. Between them and their commentators, it is true, there is an endless dispute. But if it comes to this, that you compare notes, then you are all wrong. As it is, each takes us up into the serene heavens, whither the smallest bubble rises as surely as the largest, and paints earth and sky for us. Any sincere thought is irresistible. The very austerity of the Brahmans is tempting to the devotional soul, as a more refined and nobler luxury. Wants so easily and gracefully satisfied seem like a more refined pleasure. Their conception of creation is peaceful as a dream. "When that power awakes, then has this world its full expansion; but when he slumbers with a tranquil spirit, then the whole system fades away." In the very indistinctness of their theogony a sublime truth is implied. It hardly allows the reader to rest in any supreme first cause, but directly it hints at a supremer still which created the last, and the Creator is still behind increate.

Nor will we disturb the antiquity of this Scripture; "From fire, from air, and from the sun," it was "milked out." One might as well investigate the chronology of light and heat. Let the sun shine. Menu understood this matter best, when he said, "Those best know the divisions of days and nights who understand that the day of Brahma, which endures to the end of a thousand such ages, [infinite ages, nevertheless, according to mortal reckoning,] gives rise to virtuous exertions; and that his night endures as long as his day." Indeed, the Mussulman and Tartar dynasties are beyond all dating. Methinks I have lived under them myself. In every man's

brain is the Sanscrit. The Vedas and their Angas are not so
ancient as serene contemplation. Why will we be imposed on
by antiquity? Is the babe young? When I behold it, it seems
more venerable than the oldest man; it is more ancient than
Nestor or the Sibyls, and bears the wrinkles of father Saturn
himself. And do we live but in the present? How broad a line
is that? I sit now on a stump whose rings number centuries
of growth. If I look around I see that the soil is composed of
the remains of just such stumps, ancestors to this. The earth
is covered with mould. I thrust this stick many æons deep
into its surface, and with my heel make a deeper furrow than
the elements have ploughed here for a thousand years. If I
listen, I hear the peep of frogs which is older than the slime
of Egypt, and the distant drumming of a partridge on a log,
as if it were the pulse-beat of the summer air. I raise my fairest and freshest flowers in the old mould. Why, what we
would fain call new is not skin deep; the earth is not yet
stained by it. It is not the fertile ground which we walk on,
but the leaves which flutter over our heads. The newest is but
the oldest made visible to our senses. When we dig up the
soil from a thousand feet below the surface, we call it new,
and the plants which spring from it; and when our vision
pierces deeper into space, and detects a remoter star, we call
that new also. The place where we sit is called Hudson,—
once it was Nottingham,—once—

We should read history as little critically as we consider the
landscape, and be more interested by the atmospheric tints
and various lights and shades which the intervening spaces
create, than by its groundwork and composition. It is the
morning now turned evening and seen in the west,—the
same sun, but a new light and atmosphere. Its beauty is like
the sunset; not a fresco painting on a wall, flat and bounded,
but atmospheric and roving or free. In reality, history fluc-
tuates as the face of the landscape from morning to evening.
What is of moment is its hue and color. Time hides no treasures; we want not its *then*, but its *now*. We do not complain
that the mountains in the horizon are blue and indistinct;
they are the more like the heavens.

Of what moment are facts that can be lost,—which need

to be commemorated? The monument of death will outlast the memory of the dead. The pyramids do not tell the tale which was confided to them; the living fact commemorates itself. Why look in the dark for light? Strictly speaking, the historical societies have not recovered one fact from oblivion, but are themselves, instead of the fact, that is lost. The researcher is more memorable than the researched. The crowd stood admiring the mist and the dim outlines of the trees seen through it, when one of their number advanced to explore the phenomenon, and with fresh admiration all eyes were turned on his dimly retreating figure. It is astonishing with how little co-operation of the societies the past is remembered. Its story has indeed had another muse than has been assigned it. There is a good instance of the manner in which all history began, in Alwákidis' Arabian Chronicle: "I was informed by *Ahmed Almatin Aljorhami*, who had it from *Rephâa Ebn Kais Alámiri*, who had it from *Saiph Ebn Fabalah Alchâtquarmi*, who had it from *Thabet Ebn Alkamah*, who said he was present at the action." These fathers of history were not anxious to preserve, but to learn the fact; and hence it was not forgotten. Critical acumen is exerted in vain to uncover the past; the *past* cannot be *presented*; we cannot know what we are not. But one veil hangs over past, present, and future, and it is the province of the historian to find out, not what was, but what is. Where a battle has been fought, you will find nothing but the bones of men and beasts; where a battle is being fought, there are hearts beating. We will sit on a mound and muse, and not try to make these skeletons stand on their legs again. Does Nature remember, think you, that they *were* men, or not rather that they *are* bones?

Ancient history has an air of antiquity. It should be more modern. It is written as if the spectator should be thinking of the backside of the picture on the wall, or as if the author expected that the dead would be his readers, and wished to detail to them their own experience. Men seem anxious to accomplish an orderly retreat through the centuries, earnestly rebuilding the works behind, as they are battered down by the encroachments of time; but while they loiter, they and their works both fall a prey to the arch enemy. History has neither the venerableness of antiquity, nor the freshness of the modern. It does as if it would go to the beginning of things, which natural history might with reason assume to do; but consider the Universal History, and then tell us,—when did burdock and plantain sprout first? It has been so written for the most part, that the times it describes are with remarkable propriety called *dark ages*. They are dark, as one has observed, because we are so in the dark about them. The sun rarely shines in history, what with the dust and confusion; and when we meet with any cheering fact which implies the presence of this luminary, we excerpt and modernize it. As when we read in the history of the Saxons that Edwin of Northumbria "caused stakes to be fixed in the highways where he had seen a clear spring," and "brazen dishes were chained to them to refresh the weary sojourner, whose fatigues Edwin had himself experienced." This is worth all Arthur's twelve battles.

"Through the shadow of the world we sweep into the
    younger day:
Better fifty years of Europe than a cycle of Cathay."
Than fifty years of Europe better one New England ray!

Biography, too, is liable to the same objection; it should be autobiography. Let us not, as the Germans advise, endeavor to go abroad and vex our bowels that we may be somebody else to explain him. If I am not I, who will be?

But it is fit that the Past should be dark; though the darkness is not so much a quality of the past as of tradition. It is not a distance of time, but a distance of relation, which makes thus dusky its memorials. What is near to the heart of this generation is fair and bright still. Greece lies outspread fair and sunshiny in floods of light, for there is the sun and daylight in her literature and art. Homer does not allow us to forget that the sun shone,—nor Phidias, nor the Parthenon. Yet no era has been wholly dark, nor will we too hastily submit to the historian, and congratulate ourselves on a blaze of light. If we could pierce the obscurity of those remote years, we should find it light enough; only *there* is not our day. Some creatures are made to see in the dark. There has always been the same amount of light in the world. The new and missing stars, the comets and eclipses, do not affect the general illumination, for only our glasses appreciate them. The eyes of the oldest fossil remains, they tell us, indicate that the same laws of light prevailed then as now. Always the laws of light are the same, but the modes and degrees of seeing vary. The gods are partial to no era, but steadily shines their light in the heavens, while the eye of the beholder is turned to stone. There was but the sun and the eye from the first. The ages have not added a new ray to the one, nor altered a fibre of the other.

If we will admit time into our thoughts at all, the mythologies, those vestiges of ancient poems, wrecks of poems, so to speak, the world's inheritance, still reflecting some of their original splendor, like the fragments of clouds tinted by the rays of the departed sun; reaching into the latest summer day, and allying this hour to the morning of creation; as the poet sings:—

> "Fragments of the lofty strain
> Float down the tide of years,
> As buoyant on the stormy main
> A parted wreck appears."

These are the materials and hints for a history of the rise and progress of the race; how, from the condition of ants, it arrived at the condition of men, and arts were gradually invented. Let a thousand surmises shed some light on this story. We will not be confined by historical, even geological periods which would allow us to doubt of a progress in human affairs. If we rise above this wisdom for the day, we shall expect that this morning of the race, in which it has been supplied with the simplest necessaries, with corn, and wine, and honey, and oil, and fire, and articulate speech, and agricultural and other arts, reared up by degrees from the condition of ants to men, will be succeeded by a day of equally progressive splendor; that, in the lapse of the divine periods, other divine agents and godlike men will assist to elevate the race as much above its present condition.

But we do not know much about it.

Thus did one voyageur waking dream, while his companion slumbered on the bank. Suddenly a boatman's horn was heard echoing from shore to shore, to give notice of his approach to the farmer's wife with whom he was to take his dinner, though in that place only muskrats and kingfishers seemed to hear. The current of our reflections and our slumbers being thus disturbed, we weighed anchor once more.

As we proceeded on our way in the afternoon, the western bank became lower, or receded farther from the channel in some places, leaving a few trees only to fringe the water's edge; while the eastern rose abruptly here and there into wooded hills fifty or sixty feet high. The bass, *Tilia Americana*, also called the lime or linden, which was a new tree to us, overhung the water with its broad and rounded leaf, interspersed with clusters of small hard berries now nearly ripe, and made an agreeable shade for us sailors. The inner bark of this genus is the bast, the material of the fisherman's matting, and the ropes and peasant's shoes of which the Russians make so much use, and also of nets and a coarse cloth in some places. According to poets, this was once Philyra, one of the Oceanides. The ancients are said to have used its bark for the roofs of cottages, for baskets, and for a kind of paper called Philyra. They also made bucklers of its wood, "on account of its flexibility, lightness, and resiliency." It was once much used for carving, and is still in demand for sounding-boards of piano-fortes and panels of carriages, and for various uses for which toughness and flexibility are required. Baskets and cradles are made of the twigs. Its sap affords sugar, and the honey made from its flowers is said to be preferred to any other. Its leaves are in some countries given to cattle, a kind of chocolate has been made of its fruit, a medicine has been prepared from an infusion of its flowers, and finally, the charcoal made of its wood is greatly valued for gunpowder.

The sight of this tree reminded us that we had reached a strange land to us. As we sailed under this canopy of leaves we saw the sky through its chinks, and, as it were, the meaning and idea of the tree stamped in a thousand hieroglyphics on the heavens. The universe is so aptly fitted to our organization that the eye wanders and reposes at the same time. On every side there is something to soothe and refresh this sense. Look up at the tree-tops and see how finely Nature finishes off her work there. See how the pines spire without end higher and higher, and make a graceful fringe to the earth. And who shall count the finer cobwebs that soar and float away from their utmost tops, and the myriad insects that dodge between them. Leaves are of more various forms than the alphabets of all languages put together; of the oaks alone there are hardly two alike, and each expresses its own character.

In all her products Nature only develops her simplest germs. One would say that it was no great stretch of invention to create birds. The hawk, which now takes his flight over the top of the wood, was at first, perchance, only a leaf which fluttered in its aisles. From rustling leaves she came in the course of ages to the loftier flight and clear carol of the bird.

Salmon Brook comes in from the west under the railroad, a mile and a half below the village of Nashua. We rowed up far enough into the meadows which border it to learn its piscatorial history from a haymaker on its banks. He told us that the silver eel was formerly abundant here, and pointed to some sunken creels at its mouth. This man's memory and imagination were fertile in fishermen's tales of floating isles in bottomless ponds, and of lakes mysteriously stocked with fishes, and would have kept us till nightfall to listen, but we could not afford to loiter in this roadstead, and so stood out to our sea again. Though we never trod in those meadows, but only touched their margin with our hands, we still retain a pleasant memory of them.

Salmon Brook, whose name is said to be a translation from the Indian, was a favorite haunt of the aborigines. Here, too, the first white settlers of Nashua planted, and some dents in the earth where their houses stood and the wrecks of ancient apple-trees are still visible. About one mile up this stream stood the house of old John Lovewell, who was an ensign in the army of Oliver Cromwell, and the father of "famous Captain Lovewell." He settled here before 1690, and died about 1754, at the age of one hundred and twenty years. He is thought to have been engaged in the famous Narragansett swamp fight, which took place in 1675, before he came here. The Indians are said to have spared him in succeeding wars on account of his kindness to them. Even in 1700 he was so

old and gray-headed that his scalp was worth nothing, since
the French Governor offered no bounty for such. I have
stood in the dent of his cellar on the bank of the brook, and
talked there with one whose grandfather had, whose father
might have, talked with Lovewell. Here also he had a mill in
his old age, and kept a small store. He was remembered by
some who were recently living, as a hale old man who drove
the boys out of his orchard with his cane. Consider the
triumphs of the mortal man, and what poor trophies it would
have to show, to wit:—He cobbled shoes without glasses at
a hundred, and cut a handsome swath at a hundred and five!
Lovewell's house is said to have been the first which Mrs.
Dustan reached on her escape from the Indians. Here probably the hero of Pequawket was born and bred. Close by may
be seen the cellar and the gravestone of Joseph Hassell, who,
as is elsewhere recorded, with his wife Anna, and son Benjamin, and Mary Marks, "were slain by our Indian enemies on
September 2d, [1691,] in the evening." As Gookin observed
on a previous occasion, "The Indian rod upon the English
backs had not yet done God's errand." Salmon Brook near its
mouth is still a solitary stream, meandering through woods
and meadows, while the then uninhabited mouth of the Nashua now resounds with the din of a manufacturing town.

A stream from Otternic Pond in Hudson comes in just
above Salmon Brook, on the opposite side. There was a good
view of Uncannunuc, the most conspicuous mountain in
these parts, from the bank here, seen rising over the west end
of the bridge above. We soon after passed the village of Nashua, on the river of the same name, where there is a covered
bridge over the Merrimack. The Nashua, which is one of
the largest tributaries, flows from Wachusett Mountain,
through Lancaster, Groton, and other towns, where it has
formed well-known elm-shaded meadows, but near its mouth
it is obstructed by falls and factories, and did not tempt us to
explore it.

Far away from here, in Lancaster, with another companion,
I have crossed the broad valley of the Nashua, over which we
had so long looked westward from the Concord hills without
seeing it to the blue mountains in the horizon. So many
streams, so many meadows and woods and quiet dwellings of

men had lain concealed between us and those Delectable Mountains;—from yonder hill on the road to Tyngsborough you may get a good view of them. There where it seemed uninterrupted forest to our youthful eyes, between two neighboring pines in the horizon, lay the valley of the Nashua, and this very stream was even then winding at its bottom, and then, as now, it was here silently mingling its waters with the Merrimack. The clouds which floated over its meadows and were born there, seen far in the west, gilded by the rays of the setting sun, had adorned a thousand evening skies for us. But as it were, by a turf wall this valley was concealed, and in our journey to those hills it was first gradually revealed to us. Summer and winter our eyes had rested on the dim outline of the mountains, to which distance and indistinctness lent a grandeur not their own, so that they served to interpret all the allusions of poets and travellers. Standing on the Concord Cliffs we thus spoke our mind to them:—

> With frontier strength ye stand your ground,
> With grand content ye circle round,
> Tumultuous silence for all sound,
> Ye distant nursery of rills,
> Monadnock and the Peterborough Hills;—
> Firm argument that never stirs,
> Outcircling the philosophers,—
> Like some vast fleet,
> Sailing through rain and sleet,
> Through winter's cold and summer's heat;
> Still holding on upon your high emprise,
> Until ye find a shore amid the skies;
> Not skulking close to land,
> With cargo contraband,
> For they who sent a venture out by ye
> Have set the Sun to see
> Their honesty.
> Ships of the line, each one,
> Ye westward run,
> Convoying clouds,
> Which cluster in your shrouds,
> Always before the gale,

Under a press of sail,
With weight of metal all untold,—
I seem to feel ye in my firm seat here,
Immeasurable depth of hold,
And breadth of beam, and length of running gear.

Methinks ye take luxurious pleasure
In your novel western leisure;
So cool your brows and freshly blue,
As Time had naught for ye to do;
For ye lie at your length,
An unappropriated strength,
Unhewn primeval timber,
For knees so stiff, for masts so limber;
The stock of which new earths are made,
One day to be our *western* trade,
Fit for the stanchions of a world
Which through the seas of space is hurled.

While we enjoy a lingering ray,
Ye still o'ertop the western day,
Reposing yonder on God's croft
Like solid stacks of hay;
So bold a line as ne'er was writ
On any page by human wit;
The forest glows as if
An enemy's camp-fires shone
Along the horizon,
Or the day's funeral pyre
Were lighted there;
Edged with silver and with gold,
The clouds hang o'er in damask fold,
And with such depth of amber light
The west is dight,
Where still a few rays slant,
That even Heaven seems extravagant.
Watatic Hill
Lies on the horizon's sill
Like a child's toy left overnight,
And other duds to left and right,

On the earth's edge, mountains and trees
Stand as they were on air graven,
Or as the vessels in a haven
Await the morning breeze.
I fancy even
Through your defiles windeth the way to heaven;
And yonder still, in spite of history's page,
Linger the golden and the silver age;
Upon the laboring gale
The news of future centuries is brought,
And of new dynasties of thought,
From your remotest vale.

But special I remember thee,
Wachusett, who like me
Standest alone without society.
Thy far blue eye,
A remnant of the sky,
Seen through the clearing or the gorge,
Or from the windows of the forge,
Doth leaven all it passes by.
Nothing is true
But stands 'tween me and you,
Thou western pioneer,
Who know'st not shame nor fear,
By venturous spirit driven
Under the eaves of heaven;
And canst expand thee there,
And breathe enough of air?
Even beyond the West
Thou migratest,
Into unclouded tracts,
Without a pilgrim's axe,
Cleaving thy road on high
With thy well-tempered brow,
And mak'st thyself a clearing in the sky.
Upholding heaven, holding down earth,
Thy pastime from thy birth;
Not steadied by the one, nor leaning on the other,
May I approve myself thy worthy brother!

At length, like Rasselas and other inhabitants of happy valleys, we had resolved to scale the blue wall which bounded
the western horizon, though not without misgivings that
thereafter no visible fairy-land would exist for us. But it
would be long to tell of our adventures, and we have no time
this afternoon, transporting ourselves in imagination up this
hazy Nashua valley, to go over again that pilgrimage. We have
since made many similar excursions to the principal mountains of New England and New York, and even far in the
wilderness, and have passed a night on the summit of many
of them. And now, when we look again westward from our
native hills, Wachusett and Monadnock have retreated once
more among the blue and fabulous mountains in the horizon,
though our eyes rest on the very rocks on both of them,
where we have pitched our tent for a night, and boiled our
hasty-pudding amid the clouds.

As late as 1724 there was no house on the north side of the
Nashua, but only scattered wigwams and gristly forests between this frontier and Canada. In September of that year,
two men who were engaged in making turpentine on that
side, for such were the first enterprises in the wilderness, were
taken captive and carried to Canada by a party of thirty Indians. Ten of the inhabitants of Dunstable, going to look for
them, found the hoops of their barrel cut, and the turpentine
spread on the ground. I have been told by an inhabitant of
Tyngsborough, who had the story from his ancestors, that
one of these captives, when the Indians were about to upset
his barrel of turpentine, seized a pine knot and flourishing it,
swore so resolutely that he would kill the first who touched
it, that they refrained, and when at length he returned from
Canada he found it still standing. Perhaps there was more
than one barrel. However this may have been, the scouts
knew by marks on the trees, made with coal mixed with
grease, that the men were not killed, but taken prisoners. One
of the company, named Farwell, perceiving that the turpentine had not done spreading, concluded that the Indians had
been gone but a short time, and they accordingly went in
instant pursuit. Contrary to the advice of Farwell, following
directly on their trail up the Merrimack, they fell into an am-

buscade near Thornton's Ferry, in the present town of Merrimack, and nine were killed, only one, Farwell, escaping after
a vigorous pursuit. The men of Dunstable went out and
picked up their bodies, and carried them all down to Dunstable and buried them. It is almost word for word as in the
Robin Hood ballad: —

> "They carried these foresters into fair Nottingham,
>   As many there did know,
>   They digged them graves in their churchyard,
>   And they buried them all a-row."

Nottingham is only the other side of the river, and they were
not exactly all a-row. You may read in the churchyard at
Dunstable, under the "Memento Mori," and the name of one
of them, how they "departed this life," and

> "This man with seven more that lies in
>   this grave was slew all in a day by
>   the Indians."

The stones of some others of the company stand around the
common grave· with their separate inscriptions. Eight were
buried here, but nine were killed, according to the best authorities.

> "Gentle river, gentle river,
>   Lo, thy streams are stained with gore,
>   Many a brave and noble captain
>   Floats along thy willowed shore.

> "All beside thy limpid waters,
>   All beside thy sands so bright,
>   *Indian* Chiefs and Christian warriors
>   Joined in fierce and mortal fight."

It is related in the History of Dunstable, that on the return
of Farwell the Indians were engaged by a fresh party which
they compelled to retreat, and pursued as far as the Nashua,
where they fought across the stream at its mouth. After the
departure of the Indians, the figure of an Indian's head was
found carved by them on a large tree by the shore, which
circumstance has given its name to this part of the village of

Nashville,—the "Indian Head." "It was observed by some judicious," says Gookin, referring to Philip's war, "that at the beginning of the war the English soldiers made a nothing of the Indians, and many spake words to this effect: that one Englishman was sufficient to chase ten Indians; many reckoned it was no other but *Veni, vidi, vici.*" But we may conclude that the judicious would by this time have made a different observation.

Farwell appears to have been the only one who had studied his profession, and understood the business of hunting Indians. He lived to fight another day, for the next year he was Lovewell's lieutenant at Pequawket, but that time, as we have related, he left his bones in the wilderness. His name still reminds us of twilight days and forest scouts on Indian trails, with an uneasy scalp;—an indispensable hero to New England. As the more recent poet of Lovewell's fight has sung, halting a little but bravely still:—

> "Then did the crimson streams that flowed
>   Seem like the waters of the brook,
> That brightly shine, that loudly dash,
>   Far down the cliffs of Agiochook."

These battles sound incredible to us. I think that posterity will doubt if such things ever were; if our bold ancestors who settled this land were not struggling rather with the forest shadows, and not with a copper-colored race of men. They were vapors, fever and ague of the unsettled woods. Now, only a few arrow-heads are turned up by the plough. In the Pelasgic, the Etruscan, or the British story, there is nothing so shadowy and unreal.

It is a wild and antiquated looking graveyard, overgrown with bushes, on the high-road, about a quarter of a mile from and overlooking the Merrimack, with a deserted mill-stream bounding it on one side, where lie the earthly remains of the ancient inhabitants of Dunstable. We passed it three or four miles below here. You may read there the names of Lovewell, Farwell, and many others whose families were distinguished in Indian warfare. We noticed there two large masses of granite more than a foot thick and rudely squared, lying flat on the ground over the remains of the first pastor and his wife.

It is remarkable that the dead lie everywhere under stones, —

"Strata jacent passim *suo* quæque sub" *lapide* —

corpora, we might say, if the measure allowed. When the stone is a slight one, it does not oppress the spirits of the traveller to meditate by it; but these did seem a little heathenish to us; and so are all large monuments over men's bodies, from the pyramids down. A monument should at least be "star-y-pointing," to indicate whither the spirit is gone, and not prostrate, like the body it has deserted. There have been some nations who could do nothing but construct tombs, and these are the only traces which they have left. They are the heathen. But why these stones, so upright and emphatic, like exclamation-points? What was there so remarkable that lived? Why should the monument be so much more enduring than the fame which it is designed to perpetuate, — a stone to a bone? "Here lies," — "Here lies"; — why do they not sometimes write, There rises? Is it a monument to the body only that is intended? "Having reached the term of his *natural* life"; — would it not be truer to say, Having reached the term of his *unnatural* life? The rarest quality in an epitaph is truth. If any character is given, it should be as severely true as the decision of the three judges below, and not the partial testimony of friends. Friends and contemporaries should supply only the name and date, and leave it to posterity to write the epitaph.

> Here lies an honest man,
> Rear-Admiral Van.

———

> Faith, then ye have
> Two in one grave,
> For in his favor,
> Here too lies the Engraver.

Fame itself is but an epitaph; as late, as false, as true. But they only are the true epitaphs which Old Mortality retouches.

A man might well pray that he may not taboo or curse any

portion of nature by being buried in it. For the most part, the best man's spirit makes a fearful sprite to haunt his grave, and it is therefore much to the credit of Little John, the famous follower of Robin Hood, and reflecting favorably on his character, that his grave was "long celebrous for the yielding of excellent whetstones." I confess that I have but little love for such collections as they have at the Catacombs, Père la Chaise, Mount Auburn, and even this Dunstable graveyard. At any rate, nothing but great antiquity can make graveyards interesting to me. I have no friends there. It may be that I am not competent to write the poetry of the grave. The farmer who has skimmed his farm might perchance leave his body to Nature to be ploughed in, and in some measure restore its fertility. We should not retard but forward her economies.

Soon the village of Nashua was out of sight, and the woods were gained again, and we rowed slowly on before sunset, looking for a solitary place in which to spend the night. A few evening clouds began to be reflected in the water and the surface was dimpled only here and there by a muskrat crossing the stream. We camped at length near Penichook Brook, on the confines of what is now Nashville, by a deep ravine, under the skirts of a pine wood, where the dead pine-leaves were our carpet, and their tawny boughs stretched overhead. But fire and smoke soon tamed the scene; the rocks consented to be our walls, and the pines our roof. A woodside was already the fittest locality for us.

The wilderness is near as well as dear to every man. Even the oldest villages are indebted to the border of wild wood which surrounds them, more than to the gardens of men. There is something indescribably inspiriting and beautiful in the aspect of the forest skirting and occasionally jutting into the midst of new towns, which, like the sand-heaps of fresh fox-burrows, have sprung up in their midst. The very uprightness of the pines and maples asserts the ancient rectitude and vigor of nature. Our lives need the relief of such a background, where the pine flourishes and the jay still screams.

We had found a safe harbor for our boat, and as the sun was setting carried up our furniture, and soon arranged our house upon the bank, and while the kettle steamed at the tent door, we chatted of distant friends and of the sights which we were to behold, and wondered which way the towns lay from us. Our cocoa was soon boiled, and supper set upon our chest, and we lengthened out this meal, like old voyageurs, with our talk. Meanwhile we spread the map on the ground, and read in the Gazetteer when the first settlers came here and got a township granted. Then, when supper was done and we had written the journal of our voyage, we wrapped our buffaloes about us and lay down with our heads pillowed on our arms listening awhile to the distant baying of a dog, or the murmurs of the river, or to the wind, which had not gone to rest: —

> The western wind came lumbering in,
> Bearing a faint Pacific din,
> Our evening mail, swift at the call
> Of its Postmaster General;
> Laden with news from Californ',
> Whate'er transpired hath since morn,
> How wags the world by brier and brake
> From hence to Athabasca Lake; —

or half awake and half asleep, dreaming of a star which glimmered through our cotton roof. Perhaps at midnight one was awakened by a cricket shrilly singing on his shoulder, or by a hunting spider in his eye, and was lulled asleep again by some streamlet purling its way along at the bottom of a wooded and rocky ravine in our neighborhood. It was pleasant to lie with our heads so low in the grass, and hear what a tinkling ever-busy laboratory it was. A thousand little artisans beat on their anvils all night long.

Far in the night as we were falling asleep on the bank of the Merrimack, we heard some tyro beating a drum incessantly, in preparation for a country muster, as we learned, and we thought of the line, —

"When the drum beat at dead of night."

We could have assured him that his beat would be answered, and the forces be mustered. Fear not, thou drummer of the night, we too will be there. And still he drummed on in the silence and the dark. This stray sound from a far-off sphere

came to our ears from time to time, far, sweet, and significant, and we listened with such an unprejudiced sense as if
for the first time we heard at all. No doubt he was an insignificant drummer enough, but his music afforded us a prime
and leisure hour, and we felt that we were in season wholly.
These simple sounds related us to the stars. Ay, there was a
logic in them so convincing that the combined sense of mankind could never make me doubt their conclusions. I stop my
habitual thinking, as if the plough had suddenly run deeper
in its furrow through the crust of the world. How can I go
on, who have just stepped over such a bottomless skylight in
the bog of my life. Suddenly old Time winked at me,—Ah,
you know me, you rogue,—and news had come that IT was
well. That ancient universe is in such capital health, I think
undoubtedly it will never die. Heal yourselves, doctors; by
God, I live.

> Then idle Time ran gadding by
> And left me with Eternity alone;
> I hear beyond the range of sound,
> I see beyond the verge of sight,—

I see, smell, taste, hear, feel, that everlasting Something to
which we are allied, at once our maker, our abode, our destiny, our very Selves; the one historic truth, the most remarkable fact which can become the distinct and uninvited subject
of our thought, the actual glory of the universe; the only fact
which a human being cannot avoid recognizing, or in some
way forget or dispense with.

> It doth expand my privacies
> To all, and leave me single in the crowd.

I have seen how the foundations of the world are laid, and I
have not the least doubt that it will stand a good while.

> Now chiefly is my natal hour,
> And only now my prime of life.
> I will not doubt the love untold,
> Which not my worth nor want hath bought,
> Which wooed me young and wooes me old,
> And to this evening hath me brought.

What are ears? what is Time? that this particular series of sounds called a strain of music, an invisible and fairy troop which never brushed the dew from any mead, can be wafted down through the centuries from Homer to me, and he have been conversant with that same aerial and mysterious charm which now so tingles my ears? What a fine communication from age to age, of the fairest and noblest thoughts, the aspirations of ancient men, even such as were never communicated by speech, is music! It is the flower of language, thought colored and curved, fluent and flexible, its crystal fountain tinged with the sun's rays, and its purling ripples reflecting the grass and the clouds. A strain of music reminds me of a passage of the Vedas, and I associate with it the idea of infinite remoteness, as well as of beauty and serenity, for to the senses that is farthest from us which addresses the greatest depth within us. It teaches us again and again to trust the remotest and finest as the divinest instinct, and makes a dream our only real experience. We feel a sad cheer when we hear it, perchance because we that hear are not one with that which is heard.

> Therefore a torrent of sadness deep,
> Through the strains of thy triumph is heard to sweep.

The sadness is ours. The Indian poet Calidas says in the Sacontala: "Perhaps the sadness of men on seeing beautiful forms and hearing sweet music arises from some faint remembrance of past joys, and the traces of connections in a former state of existence." As polishing expresses the vein in marble, and grain in wood, so music brings out what of heroic lurks anywhere. The hero is the sole patron of music. That harmony which exists naturally between the hero's moods and the universe the soldier would fain imitate with drum and trumpet. When we are in health all sounds fife and drum for us; we hear the notes of music in the air, or catch its echoes dying away when we awake in the dawn. Marching is when the pulse of the hero beats in unison with the pulse of Nature, and he steps to the measure of the universe; then there is true courage and invincible strength.

Plutarch says that "Plato thinks the gods never gave men music, the science of melody and harmony, for mere delecta-

tion or to tickle the ear; but that the discordant parts of the
circulations and beauteous fabric of the soul, and that of it
that roves about the body, and many times, for want of tune
and air, breaks forth into many extravagances and excesses,
might be sweetly recalled and artfully wound up to their former consent and agreement."

Music is the sound of the universal laws promulgated. It is
the only assured tone. There are in it such strains as far surpass any man's faith in the loftiness of his destiny. Things are
to be learned which it will be worth the while to learn. Formerly I heard these

RUMORS FROM AN ÆOLIAN HARP.

There is a vale which none hath seen,
Where foot of man has never been,
Such as here lives with toil and strife,
An anxious and a sinful life.

There every virtue has its birth,
Ere it descends upon the earth,
And thither every deed returns,
Which in the generous bosom burns.

There love is warm, and youth is young,
And poetry is yet unsung,
For Virtue still adventures there,
And freely breathes her native air.

And ever, if you hearken well,
You still may hear its vesper bell,
And tread of high-souled men go by,
Their thoughts conversing with the sky.

According to Jamblichus, "Pythagoras did not procure for
himself a thing of this kind through instruments or the voice,
but employing a certain ineffable divinity, and which it is difficult to apprehend, he extended his ears and fixed his intellect
in the sublime symphonies of the world, he alone hearing and
understanding, as it appears, the universal harmony and con-
sonance of the spheres, and the stars that are moved through

them, and which produce a fuller and more intense melody than anything effected by mortal sounds."

Travelling on foot very early one morning due east from here about twenty miles, from Caleb Harriman's tavern in Hampstead toward Haverhill, when I reached the railroad in Plaistow, I heard at some distance a faint music in the air like an Æolian harp, which I immediately suspected to proceed from the cord of the telegraph vibrating in the just awakening morning wind, and applying my ear to one of the posts I was convinced that it was so. It was the telegraph harp singing its message through the country, its message sent not by men, but by gods. Perchance, like the statue of Memnon, it resounds only in the morning, when the first rays of the sun fall on it. It was like the first lyre or shell heard on the seashore,—that vibrating cord high in the air over the shores of earth. So have all things their higher and their lower uses. I heard a fairer news than the journals ever print. It told of things worthy to hear, and worthy of the electric fluid to carry the news of, not of the price of cotton and flour, but it hinted at the price of the world itself and of things which are priceless, of absolute truth and beauty.

Still the drum rolled on, and stirred our blood to fresh extravagance that night. The clarion sound and clang of corselet and buckler were heard from many a hamlet of the soul, and many a knight was arming for the fight behind the encamped stars.

> "Before each van
> Prick forth the aery knights, and couch their spears
> Till thickest legions close; with feats of arms
> From either end of Heaven the welkin burns."

> Away! away! away! away!
>   Ye have not kept your secret well,
> I will abide that other day,
>   Those other lands ye tell.
>
> Has time no leisure left for these,
>   The acts that ye rehearse?
> Is not eternity a lease
>   For better deeds than verse?

'T is sweet to hear of heroes dead,
 To know them still alive,
But sweeter if we earn their bread,
 And in us they survive.

Our life should feed the springs of fame
 With a perennial wave,
As ocean feeds the babbling founts
 Which find in it their grave.

Ye skies drop gently round my breast,
 And be my corselet blue,
Ye earth receive my lance in rest,
 My faithful charger you;

Ye stars my spear-heads in the sky,
 My arrow-tips ye are;
I see the routed foemen fly,
 My bright spears fixed are.

Give me an angel for a foe,
 Fix now the place and time,
And straight to meet him I will go
 Above the starry chime.

And with our clashing bucklers' clang
 The heavenly spheres shall ring,
While bright the northern lights shall hang
 Beside our tourneying.

And if she lose her champion true,
 Tell Heaven not despair,
For I will be her champion new,
 Her fame I will repair.

There was a high wind this night, which we afterwards learned had been still more violent elsewhere, and had done much injury to the cornfields far and near; but we only heard it sigh from time to time, as if it had no license to shake the foundations of our tent; the pines murmured, the water rippled, and the tent rocked a little, but we only laid our ears closer to the ground, while the blast swept on to alarm other men, and long before sunrise we were ready to pursue our voyage as usual.

Tuesday

"On either side the river lie
Long fields of barley and of rye,
That clothe the wold and meet the sky;
And through the fields the road runs by
To many-towered Camelot."
TENNYSON.

LONG BEFORE daylight we ranged abroad, hatchet in hand, in search of fuel, and made the yet slumbering and dreaming wood resound with our blows. Then with our fire we burned up a portion of the loitering night, while the kettle sang its homely strain to the morning star. We tramped about the shore, waked all the muskrats, and scared up the bittern and birds that were asleep upon their roosts; we hauled up and upset our boat and washed it and rinsed out the clay, talking aloud as if it were broad day, until at length, by three o'clock, we had completed our preparations and were ready to pursue our voyage as usual; so, shaking the clay from our feet, we pushed into the fog.

Though we were enveloped in mist as usual, we trusted that there was a bright day behind it.

Ply the oars! away! away!
In each dew-drop of the morning
Lies the promise of a day.

Rivers from the sunrise flow,
Springing with the dewy morn;
Voyageurs 'gainst time do row,
Idle noon nor sunset know,
Ever even with the dawn.

Belknap, the historian of this State, says that, "In the neighborhood of fresh rivers and ponds, a whitish fog in the morning lying over the water is a sure indication of fair weather for that day; and when no fog is seen, rain is expected before night." That which seemed to us to invest the world was only a narrow and shallow wreath of vapor stretched over the channel of the Merrimack from the seaboard to the mountains. More extensive fogs, however, have their own limits. I once saw the day break from the top of Saddle-back Mountain in Massachusetts, above the clouds. As we cannot distinguish objects through this dense fog, let me tell this story more at length.

I had come over the hills on foot and alone in serene summer days, plucking the raspberries by the wayside, and occasionally buying a loaf of bread at a farmer's house, with a knapsack on my back which held a few traveller's books and a change of clothing, and a staff in my hand. I had that morning looked down from the Hoosack Mountain, where the road crosses it, on the village of North Adams in the valley three miles away under my feet, showing how uneven the earth may sometimes be, and making it seem an accident that it should ever be level and convenient for the feet of man. Putting a little rice and sugar and a tin cup into my knapsack at this village, I began in the afternoon to ascend the mountain, whose summit is three thousand six hundred feet above the level of the sea, and was seven or eight miles distant by the path. My route lay up a long and spacious valley called the Bellows, because the winds rush up or down it with violence in storms, sloping up to the very clouds between the principal range and a lower mountain. There were a few farms scattered along at different elevations, each commanding a fine prospect of the mountains to the north, and a stream ran down the middle of the valley on which near the head there was a mill. It seemed a road for the pilgrim to enter upon who would climb to the gates of heaven. Now I crossed a hay-field, and now over the brook on a slight bridge, still gradually ascending all the while with a sort of awe, and filled with indefinite expectations as to what kind of inhabitants and what kind of nature I should come to at last. It now seemed some advantage that the earth was uneven, for one could not imagine a more noble position for a farmhouse than this vale afforded, farther from or nearer to its head, from a glen-like seclusion overlooking the country at a great elevation between these two mountain walls.

It reminded me of the homesteads of the Huguenots, on

Staten Island, off the coast of New Jersey. The hills in the interior of this island, though comparatively low, are penetrated in various directions by similar sloping valleys on a humble scale, gradually narrowing and rising to the centre, and at the head of these the Huguenots, who were the first settlers, placed their houses quite within the land, in rural and sheltered places, in leafy recesses where the breeze played with the poplar and the gum-tree, from which, with equal security in calm and storm, they looked out through a widening vista, over miles of forest and stretching salt marsh, to the Huguenot's Tree, an old elm on the shore at whose root they had landed, and across the spacious outer bay of New York to Sandy Hook and the Highlands of Neversink, and thence over leagues of the Atlantic, perchance to some faint vessel in the horizon, almost a day's sail on her voyage to that Europe whence they had come. When walking in the interior there, in the midst of rural scenery, where there was as little to remind me of the ocean as amid the New Hampshire hills, I have suddenly, through a gap, a cleft or "clove road," as the Dutch settlers called it, caught sight of a ship under full sail, over a field of corn, twenty or thirty miles at sea. The effect was similar, since I had no means of measuring distances, to seeing a painted ship passed backwards and forwards through a magic-lantern.

But to return to the mountain. It seemed as if he must be the most singular and heavenly minded man whose dwelling stood highest up the valley. The thunder had rumbled at my heels all the way, but the shower passed off in another direction, though if it had not, I half believed that I should get above it. I at length reached the last house but one, where the path to the summit diverged to the right, while the summit itself rose directly in front. But I determined to follow up the valley to its head, and then find my own route up the steep as the shorter and more adventurous way. I had thoughts of returning to this house, which was well kept and so nobly placed, the next day, and perhaps remaining a week there, if I could have entertainment. Its mistress was a frank and hospitable young woman, who stood before me in a dishabille, busily and unconcernedly combing her long black hair while she talked, giving her head the necessary toss with each sweep of the comb, with lively, sparkling eyes, and full of interest in that lower world from which I had come, talking all the while as familiarly as if she had known me for years, and reminding me of a cousin of mine. She at first had taken me for a student from Williamstown, for they went by in parties, she said, either riding or walking, almost every pleasant day, and were a pretty wild set of fellows; but they never went by the way I was going. As I passed the last house, a man called out to know what I had to sell, for seeing my knapsack, he thought that I might be a pedler who was taking this unusual route over the ridge of the valley into South Adams. He told me that it was still four or five miles to the summit by the path which I had left, though not more than two in a straight line from where I was, but that nobody ever went this way; there was no path, and I should find it as steep as the roof of a house. But I knew that I was more used to woods and mountains than he, and went along through his cow-yard, while he, looking at the sun, shouted after me that I should not get to the top that night. I soon reached the head of the valley, but as I could not see the summit from this point, I ascended a low mountain on the opposite side, and took its bearing with my compass. I at once entered the woods, and began to climb the steep side of the mountain in a diagonal direction, taking the bearing of a tree every dozen rods. The ascent was by no means difficult or unpleasant, and occupied much less time than it would have taken to follow the path. Even country people, I have observed, magnify the difficulty of travelling in the forest, and especially among mountains. They seem to lack their usual common sense in this. I have climbed several higher mountains without guide or path, and have found, as might be expected, that it takes only more time and patience commonly than to travel the smoothest highway. It is very rare that you meet with obstacles in this world which the humblest man has not faculties to surmount. It is true we may come to a perpendicular precipice, but we need not jump off nor run our heads against it. A man may jump down his own cellar stairs or dash his brains out against his chimney, if he is mad. So far as my experience goes, travellers generally exaggerate the difficulties of the way. Like most evil, the difficulty is imaginary; for what's the

hurry? If a person lost would conclude that after all he is not
lost, he is not beside himself, but standing in his own old
shoes on the very spot where he is, and that for the time
being he will live there; but the places that have known him,
they are lost,—how much anxiety and danger would vanish.
I am not alone if I stand by myself. Who knows where in
space this globe is rolling? Yet we will not give ourselves up
for lost, let it go where it will.

I made my way steadily upward in a straight line through
a dense undergrowth of mountain laurel, until the trees began
to have a scraggy and infernal look, as if contending with
forest goblins, and at length I reached the summit, just as the
sun was setting. Several acres here had been cleared, and were
covered with rocks and stumps, and there was a rude observatory in the middle which overlooked the woods. I had one
fair view of the country before the sun went down, but I was
too thirsty to waste any light in viewing the prospect, and set
out directly to find water. First, going down a well-beaten
path for half a mile through the low scrubby wood, till I came
to where the water stood in the tracks of the horses which
had carried travellers up, I lay down flat, and drank these dry,
one after another, a pure, cold, spring-like water, but yet I
could not fill my dipper, though I contrived little siphons of
grass-stems, and ingenious aqueducts on a small scale; it was
too slow a process. Then remembering that I had passed a
moist place near the top, on my way up, I returned to find it
again, and here, with sharp stones and my hands, in the twilight, I made a well about two feet deep, which was soon
filled with pure cold water, and the birds too came and drank
at it. So I filled my dipper, and, making my way back to the
observatory, collected some dry sticks, and made a fire on
some flat stones which had been placed on the floor for that
purpose, and so I soon cooked my supper of rice, having already whittled a wooden spoon to eat it with.

I sat up during the evening, reading by the light of the fire
the scraps of newspapers in which some party had wrapped
their luncheon; the prices current in New York and Boston,
the advertisements, and the singular editorials which some
had seen fit to publish, not foreseeing under what critical circumstances they would be read. I read these things at a vast

advantage there, and it seemed to me that the advertisements, or what is called the business part of a paper, were greatly the best, the most useful, natural, and respectable. Almost all the opinions and sentiments expressed were so little considered, so shallow and flimsy, that I thought the very texture of the paper must be weaker in that part and tear the more easily. The advertisements and the prices current were more closely allied to nature, and were respectable in some measure as tide and meteorological tables are; but the reading-matter, which I remembered was most prized down below, unless it was some humble record of science, or an extract from some old classic, struck me as strangely whimsical, and crude, and one-idea'd, like a school-boy's theme, such as youths write and after burn. The opinions were of that kind that are doomed to wear a different aspect to-morrow, like last year's fashions; as if mankind were very green indeed, and would be ashamed of themselves in a few years, when they had outgrown this verdant period. There was, moreover, a singular disposition to wit and humor, but rarely the slightest real success; and the apparent success was a terrible satire on the attempt; the Evil Genius of man laughed the loudest at his best jokes. The advertisements, as I have said, such as were serious, and not of the modern quack kind, suggested pleasing and poetic thoughts; for commerce is really as interesting as nature. The very names of the commodities were poetic, and as suggestive as if they had been inserted in a pleasing poem,—Lumber, Cotton, Sugar, Hides, Guano, Logwood. Some sober, private, and original thought would have been grateful to read there, and as much in harmony with the circumstances as if it had been written on a mountain-top; for it is of a fashion which never changes, and as respectable as hides and logwood, or any natural product. What an inestimable companion such a scrap of paper would have been, containing some fruit of a mature life. What a relic! What a recipe! It seemed a divine invention, by which not mere shining coin, but shining and current thoughts, could be brought up and left there.

As it was cold, I collected quite a pile of wood and lay down on a board against the side of the building, not having any blanket to cover me, with my head to the fire, that I might look after it, which is not the Indian rule. But as it grew colder towards midnight, I at length encased myself completely in boards, managing even to put a board on top of me, with a large stone on it, to keep it down, and so slept comfortably. I was reminded, it is true, of the Irish children, who inquired what their neighbors did who had no door to put over them in winter nights as they had; but I am convinced that there was nothing very strange in the inquiry. Those who have never tried it can have no idea how far a door, which keeps the single blanket down, may go toward making one comfortable. We are constituted a good deal like chickens, which taken from the hen, and put in a basket of cotton in the chimney-corner, will often peep till they die, nevertheless, but if you put in a book, or anything heavy, which will press down the cotton, and feel like the hen, they go to sleep directly. My only companions were the mice, which came to pick up the crumbs that had been left in those scraps of paper; still, as everywhere, pensioners on man, and not unwisely improving this elevated tract for their habitation. They nibbled what was for them; I nibbled what was for me. Once or twice in the night, when I looked up, I saw a white cloud drifting through the windows, and filling the whole upper story.

This observatory was a building of considerable size, erected by the students of Williamstown College, whose buildings might be seen by daylight gleaming far down in the valley. It would be no small advantage if every college were thus located at the base of a mountain, as good at least as one well-endowed professorship. It were as well to be educated in the shadow of a mountain as in more classical shades. Some will remember, no doubt, not only that they went to the college, but that they went to the mountain. Every visit to its summit would, as it were, generalize the particular information gained below, and subject it to more catholic tests.

I was up early and perched upon the top of this tower to see the daybreak, for some time reading the names that had been engraved there, before I could distinguish more distant objects. An "untamable fly" buzzed at my elbow with the same nonchalance as on a molasses hogshead at the end of Long Wharf. Even there I must attend to his stale humdrum. But now I come to the pith of this long digression.—As the light increased I discovered around me an ocean of mist, which by chance reached up exactly to the base of the tower, and shut out every vestige of the earth, while I was left floating on this fragment of the wreck of a world, on my carved plank, in cloudland; a situation which required no aid from the imagination to render it impressive. As the light in the east steadily increased, it revealed to me more clearly the new world into which I had risen in the night, the new *terra firma* perchance of my future life. There was not a crevice left through which the trivial places we name Massachusetts or Vermont or New York could be seen, while I still inhaled the clear atmosphere of a July morning,—if it were July there. All around beneath me was spread for a hundred miles on every side, as far as the eye could reach, an undulating country of clouds, answering in the varied swell of its surface to the terrestrial world it veiled. It was such a country as we might see in dreams, with all the delights of paradise. There were immense snowy pastures, apparently smooth-shaven and firm, and shady vales between the vaporous mountains; and far in the horizon I could see where some luxurious misty timber jutted into the prairie, and trace the windings of a watercourse, some unimagined Amazon or Orinoko, by the misty trees on its brink. As there was wanting the symbol, so there was not the substance of impurity, no spot nor stain. It was a favor for which to be forever silent to be shown this vision. The earth beneath had become such a flitting thing of lights and shadows as the clouds had been before. It was not merely veiled to me, but it had passed away like the phantom of a shadow, σκιᾶς ὄναρ, and this new platform was gained. As I had climbed above storm and cloud, so by successive days' journeys I might reach the region of eternal day, beyond the tapering shadow of the earth; ay,

> "Heaven itself shall slide,
> And roll away, like melting stars that glide
> Along their oily threads."

But when its own sun began to rise on this pure world, I found myself a dweller in the dazzling halls of Aurora, into which poets have had but a partial glance over the eastern hills, drifting amid the saffron-colored clouds, and playing

with the rosy fingers of the Dawn, in the very path of the
Sun's chariot, and sprinkled with its dewy dust, enjoying the
benignant smile, and near at hand the far-darting glances of
the god. The inhabitants of earth behold commonly but the
dark and shadowy under-side of heaven's pavement; it is only
when seen at a favorable angle in the horizon, morning or
evening, that some faint streaks of the rich lining of the
clouds are revealed. But my muse would fail to convey an
impression of the gorgeous tapestry by which I was surrounded, such as men see faintly reflected afar off in the
chambers of the east. Here, as on earth, I saw the gracious
god

> "Flatter the mountain-tops with sovereign eye,
>
> .   .   .   .   .   .
>
> Gilding pale streams with heavenly alchemy."

But never here did "Heaven's sun" stain himself.

But, alas, owing, as I think, to some unworthiness in myself, my private sun did stain himself, and

> "Anon permit the basest clouds to ride
> With ugly wrack on his celestial face,"—

for before the god had reached the zenith the heavenly pavement rose and embraced my wavering virtue, or rather I sank
down again into that "forlorn world," from which the celestial sun had hid his visage,—

> "How may a worm that crawls along the dust,
>   Clamber the azure mountains, thrown so high,
>   And fetch from thence thy fair idea just,
>   That in those sunny courts doth hidden lie,
>   Clothed with such light as blinds the angel's eye?
>   How may weak mortal ever hope to file
>   His unsmooth tongue, and his deprostrate style?
>   O, raise thou from his corse thy now entombed exile!"

In the preceding evening I had seen the summits of new
and yet higher mountains, the Catskills, by which I might
hope to climb to heaven again, and had set my compass for a
fair lake in the southwest, which lay in my way, for which I

now steered, descending the mountain by my own route, on the side opposite to that by which I had ascended, and soon found myself in the region of cloud and drizzling rain, and the inhabitants affirmed that it had been a cloudy and drizzling day wholly.

But now we must make haste back before the fog disperses to the blithe Merrimack water.

> Since that first "Away! away!"
>   Many a lengthy reach we've rowed,
> Still the sparrow on the spray
> Hastes to usher in the day
>   With her simple stanza'd ode.

We passed a canal-boat before sunrise, groping its way to the seaboard, and, though we could not see it on account of the fog, the few dull, thumping, stertorous sounds which we heard, impressed us with a sense of weight and irresistible motion. One little rill of commerce already awake on this distant New Hampshire river. The fog, as it required more skill in the steering, enhanced the interest of our early voyage, and made the river seem indefinitely broad. A slight mist, through which objects are faintly visible, has the effect of expanding even ordinary streams, by a singular mirage, into arms of the sea or inland lakes. In the present instance it was even fragrant and invigorating, and we enjoyed it as a sort of earlier sunshine, or dewy and embryo light.

> Low-anchored cloud,
> Newfoundland air,
> Fountain-head and source of rivers,
> Dew-cloth, dream drapery,
> And napkin spread by fays;
> Drifting meadow of the air,
> Where bloom the daisied banks and violets,
> And in whose fenny labyrinth
> The bittern booms and heron wades;
> Spirit of lakes and seas and rivers,
> Bear only perfumes and the scent
> Of healing herbs to just men's fields!

The same pleasant and observant historian whom we quoted above says, that, "In the mountainous parts of the country, the ascent of vapors, and their formation into clouds, is a curious and entertaining object. The vapors are seen rising in small columns like smoke from many chimneys. When risen to a certain height, they spread, meet, condense, and are attracted to the mountains, where they either distil in gentle dews, and replenish the springs, or descend in showers, accompanied with thunder. After short intermissions, the process is repeated many times in the course of a summer day, affording to travellers a lively illustration of what is observed in the Book of Job, 'They are wet with the showers of the mountains.' "

Fogs and clouds which conceal the overshadowing mountains lend the breadth of the plains to mountain vales. Even a small-featured country acquires some grandeur in stormy weather when clouds are seen drifting between the beholder and the neighboring hills. When, in travelling toward Haverhill through Hampstead in this State, on the height of land between the Merrimack and the Piscataqua or the sea, you commence the descent eastward, the view toward the coast is so distant and unexpected, though the sea is invisible, that you at first suppose the unobstructed atmosphere to be a fog in the lowlands concealing hills of corresponding elevation to that you are upon; but it is the mist of prejudice alone, which the winds will not disperse. The most stupendous scenery ceases to be sublime when it becomes distinct, or in other words limited, and the imagination is no longer encouraged to exaggerate it. The actual height and breadth of a mountain or a waterfall are always ridiculously small; they are the imagined only that content us. Nature is not made after such a fashion as we would have her. We piously exaggerate her wonders, as the scenery around our home.

Such was the heaviness of the dews along this river that we were generally obliged to leave our tent spread over the bows of the boat till the sun had dried it, to avoid mildew. We passed the mouth of Penichook Brook, a wild salmon-stream, in the fog, without seeing it. At length the sun's rays struggled through the mist and showed us the pines on shore dripping with dew, and springs trickling from the moist banks,—

"And now the taller sons, whom Titan warms,
 Of unshorn mountains blown with easy winds,
 Dandle the morning's childhood in their arms,
 And, if they chanced to slip the prouder pines,
 The under corylets did catch their shines,
 To gild their leaves."

We rowed for some hours between glistening banks before the sun had dried the grass and leaves, or the day had established its character. Its serenity at last seemed the more profound and secure for the denseness of the morning's fog. The river became swifter, and the scenery more pleasing than before. The banks were steep and clayey for the most part, and trickling with water, and where a spring oozed out a few feet above the river the boatmen had cut a trough out of a slab with their axes, and placed it so as to receive the water and fill their jugs conveniently. Sometimes this purer and cooler water, bursting out from under a pine or a rock, was collected into a basin close to the edge of and level with the river, a fountain-head of the Merrimack. So near along life's stream are the fountains of innocence and youth making fertile its sandy margin; and the voyageur will do well to replenish his vessels often at these uncontaminated sources. Some youthful spring, perchance, still empties with tinkling music into the oldest river, even when it is falling into the sea, and we imagine that its music is distinguished by the river-gods from the general lapse of the stream, and falls sweeter on their ears in proportion as it is nearer to the ocean. As the evaporations of the river feed thus these unsuspected springs which filter through its banks, so, perchance, our aspirations fall back again in springs on the margin of life's stream to refresh and purify it. The yellow and tepid river may float his scow, and cheer his eye with its reflections and its ripples, but the boatman quenches his thirst at this small rill alone. It is this purer and cooler element that chiefly sustains his life. The race will long survive that is thus discreet.

Our course this morning lay between the territories of Merrimack, on the west, and Litchfield, once called Brenton's Farm, on the east, which townships were anciently the Indian Naticook. Brenton was a fur-trader among the Indians, and these lands were granted to him in 1656. The latter township contains about five hundred inhabitants, of whom, however, we saw none, and but few of their dwellings. Being on the river, whose banks are always high and generally conceal the few houses, the country appeared much more wild and primitive than to the traveller on the neighboring roads. The river is by far the most attractive highway, and those boatmen who have spent twenty or twenty-five years on it must have had a much fairer, more wild, and memorable experience than the dusty and jarring one of the teamster who has driven, during the same time, on the roads which run parallel with the stream. As one ascends the Merrimack he rarely sees a village, but for the most part alternate wood and pasture lands, and sometimes a field of corn or potatoes, of rye or oats or English grass, with a few straggling apple-trees, and, at still longer intervals, a farmer's house. The soil, excepting the best of the interval, is commonly as light and sandy as a patriot could desire. Sometimes this forenoon the country appeared in its primitive state, and as if the Indian still inhabited it, and, again, as if many free, new settlers occupied it, their slight fences straggling down to the water's edge; and the barking of dogs, and even the prattle of children, were heard, and smoke was seen to go up from some hearthstone, and the banks were divided into patches of pasture, mowing, tillage, and woodland. But when the river spread out broader, with an uninhabited islet, or a long, low sandy shore which ran on single and devious, not answering to its opposite, but far off as if it were sea-shore or single coast, and the land no longer nursed the river in its bosom, but they conversed as equals, the rustling leaves with rippling waves, and few fences were seen, but high oak woods on one side, and large herds of cattle, and all tracks seemed a point to one centre behind some statelier grove,—we imagined that the river flowed through an extensive manor, and that the few inhabitants were retainers to a lord, and a feudal state of things prevailed.

When there was a suitable reach, we caught sight of the Goffstown mountain, the Indian Uncannunuc, rising before us on the west side. It was a calm and beautiful day, with only a slight zephyr to ripple the surface of the water, and rustle the woods on shore, and just warmth enough to prove

the kindly disposition of Nature to her children. With buoyant spirits and vigorous impulses we tossed our boat rapidly
along into the very middle of this forenoon. The fish-hawk
sailed and screamed overhead. The chipping or striped squirrel, *Sciurus striatus* (*Tamias Lysteri*, Aud.), sat upon the end
of some Virginia fence or rider reaching over the stream,
twirling a green nut with one paw, as in a lathe, while the
other held it fast against its incisors as chisels. Like an independent russet leaf, with a will of its own, rustling whither it
could; now under the fence, now over it, now peeping at the
voyageurs through a crack with only its tail visible, now at its
lunch deep in the toothsome kernel, and now a rod off playing at hide-and-seek, with the nut stowed away in its chops,
where were half a dozen more besides, extending its cheeks to
a ludicrous breadth,—as if it were devising through what safe
valve of frisk or somerset to let its superfluous life escape; the
stream passing harmlessly off, even while it sits, in constant
electric flashes through its tail. And now with a chuckling
squeak it dives into the root of a hazel, and we see no more
of it. Or the larger red squirrel or chickaree, sometimes called
the Hudson Bay squirrel (*Sciurus Hudsonius*), gave warning
of our approach by that peculiar alarum of his, like the winding up of some strong clock, in the top of a pine-tree, and
dodged behind its stem, or leaped from tree to tree with such
caution and adroitness, as if much depended on the fidelity of
his scout, running along the white-pine boughs sometimes
twenty rods by our side, with such speed, and by such unerring
routes, as if it were some well-worn familiar path to him;
and presently, when we have passed, he returns to his work of
cutting off the pine-cones, and letting them fall to the ground.

We passed Cromwell's Falls, the first we met with on this
river, this forenoon, by means of locks, without using our
wheels. These falls are the Nesenkeag of the Indians. Great
Nesenkeag Stream comes in on the right just above, and Little Nesenkeag some distance below, both in Litchfield. We
read in the Gazetteer, under the head of Merrimack, that
"The first house in this town was erected on the margin of
the river [soon after 1665] for a house of traffic with the Indians. For some time one Cromwell carried on a lucrative
trade with them, weighing their furs with his foot, till, en-

raged at his supposed or real deception, they formed the resolution to murder him. This intention being communicated
to Cromwell, he buried his wealth and made his escape.
Within a few hours after his flight, a party of the Penacook
tribe arrived, and, not finding the object of their resentment,
burnt his habitation." Upon the top of the high bank here,
close to the river, was still to be seen his cellar, now overgrown with trees. It was a convenient spot for such a traffic,
at the foot of the first falls above the settlements, and commanding a pleasant view up the river, where he could see the
Indians coming down with their furs. The lock-man told us
that his shovel and tongs had been ploughed up here, and
also a stone with his name on it. But we will not vouch for
the truth of this story. In the New Hampshire Historical Collections for 1815 it says, "Some time after pewter was found in
the well, and an iron pot and trammel in the sand; the latter
are preserved." These were the traces of the white trader. On
the opposite bank, where it jutted over the stream cape-wise,
we picked up four arrow-heads and a small Indian tool made
of stone, as soon as we had climbed it, where plainly there
had once stood a wigwam of the Indians with whom Cromwell traded, and who fished and hunted here before he came.

As usual the gossips have not been silent respecting Cromwell's buried wealth, and it is said that some years ago a farmer's plough, not far from here, slid over a flat stone which
emitted a hollow sound, and, on its being raised, a small hole
six inches in diameter was discovered, stoned about, from
which a sum of money was taken. The lock-man told us another similar story about a farmer in a neighboring town,
who had been a poor man, but who suddenly bought a good
farm, and was well to do in the world, and, when he was
questioned, did not give a satisfactory account of the matter;
how few, alas, could! This caused his hired man to remember
that one day, as they were ploughing together, the plough
struck something, and his employer, going back to look, concluded not to go round again, saying that the sky looked
rather lowering, and so put up his team. The like urgency has
caused many things to be remembered which never transpired. The truth is, there is money buried everywhere, and
you have only to go to work to find it.

Not far from these falls stands an oak-tree, on the interval, about a quarter of a mile from the river, on the farm of a Mr. Lund, which was pointed out to us as the spot where French, the leader of the party which went in pursuit of the Indians from Dunstable, was killed. Farwell dodged them in the thick woods near. It did not look as if men had ever had to run for their lives on this now open and peaceful interval.

Here too was another extensive desert by the side of the road in Litchfield, visible from the bank of the river. The sand was blown off in some places to the depth of ten or twelve feet, leaving small grotesque hillocks of that height, where there was a clump of bushes firmly rooted. Thirty or forty years ago, as we were told, it was a sheep-pasture, but the sheep, being worried by the fleas, began to paw the ground, till they broke the sod, and so the sand began to blow, till now it had extended over forty or fifty acres. This evil might easily have been remedied, at first, by spreading birches with their leaves on over the sand, and fastening them down with stakes, to break the wind. The fleas bit the sheep, and the sheep bit the ground, and the sore had spread to this extent. It is astonishing what a great sore a little scratch breedeth. Who knows but Sahara, where caravans and cities are buried, began with the bite of an African flea? This poor globe, how it must itch in many places! Will no god be kind enough to spread a salve of birches over its sores? Here too we noticed where the Indians had gathered a heap of stones, perhaps for their council-fire, which, by their weight having prevented the sand under them from blowing away, were left on the summit of a mound. They told us that arrow-heads, and also bullets of lead and iron, had been found here. We noticed several other sandy tracts in our voyage; and the course of the Merrimack can be traced from the nearest mountain by its yellow sandbanks, though the river itself is for the most part invisible. Lawsuits, as we hear, have in some cases grown out of these causes. Railroads have been made through certain irritable districts, breaking their sod, and so have set the sand to blowing, till it has converted fertile farms into deserts, and the company has had to pay the damages.

This sand seemed to us the connecting link between land and water. It was a kind of water on which you could walk,

and you could see the ripple-marks on its surface, produced
by the winds, precisely like those at the bottom of a brook or
lake. We had read that Mussulmen are permitted by the Ko-
ran to perform their ablutions in sand when they cannot get
water, a necessary indulgence in Arabia, and we now understood the propriety of this provision.

Plum Island, at the mouth of this river, to whose formation, perhaps, these very banks have sent their contribution,
is a similar desert of drifting sand, of various colors, blown
into graceful curves by the wind. It is a mere sand-bar exposed, stretching nine miles parallel to the coast, and, exclusive of the marsh on the inside, rarely more than half a mile
wide. There are but half a dozen houses on it, and it is almost
without a tree, or a sod, or any green thing with which a
countryman is familiar. The thin vegetation stands half buried
in sand, as in drifting snow. The only shrub, the beach-plum,
which gives the island its name, grows but a few feet high;
but this is so abundant that parties of a hundred at once come
from the main-land and down the Merrimack, in September,
pitch their tents, and gather the plums, which are good to eat
raw and to preserve. The graceful and delicate beach-pea, too,
grows abundantly amid the sand, and several strange, moss-
like and succulent plants. The island for its whole length is
scalloped into low hills, not more than twenty feet high, by
the wind, and, excepting a faint trail on the edge of the
marsh, is as trackless as Sahara. There are dreary bluffs of sand
and valleys ploughed by the wind, where you might expect to
discover the bones of a caravan. Schooners come from Boston
to load with the sand for masons' uses, and in a few hours
the wind obliterates all traces of their work. Yet you have only
to dig a foot or two anywhere to come to fresh water; and
you are surprised to learn that woodchucks abound here, and
foxes are found, though you see not where they can burrow
or hide themselves. I have walked down the whole length of
its broad beach at low tide, at which time alone you can find
a firm ground to walk on, and probably Massachusetts does
not furnish a more grand and dreary walk. On the seaside
there are only a distant sail and a few coots to break the grand
monotony. A solitary stake stuck up, or a sharper sand-hill

than usual, is remarkable as a landmark for miles; while for music you hear only the ceaseless sound of the surf, and the dreary peep of the beach-birds.

There were several canal-boats at Cromwell's Falls passing through the locks, for which we waited. In the forward part of one stood a brawny New Hampshire man, leaning on his pole, bareheaded and in shirt and trousers only, a rude Apollo of a man, coming down from that "vast uplandish country" to the main; of nameless age, with flaxen hair, and vigorous, weather-bleached countenance, in whose wrinkles the sun still lodged, as little touched by the heats and frosts and withering cares of life as a maple of the mountain; an undressed, unkempt, uncivil man, with whom we parleyed awhile, and parted not without a sincere interest in one another. His humanity was genuine and instinctive, and his rudeness only a manner. He inquired, just as we were passing out of earshot, if we had killed anything, and we shouted after him that we had shot a *buoy*, and could see him for a long while scratching his head in vain to know if he had heard aright.

There is reason in the distinction of civil and uncivil. The manners are sometimes so rough a rind that we doubt whether they cover any core or sap-wood at all. We sometimes meet uncivil men, children of Amazons, who dwell by mountain paths, and are said to be inhospitable to strangers; whose salutation is as rude as the grasp of their brawny hands, and who deal with men as unceremoniously as they are wont to deal with the elements. They need only to extend their clearings, and let in more sunlight, to seek out the southern slopes of the hills, from which they may look down on the civil plain or ocean, and temper their diet duly with the cereal fruits, consuming less wild meat and acorns, to become like the inhabitants of cities. A true politeness does not result from any hasty and artificial polishing, it is true, but grows naturally in characters of the right grain and quality, through a long fronting of men and events, and rubbing on good and bad fortune. Perhaps I can tell a tale to the purpose while the lock is filling,—for our voyage this forenoon furnishes but few incidents of importance.

*　　　*　　　*

Early one summer morning I had left the shores of the
Connecticut, and for the livelong day travelled up the bank of
a river, which came in from the west; now looking down on
the stream, foaming and rippling through the forest a mile
off, from the hills over which the road led, and now sitting
on its rocky brink and dipping my feet in its rapids, or bathing adventurously in mid-channel. The hills grew more and
more frequent, and gradually swelled into mountains as I advanced, hemming in the course of the river, so that at last I
could not see where it came from, and was at liberty to imagine the most wonderful meanderings and descents. At noon I
slept on the grass in the shade of a maple, where the river had
found a broader channel than usual, and was spread out shallow, with frequent sand-bars exposed. In the names of the
towns I recognized some which I had long ago read on
teamsters' wagons, that had come from far up country; quiet,
uplandish towns, of mountainous fame. I walked along, musing and enchanted, by rows of sugar-maples, through the
small and uninquisitive villages, and sometimes was pleased
with the sight of a boat drawn up on a sand-bar, where there
appeared no inhabitants to use it. It seemed, however, as essential to the river as a fish, and to lend a certain dignity to
it. It was like the trout of mountain streams to the fishes of
the sea, or like the young of the land-crab born far in the
interior, who have never yet heard the sound of the ocean's
surf. The hills approached nearer and nearer to the stream,
until at last they closed behind me, and I found myself just
before nightfall in a romantic and retired valley, about half a
mile in length, and barely wide enough for the stream at its
bottom. I thought that there could be no finer site for a cottage among mountains. You could anywhere run across the
stream on the rocks, and its constant murmuring would quiet
the passions of mankind forever. Suddenly the road, which
seemed aiming for the mountain-side, turned short to the left,
and another valley opened, concealing the former, and of the
same character with it. It was the most remarkable and pleasing scenery I had ever seen. I found here a few mild and
hospitable inhabitants, who, as the day was not quite spent,
and I was anxious to improve the light, directed me four or
five miles farther on my way to the dwelling of a man whose

name was Rice, who occupied the last and highest of the valleys that lay in my path, and who, they said, was a rather rude and uncivil man. But " what is a foreign country to those who have science? Who is a stranger to those who have the habit of speaking kindly?"

At length, as the sun was setting behind the mountains in a still darker and more solitary vale, I reached the dwelling of this man. Except for the narrowness of the plain, and that the stones were solid granite, it was the counterpart of that retreat to which Belphœbe bore the wounded Timias,—

> "In a pleasant glade,
> With mountains round about environed,
> And mighty woods, which did the valley shade,
> And like a stately theatre it made,
> Spreading itself into a spacious plain;
> And in the midst a little river played
> Amongst the pumy stones which seemed to plain,
> With gentle murmur, that his course they did restrain."

I observed, as I drew near, that he was not so rude as I had anticipated, for he kept many cattle, and dogs to watch them, and I saw where he had made maple-sugar on the sides of the mountains, and above all distinguished the voices of children mingling with the murmur of the torrent before the door. As I passed his stable I met one whom I supposed to be a hired man, attending to his cattle, and I inquired if they entertained travellers at that house. "Sometimes we do," he answered, gruffly, and immediately went to the farthest stall from me, and I perceived that it was Rice himself whom I had addressed. But pardoning this incivility to the wildness of the scenery, I bent my steps to the house. There was no sign-post before it, nor any of the usual invitations to the traveller, though I saw by the road that many went and came there, but the owner's name only was fastened to the outside; a sort of implied and sullen invitation, as I thought. I passed from room to room without meeting any one, till I came to what seemed the guests' apartment, which was neat, and even had an air of refinement about it, and I was glad to find a map against the wall which would direct me on my journey on the morrow. At length I heard a step in a distant apartment, which was the first I had entered, and went to see if the land-lord had come in; but it proved to be only a child, one of those whose voices I had heard, probably his son, and be-tween him and me stood in the doorway a large watch-dog, which growled at me, and looked as if he would presently spring, but the boy did not speak to him; and when I asked for a glass of water, he briefly said, "It runs in the corner." So I took a mug from the counter and went out of doors, and searched round the corner of the house, but could find neither well nor spring, nor any water but the stream which ran all along the front. I came back, therefore, and, setting down the mug, asked the child if the stream was good to drink; whereupon he seized the mug, and, going to the cor-ner of the room, where a cool spring which issued from the mountain behind trickled through a pipe into the apartment, filled it, and drank, and gave it to me empty again, and, call-ing to the dog, rushed out of doors. Erelong some of the hired men made their appearance, and drank at the spring, and lazily washed themselves and combed their hair in silence, and some sat down as if weary, and fell asleep in their seats. But all the while I saw no women, though I sometimes heard a bustle in that part of the house from which the spring came.

At length Rice himself came in, for it was now dark, with an ox-whip in his hand, breathing hard, and he too soon set-tled down into his seat not far from me, as if, now that his day's work was done, he had no farther to travel, but only to digest his supper at his leisure. When I asked him if he could give me a bed, he said there was one ready, in such a tone as implied that I ought to have known it, and the less said about that the better. So far so good. And yet he continued to look at me as if he would fain have me say something further like a traveller. I remarked, that it was a wild and rugged country he inhabited, and worth coming many miles to see. "Not so very rough neither," said he, and appealed to his men to bear witness to the breadth and smoothness of his fields, which consisted in all of one small interval, and to the size of his crops; "and if we have some hills," added he, "there's no bet-ter pasturage anywhere." I then asked if this place was the one I had heard of, calling it by a name I had seen on the map, or if it was a certain other; and he answered, gruffly, that it was neither the one nor the other; that he had settled it and cultivated it, and made it what it was, and I could know nothing about it. Observing some guns and other implements of hunting hanging on brackets around the room, and his hounds now sleeping on the floor, I took occasion to change the discourse, and inquired if there was much game in that country, and he answered this question more graciously, having some glimmering of my drift; but when I inquired if there were any bears, he answered impatiently that he was no more in danger of losing his sheep than his neighbors; he had tamed and civilized that region. After a pause, thinking of my journey on the morrow, and the few hours of daylight in that hollow and mountainous country, which would require me to be on my way betimes, I remarked that the day must be shorter by an hour there than on the neighboring plains; at which he gruffly asked what I knew about it, and affirmed that he had as much daylight as his neighbors; he ventured to say, the days were longer there than where I lived, as I should find if I stayed; that in some way, I could not be expected to understand how, the sun came over the mountains half an hour earlier, and stayed half an hour later there than on the neighboring plains. And more of like sort he said. He was, indeed, as rude as a fabled satyr. But I suffered him to pass for what he was,—for why should I quarrel with nature?—and was even pleased at the discovery of such a singular natural phenomenon. I dealt with him as if to me all manners were indifferent, and he had a sweet, wild way with him. I would not question nature, and I would rather have him as he was than as I would have him. For I had come up here not for sympathy, or kindness, or society, but for novelty and adventure, and to see what nature had produced here. I therefore did not repel his rudeness, but quite innocently welcomed it all, and knew how to appreciate it, as if I were reading in an old drama a part well sustained. He was indeed a coarse and sensual man, and, as I have said, uncivil, but he had his just quarrel with nature and mankind, I have no doubt, only he had no artificial covering to his ill-humors. He was earthy enough, but yet there was good soil in him, and even a long-suffering Saxon probity at bottom. If you could represent the case to him, he would not let the race die out in him, like a red Indian.

At length I told him that he was a fortunate man, and I trusted that he was grateful for so much light; and, rising, said I would take a lamp, and that I would pay him then for my lodging, for I expected to recommence my journey even as early as the sun rose in his country; but he answered in haste, and this time civilly, that I should not fail to find some of his household stirring, however early, for they were no sluggards, and I could take my breakfast with them before I started, if I chose; and as he lighted the lamp I detected a gleam of true hospitality and ancient civility, a beam of pure and even gentle humanity, from his bleared and moist eyes. It was a look more intimate with me, and more explanatory, than any words of his could have been if he had tried to his dying day. It was more significant than any Rice of those parts could even comprehend, and long anticipated this man's culture,—a glance of his pure genius, which did not much enlighten him, but did impress and rule him for the moment, and faintly constrain his voice and manner. He cheerfully led the way to my apartment, stepping over the limbs of his men, who were asleep on the floor in an intervening chamber, and showed me a clean and comfortable bed. For many pleasant hours after the household was asleep I sat at the open window, for it was a sultry night, and heard the little river

"Amongst the pumy stones, which seemed to plain,
 With gentle murmur, that his course they did restrain."

But I arose as usual by starlight the next morning, before my host, or his men, or even his dogs, were awake; and, having left a ninepence on the counter, was already half-way over the mountain with the sun before they had broken their fast.

Before I had left the country of my host, while the first rays of the sun slanted over the mountains, as I stopped by the wayside to gather some raspberries, a very old man, not far from a hundred, came along with a milking-pail in his hand, and turning aside began to pluck the berries near me:—

"His reverend locks
In comelye curles did wave;
And on his aged temples grew
The blossoms of the grave."

But when I inquired the way, he answered in a low, rough
voice, without looking up or seeming to regard my presence,
which I imputed to his years; and presently, muttering to
himself, he proceeded to collect his cows in a neighboring
pasture; and when he had again returned near to the wayside,
he suddenly stopped, while his cows went on before, and,
uncovering his head, prayed aloud in the cool morning air, as
if he had forgotten this exercise before, for his daily bread,
and also that He who letteth his rain fall on the just and on
the unjust, and without whom not a sparrow falleth to the
ground, would not neglect the stranger (meaning me), and
with even more direct and personal applications, though
mainly according to the long-established formula common to
lowlanders and the inhabitants of mountains. When he had
done praying, I made bold to ask him if he had any cheese
in his hut which he would sell me, but he answered without looking up, and in the same low and repulsive voice as before, that they did not make any, and went to milking. It is
written, "The stranger who turneth away from a house with
disappointed hopes, leaveth there his own offences,
and departeth, taking with him all the good actions of the
owner."

Being now fairly in the stream of this week's commerce, we
began to meet with boats more frequently, and hailed them
from time to time with the freedom of sailors. The boatmen
appeared to lead an easy and contented life, and we thought
that we should prefer their employment ourselves to many
professions which are much more sought after. They suggested how few circumstances are necessary to the well-being
and serenity of man, how indifferent all employments are, and
that any may seem noble and poetic to the eyes of men, if
pursued with sufficient buoyancy and freedom. With liberty
and pleasant weather, the simplest occupation, any unquestioned country mode of life which detains us in the open air,

is alluring. The man who picks peas steadily for a living is more than respectable, he is even envied by his shop-worn neighbors. We are as happy as the birds when our Good Genius permits us to pursue any out-door work, without a sense of dissipation. Our penknife glitters in the sun; our voice is echoed by yonder wood; if an oar drops, we are fain to let it drop again.

The canal-boat is of very simple construction, requiring but little ship-timber, and, as we were told, costs about two hundred dollars. They are managed by two men. In ascending the stream they use poles fourteen or fifteen feet long, pointed with iron, walking about one third the length of the boat from the forward end. Going down, they commonly keep in the middle of the stream, using an oar at each end; or if the wind is favorable they raise their broad sail, and have only to steer. They commonly carry down wood or bricks,— fifteen or sixteen cords of wood, and as many thousand bricks, at a time,—and bring back stores for the country, consuming two or three days each way between Concord and Charlestown. They sometimes pile the wood so as to leave a shelter in one part where they may retire from the rain. One can hardly imagine a more healthful employment, or one more favorable to contemplation and the observation of nature. Unlike the mariner, they have the constantly varying panorama of the shore to relieve the monotony of their labor, and it seemed to us that as they thus glided noiselessly from town to town, with all their furniture about them, for their very homestead is a movable, they could comment on the character of the inhabitants with greater advantage and security to themselves than the traveller in a coach, who would be unable to indulge in such broadsides of wit and humor in so small a vessel for fear of the recoil. They are not subject to great exposure, like the lumberers of Maine, in any weather, but inhale the healthfullest breezes, being slightly encumbered with clothing, frequently with the head and feet bare. When we met them at noon as they were leisurely descending the stream, their busy commerce did not look like toil, but rather like some ancient Oriental game still played on a large scale, as the game of chess, for instance, handed down to this generation. From morning till night, unless the wind is so fair that his single sail will suffice without other labor than steering, the boatman walks back-wards and forwards on the side of his boat, now stooping with his shoulder to the pole, then drawing it back slowly to set it again, meanwhile moving steadily forward through an endless valley and an everchanging scenery, now distinguishing his course for a mile or two, and now shut in by a sudden turn of the river in a small woodland lake. All the phenomena which surround him are simple and grand, and there is something im-pressive, even majestic, in the very motion he causes, which will naturally be communicated to his own character, and he feels the slow, irresistible movement under him with pride, as if it were his own energy.

The news spread like wildfire among us youths, when for-merly, once in a year or two, one of these boats came up the Concord River, and was seen stealing mysteriously through the meadows and past the village. It came and departed as silently as a cloud, without noise or dust, and was witnessed by few. One summer day this huge traveller might be seen moored at some meadow's wharf, and another summer day it was not there. Where precisely it came from, or who these men were who knew the rocks and soundings better than we who bathed there, we could never tell. We knew some river's bay only, but they took rivers from end to end. They were a sort of fabulous river-men to us. It was inconceivable by what sort of mediation any mere landsman could hold communi-cation with them. Would they heave to, to gratify his wishes? No, it was favor enough to know faintly of their destination, or the time of their possible return. I have seen them in the summer when the stream ran low, mowing the weeds in mid-channel, and with hayers' jests cutting broad swaths in three feet of water, that they might make a passage for their scow, while the grass in long windrows was carried down the stream, undried by the rarest hay-weather. We admired unweariedly how their vessel would float, like a huge chip, sustaining so many casks of lime, and thousands of bricks, and such heaps of iron ore, with wheelbarrows aboard, and that, when we stepped on it, it did not yield to the pressure of our feet. It gave us confidence in the prevalence of the law of buoyancy, and we imagined to what infinite uses it might be put. The men appeared to lead a kind of life on it, and it was whis-

pered that they slept aboard. Some affirmed that it carried
sail, and that such winds blew here as filled the sails of vessels
on the ocean; which again others much doubted. They had
been seen to sail across our Fair Haven bay by lucky fishers
who were out, but unfortunately others were not there to see.
We might then say that our river was navigable,—why not?
In after-years I read in print, with no little satisfaction, that it
was thought by some that, with a little expense in removing
rocks and deepening the channel, "there might be a profitable
inland navigation." *I* then lived somewhere to tell of.

Such is Commerce, which shakes the cocoa-nut and bread-
fruit tree in the remotest isle, and sooner or later dawns on
the duskiest and most simple-minded savage. If we may be
pardoned the digression, who can help being affected at the
thought of the very fine and slight, but positive relation, in
which the savage inhabitants of some remote isle stand to the
mysterious white mariner, the child of the sun?—as if *we*
were to have dealings with an animal higher in the scale of
being than ourselves. It is a barely recognized fact to the natives that he exists, and has his home far away somewhere,
and is glad to buy their fresh fruits with his superfluous commodities. Under the same catholic sun glances his white ship
over Pacific waves into their smooth bays, and the poor savage's paddle gleams in the air.

> Man's little acts are grand,
> Beheld from land to land,
> There as they lie in time,
> Within their native clime.
>> Ships with the noontide weigh,
>> And glide before its ray
>> To some retired bay,
>> Their haunt,
>> Whence, under tropic sun,
>> Again they run,
>> Bearing gum Senegal and Tragicant.
> For this was ocean meant,
> For this the sun was sent,
> And moon was lent,
> And winds in distant caverns pent.

Since our voyage the railroad on the bank has been extended, and there is now but little boating on the Merrimack. All kinds of produce and stores were formerly conveyed by water, but now nothing is carried up the stream, and almost wood and bricks alone are carried down, and these are also carried on the railroad. The locks are fast wearing out, and will soon be impassable, since the tolls will not pay the expense of repairing them, and so in a few years there will be an end of boating on this river. The boating at present is principally between Merrimack and Lowell, or Hooksett and Manchester. They make two or three trips in a week, according to wind and weather, from Merrimack to Lowell and back, about twenty-five miles each way. The boatman comes singing in to shore late at night, and moors his empty boat, and gets his supper and lodging in some house near at hand, and again early in the morning, by starlight perhaps, he pushes away up stream, and, by a shout, or the fragment of a song, gives notice of his approach to the lock-man, with whom he is to take his breakfast. If he gets up to his wood-pile before noon he proceeds to load his boat, with the help of his single "hand," and is on his way down again before night. When he gets to Lowell he unloads his boat, and gets his receipt for his cargo, and, having heard the news at the public house at Middlesex or elsewhere, goes back with his empty boat and his receipt in his pocket to the owner, and to get a new load. We were frequently advertised of their approach by some faint sound behind us, and looking round saw them a mile off, creeping stealthily up the side of the stream like alligators. It was pleasant to hail these sailors of the Merrimack from time to time, and learn the news which circulated with them. We imagined that the sun shining on their bare heads had stamped a liberal and public character on their most private thoughts.

The open and sunny interval still stretched away from the river sometimes by two or more terraces, to the distant hill-country, and when we climbed the bank we commonly found an irregular copse-wood skirting the river, the primitive having floated down-stream long ago to——the "King's navy." Sometimes we saw the river-road a quarter or half a mile distant, and the particolored Concord stage, with its cloud of dust, its van of earnest travelling faces, and its rear of dusty trunks, reminding us that the country had its places of rendezvous for restless Yankee men. There dwelt along at considerable distances on this interval a quiet agricultural and pastoral people, with every house its well, as we sometimes proved, and every household, though never so still and remote it appeared in the noontide, its dinner about these times. There they lived on, those New England people, farmer lives, father and grandfather and great-grandfather, on and on without noise, keeping up tradition, and expecting, beside fair weather and abundant harvests, we did not learn what. They were contented to live, since it was so contrived for them, and where their lines had fallen.

> Our uninquiring corpses lie more low
> Than our life's curiosity doth go.

Yet these men had no need to travel to be as wise as Solomon in all his glory, so similar are the lives of men in all countries, and fraught with the same homely experiences. One half the world *knows* how the other half lives.

About noon we passed a small village in Merrimack at Thornton's Ferry, and tasted of the waters of Naticook Brook on the same side, where French and his companions, whose grave we saw in Dunstable, were ambuscaded by the Indians. The humble village of Litchfield, with its steepleless meeting-house, stood on the opposite or east bank, near where a dense grove of willows backed by maples skirted the shore. There also we noticed some shagbark-trees, which, as they do not grow in Concord, were as strange a sight to us as the palm would be, whose fruit only we have seen. Our course now curved gracefully to the north, leaving a low, flat shore on the Merrimack side, which forms a sort of harbor for canal-boats. We observed some fair elms and particularly large and handsome white-maples standing conspicuously on this interval; and the opposite shore, a quarter of a mile below, was covered with young elms and maples six inches high, which had probably sprung from the seeds which had been washed across.

Some carpenters were at work here mending a scow on the green and sloping bank. The strokes of their mallets echoed from shore to shore, and up and down the river, and their tools gleamed in the sun a quarter of a mile from us, and we realized that boat-building was as ancient and honorable an art as agriculture, and that there might be a naval as well as a pastoral life. The whole history of commerce was made manifest in that scow turned bottom upward on the shore. Thus did men begin to go down upon the sea in ships; *quæque diu steterant in montibus altis, Fluctibus ignotis insultavêre carinæ*; "and keels which had long stood on high mountains careered insultingly (*insultavêre*) over unknown waves." (Ovid, Met. I. 133.) We thought that it would be well for the traveller to build his boat on the bank of a stream, instead of finding a ferry or a bridge. In the Adventures of Henry the fur-trader, it is pleasant to read that when with his Indians he reached the shore of Ontario, they consumed two days in making two canoes of the bark of the elm-tree, in which to transport themselves to Fort Niagara. It is a worthy incident in a journey, a delay as good as much rapid travelling. A good share of our interest in Xenophon's story of his retreat is in the manœuvres to get the army safely over the rivers, whether on rafts of logs or fagots, or sheep-skins blown up. And where could they better afford to tarry meanwhile than on the banks of a river?

As we glided past at a distance, these out-door workmen appeared to have added some dignity to their labor by its very publicness. It was a part of the industry of nature, like the work of hornets and mud-wasps.

> The waves slowly beat,
> Just to keep the noon sweet,
> And no sound is floated o'er,
> Save the mallet on shore,
> Which echoing on high
> Seems a-calking the sky.

The haze, the sun's dust of travel, had a Lethean influence on the land and its inhabitants, and all creatures resigned themselves to float upon the inappreciable tides of nature.

> Woof of the sun, ethereal gauze,
> Woven of Nature's richest stuffs,
> Visible heat, air-water, and dry sea,

Last conquest of the eye;
Toil of the day displayed, sun-dust,
Aerial surf upon the shores of earth,
Ethereal estuary, frith of light,
Breakers of air, billows of heat,
Fine summer spray on inland seas;
Bird of the sun, transparent-winged
Owlet of noon, soft-pinioned,
From heath or stubble rising without song;
Establish thy serenity o'er the fields.

The routine which is in the sunshine and the finest days, as that which has conquered and prevailed, commends itself to us by its very antiquity and apparent solidity and necessity. Our weakness needs it, and our strength uses it. We cannot draw on our boots without bracing ourselves against it. If there were but one erect and solid standing tree in the woods, all creatures would go to rub against it and make sure of their footing. During the many hours which we spend in this waking sleep, the hand stands still on the face of the clock, and we grow like corn in the night. Men are as busy as the brooks or bees, and postpone everything to their busy-ness; as carpenters discuss politics between the strokes of the hammer while they are shingling a roof.

This noontide was a fit occasion to make some pleasant harbor, and there read the journal of some voyageur like ourselves, not too moral nor inquisitive, and which would not disturb the noon; or else some old classic, the very flower of all reading, which we had postponed to such a season

"Of Syrian peace, immortal leisure."

But, alas, our chest, like the cabin of a coaster, contained only its well-thumbed "Navigator" for all literature, and we were obliged to draw on our memory for these things.

We naturally remembered Alexander Henry's Adventures here, as a sort of classic among books of American travel. It contains scenery and rough sketching of men and incidents enough to inspire poets for many years, and to my fancy is as full of sounding names as any page of history,—Lake

Winnipeg, Hudson Bay, Ottaway, and portages innumerable; Chipeways, Gens de Terres, Les Pilleurs, The Weepers; with reminiscences of Hearne's journey, and the like; an immense and shaggy but sincere country, summer and winter, adorned with chains of lakes and rivers, covered with snows, with hemlocks, and fir-trees. There is a naturalness, an unpretending and cold life in this traveller, as in a Canadian winter, what life was preserved through low temperatures and frontier dangers by furs within a stout heart. He has truth and moderation worthy of the father of history, which belong only to an intimate experience, and he does not defer too much to literature. The unlearned traveller may quote his single line from the poets with as good right as the scholar. He too may speak of the stars, for he sees them shoot perhaps when the astronomer does not. The good sense of this author is very conspicuous. He is a traveller who does not exaggerate, but writes for the information of his readers, for science, and for history. His story is told with as much good faith and directness as if it were a report to his brother traders, or the Directors of the Hudson Bay Company, and is fitly dedicated to Sir Joseph Banks. It reads like the argument to a great poem on the primitive state of the country and its inhabitants, and the reader imagines what in each case, with the invocation of the Muse, might be sung, and leaves off with suspended interest, as if the full account were to follow. In what school was this fur-trader educated? He seems to travel the immense snowy country with such purpose only as the reader who accompanies him, and to the latter's imagination, it is, as it were, momentarily created to be the scene of his adventures. What is most interesting and valuable in it, however, is not the materials for the history of Pontiac, or Braddock, or the Northwest, which it furnishes; not the *annals* of the country, but the natural facts, or *perennials*, which are ever without date. When out of history the truth shall be extracted, it will have shed its dates like withered leaves.

The Souhegan, or *Crooked* River, as some translate it, comes in from the west about a mile and a half above Thornton's Ferry. Babboosuck Brook empties into it near its mouth. There are said to be some of the finest water privi-

leges in the country still unimproved on the former stream, at
a short distance from the Merrimack. One spring morning,
March 22, in the year 1677, an incident occurred on the banks
of the river here, which is interesting to us as a slight memorial of an interview between two ancient tribes of men, one
of which is now extinct, while the other, though it is still
represented by a miserable remnant, has long since disappeared from its ancient hunting-grounds. A Mr. James Parker,
at "Mr. Hinchmanne's farme ner Meremack," wrote thus "to
the Honred Governer and Council at Bostown, *Hast, Post
Hast*": —

> "Sagamore Wanalancet come this morning to informe
> me, and then went to Mr. Tyng's to informe him, that his
> son being on ye other sid of Meremack river over against
> Souhegan upon the 22 day of this instant, about tene of the
> clock in the morning, he discovered 15 Indians on this sid
> the river, which he soposed to be Mohokes by ther spech.
> He called to them; they answered, but he could not under-
> stand ther spech; and he having a conow ther in the river,
> he went to breck his conow that they might not have ani
> ues of it. In the mean time they shot about thirty guns at
> him, and he being much frighted fled, and come home
> forthwith to Nahamcock [Pawtucket Falls or Lowell], wher
> ther wigowames now stand."

Penacooks and Mohawks! *ubique gentium sunt?* In the year
1670, a Mohawk warrior scalped a Naamkeak or else a Wamesit Indian maiden near where Lowell now stands. She,
however, recovered. Even as late as 1685, John Hogkins, a
Penacook Indian, who describes his grandfather as having
lived "at place called Malamake rever, other name chef Natukkog and Panukkog, that one rever great many names," wrote
thus to the governor: —

> "May 15th, 1685.
> "Honor governor my friend, —
> "You my friend I desire your worship and your power,
> because I hope you can do som great matters this one. I
> am poor and naked and I have no men at my place because
> I afraid allwayes Mohogs he will kill me every day and

night. If your worship when please pray help me you no let Mohogs kill me at my place at Malamake river called Pannukkog and Natukkog, I will submit your worship and your power. And now I want pouder and such alminishon shatt and guns, because I have forth at my hom and I plant theare.

"This all Indian hand, but pray you do consider your humble servant,   JOHN HOGKINS."

Signed also by Simon Detogkom, King Hary, Sam Linis, Mr. Jorge Rodunnonukgus, John Owamosimmin, and nine other Indians, with their marks against their names.

But now, one hundred and fifty-four years having elapsed since the date of this letter, we went unalarmed on our way without "brecking" our "conow," reading the New England Gazetteer, and seeing no traces of "Mohogs" on the banks.

The Souhegan, though a rapid river, seemed to-day to have borrowed its character from the noon.

> Where gleaming fields of haze
> Meet the voyageur's gaze,
> And above, the heated air
> Seems to make a river there,
> The pines stand up with pride
> By the Souhegan's side,
> And the hemlock and the larch
> With their triumphal arch
> Are waving o'er its march
>   To the sea.
> No wind stirs its waves,
> But the spirits of the braves
>   Hov'ring o'er,
> Whose antiquated graves
> Its still water laves
>   On the shore.
> With an Indian's stealthy tread,
> It goes sleeping in its bed,
> Without joy or grief,
> Or the rustle of a leaf,
> Without a ripple or a billow,

Or the sigh of a willow,
From the Lyndeboro' hills
To the Merrimack mills.
With a louder din
Did its current begin,
When melted the snow
On the far mountain's brow,
And the drops came together
In that rainy weather.
Experienced river,
Hast thou flowed forever?
Souhegan soundeth old,
But the half is not told,
What names hast thou borne,
In the ages far gone,
When the Xanthus and Meander
Commenced to wander,
Ere the black bear haunted
    Thy red forest-floor,
Or Nature had planted
    The pines by thy shore?

During the heat of the day, we rested on a large island a
mile above the mouth of this river, pastured by a herd of
cattle, with steep banks and scattered elms and oaks, and a
sufficient channel for canal-boats on each side. When we
made a fire to boil some rice for our dinner, the flames
spreading amid the dry grass, and the smoke curling silently
upward and casting grotesque shadows on the ground,
seemed phenomena of the noon, and we fancied that we pro-
gressed up the stream without effort, and as naturally as the
wind and tide went down, not outraging the calm days by
unworthy bustle or impatience. The woods on the neighboring shore were alive with pigeons, which were moving south,
looking for mast, but now, like ourselves, spending their
noon in the shade. We could hear the slight, wiry, winnowing
sound of their wings as they changed their roosts from time
to time, and their gentle and tremulous cooing. They so-
journed with us during the noontide, greater travellers far
than we. You may frequently discover a single pair sitting

upon the lower branches of the white-pine in the depths of
the wood, at this hour of the day, so silent and solitary, and
with such a hermit-like appearance, as if they had never
strayed beyond its skirts, while the acorn which was gathered
in the forests of Maine is still undigested in their crops. We
obtained one of these handsome birds, which lingered too
long upon its perch, and plucked and broiled it here with
some other game, to be carried along for our supper; for,
beside the provisions which we carried with us, we depended
mainly on the river and forest for our supply. It is true, it did
not seem to be putting this bird to its right use to pluck off
its feathers, and extract its entrails, and broil its carcass on the
coals; but we heroically persevered, nevertheless, waiting for
further information. The same regard for Nature which excited our sympathy for her creatures nerved our hands to
carry through what we had begun. For we would be honorable to the party we deserted; we would fulfil fate, and so at
length, perhaps, detect the secret innocence of these incessant
tragedies which Heaven allows.

> "Too quick resolves do resolution wrong,
>   What, part so soon to be divorced so long?
>   Things to be done are long to be debated;
>   Heaven is not day'd, Repentance is not dated."

We are double-edged blades, and every time we whet our virtue the return stroke straps our vice. Where is the skilful
swordsman who can give clean wounds, and not rip up his
work with the other edge?

Nature herself has not provided the most graceful end for
her creatures. What becomes of all these birds that people the
air and forest for our solacement? The sparrows seem always
chipper, never infirm. We do not see their bodies lie about. Yet
there is a tragedy at the end of each one of their lives. They
must perish miserably; not one of them is translated. True,
"not a sparrow falleth to the ground without our Heavenly
Father's knowledge," but they do fall, nevertheless.

The carcasses of some poor squirrels, however, the same
that frisked so merrily in the morning, which we had skinned
and embowelled for our dinner, we abandoned in disgust,
with tardy humanity, as too wretched a resource for any but

starving men. It was to perpetuate the practice of a barbarous era. If they had been larger, our crime had been less. Their small red bodies, little bundles of red tissue, mere gobbets of venison, would not have "fattened fire." With a sudden impulse we threw them away, and washed our hands, and boiled some rice for our dinner. "Behold the difference between the one who eateth flesh, and him to whom it belonged! The first hath a momentary enjoyment, whilst the latter is deprived of existence!" "Who would commit so great a crime against a poor animal, who is fed only by the herbs which grow wild in the woods, and whose belly is burnt up with hunger?" We remembered a picture of mankind in the hunter age, chasing hares down the mountains; O me miserable! Yet sheep and oxen are but larger squirrels, whose hides are saved and meat is salted, whose souls perchance are not so large in proportion to their bodies.

There should always be some flowering and maturing of the fruits of nature in the cooking process. Some simple dishes recommend themselves to our imaginations as well as palates. In parched corn, for instance, there is a manifest sympathy between the bursting seed and the more perfect developments of vegetable life. It is a perfect flower with its petals, like the houstonia or anemone. On my warm hearth these cerealian blossoms expanded; here is the bank whereon they grew. Perhaps some such visible blessing would always attend the simple and wholesome repast.

Here was that "pleasant harbor" which we had sighed for, where the weary voyageur could read the journal of some other sailor, whose bark had ploughed, perchance, more famous and classic seas. At the tables of the gods, after feasting follow music and song; we will recline now under these island trees, and for our minstrel call on

ANACREON.

"Nor has he ceased his charming song, for still that lyre,
    Though he is dead, sleeps not in Hades."
                            Simonides' Epigram on Anacreon.

I lately met with an old volume from a London bookshop, containing the Greek Minor Poets, and it was a pleasure to read once more only the words, Orpheus, Linus, Musæus,—those faint poetic sounds and echoes of a name, dying away on the ears of us modern men; and those hardly more substantial sounds, Mimnermus, Ibycus, Alcæus, Stesichorus, Menander. They lived not in vain. We can converse with these bodiless fames without reserve or personality.

I know of no studies so composing as those of the classical scholar. When we have sat down to them, life seems as still and serene as if it were very far off, and I believe it is not habitually seen from any common platform so truly and unexaggerated as in the light of literature. In serene hours we contemplate the tour of the Greek and Latin authors with more pleasure than the traveller does the fairest scenery of Greece or Italy. Where shall we find a more refined society? That highway down from Homer and Hesiod to Horace and Juvenal is more attractive than the Appian. Reading the classics, or conversing with those old Greeks and Latins in their surviving works, is like walking amid the stars and constellations, a high and by way serene to travel. Indeed, the true scholar will be not a little of an astronomer in his habits. Distracting cares will not be allowed to obstruct the field of his vision, for the higher regions of literature, like astronomy, are above storm and darkness.

But passing by these rumors of bards, let us pause for a moment at the Teian poet.

There is something strangely modern about him. He is very easily turned into English. Is it that our lyric poets have resounded but that lyre, which would sound only light subjects, and which Simonides tells us does not sleep in Hades? His odes are like gems of pure ivory. They possess an ethereal and evanescent beauty like summer evenings, ὅ χρή σε νοεῖν νόου ἄνθει,—*which you must perceive with the flower of the mind,*—and show how slight a beauty could be expressed. You have to consider them, as the stars of lesser magnitude, with the side of the eye, and look aside from them to behold them. They charm us by their serenity and freedom from exaggeration and passion, and by a certain flower-like beauty, which does not propose itself, but must be approached and studied like a natural object. But perhaps their chief merit consists in the lightness and yet security of their tread;

"The young and tender stalk
    Ne'er bends when *they* do walk."

True, our nerves are never strung by them; it is too constantly the sound of the lyre, and never the note of the trumpet; but they are not gross, as has been presumed, but always
elevated above the sensual.

These are some of the best that have come down to us.

ON HIS LYRE.

I wish to sing the Atridæ,
And Cadmus I wish to sing;
But my lyre sounds
Only love with its chords.
Lately I changed the strings
And all the lyre;
And I began to sing the labors
Of Hercules; but my lyre
Resounded loves.
Farewell, henceforth, for me,
Heroes! for my lyre
Sings only loves.

TO A SWALLOW.

Thou indeed, dear swallow,
Yearly going and coming,
In summer weavest thy nest,
And in winter go'st disappearing
Either to Nile or to Memphis.
But Love always weaveth
His nest in my heart. . . . .

ON A SILVER CUP.

Turning the silver,
Vulcan, make for me,
Not indeed a panoply,
For what are battles to me?
But a hollow cup,
As deep as thou canst.

And make for me in it
Neither stars, nor wagons,
Nor sad Orion;
What are the Pleiades to me?
What the shining Bootes?
Make vines for me,
And clusters of grapes in it,
And of gold Love and Bathyllus
Treading the grapes
With the fair Lyæus.

On Himself.

Thou sing'st the affairs of Thebes,
And he the battles of Troy,
But I of my own defeats.
No horse have wasted me,
Nor foot, nor ships;
But a new and different host,
From eyes smiting me.

To a Dove.

Lovely dove,
Whence, whence dost thou fly?
Whence, running on air,
Dost thou waft and diffuse
So many sweet ointments?
Who art? What thy errand?—
Anacreon sent me
To a boy, to Bathyllus,
Who lately is ruler and tyrant of all.
Cythere has sold me
For one little song,
And I'm doing this service
For Anacreon.
And now, as you see,
I bear letters from him.
And he says that directly
He'll make me free,
But though he release me,

His slave I will tarry with him.
For why should I fly
Over mountains and fields,
And perch upon trees,
Eating some wild thing?
Now indeed I eat bread,
Plucking it from the hands
Of Anacreon himself;
And he gives me to drink
The wine which he tastes,
And drinking, I dance,
And shadow my master's
Face with my wings;
And, going to rest,
On the lyre itself I sleep.
That is all; get thee gone.
Thou hast made me more talkative,
Man, than a crow.

ON LOVE.

Love walking swiftly,
With hyacinthine staff,
Bade me to take a run with him;
And hastening through swift torrents,
And woody places, and over precipices,
A water-snake stung me.
And my heart leaped up to
My mouth, and I should have fainted;
But Love fanning my brows
With his soft wings, said,
Surely, thou art not able to love.

ON WOMEN.

Nature has given horns
To bulls, and hoofs to horses,
Swiftness to hares,
To lions yawning teeth,
To fishes swimming,
To birds flight,

To men wisdom.
For woman she had nothing beside;
What then does she give? Beauty,—
Instead of all shields,
Instead of all spears;
And she conquers even iron
And fire, who is beautiful.

ON LOVERS.

Horses have the mark
Of fire on their sides,
And some have distinguished
The Parthian men by their crests;
So I, seeing lovers,
Know them at once,
For they have a certain slight
Brand on their hearts.

TO A SWALLOW.

What dost thou wish me to do to thee,—
What, thou loquacious swallow?
Dost thou wish me taking thee
Thy light pinions to clip?
Or rather to pluck out
Thy tongue from within,
As that Tereus did?
Why with thy notes in the dawn
Hast thou plundered Bathyllus
From my beautiful dreams?

TO A COLT.

Thracian colt, why at me
Looking aslant with thy eyes,
Dost thou cruelly flee,
And think that I know nothing wise?
Know I could well
Put the bridle on thee,
And holding the reins, turn

Round the bounds of the course.
But now thou browsest the meads,
And gambolling lightly dost play,
For thou hast no skilful horseman
Mounted upon thy back.

CUPID WOUNDED.

Love once among roses
Saw not
A sleeping bee, but was stung;
And being wounded in the finger
Of his hand, cried for pain.
Running as well as flying
To the beautiful Venus,
I am killed, mother, said he,
I am killed, and I die.
A little serpent has stung me,
Winged, which they call
A bee,—the husbandmen.
And she said, If the sting
Of a bee afflicts you,
How, think you, are they afflicted,
Love, whom you smite?

———

Late in the afternoon, for we had lingered long on the island, we raised our sail for the first time, and for a short hour the southwest wind was our ally; but it did not please Heaven to abet us long. With one sail raised we swept slowly up the eastern side of the stream, steering clear of the rocks, while, from the top of a hill which formed the opposite bank, some lumberers were rolling down timber to be rafted down the stream. We could see their axes and levers gleaming in the sun, and the logs came down with a dust and a rumbling sound, which was reverberated through the woods beyond us on our side, like the roar of artillery. But Zephyr soon took us out of sight and hearing of this commerce. Having passed Read's Ferry, and another island called McGaw's Island, we reached some rapids called Moore's Falls, and entered on "that section of the river, nine miles in extent, converted, by law, into the Union Canal, comprehending in that space six distinct falls; at each of which, and at several intermediate places, work has been done." After passing Moore's Falls by means of locks, we again had recourse to our oars, and went merrily on our way, driving the small sandpiper from rock to rock before us, and sometimes rowing near enough to a cottage on the bank, though they were few and far between, to see the sunflowers, and the seed vessels of the poppy, like small goblets filled with the water of Lethe, before the door, but without disturbing the sluggish household behind. Thus we held on, sailing or dipping our way along with the paddle up this broad river, smooth and placid, flowing over concealed rocks, where we could see the pickerel lying low in the transparent water, eager to double some distant cape, to make some great bend as in the life of man, and see what new perspective would open; looking far into a new country, broad and serene, the cottages of settlers seen afar for the first time, yet with the moss of a century on their roofs, and the third or fourth generation in their shadows. Strange was it to consider how the sun and the summer, the buds of spring and the seared leaves of autumn, were related to these cabins along the shore; how all the rays which paint the landscape radiate from them, and the flight of the crow and the gyrations of the hawk have reference to their roofs. Still the ever rich and fertile shores accompanied us, fringed with vines and alive with small birds and frisking squirrels, the edge of some farmer's field or widow's woodlot, or wilder, perchance, where the muskrat, the little medicine of the river, drags itself along stealthily over the alder-leaves and muscle-shells, and man and the memory of man are banished far.

At length the unwearied, never-sinking shore, still holding on without break, with its cool copses and serene pasture-grounds, tempted us to disembark; and we adventurously landed on this remote coast, to survey it, without the knowledge of any human inhabitant probably to this day. But we still remember the gnarled and hospitable oaks which grew even there for our entertainment, and were no strangers to us, the lonely horse in his pasture, and the patient cows,

whose path to the river, so judiciously chosen to overcome
the difficulties of the way, we followed, and disturbed their
ruminations in the shade; and, above all, the cool, free aspect of the wild apple-trees, generously proffering their fruit
to us, though still green and crude,—the hard, round,
glossy fruit, which, if not ripe, still was not poison, but
New-English too, brought hither its ancestors by ours once.
These gentler trees imparted a half-civilized and twilight aspect to the otherwise barbarian land. Still farther on we
scrambled up the rocky channel of a brook, which had long
served nature for a sluice there, leaping like it from rock to
rock through tangled woods, at the bottom of a ravine,
which grew darker and darker, and more and more hoarse
the murmurs of the stream, until we reached the ruins of a
mill, where now the ivy grew, and the trout glanced through
the crumbling flume; and there we imagined what had been
the dreams and speculations of some early settler. But the
waning day compelled us to embark once more, and redeem
this wasted time with long and vigorous sweeps over the
rippling stream.

It was still wild and solitary, except that at intervals of a
mile or two the roof of a cottage might be seen over the bank.
This region, as we read, was once famous for the manufacture
of straw bonnets of the Leghorn kind, of which it claims the
invention in these parts; and occasionally some industrious
damsel tripped down to the water's edge, to put her straw a-
soak, as it appeared, and stood awhile to watch the retreating
voyageurs, and catch the fragment of a boat-song which we
had made, wafted over the water.

> Thus, perchance, the Indian hunter,
>   Many a lagging year agone,
> Gliding o'er thy rippling waters,
>   Lowly hummed a natural song.
>
> Now the sun 's behind the willows,
>   Now he gleams along the waves,
> Faintly o'er the wearied billows
>   Come the spirits of the braves.

Just before sundown we reached some more falls in the

town of Bedford, where some stone-masons were employed repairing the locks in a solitary part of the river. They were interested in our adventure, especially one young man of our own age, who inquired at first if we were bound up to " 'Skeag"; and when he had heard our story, and examined our outfit, asked us other questions, but temperately still, and always turning to his work again, though as if it were become his duty. It was plain that he would like to go with us, and, as he looked up the river, many a distant cape and wooded shore were reflected in his eye, as well as in his thoughts. When we were ready he left his work, and helped us through the locks with a sort of quiet enthusiasm, telling us that we were at Coos Falls, and we could still distinguish the strokes of his chisel for many sweeps after we had left him.

We wished to camp this night on a large rock in the middle of the stream, just above these falls, but the want of fuel, and the difficulty of fixing our tent firmly, prevented us; so we made our bed on the main-land opposite, on the west bank, in the town of Bedford, in a retired place, as we supposed, there being no house in sight.

Wednesday

"Man is man's foe and destiny."
COTTON.

EARLY THIS morning, as we were rolling up our buffaloes and loading our boat amid the dew, while our embers were still smoking, the masons who worked at the locks, and whom we had seen crossing the river in their boat the evening before while we were examining the rock, came upon us as they were going to their work, and we found that we had pitched our tent directly in the path to their boat. This was the only time that we were observed on our camping-ground. Thus, far from the beaten highways and the dust and din of travel, we beheld the country privately, yet freely, and at our leisure. Other roads do some violence to Nature, and bring the traveller to stare at her, but the river steals into the scenery it traverses without intrusion, silently creating and adorning it, and is as free to come and go as the zephyr.

As we shoved away from this rocky coast, before sunrise, the smaller bittern, the genius of the shore, was moping along its edge, or stood probing the mud for its food, with ever an eye on us, though so demurely at work, or else he ran along over the wet stones like a wrecker in his storm-coat, looking out for wrecks of snails and cockles. Now away he goes, with a limping flight, uncertain where he will alight, until a rod of clear sand amid the alders invites his feet; and now our steady approach compels him to seek a new retreat. It is a bird of the oldest Thalesian school, and no doubt believes in the priority of water to the other elements; the relic of a twilight antediluvian age which yet inhabits these bright American rivers with us Yankees. There is something venerable in this melancholy and contemplative race of birds, which may have trodden the earth while it was yet in a slimy and imperfect state. Perchance their tracks too are still visible on the stones. It still lingers into our glaring summers, bravely supporting its fate without sympathy from man, as if it looked forward to some second advent of which *he* has no assurance. One wonders if, by its patient study by rocks and sandy capes, it has wrested the whole of her secret from Nature yet. What a rich experience it must have gained, standing on one leg and looking out from its dull eye so long on sunshine and rain, moon and stars! What could it tell of stagnant pools and reeds and dank night-fogs! It would be worth the while to look closely into the eye which has been open and seeing at such hours, and in such solitudes, its dull, yellowish, greenish eye. Methinks my own soul must be a bright invisible green. I have seen these birds stand by the half-dozen together in the shallower water along the shore, with their bills thrust into the mud at the bottom, probing for food, the whole head being concealed, while the neck and body formed an arch above the water.

Cohass Brook, the outlet of Massabesic Pond,—which last is five or six miles distant, and contains fifteen hundred acres, being the largest body of fresh water in Rockingham County,—comes in near here from the east. Rowing between Manchester and Bedford, we passed, at an early hour, a ferry and some falls, called Goff's Falls, the Indian Cohasset, where there is a small village, and a handsome green islet in the middle of the stream. From Bedford and Merrimack have been boated the bricks of which Lowell is made. About twenty years before, as they told us, one Moore, of Bedford, having clay on his farm, contracted to furnish eight millions of bricks to the founders of that city within two years. He fulfilled his contract in one year, and since then bricks have been the principal export from these towns. The farmers found thus a market for their wood, and when they had brought a load to the kilns, they could cart a load of bricks to the shore, and so make a profitable day's work of it. Thus all parties were benefited. It was worth the while to see the place where Lowell was "dug out." So likewise Manchester is being built of bricks made still higher up the river at Hooksett.

There might be seen here on the bank of the Merrimack, near Goff's Falls, in what is now the town of Bedford, famous "for hops and for its fine domestic manufactures," some graves of the aborigines. The land still bears this scar here, and time is slowly crumbling the bones of a race. Yet, without fail, every spring, since they first fished and hunted here, the

brown thrasher has heralded the morning from a birch or
alder spray, and the undying race of reed-birds still rustles
through the withering grass. But these bones rustle not.
These mouldering elements are slowly preparing for another
metamorphosis, to serve new masters, and what was the Indian's will erelong be the white man's sinew.

We learned that Bedford was not so famous for hops as
formerly, since the price is fluctuating, and poles are now
scarce. Yet if the traveller goes back a few miles from the river,
the hop-kilns will still excite his curiosity.

There were few incidents in our voyage this forenoon,
though the river was now more rocky and the falls more frequent than before. It was a pleasant change, after rowing incessantly for many hours, to lock ourselves through in some
retired place,—for commonly there was no lock-man at
hand,—one sitting in the boat, while the other, sometimes
with no little labor and heave-yo-ing, opened and shut the
gates, waiting patiently to see the locks fill. We did not once
use the wheels which we had provided. Taking advantage of
the eddy, we were sometimes floated up to the locks almost
in the face of the falls; and, by the same cause, any floating
timber was carried round in a circle and repeatedly drawn
into the rapids before it finally went down the stream. These
old gray structures, with their quiet arms stretched over the
river in the sun, appeared like natural objects in the scenery,
and the kingfisher and sandpiper alighted on them as readily
as on stakes or rocks.

We rowed leisurely up the stream for several hours, until
the sun had got high in the sky, our thoughts monotonously
beating time to our oars. For outward variety there was only
the river and the receding shores, a vista continually opening
behind and closing before us, as we sat with our backs up-
stream; and, for inward, such thoughts as the muses grudg-
ingly lent us. We were always passing some low, inviting
shore, or some overhanging bank, on which, however, we
never landed.

> Such near aspects had we
> Of our life's scenery.

It might be seen by what tenure men held the earth. The

smallest stream is *mediterranean* sea, a smaller ocean creek within the land, where men may steer by their farm-bounds and cottage-lights. For my own part, but for the geographers, I should hardly have known how large a portion of our globe is water, my life has chiefly passed within so deep a cove. Yet I have sometimes ventured as far as to the mouth of my Snug Harbor. From an old ruined fort on Staten Island, I have loved to watch all day some vessel whose name I had read in the morning through the telegraph-glass, when she first came upon the coast, and her hull heaved up and glistened in the sun, from the moment when the pilot and most adventurous news-boats met her, past the Hook, and up the narrow channel of the wide outer bay, till she was boarded by the health-officer, and took her station at Quarantine, or held on her unquestioned course to the wharves of New York. It was interesting, too, to watch the less adventurous newsman, who made his assault as the vessel swept through the Narrows, defying plague and quarantine law, and, fastening his little cockboat to her huge side, clambered up and disappeared in the cabin. And then I could imagine what momentous news was being imparted by the captain, which no American ear had ever heard, that Asia, Africa, Europe—were all sunk; for which at length he pays the price, and is seen descending the ship's side with his bundle of newspapers, but not where he first got up, for these arrivers do not stand still to gossip; and he hastes away with steady sweeps to dispose of his wares to the highest bidder, and we shall erelong read something startling,—"By the latest arrival,"—"by the good ship ——." On Sunday I beheld, from some interior hill, the long procession of vessels getting to sea, reaching from the city wharves through the Narrows, and past the Hook, quite to the ocean stream, far as the eye could reach, with stately march and silken sails, all counting on lucky voyages, but each time some of the number, no doubt, destined to go to Davy's locker, and never come on this coast again. And, again, in the evening of a pleasant day, it was my amusement to count the sails in sight. But as the setting sun continually brought more and more to light, still farther in the horizon, the last count always had the advantage, till, by the time the last rays streamed over the sea, I had doubled and trebled my first number; though I could no longer class them all under the several heads of ships, barks, brigs, schooners, and sloops, but most were faint generic *vessels* only. And then the temperate twilight light, perchance, revealed the floating home of some sailor whose thoughts were already alienated from this American coast, and directed towards the Europe of our dreams. I have stood upon the same hill-top when a thunder-shower, rolling down from the Catskills and Highlands, passed over the island, deluging the land; and, when it had suddenly left us in sunshine, have seen it overtake successively, with its huge shadow and dark, descending wall of rain, the vessels in the bay. Their bright sails were suddenly drooping and dark, like the sides of barns, and they seemed to shrink before the storm; while still far beyond them on the sea, through this dark veil, gleamed the sunny sails of those vessels which the storm had not yet reached. And at midnight, when all around and overhead was darkness, I have seen a field of trembling, silvery light far out on the sea, the reflection of the moonlight from the ocean, as if beyond the precincts of our night, where the moon traversed a cloudless heaven,—and sometimes a dark speck in its midst, where some fortunate vessel was pursuing its happy voyage by night.

But to us river sailors the sun never rose out of ocean waves, but from some green coppice, and went down behind some dark mountain line. We, too, were but dwellers on the shore, like the bittern of the morning; and our pursuit, the wrecks of snails and cockles. Nevertheless, we were contented to know the better one fair particular shore.

My life is like a stroll upon the beach,
    As near the ocean's edge as I can go,
My tardy steps its waves sometimes o'erreach,
    Sometimes I stay to let them overflow.

My sole employment 't is, and scrupulous care,
    To place my gains beyond the reach of tides,
Each smoother pebble, and each shell more rare,
    Which ocean kindly to my hand confides.

I have but few companions on the shore,
   They scorn the strand who sail upon the sea,
Yet oft I think the ocean they've sailed o'er
   Is deeper known upon the strand to me.

The middle sea contains no crimson dulse,
   Its deeper waves cast up no pearls to view,
Along the shore my hand is on its pulse,
   And I converse with many a shipwrecked crew.

The small houses which were scattered along the river at intervals of a mile or more were commonly out of sight to us, but sometimes, when we rowed near the shore, we heard the peevish note of a hen, or some slight domestic sound, which betrayed them. The lock-men's houses were particularly well placed, retired, and high, always at falls or rapids, and commanding the pleasantest reaches of the river,—for it is generally wider and more lake-like just above a fall,—and there they wait for boats. These humble dwellings, homely and sincere, in which a hearth was still the essential part, were more pleasing to our eyes than palaces or castles would have been. In the noon of these days, as we have said, we occasionally climbed the banks and approached these houses, to get a glass of water and make acquaintance with their inhabitants. High in the leafy bank, surrounded commonly by a small patch of corn and beans, squashes and melons, with sometimes a graceful hop-yard on one side, and some running vine over the windows, they appeared like beehives set to gather honey for a summer. I have not read of any Arcadian life which surpasses the actual luxury and serenity of these New England dwellings. For the outward gilding, at least, the age is golden enough. As you approach the sunny doorway, awakening the echoes by your steps, still no sound from these barracks of repose, and you fear that the gentlest knock may seem rude to the Oriental dreamers. The door is opened, perchance, by some Yankee-Hindoo woman, whose small-voiced but sincere hospitality, out of the bottomless depths of a quiet nature, has travelled quite round to the opposite side, and fears only to obtrude its kindness. You step over the white-scoured floor to the bright "dresser" lightly, as if afraid to disturb the devotions of the household,—for Oriental dynasties appear to have passed away since the dinner-table was last spread here,—and thence to the frequented curb, where you see your long-forgotten, unshaven face at the bottom, in juxta-position with new-made butter and the trout in the well. "Perhaps you would like some molasses and ginger," suggests the faint noon voice. Sometimes there sits the brother who follows the sea, their representative man; who knows only how far it is to the nearest port, no more distances, all the rest is sea and distant capes,—patting the dog, or dandling the kitten in arms that were stretched by the cable and the oar, pulling against Boreas or the trade-winds. He looks up at the stranger, half pleased, half astonished, with a mariner's eye, as if he were a dolphin within cast. If men will believe it, *sua si bona nôrint*, there are no more quiet Tempes, nor more poetic and Arcadian lives, than may be lived in these New England dwellings. We thought that the employment of their inhabitants by day would be to tend the flowers and herds, and at night, like the shepherds of old, to cluster and give names to the stars from the river banks.

We passed a large and densely wooded island this forenoon, between Short's and Griffith's Falls, the fairest which we had met with, with a handsome grove of elms at its head. If it had been evening we should have been glad to camp there. Not long after, one or two more were passed. The boatmen told us that the current had recently made important changes here. An island always pleases my imagination, even the smallest, as a small continent and integral portion of the globe. I have a fancy for building my hut on one. Even a bare, grassy isle, which I can see entirely over at a glance, has some undefined and mysterious charm for me. There is commonly such a one at the junction of two rivers, whose currents bring down and deposit their respective sands in the eddy at their confluence, as it were the womb of a continent. By what a delicate and far-fetched contribution every island is made! What an enter-prise of Nature thus to lay the foundations of and to build up the future continent, of golden and silver sands and the ruins of forests, with ant-like industry! Pindar gives the following account of the origin of Thera, whence, in after times, Libyan Cyrene was settled by Battus. Triton, in the form of Eurypylus, presents a clod to Euphemus, one of the Argonauts, as they are about to return home.

"He knew of our haste,
And immediately seizing a clod
With his right hand, strove to give it
As a chance stranger's gift.
Nor did the hero disregard him, but leaping on the shore,
Stretching hand to hand,
Received the mystic clod.
But I hear it sinking from the deck,
Go with the sea brine
At evening, accompanying the watery sea.
Often indeed I urged the careless
Menials to guard it, but their minds forgot.
And now in this island the imperishable seed of spacious
    Libya
Is spilled before its hour."

It is a beautiful fable, also related by Pindar, how Helius, or the Sun, looked down into the sea one day,—when perchance his rays were first reflected from some increasing glittering sandbar,—and saw the fair and fruitful island of Rhodes

"springing up from the bottom,
Capable of feeding many men, and suitable for flocks;

and at the nod of Zeus,

"The island sprang from the watery
Sea; and the genial Father of penetrating beams,
Ruler of fire-breathing horses, has it."

The shifting islands! who would not be willing that his house should be undermined by such a foe! The inhabitant of an island can tell what currents formed the land which he cultivates; and his earth is still being created or destroyed. There before his door, perchance, still empties the stream which brought down the material of his farm ages before, and is still bringing it down or washing it away,—the graceful, gentle robber!

Not long after this we saw the Piscataquoag, or Sparkling

Water, emptying in on our left, and heard the Falls of Amoskeag above. Large quantities of lumber, as we read in the
Gazetteer, were still annually floated down the Piscataquoag
to the Merrimack, and there are many fine mill privileges on
it. Just above the mouth of this river we passed the artificial
falls where the canals of the Manchester Manufacturing Company discharge themselves into the Merrimack. They are striking enough to have a name, and, with the scenery of a
Bashpish, would be visited from far and near. The water falls
thirty or forty feet over seven or eight steep and narrow terraces of stone, probably to break its force, and is converted
into one mass of foam. This canal-water did not seem to be
the worse for the wear, but foamed and fumed as purely, and
boomed as savagely and impressively, as a mountain torrent,
and, though it came from under a factory, we saw a rainbow
here. These are now the Amoskeag Falls, removed a mile
down-stream. But we did not tarry to examine them minutely, making haste to get past the village here collected, and
out of hearing of the hammer which was laying the foundation of another Lowell on the banks. At the time of our
voyage Manchester was a village of about two thousand inhabitants, where we landed for a moment to get some cool
water, and where an inhabitant told us that he was accustomed to go across the river into Goffstown for his water.
But now, as I have been told, and indeed have witnessed, it
contains fourteen thousand inhabitants. From a hill on the
road between Goffstown and Hooksett, four miles distant, I
have seen a thunder-shower pass over, and the sun break out
and shine on a city there, where I had landed nine years before in the fields; and there was waving the flag of its Museum, where "the only perfect skeleton of a Greenland or
river whale in the United States" was to be seen, and I also
read in its directory of a "Manchester Athenæum and Gallery
of the Fine Arts."

According to the Gazetteer, the descent of Amoskeag Falls,
which are the most considerable in the Merrimack, is fifty-
four feet in half a mile. We locked ourselves through here
with much ado, surmounting the successive watery steps of
this river's staircase in the midst of a crowd of villagers, jumping into the canal to their amusement, to save our boat from

upsetting, and consuming much river-water in our service. Amoskeag, or Namaskeak, is said to mean "great fishing-place." It was hereabouts that the Sachem Wannalancet resided. Tradition says that his tribe, when at war with the Mohawks, concealed their provisions in the cavities of the rocks in the upper part of these falls. The Indians, who hid their provisions in these holes, and affirmed "that God had cut them out for that purpose," understood their origin and use better than the Royal Society, who in their Transactions, in the last century, speaking of these very holes, declare that "they seem plainly to be artificial." Similar "pot-holes" may be seen at the Stone Flume on this river, on the Ottaway, at Bellows' Falls on the Connecticut, and in the limestone rock at Shelburne Falls on Deerfield River in Massachusetts, and more or less generally about all falls. Perhaps the most remarkable curiosity of this kind in New England is the well-known Basin on the Pemigewasset, one of the head-waters of this river, twenty by thirty feet in extent and proportionably deep, with a smooth and rounded brim, and filled with a cold, pellucid, and greenish water. At Amoskeag the river is divided into many separate torrents and trickling rills by the rocks, and its volume is so much reduced by the drain of the canals that it does not fill its bed. There are many pot-holes here on a rocky island which the river washes over in high freshets. As at Shelburne Falls, where I first observed them, they are from one foot to four or five in diameter, and as many in depth, perfectly round and regular, with smooth and gracefully curved brims, like goblets. Their origin is apparent to the most careless observer. A stone which the current has washed down, meeting with obstacles, revolves as on a pivot where it lies, gradually sinking in the course of centuries deeper and deeper into the rock, and in new freshets receiving the aid of fresh stones, which are drawn into this trap and doomed to revolve there for an indefinite period, doing Sisyphus-like penance for stony sins, until they either wear out, or wear through the bottom of their prison, or else are released by some revolution of nature. There lie the stones of various sizes, from a pebble to a foot or two in diameter, some of which have rested from their labor only since the spring, and some higher up which have lain still and dry for

ages,—we noticed some here at least sixteen feet above the
present level of the water,—while others are still revolving,
and enjoy no respite at any season. In one instance, at Shelburne Falls, they have worn quite through the rock, so that
a portion of the river leaks through in anticipation of the
fall. Some of these pot-holes at Amoskeag, in a very hard
brown-stone, had an oblong, cylindrical stone of the same
material loosely fitting them. One, as much as fifteen feet
deep and seven or eight in diameter, which was worn quite
through to the water, had a huge rock of the same material,
smooth but of irregular form, lodged in it. Everywhere there
were the rudiments or the wrecks of a dimple in the rock;
the rocky shells of whirlpools. As if by force of example and
sympathy after so many lessons, the rocks, the hardest material, had been endeavoring to whirl or flow into the forms of
the most fluid. The finest workers in stone are not copper or
steel tools, but the gentle touches of air and water working
at their leisure with a liberal allowance of time.

Not only have some of these basins been forming for
countless ages, but others exist which must have been completed in a former geological period. In deepening the Pawtucket Canal, in 1822, the workmen came to ledges with pot-
holes in them, where probably was once the bed of the river,
and there are some, we are told, in the town of Canaan in
this State, with the stones still in them, on the height of land
between the Merrimack and Connecticut, and nearly a thousand feet above these rivers, proving that the mountains and
the rivers have changed places. There lie the stones which
completed their revolutions perhaps before thoughts began to
revolve in the brain of man. The periods of Hindoo and
Chinese history, though they reach back to the time when the
race of mortals is confounded with the race of gods, are as
nothing compared with the periods which these stones have
inscribed. That which commenced a rock when time was
young, shall conclude a pebble in the unequal contest. With
such expense of time and natural forces are our very paving-
stones produced. They teach us lessons, these dumb workers;
verily there are "sermons in stones, and books in the running
streams." In these very holes the Indians hid their provisions;
but now there is no bread, but only its old neighbor stones

at the bottom. Who knows how many races they have served thus? By as simple a law, some accidental by-law, perchance, our system itself was made ready for its inhabitants.

These, and such as these, must be our antiquities, for lack of human vestiges. The monuments of heroes and the temples of the gods which may once have stood on the banks of this river are now, at any rate, returned to dust and primitive soil. The murmur of unchronicled nations has died away along these shores, and once more Lowell and Manchester are on the trail of the Indian.

The fact that Romans once inhabited her reflects no little dignity on Nature herself; that from some particular hill the Roman once looked out on the sea. She need not be ashamed of the vestiges of her children. How gladly the antiquary informs us that their vessels penetrated into this frith, or up that river of some remote isle! Their military monuments still remain on the hills and under the sod of the valleys. The oft-repeated Roman story is written in still legible characters in every quarter of the Old World, and but to-day, perchance, a new coin is dug up whose inscription repeats and confirms their fame. Some *"Judæa Capta,"* with a woman mourning under a palm-tree, with silent argument and demonstration confirms the pages of history.

> "Rome living was the world's sole ornament;
>   And dead is now the world's sole monument.
>
>   .   .   .   .   .
>
> With her own weight down pressed now she lies,
>   And by her heaps her hugeness testifies."

If one doubts whether Grecian valor and patriotism are not a fiction of the poets, he may go to Athens and see still upon the walls of the temple of Minerva the circular marks made by the shields taken from the enemy in the Persian war, which were suspended there. We have not far to seek for living and unquestionable evidence. The very dust takes shape and confirms some story which we had read. As Fuller said, commenting on the zeal of Camden, "A broken urn is a whole evidence; or an old gate still surviving out of which the city is run out." When Solon endeavored to prove that Salamis had formerly belonged to the Athenians, and not to the Megareans, he caused the tombs to be opened, and showed that the inhabitants of Salamis turned the faces of their dead to the same side with the Athenians, but the Megareans to the opposite side. There they were to be interrogated.

Some minds are as little logical or argumentative as nature; they can offer no reason or "guess," but they exhibit the solemn and incontrovertible fact. If a historical question arises, they cause the tombs to be opened. Their silent and practical logic convinces the reason and the understanding at the same time. Of such sort is always the only pertinent question and the only satisfactory reply.

Our own country furnishes antiquities as ancient and durable, and as useful, as any; rocks at least as well covered with lichens, and a soil which, if it is virgin, is but virgin mould, the very dust of nature. What if we cannot read Rome, or Greece, Etruria, or Carthage, or Egypt, or Babylon, on these; are our cliffs bare? The lichen on the rocks is a rude and simple shield which beginning and imperfect Nature suspended there. Still hangs her wrinkled trophy. And here too the poet's eye may still detect the brazen nails which fastened Time's inscriptions, and if he has the gift, decipher them by this clew. The walls that fence our fields, as well as modern Rome, and not less the Parthenon itself, are all built of *ruins*. Here may be heard the din of rivers, and ancient winds which have long since lost their names sough through our woods;— the first faint sounds of spring, older than the summer of Athenian glory, the titmouse lisping in the wood, the jay's scream, and blue-bird's warble, and the hum of

> "bees that fly
> About the laughing blossoms of sallowy."

Here is the gray dawn for antiquity, and our to-morrow's future should be at least paulo-post to theirs which we have put behind us. There are the red-maple and birchen leaves, old runes which are not yet deciphered; catkins, pine-cones, vines, oak-leaves, and acorns; the very things themselves, and not their forms in stone,—so much the more ancient and venerable. And even to the current summer there has come down tradition of a hoary-headed master of all art, who once filled every field and grove with statues and god-like architecture, of every design which Greece has lately copied; whose ruins are now mingled with the dust, and not one block remains upon another. The century sun and unwearied rain have wasted them, till not one fragment from that quarry now exists; and poets perchance will feign that gods sent down the material from heaven.

What though the traveller tell us of the ruins of Egypt, are we so sick or idle, that we must sacrifice our America and to-day to some man's ill-remembered and indolent story? Carnac and Luxor are but names, or if their skeletons remain, still more desert sand, and at length a wave of the Mediterranean Sea are needed to wash away the filth that attaches to their grandeur. Carnac! Carnac! here is Carnac for me. I behold the columns of a larger and purer temple.

> This is my Carnac, whose unmeasured dome
> Shelters the measuring art and measurer's home.
> Behold these flowers, let us be up with time,
> Not dreaming of three thousand years ago,
> Erect ourselves and let those columns lie,
> Not stoop to raise a foil against the sky.
> Where is the spirit of that time but in
> This present day, perchance the present line?
> Three thousand years ago are not agone,
> They are still lingering in this summer morn,
> And Memnon's Mother sprightly greets us now,
> Wearing her youthful radiance on her brow.
> If Carnac's columns still stand on the plain,
> To enjoy our opportunities they remain.

In these parts dwelt the famous Sachem Pasaconaway, who was seen by Gookin "at Pawtucket, when he was about one hundred and twenty years old." He was reputed a wise man and a powwow, and restrained his people from going to war with the English. They believed "that he could make water burn, rocks move, and trees dance, and metamorphose himself into a flaming man; that in winter he could raise a green leaf out of the ashes of a dry one, and produce a living snake from the skin of a dead one, and many similar miracles." In 1660, according to Gookin, at a great feast and dance, he made his farewell speech to his people, in which he said, that as he was not likely to see them met together again, he would leave them this word of advice, to take heed how they quarrelled with their English neighbors, for though they might do them much mischief at first, it would prove the means of their own destruction. He himself, he said, had been as much an enemy to the English at their first coming as any, and had used all his arts to destroy them, or at least to prevent their settlement, but could by no means effect it. Gookin thought that he "possibly might have such a kind of spirit upon him as was upon Balaam, who in xxiii. Numbers, 23, said 'Surely, there is no enchantment against Jacob, neither is there any divination against Israel.' " His son Wannalancet carefully followed his advice, and when Philip's War broke out, he withdrew his followers to Penacook, now Concord in New Hampshire, from the scene of the war. On his return afterwards, he visited the minister of Chelmsford, and, as is stated in the history of that town, "wished to know whether Chelmsford had suffered much during the war; and being informed that it had not, and that God should be thanked for it, Wannalancet replied, 'Me next.' "

Manchester was the residence of John Stark, a hero of two wars, and survivor of a third, and at his death the last but one of the American generals of the Revolution. He was born in the adjoining town of Londonderry, then Nutfield, in 1728. As early as 1752, he was taken prisoner by the Indians while hunting in the wilderness near Baker's River; he performed notable service as a captain of rangers in the French war; commanded a regiment of the New Hampshire militia at the battle of Bunker Hill; and fought and won the battle of Bennington in 1777. He was past service in the last war, and died here in 1822, at the age of 94. His monument stands upon the second bank of the river, about a mile and a half above the falls, and commands a prospect several miles up and down the Merrimack. It suggested how much more impressive in the landscape is the tomb of a hero than the dwellings of the inglorious living. Who is most dead,—a hero by whose monument you stand, or his descendants of whom you have never heard?

The graves of Pasaconaway and Wannalancet are marked by no monument on the bank of their native river.

Every town which we passed, if we may believe the Gazetteer, had been the residence of some great man. But though we knocked at many doors, and even made particular inquiries, we could not find that there were any now living. Under the head of Litchfield we read:—

"The Hon. Wyseman Clagett closed his life in this town." According to another, "He was a classical scholar, a good lawyer, a wit, and a poet." We saw his old gray house just below Great Nesenkeag Brook.—Under the head of Merrimack: "Hon. Mathew Thornton, one of the signers of the Declaration of American Independence, resided many years in this town." His house too we saw from the river.—"Dr. Jonathan Gove, a man distinguished for his urbanity, his talents and professional skill, resided in this town [Goffstown]. He was one of the oldest practitioners of medicine in the county. He was many years an active member of the legislature."—"Hon. Robert Means, who died Jan. 24, 1823, at the age of 80, was for a long period a resident in Amherst. He was a native of Ireland. In 1764 he came to this country, where, by his industry and application to business, he acquired a large property, and great respect."—"William Stinson [one of the first settlers of Dunbarton], born in Ireland, came to Londonderry with his father. He was much respected and was a useful man. James Rogers was from Ireland, and father to Major Robert Rogers. He was shot in the woods, being mistaken for a bear."—"Rev. Matthew Clark, second minister of Londonderry, was a native of Ireland, who had in early life been an officer in the army, and distinguished himself in the defence of the city of Londonderry, when besieged by the army of King James II. A. D. 1688–9. He afterwards relinquished a military life for the clerical profession. He possessed a strong mind, marked by a considerable degree of eccentricity. He died Jan. 25, 1735, and was borne to the grave, at his particular request, by his former companions in arms, of whom there were a considerable number among the early settlers of this town; several of them had been made free from taxes throughout the British dominions by King William, for their bravery in that memorable siege."—Col. George Reid and Capt. David M'Clary, also citizens of Londonderry, were "distinguished and brave" officers.—"Major Andrew M'Clary, a native of this town [Epsom], fell at the battle of Breed's Hill."—Many of these heroes, like the illustrious Roman, were ploughing when the news of the massacre at Lexington arrived, and straight-way left their ploughs in the furrow, and repaired to the scene of action. Some miles from where we now were, there once stood a guide-post on which were the words, "3 miles to Squire MacGaw's."

But generally speaking, the land is now, at any rate, very bar-ren of men, and we doubt if there are as many hundreds as we read of. It may be that we stood too near.

Uncannunuc Mountain in Goffstown was visible from Amoskeag, five or six miles westward. It is the northeastern-most in the horizon, which we see from our native town, but seen from there is too ethereally blue to be the same which the like of us have ever climbed. Its name is said to mean "The Two Breasts," there being two eminences some distance apart. The highest, which is about fourteen hundred feet above the sea, probably affords a more extensive view of the Merrimack valley and the adjacent country than any other hill, though it is somewhat obstructed by woods. Only a few short reaches of the river are visible, but you can trace its course far down stream by the sandy tracts on its banks.

A little south of Uncannunuc, about sixty years ago, as the story goes, an old woman who went out to gather penny-royal, tript her foot in the bail of a small brass kettle in the dead grass and bushes. Some say that flints and charcoal and some traces of a camp were also found. This kettle, holding about four quarts, is still preserved and used to dye thread in. It is supposed to have belonged to some old French or Indian hunter, who was killed in one of his hunting or scouting excursions, and so never returned to look after his kettle.

But we were most interested to hear of the pennyroyal, it is soothing to be reminded that wild nature produces any-thing ready for the use of man. Men know that *something* is good. One says that it is yellow-dock, another that it is bittersweet, another that it is slippery-elm bark, burdock, catnip, calamint, elicampane, thoroughwort, or pennyroyal. A man may esteem himself happy when that which is his food is also his medicine. There is no kind of herb, but somebody or other says that it is good. I am very glad to hear it. It reminds me of the first chapter of Genesis. But how should they know that it is good? That is the mystery to me. I am always agree-ably disappointed; it is incredible that they should have found it out. Since all things are good, men fail at last to distinguish which is the bane, and which the antidote. There are sure to be two prescriptions diametrically opposite. Stuff a cold and starve a cold are but two ways. They are the two practices both always in full blast. Yet you must take advice of the one school as if there was no other. In respect to religion and the healing art, all nations are still in a state of barbarism. In the most civilized countries the priest is still but a Powwow, and the physician a Great Medicine. Consider the deference which is everywhere paid to a doctor's opinion. Nothing more strik-ingly betrays the credulity of mankind than medicine. Quack-ery is a thing universal, and universally successful. In this case it becomes literally true that no imposition is too great for the credulity of men. Priests and physicians should never look one another in the face. They have no common ground, nor is there any to mediate between them. When the one comes, the other goes. They could not come to-gether without laughter, or a significant silence, for the one's profession is a satire on the other's, and either's success would be the other's failure. It is wonderful that the physi-cian should ever die, and that the priest should ever live. Why is it that the priest is never called to consult with the physician? It is because men believe practically that matter is independent of spirit. But what is quackery? It is commonly an attempt to cure the diseases of a man by addressing his body alone. There is need of a physician who shall minister to both soul and body at once, that is, to man. Now he falls between two stools.

After passing through the locks, we had poled ourselves through the canal here, about half a mile in length, to the boatable part of the river. Above Amoskeag the river spreads out into a lake reaching a mile or two without a bend. There

were many canal-boats here bound up to Hooksett, about
eight miles, and as they were going up empty with a fair
wind, one boatman offered to take us in tow if we would
wait. But when we came alongside, we found that they meant
to take us on board, since otherwise we should clog their
motions too much; but as our boat was too heavy to be lifted
aboard, we pursued our way up the stream, as before, while
the boatmen were at their dinner, and came to anchor at
length under some alders on the opposite shore, where we
could take our lunch. Though far on one side, every sound
was wafted over to us from the opposite bank, and from the
harbor of the canal, and we could see everything that passed.
By and by came several canal-boats, at intervals of a quarter
of a mile, standing up to Hooksett with a light breeze, and
one by one disappeared round a point above. With their
broad sails set, they moved slowly up the stream in the sluggish and fitful breeze, like one-winged antediluvian birds, and
as if impelled by some mysterious counter-current. It was a
grand motion, so slow and stately, this "standing out," as the
phrase is, expressing the gradual and steady progress of a vessel, as if it were by mere rectitude and disposition, without
shuffling. Their sails, which stood so still, were like chips cast
into the current of the air to show which way it set. At length
the boat which we had spoken came along, keeping the middle of the stream, and when within speaking distance the
steersman called out ironically to say, that if we would come
alongside now he would take us in tow; but not heeding his
taunt, we still loitered in the shade till we had finished our
lunch, and when the last boat had disappeared round the
point with flapping sail, for the breeze had now sunk to a
zephyr, with our own sails set, and plying our oars, we shot
rapidly up the stream in pursuit, and as we glided close alongside, while they were vainly invoking Æolus to their aid, we
returned their compliment by proposing, if they would throw
us a rope, to "take them in tow," to which these Merrimack
sailors had no suitable answer ready. Thus we gradually overtook and passed each boat in succession until we had the river
to ourselves again.

Our course this afternoon was between Manchester and
Goffstown.

———

While we float here, far from that tributary stream on whose banks our Friends and kindred dwell, our thoughts, like the stars, come out of their horizon still; for there circulates a finer blood than Lavoisier has discovered the laws of,—the blood, not of kindred merely, but of kindness, whose pulse still beats at any distance and forever.

> True kindness is a pure divine affinity,
> Not founded upon human consanguinity.
> It is a spirit, not a blood relation,
> Superior to family and station.

After years of vain familiarity, some distant gesture or unconscious behavior, which we remember, speaks to us with more emphasis than the wisest or kindest words. We are sometimes made aware of a kindness long passed, and realize that there have been times when our Friends' thoughts of us were of so pure and lofty a character that they passed over us like the winds of heaven unnoticed; when they treated us not as what we were, but as what we aspired to be. There has just reached us, it may be, the nobleness of some such silent behavior, not to be forgotten, not to be remembered, and we shudder to think how it fell on us cold, though in some true but tardy hour we endeavor to wipe off these scores.

In my experience, persons, when they are made the subject of conversation, though with a Friend, are commonly the most prosaic and trivial of facts. The universe seems bankrupt as soon as we begin to discuss the character of individuals. Our discourse all runs to slander, and our limits grow narrower as we advance. How is it that we are impelled to treat our old Friends so ill when we obtain new ones? The housekeeper says, I never had any new crockery in my life but I began to break the old. I say, let us speak of mushrooms and forest trees rather. Yet we can sometimes afford to remember them in private.

> Lately, alas, I knew a gentle boy,
>   Whose features all were cast in Virtue's mould,
> As one she had designed for Beauty's toy,
>   But after manned him for her own strong-hold.

On every side he open was as day,
   That you might see no lack of strength within,
For walls and ports do only serve alway
   For a pretence to feebleness and sin.

Say not that Cæsar was victorious,
   With toil and strife who stormed the House of Fame,
In other sense this youth was glorious,
   Himself a kingdom wheresoe'er he came.

No strength went out to get him victory,
   When all was income of its own accord;
For where he went none other was to see,
   But all were parcel of their noble lord.

He forayed like the subtile haze of summer,
   That stilly shows fresh landscapes to our eyes,
And revolutions works without a murmur,
   Or rustling of a leaf beneath the skies.

So was I taken unawares by this,
   I quite forgot my homage to confess;
Yet now am forced to know, though hard it is,
   I might have loved him had I loved him less.

Each moment as we nearer drew to each,
   A stern respect withheld us farther yet,
So that we seemed beyond each other's reach,
   And less acquainted than when first we met.

We two were one while we did sympathize,
   So could we not the simplest bargain drive;
And what avails it now that we are wise,
   If absence doth this doubleness contrive?

Eternity may not the chance repeat,
   But I must tread my single way alone,
In sad remembrance that we once did meet,
   And know that bliss irrevocably gone.

The spheres henceforth my elegy shall sing,
  For elegy has other subject none;
Each strain of music in my ears shall ring
  Knell of departure from that other one.

Make haste and celebrate my tragedy;
  With fitting strain resound ye woods and fields;
Sorrow is dearer in such case to me
  Than all the joys other occasion yields.

———

Is 't then too late the damage to repair?
  Distance, forsooth, from my weak grasp hath reft
The empty husk, and clutched the useless tare,
  But in my hands the wheat and kernel left.

If I but love that virtue which he is,
  Though it be scented in the morning air,
Still shall we be truest acquaintances,
  Nor mortals know a sympathy more rare.

Friendship is evanescent in every man's experience, and re-membered like heat lightning in past summers. Fair and flit-ting like a summer cloud;—there is always some vapor in the air, no matter how long the drought; there are even April showers. Surely from time to time, for its vestiges never de-part, it floats through our atmosphere. It takes place, like veg-etation in so many materials, because there is such a law, but always without permanent form, though ancient and familiar as the sun and moon, and as sure to come again. The heart is forever inexperienced. They silently gather as by magic, these never failing, never quite deceiving visions, like the bright and fleecy clouds in the calmest and clearest days. The Friend is some fair floating isle of palms eluding the mariner in Pacific seas. Many are the dangers to be encountered, equinoctial gales and coral reefs, ere he may sail before the constant trades. But who would not sail through mutiny and storm, even over Atlantic waves, to reach the fabulous retreating shores of some continent man? The imagination still clings to the faintest tradition of

The Atlantides.

The smothered streams of love, which flow
More bright than Phlegethon, more low,
Island us ever, like the sea,
In an Atlantic mystery.
Our fabled shores none ever reach,
No mariner has found our beach,
Scarcely our mirage now is seen,
And neighboring waves with floating green,
Yet still the oldest charts contain
Some dotted outline of our main;
In ancient times midsummer days
Unto the western islands' gaze,
To Teneriffe and the Azores,
Have shown our faint and cloud-like shores.

But sink not yet, ye desolate isles,
Anon your coast with commerce smiles,
And richer freights ye'll furnish far
Than Africa or Malabar.
Be fair, be fertile evermore,
Ye rumored but untrodden shore,
Princes and monarchs will contend
Who first unto your land shall send,
And pawn the jewels of the crown
To call your distant soil their own.

Columbus has sailed westward of these isles by the mariner's compass, but neither he nor his successors have found them. We are no nearer than Plato was. The earnest seeker and hopeful discoverer of this New World always haunts the outskirts of his time, and walks through the densest crowd uninterrupted, and as it were in a straight line.

Sea and land are but his neighbors,
And companions in his labors,
Who on the ocean's verge and firm land's end
Doth long and truly seek his Friend.
Many men dwell far inland,
But he alone sits on the strand.
Whether he ponders men or books,

Always still he seaward looks,
Marine news he ever reads,
And the slightest glances heeds,
Feels the sea breeze on his cheek,
At each word the landsmen speak,
In every companion's eye
A sailing vessel doth descry;
In the ocean's sullen roar
From some distant port he hears,
Of wrecks upon a distant shore,
And the ventures of past years.

Who does not walk on the plain as amid the columns of Tadmore of the desert? There is on the earth no institution which Friendship has established; it is not taught by any religion; no scripture contains its maxims. It has no temple, nor even a solitary column. There goes a rumor that the earth is inhabited, but the shipwrecked mariner has not seen a footprint on the shore. The hunter has found only fragments of pottery and the monuments of inhabitants.

However, our fates at least are social. Our courses do not diverge; but as the web of destiny is woven it is fulled, and we are cast more and more into the centre. Men naturally, though feebly, seek this alliance, and their actions faintly foretell it. We are inclined to lay the chief stress on likeness and not on difference, and in foreign bodies we admit that there are many degrees of warmth below blood heat, but none of cold above it.

Mencius says: "If one loses a fowl or a dog, he knows well how to seek them again; if one loses the sentiments of his heart, he does not know how to seek them again. . . . . The duties of practical philosophy consist only in seeking after those sentiments of the heart which we have lost; that is all."

One or two persons come to my house from time to time, there being proposed to them the faint possibility of intercourse. They are as full as they are silent, and wait for my plectrum to stir the strings of their lyre. If they could ever come to the length of a sentence, or hear one, on that ground they are dreaming of! They speak faintly, and do not obtrude themselves. They have heard some news, which none, not even they themselves, can impart. It is a wealth they can bear about them which can be expended in various ways. What came they out to seek?

No word is oftener on the lips of men than Friendship, and indeed no thought is more familiar to their aspirations. All men are dreaming of it, and its drama, which is always a tragedy, is enacted daily. It is the secret of the universe. You may thread the town, you may wander the country, and none shall ever speak of it, yet thought is everywhere busy about it, and the idea of what is possible in this respect affects our behavior toward all new men and women, and a great many old ones. Nevertheless, I can remember only two or three essays on this subject in all literature. No wonder that the Mythology, and Arabian Nights, and Shakespeare, and Scott's novels entertain us,—we are poets and fablers and dramatists and novelists ourselves. We are continually acting a part in a more interesting drama than any written. We are dreaming that our Friends are our *Friends*, and that we are our Friends' *Friends*. Our actual Friends are but distant relations of those to whom we are pledged. We never exchange more than three words with a Friend in our lives on that level to which our thoughts and feelings almost habitually rise. One goes forth prepared to say, "Sweet Friends!" and the salutation is, "Damn your eyes!" But never mind; faint heart never won true Friend. O my Friend, may it come to pass once, that when you are my Friend I may be yours.

Of what use the friendliest dispositions even, if there are no hours given to Friendship, if it is forever postponed to unimportant duties and relations? Friendship is first, Friendship last. But it is equally impossible to forget our Friends, and to make them answer to our ideal. When they say farewell, then indeed we begin to keep them company. How often we find ourselves turning our backs on our actual Friends, that we may go and meet their ideal cousins. I would that I were worthy to be any man's Friend.

What is commonly honored with the name of Friendship is no very profound or powerful instinct. Men do not, after all, *love* their Friends greatly. I do not often see the farmers made seers and wise to the verge of insanity by their Friendship for one another. They are not often transfigured and translated by love in each other's presence. I do not observe them purified, refined, and elevated by the love of a man. If one abates a little the price of his wood, or gives a neighbor his vote at town-meeting, or a barrel of apples, or lends him his wagon frequently, it is esteemed a rare instance of Friendship. Nor do the farmers' wives lead lives consecrated to Friendship. I do not see the pair of farmer Friends of either sex prepared to stand against the world. There are only two or three couples in history. To say that a man is your Friend, means commonly no more than this, that he is not your enemy. Most contemplate only what would be the accidental and trifling advantages of Friendship, as that the Friend can assist in time of need, by his substance, or his influence, or his counsel; but he who foresees such advantages in this relation proves himself blind to its real advantage, or indeed wholly inexperienced in the relation itself. Such services are particular and menial, compared with the perpetual and all-embracing service which it is. Even the utmost good-will and harmony and practical kindness are not sufficient for Friendship, for Friends do not live in harmony merely, as some say, but in melody. We do not wish for Friends to feed and clothe our bodies,—neighbors are kind enough for that,—but to do the like office to our spirits. For this few are rich enough, however well disposed they may be. For the most part we stupidly confound one man with another. The dull distinguish only races or nations, or at most classes, but the wise man, individuals. To his Friend a man's peculiar character appears in every feature and in every action, and it is thus drawn out and improved by him.

Think of the importance of Friendship in the education of men.

> "He that hath love and judgment too,
>   Sees more than any other doe."

It will make a man honest; it will make him a hero; it will make him a saint. It is the state of the just dealing with the just, the magnanimous with the magnanimous, the sincere with the sincere, man with man.

And it is well said by another poet,

> "Why love among the virtues is not known,
> Is that love is them all contract in one."

All the abuses which are the object of reform with the philanthropist, the statesman, and the housekeeper are unconsciously amended in the intercourse of Friends. A Friend is one who incessantly pays us the compliment of expecting from us all the virtues, and who can appreciate them in us. It takes two to speak the truth,—one to speak, and another to hear. How can one treat with magnanimity mere wood and stone? If we dealt only with the false and dishonest, we should at last forget how to speak truth. Only lovers know the value and magnanimity of truth, while traders prize a cheap honesty, and neighbors and acquaintance a cheap civility. In our daily intercourse with men, our nobler faculties are dormant and suffered to rust. None will pay us the compliment to expect nobleness from us. Though we have gold to give, they demand only copper. We ask our neighbor to suffer himself to be dealt with truly, sincerely, nobly; but he answers no by his deafness. He does not even hear this prayer. He says practically, I will be content if you treat me as "no better than I should be," as deceitful, mean, dishonest, and selfish. For the most part, we are contented so to deal and to be dealt with, and we do not think that for the mass of men there is any truer and nobler relation possible. A man may have *good* neighbors, so called, and acquaintances, and even companions, wife, parents, brothers, sisters, children, who meet himself and one another on this ground only. The State does not demand justice of its members, but thinks that it succeeds very well with the least degree of it, hardly more than rogues practise; and so do the neighborhood and the family. What is commonly called Friendship even is only a little more honor among rogues.

But sometimes we are said to *love* another, that is, to stand in a true relation to him, so that we give the best to, and receive the best from, him. Between whom there is hearty truth, there is love; and in proportion to our truthfulness and confidence in one another, our lives are divine and miraculous, and answer to our ideal. There are passages of affection in our intercourse with mortal men and women, such as no prophecy had taught us to expect, which transcend our earthly life, and anticipate Heaven for us. What is this Love that may come right into the middle of a prosaic Goffstown day, equal to any of the gods? that discovers a new world, fair and fresh and eternal, occupying the place of the old one, when to the common eye a dust has settled on the universe? which world cannot else be reached, and does not exist. What other words, we may almost ask, are memorable and worthy to be repeated than those which love has inspired? It is wonderful that they were ever uttered. They are few and rare, indeed, but, like a strain of music, they are incessantly repeated and modulated by the memory. All other words crumble off with the stucco which overlies the heart. We should not dare to repeat these now aloud. We are not competent to hear them at all times.

The books for young people say a great deal about the *selection* of Friends; it is because they really have nothing to say about *Friends*. They mean associates and confidants merely. "Know that the contrariety of foe and Friend proceeds from God." Friendship takes place between those who have an affinity for one another, and is a perfectly natural and inevitable result. No professions nor advances will avail. Even speech, at first, necessarily has nothing to do with it; but it follows after silence, as the buds in the graft do not put forth into leaves till long after the graft has taken. It is a drama in which the parties have no part to act. We are all Mussulmen and fatalists in this respect. Impatient and uncertain lovers think that they must say or do something kind whenever they meet; they must never be cold. But they who are Friends do not do what they *think* they must, but what they *must*. Even their Friendship is to some extent but a sublime phenomenon to them.

The true and not despairing Friend will address his Friend in some such terms as these.

"I never asked thy leave to let me love thee,—I have a right. I love thee not as something private and personal, which is *your own*, but as something universal and worthy of love, *which I have found*. O, how I think of you! You are purely good,—you are infinitely good. I can trust you forever. I did not think that humanity was so rich. Give me an opportunity to live."

"You are the fact in a fiction,—you are the truth more strange and admirable than fiction. Consent only to be what you are. I alone will never stand in your way."

"This is what I would like,—to be as intimate with you as our spirits are intimate,—respecting you as I respect my ideal. Never to profane one another by word or action, even by a thought. Between us, if necessary, let there be no acquaintance."

"I have discovered you; how can you be concealed from me?"

The Friend asks no return but that his Friend will religiously accept and wear and not disgrace his apotheosis of him. They cherish each other's hopes. They are kind to each other's dreams.

Though the poet says, " 'T is the pre-eminence of Friendship to impute excellence," yet we can never praise our Friend, nor esteem him praiseworthy, nor let him think that he can please us by any *behavior*, or ever *treat* us well enough. That kindness which has so good a reputation elsewhere can least of all consist with this relation, and no such affront can be offered to a Friend, as a conscious good-will, a friendliness which is not a necessity of the Friend's nature.

The sexes are naturally most strongly attracted to one another, by constant constitutional differences, and are most commonly and surely the complements of each other. How natural and easy it is for man to secure the attention of woman to what interests himself. Men and women of equal culture, thrown together, are sure to be of a certain value to one another, more than men to men. There exists already a natural disinterestedness and liberality in such society, and I think that any man will more confidently carry his favorite books to read to some circle of intelligent women, than to one of his own sex. The visit of man to man is wont to be an interruption, but the sexes naturally expect one another. Yet Friendship is no respecter of sex; and perhaps it is more rare between the sexes than between two of the same sex.

Friendship is, at any rate, a relation of perfect equality. It cannot well spare any outward sign of equal obligation and advantage. The nobleman can never have a Friend among his retainers, nor the king among his subjects. Not that the parties to it are in all respects equal, but they are equal in all that respects or affects their Friendship. The one's love is exactly balanced and represented by the other's. Persons are only the vessels which contain the nectar, and the hydrostatic paradox is the symbol of love's law. It finds its level and rises to its fountain-head in all breasts, and its slenderest column balances the ocean.

> "And love as well the shepherd can
> As can the mighty nobleman."

The one sex is not, in this respect, more tender than the other. A hero's love is as delicate as a maiden's.

Confucius said, "Never contract Friendship with a man who is not better than thyself." It is the merit and preservation of Friendship, that it takes place on a level higher than the actual characters of the parties would seem to warrant. The rays of light come to us in such a curve that every man whom we meet appears to be taller than he actually is. Such foundation has civility. My Friend is that one whom I can associate with my choicest thought. I always assign to him a nobler employment in my absence than I ever find him engaged in; and I imagine that the hours which he devotes to me were snatched from a higher society. The sorest insult which I ever received from a Friend was, when he behaved with the license which only long and cheap acquaintance allows to one's faults, in my presence, without shame, and still addressed me in friendly accents. Beware, lest thy Friend learn at last to tolerate one frailty of thine, and so an obstacle be raised to the progress of thy love. There are times when we have had enough even of our Friends, when we begin inevitably to profane one another, and must withdraw religiously into solitude and silence, the better to prepare ourselves for a loftier intimacy. Silence is the ambrosial night in the intercourse of Friends, in which their sincerity is recruited and takes deeper root.

Friendship is never established as an understood relation. Do you demand that I be less your Friend that you may know

it? Yet what right have I to think that another cherishes so
rare a sentiment for me? It is a miracle which requires constant proofs. It is an exercise of the purest imagination and
the rarest faith. It says by a silent but eloquent behavior,—"I
will be so related to thee as thou canst imagine; even so thou
mayest believe. I will spend truth,—all my wealth on
thee,"—and the Friend responds silently through his nature
and life, and treats his Friend with the same divine courtesy.
He knows us literally through thick and thin. He never asks
for a sign of love, but can distinguish it by the features which
it naturally wears. We never need to stand upon ceremony
with him with regard to his visits. Wait not till I invite thee,
but observe that I am glad to see thee when thou comest. It
would be paying too dear for thy visit to ask for it. Where
my Friend lives there are all riches and every attraction, and
no slight obstacle can keep me from him. Let me never have
to tell thee what I have not to tell. Let our intercourse be
wholly above ourselves, and draw us up to it.

The language of Friendship is not words, but meanings. It
is an intelligence above language. One imagines endless conversations with his Friend, in which the tongue shall be
loosed, and thoughts be spoken without hesitancy or end; but
the experience is commonly far otherwise. Acquaintances may
come and go, and have a word ready for every occasion; but
what puny word shall he utter whose very breath is thought
and meaning? Suppose you go to bid farewell to your Friend
who is setting out on a journey; what other outward sign do
you know than to shake his hand? Have you any palaver
ready for him then? any box of salve to commit to his pocket?
any particular message to send by him? any statement which
you had forgotten to make?—as if you could forget anything.—No, it is much that you take his hand and say Farewell; that you could easily omit; so far custom has prevailed.
It is even painful, if he is to go, that he should linger so long.
If he must go, let him go quickly. Have you any *last* words?
Alas, it is only the word of words, which you have so long
sought and found not; *you* have not a *first* word yet. There
are few even whom I should venture to call earnestly by their
most proper names. A name pronounced is the recognition
of the individual to whom it belongs. He who can pronounce

my name aright, he can call me, and is entitled to my love and service. Yet reserve is the freedom and abandonment of lovers. It is the reserve of what is hostile or indifferent in their natures, to give place to what is kindred and harmonious.

The violence of love is as much to be dreaded as that of hate. When it is durable it is serene and equable. Even its famous pains begin only with the ebb of love, for few are indeed lovers, though all would fain be. It is one proof of a man's fitness for Friendship that he is able to do without that which is cheap and passionate. A true Friendship is as wise as it is tender. The parties to it yield implicitly to the guidance of their love, and know no other law nor kindness. It is not extravagant and insane, but what it says is something established henceforth, and will bear to be stereotyped. It is a truer truth, it is better and fairer news, and no time will ever shame it, or prove it false. This is a plant which thrives best in a temperate zone, where summer and winter alternate with one another. The Friend is a *necessarius*, and meets his Friend on homely ground; not on carpets and cushions, but on the ground and on rocks they will sit, obeying the natural and primitive laws. They will meet without any outcry, and part without loud sorrow. Their relation implies such qualities as the warrior prizes; for it takes a valor to open the hearts of men as well as the gates of castles. It is not an idle sympathy and mutual consolation merely, but a heroic sympathy of aspiration and endeavor.

> "When manhood shall be matched so
> That fear can take no place,
> Then weary *works* make warriors
> Each other to embrace."

The Friendship which Wawatam testified for Henry the fur-trader, as described in the latter's "Adventures," so almost bare and leafless, yet not blossomless nor fruitless, is remembered with satisfaction and security. The stern, imperturbable warrior, after fasting, solitude, and mortification of body, comes to the white man's lodge, and affirms that he is the white brother whom he saw in his dream, and adopts him henceforth. He buries the hatchet as it regards his friend, and they hunt and feast and make maple-sugar together. "Metals

unite from fluxility; birds and beasts from motives of convenience; fools from fear and stupidity; and just men at sight."
If Wawatam would taste the "white man's milk" with his
tribe, or take his bowl of human broth made of the trader's
fellow-countrymen, he first finds a place of safety for his
Friend, whom he has rescued from a similar fate. At length,
after a long winter of undisturbed and happy intercourse in
the family of the chieftain in the wilderness, hunting and fishing, they return in the spring to Michilimackinac to dispose
of their furs; and it becomes necessary for Wawatam to take
leave of his Friend at the Isle aux Outardes, when the latter,
to avoid his enemies, proceeded to the Sault de Sainte Marie,
supposing that they were to be separated for a short time
only. "We now exchanged farewells," says Henry, "with an
emotion entirely reciprocal. I did not quit the lodge without
the most grateful sense of the many acts of goodness which I
had experienced in it, nor without the sincerest respect for
the virtues which I had witnessed among its members. All the
family accompanied me to the beach; and the canoe had no
sooner put off than Wawatam commenced an address to the
Kichi Manito, beseeching him to take care of me, his brother,
till we should next meet. We had proceeded to too great a
distance to allow of our hearing his voice, before Wawatam
had ceased to offer up his prayers." We never hear of him
again.

Friendship is not so kind as is imagined; it has not much
human blood in it, but consists with a certain disregard for
men and their erections, the Christian duties and humanities,
while it purifies the air like electricity. There may be the stern-
est tragedy in the relation of two more than usually innocent
and true to their highest instincts. We may call it an essentially
heathenish intercourse, free and irresponsible in its nature,
and practising all the virtues gratuitously. It is not the highest
sympathy merely, but a pure and lofty society, a fragmentary
and godlike intercourse of ancient date, still kept up at intervals, which, remembering itself, does not hesitate to disregard
the humbler rights and duties of humanity. It requires im-
maculate and godlike qualities full-grown, and exists at all
only by condescension and anticipation of the remotest
future. We love nothing which is merely good and not fair, if

such a thing is possible. Nature puts some kind of blossom before every fruit, not simply a calyx behind it. When the Friend comes out of his heathenism and superstition, and breaks his idols, being converted by the precepts of a newer testament; when he forgets his mythology, and treats his Friend like a Christian, or as he can afford; then Friendship ceases to be Friendship, and becomes charity; that principle which established the almshouse is now beginning with its charity at home, and establishing an almshouse and pauper relations there.

As for the number which this society admits, it is at any rate to be begun with one, the noblest and greatest that we know, and whether the world will ever carry it further, whether, as Chaucer affirms,

"There be mo sterres in the skie than a pair,"

remains to be proved;

"And certaine he is well begone
Among a thousand that findeth one."

We shall not surrender ourselves heartily to any while we are conscious that another is more deserving of our love. Yet Friendship does not stand for numbers; the Friend does not count his Friends on his fingers; they are not numerable. The more there are included by this bond, if they are indeed in-cluded, the rarer and diviner the quality of the love that binds them. I am ready to believe that as private and intimate a re-lation may exist by which three are embraced, as between two. Indeed, we cannot have too many friends; the virtue which we appreciate we to some extent appropriate, so that thus we are made at last more fit for every relation of life. A base Friend-ship is of a narrowing and exclusive tendency, but a noble one is not exclusive; its very superfluity and dispersed love is the humanity which sweetens society, and sympathizes with for-eign nations; for though its foundations are private, it is, in ef-fect, a public affair and a public advantage, and the Friend, more than the father of a family, deserves well of the state.

The only danger in Friendship is that it will end. It is a

delicate plant, though a native. The least unworthiness, even if it be unknown to one's self, vitiates it. Let the Friend know that those faults which he observes in his Friend his own faults attract. There is no rule more invariable than that we are paid for our suspicions by finding what we suspected. By our narrowness and prejudices we say, I will have so much and such of you, my Friend, no more. Perhaps there are none charitable, none disinterested, none wise, noble, and heroic enough, for a true and lasting Friendship.

I sometimes hear my Friends complain finely that I do not appreciate their fineness. I shall not tell them whether I do or not. As if they expected a vote of thanks for every fine thing which they uttered or did. Who knows but it was finely appreciated. It may be that your silence was the finest thing of the two. There are some things which a man never speaks of, which are much finer kept silent about. To the highest communications we only lend a silent ear. Our finest relations are not simply kept silent about, but buried under a positive depth of silence never to be revealed. It may be that we are not even yet acquainted. In human intercourse the tragedy begins, not when there is misunderstanding about words, but when silence is not understood. Then there can never be an explanation. What avails it that another loves you, if he does not understand you? Such love is a curse. What sort of companions are they who are presuming always that their silence is more expressive than yours? How foolish, and inconsiderate, and unjust, to conduct as if you were the only party aggrieved! Has not your Friend always equal ground of complaint? No doubt my Friends sometimes speak to me in vain, but they do not know what things I hear which they are not aware that they have spoken. I know that I have frequently disappointed them by not giving them words when they expected them, or such as they expected. Whenever I see my Friend I speak to him; but the expecter, the man with the ears, is not he. They will complain too that you are hard. O ye that would have the cocoa-nut wrong side outwards, when next I weep I will let you know. They ask for words and deeds, when a true relation is word and deed. If they know not of these things, how can they be informed? We often forbear to confess our feelings, not from pride, but for fear that we could not continue to love the one who required us to give such proof of our affection.

I know a woman who possesses a restless and intelligent mind, interested in her own culture, and earnest to enjoy the highest possible advantages, and I meet her with pleasure as a natural person who not a little provokes me, and I suppose is stimulated in turn by myself. Yet our acquaintance plainly does not attain to that degree of confidence and sentiment which women, which all, in fact, covet. I am glad to help her, as I am helped by her; I like very well to know her with a sort of stranger's privilege, and hesitate to visit her often, like her other Friends. My nature pauses here, I do not well know why. Perhaps she does not make the highest demand on me, a religious demand. Some, with whose prejudices or peculiar bias I have no sympathy, yet inspire me with confidence, and I trust that they confide in me also as a religious heathen at least,—a good Greek. I, too, have principles as well founded as their own. If this person could conceive that, without wilfulness, I associate with her as far as our destinies are coincident, as far as our Good Geniuses permit, and still value such intercourse, it would be a grateful assurance to me. I feel as if I appeared careless, indifferent, and without principle to her, not expecting more, and yet not content with less. If she could know that I make an infinite demand on myself, as well as on all others, she would see that this true though incomplete intercourse, is infinitely better than a more unreserved but falsely grounded one, without the principle of growth in it. For a companion, I require one who will make an equal demand on me with my own genius. Such a one will always be rightly tolerant. It is suicide, and corrupts good manners to welcome any less than this. I value and trust those who love and praise my aspiration rather than my performance. If you would not stop to look at me, but look whither I am looking, and farther, then my education could not dispense with your company.

> My love must be as free
>   As is the eagle's wing,
> Hovering o'er land and sea
>   And everything.

I must not dim my eye
    In thy saloon,
I must not leave my sky
    And nightly moon.

Be not the fowler's net
    Which stays my flight,
And craftily is set
    T' allure the sight.

But be the favoring gale
    That bears me on,
And still doth fill my sail
    When thou art gone.

I cannot leave my sky
    For thy caprice,
True love would soar as high
    As heaven is.

The eagle would not brook
    Her mate thus won,
Who trained his eye to look
    Beneath the sun.

Few things are more difficult than to help a Friend in matters which do not require the aid of Friendship, but only a cheap and trivial service, if your Friendship wants the basis of a thorough practical acquaintance. I stand in the friendliest relation, on social and spiritual grounds, to one who does not perceive what practical skill I have, but when he seeks my assistance in such matters, is wholly ignorant of that one with whom he deals; does not use my skill, which in such matters is much greater than his, but only my hands. I know another, who, on the contrary, is remarkable for his discrimination in this respect; who knows how to make use of the talents of others when he does not possess the same; knows when not to look after or oversee, and stops short at his man. It is a rare pleasure to serve him, which all laborers know. I am not a little pained by the other kind of treat-

ment. It is as if, after the friendliest and most ennobling intercourse, your Friend should use you as a hammer, and
drive a nail with your head, all in good faith; notwithstanding that you are a tolerable carpenter, as well as his good
Friend, and would use a hammer cheerfully in his service.
This want of perception is a defect which all the virtues of
the heart cannot supply:—

> The Good how can we trust?
> Only the Wise are just.
> The Good we use,
> The Wise we cannot choose.
> These there are none above;
> The Good they know and love,
> But are not known again
> By those of lesser ken.
> They do not charm us with their eyes,
> But they transfix with their advice;
> No partial sympathy they feel,
> With private woe or private weal,
> But with the universe joy and sigh,
> Whose knowledge is their sympathy.

Confucius said: "To contract ties of Friendship with any
one, is to contract Friendship with his virtue. There ought
not to be any other motive in Friendship." But men wish us
to contract Friendship with their vice also. I have a Friend
who wishes me to see that to be right which I know to be
wrong. But if Friendship is to rob me of my eyes, if it is to
darken the day, I will have none of it. It should be expansive
and inconceivably liberalizing in its effects. True Friendship
can afford true knowledge. It does not depend on darkness
and ignorance. A want of discernment cannot be an ingredient in it. If I can see my Friend's virtues more distinctly than
another's, his faults too are made more conspicuous by contrast. We have not so good a right to hate any as our Friend.
Faults are not the less faults because they are invariably balanced by corresponding virtues, and for a fault there is no
excuse, though it may appear greater than it is in many ways.
I have never known one who could bear criticism, who could
not be flattered, who would not bribe his judge, or was

content that the truth should be loved always better than himself.

If two travellers would go their way harmoniously together, the one must take as true and just a view of things as the other, else their path will not be strewn with roses. Yet you can travel profitably and pleasantly even with a blind man, if he practises common courtesy, and when you converse about the scenery will remember that he is blind but that you can see; and you will not forget that his sense of hearing is probably quickened by his want of sight. Otherwise you will not long keep company. A blind man, and a man in whose eyes there was no defect, were walking together, when they came to the edge of a precipice. "Take care! my friend," said the latter, "here is a steep precipice; go no farther this way."—"I know better," said the other, and stepped off.

It is impossible to say all that we think, even to our truest Friend. We may bid him farewell forever sooner than complain, for our complaint is too well grounded to be uttered. There is not so good an understanding between any two, but the exposure by the one of a serious fault in the other will produce a misunderstanding in proportion to its heinousness. The constitutional differences which always exist, and are obstacles to a perfect Friendship, are forever a forbidden theme to the lips of Friends. They advise by their whole behavior. Nothing can reconcile them but love. They are fatally late when they undertake to explain and treat with one another like foes. Who will take an apology for a Friend? They must apologize like dew and frost, which are off again with the sun, and which all men know in their hearts to be beneficent. The necessity itself for explanation,—what explanation will atone for that?

True love does not quarrel for slight reasons, such mistakes as mutual acquaintances can explain away, but, alas, however slight the apparent cause, only for adequate and fatal and everlasting reasons, which can never be set aside. Its quarrel, if there is any, is ever recurring, notwithstanding the beams of affection which invariably come to gild its tears; as the rainbow, however beautiful and unerring a sign, does not promise fair weather forever, but only for a season. I have known two or three persons pretty well, and yet I have never known advice to be of use but in trivial and transient matters. One may know what another does not, but the utmost kindness cannot impart what is requisite to make the advice useful. We must accept or refuse one another as we are. I could tame a hyena more easily than my Friend. He is a material which no tool of mine will work. A naked savage will fell an oak with a firebrand, and wear a hatchet out of a rock by friction, but I cannot hew the smallest chip out of the character of my Friend, either to beautify or deform it.

The lover learns at last that there is no person quite transparent and trustworthy, but every one has a devil in him that is capable of any crime in the long run. Yet, as an Oriental philosopher has said, "Although Friendship between good men is interrupted, their principles remain unaltered. The stalk of the lotus may be broken, and the fibres remain connected."

Ignorance and bungling with love are better than wisdom and skill without. There may be courtesy, there may be even temper, and wit, and talent, and sparkling conversation, there may be good-will even,—and yet the humanest and divinest faculties pine for exercise. Our life without love is like coke and ashes. Men may be pure as alabaster and Parian marble, elegant as a Tuscan villa, sublime as Niagara, and yet if there is no milk mingled with the wine at their entertainments, better is the hospitality of Goths and Vandals.

My Friend is not of some other race or family of men, but flesh of my flesh, bone of my bone. He is my real brother. I see his nature groping yonder so like mine. We do not live far apart. Have not the fates associated us in many ways? It says, in the Vishnu Purana: "Seven paces together is sufficient for the friendship of the virtuous, but thou and I have dwelt together." Is it of no significance that we have so long partaken of the same loaf, drank at the same fountain, breathed the same air summer and winter, felt the same heat and cold; that the same fruits have been pleased to refresh us both, and we have never had a thought of different fibre the one from the other!

Nature doth have her dawn each day,
    But mine are far between;
Content, I cry, for sooth to say,
    Mine brightest are I ween.

For when my sun doth deign to rise,
    Though it be her noontide,
Her fairest field in shadow lies,
    Nor can my light abide.

Sometimes I bask me in her day,
    Conversing with my mate,
But if we interchange one ray,
    Forthwith her heats abate.

Through his discourse I climb and see,
    As from some eastern hill,
A brighter morrow rise to me
    Than lieth in her skill.

As 't were two summer days in one,
    Two Sundays come together,
Our rays united make one sun,
    With fairest summer weather.

As surely as the sunset in my latest November shall translate me to the ethereal world, and remind me of the ruddy morning of youth; as surely as the last strain of music which falls on my decaying ear shall make age to be forgotten, or, in short, the manifold influences of nature survive during the term of our natural life, so surely my Friend shall forever be my Friend, and reflect a ray of God to me, and time shall foster and adorn and consecrate our Friendship, no less than the ruins of temples. As I love nature, as I love singing birds, and gleaming stubble, and flowing rivers, and morning and evening, and summer and winter, I love thee, my Friend.

But all that can be said of Friendship, is like botany to flowers. How can the understanding take account of its friendliness?

Even the death of Friends will inspire us as much as their lives. They will leave consolation to the mourners, as the rich leave money to defray the expenses of their funerals, and their memories will be incrusted over with sublime and pleasing thoughts, as monuments of other men are overgrown with moss; for our Friends have no place in the graveyard.

This to our cis-Alpine and cis-Atlantic Friends.

Also this other word of entreaty and advice to the large and respectable nation of Acquaintances, beyond the mountains;—Greeting.

My most serene and irresponsible neighbors, let us see that we have the whole advantage of each other; we will be useful, at least, if not admirable, to one another. I know that the mountains which separate us are high, and covered with perpetual snow, but despair not. Improve the serene winter weather to scale them. If need be, soften the rocks with vinegar. For here lie the verdant plains of Italy ready to receive you. Nor shall I be slow on my side to penetrate to your Provence. Strike then boldly at head or heart or any vital part. Depend upon it, the timber is well seasoned and tough, and will bear rough usage; and if it should crack, there is plenty more where it came from. I am no piece of crockery that cannot be jostled against my neighbor without danger of being broken by the collision, and must needs ring false and jarringly to the end of my days, when once I am cracked; but rather one of the old-fashioned wooden trenchers, which one while stands at the head of the table, and at another is a milking-stool, and at another a seat for children, and finally goes down to its grave not unadorned with honorable scars, and does not die till it is worn out. Nothing can shock a brave man but dulness. Think how many rebuffs every man has experienced in his day; perhaps has fallen into a horse-pond, eaten fresh-water clams, or worn one shirt for a week without washing. Indeed, you cannot receive a shock unless you have an electric affinity for that which shocks you. Use me, then, for I am useful in my way, and stand as one of many petitioners, from toadstool and henbane up to dahlia and violet, supplicating to be put to my use, if by any means ye may find me serviceable; whether for a medicated drink or bath, as

balm and lavender; or for fragrance, as verbena and geranium; or for sight, as cactus; or for thoughts, as pansy. These
humbler, at least, if not those higher uses.

Ah, my dear Strangers and Enemies, I would not forget
you. I can well afford to welcome you. Let me subscribe myself Yours ever and truly,—your much obliged servant. We
have nothing to fear from our foes; God keeps a standing
army for that service; but we have no ally against our Friends,
those ruthless Vandals.

Once more to one and all,

> "Friends, Romans, Countrymen, and Lovers."

> Let such pure hate still underprop
> Our love, that we may be
> Each other's conscience.
> And have our sympathy
> Mainly from thence.

> We'll one another treat like gods,
> And all the faith we have
> In virtue and in truth, bestow
> On either, and suspicion leave
> To gods below.

> Two solitary stars,—
> Unmeasured systems far
> Between us roll,
> But by our conscious light we are
> Determined to one pole.

> What need confound the sphere,—
> Love can afford to wait,
> For it no hour's too late
> That witnesseth one duty's end,
> Or to another doth beginning lend.

> It will subserve no use,
> More than the tints of flowers,

Only the independent guest
Frequents its bowers,
Inherits its bequest.

No speech though kind has it,
But kinder silence doles
Unto its mates,
By night consoles,
By day congratulates.

What saith the tongue to tongue?
What heareth ear of ear?
By the decrees of fate
From year to year,
Does it communicate.

Pathless the gulf of feeling yawns,—
No trivial bridge of words,
Or arch of boldest span,
Can leap the moat that girds
The sincere man.

No show of bolts and bars
Can keep the foeman out,
Or 'scape his secret mine
Who entered with the doubt
That drew the line.

No warder at the gate
Can let the friendly in,
But, like the sun, o'er all
He will the castle win,
And shine along the wall.

There's nothing in the world I know
That can escape from love,
For every depth it goes below,
And every height above.

It waits as waits the sky,
Until the clouds go by,
Yet shines serenely on
With an eternal day,
Alike when they are gone,
And when they stay.

Implacable is Love,—
Foes may be bought or teased
From their hostile intent,
But he goes unappeased
Who is on kindness bent.

Having rowed five or six miles above Amoskeag before
sunset, and reached a pleasant part of the river, one of us
landed to look for a farm-house, where we might replenish
our stores, while the other remained cruising about the
stream, and exploring the opposite shores to find a suitable
harbor for the night. In the mean while the canal-boats began
to come round a point in our rear, poling their way along
close to the shore, the breeze having quite died away. This
time there was no offer of assistance, but one of the boatmen
only called out to say, as the truest revenge for having been
the losers in the race, that he had seen a wood-duck, which
we had scared up, sitting on a tall white-pine, half a mile
down stream; and he repeated the assertion several times, and
seemed really chagrined at the apparent suspicion with which
this information was received. But there sat the summer duck
still, undisturbed by us.

By and by the other voyageur returned from his inland expedition, bringing one of the natives with him, a little flaxen-
headed boy, with some tradition, or small edition, of Robinson Crusoe in his head, who had been charmed by the account of our adventures, and asked his father's leave to join
us. He examined, at first from the top of the bank, our boat
and furniture, with sparkling eyes, and wished himself already
his own man. He was a lively and interesting boy, and we
should have been glad to ship him; but Nathan was still his
father's boy, and had not come to years of discretion.

We had got a loaf of home-made bread, and musk and

water melons for dessert. For this farmer, a clever and well-disposed man, cultivated a large patch of melons for the Hooksett and Concord markets. He hospitably entertained us the next day, exhibiting his hop-fields and kiln and melon-patch, warning us to step over the tight rope which surrounded the latter at a foot from the ground, while he pointed to a little bower at one corner, where it connected with the lock of a gun ranging with the line, and where, as he informed us, he sometimes sat in pleasant nights to defend his premises against thieves. We stepped high over the line, and sympathized with our host's on the whole quite human, if not humane, interest in the success of his experiment. That night especially thieves were to be expected, from rumors in the atmosphere, and the priming was not wet. He was a Methodist man, who had his dwelling between the river and Uncannunuc Mountain; who there belonged, and stayed at home there, and by the encouragement of distant political organizations, and by his own tenacity, held a property in his melons, and continued to plant. We suggested melon-seeds of new varieties and fruit of foreign flavor to be added to his stock. We had come away up here among the hills to learn the impartial and unbribable beneficence of Nature. Strawberries and melons grow as well in one man's garden as another's, and the sun lodges as kindly under his hillside, —when we had imagined that she inclined rather to some few earnest and faithful souls whom we know.

We found a convenient harbor for our boat on the opposite or east shore, still in Hooksett, at the mouth of a small brook which emptied into the Merrimack, where it would be out of the way of any passing boat in the night,—for they commonly hug the shore if bound up stream, either to avoid the current, or touch the bottom with their poles,—and where it would be accessible without stepping on the clayey shore. We set one of our largest melons to cool in the still water among the alders at the mouth of this creek, but when our tent was pitched and ready, and we went to get it, it had floated out into the stream, and was nowhere to be seen. So taking the boat in the twilight, we went in pursuit of this property, and at length, after long straining of the eyes, its green disk was discovered far down the river, gently floating seaward with

many twigs and leaves from the mountains that evening, and
so perfectly balanced that it had not keeled at all, and no water had run in at the tap which had been taken out to hasten
its cooling.

As we sat on the bank eating our supper, the clear light of
the western sky fell on the eastern trees, and was reflected in
the water, and we enjoyed so serene an evening as left nothing to describe. For the most part we think that there are few
degrees of sublimity, and that the highest is but little higher
than that which we now behold; but we are always deceived.
Sublimer visions appear, and the former pale and fade away.
We are grateful when we are reminded by interior evidence of
the permanence of universal laws; for our faith is but faintly
remembered, indeed, is not a remembered assurance, but a
use and enjoyment of knowledge. It is when we do not have
to believe, but come into actual contact with Truth, and are
related to her in the most direct and intimate way. Waves of
serener life pass over us from time to time, like flakes of sunlight over the fields in cloudy weather. In some happier moment, when more sap flows in the withered stalk of our life,
Syria and India stretch away from our present as they do in
history. All the events which make the annals of the nations
are but the shadows of our private experiences. Suddenly and
silently the eras which we call history awake and glimmer in
us, and *there* is room for Alexander and Hannibal to march
and conquer. In short, the history which we read is only
a fainter memory of events which have happened in our
own experience. Tradition is a more interrupted and feebler
memory.

This world is but canvas to our imaginations. I see men
with infinite pains endeavoring to realize to their bodies,
what I, with at least equal pains, would realize to my imagination,—its capacities; for certainly there is a life of the
mind above the wants of the body, and independent of it.
Often the body is warned, but the imagination is torpid;
the body is fat, but the imagination is lean and shrunk.
But what avails all other wealth if this is wanting? "Imagination is the air of mind," in which it lives and breathes. All
things are as I am. Where is the House of Change? The past
is only so heroic as we see it. It is the canvas on which our

idea of heroism is painted, and so, in one sense, the dim prospectus of our future field. Our circumstances answer to our expectations and the demand of our natures. I have noticed that if a man thinks that he needs a thousand dollars, and cannot be convinced that he does not, he will commonly be found to have them; if he lives and thinks a thousand dollars will be forthcoming, though it be to buy shoestrings with. A thousand mills will be just as slow to come to one who finds it equally hard to convince himself that he needs *them*.

> Men are by birth equal in this, that given
> Themselves and their condition, they are even.

I am astonished at the singular pertinacity and endurance of our lives. The miracle is, that what is *is*, when it is so difficult, if not impossible, for anything else to be; that we walk on in our particular paths so far, before we fall on death and fate, merely because we must walk in some path; that every man can get a living, and so few can do anything more. So much only can I accomplish ere health and strength are gone, and yet this suffices. The bird now sits just out of gunshot. I am never rich in money, and I am never meanly poor. If debts are incurred, why, debts are in the course of events cancelled, as it were by the same law by which they were incurred. I heard that an engagement was entered into between a certain youth and a maiden, and then I heard that it was broken off, but I did not know the reason in either case. We are hedged about, we think, by accident and circumstance, now we creep as in a dream, and now again we run, as if there were a fate in it, and all things thwarted or assisted. I cannot change my clothes but when I do, and yet I do change them, and soil the new ones. It is wonderful that this gets done, when some admirable deeds which I could mention do not get done. Our particular lives seem of such fortune and confident strength and durability as piers of solid rock thrown forward into the tide of circumstance. When every other path would fail, with singular and unerring confidence we advance on our particular course. What risks we run! famine and fire and pestilence, and the thousand forms of a cruel fate,—and yet every man lives till he—dies. How did he manage that? Is there no immediate danger? We wonder superfluously when we hear of a somnambulist walking a plank securely,—we have walked a plank all our lives up to this particular string-piece where we are. My life will wait for nobody, but is being matured still without delay, while I go about the streets, and chaffer with this man and that to secure it a living. It is as indifferent and easy meanwhile as a poor man's dog, and making acquaintance with its kind. It will cut its own channel like a mountain stream, and by the longest ridge is not kept from the sea at last. I have found all things thus far, persons and inanimate matter, elements and seasons, strangely adapted to my resources. No matter what imprudent haste in my career; I am permitted to be rash. Gulfs are bridged in a twinkling, as if some unseen baggage-train carried pontoons for my convenience, and while from the heights I scan the tempting but unexplored Pacific Ocean of Futurity, the ship is being carried over the mountains piecemeal on the backs of mules and lamas, whose keel shall plough its waves, and bear me to the Indies. Day would not dawn if it were not for

The Inward Morning.

Packed in my mind lie all the clothes
    Which outward nature wears,
And in its fashion's hourly change
    It all things else repairs.

In vain I look for change abroad,
    And can no difference find,
Till some new ray of peace uncalled
    Illumes my inmost mind.

What is it gilds the trees and clouds,
    And paints the heavens so gay,
But yonder fast-abiding light
    With its unchanging ray?

Lo, when the sun streams through the wood,
    Upon a winter's morn,
Where'er his silent beams intrude
    The murky night is gone.

How could the patient pine have known
  The morning breeze would come,
Or humble flowers anticipate
  The insect's noonday hum,—

Till the new light with morning cheer
  From far streamed through the aisles,
And nimbly told the forest trees
  For many stretching miles?

I've heard within my inmost soul
  Such cheerful morning news,
In the horizon of my mind
  Have seen such orient hues,

As in the twilight of the dawn,
  When the first birds awake,
Are heard within some silent wood,
  Where they the small twigs break,

Or in the eastern skies are seen,
  Before the sun appears,
The harbingers of summer heats
  Which from afar he bears.

Whole weeks and months of my summer life slide away in
thin volumes like mist and smoke, till at length, some warm
morning, perchance, I see a sheet of mist blown down the
brook to the swamp, and I float as high above the fields
with it. I can recall to mind the stillest summer hours, in
which the grasshopper sings over the mulleins, and there is a
valor in that time the bare memory of which is armor that
can laugh at any blow of fortune. For our lifetime the strains
of a harp are heard to swell and die alternately, and death is
but "the pause when the blast is recollecting itself."

We lay awake a long while, listening to the murmurs of the
brook, in the angle formed by whose bank with the river our
tent was pitched, and there was a sort of human interest in its
story, which ceases not in freshet or in drought the livelong

summer, and the profounder lapse of the river was quite
drowned by its din. But the rill, whose

> "Silver sands and pebbles sing
> Eternal ditties with the spring,"

is silenced by the first frosts of winter, while mightier streams,
on whose bottom the sun never shines, clogged with sunken
rocks and the ruins of forests, from whose surface comes up
no murmur, are strangers to the icy fetters which bind fast a
thousand contributary rills.

I dreamed this night of an event which had occurred long
before. It was a difference with a Friend, which had not
ceased to give me pain, though I had no cause to blame myself. But in my dream ideal justice was at length done me for
his suspicions, and I received that compensation which I had
never obtained in my waking hours. I was unspeakably
soothed and rejoiced, even after I awoke, because in dreams
we never deceive ourselves, nor are deceived, and this seemed
to have the authority of a final judgment.

We bless and curse ourselves. Some dreams are divine, as
well as some waking thoughts. Donne sings of one

> "Who dreamt devoutlier than most use to pray."

Dreams are the touchstones of our characters. We are scarcely
less afflicted when we remember some unworthiness in our
conduct in a dream, than if it had been actual, and the intensity of our grief, which is our atonement, measures the degree
by which this is separated from an actual unworthiness. For
in dreams we but act a part which must have been learned
and rehearsed in our waking hours, and no doubt could discover some waking consent thereto. If this meanness had not
its foundation in us, why are we grieved at it? In dreams we
see ourselves naked and acting out our real characters, even
more clearly than we see others awake. But an unwavering
and commanding virtue would compel even its most fantastic
and faintest dreams to respect its ever-wakeful authority; as
we are accustomed to say carelessly, we should never have
dreamed of such a thing. Our truest life is when we are in
dreams awake.

"And, more to lulle him in his slumber soft,
A trickling streame from high rock tumbling downe,
And ever-drizzling raine upon the loft,
Mixt with a murmuring winde, much like the sowne
Of swarming bees, did cast him in a swowne.
No other noyse, nor people's troublous cryes,
As still are wont t' annoy the walled towne,
Might there be heard; but careless Quiet lyes
Wrapt in eternall silence farre from enemyes."

Thursday

"He trode the unplanted forest floor, whereon
The all-seeing sun for 'ages hath not shone,
Where feeds the moose, and walks the surly bear,
And up the tall mast runs the woodpecker.

.   .   .   .   .

Where darkness found him he lay glad at night;
There the red morning touched him with its light.

.   .   .   .   .

Go where he will, the wise man is at home,
His hearth the earth,—his hall the azure dome;
Where his clear spirit leads him, there 's his road,
By God's own light illumined and foreshowed."

EMERSON.

WHEN WE awoke this morning, we heard the faint, deliberate, and ominous sound of rain-drops on our cotton roof. The rain had pattered all night, and now the whole country wept, the drops falling in the river, and on the alders, and in the pastures, and instead of any bow in the heavens, there was the trill of the hair-bird all the morning. The cheery faith of this little bird atoned for the silence of the whole woodland choir beside. When we first stepped abroad, a flock of sheep, led by their rams, came rushing down a ravine in our rear, with heedless haste and unreserved frisking, as if unobserved by man, from some higher pasture where they had spent the night, to taste the herbage by the river-side; but when their leaders caught sight of our white tent through the mist, struck with sudden astonishment, with their fore-feet braced, they sustained the rushing torrent in their rear, and the whole flock stood stock-still, endeavoring to solve the mystery in their sheepish brains. At length, concluding that it boded no mischief to them, they spread themselves out quietly over the field. We learned afterward that we had pitched our tent on the very spot which a few summers before had been occupied by a party of Penobscots. We could see rising before us through the mist a dark conical eminence called Hooksett Pinnacle, a landmark to boatmen, and also Uncannunuc Mountain, broad off on the west side of the river.

This was the limit of our voyage, for a few hours more in the rain would have taken us to the last of the locks, and our boat was too heavy to be dragged around the long and numerous rapids which would occur. On foot, however, we continued up along the bank, feeling our way with a stick through the showery and foggy day, and climbing over the slippery logs in our path with as much pleasure and buoyancy as in brightest sunshine; scenting the fragrance of the pines and the wet clay under our feet, and cheered by the tones of invisible waterfalls; with visions of toadstools, and wandering frogs, and festoons of moss hanging from the spruce-trees, and thrushes flitting silent under the leaves; our road still holding together through that wettest of weather, like faith, while we confidently followed its lead. We managed to keep our thoughts dry, however, and only our clothes were wet. It was altogether a cloudy and drizzling day, with occasional brightenings in the mist, when the trill of the tree-sparrow seemed to be ushering in sunny hours.

"Nothing that naturally happens to man can *hurt* him, earthquakes and thunder-storms not excepted," said a man of genius, who at this time lived a few miles farther on our road. When compelled by a shower to take shelter under a tree, we may improve that opportunity for a more minute inspection of some of Nature's works. I have stood under a tree in the woods half a day at a time, during a heavy rain in the summer, and yet employed myself happily and profitably there prying with microscopic eye into the crevices of the bark or the leaves or the fungi at my feet. "Riches are the attendants of the miser; and the heavens rain plenteously upon the mountains." I can fancy that it would be a luxury to stand up to one's chin in some retired swamp a whole summer day, scenting the wild honeysuckle and bilberry blows, and lulled by the minstrelsy of gnats and mosquitoes! A day passed in the society of those Greek sages, such as described in the Banquet of Xenophon, would not be comparable with the dry wit of decayed cranberry vines, and the fresh Attic salt of the moss-beds. Say twelve hours of genial and familiar converse with the leopard frog; the sun to rise behind alder and dogwood, and climb buoyantly to his meridian of two hands' breadth, and finally sink to rest behind some bold western hummock. To hear the evening chant of the mosquito from a thousand green chapels, and the bittern begin to boom from some concealed fort like a sunset gun!—Surely one may as profitably be soaked in the juices of a swamp for one day as pick his way dry-shod over sand. Cold and damp,—are they not as rich experience as warmth and dryness?

At present, the drops come trickling down the stubble while we lie drenched on a bed of withered wild oats, by the side of a bushy hill, and the gathering in of the clouds, with the last rush and dying breath of the wind, and then the regular dripping of twigs and leaves the country over, enhance the sense of inward comfort and sociableness. The birds draw closer and are more familiar under the thick foliage, seemingly composing new strains upon their roosts against the sunshine. What were the amusements of the drawing-room and the library in comparison, if we had them here? We should still sing as of old,—

> My books I'd fain cast off, I cannot read,
> 'Twixt every page my thoughts go stray at large
> Down in the meadow, where is richer feed,
> And will not mind to hit their proper targe.
>
> Plutarch was good, and so was Homer too,
> Our Shakespeare's life were rich to live again,
> What Plutarch read, that was not good nor true,
> Nor Shakespeare's books, unless his books were men.
>
> Here while I lie beneath this walnut bough,
> What care I for the Greeks or for Troy town,
> If juster battles are enacted now
> Between the ants upon this hummock's crown?
>
> Bid Homer wait till I the issue learn,
> If red or black the gods will favor most,
> Or yonder Ajax will the phalanx turn,
> Struggling to heave some rock against the host.
>
> Tell Shakespeare to attend some leisure hour,
> For now I 've business with this drop of dew,

And see you not, the clouds prepare a shower,—
I'll meet him shortly when the sky is blue.

This bed of herd's-grass and wild oats was spread
Last year with nicer skill than monarchs use,
A clover tuft is pillow for my head,
And violets quite overtop my shoes.

And now the cordial clouds have shut all in,
And gently swells the wind to say all's well,
The scattered drops are falling fast and thin,
Some in the pool, some in the flower-bell.

I am well drenched upon my bed of oats;
But see that globe come rolling down its stem,
Now like a lonely planet there it floats,
And now it sinks into my garment's hem.

Drip drip the trees for all the country round,
And richness rare distils from every bough,
The wind alone it is makes every sound,
Shaking down crystals on the leaves below.

For shame the sun will never show himself,
Who could not with his beams e'er melt me so,
My dripping locks,—they would become an elf,
Who in a beaded coat does gayly go.

The Pinnacle is a small wooded hill which rises very abruptly to the height of about two hundred feet, near the shore at Hooksett Falls. As Uncannunuc Mountain is perhaps the best point from which to view the valley of the Merrimack, so this hill affords the best view of the river itself. I have sat upon its summit, a precipitous rock only a few rods long, in fairer weather, when the sun was setting and filling the river valley with a flood of light. You can see up and down the Merrimack several miles each way. The broad and straight river, full of light and life, with its sparkling and foaming falls, the islet which divides the stream, the village of Hooksett on the shore almost directly under your feet, so near that you can converse with its inhabitants or throw a stone into its yards, the woodland lake at its western base, and the mountains in the north and northeast, make a scene of rare beauty and completeness, which the traveller should take pains to behold.

We were hospitably entertained in Concord, New Hampshire, which we persisted in calling *New* Concord, as we had been wont, to distinguish it from our native town, from which we had been told that it was named and in part originally settled. This would have been the proper place to conclude our voyage, uniting Concord with Concord by these meandering rivers, but our boat was moored some miles below its port.

The richness of the intervals at Penacook, now Concord, New Hampshire, had been observed by explorers, and, according to the historian of Haverhill, in the

"year 1726, considerable progress was made in the settlement, and a road was cut through the wilderness from Haverhill to Penacook. In the fall of 1727, the first family, that of Captain Ebenezer Eastman, moved into the place. His team was driven by Jacob Shute, who was by birth a Frenchman, and he is said to have been the first person who drove a team through the wilderness. Soon after, says tradition, one Ayer, a lad of 18, drove a team consisting of ten yoke of oxen to Penacook, swam the river, and ploughed a portion of the interval. He is supposed to have been the first person who ploughed land in that place. After he had completed his work, he started on his return at sunrise, drowned a yoke of oxen while recrossing the river, and arrived at Haverhill about midnight. The crank of the first saw-mill was manufactured in Haverhill, and carried to Penacook on a horse."

But we found that the frontiers were not this way any longer. This generation has come into the world fatally late for some enterprises. Go where we will on the *surface* of things, men have been there before us. We cannot now have the pleasure of erecting the *last* house; that was long ago set up in the suburbs of Astoria City, and our boundaries have literally been run to the South Sea, according to the old patents. But the lives of men, though more extended laterally in their range, are still as shallow as ever. Undoubtedly, as a Western orator said, "Men generally live over about the same surface; some live long and narrow, and others live broad and short"; but it is all superficial living. A worm is as good a traveller as a grasshopper or a cricket, and a much wiser settler. With all their activity these do not hop away from drought nor forward to summer. We do not avoid evil by fleeing before it, but by rising above or diving below its plane; as the worm escapes drought and frost by boring a few inches deeper. The frontiers are not east or west, north or south, but wherever a man *fronts* a fact, though that fact be his neighbor, there is an unsettled wilderness between him and Canada, between him and the setting sun, or, farther still, between him and *it*. Let him build himself a log-house with the bark on where he is, *fronting* it, and wage there an Old French war for seven or seventy years, with Indians and Rangers, or whatever else may come between him and the reality, and save his scalp if he can.

We now no longer sailed or floated on the river, but trod the unyielding land like pilgrims. Sadi tells who may travel; among others, "A common mechanic, who can earn a subsistence by the industry of his hand, and shall not have to stake his reputation for every morsel of bread, as philosophers have said." He may travel who can subsist on the wild fruits and game of the most cultivated country. A man may travel fast enough and earn his living on the road. I have at times been applied to to do work when on a journey; to do tinkering and repair clocks, when I had a knapsack on my back. A man once applied to me to go into a factory, stating conditions and wages, observing that I succeeded in shutting the window of a railroad car in which we were travelling, when the other passengers had failed. "Hast thou not heard of a Sufi, who was hammering some nails into the sole of his sandal; an officer of cavalry took him by the sleeve, saying, Come along and shoe my horse." Farmers have asked me to assist them in haying, when I was passing their fields. A man once applied to me to mend his umbrella, taking me for an umbrella-mender, because, being on a journey, I carried an umbrella in my hand while the sun shone. Another wished to buy a tin cup of me, observing that I had one strapped to my belt, and a sauce-pan on my back. The cheapest way to travel, and the way to travel the farthest in the shortest distance, is to go afoot, carrying a dipper, a spoon, and a fish-line, some Indian meal, some salt, and some sugar. When you come to a brook or pond, you can catch fish and cook them; or you can boil a hasty-pudding; or you can buy a loaf of bread at a farmer's house for fourpence, moisten it in the next brook that crosses the road, and dip into it your sugar,—this alone will last you a whole day;—or, if you are accustomed to heartier living, you can buy a quart of milk for two cents, crumb your bread or cold pudding into it, and eat it with your own spoon out of your own dish. Any one of these things I mean, not all together. I have travelled thus some hundreds of miles without taking any meal in a house, sleeping on the ground when convenient, and found it cheaper, and in many respects more profitable, than staying at home. So that some have inquired why it would not be best to travel always. But I never thought of travelling simply as a means of getting a livelihood. A simple woman down in Tyngsborough, at whose house I once stopped to get a draught of water, when I said, recognizing the bucket, that I had stopped there nine years before for the same purpose, asked if I was not a traveller, supposing that I had been travelling ever since, and had now come round again; that travelling was one of the professions, more or less productive, which her husband did not follow. But continued travelling is far from productive. It begins with wearing away the soles of the shoes, and making the feet sore, and erelong it will wear a man clean up, after making his heart sore into the bargain. I have observed that the after-life of those who have travelled much is very pathetic. True and sincere travelling is no pastime, but it is as serious as the grave, or any part of the human journey, and it requires a long probation to be broken into it. I do not speak of those that travel sitting, the sedentary travellers whose legs hang dangling the while, mere idle symbols of the fact, any more than when we speak of sitting hens we mean those that sit standing, but I mean those to whom travelling is life for the legs, and death too, at last. The traveller must be born again on the road, and earn a passport from the elements, the principal powers that be for him. He shall experience at last that old threat of his mother fulfilled, that he shall be skinned alive. His sores shall gradually deepen themselves that they may heal inwardly, while he gives no rest to the sole of his foot, and at night weariness must be his pillow, that so he may acquire experience against his rainy days.—So was it with us.

Sometimes we lodged at an inn in the woods, where trout-fishers from distant cities had arrived before us, and where, to our astonishment, the settlers dropped in at nightfall to have a chat and hear the news, though there was but one road, and no other house was visible,—as if they had come out of the earth. There we sometimes read old newspapers, who never before read new ones, and in the rustle of their leaves heard the dashing of the surf along the Atlantic shore, instead of the sough of the wind among the pines. But then walking had given us an appetite even for the least palatable and nutritious food.

Some hard and dry book in a dead language, which you have found it impossible to read at home, but for which you have still a lingering regard, is the best to carry with you on a journey. At a country inn, in the barren society of ostlers and travellers, I could undertake the writers of the silver or the brazen age with confidence. Almost the last regular service which I performed in the cause of literature was to read the works of

AULUS PERSIUS FLACCUS.

If you have imagined what a divine work is spread out for the poet, and approach this author too, in the hope of finding the field at length fairly entered on, you will hardly dissent from the words of the prologue,

> "Ipse semipaganus
> Ad sacra Vatum carmen affero nostrum."

> I half pagan
> Bring my verses to the shrine of the poets.

Here is none of the interior dignity of Virgil, nor the elegance and vivacity of Horace, nor will any sibyl be needed to remind you, that from those older Greek poets there is a sad descent to Persius. You can scarcely distinguish one harmonious sound amid this unmusical bickering with the follies of men.

One sees that music has its place in thought, but hardly as yet in language. When the Muse arrives, we wait for her to remould language, and impart to it her own rhythm. Hitherto the verse groans and labors with its load, and goes not forward blithely, singing by the way. The best ode may be parodied, indeed is itself a parody, and has a poor and trivial sound, like a man stepping on the rounds of a ladder. Homer and Shakespeare and Milton and Marvell and Wordsworth are but the rustling of leaves and crackling of twigs in the forest, and there is not yet the sound of any bird. The Muse has never lifted up her voice to sing. Most of all, satire will not be sung. A Juvenal or Persius do not marry music to their verse, but are measured fault-finders at best; stand but just outside the faults they condemn, and so are concerned rather about the monster which they have escaped, than the fair prospect before them. Let them live on an age, and they will have travelled out of his shadow and reach, and found other objects to ponder.

As long as there is satire, the poet is, as it were, *particeps criminis*. One sees not but he had best let bad take care of itself, and have to do only with what is beyond suspicion. If you light on the least vestige of truth, and it is the weight of the whole body still which stamps the faintest trace, an eternity will not suffice to extol it, while no evil is so huge, but you grudge to bestow on it a moment of hate. Truth never turns to rebuke falsehood; her own straightforwardness is the severest correction. Horace would not have written satire so well if he had not been inspired by it, as by a passion, and fondly cherished his vein. In his odes, the love always exceeds the hate, so that the severest satire still sings itself, and the poet is satisfied, though the folly be not corrected.

A sort of necessary order in the development of Genius is, first, Complaint; second, Plaint; third, Love. Complaint, which is the condition of Persius, lies not in the province of poetry. Erelong the enjoyment of a superior good would have changed his disgust into regret. We can never have much sympathy with the complainer; for after searching nature through, we conclude that he must be both plaintiff and defendant too, and so had best come to a settlement without a hearing. He who receives an injury is to some extent an accomplice of the wrong-doer.

Perhaps it would be truer to say, that the highest strain of the muse is essentially plaintive. The saint's are still *tears* of joy. Who has ever heard the *Innocent* sing?

But the divinest poem, or the life of a great man, is the severest satire; as impersonal as Nature herself, and like the sighs of her winds in the woods, which convey ever a slight reproof to the hearer. The greater the genius, the keener the edge of the satire.

Hence we have to do only with the rare and fragmentary traits, which least belong to Persius, or shall we say, are the properest utterances of his muse; since that which he says best at any time is what he can best say at all times. The Spectators and Ramblers have not failed to cull some quotable sentences from this garden too, so pleasant is it to meet even the most familiar truth in a new dress, when, if our neighbor had said it, we should have passed it by as hackneyed. Out of these six satires, you may perhaps select some twenty lines, which fit so well as many thoughts, that they will recur to the scholar almost as readily as a natural image; though when translated into familiar language, they lose that insular emphasis, which fitted them for quotation. Such lines as the following, translation cannot render commonplace. Contrasting the man of true religion with those who, with jealous privacy, would fain carry on a secret commerce with the gods, he says:—

> "Haud cuivis promptum est, murmurque humilesque
>   susurros
> Tollere de templis; et aperto vivere voto."

> It is not easy for every one to take murmurs and low
> Whispers out of the temples, and live with open vow.

To the virtuous man, the universe is the only *sanctum sanctorum*, and the penetralia of the temple are the broad noon of his existence. Why should he betake himself to a subterranean crypt, as if it were the only holy ground in all the world which he had left unprofaned? The obedient soul would only the more discover and familiarize things, and escape more and more into light and air, as having henceforth done with secrecy, so that the universe shall not seem open enough for it. At length, it is neglectful even of that silence which is consistent with true modesty, but by its independence of all confidence in its disclosures, makes that which it imparts so private to the hearer, that it becomes the care of the whole world that modesty be not infringed.

To the man who cherishes a secret in his breast, there is a still greater secret unexplored. Our most indifferent acts may be matter for secrecy, but whatever we do with the utmost truthfulness and integrity, by virtue of its pureness, must be transparent as light.

In the third satire, he asks:—

> "Est aliquid quò tendis, et in quod dirigis arcum?
> An passim sequeris corvos, testâve, lutove,
> Securus quò pes ferat, atque ex tempore vivis?"

Is there anything to which thou tendest, and against which
    thou directest thy bow?
Or dost thou pursue crows, at random, with pottery or clay,
Careless whither thy feet bear thee, and live *ex tempore*?

The bad sense is always a secondary one. Language does not appear to have justice done it, but is obviously cramped and narrowed in its significance, when any meanness is described. The truest construction is not put upon it. What may readily be fashioned into a rule of wisdom, is here thrown in the teeth of the sluggard, and constitutes the front of his offence. Universally, the innocent man will come forth from the sharpest inquisition and lecturing, the combined din of reproof and commendation, with a faint sound of eulogy in his ears. Our vices always lie in the direction of our virtues, and in their best estate are but plausible imitations of the latter. Falsehood never attains to the dignity of entire falseness, but is only an inferior sort of truth; if it were more thoroughly false, it would incur danger of becoming true.

> "Securus quo pes ferat, atque ex tempore *vivit*,"

is then the motto of a wise man. For first, as the subtle discernment of the language would have taught us, with all his
negligence he is still secure; but the sluggard, notwithstanding his heedlessness, is insecure.

The life of a wise man is most of all extemporaneous, for
he lives out of an eternity which includes all time. The cunning mind travels further back than Zoroaster each instant,
and comes quite down to the present with its revelation. The
utmost thrift and industry of thinking give no man any stock
in life; his credit with the inner world is no better, his capital
no larger. He must try his fortune again to-day as yesterday.
All questions rely on the present for their solution. Time measures nothing but itself. The word that is written may be
postponed, but not that on the lip. If this is what the occasion
says, let the occasion say it. All the world is forward to
prompt him who gets up to live without his creed in his
pocket.

In the fifth satire, which is the best, I find,—

> "Stat contrà ratio, et secretam garrit in aurem,
>   Ne liceat facere id, quod quis vitiabit agendo."

> Reason opposes, and whispers in the secret ear,
>   That it is not lawful to do that which one will spoil by
>   doing.

Only they who do not see how anything might be better
done are forward to try their hand on it. Even the master
workman must be encouraged by the reflection, that his awk-
wardness will be incompetent to do that thing harm, to which
his skill may fail to do justice. Here is no apology for neglect-
ing to do many things from a sense of our incapacity,—for
what deed does not fall maimed and imperfect from our
hands?—but only a warning to bungle less.

The satires of Persius are the furthest possible from inspired; evidently a chosen, not imposed subject. Perhaps I
have given him credit for more earnestness than is apparent;
but it is certain, that that which alone we can call Persius,
which is forever independent and consistent, *was* in earnest,
and so sanctions the sober consideration of all. The artist and
his work are not to be separated. The most wilfully foolish

man cannot stand aloof from his folly, but the deed and the doer together make ever one sober fact. There is but one stage for the peasant and the actor. The buffoon cannot bribe you to laugh always at his grimaces; they shall sculpture themselves in Egyptian granite, to stand heavy as the pyramids on the ground of his character.

———

Suns rose and set and found us still on the dank forest path which meanders up the Pemigewasset, now more like an otter's or a marten's trail, or where a beaver had dragged his trap, than where the wheels of travel raise a dust; where towns begin to serve as gores, only to hold the earth together. The wild pigeon sat secure above our heads, high on the dead limbs of naval pines, reduced to a robin's size. The very yards of our hostelries inclined upon the skirts of mountains, and, as we passed, we looked up at a steep angle at the stems of maples waving in the clouds.

Far up in the country,—for we would be faithful to our experience,—in Thornton, perhaps, we met a soldier lad in the woods, going to muster in full regimentals, and holding the middle of the road; deep in the forest, with shouldered musket and military step, and thoughts of war and glory all to himself. It was a sore trial to the youth, tougher than many a battle, to get by us creditably and with soldierlike bearing. Poor man! He actually shivered like a reed in his thin military pants, and by the time we had got up with him, all the sternness that becomes the soldier had forsaken his face, and he skulked past as if he were driving his father's sheep under a sword-proof helmet. It was too much for him to carry any extra armor then, who could not easily dispose of his natural arms. And for his legs, they were like heavy artillery in boggy places; better to cut the traces and forsake them. His greaves chafed and wrestled one with another for want of other foes. But he did get by and get off with all his munitions, and lived to fight another day; and I do not record this as casting any suspicion on his honor and real bravery in the field.

Wandering on through notches which the streams had made, by the side and over the brows of hoar hills and mountains, across the stumpy, rocky, forested, and bepastured country, we at length crossed on prostrate trees over the Amonoosuck, and breathed the free air of Unappropriated Land. Thus, in fair days as well as foul, we had traced up the river to which our native stream is a tributary, until from Merrimack it became the Pemigewasset that leaped by our side, and when we had passed its fountain-head, the Wild Amonoosuck, whose puny channel was crossed at a stride, guiding us toward its distant source among the mountains, and at length, without its guidance, we were enabled to reach the summit of AGIOCOCHOOK.

> "Sweet days, so cool, so calm, so bright,
> The bridal of the earth and sky,
> Sweet dews shall weep thy fall to-night,
>   For thou must die."
>   HERBERT.

When we returned to Hooksett, a week afterward, the melon man, in whose corn-barn we had hung our tent and buffaloes and other things to dry, was already picking his hops, with many women and children to help him. We bought one watermelon, the largest in his patch, to carry with us for ballast. It was Nathan's, which he might sell if he wished, having been conveyed to him in the green state, and owned daily by his eyes. After due consultation with "Father," the bargain was concluded,—we to buy it at a venture on the vine, green or ripe, our risk, and pay "what the gentlemen pleased." It proved to be ripe; for we had had honest experience in selecting this fruit.

Finding our boat safe in its harbor, under Uncannunuc Mountain, with a fair wind and the current in our favor, we commenced our return voyage at noon, sitting at our ease and conversing, or in silence watching for the last trace of each reach in the river as a bend concealed it from our view. As the season was further advanced, the wind now blew steadily from the north, and with our sail set we could occasionally lie on our oars without loss of time. The lumbermen throwing down wood from the top of the high bank, thirty or forty feet above the water, that it might be sent down stream, paused in their work to watch our retreating sail. By this time, indeed, we were well known to the boatmen, and were hailed as the Revenue Cutter of the stream. As we sailed rapidly down the river, shut in between two mounds of earth, the sounds of this timber rolled down the bank enhanced the silence and vastness of the noon, and we fancied that only the primeval echoes were awakened. The vision of a distant scow just heaving in sight round a headland also increased by contrast the solitude.

Through the din and desultoriness of noon, even in the most Oriental city, is seen the fresh and primitive and savage nature, in which Scythians and Ethiopians and Indians dwell. What is echo, what are light and shade, day and night, ocean and stars, earthquake and eclipse, there? The works of man are everywhere swallowed up in the immensity of Nature. The Ægean Sea is but Lake Huron still to the Indian. Also there is all the refinement of civilized life in the woods under a sylvan garb. The wildest scenes have an air of domesticity and homeliness even to the citizen, and when the flicker's cackle is heard in the clearing, he is reminded that civilization has wrought but little change there. Science is welcome to the deepest recesses of the forest, for there too nature obeys the same old civil laws. The little red bug on the stump of a pine,—for it the wind shifts and the sun breaks through the clouds. In the wildest nature, there is not only the material of the most cultivated life, and a sort of anticipation of the last result, but a greater refinement already than is ever attained by man. There is papyrus by the river-side, and rushes for light, and the goose only flies overhead, ages before the studious are born or letters invented, and that literature which the former suggest, and even from the first have rudely served, it may be man does not yet use them to express. Nature is prepared to welcome into her scenery the finest work of human art, for she is herself an art so cunning that the artist never appears in his work.

Art is not tame, and Nature is not wild, in the ordinary sense. A perfect work of man's art would also be wild or natural in a good sense. Man tames Nature only that he may at last make her more free even than he found her, though he may never yet have succeeded.

*   *   *

With this propitious breeze, and the help of our oars, we soon reached the Falls of Amoskeag, and the mouth of the Piscataquoag, and recognized, as we swept rapidly by, many a fair bank and islet on which our eyes had rested in the upward passage. Our boat was like that which Chaucer describes in his Dream, in which the knight took his departure from the island,

> "To journey for his marriage,
> And return with such an host,
> That wedded might be least and most. . . . .
> Which barge was as a man's thought,
> After his pleasure to him brought,
> The queene herself accustomed aye
> In the same barge to play,
> It needed neither mast ne rother,
> I have not heard of such another,
> No master for the governance,
> Hie sayled by thought and pleasaunce,
> Without labor east and west,
> All was one, calme or tempest."

So we sailed this afternoon, thinking of the saying of Pythagoras, though we had no peculiar right to remember it, "It is beautiful when prosperity is present with intellect, and when sailing as it were with a prosperous wind, actions are performed looking to virtue; just as a pilot looks to the motions of the stars." All the world reposes in beauty to him who preserves equipoise in his life, and moves serenely on his path without secret violence; as he who sails down a stream, he has only to steer, keeping his bark in the middle, and carry it round the falls. The ripples curled away in our wake, like ringlets from the head of a child, while we steadily held on our course, and under the bows we watched

> "The swaying soft,
> Made by the delicate wave parted in front,
> As through the gentle element we move
> Like shadows gliding through untroubled dreams."

The forms of beauty fall naturally around the path of him

who is in the performance of his proper work; as the curled
shavings drop from the plane, and borings cluster round the
auger. Undulation is the gentlest and most ideal of motions,
produced by one fluid falling on another. Rippling is a more
graceful flight. From a hill-top you may detect in it the wings
of birds endlessly repeated. The two *waving* lines which represent the flight of birds appear to have been copied from the
ripple.

The trees made an admirable fence to the landscape, skirting the horizon on every side. The single trees and the groves
left standing on the interval appeared naturally disposed,
though the farmer had consulted only his convenience, for he
too falls into the scheme of Nature. Art can never match the
luxury and superfluity of Nature. In the former all is seen; it
cannot afford concealed wealth, and is niggardly in comparison; but Nature, even when she is scant and thin outwardly,
satisfies us still by the assurance of a certain generosity at the
roots. In swamps, where there is only here and there an evergreen tree amid the quaking moss and cranberry beds, the
bareness does not suggest poverty. The single-spruce, which
I had hardly noticed in gardens, attracts me in such places,
and now first I understand why men try to make them grow
about their houses. But though there may be very perfect
specimens in front-yard plots, their beauty is for the most part
ineffectual there, for there is no such assurance of kindred
wealth beneath and around them, to make them show to advantage. As we have said, Nature is a greater and more perfect
art, the art of God; though, referred to herself, she is genius;
and there is a similarity between her operations and man's art
even in the details and trifles. When the overhanging pine
drops into the water, by the sun and water, and the wind
rubbing it against the shore, its boughs are worn into fantastic shapes, and white and smooth, as if turned in a lathe.
Man's art has wisely imitated those forms into which all
matter is most inclined to run, as foliage and fruit. A ham-
mock swung in a grove assumes the exact form of a canoe,
broader or narrower, and higher or lower at the ends, as
more or fewer persons are in it, and it rolls in the air with
the motion of the body, like a canoe in the water. Our art
leaves its shavings and its dust about; her art exhibits itself

even in the shavings and the dust which we make. She has perfected herself by an eternity of practice. The world is well kept; no rubbish accumulates; the morning air is clear even at this day, and no dust has settled on the grass. Behold how the evening now steals over the fields, the shadows of the trees creeping farther and farther into the meadow, and ere-long the stars will come to bathe in these retired waters. Her undertakings are secure and never fail. If I were awakened from a deep sleep, I should know which side of the meridian the sun might be by the aspect of nature, and by the chirp of the crickets, and yet no painter can paint this difference. The landscape contains a thousand dials which indicate the natural division of time, the shadows of a thousand styles point to the hour.

> "Not only o'er the dial's face,
>   This silent phantom day by day,
> With slow, unseen, unceasing pace
>   Steals moments, months, and years away;
> From hoary rock and aged tree,
>   From proud Palmyra's mouldering walls,
> From Teneriffe, towering o'er the sea,
>   From every blade of grass it falls."

It is almost the only game which the trees play at, this tit-for-tat, now this side in the sun, now that, the drama of the day. In deep ravines under the eastern sides of cliffs, Night forwardly plants her foot even at noonday, and as Day retreats she steps into his trenches, skulking from tree to tree, from fence to fence, until at last she sits in his citadel and draws out her forces into the plain. It may be that the forenoon is brighter than the afternoon, not only because of the greater transparency of its atmosphere, but because we naturally look most into the west, as forward into the day, and so in the forenoon see the sunny side of things, but in the afternoon the shadow of every tree.

The afternoon is now far advanced, and a fresh and leisurely wind is blowing over the river, making long reaches of bright ripples. The river has done its stint, and appears not to flow, but lie at its length reflecting the light, and the haze over the woods is like the inaudible panting, or rather the gentle perspiration of resting nature, rising from a myriad of pores into the attenuated atmosphere.

On the thirty-first day of March, one hundred and forty-two years before this, probably about this time in the afternoon, there were hurriedly paddling down this part of the river, between the pine woods which then fringed these banks, two white women and a boy, who had left an island at the mouth of the Contoocook before daybreak. They were slightly clad for the season, in the English fashion, and handled their paddles unskilfully, but with nervous energy and determination, and at the bottom of their canoe lay the still bleeding scalps of ten of the aborigines. They were Hannah Dustan, and her nurse, Mary Neff, both of Haverhill, eighteen miles from the mouth of this river, and an English boy, named Samuel Lennardson, escaping from captivity among the Indians. On the 15th of March previous, Hannah Dustan had been compelled to rise from childbed, and half dressed, with one foot bare, accompanied by her nurse, commence an uncertain march, in still inclement weather, through the snow and the wilderness. She had seen her seven elder children flee with their father, but knew not of their fate. She had seen her infant's brains dashed out against an apple-tree, and had left her own and her neighbors' dwellings in ashes. When she reached the wigwam of her captor, situated on an island in the Merrimack, more than twenty miles above where we now are, she had been told that she and her nurse were soon to be taken to a distant Indian settlement, and there made to run the gauntlet naked. The family of this Indian consisted of two men, three women, and seven children, beside an English boy, whom she found a prisoner among them. Having determined to attempt her escape, she instructed the boy to inquire of one of the men, how he should despatch an enemy in the quickest manner, and take his scalp. "Strike 'em there," said he, placing his finger on his temple, and he also showed him how to take off the scalp. On the morning of the 31st she arose before daybreak, and awoke her nurse and the boy, and taking the Indians' tomahawks, they killed them all in their sleep, excepting one favorite boy, and one squaw who fled wounded with him to the woods. The English boy struck the

Indian who had given him the information, on the temple, as he had been directed. They then collected all the provision they could find, and took their master's tomahawk and gun, and scuttling all the canoes but one, commenced their flight to Haverhill, distant about sixty miles by the river. But after having proceeded a short distance, fearing that her story would not be believed if she should escape to tell it, they returned to the silent wigwam, and taking off the scalps of the dead, put them into a bag as proofs of what they had done, and then retracing their steps to the shore in the twilight, recommenced their voyage.

Early this morning this deed was performed, and now, perchance, these tired women and this boy, their clothes stained with blood, and their minds racked with alternate resolution and fear, are making a hasty meal of parched corn and moose-meat, while their canoe glides under these pine roots whose stumps are still standing on the bank. They are thinking of the dead whom they have left behind on that solitary isle far up the stream, and of the relentless living warriors who are in pursuit. Every withered leaf which the winter has left seems to know their story, and in its rustling to repeat it and betray them. An Indian lurks behind every rock and pine, and their nerves cannot bear the tapping of a woodpecker. Or they forget their own dangers and their deeds in conjecturing the fate of their kindred, and whether, if they escape the Indians, they shall find the former still alive. They do not stop to cook their meals upon the bank, nor land, except to carry their canoe about the falls. The stolen birch forgets its master and does them good service, and the swollen current bears them swiftly along with little need of the paddle, except to steer and keep them warm by exercise. For ice is floating in the river; the spring is opening; the muskrat and the beaver are driven out of their holes by the flood; deer gaze at them from the bank; a few faint-singing forest birds, perchance, fly across the river to the northernmost shore; the fish-hawk sails and screams overhead, and geese fly over with a startling clangor; but they do not observe these things, or they speedily forget them. They do not smile or chat all day. Sometimes they pass an Indian grave surrounded by its paling on the bank, or the frame of a wigwam, with a few coals left behind, or the with-

ered stalks still rustling in the Indian's solitary cornfield on
the interval. The birch stripped of its bark, or the charred
stump where a tree has been burned down to be made into a
canoe, these are the only traces of man,—a fabulous wild
man to us. On either side, the primeval forest stretches away
uninterrupted to Canada, or to the "South Sea"; to the white
man a drear and howling wilderness, but to the Indian a
home, adapted to his nature, and cheerful as the smile of the
Great Spirit.

While we loiter here this autumn evening, looking for a
spot retired enough, where we shall quietly rest to-night, they
thus, in that chilly March evening, one hundred and forty-
two years before us, with wind and current favoring, have
already glided out of sight, not to camp, as we shall, at night,
but while two sleep one will manage the canoe, and the swift
stream bear them onward to the settlements, it may be, even
to old John Lovewell's house on Salmon Brook to-night.

According to the historian, they escaped as by a miracle all
roving bands of Indians, and reached their homes in safety,
with their trophies, for which the General Court paid them
fifty pounds. The family of Hannah Dustan all assembled
alive once more, except the infant whose brains were dashed
out against the apple-tree, and there have been many who in
later times have lived to say that they had eaten of the fruit
of that apple-tree.

This seems a long while ago, and yet it happened since
Milton wrote his Paradise Lost. But its antiquity is not the
less great for that, for we do not regulate our historical time
by the English standard, nor did the English by the Roman,
nor the Roman by the Greek. "We must look a long way
back," says Raleigh, "to find the Romans giving laws to nations, and their consuls bringing kings and princes bound in
chains to Rome in triumph; to see men go to Greece for wisdom, or Ophir for gold; when now nothing remains but a
poor paper remembrance of their former condition." And yet,
in one sense, not so far back as to find the Penacooks and
Pawtuckets using bows and arrows and hatchets of stone, on
the banks of the Merrimack. From this September afternoon,
and from between these now cultivated shores, those times

seemed more remote than the dark ages. On beholding an old picture of Concord, as it appeared but seventy-five years ago, with a fair open prospect and a light on trees and river, as if it were broad noon, I find that I had not thought the sun shone in those days, or that men lived in broad daylight then. Still less do we imagine the sun shining on hill and valley during Philip's war, on the war-path of Church or Philip, or later of Lovewell or Paugus, with serene summer weather, but they must have lived and fought in a dim twilight or night.

The age of the world is great enough for our imaginations, even according to the Mosaic account, without borrowing any years from the geologist. From Adam and Eve at one leap sheer down to the deluge, and then through the ancient monarchies, through Babylon and Thebes, Brahma and Abraham, to Greece and the Argonauts; whence we might start again with Orpheus and the Trojan war, the Pyramids and the Olympic games, and Homer and Athens, for our stages; and after a breathing space at the building of Rome, continue our journey down through Odin and Christ to—America. It is a wearisome while. And yet the lives of but sixty old women, such as live under the hill, say of a century each, strung together, are sufficient to reach over the whole ground. Taking hold of hands they would span the interval from Eve to my own mother. A respectable tea-party merely,—whose gossip would be Universal History. The fourth old woman from myself suckled Columbus,—the ninth was nurse to the Norman Conqueror,—the nineteenth was the Virgin Mary,—the twenty-fourth the Cumæan Sibyl,—the thirtieth was at the Trojan war and Helen her name,—the thirty-eighth was Queen Semiramis,—the sixtieth was Eve the mother of mankind. So much for the

> "Old woman that lives under the hill,
> And if she's not gone she lives there still."

It will not take a very great-granddaughter of hers to be in at the death of Time.

We can never safely exceed the actual facts in our narratives. Of pure invention, such as some suppose, there is no instance. To write a true work of fiction even, is only to take leisure and liberty to describe some things more exactly as they are.

A true account of the actual is the rarest poetry, for common sense always takes a hasty and superficial view. Though I am not much acquainted with the works of Goethe, I should say that it was one of his chief excellences as a writer, that he was satisfied with giving an exact description of things as they appeared to him, and their effect upon him. Most travellers have not self-respect enough to do this simply, and make objects and events stand around them as the centre, but still imagine more favorable positions and relations than the actual ones, and so we get no valuable report from them at all. In his Italian Travels Goethe jogs along at a snail's pace, but always mindful that the earth is beneath and the heavens are above him. His Italy is not merely the fatherland of lazzaroni and virtuosi, and scene of splendid ruins, but a solid turf-clad soil, daily shined on by the sun, and nightly by the moon. Even the few showers are faithfully recorded. He speaks as an unconcerned spectator, whose object is faithfully to describe what he sees, and that, for the most part, in the order in which he sees it. Even his reflections do not interfere with his descriptions. In one place he speaks of himself as giving so glowing and truthful a description of an old tower to the peasants who had gathered around him, that they who had been born and brought up in the neighborhood must needs look over their shoulders, "that," to use his own words, "they might behold with their eyes, what I had praised to their ears,"—"and I added nothing, not even the ivy which for centuries had decorated the walls." It would thus be possible for inferior minds to produce invaluable books, if this very moderation were not the evidence of superiority; for the wise are not so much wiser than others as respecters of their own wisdom. Some, poor in spirit, record plaintively only what has happened to them; but others how they have happened to the universe, and the judgment which they have awarded to circumstances. Above all, he possessed a hearty good-will to all men, and never wrote a cross or even careless word. On one occasion the post-boy snivelling, "Signor perdonate, quésta è la mia patria," he confesses that "to me poor northerner came something tear-like into the eyes."

Goethe's whole education and life were those of the artist. He lacks the unconsciousness of the poet. In his autobiography he describes accurately the life of the author of Wilhelm Meister. For as there is in that book, mingled with a rare and serene wisdom, a certain pettiness or exaggeration of trifles, wisdom applied to produce a constrained and partial and merely well-bred man,—a magnifying of the theatre till life itself is turned into a stage, for which it is our duty to study our parts well, and conduct with propriety and precision,— so in the autobiography, the fault of his education is, so to speak, its merely artistic completeness. Nature is hindered, though she prevails at last in making an unusually catholic impression on the boy. It is the life of a city boy, whose toys are pictures and works of art, whose wonders are the theatre and kingly processions and crownings. As the youth studied minutely the order and the degrees in the imperial procession, and suffered none of its effect to be lost on him, so the man aimed to secure a rank in society which would satisfy his no-tion of fitness and respectability. He was defrauded of much which the savage boy enjoys. Indeed, he himself has occasion to say in this very autobiography, when at last he escapes into the woods without the gates: "Thus much is certain, that only the undefinable, wide-expanding feelings of youth and of un-cultivated nations are adapted to the sublime, which, when-ever it may be excited in us through external objects, since it is either formless, or else moulded into forms which are in-comprehensible, must surround us with a grandeur which we find above our reach." He further says of himself: "I had lived among painters from my childhood, and had accustomed my-self to look at objects, as they did, with reference to art." And this was his practice to the last. He was even too *well-bred* to be thoroughly bred. He says that he had had no intercourse with the lowest class of his towns-boys. The child should have the advantage of ignorance as well as of knowledge, and is fortunate if he gets his share of neglect and exposure.

"The laws of Nature break the rules of Art."

The Man of Genius may at the same time be, indeed is commonly, an Artist, but the two are not to be confounded. The Man of Genius, referred to mankind, is an originator, an inspired or demonic man, who produces a perfect work in obedience to laws yet unexplored. The Artist is he who detects and applies the law from observation of the works of Genius, whether of man or nature. The Artisan is he who merely applies the rules which others have detected. There has been no man of pure Genius; as there has been none wholly destitute of Genius.

Poetry is the mysticism of mankind.

The expressions of the poet cannot be analyzed; his sentence is one word, whose syllables are words. There are indeed no *words* quite worthy to be set to his music. But what matter if we do not hear the words always, if we hear the music?

Much verse fails of being poetry because it was not written exactly at the right crisis, though it may have been inconceivably near to it. It is only by a miracle that poetry is written at all. It is not recoverable thought, but a hue caught from a vaster receding thought.

A poem is one undivided unimpeded expression fallen ripe into literature, and it is undividedly and unimpededly received by those for whom it was matured.

If you can speak what you will never hear, if you can write what you will never read, you have done rare things.

> The work we choose should be our own,
> God lets alone.

The unconsciousness of man is the consciousness of God.

Deep are the foundations of sincerity. Even stone walls have their foundation below the frost.

What is produced by a free stroke charms us, like the forms of lichens and leaves. There is a certain perfection in accident which we never consciously attain. Draw a blunt quill filled with ink over a sheet of paper, and fold the paper before the ink is dry, transversely to this line, and a delicately shaded and regular figure will be produced, in some respects more pleasing than an elaborate drawing.

The talent of composition is very dangerous,—the striking out the heart of life at a blow, as the Indian takes off a scalp. I feel as if my life had grown more outward when I can express it.

On his journey from Brenner to Verona, Goethe writes:

"The Tees flows now more gently, and makes in many places broad sands. On the land, near to the water, upon the hill-sides, everything is so closely planted one to another, that you think they must choke one another,—vineyards, maize, mulberry-trees, apples, pears, quinces, and nuts. The dwarf elder throws itself vigorously over the walls. Ivy grows with strong stems up the rocks, and spreads itself wide over them, the lizard glides through the intervals, and everything that wanders to and fro reminds one of the loveliest pictures of art. The women's tufts of hair bound up, the men's bare breasts and light jackets, the excellent oxen which they drive home from market, the little asses with their loads,—everything forms a living, animated Heinrich Roos. And now that it is evening, in the mild air a few clouds rest upon the mountains, in the heavens more stand still than move, and immediately after sunset the chirping of crickets begins to grow more loud; then one feels for once at home in the world, and not as concealed or in exile. I am contented as though I had been born and brought up here, and were now returning from a Greenland or whaling voyage. Even the dust of my Father-land, which is often whirled about the wagon, and which for so long a time I had not seen, is greeted. The clock-and-bell jingling of the crickets is altogether lovely, penetrating, and agreeable. It sounds bravely when roguish boys whistle in emulation of a field of such songstresses. One fancies that they really enhance one another. Also the evening is perfectly mild as the day."

"If one who dwelt in the south, and came hither from the south, should hear of my rapture hereupon, he would deem me very childish. Alas! what I here express I have long known while I suffered under an unpropitious heaven, and now may I joyful feel this joy as an exception, which we should enjoy everforth as an eternal necessity of our nature."

Thus we "sayled by thought and pleasaunce," as Chaucer says, and all things seemed with us to flow; the shore itself, and the distant cliffs, were dissolved by the undiluted air. The hardest material seemed to obey the same law with the most fluid, and so indeed in the long run it does. Trees were but rivers of sap and woody fibre, flowing from the atmosphere, and emptying into the earth by their trunks, as their roots flowed upward to the surface. And in the heavens there were rivers of stars, and milky-ways, already beginning to gleam and ripple over our heads. There were rivers of rock on the surface of the earth, and rivers of ore in its bowels, and our thoughts flowed and circulated, and this portion of time was but the current hour. Let us wander where we will, the universe is built round about us, and we are central still. If we look into the heavens they are concave, and if we were to look into a gulf as bottomless, it would be concave also. The sky is curved downward to the earth in the horizon, because we stand on the plain. I draw down its skirts. The stars so low there seem loath to depart, but by a circuitous path to be remembering me, and returning on their steps.

We had already passed by broad daylight the scene of our encampment at Coos Falls, and at length we pitched our camp on the west bank, in the northern part of Merrimack, nearly opposite to the large island on which we had spent the noon in our way up the river.

There we went to bed that summer evening, on a sloping shelf in the bank, a couple of rods from our boat, which was drawn up on the sand, and just behind a thin fringe of oaks which bordered the river; without having disturbed any inhabitants but the spiders in the grass, which came out by the light of our lamp, and crawled over our buffaloes. When we looked out from under the tent, the trees were seen dimly through the mist, and a cool dew hung upon the grass, which seemed to rejoice in the night, and with the damp air we inhaled a solid fragrance. Having eaten our supper of hot cocoa and bread and watermelon, we soon grew weary of conversing, and writing in our journals, and, putting out the lantern which hung from the tent-pole, fell asleep.

Unfortunately, many things have been omitted which should have been recorded in our journal; for though we made it a rule to set down all our experiences therein, yet such a resolution is very hard to keep, for the important experience rarely allows us to remember such obligations, and so indifferent things get recorded, while that is frequently neglected. It is not easy to write in a journal what interests us at any time, because to write it is not what interests us.

Whenever we awoke in the night, still eking out our dreams with half-awakened thoughts, it was not till after an interval, when the wind breathed harder than usual, flapping the curtains of the tent, and causing its cords to vibrate, that we remembered that we lay on the bank of the Merrimack, and not in our chamber at home. With our heads so low in the grass, we heard the river whirling and sucking, and lapsing downward, kissing the shore as it went, sometimes rippling louder than usual, and again its mighty current making only a slight limpid, trickling sound, as if our water-pail had sprung a leak, and the water were flowing into the grass by our side. The wind, rustling the oaks and hazels, impressed us like a wakeful and inconsiderate person up at midnight, moving about, and putting things to rights, occasionally stirring up whole drawers full of leaves at a puff. There seemed to be a great haste and preparation throughout Nature, as for a distinguished visitor; all her aisles had to be swept in the night, by a thousand hand-maidens, and a thousand pots to be boiled for the next day's feasting;—such a whispering bustle, as if ten thousand fairies made their fingers fly, silently sewing at the new carpet with which the earth was to be clothed, and the new drapery which was to adorn the trees. And then the wind would lull and die away, and we like it fell asleep again.

Friday

"The Boteman strayt
Held on his course with stayed stedfastnesse,
Ne ever shroncke, ne ever sought to bayt
His tryed armes for toylesome wearinesse;
But with his oares did sweepe the watry wildernesse."
SPENSER.
"Summer's robe grows
Dusky, and like an oft-dyed garment shows."
DONNE.

As WE lay awake long before daybreak, listening to the rippling of the river, and the rustling of the leaves, in suspense whether the wind blew up or down the stream, was favorable or unfavorable to our voyage, we already suspected that there was a change in the weather, from a freshness as of autumn in these sounds. The wind in the woods sounded like an incessant waterfall dashing and roaring amid rocks, and we even felt encouraged by the unusual activity of the elements. He who hears the rippling of rivers in these degenerate days will not utterly despair. That night was the turning-point in the season. We had gone to bed in summer, and we awoke in autumn; for summer passes into autumn in some unimaginable point of time, like the turning of a leaf.

We found our boat in the dawn just as we had left it, and as if waiting for us, there on the shore, in autumn, all cool and dripping with dew, and our tracks still fresh in the wet sand around it, the fairies all gone or concealed. Before five o'clock we pushed it into the fog, and, leaping in, at one shove were out of sight of the shores, and began to sweep downward with the rushing river, keeping a sharp lookout for rocks. We could see only the yellow gurgling water, and a solid bank of fog on every side, forming a small yard around us. We soon passed the mouth of the Souhegan, and the village of Merrimack, and as the mist gradually rolled away, and we were relieved from the trouble of watching for rocks, we saw by the flitting clouds, by the first russet tinge on the hills, by the rushing river, the cottages on shore, and the shore itself, so coolly fresh and shining with dew, and later in the day, by the hue of the grape-vine, the goldfinch on the willow, the flickers flying in flocks, and when we passed near enough to the shore, as we fancied, by the faces of men, that the Fall had commenced. The cottages looked more snug and comfortable, and their inhabitants were seen only for a moment, and then went quietly in and shut the door, retreating inward to the haunts of summer.

> "And now the cold autumnal dews are seen
> To cobweb ev'ry green;
> And by the low-shorn rowens doth appear
> The fast-declining year."

We heard the sigh of the first autumnal wind, and even the water had acquired a grayer hue. The sumach, grape, and maple were already changed, and the milkweed had turned to a deep rich yellow. In all woods the leaves were fast ripening for their fall; for their full veins and lively gloss mark the ripe leaf, and not the sered one of the poets; and we knew that the maples, stripped of their leaves among the earliest, would soon stand like a wreath of smoke along the edge of the meadow. Already the cattle were heard to low wildly in the pastures and along the highways, restlessly running to and fro, as if in apprehension of the withering of the grass and of the approach of winter. Our thoughts, too, began to rustle.

As I pass along the streets of our village of Concord on the day of our annual Cattle-Show, when it usually happens that the leaves of the elms and buttonwoods begin first to strew the ground under the breath of the October wind, the lively spirits in their sap seem to mount as high as any plough-boy's let loose that day; and they lead my thoughts away to the rustling woods, where the trees are preparing for their winter campaign. This autumnal festival, when men are gathered in crowds in the streets as regularly and by as natural a law as the leaves cluster and rustle by the wayside, is naturally associated in my mind with the fall of the year. The low of cattle in the streets sounds like a hoarse symphony or running bass to the rustling of the leaves. The wind goes hurrying down the country, gleaning every loose straw that is left in the fields, while every farmer lad too appears to scud before it,—

having donned his best pea-jacket and pepper-and-salt waist-coat, his unbent trousers, outstanding rigging of duck or kerseymere or corduroy, and his furry hat withal,—to country fairs and cattle-shows, to that Rome among the villages where the treasures of the year are gathered. All the land over they go leaping the fences with their tough, idle palms, which have never learned to hang by their sides, amid the low of calves and the bleating of sheep,—Amos, Abner, Elnathan, Elbridge,—

"From steep pine-bearing mountains to the plain."

I love these sons of earth every mother's son of them, with their great hearty hearts rushing tumultuously in herds from spectacle to spectacle, as if fearful lest there should not be time between sun and sun to see them all, and the sun does not wait more than in haying-time.

"Wise Nature's darlings, they live in the world
Perplexing not themselves how it is hurled."

Running hither and thither with appetite for the coarse pastimes of the day, now with boisterous speed at the heels of the inspired negro from whose larynx the melodies of all Congo and Guinea Coast have broke loose into our streets; now to see the procession of a hundred yoke of oxen, all as august and grave as Osiris, or the droves of neat cattle and milch cows as unspotted as Isis or Io. Such as had no love for Nature

"at all,
Came lovers home from this great festival."

They may bring their fattest cattle and richest fruits to the fair, but they are all eclipsed by the show of men. These are stirring autumn days, when men sweep by in crowds, amid the rustle of leaves, like migrating finches; this is the true harvest of the year, when the air is but the breath of men, and the rustling of leaves is as the trampling of the crowd. We read now-a-days of the ancient festivals, games, and processions of the Greeks and Etruscans, with a little incredulity, or at least with little sympathy; but how natural and irrepressible in every people is some hearty and palpable greeting of Nature. The Corybantes, the Bacchantes, the rude primitive tragedians with their procession and goat-song, and the whole paraphernalia of the Panathenæa, which appear so antiquated and peculiar, have their parallel now. The husband-man is always a better Greek than the scholar is prepared to appreciate, and the old custom still survives, while antiquarians and scholars grow gray in commemorating it. The farmers crowd to the fair to-day in obedience to the same ancient law, which Solon or Lycurgus did not enact, as naturally as bees swarm and follow their queen.

It is worth the while to see the country's people, how they pour into the town, the sober farmer folk, now all agog, their very shirt and coat-collars pointing forward,—collars so broad as if they had put their shirts on wrong end upward, for the fashions always tend to superfluity,—and with an unusual springiness in their gait, jabbering earnestly to one another. The more supple vagabond, too, is sure to appear on the least rumor of such a gathering, and the next day to disappear, and go into his hole like the seventeen-year locust, in an ever-shabby coat, though finer than the farmer's best, yet never dressed; come to see the sport, and have a hand in what is going,—to know " what's the row," if there is any; to be where some men are drunk, some horses race, some cockerels fight; anxious to be shaking props under a table, and above all to see the "striped pig." He especially is the creature of the occasion. He empties both his pockets and his character into the stream, and swims in such a day. He dearly loves the social slush. There is no reserve of soberness in him.

I love to see the herd of men feeding heartily on coarse and succulent pleasures, as cattle on the husks and stalks of vegetables. Though there are many crooked and crabbled specimens of humanity among them, run all to thorn and rind, and crowded out of shape by adverse circumstances, like the third chestnut in the burr, so that you wonder to see some heads wear a whole hat, yet fear not that the race will fail or waver in them; like the crabs which grow in hedges, they furnish the stocks of sweet and thrifty fruits still. Thus is nature recruited from age to age, while the fair and palatable varieties die out, and have their period. This is that mankind. How cheap must be the material of which so many men are made.

＊   ＊   ＊

The wind blew steadily down the stream, so that we kept our sails set, and lost not a moment of the forenoon by delays, but from early morning until noon were continually dropping downward. With our hands on the steering-paddle, which was thrust deep into the river, or bending to the oar, which indeed we rarely relinquished, we felt each palpitation in the veins of our steed, and each impulse of the wings which drew us above. The current of our thoughts made as sudden bends as the river, which was continually opening new prospects to the east or south, but we are aware that rivers flow most rapidly and shallowest at these points. The steadfast shores never once turned aside for us, but still trended as they were made; why then should we always turn aside for them?

A man cannot wheedle nor overawe his Genius. It requires to be conciliated by nobler conduct than the world demands or can appreciate. These winged thoughts are like birds, and will not be handled; even hens will not let you touch them like quadrupeds. Nothing was ever so unfamiliar and startling to a man as his own thoughts.

To the rarest genius it is the most expensive to succumb and conform to the ways of the world. Genius is the worst of lumber, if the poet would float upon the breeze of popularity. The bird of paradise is obliged constantly to fly against the wind, lest its gay trappings, pressing close to its body, impede its free movements.

He is the best sailor who can steer within the fewest points of the wind, and extract a motive power out of the greatest obstacles. Most begin to veer and tack as soon as the wind changes from aft, and as within the tropics it does not blow from all points of the compass, there are some harbors which they can never reach.

The poet is no tender slip of fairy stock, who requires peculiar institutions and edicts for his defence, but the toughest son of earth and of Heaven, and by his greater strength and endurance his fainting companions will recognize the God in him. It is the worshippers of beauty, after all, who have done the real pioneer work of the world.

The poet will prevail to be popular in spite of his faults, and in spite of his beauties too. He will hit the nail on the head, and we shall not know the shape of his hammer. He makes us free of his hearth and heart, which is greater than to offer one the freedom of a city.

Great men, unknown to their generation, have their fame among the great who have preceded them, and all true worldly fame subsides from their high estimate beyond the stars.

Orpheus does not hear the strains which issue from his lyre, but only those which are breathed into it; for the original strain precedes the sound, by as much as the echo follows after. The rest is the perquisite of the rocks and trees and beasts.

When I stand in a library where is all the recorded wit of the world, but none of the recording, a mere accumulated, and not truly cumulative treasure, where immortal works stand side by side with anthologies which did not survive their month, and cobweb and mildew have already spread from these to the binding of those; and happily I am reminded of what poetry is,—I perceive that Shakespeare and Milton did not foresee into what company they were to fall. Alas! that so soon the work of a true poet should be swept into such a dust-hole!

The poet will write for his peers alone. He will remember only that he saw truth and beauty from his position, and expect the time when a vision as broad shall overlook the same field as freely.

We are often prompted to speak our thoughts to our neighbors, or the single travellers whom we meet on the road, but poetry is a communication from our home and solitude addressed to all Intelligence. It never whispers in a private ear. Knowing this, we may understand those sonnets said to be addressed to particular persons, or "To a Mistress's Eyebrow." Let none feel flattered by them. For poetry write love, and it will be equally true.

No doubt it is an important difference between men of genius or poets, and men not of genius, that the latter are unable to grasp and confront the thought which visits them. But it is because it is too faint for expression, or even conscious impression. What merely quickens or retards the blood in their veins and fills their afternoons with pleasure they know

not whence, conveys a distinct assurance to the finer organization of the poet.

We talk of genius as if it were a mere knack, and the poet
could only express what other men conceived. But in comparison with his task, the poet is the least talented of any;
the writer of prose has more skill. See what talent the smith
has. His material is pliant in his hands. When the poet is
most inspired, is stimulated by an *aura* which never even
colors the afternoons of common men, then his talent is all
gone, and he is no longer a poet. The gods do not grant
him any skill more than another. They never put their gifts
into his hands, but they encompass and sustain him with
their breath.

To say that God has given a man many and great talents,
frequently means that he has brought his heavens down
within reach of his hands.

When the poetic frenzy seizes us, we run and scratch with
our pen, intent only on worms, calling our mates around us,
like the cock, and delighting in the dust we make, but do not
detect where the jewel lies, which, perhaps, we have in the
mean time cast to a distance, or quite covered up again.

The poet's body even is not fed like other men's, but he
sometimes tastes the genuine nectar and ambrosia of the
gods, and lives a divine life. By the healthful and invigorating thrills of inspiration his life is preserved to a serene old
age.

Some poems are for holidays only. They are polished and
sweet, but it is the sweetness of sugar, and not such as toil
gives to sour bread. The breath with which the poet utters
his verse must be that by which he lives.

Great prose, of equal elevation, commands our respect
more than great verse, since it implies a more permanent and
level height, a life more pervaded with the grandeur of the
thought. The poet often only makes an irruption, like a
Parthian, and is off again, shooting while he retreats; but
the prose writer has conquered like a Roman, and settled
colonies.

The true poem is not that which the public read. There is
always a poem not printed on paper, coincident with the production of this, stereotyped in the poet's life. It is *what he has*

become through his work. Not how is the idea expressed in stone, or on canvas or paper, is the question, but how far it has obtained form and expression in the life of the artist. His true work will not stand in any prince's gallery.

> My life has been the poem I would have writ,
> But I could not both live and utter it.

THE POET'S DELAY.

> In vain I see the morning rise,
>   In vain observe the western blaze,
> Who idly look to other skies,
>   Expecting life by other ways.

> Amidst such boundless wealth without,
>   I only still am poor within,
> The birds have sung their summer out,
>   But still my spring does not begin.

> Shall I then wait the autumn wind,
>   Compelled to seek a milder day,
> And leave no curious nest behind,
>   No woods still echoing to my lay?

This raw and gusty day, and the creaking of the oaks and pines on shore, reminded us of more northern climes than Greece, and more wintry seas than the Ægean.

The genuine remains of Ossian, or those ancient poems which bear his name, though of less fame and extent, are, in many respects, of the same stamp with the Iliad itself. He asserts the dignity of the bard no less than Homer, and in his era we hear of no other priest than he. It will not avail to call him a heathen, because he personifies the sun and addresses it; and what if his heroes did "worship the ghosts of their fathers," their thin, airy, and unsubstantial forms? we worship but the ghosts of our fathers in more substantial forms. We cannot but respect the vigorous faith of those heathen, who sternly believed somewhat, and are inclined to say to the critics, who are offended by their superstitious rites,—Don't interrupt these men's prayers. As if we knew more about human life and a God, than the heathen and ancients. Does English theology contain the recent discoveries?

Ossian reminds us of the most refined and rudest eras, of Homer, Pindar, Isaiah, and the American Indian. In his poetry, as in Homer's, only the simplest and most enduring features of humanity are seen, such essential parts of a man as Stonehenge exhibits of a temple; we see the circles of stone, and the upright shaft alone. The phenomena of life acquire almost an unreal and gigantic size seen through his mists. Like all older and grander poetry, it is distinguished by the few elements in the lives of its heroes. They stand on the heath, between the stars and the earth, shrunk to the bones and sinews. The earth is a boundless plain for their deeds. They lead such a simple, dry, and everlasting life, as hardly needs depart with the flesh, but is transmitted entire from age to age. There are but few objects to distract their sight, and their life is as unencumbered as the course of the stars they gaze at.

> "The wrathful kings, on cairns apart,
> Look forward from behind their shields,
> And mark the wandering stars,
> That brilliant westward move."

It does not cost much for these heroes to live; they do not want much furniture. They are such forms of men only as can be seen afar through the mist, and have no costume nor dialect, but for language there is the tongue itself, and for costume there are always the skins of beasts and the bark of trees to be had. They live out their years by the vigor of their constitutions. They survive storms and the spears of their foes, and perform a few heroic deeds, and then

> "Mounds will answer questions of them,
> For many future years."

Blind and infirm, they spend the remnant of their days listening to the lays of the bards, and feeling the weapons which laid their enemies low, and when at length they die, by a convulsion of nature, the bard allows us a short and misty glance into futurity, yet as clear, perchance, as their lives had been. When Mac-Roine was slain,

> "His soul departed to his warlike sires,
>   To follow misty forms of boars,
>   In tempestuous islands bleak."

The hero's cairn is erected, and the bard sings a brief significant strain, which will suffice for epitaph and biography.

> "The weak will find his bow in the dwelling,
>   The feeble will attempt to bend it."

Compared with this simple, fibrous life, our civilized history appears the chronicle of debility, of fashion, and the arts of luxury. But the civilized man misses no real refinement in the poetry of the rudest era. It reminds him that civilization does but dress men. It makes shoes, but it does not toughen the soles of the feet. It makes cloth of finer texture, but it does not touch the skin. Inside the civilized man stands the savage still in the place of honor. We are those blue-eyed, yellow-haired Saxons, those slender, dark-haired Normans.

The profession of the bard attracted more respect in those days from the importance attached to fame. It was his province to record the deeds of heroes. When Ossian hears the traditions of inferior bards, he exclaims,—

> "I straightway seize the unfutile tales,
>   And send them down in faithful verse."

His philosophy of life is expressed in the opening of the third Duan of Ca-Lodin.

> "Whence have sprung the things that are?
>   And whither roll the passing years?
>   Where does Time conceal its two heads,
>   In dense impenetrable gloom,
>   Its surface marked with heroes' deeds alone?
>   I view the generations gone;
>   The past appears but dim;
>   As objects by the moon's faint beams,
>   Reflected from a distant lake.
>   I see, indeed, the thunderbolts of war,
>   But there the unmighty joyless dwell,
>   All those who send not down their deeds
>   To far, succeeding times."

The ignoble warriors die and are forgotten;

> "Strangers come to build a tower,
> And throw their ashes overhand;
> Some rusted swords appear in dust;
> One, bending forward, says,
> 'The arms belonged to heroes gone;
> We never heard their praise in song.'"

The grandeur of the similes is another feature which characterizes great poetry. Ossian seems to speak a gigantic and universal language. The images and pictures occupy even much space in the landscape, as if they could be seen only from the sides of mountains, and plains with a wide horizon, or across arms of the sea. The machinery is so massive that it cannot be less than natural. Oivana says to the spirit of her father, "Gray-haired Torkil of Torne," seen in the skies,

> "Thou glidest away like receding ships."

So when the hosts of Fingal and Starne approach to battle,

> "With murmurs loud, like rivers far,
> The race of Torne hither moved."

And when compelled to retire,

> "dragging his spear behind,
> Cudulin sank in the distant wood,
> Like a fire upblazing ere it dies."

Nor did Fingal want a proper audience when he spoke;

> "A thousand orators inclined
> To hear the lay of Fingal."

The threats too would have deterred a man. Vengeance and terror were real. Trenmore threatens the young warrior whom he meets on a foreign strand,

> "Thy mother shall find thee pale on the shore,
> While lessening on the waves she spies
> The sails of him who slew her son."

If Ossian's heroes weep, it is from excess of strength, and not from weakness, a sacrifice or libation of fertile natures, like the perspiration of stone in summer's heat. We hardly know that tears have been shed, and it seems as if weeping were proper only for babes and heroes. Their joy and their sorrow are made of one stuff, like rain and snow, the rainbow and the mist. When Fillan was worsted in fight, and ashamed in the presence of Fingal,

> "He strode away forthwith,
> And bent in grief above a stream,
> His cheeks bedewed with tears.
> From time to time the thistles gray
> He lopped with his inverted lance."

Crodar, blind and old, receives Ossian, son of Fingal, who comes to aid him in war; —

> " 'My eyes have failed,' says he, 'Crodar is blind,
> Is thy strength like that of thy fathers?
> Stretch, Ossian, thine arm to the hoary-haired.'
> I gave my arm to the king.
> The aged hero seized my hand;
> He heaved a heavy sigh;
> Tears flowed incessant down his cheek.
> 'Strong art thou, son of the mighty,
> Though not so dreadful as Morven's prince.
> .   .   .   .   .
> Let my feast be spread in the hall,
> Let every sweet-voiced minstrel sing;
> Great is he who is within my wall,
> Sons of wave-echoing Croma.' "

Even Ossian himself, the hero-bard, pays tribute to the superior strength of his father Fingal.

> "How beauteous, mighty man, was thy mind,
> Why succeeded Ossian without its strength?"

———

While we sailed fleetly before the wind, with the river gurgling under our stern, the thoughts of autumn coursed as steadily through our minds, and we observed less what was passing on the shore, than the dateless associations and impressions which the season awakened, anticipating in some measure the progress of the year.

> I hearing get, who had but ears,
>   And sight, who had but eyes before,
> I moments live, who lived but years,
>   And truth discern, who knew but learning's lore.

Sitting with our faces now up stream, we studied the landscape by degrees, as one unrolls a map, rock, tree, house, hill, and meadow, assuming new and varying positions as wind and water shifted the scene, and there was variety enough for our entertainment in the metamorphoses of the simplest objects. Viewed from this side the scenery appeared new to us.

The most familiar sheet of water viewed from a new hilltop, yields a novel and unexpected pleasure. When we have travelled a few miles, we do not recognize the profiles even of the hills which overlook our native village, and perhaps no man is quite familiar with the horizon as seen from the hill nearest to his house, and can recall its outline distinctly when in the valley. We do not commonly know, beyond a short distance, which way the hills range which take in our houses and farms in their sweep. As if our birth had at first sundered things, and we had been thrust up through into nature like a wedge, and not till the wound heals and the scar disappears, do we begin to discover where we are, and that nature is one and continuous everywhere. It is an important epoch when a man who has always lived on the east side of a mountain, and seen it in the west, travels round and sees it in the east. Yet the universe is a sphere whose centre is wherever there is intelligence. The sun is not so central as a man. Upon an isolated hill-top, in an open country, we seem to ourselves to be standing on the boss of an immense shield, the immediate landscape being apparently depressed below the more remote, and rising gradually to the horizon, which is the rim of the shield, villas, steeples, forests, mountains, one above another, till they are swallowed up in the heavens. The most distant mountains in the horizon appear to rise directly from the shore of that lake in the woods by which we chance to be standing, while from the mountain-top, not only this, but a thousand nearer and larger lakes, are equally unobserved.

Seen through this clear atmosphere, the works of the farmer, his ploughing and reaping, had a beauty to our eyes which he never saw. How fortunate were we who did not own an acre of these shores, who had not renounced our title to the whole. One who knew how to appropriate the true value of this world would be the poorest man in it. The poor rich man! all he has is what he has bought. What I see is mine. I am a large owner in the Merrimack intervals.

> Men dig and dive but cannot my wealth spend,
>   Who yet no partial store appropriate,
> Who no armed ship into the Indies send,
>   To rob me of my orient estate.

He is the rich man, and enjoys the fruits of riches, who summer and winter forever can find delight in his own thoughts. Buy a farm! What have I to pay for a farm which a farmer will take?

When I visit again some haunt of my youth, I am glad to find that nature wears so well. The landscape is indeed something real, and solid, and sincere, and I have not put my foot through it yet. There is a pleasant tract on the bank of the Concord, called Conantum, which I have in my mind;—the old deserted farm-house, the desolate pasture with its bleak cliff, the open wood, the river-reach, the green meadow in the midst, and the moss-grown wild-apple orchard,—places where one may have many thoughts and not decide anything. It is a scene which I can not only remember, as I might a vision, but when I will can bodily revisit, and find it even so, unaccountable, yet unpretending in its pleasant dreariness. When my thoughts are sensible of change, I love to see and sit on rocks which I *have* known, and pry into their moss, and see unchangeableness so established. I not yet gray on rocks forever gray, I no longer green under the evergreens. There is something even in the lapse of time by which time recovers itself.

As we have said, it proved a cool as well as breezy day, and by the time we reached Penichook Brook we were obliged to sit muffled in our cloaks, while the wind and current carried us along. We bounded swiftly over the rippling surface, far by many cultivated lands and the ends of fences which divided innumerable farms, with hardly a thought for the various lives which they separated; now by long rows of alders or groves of pines or oaks, and now by some homestead where the women and children stood outside to gaze at us, till we had swept out of their sight, and beyond the limit of their longest Saturday ramble. We glided past the mouth of the Nashua, and not long after, of Salmon Brook, without more pause than the wind.

> Salmon Brook,
> Penichook,
> Ye sweet waters of my brain,
> When shall I look,
> Or cast the hook,
> In your waves again?

> Silver eels,
> Wooden creels,
> These the baits that still allure,
> And dragon-fly
> That floated by,
> May they still endure?

The shadows chased one another swiftly over wood and meadow, and their alternation harmonized with our mood. We could distinguish the clouds which cast each one, though never so high in the heavens. When a shadow flits across the landscape of the soul, where is the substance? Probably, if we were wise enough, we should see to what virtue we are in-debted for any happier moment we enjoy. No doubt we have earned it at some time; for the gifts of Heaven are never quite gratuitous. The constant abrasion and decay of our lives makes the soil of our future growth. The wood which we now mature, when it becomes virgin mould, determines the character of our second growth, whether that be oaks or pines. Every man casts a shadow; not his body only, but his imperfectly mingled spirit. This is his grief. Let him turn which way he will, it falls opposite to the sun; short at noon, long at eve. Did you never see it?—But, referred to the sun,

it is widest at its base, which is no greater than his own opac-
ity. The divine light is diffused almost entirely around us, and
by means of the refraction of light, or else by a certain self-
luminousness, or, as some will have it, transparency, if we
preserve ourselves untarnished, we are able to enlighten our
shaded side. At any rate, our darkest grief has that bronze
color of the moon eclipsed. There is no ill which may not be
dissipated, like the dark, if you let in a stronger light upon it.
Shadows, referred to the source of light, are pyramids whose
bases are never greater than those of the substances which cast
them, but light is a spherical congeries of pyramids, whose
very apexes are the sun itself, and hence the system shines
with uninterrupted light. But if the light we use is but a paltry and narrow taper, most objects will cast a shadow wider
than themselves.

The places where we had stopped or spent the night in our
way up the river, had already acquired a slight historical interest for us; for many upward days' voyaging were unrav-
elled in this rapid downward passage. When one landed to
stretch his limbs by walking, he soon found himself falling
behind his companion, and was obliged to take advantage of
the curves, and ford the brooks and ravines in haste, to recover his ground. Already the banks and the distant meadows
wore a sober and deepened tinge, for the September air had
shorn them of their summer's pride.

> "And what's a life? The flourishing array
> Of the proud summer meadow, which to-day
> Wears her green plush, and is to-morrow hay."

The air was really the "fine element" which the poets describe. It had a finer and sharper grain, seen against the russet
pastures and meadows, than before, as if cleansed of the summer's impurities.

Having passed the New Hampshire line and reached the
Horseshoe Interval in Tyngsborough, where there is a high
and regular second bank, we climbed up this in haste to get a
nearer sight of the autumnal flowers, asters, golden-rod, and
yarrow, and blue-curls (*Trichostema dichotoma*), humble road-
side blossoms, and, lingering still, the harebell and the *Rhexia
Virginica*. The last, growing in patches of lively pink flowers

on the edge of the meadows, had almost too gay an appearance for the rest of the landscape, like a pink ribbon on the bonnet of a Puritan woman. Asters and golden-rods were the livery which nature wore at present. The latter alone expressed all the ripeness of the season, and shed their mellow lustre over the fields, as if the now declining summer's sun had bequeathed its hues to them. It is the floral solstice a little after midsummer, when the particles of golden light, the sun-dust, have, as it were, fallen like seeds on the earth, and produced these blossoms. On every hillside, and in every valley, stood countless asters, coreopses, tansies, golden-rods, and the whole race of yellow flowers, like Brahminical devotees, turning steadily with their luminary from morning till night.

"I see the golden-rod shine bright,
　　As sun-showers at the birth of day,
　A golden plume of yellow light,
　　That robs the Day-god's splendid ray.

"The aster's violet rays divide
　　The bank with many stars for me,
　And yarrow in blanch tints is dyed,
　　As moonlight floats across the sea.

"I see the emerald woods prepare
　　To shed their vestiture once more,
　And distant elm-trees spot the air
　　With yellow pictures softly o'er.

　　.　　　.　　　.　　　.　　　.

"No more the water-lily's pride
　　In milk-white circles swims content,
　No more the blue-weed's clusters ride
　　And mock the heavens' element.

　　.　　　.　　　.　　　.　　　.

"Autumn, thy wreath and mine are blent
　　With the same colors, for to me
　A richer sky than all is lent,
　　While fades my dream-like company.

"Our skies glow purple, but the wind
    Sobs chill through green trees and bright grass,
To-day shines fair, and lurk behind
    The times that into winter pass.

"So fair we seem, so cold we are,
    So fast we hasten to decay,
Yet through our night glows many a star,
    That still shall claim its sunny day."

So sang a Concord poet once.

There is a peculiar interest belonging to the still later flowers, which abide with us the approach of winter. There is something witch-like in the appearance of the witch-hazel, which blossoms late in October and in November, with its irregular and angular spray and petals like furies' hair, or small ribbon streamers. Its blossoming, too, at this irregular period, when other shrubs have lost their leaves, as well as blossoms, looks like witches' craft. Certainly it blooms in no garden of man's. There is a whole fairy-land on the hillside where it grows.

Some have thought that the gales do not at present waft to the voyager the natural and original fragrance of the land, such as the early navigators described, and that the loss of many odoriferous native plants, sweet-scented grasses and medicinal herbs, which formerly sweetened the atmosphere, and rendered it salubrious,—by the grazing of cattle and the rooting of swine, is the source of many diseases which now prevail; the earth, say they, having been long subjected to extremely artificial and luxurious modes of cultivation, to gratify the appetite, converted into a stye and hot-bed, where men for profit increase the ordinary decay of nature.

According to the record of an old inhabitant of Tyngsborough, now dead, whose farm we were now gliding past, one of the greatest freshets on this river took place in October, 1785, and its height was marked by a nail driven into an apple-tree behind his house. One of his descendants has shown this to me, and I judged it to be at least seventeen or eighteen feet above the level of the river at the time. According to Barber, the river rose twenty-one feet above the common high-water mark, at Bradford in the year 1818. Before the Lowell and Nashua railroad was built, the engineer made inquiries of the inhabitants along the banks as to how high they had known the river to rise. When he came to this house he was conducted to the apple-tree, and as the nail was not then visible, the lady of the house placed her hand on the trunk where she said that she remembered the nail to have been from her childhood. In the mean while the old man put his arm inside the tree, which was hollow, and felt the point of the nail sticking through, and it was exactly opposite to her hand. The spot is now plainly marked by a notch in the bark. But as no one else remembered the river to have risen so high as this, the engineer disregarded this statement, and I learn that there has since been a freshet which rose within nine inches of the rails at Biscuit Brook, and such a freshet as that of 1785 would have covered the railroad two feet deep.

The revolutions of nature tell as fine tales, and make as interesting revelations, on this river's banks, as on the Euphrates or the Nile. This apple-tree, which stands within a few rods of the river, is called "Elisha's apple-tree," from a friendly Indian, who was anciently in the service of Jonathan Tyng, and, with one other man, was killed here by his own race in one of the Indian wars,—the particulars of which affair were told us on the spot. He was buried close by, no one knew exactly where, but in the flood of 1785, so great a weight of water standing over the grave, caused the earth to settle where it had once been disturbed, and when the flood went down, a sunken spot, exactly of the form and size of the grave, revealed its locality; but this was now lost again, and no future flood can detect it; yet, no doubt, Nature will know how to point it out in due time, if it be necessary, by methods yet more searching and unexpected. Thus there is not only the crisis when the spirit ceases to inspire and expand the body, marked by a fresh mound in the churchyard, but there is also a crisis when the body ceases to take up room as such in nature, marked by a fainter depression in the earth.

We sat awhile to rest us here upon the brink of the western

bank, surrounded by the glossy leaves of the red variety of the mountain laurel, just above the head of Wicasuck Island, where we could observe some scows which were loading with clay from the opposite shore, and also overlook the grounds of the farmer, of whom I have spoken, who once hospitably entertained us for a night. He had on his pleasant farm, besides an abundance of the beach-plum, or *Prunus littoralis*, which grew wild, the Canada plum under cultivation, fine Porter apples, some peaches, and large patches of musk and water melons, which he cultivated for the Lowell market. Elisha's apple-tree, too, bore a native fruit, which was prized by the family. He raised the blood peach, which, as he showed us with satisfaction, was more like the oak in the color of its bark and in the setting of its branches, and was less liable to break down under the weight of the fruit, or the snow, than other varieties. It was of slower growth, and its branches strong and tough. There, also, was his nursery of native apple-trees, thickly set upon the bank, which cost but little care, and which he sold to the neighboring farmers when they were five or six years old. To see a single peach upon its stem makes an impression of paradisaical fertility and luxury. This reminded us even of an old Roman farm, as described by Varro:—"Cæsar Vopiscus Ædilicius, when he pleaded before the Censors, said that the grounds of Rosea were the garden (*sumen* the tid-bit) of Italy, in which a pole being left would not be visible the day after, on account of the growth of the herbage." This soil may not have been remarkably fertile, yet at this distance we thought that this anecdote might be told of the Tyngsborough farm.

When we passed Wicasuck Island, there was a pleasure-boat containing a youth and a maiden on the island brook, which we were pleased to see, since it proved that there were some hereabouts to whom our excursion would not be wholly strange. Before this, a canal-boatman, of whom we made some inquiries respecting Wicasuck Island, and who told us that it was disputed property, suspected that we had a claim upon it, and though we assured him that all this was news to us, and explained, as well as we could, why we had come to see it, he believed not a word of it, and seriously offered us one hundred dollars for our title. The only other small boats which we met with were used to pick up drift-wood. Some of the poorer class along the stream collect, in this way, all the fuel which they require. While one of us landed not far from this island to forage for provisions among the farm-houses whose roofs we saw, for our supply was now exhausted, the other, sitting in the boat, which was moored to the shore, was left alone to his reflections.

If there is nothing new on the earth, still the traveller always has a resource in the skies. They are constantly turning a new page to view. The wind sets the types on this blue ground, and the inquiring may always read a new truth there. There are things there written with such fine and subtile tinctures, paler than the juice of limes, that to the diurnal eye they leave no trace, and only the chemistry of night reveals them. Every man's daylight firmament answers in his mind to the brightness of the vision in his starriest hour.

These continents and hemispheres are soon run over, but an always unexplored and infinite region makes off on every side from the mind, further than to sunset, and we can make no highway or beaten track into it, but the grass immediately springs up in the path, for we travel there chiefly with our wings.

Sometimes we see objects as through a thin haze, in their eternal relations, and they stand like Palenque and the Pyramids, and we wonder who set them up, and for what purpose. If we see the reality in things, of what moment is the superficial and apparent longer? What are the earth and all its interests beside the deep surmise which pierces and scatters them? While I sit here listening to the waves which ripple and break on this shore, I am absolved from all obligation to the past, and the council of nations may reconsider its votes. The grating of a pebble annuls them. Still occasionally in my dreams I remember that rippling water.

> Oft, as I turn me on my pillow o'er,
> I hear the lapse of waves upon the shore,
> Distinct as if it were at broad noonday,
> And I were drifting down from Nashua.

With a bending sail we glided rapidly by Tyngsborough and Chelmsford, each holding in one hand half of a tart country apple-pie which we had purchased to celebrate our return, and in the other a fragment of the newspaper in which it was wrapped, devouring these with divided relish, and learning the news which had transpired since we sailed. The river here opened into a broad and straight reach of great length, which we bounded merrily over before a smacking breeze, with a devil-may-care look in our faces, and our boat a white bone in its mouth, and a speed which greatly astonished some scow boatmen whom we met. The wind in the horizon rolled like a flood over valley and plain, and every tree bent to the blast, and the mountains like school-boys turned their cheeks to it. They were great and current motions, the flowing sail, the running stream, the waving tree, the roving wind. The north-wind stepped readily into the harness which we had provided, and pulled us along with good will. Sometimes we sailed as gently and steadily as the clouds overhead, watching the receding shores and the motions of our sail; the play of its pulse so like our own lives, so thin and yet so full of life, so noiseless when it labored hardest, so noisy and impatient when least effective; now bending to some generous impulse of the breeze, and then fluttering and flapping with a kind of human suspense. It was the scale on which the varying temperature of distant atmospheres was graduated, and it was some attraction for us that the breeze it played with had been out of doors so long. Thus we sailed, not being able to fly, but as next best, making a long furrow in the fields of the Merrimack toward our home, with our wings spread, but never lifting our heel from the watery trench; gracefully ploughing homeward with our brisk and willing team, wind and stream, pulling together, the former yet a wild steer, yoked to his more sedate fellow. It was very near flying, as when the duck rushes through the water with an impulse of her wings, throwing the spray about her, before she can rise. How we had stuck fast if drawn up but a few feet on the shore!

When we reached the great bend just above Middlesex, where the river runs east thirty-five miles to the sea, we at length lost the aid of this propitious wind, though we con-trived to make one long and judicious tack carry us nearly to the locks of the canal. We were here locked through at noon by our old friend, the lover of the higher mathematics, who seemed glad to see us safe back again through so many locks; but we did not stop to consider any of his problems, though we could cheerfully have spent a whole autumn in this way another time, and never have asked what his religion was. It is so rare to meet with a man out-doors who cherishes a worthy thought in his mind, which is independent of the labor of his hands. Behind every man's busy-ness there should be a level of undisturbed serenity and industry, as within the reef encircling a coral isle there is always an expanse of still water, where the depositions are going on which will finally raise it above the surface.

The eye which can appreciate the naked and absolute beauty of a scientific truth is far more rare than that which is attracted by a moral one. Few detect the morality in the former, or the science in the latter. Aristotle defined art to be Λόγος τοῦ ἔργου ἄνευ ὕλης, *The principle of the work without the wood*; but most men prefer to have some of the wood along with the principle; they demand that the truth be clothed in flesh and blood and the warm colors of life. They prefer the partial statement because it fits and measures them and their commodities best. But science still exists everywhere as the sealer of weights and measures at least.

We have heard much about the poetry of mathematics, but very little of it has yet been sung. The ancients had a juster notion of their poetic value than we. The most distinct and beautiful statement of any truth must take at last the mathematical form. We might so simplify the rules of moral philosophy, as well as of arithmetic, that one formula would express them both. All the moral laws are readily translated into natural philosophy, for often we have only to restore the primitive meaning of the words by which they are expressed, or to attend to their literal instead of their metaphorical sense. They are already *supernatural* philosophy. The whole body of what is now called moral or ethical truth existed in the golden age as abstract science. Or, if we prefer, we may say that the laws of Nature are the purest morality. The Tree of Knowledge is a Tree of Knowledge of good and evil. He is not a true man of science who does not bring some sympathy to his studies, and expect to learn something by behavior as well as by application. It is childish to rest in the discovery of mere coincidences, or of partial and extraneous laws. The study of geometry is a petty and idle exercise of the mind, if it is applied to no larger system than the starry one. Mathematics should be mixed not only with physics but with ethics, *that* is *mixed* mathematics. The fact which interests us most is the life of the naturalist. The purest science is still biographical. Nothing will dignify and elevate science while it is sundered so wholly from the moral life of its devotee, and he professes another religion than it teaches, and worships at a foreign shrine. Anciently the faith of a philosopher was identical with his system, or, in other words, his view of the universe.

My friends mistake when they communicate facts to me with so much pains. Their presence, even their exaggerations and loose statements, are equally good facts for me. I have no respect for facts even except when I would use them, and for the most part I am independent of those which I hear, and can afford to be inaccurate, or, in other words, to substitute more present and pressing facts in their place.

The poet uses the results of science and philosophy, and generalizes their widest deductions.

The process of discovery is very simple. An unwearied and systematic application of known laws to nature, causes the unknown to reveal themselves. Almost any *mode* of observation will be successful at last, for what is most wanted is method. Only let something be determined and fixed around which observation may rally. How many new relations a foot-rule alone will reveal, and to how many things still this has not been applied! What wonderful discoveries have been, and may still be, made, with a plumb-line, a level, a surveyor's compass, a thermometer, or a barometer! Where there is an observatory and a telescope, we expect that any eyes will see new worlds at once. I should say that the most prominent scientific men of our country, and perhaps of this age, are either serving the arts and not pure science, or are performing faithful but quite subordinate labors in particular departments. They make no steady and systematic approaches to the central fact. A discovery is made, and at once the attention of all observers is distracted to that, and it draws many analogous discoveries in its train; as if their work were not already laid out for them, but they had been lying on their oars. There is wanting constant and accurate observation with enough of theory to direct and discipline it.

But, above all, there is wanting genius. Our books of science, as they improve in accuracy, are in danger of losing the freshness and vigor and readiness to appreciate the real laws of Nature, which is a marked merit in the ofttimes false theories of the ancients. I am attracted by the slight pride and satisfaction, the emphatic and even exaggerated style in which some of the older naturalists speak of the operations of Nature, though they are better qualified to appreciate than to discriminate the facts. Their assertions are not without value when disproved. If they are not facts, they are suggestions for Nature herself to act upon. "The Greeks," says Gesner, "had a common proverb (Λαγος καθευδον) a sleeping hare, for a dissembler or counterfeit; because the hare sees when she sleeps; for this is an admirable and rare work of Nature, that all the residue of her bodily parts take their rest, but the eye standeth continually sentinel."

Observation is so wide awake, and facts are being so rapidly added to the sum of human experience, that it appears as if the theorizer would always be in arrears, and were doomed forever to arrive at imperfect conclusions; but the power to perceive a law is equally rare in all ages of the world, and depends but little on the number of facts observed. The senses of the savage will furnish him with facts enough to set him up as a philosopher. The ancients can still speak to us with authority, even on the themes of geology and chemistry, though these studies are thought to have had their birth in modern times. Much is said about the progress of science in these centuries. I should say that the useful results of science had accumulated, but that there had been no accumulation of knowledge, strictly speaking, for posterity; for knowledge is to be acquired only by a corresponding experience. How can we *know* what we are *told* merely? Each man can interpret another's experience only by his own. We read that Newton discovered the law of gravitation, but how many who have heard of his famous discovery have recognized the same truth that he did? It may be not one. The revelation which was

then made to him has not been superseded by the revelation
made to any successor.

> We see the *planet* fall,
> And that is all.

In a review of Sir James Clark Ross's Antarctic Voyage of
Discovery, there is a passage which shows how far a body of
men are commonly impressed by an object of sublimity, and
which is also a good instance of the step from the sublime to
the ridiculous. After describing the discovery of the Antarctic
Continent, at first seen a hundred miles distant over fields of
ice,—stupendous ranges of mountains from seven and eight
to twelve and fourteen thousand feet high, covered with eternal snow and ice, in solitary and inaccessible grandeur, at one
time the weather being beautifully clear, and the sun shining
on the icy landscape; a continent whose islands only are accessible, and these exhibited "not the smallest trace of vegetation," only in a few places the rocks protruding through
their icy covering, to convince the beholder that land formed
the nucleus, and that it was not an iceberg;—the practical
British reviewer proceeds thus, sticking to his last, "On the
22d of January, afternoon, the Expedition made the latitude
of 74° 20′ and by 7ʰ P. M., having ground (ground! where
did they get ground?) to believe that they were then in a
higher southern latitude than had been attained by that enterprising seaman, the late Captain James Weddel, and therefore
higher than all their predecessors, an extra allowance of grog
was issued to the crews as a reward for their perseverance."
Let not us sailors of late centuries take upon ourselves any
airs on account of our Newtons and our Cuviers; we deserve
an extra allowance of grog only.

We endeavored in vain to persuade the wind to blow
through the long corridor of the canal, which is here cut
straight through the woods, and were obliged to resort to our
old expedient of drawing by a cord. When we reached the
Concord, we were forced to row once more in good earnest,
with neither wind nor current in our favor, but by this time
the rawness of the day had disappeared, and we experienced
the warmth of a summer afternoon. This change in the

weather was favorable to our contemplative mood, and disposed us to dream yet deeper at our oars, while we floated in
imagination farther down the stream of time, as we had
floated down the stream of the Merrimack, to poets of a
milder period than had engaged us in the morning. Chelmsford and Billerica appeared like old English towns, compared
with Merrimack and Nashua, and many generations of civil
poets might have lived and sung here.

What a contrast between the stern and desolate poetry of
Ossian, and that of Chaucer, and even of Shakespeare and
Milton, much more of Dryden, and Pope, and Gray. Our
summer of English poetry like the Greek and Latin before it,
seems well advanced toward its fall, and laden with the fruit
and foliage of the season, with bright autumnal tints, but
soon the winter will scatter its myriad clustering and shading
leaves, and leave only a few desolate and fibrous boughs to
sustain the snow and rime, and creak in the blasts of ages.
We cannot escape the impression that the Muse has stooped
a little in her flight, when we come to the literature of civilized eras. Now first we hear of various ages and styles of
poetry; it is pastoral, and lyric, and narrative, and didactic;
but the poetry of runic monuments is of one style, and for
every age. The bard has in a great measure lost the dignity
and sacredness of his office. Formerly he was called a *seer*,
but now it is thought that one man sees as much as another.
He has no longer the bardic rage, and only conceives the
deed, which he formerly stood ready to perform. Hosts of
warriors earnest for battle could not mistake nor dispense
with the ancient bard. His lays were heard in the pauses of
the fight. There was no danger of his being overlooked by
his contemporaries. But now the hero and the bard are of
different professions. When we come to the pleasant English
verse, the storms have all cleared away and it will never
thunder and lighten more. The poet has come within doors,
and exchanged the forest and crag for the fireside, the hut of
the Gael, and Stonehenge with its circles of stones, for the
house of the Englishman. No hero stands at the door prepared to break forth into song or heroic action, but a
homely Englishman, who cultivates the art of poetry. We see

the comfortable fireside, and hear the crackling fagots in all the verse.

Notwithstanding the broad humanity of Chaucer, and the many social and domestic comforts which we meet with in his verse, we have to narrow our vision somewhat to consider him, as if he occupied less space in the landscape, and did not stretch over hill and valley as Ossian does. Yet, seen from the side of posterity, as the father of English poetry, preceded by a long silence or confusion in history, unenlivened by any strain of pure melody, we easily come to reverence him. Passing over the earlier continental poets, since we are bound to the pleasant archipelago of English poetry, Chaucer's is the first name after that misty weather in which Ossian lived, which can detain us long. Indeed, though he represents so different a culture and society, he may be regarded as in many respects the Homer of the English poets. Perhaps he is the youthfullest of them all. We return to him as to the purest well, the fountain farthest removed from the highway of desultory life. He is so natural and cheerful, compared with later poets, that we might almost regard him as a personification of spring. To the faithful reader his muse has even given an aspect to his times, and when he is fresh from perusing him, they seem related to the golden age. It is still the poetry of youth and life, rather than of thought; and though the moral vein is obvious and constant, it has not yet banished the sun and daylight from his verse. The loftiest strains of the muse are, for the most part, sublimely plaintive, and not a carol as free as nature's. The content which the sun shines to celebrate from morning to evening, is unsung. The muse solaces herself, and is not ravished but consoled. There is a catastrophe implied, and a tragic element in all our verse, and less of the lark and morning dews, than of the nightingale and evening shades. But in Homer and Chaucer there is more of the innocence and serenity of youth than in the more modern and moral poets. The Iliad is not Sabbath but morning reading, and men cling to this old song, because they still have moments of unbaptized and uncommitted life, which give them an appetite for more. To the innocent there are neither cherubim nor angels. At rare intervals we rise above the necessity of virtue into an unchangeable morning light, in which we have only to live right on and breathe the ambrosial air. The Iliad represents no creed nor opinion, and we read it with a rare sense of freedom and irresponsibility, as if we trod on native ground, and were autochthones of the soil.

Chaucer had eminently the habits of a literary man and a scholar. There were never any times so stirring that there were not to be found some sedentary still. He was surrounded by the din of arms. The battles of Hallidon Hill and Neville's Cross, and the still more memorable battles of Cressy and Poictiers, were fought in his youth; but these did not concern our poet much, Wickliffe and his reform much more. He regarded himself always as one privileged to sit and converse with books. He helped to establish the literary class. His character as one of the fathers of the English language would alone make his works important, even those which have little poetical merit. He was as simple as Wordsworth in preferring his homely but vigorous Saxon tongue, when it was neglected by the court, and had not yet attained to the dignity of a literature, and rendered a similar service to his country to that which Dante rendered to Italy. If Greek sufficeth for Greek, and Arabic for Arabian, and Hebrew for Jew, and Latin for Latin, then English shall suffice for him, for any of these will serve to teach truth "right as divers pathes leaden divers folke the right waye to Rome." In the Testament of Love he writes, "Let then clerkes enditen in Latin, for they have the propertie of science, and the knowinge in that facultie, and lette Frenchmen in their Frenche also enditen their queinte termes, for it is kyndely to their mouthes, and let us shewe our fantasies in soche wordes as we lerneden of our dames tonge."

He will know how to appreciate Chaucer best, who has come down to him the natural way, through the meagre pastures of Saxon and ante-Chaucerian poetry; and yet, so human and wise he appears after such diet, that we are liable to misjudge him still. In the Saxon poetry extant, in the earliest English, and the contemporary Scottish poetry, there is less to remind the reader of the rudeness and vigor of youth, than of the feebleness of a declining age. It is for the most part translation of imitation merely, with only an occasional and slight tinge of poetry, oftentimes the falsehood and exaggeration of fable, without its imagination to redeem it, and we look in vain to find antiquity restored, humanized, and made blithe again by some natural sympathy between it and the present. But Chaucer is fresh and modern still, and no dust settles on his true passages. It lightens along the line, and we are reminded that flowers have bloomed, and birds sung, and hearts beaten in England. Before the earnest gaze of the reader, the rust and moss of time gradually drop off, and the original green life is revealed. He was a homely and domestic man, and did breathe quite as modern men do.

There is no wisdom that can take place of humanity, and we find *that* in Chaucer. We can expand at last in his breadth, and we think that we could have been that man's acquaintance. He was worthy to be a citizen of England, while Petrarch and Boccacio lived in Italy, and Tell and Tamerlane in Switzerland and in Asia, and Bruce in Scotland, and Wickliffe, and Gower, and Edward the Third, and John of Gaunt, and the Black Prince, were his own countrymen as well as contemporaries; all stout and stirring names. The fame of Roger Bacon came down from the preceding century, and the name of Dante still possessed the influence of a living presence. On the whole, Chaucer impresses us as greater than his reputation, and not a little like Homer and Shakespeare, for he would have held up his head in their company. Among early English poets he is the landlord and host, and has the authority of such. The affectionate mention which succeeding early poets make of him, coupling him with Homer and Virgil, is to be taken into the account in estimating his character and influence. King James and Dunbar of Scotland speak of him with more love and reverence than any modern author of his predecessors of the last century. The same childlike relation is without a parallel now. For the most part we read him without criticism, for he does not plead his own cause, but speaks for his readers, and has that greatness of trust and reliance which compels popularity. He confides in the reader, and speaks privily with him, keeping nothing back. And in return the reader has great confidence in him, that he tells no lies, and reads his story with indulgence, as if it were the circumlocution of a child, but often discovers afterwards that he has spoken with more directness and economy of words than a sage. He is never heartless,

> "For first the thing is thought within the hart,
> Er any word out from the mouth astart."

And so new was all his theme in those days, that he did not have to invent, but only to tell.

We admire Chaucer for his sturdy English wit. The easy height he speaks from in his Prologue to the Canterbury Tales, as if he were equal to any of the company there assembled, is as good as any particular excellence in it. But though it is full of good sense and humanity, it is not transcendent poetry. For picturesque description of persons it is, perhaps, without a parallel in English poetry; yet it is essentially humorous, as the loftiest genius never is. Humor, however broad and genial, takes a narrower view than enthusiasm. To his own finer vein he added all the common wit and wisdom of his time, and everywhere in his works his remarkable knowledge of the world, and nice perception of character, his rare common sense and proverbial wisdom, are apparent. His genius does not soar like Milton's, but is genial and familiar. It shows great tenderness and delicacy, but not the heroic sentiment. It is only a greater portion of humanity with all its weakness. He is not heroic, as Raleigh, nor pious, as Herbert, nor philosophical, as Shakespeare, but he is the child of the English muse, that child which is the father of the man. The charm of his poetry consists often only in an exceeding naturalness, perfect sincerity, with the behavior of a child rather than of a man.

Gentleness and delicacy of character are everywhere apparent in his verse. The simplest and humblest words come readily to his lips. No one can read the Prioress's tale, understanding the spirit in which it was written, and in which the child sings *O alma redemptoris mater*, or the account of the departure of Constance with her child upon the sea, in the Man of Lawe's tale, without feeling the native innocence and refinement of the author. Nor can we be mistaken respecting the essential purity of his character, disregarding the apology of the manners of the age. A simple pathos and feminine gentleness, which Wordsworth only occasionally approaches, but does not equal, are peculiar to him. We are tempted to say that his genius was feminine, not masculine. It was such a feminineness, however, as is rarest to find in woman, though not the appreciation of it; perhaps it is not to be found at all in woman, but is only the feminine in man.

Such pure and genuine and childlike love of Nature is hardly to be found in any poet.

Chaucer's remarkably trustful and affectionate character appears in his familiar, yet innocent and reverent, manner of speaking of his God. He comes into his thought without any false reverence, and with no more parade than the zephyr to his ear. If Nature is our mother, then God is our father. There is less love and simple, practical trust in Shakespeare and Milton. How rarely in our English tongue do we find expressed any affection for God. Certainly, there is no sentiment so rare as the love of God. Herbert almost alone expresses it, "Ah, my dear God!" Our poet uses similar words with propriety; and whenever he sees a beautiful person, or other object, prides himself on the "maistry" of his God. He even recommends Dido to be his bride,—

"if that God that heaven and yearth made,
Would have a love for beauty and goodnesse,
And womanhede, trouth, and semeliness."

But in justification of our praise, we must refer to his works themselves; to the Prologue to the Canterbury Tales, the account of Gentilesse, the Flower and the Leaf, the stories of Griselda, Virginia, Ariadne, and Blanche the Dutchesse, and much more of less distinguished merit. There are many poets of more taste, and better manners, who knew how to leave out their dulness; but such negative genius cannot detain us long; we shall return to Chaucer still with love. Some natures, which are really rude and ill-developed, have yet a higher standard of perfection than others which are refined and well balanced. Even the clown has taste, whose dictates, though he disregards them, are higher and purer than those which the artist obeys. If we have to wander through many dull and prosaic passages in Chaucer, we have at least the satisfaction of knowing that it is not an artificial dulness, but too easily matched by many passages in life. We confess that we feel a disposition commonly to concentrate sweets, and accumulate pleasures; but the poet may be presumed always to speak as a traveller, who leads us through a varied scenery, from one eminence to another, and it is, perhaps, more pleasing, after all, to meet with a fine thought in its natural setting. Surely fate has enshrined it in these circumstances for some end. Nature strews her nuts and flowers broadcast, and never collects them into heaps. This was the soil it grew in, and this the hour it bloomed in; if sun, wind, and rain came here to cherish and expand the flower, shall not we come here to pluck it?

A true poem is distinguished not so much by a felicitous expression, or any thought it suggests, as by the atmosphere which surrounds it. Most have beauty of outline merely, and are striking as the form and bearing of a stranger; but true verses come toward us indistinctly, as the very breath of all friendliness, and envelop us in their spirit and fragrance. Much of our poetry has the very best manners, but no character. It is only an unusual precision and elasticity of speech, as if its author had taken, not an intoxicating draught, but an electuary. It has the distinct outline of sculpture, and chronicles an early hour. Under the influence of passion all men speak thus distinctly, but wrath is not always divine.

There are two classes of men called poets. The one cultivates life, the other art,—one seeks food for nutriment, the other for flavor; one satisfies hunger, the other gratifies the palate. There are two kinds of writing, both great and rare; one that of genius, or the inspired, the other of intellect and taste, in the intervals of inspiration. The former is above criticism, always correct, giving the law to criticism. It vibrates and pulsates with life forever. It is sacred, and to be read with reverence, as the works of nature are studied. There are few instances of a sustained style of this kind; perhaps every man has spoken words, but the speaker is then careless of the record. Such a style removes us out of personal relations with its author; we do not take his words on our lips, but his sense into our hearts. It is the stream of inspiration, which bubbles out, now here, now there, now in this man, now in that. It matters not through what ice-crystals it is seen, now a fountain, now the ocean stream running under ground. It is in Shakespeare, Alpheus, in Burns, Arethuse; but ever the same.

The other is self-possessed and wise. It is reverent of genius, and greedy of inspiration. It is conscious in the highest and the least degree. It consists with the most perfect command of the faculties. It dwells in a repose as of the desert, and objects are as distinct in it as oases or palms in the horizon of sand. The train of thought moves with subdued and measured step, like a caravan. But the pen is only an instrument in its hand, and not instinct with life, like a longer arm. It leaves a thin varnish or glaze over all its work. The works of Goethe furnish remarkable instances of the latter.

There is no just and serene criticism as yet. Nothing is considered simply as it lies in the lap of eternal beauty, but our thoughts, as well as our bodies, must be dressed after the latest fashions. Our taste is too delicate and particular. It says nay to the poet's work, but never yea to his hope. It invites him to adorn his deformities, and not to cast them off by expansion, as the tree its bark. We are a people who live in a bright light, in houses of pearl and porcelain, and drink only light wines, whose teeth are easily set on edge by the least natural sour. If we had been consulted, the backbone of the earth would have been made, not of granite, but of Bristol spar. A modern author would have died in infancy in a ruder age. But the poet is something more than a scald, "a smoother and polisher of language"; he is a Cincinnatus in literature, and occupies no west end of the world. Like the sun, he will indifferently select his rhymes, and with a liberal taste weave into his verse the planet and the stubble.

In these old books the stucco has long since crumbled away, and we read what was sculptured in the granite. They are rude and massive in their proportions, rather than smooth and delicate in their finish. The workers in stone polish only their chimney ornaments, but their pyramids are roughly done. There is a soberness in a rough aspect, as of unhewn granite, which addresses a depth in us, but a polished surface hits only the ball of the eye. The true finish is the work of time, and the use to which a thing is put. The elements are still polishing the pyramids. Art may varnish and gild, but it can do no more. A work of genius is rough-hewn from the first, because it anticipates the lapse of time, and has an ingrained polish, which still appears when fragments are broken off, an essential quality of its substance. Its beauty is at the same time its strength, and it breaks with a lustre.

The great poem must have the stamp of greatness as well as its essence. The reader easily goes within the shallowest contemporary poetry, and informs it with all the life and promise of the day, as the pilgrim goes within the temple, and hears the faintest strains of the worshippers; but it will have to speak to posterity, traversing these deserts, through the ruins of its outmost walls, by the grandeur and beauty of its proportions.

———

But here on the stream of the Concord, where we have all the while been bodily, Nature, who is superior to all styles and ages, is now, with pensive face, composing her poem Autumn, with which no work of man will bear to be compared.

In summer we live out of doors, and have only impulses and feelings, which are all for action, and must wait commonly for the stillness and longer nights of autumn and winter before any thought will subside; we are sensible that behind the rustling leaves, and the stacks of grain, and the bare clusters of the grape, there is the field of a wholly new life, which no man has lived; that even this earth was made for more mysterious and nobler inhabitants than men and women. In the hues of October sunsets, we see the portals to other mansions than those which we occupy, not far off geographically, —

"There is a place beyond that flaming hill,
    From whence the stars their thin appearance shed,
A place beyond all place, where never ill,
    Nor impure thought was ever harbored."

Sometimes a mortal feels in himself Nature, not his Father but his Mother stirs within him, and he becomes immortal with her immortality. From time to time she claims kindredship with us, and some globule from her veins steals up into our own.

I am the autumnal sun,
With autumn gales my race is run;
When will the hazel put forth its flowers,
Or the grape ripen under my bowers?
When will the harvest or the hunter's moon,
Turn my midnight into mid-noon?
    I am all sere and yellow,
    And to my core mellow.
The mast is dropping within my woods,
The winter is lurking within my moods,
And the rustling of the withered leaf
Is the constant music of my grief.

To an unskilful rhymer the Muse thus spoke in prose:

The moon no longer reflects the day, but rises to her absolute rule, and the husbandman and hunter acknowledge her for their mistress. Asters and golden-rods reign along the way, and the life-everlasting withers not. The fields are reaped and shorn of their pride, but an inward verdure still crowns them. The thistle scatters its down on the pool, and yellow leaves clothe the vine, and naught disturbs the serious life of men. But behind the sheaves, and under the sod, there lurks a ripe fruit, which the reapers have not gathered, the true harvest of the year, which it bears forever, annually watering and maturing it, and man never severs the stalk which bears this palatable fruit.

Men nowhere, east or west, live yet a *natural* life, round which the vine clings, and which the elm willingly shadows. Man would desecrate it by his touch, and so the beauty of the world remains veiled to him. He needs not only to be spiritualized, but *naturalized*, on the soil of earth. Who shall conceive what kind of roof the heavens might extend over him, what seasons minister to him, and what employment dignify his life! Only the convalescent raise the veil of nature. An immortality in his life would confer immortality on his abode. The winds should be his breath, the seasons his moods, and he should impart of his serenity to Nature herself. But such as we know him he is ephemeral like the scenery which surrounds him, and does not aspire to an enduring existence. When we come down into the distant village, visible from the mountain-top, the nobler inhabitants with whom we peopled it have departed, and left only vermin in its desolate streets. It is the imagination of poets which puts those brave speeches into the mouths of their heroes. They may feign that Cato's last words were

> "The earth, the air, and seas I know, and all
> The joys and horrors of their peace and wars;
> And now will view the Gods' state and the stars,"

but such are not the thoughts nor the destiny of common men. What is this heaven which they expect, if it is no better than they expect? Are they prepared for a better than they can now imagine? Where is the heaven of him who dies on a stage, in a theatre? Here or nowhere is our heaven.

> "Although we see celestial bodies move
> Above the earth, the earth we till and love."

We can conceive of nothing more fair than something which we have experienced. "The remembrance of youth is a sigh." We linger in manhood to tell the dreams of our childhood, and they are half forgotten ere we have learned the language. We have need to be earth-born as well as heaven-born, γηγενεῖς, as was said of the Titans of old, or in a better sense than they. There have been heroes for whom this world seemed expressly prepared, as if creation had at last succeeded; whose daily life was the stuff of which our dreams are made, and whose presence enhanced the beauty and ampleness of Nature herself. Where they walked,

> "Largior hic campos æther et lumine vestit
> Purpureo: Solemque suum, sua sidera nôrunt."

"Here a more copious air invests the fields, and clothes with purple light; and they know their own sun and their own stars." We love to hear some men speak, though we hear not what they say; the very air they breathe is rich and perfumed, and the sound of their voices falls on the ear like the rustling of leaves or the crackling of the fire. They stand many deep. They have the heavens for their abettors, as those who have never stood from under them, and they look at the stars with an answering ray. Their eyes are like glow-worms, and their motions graceful and flowing, as if a place were already found for them, like rivers flowing through valleys. The distinctions of morality, of right and wrong, sense and nonsense, are petty, and have lost their significance, beside these pure primeval natures. When I consider the clouds stretched in stupendous masses across the sky, frowning with darkness or glowing with downy light, or gilded with the rays of the setting sun, like the battlements of a city in the heavens, their grandeur appears thrown away on the meanness of my employment; the drapery is altogether too rich for such poor acting. I am hardly worthy to be a suburban dweller outside those walls.

> "Unless above himself he can
> Erect himself, how poor a thing is man!"

With our music we would fain challenge transiently another and finer sort of intercourse than our daily toil permits. The strains come back to us amended in the echo, as when a friend reads our verse. Why have they so painted the fruits, and freighted them with such fragrance as to satisfy a more than animal appetite?

> "I asked the schoolman, his advice was free,
> But scored me out too intricate a way."

These things imply, perchance, that we live on the verge of another and purer realm, from which these odors and sounds are wafted over to us. The borders of our plot are set with flowers, whose seeds were blown from more Elysian fields adjacent. They are the pot-herbs of the gods. Some fairer fruits and sweeter fragrances wafted over to us, betray another realm's vicinity. There, too, does Echo dwell, and there is the abutment of the rainbow's arch.

> A finer race and finer fed
> Feast and revel o'er our head,
> And we titmen are only able
> To catch the fragments from their table.

> Theirs is the fragrance of the fruits,
> While we consume the pulp and roots.
> What are the moments that we stand
> Astonished on the Olympian land!

We need pray for no higher heaven than the pure senses can furnish, a *purely* sensuous life. Our present senses are but the rudiments of what they are destined to become. We are comparatively deaf and dumb and blind, and without smell or taste or feeling. Every generation makes the discovery, that its divine vigor has been dissipated, and each sense and faculty misapplied and debauched. The ears were made, not for such trivial uses as men are wont to suppose, but to hear celestial sounds. The eyes were not made for such grovelling uses as they are now put to and worn out by, but to behold beauty now invisible. May we not *see* God? Are we to be put off and amused in this life, as it were with a mere allegory? Is not Nature, rightly read, that of which she is commonly taken to be the symbol merely? When the common man looks into the sky, which he has not so much profaned, he thinks it less gross than the earth, and with reverence speaks of "the Heavens," but the seer will in the same sense speak of "the Earths," and his Father who is in them. "Did not he that made that which is *within*, make that which is *without* also?" What is it, then, to educate but to develop these divine germs called the senses? for individuals and states to deal magnanimously with the rising generation, leading it not into temptation,—not teach the eye to squint, nor attune the ear to profanity. But where is the instructed teacher? Where are the *normal* schools?

A Hindoo sage said, "As a dancer, having exhibited herself to the spectator, desists from the dance, so does Nature desist, having manifested herself to soul—. Nothing, in my opinion, is more gentle than Nature; once aware of having been seen, she does not again expose herself to the gaze of soul."

It is easier to discover another such a new world as Columbus did, than to go within one fold of this which we appear to know so well; the land is lost sight of, the compass varies,

and mankind mutiny; and still history accumulates like rubbish before the portals of nature. But there is only necessary
a moment's sanity and sound senses, to teach us that there is
a nature behind the ordinary, in which we have only some
vague pre-emption right and western reserve as yet. We live
on the outskirts of that region. Carved wood, and floating
boughs, and sunset skies, are all that we know of it. We are
not to be imposed on by the longest spell of weather. Let us
not, my friends, be wheedled and cheated into good behavior
to earn the salt of our eternal porridge, whoever they are that
attempt it. Let us wait a little, and not purchase any clearing
here, trusting that richer bottoms will soon be put up. It is
but thin soil where we stand; I have felt my roots in a richer
ere this. I have seen a bunch of violets in a glass vase, tied
loosely with a straw, which reminded me of myself.

> I am a parcel of vain strivings tied
> By a chance bond together,
> Dangling this way and that, their links
> Were made so loose and wide,
> Methinks,
> For milder weather.

> A bunch of violets without their roots,
> And sorrel intermixed,
> Encircled by a wisp of straw
> Once coiled about their shoots,
> The law
> By which I'm fixed.

> A nosegay which Time clutched from out
> Those fair Elysian fields,
> With weeds and broken stems, in haste,
> Doth make the rabble rout
> That waste
> The day he yields.

> And here I bloom for a short hour unseen,
> Drinking my juices up,
> With no root in the land

To keep my branches green,
But stand
In a bare cup.

Some tender buds were left upon my stem
In mimicry of life,
But ah! the children will not know,
Till time has withered them,
The woe
With which they're rife.

But now I see I was not plucked for naught,
And after in life's vase
Of glass set while I might survive,
But by a kind hand brought
Alive
To a strange place.

That stock thus thinned will soon redeem its hours,
And by another year,
Such as God knows, with freer air,
More fruits and fairer flowers
Will bear,
While I droop here.

This world has many rings, like Saturn, and we live now on the outmost of them all. None can say deliberately that he inhabits the same sphere, or is contemporary with, the flower which his hands have plucked, and though his feet may seem to crush it, inconceivable spaces and ages separate them, and perchance there is no danger that he will hurt it. What do the botanists know? Our lives should go between the lichen and the bark. The eye may see for the hand, but not for the mind. We are still being born, and have as yet but a dim vision of sea and land, sun, moon and stars, and shall not see clearly till after nine days at least. That is a pathetic inquiry among travellers and geographers after the site of ancient Troy. It is not near where they think it is. When a thing is decayed and gone, how indistinct must be the place it occupied!

The anecdotes of modern astronomy affect me in the same way as do those faint revelations of the Real which are vouchsafed to men from time to time, or rather from eternity to eternity. When I remember the history of that faint light in our firmament, which we call Venus, which ancient men regarded, and which most modern men still regard, as a bright spark attached to a hollow sphere revolving about our earth, but which we have discovered to be *another world*, in itself,— how Copernicus, reasoning long and patiently about the matter, predicted confidently concerning it, before yet the telescope had been invented, that if ever men came to see it more clearly than they did then, they would discover that it had phases like our moon, and that within a century after his death the telescope was invented, and that prediction verified, by Galileo,—I am not without hope that we may, even here and now obtain some accurate information concerning that OTHER WORLD which the instinct of mankind has so long predicted. Indeed, all that we call science, as well as all that we call poetry, is a particle of such information, accurate as far as it goes, though it be but to the confines of the truth. If we can reason so accurately, and with such wonderful confirmation of our reasoning, respecting so-called material objects and events infinitely removed beyond the range of our natural vision, so that the mind hesitates to trust its calculations even when they are confirmed by observation, why may not our speculations penetrate as far into the immaterial starry system, of which the former is but the outward and visible type? Surely, we are provided with senses as well fitted to penetrate the spaces of the real, the substantial, the eternal, as these outward are to penetrate the material universe. Veias, Menu, Zoroaster, Socrates, Christ, Shakespeare, Swedenborg,—these are some of our astronomers.

There are perturbations in our orbits produced by the influence of outlying spheres, and no astronomer has ever yet calculated the elements of that undiscovered world which produces them. I perceive in the common train of my thoughts a natural and uninterrupted sequence, each implying the next, or, if interruption occurs, it is occasioned by a new object being presented to my *senses*. But a steep, and sudden, and by these means unaccountable transition, is that from a comparatively narrow and partial, what is called common sense view of things, to an infinitely expanded and liberating one, from seeing things as men describe them, to seeing them as men cannot describe them. This implies a sense which is not common, but rare in the wisest man's experience; which is sensible or sentient of more than common.

In what enclosures does the astronomer loiter! His skies are shoal, and imagination, like a thirsty traveller, pants to be through their desert. The roving mind impatiently bursts the fetters of astronomical orbits, like cobwebs in a corner of its universe, and launches itself to where distance fails to follow, and law, such as science has discovered, grows weak and weary. The mind knows a distance and a space of which all those sums combined do not make a unit of measure,—the interval between that which *appears*, and that which *is*. I know that there are many stars, I know that they are far enough off, bright enough, steady enough in their orbits,— but what are they all worth? They are more waste land in the West,—star territory,—to be made slave States, perchance, if we colonize them. I have interest but for six feet of star, and that interest is transient. Then farewell to all ye bodies, such as I have known ye.

Every man, if he is wise, will stand on such bottom as will sustain him, and if one gravitates downward more strongly than another, he will not venture on those meads where the latter walks securely, but rather leave the cranberries which grow there unraked by himself. Perchance, some spring a higher freshet will float them within his reach, though they may be watery and frost-bitten by that time. Such shrivelled berries I have seen in many a poor man's garret, ay, in many a church-bin and state-coffer, and with a little water and heat they swell again to their original size and fairness, and added sugar enough, stead mankind for sauce to this world's dish.

What is called common sense is excellent in its department, and as invaluable as the virtue of conformity in the army and navy,—for there must be subordination,—but uncommon sense, that sense which is common only to the wisest, is as much more excellent as it is more rare. Some aspire to excel-

lence in the subordinate department, and may God speed
them. What Fuller says of masters of colleges is universally
applicable, that "a little alloy of dulness in a master of a college makes him fitter to manage secular affairs."

> "He that wants faith, and apprehends a grief
> Because he wants it, hath a true belief;
> And he that grieves because his grief 's so small,
> Has a true grief, and the best Faith of all."

Or be encouraged by this other poet's strain, —

> "By them went Fido marshal of the field:
>   Weak was his mother when she gave him day;
> And he at first a sick and weakly child,
>   As e'er with tears welcomed the sunny ray;
>   Yet when more years afford more growth and might,
>   A champion stout he was, and puissant knight,
> As ever came in field, or shone in armor bright.

> "Mountains he flings in seas with mighty hand;
>   Stops and turns back the sun's impetuous course;
> Nature breaks Nature's laws at his command;
>   No force of Hell or Heaven withstands his force;
>   Events to come yet many ages hence,
>   He present makes, by wondrous prescience;
> Proving the senses blind by being blind to sense."

"Yesterday, at dawn," says Hafiz, "God delivered me from
all worldly affliction; and amidst the gloom of night presented me with the water of immortality."

In the life of Sadi by Dowlat Shah occurs this sentence:
"The eagle of the immaterial soul of Shaikh Sadi shook from
his plumage the dust of his body."

Thus thoughtfully we were rowing homeward to find some
autumnal work to do, and help on the revolution of the seasons. Perhaps Nature would condescend to make use of us
even without our knowledge, as when we help to scatter her
seeds in our walks, and carry burrs and cockles on our clothes
from field to field.

All things are current found
On earthly ground,
Spirits and elements
Have their descents.

Night and day, year on year,
High and low, far and near,
These are our own aspects,
These are our own regrets.

Ye gods of the shore,
Who abide evermore,
I see your far headland,
Stretching on either hand;

I hear the sweet evening sounds
From your undecaying grounds;
Cheat me no more with time,
Take me to your clime.

As it grew later in the afternoon, and we rowed leisurely up the gentle stream, shut in between fragrant and blooming banks, where we had first pitched our tent, and drew nearer to the fields where our lives had passed, we seemed to detect the hues of our native sky in the southwest horizon. The sun was just setting behind the edge of a wooded hill, so rich a sunset as would never have ended but for some reason unknown to men, and to be marked with brighter colors than ordinary in the scroll of time. Though the shadows of the hills were beginning to steal over the stream, the whole river valley undulated with mild light, purer and more memorable than the noon. For so day bids farewell even to solitary vales uninhabited by man. Two herons, *Ardea herodias*, with their long and slender limbs relieved against the sky, were seen travelling high over our heads,—their lofty and silent flight, as they were wending their way at evening, surely not to alight in any marsh on the earth's surface, but, perchance, on the other side of our atmosphere, a symbol for the ages to study, whether impressed upon the sky, or sculptured amid the hieroglyphics of Egypt. Bound to some northern

meadow, they held on their stately, stationary flight, like the
storks in the picture, and disappeared at length behind the
clouds. Dense flocks of blackbirds were winging their way
along the river's course, as if on a short evening pilgrimage
to some shrine of theirs, or to celebrate so fair a sunset.

> "Therefore, as doth the pilgrim, whom the night
> Hastes darkly to imprison on his way,
> Think on thy home, my soul, and think aright
> Of what 's yet left thee of life's wasting day:
> Thy sun posts westward, passed is thy morn,
> And twice it is not given thee to be born."

The sun-setting presumed all men at leisure, and in a contemplative mood; but the farmer's boy only whistled the
more thoughtfully as he drove his cows home from pasture,
and the teamster refrained from cracking his whip, and
guided his team with a subdued voice. The last vestiges of
daylight at length disappeared, and as we rowed silently along
with our backs toward home through the darkness, only a few
stars being visible, we had little to say, but sat absorbed in
thought, or in silence listened to the monotonous sound of
our oars, a sort of rudimental music, suitable for the ear of
Night and the acoustics of her dimly lighted halls;

> "Pulsæ referunt ad sidera valles,"

and the valleys echoed the sound to the stars.

As we looked up in silence to those distant lights, we were
reminded that it was a rare imagination which first taught
that the stars are worlds, and had conferred a great benefit on
mankind. It is recorded in the Chronicle of Bernaldez, that in
Columbus's first voyage the natives "pointed towards the
heavens, making signs that they believed that there was all
power and holiness." We have reason to be grateful for celestial phenomena, for they chiefly answer to the ideal in man.
The stars are distant and unobtrusive, but bright and enduring as our fairest and most memorable experiences. "Let the
immortal depth of your soul lead you, but earnestly extend
your eyes upwards."

*   *   *

As the truest society approaches always nearer to solitude, so the most excellent speech finally falls into Silence. Silence is audible to all men, at all times, and in all places. She is when we hear inwardly, sound when we hear outwardly. Creation has not displaced her, but is her visible framework and foil. All sounds are her servants, and purveyors, proclaiming not only that their mistress is, but is a rare mistress, and earnestly to be sought after. They are so far akin to Silence, that they are but bubbles on her surface, which straightway burst, an evidence of the strength and prolificness of the undercurrent; a faint utterance of Silence, and then only agreeable to our auditory nerves when they contrast themselves with and relieve the former. In proportion as they do this, and are heighteners and intensifiers of the Silence, they are harmony and purest melody.

Silence is the universal refuge, the sequel to all dull discourses and all foolish acts, a balm to our every chagrin, as welcome after satiety as after disappointment; that background which the painter may not daub, be he master or bungler, and which, however awkward a figure we may have made in the foreground, remains ever our inviolable asylum, where no indignity can assail, no personality disturb us.

The orator puts off his individuality, and is then most eloquent when most silent. He listens while he speaks, and is a hearer along with his audience. Who has not hearkened to Her infinite din? She is Truth's speaking-trumpet, the sole oracle, the true Delphi and Dodona, which kings and courtiers would do well to consult, nor will they be balked by an ambiguous answer. For through Her all revelations have been made, and just in proportion as men have consulted her oracle within, they have obtained a clear insight, and their age has been marked as an enlightened one. But as often as they have gone gadding abroad to a strange Delphi and her mad priestess, their age has been dark and leaden. Such were garrulous and noisy eras, which no longer yield any sound, but the Grecian or silent and melodious era is ever sounding and resounding in the ears of men.

A good book is the plectrum with which our else silent lyres are struck. We not unfrequently refer the interest which belongs to our own unwritten sequel, to the written and com-

paratively lifeless body of the work. Of all books this sequel
is the most indispensable part. It should be the author's aim
to say once and emphatically, "He said," ἔφη, ἔ. This is the
most the book-maker can attain to. If he make his volume a
mole whereon the waves of Silence may break, it is well.

It were vain for me to endeavor to interrupt the Silence.
She cannot be done into English. For six thousand years men
have translated her with what fidelity belonged to each, and
still she is little better than a sealed book. A man may run on
confidently for a time, thinking he has her under his thumb,
and shall one day exhaust her, but he too must at last be
silent, and men remark only how brave a beginning he made;
for when he at length dives into her, so vast is the dispropor-
tion of the told to the untold, that the former will seem but
the bubble on the surface where he disappeared. Nevertheless,
we will go on, like those Chinese cliff swallows, feathering
our nests with the froth, which may one day be bread of life
to such as dwell by the sea-shore.

We had made about fifty miles this day with sail and oar,
and now, far in the evening, our boat was grating against the
bulrushes of its native port, and its keel recognized the Concord mud, where some semblance of its outline was still preserved in the flattened flags which had scarce yet erected
themselves since our departure; and we leaped gladly on
shore, drawing it up, and fastening it to the wild apple-tree,
whose stem still bore the mark which its chain had worn in
the chafing of the spring freshets.

THE END.

WALDEN

or,
Life in the Woods

I do not propose to write an ode to dejection, but to brag as lustily as chanticleer in the morning, standing on his roost, if only to wake my neighbors up. —Page 389.

Contents

Economy

WHEN I wrote the following pages, or rather the bulk of them, I lived alone, in the woods, a mile from any neighbor, in a house which I had built myself, on the shore of Walden Pond, in Concord, Massachusetts, and earned my living by the labor of my hands only. I lived there two years and two months. At present I am a sojourner in civilized life again.

I should not obtrude my affairs so much on the notice of my readers if very particular inquiries had not been made by my townsmen concerning my mode of life, which some would call impertinent, though they do not appear to me at all impertinent, but, considering the circumstances, very natural and pertinent. Some have asked what I got to eat; if I did not feel lonesome; if I was not afraid; and the like. Others have been curious to learn what portion of my income I devoted to charitable purposes; and some, who have large families, how many poor children I maintained. I will therefore ask those of my readers who feel no particular interest in me to pardon me if I undertake to answer some of these questions in this book. In most books, the *I*, or first person, is omitted; in this it will be retained; that, in respect to egotism, is the main difference. We commonly do not remember that it is, after all, always the first person that is speaking. I should not talk so much about myself if there were any body else whom I knew as well. Unfortunately, I am confined to this theme by the narrowness of my experience. Moreover, I, on my side, require of every writer, first or last, a simple and sincere account of his own life, and not merely what he has heard of other men's lives; some such account as he would send to his kindred from a distant land; for if he has lived sincerely, it must have been in a distant land to me. Perhaps these pages are more particularly addressed to poor students. As for the rest of my readers, they will accept such portions as apply to them. I trust that none will stretch the seams in putting on the coat, for it may do good service to him whom it fits.

I would fain say something, not so much concerning the

Chinese and Sandwich Islanders as you who read these pages, who are said to live in New England; something about your condition, especially your outward condition or circumstances in this world, in this town, what it is, whether it is necessary that it be as bad as it is, whether it cannot be improved as well as not. I have travelled a good deal in Concord; and every where, in shops, and offices, and fields, the inhabitants have appeared to me to be doing penance in a thousand re-markable ways. What I have heard of Bramins sitting exposed to four fires and looking in the face of the sun; or hanging suspended, with their heads downward, over flames; or look-ing at the heavens over their shoulders "until it becomes im-possible for them to resume their natural position, while from the twist of the neck nothing but liquids can pass into the stomach;" or dwelling, chained for life, at the foot of a tree; or measuring with their bodies, like caterpillars, the breadth of vast empires; or standing on one leg on the tops of pil-lars,—even these forms of conscious penance are hardly more incredible and astonishing than the scenes which I daily wit-ness. The twelve labors of Hercules were trifling in compari-son with those which my neighbors have undertaken; for they were only twelve, and had an end; but I could never see that these men slew or captured any monster or finished any labor. They have no friend Iolas to burn with a hot iron the root of the hydra's head, but as soon as one head is crushed, two spring up.

I see young men, my townsmen, whose misfortune it is to have inherited farms, houses, barns, cattle, and farming tools; for these are more easily acquired than got rid of. Better if they had been born in the open pasture and suckled by a wolf, that they might have seen with clearer eyes what field they were called to labor in. Who made them serfs of the soil? Why should they eat their sixty acres, when man is con-demned to eat only his peck of dirt? Why should they begin digging their graves as soon as they are born? They have got to live a man's life, pushing all these things before them, and get on as well as they can. How many a poor immortal soul have I met well nigh crushed and smothered under its load, creeping down the road of life, pushing before it a barn seventy-five feet by forty, its Augean stables never cleansed, and one hundred acres of land, tillage, mowing, pasture, and wood-lot! The portionless, who struggle with no such unnecessary inherited encumbrances, find it labor enough to subdue and cultivate a few cubic feet of flesh.

But men labor under a mistake. The better part of the man is soon ploughed into the soil for compost. By a seeming fate, commonly called necessity, they are employed, as it says in an old book, laying up treasures which moth and rust will corrupt and thieves break through and steal. It is a fool's life, as they will find when they get to the end of it, if not before. It is said that Deucalion and Pyrrha created men by throwing stones over their heads behind them: —

> Inde genus durum sumus, experiensque laborum,
> Et documenta damus quâ simus origine nati.

Or, as Raleigh rhymes it in his sonorous way, —

> "From thence our kind hard-hearted is, enduring pain
>   and care,
> Approving that our bodies of a stony nature are."

So much for a blind obedience to a blundering oracle, throwing the stones over their heads behind them, and not seeing where they fell.

Most men, even in this comparatively free country, through mere ignorance and mistake, are so occupied with the factitious cares and superfluously coarse labors of life that its finer fruits cannot be plucked by them. Their fingers, from excessive toil, are too clumsy and tremble too much for that. Actually, the laboring man has not leisure for a true integrity day by day; he cannot afford to sustain the manliest relations to men; his labor would be depreciated in the market. He has no time to be any thing but a machine. How can he remember well his ignorance—which his growth requires—who has so often to use his knowledge? We should feed and clothe him gratuitously sometimes, and recruit him with our cordials, before we judge of him. The finest qualities of our nature, like the bloom on fruits, can be preserved only by the most delicate handling. Yet we do not treat ourselves nor one another thus tenderly.

Some of you, we all know, are poor, find it hard to live,

are sometimes, as it were, gasping for breath. I have no doubt that some of you who read this book are unable to pay for all the dinners which you have actually eaten, or for the coats and shoes which are fast wearing or are already worn out, and have come to this page to spend borrowed or stolen time, robbing your creditors of an hour. It is very evident what mean and sneaking lives many of you live, for my sight has been whetted by experience; always on the limits, trying to get into business and trying to get out of debt, a very ancient slough, called by the Latins *æs alienum*, another's brass, for some of their coins were made of brass; still living, and dying, and buried by this other's brass; always promising to pay, promising to pay, to-morrow, and dying to-day, insolvent; seeking to curry favor, to get custom, by how many modes, only not state-prison offences; lying, flattering, voting, contracting yourselves into a nutshell of civility, or dilating into an atmosphere of thin and vaporous generosity, that you may persuade your neighbor to let you make his shoes, or his hat, or his coat, or his carriage, or import his groceries for him; making yourselves sick, that you may lay up something against a sick day, something to be tucked away in an old chest, or in a stocking behind the plastering, or, more safely, in the brick bank; no matter where, no matter how much or how little.

I sometimes wonder that we can be so frivolous, I may almost say, as to attend to the gross but somewhat foreign form of servitude called Negro Slavery, there are so many keen and subtle masters that enslave both north and south. It is hard to have a southern overseer; it is worse to have a northern one; but worst of all when you are the slave-driver of yourself. Talk of a divinity in man! Look at the teamster on the highway, wending to market by day or night; does any divinity stir within him? His highest duty to fodder and water his horses! What is his destiny to him compared with the shipping interests? Does not he drive for Squire Make-a-stir? How godlike, how immortal, is he? See how he cowers and sneaks, how vaguely all the day he fears, not being immortal nor divine, but the slave and prisoner of his own opinion of himself, a fame won by his own deeds. Public opinion is a weak tyrant compared with our own private opinion.

What a man thinks of himself, that it is which determines, or rather indicates, his fate. Self-emancipation even in the West Indian provinces of the fancy and imagination,—what Wilberforce is there to bring that about? Think, also, of the ladies of the land weaving toilet cushions against the last day, not to betray too green an interest in their fates! As if you could kill time without injuring eternity.

The mass of men lead lives of quiet desperation. What is called resignation is confirmed desperation. From the desperate city you go into the desperate country, and have to console yourself with the bravery of minks and muskrats. A stereotyped but unconscious despair is concealed even under what are called the games and amusements of mankind. There is no play in them, for this comes after work. But it is a characteristic of wisdom not to do desperate things.

When we consider what, to use the words of the catechism, is the chief end of man, and what are the true necessaries and means of life, it appears as if men had deliberately chosen the common mode of living because they preferred it to any other. Yet they honestly think there is no choice left. But alert and healthy natures remember that the sun rose clear. It is never too late to give up our prejudices. No way of thinking or doing, however ancient, can be trusted without proof. What every body echoes or in silence passes by as true to-day may turn out to be falsehood to-morrow, mere smoke of opinion, which some had trusted for a cloud that would sprinkle fertilizing rain on their fields. What old people say you cannot do you try and find that you can. Old deeds for old people, and new deeds for new. Old people did not know enough once, perchance, to fetch fresh fuel to keep the fire a-going; new people put a little dry wood under a pot, and are whirled round the globe with the speed of birds, in a way to kill old people, as the phrase is. Age is no better, hardly so well, qualified for an instructor as youth, for it has not profited so much as it has lost. One may almost doubt if the wisest man has learned any thing of absolute value by living. Practically, the old have no very important advice to give the young, their own experience has been so partial, and their lives have been such miserable failures, for private reasons, as they must believe; and it may

be that they have some faith left which belies that experience, and they are only less young than they were. I have
lived some thirty years on this planet, and I have yet to hear
the first syllable of valuable or even earnest advice from my
seniors. They have told me nothing, and probably cannot
tell me any thing, to the purpose. Here is life, an experiment
to a great extent untried by me; but it does not avail me that
they have tried it. If I have any experience which I think valuable, I am sure to reflect that this my Mentors said nothing
about.

One farmer says to me, "You cannot live on vegetable food
solely, for it furnishes nothing to make bones with;" and so
he religiously devotes a part of his day to supplying his system with the raw material of bones; walking all the while he
talks behind his oxen, which, with vegetable-made bones, jerk
him and his lumbering plough along in spite of every obstacle. Some things are really necessaries of life in some circles,
the most helpless and diseased, which in others are luxuries
merely, and in others still are entirely unknown.

The whole ground of human life seems to some to have
been gone over by their predecessors, both the heights and
the valleys, and all things to have been cared for. According
to Evelyn, "the wise Solomon prescribed ordinances for the
very distances of trees; and the Roman prætors have decided
how often you may go into your neighbor's land to gather
the acorns which fall on it without trespass, and what share
belongs to that neighbor." Hippocrates has even left directions how we should cut our nails; that is, even with the ends
of the fingers, neither shorter nor longer. Undoubtedly the
very tedium and ennui which presume to have exhausted the
variety and the joys of life are as old as Adam. But man's
capacities have never been measured; nor are we to judge of
what he can do by any precedents, so little has been tried.
Whatever have been thy failures hitherto, "be not afflicted,
my child, for who shall assign to thee what thou hast left
undone?"

We might try our lives by a thousand simple tests; as, for
instance, that the same sun which ripens my beans illumines
at once a system of earths like ours. If I had remembered this
it would have prevented some mistakes. This was not the

light in which I hoed them. The stars are the apexes of what wonderful triangles! What distant and different beings in the various mansions of the universe are contemplating the same one at the same moment! Nature and human life are as various as our several constitutions. Who shall say what prospect life offers to another? Could a greater miracle take place than for us to look through each other's eyes for an instant? We should live in all the ages of the world in an hour; ay, in all the worlds of the ages. History, Poetry, Mythology!—I know of no reading of another's experience so startling and informing as this would be.

The greater part of what my neighbors call good I believe in my soul to be bad, and if I repent of any thing, it is very likely to be my good behavior. What demon possessed me that I behaved so well? You may say the wisest thing you can old man,—you who have lived seventy years, not without honor of a kind,—I hear an irresistible voice which invites me away from all that. One generation abandons the enterprises of another like stranded vessels.

I think that we may safely trust a good deal more than we do. We may waive just so much care of ourselves as we honestly bestow elsewhere. Nature is as well adapted to our weakness as to our strength. The incessant anxiety and strain of some is a well nigh incurable form of disease. We are made to exaggerate the importance of what work we do; and yet how much is not done by us! or, what if we had been taken sick? How vigilant we are! determined not to live by faith if we can avoid it; all the day long on the alert, at night we unwillingly say our prayers and commit ourselves to uncertainties. So thoroughly and sincerely are we compelled to live, reverencing our life, and denying the possibility of change. This is the only way, we say; but there are as many ways as there can be drawn radii from one centre. All change is a miracle to contemplate; but it is a miracle which is taking place every instant. Confucius said, "To know that we know what we know, and that we do not know what we do not know, that is true knowledge." When one man has reduced a fact of the imagination to be a fact to his understanding, I foresee that all men will at length establish their lives on that basis.

✳   ✳   ✳

Let us consider for a moment what most of the trouble and anxiety which I have referred to is about, and how much it is necessary that we be troubled, or, at least, careful. It would be some advantage to live a primitive and frontier life, though in the midst of an outward civilization, if only to learn what are the gross necessaries of life and what methods have been taken to obtain them; or even to look over the old day-books of the merchants, to see what it was that men most commonly bought at the stores, what they stored, that is, what are the grossest groceries. For the improvements of ages have had but little influence on the essential laws of man's existence; as our skeletons, probably, are not to be distinguished from those of our ancestors.

By the words, *necessary of life*, I mean whatever, of all that man obtains by his own exertions, has been from the first, or from long use has become, so important to human life that few, if any, whether from savageness, or poverty, or philosophy, ever attempt to do without it. To many creatures there is in this sense but one necessary of life, Food. To the bison of the prairie it is a few inches of palatable grass, with water to drink; unless he seeks the Shelter of the forest or the mountain's shadow. None of the brute creation requires more than Food and Shelter. The necessaries of life for man in this climate may, accurately enough, be distributed under the several heads of Food, Shelter, Clothing, and Fuel; for not till we have secured these are we prepared to entertain the true problems of life with freedom and a prospect of success. Man has invented, not only houses, but clothes and cooked food; and possibly from the accidental discovery of the warmth of fire, and the consequent use of it, at first a luxury, arose the present necessity to sit by it. We observe cats and dogs acquiring the same second nature. By proper Shelter and Clothing we legitimately retain our own internal heat; but with an excess of these, or of Fuel, that is, with an external heat greater than our own internal, may not cookery properly be said to begin? Darwin, the naturalist, says of the inhabitants of Tierra del Fuego, that while his own party, who were well clothed and sitting close to a fire, were far from too warm, these naked savages, who were farther off, were observed, to his great surprise, "to be streaming with perspiration at undergoing such a roasting." So, we are told, the New Hollander goes naked with impunity, while the European shivers in his clothes. Is it impossible to combine the hardiness of these savages with the intellectualness of the civilized man? According to Liebig, man's body is a stove, and food the fuel which keeps up the internal combustion in the lungs. In cold weather we eat more, in warm less. The animal heat is the result of a slow combustion, and disease and death take place when this is too rapid; or for want of fuel, or from some defect in the draught, the fire goes out. Of course the vital heat is not to be confounded with fire; but so much for analogy. It appears, therefore, from the above list, that the expression, *animal life*, is nearly synonymous with the expression, *animal heat*; for while Food may be regarded as the Fuel which keeps up the fire within us,—and Fuel serves only to prepare that Food or to increase the warmth of our bodies by addition from without,—Shelter and Clothing also serve only to retain the *heat* thus generated and absorbed.

The grand necessity, then, for our bodies, is to keep warm, to keep the vital heat in us. What pains we accordingly take, not only with our Food, and Clothing, and Shelter, but with our beds, which are our night-clothes, robbing the nests and breasts of birds to prepare this shelter within a shelter, as the mole has its bed of grass and leaves at the end of its burrow! The poor man is wont to complain that this is a cold world; and to cold, no less physical than social, we refer directly a great part of our ails. The summer, in some climates, makes possible to man a sort of Elysian life. Fuel, except to cook his Food, is then unnecessary; the sun is his fire, and many of the fruits are sufficiently cooked by its rays; while Food generally is more various, and more easily obtained, and Clothing and Shelter are wholly or half unnecessary. At the present day, and in this country, as I find by my own experience, a few implements, a knife, an axe, a spade, a wheelbarrow, &c., and for the studious, lamplight, stationery, and access to a few books, rank next to necessaries, and can all be obtained at a trifling cost. Yet some, not wise, go to the other side of the globe, to barbarous and unhealthy regions, and devote themselves to trade for ten or twenty years, in order that they may

live,—that is, keep comfortably warm,—and die in New
England at last. The luxuriously rich are not simply kept comfortably warm, but unnaturally hot; as I implied before, they
are cooked, of course *à la mode*.

Most of the luxuries, and many of the so called comforts
of life, are not only not indispensable, but positive hinder-
ances to the elevation of mankind. With respect to luxuries
and comforts, the wisest have ever lived a more simple and
meagre life than the poor. The ancient philosophers,
Chinese, Hindoo, Persian, and Greek, were a class than
which none has been poorer in outward riches, none so rich
in inward. We know not much about them. It is remarkable
that *we* know so much of them as we do. The same is true
of the more modern reformers and benefactors of their race.
None can be an impartial or wise observer of human life but
from the vantage ground of what *we* should call voluntary
poverty. Of a life of luxury the fruit is luxury, whether in agriculture, or commerce, or literature, or art. There are nowadays professors of philosophy, but not philosophers. Yet it
is admirable to profess because it was once admirable to live.
To be a philosopher is not merely to have subtle thoughts,
nor even to found a school, but so to love wisdom as to live
according to its dictates, a life of simplicity, independence,
magnanimity, and trust. It is to solve some of the problems
of life, not only theoretically, but practically. The success of
great scholars and thinkers is commonly a courtier-like success, not kingly, not manly. They make shift to live merely
by conformity, practically as their fathers did, and are in no
sense the progenitors of a nobler race of men. But why do
men degenerate ever? What makes families run out? What is
the nature of the luxury which enervates and destroys nations? Are we sure that there is none of it in our own lives?
The philosopher is in advance of his age even in the outward
form of his life. He is not fed, sheltered, clothed, warmed,
like his contemporaries. How can a man be a philosopher
and not maintain his vital heat by better methods than other
men?

When a man is warmed by the several modes which I have
described, what does he want next? Surely not more warmth
of the same kind, as more and richer food, larger and more

splendid houses, finer and more abundant clothing, more numerous incessant and hotter fires, and the like. When he has
obtained those things which are necessary to life, there is another alternative than to obtain the superfluities; and that is,
to adventure on life now, his vacation from humbler toil having commenced. The soil, it appears, is suited to the seed, for
it has sent its radicle downward, and it may now send its
shoot upward also with confidence. Why has man rooted
himself thus firmly in the earth, but that he may rise in the
same proportion into the heavens above?—for the nobler
plants are valued for the fruit they bear at last in the air and
light, far from the ground, and are not treated like the humbler esculents, which, though they may be biennials, are cultivated only till they have perfected their root, and often cut
down at top for this purpose, so that most would not know
them in their flowering season.

I do not mean to prescribe rules to strong and valiant natures, who will mind their own affairs whether in heaven or
hell, and perchance build more magnificently and spend more
lavishly than the richest, without ever impoverishing themselves, not knowing how they live,—if, indeed, there are any
such, as has been dreamed; nor to those who find their
encouragement and inspiration in precisely the present condition of things, and cherish it with the fondness and enthusiasm of lovers,—and, to some extent, I reckon myself in this
number; I do not speak to those who are well employed, in
whatever circumstances, and they know whether they are well
employed or not;—but mainly to the mass of men who are
discontented, and idly complaining of the hardness of their
lot or of the times, when they might improve them. There are
some who complain most energetically and inconsolably of
any, because they are, as they say, doing their duty. I also
have in my mind that seemingly wealthy, but most terribly
impoverished class of all, who have accumulated dross, but
know not how to use it, or get rid of it, and thus have forged
their own golden or silver fetters.

If I should attempt to tell how I have desired to spend my
life in years past, it would probably surprise those of my readers who are somewhat acquainted with its actual history;

it would certainly astonish those who know nothing about it. I will only hint at some of the enterprises which I have cherished.

In any weather, at any hour of the day or night, I have been anxious to improve the nick of time, and notch it on my stick too; to stand on the meeting of two eternities, the past and future, which is precisely the present moment; to toe that line. You will pardon some obscurities, for there are more secrets in my trade than in most men's, and yet not voluntarily kept, but inseparable from its very nature. I would gladly tell all that I know about it, and never paint "No Admittance" on my gate.

I long ago lost a hound, a bay horse, and a turtledove, and am still on their trail. Many are the travellers I have spoken concerning them, describing their tracks and what calls they answered to. I have met one or two who had heard the hound, and the tramp of the horse, and even seen the dove disappear behind a cloud, and they seemed as anxious to recover them as if they had lost them themselves.

To anticipate, not the sunrise and the dawn merely, but, if possible, Nature herself! How many mornings, summer and winter, before yet any neighbor was stirring about his business, have I been about mine! No doubt, many of my townsmen have met me returning from this enterprise, farmers starting for Boston in the twilight, or woodchoppers going to their work. It is true, I never assisted the sun materially in his rising, but, doubt not, it was of the last importance only to be present at it.

So many autumn, ay, and winter days, spent outside the town, trying to hear what was in the wind, to hear and carry it express! I well-nigh sunk all my capital in it, and lost my own breath into the bargain, running in the face of it. If it had concerned either of the political parties, depend upon it, it would have appeared in the Gazette with the earliest intelligence. At other times watching from the observatory of some cliff or tree, to telegraph any new arrival; or waiting at evening on the hill-tops for the sky to fall, that I might catch something, though I never caught much, and that, manna-wise, would dissolve again in the sun.

For a long time I was reporter to a journal, of no very wide circulation, whose editor has never yet seen fit to print the bulk of my contributions, and, as is too common with writers, I got only my labor for my pains. However, in this case my pains were their own reward.

For many years I was self-appointed inspector of snow storms and rain storms, and did my duty faithfully; surveyor, if not of highways, then of forest paths and all across-lot routes, keeping them open, and ravines bridged and passable at all seasons, where the public heel had testified to their utility.

I have looked after the wild stock of the town, which give a faithful herdsman a good deal of trouble by leaping fences; and I have had an eye to the unfrequented nooks and corners of the farm; though I did not always know whether Jonas or Solomon worked in a particular field to-day; that was none of my business. I have watered the red huckleberry, the sand cherry and the nettle tree, the red pine and the black ash, the white grape and the yellow violet, which might have withered else in dry seasons.

In short, I went on thus for a long time, I may say it without boasting, faithfully minding my business, till it became more and more evident that my townsmen would not after all admit me into the list of town officers, nor make my place a sinecure with a moderate allowance. My accounts, which I can swear to have kept faithfully, I have, indeed, never got audited, still less accepted, still less paid and settled. However, I have not set my heart on that.

Not long since, a strolling Indian went to sell baskets at the house of a well-known lawyer in my neighborhood. "Do you wish to buy any baskets?" he asked. "No, we do not want any," was the reply. "What!" exclaimed the Indian as he went out the gate, "do you mean to starve us?" Having seen his industrious white neighbors so well off,—that the lawyer had only to weave arguments, and by some magic wealth and standing followed, he had said to himself; I will go into business; I will weave baskets; it is a thing which I can do. Thinking that when he had made the baskets he would have done his part, and then it would be the white man's to buy them. He had not discovered that it was necessary for him to make it worth the other's while to buy them, or at least make him

think that it was so, or to make something else which it
would be worth his while to buy. I too had woven a kind of
basket of a delicate texture, but I had not made it worth any
one's while to buy them. Yet not the less, in my case, did I
think it worth my while to weave them, and instead of studying how to make it worth men's while to buy my baskets, I
studied rather how to avoid the necessity of selling them. The
life which men praise and regard as successful is but one kind.
Why should we exaggerate any one kind at the expense of the
others?

Finding that my fellow-citizens were not likely to offer me
any room in the court house, or any curacy or living any
where else, but I must shift for myself, I turned my face more
exclusively than ever to the woods, where I was better known.
I determined to go into business at once, and not wait to
acquire the usual capital, using such slender means as I had
already got. My purpose in going to Walden Pond was not to
live cheaply nor to live dearly there, but to transact some private business with the fewest obstacles; to be hindered from
accomplishing which for want of a little common sense, a little enterprise and business talent, appeared not so sad as
foolish.

I have always endeavored to acquire strict business habits;
they are indispensable to every man. If your trade is with the
Celestial Empire, then some small counting house on the
coast, in some Salem harbor, will be fixture enough. You will
export such articles as the country affords, purely native products, much ice and pine timber and a little granite, always in
native bottoms. These will be good ventures. To oversee all
the details yourself in person; to be at once pilot and captain,
and owner and underwriter; to buy and sell and keep the accounts; to read every letter received, and write or read every
letter sent; to superintend the discharge of imports night and
day; to be upon many parts of the coast almost at the same
time;—often the richest freight will be discharged upon a Jersey shore;—to be your own telegraph, unweariedly sweeping
the horizon, speaking all passing vessels bound coastwise; to
keep up a steady despatch of commodities, for the supply of
such a distant and exorbitant market; to keep yourself informed of the state of the markets, prospects of war and peace

every where, and anticipate the tendencies of trade and civilization,—taking advantage of the results of all exploring expeditions, using new passages and all improvements in
navigation;—charts to be studied, the position of reefs and
new lights and buoys to be ascertained, and ever, and ever,
the logarithmic tables to be corrected, for by the error of
some calculator the vessel often splits upon a rock that should
have reached a friendly pier,—there is the untold fate of La
Perouse;—universal science to be kept pace with, studying
the lives of all great discoverers and navigators, great adven-
turers and merchants, from Hanno and the Phœnicians down
to our day; in fine, account of stock to be taken from time to
time, to know how you stand. It is a labor to task the faculties
of a man,—such problems of profit and loss, of interest, of
tare and tret, and gauging of all kinds in it, as demand a universal knowledge.

I have thought that Walden Pond would be a good place
for business, not solely on account of the railroad and the ice
trade; it offers advantages which it may not be good policy
to divulge; it is a good port and a good foundation. No Neva
marshes to be filled; though you must every where build on
piles of your own driving. It is said that a flood-tide, with a
westerly wind, and ice in the Neva, would sweep St. Peters-
burg from the face of the earth.

As this business was to be entered into without the usual
capital, it may not be easy to conjecture where those means,
that will still be indispensable to every such undertaking, were
to be obtained. As for Clothing, to come at once to the practical part of the question, perhaps we are led oftener by the
love of novelty, and a regard for the opinions of men, in pro-
curing it, than by a true utility. Let him who has work to do
recollect that the object of clothing is, first, to retain the vital
heat, and secondly, in this state of society, to cover nakedness,
and he may judge how much of any necessary or important
work may be accomplished without adding to his wardrobe.
Kings and queens who wear a suit but once, though made by
some tailor or dress-maker to their majesties, cannot know
the comfort of wearing a suit that fits. They are no better than
wooden horses to hang the clean clothes on. Every day our

garments become more assimilated to ourselves, receiving the
impress of the wearer's character, until we hesitate to lay
them aside, without such delay and medical appliances and
some such solemnity even as our bodies. No man ever stood
the lower in my estimation for having a patch in his clothes;
yet I am sure that there is greater anxiety, commonly, to have
fashionable, or at least clean and unpatched clothes, than to
have a sound conscience. But even if the rent is not mended,
perhaps the worst vice betrayed is improvidence. I sometimes
try my acquaintances by such tests as this;—who could wear
a patch, or two extra seams only, over the knee? Most behave
as if they believed that their prospects for life would be ruined
if they should do it. It would be easier for them to hobble to
town with a broken leg than with a broken pantaloon. Often
if an accident happens to a gentleman's legs, they can be
mended; but if a similar accident happens to the legs of his
pantaloons, there is no help for it; for he considers, not what
is truly respectable, but what is respected. We know but few
men, a great many coats and breeches. Dress a scarecrow in
your last shift, you standing shiftless by, who would not
soonest salute the scarecrow? Passing a cornfield the other
day, close by a hat and coat on a stake, I recognized the
owner of the farm. He was only a little more weather-beaten
than when I saw him last. I have heard of a dog that barked
at every stranger who approached his master's premises with
clothes on, but was easily quieted by a naked thief. It is an
interesting question how far men would retain their relative
rank if they were divested of their clothes. Could you, in such
a case, tell surely of any company of civilized men, which belonged to the most respected class? When Madam Pfeiffer,
in her adventurous travels round the world, from east to
west, had got so near home as Asiatic Russia, she says that
she felt the necessity of wearing other than a travelling dress,
when she went to meet the authorities, for she " was now in
a civilized country, where —— — people are judged of by
their clothes." Even in our democratic New England towns
the accidental possession of wealth, and its manifestation in
dress and equipage alone, obtain for the possessor almost
universal respect. But they who yield such respect, numerous
as they are, are so far heathen, and need to have a mission-

ary sent to them. Beside, clothes introduced sewing, a kind of work which you may call endless; a woman's dress, at least, is never done.

A man who has at length found something to do will not need to get a new suit to do it in; for him the old will do, that has lain dusty in the garret for an indeterminate period. Old shoes will serve a hero longer than they have served his valet,—if a hero ever has a valet,—bare feet are older than shoes, and he can make them do. Only they who go to soirées and legislative halls must have new coats, coats to change as often as the man changes in them. But if my jacket and trousers, my hat and shoes, are fit to worship God in, they will do; will they not? Who ever saw his old clothes,—his old coat, actually worn out, resolved into its primitive elements, so that it was not a deed of charity to bestow it on some poor boy, by him perchance to be bestowed on some poorer still, or shall we say richer, who could do with less? I say, beware of all enterprises that require new clothes, and not rather a new wearer of clothes. If there is not a new man, how can the new clothes be made to fit? If you have any enterprise before you, try it in your old clothes. All men want, not something to *do with*, but something to *do*, or rather something to *be*. Perhaps we should never procure a new suit, however ragged or dirty the old, until we have so conducted, so enterprised or sailed in some way, that we feel like new men in the old, and that to retain it would be like keeping new wine in old bottles. Our moulting season, like that of the fowls, must be a crisis in our lives. The loon retires to solitary ponds to spend it. Thus also the snake casts its slough, and the caterpillar its wormy coat, by an internal industry and expansion; for clothes are but our outmost cuticle and mortal coil. Otherwise we shall be found sailing under false colors, and be inevitably cashiered at last by our own opinion, as well as that of mankind.

We don garment after garment, as if we grew like exogenous plants by addition without. Our outside and often thin and fanciful clothes are our epidermis or false skin, which partakes not of our life, and may be stripped off here and there without fatal injury; our thicker garments, constantly worn, are our cellular integument, or cortex; but our shirts are our liber or true bark, which cannot be removed without girdling and so destroying the man. I believe that all races at some seasons wear something equivalent to the shirt. It is desirable that a man be clad so simply that he can lay his hands on himself in the dark, and that he live in all respects so compactly and preparedly, that, if an enemy take the town, he can, like the old philosopher, walk out the gate empty-handed without anxiety. While one thick garment is, for most purposes, as good as three thin ones, and cheap clothing can be obtained at prices really to suit customers; while a thick coat can be bought for five dollars, which will last as many years, thick pantaloons for two dollars, cowhide boots for a dollar and a half a pair, a summer hat for a quarter of a dollar, and a winter cap for sixty-two and a half cents, or a better be made at home at a nominal cost, where is he so poor that, clad in such a suit, *of his own earning*, there will not be found wise men to do him reverence?

When I ask for a garment of a particular form, my tailoress tells me gravely, "They do not make them so now," not emphasizing the "They" at all, as if she quoted an authority as impersonal as the Fates, and I find it difficult to get made what I want, simply because she cannot believe that I mean what I say, that I am so rash. When I hear this oracular sentence, I am for a moment absorbed in thought, emphasizing to myself each word separately that I may come at the meaning of it, that I may find out by what degree of consanguinity *They* are related to *me*, and what authority they may have in an affair which affects me so nearly; and, finally, I am inclined to answer her with equal mystery, and without any more emphasis of the "they,"—"It is true, they did not make them so recently, but they do now." Of what use this measuring of me if she does not measure my character, but only the breadth of my shoulders, as it were a peg to hang the coat on? We worship not the Graces, nor the Parcæ, but Fashion. She spins and weaves and cuts with full authority. The head monkey at Paris puts on a traveller's cap, and all the monkeys in America do the same. I sometimes despair of getting any thing quite simple and honest done in this world by the help of men. They would have to be passed through a powerful press first, to squeeze their old notions out of them, so that they would not soon get upon their legs again, and then there would be some one in the company with a maggot in his head, hatched from an egg deposited there nobody knows when, for not even fire kills these things, and you would have lost your labor. Nevertheless, we will not forget that some Egyptian wheat was handed down to us by a mummy.

On the whole, I think that it cannot be maintained that dressing has in this or any country risen to the dignity of an art. At present men make shift to wear what they can get. Like shipwrecked sailors, they put on what they can find on the beach, and at a little distance, whether of space or time, laugh at each other's masquerade. Every generation laughs at the old fashions, but follows religiously the new. We are amused at beholding the costume of Henry VIII., or Queen Elizabeth, as much as if it was that of the King and Queen of the Cannibal Islands. All costume off a man is pitiful or grotesque. It is only the serious eye peering from and the sincere life passed within it, which restrain laughter and consecrate the costume of any people. Let Harlequin be taken with a fit of the colic and his trappings will have to serve that mood too. When the soldier is hit by a cannon ball rags are as becoming as purple.

The childish and savage taste of men and women for new patterns keeps how many shaking and squinting through kaleidoscopes that they may discover the particular figure which this generation requires to-day. The manufacturers have learned that this taste is merely whimsical. Of two patterns which differ only by a few threads more or less of a particular color, the one will be sold readily, the other lie on the shelf, though it frequently happens that after the lapse of a season the latter becomes the most fashionable. Comparatively, tattooing is not the hideous custom which it is called. It is not barbarous merely because the printing is skin-deep and unalterable.

I cannot believe that our factory system is the best mode by which men may get clothing. The condition of the operatives is becoming every day more like that of the English; and it cannot be wondered at, since, as far as I have heard or observed, the principal object is, not that mankind may be

well and honestly clad, but, unquestionably, that the corpo-
rations may be enriched. In the long run men hit only what
they aim at. Therefore, though they should fail immediately,
they had better aim at something high.

As for a Shelter, I will not deny that this is now a necessary of life, though there are instances of men having done
without it for long periods in colder countries than this.
Samuel Laing says that "The Laplander in his skin dress, and
in a skin bag which he puts over his head and shoulders, will
sleep night after night on the snow——in a degree of cold
which would extinguish the life of one exposed to it in any
woollen clothing." He had seen them asleep thus. Yet he
adds, "They are not hardier than other people." But, probably, man did not live long on the earth without discovering
the convenience which there is in a house, the domestic
comforts, which phrase may have originally signified the sat-
isfactions of the house more than of the family; though
these must be extremely partial and occasional in those climates where the house is associated in our thoughts with
winter or the rainy season chiefly, and two thirds of the
year, except for a parasol, is unnecessary. In our climate, in
the summer, it was formerly almost solely a covering at
night. In the Indian gazettes a wigwam was the symbol of a
day's march, and a row of them cut or painted on the bark
of a tree signified that so many times they had camped. Man
was not made so large limbed and robust but that he must
seek to narrow his world, and wall in a space such as fitted
him. He was at first bare and out of doors; but though this
was pleasant enough in serene and warm weather, by daylight, the rainy season and the winter, to say nothing of the
torrid sun, would perhaps have nipped his race in the bud if
he had not made haste to clothe himself with the shelter of a
house. Adam and Eve, according to the fable, wore the
bower before other clothes. Man wanted a home, a place of
warmth, or comfort, first of physical warmth, then the
warmth of the affections.

We may imagine a time when, in the infancy of the human race, some enterprising mortal crept into a hollow in a
rock for shelter. Every child begins the world again, to some

extent, and loves to stay out doors, even in wet and cold. It plays house, as well as horse, having an instinct for it. Who does not remember the interest with which when young he looked at shelving rocks, or any approach to a cave? It was the natural yearning of that portion of our most primitive ancestor which still survived in us. From the cave we have advanced to roofs of palm leaves, of bark and boughs, of linen woven and stretched, of grass and straw, of boards and shingles, of stones and tiles. At last, we know not what it is to live in the open air, and our lives are domestic in more senses than we think. From the hearth to the field is a great distance. It would be well perhaps if we were to spend more of our days and nights without any obstruction between us and the celestial bodies, if the poet did not speak so much from under a roof, or the saint dwell there so long. Birds do not sing in caves, nor do doves cherish their innocence in dovecots.

However, if one designs to construct a dwelling house, it behooves him to exercise a little Yankee shrewdness, lest after all he find himself in a workhouse, a labyrinth without a clew, a museum, an almshouse, a prison, or a splendid mausoleum instead. Consider first how slight a shelter is absolutely necessary. I have seen Penobscot Indians, in this town, living in tents of thin cotton cloth, while the snow was nearly a foot deep around them, and I thought that they would be glad to have it deeper to keep out the wind. Formerly, when how to get my living honestly, with freedom left for my proper pursuits, was a question which vexed me even more than it does now, for unfortunately I am become somewhat callous, I used to see a large box by the railroad, six feet long by three wide, in which the laborers locked up their tools at night, and it suggested to me that every man who was hard pushed might get such a one for a dollar, and, having bored a few auger holes in it, to admit the air at least, get into it when it rained and at night, and hook down the lid, and so have freedom in his love, and in his soul be free. This did not appear the worst, nor by any means a despicable alternative. You could sit up as late as you pleased, and, whenever you got up, go abroad without any landlord or house-lord dogging you for rent. Many a man is harassed to death to pay the rent of a larger and more luxurious box who would not have frozen to death in such a box as this. I am far from jesting. Economy is a subject which admits of being treated with levity, but it cannot so be disposed of. A comfortable house for a rude and hardy race, that lived mostly out of doors, was once made here almost entirely of such materials as Nature furnished ready to their hands. Gookin, who was superintendent of the Indians subject to the Massachusetts Colony, writing in 1674, says, "The best of their houses are covered very neatly, tight and warm, with barks of trees, slipped from their bodies at those seasons when the sap is up, and made into great flakes, with pressure of weighty timber, when they are green. . . . The meaner sort are covered with mats which they make of a kind of bulrush, and are also indifferently tight and warm, but not so good as the former. . . . Some I have seen, sixty or a hundred feet long and thirty feet broad. . . . I have often lodged in their wigwams, and found them as warm as the best English houses." He adds, that they were commonly carpeted and lined within with well-wrought embroidered mats, and were furnished with various utensils. The Indians had advanced so far as to regulate the effect of the wind by a mat suspended over the hole in the roof and moved by a string. Such a lodge was in the first instance constructed in a day or two at most, and taken down and put up in a few hours; and every family owned one, or its apartment in one.

In the savage state every family owns a shelter as good as the best, and sufficient for its coarser and simpler wants; but I think that I speak within bounds when I say that, though the birds of the air have their nests, and the foxes their holes, and the savages their wigwams, in modern civilized society not more than one half the families own a shelter. In the large towns and cities, where civilization especially prevails, the number of those who own a shelter is a very small fraction of the whole. The rest pay an annual tax for this outside garment of all, become indispensable summer and winter, which would buy a village of Indian wigwams, but now helps to keep them poor as long as they live. I do not mean to insist here on the disadvantage of hiring compared with owning, but it is evident that the savage owns his shelter because it

costs so little, while the civilized man hires his commonly because he cannot afford to own it; nor can he, in the long run,
any better afford to hire. But, answers one, by merely paying
this tax the poor civilized man secures an abode which is a
palace compared with the savage's. An annual rent of from
twenty-five to a hundred dollars, these are the country rates,
entitles him to the benefit of the improvements of centuries,
spacious apartments, clean paint and paper, Rumford fireplace, back plastering, Venetian blinds, copper pump, spring
lock, a commodious cellar, and many other things. But how
happens it that he who is said to enjoy these things is so
commonly a *poor* civilized man, while the savage, who has
them not, is rich as a savage? If it is asserted that civilization
is a real advance in the condition of man,—and I think that
it is, though only the wise improve their advantages,—it
must be shown that it has produced better dwellings without
making them more costly; and the cost of a thing is the
amount of what I will call life which is required to be exchanged for it, immediately or in the long run. An average
house in this neighborhood costs perhaps eight hundred dollars, and to lay up this sum will take from ten to fifteen years
of the laborer's life, even if he is not encumbered with a family;—estimating the pecuniary value of every man's labor at
one dollar a day, for if some receive more, others receive
less;—so that he must have spent more than half his life commonly before *his* wigwam will be earned. If we suppose him
to pay a rent instead, this is but a doubtful choice of evils.
Would the savage have been wise to exchange his wigwam for
a palace on these terms?

It may be guessed that I reduce almost the whole advantage
of holding this superfluous property as a fund in store against
the future, so far as the individual is concerned, mainly to the
defraying of funeral expenses. But perhaps a man is not required to bury himself. Nevertheless this points to an important distinction between the civilized man and the savage;
and, no doubt, they have designs on us for our benefit, in
making the life of a civilized people an *institution*, in which
the life of the individual is to a great extent absorbed, in order
to preserve and perfect that of the race. But I wish to show
at what a sacrifice this advantage is at present obtained, and

to suggest that we may possibly so live as to secure all the advantage without suffering any of the disadvantage. What mean ye by saying that the poor ye have always with you, or that the fathers have eaten sour grapes, and the children's teeth are set on edge?

"As I live, saith the Lord God, ye shall not have occasion any more to use this proverb in Israel."

"Behold all souls are mine; as the soul of the father, so also the soul of the son is mine: the soul that sinneth it shall die."

When I consider my neighbors, the farmers of Concord, who are at least as well off as the other classes, I find that for the most part they have been toiling twenty, thirty, or forty years, that they may become the real owners of their farms, which commonly they have inherited with encumbrances, or else bought with hired money,—and we may regard one third of that toil as the cost of their houses,—but commonly they have not paid for them yet. It is true, the encumbrances sometimes outweigh the value of the farm, so that the farm itself becomes one great encumbrance, and still a man is found to inherit it, being well acquainted with it, as he says. On applying to the assessors, I am surprised to learn that they cannot at once name a dozen in the town who own their farms free and clear. If you would know the history of these homesteads, inquire at the bank where they are mortgaged. The man who has actually paid for his farm with labor on it is so rare that every neighbor can point to him. I doubt if there are three such men in Concord. What has been said of the merchants, that a very large majority, even ninety-seven in a hundred, are sure to fail, is equally true of the farmers. With regard to the merchants, however, one of them says pertinently that a great part of their failures are not genuine pecuniary failures, but merely failures to fulfil their en-gagements, because it is inconvenient; that is, it is the moral character that breaks down. But this puts an infinitely worse face on the matter, and suggests, beside, that probably not even the other three succeed in saving their souls, but are perchance bankrupt in a worse sense than they who fail hon-estly. Bankruptcy and repudiation are the spring-boards from which much of our civilization vaults and turns its somersets, but the savage stands on the unelastic plank of famine. Yet the Middlesex Cattle Show goes off here with *éclat* annually, as if all the joints of the agricultural machine were suent.

The farmer is endeavoring to solve the problem of a livelihood by a formula more complicated than the problem itself. To get his shoestrings he speculates in herds of cattle. With consummate skill he has set his trap with a hair springe to catch comfort and independence, and then, as he turned away, got his own leg into it. This is the reason he is poor; and for a similar reason we are all poor in respect to a thousand savage comforts, though surrounded by luxuries. As Chapman sings,—

> "The false society of men—
> —for earthly greatness
> All heavenly comforts rarefies to air."

And when the farmer has got his house, he may not be the richer but the poorer for it, and it be the house that has got him. As I understand it, that was a valid objection urged by Momus against the house which Minerva made, that she "had not made it movable, by which means a bad neighborhood might be avoided;" and it may still be urged, for our houses are such unwieldy property that we are often imprisoned rather than housed in them; and the bad neighborhood to be avoided is our own scurvy selves. I know one or two families, at least, in this town, who, for nearly a generation, have been wishing to sell their houses in the outskirts and move into the village, but have not been able to accomplish it, and only death will set them free.

Granted that the *majority* are able at last either to own or hire the modern house with all its improvements. While civilization has been improving our houses, it has not equally improved the men who are to inhabit them. It has created palaces, but it was not so easy to create noblemen and kings. And *if the civilized man's pursuits are no worthier than the savage's, if he is employed the greater part of his life in obtaining gross necessaries and comforts merely, why should he have a better dwelling than the former?*

But how do the poor *minority* fare? Perhaps it will be found, that just in proportion as some have been placed in

outward circumstances above the savage, others have been degraded below him. The luxury of one class is counterbalanced
by the indigence of another. On the one side is the palace, on
the other are the almshouse and "silent poor." The myriads
who built the pyramids to be the tombs of the Pharaohs were
fed on garlic, and it may be were not decently buried themselves. The mason who finishes the cornice of the palace returns at night perchance to a hut not so good as a wigwam.
It is a mistake to suppose that, in a country where the usual
evidences of civilization exist, the condition of a very large
body of the inhabitants may not be as degraded as that of
savages. I refer to the degraded poor, not now to the degraded rich. To know this I should not need to look farther
than to the shanties which every where border our railroads,
that last improvement in civilization; where I see in my daily
walks human beings living in sties, and all winter with an
open door, for the sake of light, without any visible, often
imaginable, wood pile, and the forms of both old and young
are permanently contracted by the long habit of shrinking
from cold and misery, and the development of all their limbs
and faculties is checked. It certainly is fair to look at that class
by whose labor the works which distinguish this generation
are accomplished. Such too, to a greater or less extent, is the
condition of the operatives of every denomination in England, which is the great workhouse of the world. Or I could
refer you to Ireland, which is marked as one of the white or
enlightened spots on the map. Contrast the physical condition of the Irish with that of the North American Indian, or
the South Sea Islander, or any other savage race before it was
degraded by contact with the civilized man. Yet I have no
doubt that that people's rulers are as wise as the average of
civilized rulers. Their condition only proves what squalidness
may consist with civilization. I hardly need refer now to the
laborers in our Southern States who produce the staple exports of this country, and are themselves a staple production
of the South. But to confine myself to those who are said to
be in *moderate* circumstances.

Most men appear never to have considered what a house
is, and are actually though needlessly poor all their lives because they think that they must have such a one as their

neighbors have. As if one were to wear any sort of coat which
the tailor might cut out for him, or, gradually leaving off
palmleaf hat or cap of woodchuck skin, complain of hard
times because he could not afford to buy him a crown! It is
possible to invent a house still more convenient and luxurious
than we have, which yet all would admit that man could not
afford to pay for. Shall we always study to obtain more of
these things, and not sometimes to be content with less? Shall
the respectable citizen thus gravely teach, by precept and example, the necessity of the young man's providing a certain
number of superfluous glow-shoes, and umbrellas, and empty
guest chambers for empty guests, before he dies? Why should
not our furniture be as simple as the Arab's or the Indian's?
When I think of the benefactors of the race, whom we have
apotheosized as messengers from heaven, bearers of divine
gifts to man, I do not see in my mind any retinue at their
heels, any car-load of fashionable furniture. Or what if I were
to allow—would it not be a singular allowance?—that our
furniture should be more complex than the Arab's, in proportion as we are morally and intellectually his superiors! At
present our houses are cluttered and defiled with it, and a
good housewife would sweep out the greater part into the
dust hole, and not leave her morning's work undone. Morning work! By the blushes of Aurora and the music of Memnon, what should be man's *morning work* in this world? I had
three pieces of limestone on my desk, but I was terrified to
find that they required to be dusted daily, when the furniture
of my mind was all undusted still, and I threw them out the
window in disgust. How, then, could I have a furnished
house? I would rather sit in the open air, for no dust gathers
on the grass, unless where man has broken ground.

It is the luxurious and dissipated who set the fashions
which the herd so diligently follow. The traveller who stops
at the best houses, so called, soon discovers this, for the pub-
licans presume him to be a Sardanapalus, and if he resigned
himself to their tender mercies he would soon be completely
emasculated. I think that in the railroad car we are inclined to
spend more on luxury than on safety and convenience, and it
threatens without attaining these to become no better than a
modern drawing room, with its divans, and ottomans, and

sunshades, and a hundred other oriental things, which we are taking west with us, invented for the ladies of the harem and the effeminate natives of the Celestial Empire, which Jonathan should be ashamed to know the names of. I would rather sit on a pumpkin and have it all to myself, than be crowded on a velvet cushion. I would rather ride on earth in an ox cart with a free circulation, than go to heaven in the fancy car of an excursion train and breathe a *malaria* all the way.

The very simplicity and nakedness of man's life in the primitive ages imply this advantage at least, that they left him still but a sojourner in nature. When he was refreshed with food and sleep he contemplated his journey again. He dwelt, as it were, in a tent in this world, and was either threading the valleys, or crossing the plains, or climbing the mountain tops. But lo! men have become the tools of their tools. The man who independently plucked the fruits when he was hungry is become a farmer; and he who stood under a tree for shelter, a housekeeper. We now no longer camp as for a night, but have settled down on earth and forgotten heaven. We have adopted Christianity merely as an improved method of *agri*-culture. We have built for this world a family mansion, and for the next a family tomb. The best works of art are the expression of man's struggle to free himself from this condition, but the effect of our art is merely to make this low state comfortable and that higher state to be forgotten. There is actually no place in this village for a work of *fine* art, if any had come down to us, to stand, for our lives, our houses and streets, furnish no proper pedestal for it. There is not a nail to hang a picture on, nor a shelf to receive the bust of a hero or a saint. When I consider how our houses are built and paid for, or not paid for, and their internal economy managed and sustained, I wonder that the floor does not give way under the visitor while he is admiring the gewgaws upon the mantel-piece, and let him through into the cellar, to some solid and honest though earthy foundation. I cannot but perceive that this so called rich and refined life is a thing jumped at, and I do not get on in the enjoyment of the *fine* arts which adorn it, my attention being wholly occupied with the jump; for I remember that the greatest genuine leap, due to human muscles alone, on record, is that of certain wandering Arabs, who are said to have cleared twenty-five feet on level ground. Without factitious support, man is sure to come to earth again beyond that distance. The first question which I am tempted to put to the proprietor of such great impropriety is, Who bolsters you? Are you one of the ninety-seven who fail? or of the three who succeed? Answer me these questions, and then perhaps I may look at your bawbles and find them ornamental. The cart before the horse is neither beautiful nor useful. Before we can adorn our houses with beautiful objects the walls must be stripped, and our lives must be stripped, and beautiful housekeeping and beautiful living be laid for a foundation: now, a taste for the beautiful is most cultivated out of doors, where there is no house and no housekeeper.

Old Johnson, in his "Wonder-Working Providence," speaking of the first settlers of this town, with whom he was contemporary, tells us that "they burrow themselves in the earth for their first shelter under some hillside, and, casting the soil aloft upon timber, they make a smoky fire against the earth, at the highest side." They did not "provide them houses," says he, "till the earth, by the Lord's blessing, brought forth bread to feed them," and the first year's crop was so light that "they were forced to cut their bread very thin for a long season." The secretary of the Province of New Netherland, writing in Dutch, in 1650, for the information of those who wished to take up land there, states more particularly, that "those in New Netherland, and especially in New England, who have no means to build farm houses at first according to their wishes, dig a square pit in the ground, cellar fashion, six or seven feet deep, as long and as broad as they think proper, case the earth inside with wood all round the wall, and line the wood with the bark of trees or something else to prevent the caving in of the earth; floor this cellar with plank, and wainscot it overhead for a ceiling, raise a roof of spars clear up, and cover the spars with bark or green sods, so that they can live dry and warm in these houses with their entire families for two, three, and four years, it being understood that partitions are run through those cellars which are adapted to the size of the family. The wealthy and principal men in New

England, in the beginning of the colonies, commenced their first dwelling houses in this fashion for two reasons; firstly, in order not to waste time in building, and not to want food the next season; secondly, in order not to discourage poor laboring people whom they brought over in numbers from Fatherland. In the course of three or four years, when the country became adapted to agriculture, they built themselves handsome houses, spending on them several thousands."

In this course which our ancestors took there was a show of prudence at least, as if their principle were to satisfy the more pressing wants first. But are the more pressing wants satisfied now? When I think of acquiring for myself one of our luxurious dwellings, I am deterred, for, so to speak, the country is not yet adapted to *human* culture, and we are still forced to cut our *spiritual* bread far thinner than our fore-fathers did their wheaten. Not that all architectural ornament is to be neglected even in the rudest periods; but let our houses first be lined with beauty, where they come in contact with our lives, like the tenement of the shellfish, and not overlaid with it. But, alas! I have been inside one or two of them, and know what they are lined with.

Though we are not so degenerate but that we might pos-sibly live in a cave or a wigwam or wear skins to-day, it cer-tainly is better to accept the advantages, though so dearly bought, which the invention and industry of mankind offer. In such a neighborhood as this, boards and shingles, lime and bricks, are cheaper and more easily obtained than suitable caves, or whole logs, or bark in sufficient quantities, or even well-tempered clay or flat stones. I speak understandingly on this subject, for I have made myself acquainted with it both theoretically and practically. With a little more wit we might use these materials so as to become richer than the richest now are, and make our civilization a blessing. The civilized man is a more experienced and wiser savage. But to make haste to my own experiment.

Near the end of March, 1845, I borrowed an axe and went down to the woods by Walden Pond, nearest to where I in-tended to build my house, and began to cut down some tall arrowy white pines, still in their youth, for timber. It is difficult to begin without borrowing, but perhaps it is the most generous course thus to permit your fellow-men to have an interest in your enterprise. The owner of the axe, as he released his hold on it, said that it was the apple of his eye; but I returned it sharper than I received it. It was a pleasant hillside where I worked, covered with pine woods, through which I looked out on the pond, and a small open field in the woods where pines and hickories were springing up. The ice in the pond was not yet dissolved, though there were some open spaces, and it was all dark colored and saturated with water. There were some slight flurries of snow during the days that I worked there; but for the most part when I came out on to the railroad, on my way home, its yellow sand heap stretched away gleaming in the hazy atmosphere, and the rails shone in the spring sun, and I heard the lark and pewee and other birds already come to commence another year with us. They were pleasant spring days, in which the winter of man's discontent was thawing as well as the earth, and the life that had lain torpid began to stretch itself. One day, when my axe had come off and I had cut a green hickory for a wedge, driving it with a stone, and had placed the whole to soak in a pond hole in order to swell the wood, I saw a striped snake run into the water, and he lay on the bottom, apparently without inconvenience, as long as I staid there, or more than a quarter of an hour; perhaps because he had not yet fairly come out of the torpid state. It appeared to me that for a like reason men remain in their present low and primitive condition; but if they should feel the influence of the spring of springs arousing them, they would of necessity rise to a higher and more ethereal life. I had previously seen the snakes in frosty mornings in my path with portions of their bodies still numb and inflexible, waiting for the sun to thaw them. On the 1st of April it rained and melted the ice, and in the early part of the day, which was very foggy, I heard a stray goose groping about over the pond and cackling as if lost, or like the spirit of the fog.

So I went on for some days cutting and hewing timber, and also studs and rafters, all with my narrow axe, not having many communicable or scholar-like thoughts, singing to myself, —

> Men say they know many things;
> But lo! they have taken wings,—
> The arts and sciences,
> And a thousand appliances;
> The wind that blows
> Is all that any body knows.

I hewed the main timbers six inches square, most of the studs on two sides only, and the rafters and floor timbers on one side, leaving the rest of the bark on, so that they were just as straight and much stronger than sawed ones. Each stick was carefully mortised or tenoned by its stump, for I had borrowed other tools by this time. My days in the woods were not very long ones; yet I usually carried my dinner of bread and butter, and read the newspaper in which it was wrapped, at noon, sitting amid the green pine boughs which I had cut off, and to my bread was imparted some of their fragrance, for my hands were covered with a thick coat of pitch. Before I had done I was more the friend than the foe of the pine tree, though I had cut down some of them, having become better acquainted with it. Sometimes a rambler in the wood was attracted by the sound of my axe, and we chatted pleasantly over the chips which I had made.

By the middle of April, for I made no haste in my work, but rather made the most of it, my house was framed and ready for the raising. I had already bought the shanty of James Collins, an Irishman who worked on the Fitchburg Railroad, for boards. James Collins' shanty was considered an uncommonly fine one. When I called to see it he was not at home. I walked about the outside, at first unobserved from within, the window was so deep and high. It was of small dimensions, with a peaked cottage roof, and not much else to be seen, the dirt being raised five feet all around as if it were a compost heap. The roof was the soundest part, though a good deal warped and made brittle by the sun. Door-sill there was none, but a perennial passage for the hens under the door board. Mrs. C. came to the door and asked me to view it from the inside. The hens were driven in by my approach. It was dark, and had a dirt floor for the most part, dank, clammy, and aguish, only here a board and there a board which would not bear removal. She lighted a lamp to show me the inside of the roof and the walls, and also that the board floor extended under the bed, warning me not to step into the cellar, a sort of dust hole two feet deep. In her own words, they were "good boards overhead, good boards all around, and a good window,"—of two whole squares originally, only the cat had passed out that way lately. There was a stove, a bed, and a place to sit, an infant in the house where it was born, a silk parasol, gilt-framed looking-glass, and a patent new coffee mill nailed to an oak sapling, all told. The bargain was soon concluded, for James had in the mean while returned. I to pay four dollars and twenty-five cents to-night, he to vacate at five to-morrow morning, selling to nobody else meanwhile: I to take possession at six. It were well, he said, to be there early, and anticipate certain indistinct but wholly unjust claims on the score of ground rent and fuel. This he assured me was the only encumbrance. At six I passed him and his family on the road. One large bundle held their all,—bed, coffee-mill, looking-glass, hens,—all but the cat, she took to the woods and became a wild cat, and, as I learned afterward, trod in a trap set for woodchucks, and so became a dead cat at last.

I took down this dwelling the same morning, drawing the nails, and removed it to the pond side by small cartloads, spreading the boards on the grass there to bleach and warp back again in the sun. One early thrush gave me a note or two as I drove along the woodland path. I was informed treacherously by a young Patrick that neighbor Seeley, an Irishman, in the intervals of the carting, transferred the still tolerable, straight, and drivable nails, staples, and spikes to his pocket, and then stood when I came back to pass the time of day, and look freshly up, unconcerned, with spring thoughts, at the devastation; there being a dearth of work, as he said. He was there to represent spectatordom, and help make this seemingly insignificant event one with the removal of the gods of Troy.

I dug my cellar in the side of a hill sloping to the south, where a woodchuck had formerly dug his burrow, down through sumach and blackberry roots, and the lowest stain of vegetation, six feet square by seven deep, to a fine sand where potatoes would not freeze in any winter. The sides were left shelving, and not stoned; but the sun having never shone on them, the sand still keeps its place. It was but two hours' work. I took particular pleasure in this breaking of ground, for in almost all latitudes men dig into the earth for an equable temperature. Under the most splendid house in the city is still to be found the cellar where they store their roots as of old, and long after the superstructure has disappeared posterity remark its dent in the earth. The house is still but a sort of porch at the entrance of a burrow.

At length, in the beginning of May, with the help of some of my acquaintances, rather to improve so good an occasion for neighborliness than from any necessity, I set up the frame of my house. No man was ever more honored in the character of his raisers than I. They are destined, I trust, to assist at the raising of loftier structures one day. I began to occupy my house on the 4th of July, as soon as it was boarded and roofed, for the boards were carefully feather-edged and lapped, so that it was perfectly impervious to rain; but before boarding I laid the foundation of a chimney at one end, bringing two cartloads of stones up the hill from the pond in my arms. I built the chimney after my hoeing in the fall, before a fire became necessary for warmth, doing my cooking in the mean while out of doors on the ground, early in the morning: which mode I still think is in some respects more convenient and agreeable than the usual one. When it stormed before my bread was baked, I fixed a few boards over the fire, and sat under them to watch my loaf, and passed some pleasant hours in that way. In those days, when my hands were much employed, I read but little, but the least scraps of paper which lay on the ground, my holder, or table-cloth, afforded me as much entertainment, in fact answered the same purpose as the Iliad.

It would be worth the while to build still more deliberately than I did, considering, for instance, what foundation a door, a window, a cellar, a garret, have in the nature of man, and perchance never raising any superstructure until we found a better reason for it than our temporal necessities even. There is some of the same fitness in a man's building his own house that there is in a bird's building its own nest. Who knows but if men constructed their dwellings with their own hands, and provided food for themselves and families simply and honestly enough, the poetic faculty would be universally developed, as birds universally sing when they are so engaged? But alas! we do like cowbirds and cuckoos, which lay their eggs in nests which other birds have built, and cheer no traveller with their chattering and unmusical notes. Shall we forever resign the pleasure of construction to the carpenter? What does architecture amount to in the experience of the mass of men? I never in all my walks came across a man engaged in so simple and natural an occupation as building his house. We belong to the community. It is not the tailor alone who is the ninth part of a man; it is as much the preacher, and the merchant, and the farmer. Where is this division of labor to end? and what object does it finally serve? No doubt another *may* also think for me; but it is not therefore desirable that he should do so to the exclusion of my thinking for myself.

True, there are architects so called in this country, and I have heard of one at least possessed with the idea of making architectural ornaments have a core of truth, a necessity, and hence a beauty, as if it were a revelation to him. All very well perhaps from his point of view, but only a little better than the common dilettantism. A sentimental reformer in architecture, he began at the cornice, not at the foundation. It was only how to put a core of truth within the ornaments, that every sugar plum in fact might have an almond or caraway seed in it,—though I hold that almonds are most wholesome without the sugar,—and not how the inhabitant, the indweller, might build truly within and without, and let the ornaments take care of themselves. What reasonable man ever supposed that ornaments were something outward and in the skin merely,—that the tortoise got his spotted shell, or the shellfish its mother-o'-pearl tints, by such a contract as the inhabitants of Broadway their Trinity Church? But a man has no more to do with the style of architecture of his house than a tortoise with that of its shell: nor need the soldier be so idle as to try to paint the precise *color* of his virtue on his standard. The enemy will find it out. He may turn pale when the trial comes. This man seemed to me to lean over the cornice and timidly whisper his half truth to the rude occupants who really knew it better than he. What of architectural beauty I now see, I know has gradually grown from within outward, out of the necessities and character of the indweller, who is the only builder,—out of some unconscious truthfulness, and nobleness, without ever a thought for the appearance; and whatever additional beauty of this kind is destined to be produced will be preceded by a like unconscious beauty of life. The most interesting dwellings in this country, as the painter knows, are the most unpretending, humble log huts and cottages of the poor commonly; it is the life of the inhabitants whose shells they are, and not any peculiarity in their surfaces merely, which makes them *picturesque*; and equally interesting will be the citizen's suburban box, when his life shall be as simple and as agreeable to the imagination, and there is as little straining after effect in the style of his dwelling. A great proportion of architectural ornaments are literally hollow, and a September gale would strip them off, like borrowed plumes, without injury to the substantials. They can do without *architecture* who have no olives nor wines in the cellar. What if an equal ado were made about the ornaments of style in literature, and the architects of our bibles spent as much time about their cornices as the architects of our churches do? So are made the *belles-lettres* and the *beaux-arts* and their professors. Much it concerns a man, forsooth, how a few sticks are slanted over him or under him, and what colors are daubed upon his box. It would signify somewhat, if, in any earnest sense, *he* slanted them and daubed it; but the spirit having departed out of the tenant, it is of a piece with constructing his own coffin,—the architecture of the grave, and "carpenter," is but another name for "coffin-maker." One man says, in his despair or indifference to life, take up a handful of the earth at your feet, and paint your house that color. Is he thinking of his last and narrow house? Toss up a copper for it as well. What an abundance of leisure he must have! Why do you take up a handful of dirt? Better paint your house your own complexion; let it turn pale or blush for you. An enterprise to improve the style of cottage architecture! When you have got my ornaments ready I will wear them.

Before winter I built a chimney, and shingled the sides of

my house, which were already impervious to rain, with imperfect and sappy shingles made of the first slice of the log, whose edges I was obliged to straighten with a plane.

I have thus a tight shingled and plastered house, ten feet wide by fifteen long, and eight-feet posts, with a garret and a closet, a large window on each side, two trap doors, one door at the end, and a brick fireplace opposite. The exact cost of my house, paying the usual price for such materials as I used, but not counting the work, all of which was done by myself, was as follows; and I give the details because very few are able to tell exactly what their houses cost, and fewer still, if any, the separate cost of the various materials which compose them: —

Boards,		$8 03½,	mostly shanty boards.
Refuse shingles for roof and sides,		4 00	
Laths,		1 25	
Two second-hand windows with glass,		2 43	
One thousand old brick,		4 00	
Two casks of lime,		2 40	That was high.
Hair,		0 31	More than I needed.
Mantle-tree iron,		0 15	
Nails,		3 90	
Hinges and screws,		0 14	
Latch,		0 10	
Chalk,		0 01	
Transportation,		1 40	} I carried a good part on my back
In all,		$28 12½	

These are all the materials excepting the timber stones and sand, which I claimed by squatter's right. I have also a small wood-shed adjoining, made chiefly of the stuff which was left after building the house.

I intend to build me a house which will surpass any on the main street in Concord in grandeur and luxury, as soon as it pleases me as much and will cost me no more than my present one.

I thus found that the student who wishes for a shelter can obtain one for a lifetime at an expense not greater than the rent which he now pays annually. If I seem to boast more than is becoming, my excuse is that I brag for humanity rather than for myself; and my shortcomings and inconsistencies do not affect the truth of my statement. Notwithstanding much cant and hypocrisy,—chaff which I find it difficult to separate from my wheat, but for which I am as sorry as any man,—I will breathe freely and stretch myself in this respect, it is such a relief to both the moral and physical system; and I am resolved that I will not through humility become the devil's attorney. I will endeavor to speak a good word for the truth. At Cambridge College the mere rent of a student's room, which is only a little larger than my own, is thirty dollars each year, though the corporation had the advantage of building thirty-two side by side and under one roof, and the occupant suffers the inconvenience of many and noisy neighbors, and perhaps a residence in the fourth story. I cannot but think that if we had more true wisdom in these respects, not only less education would be needed, because, forsooth, more would already have been acquired, but the pecuniary expense of getting an education would in a great measure vanish. Those conveniences which the student requires at Cambridge or elsewhere cost him or somebody else ten times as great a sacrifice of life as they would with proper management on both sides. Those things for which the most money is demanded are never the things which the student most wants. Tuition, for instance, is an important item in the term bill, while for the far more valuable education which he gets by associating with the most cultivated of his contemporaries no charge is made. The mode of founding a college is, commonly, to get up a subscription of dollars and cents, and then following blindly the principles of a division of labor to its extreme, a principle which should never be followed but with circumspection,—to call in a contractor who makes this a subject of speculation, and he employs Irishmen or other operatives actually to lay the foundations, while the students that are to be are said to be fitting themselves for it; and for these oversights successive generations have to pay. I think that it would be *better than this*, for the students, or those who desire to be benefited by it, even to lay the foundation themselves. The student who secures his coveted leisure and retirement by systematically shirking any labor necessary to man obtains but an ignoble and unprofitable leisure, defrauding himself of the experience which alone can make leisure fruitful. "But," says one, "you do not mean that the students should go to work with their hands instead of their heads?" I do not mean that exactly, but I mean something which he might think a good deal like that; I mean that they should not *play* life, or *study* it merely, while the community supports them at this expensive game, but earnestly *live* it from beginning to end. How could youths better learn to live than by at once trying the experiment of living? Methinks this would exercise their minds as much as mathematics. If I wished a boy to know something about the arts and sciences, for instance, I would not pursue the common course, which is merely to send him into the neighborhood of some professor, where any thing is professed and practised but the art of life;—to survey the world through a telescope or a microscope, and never with his natural eye; to study chemistry, and not learn how his bread is made, or mechanics, and not learn how it is earned; to discover new satellites to Neptune, and not detect the motes in his eyes, or to what vagabond he is a satellite himself; or to be devoured by the monsters that swarm all around him, while contemplating the monsters in a drop of vinegar. Which would have advanced the most at the end of a month,—the boy who had made his own jackknife from the ore which he had dug and smelted, reading as much as would be necessary for this,—or the boy who had attended the lectures on metallurgy at the Institute in the mean while, and had received a Rogers' penknife from his father? Which would be most likely to cut his fingers?—To my astonishment I was informed on leaving college that I had studied navigation!—why, if I had taken one turn down the harbor I should have known more about it. Even the *poor* student studies and is taught only *political* economy, while that economy of living which is synonymous with philosophy is not even sincerely professed in our colleges. The consequence is, that while he is reading Adam Smith, Ricardo, and Say, he runs his father in debt irretrievably.

As with our colleges, so with a hundred "modern improvements;" there is an illusion about them; there is not always a positive advance. The devil goes on exacting compound interest to the last for his early share and numerous succeeding investments in them. Our inventions are wont to be pretty toys, which distract our attention from serious things. They are but improved means to an unimproved end, an end which it was already but too easy to arrive at; as railroads lead to Boston or New York. We are in great haste to construct a magnetic telegraph from Maine to Texas; but Maine and Texas, it may be, have nothing important to communicate. Either is in such a predicament as the man who was earnest to be introduced to a distinguished deaf woman, but when he was presented, and one end of her ear trumpet was put into his hand, had nothing to say. As if the main object were to talk fast and not to talk sensibly. We are eager to tunnel under the Atlantic and bring the old world some weeks nearer to the new; but perchance the first news that will leak through into the broad, flapping American ear will be that the Princess Adelaide has the whooping cough. After all, the man whose horse trots a mile in a minute does not carry the most important messages; he is not an evangelist, nor does he come round eating locusts and wild honey. I doubt if Flying Childers ever carried a peck of corn to mill.

One says to me, "I wonder that you do not lay up money; you love to travel; you might take the cars and go to Fitchburg to-day and see the country." But I am wiser than that. I have learned that the swiftest traveller is he that goes afoot. I say to my friend, Suppose we try who will get there first. The distance is thirty miles; the fare ninety cents. That is almost a day's wages. I remember when wages were sixty cents a day for laborers on this very road. Well, I start now on foot, and get there before night; I have travelled at that rate by the week together. You will in the mean while have earned your fare, and arrive there some time to-morrow, or possibly this evening, if you are lucky enough to get a job in season. Instead of going to Fitchburg, you will be working here the greater part of the day. And so, if the railroad reached round the world, I think that I should keep ahead of you; and as for seeing the country and getting experience of that kind, I should have to cut your acquaintance altogether.

Such is the universal law, which no man can ever outwit, and with regard to the railroad even we may say it is as broad as it is long. To make a railroad round the world available to all mankind is equivalent to grading the whole surface of the planet. Men have an indistinct notion that if they keep up this activity of joint stocks and spades long enough all will at length ride somewhere, in next to no time, and for nothing; but though a crowd rushes to the depot, and the conductor shouts "All aboard!" when the smoke is blown away and the vapor condensed, it will be perceived that a few are riding, but the rest are run over,—and it will be called, and will be, "A melancholy accident." No doubt they can ride at last who shall have earned their fare, that is, if they survive so long, but they will probably have lost their elasticity and desire to travel by that time. This spending of the best part of one's life earning money in order to enjoy a questionable liberty during the least valuable part of it, reminds me of the Englishman who went to India to make a fortune first, in order that he might return to England and live the life of a poet. He should have gone up garret at once. "What!" exclaim a million Irishmen starting up from all the shanties in the land, "is not this railroad which we have built a good thing?" Yes, I answer, *comparatively* good, that is, you might have done worse; but I wish, as you are brothers of mine, that you could have spent your time better than digging in this dirt.

Before I finished my house, wishing to earn ten or twelve dollars by some honest and agreeable method, in order to meet my unusual expenses, I planted about two acres and a half of light and sandy soil near it chiefly with beans, but also a small part with potatoes, corn, peas, and turnips. The whole lot contains eleven acres, mostly growing up to pines and hickories, and was sold the preceding season for eight dollars and eight cents an acre. One farmer said that it was "good for nothing but to raise cheeping squirrels on." I put no manure on this land, not being the owner, but merely a squatter, and not expecting to cultivate so much again, and I did not quite hoe it all once. I got out several cords of stumps in ploughing, which supplied me with fuel for a long time, and left small circles of virgin mould, easily distinguishable through the summer by the greater luxuriance of the beans there. The dead and for the most part unmerchantable wood behind my house, and the driftwood from the pond, have supplied the remainder of my fuel. I was obliged to hire a team and a man for the ploughing, though I held the plough myself. My farm outgoes for the first season were, for implements, seed, work, &c., $14 72½. The seed corn was given me. This never costs any thing to speak of, unless you plant more than enough. I got twelve bushels of beans, and eighteen bushels of potatoes, beside some peas and sweet corn. The yellow corn and turnips were too late to come to any thing. My whole income from the farm was

	$23 44.
Deducting the outgoes, . . .	14 72½
there are left, ...	$8 71½,

beside produce consumed and on hand at the time this estimate was made of the value of $4 50,—the amount on hand much more than balancing a little grass which I did not raise. All things considered, that is, considering the importance of a man's soul and of to-day, notwithstanding the short time occupied by my experiment, nay, partly even because of its transient character, I believe that that was doing better than any farmer in Concord did that year.

The next year I did better still, for I spaded up all the land which I required, about a third of an acre, and I learned from the experience of both years, not being in the least awed by many celebrated works on husbandry, Arthur Young among the rest, that if one would live simply and eat only the crop which he raised, and raise no more than he ate, and not exchange it for an insufficient quantity of more luxurious and expensive things, he would need to cultivate only a few rods of ground, and that it would be cheaper to spade up that than to use oxen to plough it, and to select a fresh spot from time to time than to manure the old, and he could do all his necessary farm work as it were with his left hand at odd hours in the summer; and thus he would not be tied to an ox, or horse, or cow, or pig, as at present. I desire to speak impartially on this point, and as one not interested in the success or failure of the present economical and social arrangements. I was more independent than any farmer in Concord, for I was not anchored to a house or farm, but could follow the bent of my genius, which is a very crooked one, every moment. Beside being better off than they already, if my house had been burned or my crops had failed, I should have been nearly as well off as before.

I am wont to think that men are not so much the keepers of herds as herds are the keepers of men, the former are so much the freer. Men and oxen exchange work; but if we consider necessary work only, the oxen will be seen to have greatly the advantage, their farm is so much the larger. Man does some of his part of the exchange work in his six weeks of haying, and it is no boy's play. Certainly no nation that lived simply in all respects, that is, no nation of philosophers, would commit so great a blunder as to use the labor of animals. True, there never was and is not likely soon to be a nation of philosophers, nor am I certain it is desirable that there should be. However, *I* should never have broken a horse or bull and taken him to board for any work he might do for me, for fear I should become a horse-man or a herds-man merely; and if society seems to be the gainer by so doing, are we certain that what is one man's gain is not another's loss, and that the stable-boy has equal cause with his master to be satisfied? Granted that some public works would not have been constructed without this aid, and let man share the glory of such with the ox and horse; does it follow that he could not have accomplished works yet more worthy of himself in that case? When men begin to do, not merely unnecessary or artistic, but luxurious and idle work, with their assistance, it is inevitable that a few do all the exchange work with the oxen, or, in other words, become the slaves of the strongest. Man thus not only works for the animal within him, but, for a symbol of this, he works for the animal without him. Though we have many substantial houses of brick or stone, the prosperity of the farmer is still measured by the degree to which the barn overshadows the house. This town is said to have the largest houses for oxen cows and horses hereabouts, and it is not behindhand in its public buildings; but there are very few halls for free worship or free speech in this county. It should not be by their architecture, but why not even by their power of abstract thought, that nations should seek to commemorate themselves? How much more admirable the Bhagvat-Geeta than all the ruins of the East! Towers and temples are the luxury of princes. A simple and independent mind does not toil at the bidding of any prince. Genius is not a retainer to any emperor, nor is its material silver, or gold, or marble, except to a trifling extent. To what end, pray, is so much stone hammered? In Arcadia, when I was there, I did not see any hammering stone. Nations are possessed with an insane ambition to perpetuate the memory of themselves by the amount of hammered stone they leave. What if equal pains were taken to smooth and polish their manners? One piece of good sense would be more memorable than a monument as high as the moon. I love better to see stones in place. The grandeur of Thebes was a vulgar grandeur. More sensible is a rod of stone wall that bounds an honest man's field than a hundred-gated Thebes that has wandered farther from the true end of life. The religion and civilization which are barbaric and heathenish build splendid temples; but what you might call Christianity does not. Most of the stone a nation hammers goes toward its tomb only. It buries itself alive. As for the Pyramids, there is nothing to wonder at in them so much as the fact that so many men could be found degraded enough to spend their lives constructing a tomb for some ambitious booby, whom it would have been wiser and manlier to have drowned in the Nile, and then given his body to the dogs. I might possibly invent some excuse for them and him, but I have no time for it. As for the religion and love of art of the builders, it is much the same all the world over, whether the building be an Egyptian temple or the United States Bank. It costs more than it comes to. The mainspring is vanity, assisted by the love of garlic and bread and butter. Mr. Balcom, a promising young architect, designs it on the back of his Vitruvius, with hard pencil and ruler, and the job is let out to Dobson & Sons, stonecutters. When the thirty centuries begin to look down on it, mankind begin to look up at it. As for your high towers and monuments, there was a crazy fellow once in this town who undertook to dig through to China, and he got so far that, as he said, he heard the Chinese pots and kettles rattle; but I think that I shall not go out of my way to admire the hole which he made. Many are concerned about the monuments of the West and the East,—to know who built them. For my part,

I should like to know who in those days did not build them,—who were above such trifling. But to proceed with my statistics.

By surveying, carpentry, and day-labor of various other kinds in the village in the mean while, for I have as many trades as fingers, I had earned $13 34. The expense of food for eight months, namely, from July 4th to March 1st, the time when these estimates were made, though I lived there more than two years,—not counting potatoes, a little green corn, and some peas, which I had raised, nor considering the value of what was on hand at the last date, was

Rice, ...	$1 73½	
Molasses, . . .	1 73	Cheapest form of the saccharine.
Rye meal, . . .	1 04¾	
Indian meal, . .	0 99¾	Cheaper than rye.
Pork, ...	0 22	
Flour, ...	0 88	Costs more than Indian meal, both money and trouble.
Sugar, ...	0 80	
Lard, ...	0 65	
Apples, . . .	0 25	
Dried apple, . .	0 22	
Sweet potatoes, .	0 10	
One pumpkin, .	0 6	
One watermelon, .	0 2	
Salt, ...	0 3	

All experiments which failed.

Yes, I did eat $8 74, all told; but I should not thus unblushingly publish my guilt, if I did not know that most of my readers were equally guilty with myself, and that their deeds would look no better in print. The next year I sometimes caught a mess of fish for my dinner, and once I went so far as to slaughter a woodchuck which ravaged my bean-field,—effect his transmigration, as a Tartar would say,—and devour him, partly for experiment's sake; but though it afforded me a momentary enjoyment, notwithstanding a musky flavor, I saw that the longest use would not make that a good practice, however it might seem to have your woodchucks ready dressed by the village butcher.

Clothing and some incidental expenses within the same

dates, though little can be inferred from this item, amounted to

| | $8 | 40¾ |
| Oil and some household utensils, ... | 2 | 00 |

So that all the pecuniary outgoes, excepting for washing and mending, which for the most part were done out of the house, and their bills have not yet been received,—and these are all and more than all the ways by which money necessarily goes out in this part of the world,—were

House, ...	$28	12½
Farm one year, ...	14	72½
Food eight months, ...	8	74
Clothing, &c., eight months, ...	8	40¾
Oil, &c., eight months, ...	2	00
In all, ...	$61	99¾

I address myself now to those of my readers who have a living to get. And to meet this I have for farm produce sold

	$23	44
Earned by day-labor, ...	13	34
In all, ...	$36	78,

which subtracted from the sum of the outgoes leaves a balance of $25 21¾ on the one side,—this being very nearly the means with which I started, and the measure of expenses to be incurred,—and on the other, beside the leisure and independence and health thus secured, a comfortable house for me as long as I choose to occupy it.

These statistics, however accidental and therefore uninstructive they may appear, as they have a certain completeness, have a certain value also. Nothing was given me of which I have not rendered some account. It appears from the above estimate, that my food alone cost me in money about twenty-seven cents a week. It was, for nearly two years after this, rye and Indian meal without yeast, potatoes, rice, a very little salt pork, molasses, and salt, and my drink water. It was fit that I should live on rice, mainly, who loved so well the philosophy of India. To meet the objections of some inveterate cavillers, I may as well state, that if I dined out occasionally, as I always had done, and I trust shall have opportunities to do again, it was frequently to the detriment of my domestic arrangements. But the dining out, being, as I have stated, a constant element, does not in the least affect a comparative statement like this.

I learned from my two years' experience that it would cost incredibly little trouble to obtain one's necessary food, even in this latitude; that a man may use as simple a diet as the animals, and yet retain health and strength. I have made a satisfactory dinner, satisfactory on several accounts, simply off a dish of purslane (*Portulaca oleracea*) which I gathered in my cornfield, boiled and salted. I give the Latin on account of the savoriness of the trivial name. And pray what more can a reasonable man desire, in peaceful times, in ordinary noons, than a sufficient number of ears of green sweet-corn boiled, with the addition of salt? Even the little variety which I used was a yielding to the demands of appetite, and not of health. Yet men have come to such a pass that they frequently starve, not for want of necessaries, but for want of luxuries; and I know a good woman who thinks that her son lost his life because he took to drinking water only.

The reader will perceive that I am treating the subject rather from an economic than a dietetic point of view, and he will not venture to put my abstemiousness to the test unless he has a well-stocked larder.

Bread I at first made of pure Indian meal and salt, genuine hoe-cakes, which I baked before my fire out of doors on a shingle or the end of a stick of timber sawed off in building my house; but it was wont to get smoked and to have a piny flavor. I tried flour also; but have at last found a mixture of rye and Indian meal most convenient and agreeable. In cold weather it was no little amusement to bake several small loaves of this in succession, tending and turning them as carefully as an Egyptian his hatching eggs. They were a real cereal fruit which I ripened, and they had to my senses a fragrance like that of other noble fruits, which I kept in as long as possible by wrapping them in cloths. I made a study of the ancient and indispensable art of bread-making, consulting such authorities as offered, going back to the primitive days and first invention of the unleavened kind, when from the wildness of nuts and meats men first reached the mildness and refinement of this diet, and travelling gradually down in my studies through that accidental souring of the dough which, it is supposed, taught the leavening process, and through the various fermentations thereafter, till I came to "good, sweet, wholesome bread," the staff of life. Leaven, which some deem the soul of bread, the *spiritus* which fills its cellular tissue, which is religiously preserved like the vestal fire,—some precious bottle-full, I suppose, first brought over in the Mayflower, did the business for America, and its influence is still rising, swelling, spreading, in cerealian billows over the land,—this seed I regularly and faithfully procured from the village, till at length one morning I forgot the rules, and scalded my yeast; by which accident I discovered that even this was not indispensable,—for my discoveries were not by the synthetic but analytic process,—and I have gladly omitted it since, though most housewives earnestly assured me that safe and wholesome bread without yeast might not be, and elderly people prophesied a speedy decay of the vital forces. Yet I find it not to be an essential ingredient, and after going without it for a year am still in the land of the living; and I am glad to escape the trivialness of carrying a bottle-full in my pocket, which would sometimes pop and discharge its contents to my discomfiture. It is simpler and more respectable to omit it. Man is an animal who more than any other can adapt himself to all climates and circumstances. Neither did I put any sal soda, or other acid or alkali, into my bread. It would seem that I made it according to the recipe which Marcus Porcius Cato gave about two centuries before Christ. "Panem depsticium sic facito. Manus mortariumque bene lavato. Farinam in mortarium indito, aquæ paulatim addito, subigitoque pulchre. Ubi bene subegeris, defingito, coquitoque sub testu." Which I take to mean—"Make kneaded bread thus. Wash your hands and trough well. Put the meal into the trough, add water gradually, and knead it thoroughly. When you have kneaded it well, mould it, and bake it under a cover," that is, in a baking-kettle. Not a word about leaven. But I did not always use this staff of life. At one time, owing to the emptiness of my purse, I saw none of it for more than a month.

Every New Englander might easily raise all his own bread-

stuffs in this land of rye and Indian corn, and not depend on
distant and fluctuating markets for them. Yet so far are we
from simplicity and independence that, in Concord, fresh and
sweet meal is rarely sold in the shops, and hominy and corn
in a still coarser form are hardly used by any. For the most
part the farmer gives to his cattle and hogs the grain of his
own producing, and buys flour, which is at least no more
wholesome, at a greater cost, at the store. I saw that I could
easily raise my bushel or two of rye and Indian corn, for the
former will grow on the poorest land, and the latter does not
require the best, and grind them in a hand-mill, and so do
without rice and pork; and if I must have some concentrated
sweet, I found by experiment that I could make a very good
molasses either of pumpkins or beets, and I knew that I
needed only to set out a few maples to obtain it more easily
still, and while these were growing I could use various substitutes beside those which I have named, "For," as the Forefathers sang,—

> " we can make liquor to sweeten our lips
> Of pumpkins and parsnips and walnut-tree chips."

Finally, as for salt, that grossest of groceries, to obtain this
might be a fit occasion for a visit to the seashore, or, if I did
without it altogether, I should probably drink the less water.
I do not learn that the Indians ever troubled themselves to go
after it.

Thus I could avoid all trade and barter, so far as my food
was concerned, and having a shelter already, it would only
remain to get clothing and fuel. The pantaloons which I now
wear were woven in a farmer's family,—thank Heaven there
is so much virtue still in man; for I think the fall from the
farmer to the operative as great and memorable as that from
the man to the farmer;—and in a new country fuel is an encumbrance. As for a habitat, if I were not permitted still to
squat, I might purchase one acre at the same price for which
the land I cultivated was sold—namely, eight dollars and
eight cents. But as it was, I considered that I enhanced the
value of the land by squatting on it.

There is a certain class of unbelievers who sometimes ask
me such questions as, if I think that I can live on vegetable

food alone; and to strike at the root of the matter at once,—
for the root is faith,—I am accustomed to answer such, that
I can live on board nails. If they cannot understand that, they
cannot understand much that I have to say. For my part, I
am glad to hear of experiments of this kind being tried; as
that a young man tried for a fortnight to live on hard, raw
corn on the ear, using his teeth for all mortar. The squirrel
tribe tried the same and succeeded. The human race is interested in these experiments, though a few old women who are
incapacitated for them, or who own their thirds in mills, may
be alarmed.

My furniture, part of which I made myself, and the rest
cost me nothing of which I have not rendered an account,
consisted of a bed, a table, a desk, three chairs, a looking-
glass three inches in diameter, a pair of tongs and andirons, a
kettle, a skillet, and a frying-pan, a dipper, a wash-bowl, two
knives and forks, three plates, one cup, one spoon, a jug for
oil, a jug for molasses, and a japanned lamp. None is so poor
that he need sit on a pumpkin. That is shiftlessness. There is
a plenty of such chairs as I like best in the village garrets to
be had for taking them away. Furniture! Thank God, I can
sit and I can stand without the aid of a furniture warehouse.
What man but a philosopher would not be ashamed to see
his furniture packed in a cart and going up country exposed
to the light of heaven and the eyes of men, a beggarly account
of empty boxes? That is Spaulding's furniture. I could never
tell from inspecting such a load whether it belonged to a so
called rich man or a poor one; the owner always seemed poverty-stricken. Indeed, the more you have of such things the
poorer you are. Each load looks as if it contained the contents
of a dozen shanties; and if one shanty is poor, this is a dozen
times as poor. Pray, for what do we *move* ever but to get rid
of our furniture, our *exuviæ*; at last to go from this world to
another newly furnished, and leave this to be burned? It is the
same as if all these traps were buckled to a man's belt, and he
could not move over the rough country where our lines are
cast without dragging them,—dragging his trap. He was a
lucky fox that left his tail in the trap. The muskrat will gnaw
his third leg off to be free. No wonder man has lost his elas-

ticity. How often he is at a dead set! "Sir, if I may be so bold, what do you mean by a dead set?" If you are a seer, whenever you meet a man you will see all that he owns, ay, and much that he pretends to disown, behind him, even to his kitchen furniture and all the trumpery which he saves and will not burn, and he will appear to be harnessed to it and making what headway he can. I think that the man is at a dead set who has got through a knot hole or gateway where his sledge load of furniture cannot follow him. I cannot but feel compassion when I hear some trig, compact-looking man, seemingly free, all girded and ready, speak of his "furniture," as whether it is insured or not. "But what shall I do with my furniture?" My gay butterfly is entangled in a spider's web then. Even those who seem for a long while not to have any, if you inquire more narrowly you will find have some stored in somebody's barn. I look upon England to-day as an old gentleman who is travelling with a great deal of baggage, trumpery which has accumulated from long housekeeping, which he has not the courage to burn; great trunk, little trunk, bandbox and bundle. Throw away the first three at least. It would surpass the powers of a well man nowadays to take up his bed and walk, and I should certainly advise a sick one to lay down his bed and run. When I have met an immigrant tottering under a bundle which contained his all,—looking like an enormous wen which had grown out of the nape of his neck,—I have pitied him, not because that was his all, but because he had all *that* to carry. If I have got to drag my trap, I will take care that it be a light one and do not nip me in a vital part. But perchance it would be wisest never to put one's paw into it.

I would observe, by the way, that it costs me nothing for curtains, for I have no gazers to shut out but the sun and moon, and I am willing that they should look in. The moon will not sour milk nor taint meat of mine, nor will the sun injure my furniture or fade my carpet, and if he is sometimes too warm a friend, I find it still better economy to retreat behind some curtain which nature has provided, than to add a single item to the details of housekeeping. A lady once offered me a mat, but as I had no room to spare within the house, nor time to spare within or without to shake it, I declined it, preferring to wipe my feet on the sod before my door. It is best to avoid the beginnings of evil.

Not long since I was present at the auction of a deacon's effects, for his life had not been ineffectual:—

"The evil that men do lives after them."

As usual, a great proportion was trumpery which had begun to accumulate in his father's day. Among the rest was a dried tapeworm. And now, after lying half a century in his garret and other dust holes, these things were not burned; instead of a *bonfire*, or purifying destruction of them, there was an *auction*, or increasing of them. The neighbors eagerly collected to view them, bought them all, and carefully transported them to their garrets and dust holes, to lie there till their estates are settled, when they will start again. When a man dies he kicks the dust.

The customs of some savage nations might, perchance, be profitably imitated by us, for they at least go through the semblance of casting their slough annually; they have the idea of the thing, whether they have the reality or not. Would it not be well if we were to celebrate such a "busk," or "feast of first fruits," as Bartram describes to have been the custom of the Mucclasse Indians? "When a town celebrates the busk," says he, "having previously provided themselves with new clothes, new pots, pans, and other household utensils and furniture, they collect all their worn out clothes and other despicable things, sweep and cleanse their houses, squares, and the whole town, of their filth, which with all the remaining grain and other old provisions they cast together into one common heap, and consume it with fire. After having taken medicine, and fasted for three days, all the fire in the town is extinguished. During this fast they abstain from the gratification of every appetite and passion whatever. A general amnesty is proclaimed; all malefactors may return to their town.—"

"On the fourth morning, the high priest, by rubbing dry wood together, produces new fire in the public square, from whence every habitation in the town is supplied with the new and pure flame."

They then feast on the new corn and fruits and dance and

sing for three days, "and the four following days they receive visits and rejoice with their friends from neighboring towns who have in like manner purified and prepared themselves."

The Mexicans also practised a similar purification at the end of every fifty-two years, in the belief that it was time for the world to come to an end.

I have scarcely heard of a truer sacrament, that is, as the dictionary defines it, "outward and visible sign of an inward and spiritual grace," than this, and I have no doubt that they were originally inspired directly from Heaven to do thus, though they have no biblical record of the revelation.

For more than five years I maintained myself thus solely by the labor of my hands, and I found, that by working about six weeks in a year, I could meet all the expenses of living. The whole of my winters, as well as most of my summers, I had free and clear for study. I have thoroughly tried school-keeping, and found that my expenses were in proportion, or rather out of proportion, to my income, for I was obliged to dress and train, not to say think and believe, accordingly, and I lost my time into the bargain. As I did not teach for the good of my fellow-men, but simply for a livelihood, this was a failure. I have tried trade; but I found that it would take ten years to get under way in that, and that then I should probably be on my way to the devil. I was actually afraid that I might by that time be doing what is called a good business. When formerly I was looking about to see what I could do for a living, some sad experience in conforming to the wishes of friends being fresh in my mind to tax my ingenuity, I thought often and seriously of picking huckleberries; that surely I could do, and its small profits might suffice,—for my greatest skill has been to want but little,—so little capital it required, so little distraction from my wonted moods, I fool-ishly thought. While my acquaintances went unhesitatingly into trade or the professions, I contemplated this occupation as most like theirs; ranging the hills all summer to pick the berries which came in my way, and thereafter carelessly dis-pose of them; so, to keep the flocks of Admetus. I also dreamed that I might gather the wild herbs, or carry ever-greens to such villagers as loved to be reminded of the woods, even to the city, by hay-cart loads. But I have since learned that trade curses every thing it handles; and though you trade in messages from heaven, the whole curse of trade attaches to the business.

As I preferred some things to others, and especially valued my freedom, as I could fare hard and yet succeed well, I did not wish to spend my time in earning rich carpets or other fine furniture, or delicate cookery, or a house in the Grecian or the Gothic style just yet. If there are any to whom it is no interruption to acquire these things, and who know how to use them when acquired, I relinquish to them the pursuit. Some are "industrious," and appear to love labor for its own sake, or perhaps because it keeps them out of worse mischief; to such I have at present nothing to say. Those who would not know what to do with more leisure than they now enjoy, I might advise to work twice as hard as they do,—work till they pay for themselves, and get their free papers. For myself I found that the occupation of a day-laborer was the most independent of any, especially as it required only thirty or forty days in a year to support one. The laborer's day ends with the going down of the sun, and he is then free to devote himself to his chosen pursuit, independent of his labor; but his employer, who speculates from month to month, has no respite from one end of the year to the other.

In short, I am convinced, both by faith and experience, that to maintain one's self on this earth is not a hardship but a pastime, if we will live simply and wisely; as the pursuits of the simpler nations are still the sports of the more artificial. It is not necessary that a man should earn his living by the sweat of his brow, unless he sweats easier than I do.

One young man of my acquaintance, who has inherited some acres, told me that he thought he should live as I did, *if he had the means.* I would not have any one adopt *my* mode of living on any account; for, beside that before he has fairly learned it I may have found out another for myself, I desire that there may be as many different persons in the world as possible; but I would have each one be very careful to find out and pursue *his own* way, and not his father's or his mother's or his neighbor's instead. The youth may build or plant or sail, only let him not be hindered from doing that which he tells me he would like to do. It is by a mathematical point only that we are wise, as the sailor or the fugitive slave keeps the polestar in his eye; but that is sufficient guidance for all our life. We may not arrive at our port within a calculable period, but we would preserve the true course.

Undoubtedly, in this case, what is true for one is truer still for a thousand, as a large house is not more expensive than a small one in proportion to its size, since one roof may cover, one cellar underlie, and one wall separate several apartments. But for my part, I preferred the solitary dwelling. Moreover, it will commonly be cheaper to build the whole yourself than to convince another of the advantage of the common wall; and when you have done this, the common partition, to be much cheaper, must be a thin one, and that other may prove a bad neighbor, and also not keep his side in repair. The only coöperation which is commonly possible is exceedingly partial and superficial; and what little true coöperation there is, is as if it were not, being a harmony inaudible to men. If a man has faith he will coöperate with equal faith every where; if he has not faith, he will continue to live like the rest of the world, whatever company he is joined to. To coöperate, in the highest as well as the lowest sense, means *to get our living together*. I heard it proposed lately that two young men should travel together over the world, the one without money, earning his means as he went, before the mast and behind the plough, the other carrying a bill of exchange in his pocket. It was easy to see that they could not long be companions or coöperate, since one would not *operate* at all. They would part at the first interesting crisis in their adventures. Above all, as I have implied, the man who goes alone can start to-day; but he who travels with another must wait till that other is ready, and it may be a long time before they get off.

But all this is very selfish, I have heard some of my townsmen say. I confess that I have hitherto indulged very little in philanthropic enterprises. I have made some sacrifices to a sense of duty, and among others have sacrificed this pleasure also. There are those who have used all their arts to persuade me to undertake the support of some poor family in the town; and if I had nothing to do,—for the devil finds employment for the idle,—I might try my hand at some such pastime as that. However, when I have thought to indulge myself in this respect, and lay their Heaven under an obligation by maintaining certain poor persons in all respects as comfortably as I maintain myself, and have even ventured so far as to make them the offer, they have one and all unhesitatingly preferred to remain poor. While my townsmen and women are devoted in so many ways to the good of their fellows, I trust that one at least may be spared to other and less humane pursuits. You must have a genius for charity as well as for any thing else. As for Doing-good, that is one of the professions which are full. Moreover, I have tried it fairly, and, strange as it may seem, am satisfied that it does not agree with my constitution. Probably I should not consciously and deliberately forsake my particular calling to do the good which society demands of me, to save the universe from annihilation; and I believe that a like but infinitely greater steadfastness elsewhere is all that now preserves it. But I would not stand between any man and his genius; and to him who does this work, which I decline, with his whole heart and soul and life, I would say, Persevere, even if the world call it doing evil, as it is most likely they will.

I am far from supposing that my case is a peculiar one; no doubt many of my readers would make a similar defence. At doing something,—I will not engage that my neighbors shall pronounce it good,—I do not hesitate to say that I should be a capital fellow to hire; but what that is, it is for my employer to find out. What *good* I do, in the common sense of that word, must be aside from my main path, and for the most part wholly unintended. Men say, practically, Begin where you are and such as you are, without aiming mainly to become of more worth, and with kindness aforethought go about doing good. If I were to preach at all in this strain, I should say rather, Set about being good. As if the sun should stop when he had kindled his fires up to the splendor of a moon or a star of the sixth magnitude, and go about like a Robin Goodfellow, peeping in at every cottage window, inspiring lunatics, and tainting meats, and making darkness visible, instead of steadily increasing his genial heat and beneficence till he is of such brightness that no mortal can look him in the face, and then, and in the mean while too, going about the world in his own orbit, doing it good, or rather, as a truer philosophy has discovered, the world going about him getting good. When Phaeton, wishing to prove his heavenly birth by his beneficence, had the sun's chariot but one day, and drove out of the beaten track, he burned several blocks of houses in the lower streets of heaven, and scorched the surface of the earth, and dried up every spring, and made the great desert of Sahara, till at length Jupiter hurled him headlong to the earth with a thunderbolt, and the sun, through grief at his death, did not shine for a year.

There is no odor so bad as that which arises from goodness tainted. It is human, it is divine, carrion. If I knew for a certainty that a man was coming to my house with the conscious design of doing me good, I should run for my life, as from that dry and parching wind of the African deserts called the simoom, which fills the mouth and nose and ears and eyes with dust till you are suffocated, for fear that I should get some of his good done to me,—some of its virus mingled with my blood. No,—in this case I would rather suffer evil the natural way. A man is not a good *man* to me because he will feed me if I should be starving, or warm me if I should be freezing, or pull me out of a ditch if I should ever fall into one. I can find you a Newfoundland dog that will do as much. Philanthropy is not love for one's fellow-man in the broadest sense. Howard was no doubt an exceedingly kind and worthy man in his way, and has his reward; but, comparatively speaking, what are a hundred Howards to *us*, if their philanthropy do not help *us* in our best estate, when we are most worthy to be helped? I never heard of a philanthropic meeting in which it was sincerely proposed to do any good to me, or the like of me.

The Jesuits were quite balked by those Indians who, being burned at the stake, suggested new modes of torture to their tormentors. Being superior to physical suffering, it sometimes chanced that they were superior to any consolation which the missionaries could offer; and the law to do as you would be done by fell with less persuasiveness on the ears of those, who, for their part, did not care how they were done by, who loved their enemies after a new fashion, and came very near freely forgiving them all they did.

Be sure that you give the poor the aid they most need, though it be your example which leaves them far behind. If you give money, spend yourself with it, and do not merely abandon it to them. We make curious mistakes sometimes. Often the poor man is not so cold and hungry as he is dirty and ragged and gross. It is partly his taste, and not merely his misfortune. If you give him money, he will perhaps buy more rags with it. I was wont to pity the clumsy Irish laborers who cut ice on the pond, in such mean and ragged clothes, while I shivered in my more tidy and somewhat more fashionable garments, till, one bitter cold day, one who had slipped into the water came to my house to warm him, and I saw him strip off three pairs of pants and two pairs of stockings ere he got down to the skin, though they were dirty and ragged enough, it is true, and that he could afford to refuse the *extra* garments which I offered him, he had so many *intra* ones. This ducking was the very thing he needed. Then I began to pity myself, and I saw that it would be a greater charity to bestow on me a flannel shirt than a whole slop-shop on him. There are a thousand hacking at the branches of evil to one who is striking at the root, and it may be that he who bestows the largest amount of time and money on the needy is doing the most by his mode of life to produce that misery which he strives in vain to relieve. It is the pious slave-breeder devoting the proceeds of every tenth slave to buy a Sunday's liberty for the rest. Some show their kindness to the poor by employing them in their kitchens. Would they not be kinder if they employed themselves there? You boast of spending a tenth part of your income in charity; may be you should spend the nine tenths so, and done with it. Society recovers only a tenth part of the property then. Is this owing to the generosity of him in whose possession it is found, or to the remissness of the officers of justice?

Philanthropy is almost the only virtue which is sufficiently appreciated by mankind. Nay, it is greatly overrated; and it is our selfishness which overrates it. A robust poor man, one sunny day here in Concord, praised a fellow-townsman to me, because, as he said, he was kind to the poor; meaning

himself. The kind uncles and aunts of the race are more esteemed than its true spiritual fathers and mothers. I once
heard a reverend lecturer on England, a man of learning and
intelligence, after enumerating her scientific, literary, and political worthies, Shakspeare, Bacon, Cromwell, Milton, Newton, and others, speak next of her Christian heroes, whom, as
if his profession required it of him, he elevated to a place far
above all the rest, as the greatest of the great. They were
Penn, Howard, and Mrs. Fry. Every one must feel the falsehood and cant of this. The last were not England's best men
and women; only, perhaps, her best philanthropists.

I would not subtract any thing from the praise that is due
to philanthropy, but merely demand justice for all who by
their lives and works are a blessing to mankind. I do not value
chiefly a man's uprightness and benevolence, which are, as it
were, his stem and leaves. Those plants of whose greenness
withered we make herb tea for the sick, serve but a humble
use, and are most employed by quacks. I want the flower and
fruit of a man; that some fragrance be wafted over from him
to me, and some ripeness flavor our intercourse. His goodness must not be a partial and transitory act, but a constant
superfluity, which costs him nothing and of which he is unconscious. This is a charity that hides a multitude of sins. The
philanthropist too often surrounds mankind with the remembrance of his own cast-off griefs as an atmosphere, and calls
it sympathy. We should impart our courage, and not our despair, our health and ease, and not our disease, and take care
that this does not spread by contagion. From what southern
plains comes up the voice of wailing? Under what latitudes
reside the heathen to whom we would send light? Who is that
intemperate and brutal man whom we would redeem? If any
thing ail a man, so that he does not perform his functions, if
he have a pain in his bowels even,—for that is the seat of
sympathy,—he forthwith sets about reforming—the world.
Being a microcosm himself, he discovers, and it is a true discovery, and he is the man to make it,—that the world has
been eating green apples; to his eyes, in fact, the globe itself
is a great green apple, which there is danger awful to think of
that the children of men will nibble before it is ripe; and
straightway his drastic philanthropy seeks out the Esquimaux

and the Patagonian, and embraces the populous Indian and Chinese villages; and thus, by a few years of philanthropic activity, the powers in the mean while using him for their own ends, no doubt, he cures himself of his dyspepsia, the globe acquires a faint blush on one or both of its cheeks, as if it were beginning to be ripe, and life loses its crudity and is once more sweet and wholesome to live. I never dreamed of any enormity greater than I have committed. I never knew, and never shall know, a worse man than myself.

I believe that what so saddens the reformer is not his sympathy with his fellows in distress, but, though he be the holiest son of God, is his private ail. Let this be righted, let the spring come to him, the morning rise over his couch, and he will forsake his generous companions without apology. My excuse for not lecturing against the use of tobacco is, that I never chewed it; that is a penalty which reformed tobacco-chewers have to pay; though there are things enough I have chewed, which I could lecture against. If you should ever be betrayed into any of these philanthropies, do not let your left hand know what your right hand does, for it is not worth knowing. Rescue the drowning and tie your shoe-strings. Take your time, and set about some free labor.

Our manners have been corrupted by communication with the saints. Our hymn-books resound with a melodious cursing of God and enduring him forever. One would say that even the prophets and redeemers had rather consoled the fears than confirmed the hopes of man. There is nowhere recorded a simple and irrepressible satisfaction with the gift of life, any memorable praise of God. All health and success does me good, however far off and withdrawn it may appear; all disease and failure helps to make me sad and does me evil, however much sympathy it may have with me or I with it. If, then, we would indeed restore mankind by truly Indian, botanic, magnetic, or natural means, let us first be as simple and well as Nature ourselves, dispel the clouds which hang over our own brows, and take up a little life into our pores. Do not stay to be an overseer of the poor, but endeavor to become one of the worthies of the world.

I read in the Gulistan, or Flower Garden, of Sheik Sadi of Shiraz, that "They asked a wise man, saying; Of the many

celebrated trees which the Most High God has created lofty
and umbrageous, they call none azad, or free, excepting the
cypress, which bears no fruit; what mystery is there in this?
He replied; Each has its appropriate produce, and appointed
season, during the continuance of which it is fresh and
blooming, and during their absence dry and withered; to neither of which states is the cypress exposed, being always flourishing; and of this nature are the azads, or religious
independents.—Fix not thy heart on that which is transitory;
for the Dijlah, or Tigris, will continue to flow through Bag-
dad after the race of caliphs is extinct: if thy hand has plenty,
be liberal as the date tree; but if it affords nothing to give
away, be an azad, or free man, like the cypress."

COMPLEMENTAL VERSES.

"Thou dost presume too much, poor needy wretch,
To claim a station in the firmament,
Because thy humble cottage, or thy tub,
Nurses some lazy or pedantic virtue
In the cheap sunshine or by shady springs,
With roots and pot-herbs; where thy right hand,
Tearing those humane passions from the mind,
Upon whose stocks fair blooming virtues flourish,
Degradeth nature, and benumbeth sense,
And, Gorgon-like, turns active men to stone.
We not require the dull society
Of your necessitated temperance,
Or that unnatural stupidity
That knows nor joy nor sorrow; nor your forc'd
Falsely exalted passive fortitude
Above the active. This low abject brood,
That fix their seats in mediocrity,
Become your servile minds; but we advance
Such virtues only as admit excess,
Brave, bounteous acts, regal magnificence,
All-seeing prudence, magnanimity
That knows no bound, and that heroic virtue
For which antiquity hath left no name,
But patterns only, such as Hercules,
Achilles, Theseus. Back to thy loath'd cell;
And when thou seest the new enlightened sphere,
Study to know but what those worthies were."

T. CAREW.

Where I Lived, and What I Lived For

AT A CERTAIN season of our life we are accustomed to consider every spot as the possible site of a house. I have thus surveyed the country on every side within a dozen miles of where I live. In imagination I have bought all the farms in succession, for all were to be bought, and I knew their price. I walked over each farmer's premises, tasted his wild apples, discoursed on husbandry with him, took his farm at his price, at any price, mortgaging it to him in my mind; even put a higher price on it,—took every thing but a deed of it,—took his word for his deed, for I dearly love to talk,—cultivated it, and him too to some extent, I trust, and withdrew when I had enjoyed it long enough, leaving him to carry it on. This experience entitled me to be regarded as a sort of real-estate broker by my friends. Wherever I sat, there I might live, and the landscape radiated from me accordingly. What is a house but a *sedes*, a seat?—better if a country seat. I discovered many a site for a house not likely to be soon improved, which some might have thought too far from the village, but to my eyes the village was too far from it. Well, there I might live, I said; and there I did live, for an hour, a summer and a winter life; saw how I could let the years run off, buffet the winter through, and see the spring come in. The future inhabitants of this region, wherever they may place their houses, may be sure that they have been anticipated. An afternoon sufficed to lay out the land into orchard woodlot and pasture, and to decide what fine oaks or pines should be left to stand before the door, and whence each blasted tree could be seen to the best advantage; and then I let it lie, fallow perchance, for a man is rich in proportion to the number of things which he can afford to let alone.

My imagination carried me so far that I even had the refusal of several farms,—the refusal was all I wanted,—but I never got my fingers burned by actual possession. The nearest that I came to actual possession was when I bought the Hollowell Place, and had begun to sort my seeds, and collected materials with which to make a wheelbarrow to carry it on or off with; but before the owner gave me a deed of it, his wife—every man has such a wife—changed her mind and wished to keep it, and he offered me ten dollars to release him. Now, to speak the truth, I had but ten cents in the world, and it surpassed my arithmetic to tell, if I was that man who had ten cents, or who had a farm, or ten dollars, or all together. However, I let him keep the ten dollars and the farm too, for I had carried it far enough; or rather, to be generous, I sold him the farm for just what I gave for it, and, as he was not a rich man, made him a present of ten dollars, and still had my ten cents, and seeds, and materials for a wheelbarrow left. I found thus that I had been a rich man without any damage to my poverty. But I retained the landscape, and I have since annually carried off what it yielded without a wheelbarrow. With respect to landscapes,—

> "I am monarch of all I *survey*,
>   My right there is none to dispute."

I have frequently seen a poet withdraw, having enjoyed the most valuable part of a farm, while the crusty farmer supposed that he had got a few wild apples only. Why, the owner does not know it for many years when a poet has put his farm in rhyme, the most admirable kind of invisible fence, has fairly impounded it, milked it, skimmed it, and got all the cream, and left the farmer only the skimmed milk.

The real attractions of the Hollowell farm, to me, were; its complete retirement, being about two miles from the village, half a mile from the nearest neighbor, and separated from the highway by a broad field; its bounding on the river, which the owner said protected it by its fogs from frosts in the spring, though that was nothing to me; the gray color and ruinous state of the house and barn, and the dilapidated fences, which put such an interval between me and the last occupant; the hollow and lichen-covered apple trees, gnawed by rabbits, showing what kind of neighbors I should have; but above all, the recollection I had of it from my earliest voyages up the river, when the house was concealed behind a dense grove of red maples, through which I heard the house-dog bark. I was in haste to buy it, before the proprietor finished getting out some rocks, cutting down the hollow apple trees, and grubbing up some young birches which had sprung up in the pasture, or, in short, had made any more of his improvements. To enjoy these advantages I was ready to carry it on; like Atlas, to take the world on my shoulders,—I never heard what compensation he received for that,—and do all those things which had no other motive or excuse but that I might pay for it and be unmolested in my possession of it; for I knew all the while that it would yield the most abundant crop of the kind I wanted if I could only afford to let it alone. But it turned out as I have said.

All that I could say, then, with respect to farming on a large scale, (I have always cultivated a garden,) was, that I had had my seeds ready. Many think that seeds improve with age. I have no doubt that time discriminates between the good and the bad; and when at last I shall plant, I shall be less likely to be disappointed. But I would say to my fellows, once for all, As long as possible live free and uncommitted. It makes but little difference whether you are committed to a farm or the county jail.

Old Cato, whose "De Re Rusticâ" is my "Cultivator," says, and the only translation I have seen makes sheer nonsense of the passage, "When you think of getting a farm, turn it thus in your mind, not to buy greedily; nor spare your pains to look at it, and do not think it enough to go round it once. The oftener you go there the more it will please you, if it is good." I think I shall not buy greedily, but go round and round it as long as I live, and be buried in it first, that it may please me the more at last.

The present was my next experiment of this kind, which I purpose to describe more at length; for convenience, putting the experience of two years into one. As I have said, I do not propose to write an ode to dejection, but to brag as lustily as chanticleer in the morning, standing on his roost, if only to wake my neighbors up.

When first I took up my abode in the woods, that is, began to spend my nights as well as days there, which, by accident, was on Independence Day, or the fourth of July, 1845, my house was not finished for winter, but was merely a defence against the rain, without plastering or chimney, the walls being of rough weather-stained boards, with wide chinks, which made it cool at night. The upright white hewn studs and freshly planed door and window casings gave it a clean and airy look, especially in the morning, when its timbers were saturated with dew, so that I fancied that by noon some sweet gum would exude from them. To my imagination it retained throughout the day more or less of this auroral character, reminding me of a certain house on a mountain which I had visited the year before. This was an airy and unplastered cabin, fit to entertain a travelling god, and where a goddess might trail her garments. The winds which passed over my dwelling were such as sweep over the ridges of mountains, bearing the broken strains, or celestial parts only, of terrestrial music. The morning wind forever blows, the poem of creation is uninterrupted; but few are the ears that hear it. Olympus is but the outside of the earth every where.

The only house I had been the owner of before, if I except a boat, was a tent, which I used occasionally when making excursions in the summer, and this is still rolled up in my garret; but the boat, after passing from hand to hand, has gone down the stream of time. With this more substantial shelter about me, I had made some progress toward settling in the world. This frame, so slightly clad, was a sort of crystallization around me, and reacted on the builder. It was suggestive somewhat as a picture in outlines. I did not need to go out doors to take the air, for the atmosphere within had lost none of its freshness. It was not so much within doors as behind a door where I sat, even in the rainiest weather. The Harivansa says, "An abode without birds is like a meat without seasoning." Such was not my abode, for I found myself suddenly neighbor to the birds; not by having imprisoned one, but having caged myself near them. I was not only nearer to some of those which commonly frequent the garden and the orchard, but to those wilder and more thrilling songsters of the forest which never, or rarely, serenade a villager,—the wood-thrush, the veery, the scarlet tanager, the field-sparrow, the whippoorwill, and many others.

I was seated by the shore of a small pond, about a mile and a half south of the village of Concord and somewhat higher than it, in the midst of an extensive wood between that town and Lincoln, and about two miles south of that our only field known to fame, Concord Battle Ground; but I was so low in the woods that the opposite shore, half a mile off, like the rest, covered with wood, was my most distant horizon. For the first week, whenever I looked out on the pond it impressed me like a tarn high up on the side of a mountain, its bottom far above the surface of other lakes, and, as the sun arose, I saw it throwing off its nightly clothing of mist, and here and there, by degrees, its soft ripples or its smooth reflecting surface was revealed, while the mists, like ghosts, were stealthily withdrawing in every direction into the woods, as at the breaking up of some nocturnal conventicle. The very dew seemed to hang upon the trees later into the day than usual, as on the sides of mountains.

This small lake was of most value as a neighbor in the intervals of a gentle rain storm in August, when, both air and water being perfectly still, but the sky overcast, mid-afternoon had all the serenity of evening, and the wood-thrush sang around, and was heard from shore to shore. A lake like this is never smoother than at such a time; and the clear portion of the air above it being shallow and darkened by clouds, the water, full of light and reflections, becomes a lower heaven itself so much the more important. From a hill top near by, where the wood had been recently cut off, there was a pleasing vista southward across the pond, through a wide indentation in the hills which form the shore there, where their opposite sides sloping toward each other suggested a stream flowing out in that direction through a wooded valley, but stream there was none. That way I looked between and over the near green hills to some distant and higher ones in the horizon, tinged with blue. Indeed, by standing on tiptoe I could catch a glimpse of some of the peaks of the still bluer and more distant mountain ranges in the north-west, those true-blue coins from heaven's own mint, and also of some portion of the village. But in other directions, even from this point, I could not see over or beyond the woods which surrounded me. It is well to have some water in your neighborhood, to give buoyancy to and float the earth. One value even of the smallest well is, that when you look into it you see that earth is not continent but insular. This is as important as that it keeps butter cool. When I looked across the pond from this peak toward the Sudbury meadows, which in time of flood I distinguished elevated perhaps by a mirage in their seething valley, like a coin in a basin, all the earth beyond the pond appeared like a thin crust insulated and floated even by this small sheet of intervening water, and I was reminded that this on which I dwelt was but *dry land*.

Though the view from my door was still more contracted, I did not feel crowded or confined in the least. There was pasture enough for my imagination. The low shrub-oak plateau to which the opposite shore arose, stretched away toward the prairies of the West and the steppes of Tartary, affording ample room for all the roving families of men. "There are none happy in the world but beings who enjoy freely a vast horizon,"—said Damodara, when his herds required new and larger pastures.

Both place and time were changed, and I dwelt nearer to those parts of the universe and to those eras in history which had most attracted me. Where I lived was as far off as many a region viewed nightly by astronomers. We are wont to imagine rare and delectable places in some remote and more celestial corner of the system, behind the constellation of Cassiopeia's Chair, far from noise and disturbance. I discovered that my house actually had its site in such a withdrawn, but forever new and unprofaned, part of the universe. If it were worth the while to settle in those parts near to the Pleiades or the Hyades, to Aldebaran or Altair, then I was really there, or at an equal remoteness from the life which I had left behind, dwindled and twinkling with as fine a ray to my nearest neighbor, and to be seen only in moonless nights by him. Such was that part of creation where I had squatted;—

> "There was a shepherd that did live,
>   And held his thoughts as high
>   As were the mounts whereon his flocks
>   Did hourly feed him by."

What should we think of the shepherd's life if his flocks always wandered to higher pastures than his thoughts?

Every morning was a cheerful invitation to make my life of equal simplicity, and I may say innocence, with Nature herself. I have been as sincere a worshipper of Aurora as the Greeks. I got up early and bathed in the pond; that was a religious exercise, and one of the best things which I did. They say that characters were engraven on the bathing tub of king Tching-thang to this effect: "Renew thyself completely each day; do it again, and again, and forever again." I can understand that. Morning brings back the heroic ages. I was as much affected by the faint hum of a mosquito making its invisible and unimaginable tour through my apartment at earliest dawn, when I was sitting with door and windows open, as I could be by any trumpet that ever sang of fame. It was Homer's requiem; itself an Iliad and Odyssey in the air, singing its own wrath and wanderings. There was something cosmical about it; a standing advertisement, till forbidden, of the everlasting vigor and fertility of the world. The morning, which is the most memorable season of the day, is the awakening hour. Then there is least somnolence in us; and for an hour, at least, some part of us awakes which slumbers all the rest of the day and night. Little is to be expected of that day, if it can be called a day, to which we are not awakened by our Genius, but by the mechanical nudgings of some servitor, are not awakened by our own newly-acquired force and aspirations from within, accompanied by the undulations of celestial music, instead of factory bells, and a fragrance filling the air—to a higher life than we fell asleep from; and thus the darkness bear its fruit, and prove itself to be good, no less than the light. That man who does not believe that each day contains an earlier, more sacred, and auroral hour than he has yet profaned, has despaired of life, and is pursuing a descending and darkening way. After a partial cessation of his sensuous life, the soul of man, or its organs rather, are reinvigorated each day, and his Genius tries again what noble life it can make. All memorable events, I should say, transpire in morning time and in a morning atmosphere. The Vedas say, "All intelligences awake with the morning." Poetry and art, and the fairest and most memorable of the actions of men, date from such an hour. All poets and heroes, like Memnon, are the children of Aurora, and emit their music at sunrise. To him whose elastic and vigorous thought keeps pace with the sun, the day is a perpetual morning. It matters not

what the clocks say or the attitudes and labors of men. Morning is when I am awake and there is a dawn in me. Moral
reform is the effort to throw off sleep. Why is it that men
give so poor an account of their day if they have not been
slumbering? They are not such poor calculators. If they had
not been overcome with drowsiness they would have performed something. The millions are awake enough for physical labor; but only one in a million is awake enough for
effective intellectual exertion, only one in a hundred millions
to a poetic or divine life. To be awake is to be alive. I have
never yet met a man who was quite awake. How could I have
looked him in the face?

We must learn to reawaken and keep ourselves awake, not
by mechanical aids, but by an infinite expectation of the
dawn, which does not forsake us in our soundest sleep. I
know of no more encouraging fact than the unquestionable
ability of man to elevate his life by a conscious endeavor. It is
something to be able to paint a particular picture, or to carve
a statue, and so to make a few objects beautiful; but it is far
more glorious to carve and paint the very atmosphere and
medium through which we look, which morally we can do.
To affect the quality of the day, that is the highest of arts.
Every man is tasked to make his life, even in its details, worthy of the contemplation of his most elevated and critical
hour. If we refused, or rather used up, such paltry information as we get, the oracles would distinctly inform us how
this might be done.

I went to the woods because I wished to live deliberately,
to front only the essential facts of life, and see if I could not
learn what it had to teach, and not, when I came to die, discover that I had not lived. I did not wish to live what was
not life, living is so dear; nor did I wish to practise resignation, unless it was quite necessary. I wanted to live deep and
suck out all the marrow of life, to live so sturdily and Spartan-
like as to put to rout all that was not life, to cut a broad swath
and shave close, to drive life into a corner, and reduce it to
its lowest terms, and, if it proved to be mean, why then to
get the whole and genuine meanness of it, and publish its
meanness to the world; or if it were sublime, to know it by
experience, and be able to give a true account of it in my next

excursion. For most men, it appears to me, are in a strange uncertainty about it, whether it is of the devil or of God, and have *somewhat hastily* concluded that it is the chief end of man here to "glorify God and enjoy him forever."

Still we live meanly, like ants; though the fable tells us that we were long ago changed into men; like pygmies we fight with cranes; it is error upon error, and clout upon clout, and our best virtue has for its occasion a superfluous and evitable wretchedness. Our life is frittered away by detail. An honest man has hardly need to count more than his ten fingers, or in extreme cases he may add his ten toes, and lump the rest. Simplicity, simplicity, simplicity! I say, let your affairs be as two or three, and not a hundred or a thousand; instead of a million count half a dozen, and keep your accounts on your thumb nail. In the midst of this chopping sea of civilized life, such are the clouds and storms and quick-sands and thousand-and-one items to be allowed for, that a man has to live, if he would not founder and go to the bottom and not make his port at all, by dead reckoning, and he must be a great calculator indeed who succeeds. Simplify, simplify. Instead of three meals a day, if it be necessary eat but one; instead of a hundred dishes, five; and reduce other things in proportion. Our life is like a German Confederacy, made up of petty states, with its boundary forever fluctuating, so that even a German cannot tell you how it is bounded at any moment. The nation itself, with all its so called internal improvements, which, by the way, are all external and superficial, is just such an unwieldy and overgrown establishment, cluttered with furniture and tripped up by its own traps, ruined by luxury and heedless expense, by want of calculation and a worthy aim, as the million households in the land; and the only cure for it as for them is in a rigid economy, a stern and more than Spartan simplicity of life and elevation of purpose. It lives too fast. Men think that it is essential that the *Nation* have commerce, and export ice, and talk through a telegraph, and ride thirty miles an hour, without a doubt, whether *they* do or not; but whether we should live like baboons or like men, is a little uncertain. If we do not get out sleepers, and forge rails, and devote days and nights to the work, but go to tinkering upon our *lives* to improve *them*, who will build railroads? And if railroads are not built, how shall we get to heaven in season? But if we stay at home and mind our business, who will want railroads? We do not ride on the railroad; it rides upon us. Did you ever think what those sleepers are that underlie the railroad? Each one is a man, an Irishman, or a Yankee man. The rails are laid on them, and they are covered with sand, and the cars run smoothly over them. They are sound sleepers, I assure you. And every few years a new lot is laid down and run over; so that, if some have the pleasure of riding on a rail, others have the misfortune to be ridden upon. And when they run over a man that is walking in his sleep, a supernumerary sleeper in the wrong position, and wake him up, they suddenly stop the cars, and make a hue and cry about it, as if this were an exception. I am glad to know that it takes a gang of men for every five miles to keep the sleepers down and level in their beds as it is, for this is a sign that they may sometime get up again.

Why should we live with such hurry and waste of life? We are determined to be starved before we are hungry. Men say that a stitch in time saves nine, and so they take a thousand stitches to-day to save nine to-morrow. As for *work*, we haven't any of any consequence. We have the Saint Vitus' dance, and cannot possibly keep our heads still. If I should only give a few pulls at the parish bell-rope, as for a fire, that is, without setting the bell, there is hardly a man on his farm in the outskirts of Concord, notwithstanding that press of engagements which was his excuse so many times this morning, nor a boy, nor a woman, I might almost say, but would forsake all and follow that sound, not mainly to save property from the flames, but, if we will confess the truth, much more to see it burn, since burn it must, and we, be it known, did not set it on fire,—or to see it put out, and have a hand in it, if that is done as handsomely; yes, even if it were the parish church itself. Hardly a man takes a half hour's nap after dinner, but when he wakes he holds up his head and asks, "What's the news?" as if the rest of mankind had stood his sentinels. Some give directions to be waked every half hour, doubtless for no other purpose; and then, to pay for it, they tell what they have dreamed. After a night's sleep the news is as indispensable as the breakfast. "Pray tell me any thing new that has happened to a man any where on this globe,"—and he reads it over his coffee and rolls, that a man has had his eyes gouged out this morning on the Wachito River; never dreaming the while that he lives in the dark unfathomed mammoth cave of this world, and has but the rudiment of an eye himself.

For my part, I could easily do without the post-office. I think that there are very few important communications made through it. To speak critically, I never received more than one or two letters in my life—I wrote this some years ago—that were worth the postage. The penny-post is, commonly, an institution through which you seriously offer a man that penny for his thoughts which is so often safely offered in jest. And I am sure that I never read any memorable news in a newspaper. If we read of one man robbed, or murdered, or killed by accident, or one house burned, or one vessel wrecked, or one steamboat blown up, or one cow run over on the Western Railroad, or one mad dog killed, or one lot of grasshoppers in the winter,—we never need read of another. One is enough. If you are acquainted with the principle, what do you care for a myriad instances and applications? To a philosopher all *news*, as it is called, is gossip, and they who edit and read it are old women over their tea. Yet not a few are greedy after this gossip. There was such a rush, as I hear, the other day at one of the offices to learn the foreign news by the last arrival, that several large squares of plate glass belonging to the establishment were broken by the pressure,—news which I seriously think a ready wit might write a twelvemonth or twelve years beforehand with sufficient accuracy. As for Spain, for instance, if you know how to throw in Don Carlos and the Infanta, and Don Pedro and Seville and Granada, from time to time in the right proportions,—they may have changed the names a little since I saw the papers,—and serve up a bull-fight when other entertainments fail, it will be true to the letter, and give us as good an idea of the exact state or ruin of things in Spain as the most succinct and lucid reports under this head in the newspapers: and as for England, almost the last significant scrap of news from that quarter was the revolution of 1649; and if you have learned the history of her crops for an average year, you never need attend to that thing again, unless your speculations are of a merely pecuniary character. If one may judge who rarely looks into the newspapers, nothing new does ever happen in foreign parts, a French revolution not excepted.

What news! how much more important to know what that is which was never old! "Kieou-pe-yu (great dignitary of the state of Wei) sent a man to Khoung-tseu to know his news. Khoung-tseu caused the messenger to be seated near him, and questioned him in these terms: What is your master doing? The messenger answered with respect: My master desires to diminish the number of his faults, but he cannot come to the end of them. The messenger being gone, the philosopher remarked: What a worthy messenger! What a worthy messenger!" The preacher, instead of vexing the ears of drowsy farmers on their day of rest at the end of the week,—for Sunday is the fit conclusion of an ill-spent week, and not the fresh and brave beginning of a new one,—with this one other draggle-tail of a sermon, should shout with thundering voice,—"Pause! Avast! Why so seeming fast, but deadly slow?"

Shams and delusions are esteemed for soundest truths, while reality is fabulous. If men would steadily observe realities only, and not allow themselves to be deluded, life, to compare it with such things as we know, would be like a fairy tale and the Arabian Nights' Entertainments. If we respected only what is inevitable and has a right to be, music and poetry would resound along the streets. When we are unhurried and wise, we perceive that only great and worthy things have any permanent and absolute existence,—that petty fears and petty pleasures are but the shadow of the reality. This is always exhilarating and sublime. By closing the eyes and slumbering, and consenting to be deceived by shows, men establish and confirm their daily life of routine and habit every where, which still is built on purely illusory foundations. Children, who play life, discern its true law and relations more clearly than men, who fail to live it worthily, but who think that they are wiser by experience, that is, by failure. I have read in a Hindoo book, that "there was a king's son, who, being expelled in infancy from his native city, was brought up by a forester, and, growing up to maturity in that state, imagined himself to belong to the barbarous race with which he lived. One of his father's ministers having discovered him, revealed to him what he was, and the misconception of his character was removed, and he knew himself to be a prince. So soul," continues the Hindoo philosopher, "from the circumstances in which it is placed, mistakes its own character, until the truth is revealed to it by some holy teacher, and then it knows itself to be *Brahme*." I perceive that we inhabitants of New England live this mean life that we do because our vision does not penetrate the surface of things. We think that that *is* which *appears* to be. If a man should walk through this town and see only the reality, where, think you, would the "Mill-dam" go to? If he should give us an account of the realities he beheld there, we should not recognize the place in his description. Look at a meeting-house, or a court-house, or a jail, or a shop, or a dwelling-house, and say what that thing really is before a true gaze, and they would all go to pieces in your account of them. Men esteem truth remote, in the outskirts of the system, behind the farthest star, before Adam and after the last man. In eternity there is indeed something true and sublime. But all these times and places and occasions are now and here. God himself culminates in the present moment, and will never be more divine in the lapse of all the ages. And we are enabled to apprehend at all what is sublime and noble only by the perpetual instilling and drenching of the reality which surrounds us. The universe constantly and obediently answers to our conceptions; whether we travel fast or slow, the track is laid for us. Let us spend our lives in conceiving then. The poet or the artist never yet had so fair and noble a design but some of his posterity at least could accomplish it.

Let us spend one day as deliberately as Nature, and not be thrown off the track by every nutshell and mosquito's wing that falls on the rails. Let us rise early and fast, or break fast, gently and without perturbation; let company come and let company go, let the bells ring and the children cry,—determined to make a day of it. Why should we knock under and go with the stream? Let us not be upset and overwhelmed in that terrible rapid and whirlpool called a dinner, situated in the meridian shallows. Weather this danger and you are safe, for the rest of the way is down hill. With unrelaxed nerves, with morning vigor, sail by it, looking another way, tied to the mast like Ulysses. If the engine whistles, let it whistle till it is hoarse for its pains. If the bell rings, why should we run? We will consider what kind of music they are like. Let us settle ourselves, and work and wedge our feet downward through the mud and slush of opinion, and prejudice, and tradition, and delusion, and appearance, that alluvion which covers the globe, through Paris and London, through New York and Boston and Concord, through church and state, through poetry and philosophy and religion, till we come to a hard bottom and rocks in place, which we can call *reality*, and say, This is, and no mistake; and then begin, having a *point d'appui*, below freshet and frost and fire, a place where you might found a wall or a state, or set a lamp-post safely, or perhaps a gauge, not a Nilometer, but a Realometer, that future ages might know how deep a freshet of shams and appearances had gathered from time to time. If you stand right fronting and face to face to a fact, you will see the sun glimmer on both its surfaces, as if it were a cimeter, and feel its sweet edge dividing you through the heart and marrow, and so you will happily conclude your mortal career. Be it life or death, we crave only reality. If we are really dying, let us hear the rattle in our throats and feel cold in the extremities; if we are alive, let us go about our business.

Time is but the stream I go a-fishing in. I drink at it; but while I drink I see the sandy bottom and detect how shallow it is. Its thin current slides away, but eternity remains. I would drink deeper; fish in the sky, whose bottom is pebbly with stars. I cannot count one. I know not the first letter of the alphabet. I have always been regretting that I was not as wise as the day I was born. The intellect is a cleaver; it discerns and rifts its way into the secret of things. I do not wish to be any more busy with my hands than is necessary. My head is hands and feet. I feel all my best faculties concentrated in it. My instinct tells me that my head is an organ for burrowing, as some creatures use their snout and fore-paws, and with it I would mine and burrow my way through these hills.

I think that the richest vein is somewhere hereabouts; so by the divining rod and thin rising vapors I judge; and here I will begin to mine.

Reading

WITH A LITTLE more deliberation in the choice of their pursuits, all men would perhaps become essentially students and observers, for certainly their nature and destiny are interesting to all alike. In accumulating property for ourselves or our posterity, in founding a family or a state, or acquiring fame even, we are mortal; but in dealing with truth we are immortal, and need fear no change nor accident. The oldest Egyptian or Hindoo philosopher raised a corner of the veil from the statue of the divinity; and still the trembling robe remains raised, and I gaze upon as fresh a glory as he did, since it was I in him that was then so bold, and it is he in me that now reviews the vision. No dust has settled on that robe; no time has elapsed since that divinity was revealed. That time which we really improve, or which is improvable, is neither past, present, nor future.

My residence was more favorable, not only to thought, but to serious reading, than a university; and though I was beyond the range of the ordinary circulating library, I had more than ever come within the influence of those books which circulate round the world, whose sentences were first written on bark, and are now merely copied from time to time on to linen paper. Says the poet Mîr Camar Uddîn Mast, "Being seated to run through the region of the spiritual world; I have had this advantage in books. To be intoxicated by a single glass of wine; I have experienced this pleasure when I have drunk the liquor of the esoteric doctrines." I kept Homer's Iliad on my table through the summer, though I looked at his page only now and then. Incessant labor with my hands, at first, for I had my house to finish and my beans to hoe at the same time, made more study impossible. Yet I sustained myself by the prospect of such reading in future. I read one or two shallow books of travel in the intervals of my work, till that employment made me ashamed of myself, and I asked where it was then that *I* lived.

The student may read Homer or Æschylus in the Greek without danger of dissipation or luxuriousness, for it implies that he in some measure emulate their heroes, and consecrate morning hours to their pages. The heroic books, even if printed in the character of our mother tongue, will always be in a language dead to degenerate times; and we must laboriously seek the meaning of each word and line, conjecturing a larger sense than common use permits out of what wisdom and valor and generosity we have. The modern cheap and fertile press, with all its translations, has done little to bring us nearer to the heroic writers of antiquity. They seem as solitary, and the letter in which they are printed as rare and curious, as ever. It is worth the expense of youthful days and costly hours, if you learn only some words of an ancient language, which are raised out of the trivialness of the street, to be perpetual suggestions and provocations. It is not in vain that the farmer remembers and repeats the few Latin words which he has heard. Men sometimes speak as if the study of the classics would at length make way for more modern and practical studies; but the adventurous student will always study classics, in whatever language they may be written and however ancient they may be. For what are the classics but the noblest recorded thoughts of man? They are the only oracles which are not decayed, and there are such answers to the most modern inquiry in them as Delphi and Dodona never gave. We might as well omit to study Nature because she is old. To read well, that is, to read true books in a true spirit, is a noble exercise, and one that will task the reader more than any exercise which the customs of the day esteem. It requires a training such as the athletes underwent, the steady intention almost of the whole life to this object. Books must be read as deliberately and reservedly as they were written. It is not enough even to be able to speak the language of that nation by which they are written, for there is a memorable interval between the spoken and the written language, the language heard and the language read. The one is commonly transitory, a sound, a tongue, a dialect merely, almost brutish, and we learn it unconsciously, like the brutes, of our mothers. The other is the maturity and experience of that; if that is our mother tongue, this is our father tongue, a reserved and select expression, too significant to be heard by the ear, which we must be born again in order to speak. The crowds of men who merely *spoke* the Greek and Latin tongues in the middle ages were not entitled by the accident of birth to *read* the works of genius written in those languages; for these were not written in that Greek or Latin which they knew, but in the select language of literature. They had not learned the nobler dialects of Greece and Rome, but the very materials on which they were written were waste paper to them, and they prized instead a cheap contemporary literature. But when the several nations of Europe had acquired distinct though rude written languages of their own, sufficient for the purposes of their rising literatures, then first learning revived, and scholars were enabled to discern from that remoteness the treasures of antiquity. What the Roman and Grecian multitude could not *hear*, after the lapse of ages a few scholars *read*, and a few scholars only are still reading it.

However much we may admire the orator's occasional bursts of eloquence, the noblest written words are commonly as far behind or above the fleeting spoken language as the firmament with its stars is behind the clouds. *There* are the stars, and they who can may read them. The astronomers forever comment on and observe them. They are not exhalations like our daily colloquies and vaporous breath. What is called eloquence in the forum is commonly found to be rhetoric in the study. The orator yields to the inspiration of a transient occasion, and speaks to the mob before him, to those who can *hear* him; but the writer, whose more equable life is his occasion, and who would be distracted by the event and the crowd which inspire the orator, speaks to the intellect and heart of mankind, to all in any age who can *understand* him.

No wonder that Alexander carried the Iliad with him on his expeditions in a precious casket. A written word is the choicest of relics. It is something at once more intimate with us and more universal than any other work of art. It is the work of art nearest to life itself. It may be translated into every language, and not only be read but actually breathed from all human lips;—not be represented on canvas or in marble only, but be carved out of the breath of life itself. The symbol of an ancient man's thought becomes a modern man's speech. Two thousand summers have imparted to the monuments of Grecian literature, as to her marbles, only a maturer golden and autumnal tint, for they have carried their own serene and celestial atmosphere into all lands to protect them against the corrosion of time. Books are the treasured wealth of the world and the fit inheritance of generations and nations. Books, the oldest and the best, stand naturally and rightfully on the shelves of every cottage. They have no cause of their own to plead, but while they enlighten and sustain the reader his common sense will not refuse them. Their authors are a natural and irresistible aristocracy in every society, and, more than kings or emperors, exert an influence on mankind. When the illiterate and perhaps scornful trader has earned by enterprise and industry his coveted leisure and independence, and is admitted to the circles of wealth and fashion, he turns inevitably at last to those still higher but yet inaccessible circles of intellect and genius, and is sensible only of the imperfection of his culture and the vanity and insufficiency of all his riches, and further proves his good sense by the pains which he takes to secure for his children that intellectual culture whose want he so keenly feels; and thus it is that he becomes the founder of a family.

Those who have not learned to read the ancient classics in the language in which they were written must have a very imperfect knowledge of the history of the human race; for it is remarkable that no transcript of them has ever been made into any modern tongue, unless our civilization itself may be regarded as such a transcript. Homer has never yet been printed in English, nor Æschylus, nor Virgil even,—works as refined, as solidly done, and as beautiful almost as the morning itself; for later writers, say what we will of their genius, have rarely, if ever, equalled the elaborate beauty and finish and the lifelong and heroic literary labors of the ancients. They only talk of forgetting them who never knew them. It will be soon enough to forget them when we have the learning and the genius which will enable us to attend to and appreciate them. That age will be rich indeed when those relics which we call Classics, and the still older and more than classic but even less known Scriptures of the nations, shall have still further accumulated, when the Vaticans shall be filled with Vedas and Zendavestas and Bibles, with Homers and Dantes and Shakspeares, and all the centuries to come shall have successively deposited their trophies in the forum of the world. By such a pile we may hope to scale heaven at last.

The works of the great poets have never yet been read by mankind, for only great poets can read them. They have only been read as the multitude read the stars, at most astrologically, not astronomically. Most men have learned to read to serve a paltry convenience, as they have learned to cipher in order to keep accounts and not be cheated in trade; but of reading as a noble intellectual exercise they know little or nothing; yet this only is reading, in a high sense, not that which lulls us as a luxury and suffers the nobler faculties to sleep the while, but what we have to stand on tiptoe to read and devote our most alert and wakeful hours to.

I think that having learned our letters we should read the best that is in literature, and not be forever repeating our a b abs, and words of one syllable, in the fourth or fifth classes, sitting on the lowest and foremost form all our lives. Most men are satisfied if they read or hear read, and perchance have been convicted by the wisdom of one good book, the Bible, and for the rest of their lives vegetate and dissipate their faculties in what is called easy reading. There is a work in several volumes in our Circulating Library entitled Little Reading, which I thought referred to a town of that name which I had not been to. There are those who, like cormorants and ostriches, can digest all sorts of this, even after the fullest dinner of meats and vegetables, for they suffer nothing to be wasted. If others are the machines to provide this provender, they are the machines to read it. They read the nine thousandth tale about Zebulon and Sephronia, and how they loved as none had ever loved before, and neither did the course of their true love run smooth,—at any rate, how it did run and stumble, and get up again and go on! how some poor unfortunate got up onto a steeple, who had better never have gone up as far as the belfry; and then, having needlessly got him up there, the happy novelist rings the bell for all the world to come together and hear, O dear! how he did get down again! For my part, I think that they had better metamorphose all such aspiring heroes of universal noveldom into man weathercocks, as they used to put heroes among the constellations, and let them swing round there till they are rusty, and not come down at all to bother honest men with their pranks. The next time the novelist rings the bell I will not stir though the meeting-house burn down. "The Skip of the Tip-Toe-Hop, a Romance of the Middle Ages, by the celebrated author of 'Tittle-Tol-Tan,' to appear in monthly parts; a great rush; don't all come together." All this they read with saucer eyes, and erect and primitive curiosity, and with unwearied gizzard, whose corrugations even yet need no sharpening, just as some little four-year-old bencher his two-cent gilt-covered edition of Cinderella,—without any improvement, that I can see, in the pronunciation, or accent, or emphasis, or any more skill in extracting or inserting the moral. The result is dulness of sight, a stagnation of the vital circulations, and a general deliquium and sloughing off of all the intellectual faculties. This sort of gingerbread is baked daily and more sedulously than pure wheat or rye-and-Indian in almost every oven, and finds a surer market.

The best books are not read even by those who are called good readers. What does our Concord culture amount to? There is in this town, with a very few exceptions, no taste for the best or for very good books even in English literature, whose words all can read and spell. Even the college-bred and so called liberally educated men here and elsewhere have really little or no acquaintance with the English classics; and as for the recorded wisdom of mankind, the ancient classics and Bibles, which are accessible to all who will know of them, there are the feeblest efforts any where made to become acquainted with them. I know a woodchopper, of middle age, who takes a French paper, not for news as he says, for he is above that, but to "keep himself in practice," he being a Canadian by birth; and when I ask him what he considers the best thing he can do in this world, he says, beside this, to keep up and add to his English. This is about as much as the college bred generally do or aspire to do, and they take an English paper for the purpose. One who has just come from reading perhaps one of the best English books will find how many with whom he can converse about it? Or suppose he comes from reading a Greek or Latin classic in the original, whose praises are familiar even to the so called illiterate; he will find nobody at all to speak to, but must keep silence about it. Indeed, there is hardly the professor in our colleges, who, if he has mastered the difficulties of the language, has proportionally mastered the difficulties of the wit and poetry of a Greek poet, and has any sympathy to impart to the alert and heroic reader; and as for the sacred Scriptures, or Bibles of mankind, who in this town can tell me even their titles? Most men do not know that any nation but the Hebrews have had a scripture. A man, any man, will go considerably out of his way to pick up a silver dollar; but here are golden words, which the wisest men of antiquity have uttered, and whose worth the wise of every succeeding age have assured us of;—and yet we learn to read only as far as Easy Reading, the primers and class-books, and when we leave school, the "Little Reading," and story books, which are for boys and beginners; and our reading, our conversation and thinking, are all on a very low level, worthy only of pygmies and manikins.

I aspire to be acquainted with wiser men than this our Concord soil has produced, whose names are hardly known here. Or shall I hear the name of Plato and never read his book? As if Plato were my townsman and I never saw him,— my next neighbor and I never heard him speak or attended to the wisdom of his words. But how actually is it? His Dia- logues, which contain what was immortal in him, lie on the next shelf, and yet I never read them. We are under-bred and low-lived and illiterate; and in this respect I confess I do not make any very broad distinction between the illiterateness of my townsman who cannot read at all, and the illiterateness of him who has learned to read only what is for children and feeble intellects. We should be as good as the worthies of an- tiquity, but partly by first knowing how good they were. We are a race of tit-men, and soar but little higher in our intellec- tual flights than the columns of the daily paper.

It is not all books that are as dull as their readers. There are probably words addressed to our condition exactly, which, if we could really hear and understand, would be more salutary than the morning or the spring to our lives, and possibly put a new aspect on the face of things for us. How many a man has dated a new era in his life from the reading of a book. The book exists for us perchance which will explain our miracles and reveal new ones. The at present unutterable things we may find somewhere uttered. These same questions that disturb and puzzle and confound us have in their turn occurred to all the wise men; not one has been omitted; and each has answered them, according to his ability, by his words and his life. Moreover, with wisdom we shall learn liberality. The solitary hired man on a farm in the outskirts of Concord, who has had his second birth and peculiar religious experience, and is driven as he believes into silent gravity and exclusiveness by his faith, may think it is not true; but Zoroaster, thousands of years ago, travelled the same road and had the same experience; but he, being wise, knew it to be universal, and treated his neighbors accordingly, and is even said to have invented and established worship among men. Let him humbly commune with Zoroaster then, and, through the liberalizing influence of all the worthies, with Jesus Christ himself, and let "our church" go by the board.

We boast that we belong to the nineteenth century and are making the most rapid strides of any nation. But consider how little this village does for its own culture. I do not wish to flatter my townsmen, nor to be flattered by them, for that will not advance either of us. We need to be provoked,— goaded like oxen, as we are, into a trot. We have a comparatively decent system of common schools, schools for infants only; but excepting the half-starved Lyceum in the winter, and latterly the puny beginning of a library suggested by the state, no school for ourselves. We spend more on almost any article of bodily aliment or ailment than on our mental aliment. It is time that we had uncommon schools, that we did not leave off our education when we begin to be men and women. It is time that villages were universities, and their elder inhabitants the fellows of universities, with leisure—if they are indeed so well off—to pursue liberal studies the rest of their lives. Shall the world be confined to one Paris or one Oxford forever? Cannot students be boarded here and get a liberal education under the skies of Concord? Can we not hire some Abelard to lecture to us? Alas! what with foddering the cattle and tending the store, we are kept from school too long, and our education is sadly neglected. In this country, the village should in some respects take the place of the nobleman of Europe. It should be the patron of the fine arts. It is rich enough. It wants only the magnanimity and refinement. It can spend money enough on such things as farmers and traders value, but it is thought Utopian to propose spending money for things which more intelligent men know to be of far more worth. This town has spent seventeen thousand dollars on a town-house, thank fortune or politics, but probably it will not spend so much on living wit, the true meat to put into that shell, in a hundred years. The one hundred and twenty-five dollars annually subscribed for a Lyceum in the winter is better spent than any other equal sum raised in the town. If we live in the nineteenth century, why should we not enjoy the advantages which the nineteenth century offers? Why should our life be in any respect provincial? If we will read newspapers, why not skip the gossip of Boston and take the best newspaper in the world at once?— not be sucking the pap of "neutral family" papers, or browsing "Olive-Branches" here in New England. Let the reports of all the learned societies come to us, and we will see if they know any thing. Why should we leave it to Harper & Brothers and Redding & Co. to select our reading? As the nobleman of cultivated taste surrounds himself with whatever conduces to his culture,—genius—learning—wit—books— paintings—statuary—music—philosophical instruments, and the like; so let the village do,—not stop short at a pedagogue, a parson, a sexton, a parish library, and three selectmen, because our pilgrim forefathers got through a cold winter once on a bleak rock with these. To act collectively is according to the spirit of our institutions; and I am confident that, as our circumstances are more flourishing, our means are greater than the nobleman's. New England can hire all the wise men in the world to come and teach her, and board them round the while, and not be provincial at all. That is the *uncommon* school we want. Instead of noblemen, let us have noble villages of men. If it is necessary, omit one bridge over the river, go round a little there, and throw one arch at least over the darker gulf of ignorance which surrounds us.

Sounds

BUT WHILE we are confined to books, though the most select and classic, and read only particular written languages, which are themselves but dialects and provincial, we are in danger of forgetting the language which all things and events speak without metaphor, which alone is copious and standard. Much is published, but little printed. The rays which stream through the shutter will be no longer remembered when the shutter is wholly removed. No method nor discipline can supersede the necessity of being forever on the alert. What is a course of history, or philosophy, or poetry, no matter how well selected, or the best society, or the most admirable routine of life, compared with the discipline of looking always at what is to be seen? Will you be a reader, a student merely, or a seer? Read your fate, see what is before you, and walk on into futurity.

I did not read books the first summer; I hoed beans. Nay, I often did better than this. There were times when I could not afford to sacrifice the bloom of the present moment to any work, whether of the head or hands. I love a broad margin to my life. Sometimes, in a summer morning, having taken my accustomed bath, I sat in my sunny doorway from sunrise till noon, rapt in a revery, amidst the pines and hickories and sumachs, in undisturbed solitude and stillness, while the birds sang around or flitted noiseless through the house, until by the sun falling in at my west window, or the noise of some traveller's wagon on the distant highway, I was reminded of the lapse of time. I grew in those seasons like corn in the night, and they were far better than any work of the hands would have been. They were not time subtracted from my life, but so much over and above my usual allowance. I realized what the Orientals mean by contemplation and the forsaking of works. For the most part, I minded not how the hours went. The day advanced as if to light some work of mine; it was morning, and lo, now it is evening, and nothing memorable is accomplished. Instead of singing like the birds, I silently smiled at my incessant good fortune. As the sparrow had its trill, sitting on the hickory before my door, so had I my chuckle or suppressed warble which he might hear out of my nest. My days were not days of the week, bearing the stamp of any heathen deity, nor were they minced into hours and fretted by the ticking of a clock; for I lived like the Puri Indians, of whom it is said that "for yesterday, to-day, and to-morrow they have only one word, and they express the variety of meaning by pointing backward for yesterday, forward for to-morrow, and overhead for the passing day." This was sheer idleness to my fellow-townsmen, no doubt; but if the birds and flowers had tried me by their standard, I should not have been found wanting. A man must find his occasions in himself, it is true. The natural day is very calm, and will hardly reprove his indolence.

I had this advantage, at least, in my mode of life, over those who were obliged to look abroad for amusement, to society and the theatre, that my life itself was become my amusement and never ceased to be novel. It was a drama of many scenes and without an end. If we were always indeed getting our living, and regulating our lives according to the last and best mode we had learned, we should never be troubled with ennui. Follow your genius closely enough, and it will not fail to show you a fresh prospect every hour. Housework was a pleasant pastime. When my floor was dirty, I rose early, and, setting all my furniture out of doors on the grass, bed and bedstead making but one budget, dashed water on the floor, and sprinkled white sand from the pond on it, and then with a broom scrubbed it clean and white; and by the time the villagers had broken their fast the morning sun had dried my house sufficiently to allow me to move in again, and my meditations were almost uninterrupted. It was pleasant to see my whole household effects out on the grass, making a little pile like a gypsy's pack, and my three-legged table, from which I did not remove the books and pen and ink, standing amid the pines and hickories. They seemed glad to get out themselves, and as if unwilling to be brought in. I was sometimes tempted to stretch an awning over them and take my seat there. It was worth the while to see the sun shine on these things, and hear the free wind blow on them; so much more interesting most familiar objects look out of doors than in the house. A bird sits on the next bough, life-everlasting grows under the table, and blackberry vines run round its legs; pine cones, chestnut burs, and strawberry leaves are strewn about. It looked as if this was the way these forms came to be transferred to our furniture, to tables, chairs, and bedsteads,—because they once stood in their midst.

My house was on the side of a hill, immediately on the edge of the larger wood, in the midst of a young forest of pitch pines and hickories, and half a dozen rods from the pond, to which a narrow footpath led down the hill. In my front yard grew the strawberry, blackberry, and life-everlasting, johnswort and golden-rod, shrub-oaks and sand-cherry, blueberry and ground-nut. Near the end of May, the sand-cherry, (*Cerasus pumila,*) adorned the sides of the path with its delicate flowers arranged in umbels cylindrically about its short stems, which last, in the fall, weighed down with good sized and handsome cherries, fell over in wreaths like rays on every side. I tasted them out of compliment to Nature, though they were scarcely palatable. The sumach, (*Rhus glabra,*) grew luxuriantly about the house, pushing up through the embankment which I had made, and growing five or six feet the first season. Its broad pinnate tropical leaf was pleasant though strange to look on. The large buds, suddenly pushing out late in the spring from dry sticks which had seemed to be dead, developed themselves as by magic into graceful green and tender boughs, an inch in diameter; and sometimes, as I sat at my window, so heedlessly did they grow and tax their weak joints, I heard a fresh and tender bough suddenly fall like a fan to the ground, when there was not a breath of air stirring, broken off by its own weight. In August, the large masses of berries, which, when in flower, had attracted many wild bees, gradually assumed their bright velvety crimson hue, and by their weight again bent down and broke the tender limbs.

As I sit at my window this summer afternoon, hawks are circling about my clearing; the tantivy of wild pigeons, flying by twos and threes athwart my view, or perching restless on the white-pine boughs behind my house, gives a voice to the air; a fishhawk dimples the glassy surface of the pond and brings up a fish; a mink steals out of the marsh before my

door and seizes a frog by the shore; the sedge is bending
under the weight of the reed-birds flitting hither and thither;
and for the last half hour I have heard the rattle of railroad
cars, now dying away and then reviving like the beat of a
partridge, conveying travellers from Boston to the country.
For I did not live so out of the world as that boy, who, as I
hear, was put out to a farmer in the east part of the town,
but ere long ran away and came home again, quite down at
the heel and homesick. He had never seen such a dull and
out-of-the-way place; the folks were all gone off; why, you
couldn't even hear the whistle! I doubt if there is such a place
in Massachusetts now:—

> "In truth, our village has become a butt
> For one of those fleet railroad shafts, and o'er
> Our peaceful plain its soothing sound is—Concord."

The Fitchburg Railroad touches the pond about a hundred
rods south of where I dwell. I usually go to the village along
its causeway, and am, as it were, related to society by this
link. The men on the freight trains, who go over the whole
length of the road, bow to me as to an old acquaintance, they
pass me so often, and apparently they take me for an em-
ployee; and so I am. I too would fain be a track-repairer
somewhere in the orbit of the earth.

The whistle of the locomotive penetrates my woods summer and winter, sounding like the scream of a hawk sailing
over some farmer's yard, informing me that many restless city
merchants are arriving within the circle of the town, or adventurous country traders from the other side. As they come
under one horizon, they shout their warning to get off the
track to the other, heard sometimes through the circles of two
towns. Here come your groceries, country; your rations,
countrymen! Nor is there any man so independent on his
farm that he can say them nay. And here's your pay for them!
screams the countryman's whistle; timber like long battering
rams going twenty miles an hour against the city's walls, and
chairs enough to seat all the weary and heavy laden that dwell
within them. With such huge and lumbering civility the country hands a chair to the city. All the Indian huckleberry hills
are stripped, all the cranberry meadows are raked into the

city. Up comes the cotton, down goes the woven cloth; up comes the silk, down goes the woollen; up come the books, but down goes the wit that writes them.

When I meet the engine with its train of cars moving off with planetary motion,—or, rather, like a comet, for the beholder knows not if with that velocity and with that direction it will ever revisit this system, since its orbit does not look like a returning curve,—with its steam cloud like a banner streaming behind in golden and silver wreaths, like many a downy cloud which I have seen, high in the heavens, unfolding its masses to the light,—as if this travelling demigod, this cloud-compeller, would ere long take the sunset sky for the livery of his train; when I hear the iron horse make the hills echo with his snort like thunder, shaking the earth with his feet, and breathing fire and smoke from his nostrils, (what kind of winged horse or fiery dragon they will put into the new Mythology I don't know,) it seems as if the earth had got a race now worthy to inhabit it. If all were as it seems, and men made the elements their servants for noble ends! If the cloud that hangs over the engine were the perspiration of heroic deeds, or as beneficent to men as that which floats over the farmer's fields, then the elements and Nature herself would cheerfully accompany men on their errands and be their escort.

I watch the passage of the morning cars with the same feeling that I do the rising of the sun, which is hardly more regular. Their train of clouds stretching far behind and rising higher and higher, going to heaven while the cars are going to Boston, conceals the sun for a minute and casts my distant field into the shade, a celestial train beside which the petty train of cars which hugs the earth is but the barb of the spear. The stabler of the iron horse was up early this winter morning by the light of the stars amid the mountains, to fodder and harness his steed. Fire, too, was awakened thus early to put the vital heat in him and get him off. If the enterprise were as innocent as it is early! If the snow lies deep, they strap on his snow-shoes, and with the giant plough, plough a furrow from the mountains to the seaboard, in which the cars, like a following drill-barrow, sprinkle all the restless men and floating merchandise in the country for seed. All day the fire-steed flies over the country, stopping only that his master may rest, and I am awakened by his tramp and defiant snort at midnight, when in some remote glen in the woods he fronts the elements incased in ice and snow; and he will reach his stall only with the morning star, to start once more on his travels without rest or slumber. Or perchance, at evening, I hear him in his stable blowing off the superfluous energy of the day, that he may calm his nerves and cool his liver and brain for a few hours of iron slumber. If the enterprise were as heroic and commanding as it is protracted and unwearied!

Far through unfrequented woods on the confines of towns, where once only the hunter penetrated by day, in the darkest night dart these bright saloons without the knowledge of their inhabitants; this moment stopping at some brilliant station-house in town or city, where a social crowd is gathered, the next in the Dismal Swamp, scaring the owl and fox. The startings and arrivals of the cars are now the epochs in the village day. They go and come with such regularity and precision, and their whistle can be heard so far, that the farmers set their clocks by them, and thus one well conducted institution regulates a whole country. Have not men improved somewhat in punctuality since the railroad was invented? Do they not talk and think faster in the depot than they did in the stage-office? There is something electrifying in the atmosphere of the former place. I have been astonished at the miracles it has wrought; that some of my neighbors, who, I should have prophesied, once for all, would never get to Boston by so prompt a conveyance, are on hand when the bell rings. To do things "railroad fashion" is now the by-word; and it is worth the while to be warned so often and so sincerely by any power to get off its track. There is no stopping to read the riot act, no firing over the heads of the mob, in this case. We have constructed a fate, an *Atropos*, that never turns aside. (Let that be the name of your engine.) Men are advertised that at a certain hour and minute these bolts will be shot toward particular points of the compass; yet it interferes with no man's business, and the children go to school on the other track. We live the steadier for it. We are all educated thus to be sons of Tell. The air is full of invisible bolts. Every path but your own is the path of fate. Keep on your own track, then.

What recommends commerce to me is its enterprise and bravery. It does not clasp its hands and pray to Jupiter. I see these men every day go about their business with more or less courage and content, doing more even than they suspect, and perchance better employed than they could have consciously devised. I am less affected by their heroism who stood up for half an hour in the front line at Buena Vista, than by the steady and cheerful valor of the men who inhabit the snow-plough for their winter quarters; who have not merely the three-o'-clock in the morning courage, which Bonaparte thought was the rarest, but whose courage does not go to rest so early, who go to sleep only when the storm sleeps or the sinews of their iron steed are frozen. On this morning of the Great Snow, perchance, which is still raging and chilling men's blood, I hear the muffled tone of their engine bell from out the fog bank of their chilled breath, which announces that the cars *are coming*, without long delay, notwithstanding the veto of a New England north-east snow storm, and I behold the ploughmen covered with snow and rime, their heads peering above the mould-board which is turning down other than daisies and the nests of field-mice, like bowlders of the Sierra Nevada, that occupy an outside place in the universe.

Commerce is unexpectedly confident and serene, alert, adventurous, and unwearied. It is very natural in its methods withal, far more so than many fantastic enterprises and sentimental experiments, and hence its singular success. I am refreshed and expanded when the freight train rattles past me, and I smell the stores which go dispensing their odors all the way from Long Wharf to Lake Champlain, reminding me of foreign parts, of coral reefs, and Indian oceans, and tropical climes, and the extent of the globe. I feel more like a citizen of the world at the sight of the palm-leaf which will cover so many flaxen New England heads the next summer, the Manilla hemp and cocoa-nut husks, the old junk, gunny bags, scrap iron, and rusty nails. This car-load of torn sails is more legible and interesting now than if they should be wrought into paper and printed books. Who can write so graphically the history of the storms they have weathered as these rents have done? They are proof-sheets which need no correction. Here goes lumber from the Maine woods, which did not go

out to sea in the last freshet, risen four dollars on the thousand because of what did go out or was split up; pine, spruce,
cedar,—first, second, third and fourth qualities, so lately all
of one quality, to wave over the bear, and moose, and caribou. Next rolls Thomaston lime, a prime lot, which will get
far among the hills before it gets slacked. These rags in bales,
of all hues and qualities, the lowest condition to which cotton
and linen descend, the final result of dress,—of patterns
which are now no longer cried up, unless it be in Milwaukie,
as those splendid articles, English, French, or American
prints, ginghams, muslins, &c., gathered from all quarters
both of fashion and poverty, going to become paper of one
color or a few shades only, on which forsooth will be written
tales of real life, high and low, and founded on fact! This
closed car smells of salt fish, the strong New England and
commercial scent, reminding me of the Grand Banks and the
fisheries. Who has not seen a salt fish, thoroughly cured for
this world, so that nothing can spoil it, and putting the perseverance of the saints to the blush? with which you may
sweep or pave the streets, and split your kindlings, and the
teamster shelter himself and his lading against sun wind and
rain behind it,—and the trader, as a Concord trader once did,
hang it up by his door for a sign when he commences business, until at last his oldest customer cannot tell surely
whether it be animal, vegetable, or mineral, and yet it shall be
as pure as a snowflake, and if it be put into a pot and boiled,
will come out an excellent dun fish for a Saturday's dinner.
Next Spanish hides, with the tails still preserving their twist
and the angle of elevation they had when the oxen that wore
them were careering over the pampas of the Spanish main,—
a type of all obstinacy, and evincing how almost hopeless and
incurable are all constitutional vices. I confess, that practically
speaking, when I have learned a man's real disposition, I have
no hopes of changing it for the better or worse in this state
of existence. As the Orientals say, "A cur's tail may be
warmed, and pressed, and bound round with ligatures, and
after a twelve years' labor bestowed upon it, still it will retain
its natural form." The only effectual cure for such inveteracies
as these tails exhibit is to make glue of them, which I believe
is what is usually done with them, and then they will stay put

and stick. Here is a hogshead of molasses or of brandy directed to John Smith, Cuttingsville, Vermont, some trader among the Green Mountains, who imports for the farmers near his clearing, and now perchance stands over his bulkhead and thinks of the last arrivals on the coast, how they may affect the price for him, telling his customers this moment, as he has told them twenty times before this morning, that he expects some by the next train of prime quality. It is advertised in the Cuttingsville Times.

While these things go up other things come down. Warned by the whizzing sound, I look up from my book and see some tall pine, hewn on far northern hills, which has winged its way over the Green Mountains and the Connecticut, shot like an arrow through the township within ten minutes, and scarce another eye beholds it; going

> "to be the mast
> Of some great ammiral."

And hark! here comes the cattle-train bearing the cattle of a thousand hills, sheepcots, stables, and cow-yards in the air, drovers with their sticks, and shepherd boys in the midst of their flocks, all but the mountain pastures, whirled along like leaves blown from the mountains by the September gales. The air is filled with the bleating of calves and sheep, and the hustling of oxen, as if a pastoral valley were going by. When the old bell-weather at the head rattles his bell, the mountains do indeed skip like rams and the little hills like lambs. A carload of drovers, too, in the midst, on a level with their droves now, their vocation gone, but still clinging to their useless sticks as their badge of office. But their dogs, where are they? It is a stampede to them; they are quite thrown out; they have lost the scent. Methinks I hear them barking behind the Peterboro' Hills, or panting up the western slope of the Green Mountains. They will not be in at the death. Their vocation, too, is gone. Their fidelity and sagacity are below par now. They will slink back to their kennels in disgrace, or perchance run wild and strike a league with the wolf and the fox. So is your pastoral life whirled past and away. But the bell rings, and I must get off the track and let the cars go by;—

What's the railroad to me?
I never go to see
Where it ends.
It fills a few hollows,
And makes banks for the swallows,
It sets the sand a-blowing,
And the blackberries a-growing,

but I cross it like a cart-path in the woods. I will not have my eyes put out and my ears spoiled by its smoke and steam and hissing.

Now that the cars are gone by, and all the restless world with them, and the fishes in the pond no longer feel their rumbling, I am more alone than ever. For the rest of the long afternoon, perhaps, my meditations are interrupted only by the faint rattle of a carriage or team along the distant highway.

Sometimes, on Sundays, I heard the bells, the Lincoln, Acton, Bedford, or Concord bell, when the wind was favorable, a faint, sweet, and, as it were, natural melody, worth importing into the wilderness. At a sufficient distance over the woods this sound acquires a certain vibratory hum, as if the pine needles in the horizon were the strings of a harp which it swept. All sound heard at the greatest possible distance produces one and the same effect, a vibration of the universal lyre, just as the intervening atmosphere makes a distant ridge of earth interesting to our eyes by the azure tint it imparts to it. There came to me in this case a melody which the air had strained, and which had conversed with every leaf and needle of the wood, that portion of the sound which the elements had taken up and modulated and echoed from vale to vale. The echo is, to some extent, an original sound, and therein is the magic and charm of it. It is not merely a repetition of what was worth repeating in the bell, but partly the voice of the wood; the same trivial words and notes sung by a wood-nymph.

At evening, the distant lowing of some cow in the horizon beyond the woods sounded sweet and melodious, and at first I would mistake it for the voices of certain minstrels by whom

I was sometimes serenaded, who might be straying over hill and dale; but soon I was not unpleasantly disappointed when it was prolonged into the cheap and natural music of the cow. I do not mean to be satirical, but to express my appreciation of those youths' singing, when I state that I perceived clearly that it was akin to the music of the cow, and they were at length one articulation of Nature.

Regularly at half past seven, in one part of the summer, after the evening train had gone by, the whippoorwills chanted their vespers for half an hour, sitting on a stump by my door, or upon the ridge pole of the house. They would begin to sing almost with as much precision as a clock, within five minutes of a particular time, referred to the setting of the sun, every evening. I had a rare opportunity to become acquainted with their habits. Sometimes I heard four or five at once in different parts of the wood, by accident one a bar behind another, and so near me that I distinguished not only the cluck after each note, but often that singular buzzing sound like a fly in a spider's web, only proportionally louder. Sometimes one would circle round and round me in the woods a few feet distant as if tethered by a string, when probably I was near its eggs. They sang at intervals throughout the night, and were again as musical as ever just before and about dawn.

When other birds are still the screech owls take up the strain, like mourning women their ancient u-lu-lu. Their dismal scream is truly Ben Jonsonian. Wise midnight hags! It is no honest and blunt tu-whit tu-who of the poets, but, without jesting, a most solemn graveyard ditty, the mutual consolations of suicide lovers remembering the pangs and the delights of supernal love in the infernal groves. Yet I love to hear their wailing, their doleful responses, trilled along the wood-side, reminding me sometimes of music and singing birds; as if it were the dark and tearful side of music, the regrets and sighs that would fain be sung. They are the spirits, the low spirits and melancholy forebodings, of fallen souls that once in human shape night-walked the earth and did the deeds of darkness, now expiating their sins with their wailing hymns or threnodies in the scenery of their transgressions. They give me a new sense of the variety and capacity of that nature which is our common dwelling. *Oh-o-o-o-o that I never had been bor-r-r-r-n!* sighs one on this side of the pond, and circles with the restlessness of despair to some new perch on the gray oaks. Then—*that I never had been bor-r-r-r-n!* echoes another on the farther side with tremulous sincerity, and—*bor-r-r-r-n!* comes faintly from far in the Lincoln woods.

I was also serenaded by a hooting owl. Near at hand you could fancy it the most melancholy sound in Nature, as if she meant by this to stereotype and make permanent in her choir the dying moans of a human being,—some poor weak relic of mortality who has left hope behind, and howls like an animal, yet with human sobs, on entering the dark valley, made more awful by a certain gurgling melodiousness,—I find myself beginning with the letters gl when I try to imitate it,—expressive of a mind which has reached the gelatinous mildewy stage in the mortification of all healthy and courageous thought. It reminded me of ghouls and idiots and insane howlings. But now one answers from far woods in a strain made really melodious by distance,—*Hoo hoo hoo, hoorer hoo*; and indeed for the most part it suggested only pleasing associations, whether heard by day or night, summer or winter.

I rejoice that there are owls. Let them do the idiotic and maniacal hooting for men. It is a sound admirably suited to swamps and twilight woods which no day illustrates, suggesting a vast and undeveloped nature which men have not recognized. They represent the stark twilight and unsatisfied thoughts which all have. All day the sun has shone on the surface of some savage swamp, where the single spruce stands hung with usnea lichens, and small hawks circulate above, and the chicadee lisps amid the evergreens, and the partridge and rabbit skulk beneath; but now a more dismal and fitting day dawns, and a different race of creatures awakes to express the meaning of Nature there.

Late in the evening I heard the distant rumbling of wagons over bridges,—a sound heard farther than almost any other at night,—the baying of dogs, and sometimes again the lowing of some disconsolate cow in a distant barn-yard. In the mean while all the shore rang with the trump of bullfrogs, the sturdy spirits of ancient wine-bibbers and wassailers, still unrepentant, trying to sing a catch in their Stygian lake,—if the Walden nymphs will pardon the comparison, for though there are almost no weeds, there are frogs there,—who would fain keep up the hilarious rules of their old festal tables, though their voices have waxed hoarse and solemnly grave, mocking at mirth, and the wine has lost its flavor, and become only liquor to distend their paunches, and sweet intoxication never comes to drown the memory of the past, but mere saturation and waterloggedness and distention. The most aldermanic, with his chin upon a heart-leaf, which serves for a napkin to his drooling chaps, under this northern shore quaffs a deep draught of the once scorned water, and passes round the cup with the ejaculation *tr-r-r-oonk, tr-r-r-oonk, tr-r-r-oonk!* and straightway comes over the water from some distant cove the same password repeated, where the next in seniority and girth has gulped down to his mark; and when this observance has made the circuit of the shores, then ejaculates the master of ceremonies, with satisfaction, *tr-r-r-oonk!* and each in his turn repeats the same down to the least distended, leakiest, and flabbiest paunched, that there be no mistake; and then the bowl goes round again and again, until the sun disperses the morning mist, and only the patriarch is not under the pond, but vainly bellowing *troonk* from time to time, and pausing for a reply.

I am not sure that I ever heard the sound of cock-crowing from my clearing, and I thought that it might be worth the while to keep a cockerel for his music merely, as a singing bird. The note of this once wild Indian pheasant is certainly the most remarkable of any bird's, and if they could be naturalized without being domesticated, it would soon become the most famous sound in our woods, surpassing the clangor of the goose and the hooting of the owl; and then imagine the cackling of the hens to fill the pauses when their lords' clarions rested! No wonder that man added this bird to his tame stock,—to say nothing of the eggs and drum-sticks. To walk in a winter morning in a wood where these birds abounded, their native woods, and hear the wild cockerels crow on the trees, clear and shrill for miles over the resounding earth, drowning the feebler notes of other birds,—think of it! It would put nations on the alert. Who would not be early to rise, and rise earlier and earlier every successive day of his life, till he became unspeakably healthy, wealthy, and wise? This foreign bird's note is celebrated by the poets of all countries along with the notes of their native songsters. All climates agree with brave Chanticleer. He is more indigenous even than the natives. His health is ever good, his lungs are sound, his spirits never flag. Even the sailor on the Atlantic and Pacific is awakened by his voice; but its shrill sound never roused me from my slumbers. I kept neither dog, cat, cow, pig, nor hens, so that you would have said there was a deficiency of domestic sounds; neither the churn, nor the spinning wheel, nor even the singing of the kettle, nor the hissing of the urn, nor children crying, to comfort one. An old-fashioned man would have lost his senses or died of ennui before this. Not even rats in the wall, for they were starved out, or rather were never baited in,—only squirrels on the roof and under the floor, a whippoorwill on the ridge pole, a blue-jay screaming beneath the window, a hare or woodchuck under the house, a screech-owl or a cat-owl behind it, a flock of wild geese or a laughing loon on the pond, and a fox to bark in the night. Not even a lark or an oriole, those mild plantation birds, ever visited my clearing. No cockerels to crow nor hens to cackle in the yard. No yard! but unfenced Nature reaching up to your very sills. A young forest growing up under your windows, and wild sumachs and blackberry vines breaking through into your cellar; sturdy pitch-pines rubbing and creaking against the shingles for want of room, their roots reaching quite under the house. Instead of a scuttle or a blind blown off in the gale,—a pine tree snapped off or torn up by the roots behind your house for fuel. Instead of no path to the front-yard gate in the Great Snow,—no gate,—no front-yard,—and no path to the civilized world!

Solitude

THIS IS a delicious evening, when the whole body is one sense, and imbibes delight through every pore. I go and come with a strange liberty in Nature, a part of herself. As I walk along the stony shore of the pond in my shirt sleeves, though it is cool as well as cloudy and windy, and I see nothing special to attract me, all the elements are unusually congenial to me. The bullfrogs trump to usher in the night, and the note of the whippoorwill is borne on the rippling wind from over the water. Sympathy with the fluttering alder and poplar leaves almost takes away my breath; yet, like the lake, my serenity is rippled but not ruffled. These small waves raised by the evening wind are as remote from storm as the smooth reflecting surface. Though it is now dark, the wind still blows and roars in the wood, the waves still dash, and some creatures lull the rest with their notes. The repose is never complete. The wildest animals do not repose, but seek their prey now; the fox, and skunk, and rabbit, now roam the fields and woods without fear. They are Nature's watchmen, —links which connect the days of animated life.

When I return to my house I find that visitors have been there and left their cards, either a bunch of flowers, or a wreath of evergreen, or a name in pencil on a yellow walnut leaf or a chip. They who come rarely to the woods take some little piece of the forest into their hands to play with by the way, which they leave, either intentionally or accidentally. One has peeled a willow wand, woven it into a ring, and dropped it on my table. I could always tell if visitors had called in my absence, either by the bended twigs or grass, or the print of their shoes, and generally of what sex or age or quality they were by some slight trace left, as a flower dropped, or a bunch of grass plucked and thrown away, even as far off as the railroad, half a mile distant, or by the lingering odor of a cigar or pipe. Nay, I was frequently notified of the passage of a traveller along the highway sixty rods off by the scent of his pipe.

There is commonly sufficient space about us. Our horizon is never quite at our elbows. The thick wood is not just at

our door, nor the pond, but somewhat is always clearing, familiar and worn by us, appropriated and fenced in some way,
and reclaimed from Nature. For what reason have I this vast
range and circuit, some square miles of unfrequented forest,
for my privacy, abandoned to me by men? My nearest neighbor is a mile distant, and no house is visible from any place
but the hill-tops within half a mile of my own. I have my
horizon bounded by woods all to myself; a distant view of
the railroad where it touches the pond on the one hand, and
of the fence which skirts the woodland road on the other. But
for the most part it is as solitary where I live as on the prairies. It is as much Asia or Africa as New England. I have, as
it were, my own sun and moon and stars, and a little world
all to myself. At night there was never a traveller passed my
house, or knocked at my door, more than if I were the first
or last man; unless it were in the spring, when at long intervals some came from the village to fish for pouts,—they
plainly fished much more in the Walden Pond of their own
natures, and baited their hooks with darkness,—but they
soon retreated, usually with light baskets, and left "the world
to darkness and to me," and the black kernel of the night was
never profaned by any human neighborhood. I believe that
men are generally still a little afraid of the dark, though the
witches are all hung, and Christianity and candles have been
introduced.

Yet I experienced sometimes that the most sweet and tender, the most innocent and encouraging society may be found
in any natural object, even for the poor misanthrope and most
melancholy man. There can be no very black melancholy to
him who lives in the midst of Nature and has his senses still.
There was never yet such a storm but it was Æolian music to
a healthy and innocent ear. Nothing can rightly compel a simple and brave man to a vulgar sadness. While I enjoy the
friendship of the seasons I trust that nothing can make life a
burden to me. The gentle rain which waters my beans and
keeps me in the house to-day is not drear and melancholy,
but good for me too. Though it prevents my hoeing them, it
is of far more worth than my hoeing. If it should continue so
long as to cause the seeds to rct in the ground and destroy
the potatoes in the low lands, it would still be good for the

grass on the uplands, and, being good for the grass, it would
be good for me. Sometimes, when I compare myself with
other men, it seems as if I were more favored by the gods
than they, beyond any deserts that I am conscious of; as if I
had a warrant and surety at their hands which my fellows
have not, and were especially guided and guarded. I do not
flatter myself, but if it be possible they flatter me. I have never
felt lonesome, or in the least oppressed by a sense of solitude,
but once, and that was a few weeks after I came to the woods,
when, for an hour, I doubted if the near neighborhood of
man was not essential to a serene and healthy life. To be alone
was something unpleasant. But I was at the same time conscious of a slight insanity in my mood, and seemed to foresee
my recovery. In the midst of a gentle rain while these
thoughts prevailed, I was suddenly sensible of such sweet and
beneficent society in Nature, in the very pattering of the
drops, and in every sound and sight around my house, an
infinite and unaccountable friendliness all at once like an atmosphere sustaining me, as made the fancied advantages of
human neighborhood insignificant, and I have never thought
of them since. Every little pine needle expanded and swelled
with sympathy and befriended me. I was so distinctly made
aware of the presence of something kindred to me, even in
scenes which we are accustomed to call wild and dreary, and
also that the nearest of blood to me and humanest was not a
person nor a villager, that I thought no place could ever be
strange to me again.—

> "Mourning untimely consumes the sad;
>   Few are their days in the land of the living,
>   Beautiful daughter of Toscar."

Some of my pleasantest hours were during the long rain
storms in the spring or fall, which confined me to the house
for the afternoon as well as the forenoon, soothed by their
ceaseless roar and pelting; when an early twilight ushered in
a long evening in which many thoughts had time to take root
and unfold themselves. In those driving north-east rains
which tried the village houses so, when the maids stood ready
with mop and pail in front entries to keep the deluge out, I
sat behind my door in my little house, which was all entry,

and thoroughly enjoyed its protection. In one heavy thunder shower the lightning struck a large pitch-pine across the pond, making a very conspicuous and perfectly regular spiral groove from top to bottom, an inch or more deep, and four or five inches wide, as you would groove a walking-stick. I passed it again the other day, and was struck with awe on looking up and beholding that mark, now more distinct than ever, where a terrific and resistless bolt came down out of the harmless sky eight years ago. Men frequently say to me, "I should think you would feel lonesome down there, and want to be nearer to folks, rainy and snowy days and nights especially." I am tempted to reply to such,—This whole earth which we inhabit is but a point in space. How far apart, think you, dwell the two most distant inhabitants of yonder star, the breadth of whose disk cannot be appreciated by our instruments? Why should I feel lonely? is not our planet in the Milky Way? This which you put seems to me not to be the most important question. What sort of space is that which separates a man from his fellows and makes him solitary? I have found that no exertion of the legs can bring two minds much nearer to one another. What do we want most to dwell near to? Not to many men surely, the depot, the post-office, the bar-room, the meeting-house, the school-house, the grocery, Beacon Hill, or the Five Points, where men most congregate, but to the perennial source of our life, whence in all our experience we have found that to issue; as the willow stands near the water and sends out its roots in that direction. This will vary with different natures, but this is the place where a wise man will dig his cellar. . . . I one evening overtook one of my townsmen, who has accumulated what is called "a handsome property,"—though I never got a *fair* view of it,—on the Walden road, driving a pair of cattle to market, who inquired of me how I could bring my mind to give up so many of the comforts of life. I answered that I was very sure I liked it passably well; I was not joking. And so I went home to my bed, and left him to pick his way through the darkness and the mud to Brighton,—or Bright-town,—which place he would reach some time in the morning.

Any prospect of awakening or coming to life to a dead man makes indifferent all times and places. The place where that

may occur is always the same, and indescribably pleasant to
all our senses. For the most part we allow only outlying and
transient circumstances to make our occasions. They are, in
fact, the cause of our distraction. Nearest to all things is that
power which fashions their being. *Next* to us the grandest
laws are continually being executed. *Next* to us is not the
workman whom we have hired, with whom we love so well
to talk, but the workman whose work we are.

"How vast and profound is the influence of the subtile
powers of Heaven and of Earth!"

"We seek to perceive them, and we do not see them; we
seek to hear them, and we do not hear them; identified with
the substance of things, they cannot be separated from them."

"They cause that in all the universe men purify and sanctify
their hearts, and clothe themselves in their holiday garments
to offer sacrifices and oblations to their ancestors. It is an
ocean of subtile intelligences. They are every where, above us,
on our left, on our right; they environ us on all sides."

We are the subjects of an experiment which is not a little
interesting to me. Can we not do without the society of our
gossips a little while under these circumstances,—have our
own thoughts to cheer us? Confucius says truly, "Virtue does
not remain as an abandoned orphan; it must of necessity have
neighbors."

With thinking we may be beside ourselves in a sane sense.
By a conscious effort of the mind we can stand aloof from
actions and their consequences; and all things, good and bad,
go by us like a torrent. We are not wholly involved in Nature.
I may be either the driftwood in the stream, or Indra in the
sky looking down on it. I *may* be affected by a theatrical ex-
hibition; on the other hand, I *may not* be affected by an actual
event which appears to concern me much more. I only know
myself as a human entity; the scene, so to speak, of thoughts
and affections; and am sensible of a certain doubleness by
which I can stand as remote from myself as from another.
However intense my experience, I am conscious of the presence and criticism of a part of me, which, as it were, is not a
part of me, but spectator, sharing no experience, but taking
note of it; and that is no more I than it is you. When the
play, it may be the tragedy, of life is over, the spectator goes

his way. It was a kind of fiction, a work of the imagination only, so far as he was concerned. This doubleness may easily make us poor neighbors and friends sometimes.

I find it wholesome to be alone the greater part of the time. To be in company, even with the best, is soon wearisome and dissipating. I love to be alone. I never found the companion that was so companionable as solitude. We are for the most part more lonely when we go abroad among men than when we stay in our chambers. A man thinking or working is always alone, let him be where he will. Solitude is not measured by the miles of space that intervene between a man and his fellows. The really diligent student in one of the crowded hives of Cambridge College is as solitary as a dervis in the desert. The farmer can work alone in the field or the woods all day, hoeing or chopping, and not feel lonesome, because he is employed; but when he comes home at night he cannot sit down in a room alone, at the mercy of his thoughts, but must be where he can "see the folks," and recreate, and as he thinks remunerate, himself for his day's solitude; and hence he wonders how the student can sit alone in the house all night and most of the day without ennui and "the blues;" but he does not realize that the student, though in the house, is still at work in *his* field, and chopping in *his* woods, as the farmer in his, and in turn seeks the same recreation and society that the latter does, though it may be a more condensed form of it.

Society is commonly too cheap. We meet at very short intervals, not having had time to acquire any new value for each other. We meet at meals three times a day, and give each other a new taste of that old musty cheese that we are. We have had to agree on a certain set of rules, called etiquette and politeness, to make this frequent meeting tolerable, and that we need not come to open war. We meet at the post-office, and at the sociable, and about the fireside every night; we live thick and are in each other's way, and stumble over one another, and I think that we thus lose some respect for one another. Certainly less frequency would suffice for all important and hearty communications. Consider the girls in a factory,—never alone, hardly in their dreams. It would be better if there were but one inhabitant to a square mile, as where I live. The value of a man is not in his skin, that we should touch him.

I have heard of a man lost in the woods and dying of famine and exhaustion at the foot of a tree, whose loneliness was relieved by the grotesque visions with which, owing to bodily weakness, his diseased imagination surrounded him, and which he believed to be real. So also, owing to bodily and mental health and strength, we may be continually cheered by a like but more normal and natural society, and come to know that we are never alone.

I have a great deal of company in my house; especially in the morning, when nobody calls. Let me suggest a few comparisons, that some one may convey an idea of my situation. I am no more lonely than the loon in the pond that laughs so loud, or than Walden Pond itself. What company has that lonely lake, I pray? And yet it has not the blue devils, but the blue angels in it, in the azure tint of its waters. The sun is alone, except in thick weather, when there sometimes appear to be two, but one is a mock sun. God is alone,—but the devil, he is far from being alone; he sees a great deal of company; he is legion. I am no more lonely than a single mullein or dandelion in a pasture, or a bean leaf, or sorrel, or a horse-fly, or a humble-bee. I am no more lonely than the Mill Brook, or a weathercock, or the northstar, or the south wind, or an April shower, or a January thaw, or the first spider in a new house.

I have occasional visits in the long winter evenings, when the snow falls fast and the wind howls in the wood, from an old settler and original proprietor, who is reported to have dug Walden Pond, and stoned it, and fringed it with pine woods; who tells me stories of old time and of new eternity; and between us we manage to pass a cheerful evening with social mirth and pleasant views of things, even without apples or cider,—a most wise and humorous friend, whom I love much, who keeps himself more secret than ever did Goffe or Whalley; and though he is thought to be dead, none can show where he is buried. An elderly dame, too, dwells in my neighborhood, invisible to most persons, in whose odorous herb garden I love to stroll sometimes, gathering simples and listening to her fables; for she has a genius of unequalled fertility, and her memory runs back farther than mythology, and she can tell me the original of every fable, and on what fact every one is founded, for the incidents occurred when she was young. A ruddy and lusty old dame, who delights in all weathers and seasons, and is likely to outlive all her children yet.

The indescribable innocence and beneficence of Nature,— of sun and wind and rain, of summer and winter,—such health, such cheer, they afford forever! and such sympathy have they ever with our race, that all Nature would be affected, and the sun's brightness fade, and the winds would sigh humanely, and the clouds rain tears, and the woods shed their leaves and put on mourning in midsummer, if any man should ever for a just cause grieve. Shall I not have intelligence with the earth? Am I not partly leaves and vegetable mould myself?

What is the pill which will keep us well, serene, contented? Not my or thy great-grandfather's, but our great-grandmother Nature's universal, vegetable, botanic medicines, by which she has kept herself young always, outlived so many old Parrs in her day, and fed her health with their decaying fatness. For my panacea, instead of one of those quack vials of a mixture dipped from Acheron and the Dead Sea, which come out of those long shallow black-schooner looking wagons which we sometimes see made to carry bottles, let me have a draught of undiluted morning air. Morning air! If men will not drink of this at the fountain-head of the day, why, then, we must even bottle up some and sell it in the shops, for the benefit of those who have lost their subscription ticket to morning time in this world. But remember, it will not keep quite till noon-day even in the coolest cellar, but drive out the stopples long ere that and follow westward the steps of Aurora. I am no worshipper of Hygeia, who was the daughter of that old herb-doctor Æsculapius, and who is represented on monuments holding a serpent in one hand, and in the other a cup out of which the serpent sometimes drinks; but rather of Hebe, cupbearer to Jupiter, who was the daughter of Juno and wild lettuce, and who had the power of restoring gods and men to the vigor of youth. She was probably the only thoroughly sound-conditioned, healthy, and robust young lady that ever walked the globe, and wherever she came it was spring.

Visitors

I THINK that I love society as much as most, and am ready enough to fasten myself like a bloodsucker for the time to any full-blooded man that comes in my way. I am naturally no hermit, but might possibly sit out the sturdiest frequenter of the bar-room, if my business called me thither.

I had three chairs in my house; one for solitude, two for friendship, three for society. When visitors came in larger and unexpected numbers there was but the third chair for them all, but they generally economized the room by standing up. It is surprising how many great men and women a small house will contain. I have had twenty-five or thirty souls, with their bodies, at once under my roof, and yet we often parted without being aware that we had come very near to one another. Many of our houses, both public and private, with their almost innumerable apartments, their huge halls and their cellars for the storage of wines and other munitions of peace, appear to me extravagantly large for their inhabitants. They are so vast and magnificent that the latter seem to be only vermin which infest them. I am surprised when the herald blows his summons before some Tremont or Astor or Middlesex House, to see come creeping out over the piazza for all inhabitants a ridiculous mouse, which soon again slinks into some hole in the pavement.

One inconvenience I sometimes experienced in so small a house, the difficulty of getting to a sufficient distance from my guest when we began to utter the big thoughts in big words. You want room for your thoughts to get into sailing trim and run a course or two before they make their port. The bullet of your thought must have overcome its lateral and ricochet motion and fallen into its last and steady course before it reaches the ear of the hearer, else it may plough out again through the side of his head. Also, our sentences wanted room to unfold and form their columns in the interval. Individuals, like nations, must have suitable broad and natural boundaries, even a considerable neutral ground, between them. I have found it a singular luxury to talk across the pond to a companion on the opposite side. In my house we were so near that we could not begin to hear,—we could not speak low enough to be heard; as when you throw two stones into calm water so near that they break each other's undulations. If we are merely loquacious and loud talkers, then we can afford to stand very near together, cheek by jowl, and feel each other's breath; but if we speak reservedly and thoughtfully, we want to be farther apart, that all animal heat and moisture may have a chance to evaporate. If we would enjoy the most intimate society with that in each of us which is without, or above, being spoken to, we must not only be silent, but commonly so far apart bodily that we cannot possibly hear each other's voice in any case. Referred to this standard, speech is for the convenience of those who are hard of hearing; but there are many fine things which we cannot say if we have to shout. As the conversation began to assume a loftier and grander tone, we gradually shoved our chairs farther apart till they touched the wall in opposite corners, and then commonly there was not room enough.

My "best" room, however, my withdrawing room, always ready for company, on whose carpet the sun rarely fell, was the pine wood behind my house. Thither in summer days, when distinguished guests came, I took them, and a priceless domestic swept the floor and dusted the furniture and kept the things in order.

If one guest came he sometimes partook of my frugal meal, and it was no interruption to conversation to be stirring a hasty-pudding, or watching the rising and maturing of a loaf of bread in the ashes, in the mean while. But if twenty came and sat in my house there was nothing said about dinner, though there might be bread enough for two, more than if eating were a forsaken habit; but we naturally practised abstinence; and this was never felt to be an offence against hospitality, but the most proper and considerate course. The waste and decay of physical life, which so often needs repair, seemed miraculously retarded in such a case, and the vital vigor stood its ground. I could entertain thus a thousand as well as twenty; and if any ever went away disappointed or hungry from my house when they found me at home, they may depend upon it that I sympathized with them at least. So easy is it, though many housekeepers doubt it, to establish new and better customs in the place of the old. You need not rest your reputation on the dinners you give. For my own part, I was never so effectually deterred from frequenting a man's house, by any kind of Cerberus whatever, as by the parade one made about dining me, which I took to be a very polite and roundabout hint never to trouble him so again. I think I shall never revisit those scenes. I should be proud to have for the motto of my cabin those lines of Spenser which one of my visitors inscribed on a yellow walnut leaf for a card: —

> "Arrivéd there, the little house they fill,
>   Ne looke for entertainment where none was;
>   Rest is their feast, and all things at their will:
>   The noblest mind the best contentment has."

When Winslow, afterward governor of the Plymouth Colony, went with a companion on a visit of ceremony to Massassoit on foot through the woods, and arrived tired and hungry at his lodge, they were well received by the king, but nothing was said about eating that day. When the night arrived, to quote their own words, — "He laid us on the bed with himself and his wife, they at the one end and we at the other, it being only plank, laid a foot from the ground, and a thin mat upon them. Two more of his chief men, for want of room, pressed by and upon us; so that we were worse weary of our lodging than of our journey." At one o'clock the next day Massassoit "brought two fishes that he had shot," about thrice as big as a bream; "these being boiled, there were at least forty looked for a share in them. The most ate of them. This meal only we had in two nights and a day; and had not one of us bought a partridge, we had taken our journey fasting." Fearing that they would be light-headed for want of food and also sleep, owing to "the savages' barbarous singing, (for they used to sing themselves asleep,)" and that they might get home while they had strength to travel, they departed. As for lodging, it is true they were but poorly entertained, though what they found an inconvenience was no doubt intended for an honor; but as far as eating was concerned, I do not see how the Indians could have done better. They had nothing to eat themselves, and they were wiser than to think that apologies could supply the place of food to their guests; so they drew their belts tighter and said nothing about it. Another time when Winslow visited them, it being a season of plenty with them, there was no deficiency in this respect.

As for men, they will hardly fail one any where. I had more visitors while I lived in the woods than at any other period of my life; I mean that I had some. I met several there under more favorable circumstances than I could any where else. But fewer came to see me upon trivial business. In this respect, my company was winnowed by my mere distance from town. I had withdrawn so far within the great ocean of solitude, into which the rivers of society empty, that for the most part, so far as my needs were concerned, only the finest sediment was deposited around me. Beside, there were wafted to me evidences of unexplored and uncultivated continents on the other side.

Who should come to my lodge this morning but a true Homeric or Paphlagonian man,—he had so suitable and poetic a name that I am sorry I cannot print it here,—a Canadian, a wood-chopper and post-maker, who can hole fifty posts in a day, who made his last supper on a woodchuck which his dog caught. He, too, has heard of Homer, and, "if it were not for books," would "not know what to do rainy days," though perhaps he has not read one wholly through for many rainy seasons. Some priest who could pronounce the Greek itself taught him to read his verse in the testament in his native parish far away; and now I must translate to him, while he holds the book, Achilles' reproof to Patroclus for his sad countenance.—"Why are you in tears, Patroclus, like a young girl?"—

"Or have you alone heard some news from Phthia?
They say that Menœtius lives yet, son of Actor,
And Peleus lives, son of Æacus, among the Myrmidons,
Either of whom having died, we should greatly grieve."

He says, "That's good." He has a great bundle of white-oak bark under his arm for a sick man, gathered this Sunday morning. "I suppose there's no harm in going after such a thing to-day," says he. To him Homer was a great writer, though what his writing was about he did not know. A more simple and natural man it would be hard to find. Vice and disease, which cast such a sombre moral hue over the world, seemed to have hardly any existence for him. He was about twenty-eight years old, and had left Canada and his father's house a dozen years before to work in the States, and earn money to buy a farm with at last, perhaps in his native country. He was cast in the coarsest mould; a stout but sluggish body, yet gracefully carried, with a thick sunburnt neck, dark bushy hair, and dull sleepy blue eyes, which were occasionally lit up with expression. He wore a flat gray cloth cap, a dingy wool-colored greatcoat, and cowhide boots. He was a great consumer of meat, usually carrying his dinner to his work a couple of miles past my house,—for he chopped all summer,—in a tin pail; cold meats, often cold woodchucks, and coffee in a stone bottle which dangled by a string from his belt; and sometimes he offered me a drink. He came along early, crossing my bean-field, though without anxiety or haste to get to his work, such as Yankees exhibit. He wasn't a-going to hurt himself. He didn't care if he only earned his board. Frequently he would leave his dinner in the bushes, when his dog had caught a woodchuck by the way, and go back a mile and a half to dress it and leave it in the cellar of the house where he boarded, after deliberating first for half an hour whether he could not sink it in the pond safely till nightfall,— loving to dwell long upon these themes. He would say, as he went by in the morning, "How thick the pigeons are! If working every day were not my trade, I could get all the meat I should want by hunting,—pigeons, woodchucks, rabbits, partridges,—by gosh! I could get all I should want for a week in one day."

He was a skilful chopper, and indulged in some flourishes and ornaments in his art. He cut his trees level and close to the ground, that the sprouts which came up afterward might be more vigorous and a sled might slide over the stumps; and instead of leaving a whole tree to support his corded wood, he would pare it away to a slender stake or splinter which you could break off with your hand at last.

He interested me because he was so quiet and solitary and so happy withal; a well of good humor and contentment which overflowed at his eyes. His mirth was without alloy. Sometimes I saw him at his work in the woods, felling trees, and he would greet me with a laugh of inexpressible satisfaction, and a salutation in Canadian French, though he spoke English as well. When I approached him he would suspend his work, and with half-suppressed mirth lie along the trunk of a pine which he had felled, and, peeling off the inner bark, roll it up into a ball and chew it while he laughed and talked. Such an exuberance of animal spirits had he that he sometimes tumbled down and rolled on the ground with laughter at any thing which made him think and tickled him. Looking round upon the trees he would exclaim,—"By George! I can enjoy myself well enough here chopping; I want no better sport." Sometimes, when at leisure, he amused himself all day in the woods with a pocket pistol, firing salutes to himself at regular intervals as he walked. In the winter he had a fire by which at noon he warmed his coffee in a kettle; and as he sat on a log to eat his dinner the chicadees would sometimes come round and alight on his arm and peck at the potato in his fingers; and he said that he "liked to have the little *fellers* about him."

In him the animal man chiefly was developed. In physical endurance and contentment he was cousin to the pine and the rock. I asked him once if he was not sometimes tired at night, after working all day; and he answered, with a sincere and serious look, "Gorrappit, I never was tired in my life." But the intellectual and what is called spiritual man in him were slumbering as in an infant. He had been instructed only in that innocent and ineffectual way in which the Catholic priests teach the aborigines, by which the pupil is never educated to the degree of consciousness, but only to the degree of trust and reverence, and a child is not made a man, but kept a child. When Nature made him, she gave him a strong body and contentment for his portion, and propped him on every side with reverence and reliance, that he might live out his threescore years and ten a child. He was so genuine and unsophisticated that no introduction would serve to introduce him, more than if you introduced a woodchuck to your neighbor. He had got to find him out as you did. He would not play any part. Men paid him wages for work, and so

helped to feed and clothe him; but he never exchanged opinions with them. He was so simply and naturally humble—if
he can be called humble who never aspires—that humility
was no distinct quality in him, nor could he conceive of it.
Wiser men were demigods to him. If you told him that such
a one was coming, he did as if he thought that any thing so
grand would expect nothing of himself, but take all the responsibility on itself, and let him be forgotten still. He never
heard the sound of praise. He particularly reverenced the
writer and the preacher. Their performances were miracles.
When I told him that I wrote considerably, he thought for a
long time that it was merely the handwriting which I meant,
for he could write a remarkably good hand himself. I sometimes found the name of his native parish handsomely written
in the snow by the highway, with the proper French accent,
and knew that he had passed. I asked him if he ever wished
to write his thoughts. He said that he had read and written
letters for those who could not, but he never tried to write
thoughts,—no, he could not, he could not tell what to put
first, it would kill him, and then there was spelling to be attended to at the same time!

I heard that a distinguished wise man and reformer asked
him if he did not want the world to be changed; but he answered with a chuckle of surprise in his Canadian accent, not
knowing that the question had ever been entertained before,
"No, I like it well enough." It would have suggested many
things to a philosopher to have dealings with him. To a
stranger he appeared to know nothing of things in general;
yet I sometimes saw in him a man whom I had not seen before, and I did not know whether he was as wise as Shakspeare or as simply ignorant as a child, whether to suspect
him of a fine poetic consciousness or of stupidity. A townsman told me that when he met him sauntering through the
village in his small close-fitting cap, and whistling to himself,
he reminded him of a prince in disguise.

His only books were an almanac and an arithmetic, in
which last he was considerably expert. The former was a sort
of cyclopædia to him, which he supposed to contain an abstract of human knowledge, as indeed it does to a considerable extent. I loved to sound him on the various reforms of

the day, and he never failed to look at them in the most simple and practical light. He had never heard of such things before. Could he do without factories? I asked. He had worn the home-made Vermont gray, he said, and that was good. Could he dispense with tea and coffee? Did this country afford any beverage beside water? He had soaked hemlock leaves in water and drank it, and thought that was better than water in warm weather. When I asked him if he could do without money, he showed the convenience of money in such a way as to suggest and coincide with the most philosophical accounts of the origin of this institution, and the very derivation of the word *pecunia*. If an ox were his property, and he wished to get needles and thread at the store, he thought it would be inconvenient and impossible soon to go on mortgaging some portion of the creature each time to that amount. He could defend many institutions better than any philosopher, because, in describing them as they concerned him, he gave the true reason for their prevalence, and speculation had not suggested to him any other. At another time, hearing Plato's definition of a man,—a biped without feathers,—and that one exhibited a cock plucked and called it Plato's man, he thought it an important difference that the *knees* bent the wrong way. He would sometimes exclaim, "How I love to talk! By George, I could talk all day!" I asked him once, when I had not seen him for many months, if he had got a new idea this summer. "Good Lord," said he, "a man that has to work as I do, if he does not forget the ideas he has had, he will do well. May be the man you hoe with is inclined to race; then, by gorry, your mind must be there; you think of weeds." He would sometimes ask me first on such occasions, if I had made any improvement. One winter day I asked him if he was always satisfied with himself, wishing to suggest a substitute within him for the priest without, and some higher motive for living. "Satisfied!" said he; "some men are satisfied with one thing, and some with another. One man, perhaps, if he has got enough, will be satisfied to sit all day with his back to the fire and his belly to the table, by George!" Yet I never, by any manœuvring, could get him to take the spiritual view of things; the highest that he appeared to conceive of was a simple expediency, such as you might expect an animal to appreciate; and this, practically, is true of most men. If I suggested any improvement in his mode of life, he merely answered, without expressing any regret, that it was too late. Yet he thoroughly believed in honesty and the like virtues.

There was a certain positive originality, however slight, to be detected in him, and I occasionally observed that he was thinking for himself and expressing his own opinion, a phenomenon so rare that I would any day walk ten miles to observe it, and it amounted to the re-origination of many of the institutions of society. Though he hesitated, and perhaps failed to express himself distinctly, he always had a presentable thought behind. Yet his thinking was so primitive and immersed in his animal life, that, though more promising than a merely learned man's, it rarely ripened to any thing which can be reported. He suggested that there might be men of genius in the lowest grades of life, however permanently humble and illiterate, who take their own view always, or do not pretend to see at all; who are as bottomless even as Walden Pond was thought to be, though they may be dark and muddy.

Many a traveller came out of his way to see me and the inside of my house, and, as an excuse for calling, asked for a glass of water. I told them that I drank at the pond, and pointed thither, offering to lend them a dipper. Far off as I lived, I was not exempted from that annual visitation which occurs, methinks, about the first of April, when every body is on the move; and I had my share of good luck, though there were some curious specimens among my visitors. Half-witted men from the almshouse and elsewhere came to see me; but I endeavored to make them exercise all the wit they had, and make their confessions to me; in such cases making wit the theme of our conversation; and so was compensated. Indeed, I found some of them to be wiser than the so called *overseers* of the poor and selectmen of the town, and thought it was time that the tables were turned. With respect to wit, I learned that there was not much difference between the half and the whole. One day, in particular, an inoffensive, simple-minded pauper, whom with others I had often seen used as fencing stuff, standing or sitting on a bushel in the fields to keep cattle and himself from straying, visited me, and expressed a wish to live as I did. He told me, with the utmost simplicity and truth, quite superior, or rather *inferior*, to any thing that is called humility, that he was "deficient in intellect." These were his words. The Lord had made him so, yet he supposed the Lord cared as much for him as for another. "I have always been so," said he, "from my childhood; I never had much mind; I was not like other children; I am weak in the head. It was the Lord's will, I suppose." And there he was to prove the truth of his words. He was a metaphysical puzzle to me. I have rarely met a fellow-man on such promising ground,—it was so simple and sincere and so true all that he said. And, true enough, in proportion as he appeared to humble himself was he exalted. I did not know at first but it was the result of a wise policy. It seemed that from such a basis of truth and frankness as the poor weak-headed pauper had laid, our intercourse might go forward to something better than the intercourse of sages.

I had some guests from those not reckoned commonly among the town's poor, but who should be; who are among the world's poor, at any rate; guests who appeal, not to your hospitality, but to your *hospitalality*; who earnestly wish to be helped, and preface their appeal with the information that they are resolved, for one thing, never to help themselves. I require of a visitor that he be not actually starving, though he may have the very best appetite in the world, however he got it. Objects of charity are not guests. Men who did not know when their visit had terminated, though I went about my business again, answering them from greater and greater remoteness. Men of almost every degree of wit called on me in the migrating season. Some who had more wits than they knew what to do with; runaway slaves with plantation manners, who listened from time to time, like the fox in the fable, as if they heard the hounds a-baying on their track, and looked at me beseechingly, as much as to say,—

"O Christian, will you send me back?"

One real runaway slave, among the rest, whom I helped to forward toward the northstar. Men of one idea, like a hen with one chicken, and that a duckling; men of a thousand ideas, and unkempt heads, like those hens which are made to take charge of a hundred chickens, all in pursuit of one bug, a score of them lost in every morning's dew,—and become frizzled and mangy in consequence; men of ideas instead of legs, a sort of intellectual centipede that made you crawl all over. One man proposed a book in which visitors should write their names, as at the White Mountains; but, alas! I have too good a memory to make that necessary.

I could not but notice some of the peculiarities of my visitors. Girls and boys and young women generally seemed glad to be in the woods. They looked in the pond and at the flowers, and improved their time. Men of business, even farmers, thought only of solitude and employment, and of the great distance at which I dwelt from something or other; and though they said that they loved a ramble in the woods occasionally, it was obvious that they did not. Restless committed men, whose time was all taken up in getting a living or keeping it; ministers who spoke of God as if they enjoyed a monopoly of the subject, who could not bear all kinds of opinions; doctors, lawyers, uneasy housekeepers who pried into my cupboard and bed when I was out,—how came Mrs. —— to know that my sheets were not as clean as hers?—young men who had ceased to be young, and had concluded that it was safest to follow the beaten track of the professions,—all these generally said that it was not possible to do so much good in my position. Ay! there was the rub. The old and infirm and the timid, of whatever age or sex, thought most of sickness, and sudden accident and death; to them life seemed full of danger,—what danger is there if you don't think of any?—and they thought that a prudent man would carefully select the safest position, where Dr. B. might be on hand at a moment's warning. To them the village was literally a *com-munity*, a league for mutual defence, and you would suppose that they would not go a-huckleberrying without a medicine chest. The amount of it is, if a man is alive, there is always *danger* that he may die, though the danger must be allowed to be less in proportion as he is dead-and-alive to begin with. A man sits as many risks as he runs.

Finally, there were the self-styled reformers, the greatest bores of all, who thought that I was forever singing,—

> This is the house that I built;
> This is the man that lives in the house that I built;

but they did not know that the third line was,—

> These are the folks that worry the man
> That lives in the house that I built.

I did not fear the hen-harriers, for I kept no chickens; but I feared the men-harriers rather.

I had more cheering visitors than the last. Children come a-berrying, railroad men taking a Sunday morning walk in clean shirts, fishermen and hunters, poets and philosophers, in short, all honest pilgrims, who came out to the woods for freedom's sake, and really left the village behind, I was ready to greet with,—"Welcome, Englishmen! welcome, Englishmen!" for I had had communication with that race.

The Bean-Field

MEANWHILE my beans, the length of whose rows, added together, was seven miles already planted, were impatient to be hoed, for the earliest had grown considerably before the latest were in the ground; indeed they were not easily to be put off. What was the meaning of this so steady and self-respecting, this small Herculean labor, I knew not. I came to love my rows, my beans, though so many more than I wanted. They attached me to the earth, and so I got strength like Antæus. But why should I raise them? Only Heaven knows. This was my curious labor all summer,—to make this portion of the earth's surface, which had yielded only cinquefoil, blackberries, johnswort, and the like, before, sweet wild fruits and pleasant flowers, produce instead this pulse. What shall I learn of beans or beans of me? I cherish them, I hoe them, early and late I have an eye to them; and this is my day's work. It is a fine broad leaf to look on. My auxiliaries are the dews and rains which water this dry soil, and what fertility is in the soil itself, which for the most part is lean and effete. My enemies are worms, cool days, and most of all woodchucks. The last have nibbled for me a quarter of an acre clean. But what right had I to oust johnswort and the rest, and break up their ancient herb garden? Soon, however, the remaining beans will be too tough for them, and go forward to meet new foes.

When I was four years old, as I well remember, I was brought from Boston to this my native town, through these very woods and this field, to the pond. It is one of the oldest scenes stamped on my memory. And now to-night my flute has waked the echoes over that very water. The pines still stand here older than I; or, if some have fallen, I have cooked my supper with their stumps, and a new growth is rising all around, preparing another aspect for new infant eyes. Almost the same johnswort springs from the same perennial root in this pasture, and even I have at length helped to clothe that fabulous landscape of my infant dreams, and one of the results of my presence and influence is seen in these bean leaves, corn blades, and potato vines.

I planted about two acres and a half of upland; and as it was only about fifteen years since the land was cleared, and I myself had got out two or three cords of stumps, I did not give it any manure; but in the course of the summer it appeared by the arrow-heads which I turned up in hoeing, that an extinct nation had anciently dwelt here and planted corn and beans ere white men came to clear the land, and so, to some extent, had exhausted the soil for this very crop.

Before yet any woodchuck or squirrel had run across the road, or the sun had got above the shrub-oaks, while all the dew was on, though the farmers warned me against it,—I would advise you to do all your work if possible while the dew is on,—I began to level the ranks of haughty weeds in my bean-field and throw dust upon their heads. Early in the morning I worked barefooted, dabbling like a plastic artist in the dewy and crumbling sand, but later in the day the sun blistered my feet. There the sun lighted me to hoe beans, pacing slowly backward and forward over that yellow gravelly upland, between the long green rows, fifteen rods, the one end terminating in a shrub oak copse where I could rest in the shade, the other in a blackberry field where the green berries deepened their tints by the time I had made another bout. Removing the weeds, putting fresh soil about the bean stems, and encouraging this weed which I had sown, making the yellow soil express its summer thought in bean leaves and blossoms rather than in wormwood and piper and millet grass, making the earth say beans instead of grass,—this was my daily work. As I had little aid from horses or cattle, or hired men or boys, or improved implements of husbandry, I was much slower, and became much more intimate with my beans than usual. But labor of the hands, even when pursued to the verge of drudgery, is perhaps never the worst form of idleness. It has a constant and imperishable moral, and to the scholar it yields a classic result. A very *agricola laboriosus* was I to travellers bound westward through Lincoln and Wayland to nobody knows where; they sitting at their ease in gigs, with elbows on knees, and reins loosely hanging in festoons; I the home-staying, laborious native of the soil. But soon my homestead was out of their sight and thought. It was the only open and cultivated field for a great distance on either side of the road; so they made the most of it; and sometimes the man in the field heard more of travellers' gossip and comment than was meant for his ear: "Beans so late! peas so late!"—for I continued to plant when others had began to hoe,—the ministerial husbandman had not suspected it. "Corn, my boy, for fodder; corn for fodder." "Does he *live* there?" asks the black bonnet of the gray coat; and the hard-featured farmer reins up his grateful dobbin to inquire what you are doing where he sees no manure in the furrow, and recommends a little chip dirt, or any little waste stuff, or it may be ashes or plaster. But here were two acres and a half of furrows, and only a hoe for cart and two hands to draw it,—there being an aversion to other carts and horses,—and chip dirt far away. Fellow-travellers as they rattled by compared it aloud with the fields which they had passed, so that I came to know how I stood in the agricultural world. This was one field not in Mr. Coleman's report. And, by the way, who estimates the value of the crop which Nature yields in the still wilder fields unimproved by man? The crop of *English* hay is carefully weighed, the moisture calculated, the silicates and the potash; but in all dells and pond holes in the woods and pastures and swamps grows a rich and various crop only unreaped by man. Mine was, as it were, the connecting link between wild and cultivated fields; as some states are civilized, and others half-civilized, and others savage or barbarous, so my field was, though not in a bad sense, a half-cultivated field. They were beans cheerfully returning to their wild and primitive state that I cultivated, and my hoe played the *Rans des Vaches* for them.

Near at hand, upon the topmost spray of a birch, sings the brown-thrasher—or red mavis, as some love to call him—all the morning, glad of your society, that would find out another farmer's field if yours were not here. While you are planting the seed, he cries,—"Drop it, drop it,—cover it up, cover it up,—pull it up, pull it up, pull it up." But this was not corn, and so it was safe from such enemies as he. You may wonder what his rigmarole, his amateur Paganini performances on one string or on twenty, have to do with your planting, and yet prefer it to leached ashes or plaster. It was a cheap sort of top dressing in which I had entire faith.

As I drew a still fresher soil about the rows with my hoe, I disturbed the ashes of unchronicled nations who in primeval years lived under these heavens, and their small implements of war and hunting were brought to the light of this modern day. They lay mingled with other natural stones, some of which bore the marks of having been burned by Indian fires, and some by the sun, and also bits of pottery and glass brought hither by the recent cultivators of the soil. When my hoe tinkled against the stones, that music echoed to the woods and the sky, and was an accompaniment to my labor which yielded an instant and immeasurable crop. It was no longer beans that I hoed, nor I that hoed beans; and I remembered with as much pity as pride, if I remembered at all, my acquaintances who had gone to the city to attend the oratorios. The night-hawk circled overhead in the sunny afternoons—for I sometimes made a day of it—like a mote in the eye, or in heaven's eye, falling from time to time with a swoop and a sound as if the heavens were rent, torn at last to very rags and tatters, and yet a seamless cope remained; small imps that fill the air and lay their eggs on the ground on bare sand or rocks on the tops of hills, where few have found them; graceful and slender like ripples caught up from the pond, as leaves are raised by the wind to float in the heavens; such kindredship is in Nature. The hawk is aerial brother of the wave which he sails over and surveys, those his perfect air-inflated wings answering to the elemental unfledged pinions of the sea. Or sometimes I watched a pair of hen-hawks circling high in the sky, alternately soaring and descending, approaching and leaving one another, as if they were the imbodiment of my own thoughts. Or I was attracted by the passage of wild pigeons from this wood to that, with a slight quivering winnowing sound and carrier haste; or from under a rotten stump my hoe turned up a sluggish portentous and outlandish spotted salamander, a trace of Egypt and the Nile, yet our contemporary. When I paused to lean on my hoe, these sounds and sights I heard and saw any where in the row, a part of the inexhaustible entertainment which the country offers.

On gala days the town fires its great guns, which echo like popguns to these woods, and some waifs of martial music occasionally penetrate thus far. To me, away there in my bean-field at the other end of the town, the big guns sounded as if a puff ball had burst; and when there was a military turnout of which I was ignorant, I have sometimes had a vague sense all the day of some sort of itching and disease in the horizon, as if some eruption would break out there soon, either scarlatina or canker-rash, until at length some more favorable puff of wind, making haste over the fields and up the Wayland road, brought me information of the "trainers." It seemed by the distant hum as if somebody's bees had swarmed, and that the neighbors, according to Virgil's advice, by a faint *tintinnabulum* upon the most sonorous of their domestic utensils, were endeavoring to call them down into the hive again. And when the sound died quite away, and the hum had ceased, and the most favorable breezes told no tale, I knew that they had got the last drone of them all safely into the Middlesex hive, and that now their minds were bent on the honey with which it was smeared.

I felt proud to know that the liberties of Massachusetts and of our fatherland were in such safe keeping; and as I turned to my hoeing again I was filled with an inexpressible confidence, and pursued my labor cheerfully with a calm trust in the future.

When there were several bands of musicians, it sounded as if all the village was a vast bellows, and all the buildings expanded and collapsed alternately with a din. But sometimes it was a really noble and inspiring strain that reached these woods, and the trumpet that sings of fame, and I felt as if I could spit a Mexican with a good relish,—for why should we always stand for trifles?—and looked round for a woodchuck or a skunk to exercise my chivalry upon. These martial strains seemed as far away as Palestine, and reminded me of a march of crusaders in the horizon, with a slight tantivy and tremulous motion of the elm-tree tops which overhang the village. This was one of the *great* days; though the sky had from my clearing only the same everlastingly great look that it wears daily, and I saw no difference in it.

It was a singular experience that long acquaintance which I cultivated with beans, what with planting, and hoeing, and harvesting, and threshing, and picking over, and selling

them,—the last was the hardest of all,—I might add eating,
for I did taste. I was determined to know beans. When they
were growing, I used to hoe from five o'clock in the morning
till noon, and commonly spent the rest of the day about other
affairs. Consider the intimate and curious acquaintance one
makes with various kinds of weeds,—it will bear some iteration in the account, for there was no little iteration in the
labor,—disturbing their delicate organizations so ruthlessly,
and making such invidious distinctions with his hoe, levelling
whole ranks of one species, and sedulously cultivating another. That's Roman wormwood,—that's pigweed,—that's
sorrel,—that's piper-grass,—have at him, chop him up, turn
his roots upward to the sun, don't let him have a fibre in the
shade, if you do he'll turn himself t'other side up and be as
green as a leek in two days. A long war, not with cranes, but
with weeds, those Trojans who had sun and rain and dews on
their side. Daily the beans saw me come to their rescue armed
with a hoe, and thin the ranks of their enemies, filling up the
trenches with weedy dead. Many a lusty crest-waving Hector,
that towered a whole foot above his crowding comrades, fell
before my weapon and rolled in the dust.

Those summer days which some of my contemporaries devoted to the fine arts in Boston or Rome, and others to contemplation in India, and others to trade in London or New
York, I thus, with the other farmers of New England, devoted
to husbandry. Not that I wanted beans to eat, for I am by
nature a Pythagorean, so far as beans are concerned, whether
they mean porridge or voting, and exchanged them for rice;
but, perchance, as some must work in fields if only for the
sake of tropes and expression, to serve a parable-maker one
day. It was on the whole a rare amusement, which, continued
too long, might have become a dissipation. Though I gave
them no manure, and did not hoe them all once, I hoed them
unusually well as far as I went, and was paid for it in the end,
"there being in truth," as Evelyn says, "no compost or
lætation whatsoever comparable to this continual motion, re-
pastination, and turning of the mould with the spade." "The
earth," he adds elsewhere, "especially if fresh, has a certain
magnetism in it, by which it attracts the salt, power, or virtue
(call it either) which gives it life, and is the logic of all the

labor and stir we keep about it, to sustain us; all dungings and other sordid temperings being but the vicars succedaneous to this improvement." Moreover, this being one of those "worn-out and exhausted lay fields which enjoy their sabbath," had perchance, as Sir Kenelm Digby thinks likely, attracted "vital spirits" from the air. I harvested twelve bushels of beans.

But to be more particular; for it is complained that Mr. Coleman has reported chiefly the expensive experiments of gentlemen farmers; my outgoes were,—

For a hoe, ...	$0 54	
Ploughing, harrowing, and furrowing, ...	7 50,	Too much.
Beans for seed, ...	3 12½	
Potatoes "	1 33	
Peas "	0 40	
Turnip seed, ...	0 06	
White line for crow fence, ...	0 02	
Horse cultivator and boy three hours, ...	1 00	
Horse and cart to get crop, ...	0 75	
In all, ...	$14 72½	

My income was, (patrem familias vendacem, non emacem esse oportet,) from

Nine bushels and twelve quarts of beans sold, ...	$16 94
Five " large potatoes, ...	2 50
Nine " small "	2 25
Grass, ...	1 00
Stalks, ...	0 75
In all, ...	$23 44
Leaving a pecuniary profit, as I have elsewhere said, of	$8 71½.

This is the result of my experience in raising beans. Plant the common small white bush bean about the first of June, in rows three feet by eighteen inches apart, being careful to select fresh round and unmixed seed. First look out for worms, and supply vacancies by planting anew. Then look out for woodchucks, if it is an exposed place, for they will nibble off the earliest tender leaves almost clean as they go; and again, when the young tendrils make their appearance, they have notice of it, and will shear them off with both buds and young pods, sitting erect like a squirrel. But above all harvest as early as possible, if you would escape frosts and have a fair and salable crop; you may save much loss by this means.

This further experience also I gained. I said to myself, I will not plant beans and corn with so much industry another summer, but such seeds, if the seed is not lost, as sincerity, truth, simplicity, faith, innocence, and the like, and see if they will not grow in this soil, even with less toil and manurance, and sustain me, for surely it has not been exhausted for these crops. Alas! I said this to myself; but now another summer is gone, and another, and another, and I am obliged to say to you, Reader, that the seeds which I planted, if indeed they *were* the seeds of those virtues, were wormeaten or had lost their vitality, and so did not come up. Commonly men will only be brave as their fathers were brave, or timid. This generation is very sure to plant corn and beans each new year precisely as the Indians did centuries ago and taught the first settlers to do, as if there were a fate in it. I saw an old man the other day, to my astonishment, making the holes with a hoe for the seventieth time at least, and not for himself to lie down in! But why should not the New Englander try new adventures, and not lay so much stress on his grain, his potato and grass crop, and his orchards?— raise other crops than these? Why concern ourselves so much about our beans for seed, and not be concerned at all about a new generation of men? We should really be fed and cheered if when we met a man we were sure to see that some of the qualities which I have named, which we all prize more than those other productions, but which are for the most part broadcast and floating in the air, had taken root and grown in him. Here comes such a subtile and ineffable quality, for instance, as truth or justice, though the slightest amount or new variety of it, along the road. Our ambassadors should be instructed to send home such seeds as these, and Congress help to distribute them over all the land. We should never stand upon ceremony with sincerity. We should never cheat and insult and banish one another by our meanness, if there were present the kernel of worth and friendliness. We should not meet thus in haste. Most men I do not meet at all, for they seem not to have time; they are busy about their beans. We would not deal with a man thus plodding ever, leaning on a hoe or a spade as a staff between his work, not as a mushroom, but partially risen out of the

earth, something more than erect, like swallows alighted and
walking on the ground.—

> "And as he spake, his wings would now and then
> Spread, as he meant to fly, then close again,"

so that we should suspect that we might be conversing with
an angel. Bread may not always nourish us; but it always does
us good, it even takes stiffness out of our joints, and makes
us supple and buoyant, when we knew not what ailed us, to
recognize any generosity in man or Nature, to share any unmixed and heroic joy.

Ancient poetry and mythology suggest, at least, that husbandry was once a sacred art; but it is pursued with irreverent
haste and heedlessness by us, our object being to have large
farms and large crops merely. We have no festival, nor procession, nor ceremony, not excepting our Cattle-shows and so
called Thanksgivings, by which the farmer expresses a sense
of the sacredness of his calling, or is reminded of its sacred
origin. It is the premium and the feast which tempt him. He
sacrifices not to Ceres and the Terrestrial Jove, but to the infernal Plutus rather. By avarice and selfishness, and a grovelling habit, from which none of us is free, of regarding the soil
as property, or the means of acquiring property chiefly, the
landscape is deformed, husbandry is degraded with us, and
the farmer leads the meanest of lives. He knows Nature but
as a robber. Cato says that the profits of agriculture are particularly pious or just, (*maximeque pius quæstus,*) and according to Varro the old Romans "called the same earth Mother
and Ceres, and thought that they who cultivated it led a pious
and useful life, and that they alone were left of the race of
King Saturn."

We are wont to forget that the sun looks on our cultivated
fields and on the prairies and forests without distinction.
They all reflect and absorb his rays alike, and the former make
but a small part of the glorious picture which he beholds in
his daily course. In his view the earth is all equally cultivated
like a garden. Therefore we should receive the benefit of his
light and heat with a corresponding trust and magnanimity.
What though I value the seed of these beans, and harvest that
in the fall of the year? This broad field which I have looked

at so long looks not to me as the principal cultivator, but away from me to influences more genial to it, which water and make it green. These beans have results which are not harvested by me. Do they not grow for woodchucks partly? The ear of wheat, (in Latin *spica*, obsoletely *speca*, from *spe*, hope,) should not be the only hope of the husbandman; its kernel or grain (*granum*, from *gerendo*, bearing,) is not all that it bears. How, then, can our harvest fail? Shall I not rejoice also at the abundance of the weeds whose seeds are the granary of the birds? It matters little comparatively whether the fields fill the farmer's barns. The true husbandman will cease from anxiety, as the squirrels manifest no concern whether the woods will bear chestnuts this year or not, and finish his labor with every day, relinquishing all claim to the produce of his fields, and sacrificing in his mind not only his first but his last fruits also.

The Village

A<small>FTER HOEING</small>, or perhaps reading and writing, in the forenoon, I usually bathed again in the pond, swimming across one of its coves for a stint, and washed the dust of labor from my person, or smoothed out the last wrinkle which study had made, and for the afternoon was absolutely free. Every day or two I strolled to the village to hear some of the gossip which is incessantly going on there, circulating either from mouth to mouth, or from newspaper to newspaper, and which, taken in homœopathic doses, was really as refreshing in its way as the rustle of leaves and the peeping of frogs. As I walked in the woods to see the birds and squirrels, so I walked in the village to see the men and boys; instead of the wind among the pines I heard the carts rattle. In one direction from my house there was a colony of muskrats in the river meadows; under the grove of elms and buttonwoods in the other horizon was a village of busy men, as curious to me as if they had been prairie dogs, each sitting at the mouth of its burrow, or running over to a neighbor's to gossip. I went there frequently to observe their habits. The village appeared to me a great news room; and on one side, to support it, as once at Redding & Company's on State Street, they kept nuts and raisins, or salt and meal and other groceries. Some have such a vast appetite for the former commodity, that is, the news, and such sound digestive organs, that they can sit forever in public avenues without stirring, and let it simmer and whisper through them like the Etesian winds, or as if inhaling ether, it only producing numbness and insensibility to pain,—otherwise it would often be painful to hear,—without affecting the consciousness. I hardly ever failed, when I rambled through the village, to see a row of such worthies, either sitting on a ladder sunning themselves, with their bodies inclined forward and their eyes glancing along the line this way and that, from time to time, with a voluptuous expression, or else leaning against a barn with their hands in their pockets, like caryatides, as if to prop it up. They, being commonly out of doors, heard whatever was in the wind. These are the coarsest mills, in which all gossip is first rudely digested or cracked up before it is emptied into finer and more delicate hoppers within doors. I observed that the vitals of the village were the grocery, the bar-room, the post-office, and the bank; and, as a necessary part of the machinery, they kept a bell, a big gun, and a fire-engine, at convenient places; and the houses were so arranged as to make the most of mankind, in lanes and fronting one another, so that every traveller had to run the gantlet, and every man, woman, and child might get a lick at him. Of course, those who were stationed nearest to the head of the line, where they could most see and be seen, and have the first blow at him, paid the highest prices for their places; and the few straggling inhabitants in the outskirts, where long gaps in the line began to occur, and the traveller could get over walls or turn aside into cow paths, and so escape, paid a very slight ground or window tax. Signs were hung out on all sides to allure him; some to catch him by the appetite, as the tavern and victualling cellar; some by the fancy, as the dry goods store and the jeweller's; and others by the hair or the feet or the skirts, as the barber, the shoemaker, or the tailor. Besides, there was a still more terrible standing invitation to call at every one of these houses, and company expected about these times. For the most part I escaped wonderfully from these dangers, either by proceeding at once boldly and without deliberation to the goal, as is recommended to those who run the gantlet, or by keeping my thoughts on high things, like Orpheus, who, "loudly singing the praises of the gods to his lyre, drowned the voices of the Sirens, and kept out of danger." Sometimes I bolted suddenly, and nobody could tell my whereabouts, for I did not stand much about gracefulness, and never hesitated at a gap in a fence. I was even accustomed to make an irruption into some houses, where I was well entertained, and after learning the kernels and very last sieve-ful of news, what had subsided, the prospects of war and peace, and whether the world was likely to hold together much longer, I was let out through the rear avenues, and so escaped to the woods again.

It was very pleasant, when I staid late in town, to launch myself into the night, especially if it was dark and tempestuous, and set sail from some bright village parlor or lecture room, with a bag of rye or Indian meal upon my shoulder, for my snug harbor in the woods, having made all tight without and withdrawn under hatches with a merry crew of thoughts, leaving only my outer man at the helm, or even tying up the helm when it was plain sailing. I had many a genial thought by the cabin fire "as I sailed." I was never cast away nor distressed in any weather, though I encountered some severe storms. It is darker in the woods, even in common nights, than most suppose. I frequently had to look up at the opening between the trees above the path in order to learn my route, and, where there was no cart-path, to feel with my feet the faint track which I had worn, or steer by the known relation of particular trees which I felt with my hands, passing between two pines for instance, not more than eighteen inches apart, in the midst of the woods, invariably in the darkest night. Sometimes, after coming home thus late in a dark and muggy night, when my feet felt the path which my eyes could not see, dreaming and absent-minded all the way, until I was aroused by having to raise my hand to lift the latch, I have not been able to recall a single step of my walk, and I have thought that perhaps my body would find its way home if its master should forsake it, as the hand finds its way to the mouth without assistance. Several times, when a visitor chanced to stay into evening, and it proved a dark night, I was obliged to conduct him to the cart-path in the rear of the house, and then point out to him the direction he was to pursue, and in keeping which he was to be guided rather by his feet than his eyes. One very dark night I directed thus on their way two young men who had been fishing in the pond. They lived about a mile off through the woods, and were quite used to the route. A day or two after one of them told me that they wandered about the greater part of the night, close by their own premises, and did not get home till toward morning, by which time, as there had been several heavy showers in the mean while, and the leaves were very wet, they were drenched to their skins. I have heard of many going astray even in the village streets, when the darkness was so thick that you could cut it with a knife, as the saying is. Some who live in the outskirts, having come to town a-shopping in their wagons, have been obliged to put up for the night; and gentlemen and ladies making a call have gone half a mile out of their way, feeling the sidewalk only with their feet, and not knowing when they turned. It is a surprising and memorable, as well as valuable experience, to be lost in the woods any time. Often in a snow storm, even by day, one will come out upon a well-known road, and yet find it impossible to tell which way leads to the village. Though he knows that he has travelled it a thousand times, he cannot recognize a feature in it, but it is as strange to him as if it were a road in Siberia. By night, of course, the perplexity is infinitely greater. In our most trivial walks, we are constantly, though unconsciously, steering like pilots by certain well-known beacons and head-lands, and if we go beyond our usual course we still carry in our minds the bearing of some neighboring cape; and not till we are completely lost, or turned round,—for a man needs only to be turned round once with his eyes shut in this world to be lost,—do we appreciate the vastness and strangeness of Nature. Every man has to learn the points of compass again as often as he awakes, whether from sleep or any abstraction. Not till we are lost, in other words, not till we have lost the world, do we begin to find ourselves, and realize where we are and the infinite extent of our relations.

One afternoon, near the end of the first summer, when I went to the village to get a shoe from the cobbler's, I was seized and put into jail, because, as I have elsewhere related, I did not pay a tax to, or recognize the authority of, the state which buys and sells men, women, and children, like cattle at the door of its senate-house. I had gone down to the woods for other purposes. But, wherever a man goes, men will pursue and paw him with their dirty institutions, and, if they can, constrain him to belong to their desperate odd-fellow society. It is true, I might have resisted forcibly with more or less effect, might have run "amok" against society; but I preferred that society should run "amok" against me, it being the desperate party. However, I was released the next day, obtained my mended shoe, and returned to the woods in season to get my dinner of huckleberries on Fair-Haven Hill. I was never molested by any person but those who represented the state. I had no lock nor bolt but for the desk which held my papers, not even a nail to put over my latch or windows. I never fastened my door night or day, though I was to be absent several days; not even when the next fall I spent a fortnight in the woods of Maine. And yet my house was more respected than if it had been surrounded by a file of soldiers. The tired rambler could rest and warm himself by my fire, the literary amuse himself with the few books on my table, or the curious, by opening my closet door, see what was left of my dinner, and what prospect I had of a supper. Yet, though many people of every class came this way to the pond, I suffered no serious inconvenience from these sources, and I never missed any thing but one small book, a volume of Homer, which perhaps was improperly gilded, and this I trust a soldier of our camp has found by this time. I am convinced, that if all men were to live as simply as I then did, thieving and robbery would be unknown. These take place only in communities where some have got more than is sufficient while others have not enough. The Pope's Homers would soon get properly distributed. —

> "Nec bella fuerunt,
> Faginus astabat dum scyphus ante dapes."
> "Nor wars did men molest,
> When only beechen bowls were in request."

"You who govern public affairs, what need have you to employ punishments? Love virtue, and the people will be virtuous. The virtues of a superior man are like the wind; the virtues of a common man are like the grass; the grass, when the wind passes over it, bends."

The Ponds

SOMETIMES, having had a surfeit of human society and gossip, and worn out all my village friends, I rambled still farther westward than I habitually dwell, into yet more unfrequented parts of the town, "to fresh woods and pastures new," or, while the sun was setting, made my supper of huckleberries and blueberries on Fair Haven Hill, and laid up a store for several days. The fruits do not yield their true flavor to the purchaser of them, nor to him who raises them for the market. There is but one way to obtain it, yet few take that way. If you would know the flavor of huckleberries, ask the cow-boy or the partridge. It is a vulgar error to suppose that you have tasted huckleberries who never plucked them. A huckleberry never reaches Boston; they have not been known there since they grew on her three hills. The ambrosial and essential part of the fruit is lost with the bloom which is rubbed off in the market cart, and they become mere provender. As long as Eternal Justice reigns, not one innocent huckleberry can be transported thither from the country's hills.

Occasionally, after my hoeing was done for the day, I joined some impatient companion who had been fishing on the pond since morning, as silent and motionless as a duck or a floating leaf, and, after practising various kinds of philosophy, had concluded commonly, by the time I arrived, that he belonged to the ancient sect of Cœnobites. There was one older man, an excellent fisher and skilled in all kinds of woodcraft, who was pleased to look upon my house as a building erected for the convenience of fishermen; and I was equally pleased when he sat in my doorway to arrange his lines. Once in a while we sat together on the pond, he at one end of the boat, and I at the other; but not many words passed between us, for he had grown deaf in his later years, but he occasionally hummed a psalm, which harmonized well enough with my philosophy. Our intercourse was thus altogether one of unbroken harmony, far more pleasing to remember than if it had been carried on by speech. When, as was commonly the case, I had none to commune with, I used to raise the echoes by striking with a paddle on the side of my boat, filling the surrounding woods with circling and dilating sound, stirring them up as the keeper of a menagerie his wild beasts, until I elicited a growl from every wooded vale and hill-side.

In warm evenings I frequently sat in the boat playing the flute, and saw the perch, which I seemed to have charmed, hovering around me, and the moon travelling over the ribbed bottom, which was strewed with the wrecks of the forest. Formerly I had come to this pond adventurously, from time to time, in dark summer nights, with a companion, and making a fire close to the water's edge, which we thought attracted the fishes, we caught pouts with a bunch of worms strung on a thread; and when we had done, far in the night, threw the burning brands high into the air like skyrockets, which, coming down into the pond, were quenched with a loud hissing, and we were suddenly groping in total darkness. Through this, whistling a tune, we took our way to the haunts of men again. But now I had made my home by the shore.

Sometimes, after staying in a village parlor till the family had all retired, I have returned to the woods, and, partly with a view to the next day's dinner, spent the hours of midnight fishing from a boat by moonlight, serenaded by owls and foxes, and hearing, from time to time, the creaking note of some unknown bird close at hand. These experiences were very memorable and valuable to me,—anchored in forty feet of water, and twenty or thirty rods from the shore, surrounded sometimes by thousands of small perch and shiners, dimpling the surface with their tails in the moonlight, and communicating by a long flaxen line with mysterious nocturnal fishes which had their dwelling forty feet below, or sometimes dragging sixty feet of line about the pond as I drifted in the gentle night breeze, now and then feeling a slight vibration along it, indicative of some life prowling about its extremity, of dull uncertain blundering purpose there, and slow to make up its mind. At length you slowly raise, pulling hand over hand, some horned pout squeaking and squirming to the upper air. It was very queer, especially in dark nights, when your thoughts had wandered to vast and cosmogonal themes in other spheres, to feel this faint jerk, which came to interrupt your dreams and link you to Nature again. It seemed as if I might next cast my line upward into the air, as well as downward into this element which was scarcely more dense. Thus I caught two fishes as it were with one hook.

The scenery of Walden is on a humble scale, and, though very beautiful, does not approach to grandeur, nor can it much concern one who has not long frequented it or lived by its shore; yet this pond is so remarkable for its depth and purity as to merit a particular description. It is a clear and deep green well, half a mile long and a mile and three quarters in circumference, and contains about sixty-one and a half acres; a perennial spring in the midst of pine and oak woods, without any visible inlet or outlet except by the clouds and evaporation. The surrounding hills rise abruptly from the water to the height of forty to eighty feet, though on the southeast and east they attain to about one hundred and one hundred and fifty feet respectively, within a quarter and a third of a mile. They are exclusively woodland. All our Concord waters have two colors at least, one when viewed at a distance, and another, more proper, close at hand. The first depends more on the light, and follows the sky. In clear weather, in summer, they appear blue at a little distance, especially if agitated, and at a great distance all appear alike. In stormy weather they are sometimes of a dark slate color. The sea, however, is said to be blue one day and green another without any perceptible change in the atmosphere. I have seen our river, when, the landscape being covered with snow, both water and ice were almost as green as grass. Some consider blue "to be the color of pure water, whether liquid or solid." But, looking directly down into our waters from a boat, they are seen to be of very different colors. Walden is blue at one time and green at another, even from the same point of view. Lying between the earth and the heavens, it partakes of the color of both. Viewed from a hill-top it reflects the color of the sky, but near at hand it is of a yellowish tint next the shore where you can see the sand, then a light green, which gradually deepens to a uniform dark green in the body of the pond. In some lights, viewed even from a hill-top, it is of a vivid green next the shore. Some have referred this to the reflection of the verdure; but it is equally green there against the railroad sand-bank, and in the spring, before the leaves are expanded, and it may be simply the result of the prevailing blue mixed with the yellow of the sand. Such is the color of its iris. This is that portion, also, where in the spring, the ice being warmed by the heat of the sun reflected from the bottom, and also transmitted through the earth, melts first and forms a narrow canal about the still frozen middle. Like the rest of our waters, when much agitated, in clear weather, so that the surface of the waves may reflect the sky at the right angle, or because there is more light mixed with it, it appears at a little distance of a darker blue than the sky itself; and at such a time, being on its surface, and looking with divided vision, so as to see the reflection, I have discerned a matchless and indescribable light blue, such as watered or changeable silks and sword blades suggest, more cerulean than the sky itself, alternating with the original dark green on the opposite sides of the waves, which last appeared but muddy in comparison. It is a vitreous greenish blue, as I remember it, like those patches of the winter sky seen through cloud vistas in the west before sundown. Yet a single glass of its water held up to the light is as colorless as an equal quantity of air. It is well known that a large plate of glass will have a green tint, owing, as the makers say, to its "body," but a small piece of the same will be colorless. How large a body of Walden water would be required to reflect a green tint I have never proved. The water of our river is black or a very dark brown to one looking directly down on it, and, like that of most ponds, imparts to the body of one bathing in it a yellowish tinge; but this water is of such crystalline purity that the body of the bather appears of an alabaster whiteness, still more unnatural, which, as the limbs are magnified and distorted withal, produces a monstrous effect, making fit studies for a Michael Angelo.

The water is so transparent that the bottom can easily be discerned at the depth of twenty-five or thirty feet. Paddling over it, you may see many feet beneath the surface the schools of perch and shiners, perhaps only an inch long, yet the former easily distinguished by their transverse bars, and you think that they must be ascetic fish that find a subsistence there. Once, in the winter, many years ago, when I had been cutting holes through the ice in order to catch pickerel, as I stepped ashore I tossed my axe back on to the ice, but, as if some evil genius had directed it, it slid four or five rods directly into one of the holes, where the water was twenty-five feet deep. Out of curiosity, I lay down on the ice and looked through the hole, until I saw the axe a little on one side, standing on its head, with its helve erect and gently swaying to and fro with the pulse of the pond; and there it might have stood erect and swaying till in the course of time the handle rotted off, if I had not disturbed it. Making another hole directly over it with an ice chisel which I had, and cutting down the longest birch which I could find in the neighborhood with my knife, I made a slip-noose, which I attached to its end, and, letting it down carefully, passed it over the knob of the handle, and drew it by a line along the birch, and so pulled the axe out again.

The shore is composed of a belt of smooth rounded white stones like paving stones, excepting one or two short sand beaches, and is so steep that in many places a single leap will carry you into water over your head; and were it not for its remarkable transparency, that would be the last to be seen of its bottom till it rose on the opposite side. Some think it is bottomless. It is nowhere muddy, and a casual observer would say that there were no weeds at all in it; and of noticeable plants, except in the little meadows recently overflowed, which do not properly belong to it, a closer scrutiny does not detect a flag nor a bulrush, nor even a lily, yellow or white, but only a few small heart-leaves and potamogetons, and perhaps a water-target or two; all which however a bather might not perceive; and these plants are clean and bright like the element they grow in. The stones extend a rod or two into the water, and then the bottom is pure sand, except in the deepest parts, where there is usually a little sediment, probably from the decay of the leaves which have been wafted on to it so many successive falls, and a bright green weed is brought up on anchors even in midwinter.

We have one other pond just like this, White Pond in Nine Acre Corner, about two and a half miles westerly; but, though I am acquainted with most of the ponds within a

dozen miles of this centre, I do not know a third of this pure
and well-like character. Successive nations perchance have
drank at, admired, and fathomed it, and passed away, and still
its water is green and pellucid as ever. Not an intermitting
spring! Perhaps on that spring morning when Adam and Eve
were driven out of Eden Walden Pond was already in existence, and even then breaking up in a gentle spring rain accompanied with mist and a southerly wind, and covered with
myriads of ducks and geese, which had not heard of the fall,
when still such pure lakes sufficed them. Even then it had
commenced to rise and fall, and had clarified its waters and
colored them of the hue they now wear, and obtained a patent of heaven to be the only Walden Pond in the world and
distiller of celestial dews. Who knows in how many un-
remembered nations' literatures this has been the Castalian
Fountain? or what nymphs presided over it in the Golden
Age? It is a gem of the first water which Concord wears in
her coronet.

Yet perchance the first who came to this well have left some
trace of their footsteps. I have been surprised to detect encircling the pond, even where a thick wood has just been cut
down on the shore, a narrow shelf-like path in the steep hill-
side, alternately rising and falling, approaching and receding
from the water's edge, as old probably as the race of man
here, worn by the feet of aboriginal hunters, and still from
time to time unwittingly trodden by the present occupants of
the land. This is particularly distinct to one standing on the
middle of the pond in winter, just after a light snow has
fallen, appearing as a clear undulating white line, unobscured
by weeds and twigs, and very obvious a quarter of a mile off
in many places where in summer it is hardly distinguishable
close at hand. The snow reprints it, as it were, in clear white
type alto-relievo. The ornamented grounds of villas which
will one day be built here may still preserve some trace of this.

The pond rises and falls, but whether regularly or not, and
within what period, nobody knows, though, as usual, many
pretend to know. It is commonly higher in the winter and
lower in the summer, though not corresponding to the general wet and dryness. I can remember when it was a foot or
two lower, and also when it was at least five feet higher, than

when I lived by it. There is a narrow sand-bar running into it, with very deep water on one side, on which I helped boil a kettle of chowder, some six rods from the main shore, about the year 1824, which it has not been possible to do for twenty-five years; and on the other hand, my friends used to listen with incredulity when I told them, that a few years later I was accustomed to fish from a boat in a secluded cove in the woods, fifteen rods from the only shore they knew, which place was long since converted into a meadow. But the pond has risen steadily for two years, and now, in the summer of '52, is just five feet higher than when I lived there, or as high as it was thirty years ago, and fishing goes on again in the meadow. This makes a difference of level, at the outside, of six or seven feet; and yet the water shed by the surrounding hills is insignificant in amount, and this overflow must be referred to causes which affect the deep springs. This same summer the pond has begun to fall again. It is remarkable that this fluctuation, whether periodical or not, appears thus to require many years for its accomplishment. I have observed one rise and a part of two falls, and I expect that a dozen or fifteen years hence the water will again be as low as I have ever known it. Flints' Pond, a mile eastward, allowing for the disturbance occasioned by its inlets and outlets, and the smaller intermediate ponds also, sympathize with Walden, and recently attained their greatest height at the same time with the latter. The same is true, as far as my observation goes, of White Pond.

This rise and fall of Walden at long intervals serves this use at least; the water standing at this great height for a year or more, though it makes it difficult to walk round it, kills the shrubs and trees which have sprung up about its edge since the last rise, pitch-pines, birches, alders, aspens, and others, and, falling again, leaves an unobstructed shore; for, unlike many ponds and all waters which are subject to a daily tide, its shore is cleanest when the water is lowest. On the side of the pond next my house, a row of pitch pines fifteen feet high has been killed and tipped over as if by a lever, and thus a stop put to their encroachments; and their size indicates how many years have elapsed since the last rise to this height. By this fluctuation the pond asserts its title to a shore, and thus the *shore* is *shorn*, and the trees cannot hold it by right of possession. These are the lips of the lake on which no beard grows. It licks its chaps from time to time. When the water is at its height, the alders, willows, and maples send forth a mass of fibrous red roots several feet long from all sides of their stems in the water, and to the height of three or four feet from the ground, in the effort to maintain themselves; and I have known the high-blueberry bushes about the shore, which commonly produce no fruit, bear an abundant crop under these circumstances.

Some have been puzzled to tell how the shore became so regularly paved. My townsmen have all heard the tradition, the oldest people tell me that they heard it in their youth, that anciently the Indians were holding a pow-wow upon a hill here, which rose as high into the heavens as the pond now sinks deep into the earth, and they used much profanity, as the story goes, though this vice is one of which the Indians were never guilty, and while they were thus engaged the hill shook and suddenly sank, and only one old squaw, named Walden, escaped, and from her the pond was named. It has been conjectured that when the hill shook these stones rolled down its side and became the present shore. It is very certain, at any rate, that once there was no pond here, and now there is one; and this Indian fable does not in any respect conflict with the account of that ancient settler whom I have mentioned, who remembers so well when he first came here with his divining rod, saw a thin vapor rising from the sward, and the hazel pointed steadily downward, and he concluded to dig a well here. As for the stones, many still think that they are hardly to be accounted for by the action of the waves on these hills; but I observe that the surrounding hills are remarkably full of the same kind of stones, so that they have been obliged to pile them up in walls on both sides of the railroad cut nearest the pond; and, moreover, there are most stones where the shore is most abrupt; so that, unfortunately, it is no longer a mystery to me. I detect the paver. If the name was not derived from that of some English locality,—Saffron Walden, for instance,—one might suppose that it was called, originally, *Walled-in* Pond.

The pond was my well ready dug. For four months in the

year its water is as cold as it is pure at all times; and I think that it is then as good as any, if not the best, in the town. In the winter, all water which is exposed to the air is colder than springs and wells which are protected from it. The temperature of the pond water which had stood in the room where I sat from five o'clock in the afternoon till noon the next day, the sixth of March, 1846, the thermometer having been up to 65° or 70° some of the time, owing partly to the sun on the roof, was 42°, or one degree colder than the water of one of the coldest wells in the village just drawn. The temperature of the Boiling Spring the same day was 45°, or the warmest of any water tried, though it is the coldest that I know of in summer, when, beside, shallow and stagnant surface water is not mingled with it. Moreover, in summer, Walden never becomes so warm as most water which is exposed to the sun, on account of its depth. In the warmest weather I usually placed a pailful in my cellar, where it became cool in the night, and remained so during the day; though I also resorted to a spring in the neighborhood. It was as good when a week old as the day it was dipped, and had no taste of the pump. Whoever camps for a week in summer by the shore of a pond, needs only bury a pail of water a few feet deep in the shade of his camp to be independent on the luxury of ice.

There have been caught in Walden, pickerel, one weighing seven pounds, to say nothing of another which carried off a reel with great velocity, which the fisherman safely set down at eight pounds because he did not see him, perch and pouts, some of each weighing over two pounds, shiners, chivins or roach, (*Leuciscus pulchellus,*) a very few breams, and a couple of eels, one weighing four pounds,—I am thus particular because the weight of a fish is commonly its only title to fame, and these are the only eels I have heard of here;—also, I have a faint recollection of a little fish some five inches long, with silvery sides and a greenish back, somewhat dace-like in its character, which I mention here chiefly to link my facts to fable. Nevertheless, this pond is not very fertile in fish. Its pickerel, though not abundant, are its chief boasts. I have seen at one time lying on the ice pickerel of at least three different kinds; a long and shallow one, steel-colored, most like those caught in the river; a bright golden kind, with greenish reflections and remarkably deep, which is the most common here; and another, golden-colored, and shaped like the last, but peppered on the sides with small dark brown or black spots, intermixed with a few faint blood-red ones, very much like a trout. The specific name *reticulatus* would not apply to this; it should be *guttatus* rather. These are all very firm fish, and weigh more than their size promises. The shiners, pouts, and perch also, and indeed all the fishes which inhabit this pond, are much cleaner, handsomer, and firmer fleshed than those in the river and most other ponds, as the water is purer, and they can easily be distinguished from them. Probably many ichthyologists would make new varieties of some of them. There are also a clean race of frogs and tortoises, and a few muscles in it; muskrats and minks leave their traces about it, and occasionally a travelling mud-turtle visits it. Sometimes, when I pushed off my boat in the morning, I disturbed a great mud-turtle which had secreted himself under the boat in the night. Ducks and geese frequent it in the spring and fall, the white-bellied swallows (*Hirundo bicolor*) skim over it, the kingfishers sound their alarm around it and the peetweets (*Totanus macularius*) "teter" along its stony shores all summer. I have sometimes disturbed a fishhawk sitting on a white-pine over the water; but I doubt if it is ever profaned by the wing of a gull, like Fair Haven. At most, it tolerates one annual loon. These are all the animals of consequence which frequent it now.

You may see from a boat, in calm weather, near the sandy eastern shore, where the water is eight or ten feet deep, and also in some other parts of the pond, some circular heaps half a dozen feet in diameter by a foot in height, consisting of small stones less than a hen's egg in size, where all around is bare sand. At first you wonder if the Indians could have formed them on the ice for any purpose, and when the ice melted, they sank to the bottom; but they are too regular and some of them plainly too fresh for that. They are similar to those found in rivers; but as there are no suckers nor lampreys here, I know not by what fish they could be made. Perhaps they are the nests of the chivin. These lend a pleasing mystery to the bottom.

The shore is irregular enough not to be monotonous. I

have in my mind's eye the western indented with deep bays, the bolder northern, and the beautifully scolloped southern shore, where successive capes overlap each other and suggest unexplored coves between. The forest has never so good a setting, nor is so distinctly beautiful, as when seen from the middle of a small lake amid hills which rise from the water's edge; for the water in which it is reflected not only makes the best foreground in such a case, but, with its winding shore, the most natural and agreeable boundary to it. There is no rawness nor imperfection in its edge there, as where the axe has cleared a part, or a cultivated field abuts on it. The trees have ample room to expand on the water side, and each sends forth its most vigorous branch in that direction. There Nature has woven a natural selvage, and the eye rises by just grada-tions from the low shrubs of the shore to the highest trees. There are few traces of man's hand to be seen. The water laves the shore as it did a thousand years ago.

A lake is the landscape's most beautiful and expressive fea-ture. It is earth's eye; looking into which the beholder mea-sures the depth of his own nature. The fluviatile trees next the shore are the slender eyelashes which fringe it, and the wooded hills and cliffs around are its overhanging brows.

Standing on the smooth sandy beach at the east end of the pond, in a calm September afternoon, when a slight haze makes the opposite shore line indistinct, I have seen whence came the expression, "the glassy surface of a lake." When you invert your head, it looks like a thread of finest gossamer stretched across the valley, and gleaming against the distant pine woods, separating one stratum of the atmosphere from another. You would think that you could walk dry under it to the opposite hills, and that the swallows which skim over might perch on it. Indeed, they sometimes dive below the line, as it were by mistake, and are undeceived. As you look over the pond westward you are obliged to employ both your hands to defend your eyes against the reflected as well as the true sun, for they are equally bright; and if, between the two, you survey its surface critically, it is literally as smooth as glass, except where the skater insects, at equal intervals scat-tered over its whole extent, by their motions in the sun pro-duce the finest imaginable sparkle on it, or, perchance, a duck

plumes itself, or, as I have said, a swallow skims so low as to
touch it. It may be that in the distance a fish describes an arc
of three or four feet in the air, and there is one bright flash
where it emerges, and another where it strikes the water;
sometimes the whole silvery arc is revealed; or here and there,
perhaps, is a thistle-down floating on its surface, which the
fishes dart at and so dimple it again. It is like molten glass
cooled but not congealed, and the few motes in it are pure
and beautiful like the imperfections in glass. You may often
detect a yet smoother and darker water, separated from the
rest as if by an invisible cobweb, boom of the water nymphs,
resting on it. From a hill-top you can see a fish leap in almost
any part; for not a pickerel or shiner picks an insect from this
smooth surface but it manifestly disturbs the equilibrium of
the whole lake. It is wonderful with what elaborateness this
simple fact is advertised,—this piscine murder will out,—and
from my distant perch I distinguish the circling undulations
when they are half a dozen rods in diameter. You can even
detect a water-bug (*Gyrinus*) ceaselessly progressing over the
smooth surface a quarter of a mile off; for they furrow the
water slightly, making a conspicuous ripple bounded by two
diverging lines, but the skaters glide over it without rippling
it perceptibly. When the surface is considerably agitated there
are no skaters nor water-bugs on it, but apparently, in calm
days, they leave their havens and adventurously glide forth
from the shore by short impulses till they completely cover it.
It is a soothing employment, on one of those fine days in the
fall when all the warmth of the sun is fully appreciated, to sit
on a stump on such a height as this, overlooking the pond,
and study the dimpling circles which are incessantly inscribed
on its otherwise invisible surface amid the reflected skies and
trees. Over this great expanse there is no disturbance but it is
thus at once gently smoothed away and assuaged, as, when a
vase of water is jarred, the trembling circles seek the shore and
all is smooth again. Not a fish can leap or an insect fall on the
pond but it is thus reported in circling dimples, in lines of
beauty, as it were the constant welling up of its fountain, the
gentle pulsing of its life, the heaving of its breast. The thrills
of joy and thrills of pain are undistinguishable. How peaceful
the phenomena of the lake! Again the works of man shine as

in the spring. Ay, every leaf and twig and stone and cobweb sparkles now at mid-afternoon as when covered with dew in a spring morning. Every motion of an oar or an insect produces a flash of light; and if an oar falls, how sweet the echo!

In such a day, in September or October, Walden is a perfect forest mirror, set round with stones as precious to my eye as if fewer or rarer. Nothing so fair, so pure, and at the same time so large, as a lake, perchance, lies on the surface of the earth. Sky water. It needs no fence. Nations come and go without defiling it. It is a mirror which no stone can crack, whose quicksilver will never wear off, whose gilding Nature continually repairs; no storms, no dust, can dim its surface ever fresh;—a mirror in which all impurity presented to it sinks, swept and dusted by the sun's hazy brush,—this the light dust-cloth,—which retains no breath that is breathed on it, but sends its own to float as clouds high above its surface, and be reflected in its bosom still.

A field of water betrays the spirit that is in the air. It is continually receiving new life and motion from above. It is intermediate in its nature between land and sky. On land only the grass and trees wave, but the water itself is rippled by the wind. I see where the breeze dashes across it by the streaks or flakes of light. It is remarkable that we can look down on its surface. We shall, perhaps, look down thus on the surface of air at length, and mark where a still subtler spirit sweeps over it.

The skaters and water-bugs finally disappear in the latter part of October, when the severe frosts have come; and then and in November, usually, in a calm day, there is absolutely nothing to ripple the surface. One November afternoon, in the calm at the end of a rain storm of several days' duration, when the sky was still completely overcast and the air was full of mist, I observed that the pond was remarkably smooth, so that it was difficult to distinguish its surface; though it no longer reflected the bright tints of October, but the sombre November colors of the surrounding hills. Though I passed over it as gently as possible, the slight undulations produced by my boat extended almost as far as I could see, and gave a ribbed appearance to the reflections. But, as I was looking over the surface, I saw here and there at a distance a faint

glimmer, as if some skater insects which had escaped the
frosts might be collected there, or, perchance, the surface,
being so smooth, betrayed where a spring welled up from the
bottom. Paddling gently to one of these places, I was surprised to find myself surrounded by myriads of small perch,
about five inches long, of a rich bronze color in the green
water, sporting there and constantly rising to the surface and
dimpling it, sometimes leaving bubbles on it. In such transparent and seemingly bottomless water, reflecting the clouds,
I seemed to be floating through the air as in a balloon, and
their swimming impressed me as a kind of flight or hovering,
as if they were a compact flock of birds passing just beneath
my level on the right or left, their fins, like sails, set all around
them. There were many such schools in the pond, apparently
improving the short season before winter would draw an icy
shutter over their broad skylight, sometimes giving to the surface an appearance as if a slight breeze struck it, or a few rain-
drops fell there. When I approached carelessly and alarmed
them, they made a sudden plash and rippling with their tails,
as if one had struck the water with a brushy bough, and instantly took refuge in the depths. At length the wind rose, the
mist increased, and the waves began to run, and the perch
leaped much higher than before, half out of water, a hundred
black points, three inches long, at once above the surface.
Even as late as the fifth of December, one year, I saw some
dimples on the surface, and thinking it was going to rain hard
immediately, the air being full of mist, I made haste to take
my place at the oars and row homeward; already the rain
seemed rapidly increasing, though I felt none on my cheek,
and I anticipated a thorough soaking. But suddenly the dimples ceased, for they were produced by the perch, which the
noise of my oars had scared into the depths, and I saw their
schools dimly disappearing; so I spent a dry afternoon after
all.

An old man who used to frequent this pond nearly sixty
years ago, when it was dark with surrounding forests, tells me
that in those days he sometimes saw it all alive with ducks
and other water fowl, and that there were many eagles about
it. He came here a-fishing, and used an old log canoe which
he found on the shore. It was made of two white-pine logs

dug out and pinned together, and was cut off square at the ends. It was very clumsy, but lasted a great many years before it became water-logged and perhaps sank to the bottom. He did not know whose it was; it belonged to the pond. He used to make a cable for his anchor of strips of hickory bark tied together. An old man, a potter, who lived by the pond before the Revolution, told him once that there was an iron chest at the bottom, and that he had seen it. Sometimes it would come floating up to the shore; but when you went toward it, it would go back into deep water and disappear. I was pleased to hear of the old log canoe, which took the place of an Indian one of the same material but more graceful construction, which perchance had first been a tree on the bank, and then, as it were, fell into the water, to float there for a generation, the most proper vessel for the lake. I remember that when I first looked into these depths there were many large trunks to be seen indistinctly lying on the bottom, which had either been blown over formerly, or left on the ice at the last cutting, when wood was cheaper; but now they have mostly disappeared.

When I first paddled a boat on Walden, it was completely surrounded by thick and lofty pine and oak woods, and in some of its coves grape vines had run over the trees next the water and formed bowers under which a boat could pass. The hills which form its shores are so steep, and the woods on them were then so high, that, as you looked down from the west end, it had the appearance of an amphitheatre for some kind of sylvan spectacle. I have spent many an hour, when I was younger, floating over its surface as the zephyr willed, having paddled my boat to the middle, and lying on my back across the seats, in a summer forenoon, dreaming awake, until I was aroused by the boat touching the sand, and I arose to see what shore my fates had impelled me to; days when idleness was the most attractive and productive industry. Many a forenoon have I stolen away, preferring to spend thus the most valued part of the day; for I was rich, if not in money, in sunny hours and summer days, and spent them lavishly; nor do I regret that I did not waste more of them in the workshop or the teacher's desk. But since I left those shores the woodchoppers have still further laid them waste, and now for many a year there will be no more rambling through the aisles of the wood, with occasional vistas through which you see the water. My Muse may be excused if she is silent henceforth. How can you expect the birds to sing when their groves are cut down?

Now the trunks of trees on the bottom, and the old log canoe, and the dark surrounding woods, are gone, and the villagers, who scarcely know where it lies, instead of going to the pond to bathe or drink, are thinking to bring its water, which should be as sacred as the Ganges at least, to the village in a pipe, to wash their dishes with!—to earn their Walden by the turning of a cock or drawing of a plug! That devilish Iron Horse, whose ear-rending neigh is heard throughout the town, has muddied the Boiling Spring with his foot, and he it is that has browsed off all the woods on Walden shore; that Trojan horse, with a thousand men in his belly, introduced by mercenary Greeks! Where is the country's champion, the Moore of Moore Hall, to meet him at the Deep Cut and thrust an avenging lance between the ribs of the bloated pest?

Nevertheless, of all the characters I have known, perhaps Walden wears best, and best preserves its purity. Many men have been likened to it, but few deserve that honor. Though the woodchoppers have laid bare first this shore and then that, and the Irish have built their sties by it, and the railroad has infringed on its border, and the ice-men have skimmed it once, it is itself unchanged, the same water which my youthful eyes fell on; all the change is in me. It has not acquired one permanent wrinkle after all its ripples. It is perennially young, and I may stand and see a swallow dip apparently to pick an insect from its surface as of yore. It struck me again to-night, as if I had not seen it almost daily for more than twenty years,—Why, here is Walden, the same woodland lake that I discovered so many years ago; where a forest was cut down last winter another is springing up by its shore as lustily as ever; the same thought is welling up to its surface that was then; it is the same liquid joy and happiness to itself and its Maker, ay, and it *may* be to me. It is the work of a brave man surely, in whom there was no guile! He rounded this water with his hand, deepened and clarified it in his thought, and in his will bequeathed it to Concord. I see by its face that it is visited by the same reflection; and I can almost say, Walden, is it you?

> It is no dream of mine,
> To ornament a line;
> I cannot come nearer to God and Heaven
> Than I live to Walden even.
> I am its stony shore,
> And the breeze that passes o'er;
> In the hollow of my hand
> Are its water and its sand,
> And its deepest resort
> Lies high in my thought.

The cars never pause to look at it; yet I fancy that the engineers and firemen and brakemen, and those passengers who have a season ticket and see it often, are better men for the sight. The engineer does not forget at night, or his nature does not, that he has beheld this vision of serenity and purity once at least during the day. Though seen but once, it helps to wash out State-street and the engine's soot. One proposes that it be called "God's Drop."

I have said that Walden has no visible inlet nor outlet, but it is on the one hand distantly and indirectly related to Flints' Pond, which is more elevated, by a chain of small ponds coming from that quarter, and on the other directly and manifestly to Concord River, which is lower, by a similar chain of ponds through which in some other geological period it may have flowed, and by a little digging, which God forbid, it can be made to flow thither again. If by living thus reserved and austere, like a hermit in the woods, so long, it has acquired such wonderful purity, who would not regret that the comparatively impure waters of Flints' Pond should be mingled with it, or itself should ever go to waste its sweetness in the ocean wave?

Flints', or Sandy Pond, in Lincoln, our greatest lake and inland sea, lies about a mile east of Walden. It is much larger, being said to contain one hundred and ninety-seven acres, and is more fertile in fish; but it is comparatively shallow, and

not remarkably pure. A walk through the woods thither was
often my recreation. It was worth the while, if only to feel
the wind blow on your cheek freely, and see the waves run,
and remember the life of mariners. I went a-chestnutting
there in the fall, on windy days, when the nuts were dropping
into the water and were washed to my feet; and one day, as I
crept along its sedgy shore, the fresh spray blowing in my
face, I came upon the mouldering wreck of a boat, the sides
gone, and hardly more than the impression of its flat bottom
left amid the rushes; yet its model was sharply defined, as if
it were a large decayed pad, with its veins. It was as impressive a wreck as one could imagine on the sea-shore, and had
as good a moral. It is by this time mere vegetable mould and
undistinguishable pond shore, through which rushes and flags
have pushed up. I used to admire the ripple marks on the
sandy bottom, at the north end of this pond, made firm and
hard to the feet of the wader by the pressure of the water,
and the rushes which grew in Indian file, in waving lines,
corresponding to these marks, rank behind rank, as if the
waves had planted them. There also I have found, in considerable quantities, curious balls, composed apparently of fine
grass or roots, of pipewort perhaps, from half an inch to four
inches in diameter, and perfectly spherical. These wash back
and forth in shallow water on a sandy bottom, and are sometimes cast on the shore. They are either solid grass, or have a
little sand in the middle. At first you would say that they were
formed by the action of the waves, like a pebble; yet the
smallest are made of equally coarse materials, half an inch
long, and they are produced only at one season of the year.
Moreover, the waves, I suspect, do not so much construct as
wear down a material which has already acquired consistency.
They preserve their form when dry for an indefinite period.

Flints' Pond! Such is the poverty of our nomenclature.
What right had the unclean and stupid farmer, whose farm
abutted on this sky water, whose shores he has ruthlessly laid
bare, to give his name to it? Some skin-flint, who loved better
the reflecting surface of a dollar, or a bright cent, in which he
could see his own brazen face; who regarded even the wild
ducks which settled in it as trespassers; his fingers grown into
crooked and horny talons from the long habit of grasping

harpy-like;—so it is not named for me. I go not there to see
him nor to hear of him; who never *saw* it, who never bathed
in it, who never loved it, who never protected it, who never
spoke a good word for it, nor thanked God that he had made
it. Rather let it be named from the fishes that swim in it, the
wild fowl or quadrupeds which frequent it, the wild flowers
which grow by its shores, or some wild man or child the
thread of whose history is interwoven with its own; not from
him who could show no title to it but the deed which a like-
minded neighbor or legislature gave him,—him who thought
only of its money value; whose presence perchance cursed all
the shore; who exhausted the land around it, and would fain
have exhausted the waters within it; who regretted only that
it was not English hay or cranberry meadow,—there was
nothing to redeem it, forsooth, in his eyes,—and would have
drained and sold it for the mud at its bottom. It did not turn
his mill, and it was no *privilege* to him to behold it. I respect
not his labors, his farm where every thing has its price; who
would carry the landscape, who would carry his God, to market, if he could get any thing for him; who goes to market
for his god as it is; on whose farm nothing grows free, whose
fields bear no crops, whose meadows no flowers, whose trees
no fruits, but dollars; who loves not the beauty of his fruits,
whose fruits are not ripe for him till they are turned to dollars. Give me the poverty that enjoys true wealth. Farmers are
respectable and interesting to me in proportion as they are
poor,—poor farmers. A model farm! where the house stands
like a fungus in a muck-heap, chambers for men, horses, oxen,
and swine, cleansed and uncleansed, all contiguous to one another! Stocked with men! A great grease-spot, redolent of
manures and buttermilk! Under a high state of cultivation,
being manured with the hearts and brains of men! As if you
were to raise your potatoes in the church-yard! Such is a
model farm.

No, no; if the fairest features of the landscape are to be
named after men, let them be the noblest and worthiest men
alone. Let our lakes receive as true names at least as the Icar-
ian Sea, where "still the shore" a "brave attempt resounds."

Goose Pond, of small extent, is on my way to Flints'; Fair-

Haven, an expansion of Concord River, said to contain some
seventy acres, is a mile south-west; and White Pond, of about
forty acres, is a mile and a half beyond Fair-Haven. This is
my lake country. These, with Concord River, are my water
privileges; and night and day, year in year out, they grind
such grist as I carry to them.

Since the woodcutters, and the railroad, and I myself have
profaned Walden, perhaps the most attractive, if not the most
beautiful, of all our lakes, the gem of the woods, is White
Pond;—a poor name from its commonness, whether derived
from the remarkable purity of its waters or the color of its
sands. In these as in other respects, however, it is a lesser twin
of Walden. They are so much alike that you would say they
must be connected under ground. It has the same stony
shore, and its waters are of the same hue. As at Walden, in
sultry dog-day weather, looking down through the woods on
some of its bays which are not so deep but that the reflection
from the bottom tinges them, its waters are of a misty bluish-
green or glaucous color. Many years since I used to go there
to collect the sand by cart-loads, to make sand-paper with,
and I have continued to visit it ever since. One who frequents
it proposes to call it Virid Lake. Perhaps it might be called
Yellow-Pine Lake, from the following circumstance. About
fifteen years ago you could see the top of a pitch-pine, of the
kind called yellow-pine hereabouts, though it is not a distinct
species, projecting above the surface in deep water, many rods
from the shore. It was even supposed by some that the pond
had sunk, and this was one of the primitive forest that formerly stood there. I find that even so long ago as 1792, in a
"Topographical Description of the Town of Concord," by one
of its citizens, in the Collections of the Massachusetts Historical Society, the author, after speaking of Walden and White
Ponds, adds: "In the middle of the latter may be seen, when
the water is very low, a tree which appears as if it grew in the
place where it now stands, although the roots are fifty feet
below the surface of the water; the top of this tree is broken
off, and at that place measures fourteen inches in diameter."
In the spring of '49 I talked with the man who lives nearest
the pond in Sudbury, who told me that it was he who got
out this tree ten or fifteen years before. As near as he could

remember, it stood twelve or fifteen rods from the shore, where the water was thirty or forty feet deep. It was in the winter, and he had been getting out ice in the forenoon, and had resolved that in the afternoon, with the aid of his neighbors, he would take out the old yellow-pine. He sawed a channel in the ice toward the shore, and hauled it over and along and out on to the ice with oxen; but, before he had gone far in his work, he was surprised to find that it was wrong end upward, with the stumps of the branches pointing down, and the small end firmly fastened in the sandy bottom. It was about a foot in diameter at the big end, and he had expected to get a good saw-log, but it was so rotten as to be fit only for fuel, if for that. He had some of it in his shed then. There were marks of an axe and of woodpeckers on the but. He thought that it might have been a dead tree on the shore, but was finally blown over into the pond, and after the top had become water-logged, while the but-end was still dry and light, had drifted out and sunk wrong end up. His father, eighty years old, could not remember when it was not there. Several pretty large logs may still be seen lying on the bottom, where, owing to the undulation of the surface, they look like huge water snakes in motion.

This pond has rarely been profaned by a boat, for there is little in it to tempt a fisherman. Instead of the white lily, which requires mud, or the common sweet flag, the blue flag (*Iris versicolor*) grows thinly in the pure water, rising from the stony bottom all around the shore, where it is visited by humming birds in June, and the color both of its bluish blades and its flowers, and especially their reflections, are in singular harmony with the glaucous water.

White Pond and Walden are great crystals on the surface of the earth, Lakes of Light. If they were permanently congealed, and small enough to be clutched, they would, perchance, be carried off by slaves, like precious stones, to adorn the heads of emperors; but being liquid, and ample, and secured to us and our successors forever, we disregard them, and run after the diamond of Kohinoor. They are too pure to have a market value; they contain no muck. How much more beautiful than our lives, how much more transparent than our characters, are they! We never learned meanness of them.

How much fairer than the pool before the farmer's door, in which his ducks swim! Hither the clean wild ducks come. Nature has no human inhabitant who appreciates her. The birds with their plumage and their notes are in harmony with the flowers, but what youth or maiden conspires with the wild luxuriant beauty of Nature? She flourishes most alone, far from the towns where they reside. Talk of heaven! ye disgrace earth.

Baker Farm

SOMETIMES I rambled to pine groves, standing like temples, or like fleets at sea, full-rigged, with wavy boughs, and rippling with light, so soft and green and shady that the Druids would have forsaken their oaks to worship in them; or to the cedar wood beyond Flints' Pond, where the trees, covered with hoary blue berries, spiring higher and higher, are fit to stand before Valhalla, and the creeping juniper covers the ground with wreaths full of fruit; or to swamps where the usnea lichen hangs in festoons from the white-spruce trees, and toad-stools, round tables of the swamp gods, cover the ground, and more beautiful fungi adorn the stumps, like butterflies or shells, vegetable winkles; where the swamp-pink and dogwood grow, the red alder-berry glows like eyes of imps, the waxwork grooves and crushes the hardest woods in its folds, and the wild-holly berries make the beholder forget his home with their beauty, and he is dazzled and tempted by nameless other wild forbidden fruits, too fair for mortal taste. Instead of calling on some scholar, I paid many a visit to particular trees, of kinds which are rare in this neighborhood, standing far away in the middle of some pasture, or in the depths of a wood or swamp, or on a hill-top; such as the black-birch, of which we have some handsome specimens two feet in diameter; its cousin the yellow-birch, with its loose golden vest, perfumed like the first; the beech, which has so neat a bole and beautifully lichen-painted, perfect in all its details, of which, excepting scattered specimens, I know but one small grove of sizable trees left in the township, supposed by some to have been planted by the pigeons that were once baited with beech nuts near by; it is worth the while to see the silver grain sparkle when you split this wood; the bass; the hornbeam; the *Celtis occidentalis*, or false elm, of which we have but one well-grown; some taller mast of a pine, a shingle tree, or a more perfect hemlock than usual, standing like a pagoda in the midst of the woods; and many others I could mention. These were the shrines I visited both summer and winter.

Once it chanced that I stood in the very abutment of a

rainbow's arch, which filled the lower stratum of the atmosphere, tinging the grass and leaves around, and dazzling me
as if I looked through colored crystal. It was a lake of rainbow
light, in which, for a short while, I lived like a dolphin. If it
had lasted longer it might have tinged my employments and
life. As I walked on the railroad causeway, I used to wonder
at the halo of light around my shadow, and would fain fancy
myself one of the elect. One who visited me declared that the
shadows of some Irishmen before him had no halo about
them, that it was only natives that were so distinguished. Ben-
venuto Cellini tells us in his memoirs, that, after a certain
terrible dream or vision which he had during his confinement
in the castle of St. Angelo, a resplendent light appeared over
the shadow of his head at morning and evening, whether he
was in Italy or France, and it was particularly conspicuous
when the grass was moist with dew. This was probably the
same phenomenon to which I have referred, which is especially observed in the morning, but also at other times, and
even by moonlight. Though a constant one, it is not commonly noticed, and, in the case of an excitable imagination
like Cellini's, it would be basis enough for superstition. Beside, he tells us that he showed it to very few. But are they
not indeed distinguished who are conscious that they are regarded at all?

I set out one afternoon to go a-fishing to Fair-Haven,
through the woods, to eke out my scanty fare of vegetables.
My way led through Pleasant Meadow, an adjunct of the
Baker Farm, that retreat of which a poet has since sung, beginning,—

> "Thy entry is a pleasant field,
>   Which some mossy fruit trees yield
>   Partly to a ruddy brook,
>   By gliding musquash undertook,
>   And mercurial trout,
>   Darting about."

I thought of living there before I went to Walden. I "hooked"
the apples, leaped the brook, and scared the musquash and
the trout. It was one of those afternoons which seem indefi-

nitely long before one, in which many events may happen, a large portion of our natural life, though it was already half spent when I started. By the way there came up a shower, which compelled me to stand half an hour under a pine, piling boughs over my head, and wearing my handkerchief for a shed; and when at length I had made one cast over the pickerel-weed, standing up to my middle in water, I found myself suddenly in the shadow of a cloud, and the thunder began to rumble with such emphasis that I could do no more than listen to it. The gods must be proud, thought I, with such forked flashes to rout a poor unarmed fisherman. So I made haste for shelter to the nearest hut, which stood half a mile from any road, but so much the nearer to the pond, and had long been uninhabited: —

> "And here a poet builded,
> In the completed years,
> For behold a trivial cabin
> That to destruction steers."

So the Muse fables. But therein, as I found, dwelt now John Field, an Irishman, and his wife, and several children, from the broad-faced boy who assisted his father at his work, and now came running by his side from the bog to escape the rain, to the wrinkled, sibyl-like, cone-headed infant that sat upon its father's knee as in the palaces of nobles, and looked out from its home in the midst of wet and hunger inquisitively upon the stranger, with the privilege of infancy, not knowing but it was the last of a noble line, and the hope and cynosure of the world, instead of John Field's poor starveling brat. There we sat together under that part of the roof which leaked the least, while it showered and thundered without. I had sat there many times of old before the ship was built that floated this family to America. An honest, hard-working, but shiftless man plainly was John Field; and his wife, she too was brave to cook so many successive dinners in the recesses of that lofty stove; with round greasy face and bare breast, still thinking to improve her condition one day; with the never absent mop in one hand, and yet no effects of it visible any where. The chickens, which had also taken shelter here from the rain, stalked about the room like members of the family, too humanized methought to roast well. They stood and looked in my eye or pecked at my shoe significantly. Meanwhile my host told me his story, how hard he worked "bogging" for a neighboring farmer, turning up a meadow with a spade or bog hoe at the rate of ten dollars an acre and the use of the land with manure for one year, and his little broadfaced son worked cheerfully at his father's side the while, not knowing how poor a bargain the latter had made. I tried to help him with my experience, telling him that he was one of my nearest neighbors, and that I too, who came a-fishing here, and looked like a loafer, was getting my living like himself; that I lived in a tight light and clean house, which hardly cost more than the annual rent of such a ruin as his commonly amounts to; and how, if he chose, he might in a month or two build himself a palace of his own; that I did not use tea, nor coffee, nor butter, nor milk, nor fresh meat, and so did not have to work to get them; again, as I did not work hard, I did not have to eat hard, and it cost me but a trifle for my food; but as he began with tea, and coffee, and butter, and milk, and beef, he had to work hard to pay for them, and when he had worked hard he had to eat hard again to repair the waste of his system,—and so it was as broad as it was long, indeed it was broader than it was long, for he was discontented and wasted his life into the bargain; and yet he had rated it as a gain in coming to America, that here you could get tea, and coffee, and meat every day. But the only true America is that country where you are at liberty to pursue such a mode of life as may enable you to do without these, and where the state does not endeavor to compel you to sustain the slavery and war and other superfluous expenses which directly or indirectly result from the use of such things. For I purposely talked to him as if he were a philosopher, or desired to be one. I should be glad if all the meadows on the earth were left in a wild state, if that were the consequence of men's beginning to redeem themselves. A man will not need to study history to find out what is best for his own culture. But alas! the culture of an Irishman is an enterprise to be undertaken with a sort of moral bog hoe. I told him, that as he worked so hard at bogging, he required thick boots and stout clothing, which yet were soon soiled and worn out, but

I wore light shoes and thin clothing, which cost not half so much, though he might think that I was dressed like a gentleman, (which, however, was not the case,) and in an hour or two, without labor, but as a recreation, I could, if I wished, catch as many fish as I should want for two days, or earn enough money to support me a week. If he and his family would live simply, they might all go a-huckleberrying in the summer for their amusement. John heaved a sigh at this, and his wife stared with arms a-kimbo, and both appeared to be wondering if they had capital enough to begin such a course with, or arithmetic enough to carry it through. It was sailing by dead reckoning to them, and they saw not clearly how to make their port so; therefore I suppose they still take life bravely, after their fashion, face to face, giving it tooth and nail, not having skill to split its massive columns with any fine entering wedge, and rout it in detail;—thinking to deal with it roughly, as one should handle a thistle. But they fight at an overwhelming disadvantage,—living, John Field, alas! without arithmetic, and failing so.

"Do you ever fish?" I asked. "O yes, I catch a mess now and then when I am lying by; good perch I catch." "What's your bait?" "I catch shiners with fish-worms, and bait the perch with them." "You'd better go now, John," said his wife with glistening and hopeful face; but John demurred.

The shower was now over, and a rainbow above the eastern woods promised a fair evening; so I took my departure. When I had got without I asked for a dish, hoping to get a sight of the well bottom, to complete my survey of the premises; but there, alas! are shallows and quicksands, and rope broken withal, and bucket irrecoverable. Meanwhile the right culinary vessel was selected, water was seemingly distilled, and after consultation and long delay passed out to the thirsty one,—not yet suffered to cool, not yet to settle. Such gruel sustains life here, I thought; so, shutting my eyes, and excluding the motes by a skilfully directed under-current, I drank to genuine hospitality the heartiest draught I could. I am not squeamish in such cases when manners are concerned.

As I was leaving the Irishman's roof after the rain, bending my steps again to the pond, my haste to catch pickerel, wading in retired meadows, in sloughs and bog-holes, in forlorn and savage places, appeared for an instant trivial to me who had been sent to school and college; but as I ran down the hill toward the reddening west, with the rainbow over my shoulder, and some faint tinkling sounds borne to my ear through the cleansed air, from I know not what quarter, my Good Genius seemed to say,—Go fish and hunt far and wide day by day,—farther and wider,—and rest thee by many brooks and hearth-sides without misgiving. Remember thy Creator in the days of thy youth. Rise free from care before the dawn, and seek adventures. Let the noon find thee by other lakes, and the night overtake thee every where at home. There are no larger fields than these, no worthier games than may here be played. Grow wild according to thy nature, like these sedges and brakes, which will never become English hay. Let the thunder rumble; what if it threaten ruin to farmers' crops? that is not its errand to thee. Take shelter under the cloud, while they flee to carts and sheds. Let not to get a living be thy trade, but thy sport. Enjoy the land, but own it not. Through want of enterprise and faith men are where they are, buying and selling, and spending their lives like serfs.

O Baker Farm!

"Landscape where the richest element
  Is a little sunshine innocent." * *

"No one runs to revel
  On thy rail-fenced lea." * *

"Debate with no man hast thou,
    With questions art never perplexed,
  As tame at the first sight as now,
    In thy plain russet gabardine dressed." * *

"Come ye who love,
    And ye who hate,
  Children of the Holy Dove,
    And Guy Faux of the state,
  And hang conspiracies
  From the tough rafters of the trees!"

Men come tamely home at night only from the next field

or street, where their household echoes haunt, and their life pines because it breathes its own breath over again; their shadows morning and evening reach farther than their daily steps. We should come home from far, from adventures, and perils, and discoveries every day, with new experience and character.

Before I had reached the pond some fresh impulse had brought out John Field, with altered mind, letting go "bogging" ere this sunset. But he, poor man, disturbed only a couple of fins while I was catching a fair string, and he said it was his luck; but when we changed seats in the boat luck changed seats too. Poor John Field!—I trust he does not read this, unless he will improve by it,—thinking to live by some derivative old country mode in this primitive new country,—to catch perch with shiners. It is good bait sometimes, I allow. With his horizon all his own, yet he a poor man, born to be poor, with his inherited Irish poverty or poor life, his Adam's grandmother and boggy ways, not to rise in this world, he nor his posterity, till their wading webbed bog-trotting feet get *talaria* to their heels.

Higher Laws

As I came home through the woods with my string of fish, trailing my pole, it being now quite dark, I caught a glimpse of a woodchuck stealing across my path, and felt a strange thrill of savage delight, and was strongly tempted to seize and devour him raw; not that I was hungry then, except for that wildness which he represented. Once or twice, however, while I lived at the pond, I found myself ranging the woods, like a half-starved hound, with a strange abandonment, seeking some kind of venison which I might devour, and no morsel could have been too savage for me. The wildest scenes had become unaccountably familiar. I found in myself, and still find, an instinct toward a higher, or, as it is named, spiritual life, as do most men, and another toward a primitive rank and savage one, and I reverence them both. I love the wild not less than the good. The wildness and adventure that are in fishing still recommended it to me. I like sometimes to take rank hold on life and spend my day more as the animals do. Perhaps I have owed to this employment and to hunting, when quite young, my closest acquaintance with Nature. They early introduce us to and detain us in scenery with which otherwise, at that age, we should have little acquaintance. Fishermen, hunters, woodchoppers, and others, spending their lives in the fields and woods, in a peculiar sense a part of Nature themselves, are often in a more favorable mood for observing her, in the intervals of their pursuits, than philosophers or poets even, who approach her with expectation. She is not afraid to exhibit herself to them. The traveller on the prairie is naturally a hunter, on the head waters of the Missouri and Columbia a trapper, and at the Falls of St. Mary a fisherman. He who is only a traveller learns things at second-hand and by the halves, and is poor authority. We are most interested when science reports what those men already know practically or instinctively, for that alone is a true *humanity*, or account of human experience.

They mistake who assert that the Yankee has few amusements, because he has not so many public holidays, and men and boys do not play so many games as they do in England, for here the more primitive but solitary amusements of hunting fishing and the like have not yet given place to the former. Almost every New England boy among my contemporaries shouldered a fowling piece between the ages of ten and fourteen; and his hunting and fishing grounds were not limited like the preserves of an English nobleman, but were more boundless even than those of a savage. No wonder, then, that he did not oftener stay to play on the common. But already a change is taking place, owing, not to an increased humanity, but to an increased scarcity of game, for perhaps the hunter is the greatest friend of the animals hunted, not excepting the Humane Society.

Moreover, when at the pond, I wished sometimes to add fish to my fare for variety. I have actually fished from the same kind of necessity that the first fishers did. Whatever humanity I might conjure up against it was all factitious, and concerned my philosophy more than my feelings. I speak of fishing only now, for I had long felt differently about fowling, and sold my gun before I went to the woods. Not that I am less humane than others, but I did not perceive that my feelings were much affected. I did not pity the fishes nor the worms. This was habit. As for fowling, during the last years that I carried a gun my excuse was that I was studying ornithology, and sought only new or rare birds. But I confess that I am now inclined to think that there is a finer way of studying ornithology than this. It requires so much closer attention to the habits of the birds, that, if for that reason only, I have been willing to omit the gun. Yet notwithstanding the objection on the score of humanity, I am compelled to doubt if equally valuable sports are ever substituted for these; and when some of my friends have asked me anxiously about their boys, whether they should let them hunt, I have answered, yes,—remembering that it was one of the best parts of my education,—*make* them hunters, though sportsmen only at first, if possible, mighty hunters at last, so that they shall not find game large enough for them in this or any vegetable wilderness,—hunters as well as fishers of men. Thus far I am of the opinion of Chaucer's nun, who

> "yave not of the text a pulled hen
> That saith that hunters ben not holy men."

There is a period in the history of the individual, as of the race, when the hunters are the "best men," as the Algonquins called them. We cannot but pity the boy who has never fired a gun; he is no more humane, while his education has been sadly neglected. This was my answer with respect to those youths who were bent on this pursuit, trusting that they would soon outgrow it. No humane being, past the thought-less age of boyhood, will wantonly murder any creature, which holds its life by the same tenure that he does. The hare in its extremity cries like a child. I warn you, mothers, that my sympathies do not always make the usual phil-*anthropic* distinctions.

Such is oftenest the young man's introduction to the forest, and the most original part of himself. He goes thither at first as a hunter and fisher, until at last, if he has the seeds of a better life in him, he distinguishes his proper objects, as a poet or naturalist it may be, and leaves the gun and fish-pole behind. The mass of men are still and always young in this respect. In some countries a hunting person is no uncommon sight. Such a one might make a good shepherd's dog, but is far from being the Good Shepherd. I have been surprised to consider that the only obvious employment, except wood-chopping, ice-cutting, or the like business, which ever to my knowledge detained at Walden Pond for a whole half day any of my fellow-citizens, whether fathers or children of the town, with just one exception, was fishing. Commonly they did not think that they were lucky, or well paid for their time, unless they got a long string of fish, though they had the opportu-nity of seeing the pond all the while. They might go there a thousand times before the sediment of fishing would sink to the bottom and leave their purpose pure; but no doubt such a clarifying process would be going on all the while. The gov-ernor and his council faintly remember the pond, for they went a-fishing there when they were boys; but now they are too old and dignified to go a-fishing, and so they know it no more forever. Yet even they expect to go to heaven at last. If the legislature regards it, it is chiefly to regulate the number of hooks to be used there; but they know nothing about the hook of hooks with which to angle for the pond itself, impaling the legislature for a bait. Thus, even in civilized communities, the embryo man passes through the hunter stage of development.

I have found repeatedly, of late years, that I cannot fish without falling a little in self-respect. I have tried it again and again. I have skill at it, and, like many of my fellows, a certain instinct for it, which revives from time to time, but always when I have done I feel that it would have been better if I had not fished. I think that I do not mistake. It is a faint intimation, yet so are the first streaks of morning. There is unquestionably this instinct in me which belongs to the lower orders of creation; yet with every year I am less a fisherman, though without more humanity or even wisdom; at present I am no fisherman at all. But I see that if I were to live in a wilderness I should again be tempted to become a fisher and hunter in earnest. Beside, there is something essentially unclean about this diet and all flesh, and I began to see where housework commences, and whence the endeavor, which costs so much, to wear a tidy and respectable appearance each day, to keep the house sweet and free from all ill odors and sights. Having been my own butcher and scullion and cook, as well as the gentleman for whom the dishes were served up, I can speak from an unusually complete experience. The practical objection to animal food in my case was its uncleanness; and, besides, when I had caught and cleaned and cooked and eaten my fish, they seemed not to have fed me essentially. It was insignificant and unnecessary, and cost more than it came to. A little bread or a few potatoes would have done as well, with less trouble and filth. Like many of my contemporaries, I had rarely for many years used animal food, or tea, or coffee, &c.; not so much because of any ill effects which I had traced to them, as because they were not agreeable to my imagination. The repugnance to animal food is not the effect of experience, but is an instinct. It appeared more beautiful to live low and fare hard in many respects; and though I never did so, I went far enough to please my imagination. I believe that every man who has ever been earnest to preserve his higher or poetic faculties in the best condition has been particularly inclined to abstain from animal food, and from much food of any kind. It is a significant fact, stated by entomologists, I find it in Kirby and Spence, that "some insects in their perfect state, though furnished with organs of feeding, make no use of them;" and they lay it down as "a general rule, that almost all insects in this state eat much less than in that of larvæ. The voracious caterpillar when transformed into a butterfly," . . "and the gluttonous maggot when become a fly," content themselves with a drop or two of honey or some other sweet liquid. The abdomen under the wings of the butterfly still represents the larva. This is the tid-bit which tempts his insectivorous fate. The gross feeder is a man in the larva state; and there are whole nations in that condition, nations without fancy or imagination, whose vast abdomens betray them.

It is hard to provide and cook so simple and clean a diet as will not offend the imagination; but this, I think, is to be fed when we feed the body; they should both sit down at the same table. Yet perhaps this may be done. The fruits eaten temperately need not make us ashamed of our appetites, nor interrupt the worthiest pursuits. But put an extra condiment into your dish, and it will poison you. It is not worth the while to live by rich cookery. Most men would feel shame if caught preparing with their own hands precisely such a dinner, whether of animal or vegetable food, as is every day prepared for them by others. Yet till this is otherwise we are not civilized, and, if gentlemen and ladies, are not true men and women. This certainly suggests what change is to be made. It may be vain to ask why the imagination will not be reconciled to flesh and fat. I am satisfied that it is not. Is it not a reproach that man is a carnivorous animal? True, he can and does live, in a great measure, by preying on other animals; but this is a miserable way,—as any one who will go to snaring rabbits, or slaughtering lambs, may learn,—and he will be regarded as a benefactor of his race who shall teach man to confine himself to a more innocent and wholesome diet. Whatever my own practice may be, I have no doubt that it is a part of the destiny of the human race, in its gradual improvement, to leave off eating animals, as surely as the savage tribes have left off eating each other when they came in contact with the more civilized.

If one listens to the faintest but constant suggestions of his genius, which are certainly true, he sees not to what extremes, or even insanity, it may lead him; and yet that way, as he grows more resolute and faithful, his road lies. The faintest assured objection which one healthy man feels will at length prevail over the arguments and customs of mankind. No man ever followed his genius till it misled him. Though the result were bodily weakness, yet perhaps no one can say that the consequences were to be regretted, for these were a life in conformity to higher principles. If the day and the night are such that you greet them with joy, and life emits a fragrance like flowers and sweet-scented herbs, is more elastic, more starry, more immortal,—that is your success. All nature is your congratulation, and you have cause momentarily to bless yourself. The greatest gains and values are farthest from being appreciated. We easily come to doubt if they exist. We soon forget them. They are the highest reality. Perhaps the facts most astounding and most real are never communicated by man to man. The true harvest of my daily life is somewhat as intangible and indescribable as the tints of morning or evening. It is a little star-dust caught, a segment of the rainbow which I have clutched.

Yet, for my part, I was never unusually squeamish; I could sometimes eat a fried rat with a good relish, if it were necessary. I am glad to have drunk water so long, for the same reason that I prefer the natural sky to an opium-eater's heaven. I would fain keep sober always; and there are infinite degrees of drunkenness. I believe that water is the only drink for a wise man; wine is not so noble a liquor; and think of dashing the hopes of a morning with a cup of warm coffee, or of an evening with a dish of tea! Ah, how low I fall when I am tempted by them! Even music may be intoxicating. Such apparently slight causes destroyed Greece and Rome, and will destroy England and America. Of all ebriosity, who does not prefer to be intoxicated by the air he breathes? I have found it to be the most serious objection to coarse labors long continued, that they compelled me to eat and drink coarsely also.

But to tell the truth, I find myself at present somewhat less particular in these respects. I carry less religion to the table, ask no blessing; not because I am wiser than I was, but, I am obliged to confess, because, however much it is to be regretted, with years I have grown more coarse and indifferent. Perhaps these questions are entertained only in youth, as most believe of poetry. My practice is "nowhere," my opinion is here. Nevertheless I am far from regarding myself as one of those privileged ones to whom the Ved refers when it says, that "he who has true faith in the Omnipresent Supreme Being may eat all that exists," that is, is not bound to inquire what is his food, or who prepares it; and even in their case it is to be observed, as a Hindoo commentator has remarked, that the Vedant limits this privilege to "the time of distress."

Who has not sometimes derived an inexpressible satisfaction from his food in which appetite had no share? I have been thrilled to think that I owed a mental perception to the commonly gross sense of taste, that I have been inspired through the palate, that some berries which I had eaten on a hill-side had fed my genius. "The soul not being mistress of herself," says Thseng-tseu, "one looks, and one does not see; one listens, and one does not hear; one eats, and one does not know the savor of food." He who distinguishes the true savor of his food can never be a glutton; he who does not cannot be otherwise. A puritan may go to his brown-bread crust with as gross an appetite as ever an alderman to his turtle. Not that food which entereth into the mouth defileth a man, but the appetite with which it is eaten. It is neither the quality nor the quantity, but the devotion to sensual savors; when that which is eaten is not a viand to sustain our animal, or inspire our spiritual life, but food for the worms that possess us. If the hunter has a taste for mud-turtles, muskrats, and other such savage tid-bits, the fine lady indulges a taste for jelly made of a calf's foot, or for sardines from over the sea, and they are even. He goes to the mill-pond, she to her preserve-pot. The wonder is how they, how you and I, can live this slimy beastly life, eating and drinking.

Our whole life is startlingly moral. There is never an instant's truce between virtue and vice. Goodness is the only investment that never fails. In the music of the harp which trembles round the world it is the insisting on this which thrills us. The harp is the travelling patterer for the Universe's Insurance Company, recommending its laws, and our little goodness is all the assessment that we pay. Though the youth at last grows indifferent, the laws of the universe are not indifferent, but are forever on the side of the most sensitive. Listen to every zephyr for some reproof, for it is surely there, and he is unfortunate who does not hear it. We cannot touch a string or move a stop but the charming moral transfixes us. Many an irksome noise, go a long way off, is heard as music, a proud sweet satire on the meanness of our lives.

We are conscious of an animal in us, which awakens in proportion as our higher nature slumbers. It is reptile and sensual, and perhaps cannot be wholly expelled; like the worms which, even in life and health, occupy our bodies. Possibly we may withdraw from it, but never change its nature. I fear that it may enjoy a certain health of its own; that we may be well, yet not pure. The other day I picked up the lower jaw of a hog, with white and sound teeth and tusks, which suggested that there was an animal health and vigor distinct from the spiritual. This creature succeeded by other means than temperance and purity. "That in which men differ from brute beasts," says Mencius, "is a thing very inconsiderable; the common herd lose it very soon; superior men preserve it carefully." Who knows what sort of life would result if we had attained to purity? If I knew so wise a man as could teach me purity I would go to seek him forthwith. "A command over our passions, and over the external senses of the body, and good acts, are declared by the Ved to be indispensable in the mind's approximation to God." Yet the spirit can for the time pervade and control every member and function of the body, and transmute what in form is the grossest sensuality into purity and devotion. The generative energy, which, when we are loose, dissipates and makes us unclean, when we are continent invigorates and inspires us. Chastity is the flowering of man; and what are called Genius, Heroism, Holiness, and the like, are but various fruits which succeed it. Man flows at once to God when the channel of purity is open. By turns our purity inspires and our impurity casts us down. He is blessed who is assured that the animal is dying out in him day by day, and the divine being established. Perhaps there is none but has cause for shame on account of the inferior and brutish nature to which he is allied. I fear that we are such gods or demigods only as fauns and satyrs, the divine allied to beasts, the creatures of appetite, and that, to some extent, our very life is our disgrace.—

> "How happy's he who hath due place assigned
> To his beasts and disaforested his mind!
>
>   *   *   *   *   *
>
> Can use his horse, goat, wolf, and ev'ry beast,
> And is not ass himself to all the rest!
> Else man not only is the herd of swine,
> But he's those devils too which did incline
> Them to a headlong rage, and made them worse."

All sensuality is one, though it takes many forms; all purity is one. It is the same whether a man eat, or drink, or cohabit, or sleep sensually. They are but one appetite, and we only need to see a person do any one of these things to know how great a sensualist he is. The impure can neither stand nor sit with purity. When the reptile is attacked at one mouth of his burrow, he shows himself at another. If you would be chaste, you must be temperate. What is chastity? How shall a man know if he is chaste? He shall not know it. We have heard of this virtue, but we know not what it is. We speak conformably to the rumor which we have heard. From exertion come wisdom and purity; from sloth ignorance and sensuality. In the student sensuality is a sluggish habit of mind. An unclean person is universally a slothful one, one who sits by a stove, whom the sun shines on prostrate, who reposes without being fatigued. If you would avoid uncleanness, and all the sins, work earnestly, though it be at cleaning a stable. Nature is hard to be overcome, but she must be overcome. What avails it that you are Christian, if you are not purer than the heathen, if you deny yourself no more, if you are not more religious? I know of many systems of religion esteemed heathenish whose precepts fill the reader with shame, and provoke him to new endeavors, though it be to the performance of rites merely.

I hesitate to say these things, but it is not because of the subject,—I care not how obscene my *words* are,—but because I cannot speak of them without betraying my impurity. We discourse freely without shame of one form of sensuality, and are silent about another. We are so degraded that we cannot speak simply of the necessary functions of human nature. In earlier ages, in some countries, every function was reverently spoken of and regulated by law. Nothing was too trivial for the Hindoo lawgiver, however offensive it may be to modern taste. He teaches how to eat, drink, cohabit, void excrement and urine, and the like, elevating what is mean, and does not falsely excuse himself by calling these things trifles.

Every man is the builder of a temple, called his body, to the god he worships, after a style purely his own, nor can he get off by hammering marble instead. We are all sculptors and painters, and our material is our own flesh and blood and bones. Any nobleness begins at once to refine a man's features, any meanness or sensuality to imbrute them.

John Farmer sat at his door one September evening, after a hard day's work, his mind still running on his labor more or less. Having bathed he sat down to recreate his intellectual man. It was a rather cool evening, and some of his neighbors were apprehending a frost. He had not attended to the train of his thoughts long when he heard some one playing on a flute, and that sound harmonized with his mood. Still he thought of his work; but the burden of his thought was, that though this kept running in his head, and he found himself planning and contriving it against his will, yet it concerned him very little. It was no more than the scurf of his skin, which was constantly shuffled off. But the notes of the flute came home to his ears out of a different sphere from that he worked in, and suggested work for certain faculties which slumbered in him. They gently did away with the street, and the village, and the state in which he lived. A voice said to him,—Why do you stay here and live this mean moiling life, when a glorious existence is possible for you? Those same stars twinkle over other fields than these.—But how to come out of this condition and actually migrate thither? All that he could think of was to practise some new austerity, to let his mind descend into his body and redeem it, and treat himself with ever increasing respect.

Brute Neighbors

SOMETIMES I had a companion in my fishing, who came through the village to my house from the other side of the town, and the catching of the dinner was as much a social exercise as the eating of it.

Hermit. I wonder what the world is doing now. I have not heard so much as a locust over the sweet-fern these three hours. The pigeons are all asleep upon their roosts,—no flutter from them. Was that a farmer's noon horn which sounded from beyond the woods just now? The hands are coming in to boiled salt beef and cider and Indian bread. Why will men worry themselves so? He that does not eat need not work. I wonder how much they have reaped. Who would live there where a body can never think for the barking of Bose? And O, the housekeeping! to keep bright the devil's door-knobs, and scour his tubs this bright day! Better not keep a house. Say, some hollow tree; and then for morning calls and dinner-parties! Only a woodpecker tapping. O, they swarm; the sun is too warm there; they are born too far into life for me. I have water from the spring, and a loaf of brown bread on the shelf.—Hark! I hear a rustling of the leaves. Is it some ill-fed village hound yielding to the instinct of the chase? or the lost pig which is said to be in these woods, whose tracks I saw after the rain? It comes on apace; my sumachs and sweet-briers tremble.—Eh, Mr. Poet, is it you? How do you like the world to-day?

Poet. See those clouds; how they hang! That's the greatest thing I have seen to-day. There's nothing like it in old paintings, nothing like it in foreign lands,—unless when we were off the coast of Spain. That's a true Mediterranean sky. I thought, as I have my living to get, and have not eaten to-day, that I might go a-fishing. That's the true industry for poets. It is the only trade I have learned. Come, let's along.

Hermit. I cannot resist. My brown bread will soon be gone. I will go with you gladly soon, but I am just concluding a serious meditation. I think that I am near the end of it. Leave me alone, then, for a while. But that we may not be delayed, you shall be digging the bait meanwhile. Angleworms are rarely to be met with in these parts, where the soil was never fattened with manure; the race is nearly extinct. The sport of digging the bait is nearly equal to that of catching the fish, when one's appetite is not too keen; and this you may have all to yourself to-day. I would advise you to set in the spade down yonder among the ground-nuts, where you see the johnswort waving. I think that I may warrant you one worm to every three sods you turn up, if you look well in among the roots of the grass, as if you were weeding. Or, if you choose to go farther, it will not be unwise, for I have found the increase of fair bait to be very nearly as the squares of the distances.

Hermit alone. Let me see; where was I? Methinks I was nearly in this frame of mind; the world lay about at this angle. Shall I go to heaven or a-fishing? If I should soon bring this meditation to an end, would another so sweet occasion be likely to offer? I was as near being resolved into the essence of things as ever I was in my life. I fear my thoughts will not come back to me. If it would do any good, I would whistle for them. When they make us an offer, is it wise to say, We will think of it? My thoughts have left no track, and I cannot find the path again. What was it that I was thinking of? It was a very hazy day. I will just try these three sentences of Con-fut-see; they may fetch that state about again. I know not whether it was the dumps or a budding ecstasy. Mem. There never is but one opportunity of a kind.

Poet. How now, Hermit, is it too soon? I have got just thirteen whole ones, beside several which are imperfect or undersized; but they will do for the smaller fry; they do not cover up the hook so much. Those village worms are quite too large; a shiner may make a meal off one without finding the skewer.

Hermit. Well, then, let's be off. Shall we to the Concord? There's good sport there if the water be not too high.

Why do precisely these objects which we behold make a world? Why has man just these species of animals for his neighbors; as if nothing but a mouse could have filled this crevice? I suspect that Pilpay & Co. have put animals to their best use, for they are all beasts of burden, in a sense, made to carry some portion of our thoughts.

The mice which haunted my house were not the common ones, which are said to have been introduced into the country, but a wild native kind not found in the village. I sent one to a distinguished naturalist, and it interested him much. When I was building, one of these had its nest underneath the house, and before I had laid the second floor, and swept out the shavings, would come out regularly at lunch time and pick up the crums at my feet. It probably had never seen a man before; and it soon became quite familiar, and would run over my shoes and up my clothes. It could readily ascend the sides of the room by short impulses, like a squirrel, which it resembled in its motions. At length, as I leaned with my elbow on the bench one day, it ran up my clothes, and along my sleeve, and round and round the paper which held my dinner, while I kept the latter close, and dodged and played at bo-peep with it; and when at last I held still a piece of cheese between my thumb and finger, it came and nibbled it, sitting in my hand, and afterward cleaned its face and paws, like a fly, and walked away.

A phœbe soon built in my shed, and a robin for protection in a pine which grew against the house. In June the partridge, (*Tetrao umbellus,*) which is so shy a bird, led her brood past my windows, from the woods in the rear to the front of my house, clucking and calling to them like a hen, and in all her behavior proving herself the hen of the woods. The young suddenly disperse on your approach, at a signal from the mother, as if a whirlwind had swept them away, and they so exactly resemble the dried leaves and twigs that many a traveller has placed his foot in the midst of a brood, and heard the whir of the old bird as she flew off, and her anxious calls and mewing, or seen her trail her wings to attract his attention, without suspecting their neighborhood. The parent will sometimes roll and spin round before you in such a dishabille, that you cannot, for a few moments, detect what kind of creature it is. The young squat still and flat, often running their heads under a leaf, and mind only their mother's directions given from a distance, nor will your approach make them run again and betray themselves. You may even tread on them, or have your eyes on them for a minute, without discovering them. I have held them in my open hand at such a time, and still their only care, obedient to their mother and their instinct, was to squat there without fear or trembling. So perfect is this instinct, that once, when I had laid them on the leaves again, and one accidentally fell on its side, it was found with the rest in exactly the same position ten minutes afterward. They are not callow like the young of most birds, but more perfectly developed and precocious even than chickens. The remarkably adult yet innocent expression of their open and serene eyes is very memorable. All intelligence seems reflected in them. They suggest not merely the purity of infancy, but a wisdom clarified by experience. Such an eye was not born when the bird was, but is coeval with the sky it reflects. The woods do not yield another such a gem. The traveller does not often look into such a limpid well. The ignorant or reckless sportsman often shoots the parent at such a time, and leaves these innocents to fall a prey to some prowling beast or bird, or gradually mingle with the decaying leaves which they so much resemble. It is said that when hatched by a hen they will directly disperse on some alarm, and so are lost, for they never hear the mother's call which gathers them again. These were my hens and chickens.

It is remarkable how many creatures live wild and free though secret in the woods, and still sustain themselves in the neighborhood of towns, suspected by hunters only. How retired the otter manages to live here! He grows to be four feet long, as big as a small boy, perhaps without any human being getting a glimpse of him. I formerly saw the raccoon in the woods behind where my house is built, and probably still heard their whinnering at night. Commonly I rested an hour or two in the shade at noon, after planting, and ate my lunch, and read a little by a spring which was the source of a swamp and of a brook, oozing from under Brister's Hill, half a mile from my field. The approach to this was through a succession of descending grassy hollows, full of young pitch-pines, into a larger wood about the swamp. There, in a very secluded and shaded spot, under a spreading white-pine, there was yet a clean firm sward to sit on. I had dug out the spring and made a well of clear gray water, where I could dip up a pailful without roiling it, and thither I went for this purpose almost every day in midsummer, when the pond was warmest. Thither too the wood-cock led her brood, to probe the mud for worms, flying but a foot above them down the bank, while they ran in a troop beneath; but at last, spying me, she would leave her young and circle round and round me, nearer and nearer, till within four or five feet, pretending broken wings and legs, to attract my attention and get off her young, who would already have taken up their march, with faint wiry peep, single file through the swamp, as she directed. Or I heard the peep of the young when I could not see the parent bird. There too the turtle-doves sat over the spring, or fluttered from bough to bough of the soft white-pines over my head; or the red squirrel, coursing down the nearest bough, was particularly familiar and inquisitive. You only need sit still long enough in some attractive spot in the woods that all its inhabitants may exhibit themselves to you by turns.

I was witness to events of a less peaceful character. One day when I went out to my wood-pile, or rather my pile of stumps, I observed two large ants, the one red, the other much larger, nearly half an inch long, and black, fiercely contending with one another. Having once got hold they never let go, but struggled and wrestled and rolled on the chips incessantly. Looking farther, I was surprised to find that the chips were covered with such combatants, that it was not a *duellum*, but a *bellum*, a war between two races of ants, the red always pitted against the black, and frequently two red ones to one black. The legions of these Myrmidons covered all the hills and vales in my wood-yard, and the ground was already strewn with the dead and dying, both red and black. It was the only battle which I have ever witnessed, the only battle-field I ever trod while the battle was raging; internecine war; the red republicans on the one hand, and the black imperialists on the other. On every side they were engaged in deadly combat, yet without any noise that I could hear, and human soldiers never fought so resolutely. I watched a couple that were fast locked in each other's embraces, in a little sunny valley amid the chips, now at noon-day prepared to fight till the sun went down, or life went out. The smaller red champion had fastened himself like a vice to his adversary's front, and through all the tumblings on that field never for an instant ceased to gnaw at one of his feelers near the root, having already caused the other to go by the board; while the stronger black one dashed him from side to side, and, as I saw on looking nearer, had already divested him of several of his members. They fought with more pertinacity than bull-dogs. Neither manifested the least disposition to retreat. It was evident that their battle-cry was Conquer or die. In the mean while there came along a single red ant on the hill-side of this valley, evidently full of excitement, who either had des-patched his foe, or had not yet taken part in the battle; prob-ably the latter, for he had lost none of his limbs; whose mother had charged him to return with his shield or upon it. Or perchance he was some Achilles, who had nourished his wrath apart, and had now come to avenge or rescue his Patro-clus. He saw this unequal combat from afar,—for the blacks were nearly twice the size of the red,—he drew near with rapid pace till he stood on his guard within half an inch of the combatants; then, watching his opportunity, he sprang upon the black warrior, and commenced his operations near the root of his right fore-leg, leaving the foe to select among his own members; and so there were three united for life, as if a new kind of attraction had been invented which put all other locks and cements to shame. I should not have won-dered by this time to find that they had their respective mu-sical bands stationed on some eminent chip, and playing their national airs the while, to excite the slow and cheer the dying combatants. I was myself excited somewhat even as if they had been men. The more you think of it, the less the differ-ence. And certainly there is not the fight recorded in Concord history, at least, if in the history of America, that will bear a moment's comparison with this, whether for the numbers en-gaged in it, or for the patriotism and heroism displayed. For numbers and for carnage it was an Austerlitz or Dresden, Concord Fight! Two killed on the patriots' side, and Luther Blanchard wounded! Why here every ant was a Buttrick,— "Fire! for God's sake fire!"—and thousands shared the fate of Davis and Hosmer. There was not one hireling there. I have no doubt that it was a principle they fought for, as much as our ancestors, and not to avoid a three-penny tax on their tea;

and the results of this battle will be as important and memorable to those whom it concerns as those of the battle of
Bunker Hill, at least.

I took up the chip on which the three I have particularly
described were struggling, carried it into my house, and
placed it under a tumbler on my window-sill, in order to see
the issue. Holding a microscope to the first-mentioned red
ant, I saw that, though he was assiduously gnawing at the
near fore-leg of his enemy, having severed his remaining
feeler, his own breast was all torn away, exposing what vitals
he had there to the jaws of the black warrior, whose breast-
plate was apparently too thick for him to pierce; and the dark
carbuncles of the sufferer's eyes shone with ferocity such as
war only could excite. They struggled half an hour longer under the tumbler, and when I looked again the black soldier
had severed the heads of his foes from their bodies, and the
still living heads were hanging on either side of him like
ghastly trophies at his saddle-bow, still apparently as firmly
fastened as ever, and he was endeavoring with feeble strug-
gles, being without feelers and with only the remnant of a
leg, and I know not how many other wounds, to divest himself of them; which at length, after half an hour more, he
accomplished. I raised the glass, and he went off over the
window-sill in that crippled state. Whether he finally survived
that combat, and spent the remainder of his days in some
Hotel des Invalides, I do not know; but I thought that his
industry would not be worth much thereafter. I never learned
which party was victorious, nor the cause of the war; but I
felt for the rest of that day as if I had had my feelings excited
and harrowed by witnessing the struggle, the ferocity and carnage, of a human battle before my door.

Kirby and Spence tell us that the battles of ants have long
been celebrated and the date of them recorded, though they
say that Huber is the only modern author who appears to
have witnessed them. "Æneas Sylvius," say they, "after giving
a very circumstantial account of one contested with great obstinacy by a great and small species on the trunk of a pear
tree," adds that " 'This action was fought in the pontificate of
Eugenius the Fourth, in the presence of Nicholas Pistoriensis,
an eminent lawyer, who related the whole history of the

battle with the greatest fidelity.' A similar engagement between great and small ants is recorded by Olaus Magnus, in
which the small ones, being victorious, are said to have buried
the bodies of their own soldiers, but left those of their giant
enemies a prey to the birds. This event happened previous to
the expulsion of the tyrant Christiern the Second from Sweden." The battle which I witnessed took place in the Presidency of Polk, five years before the passage of Webster's
Fugitive-Slave Bill.

Many a village Bose, fit only to course a mud-turtle in a
victualling cellar, sported his heavy quarters in the woods,
without the knowledge of his master, and ineffectually
smelled at old fox burrows and woodchucks' holes; led perchance by some slight cur which nimbly threaded the wood,
and might still inspire a natural terror in its denizens;—now
far behind his guide, barking like a canine bull toward some
small squirrel which had treed itself for scrutiny, then, cantering off, bending the bushes with his weight, imagining that
he is on the track of some stray member of the jerbilla family.
Once I was surprised to see a cat walking along the stony
shore of the pond, for they rarely wander so far from home.
The surprise was mutual. Nevertheless the most domestic cat,
which has lain on a rug all her days, appears quite at home in
the woods, and, by her sly and stealthy behavior, proves herself more native there than the regular inhabitants. Once,
when berrying, I met with a cat with young kittens in the
woods, quite wild, and they all, like their mother, had their
backs up and were fiercely spitting at me. A few years before
I lived in the woods there was what was called a "winged
cat" in one of the farm-houses in Lincoln nearest the pond,
Mr. Gilian Baker's. When I called to see her in June, 1842,
she was gone a-hunting in the woods, as was her wont, (I am
not sure whether it was a male or female, and so use the more
common pronoun,) but her mistress told me that she came
into the neighborhood a little more than a year before, in
April, and was finally taken into their house; that she was of
a dark brownish-gray color, with a white spot on her throat,
and white feet, and had a large bushy tail like a fox; that in
the winter the fur grew thick and flatted out along her sides,
forming strips ten or twelve inches long by two and a half

wide, and under her chin like a muff, the upper side loose, the under matted like felt, and in the spring these appendages dropped off. They gave me a pair of her "wings," which I keep still. There is no appearance of a membrane about them. Some thought it was part flying-squirrel or some other wild animal, which is not impossible, for, according to naturalists, prolific hybrids have been produced by the union of the marten and domestic cat. This would have been the right kind of cat for me to keep, if I had kept any; for why should not a poet's cat be winged as well as his horse?

In the fall the loon (*Colymbus glacialis*) came, as usual, to moult and bathe in the pond, making the woods ring with his wild laughter before I had risen. At rumor of his arrival all the Mill-dam sportsmen are on the alert, in gigs and on foot, two by two and three by three, with patent rifles and conical balls and spy-glasses. They come rustling through the woods like autumn leaves, at least ten men to one loon. Some station themselves on this side of the pond, some on that, for the poor bird cannot be omnipresent; if he dive here he must come up there. But now the kind October wind rises, rustling the leaves and rippling the surface of the water, so that no loon can be heard or seen, though his foes sweep the pond with spy-glasses, and make the woods resound with their discharges. The waves generously rise and dash angrily, taking sides with all waterfowl, and our sportsmen must beat a retreat to town and shop and unfinished jobs. But they were too often successful. When I went to get a pail of water early in the morning I frequently saw this stately bird sailing out of my cove within a few rods. If I endeavored to overtake him in a boat, in order to see how he would manœuvre, he would dive and be completely lost, so that I did not discover him again, sometimes, till the latter part of the day. But I was more than a match for him on the surface. He commonly went off in a rain.

As I was paddling along the north shore one very calm October afternoon, for such days especially they settle on to the lakes, like the milkweed down, having looked in vain over the pond for a loon, suddenly one, sailing out from the shore toward the middle a few rods in front of me, set up his wild laugh and betrayed himself. I pursued with a paddle and he

dived, but when he came up I was nearer than before. He
dived again, but I miscalculated the direction he would take,
and we were fifty rods apart when he came to the surface this
time, for I had helped to widen the interval; and again he
laughed long and loud, and with more reason than before.
He manœuvred so cunningly that I could not get within half
a dozen rods of him. Each time, when he came to the surface,
turning his head this way and that, he coolly surveyed the
water and the land, and apparently chose his course so that
he might come up where there was the widest expanse of
water and at the greatest distance from the boat. It was surprising how quickly he made up his mind and put his resolve
into execution. He led me at once to the widest part of the
pond, and could not be driven from it. While he was thinking
one thing in his brain, I was endeavoring to divine his
thought in mine. It was a pretty game, played on the smooth
surface of the pond, a man against a loon. Suddenly your
adversary's checker disappears beneath the board, and the
problem is to place yours nearest to where his will appear
again. Sometimes he would come up unexpectedly on the opposite side of me, having apparently passed directly under the
boat. So long-winded was he and so unweariable, that when
he had swum farthest he would immediately plunge again,
nevertheless; and then no wit could divine where in the deep
pond, beneath the smooth surface, he might be speeding his
way like a fish, for he had time and ability to visit the bottom
of the pond in its deepest part. It is said that loons have been
caught in the New York lakes eighty feet beneath the surface,
with hooks set for trout,—though Walden is deeper than
that. How surprised must the fishes be to see this ungainly
visitor from another sphere speeding his way amid their
schools! Yet he appeared to know his course as surely under
water as on the surface, and swam much faster there. Once or
twice I saw a ripple where he approached the surface, just put
his head out to reconnoitre, and instantly dived again. I
found that it was as well for me to rest on my oars and wait
his reappearing as to endeavor to calculate where he would
rise; for again and again, when I was straining my eyes over
the surface one way, I would suddenly be startled by his
unearthly laugh behind me. But why, after displaying so

much cunning, did he invariably betray himself the moment he came up by that loud laugh? Did not his white breast enough betray him? He was indeed a silly loon, I thought. I could commonly hear the plash of the water when he came up, and so also detected him. But after an hour he seemed as fresh as ever, dived as willingly and swam yet farther than at first. It was surprising to see how serenely he sailed off with unruffled breast when he came to the surface, doing all the work with his webbed feet beneath. His usual note was this demoniac laughter, yet somewhat like that of a water-fowl; but occasionally, when he had balked me most successfully and come up a long way off, he uttered a long-drawn unearthly howl, probably more like that of a wolf than any bird; as when a beast puts his muzzle to the ground and deliberately howls. This was his looning,—perhaps the wildest sound that is ever heard here, making the woods ring far and wide. I concluded that he laughed in derision of my efforts, confident of his own resources. Though the sky was by this time overcast, the pond was so smooth that I could see where he broke the surface when I did not hear him. His white breast, the stillness of the air, and the smoothness of the water were all against him. At length, having come up fifty rods off, he uttered one of those prolonged howls, as if calling on the god of loons to aid him, and immediately there came a wind from the east and rippled the surface, and filled the whole air with misty rain, and I was impressed as if it were the prayer of the loon answered, and his god was angry with me; and so I left him disappearing far away on the tumultuous surface.

For hours, in fall days, I watched the ducks cunningly tack and veer and hold the middle of the pond, far from the sportsman; tricks which they will have less need to practise in Louisiana bayous. When compelled to rise they would sometimes circle round and round and over the pond at a considerable height, from which they could easily see to other ponds and the river, like black motes in the sky; and, when I thought they had gone off thither long since, they would settle down by a slanting flight of a quarter of a mile on to a distant part which was left free; but what beside safety they got by sailing in the middle of Walden I do not know, unless they love its water for the same reason that I do.

House-Warming

IN OCTOBER I went a-graping to the river meadows, and loaded myself with clusters more precious for their beauty and fragrance than for food. There too I admired, though I did not gather, the cranberries, small waxen gems, pendants of the meadow grass, pearly and red, which the farmer plucks with an ugly rake, leaving the smooth meadow in a snarl, heedlessly measuring them by the bushel and the dollar only, and sells the spoils of the meads to Boston and New York; destined to be *jammed*, to satisfy the tastes of lovers of Nature there. So butchers rake the tongues of bison out of the prairie grass, regardless of the torn and drooping plant. The barberry's brilliant fruit was likewise food for my eyes merely; but I collected a small store of wild apples for coddling, which the proprietor and travellers had overlooked. When chestnuts were ripe I laid up half a bushel for winter. It was very exciting at that season to roam the then boundless chestnut woods of Lincoln,—they now sleep their long sleep under the railroad,—with a bag on my shoulder, and a stick to open burrs with in my hand, for I did not always wait for the frost, amid the rustling of leaves and the loud reproofs of the red-squirrels and the jays, whose half-consumed nuts I sometimes stole, for the burrs which they had selected were sure to contain sound ones. Occasionally I climbed and shook the trees. They grew also behind my house, and one large tree which almost overshadowed it, was, when in flower, a bouquet which scented the whole neighborhood, but the squirrels and the jays got most of its fruit; the last coming in flocks early in the morning and picking the nuts out of the burrs before they fell. I relinquished these trees to them and visited the more distant woods composed wholly of chestnut. These nuts, as far as they went, were a good substitute for bread. Many other substitutes might, perhaps, be found. Digging one day for fish-worms I discovered the ground-nut (*Apios tuberosa*) on its string, the potato of the aborigines, a sort of fabulous fruit, which I had begun to doubt if I had ever dug and eaten in childhood, as I had told, and had not dreamed it. I had often since seen its crimpled red velvety blossom supported by the stems of other plants without knowing it to be the same. Cultivation has well nigh exterminated it. It has a sweetish taste, much like that of a frostbitten potato, and I found it better boiled than roasted. This tuber seemed like a faint promise of Nature to rear her own children and feed them simply here at some future period. In these days of fatted cattle and waving grain-fields, this humble root, which was once the *totem* of an Indian tribe, is quite forgotten, or known only by its flowering vine; but let wild Nature reign here once more, and the tender and luxurious English grains will probably disappear before a myriad of foes, and without the care of man the crow may carry back even the last seed of corn to the great corn-field of the Indian's God in the southwest, whence he is said to have brought it; but the now almost exterminated ground-nut will perhaps revive and flourish in spite of frosts and wildness, prove itself indigenous, and resume its ancient importance and dignity as the diet of the hunter tribe. Some Indian Ceres or Minerva must have been the inventor and bestower of it; and when the reign of poetry commences here, its leaves and string of nuts may be represented on our works of art.

Already, by the first of September, I had seen two or three small maples turned scarlet across the pond, beneath where the white stems of three aspens diverged, at the point of a promontory, next the water. Ah, many a tale their color told! And gradually from week to week the character of each tree came out, and it admired itself reflected in the smooth mirror of the lake. Each morning the manager of this gallery substituted some new picture, distinguished by more brilliant or harmonious coloring, for the old upon the walls.

The wasps came by thousands to my lodge in October, as to winter quarters, and settled on my windows within and on the walls over-head, sometimes deterring visitors from entering. Each morning, when they were numbed with cold, I swept some of them out, but I did not trouble myself much to get rid of them; I even felt complimented by their regarding my house as a desirable shelter. They never molested me seriously, though they bedded with me; and they gradually disappeared, into what crevices I do not know, avoiding winter and unspeakable cold.

Like the wasps, before I finally went into winter quarters
in November, I used to resort to the north-east side of Walden, which the sun, reflected from the pitch-pine woods and
the stony shore, made the fire-side of the pond; it is so much
pleasanter and wholesomer to be warmed by the sun while
you can be, than by an artificial fire. I thus warmed myself by
the still glowing embers which the summer, like a departed
hunter, had left.

When I came to build my chimney I studied masonry. My
bricks being second-hand ones required to be cleaned with a
trowel, so that I learned more than usual of the qualities of
bricks and trowels. The mortar on them was fifty years old,
and was said to be still growing harder; but this is one of
those sayings which men love to repeat whether they are true
or not. Such sayings themselves grow harder and adhere more
firmly with age, and it would take many blows with a trowel
to clean an old wiseacre of them. Many of the villages of Mes-
opotamia are built of second-hand bricks of a very good quality, obtained from the ruins of Babylon, and the cement on
them is older and probably harder still. However that may be,
I was struck by the peculiar toughness of the steel which bore
so many violent blows without being worn out. As my bricks
had been in a chimney before, though I did not read the
name of Nebuchadnezzar on them, I picked out as many fireplace bricks as I could find, to save work and waste, and I
filled the spaces between the bricks about the fire-place with
stones from the pond shore, and also made my mortar with
the white sand from the same place. I lingered most about
the fireplace, as the most vital part of the house. Indeed, I
worked so deliberately, that though I commenced at the
ground in the morning, a course of bricks raised a few inches
above the floor served for my pillow at night; yet I did not
get a stiff neck for it that I remember; my stiff neck is of older
date. I took a poet to board for a fortnight about those times,
which caused me to be put to it for room. He brought his
own knife, though I had two, and we used to scour them by
thrusting them into the earth. He shared with me the labors
of cooking. I was pleased to see my work rising so square and
solid by degrees, and reflected, that, if it proceeded slowly, it

was calculated to endure a long time. The chimney is to some extent an independent structure, standing on the ground and rising through the house to the heavens; even after the house is burned it still stands sometimes, and its importance and independence are apparent. This was toward the end of summer. It was now November.

The north wind had already begun to cool the pond, though it took many weeks of steady blowing to accomplish it, it is so deep. When I began to have a fire at evening, before I plastered my house, the chimney carried smoke particularly well, because of the numerous chinks between the boards. Yet I passed some cheerful evenings in that cool and airy apartment, surrounded by the rough brown boards full of knots, and rafters with the bark on high over-head. My house never pleased my eye so much after it was plastered, though I was obliged to confess that it was more comfortable. Should not every apartment in which man dwells be lofty enough to create some obscurity over-head, where flickering shadows may play at evening about the rafters? These forms are more agreeable to the fancy and imagination than fresco paintings or other the most expensive furniture. I now first began to inhabit my house, I may say, when I began to use it for warmth as well as shelter. I had got a couple of old fire-dogs to keep the wood from the hearth, and it did me good to see the soot form on the back of the chimney which I had built, and I poked the fire with more right and more satisfaction than usual. My dwelling was small, and I could hardly entertain an echo in it; but it seemed larger for being a single apartment and remote from neighbors. All the attractions of a house were concentrated in one room; it was kitchen, chamber, parlor, and keeping-room; and whatever satisfaction parent or child, master or servant, derive from living in a house, I enjoyed it all. Cato says, the master of a family (*patremfamilias*) must have in his rustic villa "cellam oleariam, vinariam, dolia multa, uti lubeat caritatem expectare, et rei, et virtuti, et gloriæ erit," that is, "an oil and wine cellar, many casks, so that it may be pleasant to expect hard times; it will be for his advantage, and virtue, and glory." I had in my cellar a firkin of potatoes, about two quarts of peas with the weevil in them, and on my shelf a little rice, a jug of molasses, and of rye and Indian meal a peck each.

I sometimes dream of a larger and more populous house, standing in a golden age, of enduring materials, and without ginger-bread work, which shall still consist of only one room, a vast, rude, substantial, primitive hall, without ceiling or plastering, with bare rafters and purlins supporting a sort of lower heaven over one's head,—useful to keep off rain and snow; where the king and queen posts stand but to receive your homage, when you have done reverence to the prostrate Saturn of an older dynasty on stepping over the sill; a cavern-ous house, wherein you must reach up a torch upon a pole to see the roof; where some may live in the fire-place, some in the recess of a window, and some on settles, some at one end of the hall, some at another, and some aloft on rafters with the spiders, if they choose; a house which you have got into when you have opened the outside door, and the cere-mony is over; where the weary traveller may wash, and eat, and converse, and sleep, without further journey; such a shel-ter as you would be glad to reach in a tempestuous night, containing all the essentials of a house, and nothing for house-keeping; where you can see all the treasures of the house at one view, and every thing hangs upon its peg that a man should use; at once kitchen, pantry, parlor, chamber, store-house, and garret; where you can see so necessary a thing as a barrel or a ladder, so convenient a thing as a cup-board, and hear the pot boil, and pay your respects to the fire that cooks your dinner and the oven that bakes your bread, and the necessary furniture and utensils are the chief orna-ments; where the washing is not put out, nor the fire, nor the mistress, and perhaps you are sometimes requested to move from off the trap-door, when the cook would descend into the cellar, and so learn whether the ground is solid or hollow beneath you without stamping. A house whose inside is as open and manifest as a bird's nest, and you cannot go in at the front door and out at the back without seeing some of its inhabitants; where to be a guest is to be presented with the freedom of the house, and not to be carefully excluded from seven eighths of it, shut up in a particular cell, and told to make yourself at home there,—in solitary confinement. Nowadays the host does not admit you to *his* hearth, but has got the mason to build one for yourself somewhere in his alley, and hospitality is the art of *keeping* you at the greatest distance. There is as much secrecy about the cooking as if he had a design to poison you. I am aware that I have been on many a man's premises, and might have been legally ordered off, but I am not aware that I have been in many men's houses. I might visit in my old clothes a king and queen who lived simply in such a house as I have described, if I were going their way; but backing out of a modern palace will be all that I shall desire to learn, if ever I am caught in one.

It would seem as if the very language of our parlors would lose all its nerve and degenerate into *parlaver* wholly, our lives pass at such remoteness from its symbols, and its metaphors and tropes are necessarily so far fetched, through slides and dumb-waiters, as it were; in other words, the parlor is so far from the kitchen and workshop. The dinner even is only the parable of a dinner, commonly. As if only the savage dwelt near enough to Nature and Truth to borrow a trope from them. How can the scholar, who dwells away in the North West Territory or the Isle of Man, tell what is parliamentary in the kitchen?

However, only one or two of my guests were ever bold enough to stay and eat a hasty-pudding with me; but when they saw that crisis approaching they beat a hasty retreat rather, as if it would shake the house to its foundations. Nevertheless, it stood through a great many hasty-puddings.

I did not plaster till it was freezing weather. I brought over some whiter and cleaner sand for this purpose from the opposite shore of the pond in a boat, a sort of conveyance which would have tempted me to go much farther if necessary. My house had in the mean while been shingled down to the ground on every side. In lathing I was pleased to be able to send home each nail with a single blow of the hammer, and it was my ambition to transfer the plaster from the board to the wall neatly and rapidly. I remembered the story of a conceited fellow, who, in fine clothes, was wont to lounge about the village once, giving advice to workmen. Venturing one day to substitute deeds for words, he turned up his cuffs, seized a plasterer's board, and having loaded his trowel without mishap, with a complacent look toward the lathing over-head, made a bold gesture thitherward; and straightway, to his complete discomfiture, received the whole contents in his ruffled bosom. I admired anew the economy and convenience of plastering, which so effectually shuts out the cold and takes a handsome finish, and I learned the various casualties to which the plasterer is liable. I was surprised to see how thirsty the bricks were which drank up all the moisture in my plaster before I had smoothed it, and how many pailfuls of water it takes to christen a new hearth. I had the previous winter made a small quantity of lime by burning the shells of the *Unio fluviatilis*, which our river affords, for the sake of the experiment; so that I knew where my materials came from. I might have got good limestone within a mile or two and burned it myself, if I had cared to do so.

The pond had in the mean while skimmed over in the shad-iest and shallowest coves, some days or even weeks before the general freezing. The first ice is especially interesting and per-fect, being hard, dark, and transparent, and affords the best opportunity that ever offers for examining the bottom where it is shallow; for you can lie at your length on ice only an inch thick, like a skater insect on the surface of the water, and study the bottom at your leisure, only two or three inches distant, like a picture behind a glass, and the water is neces-sarily always smooth then. There are many furrows in the sand where some creature has travelled about and doubled on its tracks; and, for wrecks, it is strewn with the cases of cadis worms made of minute grains of white quartz. Perhaps these have creased it, for you find some of their cases in the fur-rows, though they are deep and broad for them to make. But the ice itself is the object of most interest, though you must improve the earliest opportunity to study it. If you examine it closely the morning after it freezes, you find that the greater part of the bubbles, which at first appeared to be within it, are against its under surface, and that more are continually rising from the bottom; while the ice is as yet comparatively solid and dark, that is, you see the water through it. These bubbles are from an eightieth to an eighth of an inch in diameter, very clear and beautiful, and you see your face reflected in them through the ice. There may be thirty or forty of them to a square inch. There are also already within the ice narrow oblong perpendicular bubbles about half an inch long, sharp cones with the apex upward; or oftener, if the ice is quite fresh, minute spherical bubbles one directly above another, like a string of beads. But these within the ice are not so numerous nor obvious as those beneath. I sometimes used to cast on stones to try the strength of the ice, and those which broke through carried in air with them, which formed very large and conspicuous white bubbles beneath. One day when I came to the same place forty-eight hours afterward, I found that those large bubbles were still perfect, though an inch more of ice had formed, as I could see distinctly by the seam in the edge of a cake. But as the last two days had been very warm, like an Indian summer, the ice was not now transparent, showing the dark green color of the water, and the bottom, but opaque and whitish or gray, and though twice as thick was hardly stronger than before, for the air bubbles had greatly expanded under this heat and run together, and lost their regularity; they were no longer one directly over another, but often like silvery coins poured from a bag, one overlapping another, or in thin flakes, as if occupying slight cleavages. The beauty of the ice was gone, and it was too late to study the bottom. Being curious to know what position my great bubbles occupied with regard to the new ice, I broke out a cake containing a middling sized one, and turned it bottom upward. The new ice had formed around and under the bubble, so that it was included between the two ices. It was wholly in the lower ice, but close against the upper, and was flattish, or perhaps slightly lenticular, with a rounded edge, a quarter of an inch deep by four inches in diameter; and I was surprised to find that directly under the bubble the ice was melted with great regularity in the form of a saucer reversed, to the height of five eighths of an inch in the middle, leaving a thin partition there between the water and the bubble, hardly an eighth of an inch thick; and in many places the small bubbles in this partition had burst out downward, and probably there was no ice at all under the largest bubbles, which were a foot in diameter. I inferred that the infinite number of minute bubbles which I had first seen

against the under surface of the ice were now frozen in likewise, and that each, in its degree, had operated like a burning
glass on the ice beneath to melt and rot it. These are the little
air-guns which contribute to make the ice crack and whoop.

At length the winter set in in good earnest, just as I had
finished plastering, and the wind began to howl around the
house as if it had not had permission to do so till then. Night
after night the geese came lumbering in in the dark with a
clangor and a whistling of wings, even after the ground was
covered with snow, some to alight in Walden, and some
flying low over the woods toward Fair Haven, bound for
Mexico. Several times, when returning from the village at ten
or eleven o'clock at night, I heard the tread of a flock of
geese, or else ducks, on the dry leaves in the woods by a
pond-hole behind my dwelling, where they had come up to
feed, and the faint honk or quack of their leader as they hurried off. In 1845 Walden froze entirely over for the first time
on the night of the 22d of December, Flints' and other shallower ponds and the river having been frozen ten days or
more; in '46, the 16th; in '49, about the 31st; and in '50, about
the 27th of December; in '52, the 5th of January; in '53, the 31st
of December. The snow had already covered the ground since
the 25th of November, and surrounded me suddenly with the
scenery of winter. I withdrew yet farther into my shell, and
endeavored to keep a bright fire both within my house and
within my breast. My employment out of doors now was to
collect the dead wood in the forest, bringing it in my hands
or on my shoulders, or sometimes trailing a dead pine tree
under each arm to my shed. An old forest fence which had
seen its best days was a great haul for me. I sacrificed it to
Vulcan, for it was past serving the god Terminus. How much
more interesting an event is that man's supper who has just
been forth in the snow to hunt, nay, you might say, steal, the
fuel to cook it with! His bread and meat are sweet. There are
enough fagots and waste wood of all kinds in the forests of
most of our towns to support many fires, but which at present warm none, and, some think, hinder the growth of the
young wood. There was also the drift-wood of the pond. In
the course of the summer I had discovered a raft of pitch-pine

logs with the bark on, pinned together by the Irish when the railroad was built. This I hauled up partly on the shore. After soaking two years and then lying high six months it was perfectly sound, though waterlogged past drying. I amused myself one winter day with sliding this piece-meal across the pond, nearly half a mile, skating behind with one end of a log fifteen feet long on my shoulder, and the other on the ice; or I tied several logs together with a birch withe, and then, with a longer birch or alder which had a hook at the end, dragged them across. Though completely waterlogged and almost as heavy as lead, they not only burned long, but made a very hot fire; nay, I thought that they burned better for the soaking, as if the pitch, being confined by the water, burned longer as in a lamp.

Gilpin, in his account of the forest borderers of England, says that "the encroachments of trespassers, and the houses and fences thus raised on the borders of the forest," were "considered as great nuisances by the old forest law, and were severely punished under the name of *purprestures*, as tending *ad terrorem ferarum — ad nocumentum forestæ*, &c.," to the frightening of the game and the detriment of the forest. But I was interested in the preservation of the venison and the vert more than the hunters or wood-choppers, and as much as though I had been the Lord Warden himself; and if any part was burned, though I burned it myself by accident, I grieved with a grief that lasted longer and was more inconsolable than that of the proprietors; nay, I grieved when it was cut down by the proprietors themselves. I would that our farmers when they cut down a forest felt some of that awe which the old Romans did when they came to thin, or let in the light to, a consecrated grove, (*lucum conlucare,*) that is, would believe that it is sacred to some god. The Roman made an expiatory offering, and prayed, Whatever god or goddess thou art to whom this grove is sacred, be propitious to me, my family, and children, &c.

It is remarkable what a value is still put upon wood even in this age and in this new country, a value more permanent and universal than that of gold. After all our discoveries and inventions no man will go by a pile of wood. It is as precious to us as it was to our Saxon and Norman ancestors. If they made their bows of it, we make our gun-stocks of it. Michaux, more than thirty years ago, says that the price of wood for fuel in New York and Philadelphia "nearly equals, and sometimes exceeds, that of the best wood in Paris, though this immense capital annually requires more than three hundred thousand cords, and is surrounded to the distance of three hundred miles by cultivated plains." In this town the price of wood rises almost steadily, and the only question is, how much higher it is to be this year than it was the last. Mechanics and tradesmen who come in person to the forest on no other errand, are sure to attend the wood auction, and even pay a high price for the privilege of gleaning after the wood-chopper. It is now many years that men have resorted to the forest for fuel and the materials of the arts; the New Englander and the New Hollander, the Parisian and the Celt, the farmer and Robinhood, Goody Blake and Harry Gill, in most parts of the world the prince and the peasant, the scholar and the savage, equally require still a few sticks from the forest to warm them and cook their food. Neither could I do without them.

Every man looks at his wood-pile with a kind of affection. I loved to have mine before my window, and the more chips the better to remind me of my pleasing work. I had an old axe which nobody claimed, with which by spells in winter days, on the sunny side of the house, I played about the stumps which I had got out of my bean-field. As my driver prophesied when I was ploughing, they warmed me twice, once while I was splitting them, and again when they were on the fire, so that no fuel could give out more heat. As for the axe, I was advised to get the village blacksmith to "jump" it; but I jumped him, and, putting a hickory helve from the woods into it, made it do. If it was dull, it was at least hung true.

A few pieces of fat pine were a great treasure. It is interesting to remember how much of this food for fire is still concealed in the bowels of the earth. In previous years I had often gone "prospecting" over some bare hill-side, where a pitch-pine wood had formerly stood, and got out the fat pine roots. They are almost indestructible. Stumps thirty or forty years old, at least, will still be sound at the core, though the sapwood has all become vegetable mould, as appears by the scales of the thick bark forming a ring level with the earth four or five inches distant from the heart. With axe and shovel you explore this mine, and follow the marrowy store, yellow as beef tallow, or as if you had struck on a vein of gold, deep into the earth. But commonly I kindled my fire with the dry leaves of the forest, which I had stored up in my shed before the snow came. Green hickory finely split makes the woodchopper's kindlings, when he has a camp in the woods. Once in a while I got a little of this. When the villagers were lighting their fires beyond the horizon, I too gave notice to the various wild inhabitants of Walden vale, by a smoky streamer from my chimney, that I was awake.—

> Light-winged Smoke, Icarian bird,
> Melting thy pinions in thy upward flight,
> Lark without song, and messenger of dawn,
> Circling above the hamlets as thy nest;
> Or else, departing dream, and shadowy form
> Of midnight vision, gathering up thy skirts;
> By night star-veiling, and by day
> Darkening the light and blotting out the sun;
> Go thou my incense upward from this hearth,
> And ask the gods to pardon this clear flame.

Hard green wood just cut, though I used but little of that, answered my purpose better than any other. I sometimes left a good fire when I went to take a walk in a winter afternoon; and when I returned, three or four hours afterward, it would be still alive and glowing. My house was not empty though I was gone. It was as if I had left a cheerful housekeeper behind. It was I and Fire that lived there; and commonly my housekeeper proved trustworthy. One day, however, as I was splitting wood, I thought that I would just look in at the window and see if the house was not on fire; it was the only time I remember to have been particularly anxious on this score; so I looked and saw that a spark had caught my bed, and I went in and extinguished it when it had burned a place as big as my hand. But my house occupied so sunny and sheltered a position, and its roof was so low, that I could afford to let the fire go out in the middle of almost any winter day.

The moles nested in my cellar, nibbling every third potato, and making a snug bed even there of some hair left after plastering and of brown paper; for even the wildest animals love comfort and warmth as well as man, and they survive the winter only because they are so careful to secure them. Some of my friends spoke as if I was coming to the woods on purpose to freeze myself. The animal merely makes a bed, which he warms with his body in a sheltered place; but man, having discovered fire, boxes up some air in a spacious apartment, and warms that, instead of robbing himself, makes that his bed, in which he can move about divested of more cumbrous clothing, maintain a kind of summer in the midst of winter, and by means of windows even admit the light, and with a lamp lengthen out the day. Thus he goes a step or two beyond instinct, and saves a little time for the fine arts. Though, when I had been exposed to the rudest blasts a long time, my whole body began to grow torpid, when I reached the genial atmosphere of my house I soon recovered my faculties and prolonged my life. But the most luxuriously housed has little to boast of in this respect, nor need we trouble ourselves to speculate how the human race may be at last destroyed. It would be easy to cut their threads any time with a little sharper blast from the north. We go on dating from Cold Fridays and Great Snows; but a little colder Friday, or greater snow, would put a period to man's existence on the globe.

The next winter I used a small cooking-stove for economy, since I did not own the forest; but it did not keep fire so well as the open fire-place. Cooking was then, for the most part, no longer a poetic, but merely a chemic process. It will soon be forgotten, in these days of stoves, that we used to roast potatoes in the ashes, after the Indian fashion. The stove not only took up room and scented the house, but it concealed the fire, and I felt as if I had lost a companion. You can always see a face in the fire. The laborer, looking into it at evening, purifies his thoughts of the dross and earthiness which they have accumulated during the day. But I could no longer sit and look into the fire, and the pertinent words of a poet recurred to me with new force.—

"Never, bright flame, may be denied to me
Thy dear, life imaging, close sympathy.
What but my hopes shot upward e'er so bright?
What but my fortunes sunk so low in night?

Why art thou banished from our hearth and hall,
Thou who art welcomed and beloved by all?
Was thy existence then too fanciful
For our life's common light, who are so dull?
Did thy bright gleam mysterious converse hold
With our congenial souls? secrets too bold?
Well, we are safe and strong, for now we sit
Beside a hearth where no dim shadows flit,
Where nothing cheers nor saddens, but a fire
Warms feet and hands—nor does to more aspire;
By whose compact utilitarian heap
The present may sit down and go to sleep,
Nor fear the ghosts who from the dim past walked,
And with us by the unequal light of the old wood fire
    talked."

Former Inhabitants; and Winter Visitors

I WEATHERED some merry snow storms, and spent some cheerful winter evenings by my fire-side, while the snow whirled wildly without, and even the hooting of the owl was hushed. For many weeks I met no one in my walks but those who came occasionally to cut wood and sled it to the village. The elements, however, abetted me in making a path through the deepest snow in the woods, for when I had once gone through the wind blew the oak leaves into my tracks, where they lodged, and by absorbing the rays of the sun melted the snow, and so not only made a dry bed for my feet, but in the night their dark line was my guide. For human society I was obliged to conjure up the former occupants of these woods. Within the memory of many of my townsmen the road near which my house stands resounded with the laugh and gossip of inhabitants, and the woods which border it were notched and dotted here and there with their little gardens and dwell-ings, though it was then much more shut in by the forest than now. In some places, within my own remembrance, the pines would scrape both sides of a chaise at once, and women and children who were compelled to go this way to Lincoln alone and on foot did it with fear, and often ran a good part of the distance. Though mainly but a humble route to neighboring villages, or for the woodman's team, it once amused the trav-eller more than now by its variety, and lingered longer in his memory. Where now firm open fields stretch from the village to the woods, it then ran through a maple swamp on a foun-dation of logs, the remnants of which, doubtless, still underlie the present dusty highway, from the Stratten, now the Alms House, Farm, to Brister's Hill.

East of my bean-field, across the road, lived Cato In-graham, slave of Duncan Ingraham, Esquire, gentleman of Concord village; who built his slave a house, and gave him permission to live in Walden Woods;—Cato, not Uticensis, but Concordiensis. Some say that he was a Guinea Negro. There are a few who remember his little patch among the walnuts, which he let grow up till he should be old and need them; but a younger and whiter speculator got them at last.

He too, however, occupies an equally narrow house at present. Cato's half-obliterated cellar hole still remains, though known to few, being concealed from the traveller by a fringe of pines. It is now filled with the smooth sumach, (*Rhus glabra,*) and one of the earliest species of golden-rod (*Solidago stricta*) grows there luxuriantly.

Here, by the very corner of my field, still nearer to town, Zilpha, a colored woman, had her little house, where she spun linen for the townsfolk, making the Walden Woods ring with her shrill singing, for she had a loud and notable voice. At length, in the war of 1812, her dwelling was set on fire by English soldiers, prisoners on parole, when she was away, and her cat and dog and hens were all burned up together. She led a hard life, and somewhat inhumane. One old frequenter of these woods remembers, that as he passed her house one noon he heard her muttering to herself over her gurgling pot,—"Ye are all bones, bones!" I have seen bricks amid the oak copse there.

Down the road, on the right hand, on Brister's Hill, lived Brister Freeman, "a handy Negro," slave of Squire Cummings once,—there where grow still the apple-trees which Brister planted and tended; large old trees now, but their fruit still wild and ciderish to my taste. Not long since I read his epitaph in the old Lincoln burying-ground, a little on one side, near the unmarked graves of some British grenadiers who fell in the retreat from Concord,—where he is styled "Sippio Brister,"—Scipio Africanus he had some title to be called,—"a man of color," as if he were discolored. It also told me, with staring emphasis, when he died; which was but an indirect way of informing me that he ever lived. With him dwelt Fenda, his hospitable wife, who told fortunes, yet pleasantly,—large, round, and black, blacker than any of the children of night, such a dusky orb as never rose on Concord before or since.

Farther down the hill, on the left, on the old road in the woods, are marks of some homestead of the Stratten family; whose orchard once covered all the slope of Brister's Hill, but was long since killed out by pitch-pines, excepting a few stumps, whose old roots furnish still the wild stocks of many a thrifty village tree.

Nearer yet to town, you come to Breed's location, on the other side of the way, just on the edge of the wood; ground famous for the pranks of a demon not distinctly named in old mythology, who has acted a prominent and astounding part in our New England life, and deserves, as much as any mythological character, to have his biography written one day; who first comes in the guise of a friend or hired man, and then robs and murders the whole family,—New-England Rum. But history must not yet tell the tragedies enacted here; let time intervene in some measure to assuage and lend an azure tint to them. Here the most indistinct and dubious tradition says that once a tavern stood; the well the same, which tempered the traveller's beverage and refreshed his steed. Here then men saluted one another, and heard and told the news, and went their ways again.

Breed's hut was standing only a dozen years ago, though it had long been unoccupied. It was about the size of mine. It was set on fire by mischievous boys, one Election night, if I do not mistake. I lived on the edge of the village then, and had just lost myself over Davenant's Gondibert, that winter that I labored with a lethargy,—which, by the way, I never knew whether to regard as a family complaint, having an uncle who goes to sleep shaving himself, and is obliged to sprout potatoes in a cellar Sundays, in order to keep awake and keep the Sabbath, or as the consequence of my attempt to read Chalmers' collection of English poetry without skipping. It fairly overcame my Nervii. I had just sunk my head on this when the bells rung fire, and in hot haste the engines rolled that way, led by a straggling troop of men and boys, and I among the foremost, for I had leaped the brook. We thought it was far south over the woods,—we who had run to fires before,—barn, shop, or dwelling-house, or all together. "It's Baker's barn," cried one. "It is the Codman Place," affirmed another. And then fresh sparks went up above the wood, as if the roof fell in, and we all shouted "Concord to the rescue!" Wagons shot past with furious speed and crushing loads, bearing, perchance, among the rest, the agent of the Insurance Company, who was bound to go however far; and ever and anon the engine bell tinkled behind, more slow and sure, and rearmost of all, as it was afterward whispered, came they who set the fire and gave the alarm. Thus we kept on like true idealists, rejecting the evidence of our senses, until at a turn in the road we heard the crackling and actually felt the heat of the fire from over the wall, and realized, alas! that we were there. The very nearness of the fire but cooled our ardor. At first we thought to throw a frog-pond on to it; but concluded to let it burn, it was so far gone and so worthless. So we stood round our engine, jostled one another, expressed our sentiments through speaking trumpets, or in lower tone referred to the great conflagrations which the world has witnessed, including Bascom's shop, and, between ourselves, we thought that, were we there in season with our "tub," and a full frog-pond by, we could turn that threatened last and universal one into another flood. We finally retreated without doing any mischief,—returned to sleep and Gondibert. But as for Gondibert, I would except that passage in the preface about wit being the soul's powder,—"but most of mankind are strangers to wit, as Indians are to powder."

It chanced that I walked that way across the fields the following night, about the same hour, and hearing a low moaning at this spot, I drew near in the dark, and discovered the only survivor of the family that I know, the heir of both its virtues and its vices, who alone was interested in this burning, lying on his stomach and looking over the cellar wall at the still smouldering cinders beneath, muttering to himself, as is his wont. He had been working far off in the river meadows all day, and had improved the first moments that he could call his own to visit the home of his fathers and his youth. He gazed into the cellar from all sides and points of view by turns, always lying down to it, as if there was some treasure, which he remembered, concealed between the stones, where there was absolutely nothing but a heap of bricks and ashes. The house being gone, he looked at what there was left. He was soothed by the sympathy which my mere presence implied, and showed me, as well as the darkness permitted, where the well was covered up; which, thank Heaven, could never be burned; and he groped long about the wall to find the well-sweep which his father had cut and mounted, feeling for the iron hook or staple by which a burden had been fastened to the heavy end,—all that he could now cling to,—to convince me that it was no common "rider." I felt it, and still remark it almost daily in my walks, for by it hangs the history of a family.

Once more, on the left, where are seen the well and lilac bushes by the wall, in the now open field, lived Nutting and Le Grosse. But to return toward Lincoln.

Farther in the woods than any of these, where the road approaches nearest to the pond, Wyman the potter squatted, and furnished his townsmen with earthen ware, and left descendants to succeed him. Neither were they rich in worldly goods, holding the land by sufferance while they lived; and there often the sheriff came in vain to collect the taxes, and "attached a chip," for form's sake, as I have read in his accounts, there being nothing else that he could lay his hands on. One day in midsummer, when I was hoeing, a man who was carrying a load of pottery to market stopped his horse against my field and inquired concerning Wyman the younger. He had long ago bought a potter's wheel of him, and wished to know what had become of him. I had read of the potter's clay and wheel in Scripture, but it had never occurred to me that the pots we use were not such as had come down unbroken from those days, or grown on trees like gourds somewhere, and I was pleased to hear that so fictile an art was ever practised in my neighborhood.

The last inhabitant of these woods before me was an Irishman, Hugh Quoil, (if I have spelt his name with coil enough,) who occupied Wyman's tenement,—Col. Quoil, he was called. Rumor said that he had been a soldier at Waterloo. If he had lived I should have made him fight his battles over again. His trade here was that of a ditcher. Napoleon went to St. Helena; Quoil came to Walden Woods. All I know of him is tragic. He was a man of manners, like one who had seen the world, and was capable of more civil speech than you could well attend to. He wore a great coat in midsummer, being affected with the trembling delirium, and his face was the color of carmine. He died in the road at the foot of Brister's Hill shortly after I came to the woods, so that I have not remembered him as a neighbor. Before his house was pulled down, when his comrades avoided it as "an unlucky castle," I visited it. There lay his old clothes curled up by use, as if they were himself, upon his raised plank bed. His pipe lay broken on the hearth, instead of a bowl broken at the fountain. The last could never have been the symbol of his death, for he confessed to me that, though he had heard of Brister's Spring, he had never seen it; and soiled cards, kings of diamonds spades and hearts, were scattered over the floor. One black chicken which the administrator could not catch, black as night and as silent, not even croaking, awaiting Reynard, still went to roost in the next apartment. In the rear there was the dim outline of a garden, which had been planted but had never received its first hoeing, owing to those terrible shaking fits, though it was now harvest time. It was over-run with Roman wormwood and beggar-ticks, which last stuck to my clothes for all fruit. The skin of a woodchuck was freshly stretched upon the back of the house, a trophy of his last Waterloo; but no warm cap or mittens would he want more.

Now only a dent in the earth marks the site of these dwell-ings, with buried cellar stones, and strawberries, raspberries, thimble-berries, hazel-bushes, and sumachs growing in the sunny sward there; some pitch-pine or gnarled oak occupies what was the chimney nook, and a sweet-scented black-birch, perhaps, waves where the door-stone was. Sometimes the well dent is visible, where once a spring oozed; now dry and tear-less grass; or it was covered deep,—not to be discovered till some late day,—with a flat stone under the sod, when the last of the race departed. What a sorrowful act must that be,—the covering up of wells! coincident with the opening of wells of tears. These cellar dents, like deserted fox burrows, old holes, are all that is left where once were the stir and bustle of human life, and "fate, free-will, foreknowledge ab-solute," in some form and dialect or other were by turns dis-cussed. But all I can learn of their conclusions amounts to just this, that "Cato and Brister pulled wool;" which is about as edifying as the history of more famous schools of philosophy.

Still grows the vivacious lilac a generation after the door and lintel and the sill are gone, unfolding its sweet-scented flowers each spring, to be plucked by the musing traveller; planted and tended once by children's hands, in front-yard plots,—now standing by wall-sides in retired pastures, and giving place to new-rising forests;—the last of that stirp, sole survivor of that family. Little did the dusky children think that the puny slip with its two eyes only, which they stuck in the ground in the shadow of the house and daily watered, would root itself so, and outlive them and house itself in the rear that shaded it, and grown man's garden and orchard, and tell their story faintly to the lone wanderer a half century after they had grown up and died,—blossoming as fair, and smelling as sweet, as in that first spring. I mark its still tender, civil, cheerful, lilac colors.

But this small village, germ of something more, why did it fail while Concord keeps its ground? Were there no natural advantages,—no water privileges, forsooth? Ay, the deep Walden Pond and cool Brister's Spring,—privilege to drink long and healthy draughts at these, all unimproved by these men but to dilute their glass. They were universally a thirsty race. Might not the basket, stable-broom, mat-making, corn-parching, linen-spinning, and pottery business have thrived here, making the wilderness to blossom like the rose, and a numerous posterity have inherited the land of their fathers? The sterile soil would at least have been proof against a low-land degeneracy. Alas! how little does the memory of these human inhabitants enhance the beauty of the landscape! Again, perhaps, Nature will try, with me for a first settler, and my house raised last spring to be the oldest in the hamlet.

I am not aware that any man has ever built on the spot which I occupy. Deliver me from a city built on the site of a more ancient city, whose materials are ruins, whose gardens cemeteries. The soil is blanched and accursed there, and before that becomes necessary the earth itself will be destroyed. With such reminiscences I repeopled the woods and lulled myself asleep.

At this season I seldom had a visitor. When the snow lay deepest no wanderer ventured near my house for a week or fortnight at a time, but there I lived as snug as a meadow mouse, or as cattle and poultry which are said to have survived for a long time buried in drifts, even without food; or like that early settler's family in the town of Sutton, in this state, whose cottage was completely covered by the great snow of 1717 when he was absent, and an Indian found it only by the hole which the chimney's breath made in the drift, and so relieved the family. But no friendly Indian concerned himself about me; nor needed he, for the master of the house was at home. The Great Snow! How cheerful it is to hear of! When the farmers could not get to the woods and swamps with their teams, and were obliged to cut down the shade trees before their houses, and when the crust was harder cut off the trees in the swamps ten feet from the ground, as it appeared the next spring.

In the deepest snows, the path which I used from the highway to my house, about half a mile long, might have been represented by a meandering dotted line, with wide intervals between the dots. For a week of even weather I took exactly the same number of steps, and of the same length, coming and going, stepping deliberately and with the precision of a pair of dividers in my own deep tracks,—to such routine the winter reduces us,—yet often they were filled with heaven's own blue. But no weather interfered fatally with my walks, or rather my going abroad, for I frequently tramped eight or ten miles through the deepest snow to keep an appointment with a beech-tree, or a yellow-birch, or an old acquaintance among the pines; when the ice and snow causing their limbs to droop, and so sharpening their tops, had changed the pines into fir-trees; wading to the tops of the highest hills when the snow was nearly two feet deep on a level, and shaking down another snow-storm on my head at every step; or sometimes creeping and floundering thither on my hands and knees, when the hunters had gone into winter quarters. One afternoon I amused myself by watching a barred owl (*Strix nebulosa*) sitting on one of the lower dead limbs of a white-pine, close to the trunk, in broad daylight, I standing within a rod of him. He could hear me when I moved and cronched the snow with my feet, but could not plainly see me. When I made most noise he would stretch out his neck, and erect his neck feathers, and open his eyes wide; but their lids soon fell again, and he began to nod. I too felt a slumberous influence after watching him half an hour, as he sat thus with his eyes half open, like a cat, winged brother of the cat. There was only a narrow slit left between their lids, by which he preserved a peninsular relation to me; thus, with half-shut eyes, looking out from the land of dreams, and endeavoring to realize me, vague object or mote that interrupted his visions. At length, on some louder noise or my nearer approach, he would grow uneasy and sluggishly turn about on his perch, as if impatient at having his dreams disturbed; and when he launched himself off and flapped through the pines, spreading his wings to unexpected breadth, I could not hear the slightest sound from them. Thus, guided amid the pine boughs rather by a delicate sense of their neighborhood than by sight, feeling his twilight way as it were with his sensitive pinions, he found a new perch, where he might in peace await the dawning of his day.

As I walked over the long causeway made for the railroad through the meadows, I encountered many a blustering and nipping wind, for nowhere has it freer play; and when the frost had smitten me on one cheek, heathen as I was, I turned to it the other also. Nor was it much better by the carriage road from Brister's Hill. For I came to town still, like a friendly Indian, when the contents of the broad open fields were all piled up between the walls of the Walden road, and half an hour sufficed to obliterate the tracks of the last traveller. And when I returned new drifts would have formed, through which I floundered, where the busy north-west wind had been depositing the powdery snow round a sharp angle in the road, and not a rabbit's track, nor even the fine print, the small type, of a meadow mouse was to be seen. Yet I rarely failed to find, even in mid-winter, some warm and springy swamp where the grass and the skunk-cabbage still put forth with perennial verdure, and some hardier bird occasionally awaited the return of spring.

Sometimes, notwithstanding the snow, when I returned from my walk at evening I crossed the deep tracks of a wood-chopper leading from my door, and found his pile of whittlings on the hearth, and my house filled with the odor of his pipe. Or on a Sunday afternoon, if I chanced to be at home, I heard the cronching of the snow made by the step of a long-headed farmer, who from far through the woods sought my house, to have a social "crack;" one of the few of his vocation who are "men on their farms;" who donned a frock instead of a professor's gown, and is as ready to extract the moral out of church or state as to haul a load of manure from his barn-yard. We talked of rude and simple times, when men sat about large fires in cold bracing weather, with clear heads; and when other dessert failed, we tried our teeth on many a nut which wise squirrels have long since abandoned, for those which have the thickest shells are commonly empty.

The one who came from farthest to my lodge, through deepest snows and most dismal tempests, was a poet. A farmer, a hunter, a soldier, a reporter, even a philosopher, may be daunted; but nothing can deter a poet, for he is actuated by pure love. Who can predict his comings and goings? His business calls him out at all hours, even when doctors sleep. We made that small house ring with boisterous mirth and resound with the murmur of much sober talk, making amends then to Walden vale for the long silences. Broadway was still and deserted in comparison. At suitable intervals there were regular salutes of laughter, which might have been referred indifferently to the last uttered or the forth-coming jest. We made many a "bran new" theory of life over a thin dish of gruel, which combined the advantages of conviviality with the clear-headedness which philosophy requires.

I should not forget that during my last winter at the pond there was another welcome visitor, who at one time came through the village, through snow and rain and darkness, till he saw my lamp through the trees, and shared with me some long winter evenings. One of the last of the philosophers,— Connecticut gave him to the world,—he peddled first her wares, afterwards, as he declares, his brains. These he peddles still, prompting God and disgracing man, bearing for fruit his brain only, like the nut its kernel. I think that he must be the man of the most faith of any alive. His words and attitude always suppose a better state of things than other men are acquainted with, and he will be the last man to be disappointed as the ages revolve. He has no venture in the present. But though comparatively disregarded now, when his day comes, laws unsuspected by most will take effect, and masters of families and rulers will come to him for advice.—

"How blind that cannot see serenity!"

A true friend of man; almost the only friend of human progress. An Old Mortality, say rather an Immortality, with unwearied patience and faith making plain the image engraven
in men's bodies, the God of whom they are but defaced and
leaning monuments. With his hospitable intellect he embraces
children, beggars, insane, and scholars, and entertains the
thought of all, adding to it commonly some breadth and elegance. I think that he should keep a caravansary on the
world's highway, where philosophers of all nations might put
up, and on his sign should be printed, "Entertainment for
man, but not for his beast. Enter ye that have leisure and a
quiet mind, who earnestly seek the right road." He is perhaps
the sanest man and has the fewest crotchets of any I chance
to know; the same yesterday and to-morrow. Of yore we had
sauntered and talked, and effectually put the world behind us;
for he was pledged to no institution in it, freeborn, *ingenuus*.
Whichever way we turned, it seemed that the heavens and the
earth had met together, since he enhanced the beauty of the
landscape. A blue-robed man, whose fittest roof is the over-
arching sky which reflects his serenity. I do not see how he
can ever die; Nature cannot spare him.

Having each some shingles of thought well dried, we sat
and whittled them, trying our knives, and admiring the clear
yellowish grain of the pumpkin pine. We waded so gently and
reverently, or we pulled together so smoothly, that the fishes
of thought were not scared from the stream, nor feared any
angler on the bank, but came and went grandly, like the
clouds which float through the western sky, and the mother-
o'-pearl flocks which sometimes form and dissolve there.
There we worked, revising mythology, rounding a fable here
and there, and building castles in the air for which earth offered no worthy foundation. Great Looker! Great Expecter!
to converse with whom was a New England Night's Entertainment. Ah! such discourse we had, hermit and philosopher, and the old settler I have spoken of,—we three,—it
expanded and racked my little house; I should not dare to say
how many pounds' weight there was above the atmospheric
pressure on every circular inch; it opened its seams so that

they had to be calked with much dulness thereafter to stop the consequent leak;—but I had enough of that kind of oakum already picked.

There was one other with whom I had "solid seasons," long to be remembered, at his house in the village, and who looked in upon me from time to time; but I had no more for society there.

There too, as every where, I sometimes expected the Visitor who never comes. The Vishnu Purana says, "The householder is to remain at eventide in his court-yard as long as it takes to milk a cow, or longer if he pleases, to await the arrival of a guest." I often performed this duty of hospitality, waited long enough to milk a whole herd of cows, but did not see the man approaching from the town.

Winter Animals

WHEN THE PONDS were firmly frozen, they afforded not only new and shorter routes to many points, but new views from their surfaces of the familiar landscape around them. When I crossed Flints' Pond, after it was covered with snow, though I had often paddled about and skated over it, it was so unexpectedly wide and so strange that I could think of nothing but Baffin's Bay. The Lincoln hills rose up around me at the extremity of a snowy plain, in which I did not remember to have stood before; and the fishermen, at an indeterminable distance over the ice, moving slowly about with their wolfish dogs, passed for sealers or Esquimaux, or in misty weather loomed like fabulous creatures, and I did not know whether they were giants or pygmies. I took this course when I went to lecture in Lincoln in the evening, travelling in no road and passing no house between my own hut and the lecture room. In Goose Pond, which lay in my way, a colony of muskrats dwelt, and raised their cabins high above the ice, though none could be seen abroad when I crossed it. Walden, being like the rest usually bare of snow, or with only shallow and interrupted drifts on it, was my yard, where I could walk freely when the snow was nearly two feet deep on a level elsewhere and the villagers were confined to their streets. There, far from the village street, and except at very long intervals, from the jingle of sleigh-bells, I slid and skated, as in a vast moose-yard well trodden, overhung by oak woods and solemn pines bent down with snow or bristling with icicles.

For sounds in winter nights, and often in winter days, I heard the forlorn but melodious note of a hooting owl indefinitely far; such a sound as the frozen earth would yield if struck with a suitable plectrum, the very *lingua vernacula* of Walden Wood, and quite familiar to me at last, though I never saw the bird while it was making it. I seldom opened my door in a winter evening without hearing it; *Hoo hoo hoo, hoorer hoo,* sounded sonorously, and the first three syllables accented somewhat like *how der do*; or sometimes *hoo hoo* only. One night in the beginning of winter, before the pond froze over, about nine o'clock, I was startled by the loud honking of a goose, and, stepping to the door, heard the sound of their wings like a tempest in the woods as they flew low over my house. They passed over the pond toward Fair Haven, seemingly deterred from settling by my light, their commodore honking all the while with a regular beat. Suddenly an unmistakable cat-owl from very near me, with the most harsh and tremendous voice I ever heard from any inhabitant of the woods, responded at regular intervals to the goose, as if determined to expose and disgrace this intruder from Hudson's Bay by exhibiting a greater compass and volume of voice in a native, and *boo-hoo* him out of Concord horizon. What do you mean by alarming the citadel at this time of night consecrated to me? Do you think I am ever caught napping at such an hour, and that I have not got lungs and a larynx as well as yourself? *Boo-hoo, boo-hoo, boo-hoo!* It was one of the most thrilling discords I ever heard. And yet, if you had a discriminating ear, there were in it the elements of a concord such as these plains never saw nor heard.

I also heard the whooping of the ice in the pond, my great bed-fellow in that part of Concord, as if it were restless in its bed and would fain turn over, were troubled with flatulency and bad dreams; or I was waked by the cracking of the ground by the frost, as if some one had driven a team against my door, and in the morning would find a crack in the earth a quarter of a mile long and a third of an inch wide.

Sometimes I heard the foxes as they ranged over the snow crust, in moonlight nights, in search of a partridge or other game, barking raggedly and demoniacally like forest dogs, as if laboring with some anxiety, or seeking expression, struggling for light and to be dogs outright and run freely in the streets; for if we take the ages into our account, may there not be a civilization going on among brutes as well as men? They seemed to me to be rudimental, burrowing men, still standing on their defence, awaiting their transformation. Sometimes one came near to my window, attracted by my light, barked a vulpine curse at me, and then retreated.

Usually the red squirrel (*Sciurus Hudsonius*) waked me in the dawn, coursing over the roof and up and down the sides of the house, as if sent out of the woods for this purpose. In the course of the winter I threw out half a bushel of ears of sweet-corn, which had not got ripe, on to the snow crust by my door, and was amused by watching the motions of the various animals which were baited by it. In the twilight and the night the rabbits came regularly and made a hearty meal. All day long the red squirrels came and went, and afforded me much entertainment by their manœuvres. One would approach at first warily through the shrub-oaks, running over the snow crust by fits and starts like a leaf blown by the wind, now a few paces this way, with wonderful speed and waste of energy, making inconceivable haste with his "trotters," as if it were for a wager, and now as many paces that way, but never getting on more than half a rod at a time; and then suddenly pausing with a ludicrous expression and a gratuitous somerset, as if all the eyes in the universe were fixed on him,—for all the motions of a squirrel, even in the most solitary recesses of the forest, imply spectators as much as those of a dancing girl,—wasting more time in delay and circumspection than would have sufficed to walk the whole distance,—I never saw one walk,—and then suddenly, before you could say Jack Robinson, he would be in the top of a young pitch-pine, winding up his clock and chiding all imaginary spectators, soliloquizing and talking to all the universe at the same time,—for no reason that I could ever detect, or he himself was aware of, I suspect. At length he would reach the corn, and selecting a suitable ear, frisk about in the same uncertain trigonometrical way to the topmost stick of my wood-pile, before my window, where he looked me in the face, and there sit for hours, supplying himself with a new ear from time to time, nibbling at first voraciously and throwing the half-naked cobs about; till at length he grew more dainty still and played with his food, tasting only the inside of the kernel, and the ear, which was held balanced over the stick by one paw, slipped from his careless grasp and fell to the ground, when he would look over at it with a ludicrous expression of uncertainty, as if suspecting that it had life, with a mind not made up whether to get it again, or a new one, or be off; now thinking of corn, then listening to hear what was in the wind. So the

little impudent fellow would waste many an ear in a forenoon; till at last, seizing some longer and plumper one, considerably bigger than himself, and skilfully balancing it, he
would set out with it to the woods, like a tiger with a buffalo, by the same zig-zag course and frequent pauses,
scratching along with it as if it were too heavy for him and
falling all the while, making its fall a diagonal between a perpendicular and horizontal, being determined to put it
through at any rate;—a singularly frivolous and whimsical
fellow;—and so he would get off with it to where he lived,
perhaps carry it to the top of a pine tree forty or fifty rods
distant, and I would afterwards find the cobs strewn about
the woods in various directions.

At length the jays arrive, whose discordant screams were
heard long before, as they were warily making their approach an eighth of a mile off, and in a stealthy and sneaking manner they flit from tree to tree, nearer and nearer, and
pick up the kernels which the squirrels have dropped. Then,
sitting on a pitch-pine bough, they attempt to swallow in
their haste a kernel which is too big for their throats and
chokes them; and after great labor they disgorge it, and
spend an hour in the endeavor to crack it by repeated blows
with their bills. They were manifestly thieves, and I had not
much respect for them; but the squirrels, though at first shy,
went to work as if they were taking what was their own.

Meanwhile also came the chicadees in flocks, which picking up the crums the squirrels had dropped, flew to the
nearest twig, and placing them under their claws, hammered
away at them with their little bills, as if it were an insect in
the bark, till they were sufficiently reduced for their slender
throats. A little flock of these tit-mice came daily to pick a
dinner out of my wood-pile, or the crums at my door, with
faint flitting lisping notes, like the tinkling of icicles in the
grass, or else with sprightly *day day day*, or more rarely, in
spring-like days, a wiry summery *phe-be* from the wood-side.
They were so familiar that at length one alighted on an armful of wood which I was carrying in, and pecked at the
sticks without fear. I once had a sparrow alight upon my
shoulder for a moment while I was hoeing in a village garden, and I felt that I was more distinguished by that circum-

stance than I should have been by any epaulet I could have worn. The squirrels also grew at last to be quite familiar, and occasionally stepped upon my shoe, when that was the nearest way.

When the ground was not yet quite covered, and again near the end of winter, when the snow was melted on my south hill-side and about my wood-pile, the partridges came out of the woods morning and evening to feed there. Whichever side you walk in the woods the partridge bursts away on whirring wings, jarring the snow from the dry leaves and twigs on high, which comes sifting down in the sun-beams like golden dust; for this brave bird is not to be scared by winter. It is frequently covered up by drifts, and, it is said, "sometimes plunges from on wing into the soft snow, where it remains concealed for a day or two." I used to start them in the open land also, where they had come out of the woods at sunset to "bud" the wild apple-trees. They will come regularly every evening to particular trees, where the cunning sportsman lies in wait for them, and the distant orchards next the woods suffer thus not a little. I am glad that the partridge gets fed, at any rate. It is Nature's own bird which lives on buds and diet-drink.

In dark winter mornings, or in short winter afternoons, I sometimes heard a pack of hounds threading all the woods with hounding cry and yelp, unable to resist the instinct of the chase, and the note of the hunting horn at intervals, proving that man was in the rear. The woods ring again, and yet no fox bursts forth on to the open level of the pond, nor following pack pursuing their Actæon. And perhaps at evening I see the hunters returning with a single brush trailing from their sleigh for a trophy, seeking their inn. They tell me that if the fox would remain in the bosom of the frozen earth he would be safe, or if he would run in a straight line away no fox-hound could overtake him; but, having left his pursuers far behind, he stops to rest and listen till they come up, and when he runs he circles round to his old haunts, where the hunters await him. Sometimes, however, he will run upon a wall many rods, and then leap off far to one side, and he appears to know that water will not retain his scent. A hunter told me that he once saw a fox pursued by hounds burst out on to Walden when the ice was covered with shallow puddles, run part way across, and then return to the same shore. Ere long the hounds arrived, but here they lost the scent. Sometimes a pack hunting by themselves would pass my door, and circle round my house, and yelp and hound without regarding me, as if afflicted by a species of madness, so that nothing could divert them from the pursuit. Thus they circle until they fall upon the recent trail of a fox, for a wise hound will forsake every thing else for this. One day a man came to my hut from Lexington to inquire after his hound that made a large track, and had been hunting for a week by himself. But I fear that he was not the wiser for all I told him, for every time I attempted to answer his questions he interrupted me by asking, "What do you do here?" He had lost a dog, but found a man.

One old hunter who has a dry tongue, who used to come to bathe in Walden once every year when the water was warmest, and at such times looked in upon me, told me, that many years ago he took his gun one afternoon and went out for a cruise in Walden Wood; and as he walked the Wayland road he heard the cry of hounds approaching, and ere long a fox leaped the wall into the road, and as quick as thought leaped the other wall out of the road, and his swift bullet had not touched him. Some way behind came an old hound and her three pups in full pursuit, hunting on their own account, and disappeared again in the woods. Late in the afternoon, as he was resting in the thick woods south of Walden, he heard the voice of the hounds far over toward Fair Haven still pursuing the fox; and on they came, their hounding cry which made all the woods ring sounding nearer and nearer, now from Well-Meadow, now from the Baker Farm. For a long time he stood still and listened to their music, so sweet to a hunter's ear, when suddenly the fox appeared, threading the solemn aisles with an easy coursing pace, whose sound was concealed by a sympathetic rustle of the leaves, swift and still, keeping the ground, leaving his pursuers far behind; and, leaping upon a rock amid the woods, he sat erect and listening, with his back to the hunter. For a moment compassion restrained the latter's arm; but that was a short-lived mood, and as quick as thought can follow thought his piece was levelled, and *whang!*—the fox rolling over the rock lay dead on the ground. The hunter still kept his place and listened to the hounds. Still on they came, and now the near woods resounded through all their aisles with their demoniac cry. At length the old hound burst into view with muzzle to the ground, and snapping the air as if possessed, and ran directly to the rock; but spying the dead fox she suddenly ceased her hounding, as if struck dumb with amazement, and walked round and round him in silence; and one by one her pups arrived, and, like their mother, were sobered into silence by the mystery. Then the hunter came forward and stood in their midst, and the mystery was solved. They waited in silence while he skinned the fox, then followed the brush a while, and at length turned off into the woods again. That evening a Weston Squire came to the Concord hunter's cottage to inquire for his hounds, and told how for a week they had been hunting on their own account from Weston woods. The Concord hunter told him what he knew and offered him the skin; but the other declined it and departed. He did not find his hounds that night, but the next day learned that they had crossed the river and put up at a farm-house for the night, whence, having been well fed, they took their departure early in the morning.

The hunter who told me this could remember one Sam Nutting, who used to hunt bears on Fair Haven Ledges, and exchange their skins for rum in Concord village; who told him, even, that he had seen a moose there. Nutting had a famous fox-hound named Burgoyne,—he pronounced it Bugine,—which my informant used to borrow. In the "Wast Book" of an old trader of this town, who was also a captain, town-clerk, and representative, I find the following entry. Jan. 18th, 1742–3, "John Melven Cr. by 1 Grey Fox 0—2—3;" they are not now found here; and in his leger, Feb. 7th, 1743, Hezekiah Stratton has credit "by ½ a Catt skin 0—1—4½;" of course, a wild-cat, for Stratton was a sergeant in the old French war, and would not have got credit for hunting less noble game. Credit is given for deer skins also, and they were daily sold. One man still preserves the horns of the last deer that was killed in this vicinity, and another has told me the particulars of the hunt in which his uncle was engaged. The hunters were formerly a numerous and merry crew here. I remember well one gaunt Nimrod who would catch up a leaf by the road-side and play a strain on it wilder and more melodious, if my memory serves me, than any hunting horn.

At midnight, when there was a moon, I sometimes met with hounds in my path prowling about the woods, which would skulk out of my way, as if afraid, and stand silent amid the bushes till I had passed.

Squirrels and wild mice disputed for my store of nuts. There were scores of pitch-pines around my house, from one to four inches in diameter, which had been gnawed by mice the previous winter,—a Norwegian winter for them, for the snow lay long and deep, and they were obliged to mix a large proportion of pine bark with their other diet. These trees were alive and apparently flourishing at mid-summer, and many of them had grown a foot, though completely girdled; but after another winter such were without exception dead. It is remarkable that a single mouse should thus be allowed a whole pine tree for its dinner, gnawing round instead of up and down it; but perhaps it is necessary in order to thin these trees, which are wont to grow up densely.

The hares (*Lepus Americanus*) were very familiar. One had her form under my house all winter, separated from me only by the flooring, and she startled me each morning by her hasty departure when I began to stir,—thump, thump, thump, striking her head against the floor timbers in her hurry. They used to come round my door at dusk to nibble the potato parings which I had thrown out, and were so nearly the color of the ground that they could hardly be distinguished when still. Sometimes in the twilight I alternately lost and recovered sight of one sitting motionless under my window. When I opened my door in the evening, off they would go with a squeak and a bounce. Near at hand they only excited my pity. One evening one sat by my door two paces from me, at first trembling with fear, yet unwilling to move; a poor wee thing, lean and bony, with ragged ears and sharp nose, scant tail and slender paws. It looked as if Nature no longer contained the breed of nobler bloods, but

stood on her last toes. Its large eyes appeared young and unhealthy, almost dropsical. I took a step, and lo, away it scud
with an elastic spring over the snow crust, straightening its
body and its limbs into graceful length, and soon put the
forest between me and itself,—the wild free venison, assert-
ing its vigor and the dignity of Nature. Not without reason
was its slenderness. Such then was its nature. (*Lepus*, *levipes*,
light-foot, some think.)

What is a country without rabbits and partridges? They
are among the most simple and indigenous animal products;
ancient and venerable families known to antiquity as to
modern times; of the very hue and substance of Nature,
nearest allied to leaves and to the ground,—and to one another; it is either winged or it is legged. It is hardly as if you
had seen a wild creature when a rabbit or a partridge bursts
away, only a natural one, as much to be expected as rustling
leaves. The partridge and the rabbit are still sure to thrive,
like true natives of the soil, whatever revolutions occur. If
the forest is cut off, the sprouts and bushes which spring up
afford them concealment, and they become more numerous
than ever. That must be a poor country indeed that does not
support a hare. Our woods teem with them both, and
around every swamp may be seen the partridge or rabbit
walk, beset with twiggy fences and horse-hair snares, which
some cow-boy tends.

The Pond in Winter

A̲FTER A STILL winter night I awoke with the impression that some question had been put to me, which I had been endeavoring in vain to answer in my sleep, as what—how—when—where? But there was dawning Nature, in whom all creatures live, looking in at my broad windows with serene and satisfied face, and no question on *her* lips. I awoke to an answered question, to Nature and daylight. The snow lying deep on the earth dotted with young pines, and the very slope of the hill on which my house is placed, seemed to say, Forward! Nature puts no question and answers none which we mortals ask. She has long ago taken her resolution. "O Prince, our eyes contemplate with admiration and transmit to the soul the wonderful and varied spectacle of this universe. The night veils without doubt a part of this glorious creation; but day comes to reveal to us this great work, which extends from earth even into the plains of the ether."

Then to my morning work. First I take an axe and pail and go in search of water, if that be not a dream. After a cold and snowy night it needed a divining rod to find it. Every winter the liquid and trembling surface of the pond, which was so sensitive to every breath, and reflected every light and shadow, becomes solid to the depth of a foot or a foot and a half, so that it will support the heaviest teams, and perchance the snow covers it to an equal depth, and it is not to be distinguished from any level field. Like the marmots in the surrounding hills, it closes its eye-lids and becomes dormant for three months or more. Standing on the snow-covered plain, as if in a pasture amid the hills, I cut my way first through a foot of snow, and then a foot of ice, and open a window under my feet, where, kneeling to drink, I look down into the quiet parlor of the fishes, pervaded by a softened light as through a window of ground glass, with its bright sanded floor the same as in summer; there a perennial waveless serenity reigns as in the amber twilight sky, corresponding to the cool and even temperament of the inhabitants. Heaven is under our feet as well as over our heads.

Early in the morning, while all things are crisp with frost, men come with fishing reels and slender lunch, and let down their fine lines through the snowy field to take pickerel and perch; wild men, who instinctively follow other fashions and trust other authorities than their townsmen, and by their goings and comings stitch towns together in parts where else they would be ripped. They sit and eat their luncheon in stout fear-naughts on the dry oak leaves on the shore, as wise in natural lore as the citizen is in artificial. They never consulted with books, and know and can tell much less than they have done. The things which they practise are said not yet to be known. Here is one fishing for pickerel with grown perch for bait. You look into his pail with wonder as into a summer pond, as if he kept summer locked up at home, or knew where she had retreated. How, pray, did he get these in mid-winter? O, he got worms out of rotten logs since the ground froze, and so he caught them. His life itself passes deeper in Nature than the studies of the naturalist penetrate; himself a subject for the naturalist. The latter raises the moss and bark gently with his knife in search of insects; the former lays open logs to their core with his axe, and moss and bark fly far and wide. He gets his living by barking trees. Such a man has some right to fish, and I love to see Nature carried out in him. The perch swallows the grub-worm, the pickerel swallows the perch, and the fisherman swallows the pickerel; and so all the chinks in the scale of being are filled.

When I strolled around the pond in misty weather I was sometimes amused by the primitive mode which some ruder fisherman had adopted. He would perhaps have placed alder branches over the narrow holes in the ice, which were four or five rods apart and an equal distance from the shore, and having fastened the end of the line to a stick to prevent its being pulled through, have passed the slack line over a twig of the alder, a foot or more above the ice, and tied a dry oak leaf to it, which, being pulled down, would show when he had a bite. These alders loomed through the mist at regular intervals as you walked half way round the pond.

Ah, the pickerel of Walden! when I see them lying on the ice, or in the well which the fisherman cuts in the ice, making a little hole to admit the water, I am always surprised by their rare beauty, as if they were fabulous fishes, they are so foreign

to the streets, even to the woods, foreign as Arabia to our
Concord life. They possess a quite dazzling and transcendent
beauty which separates them by a wide interval from the ca-
daverous cod and haddock whose fame is trumpeted in our
streets. They are not green like the pines, nor gray like the
stones, nor blue like the sky; but they have, to my eyes, if
possible, yet rarer colors, like flowers and precious stones, as
if they were the pearls, the animalized *nuclei* or crystals of the
Walden water. They, of course, are Walden all over and all
through; are themselves small Waldens in the animal kingdom, Waldenses. It is surprising that they are caught here,—
that in this deep and capacious spring, far beneath the rattling
teams and chaises and tinkling sleighs that travel the Walden
road, this great gold and emerald fish swims. I never chanced
to see its kind in any market; it would be the cynosure of all
eyes there. Easily, with a few convulsive quirks, they give up
their watery ghosts, like a mortal translated before his time to
the thin air of heaven.

As I was desirous to recover the long lost bottom of Walden Pond, I surveyed it carefully, before the ice broke up,
early in '46, with compass and chain and sounding line. There
have been many stories told about the bottom, or rather no
bottom, of this pond, which certainly had no foundation for
themselves. It is remarkable how long men will believe in the
bottomlessness of a pond without taking the trouble to sound
it. I have visited two such Bottomless Ponds in one walk in
this neighborhood. Many have believed that Walden reached
quite through to the other side of the globe. Some who have
lain flat on the ice for a long time, looking down through the
illusive medium, perchance with watery eyes into the bargain,
and driven to hasty conclusions by the fear of catching cold
in their breasts, have seen vast holes "into which a load of hay
might be driven," if there were any body to drive it, the un-
doubted source of the Styx and entrance to the Infernal Regions from these parts. Others have gone down from the
village with a "fifty-six" and a wagon load of inch rope, but
yet have failed to find any bottom; for while the "fifty-six"
was resting by the way, they were paying out the rope in the
vain attempt to fathom their truly immeasurable capacity for

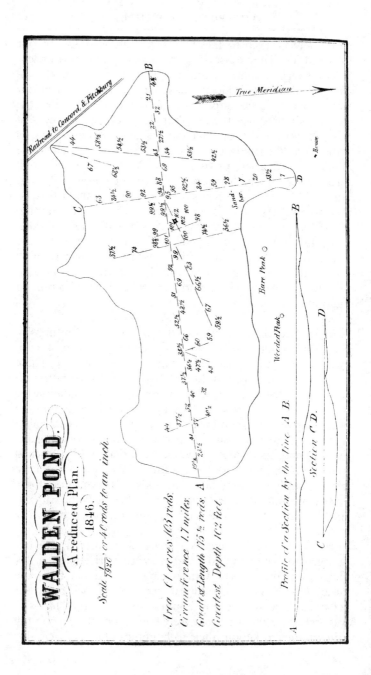

WALDEN POND.

A reduced Plan.

1846.

Scale 7920, or 40 rods to an inch.

Railroad to Concord & Fitchburg

True Meridian

House

Sand-bar

Bare Peak

Wooded Peak

Area 61 acres 103 rds.
Circumference 1.7 miles.
Greatest Length 175½ rds.
Greatest Depth 102 feet.

Profile of a Section by the line A B.

Section C D.

marvellousness. But I can assure my readers that Walden has a reasonably tight bottom at a not unreasonable, though at an unusual, depth. I fathomed it easily with a cod-line and a stone weighing about a pound and a half, and could tell accurately when the stone left the bottom, by having to pull so much harder before the water got underneath to help me. The greatest depth was exactly one hundred and two feet; to which may be added the five feet which it has risen since, making one hundred and seven. This is a remarkable depth for so small an area; yet not an inch of it can be spared by the imagination. What if all ponds were shallow? Would it not react on the minds of men? I am thankful that this pond was made deep and pure for a symbol. While men believe in the infinite some ponds will be thought to be bottomless.

A factory owner, hearing what depth I had found, thought that it could not be true, for, judging from his acquaintance with dams, sand would not lie at so steep an angle. But the deepest ponds are not so deep in proportion to their area as most suppose, and, if drained, would not leave very remarkable valleys. They are not like cups between the hills; for this one, which is so unusually deep for its area, appears in a vertical section through its centre not deeper than a shallow plate. Most ponds, emptied, would leave a meadow no more hollow than we frequently see. William Gilpin, who is so admirable in all that relates to landscapes, and usually so correct, standing at the head of Loch Fyne, in Scotland, which he describes as "a bay of salt water, sixty or seventy fathoms deep, four miles in breadth," and about fifty miles long, surrounded by mountains, observes, "If we could have seen it immediately after the diluvian crash, or whatever convulsion of Nature occasioned it, before the waters gushed in, what a horrid chasm it must have appeared!

> So high as heaved the tumid hills, so low
> Down sunk a hollow bottom, broad, and deep,
> Capacious bed of waters——."

But if, using the shortest diameter of Loch Fyne, we apply these proportions to Walden, which, as we have seen, appears already in a vertical section only like a shallow plate, it will appear four times as shallow. So much for the *increased* horrors of the chasm of Loch Fyne when emptied. No doubt many a smiling valley with its stretching cornfields occupies exactly such a "horrid chasm," from which the waters have receded, though it requires the insight and the far sight of the geologist to convince the unsuspecting inhabitants of this fact. Often an inquisitive eye may detect the shores of a primitive lake in the low horizon hills, and no subsequent elevation of the plain has been necessary to conceal their history. But it is easiest, as they who work on the highways know, to find the hollows by the puddles after a shower. The amount of it is, the imagination, give it the least license, dives deeper and soars higher than Nature goes. So, probably, the depth of the ocean will be found to be very inconsiderable compared with its breadth.

As I sounded through the ice I could determine the shape of the bottom with greater accuracy than is possible in surveying harbors which do not freeze over, and I was surprised at its general regularity. In the deepest part there are several acres more level than almost any field which is exposed to the sun wind and plough. In one instance, on a line arbitrarily chosen, the depth did not vary more than one foot in thirty rods; and generally, near the middle, I could calculate the variation for each one hundred feet in any direction beforehand within three or four inches. Some are accustomed to speak of deep and dangerous holes even in quiet sandy ponds like this, but the effect of water under these circumstances is to level all inequalities. The regularity of the bottom and its conformity to the shores and the range of the neighboring hills were so perfect that a distant promontory betrayed itself in the soundings quite across the pond, and its direction could be determined by observing the opposite shore. Cape becomes bar, and plain shoal, and valley and gorge deep water and channel.

When I had mapped the pond by the scale of ten rods to an inch, and put down the soundings, more than a hundred in all, I observed this remarkable coincidence. Having noticed that the number indicating the greatest depth was apparently in the centre of the map, I laid a rule on the map lengthwise, and then breadthwise, and found, to my surprise, that the line of greatest length intersected the line of greatest breadth *exactly* at the point of greatest depth, notwithstanding that the middle is so nearly level, the outline of the pond far from regular, and the extreme length and breadth were got by measuring into the coves; and I said to myself, Who knows but this hint would conduct to the deepest part of the ocean as well as of a pond or puddle? Is not this the rule also for the height of mountains, regarded as the opposite of valleys? We know that a hill is not highest at its narrowest part.

Of five coves, three, or all which had been sounded, were observed to have a bar quite across their mouths and deeper water within, so that the bay tended to be an expansion of water within the land not only horizontally but vertically, and to form a basin or independent pond, the direction of the two capes showing the course of the bar. Every harbor on the sea-coast, also, has its bar at its entrance. In proportion as the mouth of the cove was wider compared with its length, the water over the bar was deeper compared with that in the basin. Given, then, the length and breadth of the cove, and the character of the surrounding shore, and you have almost elements enough to make out a formula for all cases.

In order to see how nearly I could guess, with this experience, at the deepest point in a pond, by observing the outlines of its surface and the character of its shores alone, I made a plan of White Pond, which contains about forty-one acres, and, like this, has no island in it, nor any visible inlet or outlet; and as the line of greatest breadth fell very near the line of least breadth, where two opposite capes approached each other and two opposite bays receded, I ventured to mark a point a short distance from the latter line, but still on the line of greatest length, as the deepest. The deepest part was found to be within one hundred feet of this, still farther in the direction to which I had inclined, and was only one foot deeper, namely, sixty feet. Of course, a stream running through, or an island in the pond, would make the problem much more complicated.

If we knew all the laws of Nature, we should need only one fact, or the description of one actual phenomenon, to infer all the particular results at that point. Now we know only a few laws, and our result is vitiated, not, of course, by any confusion or irregularity in Nature, but by our ignorance of essential elements in the calculation. Our notions of law and harmony are commonly confined to those instances which we detect; but the harmony which results from a far greater number of seemingly conflicting, but really concurring, laws, which we have not detected, is still more wonderful. The particular laws are as our points of view, as, to the traveller, a mountain outline varies with every step, and it has an infinite number of profiles, though absolutely but one form. Even when cleft or bored through it is not comprehended in its entireness.

What I have observed of the pond is no less true in ethics. It is the law of average. Such a rule of the two diameters not only guides us toward the sun in the system and the heart in man, but draw lines through the length and breadth of the aggregate of a man's particular daily behaviors and waves of life into his coves and inlets, and where they intersect will be the height or depth of his character. Perhaps we need only to know how his shores trend and his adjacent country or circumstances, to infer his depth and concealed bottom. If he is surrounded by mountainous circumstances, an Achillean shore, whose peaks overshadow and are reflected in his bosom, they suggest a corresponding depth in him. But a low and smooth shore proves him shallow on that side. In our bodies, a bold projecting brow falls off to and indicates a corresponding depth of thought. Also there is a bar across the entrance of our every cove, or particular inclination; each is our harbor for a season, in which we are detained and partially land-locked. These inclinations are not whimsical usually, but their form, size, and direction are determined by the promontories of the shore, the ancient axes of elevation. When this bar is gradually increased by storms, tides, or currents, or there is a subsidence of the waters, so that it reaches to the surface, that which was at first but an inclination in the shore in which a thought was harbored becomes an individual lake, cut off from the ocean, wherein the thought secures its own conditions, changes, perhaps, from salt to fresh, becomes a sweet sea, dead sea, or a marsh. At the advent of each individual into this life, may we not suppose that such a bar has risen to the surface somewhere? It is true, we are such poor navigators that our thoughts, for the most part, stand off and on upon a harborless coast, are conversant only with the bights of the bays of poesy, or steer for the public ports of entry, and go into the dry docks of science, where they merely refit for this world, and no natural currents concur to individualize them.

As for the inlet or outlet of Walden, I have not discovered any but rain and snow and evaporation, though perhaps, with a thermometer and a line, such places may be found, for where the water flows into the pond it will probably be coldest in summer and warmest in winter. When the ice-men were at work here in '46–7, the cakes sent to the shore were one day rejected by those who were stacking them up there, not being thick enough to lie side by side with the rest; and the cutters thus discovered that the ice over a small space was two or three inches thinner than elsewhere, which made them think that there was an inlet there. They also showed me in another place what they thought was a "leach hole," through which the pond leaked out under a hill into a neighboring meadow, pushing me out on a cake of ice to see it. It was a small cavity under ten feet of water; but I think that I can warrant the pond not to need soldering till they find a worse leak than that. One has suggested, that if such a "leach hole" should be found, its connection with the meadow, if any existed, might be proved by conveying some colored powder or sawdust to the mouth of the hole, and then putting a strainer over the spring in the meadow, which would catch some of the particles carried through by the current.

While I was surveying, the ice, which was sixteen inches thick, undulated under a slight wind like water. It is well known that a level cannot be used on ice. At one rod from the shore its greatest fluctuation, when observed by means of a level on land directed toward a graduated staff on the ice, was three quarters of an inch, though the ice appeared firmly attached to the shore. It was probably greater in the middle. Who knows but if our instruments were delicate enough we might detect an undulation in the crust of the earth? When two legs of my level were on the shore and the third on the ice, and the sights were directed over the latter, a rise or fall of the ice of an almost infinitesimal amount made a difference of several feet on a tree across the pond. When I began to cut holes for sounding, there were three or four inches of water on the ice under a deep snow which had sunk it thus far; but the water began immediately to run into these holes, and continued to run for two days in deep streams, which wore away the ice on every side, and contributed essentially, if not mainly, to dry the surface of the pond; for, as the water ran in, it raised and floated the ice. This was somewhat like cutting a hole in the bottom of a ship to let the water out. When such holes freeze, and a rain succeeds, and finally a new freezing forms a fresh smooth ice over all, it is beautifully mottled internally by dark figures, shaped somewhat like a spider's web, what you may call ice rosettes, produced by the channels worn by the water flowing from all sides to a centre. Sometimes, also, when the ice was covered with shallow puddles, I saw a double shadow of myself, one standing on the head of the other, one on the ice, the other on the trees or hill-side.

While yet it is cold January, and snow and ice are thick and solid, the prudent landlord comes from the village to get ice to cool his summer drink; impressively, even pathetically wise, to foresee the heat and thirst of July now in January,— wearing a thick coat and mittens! when so many things are not provided for. It may be that he lays up no treasures in this world which will cool his summer drink in the next. He cuts and saws the solid pond, unroofs the house of fishes, and carts off their very element and air, held fast by chains and stakes like corded wood, through the favoring winter air, to wintry cellars, to underlie the summer there. It looks like solidified azure, as, far off, it is drawn through the streets. These ice-cutters are a merry race, full of jest and sport, and when I went among them they were wont to invite me to saw pit-fashion with them, I standing underneath.

In the winter of '46—7 there came a hundred men of Hyperborean extraction swoop down on to our pond one morning, with many car-loads of ungainly-looking farming tools, sleds, ploughs, drill-barrows, turf-knives, spades, saws, rakes, and each man was armed with a double-pointed pike-staff, such as is not described in the New-England Farmer or the Cultivator. I did not know whether they had come to sow a crop of winter rye, or some other kind of grain recently introduced from Iceland. As I saw no manure, I judged that they meant to skim the land, as I had done, thinking the soil was deep and had lain fallow long enough. They said that a gentleman farmer, who was behind the scenes, wanted to double his money, which, as I understood, amounted to half a million already; but in order to cover each one of his dollars with another, he took off the only coat, ay, the skin itself, of Walden Pond in the midst of a hard winter. They went to work at once, ploughing, harrowing, rolling, furrowing, in admirable order, as if they were bent on making this a model farm; but when I was looking sharp to see what kind of seed they dropped into the furrow, a gang of fellows by my side suddenly began to hook up the virgin mould itself, with a peculiar jerk, clean down to the sand, or rather the water,—for it was a very springy soil,—indeed all the *terra firma* there was, and haul it away on sleds, and then I guessed that they must be cutting peat in a bog. So they came and went every day, with a peculiar shriek from the locomotive, from and to some point of the polar regions, as it seemed to me, like a flock of arctic snow-birds. But sometimes Squaw Walden had her revenge, and a hired man, walking behind his team, slipped through a crack in the ground down toward Tartarus, and he who was so brave before suddenly became but the ninth part of a man, almost gave up his animal heat, and was glad to take refuge in my house, and acknowledged that there was some virtue in a stove; or sometimes the frozen soil took a piece of steel out of a ploughshare, or a plough got set in the furrow and had to be cut out.

To speak literally, a hundred Irishmen, with Yankee overseers, came from Cambridge every day to get out the ice. They divided it into cakes by methods too well known to require description, and these, being sledded to the shore, were rapidly hauled off on to an ice platform, and raised by grappling irons and block and tackle, worked by horses, on to a stack, as surely as so many barrels of flour, and there placed evenly side by side, and row upon row, as if they formed the solid base of an obelisk designed to pierce the clouds. They told me that in a good day they could get out a thousand tons, which was the yield of about one acre. Deep ruts and "cradle holes" were worn in the ice, as on *terra firma*, by the passage of the sleds over the same track, and the horses invariably ate their oats out of cakes of ice hollowed out like buckets. They stacked up the cakes thus in the open air in a pile thirty-five feet high on one side and six or seven rods square, putting hay between the outside layers to exclude the air; for when the wind, though never so cold, finds a passage through, it will wear large cavities, leaving slight supports or studs only here and there, and finally topple it down. At first it looked like a vast blue fort or Valhalla; but when they began to tuck the coarse meadow hay into the crevices, and this became covered with rime and icicles, it looked like a venerable moss-grown and hoary ruin, built of azure-tinted marble, the abode of Winter, that old man we see in the almanac,—his shanty, as if he had a design to estivate with us. They calculated that not twenty-five per cent. of this would reach its destination, and that two or three per cent. would be wasted in the cars. However, a still greater part of this heap had a different destiny from what was intended; for, either because the ice was found not to keep so well as was expected, containing more air than usual, or for some other reason, it never got to market. This heap, made in the winter of '46–7 and estimated to contain ten thousand tons, was finally covered with hay and boards; and though it was unroofed the following July, and a part of it carried off, the rest remaining exposed to the sun, it stood over that summer and the next winter, and was not quite melted till September 1848. Thus the pond recovered the greater part.

Like the water, the Walden ice, seen near at hand, has a green tint, but at a distance is beautifully blue, and you can easily tell it from the white ice of the river, or the merely greenish ice of some ponds, a quarter of a mile off. Sometimes one of those great cakes slips from the ice-man's sled into the village street, and lies there for a week like a great emerald, an object of interest to all passers. I have noticed that a portion of Walden which in the state of water was green will often, when frozen, appear from the same point of view blue. So the hollows about this pond will, sometimes, in the winter, be filled with a greenish water somewhat like its own, but the next day will have frozen blue. Perhaps the blue color of water and ice is due to the light and air they contain, and the most transparent is the bluest. Ice is an interesting subject for contemplation. They told me that they had some in the ice-houses at Fresh Pond five years old which was as good as ever. Why is it that a bucket of water soon becomes putrid, but frozen remains sweet forever? It is commonly said that this is the difference between the affections and the intellect.

Thus for sixteen days I saw from my window a hundred men at work like busy husbandmen, with teams and horses and apparently all the implements of farming, such a picture as we see on the first page of the almanac; and as often as I looked out I was reminded of the fable of the lark and the reapers, or the parable of the sower, and the like; and now they are all gone, and in thirty days more, probably, I shall look from the same window on the pure sea-green Walden water there, reflecting the clouds and the trees, and sending up its evaporations in solitude, and no traces will appear that a man has ever stood there. Perhaps I shall hear a solitary loon laugh as he dives and plumes himself, or shall see a lonely fisher in his boat, like a floating leaf, beholding his form reflected in the waves, where lately a hundred men securely labored.

Thus it appears that the sweltering inhabitants of Charleston and New Orleans, of Madras and Bombay and Calcutta, drink at my well. In the morning I bathe my intellect in the stupendous and cosmogonal philosophy of the Bhagvat Geeta, since whose composition years of the gods have elapsed, and in comparison with which our modern world and its literature seem puny and trivial; and I doubt if that philosophy is not to be referred to a previous state of existence, so remote is its sublimity from our conceptions. I lay down the book and go to my well for water, and lo! there I meet the servant of the Bramin, priest of Brahma and Vishnu and Indra, who still sits in his temple on the Ganges reading the Vedas, or dwells at the root of a tree with his crust and water jug. I meet his servant come to draw water for his master, and our buckets as it were grate together in the same well. The pure Walden water is mingled with the sacred water of the Ganges. With favoring winds it is wafted past the site of the fabulous islands of Atlantis and the Hesperides, makes the periplus of Hanno, and, floating by Ternate and Tidore and the mouth of the Persian Gulf, melts in the tropic gales of the Indian seas, and is landed in ports of which Alexander only heard the names.

Spring

THE OPENING of large tracts by the ice-cutters commonly causes a pond to break up earlier; for the water, agitated by the wind, even in cold weather, wears away the surrounding ice. But such was not the effect on Walden that year, for she had soon got a thick new garment to take the place of the old. This pond never breaks up so soon as the others in this neighborhood, on account both of its greater depth and its having no stream passing through it to melt or wear away the ice. I never knew it to open in the course of a winter, not excepting that of '52–3, which gave the ponds so severe a trial. It commonly opens about the first of April, a week or ten days later than Flints' Pond and Fair-Haven, beginning to melt on the north side and in the shallower parts where it began to freeze. It indicates better than any water hereabouts the absolute progress of the season, being least affected by transient changes of temperature. A severe cold of a few days' duration in March may very much retard the opening of the former ponds, while the temperature of Walden increases almost uninterruptedly. A thermometer thrust into the middle of Walden on the 6th of March, 1847, stood at 32°, or freezing point; near the shore at 33°; in the middle of Flints' Pond, the same day, at 32½°; at a dozen rods from the shore, in shallow water, under ice a foot thick, at 36°. This difference of three and a half degrees between the temperature of the deep water and the shallow in the latter pond, and the fact that a great proportion of it is comparatively shallow, show why it should break up so much sooner than Walden. The ice in the shallowest part was at this time several inches thinner than in the middle. In mid-winter the middle had been the warmest and the ice thinnest there. So, also, every one who has waded about the shores of a pond in summer must have perceived how much warmer the water is close to the shore, where only three or four inches deep, than a little distance out, and on the surface where it is deep, than near the bottom. In spring the sun not only exerts an influence through the increased temperature of the air and earth, but its heat passes through ice a foot or more thick, and is reflected from the bottom in shallow water, and so also warms the water and melts the under side of the ice, at the same time that it is melting it more directly above, making it uneven, and causing the air bubbles which it contains to extend themselves upward and downward until it is completely honey-combed, and at last disappears suddenly in a single spring rain. Ice has its grain as well as wood, and when a cake begins to rot or "comb," that is, assume the appearance of honey-comb, whatever may be its position, the air cells are at right angles with what was the water surface. Where there is a rock or a log rising near to the surface the ice over it is much thinner, and is frequently quite dissolved by this reflected heat; and I have been told that in the experiment at Cambridge to freeze water in a shallow wooden pond, though the cold air circulated underneath, and so had access to both sides, the reflection of the sun from the bottom more than counterbalanced this advantage. When a warm rain in the middle of the winter melts off the snow-ice from Walden, and leaves a hard dark or transparent ice on the middle, there will be a strip of rotten though thicker white ice, a rod or more wide, about the shores, created by this reflected heat. Also, as I have said, the bubbles themselves within the ice operate as burning glasses to melt the ice beneath.

The phenomena of the year take place every day in a pond on a small scale. Every morning, generally speaking, the shallow water is being warmed more rapidly than the deep, though it may not be made so warm after all, and every evening it is being cooled more rapidly until the morning. The day is an epitome of the year. The night is the winter, the morning and evening are the spring and fall, and the noon is the summer. The cracking and booming of the ice indicate a change of temperature. One pleasant morning after a cold night, February 24th, 1850, having gone to Flints' Pond to spend the day, I noticed with surprise, that when I struck the ice with the head of my axe, it resounded like a gong for many rods around, or as if I had struck on a tight drum-head. The pond began to boom about an hour after sunrise, when it felt the influence of the sun's rays slanted upon it from over the hills; it stretched itself and yawned like a waking man with a gradually increasing tumult, which was kept up three or four hours. It took a short siesta at noon, and boomed once more toward night, as the sun was withdrawing his influence. In the right stage of the weather a pond fires its evening gun with great regularity. But in the middle of the day, being full of cracks, and the air also being less elastic, it had completely lost its resonance, and probably fishes and musk-rats could not then have been stunned by a blow on it. The fishermen say that the "thundering of the pond" scares the fishes and prevents their biting. The pond does not thunder every evening, and I cannot tell surely when to expect its thundering; but though I may perceive no difference in the weather, it does. Who would have suspected so large and cold and thick-skinned a thing to be so sensitive? Yet it has its law to which it thunders obedience when it should as surely as the buds expand in the spring. The earth is all alive and covered with papillæ. The largest pond is as sensitive to atmospheric changes as the globule of mercury in its tube.

One attraction in coming to the woods to live was that I should have leisure and opportunity to see the spring come in. The ice in the pond at length begins to be honey-combed, and I can set my heel in it as I walk. Fogs and rains and warmer suns are gradually melting the snow; the days have grown sensibly longer; and I see how I shall get through the winter without adding to my wood-pile, for large fires are no longer necessary. I am on the alert for the first signs of spring, to hear the chance note of some arriving bird, or the striped squirrel's chirp, for his stores must be now nearly exhausted, or see the woodchuck venture out of his winter quarters. On the 13th of March, after I had heard the bluebird, song-spar-row, and red-wing, the ice was still nearly a foot thick. As the weather grew warmer, it was not sensibly worn away by the water, nor broken up and floated off as in rivers, but, though it was completely melted for half a rod in width about the shore, the middle was merely honey-combed and saturated with water, so that you could put your foot through it when six inches thick; but by the next day evening, perhaps, after a warm rain followed by fog, it would have wholly disappeared, all gone off with the fog, spirited away. One year I went across the middle only five days before it disappeared entirely.

In 1845 Walden was first completely open on the 1st of April; in '46, the 25th of March; in '47, the 8th of April; in '51, the 28th of March; in '52, the 18th of April; in '53, the 23d of March; in '54, about the 7th of April.

Every incident connected with the breaking up of the rivers and ponds and the settling of the weather is particularly interesting to us who live in a climate of so great extremes. When the warmer days come, they who dwell near the river hear the ice crack at night with a startling whoop as loud as artillery, as if its icy fetters were rent from end to end, and within a few days see it rapidly going out. So the alligator comes out of the mud with quakings of the earth. One old man, who has been a close observer of Nature, and seems as thoroughly wise in regard to all her operations as if she had been put upon the stocks when he was a boy, and he had helped to lay her keel,—who has come to his growth, and can hardly acquire more of natural lore if he should live to the age of Methuselah,—told me, and I was surprised to hear him express wonder at any of Nature's operations, for I thought that there were no secrets between them, that one spring day he took his gun and boat, and thought that he would have a little sport with the ducks. There was ice still on the meadows, but it was all gone out of the river, and he dropped down without obstruction from Sudbury, where he lived, to Fair-Haven Pond, which he found, unexpectedly, covered for the most part with a firm field of ice. It was a warm day, and he was surprised to see so great a body of ice remaining. Not seeing any ducks, he hid his boat on the north or back side of an island in the pond, and then concealed himself in the bushes on the south side, to await them. The ice was melted for three or four rods from the shore, and there was a smooth and warm sheet of water, with a muddy bottom, such as the ducks love, within, and he thought it likely that some would be along pretty soon. After he had lain still there about an hour he heard a low and seemingly very distant sound, but singularly grand and impressive, unlike any thing he had ever heard, gradually swelling and increasing as if it would have a universal and memorable ending, a sullen rush and roar, which seemed to him all at once like the sound of a vast body of fowl coming in to settle there, and, seizing

his gun, he started up in haste and excited; but he found, to
his surprise, that the whole body of the ice had started while
he lay there, and drifted in to the shore, and the sound he
had heard was made by its edge grating on the shore,—at
first gently nibbled and crumbled off, but at length heaving
up and scattering its wrecks along the island to a considerable
height before it came to a stand still.

At length the sun's rays have attained the right angle, and
warm winds blow up mist and rain and melt the snow banks,
and the sun dispersing the mist smiles on a checkered landscape of russet and white smoking with incense, through
which the traveller picks his way from islet to islet, cheered
by the music of a thousand tinkling rills and rivulets whose
veins are filled with the blood of winter which they are bearing off.

Few phenomena gave me more delight than to observe the
forms which thawing sand and clay assume in flowing down
the sides of a deep cut on the railroad through which I passed
on my way to the village, a phenomenon not very common
on so large a scale, though the number of freshly exposed
banks of the right material must have been greatly multiplied
since railroads were invented. The material was sand of every
degree of fineness and of various rich colors, commonly
mixed with a little clay. When the frost comes out in the
spring, and even in a thawing day in the winter, the sand
begins to flow down the slopes like lava, sometimes bursting
out through the snow and overflowing it where no sand was
to be seen before. Innumerable little streams overlap and in-
terlace one with another, exhibiting a sort of hybrid product,
which obeys half way the law of currents, and half way that
of vegetation. As it flows it takes the forms of sappy leaves or
vines, making heaps of pulpy sprays a foot or more in depth,
and resembling, as you look down on them, the laciniated
lobed and imbricated thalluses of some lichens; or you are
reminded of coral, of leopards' paws or birds' feet, of brains
or lungs or bowels, and excrements of all kinds. It is a truly
grotesque vegetation, whose forms and color we see imitated
in bronze, a sort of architectural foliage more ancient and typical than acanthus, chiccory, ivy, vine, or any vegetable leaves;
destined perhaps, under some circumstances, to become a

puzzle to future geologists. The whole cut impressed me as if it were a cave with its stalactites laid open to the light. The various shades of the sand are singularly rich and agreeable, embracing the different iron colors, brown, gray, yellowish, and reddish. When the flowing mass reaches the drain at the foot of the bank it spreads out flatter into *strands*, the separate streams losing their semi-cylindrical form and gradually becoming more flat and broad, running together as they are more moist, till they form an almost flat *sand*, still variously and beautifully shaded, but in which you can trace the original forms of vegetation; till at length, in the water itself, they are converted into *banks*, like those formed off the mouths of rivers, and the forms of vegetation are lost in the ripple marks on the bottom.

The whole bank, which is from twenty to forty feet high, is sometimes overlaid with a mass of this kind of foliage, or sandy rupture, for a quarter of a mile on one or both sides, the produce of one spring day. What makes this sand foliage remarkable is its springing into existence thus suddenly. When I see on the one side the inert bank,—for the sun acts on one side first,—and on the other this luxuriant foliage, the creation of an hour, I am affected as if in a peculiar sense I stood in the laboratory of the Artist who made the world and me,—had come to where he was still at work, sporting on this bank, and with excess of energy strewing his fresh designs about. I feel as if I were nearer to the vitals of the globe, for this sandy overflow is something such a foliaceous mass as the vitals of the animal body. You find thus in the very sands an anticipation of the vegetable leaf. No wonder that the earth expresses itself outwardly in leaves, it so labors with the idea inwardly. The atoms have already learned this law, and are pregnant by it. The overhanging leaf sees here its prototype. *Internally*, whether in the globe or animal body, it is a moist thick *lobe*, a word especially applicable to the liver and lungs and the *leaves* of fat, (λείβω, *labor, lapsus*, to flow or slip downward, a lapsing; λοβος, *globus*, lobe, globe; also lap, flap, and many other words,) *externally* a dry thin *leaf*, even as the *f* and *v* are a pressed and dried *b*. The radicals of lobe are *lb*, the soft mass of the *b* (single lobed, or B, double lobed,) with a liquid *l* behind it pressing it forward. In globe, *glb*, the guttural *g* adds to the meaning the capacity of the throat. The feathers and wings of birds are still drier and thinner leaves. Thus, also, you pass from the lumpish grub in the earth to the airy and fluttering butterfly. The very globe continually transcends and translates itself, and becomes winged in its orbit. Even ice begins with delicate crystal leaves, as if it had flowed into moulds which the fronds of water plants have impressed on the watery mirror. The whole tree itself is but one leaf, and rivers are still vaster leaves whose pulp is intervening earth, and towns and cities are the ova of insects in their axils.

When the sun withdraws the sand ceases to flow, but in the morning the streams will start once more and branch and branch again into a myriad of others. You here see perchance how blood vessels are formed. If you look closely you observe that first there pushes forward from the thawing mass a stream of softened sand with a drop-like point, like the ball of the finger, feeling its way slowly and blindly downward, until at last with more heat and moisture, as the sun gets higher, the most fluid portion, in its effort to obey the law to which the most inert also yields, separates from the latter and forms for itself a meandering channel or artery within that, in which is seen a little silvery stream glancing like lightning from one stage of pulpy leaves or branches to another, and ever and anon swallowed up in the sand. It is wonderful how rapidly yet perfectly the sand organizes itself as it flows, using the best material its mass affords to form the sharp edges of its channel. Such are the sources of rivers. In the silicious matter which the water deposits is perhaps the bony system, and in the still finer soil and organic matter the fleshy fibre or cellular tissue. What is man but a mass of thawing clay? The ball of the human finger is but a drop congealed. The fingers and toes flow to their extent from the thawing mass of the body. Who knows what the human body would expand and flow out to under a more genial heaven? Is not the hand a spreading *palm* leaf with its lobes and veins? The ear may be regarded, fancifully, as a lichen, *umbilicaria*, on the side of the head, with its lobe or drop. The lip (*labium*, from *labor* (?)) laps or lapses from the sides of the cavernous mouth. The nose is a manifest congealed drop or stalactite.

The chin is a still larger drop, the confluent dripping of the face. The cheeks are a slide from the brows into the valley of the face, opposed and diffused by the cheek bones. Each rounded lobe of the vegetable leaf, too, is a thick and now loitering drop, larger or smaller; the lobes are the fingers of the leaf; and as many lobes as it has, in so many directions it tends to flow, and more heat or other genial influences would have caused it to flow yet farther.

Thus it seemed that this one hillside illustrated the principle of all the operations of Nature. The Maker of this earth but patented a leaf. What Champollion will decipher this hiero-glyphic for us, that we may turn over a new leaf at last? This phenomenon is more exhilarating to me than the luxuriance and fertility of vineyards. True, it is somewhat excrementi-tious in its character, and there is no end to the heaps of liver lights and bowels, as if the globe were turned wrong side outward; but this suggests at least that Nature has some bow-els, and there again is mother of humanity. This is the frost coming out of the ground; this is Spring. It precedes the green and flowery spring, as mythology precedes regular po-etry. I know of nothing more purgative of winter fumes and indigestions. It convinces me that Earth is still in her swad-dling clothes, and stretches forth baby fingers on every side. Fresh curls spring from the baldest brow. There is nothing inorganic. These foliaceous heaps lie along the bank like the slag of a furnace, showing that Nature is "in full blast" within. The earth is not a mere fragment of dead history, stratum upon stratum like the leaves of a book, to be studied by geologists and antiquaries chiefly, but living poetry like the leaves of a tree, which precede flowers and fruit,—not a fossil earth, but a living earth; compared with whose great central life all animal and vegetable life is merely parasitic. Its throes will heave our exuviæ from their graves. You may melt your metals and cast them into the most beautiful moulds you can; they will never excite me like the forms which this molten earth flows out into. And not only it, but the institutions upon it, are plastic like clay in the hands of the potter.

Ere long, not only on these banks, but on every hill and plain and in every hollow, the frost comes out of the ground like a dormant quadruped from its burrow, and seeks the sea with music, or migrates to other climes in clouds. Thaw with his gentle persuasion is more powerful than Thor with his hammer. The one melts, the other but breaks in pieces.

When the ground was partially bare of snow, and a few warm days had dried its surface somewhat, it was pleasant to compare the first tender signs of the infant year just peeping forth with the stately beauty of the withered vegetation which had withstood the winter,—life-everlasting, golden-rods, pinweeds, and graceful wild grasses, more obvious and interesting frequently than in summer even, as if their beauty was not ripe till then; even cotton-grass, cat-tails, mulleins, johnswort, hard-hack, meadow-sweet, and other strong stemmed plants, those unexhausted granaries which entertain the earliest birds,—decent weeds, at least, which widowed Nature wears. I am particularly attracted by the arching and sheaf-like top of the wool-grass; it brings back the summer to our winter memories, and is among the forms which art loves to copy, and which, in the vegetable kingdom, have the same relation to types already in the mind of man that astronomy has. It is an antique style older than Greek or Egyptian. Many of the phenomena of Winter are suggestive of an inexpressible tenderness and fragile delicacy. We are accustomed to hear this king described as a rude and boisterous tyrant; but with the gentleness of a lover he adorns the tresses of Summer.

At the approach of spring the red-squirrels got under my house, two at a time, directly under my feet as I sat reading or writing, and kept up the queerest chuckling and chirruping and vocal pirouetting and gurgling sounds that ever were heard; and when I stamped they only chirruped the louder, as if past all fear and respect in their mad pranks, defying humanity to stop them. No you don't—chickaree—chickaree. They were wholly deaf to my arguments, or failed to perceive their force, and fell into a strain of invective that was irresistible.

The first sparrow of spring! The year beginning with younger hope than ever! The faint silvery warblings heard over the partially bare and moist fields from the blue-bird, the song-sparrow, and the red-wing, as if the last flakes of winter tinkled as they fell! What at such a time are histories, chronologies, traditions, and all written revelations? The brooks sing carols and glees to the spring. The marsh-hawk sailing low over the meadow is already seeking the first slimy life that awakes. The sinking sound of melting snow is heard in all dells, and the ice dissolves apace in the ponds. The grass flames up on the hillsides like a spring fire,—"et primitus oritur herba imbribus primoribus evocata,"—as if the earth sent forth an inward heat to greet the returning sun; not yellow but green is the color of its flame;—the symbol of perpetual youth, the grass-blade, like a long green ribbon, streams from the sod into the summer, checked indeed by the frost, but anon pushing on again, lifting its spear of last year's hay with the fresh life below. It grows as steadily as the rill oozes out of the ground. It is almost identical with that, for in the growing days of June, when the rills are dry, the grass blades are their channels, and from year to year the herds drink at this perennial green stream, and the mower draws from it betimes their winter supply. So our human life but dies down to its root, and still puts forth its green blade to eternity.

Walden is melting apace. There is a canal two rods wide along the northerly and westerly sides, and wider still at the east end. A great field of ice has cracked off from the main body. I hear a song-sparrow singing from the bushes on the shore,— *olit, olit, olit,* — *chip, chip, chip, che char,* — *che wiss, wiss, wiss.* He too is helping to crack it. How handsome the great sweeping curves in the edge of the ice, answering somewhat to those of the shore, but more regular! It is unusually hard, owing to the recent severe but transient cold, and all watered or waved like a palace floor. But the wind slides eastward over its opaque surface in vain, till it reaches the living surface beyond. It is glorious to behold this ribbon of water sparkling in the sun, the bare face of the pond full of glee and youth, as if it spoke the joy of the fishes within it, and of the sands on its shore,—a silvery sheen as from the scales of a *leuciscus*, as it were all one active fish. Such is the contrast between winter and spring. Walden was dead and is alive again. But this spring it broke up more steadily, as I have said.

The change from storm and winter to serene and mild

weather, from dark and sluggish hours to bright and elastic ones, is a memorable crisis which all things proclaim. It is seemingly instantaneous at last. Suddenly an influx of light filled my house, though the evening was at hand, and the clouds of winter still overhung it, and the eaves were dripping with sleety rain. I looked out the window, and lo! where yesterday was cold gray ice there lay the transparent pond already calm and full of hope as on a summer evening, reflecting a summer evening sky in its bosom, though none was visible overhead, as if it had intelligence with some remote horizon. I heard a robin in the distance, the first I had heard for many a thousand years, methought, whose note I shall not forget for many a thousand more,—the same sweet and powerful song as of yore. O the evening robin, at the end of a New England summer day! If I could ever find the twig he sits upon! I mean *he*; I mean *the twig*. This at least is not the *Turdus migratorius*. The pitch-pines and shrub-oaks about my house, which had so long drooped, suddenly resumed their several characters, looked brighter, greener, and more erect and alive, as if effectually cleansed and restored by the rain. I knew that it would not rain any more. You may tell by looking at any twig of the forest, ay, at your very wood-pile, whether its winter is past or not. As it grew darker, I was startled by the *honking* of geese flying low over the woods, like weary travellers getting in late from southern lakes, and indulging at last in unrestrained complaint and mutual consolation. Standing at my door, I could hear the rush of their wings; when, driving toward my house, they suddenly spied my light, and with hushed clamor wheeled and settled in the pond. So I came in, and shut the door, and passed my first spring night in the woods.

In the morning I watched the geese from the door through the mist, sailing in the middle of the pond, fifty rods off, so large and tumultuous that Walden appeared like an artificial pond for their amusement. But when I stood on the shore they at once rose up with a great flapping of wings at the signal of their commander, and when they had got into rank circled about over my head, twenty-nine of them, and then steered straight to Canada, with a regular *honk* from the leader at intervals, trusting to break their fast in muddier

pools. A "plump" of ducks rose at the same time and took
the route to the north in the wake of their noisier cousins.

For a week I heard the circling groping clangor of some
solitary goose in the foggy mornings, seeking its companion,
and still peopling the woods with the sound of a larger life
than they could sustain. In April the pigeons were seen again
flying express in small flocks, and in due time I heard the
martins twittering over my clearing, though it had not
seemed that the township contained so many that it could
afford me any, and I fancied that they were peculiarly of the
ancient race that dwelt in hollow trees ere white men came.
In almost all climes the tortoise and the frog are among the
precursors and heralds of this season, and birds fly with song
and glancing plumage, and plants spring and bloom, and
winds blow, to correct this slight oscillation of the poles and
preserve the equilibrium of Nature.

As every season seems best to us in its turn, so the coming
in of spring is like the creation of Cosmos out of Chaos and
the realization of the Golden Age. —

> "Eurus ad Auroram, Nabathæaque regna recessit,
>   Persidaque, et radiis juga subdita matutinis."

> "The East-Wind withdrew to Aurora and the Nabathæan
>   kingdom,
>   And the Persian, and the ridges placed under the morning
>   rays.
>
> *   *   *   *
>
> Man was born. Whether that Artificer of things,
>   The origin of a better world, made him from the divine
>   seed;
>   Or the earth being recent and lately sundered from the
>   high
>   Ether, retained some seeds of cognate heaven."

A single gentle rain makes the grass many shades greener.
So our prospects brighten on the influx of better thoughts.
We should be blessed if we lived in the present always, and
took advantage of every accident that befell us, like the grass
which confesses the influence of the slightest dew that falls on

it; and did not spend our time in atoning for the neglect of past opportunities, which we call doing our duty. We loiter in winter while it is already spring. In a pleasant spring morning all men's sins are forgiven. Such a day is a truce to vice. While such a sun holds out to burn, the vilest sinner may return. Through our own recovered innocence we discern the innocence of our neighbors. You may have known your neighbor yesterday for a thief, a drunkard, or a sensualist, and merely pitied or despised him, and despaired of the world; but the sun shines bright and warm this first spring morning, recreating the world, and you meet him at some serene work, and see how his exhausted and debauched veins expand with still joy and bless the new day, feel the spring influence with the innocence of infancy, and all his faults are forgotten. There is not only an atmosphere of good will about him, but even a savor of holiness groping for expression, blindly and ineffectually perhaps, like a new-born instinct, and for a short hour the south hill-side echoes to no vulgar jest. You see some innocent fair shoots preparing to burst from his gnarled rind and try another year's life, tender and fresh as the youngest plant. Even he has entered into the joy of his Lord. Why the jailer does not leave open his prison doors,—why the judge does not dismiss his case,—why the preacher does not dismiss his congregation! It is because they do not obey the hint which God gives them, nor accept the pardon which he freely offers to all.

"A return to goodness produced each day in the tranquil and beneficent breath of the morning, causes that in respect to the love of virtue and the hatred of vice, one approaches a little the primitive nature of man, as the sprouts of the forest which has been felled. In like manner the evil which one does in the interval of a day prevents the germs of virtues which began to spring up again from developing themselves and destroys them.

"After the germs of virtue have thus been prevented many times from developing themselves, then the beneficent breath of evening does not suffice to preserve them. As soon as the breath of evening does not suffice longer to preserve them, then the nature of man does not differ much from that of the brute. Men seeing the nature of this man like that of the brute, think that he has never possessed the innate faculty of reason. Are those the true and natural sentiments of man?"

"The Golden Age was first created, which without any
    avenger
Spontaneously without law cherished fidelity and rectitude.
Punishment and fear were not; nor were threatening words
    read
On suspended brass; nor did the suppliant crowd fear
The words of their judge; but were safe without an
    avenger.
Not yet the pine felled on its mountains had descended
To the liquid waves that it might see a foreign world,
And mortals knew no shores but their own.
       *   *   *   *
There was eternal spring, and placid zephyrs with warm
Blasts soothed the flowers born without seed."

On the 29th of April, as I was fishing from the bank of the river near the Nine-Acre-Corner bridge, standing on the quaking grass and willow roots, where the muskrats lurk, I heard a singular rattling sound, somewhat like that of the sticks which boys play with their fingers, when, looking up, I observed a very slight and graceful hawk, like a night-hawk, alternately soaring like a ripple and tumbling a rod or two over and over, showing the underside of its wings, which gleamed like a satin ribbon in the sun, or like the pearly inside of a shell. This sight reminded me of falconry and what nobleness and poetry are associated with that sport. The Merlin it seemed to me it might be called: but I care not for its name. It was the most ethereal flight I had ever witnessed. It did not simply flutter like a butterfly, nor soar like the larger hawks, but it sported with proud reliance in the fields of air; mounting again and again with its strange chuckle, it repeated its free and beautiful fall, turning over and over like a kite, and then recovering from its lofty tumbling, as if it had never set its foot on *terra firma*. It appeared to have no companion in the universe,—sporting there alone,—and to need none but the morning and the ether with which it played. It was not lonely, but made all the earth lonely beneath it. Where was the parent which hatched it, its kindred, and its father in the heavens? The tenant of the air, it seemed related to the earth but by an egg hatched some time in the crevice of a crag;— or was its native nest made in the angle of a cloud, woven of the rainbow's trimmings and the sunset sky, and lined with some soft midsummer haze caught up from earth? Its eyry now some cliffy cloud.

Beside this I got a rare mess of golden and silver and bright cupreous fishes, which looked like a string of jewels. Ah! I have penetrated to those meadows on the morning of many a first spring day, jumping from hummock to hummock, from willow root to willow root, when the wild river valley and the woods were bathed in so pure and bright a light as would have waked the dead, if they had been slumbering in their graves, as some suppose. There needs no stronger proof of immortality. All things must live in such a light. O Death, where was thy sting? O Grave, where was thy victory, then?

Our village life would stagnate if it were not for the unexplored forests and meadows which surround it. We need the tonic of wildness,—to wade sometimes in marshes where the bittern and the meadow-hen lurk, and hear the booming of the snipe; to smell the whispering sedge where only some wilder and more solitary fowl builds her nest, and the mink crawls with its belly close to the ground. At the same time that we are earnest to explore and learn all things, we require that all things be mysterious and unexplorable, that land and sea be infinitely wild, unsurveyed and unfathomed by us because unfathomable. We can never have enough of Nature. We must be refreshed by the sight of inexhaustible vigor, vast and Titanic features, the sea-coast with its wrecks, the wilderness with its living and its decaying trees, the thunder cloud, and the rain which lasts three weeks and produces freshets. We need to witness our own limits transgressed, and some life pasturing freely where we never wander. We are cheered when we observe the vulture feeding on the carrion which disgusts and disheartens us and deriving health and strength from the repast. There was a dead horse in the hollow by the path to my house, which compelled me sometimes to go out of my way, especially in the night when the air was heavy, but the assurance it gave me of the strong appetite and inviolable health of Nature was my compensation for this. I love to see that Nature is so rife with life that myriads can be afforded to be sacrificed and suffered to prey on one another; that tender organizations can be so serenely squashed out of existence like pulp,—tadpoles which herons gobble up, and tortoises and toads run over in the road; and that sometimes it has rained flesh and blood! With the liability to accident, we must see how little account is to be made of it. The impression made on a wise man is that of universal innocence. Poison is not poisonous after all, nor are any wounds fatal. Compassion is a very untenable ground. It must be expeditious. Its pleadings will not bear to be stereotyped.

Early in May, the oaks, hickories, maples, and other trees, just putting out amidst the pine woods around the pond, imparted a brightness like sunshine to the landscape, especially in cloudy days, as if the sun were breaking through mists and shining faintly on the hill-sides here and there. On the third or fourth of May I saw a loon in the pond, and during the first week of the month I heard the whippoorwill, the brown-thrasher, the veery, the wood-pewee, the chewink, and other birds. I had heard the wood-thrush long before. The phœbe had already come once more and looked in at my door and window, to see if my house was cavern-like enough for her, sustaining herself on humming wings with clinched talons, as if she held by the air, while she surveyed the premises. The sulphur-like pollen of the pitch-pine soon covered the pond and the stones and rotten wood along the shore, so that you could have collected a barrel-ful. This is the "sulphur showers" we hear of. Even in Calidas' drama of Sacontala, we read of "rills dyed yellow with the golden dust of the lotus." And so the seasons went rolling on into summer, as one rambles into higher and higher grass.

Thus was my first year's life in the woods completed; and the second year was similar to it. I finally left Walden September 6th, 1847.

Conclusion

To the sick the doctors wisely recommend a change of air and scenery. Thank Heaven, here is not all the world. The buck-eye does not grow in New England, and the mocking-bird is rarely heard here. The wild-goose is more of a cosmopolite than we; he breaks his fast in Canada, takes a luncheon in the Ohio, and plumes himself for the night in a southern bayou. Even the bison, to some extent, keeps pace with the seasons, cropping the pastures of the Colorado only till a greener and sweeter grass awaits him by the Yellowstone. Yet we think that if rail-fences are pulled down, and stone-walls piled up on our farms, bounds are henceforth set to our lives and our fates decided. If you are chosen town-clerk, forsooth, you cannot go to Tierra del Fuego this summer: but you may go to the land of infernal fire nevertheless. The universe is wider than our views of it.

Yet we should oftener look over the tafferel of our craft, like curious passengers, and not make the voyage like stupid sailors picking oakum. The other side of the globe is but the home of our correspondent. Our voyaging is only great-circle sailing, and the doctors prescribe for diseases of the skin merely. One hastens to Southern Africa to chase the giraffe; but surely that is not the game he would be after. How long, pray, would a man hunt giraffes if he could? Snipes and woodcocks also may afford rare sport; but I trust it would be nobler game to shoot one's self.—

> "Direct your eye sight inward, and you'll find
> A thousand regions in your mind
> Yet undiscovered. Travel them, and be
> Expert in home-cosmography."

What does Africa,—what does the West stand for? Is not our own interior white on the chart? black though it may prove, like the coast, when discovered. Is it the source of the Nile, or the Niger, or the Mississippi, or a North-West Passage around this continent, that we would find? Are these the problems which most concern mankind? Is Franklin the only man who is lost, that his wife should be so earnest to find him? Does Mr. Grinnell know where he himself is? Be rather the Mungo Park, the Lewis and Clarke and Frobisher, of your own streams and oceans; explore your own higher latitudes,—with shiploads of preserved meats to support you, if they be necessary; and pile the empty cans sky-high for a sign. Were preserved meats invented to preserve meat merely? Nay, be a Columbus to whole new continents and worlds within you, opening new channels, not of trade, but of thought. Every man is the lord of a realm beside which the earthly empire of the Czar is but a petty state, a hummock left by the ice. Yet some can be patriotic who have no *self*-respect, and sacrifice the greater to the less. They love the soil which makes their graves, but have no sympathy with the spirit which may still animate their clay. Patriotism is a maggot in their heads. What was the meaning of that South-Sea Exploring Expedition, with all its parade and expense, but an indirect recognition of the fact, that there are continents and seas in the moral world, to which every man is an isthmus or an inlet, yet unexplored by him, but that it is easier to sail many thousand miles through cold and storm and cannibals, in a government ship, with five hundred men and boys to assist one, than it is to explore the private sea, the Atlantic and Pacific Ocean of one's being alone.—

> "Erret, et extremos alter scrutetur Iberos.
> Plus habet hic vitæ, plus habet ille viæ."

Let them wander and scrutinize the outlandish Australians. I have more of God, they more of the road.

It is not worth the while to go round the world to count the cats in Zanzibar. Yet do this even till you can do better, and you may perhaps find some "Symmes' Hole" by which to get at the inside at last. England and France, Spain and Portugal, Gold Coast and Slave Coast, all front on this private sea; but no bark from them has ventured out of sight of land, though it is without doubt the direct way to India. If you would learn to speak all tongues and conform to the customs of all nations, if you would travel farther than all travellers, be naturalized in all climes, and cause the Sphinx to dash her head against a stone, even obey the precept of the old philosopher, and Explore thyself. Herein are demanded the eye and the nerve. Only the defeated and deserters go to the wars, cowards that run away and enlist. Start now on that farthest western way, which does not pause at the Mississippi or the Pacific, nor conduct toward a worn-out China or Japan, but leads on direct a tangent to this sphere, summer and winter, day and night, sun down, moon down, and at last earth down too.

It is said that Mirabeau took to highway robbery "to ascertain what degree of resolution was necessary in order to place one's self in formal opposition to the most sacred laws of society." He declared that "a soldier who fights in the ranks does not require half so much courage as a foot-pad,"—"that honor and religion have never stood in the way of a well-considered and a firm resolve." This was manly, as the world goes; and yet it was idle, if not desperate. A saner man would have found himself often enough "in formal opposition" to what are deemed "the most sacred laws of society," through obedience to yet more sacred laws, and so have tested his resolution without going out of his way. It is not for a man to put himself in such an attitude to society, but to maintain himself in whatever attitude he find himself through obedience to the laws of his being, which will never be one of opposition to a just government, if he should chance to meet with such.

I left the woods for as good a reason as I went there. Perhaps it seemed to me that I had several more lives to live, and could not spare any more time for that one. It is remarkable how easily and insensibly we fall into a particular route, and make a beaten track for ourselves. I had not lived there a week before my feet wore a path from my door to the pond-side; and though it is five or six years since I trod it, it is still quite distinct. It is true, I fear that others may have fallen into it, and so helped to keep it open. The surface of the earth is soft and impressible by the feet of men; and so with the paths which the mind travels. How worn and dusty, then, must be the highways of the world, how deep the ruts of tradition and conformity! I did not wish to take a cabin passage, but rather to go before the mast and on the deck of the world, for there I could best see the moonlight amid the mountains. I do not wish to go below now.

I learned this, at least, by my experiment; that if one advances confidently in the direction of his dreams, and endeavors to live the life which he has imagined, he will meet with a success unexpected in common hours. He will put some things behind, will pass an invisible boundary; new, universal, and more liberal laws will begin to establish themselves around and within him; or the old laws be expanded, and interpreted in his favor in a more liberal sense, and he will live with the license of a higher order of beings. In proportion as he simplifies his life, the laws of the universe will appear less complex, and solitude will not be solitude, nor poverty poverty, nor weakness weakness. If you have built castles in the air, your work need not be lost; that is where they should be. Now put the foundations under them.

It is a ridiculous demand which England and America make, that you shall speak so that they can understand you. Neither men nor toad-stools grow so. As if that were important, and there were not enough to understand you without them. As if Nature could support but one order of understandings, could not sustain birds as well as quadrupeds, flying as well as creeping things, and *hush* and *who*, which Bright can understand, were the best English. As if there were safety in stupidity alone. I fear chiefly lest my expression may not be *extra- vagant* enough, may not wander far enough beyond the narrow limits of my daily experience, so as to be adequate to the truth of which I have been convinced. *Extra vagance!* it depends on how you are yarded. The migrating buffalo, which seeks new pastures in another latitude, is not extravagant like the cow which kicks over the pail, leaps the cow-yard fence, and runs after her calf, in milking time. I desire to speak somewhere *without* bounds; like a man in a waking moment, to men in their waking moments; for I am convinced that I cannot exaggerate enough even to lay the foundation of a true expression. Who that has heard a strain of music feared then lest he should speak extravagantly any more forever? In view of the future or possible, we should live quite laxly and undefined in front, our outlines dim and misty on that side; as our shadows reveal an insensible perspiration toward the sun. The volatile truth of our words should continually betray the inadequacy of the residual statement. Their truth is instantly *translated*; its literal monument alone remains. The words which express our faith and piety are not definite; yet they are significant and fragrant like frankincense to superior natures.

Why level downward to our dullest perception always, and praise that as common sense? The commonest sense is the sense of men asleep, which they express by snoring. Sometimes we are inclined to class those who are once-and-a-half witted with the half-witted, because we appreciate only a third part of their wit. Some would find fault with the morning-red, if they ever got up early enough. "They pretend," as I hear, "that the verses of Kabir have four different senses; illusion, spirit, intellect, and the exoteric doctrine of the Vedas;" but in this part of the world it is considered a ground for complaint if a man's writings admit of more than one interpretation. While England endeavors to cure the potato-rot, will not any endeavor to cure the brain-rot, which prevails so much more widely and fatally?

I do not suppose that I have attained to obscurity, but I should be proud if no more fatal fault were found with my pages on this score than was found with the Walden ice. Southern customers objected to its blue color, which is the evidence of its purity, as if it were muddy, and preferred the Cambridge ice, which is white, but tastes of weeds. The purity men love is like the mists which envelop the earth, and not like the azure ether beyond.

Some are dinning in our ears that we Americans, and moderns generally, are intellectual dwarfs compared with the ancients, or even the Elizabethan men. But what is that to the purpose? A living dog is better than a dead lion. Shall a man go and hang himself because he belongs to the race of pygmies, and not be the biggest pygmy that he can? Let every one mind his own business, and endeavor to be what he was made.

Why should we be in such desperate haste to succeed, and in such desperate enterprises? If a man does not keep pace with his companions, perhaps it is because he hears a different drummer. Let him step to the music which he hears, however measured or far away. It is not important that he should mature as soon as an apple-tree or an oak. Shall he turn his spring into summer? If the condition of things which we were made for is not yet, what were any reality which we can substitute? We will not be shipwrecked on a vain reality. Shall we with pains erect a heaven of blue glass over ourselves, though when it is done we shall be sure to gaze still at the true ethereal heaven far above, as if the former were not?

There was an artist in the city of Kouroo who was disposed to strive after perfection. One day it came into his mind to make a staff. Having considered that in an imperfect work time is an ingredient, but into a perfect work time does not enter, he said to himself, It shall be perfect in all respects, though I should do nothing else in my life. He proceeded instantly to the forest for wood, being resolved that it should not be made of unsuitable material; and as he searched for and rejected stick after stick, his friends gradually deserted him, for they grew old in their works and died, but he grew not older by a moment. His singleness of purpose and resolution, and his elevated piety, endowed him, without his knowledge, with perennial youth. As he made no compromise with Time, Time kept out of his way, and only sighed at a distance because he could not overcome him. Before he had found a stock in all respects suitable the city of Kouroo was a hoary ruin, and he sat on one of its mounds to peel the stick. Before he had given it the proper shape the dynasty of the Candahars was at an end, and with the point of the stick he wrote the name of the last of that race in the sand, and then resumed his work. By the time he had smoothed and polished the staff Kalpa was no longer the pole-star; and ere he had put on the ferule and the head adorned with precious stones, Brahma had awoke and slumbered many times. But why do I stay to mention these things? When the finishing stroke was put to his work, it suddenly expanded before the eyes of the astonished artist into the fairest of all the creations of Brahma. He had made a new system in making a staff, a world with full and fair proportions; in which, though the old cities and dynasties had passed away, fairer and more glorious ones had taken their places. And now he saw by the heap of shavings still fresh at his feet, that, for him and his work, the former lapse of time had been an illusion, and that no more time had elapsed than is required for a single scintillation from the brain of Brahma to fall on and inflame the tinder of a mortal brain. The material was pure, and his art was pure; how could the result be other than wonderful?

No face which we can give to a matter will stead us so well at last as the truth. This alone wears well. For the most part, we are not where we are, but in a false position. Through an infirmity of our natures, we suppose a case, and put ourselves into it, and hence are in two cases at the same time, and it is doubly difficult to get out. In sane moments we regard only the facts, the case that is. Say what you have to say, not what you ought. Any truth is better than make-believe. Tom Hyde, the tinker, standing on the gallows, was asked if he had any thing to say. "Tell the tailors," said he, "to remember to make a knot in their thread before they take the first stitch." His companion's prayer is forgotten.

However mean your life is, meet it and live it; do not shun it and call it hard names. It is not so bad as you are. It looks poorest when you are richest. The fault-finder will find faults even in paradise. Love your life, poor as it is. You may per-haps have some pleasant, thrilling, glorious hours, even in a poor-house. The setting sun is reflected from the windows of the alms-house as brightly as from the rich man's abode; the snow melts before its door as early in the spring. I do not see but a quiet mind may live as contentedly there, and have as cheering thoughts, as in a palace. The town's poor seem to me often to live the most independent lives of any. May be they are simply great enough to receive without misgiving. Most think that they are above being supported by the town; but it oftener happens that they are not above supporting themselves by dishonest means, which should be more disrep-utable. Cultivate poverty like a garden herb, like sage. Do not trouble yourself much to get new things, whether clothes or friends. Turn the old; return to them. Things do not change; we change. Sell your clothes and keep your thoughts. God will see that you do not want society. If I were confined to a corner of a garret all my days, like a spider, the world would be just as large to me while I had my thoughts about me. The philosopher said: "From an army of three divisions one can take away its general, and put it in disorder; from the man the most abject and vulgar one cannot take away his thought." Do not seek so anxiously to be developed, to subject yourself to many influences to be played on; it is all dissipation. Humility like darkness reveals the heavenly lights. The shadows of poverty and meanness gather around us, "and lo! creation widens to our view." We are often reminded that if there were bestowed on us the wealth of Crœsus, our aims must still be the same, and our means essentially the same. Moreover, if you are restricted in your range by poverty, if you cannot buy books and newspapers, for instance, you are but confined to the most significant and vital experiences; you are compelled to deal with the material which yields the most sugar and the most starch. It is life near the bone where it is sweetest. You are defended from being a trifler. No man loses ever on a lower level by magnanimity on a higher. Superfluous wealth can buy superfluities only. Money is not required to buy one necessary of the soul.

I live in the angle of a leaden wall, into whose composition was poured a little alloy of bell metal. Often, in the repose of my mid-day, there reaches my ears a confused *tintinnabulum* from without. It is the noise of my contemporaries. My neighbors tell me of their adventures with famous gentlemen and ladies, what notabilities they met at the dinner-table; but I am no more interested in such things than in the contents of the Daily Times. The interest and the conversation are about costume and manners chiefly; but a goose is a goose still, dress it as you will. They tell me of California and Texas, of England and the Indies, of the Hon. Mr. —— of Georgia or of Massachusetts, all transient and fleeting phenomena, till I am ready to leap from their court-yard like the Mameluke bey. I delight to come to my bearings,—not walk in procession with pomp and parade, in a conspicuous place, but to walk even with the Builder of the universe, if I may,—not to live in this restless, nervous, bustling, trivial Nineteenth Century, but stand or sit thoughtfully while it goes by. What are men celebrating? They are all on a committee of arrangements, and hourly expect a speech from somebody. God is only the president of the day, and Webster is his orator. I love to weigh, to settle, to gravitate toward that which most strongly and rightfully attracts me;—not hang by the beam of the scale and try to weigh less,—not suppose a case, but take the case that is; to travel the only path I can, and that on which no power can resist me. It affords me no satisfaction to commence to spring an arch before I have got a solid foundation. Let us not play at kittlybenders. There is a solid bottom every where. We read that the traveller asked the boy if the swamp before him had a hard bottom. The boy replied that it had. But presently the traveller's horse sank in up to the girths, and he observed to the boy, "I thought you said that this bog had a hard bottom." "So it has," answered the latter, "but you have not got half way to it yet." So it is with the bogs and quicksands of society; but he is an old boy that knows it. Only what is thought said or done at a certain rare coincidence is good. I would not be one of those who will foolishly drive a nail into mere lath and plastering; such a deed would keep me awake nights. Give me a hammer, and let me feel for the furrowing. Do not depend on the putty. Drive a nail home and clinch it so faithfully that you can wake up in the night and think of your work with satisfaction,—a work at which you would not be ashamed to invoke the Muse. So will help you God, and so only. Every nail driven should be as another rivet in the machine of the universe, you carrying on the work.

Rather than love, than money, than fame, give me truth. I sat at a table where were rich food and wine in abundance, and obsequious attendance, but sincerity and truth were not; and I went away hungry from the inhospitable board. The hospitality was as cold as the ices. I thought that there was no need of ice to freeze them. They talked to me of the age of the wine and the fame of the vintage; but I thought of an older, a newer, and purer wine, of a more glorious vintage, which they had not got, and could not buy. The style, the house and grounds and "entertainment" pass for nothing with me. I called on the king, but he made me wait in his hall, and conducted like a man incapacitated for hospitality. There was a man in my neighborhood who lived in a hollow tree. His manners were truly regal. I should have done better had I called on him.

How long shall we sit in our porticoes practising idle and musty virtues, which any work would make impertinent? As if one were to begin the day with long-suffering, and hire a man to hoe his potatoes; and in the afternoon go forth to practise Christian meekness and charity with goodness afore-thought! Consider the China pride and stagnant self-complacency of mankind. This generation reclines a little to congratulate itself on being the last of an illustrious line; and in Boston and London and Paris and Rome, thinking of its long descent, it speaks of its progress in art and science and literature with satisfaction. There are the Records of the Philosophical Societies, and the public Eulogies of *Great Men!* It is the good Adam contemplating his own virtue. "Yes, we have done great deeds, and sung divine songs, which shall never die,"—that is, as long as *we* can remember them. The learned societies and great men of Assyria,—where are they? What youthful philosophers and experimentalists we are! There is not one of my readers who has yet lived a whole human life. These may be but the spring months in the life of the race. If we have had the seven-years' itch, we have not seen the seventeen-year locust yet in Concord. We are acquainted with a mere pellicle of the globe on which we live. Most have not delved six feet beneath the surface, nor leaped as many above it. We know not where we are. Beside, we are sound asleep nearly half our time. Yet we esteem ourselves wise, and have an established order on the surface. Truly, we are deep thinkers, we are ambitious spirits! As I stand over the insect crawling amid the pine needles on the forest floor, and endeavoring to conceal itself from my sight, and ask myself why it will cherish those humble thoughts, and hide its head from me who might perhaps be its benefactor, and impart to its race some cheering information, I am reminded of the greater Benefactor and Intelligence that stands over me the human insect.

There is an incessant influx of novelty into the world, and yet we tolerate incredible dulness. I need only suggest what kind of sermons are still listened to in the most enlightened countries. There are such words as joy and sorrow, but they are only the burden of a psalm, sung with a nasal twang, while we believe in the ordinary and mean. We think that we can change our clothes only. It is said that the British Empire is very large and respectable, and that the United States are a first-rate power. We do not believe that a tide rises and falls behind every man which can float the British Empire like a chip, if he should ever harbor it in his mind. Who knows what sort of seventeen-year locust will next come out of the ground? The government of the world I live in was not framed, like that of Britain, in after-dinner conversations over the wine.

The life in us is like the water in the river. It may rise this year higher than man has ever known it, and flood the parched uplands; even this may be the eventful year, which will drown out all our muskrats. It was not always dry land where we dwell. I see far inland the banks which the stream anciently washed, before science began to record its freshets. Every one has heard the story which has gone the rounds of New England, of a strong and beautiful bug which came out of the dry leaf of an old table of apple-tree wood, which had stood in a farmer's kitchen for sixty years, first in Connecticut, and afterward in Massachusetts,—from an egg deposited in the living tree many years earlier still, as appeared by counting the annual layers beyond it; which was heard gnawing out for several weeks, hatched perchance by the heat of an urn. Who does not feel his faith in a resurrection and immortality strengthened by hearing of this? Who knows what beautiful and winged life, whose egg has been buried for ages under many concentric layers of woodenness in the dead dry life of society, deposited at first in the alburnum of the green and living tree, which has been gradually converted into the semblance of its well-seasoned tomb,—heard perchance gnawing out now for years by the astonished family of man, as they sat round the festive board,—may unexpectedly come forth from amidst society's most trivial and handselled furniture, to enjoy its perfect summer life at last!

I do not say that John or Jonathan will realize all this; but such is the character of that morrow which mere lapse of time can never make to dawn. The light which puts out our eyes is darkness to us. Only that day dawns to which we are awake. There is more day to dawn. The sun is but a morning star.

THE END.

THE MAINE WOODS

Contents

Ktaadn

O<small>N THE</small> 31st of August, 1846, I left Concord in Massachusetts for Bangor and the backwoods of Maine, by way of the railroad and steamboat, intending to accompany a relative of mine engaged in the lumber-trade in Bangor, as far as a dam on the west branch of the Penobscot, in which property he was interested. From this place, which is about one hundred miles by the river above Bangor, thirty miles from the Houlton military road, and five miles beyond the last log-hut, I proposed to make excursions to Mount Ktaadn, the second highest mountain in New England, about thirty miles distant, and to some of the lakes of the Penobscot, either alone or with such company as I might pick up there. It is unusual to find a camp so far in the woods at that season, when lumbering operations have ceased, and I was glad to avail myself of the circumstance of a gang of men being employed there at that time in repairing the injuries caused by the great freshet in the spring. The mountain may be approached more easily and directly on horseback and on foot from the northeast side, by the Aroostook road, and the Wassataquoik River; but in that case you see much less of the wilderness, none of the glorious river and lake scenery, and have no experience of the batteau and the boatman's life. I was fortunate also in the season of the year, for in the summer myriads of black flies, mosquitoes, and midges, or, as the Indians call them, "no-see-ems," make travelling in the woods almost impossible; but now their reign was nearly over.

Ktaadn, whose name is an Indian word signifying highest land, was first ascended by white men in 1804. It was visited by Professor J. W. Bailey of West Point in 1836; by Dr. Charles T. Jackson, the State Geologist, in 1837; and by two young men from Boston in 1845. All these have given accounts of their expeditions. Since I was there, two or three other parties have made the excursion, and told their stories. Besides these, very few, even among backwoodsmen and hunters, have ever climbed it, and it will be a long time before the tide of fashionable travel sets that way. The mountainous region of the State of Maine stretches from near the White

Mountains, northeasterly one hundred and sixty miles, to the head of the Aroostook River, and is about sixty miles wide. The wild or unsettled portion is far more extensive. So that some hours only of travel in this direction will carry the curious to the verge of a primitive forest, more interesting, perhaps, on all accounts, than they would reach by going a thousand miles westward.

The next forenoon, Tuesday, September 1st, I started with my companion in a buggy from Bangor for "up river," expecting to be overtaken the next day night at Mattawamkeag Point, some sixty miles off, by two more Bangoreans, who had decided to join us in a trip to the mountain. We had each a knapsack or bag filled with such clothing and articles as were indispensable, and my companion carried his gun.

Within a dozen miles of Bangor we passed through the villages of Stillwater and Oldtown, built at the falls of the Penobscot; which furnish the principal power by which the Maine woods are converted into lumber. The mills are built directly over and across the river. Here is a close jam, a hard rub, at all seasons; and then the once green tree, long since white, I need not say as the driven snow, but as a driven log, becomes lumber merely. Here your inch, your two and your three inch stuff begin to be, and Mr. Sawyer marks off those spaces which decide the destiny of so many prostrate forests. Through this steel riddle, more or less coarse, is the arrowy Maine forest, from Ktaadn and Chesuncook, and the head-waters of the St. John, relentlessly sifted, till it comes out boards, clapboards, laths, and shingles such as the wind can take, still perchance to be slit and slit again, till men get a size that will suit. Think how stood the white-pine tree on the shore of Chesuncook, its branches soughing with the four winds, and every individual needle trembling in the sunlight,—think how it stands with it now,—sold, perchance, to the New England Friction-Match Company! There were in 1837, as I read, two hundred and fifty saw-mills on the Penobscot and its tributaries above Bangor, the greater part of them in this immediate neighborhood, and they sawed two hundred millions of feet of boards annually. To this is to be added the lumber of the Kennebec, Androscoggin, Saco, Passamaquoddy, and other streams. No wonder that we hear so

often of vessels which are becalmed off our coast, being surrounded a week at a time by floating lumber from the Maine
woods. The mission of men there seems to be, like so many
busy demons, to drive the forest all out of the country, from
every solitary beaver-swamp and mountain-side, as soon as
possible.

At Oldtown we walked into a batteau-manufactory. The
making of batteaux is quite a business here for the supply of
the Penobscot River. We examined some on the stocks. They
are light and shapely vessels, calculated for rapid and rocky
streams, and to be carried over long portages on men's shoulders, from twenty to thirty feet long, and only four or four
and a half wide, sharp at both ends like a canoe, though
broadest forward on the bottom, and reaching seven or eight
feet over the water, in order that they may slip over rocks as
gently as possible. They are made very slight, only two boards
to a side, commonly secured to a few light maple or other
hard-wood knees, but inward are of the clearest and widest
white-pine stuff, of which there is a great waste on account
of their form, for the bottom is left perfectly flat, not only
from side to side, but from end to end. Sometimes they become "hogging" even, after long use, and the boatmen then
turn them over and straighten them by a weight at each end.
They told us that one wore out in two years, or often in a
single trip, on the rocks, and sold for from fourteen to sixteen
dollars. There was something refreshing and wildly musical to
my ears in the very name of the white man's canoe, reminding
me of Charlevoix and Canadian Voyageurs. The batteau is
a sort of mongrel between the canoe and the boat, a fur-
trader's boat.

The ferry here took us past the Indian island. As we left
the shore, I observed a short, shabby, washerwoman-looking
Indian—they commonly have the woe-begone look of the
girl that cried for spilt milk—just from "up river"—land on
the Oldtown side near a grocery, and, drawing up his canoe,
take out a bundle of skins in one hand, and an empty keg or
half-barrel in the other, and scramble up the bank with them.
This picture will do to put before the Indian's history, that is,
the history of his extinction. In 1837 there were three hundred
and sixty-two souls left of this tribe. The island seemed

deserted to-day, yet I observed some new houses among the weather-stained ones, as if the tribe had still a design upon life; but generally they have a very shabby, forlorn, and cheerless look, being all back side and woodshed, not homesteads, even Indian homesteads, but instead of home or abroadsteads, for their life is *domi aut militiæ*, at home or at war, or now rather *venatus*, that is, a hunting, and most of the latter. The church is the only trim-looking building, but that is not Abenaki, that was Rome's doings. Good Canadian it may be, but it is poor Indian. These were once a powerful tribe. Politics are all the rage with them now. I even thought that a row of wigwams, with a dance of powwows, and a prisoner tortured at the stake, would be more respectable than this.

We landed in Milford, and rode along on the east side of the Penobscot, having a more or less constant view of the river, and the Indian islands in it, for they retain all the islands as far up as Nickatow, at the mouth of the East Branch. They are generally well-timbered, and are said to be better soil than the neighboring shores. The river seemed shallow and rocky, and interrupted by rapids, rippling and gleaming in the sun. We paused a moment to see a fish-hawk dive for a fish down straight as an arrow, from a great height, but he missed his prey this time. It was the Houlton road on which we were now travelling, over which some troops were marched once towards Mars' Hill, though not to Mars' *field*, as it proved. It is the main, almost the only, road in these parts, as straight and well made, and kept in as good repair, as almost any you will find anywhere. Everywhere we saw signs of the great freshet,—this house standing awry, and that where it was not founded, but where it was found, at any rate, the next day; and that other with a water-logged look, as if it were still airing and drying its basement, and logs with everybody's marks upon them, and sometimes the marks of their having served as bridges, strewn along the road. We crossed the Sunkhaze, a summery Indian name, the Olemmon, Passadumkeag, and other streams, which make a greater show on the map than they now did on the road. At Passadumkeag we found anything but what the name implies,—earnest politicians, to wit,—white ones, I mean,—on the alert, to know how the election was likely to go; men who talked rapidly, with subdued voice, and a sort of factitious earnestness, you could not help believing, hardly waiting for an introduction, one on each side of your buggy, endeavoring to say much in little, for they see you hold the whip impatiently, but always saying little in much. Caucuses they have had, it seems, and caucuses they are to have again,—victory and defeat. Somebody may be elected, somebody may not. One man, a total stranger, who stood by our carriage in the dusk, actually frightened the horse with his asseverations, growing more solemnly positive as there was less in him to be positive about. So Passadumkeag did not look on the map. At sundown, leaving the river-road awhile for shortness, we went by way of Enfield, where we stopped for the night. This, like most of the localities bearing names on this road, was a place to name, which, in the midst of the unnamed and unincorporated wilderness, was to make a distinction without a difference, it seemed to me. Here, however, I noticed quite an orchard of healthy and well-grown apple-trees, in a bearing state, it being the oldest settler's house in this region, but all natural fruit, and comparatively worthless for want of a grafter. And so it is generally, lower down the river. It would be a good speculation, as well as a favor conferred on the settlers, for a Massachusetts boy to go down there with a trunk full of choice scions, and his grafting apparatus, in the spring.

The next morning we drove along through a high and hilly country, in view of Cold-Stream Pond, a beautiful lake four or five miles long, and came into the Houlton road again, here called the military road, at Lincoln, forty-five miles from Bangor, where there is quite a village for this country,—the principal one above Oldtown. Learning that there were several wigwams here, on one of the Indian islands, we left our horse and wagon, and walked through the forest half a mile to the river, to procure a guide to the mountain. It was not till after considerable search that we discovered their habitations,—small huts, in a retired place, where the scenery was unusually soft and beautiful, and the shore skirted with pleasant meadows and graceful elms. We paddled ourselves across to the island-side in a canoe, which we found on the shore. Near where we landed sat an Indian girl ten or twelve years old, on a rock in the water, in the sun, washing, and humming or moaning a song meanwhile. It was an aboriginal strain. A salmon-spear, made wholly of wood, lay on the shore, such as they might have used before white men came. It had an elastic piece of wood fastened to one side of its point, which slipped over and closed upon the fish, somewhat like the contrivance for holding a bucket at the end of a well-pole. As we walked up to the nearest house, we were met by a sally of a dozen wolfish-looking dogs, which may have been lineal descendants from the ancient Indian dogs, which the first voyageurs describe as "their wolves." I suppose they were. The occupant soon appeared, with a long pole in his hand, with which he beat off the dogs, while he parleyed with us. A stalwart, but dull and greasy-looking fellow, who told us, in his sluggish way, in answer to our questions, as if it were the first serious business he had to do that day, that there *were* Indians going "up river"—he and one other—to-day, before noon. And who was the other? Louis Neptune, who lives in the next house. Well, let us go over and see Louis together. The same doggish reception, and Louis Neptune makes his appearance,—a small, wiry man, with puckered and wrinkled face, yet he seemed the chief man of the two; the same, as I remembered, who had accompanied Jackson to the mountain in '37. The same questions were put to Louis, and the same information obtained, while the other Indian stood by. It appeared that they were going to start by noon, with two canoes, to go up to Chesuncook to hunt moose,—to be gone a month. "Well, Louis, suppose you get to the Point [to the Five Islands, just below Mattawamkeag], to camp, we walk on up the West Branch to-morrow,—four of us,—and wait for you at the dam, or this side. You overtake us to-morrow or next day, and take us into your canoes. We stop for you, you stop for us. We pay you for your trouble." "Ye!" replied Louis, "may be you carry some provision for all,—some pork,—some bread,—and so pay." He said, "Me sure get some moose"; and when I asked if he thought Pomola would let us go up, he answered that we must plant one bottle of rum on the top; he had planted good many; and when he looked again, the rum was all gone. He had been up two or three times: he had planted letter,—English, German, French, &c. These men were slightly clad in shirt and pantaloons, like laborers with us in warm weather. They did not invite us into their houses, but met us outside. So we left the Indians, thinking ourselves lucky to have secured such guides and companions.

There were very few houses along the road, yet they did not altogether fail, as if the law by which men are dispersed over the globe were a very stringent one, and not to be resisted with impunity or for slight reasons. There were even the germs of one or two villages just beginning to expand. The beauty of the road itself was remarkable. The various evergreens, many of which are rare with us,—delicate and beautiful specimens of the larch, arbor-vitæ, ball-spruce, and fir-balsam, from a few inches to many feet in height,—lined its sides, in some places like a long, front yard, springing up from the smooth grass-plots which uninterruptedly border it, and are made fertile by its wash; while it was but a step on either hand to the grim, untrodden wilderness, whose tangled labyrinth of living, fallen, and decaying trees only the deer and moose, the bear and wolf, can easily penetrate. More perfect specimens than any front-yard plot can show, grew there to grace the passage of the Houlton teams.

About noon we reached the Mattawamkeag, fifty-six miles from Bangor by the way we had come, and put up at a frequented house still on the Houlton road, where the Houlton stage stops. Here was a substantial covered bridge over the Mattawamkeag, built, I think they said, some seventeen years before. We had dinner,—where, by the way, and even at breakfast, as well as supper, at the public-houses on this road, the front rank is composed of various kinds of "sweet cakes," in a continuous line from one end of the table to the other. I think I may safely say that there was a row of ten or a dozen plates of this kind set before us two here. To account for which, they say that, when the lumberers come out of the woods, they have a craving for cakes and pies, and such sweet things, which there are almost unknown, and this is the *supply* to satisfy that *demand*. The supply is always equal to the demand, and these hungry men think a good deal of getting their money's worth. No doubt the balance of victuals is restored by the time they reach Bangor,—Mattawamkeag takes off the raw edge. Well, over this front rank, I say, you, coming from the "sweet cake" side, with a cheap philosophic indifference though it may be, have to assault what there is behind, which I do not by any means mean to insinuate is insufficient in quantity or quality to supply that other demand, of men, not from the woods, but from the towns, for venison and strong country fare. After dinner we strolled down to the "Point," formed by the junction of the two rivers, which is said to be the scene of an ancient battle between the Eastern Indians and the Mohawks, and searched there carefully for relics, though the men at the bar-room had never heard of such things; but we found only some flakes of arrow-head stone, some points of arrow-heads, one small leaden bullet, and some colored beads, the last to be referred, perhaps, to early fur-trader days. The Mattawamkeag, though wide, was a mere river's bed, full of rocks and shallows at this time, so that you could cross it almost dry-shod in boots; and I could hardly believe my companion, when he told me that he had been fifty or sixty miles up it in a batteau, through distant and still uncut forests. A batteau could hardly find a harbor now at its mouth. Deer and carribou, or reindeer, are taken here in the winter, in sight of the house.

Before our companions arrived, we rode on up the Houlton road seven miles, to Molunkus, where the Aroostook road comes into it, and where there is a spacious public house in the woods, called the "Molunkus House," kept by one Libbey, which looked as if it had its hall for dancing and for military drills. There was no other evidence of man but this huge shingle palace in this part of the world; but sometimes even this is filled with travellers. I looked off the piazza round the corner of the house up the Aroostook road, on which there was no clearing in sight. There was a man just adventuring upon it this evening in a rude, original, what you may call Aroostook wagon,—a mere seat, with a wagon swung under it, a few bags on it, and a dog asleep to watch them. He offered to carry a message for us to anybody in that country, cheerfully. I suspect that, if you should go to the end of the world, you would find somebody there going farther, as if just starting for home at sundown, and having a last word before he drove off. Here, too, *was* a small trader, whom I did not see at first, who kept a store—but no great store, certainly—in a small box over the way, behind the Molunkus sign-post. It looked like the balance-box of a patent hay-scales. As for his house, we could only conjecture where that was; he may have been a boarder in the Molunkus House. I saw him standing in his shop-door,—his shop was so small, that, if a traveller should make demonstrations of entering in, *he* would have to go out by the back way, and confer with his customer through a window, about his goods in the cellar, or, more probably, bespoken, and yet on the way. I should have gone in, for I felt a real impulse to trade, if I had not stopped to consider what would become of him. The day before, we had walked into a shop, over against an inn where we stopped, the puny beginning of trade, which would grow at last into a firm copartnership in the future town or city,— indeed, it was already "Somebody & Co.," I forget who. The woman came forward from the penetralia of the attached house, for "Somebody & Co." was in the burning, and she sold us percussion-caps, canalés and smooth, and knew their prices and qualities, and which the hunters preferred. Here was a little of everything in a small compass to satisfy the wants and the ambition of the woods,—a stock selected with what pains and care, and brought home in the wagon-box, or a corner of the Houlton team; but there seemed to me, as usual, a preponderance of children's toys,—dogs to bark, and cats to mew, and trumpets to blow, where natives there hardly are yet. As if a child, born into the Maine woods, among the pine-cones and cedar-berries, could not do without such a sugar-man, or skipping-jack, as the young Rothschild has.

I think that there was not more than one house on the road to Molunkus, or for seven miles. At that place we got over the fence into a new field, planted with potatoes, where the logs were still burning between the hills; and, pulling up the vines, found good-sized potatoes, nearly ripe, growing like weeds, and turnips mixed with them. The mode of clearing and planting is, to fell the trees, and burn once what will burn, then cut them up into suitable lengths, roll into heaps, and burn again; then, with a hoe, plant potatoes where you can come at the ground between the stumps and charred logs; for a first crop the ashes sufficing for manure, and no hoeing being necessary the first year. In the fall, cut, roll, and burn again, and so on, till the land is cleared; and soon it is ready for grain, and to be laid down. Let those talk of poverty and hard times who will in the towns and cities; cannot the emigrant who can pay his fare to New York or Boston pay five dollars more to get here,—I paid three, all told, for my passage from Boston to Bangor, two hundred and fifty miles,—and be as rich as he pleases, where land virtually costs nothing, and houses only the labor of building, and he may begin life as Adam did? If he will still remember the distinction of poor and rich, let him bespeak him a narrower house forthwith.

When we returned to the Mattawamkeag, the Houlton stage had already put up there; and a Province man was betraying his greenness to the Yankees by his questions. Why Province money won't pass here at par, when States' money is good at Frederickton,—though this, perhaps, was sensible enough. From what I saw then, it appears that the Province man was now the only real Jonathan, or raw country bumpkin, left so far behind by his enterprising neighbors that he did n't know enough to put a question to them. No people can long continue provincial in character who have the propensity for politics and whittling, and rapid travelling, which the Yankees have, and who are leaving the mother country behind in the variety of their notions and inventions. The possession and exercise of practical talent merely are a sure and rapid means of intellectual culture and independence.

The last edition of Greenleaf's Map of Maine hung on the wall here, and, as we had no pocket-map, we resolved to trace a map of the lake country. So, dipping a wad of tow into the lamp, we oiled a sheet of paper on the oiled table-cloth, and, in good faith, traced what we afterwards ascertained to be a labyrinth of errors, carefully following the outlines of the imaginary lakes which the map contains. The Map of the Public Lands of Maine and Massachusetts is the only one I have seen that at all deserves the name. It was while we were engaged in this operation that our companions arrived. They had seen the Indians' fire on the Five Islands, and so we concluded that all was right.

Early the next morning we had mounted our packs, and

prepared for a tramp up the West Branch, my companion having turned his horse out to pasture for a week or ten days, thinking that a bite of fresh grass, and a taste of running water, would do him as much good as backwoods fare and new country influences his master. Leaping over a fence, we began to follow an obscure trail up the northern bank of the Penobscot. There was now no road further, the river being the only highway, and but half a dozen log-huts confined to its banks, to be met with for thirty miles. On either hand, and beyond, was a wholly uninhabited wilderness, stretching to Canada. Neither horse nor cow, nor vehicle of any kind, had ever passed over this ground; the cattle, and the few bulky articles which the loggers use, being got up in the winter on the ice, and down again before it breaks up. The evergreen woods had a decidedly sweet and bracing fragrance; the air was a sort of diet-drink, and we walked on buoyantly in Indian file, stretching our legs. Occasionally there was a small opening on the bank, made for the purpose of log-rolling, where we got a sight of the river,—always a rocky and rippling stream. The roar of the rapids, the note of a whistler-duck on the river, of the jay and chickadee around us, and of the pigeon-woodpecker in the openings, were the sounds that we heard. This was what you might call a bran-new country; the only roads were of Nature's making, and the few houses were camps. Here, then, one could no longer accuse institutions and society, but must front the true source of evil.

There are three classes of inhabitants who either frequent or inhabit the country which we had now entered;—first, the loggers, who, for a part of the year, the winter and spring, are far the most numerous, but in the summer, except a few explorers for timber, completely desert it; second, the few settlers I have named, the only permanent inhabitants, who live on the verge of it, and help raise supplies for the former; third, the hunters, mostly Indians, who range over it in their season.

At the end of three miles, we came to the Mattaseunk stream and mill, where there was even a rude wooden railroad running down to the Penobscot, the last railroad we were to see. We crossed one tract, on the bank of the river, of more than a hundred acres of heavy timber, which had just been felled and burnt over, and was still smoking. Our trail lay through the midst of it, and was wellnigh blotted out. The trees lay at full length, four or five feet deep, and crossing each other in all directions, all black as charcoal, but perfectly sound within, still good for fuel or for timber; soon they would be cut into lengths and burnt again. Here were thousands of cords, enough to keep the poor of Boston and New York amply warm for a winter, which only cumbered the ground and were in the settler's way. And the whole of that solid and interminable forest is doomed to be gradually devoured thus by fire, like shavings, and no man be warmed by it. At Crocker's log-hut, at the mouth of Salmon River, seven miles from the Point, one of the party commenced distributing a store of small cent picture-books among the children, to teach them to read, and also newspapers, more or less recent, among the parents, than which nothing can be more acceptable to a backwoods people. It was really an important item in our outfit, and, at times, the only currency that would circulate. I walked through Salmon River with my shoes on, it being low water, but not without wetting my feet. A few miles farther we came to "Marm Howard's," at the end of an extensive clearing, where there were two or three log-huts in sight at once, one on the opposite side of the river, and a few graves, even surrounded by a wooden paling, where already the rude forefathers of *a* hamlet lie, and a thousand years hence, perchance, some poet will write his "Elegy in a Country Churchyard." The "Village Hampdens," the "mute, inglorious Miltons," and Cromwells, "guiltless of" their "country's blood," were yet unborn.

> "Perchance in this *wild* spot *there will be* laid
> Some heart once pregnant with celestial fire;
> Hands that the rod of empire might have swayed,
> Or waked to ecstasy the living lyre."

The next house was Fisk's, ten miles from the Point, at the mouth of the East Branch, opposite to the island Nickatow, or the Forks, the last of the Indian islands. I am particular to give the names of the settlers and the distances, since every log-hut in these woods is a public house, and such information is of no little consequence to those who may have occasion to travel this way. Our course here crossed the Penobscot, and followed the southern bank. One of the party, who entered the house in search of some one to set us over, reported a very neat dwelling, with plenty of books, and a new wife, just imported from Boston, wholly new to the woods. We found the East Branch a large and rapid stream at its mouth, and much deeper than it appeared. Having with some difficulty discovered the trail again, we kept up the south side of the West Branch, or main river, passing by some rapids called Rock-Ebeeme, the roar of which we heard through the woods, and, shortly after, in the thickest of the wood, some empty loggers' camps, still new, which were occupied the previous winter. Though we saw a few more afterwards, I will make one account serve for all. These were such houses as the lumberers of Maine spend the winter in, in the wilderness. There were the camps and the hovels for the cattle, hardly distinguishable, except that the latter had no chimney. These camps were about twenty feet long by fifteen wide, built of logs,—hemlock, cedar, spruce, or yellow birch,—one kind alone, or all together, with the bark on; two or three large ones first, one directly above another, and notched together at the ends, to the height of three or four feet, then of smaller logs resting upon transverse ones at the ends, each of the last successively shorter than the other, to form the roof. The chimney was an oblong square hole in the middle, three or four feet in diameter, with a fence of logs as high as the ridge. The interstices were filled with moss, and the roof was shingled with long and handsome splints of cedar, or spruce, or pine, rifted with a sledge and cleaver. The fire-place, the most important place of all, was in shape and size like the chimney, and directly under it, defined by a log fence or fender on the ground, and a heap of ashes, a foot or two deep, within, with solid benches of split logs running round it. Here the fire usually melts the snow, and dries the rain before it can descend to quench it. The faded beds of arbor-vitæ leaves extended under the eaves on either hand. There was the place for the water-pail, pork-barrel, and wash-basin, and generally a dingy pack of cards left on a log. Usually a good deal of whittling was expended on the latch, which was made of wood, in the form of an iron one. These houses are made comfortable by the huge fires, which can be afforded night and day. Usually the scenery about them is drear and savage enough; and the loggers' camp is as completely in the woods as a fungus at the foot of a pine in a swamp; no outlook but to the sky overhead; no more clearing than is made by cutting down the trees of which it is built, and those which are necessary for fuel. If only it be well sheltered and convenient to his work, and near a spring, he wastes no thought on the prospect. They are very proper forest houses, the stems of the trees collected together and piled up around a man to keep out wind and rain,—made of living green logs, hanging with moss and lichen, and with the curls and fringes of the yellow-birch bark, and dripping with resin, fresh and moist, and redolent of swampy odors, with that sort of vigor and perennialness even about them that toadstools suggest.* The logger's fare consists of tea, molasses, flour, pork (sometimes beef), and beans. A great proportion of the beans raised in Massachusetts find their market here. On expeditions it is only hard bread and pork, often raw, slice upon slice, with tea or water, as the case may be.

The primitive wood is always and everywhere damp and mossy, so that I travelled constantly with the impression that I was in a swamp; and only when it was remarked that this or that tract, judging from the quality of the timber on it, would make a profitable clearing, was I reminded, that if the sun were let in it would make a dry field, like the few I had seen, at once. The best shod for the most part travel with wet feet. If the ground was so wet and spongy at this, the dryest part of a dry season, what must it be in the spring? The woods hereabouts abounded in beech and yellow birch, of

---

*Springer, in his "Forest Life" (1851), says that they first remove the leaves and turf from the spot where they intend to build a camp, for fear of fire; also, that "the spruce-tree is generally selected for camp-building, it being light, straight, and quite free from sap"; that "the roof is finally covered with the boughs of the fir, spruce, and hemlock, so that when the snow falls upon the whole, the warmth of the camp is preserved in the coldest weather"; and that they make the log seat before the fire, called the "Deacon's Seat," of a spruce or fir split in halves, with three or four stout limbs left on one side for legs, which are not likely to get loose.

which last there were some very large specimens; also spruce, cedar, fir, and hemlock; but we saw only the stumps of the white pine here, some of them of great size, these having been already culled out, being the only tree much sought after, even as low down as this. Only a little spruce and hemlock beside had been logged here. The Eastern wood which is sold for fuel in Massachusetts all comes from below Bangor. It was the pine alone, chiefly the white pine, that had tempted any but the hunter to precede us on this route.

Waite's farm, thirteen miles from the Point, is an extensive and elevated clearing, from which we got a fine view of the river, rippling and gleaming far beneath us. My companions had formerly had a good view of Ktaadn and the other mountains here, but to-day it was so smoky that we could see nothing of them. We could overlook an immense country of uninterrupted forest, stretching away up the East Branch toward Canada, on the north and northwest, and toward the Aroostook valley on the northeast; and imagine what wild life was stirring in its midst. Here was quite a field of corn for this region, whose peculiar dry scent we perceived a third of a mile off, before we saw it.

Eighteen miles from the Point brought us in sight of McCauslin's, or "Uncle George's," as he was familiarly called by my companions, to whom he was well known, where we intended to break our long fast. His house was in the midst of an extensive clearing of intervale, at the mouth of the Little Schoodic River, on the opposite or north bank of the Penobscot. So we collected on a point of the shore, that we might be seen, and fired our gun as a signal, which brought out his dogs forthwith, and thereafter their master, who in due time took us across in his batteau. This clearing was bounded abruptly, on all sides but the river, by the naked stems of the forest, as if you were to cut only a few feet square in the midst of a thousand acres of mowing, and set down a thimble therein. He had a whole heaven and horizon to himself, and the sun seemed to be journeying over his clearing only the livelong day. Here we concluded to spend the night, and wait for the Indians, as there was no stopping-place so convenient above. He had seen no Indians pass, and this did not often happen without his knowledge. He thought that his dogs sometimes gave notice of the approach of Indians half an hour before they arrived.

McCauslin was a Kennebec man, of Scotch descent, who had been a waterman twenty-two years, and had driven on the lakes and head-waters of the Penobscot five or six springs in succession, but was now settled here to raise supplies for the lumberers and for himself. He entertained us a day or two with true Scotch hospitality, and would accept no recompense for it. A man of a dry wit and shrewdness, and a general intelligence which I had not looked for in the backwoods. In fact, the deeper you penetrate into the woods, the more intelligent, and, in one sense, less countrified do you find the inhabitants; for always the pioneer has been a traveller, and, to some extent, a man of the world; and, as the distances with which he is familiar are greater, so is his information more general and far reaching than the villager's. If I were to look for a narrow, uninformed, and countrified mind, as opposed to the intelligence and refinement which are thought to emanate from cities, it would be among the rusty inhabitants of an old-settled country, on farms all run out and gone to seed with life-everlasting, in the towns about Boston, even on the high-road in Concord, and not in the backwoods of Maine.

Supper was got before our eyes in the ample kitchen, by a fire which would have roasted an ox; many whole logs, four feet long, were consumed to boil our tea-kettle,—birch, or beech, or maple, the same summer and winter; and the dishes were soon smoking on the table, late the arm-chair, against the wall, from which one of the party was expelled. The arms of the chair formed the frame on which the table rested; and, when the round top was turned up against the wall, it formed the back of the chair, and was no more in the way than the wall itself. This, we noticed, was the prevailing fashion in these log-houses, in order to economize in room. There were piping-hot wheaten cakes, the flour having been brought up the river in batteaux,—no Indian bread, for the upper part of Maine, it will be remembered, is a wheat country,—and ham, eggs, and potatoes, and milk and cheese, the produce of the farm; and also shad and salmon, tea sweetened with molasses, and sweet cakes, in contradistinction to the hot cakes not sweetened, the one white, the other yellow, to wind up with.

Such we found was the prevailing fare, ordinary and extraordinary, along this river. Mountain cranberries (*Vaccinium Vitis-Idæa*), stewed and sweetened, were the common dessert. Everything here was in profusion, and the best of its kind. Butter was in such plenty that it was commonly used, before it was salted, to grease boots with.

In the night we were entertained by the sound of raindrops on the cedar-splints which covered the roof, and awaked the next morning with a drop or two in our eyes. It had set in for a storm, and we made up our minds not to forsake such comfortable quarters with this prospect, but wait for Indians and fair weather. It rained and drizzled and gleamed by turns, the livelong day. What we did there, how we killed the time, would perhaps be idle to tell; how many times we buttered our boots, and how often a drowsy one was seen to sidle off to the bedroom. When it held up, I strolled up and down the bank, and gathered the harebell and cedar-berries, which grew there; or else we tried by turns the long-handled axe on the logs before the door. The axe-helves here were made to chop standing on the log,—a primitive log of course,—and were, therefore, nearly a foot longer than with us. One while we walked over the farm and visited his well-filled barns with McCauslin. There were one other man and two women only here. He kept horses, cows, oxen, and sheep. I think he said that he was the first to bring a plough and a cow so far; and he might have added the last, with only two exceptions. The potato-rot had found him out here, too, the previous year, and got half or two thirds of his crop, though the seed was of his own raising. Oats, grass, and potatoes were his staples; but he raised, also, a few carrots and turnips, and "a little corn for the hens," for this was all that he dared risk, for fear that it would not ripen. Melons, squashes, sweet-corn, beans, tomatoes, and many other vegetables, could not be ripened there.

The very few settlers along this stream were obviously tempted by the cheapness of the land mainly. When I asked McCauslin why more settlers did not come in, he answered, that one reason was, they could not buy the land, it belonged to individuals or companies who were afraid that their wild lands would be settled, and so incorporated into towns, and they be taxed for them; but to settling on the States' land there was no such hinderance. For his own part, he wanted no neighbors,—he did n't wish to see any road by his house. Neighbors, even the best, were a trouble and expense, especially on the score of cattle and fences. They might live across the river, perhaps, but not on the same side.

The chickens here were protected by the dogs. As Mc-Causlin said, "The old one took it up first, and she taught the pup, and now they had got it into their heads that it would n't do to have anything of the bird kind on the premises." A hawk hovering over was not allowed to alight, but barked off by the dogs circling underneath; and a pigeon, or a "yellow-hammer," as they called the pigeon-woodpecker, on a dead limb or stump, was instantly expelled. It was the main business of their day, and kept them constantly coming and going. One would rush out of the house on the least alarm given by the other.

When it rained hardest, we returned to the house, and took down a tract from the shelf. There was the Wandering Jew, cheap edition, and fine print, the Criminal Calendar, and Parish's Geography, and flash novels two or three. Under the pressure of circumstances, we read a little in these. With such aid, the press is not so feeble an engine, after all. This house, which was a fair specimen of those on this river, was built of huge logs, which peeped out everywhere, and were chinked with clay and moss. It contained four or five rooms. There were no sawed boards, or shingles, or clapboards, about it; and scarcely any tool but the axe had been used in its construction. The partitions were made of long clapboard-like splints, of spruce or cedar, turned to a delicate salmon color by the smoke. The roof and sides were covered with the same, instead of shingles and clapboards, and some of a much thicker and larger size were used for the floor. These were all so straight and smooth, that they answered the purpose admirably; and a careless observer would not have suspected that they were not sawed and planed. The chimney and hearth were of vast size, and made of stone. The broom was a few twigs of arbor-vitæ tied to a stick; and a pole was suspended over the hearth, close to the ceiling, to dry stockings and clothes on. I noticed that the floor was full of small, dingy holes, as if made with a gimlet, but which were, in fact, made by the spikes, nearly an inch long, which the lumberers wear in their boots to prevent their slipping on wet logs. Just above McCauslin's, there is a rocky rapid, where logs jam in the spring; and many "drivers" are there collected, who frequent his house for supplies; these were their tracks which I saw.

At sundown McCauslin pointed away over the forest, across the river, to signs of fair weather amid the clouds,— some evening redness there. For even there the points of compass held; and there was a quarter of the heavens appropriated to sunrise and another to sunset.

The next morning, the weather proving fair enough for our purpose, we prepared to start, and, the Indians having failed us, persuaded McCauslin, who was not unwilling to revisit the scenes of his driving, to accompany us in their stead, intending to engage one other boatman on the way. A strip of cotton cloth for a tent, a couple of blankets, which would suffice for the whole party, fifteen pounds of hard bread, ten pounds of "clear" pork, and a little tea, made up "Uncle George's" pack. The last three articles were calculated to be provision enough for six men for a week, with what we might pick up. A tea-kettle, a frying-pan, and an axe, to be obtained at the last house, would complete our outfit.

We were soon out of McCauslin's clearing, and in the ever green woods again. The obscure trail made by the two settlers above, which even the woodman is sometimes puzzled to discern, erelong crossed a narrow, open strip in the woods overrun with weeds, called the Burnt Land, where a fire had raged formerly, stretching northward nine or ten miles, to Millinocket Lake. At the end of three miles, we reached Shad Pond, or Noliseemack, an expansion of the river. Hodge, the Assistant State Geologist, who passed through this on the 25th of June, 1837, says, "We pushed our boat through an acre or more of buck-beans, which had taken root at the bottom, and bloomed above the surface in the greatest profusion and beauty." Thomas Fowler's house is four miles from McCauslin's, on the shore of the pond, at the mouth of the Millinocket River, and eight miles from the lake of the same name, on the latter stream. This lake affords a more direct course to Ktaadn, but we preferred to follow the Penobscot and the Pamadumcook lakes. Fowler was just completing a new log-hut, and was sawing out a window through the logs, nearly two feet thick, when we arrived. He had begun to paper his house with spruce-bark, turned inside out, which had a good effect, and was in keeping with the circumstances. Instead of water we got here a draught of beer, which, it was allowed, would be better; clear and thin, but strong and stringent as the cedar-sap. It was as if we sucked at the very teats of Nature's pine-clad bosom in these parts,—the sap of all Millinocket botany commingled,—the topmost, most fantastic, and spiciest sprays of the primitive wood, and whatever invigorating and stringent gum or essence it afforded steeped and dissolved in it,—a lumberer's drink, which would acclimate and naturalize a man at once,—which would make him see green, and, if he slept, dream that he heard the wind sough among the pines. Here was a fife, praying to be played on, through which we breathed a few tuneful strains,—brought hither to tame wild beasts. As we stood upon the pile of chips by the door, fish-hawks were sailing overhead; and here, over Shad Pond, might daily be witnessed the tyranny of the bald-eagle over that bird. Tom pointed away over the lake to a bald-eagle's nest, which was plainly visible more than a mile off, on a pine, high above the surrounding forest, and was frequented from year to year by the same pair, and held sacred by him. There were these two houses only there, his low hut and the eagles' airy cart-load of fagots. Thomas Fowler, too, was persuaded to join us, for two men were necessary to manage the batteau, which was soon to be our carriage, and these men needed to be cool and skilful for the navigation of the Penobscot. Tom's pack was soon made, for he had not far to look for his waterman's boots, and a red-flannel shirt. This is the favorite color with lumbermen; and red flannel is reputed to possess some mysterious virtues, to be most healthful and convenient in respect to perspiration. In every gang there will be a large proportion of red birds. We took here a poor and leaky batteau, and began to pole up the Millinocket two miles, to the elder Fowler's, in order to avoid the Grand Falls of the Penobscot, intending to exchange our batteau there for a better. The Millinocket is a small, shallow, and sandy stream, full of what I took to be lamprey-eels' or suckers' nests, and lined with musquash cabins, but free from rapids, according to Fowler, excepting at its outlet from the lake. He was at this time engaged in cutting the native grass,—rush-grass and meadow-clover, as he called it,—on the meadows and small, low islands of this stream. We noticed flattened places in the grass on either side, where, he said, a moose had laid down the night before, adding, that there were thousands in these meadows.

Old Fowler's, on the Millinocket, six miles from Mc-Causlin's, and twenty-four from the Point, is the last house. Gibson's, on the Sowadnehunk, is the only clearing above, but that had proved a failure, and was long since deserted. Fowler is the oldest inhabitant of these woods. He formerly lived a few miles from here, on the south side of the West Branch, where he built his house sixteen years ago, the first house built above the Five Islands. Here our new batteau was to be carried over the first portage of two miles, round the Grand Falls of the Penobscot, on a horse-sled made of saplings, to jump the numerous rocks in the way; but we had to wait a couple of hours for them to catch the horses, which were pastured at a distance, amid the stumps, and had wandered still farther off. The last of the salmon for this season had just been caught, and were still fresh in pickle, from which enough was extracted to fill our empty kettle, and so graduate our introduction to simpler forest fare. The week before they had lost nine sheep here out of their first flock, by the wolves. The surviving sheep came round the house, and seemed frightened, which induced them to go and look for the rest, when they found seven dead and lacerated, and two still alive. These last they carried to the house, and, as Mrs. Fowler said, they were merely scratched in the throat, and had no more visible wound than would be produced by the prick of a pin. She sheared off the wool from their throats, and washed them, and put on some salve, and turned them out, but in a few moments they were missing, and had not been found since. In fact, they were all poisoned, and those that were found swelled up at once, so that they saved neither skin nor wool. This realized the old fables of the wolves and the sheep, and convinced me that that ancient

hostility still existed. Verily, the shepherd-boy did not need to
sound a false alarm this time. There were steel traps by the
door, of various sizes, for wolves, otter, and bears, with large
claws instead of teeth, to catch in their sinews. Wolves are
frequently killed with poisoned bait.

At length, after we had dined here on the usual backwoods
fare, the horses arrived, and we hauled our batteau out of the
water, and lashed it to its wicker carriage, and, throwing in
our packs, walked on before, leaving the boatmen and driver,
who was Tom's brother, to manage the concern. The route,
which led through the wild pasture where the sheep were
killed, was in some places the roughest ever travelled by
horses, over rocky hills, where the sled bounced and slid
along, like a vessel pitching in a storm; and one man was as
necessary to stand at the stern, to prevent the boat from being
wrecked, as a helmsman in the roughest sea. The philosophy
of our progress was something like this: when the runners
struck a rock three or four feet high, the sled bounced back
and upwards at the same time; but, as the horses never ceased
pulling, it came down on the top of the rock, and so we got
over. This portage probably followed the trail of an ancient
Indian carry round these falls. By two o'clock we, who had
walked on before, reached the river above the falls, not far
from the outlet of Quakish Lake, and waited for the batteau
to come up. We had been here but a short time, when a thunder-shower was seen coming up from the west, over the still
invisible lakes, and that pleasant wilderness which we were so
eager to become acquainted with; and soon the heavy drops
began to patter on the leaves around us. I had just selected
the prostrate trunk of a huge pine, five or six feet in diameter,
and was crawling under it, when, luckily, the boat arrived. It
would have amused a sheltered man to witness the manner in
which it was unlashed, and whirled over, while the first waterspout burst upon us. It was no sooner in the hands of the
eager company than it was abandoned to the first revolutionary impulse, and to gravity, to adjust it; and they might have
been seen all stooping to its shelter, and wriggling under like
so many eels, before it was fairly deposited on the ground.
When all were under, we propped up the lee side, and busied
ourselves there whittling thole-pins for rowing, when we

should reach the lakes; and made the woods ring, between the claps of thunder, with such boat-songs as we could remember. The horses stood sleek and shining with the rain, all drooping and crestfallen, while deluge after deluge washed over us; but the bottom of a boat may be relied on for a tight roof. At length, after two hours' delay at this place, a streak of fair weather appeared in the northwest, whither our course now lay, promising a serene evening for our voyage; and the driver returned with his horses, while we made haste to launch our boat, and commence our voyage in good earnest.

There were six of us, including the two boatmen. With our packs heaped up near the bows, and ourselves disposed as baggage to trim the boat, with instructions not to move in case we should strike a rock, more than so many barrels of pork, we pushed out into the first rapid, a slight specimen of the stream we had to navigate. With Uncle George in the stern, and Tom in the bows, each using a spruce pole about twelve feet long, pointed with iron,* and poling on the same side, we shot up the rapids like a salmon, the water rushing and roaring around, so that only a practised eye could distinguish a safe course, or tell what was deep water and what rocks, frequently grazing the latter on one or both sides, with a hundred as narrow escapes as ever the Argo had in passing through the Symplegades. I, who had had some experience in boating, had never experienced any half so exhilarating before. We were lucky to have exchanged our Indians, whom we did not know, for these men, who, together with Tom's brother, were reputed the best boatmen on the river, and were at once indispensable pilots and pleasant companions. The canoe is smaller, more easily upset, and sooner worn out; and the Indian is said not to be so skilful in the management of the batteau. He is, for the most part, less to be relied on, and more disposed to sulks and whims. The utmost familiarity with dead streams, or with the ocean, would not prepare a man for this peculiar navigation; and the most skilful boatman anywhere else would here be obliged to take out his boat and carry round a hundred times, still with great risk, as well as delay, where the practised batteau-man poles up with

---

*The Canadians call it *picquer de fond.*

comparative ease and safety. The hardy "voyageur" pushes with incredible perseverance and success quite up to the foot of the falls, and then only carries round some perpendicular ledge, and launches again in

"The torrent's smoothness, ere it dash below,"

to struggle with the boiling rapids above. The Indians say that the river once ran both ways, one half up and the other down, but that, since the white man came, it all runs down, and now they must laboriously pole their canoes against the stream, and carry them over numerous portages. In the summer, all stores—the grindstone and the plough of the pioneer, flour, pork, and utensils for the explorer—must be conveyed up the river in batteaux; and many a cargo and many a boatman is lost in these waters. In the winter, however, which is very equable and long, the ice is the great highway, and the loggers' team penetrates to Chesuncook Lake, and still higher up, even two hundred miles above Bangor. Imagine the solitary sled-track running far up into the snowy and evergreen wilderness, hemmed in closely for a hundred miles by the forest, and again stretching straight across the broad surfaces of concealed lakes!

We were soon in the smooth water of the Quakish Lake, and took our turns at rowing and paddling across it. It is a small, irregular, but handsome lake, shut in on all sides by the forest, and showing no traces of man but some low boom in a distant cove, reserved for spring use. The spruce and cedar on its shores, hung with gray lichens, looked at a distance like the ghosts of trees. Ducks were sailing here and there on its surface, and a solitary loon, like a more living wave,—a vital spot on the lake's surface,—laughed and frolicked, and showed its straight leg, for our amusement. Joe Merry Mountain appeared in the northwest, as if it were looking down on this lake especially; and we had our first, but a partial view of Ktaadn, its summit veiled in clouds, like a dark isthmus in that quarter, connecting the heavens with the earth. After two miles of smooth rowing across this lake, we found ourselves in the river again, which was a continuous rapid for one mile, to the dam, requiring all the strength and skill of our boatmen to pole up it.

This dam is a quite important and expensive work for this country, whither cattle and horses cannot penetrate in the summer, raising the whole river ten feet, and flooding, as they said, some sixty square miles by means of the innumerable lakes with which the river connects. It is a lofty and solid structure, with sloping piers some distance above, made of frames of logs filled with stones, to break the ice.* Here every log pays toll as it passes through the sluices.

We filed into the rude logger's camp at this place, such as I have described, without ceremony, and the cook, at that moment the sole occupant, at once set about preparing tea for his visitors. His fireplace, which the rain had converted into a mud-puddle, was soon blazing again, and we sat down on the log benches around it to dry us. On the well-flattened and somewhat faded beds of arbor-vitæ leaves, which stretched on either hand under the eaves behind us, lay an odd leaf of the Bible, some genealogical chapter out of the Old Testament; and, half buried by the leaves, we found Emerson's Address on West India Emancipation, which had been left here formerly by one of our company, and *had made two converts to the Liberty party here*, as I was told; also, an odd number of the Westminster Review, for 1834, and a pamphlet entitled History of the Erection of the Monument on the grave of Myron Holly. This was the readable, or reading matter, in a lumberer's camp in the Maine woods, thirty miles from a road, which would be given up to the bears in a fortnight. These things were well thumbed and soiled. This gang was headed by one John Morrison, a good specimen of a Yankee; and was necessarily composed of men not bred to the business of dam-building, but who were Jacks-at-all-trades, handy with the axe, and other simple implements, and well skilled in wood and water craft. We had hot cakes for our supper even here, white as snow-balls, but without butter, and the never-failing sweet cakes, with which we filled our pockets, foreseeing that we should not soon meet with the like again. Such delicate puff-balls seemed a singular diet for back-

---

*Even the Jesuit missionaries, accustomed to the St. Lawrence and other rivers of Canada, in their first expeditions to the Abenaquinois, speak of rivers *ferrées de rochers*, shod with rocks. See also No. 10 Relations, for 1647, p. 185.

woodsmen. There was also tea without milk, sweetened with molasses. And so, exchanging a word with John Morrison and his gang when we had returned to the shore, and also exchanging our batteau for a better still, we made haste to improve the little daylight that remained. This camp, exactly twenty-nine miles from Mattawamkeag Point, by the way we had come, and about one hundred from Bangor by the river, was the last human habitation of any kind in this direction. Beyond, there was no trail; and the river and lakes, by batteaux and canoes, was considered the only practicable route. We were about thirty miles by the river from the summit of Ktaadn, which was in sight, though not more than twenty, perhaps, in a straight line.

It being about the full of the moon, and a warm and pleasant evening, we decided to row five miles by moonlight to the head of the North Twin Lake, lest the wind should rise on the morrow. After one mile of river, or what the boatmen call "thoroughfare,"—for the river becomes at length only the connecting link between the lakes,—and some slight rapid which had been mostly made smooth water by the dam, we entered the North Twin Lake just after sundown, and steered across for the river "thoroughfare," four miles distant. This is a noble sheet of water, where one may get the impression which a new country and a "lake of the woods" are fitted to create. There was the smoke of no log-hut nor camp of any kind to greet us, still less was any lover of nature or musing traveller watching our batteau from the distant hills; not even the Indian hunter was there, for he rarely climbs them, but hugs the river like ourselves. No face welcomed us but the fine fantastic sprays of free and happy evergreen trees, waving one above another in their ancient home. At first the red clouds hung over the western shore as gorgeously as if over a city, and the lake lay open to the light with even a civilized aspect, as if expecting trade and commerce, and towns and villas. We could distinguish the inlet to the South Twin, which is said to be the larger, where the shore was misty and blue, and it was worth the while to look thus through a narrow opening across the entire expanse of a concealed lake to its own yet more dim and distant shore. The shores rose gently to ranges of low hills covered with forests; and though, in fact, the most valuable white pine timber, even about this lake, had been culled out, this would never have been suspected by the voyager. The impression, which indeed corresponded with the fact, was, as if we were upon a high table-land between the States and Canada, the northern side of which is drained by the St. John and Chaudiere, the southern by the Penobscot and Kennebec. There was no bold mountainous shore, as we might have expected, but only isolated hills and mountains rising here and there from the plateau. The country is an archipelago of lakes,—the lake-country of New England. Their levels vary but a few feet, and the boatmen, by short portages, or by none at all, pass easily from one to another. They say that at very high water the Penobscot and the Kennebec flow into each other, or at any rate, that you may lie with your face in the one and your toes in the other. Even the Penobscot and St. John have been connected by a canal, so that the lumber of the Allegash, instead of going down the St. John, comes down the Penobscot; and the Indian's tradition, that the Penobscot once ran both ways for his convenience, is, in one sense, partially realized to-day.

None of our party but McCauslin had been above this lake, so we trusted to him to pilot us, and we could not but confess the importance of a pilot on these waters. While it is river, you will not easily forget which way is up stream; but when you enter a lake, the river is completely lost, and you scan the distant shores in vain to find where it comes in. A stranger is, for the time at least, lost, and must set about a voyage of discovery first of all to find the river. To follow the windings of the shore when the lake is ten miles, or even more, in length, and of an irregularity which will not soon be mapped, is a wearisome voyage, and will spend his time and his provisions. They tell a story of a gang of experienced woodmen sent to a location on this stream, who were thus lost in the wilderness of lakes. They cut their way through thickets, and carried their baggage and their boats over from lake to lake, sometimes several miles. They carried into Millinocket Lake, which is on another stream, and is ten miles square, and contains a hundred islands. They explored its shores thoroughly, and then carried into another, and another, and it was a week of toil and anxiety before they found the Penobscot River again, and then their provisions were exhausted, and they were obliged to return.

While Uncle George steered for a small island near the head of the lake, now just visible, like a speck on the water, we rowed by turns swiftly over its surface, singing such boat-songs as we could remember. The shores seemed at an indefinite distance in the moonlight. Occasionally we paused in our singing and rested on our oars, while we listened to hear if the wolves howled, for this is a common serenade, and my companions affirmed that it was the most dismal and unearthly of sounds; but we heard none this time. If we did not *hear*, however, we did *listen*, not without a reasonable expectation; that at least I have to tell,—only some utterly uncivilized, big-throated owl hooted loud and dismally in the drear and boughy wilderness, plainly not nervous about his solitary life, nor afraid to hear the echoes of his voice there. We remembered also that possibly moose were silently watching us from the distant coves, or some surly bear or timid caribou had been startled by our singing. It was with new emphasis that we sang there the Canadian boat-song,—

> "Row, brothers, row, the stream runs fast,
>   The Rapids are near and the daylight's past!"—

which describes precisely our own adventure, and was inspired by the experience of a similar kind of life,—for the rapids were ever near, and the daylight long past; the woods on shore looked dim, and many an Utawas' tide here emptied into the lake.

> "Why should we yet our sail unfurl?
>   There is not a breath the blue wave to curl!
>   But, when the wind blows off the shore,
>   O sweetly we'll rest our weary oar."

> "Utawas' tide! this trembling moon,
>   Shall see us float o'er thy surges soon."

At last we glided past the "green isle" which had been our landmark, all joining in the chorus; as if by the watery links of rivers and of lakes we were about to float over unmeasured zones of earth, bound on unimaginable adventures,—

"Saint of this green isle! hear our prayers,
     O grant us cool heavens and favoring airs!"

About nine o'clock we reached the river, and ran our boat
into a natural haven between some rocks, and drew her out
on the sand. This camping-ground McCauslin had been familiar with in his lumbering days, and he now struck it un-
erringly in the moonlight, and we heard the sound of the rill
which would supply us with cool water emptying into the
lake. The first business was to make a fire, an operation which
was a little delayed by the wetness of the fuel and the ground,
owing to the heavy showers of the afternoon. The fire is the
main comfort of the camp, whether in summer or winter, and
is about as ample at one season as at another. It is as well for
cheerfulness as for warmth and dryness. It forms one side of
the camp; one bright side at any rate. Some were dispersed
to fetch in dead trees and boughs, while Uncle George felled
the birches and beeches which stood convenient, and soon we
had a fire some ten feet long by three or four high, which
rapidly dried the sand before it. This was calculated to burn
all night. We next proceeded to pitch our tent; which operation was performed by sticking our two spike-poles into the
ground in a slanting direction, about ten feet apart, for rafters, and then drawing our cotton cloth over them, and tying
it down at the ends, leaving it open in front, shed-fashion.
But this evening the wind carried the sparks on to the tent
and burned it. So we hastily drew up the batteau just within
the edge of the woods before the fire, and propping up one
side three or four feet high, spread the tent on the ground to
lie on; and with the corner of a blanket, or what more or less
we could get to put over us, lay down with our heads and
bodies under the boat, and our feet and legs on the sand toward the fire. At first we lay awake, talking of our course, and
finding ourselves in so convenient a posture for studying the
heavens, with the moon and stars shining in our faces, our
conversation naturally turned upon astronomy, and we re-
counted by turns the most interesting discoveries in that science. But at length we composed ourselves seriously to sleep.
It was interesting, when awakened at midnight, to watch the
grotesque and fiend-like forms and motions of some one of

the party, who, not being able to sleep, had got up silently to arouse the fire, and add fresh fuel, for a change; now stealthily lugging a dead tree from out the dark, and heaving it on, now stirring up the embers with his fork, or tiptoeing about to observe the stars, watched, perchance, by half the prostrate party in breathless silence; so much the more intense because they were awake, while each supposed his neighbor sound asleep. Thus aroused, I too brought fresh fuel to the fire, and then rambled along the sandy shore in the moonlight, hoping to meet a moose, come down to drink, or else a wolf. The little rill tinkled the louder, and peopled all the wilderness for me; and the glassy smoothness of the sleeping lake, laving the shores of a new world, with the dark, fantastic rocks rising here and there from its surface, made a scene not easily described. It has left such an impression of stern, yet gentle, wildness on my memory as will not soon be effaced. Not far from midnight we were one after another awakened by rain falling on our extremities; and as each was made aware of the fact by cold or wet, he drew a long sigh and then drew up his legs, until gradually we had all sidled round from lying at right angles with the boat, till our bodies formed an acute angle with it, and were wholly protected. When next we awoke, the moon and stars were shining again, and there were signs of dawn in the east. I have been thus particular in order to convey some idea of a night in the woods.

We had soon launched and loaded our boat, and, leaving our fire blazing, were off again before breakfast. The lumberers rarely trouble themselves to put out their fires, such is the dampness of the primitive forest; and this is one cause, no doubt, of the frequent fires in Maine, of which we hear so much on smoky days in Massachusetts. The forests are held cheap after the white pine has been culled out; and the explorers and hunters pray for rain only to clear the atmosphere of smoke. The woods were so wet to-day, however, that there was no danger of our fire spreading. After poling up half a mile of river, or thoroughfare, we rowed a mile across the foot of Pamadumcook Lake, which is the name given on the map to this whole chain of lakes, as if there was but one, though they are, in each instance, distinctly separated by a reach of the river, with its narrow and rocky channel and its rapids. This lake, which is one of the largest, stretched north-west ten miles, to hills and mountains in the distance. Mc-Causlin pointed to some distant, and as yet inaccessible, forests of white pine, on the sides of a mountain in that direction. The Joe Merry Lakes, which lay between us and Moosehead, on the west, were recently, if they are not still, "surrounded by some of the best timbered land in the State." By another thoroughfare we passed into Deep Cove, a part of the same lake, which makes up two miles, toward the northeast, and rowing two miles across this, by another short thoroughfare, entered Ambejijis Lake.

At the entrance to a lake we sometimes observed what is technically called "fencing stuff," or the unhewn timbers of which booms are formed, either secured together in the water, or laid up on the rocks and lashed to trees, for spring use. But it was always startling to discover so plain a trail of civilized man there. I remember that I was strangely affected, when we were returning, by the sight of a ring-bolt well drilled into a rock, and fastened with lead, at the head of this solitary Ambejijis Lake.

It was easy to see that driving logs must be an exciting as well as arduous and dangerous business. All winter long the logger goes on piling up the trees which he has trimmed and hauled in some dry ravine at the head of a stream, and then in the spring he stands on the bank and whistles for Rain and Thaw, ready to wring the perspiration out of his shirt to swell the tide, till suddenly, with a whoop and halloo from him, shutting his eyes, as if to bid farewell to the existing state of things, a fair proportion of his winter's work goes scrambling down the country, followed by his faithful dogs, Thaw and Rain and Freshet and Wind, the whole pack in full cry, toward the Orono Mills. Every log is marked with the owner's name, cut in the sapwood with an axe or bored with an auger, so deep as not to be worn off in the driving, and yet not so as to injure the timber; and it requires considerable ingenuity to invent new and simple marks where there are so many owners. They have quite an alphabet of their own, which only the practised can read. One of my companions read off from his memorandum-book some marks of his own logs, among which there were crosses, belts, crow's feet, girdles, &c., as, "Y—girdle—crow-foot," and various other devices. When the logs have run the gauntlet of innumerable rapids and falls, each on its own account, with more or less jamming and bruising, those bearing various owners' marks being mixed up together,—since all must take advantage of the same freshet,—they are collected together at the heads of the lakes, and surrounded by a boom fence of floating logs, to prevent their being dispersed by the wind, and are thus towed altogether, like a flock of sheep, across the lake, where there is no current, by a windlass, or boom-head, such as we sometimes saw standing on an island or head-land, and, if circumstances permit, with the aid of sails and oars. Sometimes, notwithstanding, the logs are dispersed over many miles of lake surface in a few hours by winds and freshets, and thrown up on distant shores, where the driver can pick up only one or two at a time, and return with them to the thoroughfare; and before he gets his flock well through Ambejijis or Pamadumcook, he makes many a wet and uncomfortable camp on the shore. He must be able to navigate a log as if it were a canoe, and be as indifferent to cold and wet as a muskrat. He uses a few efficient tools,—a lever commonly of rock-maple, six or seven feet long, with a stout spike in it, strongly feruled on, and a long spike-pole, with a screw at the end of the spike to make it hold. The boys along shore learn to walk on floating logs as city boys on sidewalks. Sometimes the logs are thrown up on rocks in such positions as to be irrecoverable but by another freshet as high, or they jam together at rapids and falls, and accumulate in vast piles, which the driver must start at the risk of his life. Such is the lumber business, which depends on many accidents, as the early freezing of the rivers, that the teams may get up in season, a sufficient freshet in the spring, to fetch the logs down, and many others.* I quote Michaux on Lumbering on the Kennebec, then the source of the best white-pine lumber car-

---

*"A steady current or pitch of water is preferable to one either rising or diminishing; as, when rising rapidly, the water at the middle of the river is considerably higher than at the shores,—so much so as to be distinctly perceived by the eye of a spectator on the banks, presenting an appearance like a turnpike road. The lumber, therefore, is always sure to incline from the centre of the channel toward either shore."—Springer.

ried to England. "The persons engaged in this branch of industry are generally emigrants from New Hampshire. . . . .
In the summer they unite in small companies, and traverse
these vast solitudes in every direction, to ascertain the places
in which the pines abound. After cutting the grass and converting it into hay for the nourishment of the cattle to be
employed in their labor, they return home. In the beginning
of the winter they enter the forests again, establish themselves
in huts covered with the bark of the canoe-birch, or the
arbor-vitæ; and, though the cold is so intense that the mercury
sometimes remains for several weeks from 40° to 50° [Fahr.]
below the point of congelation, they persevere, with unabated
courage, in their work." According to Springer, the company
consists of choppers, swampers,—who make roads,—barker
and loader, teamster, and cook. "When the trees are felled,
they cut them into logs from fourteen to eighteen feet long,
and, by means of their cattle, which they employ with great
dexterity, drag them to the river, and after stamping on them
a mark of property, roll them on its frozen bosom. At the
breaking of the ice, in the spring, they float down with the
current. . . . . The logs that are not drawn the first year,"
adds Michaux, "are attacked by large worms, which form
holes about two lines in diameter, in every direction; but, if
stripped of their bark, they will remain uninjured for thirty
years."

Ambejijis, this quiet Sunday morning, struck me as the
most beautiful lake we had seen. It is said to be one of the
deepest. We had the fairest view of Joe Merry, Double Top,
and Ktaadn, from its surface. The summit of the latter had a
singularly flat, table-land appearance, like a short highway,
where a demigod might be let down to take a turn or two in
an afternoon, to settle his dinner. We rowed a mile and a half
to near the head of the lake, and, pushing through a field of
lily-pads, landed, to cook our breakfast, by the side of a large
rock, known to McCauslin. Our breakfast consisted of tea,
with hard bread and pork, and fried salmon, which we ate
with forks neatly whittled from alder-twigs, which grew
there, off strips of birch-bark for plates. The tea was black tea,
without milk to color or sugar to sweeten it, and two tin
dippers were our tea-cups. This beverage is as indispensable

to the loggers as to any gossiping old women in the land, and they, no doubt, derive great comfort from it. Here was the site of an old logger's camp, remembered by McCauslin, now overgrown with weeds and bushes. In the midst of a dense underwood we noticed a whole brick, on a rock, in a small run, clean and red and square as in a brick-yard, which had been brought thus far formerly for tamping. Some of us afterward regretted that we had not carried this on with us to the top of the mountain, to be left there for our mark. It would certainly have been a simple evidence of civilized man. McCauslin said, that large wooden crosses, made of oak, still sound, were sometimes found standing in this wilderness, which were set up by the first Catholic missionaries who came through to the Kennebec.

In the next nine miles, which were the extent of our voyage, and which it took us the rest of the day to get over, we rowed across several small lakes, poled up numerous rapids and thoroughfares, and carried over four portages. I will give the names and distances, for the benefit of future tourists. First, after leaving Ambejijis Lake, we had a quarter of a mile of rapids to the portage, or carry of ninety rods around Ambejijis Falls; then a mile and a half through Passamagamet Lake, which is narrow and river-like, to the falls of the same name,—Ambejijis stream coming in on the right; then two miles through Katepskonegan Lake to the portage of ninety rods around Katepskonegan Falls, which name signifies "carrying-place,"—Passamagamet stream coming in on the left; then three miles through Pockwockomus Lake, a slight expansion of the river, to the portage of forty rods around the falls of the same name,—Katepskonegan stream coming in on the left; then three quarters of a mile through Aboljacarmegus Lake, similar to the last, to the portage of forty rods around the falls of the same name; then half a mile of rapid water to the Sowadnehunk dead-water, and the Aboljacknagesic stream.

This is generally the order of names as you ascend the river: First, the lake, or, if there is no expansion, the dead-water; then the falls; then the stream emptying into the lake, or river above, all of the same name. First we came to Passamagamet Lake, then to Passamagamet Falls, then to Passamagamet stream, emptying in. This order and identity of names, it will be perceived, is quite philosophical, since the dead-water or lake is always at least partially produced by the stream emptying in above; and the first fall below, which is the outlet of that lake, and where that tributary water makes its first plunge, also naturally bears the same name.

At the portage around Ambejijis Falls I observed a pork-barrel on the shore, with a hole eight or nine inches square cut in one side, which was set against an upright rock; but the bears, without turning or upsetting the barrel, had gnawed a hole in the opposite side, which looked exactly like an enormous rat hole, big enough to put their heads in; and at the bottom of the barrel were still left a few mangled and slabbered slices of pork. It is usual for the lumberers to leave such supplies as they cannot conveniently carry along with them at carries or camps, to which the next comers do not scruple to help themselves, they being the property, commonly, not of an individual, but a company, who can afford to deal liberally.

I will describe particularly how we got over some of these portages and rapids, in order that the reader may get an idea of the boatman's life. At Ambejijis Falls, for instance, there was the roughest path imaginable cut through the woods; at first up hill, at an angle of nearly forty-five degrees, over rocks and logs without end. This was the manner of the portage. We first carried over our baggage, and deposited it on the shore at the other end; then returning to the batteau, we dragged it up the hill by the painter, and onward, with frequent pauses, over half the portage. But this was a bungling way, and would soon have worn out the boat. Commonly, three men walk over with a batteau weighing from three to five or six hundred pounds on their heads and shoulders, the tallest standing under the middle of the boat, which is turned over, and one at each end, or else there are two at the bows. More cannot well take hold at once. But this requires some practice, as well as strength, and is in any case extremely laborious, and wearing to the constitution, to follow. We were, on the whole, rather an invalid party, and could render our boatmen but little assistance. Our two men at length took the batteau upon their shoulders, and, while two of us steadied it, to prevent it from rocking and wearing into their shoulders, on which they placed their hats folded, walked bravely over the remaining distance, with two or three pauses. In the same manner they accomplished the other portages. With this crushing weight they must climb and stumble along over fallen trees and slippery rocks of all sizes, where those who walked by the sides were continually brushed off, such was the narrowness of the path. But we were fortunate not to have to cut our path in the first place. Before we launched our boat, we scraped the bottom smooth again, with our knives, where it had rubbed on the rocks, to save friction.

To avoid the difficulties of the portage, our men determined to "warp up" the Passamagamet Falls; so while the rest walked over the portage with the baggage, I remained in the batteau, to assist in warping up. We were soon in the midst of the rapids, which were more swift and tumultuous than any we had poled up, and had turned to the side of the stream for the purpose of warping, when the boatmen, who felt some pride in their skill, and were ambitious to do something more than usual, for my benefit, as I surmised, took one more view of the rapids, or rather the falls; and, in answer to one's question, whether we couldn't get up there, the other answered that he guessed he'd try it. So we pushed again into the midst of the stream, and began to struggle with the current. I sat in the middle of the boat to trim it, moving slightly to the right or left as it grazed a rock. With an uncertain and wavering motion we wound and bolted our way up, until the bow was actually raised two feet above the stern at the steepest pitch; and then, when everything depended upon his exertions, the bowman's pole snapped in two; but before he had time to take the spare one, which I reached him, he had saved himself with the fragment upon a rock; and so we got up by a hair's breadth; and Uncle George exclaimed that that was never done before, and he had not tried it if he had not known whom he had got in the bow, nor he in the bow, if he had not known him in the stern. At this place there was a regular portage cut through the woods, and our boatmen had never known a batteau to ascend the falls. As near as I can remember, there was a perpendicular fall here, at the worst place of the whole Penobscot River, two or three feet at least.

I could not sufficiently admire the skill and coolness with which they performed this feat, never speaking to each other. The bowman, not looking behind, but knowing exactly what the other is about, works as if he worked alone. Now sounding in vain for a bottom in fifteen feet of water, while the boat falls back several rods, held straight only with the greatest skill and exertion; or, while the sternman obstinately holds his ground, like a turtle, the bowman springs from side to side with wonderful suppleness and dexterity, scanning the rapids and the rocks with a thousand eyes; and now, having got a bite at last, with a lusty shove, which makes his pole bend and quiver, and the whole boat tremble, he gains a few feet upon the river. To add to the danger, the poles are liable at any time to be caught between the rocks, and wrenched out of their hands, leaving them at the mercy of the rapids,— the rocks, as it were, lying in wait, like so many alligators, to catch them in their teeth, and jerk them from your hands, before you have stolen an effectual shove against their palates. The pole is set close to the boat, and the prow is made to overshoot, and just turn the corners of the rocks, in the very teeth of the rapids. Nothing but the length and lightness, and the slight draught of the batteau, enables them to make any headway. The bowman must quickly choose his course; there is no time to deliberate. Frequently the boat is shoved between rocks where both sides touch, and the waters on either hand are a perfect maelstrom.

Half a mile above this, two of us tried our hands at poling up a slight rapid; and we were just surmounting the last difficulty when an unlucky rock confounded our calculations; and while the batteau was sweeping round irrecoverably amid the whirlpool, we were obliged to resign the poles to more skilful hands.

Katepskonegan is one of the shallowest and weediest of the lakes, and looked as if it might abound in pickerel. The falls of the same name, where we stopped to dine, are considerable and quite picturesque. Here Uncle George had seen trout caught by the barrelful; but they would not rise to our bait at this hour. Half-way over this carry, thus far in the Maine wilderness on its way to the Provinces, we noticed a large, flaming, Oak Hall hand-bill, about two feet long, wrapped round the trunk of a pine, from which the bark had been stript, and to which it was fast glued by the pitch. This should be recorded among the advantages of this mode of advertising, that so, possibly, even the bears and wolves, moose, deer, otter, and beaver, not to mention the Indian, may learn where they can fit themselves according to the latest fashion, or, at least, recover some of their own lost garments. We christened this, the Oak Hall carry.

The forenoon was as serene and placid on this wild stream in the woods, as we are apt to imagine that Sunday in summer usually is in Massachusetts. We were occasionally startled by the scream of a bald-eagle, sailing over the stream in front of our batteau; or of the fish-hawks, on whom he levies his contributions. There were, at intervals, small meadows of a few acres on the sides of the stream, waving with uncut grass, which attracted the attention of our boatmen, who regretted that they were not nearer to their clearings, and calculated how many stacks they might cut. Two or three men sometimes spend the summer by themselves, cutting the grass in these meadows, to sell to the loggers in the winter, since it will fetch a higher price on the spot than in any market in the State. On a small isle, covered with this kind of rush, or cut grass, on which we landed, to consult about our further course, we noticed the recent track of a moose, a large, roundish hole, in the soft wet ground, evincing the great size and weight of the animal that made it. They are fond of the water, and visit all these island-meadows, swimming as easily from island to island as they make their way through the thickets on land. Now and then we passed what McCauslin called a pokelogan, an Indian term for what the drivers might have reason to call a poke-logs-in, an inlet that leads nowhere. If you get in, you have got to get out again the same way. These, and the frequent "run-rounds" which come into the river again, would embarrass an inexperienced voyager not a little.

The carry around Pockwockomus Falls was exceedingly rough and rocky, the batteau having to be lifted directly from the water up four or five feet on to a rock, and launched again down a similar bank. The rocks on this portage were covered with the *dents* made by the spikes in the lumberers' boots while staggering over under the weight of their batteaux; and you could see where the surface of some large rocks on which they had rested their batteaux was worn quite smooth with use. As it was, we had carried over but half the usual portage at this place for this stage of the water, and launched our boat in the smooth wave just curving to the fall, prepared to struggle with the most violent rapid we had to encounter. The rest of the party walked over the remainder of the portage, while I remained with the boatmen to assist in warping up. One had to hold the boat while the others got in to prevent it from going over the falls. When we had pushed up the rapids as far as possible, keeping close to the shore, Tom seized the painter and leaped out upon a rock just visible in the water, but he lost his footing, notwithstanding his spiked boots, and was instantly amid the rapids; but recovering himself by good luck, and reaching another rock, he passed the painter to me, who had followed him, and took his place again in the bows. Leaping from rock to rock in the shoal water, close to the shore, and now and then getting a bite with the rope round an upright one, I held the boat while one reset his pole, and then all three forced it upward against any rapid. This was "warping up." When a part of us walked round at such a place, we generally took the precaution to take out the most valuable part of the baggage, for fear of being swamped.

As we poled up a swift rapid for half a mile above Abolja-carmegus Falls, some of the party read their own marks on the huge logs which lay piled up high and dry on the rocks on either hand, the relics probably of a jam which had taken place here in the Great Freshet in the spring. Many of these would have to wait for another great freshet, perchance, if they lasted so long, before they could be got off. It was singular enough to meet with property of theirs which they had never seen, and where they had never been before, thus detained by freshets and rocks when on its way to them. Methinks that must be where all my property lies, cast up on the rocks on some distant and unexplored stream, and waiting for an unheard-of freshet to fetch it down. O make haste, ye gods, with your winds and rains, and start the jam before it rots!

The last half-mile carried us to the Sowadnehunk dead-water, so called from the stream of the same name, signifying "running between mountains," an important tributary which comes in a mile above. Here we decided to camp, about twenty miles from the Dam, at the mouth of Murch Brook and the Aboljacknagesic, mountain streams, broad off from Ktaadn, and about a dozen miles from its summit; having made fifteen miles this day.

We had been told by McCauslin that we should here find trout enough: so, while some prepared the camp, the rest fell to fishing. Seizing the birch-poles which some party of Indians, or white hunters, had left on the shore, and baiting our hooks with pork, and with trout, as soon as they were caught, we cast our lines into the mouth of the Aboljacknagesic, a clear, swift, shallow stream, which came in from Ktaadn. Instantly a shoal of white chivin (*Leucisci pulchelli*), silvery roaches, cousin-trout, or what not, large and small, prowling thereabouts, fell upon our bait, and one after another were landed amidst the bushes. Anon their cousins, the true trout, took their turn, and alternately the speckled trout, and the silvery roaches, swallowed the bait as fast as we could throw in; and the finest specimens of both that I have ever seen, the largest one weighing three pounds, were heaved upon the shore, though at first in vain, to wriggle down into the water again, for we stood in the boat; but soon we learned to remedy this evil: for one, who had lost his hook, stood on shore to catch them as they fell in a perfect shower around him,— sometimes, wet and slippery, full in his face and bosom, as his arms were outstretched to receive them. While yet alive, before their tints had faded, they glistened like the fairest flowers, the product of primitive rivers; and he could hardly trust his senses, as he stood over them, that these jewels should have swam away in that Aboljacknagesic water for so long, so many dark ages;—these bright fluviatile flowers, seen of Indians only, made beautiful, the Lord only knows why, to swim there! I could understand better, for this, the truth of mythology, the fables of Proteus, and all those beautiful sea-monsters,—how all history, indeed, put to a terrestrial use, is mere history; but put to a celestial, is mythology always.

But there is the rough voice of Uncle George, who commands at the frying-pan, to send over what you've got, and then you may stay till morning. The pork sizzles, and cries for fish. Luckily for the foolish race, and this particularly foolish generation of trout, the night shut down at last, not a little deepened by the dark side of Ktaadn, which, like a permanent shadow, reared itself from the eastern bank. Lescarbot, writing in 1609, tells us that the Sieur Champdoré, who, with one of the people of the Sieur de Monts, ascended some fifty leagues up the St. John in 1608, found the fish so plenty, "qu'en mettant la chaudière sur le feu ils en avoient pris suffisamment pour eux dîsner avant que l'eau fust chaude." Their descendants here are no less numerous. So we accompanied Tom into the woods to cut cedar-twigs for our bed. While he went ahead with the axe, and lopt off the smallest twigs of the flat-leaved cedar, the arbor-vitæ of the gardens, we gathered them up, and returned with them to the boat, until it was loaded. Our bed was made with as much care and skill as a roof is shingled; beginning at the foot, and laying the twig end of the cedar upward, we advanced to the head, a course at a time, thus successively covering the stub-ends, and producing a soft and level bed. For us six it was about ten feet long by six in breadth. This time we lay under our tent, having pitched it more prudently with reference to the wind and the flame, and the usual huge fire blazed in front. Supper was eaten off a large log, which some freshet had thrown up. This night we had a dish of arbor-vitæ, or cedar-tea, which the lumberer sometimes uses when other herbs fail,—

> "A quart of arbor-vitæ,
> To make him strong and mighty,"

but I had no wish to repeat the experiment. It had too medicinal a taste for my palate. There was the skeleton of a moose here, whose bones some Indian hunters had picked on this very spot.

In the night I dreamed of trout-fishing; and, when at length I awoke, it seemed a fable that this painted fish swam there so near my couch, and rose to our hooks the last evening, and I doubted if I had not dreamed it all. So I arose before dawn to test its truth, while my companions were still sleeping. There stood Ktaadn with distinct and cloudless outline in the moonlight; and the rippling of the rapids was the only sound to break the stillness. Standing on the shore, I once more cast my line into the stream, and found the dream to be real and the fable true. The speckled trout and silvery roach, like flying-fish, sped swiftly through the moonlight air, describing bright arcs on the dark side of Ktaadn, until moonlight, now fading into daylight, brought satiety to my mind, and the minds of my companions, who had joined me.

By six o'clock, having mounted our packs and a good blanketful of trout, ready dressed, and swung up such baggage and provision as we wished to leave behind, upon the tops of saplings, to be out of the reach of bears, we started for the summit of the mountain, distant, as Uncle George said the boatmen called it, about four miles, but as I judged, and as it proved, nearer fourteen. He had never been any nearer the mountain than this, and there was not the slightest trace of man to guide us farther in this direction. At first, pushing a few rods up the Aboljacknagesic, or "open-land stream," we fastened our batteau to a tree, and travelled up the north side, through burnt lands, now partially overgrown with young aspens, and other shrubbery; but soon, recrossing this stream, where it was about fifty or sixty feet wide, upon a jam of logs and rocks,—and you could cross it by this means almost anywhere,—we struck at once for the highest peak, over a mile or more of comparatively open land still, very gradually ascending the while. Here it fell to my lot, as the oldest mountain-climber, to take the lead. So, scanning the woody side of the mountain, which lay still at an indefinite distance, stretched out some seven or eight miles in length before us, we determined to steer directly for the base of the highest peak, leaving a large slide, by which, as I have since learned, some of our predecessors ascended, on our left. This course would lead us parallel to a dark seam in the forest, which marked the bed of a torrent, and over a slight spur, which extended southward from the main mountain, from whose bare summit we could get an outlook over the country, and climb directly up the peak, which would then be close at hand. Seen from this point, a bare ridge at the extremity of the open land, Ktaadn presented a different aspect from any mountain I have seen, there being a greater proportion of naked rock rising abruptly from the forest; and we looked up at this blue barrier as if it were some fragment of a wall which anciently bounded the earth in that direction. Setting the compass for a northeast course, which was the bearing of the southern base of the highest peak, we were soon buried in the woods.

We soon began to meet with traces of bears and moose, and those of rabbits were everywhere visible. The tracks of moose, more or less recent, to speak literally, covered every square rod on the sides of the mountain; and these animals are probably more numerous there now than ever before, being driven into this wilderness, from all sides, by the settlements. The track of a full-grown moose is like that of a cow, or larger, and of the young, like that of a calf. Sometimes we found ourselves travelling in faint paths, which they had made, like cow-paths in the woods, only far more indistinct, being rather openings, affording imperfect vistas through the dense underwood, than trodden paths; and everywhere the twigs had been browsed by them, clipt as smoothly as if by a knife. The bark of trees was stript up by them to the height of eight or nine feet, in long, narrow strips, an inch wide, still showing the distinct marks of their teeth. We expected nothing less than to meet a herd of them every moment, and our Nimrod held his shooting-iron in readiness; but we did not go out of our way to look for them, and, though numerous, they are so wary that the unskilful hunter might range the forest a long time before he could get sight of one. They are sometimes dangerous to encounter, and will not turn out for the hunter, but furiously rush upon him and trample him to death, unless he is lucky enough to avoid them by dodging round a tree. The largest are nearly as large as a horse, and weigh sometimes one thousand pounds; and it is said that they can step over a five-feet gate in their ordinary walk. They are described as exceedingly awkward-looking animals, with their long legs and short bodies, making a ludicrous figure when in full run, but making great headway nevertheless. It seemed a mystery to us how they could thread these woods, which it required all our suppleness to accomplish,—climbing, stooping, and winding, alternately. They are said to drop their long and branching horns, which usually spread five or six feet, on their backs, and make their way easily by the weight of their bodies. Our boatmen said, but I know not with how much truth, that their horns are apt to be gnawed away by vermin while they sleep. Their flesh, which is more like beef than venison, is common in Bangor market.

We had proceeded on thus seven or eight miles, till about noon, with frequent pauses to refresh the weary ones, crossing a considerable mountain stream, which we conjectured to be Murch Brook, at whose mouth we had camped, all the time in woods, without having once seen the summit, and rising very gradually, when the boatmen, beginning to despair a little, and fearing that we were leaving the mountain on one side of us, for they had not entire faith in the compass, McCauslin climbed a tree, from the top of which he could see the peak, when it appeared that we had not swerved from a right line, the compass down below still ranging with his arm, which pointed to the summit. By the side of a cool mountain rill, amid the woods, where the water began to partake of the purity and transparency of the air, we stopped to cook some of our fishes, which we had brought thus far in order to save our hard bread and pork, in the use of which we had put ourselves on short allowance. We soon had a fire blazing, and stood around it, under the damp and sombre forest of firs and birches, each with a sharpened stick, three or four feet in length, upon which he had spitted his trout, or roach, previously well gashed and salted, our sticks radiating like the spokes of a wheel from one centre, and each crowding his particular fish into the most desirable exposure, not with the truest regard always to his neighbor's rights. Thus we regaled ourselves, drinking meanwhile at the spring, till one man's pack, at least, was considerably lightened, when we again took up our line of march.

At length we reached an elevation sufficiently bare to afford a view of the summit, still distant and blue, almost as if retreating from us. A torrent, which proved to be the same we had crossed, was seen tumbling down in front, literally from out of the clouds. But this glimpse at our whereabouts was soon lost, and we were buried in the woods again. The wood was chiefly yellow birch, spruce, fir, mountain-ash, or roundwood, as the Maine people call it, and moose-wood. It was the worst kind of travelling; sometimes like the densest scrub-oak patches with us. The cornel, or bunch-berries, were very abundant, as well as Solomon's seal and moose-berries. Blue-berries were distributed along our whole route; and in one place the bushes were drooping with the weight of the fruit, still as fresh as ever. It was the 7th of September. Such patches afforded a grateful repast, and served to bait the tired party forward. When any lagged behind, the cry of "blue-berries" was most effectual to bring them up. Even at this elevation we passed through a moose-yard, formed by a large flat rock, four or five rods square, where they tread down the snow in winter. At length, fearing that if we held the direct course to the summit, we should not find any water near our camping-ground, we gradually swerved to the west, till, at four o'clock, we struck again the torrent which I have mentioned, and here, in view of the summit, the weary party decided to camp that night.

While my companions were seeking a suitable spot for this purpose, I improved the little daylight that was left, in climbing the mountain alone. We were in a deep and narrow ravine, sloping up to the clouds, at an angle of nearly forty-five degrees, and hemmed in by walls of rock, which were at first covered with low trees, then with impenetrable thickets of scraggy birches and spruce-trees, and with moss, but at last bare of all vegetation but lichens, and almost continually draped in clouds. Following up the course of the torrent which occupied this,—and I mean to lay some emphasis on this word *up*,—pulling myself up by the side of perpendicular falls of twenty or thirty feet, by the roots of firs and birches, and then, perhaps, walking a level rod or two in the thin stream, for it took up the whole road, ascending by huge steps, as it were, a giant's stairway, down which a river flowed, I had soon cleared the trees, and paused on the successive shelves, to look back over the country. The torrent was from fifteen to thirty feet wide, without a tributary, and seemingly not diminishing in breadth as I advanced; but still it came rushing and roaring down, with a copious tide, over and amidst masses of bare rock, from the very clouds, as though a waterspout had just burst over the mountain. Leaving this at last, I began to work my way, scarcely less arduous than Satan's anciently through Chaos, up the nearest, though not the highest peak. At first scrambling on all fours over the tops of ancient black spruce-trees (*Abies nigra*), old as the flood, from two to ten or twelve feet in height, their tops flat and spreading, and their foliage blue, and nipt with cold, as if for centuries they had ceased growing upward against the bleak sky, the solid cold. I walked some good rods erect upon the tops of these trees, which were overgrown with moss and mountain-cranberries. It seemed that in the course of time they had filled up the intervals between the huge rocks, and the cold wind had uniformly levelled all over. Here the principle of vegetation was hard put to it. There was apparently a belt of this kind running quite round the mountain, though, perhaps, nowhere so remarkable as here. Once, slumping through, I looked down ten feet, into a dark and cavernous region, and saw the stem of a spruce, on whose top I stood, as on a mass of coarse basket-work, fully nine inches in diameter at the ground. These holes were bears' dens, and the bears were even then at home. This was the sort of garden I made my way *over*, for an eighth of a mile, at the risk, it is true, of treading on some of the plants, not seeing any path *through* it,—certainly the most treacherous and porous country I ever travelled.

> "Nigh foundered on he fares,
> Treading the crude consistence, half on foot,
> Half flying."

But nothing could exceed the toughness of the twigs,—not one snapped under my weight, for they had slowly grown. Having slumped, scrambled, rolled, bounced, and walked, by turns, over this scraggy country, I arrived upon a side-hill, or rather side-mountain, where rocks, gray, silent rocks, were the flocks and herds that pastured, chewing a rocky cud at sunset. They looked at me with hard gray eyes, without a bleat or a low. This brought me to the skirt of a cloud, and bounded my walk that night. But I had already seen that Maine country when I turned about, waving, flowing, rippling, down below.

When I returned to my companions, they had selected a camping-ground on the torrent's edge, and were resting on the ground; one was on the sick list, rolled in a blanket, on a damp shelf of rock. It was a savage and dreary scenery enough; so wildly rough, that they looked long to find a level and open space for the tent. We could not well camp higher, for want of fuel; and the trees here seemed so evergreen and sappy, that we almost doubted if they would acknowledge the influence of fire; but fire prevailed at last, and blazed here, too, like a good citizen of the world. Even at this height we met with frequent traces of moose, as well as of bears. As here was no cedar, we made our bed of coarser feathered spruce; but at any rate the feathers were plucked from the live tree. It was, perhaps, even a more grand and desolate place for a night's lodging than the summit would have been, being in the neighborhood of those wild trees, and of the torrent. Some more aerial and finer-spirited winds rushed and roared through the ravine all night, from time to time arousing our fire, and dispersing the embers about. It was as if we lay in the very nest of a young whirlwind. At midnight, one of my bedfellows, being startled in his dreams by the sudden blazing up to its top of a fir-tree, whose green boughs were dried by the heat, sprang up, with a cry, from his bed, thinking the world on fire, and drew the whole camp after him.

In the morning, after whetting our appetite on some raw pork, a wafer of hard bread, and a dipper of condensed cloud or waterspout, we all together began to make our way up the falls, which I have described; this time choosing the right hand, or highest peak, which was not the one I had approached before. But soon my companions were lost to my sight behind the mountain ridge in my rear, which still seemed ever retreating before me, and I climbed alone over huge rocks, loosely poised, a mile or more, still edging toward the clouds; for though the day was clear elsewhere, the summit was concealed by mist. The mountain seemed a vast aggregation of loose rocks, as if some time it had rained rocks, and they lay as they fell on the mountain sides, nowhere fairly at rest, but leaning on each other, all rocking-stones, with cavities between, but scarcely any soil or smoother shelf. They were the raw materials of a planet dropped from an unseen quarry, which the vast chemistry of nature would anon work up, or work down, into the smiling and verdant plains and valleys of earth. This was an undone extremity of the globe; as in lignite, we see coal in the process of formation.

At length I entered within the skirts of the cloud which seemed forever drifting over the summit, and yet would never be gone, but was generated out of that pure air as fast as it flowed away; and when, a quarter of a mile farther, I reached the summit of the ridge, which those who have seen in clearer weather say is about five miles long, and contains a thousand acres of table-land, I was deep within the hostile ranks of clouds, and all objects were obscured by them. Now the wind would blow me out a yard of clear sunlight, wherein I stood; then a gray, dawning light was all it could accomplish, the cloud-line ever rising and falling with the wind's intensity. Sometimes it seemed as if the summit would be cleared in a few moments, and smile in sunshine: but what was gained on one side was lost on another. It was like sitting in a chimney and waiting for the smoke to blow away. It was, in fact, a cloud-factory,—these were the cloud-works, and the wind turned them off done from the cool, bare rocks. Occasionally, when the windy columns broke in to me, I caught sight of a dark, damp crag to the right or left; the mist driving ceaselessly between it and me. It reminded me of the creations of the old epic and dramatic poets, of Atlas, Vulcan, the Cyclops, and Prometheus. Such was Caucasus and the rock where Prometheus was bound. Æschylus had no doubt visited such scenery as this. It was vast, Titanic, and such as man never inhabits. Some part of the beholder, even some vital part, seems to escape through the loose grating of his ribs as he ascends. He is more lone than you can imagine. There is less of substantial thought and fair understanding in him, than in the plains where men inhabit. His reason is dispersed and shadowy, more thin and subtile, like the air. Vast, Titanic, inhuman Nature has got him at disadvantage, caught him alone, and pilfers him of some of his divine faculty. She does not smile on him as in the plains. She seems to say sternly, why came ye here before your time? This ground is not prepared for you. Is it not enough that I smile in the valleys? I have never made this soil for thy feet, this air for thy breathing, these rocks for thy neighbors. I cannot pity nor fondle thee here, but forever relentlessly drive thee hence to where I *am* kind. Why seek me where I have not called thee, and then complain because you find me but a stepmother? Shouldst thou freeze or starve, or shudder thy life away, here is no shrine, nor altar, nor any access to my ear.

> "Chaos and ancient Night, I come no spy
> With purpose to explore or to disturb
> The secrets of your realm, but . . .
> .   .   .   .   .   as my way
> Lies through your spacious empire up to light."

The tops of mountains are among the unfinished parts of the globe, whither it is a slight insult to the gods to climb and pry into their secrets, and try their effect on our humanity. Only daring and insolent men, perchance, go there. Simple races, as savages, do not climb mountains,—their tops are sacred and mysterious tracts never visited by them. Pomola is always angry with those who climb to the summit of Ktaadn.

According to Jackson, who, in his capacity of geological surveyor of the State, has accurately measured it,—the altitude of Ktaadn is 5,300 feet, or a little more than one mile above the level of the sea,—and he adds, "It is then evidently the highest point in the State of Maine, and is the most abrupt granite mountain in New England." The peculiarities of that spacious table-land on which I was standing, as well as the remarkable semi-circular precipice or basin on the eastern side, were all concealed by the mist. I had brought my whole pack to the top, not knowing but I should have to make my descent to the river, and possibly to the settled portion of the State alone, and by some other route, and wishing to have a complete outfit with me. But at length, fearing that my companions would be anxious to reach the river before night, and knowing that the clouds might rest on the mountain for days, I was compelled to descend. Occasionally, as I came down, the wind would blow me a vista open, through which I could see the country eastward, boundless forests, and lakes, and streams, gleaming in the sun, some of them emptying into the East Branch. There were also new mountains in sight in that direction. Now and then some small bird of the sparrow family would flit away before me, unable to command its course, like a fragment of the gray rock blown off by the wind.

I found my companions where I had left them, on the side of the peak, gathering the mountain cranberries, which filled every crevice between the rocks, together with blueberries, which had a spicier flavor the higher up they grew, but were not the less agreeable to our palates. When the country is settled, and roads are made, these cranberries will perhaps become an article of commerce. From this elevation, just on the skirts of the clouds, we could overlook the country, west and south, for a hundred miles. There it was, the State of Maine, which we had seen on the map, but not much like that,— immeasurable forest for the sun to shine on, that eastern *stuff* we hear of in Massachusetts. No clearing, no house. It did not look as if a solitary traveller had cut so much as a walking-stick there. Countless lakes,—Moosehead in the southwest, forty miles long by ten wide, like a gleaming silver platter at the end of the table; Chesuncook, eighteen long by three wide, without an island; Millinocket, on the south, with its hundred islands; and a hundred others without a name; and mountains also, whose names, for the most part, are known only to the Indians. The forest looked like a firm grass sward, and the effect of these lakes in its midst has been well compared, by one who has since visited this same spot, to that of a "mirror broken into a thousand fragments, and wildly scattered over the grass, reflecting the full blaze of the sun." It was a large farm for somebody, when cleared. According to the Gazetteer, which was printed before the boundary question was settled, this single Penobscot county, in which we were, was larger than the whole State of Vermont, with its fourteen counties; and this was only a part of the wild lands of Maine. We are concerned now, however, about natural, not political limits. We were about eighty miles, as the bird flies, from Bangor, or one hundred and fifteen, as we had rode, and walked, and paddled. We had to console ourselves with the reflection that this view was probably as good as that from the peak, as far as it went; and what were a mountain without its attendant clouds and mists? Like ourselves, neither Bailey nor Jackson had obtained a clear view from the summit.

Setting out on our return to the river, still at an early hour
in the day, we decided to follow the course of the torrent,
which we supposed to be Murch Brook, as long as it would
not lead us too far out of our way. We thus travelled about
four miles in the very torrent itself, continually crossing and
recrossing it, leaping from rock to rock, and jumping with
the stream down falls of seven or eight feet, or sometimes
sliding down on our backs in a thin sheet of water. This ravine had been the scene of an extraordinary freshet in the
spring, apparently accompanied by a slide from the mountain.
It must have been filled with a stream of stones and water, at
least twenty feet above the present level of the torrent. For a
rod or two, on either side of its channel, the trees were
barked and splintered up to their tops, the birches bent over,
twisted, and sometimes finely split, like a stable-broom; some,
a foot in diameter, snapped off, and whole clumps of trees
bent over with the weight of rocks piled on them. In one
place we noticed a rock, two or three feet in diameter, lodged
nearly twenty feet high in the crotch of a tree. For the whole
four miles, we saw but one rill emptying in, and the volume
of water did not seem to be increased from the first. We travelled thus very rapidly with a downward impetus, and grew
remarkably expert at leaping from rock to rock, for leap we
must, and leap we did, whether there was any rock at the
right distance or not. It was a pleasant picture when the foremost turned about and looked up the winding ravine, walled
in with rocks and the green forest, to see, at intervals of a rod
or two, a red-shirted or green-jacketed mountaineer against
the white torrent, leaping down the channel with his pack on
his back, or pausing upon a convenient rock in the midst of
the torrent to mend a rent in his clothes, or unstrap the dipper at his belt to take a draught of the water. At one place we
were startled by seeing, on a little sandy shelf by the side of
the stream, the fresh print of a man's foot, and for a moment
realized how Robinson Crusoe felt in a similar case; but at
last we remembered that we had struck this stream on our
way up, though we could not have told where, and one had
descended into the ravine for a drink. The cool air above, and
the continual bathing of our bodies in mountain water, alternate foot, sitz, douche, and plunge baths, made this walk

exceedingly refreshing, and we had travelled only a mile or two, after leaving the torrent, before every thread of our clothes was as dry as usual, owing perhaps to a peculiar quality in the atmosphere.

After leaving the torrent, being in doubt about our course, Tom threw down his pack at the foot of the loftiest spruce tree at hand, and shinned up the bare trunk, some twenty feet, and then climbed through the green tower, lost to our sight, until he held the topmost spray in his hand.* Mc-Causlin, in his younger days, had marched through the wilderness with a body of troops, under General Somebody, and with one other man did all the scouting and spying service. The General's word was, "Throw down the top of that tree," and there was no tree in the Maine woods so high that it did not lose its top in such a case. I have heard a story of two men being lost once in these woods, nearer to the settlements than this, who climbed the loftiest pine they could find, some six feet in diameter at the ground, from whose top they discovered a solitary clearing and its smoke. When at this height, some two hundred feet from the ground, one of them became dizzy, and fainted in his companion's arms, and the latter had to accomplish the descent with him, alternately fainting and reviving, as best he could. To Tom we cried, Where away does the summit bear? where the burnt lands? The last he could only conjecture; he descried, however, a little meadow and pond, lying probably in our course, which we concluded to steer for. On reaching this secluded meadow, we found fresh tracks of moose on the shore of the pond, and the water was still unsettled as if they had fled before us. A little farther, in a dense thicket, we seemed to be still on their trail. It was a small meadow, of a few acres, on the mountain side, concealed by the forest, and perhaps never seen by a white man

---

*"The spruce-tree," says Springer in '51, "is generally selected, principally for the superior facilities which its numerous limbs afford the climber. To gain the first limbs of this tree, which are from twenty to forty feet from the ground, a smaller tree is undercut and lodged against it, clambering up which the top of the spruce is reached. In some cases, when a very elevated position is desired, the spruce-tree is lodged against the trunk of some lofty pine, up which we ascend to a height twice that of the surrounding forest."

To indicate the direction of pines, he throws down a branch, and a man at the ground takes the bearing.

before, where one would think that the moose might browse and bathe, and rest in peace. Pursuing this course, we soon reached the open land, which went sloping down some miles toward the Penobscot.

Perhaps I most fully realized that this was primeval, untamed, and forever untameable *Nature*, or whatever else men call it, while coming down this part of the mountain. We were passing over "Burnt Lands," burnt by lightning, perchance, though they showed no recent marks of fire, hardly so much as a charred stump, but looked rather like a natural pasture for the moose and deer, exceedingly wild and desolate, with occasional strips of timber crossing them, and low poplars springing up, and patches of blueberries here and there. I found myself traversing them familiarly, like some pasture run to waste, or partially reclaimed by man; but when I reflected what man, what brother or sister or kinsman of our race made it and claimed it, I expected the proprietor to rise up and dispute my passage. It is difficult to conceive of a region uninhabited by man. We habitually presume his presence and influence everywhere. And yet we have not seen pure Nature, unless we have seen her thus vast and drear and inhuman, though in the midst of cities. Nature was here something savage and awful, though beautiful. I looked with awe at the ground I trod on, to see what the Powers had made there, the form and fashion and material of their work. This was that Earth of which we have heard, made out of Chaos and Old Night. Here was no man's garden, but the unhandselled globe. It was not lawn, nor pasture, nor mead, nor woodland, nor lea, nor arable, nor waste-land. It was the fresh and natural surface of the planet Earth, as it was made for ever and ever,—to be the dwelling of man, we say,—so Nature made it, and man may use it if he can. Man was not to be associated with it. It was Matter, vast, terrific,—not his Mother Earth that we have heard of, not for him to tread on, or be buried in,—no, it were being too familiar even to let his bones lie there,—the home, this, of Necessity and Fate. There was there felt the presence of a force not bound to be kind to man. It was a place for heathenism and superstitious rites,—to be inhabited by men nearer of kin to the rocks and to wild animals than we. We walked over it with a certain awe, stopping, from time to time, to pick the blueberries which grew there, and had a smart and spicy taste. Perchance where *our* wild pines stand, and leaves lie on their forest floor, in Concord, there were once reapers, and husbandmen planted grain; but here not even the surface had been scarred by man, but it was a specimen of what God saw fit to make this world. What is it to be admitted to a museum, to see a myriad of particular things, compared with being shown some star's surface, some hard matter in its home! I stand in awe of my body, this matter to which I am bound has become so strange to me. I fear not spirits, ghosts, of which I am one,—*that* my body might,—but I fear bodies, I tremble to meet them. What is this Titan that has possession of me? Talk of mysteries!—Think of our life in nature,—daily to be shown matter, to come in contact with it,—rocks, trees, wind on our cheeks! the *solid* earth! the *actual* world! the *common sense! Contact! Contact! Who* are we? *where* are we?

Erelong we recognized some rocks and other features in the landscape which we had purposely impressed on our memories, and, quickening our pace, by two o'clock we reached the batteau.* Here we had expected to dine on trout, but in this glaring sunlight they were slow to take the bait, so we were compelled to make the most of the crumbs of our hard bread and our pork, which were both nearly exhausted. Meanwhile we deliberated whether we should go up the river a mile farther, to Gibson's clearing, on the Sowadnehunk, where there was a deserted log-hut, in order to get a half-inch auger, to mend one of our spike-poles with. There were young spruce-trees enough around us, and we had a spare spike, but nothing to make a hole with. But as it was uncertain whether we should find any tools left there, we patched up the broken pole, as well as we could, for the downward voyage, in which there would be but little use for it. Moreover, we were unwilling to lose any time in this expedition, lest the wind should rise before we reached the larger lakes, and detain us; for a moderate wind produces quite a sea on these waters, in which a batteau will not live for a moment; and on one

*The bears had not touched things on our possessions. They sometimes tear a batteau to pieces for the sake of the tar with which it is besmeared.

occasion McCauslin had been delayed a week at the head of the North Twin, which is only four miles across. We were nearly out of provisions, and ill prepared in this respect for what might possibly prove a week's journey round by the shore, fording innumerable streams, and threading a trackless forest, should any accident happen to our boat.

It was with regret that we turned our backs on Chesuncook, which McCauslin had formerly logged on, and the Allegash lakes. There were still longer rapids and portages above; among the last the Rippogenus Portage, which he described as the most difficult on the river, and three miles long. The whole length of the Penobscot is two hundred and seventy-five miles, and we are still nearly one hundred miles from its source. Hodge, the assistant State Geologist, passed up this river in 1837, and by a portage of only one mile and three-quarters crossed over into the Allegash, and so went down that into the St. John, and up the Madawaska to the Grand Portage across to the St. Lawrence. His is the only account that I know, of an expedition through to Canada in this direction. He thus describes his first sight of the latter river, which, to compare small things with great, is like Balboa's first sight of the Pacific from the mountains of the Isthmus of Darien. "When we first came in sight of the St. Lawrence," he says, "from the top of a high hill, the view was most striking, and much more interesting to me from having been shut up in the woods for the two previous months. Directly before us lay the broad river, extending across nine or ten miles, its surface broken by a few islands and reefs, and two ships riding at anchor near the shore. Beyond, extended ranges of uncultivated hills, parallel with the river. The sun was just going down behind them, and gilding the whole scene with its parting rays."

About four o'clock, the same afternoon, we commenced our return voyage, which would require but little if any poling. In shooting rapids the boatmen use large and broad paddles, instead of poles, to guide the boat with. Though we glided so swiftly, and often smoothly, down, where it had cost us no slight effort to get up, our present voyage was attended with far more danger: for if we once fairly struck one of the thousand rocks by which we were surrounded the boat would be swamped in an instant. When a boat is swamped under these circumstances, the boatmen commonly find no difficulty in keeping afloat at first, for the current keeps both them and their cargo up for a long way down the stream; and if they can swim, they have only to work their way gradually to the shore. The greatest danger is of being caught in an eddy behind some larger rock, where the water rushes up stream faster than elsewhere it does down, and being carried round and round under the surface till they are drowned. McCauslin pointed out some rocks which had been the scene of a fatal accident of this kind. Sometimes the body is not thrown out for several hours. He himself had performed such a circuit once, only his legs being visible to his companions; but he was fortunately thrown out in season to recover his breath.* In shooting the rapids, the boatman has this problem to solve: to choose a circuitous and safe course amid a thousand sunken rocks, scattered over a quarter or half a mile, at the same time that he is moving steadily on at the rate of fifteen miles an hour. Stop he cannot; the only question is, where will he go? The bow-man chooses the course with all his eyes about him, striking broad off with his paddle, and drawing the boat by main force into her course. The stern-man faithfully follows the bow.

We were soon at the Aboljacarmegus Falls. Anxious to avoid the delay, as well as the labor, of the portage here, our boatmen went forward first to reconnoitre, and concluded to let the batteau down the falls, carrying the baggage only over the portage. Jumping from rock to rock until nearly in the middle of the stream, we were ready to receive the boat and let her down over the first fall, some six or seven feet perpendicular. The boatmen stand upon the edge of a shelf of rock, where the fall is perhaps nine or ten feet perpendicular, in from one to two feet of rapid water, one on each side of the boat, and let it slide gently over, till the bow is run out ten or twelve feet in the air; then, letting it drop squarely, while

---

*I cut this from a newspaper. "On the 11th (instant?) [May, '49], on Rappogenes Falls, Mr. John Delantee, of Orono, Me., was drowned while running logs. He was a citizen of Orono, and was twenty-six years of age. His companions found his body, enclosed it in bark, and buried it in the solemn woods."

one holds the painter, the other leaps in, and his companion following, they are whirled down the rapids to a new fall, or to smooth water. In a very few minutes they had accomplished a passage in safety, which would be as foolhardy for the unskilful to attempt as the descent of Niagara itself. It seemed as if it needed only a little familiarity, and a little more skill, to navigate down such falls as Niagara itself with safety. At any rate, I should not despair of such men in the rapids above table-rock, until I saw them actually go over the falls, so cool, so collected, so fertile in resources are they. One might have thought that these were falls, and that falls were not to be waded through with impunity, like a mud-puddle. There was really danger of their losing their sublimity in losing their power to harm us. Familiarity breeds contempt. The boatman pauses, perchance, on some shelf beneath a table-rock under the fall, standing in some cove of back-water two feet deep, and you hear his rough voice come up through the spray, coolly giving directions how to launch the boat this time.

Having carried round Pockwockomus Falls, our oars soon brought us to the Katepskonegan, or Oak Hall carry, where we decided to camp half way over, leaving our batteau to be carried over in the morning on fresh shoulders. One shoulder of each of the boatmen showed a red spot as large as one's hand, worn by the batteau on this expedition; and this shoulder, as it did all the work, was perceptibly lower than its fellow, from long service. Such toil soon wears out the strongest constitution. The drivers are accustomed to work in the cold water in the spring, rarely ever dry; and if one falls in all over he rarely changes his clothes till night, if then, even. One who takes this precaution is called by a particular nickname, or is turned off. None can lead this life who are not almost amphibious. McCauslin said soberly, what is at any rate a good story to tell, that he had seen where six men were wholly under water at once, at a jam, with their shoulders to handspikes. If the log did not start, then they had to put out their heads to breathe. The driver works as long as he can see, from dark to dark, and at night has not time to eat his supper and dry his clothes fairly, before he is asleep on his cedar bed. We lay that night on the very bed made by such a party, stretching our tent over the poles which were still standing, but reshingling the damp and faded bed with fresh leaves.

In the morning we carried our boat over and launched it, making haste lest the wind should rise. The boatmen ran down Passamagamet, and, soon after, Ambejijis Falls, while we walked round with the baggage. We made a hasty breakfast at the head of Ambejijis Lake, on the remainder of our pork, and were soon rowing across its smooth surface again, under a pleasant sky, the mountain being now clear of clouds, in the northeast. Taking turns at the oars, we shot rapidly across Deep Cove, the foot of Pamadumcook, and the North Twin, at the rate of six miles an hour, the wind not being high enough to disturb us, and reached the Dam at noon. The boatmen went through one of the log sluices in the batteau, where the fall was ten feet at the bottom, and took us in below. Here was the longest rapid in our voyage, and perhaps the running this was as dangerous and arduous a task as any. Shooting down sometimes at the rate, as we judged, of fifteen miles an hour, if we struck a rock we were split from end to end in an instant. Now, like a bait bobbing for some river monster, amid the eddies, now darting to this side of the stream, now to that, gliding swift and smooth near to our destruction, or striking broad off with the paddle and drawing the boat to right or left with all our might, in order to avoid a rock. I suppose that it was like running the rapids of the Saute de St. Marie, at the outlet of Lake Superior, and our boatmen probably displayed no less dexterity than the Indians there do. We soon ran through this mile, and floated in Quakish Lake.

After such a voyage, the troubled and angry waters, which once had seemed terrible and not to be trifled with, appeared tamed and subdued; they had been bearded and worried in their channels, pricked and whipped into submission with the spike-pole and paddle, gone through and through with impunity, and all their spirit and their danger taken out of them, and the most swollen and impetuous rivers seemed but playthings henceforth. I began, at length, to understand the boatman's familiarity with, and contempt for, the rapids. "Those Fowler boys," said Mrs. McCauslin, "are perfect ducks for the water." They had run down to Lincoln, according to her, thirty or forty miles, in a batteau, in the night, for a doctor, when it was so dark that they could not see a rod before them, and the river was swollen so as to be almost a continuous rapid, so that the doctor *cried*, when they brought him up by daylight, "Why, Tom, how did you see to steer?" "We did n't steer much,—only kept her straight." And yet they met with no accident. It is true, the more difficult rapids are higher up than this.

When we reached the Millinocket opposite to Tom's house, and were waiting for his folks to set us over, for we had left our batteau above the Grand Falls, we discovered two canoes, with two men in each, turning up this stream from Shad Pond, one keeping the opposite side of a small island before us, while the other approached the side where we were standing, examining the banks carefully for muskrats as they came along. The last proved to be Louis Neptune and his companion, now, at last, on their way up to Chesuncook after moose; but they were so disguised that we hardly knew them. At a little distance they might have been taken for Quakers, with their broad-brimmed hats, and overcoats with broad capes, the spoils of Bangor, seeking a settlement in this Sylvania,— or, nearer at hand, for fashionable gentlemen the morning after a spree. Met face to face, these Indians in their native woods looked like the sinister and slouching fellows whom you meet picking up strings and paper in the streets of a city. There is, in fact, a remarkable and unexpected resemblance between the degraded savage and the lowest classes in a great city. The one is no more a child of nature than the other. In the progress of degradation the distinction of races is soon lost. Neptune at first was only anxious to know what we "kill," seeing some partridges in the hands of one of the party, but we had assumed too much anger to permit of a reply. We thought Indians had some honor before. But—"Me been sick. O, me unwell now. You make bargain, then me go." They had in fact been delayed so long by a drunken frolic at the Five Islands, and they had not yet recovered from its effects. They had some young musquash in their canoes, which they dug out of the banks with a hoe, for food, not for their skins, for musquash are their principal food on these expeditions. So they went on up the Millinocket, and we kept down the bank of the Penobscot, after recruiting ourselves with a draught of Tom's beer, leaving Tom at his home.

Thus a man shall lead his life away here on the edge of the wilderness, on Indian Millinocket stream, in a new world, far in the dark of a continent, and have a flute to play at evening here, while his strains echo to the stars, amid the howling of wolves; shall live, as it were, in the primitive age of the world, a primitive man. Yet he shall spend a sunny day, and in this century be my contemporary; perchance shall read some scattered leaves of literature, and sometimes talk with me. Why read history, then, if the ages and the generations are now? He lives three thousand years deep into time, an age not yet described by poets. Can you well go further back in history than this? Ay! ay!—for there turns up but now into the mouth of Millinocket stream a still more ancient and primitive man, whose history is not brought down even to the former. In a bark vessel sewn with the roots of the spruce, with hornbeam paddles, he dips his way along. He is but dim and misty to me, obscured by the æons that lie between the bark-canoe and the batteau. He builds no house of logs, but a wigwam of skins. He eats no hot bread and sweet cake, but musquash and moose-meat and the fat of bears. He glides up the Millinocket and is lost to my sight, as a more distant and misty cloud is seen flitting by behind a nearer, and is lost in space. So he goes about his destiny, the red face of man.

After having passed the night, and buttered our boots for the last time, at Uncle George's, whose dogs almost devoured him for joy at his return, we kept on down the river the next day, about eight miles on foot, and then took a batteau, with a man to pole it, to Mattawamkeag, ten more. At the middle of that very night, to make a swift conclusion to a long story, we dropped our buggy over the half-finished bridge at Oldtown, where we heard the confused din and clink of a hundred saws, which never rest, and at six o'clock the next morning one of the party was steaming his way to Massachusetts.

What is most striking in the Maine wilderness is the continuousness of the forest, with fewer open intervals or glades than you had imagined. Except the few burnt-lands, the narrow intervals on the rivers, the bare tops of the high mountains, and the lakes and streams, the forest is uninterrupted. It is even more grim and wild than you had anticipated, a damp and intricate wilderness, in the spring everywhere wet and miry. The aspect of the country, indeed, is universally stern and savage, excepting the distant views of the forest from hills, and the lake prospects, which are mild and civilizing in a degree. The lakes are something which you are unprepared for; they lie up so high, exposed to the light, and the forest is diminished to a fine fringe on their edges, with here and there a blue mountain, like amethyst jewels set around some jewel of the first water,—so anterior, so superior, to all the changes that are to take place on their shores, even now civil and refined, and fair as they can ever be. These are not the artificial forests of an English king,—a royal preserve merely. Here prevail no forest laws but those of nature. The aborigines have never been dispossessed, nor nature disforested.

It is a country full of evergreen trees, of mossy silver birches and watery maples, the ground dotted with insipid, small, red berries, and strewn with damp and moss-grown rocks,—a country diversified with innumerable lakes and rapid streams, peopled with trout and various species of *leucisci*, with salmon, shad, and pickerel, and other fishes; the forest resounding at rare intervals with the note of the chicadee, the blue-jay, and the woodpecker, the scream of the fishhawk and the eagle, the laugh of the loon, and the whistle of ducks along the solitary streams; at night, with the hooting of owls and howling of wolves; in summer, swarming with myriads of black flies and mosquitoes, more formidable than wolves to the white man. Such is the home of the moose, the bear, the caribou, the wolf, the beaver, and the Indian. Who shall describe the inexpressible tenderness and immortal life of the grim forest, where Nature, though it be mid-winter, is ever in her spring, where the moss-grown and decaying trees are not old, but seem to enjoy a perpetual youth; and blissful, innocent Nature, like a serene infant, is too happy to make a noise, except by a few tinkling, lisping birds and trickling rills?

What a place to live, what a place to die and be buried in!

There certainly men would live forever, and laugh at death and the grave. There they could have no such thoughts as are associated with the village graveyard,—that make a grave out of one of those moist evergreen hummocks!

> Die and be buried who will,
>   I mean to live here still;
> My nature grows ever more young
>   The primitive pines among.

I am reminded by my journey how exceedingly new this country still is. You have only to travel for a few days into the interior and back parts even of many of the old States, to come to that very America which the Northmen, and Cabot, and Gosnold, and Smith, and Raleigh visited. If Columbus was the first to discover the islands, Americus Vespucius and Cabot, and the Puritans, and we their descendants, have discovered only the shores of America. While the republic has already acquired a history world-wide, America is still unsettled and unexplored. Like the English in New Holland, we live only on the shores of a continent even yet, and hardly know where the rivers come from which float our navy. The very timber and boards and shingles of which our houses are made, grew but yesterday in a wilderness where the Indian still hunts and the moose runs wild. New York has her wilderness within her own borders; and though the sailors of Europe are familiar with the soundings of her Hudson, and Fulton long since invented the steamboat on its waters, an Indian is still necessary to guide her scientific men to its head-waters in the Adirondac country.

Have we even so much as discovered and settled the shores? Let a man travel on foot along the coast, from the Passamaquoddy to the Sabine, or to the Rio Bravo, or to wherever the end is now, if he is swift enough to overtake it, faithfully following the windings of every inlet and of every cape, and stepping to the music of the surf,—with a desolate fishing-town once a week, and a city's port once a month to cheer him, and putting up at the light-houses, when there are any,—and tell me if it looks like a discovered and settled country, and not rather, for the most part, like a desolate island, and No-man's Land.

We have advanced by leaps to the Pacific, and left many a lesser Oregon and California unexplored behind us. Though the railroad and the telegraph have been established on the shores of Maine, the Indian still looks out from her interior mountains over all these to the sea. There stands the city of Bangor, fifty miles up the Penobscot, at the head of navigation for vessels of the largest class, the principal lumber depot on this continent, with a population of twelve thousand, like a star on the edge of night, still hewing at the forests of which it is built, already overflowing with the luxuries and refinement of Europe, and sending its vessels to Spain, to England, and to the West Indies for its groceries,—and yet only a few axe-men have gone "up river," into the howling wilderness which feeds it. The bear and deer are still found within its limits; and the moose, as he swims the Penobscot, is entangled amid its shipping, and taken by foreign sailors in its harbor. Twelve miles in the rear, twelve miles of railroad, are Orono and the Indian Island, the home of the Penobscot tribe, and then commence the batteau and the canoe, and the military road; and sixty miles above, the country is virtually unmapped and unexplored, and there still waves the virgin forest of the New World.

Chesuncook

At 5 p. m., September 13th, 1853, I left Boston, in the steamer, for Bangor, by the outside course. It was a warm and still night,—warmer, probably, on the water than on the land, —and the sea was as smooth as a small lake in summer, merely rippled. The passengers went singing on the deck, as in a parlor, till ten o'clock. We passed a vessel on her beamends on a rock just outside the islands, and some of us thought that she was the "rapt ship" which ran

> "on her side so low
> That she drank water, and her keel ploughed air,"

not considering that there was no wind, and that she was under bare poles. Now we have left the islands behind and are off Nahant. We behold those features which the discoverers saw, apparently unchanged. Now we see the Cape Ann lights, and now pass near a small village-like fleet of mackerel-fishers at anchor, probably off Gloucester. They salute us with a shout from their low decks; but I understand their "Good evening" to mean, "Don't run against me, Sir." From the wonders of the deep we go below to yet deeper sleep. And then the absurdity of being waked up in the night by a man who wants the job of blacking your boots! It is more inevitable than sea-sickness, and may have something to do with it. It is like the ducking you get on crossing the line the first time. I trusted that these old customs were abolished. They might with the same propriety insist on blacking your face. I heard of one man who complained that somebody had stolen his boots in the night; and when he found them, he wanted to know what they had done to them,—they had spoiled them,—he never put that stuff on them; and the boot-black narrowly escaped paying damages.

Anxious to get out of the whale's belly, I rose early, and joined some old salts, who were smoking by a dim light on a sheltered part of the deck. We were just getting into the river. They knew all about it, of course. I was proud to find that I had stood the voyage so well, and was not in the least digested. We brushed up and watched the first signs of dawn through an open port; but the day seemed to hang fire. We inquired the time; none of my companions had a chronometer. At length an African prince rushed by, observing, "Twelve o'clock, gentlemen!" and blew out the light. It was moon-rise. So I slunk down into the monster's bowels again.

The first land we make is Monhegan Island, before dawn, and next St. George's Islands, seeing two or three lights. Whitehead, with its bare rocks and funereal bell, is interesting. Next I remember that the Camden Hills attracted my eyes, and afterward the hills about Frankfort. We reached Bangor about noon.

When I arrived, my companion that was to be had gone up river, and engaged an Indian, Joe Aitteon, a son of the Governor, to go with us to Chesuncook Lake. Joe had conducted two white men a-moose-hunting in the same direction the year before. He arrived by cars at Bangor that evening, with his canoe and a companion, Sabattis Solomon, who was going to leave Bangor the following Monday with Joe's father, by way of the Penobscot, and join Joe in moose-hunting at Chesuncook, when we had done with him. They took supper at my friend's house and lodged in his barn, saying that they should fare worse than that in the woods. They only made Watch bark a little, when they came to the door in the night for water, for he does not like Indians.

The next morning Joe and his canoe were put on board the stage for Moosehead Lake, sixty and odd miles distant, an hour before we started in an open wagon. We carried hard bread, pork, smoked beef, tea, sugar, etc., seemingly enough for a regiment; the sight of which brought together reminded me by what ignoble means we had maintained our ground hitherto. We went by the Avenue Road, which is quite straight and very good, north-westward toward Moosehead Lake, through more than a dozen flourishing towns, with almost every one its academy,—not one of which, however, is on my General Atlas, published, alas! in 1824; so much are they before the age, or I behind it! The earth must have been considerably lighter to the shoulders of General Atlas then.

It rained all this day and till the middle of the next forenoon, concealing the landscape almost entirely; but we had hardly got out of the streets of Bangor before I began to be exhilarated by the sight of the wild fir and spruce-tops, and those of other primitive evergreens, peering through the mist in the horizon. It was like the sight and odor of cake to a schoolboy. He who rides and keeps the beaten track studies the fences chiefly. Near Bangor, the fence-posts, on account of the frost's heaving them in the clayey soil, were not planted in the ground, but were mortised into a transverse horizontal beam lying on the surface. Afterwards, the prevailing fences were log ones, with sometimes a Virginia fence, or else rails slanted over crossed stakes,—and these zigzagged or played leap-frog all the way to the lake, keeping just ahead of us. After getting out of the Penobscot Valley, the country was unexpectedly level, or consisted of very even and equal swells, for twenty or thirty miles, never rising above the general level, but affording, it is said, a very good prospect in clear weather, with frequent views of Ktaadn,—straight roads and long hills. The houses were far apart, commonly small and of one story, but framed. There was very little land under cultivation, yet the forest did not often border the road. The stumps were frequently as high as one's head, showing the depth of the snows. The white hay-caps, drawn over small stacks of beans or corn in the fields, on account of the rain, were a novel sight to me. We saw large flocks of pigeons, and several times came within a rod or two of partridges in the road. My companion said, that, in one journey out of Bangor, he and his son had shot sixty partridges from his buggy. The mountain-ash was now very handsome, as also the wayfarer's-tree or hobble-bush, with its ripe purple berries mixed with red. The Canada thistle, an introduced plant, was the prevailing weed all the way to the lake,—the road-side in many places, and fields not long cleared, being densely filled with it as with a crop, to the exclusion of everything else. There were also whole fields full of ferns, now rusty and withering, which in older countries are commonly confined to wet ground. There were very few flowers, even allowing for the lateness of the season. It chanced that I saw no asters in bloom along the road for fifty miles, though they were so abundant then in Massachusetts,—except in one place one or two of the Aster acuminatus,—and no golden-rods till within twenty miles of Monson, where I saw a three-ribbed one. There were many late buttercups, however, and the two fire-weeds, Erechthites and Epilobium, commonly where there had been a burning, and at last the pearly everlasting. I noticed occasionally very long troughs which supplied the road with water, and my companion said that three dollars annually were granted by the State to one man in each school-district, who provided and maintained a suitable water-trough by the road-side, for the use of travellers,—a piece of intelligence as refreshing to me as the water itself. That legislature did not sit in vain. It was an Oriental act, which made me wish that I was still farther down East,—another Maine law, which I hope we may get in Massachusetts. That State is banishing bar-rooms from its highways, and conducting the mountain-springs thither.

The country was first decidedly mountainous in Garland, Sangerville, and onwards, twenty-five or thirty miles from Bangor. At Sangerville, where we stopped at mid-afternoon to warm and dry ourselves, the landlord told us that he had found a wilderness where we found him. At a fork in the road between Abbot and Monson, about twenty miles from Moosehead Lake, I saw a guide-post surmounted by a pair of moose-horns, spreading four or five feet, with the word "Monson" painted on one blade, and the name of some other town on the other. They are sometimes used for ornamental hat-trees, together with deers' horns, in front entries; but, after the experience which I shall relate, I trust that I shall have a better excuse for killing a moose than that I may hang my hat on his horns. We reached Monson, fifty miles from Bangor, and thirteen from the lake, after dark.

At four o'clock the next morning, in the dark, and still in the rain, we pursued our journey. Close to the academy in this town they have erected a sort of gallows for the pupils to practice on. I thought that they might as well hang at once all who need to go through such exercises in so new a country, where there is nothing to hinder their living an out-door life. Better omit Blair, and take the air. The country about the south end of the lake is quite mountainous, and the road began to feel the effects of it. There is one hill which, it is calculated, it takes twenty-five minutes to ascend. In many places the road was in that condition called *repaired*, having just been whittled into the required semi-cylindrical form with the shovel and scraper, with all the softest inequalities in the middle, like a hog's back with the bristles up, and Jehu was expected to keep astride of the spine. As you looked off each side of the bare sphere into the horizon, the ditches were awful to behold,—a vast hollowness, like that between Saturn and his ring. At a tavern hereabouts the hostler greeted our horse as an old acquaintance, though he did not remember the driver. He said that he had taken care of that little mare for a short time, a year or two before, at the Mount Kineo House, and thought she was not in as good condition as then. Every man to his trade. I am not acquainted with a single horse in the world, not even the one that kicked me.

Already we had thought that we saw Moosehead Lake from a hill-top, where an extensive fog filled the distant lowlands, but we were mistaken. It was not till we were within a mile or two of its south end that we got our first view of it,—a suitably wild-looking sheet of water, sprinkled with small, low islands, which were covered with shaggy spruce and other wild wood,—seen over the infant port of Greenville, with mountains on each side and far in the north, and a steamer's smoke-pipe rising above a roof. A pair of moose-horns ornamented a corner of the public-house where we left our horse, and a few rods distant lay the small steamer Moosehead, Captain King. There was no village, and no summer road any farther in this direction,—but a winter road, that is, one passable only when deep snow covers its inequalities, from Greenville up the east side of the lake to Lily Bay, about twelve miles.

I was here first introduced to Joe. He had ridden all the way on the outside of the stage, the day before, in the rain, giving way to ladies, and was well wetted. As it still rained, he asked if we were going to "put it through." He was a good-looking Indian, twenty-four years old, apparently of unmixed blood, short and stout, with a broad face and reddish complexion, and eyes, methinks, narrower and more turned-up at the outer corners than ours, answering to the description of his race. Beside his under-clothing, he wore a red-flannel shirt, woollen pants, and a black Kossuth hat, the ordinary dress of the lumberman, and, to a considerable extent, of the Penobscot Indian. When, afterward, he had occasion to take off his shoes and stockings, I was struck with the smallness of his feet. He had worked a good deal as a lumberman, and appeared to identify himself with that class. He was the only one of the party who possessed an India-rubber jacket. The top strip or edge of his canoe was worn nearly through by friction on the stage.

At eight o'clock the steamer, with her bell and whistle, scaring the moose, summoned us on board. She was a well-appointed little boat, commanded by a gentlemanly captain, with patent life-seats and metallic life-boat, and dinner on board, if you wish. She is chiefly used by lumberers for the transportation of themselves, their boats, and supplies, but also by hunters and tourists. There was another steamer, named Amphitrite, laid up close by; but, apparently, her name was not more trite than her hull. There were also two or three large sail-boats in port. These beginnings of commerce on a lake in the wilderness are very interesting,—these larger white birds that come to keep company with the gulls. There were but few passengers, and not one female among them: a St. Francis Indian, with his canoe and moose-hides, two explorers for lumber, three men who landed at Sandbar Island, and a gentleman who lives on Deer Island, eleven miles up the lake, and owns also Sugar Island, between which and the former the steamer runs; these, I think, were all beside ourselves. In the saloon was some kind of musical instrument, cherubim, or seraphim, to soothe the angry waves; and there, very properly, was tacked up the map of the public lands of Maine and Massachusetts, a copy of which I had in my pocket.

The heavy rain confining us to the saloon awhile, I discoursed with the proprietor of Sugar Island on the condition of the world in Old Testament times. But at length, leaving this subject as fresh as we found it, he told me that he had lived about this lake twenty or thirty years, and yet had not been to the head of it for twenty-one years. He faces the other way. The explorers had a fine new birch on board, larger than ours, in which they had come up the Piscataquis from Howland, and they had had several messes of trout already. They were going to the neighborhood of Eagle and Chamberlain Lakes, or the head-waters of the St. John, and offered to keep us company as far as we went. The lake to-day was rougher than I found the ocean, either going or returning, and Joe remarked that it would swamp his birch. Off Lily Bay it is a dozen miles wide, but it is much broken by islands. The scenery is not merely wild, but varied and interesting; mountains were seen, farther or nearer, on all sides but the northwest, their summits now lost in the clouds; but Mount Kineo is the principal feature of the lake, and more exclusively belongs to it. After leaving Greenville, at the foot, which is the nucleus of a town some eight or ten years old, you see but three or four houses for the whole length of the lake, or about forty miles, three of them the public houses at which the steamer is advertised to stop, and the shore is an unbroken wilderness. The prevailing wood seemed to be spruce, fir, birch, and rock-maple. You could easily distinguish the hard wood from the soft, or "black growth," as it is called, at a great distance,—the former being smooth, round-topped, and light green, with a bowery and cultivated look.

Mount Kineo, at which the boat touched, is a peninsula with a narrow neck, about midway the lake on the east side. The celebrated precipice is on the east or land side of this, and is so high and perpendicular that you can jump from the top, many hundred feet, into the water, which makes up behind the point. A man on board told us that an anchor had been sunk ninety fathoms at its base before reaching bottom! Probably it will be discovered erelong that some Indian maiden jumped off it for love once, for true love never could have found a path more to its mind. We passed quite close to the rock here, since it is a very bold shore, and I observed marks of a rise of four or five feet on it. The St. Francis Indian expected to take in his boy here, but he was not at the landing. The father's sharp eyes, however, detected a canoe with his boy in it far away under the mountain, though no one else could see it. "Where is the canoe?" asked the captain, "I don't see it"; but he held on, nevertheless, and by and by it hove in sight.

We reached the head of the lake about noon. The weather had, in the meanwhile, cleared up, though the mountains were still capped with clouds. Seen from this point, Mount Kineo, and two other allied mountains ranging with it northeasterly, presented a very strong family likeness, as if all cast in one mould. The steamer here approached a long pier projecting from the northern wilderness, and built of some of its logs,—and whistled, where not a cabin nor a mortal was to be seen. The shore was quite low, with flat rocks on it, overhung with black ash, arbor-vitæ, etc., which at first looked as if they did not care a whistle for us. There was not a single cabman to cry "Coach!" or inveigle us to the United States Hotel. At length a Mr. Hinckley, who has a camp at the other end of the "carry," appeared with a truck drawn by an ox and a horse over a rude log-railway through the woods. The next thing was to get our canoe and effects over the carry from this lake, one of the heads of the Kennebec, into the Penobscot River. This railway from the lake to the river occupied the middle of a clearing two or three rods wide and perfectly straight through the forest. We walked across while our baggage was drawn behind. My companion went ahead to be ready for partridges, while I followed, looking at the plants.

This was an interesting botanical locality for one coming from the South to commence with; for many plants which are rather rare, and one or two which are not found at all, in the eastern part of Massachusetts, grew abundantly between the rails,—as Labrador tea, Kalmia glauca, Canada blueberry (which was still in fruit, and a second time in bloom), Clintonia and Linnæa borealis, which last a lumberer called *moxon*, creeping snowberry, painted trillium, large-flowered bellwort, etc. I fancied that the Aster radula, Diplopappus umbellatus, Solidago lanceolatus, red trumpet-weed, and many others which were conspicuously in bloom on the shore of the lake and on the carry, had a peculiarly wild and primitive look there. The spruce and fir trees crowded to the track on each side to welcome us, the arbor-vitæ, with its changing leaves, prompted us to make haste, and the sight of the canoe-birch gave us spirits to do so. Sometimes an evergreen just fallen lay across the track with its rich burden of cones, looking, still, fuller of life than our trees in the most favorable positions. You did not expect to find such *spruce* trees in the wild woods, but they evidently attend to their toilets each morning even there. Through such a front-yard did we enter that wilderness.

There was a very slight rise above the lake,—the country appearing like, and perhaps being, partly a swamp,—and at length a gradual descent to the Penobscot, which I was surprised to find here a large stream, from twelve to fifteen rods wide, flowing from west to east, or at right angles with the lake, and not more than two and a half miles from it. The distance is nearly twice too great on the Map of the Public Lands, and on Colton's Map of Maine, and Russell Stream is placed too far down. Jackson makes Moosehead Lake to be nine hundred and sixty feet above high water in Portland harbor. It is higher than Chesuncook, for the lumberers consider the Penobscot, where we struck it, twenty-five feet lower than Moosehead,—though eight miles above it is said to be the highest, so that the water can be made to flow either way, and the river falls a good deal between here and Chesuncook. The carryman called this about one hundred and forty miles above Bangor by the river, or two hundred from the ocean, and fifty-five miles below Hilton's, on the Canada road, the first clearing above, which is four and a half miles from the source of the Penobscot.

At the north end of the carry, in the midst of a clearing of sixty acres or more, there was a log camp of the usual construction, with something more like a house adjoining, for the accommodation of the carryman's family and passing lumberers. The bed of withered fir-twigs smelled very sweet, though really very dirty. There was also a store-house on the bank of the river, containing pork, flour, iron, batteaux, and birches, locked up.

We now proceeded to get our dinner, which always turned out to be tea, and to pitch canoes, for which purpose a large iron pot lay permanently on the bank. This we did in company with the explorers. Both Indians and whites use a mixture of rosin and grease for this purpose,—that is, for the pitching, not the dinner. Joe took a small brand from the fire and blew the heat and flame against the pitch on his birch, and so melted and spread it. Sometimes he put his mouth over the suspected spot and sucked, to see if it admitted air; and at one place, where we stopped, he set his canoe high on crossed stakes, and poured water into it. I narrowly watched his motions, and listened attentively to his observations, for we had employed an Indian mainly that I might have an opportunity to study his ways. I heard him swear once, mildly, during this operation, about his knife being as dull as a hoe,—an accomplishment which he owed to his intercourse with the whites; and he remarked, "We ought to have some tea before we start; we shall be hungry before we kill that moose."

At mid-afternoon we embarked on the Penobscot. Our birch was nineteen and a half feet long by two and a half at the widest part, and fourteen inches deep within, both ends alike, and painted green, which Joe thought affected the pitch and made it leak. This, I think, was a middling-sized one. That of the explorers was much larger, though probably not much longer. This carried us three with our baggage, weighing in all between five hundred and fifty and six hundred pounds. We had two heavy, though slender, rock-maple paddles, one of them of bird's-eye maple. Joe placed birch-bark on the bottom for us to sit on, and slanted cedar splints against the cross-bars to protect our backs, while he himself sat upon a cross-bar in the stern. The baggage occupied the middle or widest part of the canoe. We also paddled by turns in the bows, now sitting with our legs extended, now sitting upon our legs, and now rising upon our knees; but I found none of these positions endurable, and was reminded of the complaints of the old Jesuit missionaries of the torture they endured from long confinement in constrained positions in canoes, in their long voyages from Quebec to the Huron country; but afterwards I sat on the cross-bars, or stood up, and experienced no inconvenience.

It was dead water for a couple of miles. The river had been raised about two feet by the rain, and lumberers were hoping for a flood sufficient to bring down the logs that were left in the spring. Its banks were seven or eight feet high, and densely covered with white and black spruce,—which, I think, must be the commonest trees thereabouts,—fir, arbor-vitæ, canoe, yellow, and black birch, rock, mountain, and a few red maples, beech, black and mountain ash, the large-toothed aspen, many civil looking elms, now imbrowned, along the stream, and at first a few hemlocks also. We had not gone far before I was startled by seeing what I thought was an Indian encampment, covered with a red flag, on the bank, and exclaimed, "Camp!" to my comrades. I was slow to discover that it was a red maple changed by the frost. The immediate shores were also densely covered with the speckled alder, red osier, shrubby-willows or sallows, and the like. There were a few yellow-lily-pads still left, half-drowned, along the sides, and sometimes a white one. Many fresh tracks of moose were visible where the water was shallow, and on the shore, and the lily-stems were freshly bitten off by them.

After paddling about two miles, we parted company with the explorers, and turned up Lobster Stream, which comes in on the right, from the southeast. This was six or eight rods wide, and appeared to run nearly parallel with the Penobscot. Joe said that it was so called from small fresh-water lobsters found in it. It is the Matahumkeag of the maps. My companion wished to look for moose signs, and intended, if it proved worth the while, to camp up that way, since the Indian advised it. On account of the rise of the Penobscot the water ran up this stream quite to the pond of the same name, or two miles. The Spencer Mountains, east of the north end of Moosehead Lake, were now in plain sight in front of us. The kingfisher flew before us, the pigeon woodpecker was seen and heard, and nuthatches and chicadees close at hand. Joe said that they called the chicadee *kecunnilessu* in his language. I will not vouch for the spelling of what possibly was never spelt before, but I pronounced after him till he said it would do. We passed close to a woodcock, which stood perfectly still on the shore, with feathers puffed up, as if sick. This Joe said they called *nipsquecohossus*. The kingfisher was *skuscumonsuck*; bear was *wassus*; Indian Devil, *lunxus*; the mountain-ash, *upahsis*. This was very abundant and beautiful. Moose-tracks were not so fresh along this stream, except in a small creek about a mile up it, where a large log had lodged in the spring, marked "W-cross-girdle-crow-foot." We saw a pair of moose-horns on the shore, and I asked Joe if a moose had shed them; but he said there was a head attached to them, and I knew that they did not shed their heads more than once in their lives.

After ascending about a mile and a half, to within a short distance of Lobster Lake, we returned to the Penobscot. Just below the mouth of the Lobster we found quick water, and the river expanded to twenty or thirty rods in width. The moose-tracks were quite numerous and fresh here. We noticed in a great many places narrow and well-trodden paths by which they had come down to the river, and where they had slid on the steep and clayey bank. Their tracks were either close to the edge of the stream, those of the calves distinguishable from the others, or in shallow water; the holes made by their feet in the soft bottom being visible for a long time. They were particularly numerous where there was a small bay, or *pokelogan*, as it is called, bordered by a strip of meadow, or separated from the river by a low peninsula covered with coarse grass, wool-grass, etc., wherein they had waded back and forth and eaten the pads. We detected the remains of one in such a spot. At one place, where we landed to pick up a summer duck, which my companion had shot, Joe peeled a canoe-birch for bark for his hunting-horn. He then asked if we were not going to get the other duck, for his sharp eyes had seen another fall in the bushes a little farther along, and my companion obtained it. I now began to notice the bright red berries of the tree-cranberry, which grows eight or ten feet high, mingled with the alders and cornel along the shore. There was less hard wood than at first.

After proceeding a mile and three quarters below the mouth of the Lobster, we reached, about sundown, a small island at the head of what Joe called the Moosehorn Deadwater, (the Moosehorn, in which he was going to hunt that night, coming in about three miles below,) and on the upper end of this we decided to camp. On a point at the lower end lay the carcass of a moose killed a month or more before. We concluded merely to prepare our camp, and leave our baggage here, that all might be ready when we returned from moose-hunting. Though I had not come a-hunting, and felt some compunctions about accompanying the hunters, I wished to see a moose near at hand, and was not sorry to learn how the Indian managed to kill one. I went as reporter or chaplain to the hunters,—and the chaplain has been known to carry a gun himself. After clearing a small space amid the dense spruce and fir trees, we covered the damp ground with a shingling of fir-twigs, and, while Joe was preparing his birch-horn and pitching his canoe,—for this had to be done whenever we stopped long enough to build a fire, and was the principal labor which he took upon himself at such times,—we collected fuel for the night, large wet and rotting logs, which had lodged at the head of the island, for our hatchet was too small for effective chopping; but we did not kindle a fire, lest the moose should smell it. Joe set up a couple of forked stakes, and prepared half a dozen poles, ready to cast one of our blankets over in case it rained in the night, which precaution, however, was omitted the next night. We also plucked the ducks which had been killed for breakfast.

While we were thus engaged in the twilight, we heard faintly, from far down the stream, what sounded like two strokes of a woodchopper's axe, echoing dully through the grim solitude. We are wont to liken many sounds, heard at a distance in the forest, to the stroke of an axe, because they resemble each other under those circumstances, and that is the one we commonly hear there. When we told Joe of this, he exclaimed, "By George, I 'll bet that was a moose! They make a noise like that." These sounds affected us strangely, and by their very resemblance to a familiar one, where they probably had so different an origin, enhanced the impression of solitude and wildness.

At starlight we dropped down the stream, which was a dead-water for three miles, or as far as the Moosehorn; Joe telling us that we must be very silent, and he himself making no noise with his paddle, while he urged the canoe along with effective impulses. It was a still night, and suitable for this purpose,—for if there is wind, the moose will smell you,—and Joe was very confident that he should get some. The harvest moon had just risen, and its level rays began to light up the forest on our right, while we glided downward in the shade on the same side, against the little breeze that was stirring. The lofty, spiring tops of the spruce and fir were very black against the sky, and more distinct than by day, close bordering this broad avenue on each side; and the beauty of the scene, as the moon rose above the forest, it would not be easy to describe. A bat flew over our heads, and we heard a few faint notes of birds from time to time, perhaps the myrtle-bird for one, or the sudden plunge of a musquash, or saw one crossing the stream before us, or heard the sound of a rill emptying in, swollen by the recent rain. About a mile below the island, when the solitude seemed to be growing more complete every moment, we suddenly saw the light and heard the crackling of a fire on the bank, and discovered the camp of the two explorers; they standing before it in their red shirts, and talking aloud of the adventures and profits of the day. They were just then speaking of a bargain, in which, as I understood, somebody had cleared twenty-five dollars. We glided by without speaking, close under the bank, within a couple of rods of them; and Joe, taking his horn, imitated the call of the moose, till we suggested that they might fire on us. This was the last we saw of them, and we never knew whether they detected or suspected us.

I have often wished since that I was with them. They search for timber over a given section, climbing hills and often high trees to look off,—explore the streams by which it is to be driven, and the like,—spend five or six weeks in the woods, they two alone, a hundred miles or more from any town,—roaming about, and sleeping on the ground where night overtakes them,—depending chiefly on the provisions they carry with them, though they do not decline what game they come across,—and then in the fall they return and make report to their employers, determining the number of teams that will be required the following winter. Experienced men get three or four dollars a day for this work. It is a solitary and adventurous life, and comes nearest to that of the trapper of the West, perhaps. They work ever with a gun as well as an axe, let their beards grow, and live without neighbors, not on an open plain, but far within a wilderness.

This discovery accounted for the sounds which we had heard, and destroyed the prospect of seeing moose yet awhile. At length, when we had left the explorers far behind, Joe laid down his paddle, drew forth his birch horn,—a straight one, about fifteen inches long and three or four wide at the mouth, tied round with strips of the same bark,—and standing up, imitated the call of the moose,— *ugh-ugh-ugh*, or *oo-oo-oo-oo*, and then a prolonged *oo-o-o-o-o-o-o*, and listened attentively for several minutes. We asked him what kind of noise he expected to hear. He said, that, if a moose heard it, he guessed we should find out; we should hear him coming half a mile off; he would come close to, perhaps into, the water, and my companion must wait till he got fair sight, and then aim just behind the shoulder.

The moose venture out to the river-side to feed and drink at night. Earlier in the season the hunters do not use a horn to call them out, but steal upon them as they are feeding along the sides of the stream, and often the first notice they have of one is the sound of the water dropping from its muzzle. An Indian whom I heard imitate the voice of the moose, and also that of the caribou and the deer, using a much longer horn than Joe's, told me that the first could be heard eight or ten miles, sometimes; it was a loud sort of bellowing sound, clearer and more sonorous than the lowing of cattle,—the caribou's a sort of snort,—and the small deer's like that of a lamb.

At length we turned up the Moosehorn, where the Indians at the carry had told us that they killed a moose the night before. This is a very meandering stream, only a rod or two in width, but comparatively deep, coming in on the right, fitly enough named Moosehorn, whether from its windings or its inhabitants. It was bordered here and there by narrow meadows between the stream and the endless forest, affording favorable places for the moose to feed, and to call them out on. We proceeded half a mile up this, as through a narrow, winding canal, where the tall, dark spruce and firs and arbor-vitæ towered on both sides in the moonlight, forming a perpendicular forest-edge of great height, like the spires of a Venice in the forest. In two places stood a small stack of hay on the bank, ready for the lumberer's use in the winter, looking strange enough there. We thought of the day when this might be a brook winding through smooth-shaven meadows on some gentleman's grounds; and seen by moonlight then, excepting the forest that now hems it in, how little changed it would appear!

Again and again Joe called the moose, placing the canoe close by some favorable point of meadow for them to come out on, but listened in vain to hear one come rushing through the woods, and concluded that they had been hunted too much thereabouts. We saw, many times, what to our imaginations looked like a gigantic moose, with his horns peering from out the forest-edge; but we saw the forest only, and not its inhabitants, that night. So at last we turned about. There was now a little fog on the water, though it was a fine, clear night above. There were very few sounds to break the stillness of the forest. Several times we heard the hooting of a great horned-owl, as at home, and told Joe that he would call out the moose for him, for he made a sound considerably like the horn,—but Joe answered, that the moose had heard that sound a thousand times, and knew better; and oftener still we were startled by the plunge of a musquash. Once, when Joe had called again, and we were listening for moose, we heard, come faintly echoing, or creeping from far, through the moss-clad aisles, a dull, dry, rushing sound, with a solid core to it, yet as if half smothered under the grasp of the luxuriant and fungus-like forest, like the shutting of a door in some distant entry of the damp and shaggy wilderness. If we had not been there, no mortal had heard it. When we asked Joe in a whisper what it was, he answered,—"Tree fall." There is something singularly grand and impressive in the sound of a tree falling in a perfectly calm night like this, as if the agencies which overthrow it did not need to be excited, but worked with a subtle, deliberate, and conscious force, like a boa-constrictor, and more effectively then than even in a windy day. If there is any such difference, perhaps it is because trees with the dews of the night on them are heavier than by day.

Having reached the camp, about ten o'clock, we kindled our fire and went to bed. Each of us had a blanket, in which he lay on the fir-twigs, with his extremities toward the fire, but nothing over his head. It was worth the while to lie down in a country where you could afford such great fires; that was one whole side, and the bright side, of our world. We had first rolled up a large log some eighteen inches through and ten feet long, for a back-log, to last all night, and then piled on the trees to the height of three or four feet, no matter how green or damp. In fact, we burned as much wood that night as would, with economy and an air-tight stove, last a poor family in one of our cities all winter. It was very agreeable, as well as independent, this lying in the open air, and the fire kept our uncovered extremities warm enough. The Jesuit missionaries used to say, that, in their journeys with the Indians in Canada, they lay on a bed which had never been shaken up since the creation, unless by earthquakes. It is surprising with what impunity and comfort one who has always lain in a warm bed in a close apartment, and studiously avoided drafts of air, can lie down on the ground without a shelter, roll himself in a blanket, and sleep before a fire, in a frosty, autumn night, just after a long rain-storm, and even come soon to enjoy and value the fresh air.

I lay awake awhile, watching the ascent of the sparks through the firs, and sometimes their descent in half-extinguished cinders on my blanket. They were as interesting as fireworks, going up in endless, successive crowds, each after an explosion, in an eager, serpentine course, some to five or six rods above the tree-tops before they went out. We do not suspect how much our chimneys have concealed; and now air-tight stoves have come to conceal all the rest. In the course of the night, I got up once or twice and put fresh logs on the fire, making my companions curl up their legs.

When we awoke in the morning, (Saturday, September 17,) there was considerable frost whitening the leaves. We heard the sound of the chickaree, and a few faintly lisping birds, and also of ducks in the water about the island. I took a botanical account of stock of our domains before the dew was off, and found that the ground-hemlock, or American yew, was the prevailing under-shrub. We breakfasted on tea, hard bread, and ducks.

Before the fog had fairly cleared away, we paddled down the stream again, and were soon past the mouth of the Moosehorn. These twenty miles of the Penobscot, between Moosehead and Chesuncook Lakes, are comparatively smooth, and a great part dead-water; but from time to time it is shallow and rapid, with rocks or gravel-beds, where you can wade across. There is no expanse of water, and no break in the forest, and the meadow is a mere edging here and there. There are no hills near the river nor within sight, except one or two distant mountains seen in a few places. The banks are from six to ten feet high, but once or twice rise gently to higher ground. In many places the forest on the bank was but a thin strip, letting the light through from some alder-swamp or meadow behind. The conspicuous berry-bearing bushes and trees along the shore were the red osier, with its whitish fruit, hobble-bush, mountain-ash, tree-cranberry, choke-cherry, now ripe, alternate cornel, and naked viburnum. Following Joe's example, I ate the fruit of the last, and also of the hobble-bush, but found them rather insipid and seedy. I looked very narrowly at the vegetation, as we glided along close to the shore, and frequently made Joe turn aside for me to pluck a plant, that I might see by comparison what was primitive about my native river. Horehound, horsemint, and the sensitive fern grew close to the edge, under the willows and alders, and wool-grass on the islands, as along the Assabet River in Concord. It was too late for flowers, except a few asters, golden-rods, etc. In several places we noticed the slight frame of a camp, such as we had prepared to set up, amid the forest by the river-side, where some lumberers or hunters had passed a night,—and sometimes steps cut in the muddy or clayey bank in front of it.

We stopped to fish for trout at the mouth of a small stream called Ragmuff, which came in from the west, about two miles below the Moosehorn. Here were the ruins of an old lumbering-camp, and a small space, which had formerly been cleared and burned over, was now densely overgrown with the red cherry and raspberries. While we were trying for trout, Joe, Indian-like, wandered off up the Ragmuff on his own errands, and when we were ready to start was far beyond call. So we were compelled to make a fire and get our dinner here, not to lose time. Some dark reddish birds, with grayer females, (perhaps purple finches,) and myrtle-birds in their summer dress, hopped within six or eight feet of us and our smoke. Perhaps they smelled the frying pork. The latter bird, or both, made the lisping notes which I had heard in the forest. They suggested that the few small birds found in the wilderness are on more familiar terms with the lumberman and hunter than those of the orchard and clearing with the farmer. I have since found the Canada jay, and partridges, both the black and the common, equally tame there, as if they had not yet learned to mistrust man entirely. The chicadee, which is at home alike in the primitive woods and in our

wood-lots, still retains its confidence in the towns to a remarkable degree.

Joe at length returned, after an hour and a half, and said
that he had been two miles up the stream exploring, and had
seen a moose, but, not having the gun, he did not get him.
We made no complaint, but concluded to look out for Joe the
next time. However, this may have been a mere mistake, for
we had no reason to complain of him afterwards. As we continued down the stream, I was surprised to hear him whistling "O Susanna," and several other such airs, while his
paddle urged us along. Once he said, "Yes, Sir-ee." His common word was "Sartain." He paddled, as usual, on one side
only, giving the birch an impulse by using the side as a ful-
crum. I asked him how the ribs were fastened to the side rails.
He answered, "I don't know, I never noticed." Talking with
him about subsisting wholly on what the woods yielded,
game, fish, berries, etc., I suggested that his ancestors did so;
but he answered, that he had been brought up in such a way
that he could not do it. "Yes," said he, "that 's the way they
got a living, like wild fellows, wild as bears. By George! I
shan't go into the woods without provision,—hard bread,
pork, etc." He had brought on a barrel of hard bread and
stored it at the carry for his hunting. However, though he
was a Governor's son, he had not learned to read.

At one place below this, on the east side, where the bank
was higher and drier than usual, rising gently from the shore
to a slight elevation, some one had felled the trees over
twenty or thirty acres, and left them drying in order to burn.
This was the only preparation for a house between the
Moosehead carry and Chesuncook, but there was no hut nor
inhabitants there yet. The pioneer thus selects a site for his
house, which will, perhaps, prove the germ of a town.

My eyes were all the while on the trees, distinguishing between the black and white spruce and the fir. You paddle
along in a narrow canal through an endless forest, and the
vision I have in my mind's eye, still, is of the small, dark, and
sharp tops of tall fir and spruce trees, and pagoda-like arbor-
vitæs, crowded together on each side, with various hard
woods, intermixed. Some of the arbor-vitæs were at least sixty
feet high. The hard woods, occasionally occurring exclusively,

were less wild to my eye. I fancied them ornamental grounds, with farm-houses in the rear. The canoe and yellow birch, beech, maple, and elm are Saxon and Norman; but the spruce and fir, and pines generally, are Indian. The soft engravings which adorn the annuals give no idea of a stream in such a wilderness as this. The rough sketches in Jackson's Reports on the Geology of Maine answer much better. At one place we saw a small grove of slender sapling white-pines, the only collection of pines that I saw on this voyage. Here and there, however, was a full-grown, tall, and slender, but defective one, what lumbermen call a *konchus* tree, which they ascertain with their axes, or by the knots. I did not learn whether this word was Indian or English. It reminded me of the Greek κόγχη, a conch or shell, and I amused myself with fancying that it might signify the dead sound which the trees yield when struck. All the rest of the pines had been driven off.

How far men go for the material of their houses! The inhabitants of the most civilized cities, in all ages, send into far, primitive forests, beyond the bounds of their civilization, where the moose and bear and savage dwell, for their pine-boards for ordinary use. And, on the other hand, the savage soon receives from cities, iron arrow-points, hatchets, and guns, to point his savageness with.

The solid and well-defined fir-tops, like sharp and regular spear-heads, black against the sky, gave a peculiar, dark, and sombre look to the forest. The spruce-tops have a similar, but more ragged outline,—their shafts also merely feathered below. The firs were somewhat oftener regular and dense pyramids. I was struck by this universal spiring upward of the forest evergreens. The tendency is to slender, spiring tops, while they are narrower below. Not only the spruce and fir, but even the arbor-vitæ and white-pine, unlike the soft, spreading second-growth, of which I saw none, all spire upwards, lifting a dense spear-head of cones to the light and air, at any rate, while their branches straggle after as they may; as Indians lift the ball over the heads of the crowd in their desperate game. In this they resemble grasses, as also palms somewhat. The hemlock is commonly a tent-like pyramid from the ground to its summit.

After passing through some long rips, and by a large island, we reached an interesting part of the river called the Pine-Stream Dead-Water, about six miles below Ragmuff, where the river expanded to thirty rods in width and had many islands in it, with elms and canoe-birches, now yellowing, along the shore, and we got our first sight of Ktaadn.

Here, about two o'clock, we turned up a small branch three or four rods wide, which comes in on the right from the south, called Pine-Stream, to look for moose signs. We had gone but a few rods before we saw very recent signs along the water's edge, the mud lifted up by their feet being quite fresh, and Joe declared that they had gone along there but a short time before. We soon reached a small meadow on the east side, at an angle in the stream, which was, for the most part, densely covered with alders. As we were advancing along the edge of this, rather more quietly than usual, perhaps, on account of the freshness of the signs,—the design being to camp up this stream, if it promised well,—I heard a slight crackling of twigs deep in the alders, and turned Joe's attention to it; whereupon he began to push the canoe back rapidly; and we had receded thus half a dozen rods, when we suddenly spied two moose standing just on the edge of the open part of the meadow which we had passed, not more than six or seven rods distant, looking round the alders at us. They made me think of great frightened rabbits, with their long ears and half-inquisitive, half-frightened looks; the true denizens of the forest, (I saw at once,) filling a vacuum which now first I discovered had not been filled for me,— *moose-men*, *wood-eaters*, the word is said to mean,—clad in a sort of Vermont gray, or homespun. Our Nimrod, owing to the retrograde movement, was now the farthest from the game; but being warned of its neighborhood, he hastily stood up, and, while we ducked, fired over our heads one barrel at the foremost, which alone he saw, though he did not know what kind of creature it was; whereupon this one dashed across the meadow and up a high bank on the northeast, so rapidly as to leave but an indistinct impression of its outlines on my mind. At the same instant, the other, a young one, but as tall as a horse, leaped out into the stream, in full sight, and there stood cowering for a moment, or rather its disproportionate lowness behind gave it that appearance, and uttering two or three trumpeting squeaks. I have an indistinct recollection of seeing the old one pause an instant on the top of the bank in the woods, look toward its shivering young, and then dash away again. The second barrel was levelled at the calf, and when we expected to see it drop in the water, after a little hesitation, it, too, got out of the water, and dashed up the hill, though in a somewhat different direction. All this was the work of a few seconds, and our hunter, having never seen a moose before, did not know but they were deer, for they stood partly in the water, nor whether he had fired at the same one twice or not. From the style in which they went off, and the fact that he was not used to standing up and firing from a canoe, I judged that we should not see anything more of them. The Indian said that they were a cow and her calf,— a yearling, or perhaps two years old, for they accompany their dams so long; but, for my part, I had not noticed much difference in their size. It was but two or three rods across the meadow to the foot of the bank, which, like all the world thereabouts, was densely wooded; but I was surprised to notice, that, as soon as the moose had passed behind the veil of the woods, there was no sound of footsteps to be heard from the soft, damp moss which carpets that forest, and long before we landed, perfect silence reigned. Joe said, "If you wound 'em moose, me sure get 'em."

We all landed at once. My companion reloaded; the Indian fastened his birch, threw off his hat, adjusted his waistband, seized the hatchet, and set out. He told me afterward, casually, that before we landed he had seen a drop of blood on the bank, when it was two or three rods off. He proceeded rapidly up the bank and through the woods, with a peculiar, elastic, noiseless, and stealthy tread, looking to right and left on the ground, and stepping in the faint tracks of the wounded moose, now and then pointing in silence to a single drop of blood on the handsome, shining leaves of the Clintonia Borealis, which, on every side, covered the ground, or to a dry fern-stem freshly broken, all the while chewing some leaf or else the spruce gum. I followed, watching his motions more than the trail of the moose. After following the trail about forty rods in a pretty direct course, stepping over fallen trees and winding between standing ones, he at length lost it, for there were many other moose-tracks there, and, returning once more to the last blood-stain, traced it a little way and lost it again, and, too soon, I thought, for a good hunter, gave it up entirely. He traced a few steps, also, the tracks of the calf; but, seeing no blood, soon relinquished the search.

I observed, while he was tracking the moose, a certain reticence or moderation in him. He did not communicate several observations of interest which he made, as a white man would have done, though they may have leaked out afterward. At another time, when we heard a slight crackling of twigs and he landed to reconnoitre, he stepped lightly and gracefully, stealing through the bushes with the least possible noise, in a way in which no white man does,—as it were, finding a place for his foot each time.

About half an hour after seeing the moose, we pursued our voyage up Pine-Stream, and, soon, coming to a part which was very shoal and also rapid, we took out the baggage, and proceeded to carry it round, while Joe got up with the canoe alone. We were just completing our portage and I was absorbed in the plants, admiring the leaves of the aster macrophyllus, ten inches wide, and plucking the seeds of the great round-leaved orchis, when Joe exclaimed from the stream that he had killed a moose. He had found the cow-moose lying dead, but quite warm, in the middle of the stream, which was so shallow that it rested on the bottom, with hardly a third of its body above water. It was about an hour after it was shot, and it was swollen with water. It had run about a hundred rods and sought the stream again, cutting off a slight bend. No doubt, a better hunter would have tracked it to this spot at once. I was surprised at its great size, horse-like, but Joe said it was not a large cow-moose. My companion went in search of the calf again. I took hold of the ears of the moose, while Joe pushed his canoe down stream toward a favorable shore, and so we made out, though with some difficulty, its long nose frequently sticking in the bottom, to drag it into still shallower water. It was a brownish black, or perhaps a dark iron-gray, on the back and sides, but lighter beneath and in front. I took the cord which served for the canoe's painter, and with Joe's assistance measured it carefully, the greatest distances first, making a knot each time.

The painter being wanted, I reduced these measures that night with equal care to lengths and fractions of my umbrella, beginning with the smallest measures, and untying the knots as I proceeded; and when we arrived at Chesuncook the next day, finding a two-foot rule there, I reduced the last to feet and inches; and, moreover, I made myself a two-foot rule of a thin and narrow strip of black ash which would fold up conveniently to six inches. All this pains I took because I did not wish to be obliged to say merely that the moose was very large. Of the various dimensions which I obtained I will mention only two. The distance from the tips of the hoofs of the fore-feet, stretched out, to the top of the back between the shoulders, was seven feet and five inches. I can hardly believe my own measure, for this is about two feet greater than the height of a tall horse. [Indeed, I am now satisfied that this measurement was incorrect, but the other measures given here I can warrant to be correct, having proved them in a more recent visit to those woods.] The extreme length was eight feet and two inches. Another cow-moose, which I have since measured in those woods with a tape, was just six feet from the tip of the hoof to the shoulders, and eight feet long as she lay.

When afterward I asked an Indian at the carry how much taller the male was, he answered, "Eighteen inches," and made me observe the height of a cross-stake over the fire, more than four feet from the ground, to give me some idea of the depth of his chest. Another Indian, at Oldtown, told me that they were nine feet high to the top of the back, and that one which he tried weighed eight hundred pounds. The length of the spinal projections between the shoulders is very great. A white hunter, who was the best authority among hunters that I could have, told me that the male was *not* eighteen inches taller than the female; yet he agreed that he was sometimes nine feet high to the top of the back, and weighed a thousand pounds. Only the male has horns, and they rise two feet or more above the shoulders,—spreading three or four, and sometimes six feet,—which would make him in all, sometimes, eleven feet high! According to this calculation, the moose is as tall, though it may not be as large, as the great Irish elk, Megaceros Hibernicus, of a former period, of which

Mantell says that it "very far exceeded in magnitude any living species, the skeleton" being "upward of ten feet high from the ground to the highest point of the antlers." Joe said, that, though the moose shed the whole horn annually, each new horn has an additional prong; but I have noticed that they sometimes have more prongs on one side than on the other. I was struck with the delicacy and tenderness of the hoofs, which divide very far up, and the one half could be pressed very much behind the other, thus probably making the animal surer-footed on the uneven ground and slippery moss-covered logs of the primitive forest. They were very unlike the stiff and battered feet of our horses and oxen. The bare, horny part of the fore-foot was just six inches long, and the two portions could be separated four inches at the extremities.

The moose is singularly grotesque and awkward to look at. Why should it stand so high at the shoulders? Why have so long a head? Why have no tail to speak of? for in my examination I overlooked it entirely. Naturalists say it is an inch and a half long. It reminded me at once of the camelopard, high before and low behind,—and no wonder, for, like it, it is fitted to browse on trees. The upper lip projected two inches beyond the lower for this purpose. This was the kind of man that was at home there; for, as near as I can learn, that has never been the residence, but rather the hunting-ground of the Indian. The moose will perhaps one day become extinct; but how naturally then, when it exists only as a fossil relic, and unseen as that, may the poet or sculptor invent a fabulous animal with similar branching and leafy horns,—a sort of fucus or lichen in bone,—to be the inhabitant of such a forest as this!

Here, just at the head of the murmuring rapids, Joe now proceeded to skin the moose with a pocket-knife, while I looked on; and a tragical business it was,—to see that still warm and palpitating body pierced with a knife, to see the warm milk stream from the rent udder, and the ghastly naked red carcass appearing from within its seemly robe, which was made to hide it. The ball had passed through the shoulder-blade diagonally and lodged under the skin on the opposite side, and was partially flattened. My companion keeps it to show to his grandchildren. He has the shanks of another moose which he has since shot, skinned and stuffed, ready to be made into boots by putting in a thick leather sole. Joe said, if a moose stood fronting you, you must not fire, but advance toward him, for he will turn slowly and give you a fair shot. In the bed of this narrow, wild, and rocky stream, between two lofty walls of spruce and firs, a mere cleft in the forest which the stream had made, this work went on. At length Joe had stripped off the hide and dragged it trailing to the shore, declaring that it weighed a hundred pounds, though probably fifty would have been nearer the truth. He cut off a large mass of the meat to carry along, and another, together with the tongue and nose, he put with the hide on the shore to lie there all night, or till we returned. I was surprised that he thought of leaving this meat thus exposed by the side of the carcass, as the simplest course, not fearing that any creature would touch it; but nothing did. This could hardly have happened on the bank of one of our rivers in the eastern part of Massachusetts; but I suspect that fewer small wild animals are prowling there than with us. Twice, however, in this excursion I had a glimpse of a species of large mouse.

This stream was so withdrawn, and the moose-tracks were so fresh, that my companions, still bent on hunting, concluded to go farther up it and camp, and then hunt up or down at night. Half a mile above this, at a place where I saw the aster puniceus and the beaked hazel, as we paddled along, Joe, hearing a slight rustling amid the alders, and seeing something black about two rods off, jumped up and whispered, "Bear!" but before the hunter had discharged his piece, he corrected himself to "Beaver!"—"Hedgehog!" The bullet killed a large hedgehog more than two feet and eight inches long. The quills were rayed out and flattened on the hinder part of its back, even as if it had lain on that part, but were erect and long between this and the tail. Their points, closely examined, were seen to be finely bearded or barbed, and shaped like an awl, that is, a little concave, to give the barbs effect. After about a mile of still water, we prepared our camp on the right side, just at the foot of a considerable fall. Little chopping was done that night, for fear of scaring the moose. We had moose-meat fried for supper. It tasted like tender beef, with perhaps more flavor,—sometimes like veal.

After supper, the moon having risen, we proceeded to hunt a mile up this stream, first "carrying" about the falls. We made a picturesque sight, wending single-file along the shore, climbing over rocks and logs,—Joe, who brought up the rear, twirling his canoe in his hands as if it were a feather, in places where it was difficult to get along without a burden. We launched the canoe again from the ledge over which the stream fell, but after half a mile of still water, suitable for hunting, it became rapid again, and we were compelled to make our way along the shore, while Joe endeavored to get up in the birch alone, though it was still very difficult for him to pick his way amid the rocks in the night. We on the shore found the worst of walking, a perfect chaos of fallen and drifted trees, and of bushes projecting far over the water, and now and then we made our way across the mouth of a small tributary on a kind of net-work of alders. So we went tumbling on in the dark, being on the shady side, effectually scaring all the moose and bears that might be thereabouts. At length we came to a standstill, and Joe went forward to reconnoitre; but he reported that it was still a continuous rapid as far as he went, or half a mile, with no prospect of improvement, as if it were coming down from a mountain. So we turned about, hunting back to the camp through the still water. It was a splendid moonlight night, and I, getting sleepy as it grew late,—for I had nothing to do,—found it difficult to realize where I was. This stream was much more unfrequented than the main one, lumbering operations being no longer carried on in this quarter. It was only three or four rods wide, but the firs and spruce through which it trickled seemed yet taller by contrast. Being in this dreamy state, which the moonlight enhanced, I did not clearly discern the shore, but seemed, most of the time, to be floating through ornamental grounds,—for I associated the fir-tops with such scenes;—very high up some Broadway, and beneath or between their tops, I thought I saw an endless succession of porticos and columns, cornices and façades, verandas and churches. I did not merely fancy this, but in my drowsy state such was the illusion. I fairly lost myself in sleep several times, still dreaming of that architecture and the nobility that dwelt behind and might issue from it; but all at once I would be aroused and brought back to a sense of my actual position by the sound of Joe's birch horn in the midst of all this silence calling the moose, *ugh, ugh, oo-oo-oo-oo-oo-oo*, and I prepared to hear a furious moose come rushing and crashing through the forest, and see him burst out on to the little strip of meadow by our side.

But, on more accounts than one, I had had enough of moose-hunting. I had not come to the woods for this purpose, nor had I foreseen it, though I had been willing to learn how the Indian manœuvred; but one moose killed was as good, if not as bad, as a dozen. The afternoon's tragedy, and my share in it, as it affected the innocence, destroyed the pleasure of my adventure. It is true, I came as near as is possible to come to being a hunter and miss it, myself; and as it is, I think that I could spend a year in the woods, fishing and hunting, just enough to sustain myself, with satisfaction. This would be next to living like a philosopher on the fruits of the earth which you had raised, which also attracts me. But this hunting of the moose merely for the satisfaction of killing him,—not even for the sake of his hide,—without making any extraordinary exertion or running any risk yourself, is too much like going out by night to some wood-side pasture and shooting your neighbor's horses. These are God's own horses, poor, timid creatures, that will run fast enough as soon as they smell you, though they *are* nine feet high. Joe told us of some hunters who a year or two before had shot down several oxen by night, somewhere in the Maine woods, mistaking them for moose. And so might any of the hunters; and what is the difference in the sport, but the name? In the former case, having killed one of God's and *your own* oxen, you strip off its hide,—because that is the common trophy, and, moreover, you have heard that it may be sold for moccasins,—cut a steak from its haunches, and leave the huge carcass to smell to heaven for you. It is no better, at least, than to assist at a slaughter-house.

This afternoon's experience suggested to me how base or coarse are the motives which commonly carry men into the wilderness. The explorers and lumberers generally are all hirelings, paid so much a day for their labor, and as such they have no more love for wild nature than wood-sawyers have for forests. Other white men and Indians who come here are for the most part hunters, whose object is to slay as many moose and other wild animals as possible. But, pray, could not one spend some weeks or years in the solitude of this vast wilderness with other employments than these,—employments perfectly sweet and innocent and ennobling? For one that comes with a pencil to sketch or sing, a thousand come with an axe or rifle. What a coarse and imperfect use Indians and hunters make of Nature! No wonder that their race is so soon exterminated. I already, and for weeks afterward, felt my nature the coarser for this part of my woodland experience, and was reminded that our life should be lived as tenderly and daintily as one would pluck a flower.

With these thoughts, when we reached our camping-ground, I decided to leave my companions to continue moose-hunting down the stream, while I prepared the camp, though they requested me not to chop much nor make a large fire, for fear I should scare their game. In the midst of the damp fir-wood, high on the mossy bank, about nine o'clock of this bright moonlight night, I kindled a fire, when they were gone, and, sitting on the fir-twigs, within sound of the falls, examined by its light the botanical specimens which I had collected that afternoon, and wrote down some of the reflections which I have here expanded; or I walked along the shore and gazed up the stream, where the whole space above the falls was filled with mellow light. As I sat before the fire on my fir-twig seat, without walls above or around me, I remembered how far on every hand that wilderness stretched, before you came to cleared or cultivated fields, and wondered if any bear or moose was watching the light of my fire; for Nature looked sternly upon me on account of the murder of the moose.

Strange that so few ever come to the woods to see how the pine lives and grows and spires, lifting its evergreen arms to the light,—to see its perfect success; but most are content to behold it in the shape of many broad boards brought to market, and deem *that* its true success! But the pine is no more lumber than man is, and to be made into boards and houses is no more its true and highest use than the truest use of a man is to be cut down and made into manure. There is a higher law affecting our relation to pines as well as to men. A pine cut down, a dead pine, is no more a pine than a dead human carcass is a man. Can he who has discovered only some of the values of whalebone and whale oil be said to have discovered the true use of the whale? Can he who slays the elephant for his ivory be said to have "seen the elephant"? These are petty and accidental uses; just as if a stronger race were to kill us in order to make buttons and flageolets of our bones; for everything may serve a lower as well as a higher use. Every creature is better alive than dead, men and moose and pine-trees, and he who understands it aright will rather preserve its life than destroy it.

Is it the lumberman, then, who is the friend and lover of the pine, stands nearest to it, and understands its nature best? Is it the tanner who has barked it, or he who has boxed it for turpentine, whom posterity will fable to have been changed into a pine at last? No! no! it is the poet; he it is who makes the truest use of the pine,—who does not fondle it with an axe, nor tickle it with a saw, nor stroke it with a plane,—who knows whether its heart is false without cutting into it,— who has not bought the stumpage of the township on which it stands. All the pines shudder and heave a sigh when *that* man steps on the forest floor. No, it is the poet, who loves them as his own shadow in the air, and lets them stand. I have been into the lumber-yard, and the carpenter's shop, and the tannery, and the lampblack-factory, and the turpentine clearing; but when at length I saw the tops of the pines waving and reflecting the light at a distance high over all the rest of the forest, I realized that the former were not the highest use of the pine. It is not their bones or hide or tallow that I love most. It is the living spirit of the tree, not its spirit of turpentine, with which I sympathize, and which heals my cuts. It is as immortal as I am, and perchance will go to as high a heaven, there to tower above me still.

Erelong, the hunters returned, not having seen a moose, but, in consequence of my suggestions, bringing a quarter of the dead one, which, with ourselves, made quite a load for the canoe.

After breakfasting on moose-meat, we returned down Pine Stream on our way to Chesuncook Lake, which was about five miles distant. We could see the red carcass of the moose lying in Pine Stream when nearly half a mile off. Just below the mouth of this stream were the most considerable rapids between the two lakes, called Pine-Stream Falls, where were large flat rocks washed smooth, and at this time you could easily wade across above them. Joe ran down alone while we walked over the portage, my companion collecting spruce gum for his friends at home, and I looking for flowers. Near the lake, which we were approaching with as much expectation as if it had been a university,—for it is not often that the stream of our life opens into such expansions,—were islands, and a low and meadowy shore with scattered trees, birches, white and yellow, slanted over the water, and maples,—many of the white birches killed, apparently by inundations. There was considerable native grass; and even a few cattle—whose movements we heard, though we did not see them, mistaking them at first for moose—were pastured there.

On entering the lake, where the stream runs southeasterly, and for some time before, we had a view of the mountains about Ktaadn, (*Katahdinauguoh* one says they are called,) like a cluster of blue fungi of rank growth, apparently twenty-five or thirty miles distant, in a southeast direction, their summits concealed by clouds. Joe called some of them the *Souadneunk* mountains. This is the name of a stream there, which another Indian told us meant "Running between mountains." Though some lower summits were afterward uncovered, we got no more complete view of Ktaadn while we were in the woods. The clearing to which we were bound was on the right of the mouth of the river, and was reached by going round a low point, where the water was shallow to a great distance from the shore. Chesuncook Lake extends northwest and southeast, and is called eighteen miles long and three wide, without an island. We had entered the northwest corner of it, and when near the shore could see only part way down it. The principal mountains visible from the land here were those already mentioned, between southeast and east, and a few summits a little west of north, but generally the north and northwest horizon about the St. John and the British boundary was comparatively level.

Ansell Smith's, the oldest and principal clearing about this lake, appeared to be quite a harbor for *bateaux* and canoes; seven or eight of the former were lying about, and there was a small scow for hay, and a capstan on a platform, now high and dry, ready to be floated and anchored to tow rafts with. It was a very primitive kind of harbor, where boats were drawn up amid the stumps,—such a one, methought, as the Argo might have been launched in. There were five other huts with small clearings on the opposite side of the lake, all at this end and visible from this point. One of the Smiths told me that it was so far cleared that they came here to live and built the present house four years before, though the family had been here but a few months.

I was interested to see how a pioneer lived on this side of the country. His life is in some respects more adventurous than that of his brother in the West; for he contends with winter as well as the wilderness, and there is a greater interval of time at least between him and the army which is to follow. Here immigration is a tide which may ebb when it has swept away the pines; there it is not a tide, but an inundation, and roads and other improvements come steadily rushing after.

As we approached the log-house, a dozen rods from the lake, and considerably elevated above it, the projecting ends of the logs lapping over each other irregularly several feet at the corners gave it a very rich and picturesque look, far removed from the meanness of weather-boards. It was a very spacious, low building, about eighty feet long, with many large apartments. The walls were well clayed between the logs, which were large and round, except on the upper and under sides, and as visible inside as out, successive bulging cheeks gradually lessening upwards and tuned to each other with the axe, like Pandean pipes. Probably the musical forest-gods had not yet cast them aside; they never do till they are split or the bark is gone. It was a style of architecture not described by Vitruvius, I suspect, though possibly hinted at in the biography of Orpheus; none of your frilled or fluted columns, which have cut such a false swell, and support nothing but a gable end and their builder's pretensions,— that is, with the multitude; and as for "ornamentation," one of those words with a dead tail which architects very properly use to describe their flourishes, there were the lichens and mosses and fringes of bark, which nobody troubled himself about. We certainly leave the handsomest paint and clapboards behind in the woods, when we strip off the bark and poison ourselves with white-lead in the towns. We get but half the spoils of the forest. For beauty, give me trees with the fur on. This house was designed and constructed with the freedom of stroke of a forester's axe, without other compass and square than Nature uses. Wherever the logs were cut off by a window or door, that is, were not kept in place by alternate overlapping, they were held one upon another by very large pins, driven in diagonally on each side, where branches might have been, and then cut off so close up and down as not to project beyond the bulge of the log, as if the logs clasped each other in their arms. These logs were posts, studs, boards, clapboards, laths, plaster, and nails, all in one. Where the citizen uses a mere sliver or board, the pioneer uses the whole trunk of a tree. The house had large stone chimneys, and was roofed with spruce-bark. The windows were imported, all but the casings. One end was a regular logger's camp, for the boarders, with the usual fir floor and log benches. Thus this house was but a slight departure from the hollow tree, which the bear still inhabits,—being a hollow made with trees piled up, with a coating of bark like its original.

The cellar was a separate building, like an ice-house, and it answered for a refrigerator at this season, our moose-meat being kept there. It was a potato-hole with a permanent roof. Each structure and institution here was so primitive that you could at once refer it to its source; but our buildings commonly suggest neither their origin nor their purpose. There was a large, and what farmers would call handsome, barn, part of whose boards had been sawed by a whip-saw; and the saw-pit, with its great pile of dust, remained before the house. The long split shingles on a portion of the barn were laid a foot to the weather, suggesting what kind of weather they have there. Grant's barn at Caribou Lake was said to be still larger, the biggest ox-nest in the woods, fifty feet by a hundred. Think of a monster barn in that primitive forest lifting its gray back above the tree-tops! Man makes very much such a nest for his domestic animals, of withered grass and fodder, as the squirrels and many other wild creatures do for themselves.

There was also a blacksmith's shop, where plainly a good deal of work was done. The oxen and horses used in lumbering operations were shod, and all the iron-work of sleds, etc., was repaired or made here. I saw them load a *bateau* at the Moosehead carry, the next Tuesday, with about thirteen hundred weight of bar iron for this shop. This reminded me how primitive and honorable a trade was Vulcan's. I do not hear that there was any carpenter or tailor among the gods. The smith seems to have preceded these and every other mechanic at Chesuncook as well as on Olympus, and his family is the most widely dispersed, whether he be christened John or Ansell.

Smith owned two miles down the lake by half a mile in width. There were about one hundred acres cleared here. He cut seventy tons of English hay this year on this ground, and twenty more on another clearing, and he uses it all himself in lumbering operations. The barn was crowded with pressed hay and a machine to press it. There was a large garden full of roots, turnips, beets, carrots, potatoes, etc., all of great size. They said that they were worth as much here as in New York. I suggested some currants for sauce, especially as they had no apple-trees set out, and showed how easily they could be obtained.

There was the usual long-handled axe of the primitive woods by the door, three and a half feet long,—for my new black-ash rule was in constant use,—and a large, shaggy dog, whose nose, report said, was full of porcupine quills. I can testify that he looked very sober. This is the usual fortune of pioneer dogs, for they have to face the brunt of the battle for their race, and act the part of Arnold Winkelried without intending it. If he should invite one of his town friends up this way, suggesting moose-meat and unlimited freedom, the latter might pertinently inquire, "What is that sticking in your nose?" When a generation or two have used up all the enemies' darts, their successors lead a comparatively easy life. We owe to our fathers analogous blessings. Many old people receive pensions for no other reason, it seems to me, but as a compensation for having lived a long time ago. No doubt our town dogs still talk, in a snuffling way, about the days that tried dogs' noses. How they got a cat up there I do not know, for they are as shy as my aunt about entering a canoe. I wondered that she did not run up a tree on the way; but perhaps she was bewildered by the very crowd of opportunities.

Twenty or thirty lumberers, Yankee and Canadian, were coming and going,—Aleck among the rest,—and from time to time an Indian touched here. In the winter there are sometimes a hundred men lodged here at once. The most interesting piece of news that circulated among them appeared to be, that four horses belonging to Smith, worth seven hundred dollars, had passed by farther into the woods a week before.

The white-pine-tree was at the bottom or farther end of all this. It is a war against the pines, the only real Aroostook or Penobscot war. I have no doubt that they lived pretty much the same sort of life in the Homeric age, for men have always thought more of eating than of fighting; then, as now, their minds ran chiefly on the "hot bread and sweet cakes"; and the fur and lumber trade is an old story to Asia and Europe. I doubt if men ever made a trade of heroism. In the days of Achilles, even, they delighted in big barns, and perchance in pressed hay, and he who possessed the most valuable team was the best fellow.

We had designed to go on at evening up the Caucomgomoc, whose mouth was a mile or two distant, to the lake of the same name, about ten miles off; but some Indians of Joe's acquaintance, who were making canoes on the Caucomgomoc, came over from that side, and gave so poor an account of the moose-hunting, so many had been killed there lately, that my companions concluded not to go there. Joe spent this Sunday and the night with his acquaintances. The lumberers told me that there were many moose hereabouts, but no caribou or deer. A man from Oldtown had killed ten or twelve moose, within a year, so near the house that they heard all his guns. His name may have been Hercules, for aught I know, though I should rather have expected to hear the rattling of his club; but, no doubt, he keeps pace with the improvements of the age, and uses a Sharpe's rifle now; probably he gets all his armor made and repaired at Smith's shop. One moose had been killed and another shot at within sight of the house within two years. I do not know whether Smith has yet got a poet to look after the cattle, which, on account of the early breaking up of the ice, are compelled to summer in the woods, but I would suggest this office to such of my acquaintances as love to write verses and go a-gunning.

After a dinner, at which apple-sauce was the greatest luxury to me, but our moose-meat was oftenest called for by the lumberers, I walked across the clearing into the forest, southward, returning along the shore. For my dessert, I helped myself to a large slice of the Chesuncook woods, and took a hearty draught of its waters with all my senses. The woods were as fresh and full of vegetable life as lichen in wet weather, and contained many interesting plants; but unless they are of white pine, they are treated with as little respect here as a mildew, and in the other case they are only the more quickly cut down. The shore was of coarse, flat, slate rocks, often in slabs, with the surf beating on it. The rocks and bleached drift-logs, extending some way into the shaggy woods, showed a rise and fall of six or eight feet, caused partly by the dam at the outlet. They said that in winter the snow was three feet deep on a level here, and sometimes four or five,—that the ice on the lake was two feet thick, clear, and four feet including the snow-ice. Ice had already formed in vessels.

We lodged here this Sunday night in a comfortable bed-room, apparently the best one; and all that I noticed unusual in the night—for I still kept taking notes, like a spy in the camp—was the creaking of the thin split boards, when any of our neighbors stirred.

Such were the first rude beginnings of a town. They spoke of the practicability of a winter-road to the Moosehead carry, which would not cost much, and would connect them with steam and staging and all the busy world. I almost doubted if the lake would be then the self-same lake,—preserve its form and identity, when the shores should be cleared and settled; as if these lakes and streams which explorers report never awaited the advent of the citizen.

The sight of one of these frontier-houses, built of these

great logs, whose inhabitants have unflinchingly maintained
their ground many summers and winters in the wilderness,
reminds me of famous forts, like Ticonderoga or Crown
Point, which have sustained memorable sieges. They are especially winter-quarters, and at this season this one had a partially deserted look, as if the siege were raised a little, the
snow-banks being melted from before it, and its garrison accordingly reduced. I think of their daily food as rations,—it
is called "supplies"; a Bible and a great-coat are munitions of
war, and a single man seen about the premises is a sentinel
on duty. You expect that he will require the countersign, and
will perchance take you for Ethan Allen, come to demand the
surrender of his fort in the name of the Continental Congress.
It is a sort of ranger service. Arnold's expedition is a daily
experience with these settlers. They can prove that they were
out at almost any time; and I think that all the first generation
of them deserve a pension more than any that went to the
Mexican war.

Early the next morning we started on our return up the
Penobscot, my companion wishing to go about twenty-five
miles above the Moosehead carry to a camp near the junction
of the two forks, and look for moose there. Our host allowed
us something for the quarter of the moose which we had
brought, and which he was glad to get. Two explorers from
Chamberlain Lake started at the same time that we did. Red-
flannel shirts should be worn in the woods, if only for the
fine contrast which this color makes with the evergreens and
the water. Thus I thought when I saw the forms of the explorers in their birch, poling up the rapids before us, far off
against the forest. It is the surveyor's color also, most distinctly seen under all circumstances. We stopped to dine at
Ragmuff, as before. My companion it was who wandered up
the stream to look for moose this time, while Joe went to
sleep on the bank, so that we felt sure of him; and I improved
the opportunity to botanize and bathe. Soon after starting
again, while Joe was gone back in the canoe for the frying-
pan, which had been left, we picked a couple of quarts of
tree-cranberries for a sauce.

I was surprised by Joe's asking me how far it was to the
Moosehorn. He was pretty well acquainted with this stream,

but he had noticed that I was curious about distances, and had several maps. He, and Indians generally, with whom I have talked, are not able to describe dimensions or distances in our measures with any accuracy. He could tell perhaps, at what time we should arrive, but not how far it was. We saw a few wood-ducks, sheldrakes, and black ducks, but they were not so numerous there at that season as on our river at home. We scared the same family of wood-ducks before us, going and returning. We also heard the note of one fish-hawk, somewhat like that of a pigeon-woodpecker, and soon after saw him perched near the top of a dead white-pine against the island where we had first camped, while a company of peetweets were twittering and teetering about over the carcass of a moose on a low sandy spit just beneath. We drove the fish-hawk from perch to perch, each time eliciting a scream or whistle, for many miles before us. Our course being up-stream, we were obliged to work much harder than before, and had frequent use for a pole. Sometimes all three of us paddled together, standing up, small and heavily laden as the canoe was. About six miles from Moosehead, we began to see the mountains east of the north end of the lake, and at four o'clock we reached the carry.

The Indians were still encamped here. There were three, including the St. Francis Indian who had come in the steamer with us. One of the others was called Sabattis. Joe and the St. Francis Indian were plainly clear Indian, the other two apparently mixed Indian and white; but the difference was confined to their features and complexions, for all that I could see. We here cooked the tongue of the moose for supper,—having left the nose, which is esteemed the choicest part, at Chesuncook, boiling, it being a good deal of trouble to prepare it. We also stewed our tree-cranberries, (*Viburnum opulus*,) sweetening them with sugar. The lumberers sometimes cook them with molasses. They were used in Arnold's expedition. This sauce was very grateful to us who had been confined to hard bread, pork, and moose-meat, and, notwithstanding their seeds, we all three pronounced them equal to the common cranberry; but perhaps some allowance is to be made for our forest appetites. It would be worth the while to cultivate them, both for beauty and for food. I afterward saw them in a garden in Bangor. Joe said that they were called *ebeemenar*.

While we were getting supper, Joe commenced curing the moose-hide, on which I had sat a good part of the voyage, he having already cut most of the hair off with his knife at the Caucomgomoc. He set up two stout forked poles on the bank, seven or eight feet high, and as much asunder east and west, and having cut slits eight or ten inches long, and the same distance apart, close to the edge, on the sides of the hide, he threaded poles through them, and then, placing one of the poles on the forked stakes, tied the other down tightly at the bottom. The two ends also were tied with cedar-bark, their usual string, to the upright poles, through small holes at short intervals. The hide, thus stretched, and slanted a little to the north, to expose its flesh side to the sun, measured, in the extreme, eight feet long by six high. Where any flesh still adhered, Joe boldly scored it with his knife to lay it open to the sun. It now appeared somewhat spotted and injured by the duck shot. You may see the old frames on which hides have been stretched at many camping-places in these woods.

For some reason or other, the going to the forks of the Penobscot was given up, and we decided to stop here, my companion intending to hunt down the stream at night. The Indians invited us to lodge with them, but my companion inclined to go to the log-camp on the carry. This camp was close and dirty, and had an ill smell, and I preferred to accept the Indians' offer, if we did not make a camp for ourselves; for, though they were dirty, too, they were more in the open air, and were much more agreeable, and even refined company, than the lumberers. The most interesting question entertained at the lumberers' camp was, which man could "handle" any other on the carry; and, for the most part, they possessed no qualities which you could not lay hands on. So we went to the Indians' camp or wigwam.

It was rather windy, and therefore Joe concluded to hunt after midnight, if the wind went down, which the other Indians thought it would not do, because it was from the south. The two mixed-bloods, however, went off up the river for moose at dark, before we arrived at their camp. This Indian camp was a slight, patched-up affair, which had stood there several weeks, built shed-fashion, open to the fire on the west. If the wind changed, they could turn it round. It was formed by two forked stakes and a cross-bar, with rafters slanted from this to the ground. The covering was partly an old sail, partly birch-bark, quite imperfect, but securely tied on, and coming down to the ground on the sides. A large log was rolled up at the back side for a head-board, and two or three moose-hides were spread on the ground with the hair up. Various articles of their wardrobe were tucked around the sides and corners, or under the roof. They were smoking moose-meat on just such a crate as is represented by With, in De Bry's "Collectio Peregrinationum," published in 1588, and which the natives of Brazil called *boucan*, (whence buccaneer,) on which were frequently shown pieces of human flesh drying along with the rest. It was erected in front of the camp over the usual large fire, in the form of an oblong square. Two stout forked stakes, four or five feet apart and five feet high, were driven into the ground at each end, and then two poles ten feet long were stretched across over the fire, and smaller ones laid transversely on these a foot apart. On the last hung large, thin slices of moose-meat smoking and drying, a space being left open over the centre of the fire. There was the whole heart, black as a thirty-two pound ball, hanging at one corner. They said, that it took three or four days to cure this meat, and it would keep a year or more. Refuse pieces lay about on the ground in different stages of decay, and some pieces also in the fire, half buried and sizzling in the ashes, as black and dirty as an old shoe. These last I at first thought were thrown away, but afterwards found that they were being cooked. Also a tremendous rib-piece was roasting before the fire, being impaled on an upright stake forced in and out between the ribs. There was a moose-hide stretched and curing on poles like ours, and quite a pile of cured skins close by. They had killed twenty-two moose within two months, but, as they could use but very little of the meat, they left the carcasses on the ground. Altogether it was about as savage a sight as was ever witnessed, and I was carried back at once three hundred years. There were many torches of birch-bark, shaped like straight tin horns, lying ready for use on a stump outside.

For fear of dirt, we spread our blankets over their hides, so as not to touch them anywhere. The St. Francis Indian and Joe alone were there at first, and we lay on our backs talking with them till midnight. They were very sociable, and, when they did not talk with us, kept up a steady chatting in their own language. We heard a small bird just after dark, which, Joe said, sang at a certain hour in the night,—at ten o'clock, he believed. We also heard the hylodes and tree-toads, and the lumberers singing in their camp a quarter of a mile off. I told them that I had seen pictured in old books pieces of human flesh drying on these crates; whereupon they repeated some tradition about the Mohawks eating human flesh, what parts they preferred, etc., and also of a battle with the Mohawks near Moosehead, in which many of the latter were killed; but I found that they knew but little of the history of their race, and could be entertained by stories about their ancestors as readily as any way. At first I was nearly roasted out, for I lay against one side of the camp, and felt the heat reflected not only from the birch-bark above, but from the side; and again I remembered the sufferings of the Jesuit missionaries, and what extremes of heat and cold the Indians were said to endure. I struggled long between my desire to remain and talk with them, and my impulse to rush out and stretch myself on the cool grass; and when I was about to take the last step, Joe, hearing my murmurs, or else being uncomfortable himself, got up and partially dispersed the fire. I suppose that that is Indian manners,—to defend yourself.

While lying there listening to the Indians, I amused myself with trying to guess at their subject by their gestures, or some proper name introduced. There can be no more startling evidence of their being a distinct and comparatively aboriginal race, than to hear this unaltered Indian language, which the white man cannot speak nor understand. We may suspect change and deterioration in almost every other particular, but the language which is so wholly unintelligible to us. It took me by surprise, though I had found so many arrow-heads, and convinced me that the Indian was not the invention of historians and poets. It was a purely wild and primitive American sound, as much as the barking of a *chickaree*, and I could not understand a syllable of it; but Paugus, had he been there, would have understood it. These Abenakis gossiped, laughed, and jested, in the language in which Eliot's Indian Bible is written, the language which has been spoken in New England who shall say how long? These were the sounds that issued from the wigwams of this country before Columbus was born; they have not yet died away; and, with remarkably few exceptions, the language of their forefathers is still copious enough for them. I felt that I stood, or rather lay, as near to the primitive man of America, that night, as any of its discoverers ever did.

In the midst of their conversation, Joe suddenly appealed to me to know how long Moosehead Lake was.

Meanwhile, as we lay there, Joe was making and trying his horn, to be ready for hunting after midnight. The St. Francis Indian also amused himself with sounding it, or rather calling through it; for the sound is made with the voice, and not by blowing through the horn. The latter appeared to be a speculator in moose-hides. He bought my companion's for two dollars and a quarter, green. Joe said that it was worth two and a half at Oldtown. Its chief use is for moccasins. One or two of these Indians wore them. I was told, that, by a recent law of Maine, foreigners are not allowed to kill moose there at any season; white Americans can kill them only at a particular season, but the Indians of Maine at all seasons. The St. Francis Indian accordingly asked my companion for a *wighiggin*, or bill, to show, since he was a foreigner. He lived near Sorel. I found that he could write his name very well, *Tahmunt Swasen*. One Ellis, an old white man of Guilford, a town through which we passed, not far from the south end of Moosehead, was the most celebrated moose-hunter of those parts. Indians and whites spoke with equal respect of him. Tahmunt said, that there were more moose here than in the Adirondack country in New York, where he had hunted; that three years before there were a great many about, and there were a great many now in the woods, but they did not come out to the water. It was of no use to hunt them at midnight,—they would not come out then. I asked Sabattis, after he came home, if the moose never attacked him. He answered, that you must not fire many times so as to mad him. "I fire once and hit him in the right place, and in the morning

I find him. He won't go far. But if you keep firing, you mad him. I fired once five bullets, every one through the heart, and he did not mind 'em at all; it only made him more mad." I asked him if they did not hunt them with dogs. He said, that they did so in winter, but never in the summer, for then it was of no use; they would run right off straight and swiftly a hundred miles.

Another Indian said, that the moose, once scared, would run all day. A dog will hang to their lips, and be carried along till he is swung against a tree and drops off. They cannot run on a "glaze," though they can run in snow four feet deep; but the caribou can run on ice. They commonly find two or three moose together. They cover themselves with water, all but their noses, to escape flies. He had the horns of what he called "the black moose that goes in low lands." These spread three or four feet. The "red moose" was another kind, "running on mountains," and had horns which spread six feet. Such were his distinctions. Both can move their horns. The broad flat blades are covered with hair, and are so soft, when the animal is alive, that you can run a knife through them. They regard it as a good or bad sign, if the horns turn this way or that. His caribou horns had been gnawed by mice in his wigwam, but he thought that the horns neither of the moose nor of the caribou were ever gnawed while the creature was alive, as some have asserted. An Indian, whom I met after this at Old-town, who had carried about a bear and other animals of Maine to exhibit, told me that thirty years ago there were not so many moose in Maine as now; also, that the moose were very easily tamed, and would come back when once fed, and so would deer, but not caribou. The Indians of this neighborhood are about as familiar with the moose as we are with the ox, having associated with them for so many generations. Father Rasles, in his Dictionary of the Abenaki Language, gives not only a word for the male moose, (*aianbé,*) and another for the female, (*hèrar,*) but for the bone which is in the middle of the heart of the moose (!), and for his left hind-leg.

There were none of the small deer up there; they are more common about the settlements. One ran into the city of Bangor two years before, and jumped through a window of costly plate glass, and then into a mirror, where it thought it recognized one of its kind, and out again, and so on, leaping over the heads of the crowd, until it was captured. This the inhabitants speak of as the deer that went a-shopping. The last-mentioned Indian spoke of the *lunxus* or Indian devil, (which I take to be the cougar, and not the *Gulo luscus*,) as the only animal in Maine which man need fear; it would follow a man, and did not mind a fire. He also said, that beavers were getting to be pretty numerous again, where we went, but their skins brought so little now that it was not profitable to hunt them.

I had put the ears of our moose, which were ten inches long, to dry along with the moose-meat over the fire, wishing to preserve them; but Sabattis told me that I must skin and cure them, else the hair would all come off. He observed, that they made tobacco-pouches of the skins of their ears, putting the two together inside to inside. I asked him how he got fire; and he produced a little cylindrical box of friction-matches. He also had flints and steel, and some punk, which was not dry; I think it was from the yellow birch. "But suppose you upset, and all these and your powder get wet." "Then," said he, " we wait till we get to where there is some fire." I produced from my pocket a little vial, containing matches, stoppled water-tight, and told him, that, though we were upset, we should still have some dry matches; at which he stared without saying a word.

We lay awake thus a long while talking, and they gave us the meaning of many Indian names of lakes and streams in the vicinity,—especially Tahmunt. I asked the Indian name of Moosehead Lake. Joe answered, *Sebamook*; Tahmunt pronounced it *Sebemook*. When I asked what it meant, they answered, Moosehead Lake. At length, getting my meaning, they alternately repeated the word over to themselves, as a philologist might,—*Sebamook*,—*Sebamook*,—now and then comparing notes in Indian; for there was a slight difference in their dialects; and finally Tahmunt said, "Ugh! I know,"— and he rose up partly on the moose-hide,—"like as here is a place, and there is a place," pointing to different parts of the hide, "and you take water from there and fill this, and it stays here; that is *Sebamook*." I understood him to mean that it was a reservoir of water which did not run away, the river coming in on one side and passing out again near the same place, leaving a permanent bay. Another Indian said, that it meant Large-Bay Lake, and that *Sebago* and *Sebec*, the names of other lakes, were kindred words, meaning large open water. Joe said that *Seboois* meant Little River. I observed their inability, often described, to convey an abstract idea. Having got the idea, though indistinctly, they groped about in vain for words with which to express it. Tahmunt thought that the whites called it Moosehead Lake, because Mount Kineo, which commands it, is shaped like a moose's head, and that Moose River was so called "because the mountain points right across the lake to its mouth." John Josselyn, writing about 1673, says, "Twelve miles from Casco Bay, and passable for men and horses, is a lake, called by the Indians Sebug. On the brink thereof, at one end, is the famous rock, shaped like a moose deer or helk, diaphanous, and called the Moose Rock." He appears to have confounded Sebamook with Sebago, which is nearer, but has no "diaphanous" rock on its shore.

I give more of their definitions, for what they are worth,— partly *because* they differ sometimes from the commonly received ones. They never analyzed these words before. After long deliberation and repeating of the word, for it gave much trouble, Tahmunt said that *Chesuncook* meant a place where many streams emptied in (?), and he enumerated them,— Penobscot, Umbazookskus, Cusabesex, Red Brook, etc.— "*Caucomgomoc*,—what does that mean?" "What are those large white birds?" he asked. "Gulls," said I. "Ugh! Gull Lake."—*Pammadumcook*, Joe thought, meant the Lake with Gravelly Bottom or Bed.—*Kenduskeag*, Tahmunt concluded at last, after asking if birches went up it, for he said that he was not much acquainted with it, meant something like this: "You go up Penobscot till you come to *Kenduskeag*, and you go by, you don't turn up there. That is *Kenduskeag*." (?) Another Indian, however, who knew the river better, told us afterward that it meant Little Eel River.—*Mattawamkeag* was a place where two rivers meet. (?)—*Penobscot* was Rocky River. One writer says, that this was "originally the name of only a section of the main channel, from the head of the tide-water to a short distance above Oldtown."

A very intelligent Indian, whom we afterward met, son-in-law of Neptune, gave us also these other definitions: — *Umbazookskus*, Meadow Stream; *Millinoket*, Place of Islands; *Aboljacarmegus*, Smooth-Ledge Falls (and Dead-Water); *Aboljacarmeguscook*, the stream emptying in; (the last was the word he gave when I asked about *Aboljacknagesic*, which he did not recognize;) *Mattahumkeag*, Sand-Creek Pond; *Piscataquis*, Branch of a River.

I asked our hosts what *Musketaquid*, the Indian name of Concord, Massachusetts, meant; but they changed it to *Musketicook*, and repeated that, and Tahmunt said that it meant Dead Stream, which is probably true. *Cook* appears to mean stream, and perhaps *quid* signifies the place or ground. When I asked the meaning of the names of two of our hills, they answered that they were another language. As Tahmunt said that he traded at Quebec, my companion inquired the meaning of the word *Quebec*, about which there has been so much question. He did not know, but began to conjecture. He asked what those great ships were called that carried soldiers. "Men-of-war," we answered. "Well," he said, " when the English ships came up the river, they could not go any farther, it was so narrow there; they must go back,—go-back,— that's Que-bec." I mention this to show the value of his authority in the other cases.

Late at night the other two Indians came home from moose-hunting, not having been successful, aroused the fire again, lighted their pipes, smoked awhile, took something strong to drink, and ate some moose-meat, and, finding what room they could, lay down on the moose-hides; and thus we passed the night, two white men and four Indians, side by side.

When I awoke in the morning the weather was drizzling. One of the Indians was lying outside, rolled in his blanket, on the opposite side of the fire, for want of room. Joe had neglected to awake my companion, and he had done no hunting that night. Tahmunt was making a cross-bar for his canoe with a singularly shaped knife, such as I have since seen other Indians using. The blade was thin, about three quarters of an inch wide, and eight or nine inches long, but curved out of its plane into a hook, which he said made it more convenient to shave with. As the Indians very far north and northwest use the same kind of knife, I suspect that it was made according to an aboriginal pattern, though some white artisans may use a similar one. The Indians baked a loaf of flour bread in a spider on its edge before the fire for their breakfast; and while my companion was making tea, I caught a dozen sizable fishes in the Penobscot, two kinds of sucker and one trout. After we had breakfasted by ourselves, one of our bedfellows, who had also breakfasted, came along, and, being invited, took a cup of tea, and finally, taking up the common platter, licked it clean. But he was nothing to a white fellow, a lumberer, who was continually stuffing himself with the Indians' moose-meat, and was the butt of his companions accordingly. He seems to have thought that it was a feast "to eat all." It is commonly said that the white man finally surpasses the Indian on his own ground, and it was proved true in this case. I cannot swear to his employment during the hours of darkness, but I saw him at it again as soon as it was light, though he came a quarter of a mile to his work.

The rain prevented our continuing any longer in the woods; so giving some of our provisions and utensils to the Indians, we took leave of them. This being the steamer's day, I set out for the lake at once.

I walked over the carry alone and waited at the head of the lake. An eagle, or some other large bird, flew screaming away from its perch by the shore at my approach. For an hour after I reached the shore there was not a human being to be seen, and I had all that wide prospect to myself. I thought that I heard the sound of the steamer before she came in sight on the open lake. I noticed at the landing, when the steamer came in, one of our bedfellows, who had been a-moose-hunting the night before, now very sprucely dressed in a clean white shirt and fine black pants, a true Indian dandy, who had evidently come over the carry to show himself to any arrivers on the north shore of Moosehead Lake, just as New York dandies take a turn up Broadway and stand on the steps of a hotel.

Midway the lake we took on board two manly-looking middle-aged men, with their *bateau*, who had been exploring for six weeks as far as the Canada line, and had let their beards grow. They had the skin of a beaver, which they had recently caught, stretched on an oval hoop, though the fur was not good at that season. I talked with one of them, telling him that I had come all this distance partly to see where the white-pine, the Eastern stuff of which our houses are built, grew, but that on this and a previous excursion into another part of Maine I had found it a scarce tree; and I asked him where I must look for it. With a smile, he answered, that he could hardly tell me. However, he said that he had found enough to employ two teams the next winter in a place where there was thought to be none left. What was considered a "top-top" tree now was not looked at twenty years ago, when he first went into the business; but they succeeded very well now with what was considered quite inferior timber then. The explorer used to cut into a tree higher and higher up, to see if it was false-hearted, and if there was a rotten heart as big as his arm, he let it alone; but now they cut such a tree, and sawed it all around the rot, and it made the very best of boards, for in such a case they were never shaky.

One connected with lumbering operations at Bangor told me that the largest pine belonging to his firm, cut the previous winter, "scaled" in the woods four thousand five hundred feet, and was worth ninety dollars in the log at the Bangor boom in Oldtown. They cut a road three and a half miles long for this tree alone. He thought that the principal locality for the white-pine that came down the Penobscot now was at the head of the East Branch and the Allegash, about Webster Stream and Eagle and Chamberlain Lakes. Much timber has been stolen from the public lands. (Pray, what kind of forest-warden is the Public itself?) I heard of one man who, having discovered some particularly fine trees just within the boundaries of the public lands, and not daring to employ an accomplice, cut them down, and by means of block and tackle, without cattle, tumbled them into a stream, and so succeeded in getting off with them without the least assistance. Surely, stealing pine-trees in this way is not so mean as robbing hen-roosts.

We reached Monson that night, and the next day rode to Bangor, all the way in the rain again, varying our route a little. Some of the taverns on this road, which were particularly dirty, were plainly in a transition state from the camp to the house.

The next forenoon we went to Oldtown. One slender old Indian on the Oldtown shore, who recognized my companion, was full of mirth and gestures, like a Frenchman. A Catholic priest crossed to the island in the same *bateau* with us. The Indian houses are framed, mostly of one story, and in rows one behind another, at the south end of the island, with a few scattered ones. I counted about forty, not including the church and what my companion called the council-house. The last, which I suppose is their town-house, was regularly framed and shingled like the rest. There were several of two stories, quite neat, with front-yards enclosed, and one at least had green blinds. Here and there were moose-hides stretched and drying about them. There were no cart-paths, nor tracks of horses, but foot-paths; very little land cultivated, but an abundance of weeds, indigenous and naturalized; more introduced weeds than useful vegetables, as the Indian is said to cultivate the vices rather than the virtues of the white man. Yet this village was cleaner than I expected, far cleaner than such Irish villages as I have seen. The children were not particularly ragged nor dirty. The little boys met us with bow in hand and arrow on string, and cried, "Put up a cent." Verily, the Indian has but a feeble hold on his bow now; but the curiosity of the white man is insatiable, and from the first he has been eager to witness this forest accomplishment. That elastic piece of wood with its feathered dart, so sure to be unstrung by contact with civilization, will serve for the type, the coat-of-arms of the savage. Alas for the Hunter Race! the white man has driven off their game, and substituted a cent in its place. I saw an Indian woman washing at the water's edge. She stood on a rock, and, after dipping the clothes in the stream, laid them on the rock, and beat them with a short club. In the graveyard, which was crowded with graves, and overrun with weeds, I noticed an inscription in Indian, painted on a wooden grave-board. There was a large wooden cross on the island.

Since my companion knew him, we called on Governor Neptune, who lived in a little "ten-footer," one of the humblest of them all. Personalities are allowable in speaking of public men, therefore I will give the particulars of our visit. He was a-bed. When we entered the room, which was one half of the house, he was sitting on the side of the bed. There was a clock hanging in one corner. He had on a black frock-coat, and black pants, much worn, white cotton shirt, socks, a red silk handkerchief about his neck, and a straw hat. His black hair was only slightly grayed. He had very broad cheeks, and his features were decidedly and refreshingly different from those of any of the upstart Native American party whom I have seen. He was no darker than many old white men. He told me that he was eighty-nine; but he was going a-moose-hunting that fall, as he had been the previous one. Probably his companions did the hunting. We saw various squaws dodging about. One sat on the bed by his side and helped him out with his stories. They were remarkably corpulent, with smooth, round faces, apparently full of good-humor. Certainly our much-abused climate had not dried up their adipose substance. While we were there,—for we stayed a good while,—one went over to Oldtown, returned and cut out a dress, which she had bought, on another bed in the room. The Governor said, that "he could remember when the moose were much larger; that they did not use to be in the woods, but came out of the water, as all deer did. Moose was whale once. Away down Merrimack way, a whale came ashore in a shallow bay. Sea went out and left him, and he came up on land a moose. What made them know he was a whale was, that at first, before he began to run in bushes, he had no bowels inside, but"——and then the squaw who sat on the bed by his side, as the Governor's aid, and had been putting in a word now and then and confirming the story, asked me what we called that soft thing we find along the sea-shore. "Jelly-fish," I suggested. "Yes," said he, "no bowels, but jelly-fish."

There may be some truth in what he said about the moose growing larger formerly; for the quaint John Josselyn, a physician who spent many years in this very district of Maine in the seventeenth century, says, that the tips of their horns "are sometimes found to be two fathoms asunder,"—and he is particular to tell us that a fathom is six feet,—"and [they are] in height, from the toe of the fore foot to the pitch of the shoulder, twelve foot, both which hath been taken by some of my sceptique readers to be monstrous lies"; and he adds, "There are certain transcendentia in every creature, which are the indelible characters of God, and which discover God." This is a greater dilemma to be caught in than is presented by the cranium of the young Bechuana ox, apparently another of the *transcendentia*, in the collection of Thomas Steel, Upper Brook Street, London, whose "entire length of horn, from tip to tip, along the curve, is 13 ft. 5 in.; distance (straight) between the tips of the horns, 8 ft. 8½ in." However, the size both of the moose and the cougar, as I have found, is generally rather underrated than overrated, and I should be inclined to add to the popular estimate a part of what I subtracted from Josselyn's.

But we talked mostly with the Governor's son-in-law, a very sensible Indian; and the Governor, being so old and deaf, permitted himself to be ignored, while we asked questions about him. The former said, that there were two political parties among them,—one in favor of schools, and the other opposed to them, or rather they did not wish to resist the priest, who was opposed to them. The first had just prevailed at the election and sent their man to the legislature. Neptune and Aitteon and he himself were in favor of schools. He said, "If Indians got learning, they would keep their money." When we asked where Joe's father, Aitteon, was, he knew that he must be at Lincoln, though he was about going a-moose-hunting, for a messenger had just gone to him there to get his signature to some papers. I asked Neptune if they had any of the old breed of dogs yet. He answered, "Yes." "But that," said I, pointing to one that had just come in, "is a Yankee dog." He assented. I said that he did not look like a good one. "O yes!" he said, and he told, with much gusto, how, the year before, he had caught and held by the throat a wolf. A very small black puppy rushed into the room and made at the Governor's feet, as he sat in his stockings with his legs dangling from the bedside. The Governor rubbed his hands and dared him to come on, entering into the sport with spirit. Nothing more that was significant transpired, to my knowledge, during this interview. This was the first time that

I ever called on a governor, but, as I did not ask for an office, I can speak of it with the more freedom.

An Indian who was making canoes behind a house, looking up pleasantly from his work,—for he knew my companion,—said that his name was Old John Pennyweight. I had heard of him long before, and I inquired after one of his contemporaries, Joe Four-pence-ha'penny; but, alas! he no longer circulates. I made a faithful study of canoe-building, and I thought that I should like to serve an apprenticeship at that trade for one season, going into the woods for bark with my "boss," making the canoe there, and returning in it at last.

While the *bateau* was coming over to take us off, I picked up some fragments of arrow-heads on the shore, and one broken stone chisel, which were greater novelties to the Indians than to me. After this, on Old Fort Hill, at the bend of the Penobscot, three miles above Bangor, looking for the site of an Indian town which some think stood thereabouts, I found more arrow-heads, and two little dark and crumbling fragments of Indian earthenware, in the ashes of their fires. The Indians on the Island appeared to live quite happily and to be well treated by the inhabitants of Oldtown.

We visited Veazie's mills, just below the Island, where were sixteen sets of saws,—some gang saws, sixteen in a gang, not to mention circular saws. On one side, they were hauling the logs up an inclined plane by water-power; on the other, passing out the boards, planks, and sawed timber, and forming them into rafts. The trees were literally drawn and quartered there. In forming the rafts, they use the lower three feet of hard-wood saplings, which have a crooked and knobbed but-end, for bolts, passing them up through holes bored in the corners and sides of the rafts, and keying them. In another apartment they were making fence-slats, such as stand all over New England, out of odds and ends,—and it may be that I saw where the picket-fence behind which I dwell at home came from. I was surprised to find a boy collecting the long edgings of boards as fast as cut off, and thrusting them down a hopper, where they were *ground up* beneath the mill, that they might be out of the way; otherwise they accumulate in vast piles by the side of the building, increasing the danger from fire, or, floating off, they obstruct the river. This was not only a saw-mill, but a grist-mill, then. The inhabitants of Oldtown, Stillwater, and Bangor cannot suffer for want of kindling stuff, surely. Some get their living exclusively by picking up the drift-wood and selling it by the cord in the winter. In one place I saw where an Irishman, who keeps a team and a man for the purpose, had covered the shore for a long distance with regular piles, and I was told that he had sold twelve hundred dollars' worth in a year. Another, who lived by the shore, told me that he got all the material of his out-buildings and fences from the river; and in that neighborhood I perceived that this refuse wood was frequently used instead of sand to fill hollows with, being apparently cheaper than dirt.

I got my first clear view of Ktaadn, on this excursion, from a hill about two miles northwest of Bangor, whither I went for this purpose. After this I was ready to return to Massachusetts.

Humboldt has written an interesting chapter on the primitive forest, but no one has yet described for me the difference between that wild forest which once occupied our oldest townships, and the tame one which I find there to-day. It is a difference which would be worth attending to. The civilized man not only clears the land permanently to a great extent, and cultivates open fields, but he tames and cultivates to a certain extent the forest itself. By his mere presence, almost, he changes the nature of the trees as no other creature does. The sun and air, and perhaps fire, have been introduced, and grain raised where it stands. It has lost its wild, damp, and shaggy look, the countless fallen and decaying trees are gone, and consequently that thick coat of moss which lived on them is gone too. The earth is comparatively bare and smooth and dry. The most primitive places left with us are the swamps, where the spruce still grows shaggy with usnea. The surface of the ground in the Maine woods is everywhere spongy and saturated with moisture. I noticed that the plants which cover the forest floor there are such as are commonly confined to swamps with us,—the *Clintonia borealis*, orchises, creeping snowberry, and others; and the prevailing aster there is the

Aster acuminatus, which with us grows in damp and shady woods. The asters *cordifolius* and *macrophyllus* also are common, asters of little or no color, and sometimes without petals. I saw no soft, spreading, second-growth white-pines, with smooth bark, acknowledging the presence of the wood-chopper, but even the young white-pines were all tall and slender rough-barked trees.

Those Maine woods differ essentially from ours. There you are never reminded that the wilderness which you are threading is, after all, some villager's familiar wood-lot, some widow's thirds, from which her ancestors have sledded fuel for generations, minutely described in some old deed which is recorded, of which the owner has got a plan too, and old bound-marks may be found every forty rods, if you will search. 'T is true, the map may inform you that you stand on land granted by the State to some academy, or on Bingham's purchase; but these names do not impose on you, for you see nothing to remind you of the academy or of Bingham. What were the "forests" of England to these? One writer relates of the Isle of Wight, that in Charles the Second's time "there were woods in the island so complete and extensive, that it is said a squirrel might have travelled in several parts many leagues together on the top of the trees." If it were not for the rivers, (and he might go round their heads,) a squirrel could here travel thus the whole breadth of the country.

We have as yet had no adequate account of a primitive pine-forest. I have noticed that in a physical atlas lately published in Massachusetts, and used in our schools, the " wood land" of North America is limited almost solely to the valleys of the Ohio and some of the Great Lakes, and the great pine-forests of the globe are not represented. In our vicinity, for instance, New Brunswick and Maine are exhibited as bare as Greenland. It may be that the children of Greenville, at the foot of Moosehead Lake, who surely are not likely to be scared by an owl, are referred to the valley of the Ohio to get an idea of a forest; but they would not know what to do with their moose, bear, caribou, beaver, etc., there. Shall we leave it to an Englishman to inform us, that "in North America, both in the United States and Canada, are the most extensive pine-forests in the world"? The greater part of New Brunswick, the northern half of Maine, and adjacent parts of Canada, not to mention the northeastern part of New York and other tracts farther off, are still covered with an almost unbroken pine-forest.

But Maine, perhaps, will soon be where Massachusetts is. A good part of her territory is already as bare and commonplace as much of our neighborhood, and her villages generally are not so well shaded as ours. We seem to think that the earth must go through the ordeal of sheep-pasturage before it is habitable by man. Consider Nahant, the resort of all the fashion of Boston,—which peninsula I saw but indistinctly in the twilight, when I steamed by it, and thought that it was unchanged since the discovery. John Smith described it in 1614 as "the Mattahunts, two pleasant isles of groves, gardens, and cornfields"; and others tell us that it was once well wooded, and even furnished timber to build the wharves of Boston. Now it is difficult to make a tree grow there, and the visitor comes away with a vision of Mr. Tudor's ugly fences, a rod high, designed to protect a few pear-shrubs. And what are we coming to in our Middlesex towns?—a bald, staring town-house, or meeting-house, and a bare liberty-pole, as leafless as it is fruitless, for all I can see. We shall be obliged to import the timber for the last, hereafter, or splice such sticks as we have;—and our ideas of liberty are equally mean with these. The very willow-rows lopped every three years for fuel or powder,—and every sizable pine and oak, or other forest tree, cut down within the memory of man! As if individual speculators were to be allowed to export the clouds out of the sky, or the stars out of the firmament, one by one. We shall be reduced to gnaw the very crust of the earth for nutriment.

They have even descended to smaller game. They have lately, as I hear, invented a machine for chopping up huckleberry-bushes fine, and so converting them into fuel!—bushes which, for fruit alone, are worth all the pear-trees in the country many times over. (I can give you a list of the three best kinds, if you want it.) At this rate, we shall all be obliged to let our beards grow at least, if only to hide the nakedness of the land and make a sylvan appearance. The farmer sometimes talks of "brushing up," simply as if bare ground looked better than clothed ground, than that which wears its natural vesture,—as if the wild hedges, which, perhaps, are more to his children than his whole farm beside, were *dirt*. I know of one who deserves to be called the Tree-hater, and, perhaps, to leave this for a new patronymic to his children. You would think that he had been warned by an oracle that he would be killed by the fall of a tree, and so was resolved to anticipate them. The journalists think that they cannot say too much in favor of such "improvements" in husbandry; it is a safe theme, like piety; but as for the beauty of one of these "model farms," I would as lief see a patent churn and a man turning it. They are, commonly, places merely where somebody is making money, it may be counterfeiting. The virtue of making two blades of grass grow where only one grew before does not begin to be superhuman.

Nevertheless, it was a relief to get back to our smooth, but still varied landscape. For a permanent residence, it seemed to me that there could be no comparison between this and the wilderness, necessary as the latter is for a resource and a background, the raw material of all our civilization. The wilderness is simple, almost to barrenness. The partially cultivated country it is which chiefly has inspired, and will continue to inspire, the strains of poets, such as compose the mass of any literature. Our woods are sylvan, and their inhabitants woodmen and rustics,—that is, *selvaggia*, and the inhabitants are *salvages*. A civilized man, using the word in the ordinary sense, with his ideas and associations, must at length pine there, like a cultivated plant, which clasps its fibres about a crude and undissolved mass of peat. At the extreme North, the voyagers are obliged to dance and act plays for employment. Perhaps our own woods and fields,—in the best wooded towns, where we need not quarrel about the huckleberries,—with the primitive swamps scattered here and there in their midst, but not prevailing over them, are the perfection of parks and groves, gardens, arbors, paths, vistas, and landscapes. They are the natural consequence of what art and refinement we as a people have,—the common which each village possesses, its true paradise, in comparison with which all elaborately and wilfully wealth-constructed parks and gardens are paltry imitations. Or, I would rather say, such *were* our groves twenty years ago. The poet's, commonly, is not a logger's path, but a woodman's. The logger and pioneer have preceded him, like John the Baptist; eaten the wild honey, it may be, but the locusts also; banished decaying wood and the spongy mosses which feed on it, and built hearths and humanized Nature for him.

But there are spirits of a yet more liberal culture, to whom no simplicity is barren. There are not only stately pines, but fragile flowers, like the orchises, commonly described as too delicate for cultivation, which derive their nutriment from the crudest mass of peat. These remind us, that, not only for strength, but for beauty, the poet must, from time to time, travel the logger's path and the Indian's trail, to drink at some new and more bracing fountain of the Muses, far in the recesses of the wilderness.

The kings of England formerly had their forests "to hold the king's game," for sport or food, sometimes destroying villages to create or extend them; and I think that they were impelled by a true instinct. Why should not we, who have renounced the king's authority, have our national preserves, where no villages need be destroyed, in which the bear and panther, and some even of the hunter race, may still exist, and not be "civilized off the face of the earth,"—our forests, not to hold the king's game merely, but to hold and preserve the king himself also, the lord of creation,—not for idle sport or food, but for inspiration and our own true re-creation? or shall we, like villains, grub them all up, poaching on our own national domains?

The Allegash and East Branch

I STARTED on my third excursion to the Maine woods Monday, July 20th, 1857, with one companion, arriving at Bangor the next day at noon. We had hardly left the steamer, when we passed Molly Molasses in the street. As long as she lives the Penobscots may be considered extant as a tribe. The succeeding morning, a relative of mine, who is well acquainted with the Penobscot Indians, and who had been my companion in my two previous excursions into the Maine woods, took me in his wagon to Oldtown, to assist me in obtaining an Indian for this expedition. We were ferried across to the Indian Island in a batteau. The ferryman's boy had got the key to it, but the father who was a blacksmith, after a little hesitation, cut the chain with a cold-chisel on a rock. He told us that the Indians were nearly all gone to the seaboard and to Massachusetts, partly on account of the small-pox, of which they are very much afraid, having broken out in Oldtown, and it was doubtful whether we should find a suitable one at home. The old chief Neptune, however, was there still. The first man we saw on the island was an Indian named Joseph Polis, whom my relative had known from a boy, and now addressed familiarly as "Joe." He was dressing a deerskin in his yard. The skin was spread over a slanting log, and he was scraping it with a stick, held by both hands. He was stoutly built, perhaps a little above the middle height, with a broad face, and, as others said, perfect Indian features and complexion. His house was a two-story white one with blinds, the best looking that I noticed there, and as good as an average one on a New England village street. It was surrounded by a garden and fruit-trees, single cornstalks standing thinly amid the beans. We asked him if he knew any good Indian who would like to go into the woods with us, that is, to the Allegash Lakes, by way of Moosehead, and return by the East Branch of the Penobscot, or vary from this as we pleased. To which he answered, out of that strange remoteness in which the Indian ever dwells to the white man, "Me like to go myself; me want to get some moose"; and kept on scraping the skin. His brother had

been into the woods with my relative only a year or two before, and the Indian now inquired what the latter had done
to him, that he did not come back, for he had not seen nor
heard from him since.

At length we got round to the more interesting topic again.
The ferryman had told us that all the best Indians were gone
except Polis, who was one of the aristocracy. He to be sure
would be the best man we could have, but if he went at all
would want a great price; so we did not expect to get him.
Polis asked at first two dollars a day, but agreed to go for a
dollar and a half, and fifty cents a week for his canoe. He
would come to Bangor with his canoe by the seven o'clock
train that evening,—we might depend on him. We thought
ourselves lucky to secure the services of this man, who was
known to be particularly steady and trustworthy.

I spent the afternoon with my companion, who had remained in Bangor, in preparing for our expedition, purchas-
ing provisions, hard bread, pork, coffee, sugar, &c., and some
India-rubber clothing.

We had at first thought of exploring the St. John from its
source to its mouth, or else to go up the Penobscot by its
East Branch to the lakes of the St. John, and return by way
of Chesuncook and Moosehead. We had finally inclined to the
last route, only reversing the order of it, going by way of
Moosehead, and returning by the Penobscot, otherwise it
would have been all the way up stream and taken twice as
long.

At evening the Indian arrived in the cars, and I led the way
while he followed me three quarters of a mile to my friend's
house, with the canoe on his head. I did not know the exact
route myself, but steered by the lay of the land, as I do in
Boston, and I tried to enter into conversation with him, but
as he was puffing under the weight of his canoe, not having
the usual apparatus for carrying it, but, above all, was an Indian, I might as well have been thumping on the bottom of
his birch the while. In answer to the various observations
which I made by way of breaking the ice, he only grunted
vaguely from beneath his canoe once or twice, so that I knew
he was there.

Early the next morning (July 23d) the stage called for us,

the Indian having breakfasted with us, and already placed the baggage in the canoe to see how it would go. My companion and I had each a large knapsack as full as it would hold, and we had two large India-rubber bags which held our provision and utensils. As for the Indian, all the baggage he had, beside his axe and gun, was a blanket, which he brought loose in his hand. However, he had laid in a store of tobacco and a new pipe for the excursion. The canoe was securely lashed diagonally across the top of the stage, with bits of carpet tucked under the edge to prevent its chafing. The very accommodating driver appeared as much accustomed to carrying canoes in this way as bandboxes.

At the Bangor House we took in four men bound on a hunting excursion, one of the men going as cook. They had a dog, a middling-sized brindled cur, which ran by the side of the stage, his master showing his head and whistling from time to time; but after we had gone about three miles the dog was suddenly missing, and two of the party went back for him, while the stage, which was full of passengers, waited. I suggested that he had taken the back track for the Bangor House. At length one man came back, while the other kept on. This whole party of hunters declared their intention to stop till the dog was found; but the very obliging driver was ready to wait a spell longer. He was evidently unwilling to lose so many passengers, who would have taken a private conveyance, or perhaps the other line of stages, the next day. Such progress did we make with a journey of over sixty miles, to be accomplished that day, and a rain-storm just setting in. We discussed the subject of dogs and their instincts till it was threadbare, while we waited there, and the scenery of the suburbs of Bangor is still distinctly impressed on my memory. After full half an hour the man returned, leading the dog by a rope. He had overtaken him just as he was entering the Bangor House. He was then tied on the top of the stage, but being wet and cold, several times in the course of the journey he jumped off, and I saw him dangling by his neck. This dog was depended on to stop bears with. He had already stopped one somewhere in New Hampshire, and I can testify that he stopped a stage in Maine. This party of four probably paid nothing for the dog's ride, nor for his run, while our party of three paid two dollars, and were charged four for the light canoe which lay still on the top.

It soon began to rain, and grew more and more stormy as the day advanced. This was the third time that I had passed over this route, and it rained steadily each time all day. We accordingly saw but little of the country. The stage was crowded all the way, and I attended the more to my fellow-travellers. If you had looked inside this coach you would have thought that we were prepared to run the gauntlet of a band of robbers, for there were four or five guns on the front seat, the Indian's included, and one or two on the back one, each man holding his darling in his arms. One had a gun which carried twelve to a pound. It appeared that this party of hunters was going our way, but much farther down the Allegash and St. John, and thence up some other stream, and across to the Ristigouche and the Bay of Chaleur, to be gone six weeks. They had canoes, axes, and supplies deposited some distance along the route. They carried flour, and were to have new bread made every day. Their leader was a handsome man about thirty years old, of good height, but not apparently robust, of gentlemanly address and faultless toilet; such a one as you might expect to meet on Broadway. In fact, in the popular sense of the word, he was the most "gentlemanly" appearing man in the stage, or that we saw on the road. He had a fair white complexion, as if he had always lived in the shade, and an intellectual face, and with his quiet manners might have passed for a divinity student who had seen something of the world. I was surprised to find, on talking with him in the course of the day's journey, that he was a hunter at all,—for his gun was not much exposed,—and yet more to find that he was probably the chief white hunter of Maine, and was known all along the road. He had also hunted in some of the States farther south and west. I afterwards heard him spoken of as one who could endure a great deal of exposure and fatigue without showing the effect of it; and he could not only use guns, but make them, being himself a gunsmith. In the spring, he had saved a stage-driver and two passengers from drowning in the backwater of the Piscataquis in Foxcroft on this road, having swum ashore in the freezing water and made a raft and got them off,—though the horses were drowned,—at great risk to himself, while the only other man who could swim withdrew to the nearest house to prevent freezing. He could now ride over this road for nothing. He knew our man, and remarked that we had a good Indian there, a good hunter; adding that he was said to be worth $6,000. The Indian also knew him, and said to me, "the great hunter."

The former told me that he practised a kind of still hunting, new or uncommon in those parts, that the caribou, for instance, fed round and round the same meadow, returning on the same path, and he lay in wait for them.

The Indian sat on the front seat, saying nothing to anybody, with a stolid expression of face, as if barely awake to what was going on. Again I was struck by the peculiar vagueness of his replies when addressed in the stage, or at the taverns. He really never said anything on such occasions. He was merely stirred up, like a wild beast, and passively muttered some insignificant response. His answer, in such cases, was never the consequence of a positive mental energy, but vague as a puff of smoke, suggesting no *responsibility*, and if you considered it, you would find that you had got nothing out of him. This was instead of the conventional palaver and smartness of the white man, and equally profitable. Most get no more than this out of the Indian, and pronounce him stolid accordingly. I was surprised to see what a foolish and impertinent style a Maine man, a passenger, used in addressing him, as if he were a child, which only made his eyes glisten a little. A tipsy Canadian asked him at a tavern, in a drawling tone, if he smoked, to which he answered with an indefinite "yes." "Won't you lend me your pipe a little while?" asked the other. He replied, looking straight by the man's head, with a face singularly vacant to all neighboring interests, "Me got no pipe"; yet I had seen him put a new one, with a supply of tobacco, into his pocket that morning.

Our little canoe, so neat and strong, drew a favorable criticism from all the wiseacres among the tavern loungers along the road. By the roadside, close to the wheels, I noticed a splendid great purple-fringed orchis with a spike as big as an epilobium, which I would fain have stopped the stage to pluck, but as this had never been known to stop a bear, like the cur on the stage, the driver would probably have thought it a waste of time.

When we reached the lake, about half past eight in the evening, it was still steadily raining, and harder than before; and, in that fresh, cool atmosphere, the hylodes were peeping and the toads ringing about the lake universally, as in the spring with us. It was as if the seasons had revolved backward two or three months, or I had arrived at the abode of perpetual spring.

We had expected to go upon the lake at once, and after paddling up two or three miles, to camp on one of its islands; but on account of the steady and increasing rain, we decided to go to one of the taverns for the night, though, for my own part, I should have preferred to camp out.

About four o'clock the next morning, (July 24th,) though it was quite cloudy, accompanied by the landlord to the water's edge, in the twilight, we launched our canoe from a rock on the Moosehead Lake. When I was there four years before we had a rather small canoe for three persons, and I had thought that this time I would get a larger one, but the present one was even smaller than that. It was 18¼ feet long by 2 feet 6½ inches wide in the middle, and one foot deep within, as I found by measurement, and I judged that it would weigh not far from eighty pounds. The Indian had recently made it himself, and its smallness was partly compensated for by its newness, as well as stanchness and solidity, it being made of very thick bark and ribs. Our baggage weighed about 166 pounds, so that the canoe carried about 600 pounds in all, or the weight of four men. The principal part of the baggage was, as usual, placed in the middle of the broadest part, while we stowed ourselves in the chinks and crannies that were left before and behind it, where there was no room to extend our legs, the loose articles being tucked into the ends. The canoe was thus as closely packed as a market-basket, and might possibly have been upset without spilling any of its contents. The Indian sat on a cross-bar in the stern, but we flat on the bottom, with a splint or chip behind our backs, to protect them from the cross-bar, and one of us commonly paddled with the Indian. He foresaw that we should not want a pole till we reached the Umbazookskus River, it being either dead water or down stream so far, and he was prepared to make a sail of his blanket in the bows, if the wind should be fair; but we never used it.

It had rained more or less the four previous days, so that we thought we might count on some fair weather. The wind was at first southwesterly.

Paddling along the eastern side of the lake in the still of the morning, we soon saw a few sheldrakes, which the Indian called *Shecorways*, and some peetweets *Naramekechus*, on the rocky shore; we also saw and heard loons, *medawisla*, which he said was a sign of wind. It was inspiriting to hear the regular dip of the paddles, as if they were our fins or flippers, and to realize that we were at length fairly embarked. We who had felt strangely as stage-passengers and tavern-lodgers were suddenly naturalized there and presented with the freedom of the lakes and the woods. Having passed the small rocky isles within two or three miles of the foot of the lake, we had a short consultation respecting our course, and inclined to the western shore for the sake of its lee; for otherwise, if the wind should rise, it would be impossible for us to reach Mount Kineo, which is about midway up the lake on the east side, but at its narrowest part, where probably we could recross if we took the western side. The wind is the chief obstacle to crossing the lakes, especially in so small a canoe. The Indian remarked several times that he did not like to cross the lakes "in littlum canoe," but nevertheless, "just as we say, it made no odds to him." He sometimes took a straight course up the middle of the lake between Sugar and Deer Islands, when there was no wind.

Measured on the map, Moosehead Lake is twelve miles wide at the widest place, and thirty miles long in a direct line, but longer as it lies. The captain of the steamer called it thirty-eight miles as he steered. We should probably go about forty. The Indian said that it was called "*Mspame*, because large water." Squaw Mountain rose darkly on our left, near the outlet of the Kennebec, and what the Indian called Spencer Bay Mountain, on the east, and already we saw Mount Kineo before us in the north.

Paddling near the shore, we frequently heard the *pe-pe* of the olive-sided fly-catcher, also the wood-pewee, and the kingfisher, thus early in the morning. The Indian reminding us that he could not work without eating, we stopped to breakfast on the main shore, southwest of Deer Island, at a spot where the *Mimulus ringens* grew abundantly. We took out our bags, and the Indian made a fire under a very large bleached log, using white-pine bark from a stump, though he said that hemlock was better, and kindling with canoe-birch bark. Our table was a large piece of freshly peeled birch-bark, laid wrong-side-up, and our breakfast consisted of hard bread, fried pork, and strong coffee, well sweetened, in which we did not miss the milk.

While we were getting breakfast a brood of twelve black dippers, half grown, came paddling by within three or four rods, not at all alarmed; and they loitered about as long as we stayed, now huddled close together, within a circle of eighteen inches in diameter, now moving off in a long line, very cunningly. Yet they bore a certain proportion to the great Moosehead Lake on whose bosom they floated, and I felt as if they were under its protection.

Looking northward from this place it appeared as if we were entering a large bay, and we did not know whether we should be obliged to diverge from our course and keep outside a point which we saw, or should find a passage between this and the mainland. I consulted my map and used my glass, and the Indian did the same, but we could not find our place exactly on the map, nor could we detect any break in the shore. When I asked the Indian the way, he answered "I don't know," which I thought remarkable, since he had said that he was familiar with the lake; but it appeared that he had never been up this side. It was misty dog-day weather, and we had already penetrated a smaller bay of the same kind, and knocked the bottom out of it, though we had been obliged to pass over a small bar, between an island and the shore, where there was but just breadth and depth enough to float the canoe, and the Indian had observed, "Very easy makum bridge here," but now it seemed that, if we held on, we should be fairly embayed. Presently, however, though we had not stirred, the mist lifted somewhat, and revealed a break in the shore northward, showing that the point was a portion of Deer Island, and that our course lay westward of it. Where it had seemed a continuous shore even through a glass, one portion was now seen by the naked eye to be much more distant than the other which overlapped it, merely by the greater thickness of the mist which still rested on it, while the nearer or island portion was comparatively bare and green. The line of separation was very distinct, and the Indian immediately remarked, "I guess you and I go there,—I guess there's room for my canoe there." This was his common expression instead of saying we. He never addressed us by our names, though curious to know how they were spelled and what they meant, while we called him Polis. He had already guessed very accurately at our ages, and said that he was forty-eight.

After breakfast I emptied the melted pork that was left into the lake, making what sailors call a "slick," and watching to see how much it spread over and smoothed the agitated surface. The Indian looked at it a moment and said, "That make hard paddlum thro'; hold 'em canoe. So say old times."

We hastily reloaded, putting the dishes loose in the bows, that they might be at hand when wanted, and set out again. The western shore, near which we paddled along, rose gently to a considerable height, and was everywhere densely covered with the forest, in which was a large proportion of hard wood to enliven and relieve the fir and spruce.

The Indian said that the usnea lichen which we saw hanging from the trees was called *chorchorque*. We asked him the names of several small birds which we heard this morning. The wood-thrush, which was quite common, and whose note he imitated, he said was called *Adelungquamooktum*; but sometimes he could not tell the name of some small bird which I heard and knew, but he said, "I tell all the birds about here,—this country; can't tell littlum noise, but I see 'em, then I can tell."

I observed that I should like to go to school to him to learn his language, living on the Indian island the while; could not that be done? "O, yer," he replied, "good many do so." I asked how long he thought it would take. He said one week. I told him that in this voyage I would tell him all I knew, and he should tell me all he knew, to which he readily agreed.

The birds sang quite as in our woods,—the red-eye, redstart, veery, wood-pewee, etc., but we saw no bluebirds in all our journey, and several told me in Bangor that they had not the bluebird there. Mt. Kineo, which was generally visible, though occasionally concealed by islands or the mainland in front, had a level bar of cloud concealing its summit, and all the mountain-tops about the lake were cut off at the same height. Ducks of various kinds—sheldrake, summer ducks, etc.—were quite common, and ran over the water before us as fast as a horse trots. Thus they were soon out of sight.

The Indian asked the meaning of *realility*, as near as I could make out the word, which he said one of us had used; also of "*interrent*," that is intelligent. I observed that he could rarely sound the letter r, but used l, as also r for l sometimes; as *load* for road, *pickelel* for pickerel, *Soogle* Island for Sugar Island, *lock* for rock, etc. Yet he trilled the r pretty well after me.

He generally added the syllable *um* to his words when he could,—as padl*um*, etc. I have once heard a Chippewa lecture, who made his audience laugh unintentionally by putting *m* after the word *too*, which word he brought in continually and unnecessarily, accenting and prolonging this sound into *m ar* sonorously as if it were necessary to bring in so much of his vernacular as a relief to his organs, a compensation for twisting his jaws about, and putting his tongue into every corner of his mouth, as he complained that he was obliged to do when he spoke English. There was so much of the Indian accent resounding through his English, so much of the "bow-arrow tang" as my neighbor calls it, and I have no doubt that word seemed to him the best pronounced. It was a wild and refreshing sound, like that of the wind among the pines, or the booming of the surf on the shore.

I asked him the meaning of the word *Musketicook*, the Indian name of Concord River. He pronounced it *Muskéeticook*, emphasizing the second syllable with a peculiar guttural sound, and said that it meant "Dead-water," which it is, and in this definition he agreed exactly with the St. Francis Indian with whom I talked in 1853.

On a point on the mainland some miles southwest of Sandbar Island, where we landed to stretch our legs and look at the vegetation, going inland a few steps, I discovered a fire still glowing beneath its ashes, where somebody had breakfasted, and a bed of twigs prepared for the following night. So I knew not only that they had just left, but that they designed to return, and by the breadth of the bed that there was more than one in the party. You might have gone within six feet of these signs without seeing them. There grew the beaked hazel, the only hazel which I saw on this journey, the *Diervilla*, rue seven feet high, which was very abundant on all the lake and river shores, and *Cornus stolonifera*, or red osier, whose bark, the Indian said, was good to smoke, and was called *maquoxigill*, "tobacco before white people came to this country, Indian tobacco."

The Indian was always very careful in approaching the shore, lest he should injure his canoe on the rocks, letting it swing round slowly sidewise, and was still more particular that we should not step into it on shore, nor till it floated free, and then should step gently lest we should open its seams, or make a hole in the bottom. He said that he would tell us when to jump.

Soon after leaving this point we passed the mouth of the Kennebec, and heard and saw the falls at the dam there, for even Moosehead Lake is dammed. After passing Deer Island, we saw the little steamer from Greenville, far east in the middle of the lake, and she appeared nearly stationary. Sometimes we could hardly tell her from an island which had a few trees on it. Here we were exposed to the wind from over the whole breadth of the lake, and ran a little risk of being swamped. While I had my eye fixed on the spot where a large fish had leaped, we took in a gallon or two of water, which filled my lap; but we soon reached the shore and took the canoe over the bar, at Sand-bar Island, a few feet wide only, and so saved a considerable distance. One landed first at a more sheltered place, and walking round caught the canoe by the prow, to prevent it being injured against the shore.

Again we crossed a broad bay opposite the mouth of Moose River, before reaching the narrow strait at Mount Kineo, made what the voyageurs call a *traverse*, and found the water quite rough. A very little wind on these broad lakes raises a sea which will swamp a canoe. Looking off from a lee shore, the surface may appear to be very little agitated, almost smooth, a mile distant, or if you see a few white crests they appear nearly level with the rest of the lake; but when you get out so far, you may find quite a sea running, and erelong, before you think of it, a wave will gently creep up the side of the canoe and fill your lap, like a monster deliberately covering you with its slime before it swallows you, or it will strike the canoe violently and break into it. The same thing may happen when the wind rises suddenly, though it were perfectly calm and smooth there a few minutes before; so that nothing can save you, unless you can swim ashore, for it is impossible to get into a canoe again when it is upset. Since you sit flat on the bottom, though the danger should not be imminent, a little water is a great inconvenience, not to mention the wetting of your provisions. We rarely crossed even a bay directly, from point to point, when there was wind, but made a slight curve corresponding somewhat to the shore, that we might the sooner reach it if the wind increased.

When the wind is aft, and not too strong, the Indian makes a spritsail of his blanket. He thus easily skims over the whole length of this lake in a day.

The Indian paddled on one side, and one of us on the other, to keep the canoe steady, and when he wanted to change hands he would say "t'other side." He asserted, in answer to our questions, that he had never upset a canoe himself, though he may have been upset by others.

Think of our little egg-shell of a canoe tossing across that great lake, a mere black speck to the eagle soaring above it.

My companion trailed for trout as we paddled along, but the Indian warning him that a big fish might upset us, for there are some very large ones there, he agreed to pass the line quickly to him in the stern if he had a bite. Beside trout, I heard of cusk, white-fish, &c., as found in this lake.

While we were crossing this bay, where Mount Kineo rose dark before us, within two or three miles, the Indian repeated the tradition respecting this mountain's having anciently been a cow moose,—how a mighty Indian hunter, whose name I forget, succeeding in killing this queen of the moose tribe with great difficulty, while her calf was killed somewhere among the islands in Penobscot Bay, and, to his eyes, this mountain had still the form of the moose in a reclining posture, its precipitous side presenting the outline of her head.

He told this at some length, though it did not amount to much, and with apparent good faith, and asked us how we supposed the hunter could have killed such a mighty moose as that,—how we could do it. Whereupon a man-of-war to fire broadsides into her was suggested, etc. An Indian tells such a story as if he thought it deserved to have a good deal said about it, only he has not got it to say, and so he makes up for the deficiency by a drawling tone, long-windedness, and a dumb wonder which he hopes will be contagious.

We approached the land again through pretty rough water, and then steered directly across the lake, at its narrowest part, to the eastern side, and were soon partly under the lee of the mountain, about a mile north of the Kineo House, having paddled about twenty miles. It was now about noon.

We designed to stop there that afternoon and night, and spent half an hour looking along the shore northward for a suitable place to camp. We took out all our baggage at one place in vain, it being too rocky and uneven, and while engaged in this search we made our first acquaintance with the moose-fly. At length, half a mile farther north, by going half a dozen rods into the dense spruce and fir wood on the side of the mountain, almost as dark as a cellar, we found a place sufficiently clear and level to lie down on, after cutting away a few bushes. We required a space only seven feet by six for our bed, the fire being four or five feet in front, though it made no odds how rough the hearth was; but it was not always easy to find this in those woods. The Indian first cleared a path to it from the shore with his axe, and we then carried up all our baggage, pitched our tent, and made our bed, in order to be ready for foul weather, which then threatened us, and for the night. He gathered a large armful of fir twigs, breaking them off, which he said were the best for our bed, partly, I thought, because they were the largest and could be most rapidly collected. It had been raining more or less for four or five days, and the wood was even damper than usual, but he got dry bark for the fire from the under-side of a dead leaning hemlock, which, he said, he could always do.

This noon his mind was occupied with a law question, and I referred him to my companion, who was a lawyer. It appeared that he had been buying land lately, (I think it was a hundred acres,) but there was probably an incumbrance to it, somebody else claiming to have bought some grass on it for this year. He wished to know to whom the grass belonged, and was told that if the other man could prove that he bought the grass before he, Polis, bought the land, the former could take it, whether the latter knew it or not. To which he only answered, "Strange!" He went over this several times, fairly sat down to it, with his back to a tree, as if he meant to confine us to this topic henceforth; but as he made no headway, only reached the jumping-off place of his wonder at white men's institutions after each explanation, we let the subject die.

He said that he had fifty acres of grass, potatoes, &c., somewhere above Oldtown, beside some about his house; that he hired a good deal of his work, hoeing, &c., and preferred white men to Indians, because "they keep steady, and know how."

After dinner we returned southward along the shore, in the canoe, on account of the difficulty of climbing over the rocks and fallen trees, and began to ascend the mountain along the edge of the precipice. But a smart shower coming up just then, the Indian crept under his canoe, while we, being protected by our rubber coats, proceeded to botanize. So we sent him back to the camp for shelter, agreeing that he should come there for us with his canoe toward night. It had rained a little in the forenoon, and we trusted that this would be the clearing-up shower, which it proved; but our feet and legs were thoroughly wet by the bushes. The clouds breaking away a little, we had a glorious wild view, as we ascended, of the broad lake with its fluctuating surface and numerous forest-clad islands, extending beyond our sight both north and south, and the boundless forest undulating away from its shores on every side, as densely packed as a rye-field, and enveloping nameless mountains in succession; but above all, looking westward over a large island was visible a very distant part of the lake, though we did not then suspect it to be Moosehead,—at first a mere broken white line seen through the tops of the island trees, like hay-caps, but spreading to a lake when we got higher. Beyond this we saw what appears to be called Bald Mountain on the map, some twenty-five miles distant, near the sources of the Penobscot. It was a perfect lake of the woods. But this was only a transient gleam, for the rain was not quite over.

Looking southward, the heavens were completely overcast, the mountains capped with clouds, and the lake generally wore a dark and stormy appearance, but from its surface just north of Sugar Island, six or eight miles distant, there was reflected upward to us through the misty air a bright blue tinge from the distant unseen sky of another latitude beyond. They probably had a clear sky then at Greenville, the south end of the lake. Standing on a mountain in the midst of a lake, where would you look for the first sign of approaching fair weather? Not into the heavens, it seems, but into the lake.

Again we mistook a little rocky islet seen through the "drisk," with some taller bare trunks or stumps on it, for the steamer with its smoke-pipes, but as it had not changed its position after half an hour, we were undeceived. So much do the works of man resemble the works of nature. A moose might mistake a steamer for a floating isle, and not be scared till he heard its puffing or its whistle.

If I wished to see a mountain or other scenery under the most favorable auspices, I would go to it in foul weather, so as to be there when it cleared up; we are then in the most suitable mood, and nature is most fresh and inspiring. There is no serenity so fair as that which is just established in a tearful eye.

Jackson, in his Report on the Geology of Maine, in 1838, says of this mountain: "Hornstone, which will answer for flints, occurs in various parts of the State, where trap-rocks have acted upon silicious slate. The largest mass of this stone known in the world is Mount Kineo, upon Moosehead Lake, which appears to be entirely composed of it, and rises seven hundred feet above the lake level. This variety of hornstone I have seen in every part of New England in the form of Indian arrow-heads, hatchets, chisels, etc., which were probably obtained from this mountain by the aboriginal inhabitants of the country." I have myself found hundreds of arrow-heads made of the same material. It is generally slate-colored, with white specks, becoming a uniform white where exposed to the light and air, and it breaks with a conchoidal fracture, producing a ragged cutting edge. I noticed some conchoidal hollows more than a foot in diameter. I picked up a small thin piece which had so sharp an edge that I used it as a dull knife, and to see what I could do, fairly cut off an aspen one inch thick with it, by bending it and making many cuts; though I cut my fingers badly with the back of it in the meanwhile.

From the summit of the precipice which forms the southern and eastern sides of this mountain peninsula, and is its most remarkable feature, being described as five or six hundred feet high, we looked, and probably might have jumped down to the water, or to the seemingly dwarfish trees on the narrow neck of land which connects it with the main. It is a dangerous place to try the steadiness of your nerves. Hodge says that these cliffs descend "perpendicularly ninety feet" below the surface of the water.

The plants which chiefly attracted our attention on this mountain were the mountain cinquefoil (*Potentilla tridentata*), abundant and in bloom still at the very base, by the water-side, though it is usually confined to the summits of mountains in our latitude; very beautiful harebells overhanging the precipice; bear-berry; the Canada blueberry (*Vaccinium Canadense*), similar to the *V. Pennsylvanicum* our earliest one, but entire leaved and with a downy stem and leaf; I have not seen it in Massachusetts; *Diervilla trifida*; *Microstylis ophioglossoides*, an orchidaceous plant new to us; wild holly (*Nemopanthes Canadensis*); the great round-leaved orchis (*Platanthera orbiculata*), not long in bloom; *Spiranthes cernua*, at the top; bunch-berry, reddening as we ascended, green at the base of the mountain, red at the top; and the small fern, *Woodsia ilvensis*, growing in tufts, now in fruit. I have also received *Liparis liliifolia*, or twayblade, from this spot. Having explored the wonders of the mountain, and the weather being now entirely cleared up, we commenced the descent. We met the Indian, puffing and panting, about one third of the way up, but thinking that he must be near the top, and saying that it took his breath away. I thought that superstition had something to do with his fatigue. Perhaps he believed that he was climbing over the back of a tremendous moose. He said that he had never ascended Kineo. On reaching the canoe we found that he had caught a lake trout weighing about three pounds, at the depth of twenty-five or thirty feet, while we were on the mountain.

When we got to the camp, the canoe was taken out and turned over, and a log laid across it to prevent its being blown away. The Indian cut some large logs of damp and rotten hard wood to smoulder and keep fire through the night. The trout was fried for supper. Our tent was of thin cotton cloth and quite small, forming with the ground a triangular prism closed at the rear end, six feet long, seven wide, and four high, so that we could barely sit up in the middle. It required two forked stakes, a smooth ridge-pole, and a dozen or more pins to pitch it. It kept off dew and wind, and an ordinary rain, and answered our purpose well enough. We reclined within it till bedtime, each with his baggage at his head, or else sat about the fire, having hung our wet clothes on a pole before the fire for the night.

As we sat there, just before night, looking out through the dusky wood, the Indian heard a noise which he said was made by a snake. He imitated it at my request, making a low whistling note,—*pheet—pheet*,—two or three times repeated, somewhat like the peep of the hylodes, but not so loud. In answer to my inquiries, he said that he had never seen them while making it, but going to the spot he finds the snake. This, he said on another occasion, was a sign of rain. When I had selected this place for our camp, he had remarked that there were snakes there,—he saw them. But they won't do any hurt, I said. "O no," he answered, "just as you say, it makes no difference to me."

He lay on the right side of the tent, because, as he said, he was partly deaf in one ear, and he wanted to lie with his good ear up. As we lay there, he inquired if I ever heard "Indian sing." I replied that I had not often, and asked him if he would not favor us with a song. He readily assented, and lying on his back, with his blanket wrapped around him, he commenced a slow, somewhat nasal, yet musical chant, in his own language, which probably was taught his tribe long ago by the Catholic missionaries. He translated it to us, sentence by sentence, afterward, wishing to see if we could remember it. It proved to be a very simple religious exercise or hymn, the burden of which was, that there was only one God who ruled all the world. This was hammered (or sung) out very thin, so that some stanzas wellnigh meant nothing at all, merely keeping up the idea. He then said that he would sing us a Latin song; but we did not detect any Latin, only one or two Greek words in it,—the rest may have been Latin with the Indian pronunciation.

His singing carried me back to the period of the discovery of America, to San Salvador and the Incas, when Europeans first encountered the simple faith of the Indian. There was, indeed, a beautiful simplicity about it; nothing of the dark and savage, only the mild and infantile. The sentiments of humility and reverence chiefly were expressed.

It was a dense and damp spruce and fir wood in which we lay, and, except for our fire, perfectly dark; and when I awoke in the night, I either heard an owl from deeper in the forest behind us, or a loon from a distance over the lake. Getting up some time after midnight to collect the scattered brands together, while my companions were sound asleep, I observed, partly in the fire, which had ceased to blaze, a perfectly regular elliptical ring of light, about five inches in its shortest diameter, six or seven in its longer, and from one eighth to one quarter of an inch wide. It was fully as bright as the fire, but not reddish or scarlet like a coal, but a white and slumbering light, like the glowworm's. I could tell it from the fire only by its whiteness. I saw at once that it must be phosphorescent wood, which I had so often heard of, but never chanced to see. Putting my finger on it, with a little hesitation, I found that it was a piece of dead moose-wood (*Acer striatum*) which the Indian had cut off in a slanting direction the evening before. Using my knife, I discovered that the light proceeded from that portion of the sap-wood immediately under the bark, and thus presented a regular ring at the end, which, indeed, appeared raised above the level of the wood, and when I pared off the bark and cut into the sap, it was all aglow along the log. I was surprised to find the wood quite hard and apparently sound, though probably decay had commenced in the sap, and I cut out some little triangular chips, and placing them in the hollow of my hand, carried them into the camp, waked my companion, and showed them to him. They lit up the inside of my hand, revealing the lines and wrinkles, and appearing exactly like coals of fire raised to a white heat, and I saw at once how, probably, the Indian jugglers had imposed on their people and on travellers, pretending to hold coals of fire in their mouths.

I also noticed that part of a decayed stump within four or five feet of the fire, an inch wide and six inches long, soft and shaking wood, shone with equal brightness.

I neglected to ascertain whether our fire had anything to do with this, but the previous day's rain and long-continued wet weather undoubtedly had.

I was exceedingly interested by this phenomenon, and already felt paid for my journey. It could hardly have thrilled me more if it had taken the form of letters, or of the human face. If I had met with this ring of light while groping in this forest alone, away from any fire, I should have been still more surprised. I little thought that there was such a light shining in the darkness of the wilderness for me.

The next day the Indian told me their name for this light,—*Artoosoqu'*,—and on my inquiring concerning the will-o'-the-wisp, and the like phenomena, he said that his "folks" sometimes saw fires passing along at various heights, even as high as the trees, and making a noise. I was prepared after this to hear of the most startling and unimagined phenomena witnessed by "his folks," they are abroad at all hours and seasons in scenes so unfrequented by white men. Nature must have made a thousand revelations to them which are still secrets to us.

I did not regret my not having seen this before, since I now saw it under circumstances so favorable. I was in just the frame of mind to see something wonderful, and this was a phenomenon adequate to my circumstances and expectation, and it put me on the alert to see more like it. I exulted like "a pagan suckled in a creed" that had never been worn at all, but was bran new, and adequate to the occasion. I let science slide, and rejoiced in that light as if it had been a fellow-creature. I saw that it was excellent, and was very glad to know that it was so cheap. A scientific *explanation*, as it is called, would have been altogether out of place there. That is for pale daylight. Science with its retorts would have put me to sleep; it was the opportunity to be ignorant that I improved. It suggested to me that there was something to be seen if one had eyes. It made a believer of me more than before. I believed that the woods were not tenantless, but choke-full of honest spirits as good as myself any day,—not an empty chamber, in which chemistry was left to work alone, but an inhabited house,—and for a few moments I enjoyed fellowship with them. Your so-called wise man goes trying to persuade himself that there is no entity there but himself and his traps, but it is a great deal easier to believe the truth. It suggested, too, that the same experience always gives birth to the same sort of belief or religion. One revelation has been made to the Indian, another to the white man. I have much to learn of the Indian, nothing of the missionary. I am not sure but all that would tempt me to teach the Indian my religion would be his promise to teach me *his*. Long enough I had heard of irrelevant things; now at length I was glad to make acquaintance with the light that dwells in rotten wood. Where is all your knowledge gone to? It evaporates completely, for it has no depth.

I kept those little chips and wet them again the next night, but they emitted no light.

SATURDAY, July 25.

At breakfast this Saturday morning, the Indian, evidently curious to know what would be expected of him the next day, whether we should go along or not, asked me how I spent the Sunday when at home. I told him that I commonly sat in my chamber reading, etc., in the forenoon, and went to walk in the afternoon. At which he shook his head and said, "Er, that is ver bad." "How do you spend it?" I asked. He said that he did no work, that he went to church at Oldtown when he was at home; in short, he did as he had been taught by the whites. This led to a discussion in which I found myself in the minority. He stated that he was a Protestant, and asked me if I was. I did not at first know what to say, but I thought that I could answer with truth that I was.

When we were washing the dishes in the lake, many fishes,

apparently chivin, came close up to us to get the particles of grease.

The weather seemed to be more settled this morning, and we set out early in order to finish our voyage up the lake before the wind arose. Soon after starting the Indian directed our attention to the Northeast Carry, which we could plainly see, about thirteen miles distant in that direction as measured on the map, though it is called much farther. This carry is a rude wooden railroad, running north and south about two miles, perfectly straight, from the lake to the Penobscot, through a low tract, with a clearing three or four rods wide; but low as it is, it passes over the height of land there. This opening appeared as a clear bright, or light point in the horizon, resting on the edge of the lake, whose breadth a hair could have covered at a considerable distance from the eye, and of no appreciable height. We should not have suspected it to be visible if the Indian had not drawn our attention to it. It was a remarkable kind of light to steer for,—daylight seen through a vista in the forest,—but visible as far as an ordinary beacon by night.

We crossed a deep and wide bay which makes eastward north of Kineo, leaving an island on our left, and keeping up the eastern side of the lake. This way or that led to some Tomhegan or *Socatarian* stream, up which the Indian had hunted, and whither I longed to go. The last name, however, had a bogus sound, too much like sectarian for me, as if a missionary had tampered with it; but I know that the Indians were very liberal. I think I should have inclined to the Tomhegan first.

We then crossed another broad bay, which, as we could no longer observe the shore particularly, afforded ample time for conversation. The Indian said that he had got his money by hunting, mostly high up the west branch of the Penobscot, and toward the head of the St. John; he had hunted there from a boy, and knew all about that region. His game had been, beaver, otter, black cat (or fisher), sable, moose, &c. Loup cervier (or Canada lynx) were plenty yet in burnt grounds. For food in the woods, he uses partridges, ducks, dried moose-meat, hedge-hog, &c. Loons, too, were good, only "bile 'em good." He told us at some length how he had suffered from starvation when a mere lad, being overtaken by winter when hunting with two grown Indians in the northern part of Maine, and obliged to leave their canoe on account of ice.

Pointing into the bay, he said that it was the way to various lakes which he knew. Only solemn bear-haunted mountains, with their great wooded slopes, were visible; where, as man is not, we suppose some other power to be. My imagination personified the slopes themselves, as if by their very length they would waylay you, and compel you to camp again on them before night. Some invisible glutton would seem to drop from the trees and gnaw at the heart of the solitary hunter who threaded those woods; and yet I was tempted to walk there. The Indian said that he had been along there several times.

I asked him how he guided himself in the woods. "O," said he, "I can tell good many ways." When I pressed him further, he answered, "Sometimes I lookum side-hill," and he glanced toward a high hill or mountain on the eastern shore, "great difference between the north and south, see where the sun has shone most. So trees,—the large limbs bend toward south. Sometimes I lookum locks" (rocks). I asked what he saw on the rocks, but he did not describe anything in particular, answering vaguely, in a mysterious or drawling tone, "Bare locks on lake shore,—great difference between N. S. E. W. side,—can tell what the sun has shone on." "Suppose," said I, "that I should take you in a dark night, right up here into the middle of the woods a hundred miles, set you down, and turn you round quickly twenty times, could you steer straight to Oldtown?" "O yer," said he, "have done pretty much same thing. I will tell you. Some years ago I met an old white hunter at Millinocket; very good hunter. He said he could go anywhere in the woods. He wanted to hunt with me that day, so we start. We chase a moose all the forenoon, round and round, till middle of afternoon, when we kill him. Then I said to him, now you go straight to camp. Don't go round and round where we 've been, but go straight. He said, I can't do that, I don't know where I am. Where you think camp? I asked. He pointed so. Then I laugh at him. I take the lead and go right off the other way, cross our tracks many times, straight camp." "How do you do that?" asked I. "O, I can't tell *you*," he replied. "Great difference between me and white man."

It appeared as if the sources of information were so various that he did not give a distinct, conscious attention to any one, and so could not readily refer to any when questioned about it, but he found his way very much as an animal does. Perhaps what is commonly called instinct in the animal, in this case is merely a sharpened and educated sense. Often, when an Indian says, "I don't know," in regard to the route he is to take, he does not mean what a white man would by those words, for his Indian instinct may tell him still as much as the most confident white man knows. He does not carry things in his head, nor remember the route exactly, like a white man, but relies on himself at the moment. Not having experienced the need of the other sort of knowledge, all labelled and arranged, he has not acquired it.

The white hunter with whom I talked in the stage knew some of the resources of the Indian. He said that he steered by the wind, or by the limbs of the hemlocks, which were largest on the south side; also sometimes, when he knew that there was a lake near, by firing his gun and listening to hear the direction and distance of the echo from over it.

The course we took over this lake, and others afterward, was rarely direct, but a succession of curves from point to point, digressing considerably into each of the bays; and this was not merely on account of the wind, for the Indian, looking toward the middle of the lake, said it was hard to go there, easier to keep near the shore, because he thus got over it by successive reaches and saw by the shore how he got along.

The following will suffice for a common experience in crossing lakes in a canoe. As the forenoon advanced the wind increased. The last bay which we crossed before reaching the desolate pier at the northeast carry, was two or three miles over, and the wind was southwesterly. After going a third of the way, the waves had increased so as occasionally to wash into the canoe, and we saw that it was worse and worse ahead. At first we might have turned about, but were not willing to. It would have been of no use to follow the course of the shore, for not only the distance would have been much greater, but the waves ran still higher there on account of the greater sweep the wind had. At any rate it would have been dangerous now to alter our course, because the waves would have struck us at an advantage. It will not do to meet them at right angles, for then they will wash in both sides, but you must take them quartering. So the Indian stood up in the canoe, and exerted all his skill and strength for a mile or two, while I paddled right along in order to give him more steerage-way. For more than a mile he did not allow a single wave to strike the canoe as it would, but turned it quickly from this side to that, so that it would always be on or near the crest of a wave when it broke, where all its force was spent, and we merely settled down with it. At length I jumped out on to the end of the pier, against which the waves were dashing violently, in order to lighten the canoe, and catch it at the landing, which was not much sheltered; but just as I jumped we took in two or three gallons of water. I remarked to the Indian, "You managed that well," to which he replied: "Ver few men do that. Great many waves; when I look out for one, another come quick."

While the Indian went to get cedar-bark, &c., to carry his canoe with, we cooked the dinner on the shore, at this end of the carry, in the midst of a sprinkling rain.

He prepared his canoe for carrying in this wise. He took a cedar shingle or splint eighteen inches long and four or five wide, rounded at one end, that the corners might not be in the way, and tied it with cedar-bark by two holes made midway, near the edge on each side, to the middle crossbar of the canoe. When the canoe was lifted upon his head bottom up, this shingle, with its rounded end uppermost, distributed the weight over his shoulders and head, while a band of cedar-bark, tied to the cross-bar on each side of the shingle, passed round his breast, and another longer one, outside of the last, round his forehead; also a hand on each side rail served to steer the canoe and keep it from rocking. He thus carried it with his shoulders, head, breast, forehead, and both hands, as if the upper part of his body were all one hand to clasp and hold it. If you know of a better way, I should like to hear of it. A cedar-tree furnished all the gear in this case, as it had the woodwork of the canoe. One of the paddles rested on the crossbars in the bows. I took the canoe upon my head and found that I could carry it with ease, though the straps were not fitted to my shoulders; but I let him carry it, not caring to establish a different precedent, though he said that if I would carry the canoe, he would take all the rest of the baggage, except my companion's. This shingle remained tied to the crossbar throughout the voyage, was always ready for the carries, and also served to protect the back of one passenger.

We were obliged to go over this carry twice, our load was so great. But the carries were an agreeable variety, and we improved the opportunity to gather the rare plants which we had seen, when we returned empty-handed.

We reached the Penobscot about four o'clock, and found there some St. Francis Indians encamped on the bank, in the same place where I camped with four Indians four years before. They were making a canoe, and, as then, drying moose-meat. The meat looked very suitable to make a *black* broth at least. Our Indian said it was not good. Their camp was covered with spruce-bark. They had got a young moose, taken in the river a fortnight before, confined in a sort of cage of logs piled up cob-fashion, seven or eight feet high. It was quite tame, about four feet high, and covered with moose-flies. There was a large quantity of cornel (*C. stolonifera*), red maple, and also willow and aspen boughs, stuck through between the logs on all sides, but-ends out, and on their leaves it was browsing. It looked at first as if it were in a bower rather than a pen.

Our Indian said that *he* used *black* spruce-roots to sew canoes with, obtaining it from high lands or mountains. The St. Francis Indian thought that *white* spruce-roots might be best. But the former said, "No good, break, can't split 'em"; also that they were hard to get, deep in ground, but the black were near the surface, on higher land, as well as tougher. He said that the white spruce was *subekoondark*, black, *skusk*. I told him I thought that I could make a canoe, but he expressed great doubt of it; at any rate, he thought that my work would not be "neat" the first time. An Indian at Greenville had told me that the winter bark, that is, bark taken off before the sap flows in May, was harder and much better than summer bark.

Having reloaded, we paddled down the Penobscot, which, as the Indian remarked, and even I detected, remembering how it looked before, was uncommonly full. We soon after saw a splended yellow lily (*Lilium Canadense*) by the shore, which I plucked. It was six feet high, and had twelve flowers, in two whorls, forming a pyramid, such as I have seen in Concord. We afterward saw many more thus tall along this stream, and also still more numerous on the East Branch, and, on the latter, one which I thought approached yet nearer to the *Lilium superbum*. The Indian asked what we called it, and said that the "loots" (roots) were good for soup, that is, to cook with meat, to thicken it, taking the place of flour. They get them in the fall. I dug some, and found a mass of bulbs pretty deep in the earth, two inches in diameter, looking, and even tasting, somewhat like raw green corn on the ear.

When we had gone about three miles down the Penobscot, we saw through the tree-tops a thunder-shower coming up in the west, and we looked out a camping-place in good season, about five o'clock, on the west side, not far below the mouth of what Joe Aitteon, in '53, called Lobster Stream, coming from Lobster Pond. Our present Indian, however, did not admit this name, nor even that of *Matahumkeag*, which is on the map, but called the lake *Beskabekuk*.

I will describe, once for all, the routine of camping at this season. We generally told the Indian that we would stop at the first suitable place, so that he might be on the lookout for it. Having observed a clear, hard, and flat beach to land on, free from mud, and from stones which would injure the canoe, one would run up the bank to see if there were open and level space enough for the camp between the trees, or if it could be easily cleared, preferring at the same time a cool place, on account of insects. Sometimes we paddled a mile or more before finding one to our minds, for where the shore was suitable, the bank would often be too steep, or else too low and grassy, and therefore mosquitoey. We then took out the baggage and drew up the canoe, sometimes turning it over on shore for safety. The Indian cut a path to the spot we had selected, which was usually within two or three rods of the water, and we carried up our baggage. One, perhaps, takes canoe-birch bark, always at hand, and dead dry wood or bark, and kindles a fire five or six feet in front of where we intend to lie. It matters not, commonly, on which side this is, because there is little or no wind in so dense a wood at that season; and then he gets a kettle of water from the river, and takes out the pork, bread, coffee, &c., from their several packages.

Another, meanwhile, having the axe, cuts down the nearest dead rock-maple or other dry hard wood, collecting several large logs to last through the night, also a green stake, with a notch or fork to it, which is slanted over the fire, perhaps resting on a rock or forked stake, to hang the kettle on, and two forked stakes and a pole for the tent.

The third man pitches the tent, cuts a dozen or more pins with his knife, usually of moose-wood, the common under-wood, to fasten it down with, and then collects an armful or two of fir-twigs,* arbor-vitæ, spruce, or hemlock, whichever is at hand, and makes the bed, beginning at either end, and laying the twigs wrong-side up, in regular rows, covering the stub-ends of the last row; first, however, filling the hollows, if there are any, with coarser material. Wrangel says that his guides in Siberia first strewed a quantity of dry brushwood on the ground, and then cedar twigs on that.

Commonly, by the time the bed is made, or within fifteen or twenty minutes, the water boils, the pork is fried, and sup-per is ready. We eat this sitting on the ground, or a stump, if there is any, around a large piece of birch-bark for a table, each holding a dipper in one hand and a piece of ship-bread or fried pork in the other, frequently making a pass with his hand, or thrusting his head into the smoke, to avoid the mosquitoes.

Next, pipes are lit by those who smoke, and veils are donned by those who have them, and we hastily examine and dry our plants, anoint our faces and hands, and go to bed,— and—the mosquitoes.

Though you have nothing to do but see the country, there's rarely any time to spare, hardly enough to examine a

*These twigs are called in Rasle's Dictionary, *Sediak.*

plant, before the night or drowsiness is upon you.

Such was the ordinary experience, but this evening we had camped earlier on account of the rain, and had more time.

We found that our camp to-night was on an old, and now more than usually indistinct, supply-road, running along the river. What is called a road there shows no ruts or trace of wheels, for they are not used; nor, indeed, of runners, since they are used only in the winter, when the snow is several feet deep. It is only an indistinct vista through the wood, which it takes an experienced eye to detect.

We had no sooner pitched our tent than the thunder-shower burst on us, and we hastily crept under it, drawing our bags after us, curious to see how much of a shelter our thin cotton roof was going to be in this excursion. Though the violence of the rain forced a fine shower through the cloth before it was fairly wetted and shrunk, with which we were well bedewed, we managed to keep pretty dry, only a box of matches having been left out and spoiled, and before we were aware of it the shower was over, and only the dripping trees imprisoned us.

Wishing to see what fishes there were in the river there, we cast our lines over the wet bushes on the shore, but they were repeatedly swept down the swift stream in vain. So, leaving the Indian, we took the canoe just before dark, and dropped down the river a few rods to fish at the mouth of a sluggish brook on the opposite side. We pushed up this a rod or two, where, perhaps, only a canoe had been before. But though there were a few small fishes, mostly *chivin*, there, we were soon driven off by the mosquitoes. While there we heard the Indian fire his gun twice in such rapid succession that we thought it must be double-barrelled, though we observed afterward that it was single. His object was to clean out and dry it after the rain, and he then loaded it with ball, being now on ground where he expected to meet with large game. This sudden, loud, crashing noise in the still aisles of the forest, affected me like an insult to nature, or ill manners at any rate, as if you were to fire a gun in a hall or temple. It was not heard far, however, except along the river, the sound being rapidly hushed up or absorbed by the damp trees and mossy ground.

The Indian made a little smothered fire of damp leaves close to the back of the camp, that the smoke might drive through and keep out the mosquitoes; but just before we fell asleep this suddenly blazed up, and came near setting fire to the tent. We were considerably molested by mosquitoes at this camp.

SUNDAY, July 26.

The note of the white-throated sparrow, a very inspiriting but almost wiry sound, was the first heard in the morning, and with this all the woods rang. This was the prevailing bird in the northern part of Maine. The forest generally was all alive with them at this season, and they were proportionally numerous and musical about Bangor. They evidently breed in that State. Wilson did not know where they bred, and says, "Their only note is a kind of chip." Though commonly unseen, their simple *ah, te-te-te, te-te-te, te-te-te,* so sharp and piercing, was as distinct to the ear as the passage of a spark of fire shot into the darkest of the forest would be to the eye. I thought that they commonly uttered it as they flew. I hear this note for a few days only in the spring, as they go through Concord, and in the fall see them again going southward, but then they are mute. We were commonly aroused by their lively strain very early. What a glorious time they must have in that wilderness, far from mankind and election day!

I told the Indian that we would go to church to Chesuncook this (Sunday) morning, some fifteen miles. It was settled weather at last. A few swallows flitted over the water, we heard the white throats along the shore, the phebe notes of the chicadee, and, I believe, red-starts, and moose-flies of large size pursued us in mid-stream.

The Indian thought that we should lie by on Sunday. Said he, "We come here lookum things, look all round; but come Sunday, lock up all that, and then Monday look again." He spoke of an Indian of his acquaintance who had been with some ministers to Ktaadn, and had told him how they conducted. This he described in a low and solemn voice. "They make a long prayer every morning and night, and at every meal. Come Sunday," said he, "they stop 'em, no go at all that day,—keep still,—preach all day,—first one then another, just like church. O, ver good men." "One day," said he, "going along a river, they came to the body of a man in the water, drowned good while, all ready fall to pieces. They go right ashore,—stop there, go no farther that day,—they have meeting there, preach and pray just like Sunday. Then they get poles and lift up the body, and they go back and carry the body with them. O, they ver good men."

I judged from this account that their every camp was a camp-meeting, and they had mistaken their route,—they should have gone to Eastham; that they wanted an opportunity to preach somewhere more than to see Ktaadn. I read of another similar party that seem to have spent their time there singing the songs of Zion. I was glad that I did not go to that mountain with such slow coaches.

However, the Indian added, plying the paddle all the while, that if we would go along, he must go with us, he our man, and he suppose that if he no takum pay for what he do Sunday, then ther 's no harm, but if he takum pay, then wrong. I told him that he was stricter than white men. Nevertheless, I noticed that he did not forget to reckon in the Sundays at last.

He appeared to be a very religious man, and said his prayers in a loud voice, in Indian, kneeling before the camp, morning and evening,—sometimes scrambling up again in haste when he had forgotten this, and saying them with great rapidity. In the course of the day, he remarked, not very originally, "Poor man rememberum God more than rich."

We soon passed the island where I had camped four years before, and I recognized the very spot. The dead water, a mile or two below it, the Indian called, *Beska bekukskishtuk*, from the lake *Beskabekuk*, which empties in above. This dead water, he said, was "a great place for moose always." We saw the grass bent where a moose came out the night before, and the Indian said that he could smell one as far as he could see him; but, he added, that if he should see five or six to-day close by canoe, he no shoot 'em. Accordingly, as he was the only one of the party who had a gun, or had come a-hunting, the moose were safe.

Just below this, a cat-owl flew heavily over the stream, and he, asking if I knew what it was, imitated very well the common *hoo, hoo, hoo, hoorer, hoo*, of our woods; making a hard, guttural sound, "Ugh, ugh, ugh,—ugh, ugh." When we passed the Moose-horn, he said that it had no name. What Joe Aitteon had called Ragmuff, he called *Pay tay te quick*, and said that it meant Burnt Ground Stream. We stopped there, where I had stopped before, and I bathed in this tributary. It was shallow but cold, apparently too cold for the Indian, who stood looking on. As we were pushing away again, a white-headed eagle sailed over our heads. A reach some miles above Pine Stream, where there were several islands, the Indian said was *Nonglangyis*, dead-water. Pine Stream he called Black River, and said that its Indian name was *Karsaootuk*. He could go to Caribou Lake that way.

We carried a part of the baggage about Pine Stream Falls, while the Indian went down in the canoe. A Bangor merchant had told us that two men in his employ were drowned some time ago while passing these falls in a bateau, and a third clung to a rock all night, and was taken off in the morning. There were magnificent great purple-fringed orchises on this carry and the neighboring shores. I measured the largest canoe-birch which I saw in this journey near the end of the carry. It was 14½ feet in circumference at two feet from the ground, but at five feet divided into three parts. The canoe-birches thereabouts were commonly marked by conspicuous dark spiral ridges, with a groove between, so that I thought at first that they had been struck by lightning, but, as the Indian said, it was evidently caused by the grain of the tree. He cut a small, woody knob, as big as a filbert, from the trunk of a fir, apparently an old balsam vesicle filled with wood, which he said was good medicine.

After we had embarked and gone half a mile, my companion remembered that he had left his knife, and we paddled back to get it, against the strong and swift current. This taught us the difference between going up and down the stream, for while we were working our way back a quarter of a mile, we should have gone down a mile and a half at least. So we landed, and while he and the Indian were gone back for it, I watched the motions of the foam, a kind of white water-fowl near the shore, forty or fifty rods below. It alternately appeared and disappeared behind the rock, being carried round by an eddy. Even this semblance of life was interesting on that lonely river.

Immediately below these falls was the Chesuncook dead-water, caused by the flowing back of the lake. As we paddled slowly over this, the Indian told us a story of his hunting thereabouts, and something more interesting about himself. It appeared that he had represented his tribe at Augusta, and also once at Washington, where he had met some Western chiefs. He had been consulted at Augusta, and gave advice, which he said was followed, respecting the eastern boundary of Maine, as determined by highlands and streams, at the time of the difficulties on that side. He was employed with the surveyors on the line. Also he had called on Daniel Webster in Boston, at the time of his Bunker Hill oration.

I was surprised to hear him say that he liked to go to Boston, New York, Philadelphia, &c., &c.; that he would like to live there. But then, as if relenting a little, when he thought what a poor figure he would make there, he added, "I suppose, I live in New York, I be poorest hunter, I expect." He understood very well both his superiority and his inferiority to the whites. He criticised the people of the United States as compared with other nations, but the only distinct idea with which he labored was, that they were "very strong," but, like some individuals, "too fast." He must have the credit of saying this just before the general breaking down of railroads and banks. He had a great idea of education, and would occasionally break out into such expressions as this, "Kademy— a-cad-e-my—good thing—I suppose they usum Fifth Reader there. . . . . . You been college?"

From this dead-water the outlines of the mountains about Ktaadn were visible. The top of Ktaadn was concealed by a cloud, but the Souneunk Mountains were nearer, and quite visible. We steered across the northwest end of the lake, from which we looked down south-southeast, the whole length to Joe Merry Mountain, seen over its extremity. It is an agreeable change to cross a lake, after you have been shut up in the woods, not only on account of the greater expanse of water, but also of sky. It is one of the surprises which Nature has in store for the traveller in the forest. To look down, in this case, over eighteen miles of water, was liberating and civilizing even. No doubt, the short distance to which you can see in the woods, and the general twilight, would at length react on the inhabitants, and make them *salvages*. The lakes also reveal the mountains, and give ample scope and range to our thought. The very gulls which we saw sitting on the rocks, like white specks, or circling about, reminded me of custom-house officers. Already there were half a dozen log-huts about this end of the lake, though so far from a road. I perceive that in these woods the earliest settlements are, for various reasons, clustering about the lakes, but partly, I think, for the sake of the neighborhood as the oldest clearings. They are forest schools already established,—great centres of light. Water is a pioneer which the settler follows, taking advantage of its improvements.

Thus far only I had been before. About noon we turned northward, up a broad kind of estuary, and at its northeast corner found the Caucomgomoc River, and after going about a mile from the lake, reached the Umbazookskus, which comes in on the right at a point where the former river, coming from the west, turns short to the south. Our course was up the Umbazookskus, but as the Indian knew of a good camping-place, that is, a cool place where there were few mosquitoes, about half a mile farther up the Caucomgomoc, we went thither. The latter river, judging from the map, is the longer and principal stream, and, therefore, its name must prevail below the junction. So quickly we changed the civilizing sky of Chesuncook for the dark wood of the Caucomgomoc. On reaching the Indian's camping-ground, on the south side, where the bank was about a dozen feet high, I read on the trunk of a fir-tree blazed by an axe an inscription in charcoal which had been left by him. It was surmounted by a drawing of a bear paddling a canoe, which he said was the sign which had been used by his family always. The drawing, though rude, could not be mistaken for anything but a bear, and he doubted my ability to copy it. The inscription ran thus, *verbatim et literatim*. I interline the English of his Indian as he gave it to me.

July 26,
1853.

Niasoseb	
We alone	Joseph
Polis	*elioi*
Polis	start
sia	*olta*
for	Oldtown
onke	*ni*
right	away.
quambi	

July 15,
1855.
Niasoseb.

He added now below: —

1857,
July 26.
Io.   Polis.

This was one of his homes. I saw where he had sometimes stretched his moose-hides on the opposite or sunny north side of the river, where there was a narrow meadow.

After we had selected a place for our camp, and kindled our fire, almost exactly on the site of the Indian's last camp here, he, looking up, observed, "That tree danger." It was a dead part, more than a foot in diameter, of a large canoe-birch, which branched at the ground. This branch, rising thirty feet or more, slanted directly over the spot which we had chosen for our bed. I told him to try it with his axe; but he could not shake it perceptibly, and, therefore, seemed inclined to disregard it, and my companion expressed his willingness to run the risk. But it seemed to me that we should be fools to lie under it, for though the lower part was firm, the top, for aught we knew, might be just ready to fall, and we should at any rate be very uneasy if the wind arose in the night. It is a common accident for men camping in the woods to be killed by a falling tree. So the camp was moved to the other side of the fire.

It was, as usual, a damp and shaggy forest, that Caucomgomoc one, and the most you knew about it was, that on this side it stretched toward the settlements, and on that to still more unfrequented regions. You carried so much topography in your mind always,—and sometimes it seemed to make a considerable difference whether you sat or lay nearer the settlements, or farther off, than your companions,—were the rear or frontier man of the camp. But there is really the same difference between our positions wherever we may be camped, and some are nearer the frontiers on feather-beds in the towns than others on fir-twigs in the backwoods.

The Indian said that the Umbazookskus, being a dead stream with broad meadows, was a good place for moose, and he frequently came a-hunting here, being out alone three weeks or more from Oldtown. He sometimes, also, went a-hunting to the Seboois Lakes, taking the stage, with his gun and ammunition, axe and blankets, hard bread and pork, perhaps for a hundred miles of the way, and jumped off at the wildest place on the road, where he was at once at home, and every rod was a tavern-site for him. Then, after a short journey through the woods, he would build a spruce-bark canoe in one day, putting but few ribs into it, that it might be light, and after doing his hunting with it on the lakes, would return with his furs the same way he had come. Thus you have an Indian availing himself cunningly of the advantages of civilization, without losing any of his woodcraft, but proving himself the more successful hunter for it.

This man was very clever and quick to learn anything in his line. Our tent was of a kind new to him; but when he had once seen it pitched it was surprising how quickly he would find and prepare the pole and forked stakes to pitch it with, cutting and placing them right the first time, though I am sure that the majority of white men would have blundered several times.

This river came from Caucomgomoc Lake, about ten miles farther up. Though it was sluggish here, there were falls not far above us, and we saw the foam from them go by from time to time. The Indian said that *Caucomgomoc* meant Big-

gull Lake, (i. e. Herring-gull, I suppose,) *gomoc* meaning lake.
Hence this was *Caucomgomoctook*, or the river from that lake.
This was the Penobscot *Caucomgomoc-took*. There was another
St. John one not far north. He finds the eggs of this gull,
sometimes twenty together, as big as hen's eggs, on rocky
ledges on the west side of Millinocket River, for instance, and
eats them.

Now I thought I would observe how he spent his Sunday.
While I and my companion were looking about at the trees
and river, he went to sleep. Indeed, he improved every opportunity to get a nap, whatever the day.

Rambling about the woods at this camp, I noticed that
they consisted chiefly of firs, black spruce, and some white,
red maple, canoe-birch, and, along the river, the hoary alder,
Alnus incana. I name them in the order of their abundance.
The *Viburnum nudum* was a common shrub, and of smaller
plants, there were the dwarf-cornel, great round-leaved orchis, abundant and in bloom (a greenish-white flower growing in little communities), *Uvularia grandiflora*, whose stem
tasted like a cucumber, *Pyrola secunda*, apparently the commonest Pyrola in those woods, now out of bloom, *Pyrola elliptica*, and *Chiogenes hispidula*. The *Clintonia borealis*, with
ripe berries, was very abundant, and perfectly at home there.
Its leaves, disposed commonly in triangles about its stem,
were just as handsomely formed and green, and its berries as
blue and glossy, as if it grew by some botanist's favorite path.

I could trace the outlines of large birches that had fallen
long ago, collapsed and rotted and turned to soil, by faint
yellowish-green lines of feather-like moss, eighteen inches wide
and twenty or thirty feet long, crossed by other similar lines.

I heard a Maryland yellow-throat's midnight strain, wood-
thrush, kingfisher (tweezer bird), or parti-colored warbler,
and a night-hawk. I also heard and saw red squirrels, and
heard a bull-frog. The Indian said that he heard a snake.

Wild as it was, it was hard for me to get rid of the associations of the settlements. Any steady and monotonous sound,
to which I did not distinctly attend, passed for a sound of
human industry. The waterfalls which I heard were not without their dams and mills to my imagination,—and several
times I found that I had been regarding the steady rushing

sound of the wind from over the woods beyond the rivers as that of a train of cars,—the cars at Quebec. Our minds anywhere, when left to themselves, are always thus busily drawing conclusions from false premises.

I asked the Indian to make us a sugar-bowl of birch-bark, which he did, using the great knife which dangled in a sheath from his belt; but the bark broke at the corners when he bent it up, and he said it was not good; that there was a great difference in this respect between the bark of one canoe-birch and that of another, i. e. one cracked more easily than another. I used some thin and delicate sheets of this bark which he split and cut, in my flower-book; thinking it would be good to separate the dried specimens from the green.

My companion, wishing to distinguish between the black and white spruce, asked Polis to show him a twig of the latter, which he did at once, together with the black; indeed, he could distinguish them about as far as he could see them; but as the two twigs appeared very much alike, my companion asked the Indian to point out the difference; whereupon the latter, taking the twigs, instantly remarked, as he passed his hand over them successively in a stroking manner, that the white was rough (i. e. the needles stood up nearly perpendicular), but the black smooth (i. e. as if bent or combed down). This was an obvious difference, both to sight and touch. However, if I remember rightly, this would not serve to distinguish the white spruce from the light-colored variety of the black.

I asked him to let me see him get some black spruce root, and make some thread. Whereupon, without looking up at the trees overhead, he began to grub in the ground, instantly distinguishing the black spruce roots, and cutting off a slender one, three or four feet long, and as big as a pipe-stem, he split the end with his knife, and taking a half between the thumb and forefinger of each hand, rapidly separated its whole length into two equal semi-cylindrical halves; then giving me another root, he said, "You try." But in my hands it immediately ran off one side, and I got only a very short piece. In short, though it looked very easy, I found that there was a great art in splitting these roots. The split is skilfully humored by bending short with this hand or that, and so kept in the middle. He then took off the bark from each half, pressing a short piece of cedar bark against the convex side with both hands, while he drew the root upward with his teeth. An Indian's teeth are strong, and I noticed that he used his often where we should have used a hand. They amounted to a third hand. He thus obtained, in a moment, a very neat, tough, and flexible string, which he could tie into a knot, or make into a fish-line even. It is said that in Norway and Sweden the roots of the Norway spruce (*Abies excelsa*) are used in the same way for the same purpose. He said that you would be obliged to give half a dollar for spruce root enough for a canoe, thus prepared. He had hired the sewing of his own canoe, though he made all the rest. The root in his canoe was of a pale slate color, probably acquired by exposure to the weather, or perhaps from being boiled in water first.

He had discovered the day before that his canoe leaked a little, and said that it was owing to stepping into it violently, which forced the water under the edge of the horizontal seams on the side. I asked him where he would get pitch to mend it with, for they commonly use hard-pitch, obtained of the whites at Oldtown. He said that he could make something very similar, and equally good, not of spruce gum, or the like, but of material which we had with us; and he wished me to guess what. But I could not, and he would not tell me, though he showed me a ball of it when made, as big as a pea, and like black pitch, saying, at last, that there were some things which a man did not tell even his wife. It may have been his own discovery. In Arnold's expedition the pioneers used for their canoe "the turpentine of the pine, and the scrapings of the pork-bag."

Being curious to see what kind of fishes there were in this dark, deep, sluggish river, I cast in my line just before night, and caught several small somewhat yellowish sucker-like fishes, which the Indian at once rejected, saying that they were *Michigan* fish (i. e. *soft* and *stinking* fish) and good for nothing. Also, he would not touch a pout, which I caught, and said that neither Indians nor whites thereabouts ever ate them, which I thought was singular, since they are esteemed in Massachusetts, and he had told me that he ate hedgehogs, loons, &c. But he said that some small silvery fishes, which I called white chivin, which were similar in size and form to the first, were the best fish in the Penobscot waters, and if I would toss them up the bank to him, he would cook them for me. After cleaning them, not very carefully, leaving the heads on, he laid them on the coals and so broiled them.

Returning from a short walk, he brought a vine in his hand, and asked me if I knew what it was, saying that it made the best tea of anything in the woods. It was the Creeping Snowberry (*Chiogenes hispidula*), which was quite common there, its berries just grown. He called it *cowosnebagosar*, which name implies that it grows where old prostrate trunks have collapsed and rotted. So we determined to have some tea made of this to-night. It had a slight checkerberry flavor, and we both agreed that it was really better than the black tea which we had brought. We thought it quite a discovery, and that it might well be dried, and sold in the shops. I, for one, however, am not an old tea-drinker, and cannot speak with authority to others. It would have been particularly good to carry along for a cold drink during the day, the water thereabouts being invariably warm. The Indian said that they also used for tea a certain herb which grew in low ground, which he did not find there, and *Ledum*, or Labrador tea, which I have since found and tried in Concord; also hemlock leaves, the last especially in the winter, when the other plants were covered with snow; and various other things; but he did not approve of *arbor vitæ*, which I said I had drunk in those woods. We could have had a new kind of tea every night.

Just before night we saw a *musquash*, (he did not say musk-rat,) the only one we saw in this voyage, swimming downward on the opposite side of the stream. The Indian, wishing to get one to eat, hushed us, saying, "Stop, me call 'em"; and sitting flat on the bank, he began to make a curious squeaking, wiry sound with his lips, exerting himself considerably. I was greatly surprised,—thought that I had at last got into the wilderness, and that he was a wild man indeed, to be talking to a musquash! I did not know which of the two was the strangest to me. He seemed suddenly to have quite forsaken humanity, and gone over to the musquash side. The musquash, however, as near as I could see, did not turn aside, though he may have hesitated a little, and the Indian said that he saw our fire; but it was evident that he was in the habit of calling the musquash to him, as he said. An acquaintance of mine who was hunting moose in the woods a month after this, tells me that his Indian in this way repeatedly called the musquash within reach of his paddle in the moonlight, and struck at them.

The Indian said a particularly long prayer this Sunday evening, as if to atone for working in the morning.

MONDAY, July 27.

Having rapidly loaded the canoe, which the Indian always carefully attended to, that it might be well trimmed, and each having taken a look, as usual, to see that nothing was left, we set out again, descending the Caucomgomoc, and turning northeasterly up the *Umbazookskus*. This name, the Indian said, meant *Much Meadow River*. We found it a very meadowy stream, and dead water, and now very wide on account of the rains, though, he said, it was sometimes quite narrow. The space between the woods, chiefly bare meadow, was from fifty to two hundred rods in breadth, and is a rare place for moose. It reminded me of the Concord; and what increased the resemblance, was one old musquash house almost afloat.

In the water on the meadows grew sedges, wool-grass, the common blue-flag abundantly, its flower just showing itself above the high water, as if it were a blue water-lily, and higher in the meadows a great many clumps of a peculiar narrow-leaved willow (*Salix petiolaris*), which is common in our river meadows. It was the prevailing one here, and the Indian said that the musquash ate much of it; and here also grew the red osier (*Cornus stolonifera*), its large fruit now whitish.

Though it was still early in the morning, we saw night-hawks circling over the meadow, and as usualy heard the *Pepe* (*Muscicapa Cooperi*), which is one of the prevailing birds in these woods, and the robin.

It was unusual for the woods to be so distant from the shore, and there was quite an echo from them, but when I was shouting in order to awake it, the Indian reminded me that I should scare the moose, which he was looking out for, and which we all wanted to see. The word for echo was *Pocka-dunkquaywayle*.

A broad belt of dead larch-trees along the distant edge of the meadow, against the forest on each side, increased the usual wildness of the scenery. The Indian called these juniper, and said that they had been killed by the back water caused by the dam at the outlet of Chesuncook Lake, some twenty miles distant. I plucked at the water's edge the *Asclepias incarnata*, with quite handsome flowers, a brighter red than our variety (the *pulchra*). It was the only form of it which I saw there.

Having paddled several miles up the Umbazookskus, it suddenly contracted to a mere brook, narrow and swift, the larches and other trees approaching the bank and leaving no open meadow, and we landed to get a black-spruce pole for pushing against the stream. This was the first occasion for one. The one selected was quite slender, cut about ten feet long, merely whittled to a point, and the bark shaved off. The stream, though narrow and swift, was still deep, with a muddy bottom, as I proved by diving to it. Beside the plants which I have mentioned, I observed on the bank here the *Salix cordata* and *rostrata*, *Ranunculus recurvatus*, and *Rubus triflorus* with ripe fruit.

While we were thus employed, two Indians in a canoe hove in sight round the bushes, coming down stream. Our Indian knew one of them, an old man, and fell into conversation with him in Indian. He belonged at the foot of Moosehead. The other was of another tribe. They were returning from hunting. I asked the younger if they had seen any moose, to which he said no; but I, seeing the moose-hides sticking out from a great bundle made with their blankets in the middle of the canoe, added, "Only their hides." As he was a foreigner, he may have wished to deceive me, for it is against the law for white men and foreigners to kill moose in Maine at this season. But, perhaps, he need not have been alarmed, for the moose-wardens are not very particular. I heard quite directly of one, who being asked by a white man going into the woods what he would say if he killed a moose, answered, "If you bring me a quarter of it, I guess you won't be troubled." His duty being, as he said, only to prevent the "indiscriminate" slaughter of them for their hides. I suppose that he would consider it an *indiscriminate* slaughter when a quarter was not reserved for himself. Such are the perquisites of this office.

We continued along through the most extensive larch wood which I had seen,—tall and slender trees with fantastic branches. But though this was the prevailing tree here, I do not remember that we saw any afterward. You do not find straggling trees of this species here and there throughout the wood, but rather a little forest of them. The same is the case with the white and red pines, and some other trees, greatly to the convenience of the lumberer. They are of a social habit, growing in "veins," "clumps," "groups," or "communities," as the explorers call them, distinguishing them far away, from the top of a hill or a tree, the white pines towering above the surrounding forest, or else they form extensive forests by themselves. I would have liked to come across a large community of pines, which had never been invaded by the lumbering army.

We saw some fresh moose tracks along the shore, but the Indian said that the moose were not driven out of the woods by the flies, as usual at this season, on account of the abundance of water everywhere. The stream was only from one and one half to three rods wide, quite winding, with occasional small islands, meadows, and some very swift and shallow places. When we came to an island, the Indian never hesitated which side to take, as if the current told him which was the shortest and deepest. It was lucky for us that the water was so high. We had to walk but once on this stream, carrying a part of the load, at a swift and shallow reach, while he got up with the canoe, not being obliged to take out, though he said it was very strong water. Once or twice we passed the red wreck of a bateau which had been stove some spring.

While making this portage I saw many splendid specimens of the great purple-fringed orchis, three feet high. It is remarkable that such delicate flowers should here adorn these wilderness paths.

Having resumed our seats in the canoe, I felt the Indian wiping my back, which he had acccidentally spat upon. He said it was a sign that I was going to be married.

The Umbazookskus River is called ten miles long. Having polled up the narrowest part some three or four miles, the next opening in the sky was over Umbazookskus Lake, which we suddenly entered about eleven o'clock in the forenoon. It stretches northwesterly four or five miles, with what the Indian called the Caucomgomoc Mountain seen far beyond it. It was an agreeable change.

This lake was very shallow a long distance from the shore, and I saw stone heaps on the bottom, like those in the Assabet at home. The canoe ran into one. The Indian thought that they were made by an eel. Joe Aitteon in 1853 thought that they were made by chub. We crossed the southeast end of the lake to the carry into Mud Pond.

Umbazookskus Lake is the head of the Penobscot in this direction, and Mud Pond is the nearest head of the Allegash, one of the chief sources of the St. John. Hodge, who went through this way to the St. Lawrence in the service of the State, calls the portage here a mile and three quarters long, and states that Mud Pond has been found to be fourteen feet higher than Umbazookskus Lake. As the west branch of the Penobscot at the Moosehead carry is considered about twenty-five feet lower than Moosehead Lake, it appears that the Penobscot in the upper part of its course runs in a broad and shallow valley, between the Kennebec and St. Johns, and lower than either of them, though, judging from the map, you might expect it to be the highest.

Mud Pond is about half-way from Umbazookskus to Chamberlain Lake, into which it empties, and to which we were bound. The Indian said that this was the wettest carry in the State, and as the season was a very wet one, we anticipated an unpleasant walk. As usual he made one large bundle of the pork-keg, cooking utensils, and other loose traps, by tying them up in his blanket. We should be obliged to go over the carry twice, and our method was to carry one half part way, and then go back for the rest.

Our path ran close by the door of a log-hut in a clearing at this end of the carry, which the Indian, who alone entered it, found to be occupied by a Canadian and his family, and that the man had been blind for a year. He seemed peculiarly unfortunate to be taken blind there, where there were so few eyes to see for him. He could not even be led out of that country by a dog, but must be taken down the rapids as passively as a barrel of flour. This was the first house above Chesuncook, and the last on the Penobscot waters, and was built here, no doubt, because it was the route of the lumberers in the winter and spring.

After a slight ascent from the lake through the springy soil of the Canadian's clearing, we entered on a level and very wet and rocky path through the universal dense evergreen forest, a loosely paved gutter merely, where we went leaping from rock to rock and from side to side, in the vain attempt to keep out of the water and mud. We concluded that it was yet Penobscot water, though there was no flow to it. It was on this carry that the white hunter whom I met in the stage, as he told me, had shot two bears a few months before. They stood directly in the path, and did not turn out for him. They might be excused for not turning out there, or only taking the right as the law directs. He said that at this season bears were found on the mountains and hillsides, in search of berries, and were apt to be saucy,—that we might come across them up Trout Stream; and he added, what I hardly credited, that many Indians slept in their canoes, not daring to sleep on land, on account of them.

Here commences what was called, twenty years ago, the best timber land in the State. This very spot was described as "covered with the greatest abundance of pine," but now this appeared to me, comparatively, an uncommon tree there,— and yet you did not see where any more could have stood, amid the dense growth of cedar, fir, &c. It was then proposed to cut a canal from lake to lake here, but the outlet was finally made farther east, at Telos Lake, as we shall see.

The Indian with his canoe soon disappeared before us; but erelong he came back and told us to take a path which turned off westward, it being better walking, and, at my suggestion, he agreed to leave a bough in the regular carry at that place, that we might not pass it by mistake. Thereafter, he said, we were to keep the main path, and he added, "You see 'em my tracks." But I had not much faith that we could distinguish his tracks, since others had passed over the carry within a few days.

We turned off at the right place, but were soon confused by numerous logging-paths, coming into the one we were on, by which lumberers had been to pick out those pines which I have mentioned. However, we kept what we considered the main path, though it was a winding one, and in this, at long intervals, we distinguished a faint trace of a footstep. This, though comparatively unworn, was at first a better, or, at least, a drier road, than the regular carry which we had left. It led through an arbor-vitæ wilderness of the grimmest character. The great fallen and rotting trees had been cut through and rolled aside, and their huge trunks abutted on the path on each side, while others still lay across it two or three feet high. It was impossible for us to discern the Indian's trail in the elastic moss, which, like a thick carpet, covered every rock and fallen tree, as well as the earth. Nevertheless, I did occasionally detect the track of a man, and I gave myself some credit for it. I carried my whole load at once, a heavy knapsack, and a large India-rubber bag, containing our bread and a blanket, swung on a paddle; in all, about sixty pounds; but my companion preferred to make two journeys, by short stages, while I waited for him. We could not be sure that we were not depositing our loads each time farther off from the true path.

As I sat waiting for my companion, he would seem to be gone a long time, and I had ample opportunity to make observations on the forest. I now first began to be seriously molested by the black-fly, a very small but perfectly formed fly of that color, about one tenth of an inch long, which I first felt, and then saw, in swarms about me, as I sat by a wider and more than usually doubtful fork in this dark forest-path. The hunters tell bloody stories about them,—how they settle in a ring about your neck, before you know it, and are wiped off in great numbers with your blood. But remembering that I had a wash in my knapsack, prepared by a thoughtful hand in Bangor, I made haste to apply it to my face and hands, and was glad to find it effectual, as long as it was fresh, or for twenty minutes, not only against black-flies, but all the insects that molested us. They would not alight on the part thus defended. It was composed of sweet-oil and oil of turpentine, with a little oil of spearmint, and camphor. However, I finally concluded that the remedy was worse than the disease. It was so disagreeable and inconvenient to have your face and hands covered with such a mixture.

Three large slate-colored birds of the jay genus (*Garrulus Canadensis*), the Canada-jay, moose-bird, meat-bird, or what not, came flitting silently and by degrees toward me, and hopped down the limbs inquisitively to within seven or eight feet. They were more clumsy and not nearly so handsome as the blue-jay. Fish-hawks, from the lake, uttered their sharp whistling notes low over the top of the forest near me, as if they were anxious about a nest there.

After I had sat there some time, I noticed at this fork in the path a tree which had been blazed, and the letters "Chamb. L." written on it with red chalk. This I knew to mean Chamberlain Lake. So I concluded that on the whole we were on the right course, though as we had come nearly two miles, and saw no signs of Mud Pond, I did harbor the suspicion that we might be on a direct course to Chamberlain Lake, leaving out Mud Pond. This I found by my map would be about five miles northeasterly, and I then took the bearing by my compass.

My companion having returned with his bag, and also defended his face and hands with the insect-wash, we set forward again. The walking rapidly grew worse, and the path more indistinct, and at length, after passing through a patch of *calla palustris*, still abundantly in bloom, we found ourselves in a more open and regular swamp, made less passable than ordinary by the unusual wetness of the season. We sank a foot deep in water and mud at every step, and sometimes up to our knees, and the trail was almost obliterated, being no more than that a musquash leaves in similar places, when he parts the floating sedge. In fact, it probably was a musquash trail in some places. We concluded that if Mud Pond was as muddy as the approach to it was wet, it certainly deserved its name. It would have been amusing to behold the dogged and deliberate pace at which we entered that swamp, without interchanging a word, as if determined to go through it, though it should come up to our necks. Having penetrated a considerable distance into this, and found a tussuck on which we could deposit our loads, though there was no place to sit, my companion went back for the rest of his pack. I had thought to observe on this carry when we crossed the dividing line between the Penobscot and St. John, but as my feet had hardly been out of water the whole distance, and it was all level and stagnant, I began to despair of finding it. I remembered hearing a good deal about the "highlands" dividing the waters of the Penobscot from those of the St. John, as well as the St. Lawrence, at the time of the northeast boundary dispute, and I observed by my map, that the line claimed by Great Britain as the boundary prior to 1842 passed between Umbazookskus Lake and Mud Pond, so that we had either crossed or were then on it. These, then, according to *her* interpretation of the treaty of '83, were the "highlands which divide those rivers that empty themselves into the St. Lawrence from those which fall into the Atlantic Ocean." Truly an interesting spot to stand on,— if that were it,—though you could not sit down there. I thought that if the commissioners themselves, and the king of Holland with them, had spent a few days here, with their packs upon their backs, looking for that "highland," they would have had an interesting time, and perhaps it would have modified their views of the question somewhat. The king of Holland would have been in his element. Such were my meditations while my companion was gone back for his bag.

It was a cedar swamp, through which the peculiar note of the white-throated sparrow rang loud and clear. There grew the side-saddle flower, Labrador tea, *Kalmia glauca*, and, what was new to me, the Low Birch (*Betula pumila*), a little round-leafed shrub, two or three feet high only. We thought to name this swamp after the latter.

After a long while my companion came back, and the Indian with him. We had taken the wrong road, and the Indian had lost us. He had very wisely gone back to the Canadian's camp, and asked him which way we had probably gone, since he could better understand the ways of white men, and he told him correctly that we had undoubtedly taken the supply road to Chamberlain Lake (slender supplies they would get over such a road at this season). The Indian was greatly surprised that we should have taken what he called a "tow"

(i. e. tote or toting or supply) road, instead of a carry path,—
that we had not followed his tracks,—said it was "strange,"
and evidently thought little of our woodcraft.

Having held a consultation, and eaten a mouthful of
bread, we concluded that it would, perhaps, be nearer for us
two now to keep on to Chamberlain Lake, omitting Mud
Pond, than to go back and start anew for the last place,
though the Indian had never been through this way, and
knew nothing about it. In the meanwhile he would go back
and finish carrying over his canoe and bundle to Mud Pond,
cross that, and go down its outlet and up Chamberlain Lake,
and trust to meet us there before night. It was now a little
after noon. He supposed that the water in which we stood
had flowed back from Mud Pond, which could not be far off
eastward, but was unapproachable through the dense cedar
swamp.

Keeping on, we were erelong agreeably disappointed by
reaching firmer ground, and we crossed a ridge where the
path was more distinct, but there was never any outlook
over the forest. While descending the last, I saw many specimens of the great round-leaved orchis, of large size; one
which I measured had leaves, as usual, flat on the ground,
nine and a half inches long, and nine wide, and was two feet
high. The dark, damp wilderness is favorable to some of
these orchidaceous plants, though they are too delicate for
cultivation. I also saw the swamp gooseberry (*Ribes lacustre*),
with green fruit, and in all the low ground, where it was not
too wet, the *Rubus triflorus* in fruit. At one place I heard a
very clear and piercing note from a small hawk, like a single
note from a white-throated sparrow, only very much louder,
as he dashed through the tree-tops over my head. I wondered that he allowed himself to be disturbed by our presence, since it seemed as if he could not easily find his nest
again himself in that wilderness. We also saw and heard several times the red squirrel, and often, as before observed, the
bluish scales of the fir cones which it had left on a rock or
fallen tree. This, according to the Indian, is the only squirrel
found in those woods, except a very few striped ones. It
must have a solitary time in that dark evergreen forest,

where there is so little life, seventy-five miles from a road as we had come. I wondered how he could call any particular tree there his home; and yet he would run up the stem of one out of the myriads, as if it were an old road to him. How can a hawk ever find him there? I fancied that he must be glad to see us, though he did seem to chide us. One of those sombre fir and spruce woods is not complete unless you hear from out its cavernous mossy and twiggy recesses his fine alarum,—his spruce voice, like the working of the sap through some crack in a tree,—the working of the spruce-beer. Such an impertinent fellow would occasionally try to alarm the wood about me. "O," said I, "I am well acquainted with your family, I know your cousins in Concord very well. Guess the mail 's irregular in these parts, and you 'd like to hear from 'em." But my overtures were vain, for he would withdraw by his aerial turnpikes into a more distant cedar-top, and spring his rattle again.

We then entered another swamp, at a necessarily slow pace, where the walking was worse than ever, not only on account of the water, but the fallen timber, which often obliterated the indistinct trail entirely. The fallen trees were so numerous, that for long distances the route was through a succession of small yards, where we climbed over fences as high as our heads, down into water often up to our knees, and then over another fence into a second yard, and so on; and going back for his bag my companion once lost his way and came back without it. In many places the canoe would have run if it had not been for the fallen timber. Again it would be more open, but equally wet, too wet for trees to grow, and no place to sit down. It was a mossy swamp, which it required the long legs of a moose to traverse, and it is very likely that we scared some of them in our transit, though we saw none. It was ready to echo the growl of a bear, the howl of a wolf, or the scream of a panther; but when you get fairly into the middle of one of these grim forests, you are surprised to find that the larger inhabitants are not at home commonly, but have left only a puny red squirrel to bark at you. Generally speaking, a howling wilderness does not howl: it is the imagination of the traveller that does the howling. I did, however, see one dead porcupine; perhaps he had succumbed to the difficulties of the way. These bristly fellows are a very suitable small fruit of such unkempt wildernesses.

Making a logging-road in the Maine woods is called "swamping it," and they who do the work are called "swampers." I now perceived the fitness of the term. This was the most perfectly swamped of all the roads I ever saw. Nature must have co-operated with art here. However, I suppose they would tell you that this name took its origin from the fact that the chief work of road-makers in those woods is to make the swamps passable. We came to a stream where the bridge, which had been made of logs tied together with cedar bark, had been broken up, and we got over as we could. This probably emptied into Mud Pond, and perhaps the Indian might have come up it and taken us in there if he had known it. Such as it was, this ruined bridge was the chief evidence that we were on a path of any kind.

We then crossed another low rising ground, and I, who wore shoes, had an opportunity to wring out my stockings, but my companion, who used boots, had found that this was not a safe experiment for him, for he might not be able to get his wet boots on again. He went over the whole ground, or water, three times, for which reason our progress was very slow; beside that the water softened our feet, and to some extent unfitted them for walking. As I sat waiting for him, it would naturally seem an unaccountable time that he was gone. Therefore, as I could see through the woods that the sun was getting low, and it was uncertain how far the lake might be, even if we were on the right course, and in what part of the world we should find ourselves at nightfall, I proposed that I should push through with what speed I could, leaving boughs to mark my path, and find the lake and the Indian, if possible, before night, and send the latter back to carry my companion's bag.

Having gone about a mile, and got into low ground again, I heard a noise like the note of an owl, which I soon discovered to be made by the Indian, and answering him, we soon came together. He had reached the lake, after crossing Mud Pond, and running some rapids below it, and had come up about a mile and a half on our path. If he had not come back to meet us, we probably should not have found him that night, for the path branched once or twice before reaching this particular part of the lake. So he went back for my companion and his bag, while I kept on. Having waded through another stream where the bridge of logs had been broken up and half floated away,—and this was not altogether worse than our ordinary walking, since it was less muddy,—we continued on, through alternate mud and water, to the shore of Apmoojenegamook Lake, which we reached in season for a late supper, instead of dining there, as we had expected, having gone without our dinner. It was at least five miles by the way we had come, and as my companion had gone over most of it three times, he had walked full a dozen miles, bad as it was. In the winter, when the water is frozen, and the snow is four feet deep, it is no doubt a tolerable path to a footman. As it was, I would not have missed that walk for a good deal. If you want an exact recipe for making such a road, take one part Mud Pond, and dilute it with equal parts of Umbazookskus and Apmoojenegamook; then send a family of musquash through to locate it, look after the grades and culverts, and finish it to their minds, and let a hurricane follow to do the fencing.

We had come out on a point extending into Apmoojenegamook, or Chamberlain Lake, west of the outlet of Mud Pond, where there was a broad, gravelly, and rocky shore, encumbered with bleached logs and trees. We were rejoiced to see such dry things in that part of the world. But at first we did not attend to dryness so much as to mud and wetness. We all three walked into the lake up to our middle to wash our clothes.

This was another noble lake, called twelve miles long, east and west; if you add Telos Lake, which, since the dam was built, has been connected with it by dead water, it will be twenty; and it is apparently from a mile and a half to two miles wide. We were about midway its length, on the south side. We could see the only clearing in these parts, called the "Chamberlain Farm," with two or three log buildings close together, on the opposite shore, some two and a half miles distant. The smoke of our fire on the shore brought over two men in a canoe from the farm, that being a common signal agreed on when one wishes to cross. It took them about half an hour to come over, and they had their labor for their pains this time. Even the English name of the lake had a wild, woodland sound, reminding me of that Chamberlain who killed Paugus at Lovewell's fight.

After putting on such dry clothes as we had, and hanging the others to dry on the pole which the Indian arranged over the fire, we ate our supper, and lay down on the pebbly shore with our feet to the fire, without pitching our tent, making a thin bed of grass to cover the stones.

Here first I was molested by the little midge called the No-see-em (*Simulium nocivum*, the latter word is not the Latin for no-see-em), especially over the sand at the water's edge, for it is a kind of sand-fly. You would not observe them but for their light-colored wings. They are said to get under your clothes, and produce a feverish heat, which I suppose was what I felt that night.

Our insect foes in this excursion, to sum them up, were, first, mosquitoes, the chief ones, but only troublesome at night, or when we sat still on shore by day; second, black flies (*Simulium molestum*), which molested us more or less on the carries by day, as I have before described, and sometimes in narrower parts of the stream. Harris mistakes when he says that they are not seen after June. Third, moose-flies. The big ones, Polis said, were called *Bososquasis*. It is a stout brown fly, much like a horse-fly, about eleven sixteenths of an inch long, commonly rusty colored beneath, with unspotted wings. They can bite smartly, according to Polis, but are easily avoided or killed. Fourth, the No-see-ems above mentioned. Of all these, the mosquitoes are the only ones that troubled me seriously; but, as I was provided with a wash and a veil, they have not made any deep impression.

The Indian would not use our wash to protect his face and hands, for fear that it would hurt his skin, nor had he any veil; he, therefore, suffered from insects now, and throughout this journey, more than either of us. I think that he suffered more than I did, when neither of us was protected. He regularly tied up his face in his handkerchief, and buried it in his blanket, and he now finally lay down on the sand between us and the fire for the sake of the smoke, which he tried to make enter his blanket about his face, and for the same purpose he lit his pipe and breathed the smoke into his blanket.

As we lay thus on the shore, with nothing between us and the stars, I inquired what stars he was acquainted with, or had names for. They were the Great Bear, which he called by this name, the Seven Stars, which he had no English name for, "the morning star," and "the north star."

In the middle of the night, as indeed each time that we lay on the shore of a lake, we heard the voice of the loon, loud and distinct, from far over the lake. It is a very wild sound, quite in keeping with the place and the circumstances of the traveller, and very unlike the voice of a bird. I could lie awake for hours listening to it, it is so thrilling. When camping in such a wilderness as this, you are prepared to hear sounds from some of its inhabitants which will give voice to its wildness. Some idea of bears, wolves, or panthers runs in your head naturally, and when this note is first heard very far off at midnight, as you lie with your ear to the ground,—the forest being perfectly still about you, you take it for granted that it is the voice of a wolf or some other wild beast, for only the last part is heard when at a distance,—you conclude that it is a pack of wolves baying the moon, or, perchance, cantering after a moose. Strange as it may seem, the "mooing" of a cow on a mountain-side comes nearest to my idea of the voice of a bear; and this bird's note resembled that. It was the unfailing and characteristic sound of those lakes. We were not so lucky as to hear wolves howl, though that is an occasional serenade. Some friends of mine, who two years ago went up the Caucomgomoc River, were serenaded by wolves while moose-hunting by moonlight. It was a sudden burst, as if a hundred demons had broke loose,—a startling sound enough, which, if any, would make your hair stand on end, and all was still again. It lasted but a moment, and you 'd have thought there were twenty of them, when probably there were only two or three. They heard it twice only, and they said that it gave expression to the wilderness which it lacked before. I heard of some men who, while skinning a moose lately in those woods, were driven off from the carcass by a pack of wolves, which ate it up.

This of the loon—I do not mean its laugh, but its

looning—is a long-drawn call, as it were, sometimes singularly human to my ear,— *hoo-hoo-ooooo*, like the hallooing of a man on a very high key, having thrown his voice into his head. I have heard a sound exactly like it when breathing heavily through my own nostrils, half awake at ten at night, suggesting my affinity to the loon; as if its language were but a dialect of my own, after all. Formerly, when lying awake at midnight in those woods, I had listened to hear some words or syllables of their language, but it chanced that I listened in vain until I heard the cry of the loon. I have heard it occasionally on the ponds of my native town, but there its wildness is not enhanced by the surrounding scenery.

I was awakened at midnight by some heavy, low-flying bird, probably a loon, flapping by close over my head, along the shore. So, turning the other side of my half-clad body to the fire, I sought slumber again.

TUESDAY, July 28.

When we awoke we found a heavy dew on our blankets. I lay awake very early, and listened to the clear, shrill *ah-tette-tette-te*, of the white-throated sparrow, repeated at short intervals, without the least variation, for half an hour, as if it could not enough express its happiness. Whether my companions heard it or not, I know not, but it was a kind of matins to me, and the event of that forenoon.

It was a pleasant sunrise, and we had a view of the mountains in the southeast. Ktaadn appeared about southeast by south. A double-topped mountain, about southeast by east, and another portion of the same, east-southeast. The last the Indian called Nerlumskeechticook, and said that it was at the head of the East Branch, and we should pass near it on our return that way.

We did some more washing in the lake this morning, and with our clothes hung about on the dead trees and rocks, the shore looked like washing-day at home. The Indian, taking the hint, borrowed the soap, and walking into the lake, washed his only cotton shirt on his person, then put on his pants and let it dry on him.

I observed that he wore a cotton shirt, originally white, a greenish flannel one over it, but no waistcoat, flannel drawers, and strong linen or duck pants, which also had been white, blue woollen stockings, cowhide boots, and a Kossuth hat. He carried no change of clothing, but putting on a stout, thick jacket, which he laid aside in the canoe, and seizing a full-sized axe, his gun and ammunition, and a blanket, which would do for a sail or knapsack, if wanted, and strapping on his belt, which contained a large sheath-knife, he walked off at once, ready to be gone all summer. This looked very independent; a few simple and effective tools, and no India-rubber clothing. He was always the first ready to start in the morning, and if it had not held some of our property would not have been obliged to roll up his blanket. Instead of carrying a large bundle of his own extra clothing, &c., he brought back the great-coats of moose tied up in his blanket. I found that his outfit was the result of a long experience, and in the main was hardly to be improved on, unless by washing or an extra shirt. Wanting a button here, he walked off to a place where some Indians had recently encamped, and searched for one, but I believe in vain.

Having softened our stiffened boots and shoes with the pork fat, the usual disposition of what was left at breakfast, we crossed the lake early, steering in a diagonal direction northwesterly about four miles, to the outlet, which was not to be discovered till we were close to it. The Indian name, Apmoojenegamook, means lake that is crossed, because the usual course lies across, and not along it. This is the largest of the Allegash lakes, and was the first St. John's water that we floated on. It is shaped in the main like Chesuncook. There are no mountains or high hills very near it. At Bangor we had been told of a township many miles farther northwest; it was indicated to us as containing the highest land thereabouts, where, by climbing a particular tree in the forest, we could get a general idea of the country. I have no doubt that the last was good advice, but we did not go there. We did not now intend to go far down the Allegash, but merely to get a view of the great lakes which are its source, and then return this way to the East Branch of the Penobscot. The water now, by good rights, flowed northward, if it could be said to flow at all.

After reaching the middle of the lake, we found the waves

as usual pretty high, and the Indian warned my companion, who was nodding, that he must not allow himself to fall asleep in the canoe lest he should upset us; adding, that when Indians want to sleep in a canoe, they lie down straight on the bottom. But in this crowded one that was impossible. However, he said that he would nudge him if he saw him nodding.

A belt of dead trees stood all around the lake, some far out in the water, with others prostrate behind them, and they made the shore, for the most part, almost inaccessible. This is the effect of the dam at the outlet. Thus the natural sandy or rocky shore, with its green fringe, was concealed and destroyed. We coasted westward along the north side, searching for the outlet, about one quarter of a mile distant from this savage-looking shore, on which the waves were breaking violently, knowing that it might easily be concealed amid this rubbish, or by the over-lapping of the shore. It is remarkable how little these important gates to a lake are blazoned. There is no triumphal arch over the modest inlet or outlet, but at some undistinguished point it trickles in or out through the uninterrupted forest, almost as through a sponge.

We reached the outlet in about an hour, and carried over the dam there, which is quite a solid structure, and about one quarter of a mile farther there was a second dam. The reader will perceive that the result of this particular damming about Chamberlain Lake is, that the head-waters of the St. John are made to flow by Bangor. They have thus dammed all the larger lakes, raising their broad surfaces many feet; Moosehead, for instance, some forty miles long, with its steamer on it; thus turning the forces of nature against herself, that they might float their spoils out of the country. They rapidly run out of these immense forests all the finer, and more accessible pine timber, and then leave the bears to watch the decaying dams, not clearing nor cultivating the land, nor making roads, nor building houses, but leaving it a wilderness, as they found it. In many parts, only these dams remain, like deserted beaver-dams. Think how much land they have flowed, without asking Nature's leave! When the State wishes to endow an academy or university, it grants it a tract of forest land: one saw represents an academy; a gang, a university.

The wilderness experiences a sudden rise of all her streams and lakes, she feels ten thousand vermin gnawing at the base of her noblest trees, many combining, drag them off, jarring over the roots of the survivors, and tumble them into the nearest stream, till the fairest having fallen, they scamper off to ransack some new wilderness, and all is still again. It is as when a migrating army of mice girdles a forest of pines. The chopper fells trees from the same motive that the mouse gnaws them,—to get his living. You tell me that he has a more interesting family than the mouse. That is as it happens. He speaks of a "berth" of timber, a good place for him to get into, just as a worm might. When the chopper would praise a pine, he will commonly tell you that the one he cut was so big that a yoke of oxen stood on its stump; as if that were what the pine had grown for, to become the footstool of oxen. In my mind's eye, I can see these unwieldy tame deer, with a yoke binding them together, and brazen-tipped horns betraying their servitude, taking their stand on the stump of each giant pine in succession throughout this whole forest, and chewing their cud there, until it is nothing but an ox-pasture, and run out at that. As if it were good for the oxen, and some terebinthine or other medicinal quality ascended into their nostrils. Or is their elevated position intended merely as a symbol of the fact that the pastoral comes next in order to the sylvan or hunter life?

The character of the logger's admiration is betrayed by his very mode of expressing it. If he told all that was in his mind, he would say, it was so big that I cut it down and then a yoke of oxen could stand on its stump. He admires the log, the carcass or corpse, more than the tree. Why, my dear sir, the tree might have stood on its own stump, and a great deal more comfortably and firmly than a yoke of oxen can, if you had not cut it down. What right have you to celebrate the virtues of the man you murdered?

The Anglo-American can indeed cut down, and grub up all this waving forest, and make a stump speech, and vote for Buchanan on its ruins, but he cannot converse with the spirit of the tree he fells, he cannot read the poetry and mythology which retire as he advances. He ignorantly erases mythological tablets in order to print his handbills and town-meeting warrants on them. Before he has learned his a b c in the beautiful but mystic lore of the wilderness which Spenser and Dante had just begun to read, he cuts it down, coins a *pine-tree* shilling, (as if to signify the pine's value to him,) puts up a *dee*strict school-house, and introduces Webster's spelling-book.

Below the last dam, the river being swift and shallow, though broad enough, we two walked about half a mile to lighten the canoe. I made it a rule to carry my knapsack when I walked, and also to keep it tied to a cross-bar when in the canoe, that it might be found with the canoe if we should upset.

I heard the dog-day locust here, and afterward on the carries, a sound which I had associated only with more open, if not settled countries. The area for locusts must be small in the Maine woods.

We were now fairly on the Allegash River, which name our Indian said meant hemlock bark. These waters flow northward about 100 miles, at first very feebly, then southeasterly 250 more to the Bay of Fundy. After perhaps two miles of river, we entered Heron Lake, called on the map *Pongokwahem*, scaring up forty or fifty young *shecorways*, sheldrakes, at the entrance, which ran over the water with great rapidity, as usual in a long line.

This was the fourth great lake, lying northwest and southeast, like Chesuncook, and most of the long lakes in that neighborhood, and, judging from the map, it is about ten miles long. We had entered it on the southwest side, and saw a dark mountain northeast over the lake, not very far off nor high, which the Indian said was called *Peaked Mountain*, and used by explorers to look for timber from. There was also some other high land more easterly. The shores were in the same ragged and unsightly condition, encumbered with dead timber, both fallen and standing, as in the last lake, owing to the dam on the Allegash below. Some low points or islands were almost drowned.

I saw something white a mile off on the water, which turned out to be a great gull on a rock in the middle, which the Indian would have been glad to kill and eat, but it flew away long before we were near; and also a flock of summer ducks that were about the rock with it. I asking him about herons, since this was Heron Lake, he said that he found the blue heron's nests in the hard-wood trees. I thought that I saw a light-colored object move along the opposite or northern shore, four or five miles distant. He did not know what it could be, unless it were a moose, though he had never seen a white one; but he said that he could distinguish a moose "anywhere on shore, clear across the lake."

Rounding a point, we stood across a bay for a mile and a half or two miles, toward a large island, three or four miles down the lake. We met with ephemeræ (shad-fly) midway, about a mile from the shore, and they evidently fly over the whole lake. On Moosehead I had seen a large devil's-needle half a mile from the shore, coming from the middle of the lake, where it was three or four miles wide at least. It had probably crossed. But at last, of course, you come to lakes so large that an insect cannot fly across them; and this, perhaps, will serve to distinguish a large lake from a small one.

We landed on the southeast side of the island, which was rather elevated, and densely wooded, with a rocky shore, in season for an early dinner. Somebody had camped there not long before, and left the frame on which they stretched a moose-hide, which our Indian criticised severely, thinking it showed but little woodcraft. Here were plenty of the shells of crayfish, or fresh-water lobsters, which had been washed ashore, such as have given a name to some ponds and streams. They are commonly four or five inches long. The Indian proceeded at once to cut a canoe-birch, slanted it up against another tree on the shore, tying it with a withe, and lay down to sleep in its shade.

When we were on the Caucomgomoc, he recommended to us a new way home, the very one which we had first thought of, by the St. John. He even said that it was easier, and would take but little more time than the other, by the east branch of the Penobscot, though very much farther round; and taking the map, he showed where we should be each night, for he was familiar with the route. According to his calculation, we should reach the French settlements the next night after this, by keeping northward down the Allegash, and when we got into the main St. John the banks would be more or less settled all the way; as if that were a recommendation. There would be but one or two falls, with short carrying-places, and we should go down the stream very fast, even a hundred miles a day, if the wind allowed; and he indicated where we should carry over into Eel River to save a bend below Woodstock in New Brunswick, and so into the Schoodic Lake, and thence to the Mattawamkeag. It would be about three hundred and sixty miles to Bangor this way, though only about one hundred and sixty by the other; but in the former case we should explore the St. John from its source through two thirds of its course, as well as the Schoodic Lake and Mattawamkeag,—and we were again tempted to go that way. I feared, however, that the banks of the St. John were too much settled. When I asked him which course would take us through the wildest country, he said the route by the East Branch. Partly from this consideration, as also from its shortness, we resolved to adhere to the latter route, and perhaps ascend Ktaadn on the way. We made this island the limit of our excursion in this direction.

We had now seen the largest of the Allegash Lakes. The next dam " was about fifteen miles" farther north, down the Allegash, and it was dead water so far. We had been told in Bangor of a man who lived alone, a sort of hermit, at that dam, to take care of it, who spent his time tossing a bullet from one hand to the other, for want of employment,—as if we might want to call on him. This sort of tit-for-tat intercourse between his two hands, bandying to and fro a leaden subject, seems to have been his symbol for society.

This island, according to the map, was about a hundred and ten miles in a straight line north-northwest from Bangor, and about ninety-nine miles east-southeast from Quebec. There was another island visible toward the north end of the lake, with an elevated clearing on it; but we learned afterward that it was not inhabited, had only been used as a pasture for cattle which summered in these woods, though our informant said that there was a hut on the mainland near the outlet of the lake. This unnaturally smooth-shaven, squarish spot, in the midst of the otherwise uninterrupted forest, only reminded us how uninhabited the country was. You would sooner expect to meet with a bear than an ox in such a clearing. At any rate, it must have been a surprise to the bears when they came across it. Such, seen far or near, you know at once to be man's work, for Nature never does it. In order to let in the light to the earth as on a lake, he clears off the forest on the hillsides and plains, and sprinkles fine grass-seed, like an enchanter, and so carpets the earth with a firm sward.

Polis had evidently more curiosity respecting the few settlers in those woods than we. If nothing was said, he took it for granted that we wanted to go straight to the next log-hut. Having observed that we came by the log-huts at Chesuncook, and the blind Canadian's at the Mud Pond carry, without stopping to communicate with the inhabitants, he took occasion now to suggest that the usual way was, when you came near a house, to go to it, and tell the inhabitants what you had seen or heard, and then they tell you what they had seen; but we laughed, and said that we had had enough of houses for the present, and had come here partly to avoid them.

In the mean while, the wind, increasing, blew down the Indian's birch and created such a sea that we found ourselves prisoners on the island, the nearest shore, which was the western, being perhaps a mile distant, and we took the canoe out to prevent its drifting away. We did not know but we should be compelled to spend the rest of the day and the night there. At any rate, the Indian went to sleep again in the shade of his birch, my companion busied himself drying his plants, and I rambled along the shore westward, which was quite stony, and obstructed with fallen bleached or drifted trees for four or five rods in width. I found growing on this broad rocky and gravelly shore the *Salix rostrata, discolor,* and *lucida, Ranunculus recurvatus, Potentilla Norvegica, Scutellaria lateriflora, Eupatorium purpureum, Aster Tradescanti, Mentha Canadensis, Epilobium angustifolium,* abundant, *Lycopus sinuatus, Solidago lanceolata, Spiræa salicifolia, Antennaria margaritacea, Prunella, Rumex acetosella,* Raspberries, Wool-grass, *Onoclea,* &c. The nearest trees were *Betula papyracea* and *excelsa,* and *Populus tremuloides.* I give these names because it was my farthest northern point.

Our Indian said that he was a doctor, and could tell me some medicinal use for every plant I could show him. I immediately tried him. He said that the inner bark of the aspen (*Populus tremuloides*) was good for sore eyes; and so with various other plants, proving himself as good as his word. According to his account, he had acquired such knowledge in his youth from a wise old Indian with whom he associated, and he lamented that the present generation of Indians "had lost a great deal."

He said that the caribou was a "very great runner," that there was none about this lake now, though there used to be many, and pointing to the belt of dead trees caused by the dams, he added, "No likum stump,—when he sees that he scared."

Pointing southeasterly over the lake and distant forest, he observed, "Me go Oldtown in three days." I asked how he would get over the swamps and fallen trees. "O," said he, "in winter all covered, go anywhere on snow-shoes, right across lakes." When I asked how he went, he said, "First I go Ktaadn, west side, then I go Millinocket, then Pamadumcook, then Nickatou, then Lincoln, then Oldtown," or else he went a shorter way by the Piscataquis. What a wilderness walk for a man to take alone! None of your half-mile swamps, none of your mile-wide woods merely, as on the skirts of our towns, without hotels, only a dark mountain or a lake for guide-board and station, over ground much of it impassable in summer!

It reminded me of Prometheus Bound. Here was travelling of the old heroic kind over the unaltered face of nature. From the Allegash, or Hemlock River, and Pongoquahem Lake, across great Apmoojenegamook, and leaving the Nerlum-skeechticook Mountain on his left, he takes his way under the bear-haunted slopes of Souneunk and Ktaadn Mountains to Pamadumcook and Millinocket's inland seas, (where often gulls'-eggs may increase his store,) and so on to the forks of the Nickatou, (*nia soseb* "we alone Joseph" seeing what our folks see,) ever pushing the boughs of the fir and spruce aside, with his load of furs, contending day and night, night and day, with the shaggy demon vegetation, travelling through the mossy graveyard of trees. Or he could go by "that rough tooth of the sea," Kineo, great source of arrows and of spears to the ancients, when weapons of stone were used. Seeing and hearing moose, caribou, bears, porcupines, lynxes, wolves, and panthers. Places where he might live and die and never hear of the United States, which make such a noise in the world,—never hear of America, so called from the name of a European gentleman.

There is a lumberer's road called the Eagle Lake road, from the Seboois to the east side of this lake. It may seem strange that any road through such a wilderness should be passable, even in winter, when the snow is three or four feet deep, but at that season, wherever lumbering operations are actively carried on, teams are continually passing on the single track, and it becomes as smooth almost as a railway. I am told that in the Aroostook country the sleds are required by law to be of one width, (four feet,) and sleighs must be altered to fit the track, so that one runner may go in one rut and the other follow the horse. Yet it is very bad turning out.

We had for some time seen a thunder-shower coming up from the west over the woods of the island, and heard the muttering of the thunder, though we were in doubt whether it would reach us; but now the darkness rapidly increasing, and a fresh breeze rustling the forest, we hastily put up the plants which we had been drying, and with one consent made a rush for the tent material and set about pitching it. A place was selected and stakes and pins cut in the shortest possible time, and we were pinning it down lest it should be blown away, when the storm suddenly burst over us.

As we lay huddled together under the tent, which leaked considerably about the sides, with our baggage at our feet, we listened to some of the grandest thunder which I ever heard,—rapid peals, round and plump, bang, bang, bang, in succession, like artillery from some fortress in the sky; and the lightning was proportionally brilliant. The Indian said, "It must be good powder." All for the benefit of the moose and us, echoing far over the concealed lakes. I thought it must be a place which the thunder loved, where the lightning practised to keep its hand in, and it would do no harm to shatter a few pines. What had become of the ephemeræ and devil's-needles then? Were they prudent enough to seek harbor before the storm? Perhaps their motions might guide the voyageur.

Looking out I perceived that the violent shower falling on the lake had almost instantaneously flattened the waves,—the commander of that fortress had smoothed it for us so,—and it clearing off, we resolved to start immediately, before the wind raised them again.

Going outside, I said that I saw clouds still in the southwest, and heard thunder there. The Indian asked if the thunder went "lound" (round), saying that if it did we should have more rain. I thought that it did. We embarked, nevertheless, and paddled rapidly back toward the dams. The white-throated sparrows on the shore were about, singing, *Ah te, e, e, te, e, e, te,* or else *ah te, e, e, te, e, e, te, e, e, te, e, e.*

At the outlet of Chamberlain Lake we were overtaken by another gusty rain-storm, which compelled us to take shelter, the Indian under his canoe on the bank, and we ran under the edge of the dam. However, we were more scared than wet. From my covert I could see the Indian peeping out from beneath his canoe to see what had become of the rain. When we had taken our respective places thus once or twice, the rain not coming down in earnest, we commenced rambling about the neighborhood, for the wind had by this time raised such waves on the lake that we could not stir, and we feared that we should be obliged to camp there. We got an early supper on the dam and tried for fish there, while waiting for the tumult to subside. The fishes were not only few, but small and worthless, and the Indian declared that there were no good fishes in the St. John's waters; that we must wait till we got to the Penobscot waters.

At length, just before sunset, we set out again. It was a wild evening when we coasted up the north side of this Apmoojenegamook Lake. One thunder-storm was just over, and the waves which it had raised still running with violence, and another storm was now seen coming up in the southwest, far over the lake; but it might be worse in the morning, and we wished to get as far as possible on our way up the lake while we might. It blowed hard against the northern shore about an eighth of a mile distant on our left, and there was just as much sea as our shallow canoe would bear, without our taking unusual care. That which we kept off, and toward which the waves were driving, was as dreary and harborless a shore as you can conceive. For half a dozen rods in width it was a perfect maze of submerged trees, all dead and bare and bleaching, some standing half their original height, others prostrate, and criss-across, above or beneath the surface, and mingled with them were loose trees and limbs and stumps, beating about. Imagine the wharves of the largest city in the world, decayed, and the earth and planking washed away, leaving the spiles standing in loose order, but often of twice the ordinary height, and mingled with and beating against them the wreck of ten thousand navies, all their spars and timbers, while there rises from the water's edge the densest and grimmest wilderness, ready to supply more material when the former fails, and you may get a faint idea of that coast. We could not have landed if we would, without the greatest danger of being swamped; so blow as it might, we must depend on coasting by it. It was twilight, too, and that stormy cloud was advancing rapidly in our rear. It was a pleasant excitement, yet we were glad to reach, at length, in the dusk, the cleared shore of the Chamberlain Farm.

We landed on a low and thinly wooded point there, and while my companions were pitching the tent, I ran up to the house to get some sugar, our six pounds being gone;—it was no wonder they were, for Polis had a sweet tooth. He would first fill his dipper nearly a third full of sugar, and then add the coffee to it. Here was a clearing extending back from the lake to a hill-top, with some dark-colored log buildings and a storehouse in it, and half a dozen men standing in front of the principal hut, greedy for news. Among them was the man who tended the dam on the Allegash and tossed the bullet. He having charge of the dams, and learning that we were going to Webster Stream the next day, told me that some of their men, who were haying at Telos Lake, had shut the dam at the canal there in order to catch trout, and if we wanted more water to take us through the canal we might raise the gate, for he would like to have it raised. The Chamberlain Farm is no doubt a cheerful opening in the woods, but such was the lateness of the hour that it has left but a dusky impression on my mind. As I have said, the influx of light merely is civilizing, yet I fancied that they walked about on Sundays in their clearing somewhat as in a prison-yard.

They were unwilling to spare more than four pounds of brown sugar,—unlocking the storehouse to get it,—since they only kept a little for such cases as this, and they charged twenty cents a pound for it, which certainly it was worth to get it up there.

When I returned to the shore it was quite dark, but we had a rousing fire to warm and dry us by, and a snug apartment behind it. The Indian went up to the house to inquire after a brother who had been absent hunting a year or two, and while another shower was beginning, I groped about cutting spruce and arbor-vitæ twigs for a bed. I preferred the arbor-vitæ on account of its fragrance, and spread it particularly thick about the shoulders. It is remarkable with what pure satisfaction the traveller in these woods will reach his camping-ground on the eve of a tempestuous night like this, as if he had got to his inn, and, rolling himself in his blanket, stretch himself on his six feet by two bed of dripping fir-twigs, with a thin sheet of cotton for roof, snug as a meadow-mouse in its nest. Invariably our best nights were those when it rained, for then we were not troubled with mosquitoes.

You soon come to disregard rain on such excursions, at least in the summer, it is so easy to dry yourself, supposing a dry change of clothing is not to be had. You can much sooner dry you by such a fire as you can make in the woods than in anybody's kitchen, the fireplace is so much larger, and wood so much more abundant. A shed-shaped tent will catch and reflect the heat like a Yankee-baker, and you may be drying while you are sleeping.

Some who have leaky roofs in the towns may have been kept awake, but we were soon lulled asleep by a steady, soaking rain, which lasted all night. To-night, the rain not coming at once with violence, the twigs were soon dried by the reflected heat.

WEDNESDAY, July 29.

When we awoke it had done raining, though it was still cloudy. The fire was put out, and the Indian's boots, which stood under the eaves of the tent, were half full of water. He was much more improvident in such respects than either of us, and he had to thank us for keeping his powder dry. We decided to cross the lake at once, before breakfast, or while we could; and before starting I took the bearing of the shore which we wished to strike, S. S. E. about three miles distant, lest a sudden misty rain should conceal it when we were midway. Though the bay in which we were was perfectly quiet and smooth, we found the lake already wide awake outside, but not dangerously or unpleasantly so; nevertheless, when you get out on one of those lakes in a canoe like this, you do not forget that you are completely at the mercy of the wind, and a fickle power it is. The playful waves may at any time become too rude for you in their sport, and play right on over you. We saw a few *she-cor-ways* and a *fish-hawk* thus early, and after much steady paddling and dancing over the dark waves of Apmoojenegamook, we found ourselves in the neighborhood of the southern land, heard the waves breaking on it, and turned our thoughts wholly to that side. After coasting eastward along this shore a mile or two, we breakfasted on a rocky point, the first convenient place that offered.

It was well enough that we crossed thus early, for the waves now ran quite high, and we should have been obliged to go round somewhat, but beyond this point we had comparatively smooth water. You can commonly go along one side or the other of a lake, when you cannot cross it.

The Indian was looking at the hard-wood ridges from time to time, and said that he would like to buy a few hundred acres somewhere about this lake, asking our advice. It was to buy as near the crossing place as possible.

My companion and I having a minute's discussion on some point of ancient history, were amused by the attitude which the Indian, who could not tell what we were talking about, assumed. He constituted himself umpire, and, judging by our air and gesture, he very seriously remarked from time to time, "you beat," or "he beat."

Leaving a spacious bay, a northeasterly prolongation of Chamberlain Lake, on our left, we entered through a short strait into a small lake a couple of miles over, called on the map *Telasinis*, but the Indian had no distinct name for it, and thence into *Telos* Lake, which he called *Paytaywecomgomoc*, or Burnt-Ground Lake. This curved round toward the northeast, and may have been three or four miles long as we paddled.

He had not been here since 1825. He did not know what Telos meant; thought it was not Indian. He used the word "*Spoke-logan*" (for an inlet in the shore which led nowhere), and when I asked its meaning said that there was "no Indian in 'em." There was a clearing, with a house and barn, on the southwest shore, temporarily occupied by some men who were getting the hay, as we had been told; also a clearing for a pasture on a hill on the west side of the lake.

We landed on a rocky point on the northeast side, to look at some Red Pines (*Pinus resinosa*), the first we had noticed, and get some cones, for our few which grow in Concord do not bear any.

The outlet from the lake into the East Branch of the Penobscot is an artificial one, and it was not very apparent where it was exactly, but the lake ran curving far up northeasterly into two narrow valleys or ravines, as if it had for a long time been groping its way toward the Penobscot waters, or remembered when it anciently flowed there; by observing where the horizon was lowest, and following the longest of these, we at length reached the dam, having come about a dozen miles from the last camp. Somebody had left a line set for trout, and the jackknife with which the bait had been cut on the dam beside it, an evidence that man was near, and on a deserted log close by a loaf of bread baked in a Yankee-baker. These proved the property of a solitary hunter, whom we soon met, and canoe and gun and traps were not far off. He told us that it was twenty miles farther on our route to the foot of Grand Lake, where you could catch as many trout as you wanted, and that the first house below the foot of the lake, on the East Branch, was Hunt's, about forty-five miles farther; though there was one about a mile and a half up Trout stream, some fifteen miles ahead, but it was rather a blind route to it. It turned out that, though the stream was in our favor, we did not reach the next house till the morning of the third day after this. The nearest permanently inhabited house behind us was now a dozen miles distant, so that the interval between the two nearest houses on our route was about sixty miles.

This hunter, who was a quite small, sunburnt man, having already carried his canoe over, and baked his loaf, had nothing so interesting and pressing to do as to observe our transit. He had been out a month or more alone. How much more wild and adventurous his life than that of the hunter in Concord woods, who gets back to his house and the mill-dam every night! Yet they in the towns who have wild oats to sow commonly sow them on cultivated and comparatively exhausted ground. And as for the rowdy world in the large cities, so little enterprise has it that it never adventures in this direction, but like vermin clubs together in alleys and drinking-saloons, its highest accomplishment, perchance, to run beside a fire-engine and throw brickbats. But the former is comparatively an independent and successful man, getting his living in a way that he likes, without disturbing his human neighbors. How much more respectable also is the life of the solitary pioneer or settler in these, or any woods,—having real difficulties, not of his own creation, drawing his subsistence directly from nature,—than that of the helpless multitudes in the towns who depend on gratifying the extremely artificial wants of society and are thrown out of employment by hard times!

Here for the first time we found the raspberries really plenty,—that is, on passing the height of land between the Allegash and the East Branch of the Penobscot; the same was true of the blueberries.

Telos Lake, the head of the St. John on this side, and Webster Pond, the head of the East Branch of the Penobscot, are only about a mile apart, and they are connected by a ravine, in which but little digging was required to make the water of the former, which is the highest, flow into the latter. This canal, which is something less than a mile long and about four rods wide, was made a few years before my first visit to Maine. Since then the lumber of the upper Allegash and its lakes has been run down the Penobscot, that is, up the Allegash, which here consists principally of a chain of large and stagnant lakes, whose thoroughfares, or river-links, have been made nearly equally stagnant by damming, and then down the Penobscot. The rush of the water has produced such changes in the canal that it has now the appearance of a very rapid mountain stream flowing through a ravine, and you would not suspect that any digging had been required to persuade the waters of the St. John to flow into the Penobscot here. It was so winding that one could see but little way down.

It is stated by Springer, in his "Forest Life," that the cause of this canal being dug was this. According to the treaty of 1842 with Great Britain, it was agreed that all the timber run down the St. John, which rises in Maine, "when within the Province of New Brunswick . . . . shall be dealt with as if it were the produce of the said Province," which was thought by our side to mean that it should be free from taxation. Immediately, the Province, wishing to get something out of the Yankees, levied a duty on all the timber that passed down the St. John; but to satisfy its own subjects "made a corresponding discount on the stumpage charged those hauling timber from the crown lands." The result was that the Yankees made the St. John run the other way, or down the Penobscot, so that the Province lost both its duty and its water, while the Yankees, being greatly enriched, had reason to thank it for the suggestion.

It is wonderful how well watered this country is. As you paddle across a lake, bays will be pointed out to you, by following up which, and perhaps the tributary stream which empties in, you may, after a short portage, or possibly, at some seasons, none at all, get into another river, which empties far away from the one you are on. Generally, you may go in any direction in a canoe, by making frequent but not very long portages. You are only realizing once more what all nature distinctly remembers here, for no doubt the waters flowed thus in a former geological period, and instead of being a lake country, it was an archipelago. It seems as if the more youthful and impressible streams can hardly resist the numerous invitations and temptations to leave their native beds and run down their neighbors' channels. Your carries are often over half-submerged ground, on the dry channels of a former period. In carrying from one river to another, I did not go over such high and rocky ground as in going about the falls of the same river. For in the former case I was once lost in a swamp, as I have related, and, again, found an artificial canal which appeared to be natural.

I remember once dreaming of pushing a canoe up the rivers

of Maine, and that, when I had got so high that the channels were dry, I kept on through the ravines and gorges, nearly as well as before, by pushing a little harder, and now it seemed to me that my dream was partially realized.

Wherever there is a channel for water, there is a road for the canoe. The pilot of the steamer which ran from Oldtown up the Penobscot in 1854 told me that she drew only fourteen inches, and would run easily in two feet of water, though they did not like to. It is said that some Western steamers can run on a heavy dew, whence we can imagine what a canoe may do. Montresor, who was sent from Quebec by the English about 1760 to explore the route to the Kennebec, over which Arnold afterward passed, supplied the Penobscot near its source with water by opening the beaver-dams, and he says, "This is often done." He afterward states that the Governor of Canada had forbidden to molest the beaver about the outlet of the Kennebec from Moosehead Lake, on account of the service which their dams did by raising the water for navigation.

This canal, so called, was a considerable and extremely rapid and rocky river. The Indian decided that there was water enough in it without raising the dam, which would only make it more violent, and that he would run down it alone, while we carried the greater part of the baggage. Our provision being about half consumed, there was the less left in the canoe. We had thrown away the pork-keg, and wrapt its contents in birch bark, which is the unequalled wrapping-paper of the woods.

Following a moist trail through the forest, we reached the head of Webster Pond about the same time with the Indian, notwithstanding the velocity with which he moved, our route being the most direct. The Indian name of Webster Stream, of which this pond is the source, is, according to him, *Madunkehunk*, i. e. Height of Land, and of the pond, *Madunke-hunk-gamooc*, or Height of Land Pond. The latter was two or three miles long. We passed near a pine on its shore which had been splintered by lightning, perhaps the day before. This was the first proper East Branch Penobscot water that we came to.

At the outlet of Webster Lake was another dam, at which

we stopped and picked raspberries, while the Indian went down the stream a half-mile through the forest, to see what he had got to contend with. There was a deserted log camp here, apparently used the previous winter, with its "hovel" or barn for cattle. In the hut was a large fir-twig bed, raised two feet from the floor, occupying a large part of the single apartment, a long narrow table against the wall, with a stout log bench before it, and above the table a small window, the only one there was, which admitted a feeble light. It was a simple and strong fort erected against the cold, and suggested what valiant trencher work had been done there. I discovered one or two curious wooden traps, which had not been used for a long time, in the woods near by. The principal part consisted of a long and slender pole.

We got our dinner on the shore, on the upper side of the dam. As we were sitting by our fire, concealed by the earth bank of the dam, a long line of sheldrake, half grown, came waddling over it from the water below, passing within about a rod of us, so that we could almost have caught them in our hands. They were very abundant on all the streams and lakes which we visited, and every two or three hours they would rush away in a long string over the water before us, twenty to fifty of them at once, rarely ever flying, but running with great rapidity up or down the stream, even in the midst of the most violent rapids, and apparently as fast up as down, or else crossing diagonally, the old, as it appeared, behind, and driving them, and flying to the front from time to time, as if to direct them. We also saw many small black dippers, which behaved in a similar manner, and, once or twice, a few black ducks.

An Indian at Oldtown had told us that we should be obliged to carry ten miles between Telos Lake on the St. John's and Second Lake on the East Branch of the Penobscot; but the lumberers whom we met assured us that there would not be more than a mile of carry. It turned out that the Indian, who had lately been over this route, was nearest right, as far as we were concerned. However, if one of us could have assisted the Indian in managing the canoe in the rapids, we might have run the greater part of the way; but as he was alone in the management of the canoe in such places, we were obliged to walk the greater part. I did not feel quite ready to try such an experiment on Webster Stream, which has so bad a reputation. According to my observation, a bateau, properly manned, shoots rapids as a matter of course, which a single Indian with a canoe carries round.

My companion and I carried a good part of the baggage on our shoulders, while the Indian took that which would be least injured by wet in the canoe. We did not know when we should see him again, for he had not been this way since the canal was cut, nor for more than thirty years. He agreed to stop when he got to smooth water, come up and find our path if he could, and halloo for us, and after waiting a reasonable time go on and try again,—and we were to look out in like manner for him.

He commenced by running through the sluice-way and over the dam, as usual, standing up in his tossing canoe, and was soon out of sight behind a point in a wild gorge. This Webster Stream is well known to lumbermen as a difficult one. It is exceedingly rapid and rocky, and also shallow, and can hardly be considered navigable, unless that may mean that what is launched in it is sure to be carried swiftly down it, though it may be dashed to pieces by the way. It is somewhat like navigating a thunder-spout. With commonly an irresistible force urging you on, you have got to choose your own course each moment, between the rocks and shallows, and to get into it, moving forward always with the utmost possible moderation, and often holding on, if you can, that you may inspect the rapids before you.

By the Indian's direction we took an old path on the south side, which appeared to keep down the stream, though at a considerable distance from it, cutting off bends, perhaps to Second Lake, having first taken the course from the map with a compass, which was northeasterly, for safety. It was a wild wood-path, with a few tracks of oxen which had been driven over it, probably to some old camp clearing, for pasturage, mingled with the tracks of moose which had lately used it. We kept on steadily for about an hour without putting down our packs, occasionally winding around or climbing over a fallen tree, for the most part far out of sight and hearing of the river; till, after walking about three miles, we were glad to find that the path came to the river again at an old camp ground, where there was a small opening in the forest, at which we paused. Swiftly as the shallow and rocky river ran here, a continuous rapid with dancing waves, I saw, as I sat on the shore, a long string of sheldrakes, which something scared, run up the opposite side of the stream by me, with the same ease that they commonly did down it, just touching the surface of the waves, and getting an impulse from them as they flowed from under them; but they soon came back, driven by the Indian, who had fallen a little behind us, on account of the windings. He shot round a point just above, and came to land by us with considerable water in his canoe. He had found it, as he said, "very strong water," and had been obliged to land once before to empty out what he had taken in. He complained that it strained him to paddle so hard in order to keep his canoe straight in its course, having no one in the bows to aid him, and, shallow as it was, said that it would be no joke to upset there, for the force of the water was such that he had as lief I would strike him over the head with a paddle as have that water strike him. Seeing him come out of that gap was as if you should pour water down an inclined and zigzag trough, then drop a nutshell into it, and taking a short cut to the bottom, get there in time to see it come out, notwithstanding the rush and tumult, right side up, and only partly full of water.

After a moment's breathing space, while I held his canoe, he was soon out of sight again around another bend, and we, shouldering our packs, resumed our course.

We did not at once fall into our path again, but made our way with difficulty along the edge of the river, till at length, striking inland through the forest, we recovered it. Before going a mile we heard the Indian calling to us. He had come up through the woods and along the path to find us, having reached sufficiently smooth water to warrant his taking us in. The shore was about one fourth of a mile distant, through a dense, dark forest, and as he led us back to it, winding rapidly about to the right and left, I had the curiosity to look down carefully, and found that he was following his steps backward. I could only occasionally perceive his trail in the moss, and yet he did not appear to look down nor hesitate an instant, but led us out exactly to his canoe. This surprised me, for without a compass, or the sight or noise of the river to guide us, we could not have kept our course many minutes, and could have retraced our steps but a short distance, with a great deal of pains and very slowly, using a laborious circumspection. But it was evident that he could go back through the forest wherever he had been during the day.

After this rough walking in the dark woods it was an agreeable change to glide down the rapid river in the canoe once more. This river, which was about the size of our Assabet (in Concord), though still very swift, was almost perfectly smooth here, and showed a very visible declivity, a regularly inclined plane, for several miles, like a mirror set a little aslant, on which we coasted down. This very obvious regular descent, particularly plain when I regarded the water-line against the shores, made a singular impression on me, which the swiftness of our motion probably enhanced, so that we seemed to be gliding down a much steeper declivity than we were, and that we could not save ourselves from rapids and falls if we should suddenly come to them. My companion did not perceive this slope, but I have a surveyor's eyes, and I satisfied myself that it was no ocular illusion. You could tell at a glance on approaching such a river, which way the water flowed, though you might perceive no motion. I observed the angle at which a level line would strike the surface, and calculated the amount of fall in a rod, which did not need to be remarkably great to produce this effect.

It was very exhilarating, and the perfection of travelling, quite unlike floating on our dead Concord River, the coasting down this inclined mirror, which was now and then gently winding, down a mountain, indeed, between two evergreen forests, edged with lofty dead white pines, sometimes slanted half-way over the stream, and destined soon to bridge it. I saw some monsters there, nearly destitute of branches, and scarcely diminishing in diameter for eighty or ninety feet.

As we thus swept along, our Indian repeated in a deliberate and drawling tone the words "Daniel Webster, great lawyer," apparently reminded of him by the name of the stream, and he described his calling on him once in Boston, at what he supposed was his boarding-house. He had no business with him, but merely went to pay his respects, as we should say. In answer to our questions, he described his person well enough. It was on the day after Webster delivered his Bunker Hill oration, which I believe Polis heard. The first time he called he waited till he was tired without seeing him, and then went away. The next time, he saw him go by the door of the room in which he was waiting several times, in his shirt-sleeves, without noticing him. He thought that if he had come to see Indians, they would not have treated him so. At length, after very long delay, he came in, walked toward him, and asked in a loud voice, gruffly, "What do you want?" and he, thinking at first, by the motion of his hand, that he was going to strike him, said to himself, "You'd better take care, if you try that I shall know what to do." He did not like him, and declared that all he said "was not worth talk about a musquash." We suggested that probably Mr. Webster was very busy, and had a great many visitors just then.

Coming to falls and rapids, our easy progress was suddenly terminated. The Indian went along shore to inspect the water, while we climbed over the rocks, picking berries. The peculiar growth of blueberries on the tops of large rocks here made the impression of high land, and indeed this was the Height-of-land stream. When the Indian came back, he remarked, "You got to walk; ver strong water." So, taking out his canoe, he launched it again below the falls, and was soon out of sight. At such times, he would step into the canoe, take up his paddle, and, with an air of mystery, start off, looking far down stream, and keeping his own counsel, as if absorbing all the intelligence of forest and stream into himself; but I sometimes detected a little fun in his face, which could yield to my sympathetic smile, for he was thoroughly good-humored. We meanwhile scrambled along the shore with our packs, without any path. This was the last of *our* boating for the day.

The prevailing rock here was a kind of slate, standing on its edges, and my companion, who was recently from California, thought it exactly like that in which the gold is found, and said that if he had had a pan he would have liked to wash a little of the sand here.

The Indian now got along much faster than we, and waited

for us from time to time. I found here the only cool spring that I drank at anywhere on this excursion, a little water filling a hollow in the sandy bank. It was a quite memorable event, and due to the elevation of the country, for wherever else we had been the water in the rivers and the streams emptying in was dead and warm, compared with that of a mountainous region. It was very bad walking along the shore over fallen and drifted trees and bushes, and rocks, from time to time swinging ourselves round over the water, or else taking to a gravel bar or going inland. At one place, the Indian being ahead, I was obliged to take off all my clothes in order to ford a small but deep stream emptying in, while my companion, who was inland, found a rude bridge, high up in the woods, and I saw no more of him for some time. I saw there very fresh moose tracks, found a new golden-rod to me (perhaps *Solidago thyrsoidea*), and I passed one white-pine log, which had lodged, in the forest near the edge of the stream, which was quite five feet in diameter at the but. Probably its size detained it.

Shortly after this, I overtook the Indian at the edge of some burnt land, which extended three or four miles at least, beginning about three miles above Second Lake, which we were expecting to reach that night, and which is about ten miles from Telos Lake. This burnt region was still more rocky than before, but, though comparatively open, we could not yet see the lake. Not having seen my companion for some time, I climbed, with the Indian, a singular high rock on the edge of the river, forming a narrow ridge only a foot or two wide at top, in order to look for him; and after calling many times, I at length heard him answer from a considerable distance inland, he having taken a trail which led off from the river, perhaps directly to the lake, and was now in search of the river again. Seeing a much higher rock, of the same character, about one third of a mile farther east, or down stream, I proceeded toward it, through the burnt land, in order to look for the lake from its summit, supposing that the Indian would keep down the stream in his canoe, and hallooing all the while that my companion might join me on the way. Before we came together, I noticed where a moose, which possibly I had scared by my shouting, had apparently just run along a large rotten trunk of a pine, which made a bridge, thirty or forty feet long, over a hollow, as convenient for him as for me. The tracks were as large as those of an ox, but an ox could not have crossed there. This burnt land was an exceedingly wild and desolate region. Judging by the weeds and sprouts, it appeared to have been burnt about two years before. It was covered with charred trunks, either prostrate or standing, which crocked our clothes and hands, and we could not easily have distinguished a bear there by his color. Great shells of trees, sometimes unburnt without, or burnt on one side only, but black within, stood twenty or forty feet high. The fire had run up inside, as in a chimney, leaving the sapwood. Sometimes we crossed a rocky ravine fifty feet wide, on a fallen trunk; and there were great fields of fire-weed (*Epilobium angustifolium*) on all sides, the most extensive that I ever saw, which presented great masses of pink. Intermixed with these were blueberry and raspberry bushes.

Having crossed a second rocky ridge, like the first, when I was beginning to ascend the third, the Indian, whom I had left on the shore some fifty rods behind, beckoned to me to come to him, but I made sign that I would first ascend the highest rock before me, whence I expected to see the lake. My companion accompanied me to the top. This was formed just like the others. Being struck with the perfect parallelism of these singular rock-hills, however much one might be in advance of another, I took out my compass and found that they lay northwest and southeast, the rock being on its edge, and sharp edges they were. This one, to speak from memory, was perhaps a third of a mile in length, but quite narrow, rising gradually from the northwest to the height of about eighty feet, but steep on the southeast end. The southwest side was as steep as an ordinary roof, or as we could safely climb; the northeast was an abrupt precipice from which you could jump clean to the bottom, near which the river flowed; while the level top of the ridge, on which you walked along, was only from one to three or four feet in width. For a rude illustration, take the half of a pear cut in two lengthwise, lay it on its flat side, the stem to the northwest, and then halve it vertically in the direction of its length, keeping the southwest half. Such was the general form.

There was a remarkable series of these great rock-waves revealed by the burning; breakers, as it were. No wonder that
the river that found its way through them was rapid and obstructed by falls. No doubt the absence of soil on these rocks,
or its dryness where there was any, caused this to be a very
thorough burning. We could see the lake over the woods, two
or three miles ahead, and that the river made an abrupt turn
southward around the northwest end of the cliff on which we
stood, or a little above us, so that we had cut off a bend, and
that there was an important fall in it a short distance below
us. I could see the canoe a hundred rods behind, but now on
the opposite shore, and supposed that the Indian had concluded to take out and carry round some bad rapids on that
side, and that that might be what he had beckoned to me for;
but after waiting a while I could still see nothing of him, and
I observed to my companion that I wondered where he was,
though I began to suspect that he had gone inland to look
for the lake from some hill-top on that side, as we had done.
This proved to be the case; for after I had started to return
to the canoe, I heard a faint halloo, and descried him on the
top of a distant rocky hill on that side. But as, after a long
time had elapsed, I still saw his canoe in the same place, and
he had not returned to it, and appeared in no hurry to do so,
and, moreover, as I remembered that he had previously beckoned to me, I thought that there might be something more
to delay him than I knew, and began to return northwest,
along the ridge, toward the angle in the river. My companion,
who had just been separated from us, and had even contemplated the necessity of camping alone, wishing to husband his
steps, and yet to keep with us, inquired where I was going;
to which I answered, that I was going far enough back to
communicate with the Indian, and that then I thought we
had better go along the shore together, and keep him in sight.

When we reached the shore, the Indian appeared from out
the woods on the opposite side, but on account of the roar
of the water it was difficult to communicate with him. He
kept along the shore westward to his canoe, while we stopped
at the angle where the stream turned southward around the
precipice. I again said to my companion, that we would keep
along the shore and keep the Indian in sight. We started to

do so, being close together, the Indian behind us having launched his canoe again, but just then I saw the latter, who had crossed to our side, forty or fifty rods behind, beckoning to me, and I called to my companion, who had just disappeared behind large rocks at the point of the precipice, three or four rods before me, on his way down the stream, that I was going to help the Indian a moment. I did so,—helped get the canoe over a fall, lying with my breast over a rock, and holding one end while he received it below,—and within ten or fifteen minutes at most I was back again at the point where the river turned southward, in order to catch up with my companion, while Polis glided down the river alone, parallel with me. But to my surprise, when I rounded the precipice, though the shore was bare of trees, not of rocks, for a quarter of a mile at least, my companion was not to be seen. It was as if he had sunk into the earth. This was the more unaccountable to me, because I knew that his feet were since our swamp walk very sore, and that he wished to keep with the party; and besides this was very bad walking, climbing over or about the rocks. I hastened along, hallooing and searching for him, thinking he might be concealed behind a rock, yet doubting if he had not taken the other side of the precipice, but the Indian had got along still faster in his canoe, till he was arrested by the falls, about a quarter of a mile below. He then landed, and said that we could go no farther that night. The sun was setting, and on account of falls and rapids we should be obliged to leave this river and carry a good way into another farther east. The first thing then was to find my companion, for I was now very much alarmed about him, and I sent the Indian along the shore down stream, which began to be covered with unburnt wood again just below the falls, while I searched backward about the precipice which we had passed. The Indian showed some unwillingness to exert himself, complaining that he was very tired, in consequence of his day's work, that it had strained him very much getting down so many rapids alone; but he went off calling somewhat like an owl. I remembered that my companion was near-sighted, and I feared that he had either fallen from the precipice, or fainted and sunk down amid the rocks beneath it. I shouted and searched above and below this precipice in the twilight till I could not see, expecting nothing less than to find his body beneath it. For half an hour I anticipated and believed only the worst. I thought what I should do the next day, if I did not find him, what I *could* do in such a wilderness, and how his relatives would feel, if I should return without him. I felt that if he were really lost away from the river there, it would be a desperate undertaking to find him; and where were they who could help you? What would it be to raise the country, where there were only two or three camps, twenty or thirty miles apart, and no road, and perhaps nobody at home? Yet we must try the harder, the less the prospect of success.

I rushed down from this precipice to the canoe in order to fire the Indian's gun, but found that my companion had the caps. I was still thinking of getting it off when the Indian returned. He had not found him, but he said that he had seen his tracks once or twice along the shore. This encouraged me very much. He objected to firing the gun, saying that if my companion heard it, which was not likely, on account of the roar of the stream, it would tempt him to come toward us, and he might break his neck in the dark. For the same reason we refrained from lighting a fire on the highest rock. I proposed that we should both keep down the stream to the lake, or that I should go at any rate, but the Indian said, "No use, can't do anything in the dark; come morning, then we find 'em. No harm,—he make 'em camp. No bad animals here, no gristly bears, such as in California, where he 's been,—warm night,—he well off as you and I." I considered that if he was well he could do without us. He had just lived eight years in California, and had plenty of experience with wild beasts and wilder men, was peculiarly accustomed to make journeys of great length, but if he were sick or dead, he was near where we were. The darkness in the woods was by this so thick that it alone decided the question. We must camp where we were. I knew that he had his knapsack, with blankets and matches, and, if well, would fare no worse than we, except that he would have no supper nor society.

This side of the river being so encumbered with rocks, we crossed to the eastern or smoother shore, and proceeded to camp there, within two or three rods of the Falls. We pitched no tent, but lay on the sand, putting a few handfuls of grass and twigs under us, there being no evergreen at hand. For fuel we had some of the charred stumps. Our various bags of provisions had got quite wet in the rapids, and I arranged them about the fire to dry. The fall close by was the principal one on this stream, and it shook the earth under us. It was a cool, because dewy, night; the more so, probably, owing to the nearness of the falls. The Indian complained a good deal, and thought afterward that he got a cold there which occasioned a more serious illness. We were not much troubled by mosquitoes at any rate. I lay awake a good deal from anxiety, but, unaccountably to myself, was at length comparatively at ease respecting him. At first I had apprehended the worst, but now I had little doubt but that I should find him in the morning. From time to time I fancied that I heard his voice calling through the roar of the falls from the opposite side of the river; but it is doubtful if we could have heard him across the stream there. Sometimes I doubted whether the Indian had really seen his tracks, since he manifested an unwillingness to make much of a search, and then my anxiety returned.

It was the most wild and desolate region we had camped in, where, if anywhere, one might expect to meet with befitting inhabitants, but I heard only the squeak of a night-hawk flitting over. The moon in her first quarter, in the fore part of the night, setting over the bare rocky hills, garnished with tall, charred, and hollow stumps or shells of trees, served to reveal the desolation.

THURSDAY, July 30.

I aroused the Indian early this morning to go in search of our companion, expecting to find him within a mile or two, farther down the stream. The Indian wanted his breakfast first, but I reminded him that my companion had had neither breakfast nor supper. We were obliged first to carry our canoe and baggage over into another stream, the main East Branch, about three fourths of a mile distant, for Webster Stream was no farther navigable. We went twice over this carry, and the dewy bushes wet us through like water up to the middle; I hallooed in a high key from time to time, though I had little expectation that I could be heard over the roar of the rapids, and moreover we were necessarily on the opposite side of the stream to him. In going over this portage the last time, the Indian, who was before me with the canoe on his head, stumbled and fell heavily once, and lay for a moment silent, as if in pain. I hastily stepped forward to help him, asking if he was much hurt, but after a moment's pause, without replying, he sprang up and went forward. He was all the way subject to taciturn fits, but they were harmless ones.

We had launched our canoe and gone but little way down the East Branch, when I heard an answering shout from my companion, and soon after saw him standing on a point where there was a clearing a quarter of a mile below, and the smoke of his fire was rising near by. Before I saw him I naturally shouted again and again, but the Indian curtly remarked, "He hears you," as if once was enough. It was just below the mouth of Webster Stream. When we arrived, he was smoking his pipe, and said that he had passed a pretty comfortable night, though it was rather cold, on account of the dew.

It appeared that when we stood together the previous evening, and I was shouting to the Indian across the river, he, being near-sighted, had not seen the Indian nor his canoe, and when I went back to the Indian's assistance, did not see which way I went, and supposed that we were below and not above him, and so, making haste to catch up, he ran away from us. Having reached this clearing, a mile or more below our camp, the night overtook him, and he made a fire in a little hollow, and lay down by it in his blanket, still thinking that we were ahead of him. He thought it likely that he had heard the Indian call once the evening before, but mistook it for an owl. He had seen one botanical rarity before it was dark,—pure white *Epilobium angustifolium* amidst the fields of pink ones, in the burnt lands. He had already stuck up the remnant of a lumberer's shirt, found on the point, on a pole by the water-side, for a signal, and attached a note to it, to inform us that he had gone on to the lake, and that if he did not find us there, he would be back in a couple of hours. If he had not found us soon, he had some thoughts of going back in search of the solitary hunter whom we had met at Telos Lake, ten miles behind, and, if successful, hire him to take him to Bangor. But if this hunter had moved as fast as we, he would have been twenty miles off by this time, and who could guess in what direction? It would have been like looking for a needle in a hay-mow, to search for him in these woods. He had been considering how long he could live on berries alone.

We substituted for his note a card containing our names and destination, and the date of our visit, which Polis neatly enclosed in a piece of birch-bark to keep it dry. This has probably been read by some hunter or explorer ere this.

We all had good appetites for the breakfast which we made haste to cook here, and then, having partially dried our clothes, we glided swiftly down the winding stream toward Second Lake.

As the shores became flatter with frequent gravel and sand bars, and the stream more winding in the lower land near the lake, elms and ash trees made their appearance; also the wild yellow lily (*Lilium Canadense*), some of whose bulbs I collected for a soup. On some ridges the burnt land extended as far as the lake. This was a very beautiful lake, two or three miles long, with high mountains on the southwest side, the (as our Indian said) *Nerlumskeechticook*, i. e. Dead-Water Mountain. It appears to be the same called Carbuncle Mountain on the map. According to Polis, it extends in separate elevations all along this and the next lake, which is much larger. The lake, too, I think, is called by the same name, or perhaps with the addition of *gamoc* or *mooc*. The morning was a bright one, and perfectly still and serene, the lake as smooth as glass, we making the only ripples as we paddled into it. The dark mountains about it were seen through a glaucous mist, and the brilliant white stems of canoe-birches mingled with the other woods around it. The wood-thrush sang on the distant shore, and the laugh of some loons, sporting in a concealed western bay, as if inspired by the morning, came distinct over the lake to us, and, what was remarkable, the echo which ran round the lake was much louder than the original note; probably because, the loons being in a regularly curving bay under the mountain, we were exactly in the focus of many echoes, the sound being reflected like light from a concave mirror. The beauty of the scene may have been enhanced to our eyes by the fact that we had just come together again after a night of some anxiety. This reminded me of the Ambejijis Lake on the West Branch, which I crossed in my first coming to Maine. Having paddled down three quarters of the lake, we came to a stand still, while my companion let down for fish. A white (or whitish) gull sat on a rock which rose above the surface in mid-lake not far off, quite in harmony with the scene; and as we rested there in the warm sun, we heard one loud crashing or crackling sound from the forest, forty or fifty rods distant, as of a stick broken by the foot of some large animal. Even this was an interesting incident there. In the midst of our dreams of giant lake-trout, even then supposed to be nibbling, our fisherman drew up a diminutive red perch, and we took up our paddles again in haste.

It was not apparent where the outlet of this lake was, and while the Indian thought it was in one direction, I thought it was in another. He said, "I bet you fourpence it is there," but he still held on in my direction, which proved to be the right one. As we were approaching the outlet, it being still early in the forenoon, he suddenly exclaimed, "Moose! moose!" and told us to be still. He put a cap on his gun, and standing up in the stern, rapidly pushed the canoe straight toward the shore and the moose. It was a cow-moose, about thirty rods off, standing in the water by the side of the outlet, partly behind some fallen timber and bushes, and at that distance she did not look very large. She was flapping her large ears, and from time to time poking off the flies with her nose from some part of her body. She did not appear much alarmed by our neighborhood, only occasionally turned her head and looked straight at us, and then gave her attention to the flies again. As we approached nearer, she got out of the water, stood higher and regarded us more suspiciously. Polis pushed the canoe steadily forward in the shallow water, and I for a moment forgot the moose in attending to some pretty rose-colored Polygonums just rising above the surface, but the canoe soon grounded in the mud eight or ten rods distant from the moose, and the Indian seized his gun and prepared to fire. After standing still a moment, she turned slowly, as usual, so as to expose her side, and he improved this moment to fire, over our heads. She thereupon moved off eight or ten rods at a moderate pace, across a shallow bay, to an old standing-place of hers, behind some fallen red maples, on the opposite shore, and there she stood still again a dozen or fourteen rods from us, while the Indian hastily loaded and fired twice at her, without her moving. My companion, who passed him his caps and bullets, said that Polis was as excited as a boy of fifteen, that his hand trembled, and he once put his ramrod back up-side down. This was remarkable for so experienced a hunter. Perhaps he was anxious to make a good shot before us. The white hunter had told me that the Indians were not good shots, because they were excited, though he said that we had got a good hunter with us.

The Indian now pushed quickly and quietly back, and a long distance round, in order to get into the outlet,—for he had fired over the neck of a peninsula between it and the lake,—till we approached the place where the moose had stood, when he exclaimed, "She is a goner," and was surprised that we did not see her as soon as he did. There, to be sure, she lay perfectly dead, with her tongue hanging out, just where she had stood to receive the last shots, looking unexpectedly large and horse-like, and we saw where the bullets had scored the trees.

Using a tape, I found that the moose measured just six feet from the shoulder to the tip of the hoof, and was eight feet long as she lay. Some portions of the body, for a foot in diameter, were almost covered with flies, apparently the common fly of our woods, with a dark spot on the wing, and not the very large ones which occasionally pursued us in midstream, though both are called moose-flies.

Polis, preparing to skin the moose, asked me to help him find a stone on which to sharpen his large knife. It being all a flat alluvial ground where the moose had fallen, covered with red maples, &c., this was no easy matter; we searched far and wide, a long time, till at length I found a flat kind of slate-stone, and soon after he returned with a similar one, on which he soon made his knife very sharp.

While he was skinning the moose, I proceeded to ascertain what kind of fishes were to be found in the sluggish and muddy outlet. The greatest difficulty was to find a pole. It was almost impossible to find a slender, straight pole ten or twelve feet long in those woods. You might search half an hour in vain. They are commonly spruce, arbor-vitæ, fir, &c., short, stout, and branchy, and do not make good fish-poles, even after you have patiently cut off all their tough and scraggy branches. The fishes were red perch and chivin.

The Indian having cut off a large piece of sirloin, the upper lip and the tongue, wrapped them in the hide, and placed them in the bottom of the canoe, observing that there was "one man," meaning the weight of one. Our load had previously been reduced some thirty pounds, but a hundred pounds were now added, a serious addition, which made our quarters still more narrow, and considerably increased the danger on the lakes and rapids, as well as the labor of the carries. The skin was ours according to custom, since the Indian was in our employ, but we did not think of claiming it. He being a skilful dresser of moose-hides, would make it worth seven or eight dollars to him, as I was told. He said that he sometimes earned fifty or sixty dollars in a day at them; he had killed ten moose in one day, though the skinning and all took two days. This was the way he had got his property. There were the tracks of a calf thereabouts, which he said would come "by, by," and he could get it if we cared to wait, but I cast cold water on the project.

We continued along the outlet toward Grand Lake, through a swampy region, by a long, winding, and narrow dead water, very much choked up by wood, where we were obliged to land sometimes in order to get the canoe over a log. It was hard to find any channel, and we did not know but we should be lost in the swamp. It abounded in ducks, as usual. At length we reached Grand Lake, which the Indian called *Matungamook*.

At the head of this we saw, coming in from the southwest, with a sweep apparently from a gorge in the mountains, Trout Stream, or *Uncardnerheese*, which name, the Indian said, had something to do with mountains.

We stopped to dine on an interesting high rocky island, soon after entering Matungamook Lake, securing our canoe to the cliffy shore. It is always pleasant to step from a boat on to a large rock or cliff. Here was a good opportunity to dry our dewy blankets on the open sunny rock. Indians had recently camped here, and accidentally burned over the western end of the island, and Polis picked up a gun-case of blue broadcloth, and said that he knew the Indian it belonged to, and would carry it to him. His tribe is not so large but he may know all its effects. We proceeded to make a fire and cook our dinner amid some pines, where our predecessors had done the same, while the Indian busied himself about his moose-hide on the shore, for he said that he thought it a good plan for one to do all the cooking, i. e. I suppose if that one were not himself. A peculiar evergreen overhung our fire, which at first glance looked like a pitch pine (*P. rigida*), with leaves little more than an inch long, spruce-like, but we found it to be the *Pinus Banksiana*,—"Banks's, or the Labrador Pine," also called Scrub Pine, Gray Pine, &c., a new tree to us. These must have been good specimens, for several were thirty or thirty-five feet high, which is 2 or 3 times the height commonly assigned them. Michaux says that it grows further north than any of our pines, but he did not find it any where more than 10 feet high. Richardson found it forty feet high and upward, and states that the porcupine feeds on its bark. Here also grew the Red Pine (*Pinus resinosa*).

I saw where the Indians had made canoes in a little secluded hollow in the woods, on the top of the rock, where they were out of the wind, and large piles of whittlings remained. This must have been a favorite resort for their ancestors, and, indeed, we found here the point of an arrow-head, such as they have not used for two centuries and now know not how to make. The Indian, picking up a stone, remarked to me, "That very strange lock (rock)." It was a piece of hornstone, which I told him his tribe had probably brought here centuries before to make arrow-heads of. He also picked up a yellowish curved bone by the side of our fireplace and asked me to guess what it was. It was one of the upper incisors of a beaver, on which some party had feasted within a year or two. I found also most of the teeth, and the skull, &c. We here dined on fried moose-meat.

One who was my companion in my two previous excursions to these woods, tells me that when hunting up the Caucomgomoc, about two years ago, he found himself dining one day on moose-meat, mud-turtle, trout, and beaver, and he thought that there were few places in the world where these dishes could easily be brought together on one table.

After the almost incessant rapids and falls of the Madunkehunk (Height-of-Land, or Webster Stream), we had just passed through the dead-water of Second Lake, and were now in the much larger dead-water of Grand Lake, and I thought the Indian was entitled to take an extra nap here. Ktaadn, near which we were to pass the next day, is said to mean "Highest Land." So much geography is there in their names. The Indian navigator naturally distinguishes by a name those parts of a stream where he has encountered quick water and falls, and again, the lakes and smooth water where he can rest his weary arms, since those are the most interesting and memorable parts to him. The very sight of the *Nerlumskeechticook*, or Dead-Water Mountains, a day's journey off over the forest, as we first saw them, must awaken in him pleasing memories. And not less interesting is it to the white traveller, when he is crossing a placid lake in these out-of-the-way woods, perhaps thinking that he is in some sense one of the earlier discoverers of it, to be reminded that it was thus well known and suitably named by Indian hunters perhaps a thousand years ago.

Ascending the precipitous rock which formed this long narrow island, I was surprised to find that its summit was a narrow ridge, with a precipice on one side, and that its axis of elevation extended from northwest to southeast, exactly like that of the great rocky ridges at the commencement of the Burnt Ground, ten miles northwesterly. The same arrangement prevailed here, and we could plainly see that the mountain ridges on the west of the lake trended the same way. Splendid large harebells nodded over the edge and in the clefts of the cliff, and the blueberries (*Vaccinium Canadense*) were for the first time really abundant in the thin soil on its top. There was no lack of them henceforward on the East Branch. There was a fine view hence over the sparkling lake, which looked pure and deep, and had two or three, in all, rocky islands in it. Our blankets being dry, we set out again, the Indian as usual having left his gazette on a tree. This time it was we three in a canoe, my companion smoking. We paddled southward down this handsome lake, which appeared to extend nearly as far east as south, keeping near the western shore, just outside a small island, under the dark *Nerlumskeechticook* mountain. For I had observed on my map that this was the course. It was three or four miles across it. It struck me that the outline of this mountain on the southwest of the lake, and of another beyond it, was not only like that of the huge rock waves of Webster Stream, but in the main like Kineo, on Moosehead Lake, having a similar but less abrupt precipice at the southeast end; in short, that all the prominent hills and ridges hereabouts were larger or smaller Kineos, and that possibly there was such a relation between Kineo and the rocks of Webster Stream.

The Indian did not know exactly where the outlet was, whether at the extreme southwest angle or more easterly, and had asked to see my plan at the last stopping-place, but I had forgotten to show it to him. As usual, he went feeling his way by a middle course between two probable points, from which he could diverge either way at last without losing much distance. In approaching the south shore, as the clouds looked gusty, and the waves ran pretty high, we so steered as to get partly under the lee of an island, though at a great distance from it.

I could not distinguish the outlet till we were almost in it, and heard the water falling over the dam there.

Here was a considerable fall, and a very substantial dam, but no sign of a cabin or camp. The hunter whom we met at Telos Lake had told us that there were plenty of trout here, but at this hour they did not rise to the bait, only cousin trout, from the very midst of the rushing waters. There are not so many fishes in these rivers as in the Concord.

While we loitered here, Polis took occasion to cut with his big knife some of the hair from his moose-hide, and so lightened and prepared it for drying. I noticed at several old Indian camps in the woods the pile of hair which they had cut from their hides.

Having carried over the dam, he darted down the rapids, leaving us to walk for a mile or more, where for the most part there was no path, but very thick and difficult travelling near the stream. At length he would call to let us know where he was waiting for us with his canoe, when, on account of the windings of the stream, we did not know where the shore was, but he did not call often enough, forgetting that we were not Indians. He seemed to be very saving of his breath,—yet he would be surprised if we went by, or did not strike the right spot. This was not because he was unaccommodating, but a proof of superior manners. Indians like to get along with the least possible communication and ado. He was really paying us a great compliment all the while, thinking that we preferred a hint to a kick.

At length, climbing over the willows and fallen trees, when this was easier than to go round or under them, we overtook the canoe, and glided down the stream in smooth but swift water for several miles. I here observed again, as at Webster Stream, and on a still larger scale the next day, that the river was a smooth and regularly inclined plane down which we coasted. As we thus glided along we started the first black ducks which we had distinguished.

We decided to camp early to-night, that we might have ample time before dark; so we stopped at the first favorable shore, where there was a narrow gravelly beach on the western side, some five miles below the outlet of the lake. It was an interesting spot, where the river began to make a great bend to the east, and the last of the peculiar moose-faced *Nerlumskeechticook* mountains not far southwest of Grand Lake rose dark in the northwest a short distance behind, displaying its gray precipitous southeast side, but we could not see this without coming out upon the shore.

Two steps from the water on either side, and you come to the abrupt bushy and rooty if not turfy edge of the bank, four or five feet high, where the interminable forest begins, as if the stream had but just cut its way through it.

It is surprising on stepping ashore anywhere into this unbroken wilderness to see so often, at least within a few rods of the river, the marks of the axe, made by lumberers who have either camped here, or driven logs past in previous springs. You will see perchance where, going on the same errand that you do, they have cut large chips from a tall white-pine stump for their fire. While we were pitching the camp and getting supper, the Indian cut the rest of the hair from his moose-hide, and proceeded to extend it vertically on a temporary frame between two small trees, half a dozen feet from the opposite side of the fire, lashing and stretching it with arbor-vitæ bark, which was always at hand, and in this case was stripped from one of the trees it was tied to. Asking for a new kind of tea, he made us some, pretty good, of the checkerberry (*Gaultheria procumbens*), which covered the ground, dropping a little bunch of it tied up with cedar bark into the kettle; but it was not quite equal to the *Chiogenes*. We called this therefore Checkerberry-tea Camp.

I was struck with the abundance of the *Linnæa borealis*, checkerberry, and *Chiogenes hispidula*, almost everywhere in the Maine woods. The wintergreen (*Chimaphila umbellata*) was still in bloom here, and *Clintonia* berries were abundant and ripe. This handsome plant is one of the most common in that forest. We here first noticed the moose-wood in fruit on the banks. The prevailing trees were spruce (commonly black), arbor-vitæ, canoe-birch, (black ash and elms beginning to appear,) yellow birch, red maple, and a little hemlock skulking in the forest. The Indian said that the white-maple punk was the best for tinder, that yellow-birch punk was pretty good, but hard. After supper he put on the moose tongue and lips to boil, cutting out the *septum*. He showed me how to write on the under side of birch bark, with a black spruce twig, which is hard and tough and can be brought to a point.

The Indian wandered off into the woods a short distance just before night, and, coming back, said, "Me found great treasure—fifty, sixty dollars worth." "What 's that?" we asked. "Steel traps, under a log, thirty or forty, I did n't count 'em. I guess Indian work—worth three dollars apiece." It was a singular coincidence that he should have chanced to walk to and look under that particular log, in that trackless forest.

I saw chivin and chub in the stream when washing my hands, but my companion tried in vain to catch them. I also heard the sound of bull-frogs from a swamp on the opposite side, thinking at first that they were moose; a duck paddled swiftly by; and sitting in that dusky wilderness, under that dark mountain, by the bright river which was full of reflected light, still I heard the wood-thrush sing, as if no higher civilization could be attained. By this time the night was upon us.

You commonly make your camp just at sundown, and are collecting wood, getting your supper, or pitching your tent while the shades of night are gathering around and adding to the already dense gloom of the forest. You have no time to explore or look around you before it is dark. You may penetrate half a dozen rods farther into that twilight wilderness, after some dry bark to kindle your fire with, and wonder what mysteries lie hidden still deeper in it, say at the end of a long day's walk; or you may run down to the shore for a dipper of water, and get a clearer view for a short distance up or down the stream, and while you stand there, see a fish leap, or duck alight in the river, or hear a wood-thrush or robin sing in the woods. That is as if you had been to town or civilized parts. But there is no sauntering off to see the country, and ten or fifteen rods seems a great way from your companions, and you come back with the air of a much travelled man, as from a long journey, with adventures to relate, though you may have heard the crackling of the fire all the while,—and at a hundred rods you might be lost past recovery, and have to camp out. It is all mossy and *moosey*. In some of those dense fir and spruce woods there is hardly room for the smoke to go up. The trees are a *standing* night, and every fir and spruce which you fell is a plume plucked from night's raven wing. Then at night the general stillness is more impressive than any sound, but occasionally you hear the note of an owl farther or nearer in the woods, and if near a lake, the semi-human cry of the loons at their unearthly revels.

To-night the Indian lay between the fire and his stretched moose-hide, to avoid the mosquitoes. Indeed, he also made a small smoky fire of damp leaves at his head and his feet, and then as usual rolled up his head in his blanket. We with our veils and our wash were tolerably comfortable, but it would be difficult to pursue any sedentary occupation in the woods at this season: you cannot see to read much by the light of a fire through a veil in the evening, nor handle pencil and paper well with gloves or anointed fingers.

The Indian said, "You and I kill moose last night, therefore use 'em best wood. Always use hard wood to cook moose-meat." His "best wood" was rock-maple. He cast the moose's lip into the fire, to burn the hair off, and then rolled it up with the meat to carry along. Observing that we were sitting down to breakfast without any pork, he said, with a very grave look, "Me want some fat," so he was told that he might have as much as he would fry.

We had smooth but swift water for a considerable distance, where we glided rapidly along, scaring up ducks and kingfish-ers. But as usual, our smooth progress erelong came to an end, and we were obliged to carry canoe and all about half a mile down the right bank, around some rapids or falls. It re-quired sharp eyes sometimes to tell which side was the carry, before you went over the falls, but Polis never failed to land us rightly. The raspberries were particularly abundant and large here, and all hands went to eating them, the Indian re-marking on their size.

Often on bare rocky carries the trail was so indistinct that I repeatedly lost it, but when I walked behind him I observed that he could keep it almost like a hound, and rarely hesitated, or, if he paused a moment on a bare rock, his eye immediately detected some sign which would have escaped me. Frequently *we* found no path at all at these places, and were to him un-accountably delayed. He would only say it was "ver strange."

We had heard of a Grand Fall on this stream, and thought that each fall we came to must be it, but after christening several in succession with this name, we gave up the search. There were more Grand or Petty Falls than I can remember.

I cannot tell how many times we had to walk on account of falls or rapids. We were expecting all the while that the river would take a final leap and get to smooth water, but there was no improvement this forenoon. However, the car-ries were an agreeable variety. So surely as we stepped out of the canoe and stretched our legs we found ourselves in a blue-berry and raspberry garden, each side of our rocky trail around the falls being lined with one or both. There was not a carry on the main East Branch where we did not find an abundance of both these berries, for these were the rockiest

places, and partially cleared, such as these plants prefer, and
there had been none to gather the finest before us.

In our three journeys over the carries, for we were obliged
to go over the ground three times whenever the canoe was
taken out, we did full justice to the berries, and they were just
what we wanted to correct the effect of our hard bread and
pork diet. Another name for making a portage would have
been going a berrying. We also found a few *Amelanchier*, or
service berries, though most were abortive, but they held on
rather more generally than they do in Concord. The Indian
called them *Pemoymenuk*, and said that they bore much fruit
in some places. He sometimes also ate the northern wild red
cherries, saying that they were good medicine, but they were
scarcely edible.

We bathed and dined at the foot of one of these carries. It
was the Indian who commonly reminded us that it was din-
ner-time, sometimes even by turning the prow to the shore.
He once made an indirect, but lengthy apology, by saying
that we might think it strange, but that one who worked hard
all day was very particular to have his dinner in good season.
At the most considerable fall on this stream, when I was walking over the carry, close behind the Indian, he observed a
track on the rock, which was but slightly covered with soil,
and, stooping, muttered "caribou." When we returned, he
observed a much larger track near the same place, where some
animal's foot had sunk into a small hollow in the rock, partly
filled with grass and earth, and he exclaimed with surprise,
"What that?" "Well, what is it?" I asked. Stooping and laying
his hand in it, he answered with a mysterious air, and in a
half whisper, "Devil [that is, Indian Devil, or cougar] ledges
about here—very bad animal—pull 'em *locks* all to pieces."
"How long since it was made?" I asked. "To-day or yesterday," said he. But when I asked him afterward if he was sure
it was the devil's track, he said he did not know. I had been
told that the scream of a cougar was heard about Ktaadn recently, and we were not far from that mountain.

We spent at least half the time in walking to-day, and the
walking was as bad as usual, for the Indian being alone, commonly ran down far below the foot of the carries before he
waited for us. The carry-paths themselves were more than

usually indistinct, often the route being revealed only by the countless small holes in the fallen timber made by the tacks in the drivers' boots, or where there *was* a slight trail we did not find it. It was a tangled and perplexing thicket, through which we stumbled and threaded our way, and when we had finished a mile of it, our starting-point seemed far away. We were glad that we had not got to walk to Bangor along the banks of this river, which would be a journey of more than a hundred miles. Think of the denseness of the forest, the fallen trees and rocks, the windings of the river, the streams emptying in and the frequent swamps to be crossed. It made you shudder. Yet the Indian from time to time pointed out to us where he had thus crept along day after day when he was a boy of ten, and in a starving condition. He had been hunting far north of this with two grown Indians. The winter came on unexpectedly early, and the ice compelled them to leave their canoe at Grand Lake, and walk down the bank. They shouldered their furs and started for Oldtown. The snow was not deep enough for snow-shoes, or to cover the inequalities of the ground. Polis was soon too weak to carry any burden; but he managed to catch one otter. This was the most they all had to eat on this journey, and he remembered how good the yellow-lily roots were, made into a soup with the otter oil. He shared this food equally with the other two, but being so small he suffered much more than they. He waded through the Mattawamkeag at its mouth, when it was freezing cold and came up to his chin, and he, being very weak and emaciated, expected to be swept away. The first house which they reached was at Lincoln, and thereabouts they met a white teamster with supplies, who seeing their condition gave them as much of his load as they could eat. For six months after getting home he was very low, and did not expect to live, and was perhaps always the worse for it.

We could not find much more than half of this day's journey on our maps (the "Map of the Public Lands of Maine and Massachusetts," and "Colton's Railroad and Township Map of Maine," which copies the former). By the maps there was not more than fifteen miles between camps, at the outside, and yet we had been busily progressing all day, and much of the time very rapidly.

For seven or eight miles below that succession of "Grand" falls, the aspect of the banks as well as the character of the stream was changed. After passing a tributary from the northeast, perhaps Bowlin Stream, we had good swift smooth water, with a regular slope, such as I have described. Low, grassy banks and muddy shores began. Many elms, as well as maples, and more ash trees overhung the stream, and supplanted the spruce.

My lily-roots having been lost when the canoe was taken out at a carry, I landed late in the afternoon, at a low and grassy place amid maples, to gather more. It was slow work grubbing them up amid the sand, and the mosquitoes were all the while feasting on me. Mosquitoes, black flies, &c., pursued us in mid-channel, and we were glad sometimes to get into violent rapids, for then we escaped them.

A red-headed woodpecker flew across the river, and the Indian remarked that it was good to eat. As we glided swiftly down the inclined plane of the river, a great cat-owl launched itself away from a stump on the bank, and flew heavily across the stream, and the Indian, as usual, imitated its note. Soon the same bird flew back in front of us, and we afterwards passed it perched on a tree. Soon afterward a white-headed eagle sailed down the stream before us. We drove him several miles, while we were looking for a good place to camp, for we expected to be overtaken by a shower,—and still we could distinguish him by his white tail, sailing away from time to time from some tree by the shore still farther down the stream. Some shecorways, being surprised by us, a part of them dived, and we passed directly over them, and could trace their course here and there by a bubble on the surface, but we did not see them come up. Polis detected once or twice what he called a "tow" road, an indistinct path leading into the forest. In the mean while we passed the mouth of the Seboois on our left. This did not look so large as our stream, which was indeed the main one. It was some time before we found a camping-place, for the shore was either too grassy and muddy, where mosquitoes abounded, or too steep a hillside. The Indian said that there were but few mosquitoes on a steep hillside. We examined a good place, where somebody had camped a long time; but it seemed pitiful to occupy an old site, where there was so much room to choose, so we continued on. We at length found a place to our minds, on the west bank, about a mile below the mouth of the Seboois, where, in a very dense spruce wood above a gravelly shore, there seemed to be but few insects. The trees were so thick that we were obliged to clear a space to build our fire and lie down in, and the young spruce trees that were left were like the wall of an apartment rising around us. We were obliged to pull ourselves up a steep bank to get there. But the place which you have selected for your camp, though never so rough and grim, begins at once to have its attractions, and becomes a very centre of civilization to you: "Home is home, be it never so homely."

It turned out that the mosquitoes were more numerous here than we had found them before, and the Indian complained a good deal, though he lay, as the night before, between three fires and his stretched hide. As I sat on a stump by the fire, with a veil and gloves on trying to read, he observed, "I make you candle," and in a minute he took a piece of birch bark about two inches wide and rolled it hard, like an allumette fifteen inches long, lit it, and fixed it by the other end horizontally in a split stick three feet high, stuck it in the ground, turning the blazing end to the wind, and telling me to snuff it from time to time. It answered the purpose of a candle pretty well.

I noticed, as I had done before, that there was a lull among the mosquitoes about midnight, and that they began again in the morning. Nature is thus merciful. But apparently they need rest as well as we. Few if any creatures are equally active all night. As soon as it was light I saw, through my veil, that the inside of the tent about our heads was quite blackened with myriads, each one of their wings when flying, as has been calculated, vibrating some three thousand times in a minute, and their combined hum was almost as bad to endure as their stings. I had an uncomfortable night on this account, though I am not sure that one succeeded in his attempt to sting me. We did not suffer so much from insects on this excursion as the statements of some who have explored these woods in midsummer led us to anticipate. Yet I have no doubt that at some seasons and in some places they are a much more serious pest. The Jesuit Hierome Lalemant, of Quebec, reporting the death of Father Reni Menard, who was abandoned, lost his way, and died in the woods, among the Ontarios near Lake Superior, in 1661, dwells chiefly on his probable sufferings from the attacks of mosquitoes when too weak to defend himself, adding that there was a frightful number of them in those parts, "and so insupportable," says he, "that the three Frenchmen who have made that voyage, affirm that there was no other means of defending one's self but to run always without stopping, and it was even necessary for two of them to be employed in driving off these creatures while the third wanted to drink, otherwise he could not have done it." I have no doubt that this was said in good faith.

August 1.

I caught two or three large red chivin (*Leuciscus pulchellus*) early this morning, within twenty feet of the camp, which, added to the moose-tongue, that had been left in the kettle boiling over night, and to our other stores, made a sumptuous breakfast. The Indian made us some hemlock tea instead of coffee, and we were not obliged to go as far as China for it; indeed, not quite so far as for the fish. This was tolerable, though he said it was not strong enough. It was interesting to see so simple a dish as a kettle of water with a handful of green hemlock sprigs in it, boiling over the huge fire in the open air, the leaves fast losing their lively green color, and know that it was for our breakfast.

We were glad to embark once more, and leave some of the mosquitoes behind. We had passed the *Wassataquoik* without perceiving it. This, according to the Indian, is the name of the main East Branch itself, and not properly applied to this small tributary alone, as on the maps.

We found that we had camped about a mile above Hunt's, which is on the east bank, and is the last house for those who ascend Ktaadn on this side.

We also had expected to ascend it from this point, but omitted it on account of the chafed feet of one of my companions. The Indian, however, suggested that perhaps he might get a pair of moccasins at this place, and that he could walk very easily in them without hurting his feet, wearing several pairs of stockings, and he said beside that they were so porous that when you had taken in water it all drained out again in a little while. We stopped to get some sugar, but found that the family had moved away, and the house was unoccupied, except temporarily by some men who were getting the hay. They told us that the road to Ktaadn left the river eight miles above; also that perhaps we could get some sugar at Fisk's, fourteen miles below. I do not remember that we saw the mountain at all from the river. I noticed a seine here stretched on the bank, which probably had been used to catch salmon. Just below this, on the west bank, we saw a moose-hide stretched, and with it a bearskin, which was comparatively very small. I was the more interested in this sight, because it was near here that a townsman of ours, then quite a lad, and alone, killed a large bear some years ago. The Indian said that they belonged to Joe Aitteon, my last guide, but how he told I do not know. He was probably hunting near, and had left them for the day. Finding that we were going directly to Oldtown, he regretted that he had not taken more of the moose-meat to his family, saying that in a short time, by drying it, he could have made it so light as to have brought away the greater part, leaving the bones. We once or twice inquired after the lip, which is a famous tit-bit, but he said, "That go Oldtown for my old woman; don't get it every day."

Maples grew more and more numerous. It was lowering, and rained a little during the forenoon, and, as we expected a wetting, we stopped early and dined on the east side of a small expansion of the river, just above what are probably called Whetstone Falls, about a dozen miles below Hunt's. There were pretty fresh moose-tracks by the water-side. There were singular long ridges hereabouts, called "horsebacks," covered with ferns. My companion having lost his pipe asked the Indian if he could not make him one. "O yer," said he, and in a minute rolled up one of birch-bark, telling him to wet the bowl from time to time. Here also he left his gazette on a tree.

We carried round the falls just below, on the west side. The rocks were on their edges, and very sharp. The distance was about three fourths of a mile. When we had carried over one load, the Indian returned by the shore, and I by the path; and though I made no particular haste, I was nevertheless surprised to find him at the other end as soon as I. It was remarkable how easily he got along over the worst ground. He said to me, "I take canoe and you take the rest, suppose you can keep along with me?" I thought that he meant, that while he ran down the rapids I should keep along the shore, and be ready to assist him from time to time, as I had done before; but as the walking would be very bad, I answered, "I suppose you will go too fast for me, but I will try." But I was to go by the path, he said. This I thought would not help the matter, I should have so far to go to get to the river-side when he wanted me. But neither was this what he meant. He was proposing a race over the carry, and asked me if I thought I could keep along with him by the same path, adding that I must be pretty smart to do it. As his load, the canoe, would be much the heaviest and bulkiest, though the simplest, I thought that I ought to be able to do it, and said that I would try. So I proceeded to gather up the gun, axe, paddle, kettle, frying-pan, plates, dippers, carpets, &c., &c., and while I was thus engaged he threw me his cow-hide boots. "What, are these in the bargain?" I asked. "O yer," said he; but before I could make a bundle of my load I saw him disappearing over a hill with the canoe on his head; so, hastily scraping the various articles together, I started on the run, and immediately went by him in the bushes, but I had no sooner left him out of sight in a rocky hollow, than the greasy plates, dippers, &c., took to themselves wings, and while I was employed in gathering them up again, he went by me; but hastily pressing the sooty kettle to my side, I started once more, and soon passing him again, I saw him no more on the carry. I do not mention this as anything of a feat, for it was but poor running on my part, and he was obliged to move with great caution for fear of breaking his canoe as well as his neck. When he made his appearance, puffing and panting like myself, in answer to my inquiries where he had been, he said, "Locks (rocks) cut 'em feet," and laughing added, "O, me love to play sometimes." He said that he and his companions when they came to carries several miles long used to try who would get over first; each perhaps with a canoe on his head.

I bore the sign of the kettle on my brown linen sack for the rest of the voyage.

We made a second carry on the west side, around some falls about a mile below this. On the mainland were Norway pines, indicating a new geological formation, and it was such a dry and sandy soil as we had not noticed before.

As we approached the mouth of the East Branch, we passed two or three huts, the first sign of civilization after Hunt's, though we saw no road as yet; we heard a cow-bell, and even saw an infant held up to a small square window to see us pass, but apparently the infant and the mother that held it were the only inhabitants then at home for several miles. This took the wind out of our sails, reminding us that we were travellers surely, while it was a native of the soil, and had the advantage of us. Conversation flagged. I would only hear the Indian, perhaps, ask my companion, "You load my pipe?" He said that he smoked alder bark, for medicine. On entering the West Branch at Nickertow it appeared much larger than the East. Polis remarked that the former was all gone and lost now, that it was all smooth water hence to Oldtown, and he threw away his pole which was cut on the Umbazookskus. Thinking of the rapids, he said once or twice, that you would n't catch him to go East Branch again; but he did not by any means mean all that he said.

Things are quite changed since I was here eleven years ago. Where there were but one or two houses, I now found quite a village, with saw-mills and a store (the latter was locked, but its contents were so much the more safely stored), and there was a stage-road to Mattawamkeag, and the rumor of a stage. Indeed, a steamer had ascended thus far once, when the water was very high. But we were not able to get any sugar, only a better shingle to lean our backs against.

We camped about two miles below Nickertow, on the south side of the West Branch, covering with fresh twigs the withered bed of a former traveller, and feeling that we were now in a settled country, especially when in the evening we heard an ox sneeze in its wild pasture across the river. Wherever you land along the frequented part of the river, you have not far to go to find these sites of temporary inns, the withered bed of flattened twigs, the charred sticks, and perhaps the tent-poles. And not long since, similar beds were spread along the Connecticut, the Hudson, and the Delaware, and longer still ago, by the Thames and Seine, and they now help to make the soil where private and public gardens, mansions and palaces are. We could not get fir twigs for our bed here, and the spruce was harsh in comparison, having more twig in proportion to its leaf, but we improved it somewhat with hemlock. The Indian remarked as before, "Must have hard wood to cook moose-meat," as if that were a maxim, and proceeded to get it. My companion cooked some in California fashion, winding a long string of the meat round a stick and slowly turning it in his hand before the fire. It was very good. But the Indian not approving of the mode, or because he was not allowed to cook it his own way, would not taste it. After the regular supper we attempted to make a lily soup of the bulbs which I had brought along, for I wished to learn all I could before I got out of the woods. Following the Indian's directions, for he began to be sick, I washed the bulbs carefully, minced some moose-meat and some pork, salted and boiled all together, but we had not patience to try the experiment fairly, for he said it must be boiled till the roots were completely softened so as to thicken the soup like flour; but though we left it on all night, we found it dried to the kettle in the morning, and not yet boiled to a flour. Perhaps the roots were not ripe enough, for they commonly gather them in the fall. As it was, it was palatable enough, but it reminded me of the Irishman's limestone broth. The other ingredients were enough alone. The Indian's name for these bulbs was *Sheepnoc*. I stirred the soup by accident with a striped maple or moose-wood stick, which I had peeled, and he remarked that its bark was an emetic.

He prepared to camp as usual between his moose-hide and the fire, but it beginning to rain suddenly, he took refuge under the tent with us, and gave us a song before falling asleep. It rained hard in the night and spoiled another box of matches for us, which the Indian had left out, for he was very careless; but, as usual, we had so much the better night for the rain, since it kept the mosquitoes down.

SUNDAY, August 2,—

Was a cloudy and unpromising morning. One of us observed to the Indian, "You did not stretch your moose-hide last night, did you, Mr. Polis?" Whereat he replied, in a tone of surprise, though perhaps not of ill humor: "What you ask me that question for? Suppose I stretch 'em, you see 'em. May be your way talking, may be all right, no Indian way." I had observed that he did not wish to answer the same question more than once, and was often silent when it was put again for the sake of certainty, as if he were moody. Not that he was incommunicative, for he frequently commenced a long-winded narrative of his own accord,—repeated at length the tradition of some old battle, or some passage in the recent history of his tribe in which he had acted a prominent part, from time to time drawing a long breath, and resuming the thread of his tale, with the true story-teller's leisureliness, perhaps after shooting a rapid,—prefacing with " we-ll-by-by," &c., as he paddled along. Especially after the day's work was over, and he had put himself in posture for the night, he would be unexpectedly sociable, exhibit even the *bonhommie* of a Frenchman, and we would fall asleep before he got through his periods.

Nickertow is called eleven miles from Mattawamkeag by the river. Our camp was, therefore, about nine miles from the latter place.

The Indian was quite sick this morning with the colic. I thought that he was the worse for the moose-meat he had eaten.

We reached the Mattawamkeag at half past eight in the morning, in the midst of a drizzling rain, and after buying some sugar set out again.

The Indian growing much worse, we stopped in the north part of Lincoln to get some brandy for him, but failing in this, an apothecary recommended Brandreth's pills, which he refused to take, because he was not acquainted with them. He said to me, "Me doctor—first study my case, find out what ail 'em—then I know what to take." We dropped down a little farther, and stopped at mid-forenoon on an island and made him a dipper of tea. Here too we dined and did some washing and botanizing, while he lay on the bank. In the afternoon we went on a little farther, though the Indian was no better. *"Burntibus,"* as he called it, was a long smooth lake-like reach below the Five Islands. He said that he owned a hundred acres somewhere up this way. As a thunder-shower appeared to be coming up, we stopped opposite a barn on the west bank, in Chester, about a mile above Lincoln. Here at last we were obliged to spend the rest of the day and night, on account of our patient, whose sickness did not abate. He lay groaning under his canoe on the bank, looking very woe-begone, yet it was only a common case of colic. You would not have thought, if you had seen him lying about thus, that he was the proprietor of so many acres in that neighborhood, was worth $6,000, and had been to Washington. It seemed to me that, like the Irish, he made a greater ado about his sickness than a Yankee does, and was more alarmed about himself. We talked somewhat of leaving him with his people in Lincoln,—for that is one of their homes,—and taking the stage the next day, but he objected on account of the expense, saying, "Suppose me well in morning, you and I go Oldtown by noon."

As we were taking our tea at twilight, while he lay groaning still under his canoe, having at length found out " what ail him," he asked me to get him a dipper of water. Taking the dipper in one hand, he seized his powder-horn with the other, and pouring into it a charge or two of powder, stirred it up with his finger, and drank it off. This was all he took to-day after breakfast beside his tea.

To save the trouble of pitching our tent, when we had secured our stores from wandering dogs, we camped in the solitary half-open barn near the bank, with the permission of the owner, lying on new-mown hay four feet deep. The fragrance of the hay, in which many ferns, &c. were mingled, was agreeable, though it was quite alive with grasshoppers which you could hear crawling through it. This served to graduate our approach to houses and feather-beds. In the night some large bird, probably an owl, flitted through over our heads, and very early in the morning we were awakened by the twittering of swallows which had their nests there.

MONDAY, August 3.

We started early before breakfast, the Indian being considerably better, and soon glided by Lincoln, and after another long and handsome lake-like reach, we stopped to breakfast on the west shore, two or three miles below this town.

We frequently passed Indian Islands with their small houses on them. The Governor, Aitteon, lives in one of them, in Lincoln.

The Penobscot Indians seem to be more social, even, than the whites. Ever and anon in the deepest wilderness of Maine you come to the log-hut of a Yankee or Canada settler, but a Penobscot never takes up his residence in such a solitude. They are not even scattered about on their islands in the Penobscot, which are all within the settlements, but gathered together on two or three,—though not always on the best soil,—evidently for the sake of society. I saw one or two houses not now used by them, because, as our Indian Polis said, they were too solitary.

The small river emptying in at Lincoln is the Matanawcook, which also, we noticed, was the name of a steamer moored there. So we paddled and floated along, looking into the mouths of rivers. When passing the Mohawk Rips, or, as the Indian called them, "Mohog lips," four or five miles below Lincoln, he told us at length the story of a fight between his tribe and the Mohawks there, anciently,—how the latter were overcome by stratagem, the Penobscots using concealed knives,—but they could not for a long time kill the Mohawk chief, who was a very large and strong man, though he was attacked by several canoes at once, when swimming alone in the river.

From time to time we met Indians in their canoes, going up river. Our man did not commonly approach them, but exchanged a few words with them at a distance in his tongue. These were the first Indians we had met since leaving the *Umbazookskus.*

At Piscataquis Falls, just above the river of that name, we walked over the wooden railroad on the eastern shore, about one and a half miles long, while the Indian glided down the rapids. The steamer from Oldtown stops here, and passengers take a new boat above. Piscataquis, whose mouth we here passed, means "branch." It is obstructed by falls at its mouth, but can be navigated with bateaux or canoes above through a settled country, even to the neighborhood of Moosehead Lake, and we had thought at first of going that way. We were not obliged to get out of the canoe after this on account of falls or rapids, nor, indeed, was it quite necessary here. We took less notice of the scenery to-day, because we were in quite a settled country. The river became broad and sluggish, and we saw a blue heron winging its way slowly down the stream before us.

We passed the Passadumkeag River on our left and saw the blue *Olamon* mountains at a distance in the southeast. Here-abouts our Indian told us at length the story of their contention with the priest respecting schools. He thought a great deal of education and had recommended it to his tribe. His argument in its favor was, that if you had been to college and learnt to calculate, you could "keep 'em property,—no other way." He said that his boy was the best scholar in the school at Oldtown, to which he went with whites. He himself is a Protestant, and goes to church regularly in Oldtown. According to his account, a good many of his tribe are Protestants, and many of the Catholics also are in favor of schools. Some years ago they had a schoolmaster, a Protestant, whom they liked very well. The priest came and said that they must send him away, and finally he had such influence, telling them that they would go to the bad place at last if they retained him, that they sent him away. The school party, though numerous, were about giving up. Bishop Fenwick came from Boston and used his influence against them. But our Indian told his side that they must not give up, must hold on, they were the strongest. If they gave up, then they would have no party. But they answered that it was "no use, priest too strong, we'd better give up." At length he persuaded them to make a stand.

The priest was going for a sign to cut down the liberty-pole. So Polis and his party had a secret meeting about it; he got ready fifteen or twenty stout young men, "strip 'em na-ked, and painted 'em like old times," and told them that when the priest and his party went to cut down the liberty-pole, they were to rush up, take hold of it and prevent them, and he assured them that there would be no war, only a noise, "no war where priest is." He kept his men concealed in a house near by, and when the priest's party were about to cut down the liberty-pole, the fall of which would have been a death-blow to the school party, he gave a signal, and his young men rushed out and seized the pole. There was a great uproar, and they were about coming to blows, but the priest interfered, saying, "No war, no war," and so the pole stands, and the school goes on still.

We thought that it showed a good deal of tact in him, to seize this occasion and take his stand on it; proving how well he understood those with whom he had to deal.

The Olamon River comes in from the east in Greenbush a few miles below the Passadumkeag. When we asked the meaning of this name, the Indian said that there was an island opposite its mouth which was called *Olarmon*. That in old times, when visitors were coming to Oldtown, they used to stop there to dress and fix up or paint themselves. "What is that which ladies used?" he asked. Rouge? Red vermilion? "Yer," he said, "that is *larmon*, a kind of clay or red paint, which they used to get here."

We decided that we too would stop at this island, and fix up our inner man, at least, by dining.

It was a large island with an abundance of hemp-nettle, but I did not notice any kind of red paint there. The Olarmon River, at its mouth at least, is a dead stream. There was another large island in that neighborhood, which the Indian called *"Soogle"* (i. e. Sugar) Island.

About a dozen miles before reaching Oldtown he inquired, "How you like 'em your pilot?" But we postponed an answer till we had got quite back again.

The *Sunkhaze*, another short dead stream, comes in from the east two miles above Oldtown. There is said to be some of the best deer ground in Maine on this stream. Asking the meaning of this name, the Indian said, "Suppose you are going down Penobscot, just like we, and you see a canoe come out of bank and go along before you, but you no see 'em stream. That is *Sunkhaze*."

He had previously complimented me on my paddling, saying that I paddled "just like anybody," giving me an Indian name which meant "great paddler." When off this stream he said to me, who sat in the bows, "Me teach you paddle." So turning toward the shore he got out, came forward and placed my hands as he wished. He placed one of them quite outside the boat, and the other parallel with the first, grasping the paddle near the end, not over the flat extremity, and told me to slide it back and forth on the side of the canoe. This, I found, was a great improvement which I had not thought of, saving me the labor of lifting the paddle each time, and I wondered that he had not suggested it before. It is true, before our baggage was reduced we had been obliged to sit with our legs drawn up, and our knees above the side of the canoe, which would have prevented our paddling thus, or perhaps he was afraid of wearing out his canoe, by constant friction on the side.

I told him that I had been accustomed to sit in the stern, and lifting my paddle at each stroke, getting a pry on the side each time, and I still paddled partly as if in the stern. He then wanted to see me paddle in the stern. So, changing paddles, for he had the longer and better one, and turning end for end, he sitting flat on the bottom and I on the crossbar, he began to paddle very hard, trying to turn the canoe, looking over his shoulder and laughing, but finding it in vain he relaxed his efforts, though we still sped along a mile or two very swiftly. He said that he had no fault to find with my paddling in the stern, but I complained that he did not paddle according to his own directions in the bows.

Opposite the Sunkhaze is the main boom of the Penobscot, where the logs from far up the river are collected and assorted.

As we drew near to Oldtown I asked Polis if he was not glad to get home again; but there was no relenting to his wildness, and he said, "It makes no difference to me where I am." Such is the Indian's pretence always.

We approached the Indian Island through the narrow strait called "Cook." He said, "I 'xpect we take in some water there, river so high,—never see it so high at this season. Very rough water there, but short; swamp steamboat once. Don't you paddle till I tell you, then you paddle right along." It was a very short rapid. When we were in the midst of it he shouted "paddle," and we shot through without taking in a drop.

Soon after the Indian houses came in sight, but I could not at first tell my companion which of two or three large white ones was our guide's. He said it was the one with blinds.

We landed opposite his door at about four in the afternoon, having come some forty miles this day. From the Piscataquis we had come remarkably and unaccountably quick, probably as fast as the stage on the bank, though the last dozen miles was dead water.

Polis wanted to sell us his canoe, said it would last seven or eight years, or with care, perhaps ten; but we were not ready to buy it.

We stopped for an hour at his house, where my companion shaved with his razor, which he pronounced in very good condition. Mrs. P. wore a hat and had a silver brooch on her breast, but she was not introduced to us. The house was roomy and neat. A large new map of Oldtown and the Indian Island hung on the wall, and a clock opposite to it. Wishing to know when the cars left Oldtown, Polis's son brought one of the last Bangor papers, which I saw was directed to "Joseph Polis," from the office.

This was the last that I saw of Joe Polis. We took the last train, and reached Bangor that night.

Appendix

I. TREES.

THE prevailing trees (I speak only of what I saw) on the east and west branches of the Penobscot and on the upper part of the Allegash were the fir, spruce (both black and white), and arbor-vitæ, or "cedar." The fir has the darkest foliage, and, together with the spruce, makes a very dense "black growth," especially on the upper parts of the rivers. A dealer in lumber with whom I talked called the former a weed, and it is commonly regarded as fit neither for timber nor fuel. But it is more sought after as an ornamental tree than any other evergreen of these woods except the arbor-vitæ. The black spruce is much more common than the white. Both are tall and slender trees. The arbor-vitæ, which is of a more cheerful hue, with its light-green fans, is also tall and slender, though sometimes two feet in diameter. It often fills the swamps.

Mingled with the former, and also here and there forming extensive and more open woods by themselves, indicating, it is said, a better soil, were canoe and yellow birches (the former was always at hand for kindling a fire,—we saw no small white-birches in that wilderness), and sugar and red maples.

The Aspen (*Populus tremuloides*) was very common on burnt grounds. We saw many straggling white pines, commonly unsound trees, which had therefore been skipped by the choppers; these were the largest trees we saw; and we occasionally passed a small wood in which this was the prevailing tree; but I did not notice nearly so many of these trees as I can see in a single walk in Concord. The speckled or hoary alder (*Alnus incana*) abounds everywhere along the muddy banks of rivers and lakes, and in swamps. Hemlock could commonly be found for tea, but was nowhere abundant. Yet F. A. Michaux states that in Maine, Vermont, and the upper part of New Hampshire, &c., the hemlock forms three fourths of the evergreen woods, the rest being black spruce. It belongs to cold hillsides.

The elm and black ash were very common along the lower and stiller parts of the streams, where the shores were flat and grassy or there were low gravelly islands. They made a pleasing variety in the scenery, and we felt as if nearer home while gliding past them.

The above fourteen trees made the bulk of the woods which we saw.

The larch (Juniper), beech, and Norway pine (*Pinus resinosa*, red pine), were only occasionally seen in particular places. The *Pinus Banksiana* (gray or Northern scrub-pine), and a single small red oak (*Quercus rubra*) only, are on islands in Grand Lake, on the East Branch.

The above are almost all peculiarly Northern trees, and found chiefly, if not solely, on mountains southward.

II. FLOWERS AND SHRUBS.

IT appears that in a forest like this the great majority of flowers, shrubs, and grasses are confined to the banks of the rivers and lakes, and to the meadows, more open swamps, burnt lands, and mountain-tops; comparatively very few indeed penetrate the woods. There is no such dispersion even of wild-flowers as is commonly supposed, or as exists in a cleared and settled country. Most of our wild-flowers, so called, may be considered as naturalized in the localities where they grow. Rivers and lakes are the great protectors of such plants against the aggressions of the forest, by their annual rise and fall keeping open a narrow strip where these more delicate plants have light and space in which to grow. They are the *protégés* of the rivers. These narrow and straggling bands and isolated groups are, in a sense, the pioneers of civilization. Birds, quadrupeds, insects, and man also, in the main, follow the flowers, and the latter in his turn makes more room for them and for berry-bearing shrubs, birds, and small quadrupeds. One settler told me that not only blackberries and raspberries, but mountain-maples came in, in the clearing and burning.

Though plants are often referred to primitive woods as

their locality, it cannot be true of very many, unless the woods are supposed to include such localities as I have mentioned. Only those which require but little light, and can bear the drip of the trees, penetrate the woods, and these have commonly more beauty in their leaves than in their pale and almost colorless blossoms.

The prevailing flowers and conspicuous small plants of the *woods*, which I noticed, were: *Clintonia borealis*, *Linnæa*, checkerberry (*Gaultheria procumbens*), *Aralia nudicaulis* (wild sarsaparilla), great round-leaved orchis, *Dalibarda repens*, *Chiogenes hispidula* (creeping snowberry), *Oxalis acetosella* (common wood-sorrel), *Aster acuminatus*, *Pyrola secunda* (one-sided pyrola), *Medeola Virginica* (Indian cucumber-root), small *Circæa* (enchanter's nightshade), and perhaps *Cornus Canadensis* (dwarf cornel).

Of these, the last of July, 1857, only the *Aster acuminatus* and great round-leaved *orchis* were conspicuously in bloom.

The most common flowers of the *river* and *lake shores* were: *Thalictrum cornuti* (meadow-rue), *Hypericum ellipticum*, *mutilum*, and *Canadense* (St. John's-wort), horsemint, horehound, *Lycopus Virginicus* and *Europæus*, var. *sinuatus* (bugleweed), *Scutellaria galericulata* (skull-cap), *Solidago lanceolata* and *squarrosa* East Branch (golden-rod), *Diplopappus umbellatus* (double-bristled aster), *Aster radula*, *Cicuta maculata* and *bulbifera* (water-hemlock), meadow-sweet, *Lysimachia stricta* and *ciliata* (loose-strife), *Galium trifidum* (small bedstraw), *Lilium Canadense* (wild yellow-lily), *Platanthera peramœna* and *psycodes* (great purple orchis and small purple-fringed orchis), *Mimulus ringens* (monkey-flower), dock (water), blue flag, *Hydrocotyle Americana* (marsh pennywort), *Sanicula Canadensis*? (black snake-root), *Clematis Virginiana*? (common virgin's-bower), *Nasturtium palustre* (marsh cress), *Ranunculus recurvatus* (hooked crowfoot), *Asclepias incarnata* (swamp milkweed), *Aster Tradescanti* (Tradescant's aster), *Aster miser*, also *longifolius*, *Eupatorium purpureum* apparently, lake shores (Joe-Pye-weed), *Apocynum Cannabinum* East Branch (Indian hemp), *Polygonum cilinode* (bind-weed), and others. Not to mention among inferior orders wool-grass and the sensitive fern.

In the water, *Nuphar advena* (yellow pond-lily), some *potamogetons* (pond-weed), *Sagittaria variabilis* (arrow-head), *Sium lineare*? (water-parsnip).

Of these, those conspicuously in flower the last of July, 1857, were: rue, *Solidago lanceolata* and *squarrosa*, *Diplopappus umbellatus*, *Aster radula*, *Lilium Canadense*, great and small purple orchis, *Mimulus ringens*, blue flag, virgin's-bower, &c.

The characteristic flowers in *swamps* were: *Rubus triflorus* (dwarf raspberry), *Calla palustris* (water-arum), and *Sarracenia purpurea* (pitcher-plant). On *burnt grounds*: *Epilobium angustifolium*, in full bloom (great willow-herb), and *Erechthites hieracifolia* (fire-weed). On *cliffs*: *Campanula rotundifolia* (harebell), *Cornus Canadensis* (dwarf cornel), *Arctostaphylos uva-ursi* (bearberry), *Potentilla tridentata* (mountain cinquefoil), *Pteris aquilina* (common brake). At *old camps, carries, and logging-paths*: *Cirsium arvense* (Canada thistle), *Prunella vulgaris* (common self-heal), clover, herds-grass, *Achillea millefolium* (common yarrow), *Leucanthemum vulgare* (whiteweed), *Aster macrophyllus*, *Halenia deflexa* East Branch (spurred gentian), *Antennaria margaritacea* (pearly everlasting), *Actæa rubra* and *alba*, wet carries (red and white cohosh), *Desmodium Canadense* (tick-trefoil), sorrel.

The handsomest and most interesting flowers were the great purple orchises, rising ever and anon, with their great purple spikes perfectly erect, amid the shrubs and grasses of the shore. It seemed strange that they should be made to grow there in such profusion, seen of moose and moose-hunters only, while they are so rare in Concord. I have never seen this species flowering nearly so late with us, or with the small one.

The prevailing underwoods were: *Dirca palustris* (moose-wood), *Acer spicatum* (mountain maple), *Viburnum lantanoides* (hobble-bush), and frequently *Taxus baccata*, var. *Canadensis* (American yew).

The prevailing shrubs and small trees along the shore were: *osier rouge* and alders (before mentioned); sallows, or small willows, of two or three kinds, as *Salix humilis*, *rostrata*, and *discolor*?, *Sambucus Canadensis* (black elder), rose, *Viburnum opulus* and *nudum* (cranberry-tree and withe-rod), *Pyrus*

Americana (American mountain-ash), *Corylus rostrata* (beaked hazel-nut), *Diervilla trifida* (bush-honeysuckle), *Prunus Virginiana* (choke-cherry), *Myrica gale* (sweet-gale), *Nemopanthes Canadensis* (mountain holly), *Cephalanthus occidentalis* (button-bush), *Ribes prostratum*, in some places (fetid currant).

More particularly of shrubs and small trees in *swamps*: some willows, *Kalmia glauca* (pale laurel), *Ledum latifolium* and *palustre* (Labrador tea), *Ribes lacustre* (swamp gooseberry), and in one place *Betula pumila* (low birch). At *camps and carries*: raspberry, *Vaccinium Canadense* (Canada blueberry), *Prunus Pennsylvanica* also along shore (wild red cherry), *Amelanchier Canadensis* (shad-bush), *Sambucus pubens* (red-berried elder). Among those peculiar to the *mountains* would be the *Vaccinium vitis-idæa* (cow-berry).

Of plants commonly regarded as *introduced* from Europe, I observed at Ansel Smith's clearing, Chesuncook, abundant in 1857: *Ranunculus acris* (buttercups), *Plantago major* (common plantain), *Chenopodium album* (lamb's-quarters), *Capsella bursa-pastoris*, 1853 (shepherd's-purse), *Spergula arvensis*, also, north shore of Moosehead, in 1853, and elsewhere, 1857 (corn-spurrey), *Taraxacum dens-leonis*—regarded as indigenous by Gray, but evidently introduced there—(common dandelion), *Polygonum Persicaria* and *hydropiper*, by a logging-path in woods at Smith's (lady's-thumb and smart-weed), *Rumex acetosella*, common at carries (sheep-sorrel), *Trifolium pratense*, 1853, and carries frequent (red clover), *Leucanthemum vulgare*, carries (white weed), *Phleum pratense*, carries, 1853–7 (herd's-grass), *Verbena hastata* (blue vervain), *Cirsium arvense*, abundant at camps 1857 (Canada thistle), *Rumex crispus*?, West Branch, 1853? (curled dock), *Verbascum thapsus*, between Bangor and lake, 1853 (common mullein).

It appears that I saw about a dozen plants which had accompanied man as far into the woods as Chesuncook, and had naturalized themselves there, in 1853. Plants begin thus early to spring by the side of a logging-path,—a mere vista through the woods, which can only be used in the winter, on account of the stumps and fallen trees,—which at length are the roadside plants in old settlements. The pioneers of such are planted in part by the first cattle, which cannot be summered in the woods.

III. LIST OF PLANTS.

THE following is a list of the plants which I noticed in the Maine woods, in the years 1853 and 1857. (Those marked * not in woods.)

1. THOSE WHICH ATTAINED THE HEIGHT OF TREES.

Alnus incana (speckled or hoary alder), abundant along streams, &c.

Thuja occidentalis (American arbor-vitæ), one of the prevailing.

Fraxinus sambucifolia (black ash), very common, especially near dead water. The Indian spoke of "yellow ash" as also found there.

Populus tremuloides (American aspen), very common, especially on burnt lands, almost as white as birches.

Populus grandidentata (large-toothed aspen), perhaps two or three.

Fagus ferruginea (American beech), not uncommon, at least on the West Branch (saw more in 1846).

Betula papyracea (canoe-birch), prevailing everywhere and about Bangor.

Betula excelsa (yellow birch), very common.

Betula lenta (black birch), on the West Branch, in 1853.

Betula alba (American white birch), about Bangor only.

Ulmus Americana (American or white elm), West Branch and low down the East Branch, i. e. on the lower and alluvial part of the river, very common.

Larix Americana (American or black larch), very common on the Umbazookskus, some elsewhere.

Abies Canadensis (hemlock-spruce), not abundant, some on the West Branch, and a little everywhere.

Acer saccharinum (sugar maple), very common.

Acer rubrum (red or swamp maple), very common.

Acer dasycarpum (white or silver maple), a little low on East Branch and in Chesuncook woods.

Quercus rubra (red oak), one on an island in Grand Lake, East Branch, and, according to a settler, a few on the east side of Chesuncook Lake; a few also about Bangor in 1853.

Pinus strobus (white pine), scattered along, most abundant at Heron Lake.

Pinus resinosa (red pine), Telos and Grand Lake, a little afterwards here and there.

Abies balsamea (balsam fir), perhaps the most common tree, especially in the upper parts of rivers.

Abies nigra (black or double spruce), next to the last the most common, if not equally common, and on mountains.

Abies alba (white or single spruce), common with the last along the rivers.

Pinus Banksiana (gray or Northern scrub-pine), a few on an island in Grand Lake.

Twenty-three in all (23).

2. SMALL TREES AND SHRUBS.

Prunus depressa (dwarf-cherry), on gravel bars, East Branch, near Hunt's, with green fruit, obviously distinct from the *pumila* of river and meadows.

Vaccinium corymbosum (common swamp blueberry), Bucksport.

Vaccinium Canadense (Canada blueberry), carries and rocky hills everywhere as far south as Bucksport.

Vaccinium Pennsylvanicum (dwarf-blueberry?), Whetstone Falls.

Betula pumila (low birch), Mud Pond Swamp.

Prinos verticillata (black alder, '57), now placed with *Ilex* by Gray, 2d ed.

Cephalanthus occidentalis (button-bush).

Prunus Pennsylvanica (wild red cherry), very common at camps, carries, &c., along rivers; fruit ripe August 1, 1857.

Prunus Virginiana (choke-cherry), river-side, common.

Cornus alternifolia (alternate-leaved cornel), West Branch, 1853.

Ribes prostratum (fetid currant), common along streams, on Webster Stream.

Sambucus Canadensis (common elder), common along river-sides.

Sambucus pubens (red-berried elder), not quite so common, roadsides toward Moosehead, and on carries afterward, fruit beautiful.

Ribes lacustre (swamp-gooseberry), swamps, common, Mud Pond Swamp and Webster Stream; not ripe July 29, 1857.

Corylus rostrata (beaked hazel-nut), common.

Taxus baccata, var. *Canadensis* (American yew), a common under-shrub at an island in West Branch and Chesuncook woods.

Viburnum lantanoides (hobble-bush), common, especially in Chesuncook woods; fruit ripe in September, 1853, not in July, 1857.

Viburnum opulus (cranberry-tree), on West Branch; one in flower still, July 25, 1857.

Viburnum nudum (withe-rod), common along rivers.

Kalmia glauca (pale laurel), swamps, common, as at Moosehead carry and Chamberlain swamp.

Kalmia angustifolia (lamb-kill), with *Kalmia glauca*.

Acer spicatum (mountain maple), a prevailing underwood.

Acer striatum (striped maple), in fruit July 30, 1857; green the first year; green, striped with white, the second; darker, the third, with dark blotches.

Cornus stolonifera (red-osier dogwood), prevailing shrub on shore of West Branch; fruit still white in August, 1857.

Pyrus Americana (American mountain ash), common along shores.

Amelanchier Canadensis (shad-bush), rocky carries, &c.; considerable fruit in 1857.

Rubus strigosus (wild red raspberry), very abundant, burnt grounds, camps, and carries, but not ripe till we got to Chamberlain dam and on East Branch.

Rosa Carolina (swamp-rose), common on the shores of lakes, &c.

*Rhus typhina** (stag-horn sumac).

Myrica gale (sweet-gale), common.

Nemopanthes Canadensis (mountain holly), common in low ground, Moosehead carry, and on Mount Kineo.

Cratægus (*coccinea*? scarlet-fruited thorn), not uncommon; with hard fruit in September, 1853.

Salix (near to *petiolaris*, petioled willow), very common in Umbazookskus meadows.

Salix rostrata (long-beaked willow), common.

Salix humilis (low bush-willow), common.

Salix discolor (glaucous willow?).
Salix lucida (shining willow), at island in Heron lake.
Dirca palustris (moose-wood), common.
In all, 38.

3. SMALL SHRUBS AND HERBACEOUS PLANTS.

Agrimonia Eupatoria (common agrimony), not uncommon.
Circæa Alpina (enchanter's nightshade), very common in woods.
Nasturtium palustre (marsh cress), var. *hispidum*, common as at A. Smith's.
Aralia hispida (bristly sarsaparilla), on West Branch, both years.
Aralia nudicaulis (wild sarsaparilla), Chesuncook woods.
Sagittaria variabilis (arrow-head), common at Moosehead and afterward.
Arum triphyllum (Indian turnip), now *arisæma*, Moosehead carry in 1853.
Asclepias incarnata (swamp milk-weed), Umbazookskus River and after, redder than ours, and a different variety from our var. *pulchra*.
Aster acuminatus (pointed-leaved aster), the prevailing aster in woods, not long open on South Branch July 31st; two or more feet high.
Aster macrophyllus (large-leaved aster), common, and the whole plant surprisingly fragrant, like a medicinal herb, just out at Telos Dam July 29, 1857, and after to Bangor and Bucksport; bluish flower (in woods on Pine Stream and at Chesuncook in 1853).
Aster radula (rough-leaved aster), common, Moosehead carry and after.
Aster miser (petty aster), in 1853 on West Branch, and common on Chesuncook shore.
Aster longifolius (willow-leaved blue aster), 1853, Moosehead and Chesuncook shores.
Aster cordifolius (heart-leaved aster), 1853, West Branch.
Aster Tradescanti (Tradescant's aster), 1857. A narrow-leaved one Chesuncook shore, 1853.
Aster, *longifolius* like, with small flowers, West Branch, 1853.

Aster puniceus (rough-stemmed aster), Pine Stream.

Diplopappus umbellatus (large *diplopappus* aster), common along river.

Arctostaphylos uva-ursi (bear-berry), Kineo, &c., 1857.

Polygonum cilinode (fringe-jointed false buckwheat), common.

Bidens cernua (bur-marigold), 1853, West Branch.

Ranunculus acris (buttercups), abundant at Smith's dam, Chesuncook, 1853.

Rubus triflorus (dwarf-raspberry), low grounds and swamps, common.

*Utricularia vulgaris** (greater bladder-wort), Pushaw.

Iris versicolor (larger blue-flag), common Moosehead, West Branch, Umbazookskus, &c.

Sparganium (bur-reed).

Calla palustris (water-arum), in bloom July 27, 1857, Mud Pond Swamp.

Lobelia cardinalis (cardinal-flower), apparently common, but out of bloom August, 1857.

Cerastium nutans (clammy wild chickweed?).

Gaultheria procumbens (checkerberry), prevailing everywhere in woods along banks of rivers.

*Stellaria media** (common chickweed), Bangor.

Chiogenes hispidula (creeping snowberry), very common in woods.

Cicuta maculata (water-hemlock).

Cicuta bulbifera (bulb-bearing water-hemlock), Penobscot and Chesuncook shore, 1853.

Galium trifidum (small bed-straw), common.

Galium Aparine (cleavers?), Chesuncook, 1853.

Galium, one kind on Pine Stream, 1853.

Trifolium pratense (red-clover), on carries, &c.

Actæa spicata, var. *alba* (white cohosh), Chesuncook woods 1853, and East Branch 1857.

Actæa var. *rubra* (red cohosh), East Branch 1857.

Vaccinium vitis-idæa (cow-berry), Ktaadn, very abundant.

Cornus Canadensis (dwarf-cornel), in woods Chesuncook 1853; just ripe at Kineo July 24, 1857, common; still in bloom, Moosehead carry September 16, 1853.

Medeola Virginica (Indian cucumber-root), West Branch and Chesuncook woods.

Dalibarda repens (Dalibarda), Moosehead carry and after, common. In flower still, August 1, 1857.

Taraxacum dens-leonis (common dandelion), Smith's 1853, only there. Is it not foreign?

Diervilla trifida (bush honeysuckle), very common.

Rumex hydrolapathum? (great water-dock), in 1857; noticed it was large seeded in 1853, common.

Rumex crispus? (curled-dock), West Branch 1853.

Apocynum cannabinum (Indian hemp), Kineo, *Bradford*, and East Branch 1857, at Whetstone Falls.

Apocynum androsæmifolium (spreading dogbane), Kineo, *Bradford*.

Clintonia borealis (Clintonia), all over woods; fruit just ripening July 25, 1857.

A lemna (duckweed), Pushaw 1857.

Elodea Virginica (marsh St. John's-wort), Moosehead 1853.

Epilobium angustifolium (great willow-herb), great fields on burnt lands; some white at Webster Stream.

Epilobium coloratum (purple-veined willow-herb), once in 1857.

Eupatorium purpureum (Joe-Pye-weed), Heron, Moosehead, and Chesuncook lake-shores, common.

Allium (onion), a new kind to me in bloom, without bulbs above, on rocks near Whetstone Falls? East Branch.

Halenia deflexa (spurred gentian), carries on East Branch, common.

Geranium Robertianum (Herb Robert).

Solidago lanceolata (bushy golden-rod), very common.

Solidago, one of the three-ribbed, in both years.

Solidago thyrsoidea (large mountain golden-rod), one on Webster Stream.

Solidago squarrosa (large-spiked golden-rod), the most common on East Branch.

Solidago altissima (rough hairy golden-rod), not uncommon both years.

Coptis trifolia (three-leaved gold-thread).

Smilax herbacea (carrion-flower), not uncommon both years.

*Spiræa tomentosa** (hardhack), Bangor.

Campanula rotundifolia (harebell), cliffs Kineo, Grand Lake, &c.

Hieracium (hawk-weed), not uncommon.

Veratrum viride (American white hellebore).

Lycopus Virginicus (bugle-weed), 1857.

Lycopus Europæus (water-horehound), var. *sinuatus*, Heron Lake shore.

Chenopodium album (lamb's-quarters), Smith's.

Mentha Canadensis (wild mint), very common.

Galeopsis tetrahit (common hemp-nettle), Olarmon Isle, abundant, and below, in prime August 3, 1857.

Houstonia cærulea (bluets), now *Oldenlandia* (Gray, 2d ed.), 1857.

Hydrocotyle Americana (marsh pennywort), common.

Hypericum ellipticum (elliptical-leaved St. John's-wort), common.

Hypericum mutilum (small St. John's-wort), both years, common.

Hypericum Canadense (Canadian St. John's-wort), Moosehead Lake and Chesuncook shores, 1853.

Trientalis Americana (star-flower), Pine Stream, 1853.

Lobelia inflata (Indian tobacco).

Spiranthes cernuus (ladies' tresses), Kineo and after.

Nabalus (rattlesnake root), 1857; *altissimus* (tall white lettuce), Chesuncook woods, 1853.

Antennaria margaritacea (pearly everlasting), common, Moosehead, Smith's, &c.

Lilium Canadense (wild yellow lily), very common and large, West and East Branch; one on East Branch, 1857, with strongly revolute petals, and leaves perfectly smooth beneath, but not larger than the last, and apparently only a variety.

Linnæa borealis (Linnæa), almost everywhere in woods.

Lobelia Dortmanna (water-lobelia), pond in Bucksport.

Lysimachia ciliata (hairy-stalked loosestrife), very common, Chesuncook shore and East Branch.

Lysimachia stricta (upright loosestrife), very common.

Microstylis ophioglossoides (adder's-mouth), Kineo.

Spiræa salicifolia (common meadow-sweet), common.

Mimulus ringens (monkey-flower), common, lake-shores, &c.

Scutellaria galericulata (skullcap), very common.

Scutellaria lateriflora (mad-dog skullcap), Heron Lake, 1857, Chesuncook, 1853.

Platanthera psycodes (small purple-fringed orchis), very common, East Branch and Chesuncook, 1853.

Platanthera fimbriata (large purple-fringed orchis), very common, West Branch and Umbazookskus, 1857.

Platanthera orbiculata (large round-leaved orchis), very common in woods, Moosehead and Chamberlain carries, Caucomgomoc, &c.

Amphicarpæa monoica (hog peanut).

Aralia racemosa (spikenard), common, Moosehead carry, Telos Lake, &c., and after; out about August 1, 1857.

Plantago major (common plantain), common in open land at Smith's in 1853.

*Pontederia cordata** (pickerel-weed), only near Oldtown, 1857.

Potamogeton (pond-weed), not common.

Potentilla tridentata (mountain cinquefoil), Kineo.

Potentilla Norvegica (cinquefoil), Heron Lake shore and Smith's.

Polygonum amphibium (water-persicaria), var. *aquaticum*, Second Lake.

Polygonum Persicaria (lady's-thumb), log-path Chesuncook, 1853.

Nuphar advena (yellow pond-lily), not abundant.

Nymphæa odorata (sweet water-lily), a few in West Branch, 1853.

Polygonum hydropiper (smart-weed), log-path, Chesuncook.

Pyrola secunda (one-sided pyrola), very common, Caucomgomoc.

Pyrola elliptica (shin-leaf), Caucomgomoc River.

Ranunculus Flammula (spearwort, var. *reptans*).

Ranunculus recurvatus (hooked crowfoot), Umbazookskus landing, &c.

*Typha latifolia** (common cat-tail or reed-mace), extremely abundant between Bangor and Portland.

Sanicula Marylandica (black snake-root), Moosehead carry and after.

Aralia nudicaulis (wild sarsaparilla).

Capsella bursa-pastoris (shepherd's-purse), Smith's, 1853.

Prunella vulgaris (self-heal), very common everywhere.

Erechthites hieracifolia (fireweed), 1857, and Smith's open land, 1853.

Sarracenia purpurea (pitcher-plant), Mud Pond swamp.

Smilacina bifolia (false Solomon's-seal), 1857, and Chesuncook woods, 1853.

Smilacina racemosa (false spikenard?), Umbazookskus carry (July 27, 1853).

Veronica scutellata (marsh speedwell).

Spergula arvensis (corn spurrey), 1857, not uncommon, 1853, Moosehead and Smith's.

Fragaria (strawberry), 1853 Smith's, 1857 Bucksport.

Thalictrum Cornuti (meadow-rue), very common, especially along rivers, tall, and conspicuously in bloom in July, 1857.

Cirsium arvense (Canada thistle), abundant at camps and highway sides in the north of Maine.

Cirsium muticum (swamp-thistle), well in bloom Webster Stream, August 31.

Rumex acetosella (sheep-sorrel), common by river and log-paths, as Chesuncook log-path.

Impatiens fulva (spotted touch-me-not).

Trillium erythrocarpum (painted trillium), common West Branch and Moosehead carry.

Verbena hastata (blue vervain).

Clematis Virginiana (common virgin's-bower), common on river banks, feathered in September, 1853, in bloom July, 1857.

Leucanthemum vulgare (white-weed).

Sium lineare (water-parsnip), 1857, and Chesuncook shore, 1853.

Achillea millefolium (common yarrow), by river and log-paths, and Smith's.

Desmodium Canadense (Canadian tick-trefoil), not uncommon.

Oxalis acetosella (common wood-sorrel), still out July 25, 1853, at Moosehead carry and after.

Oxalis stricta (yellow wood-sorrel), 1853, at Smith's and his wood-path.

Liparis liliifolia (tway-blade), Kineo, *Bradford*.

Uvularia grandiflora (large-flowered bellwort), woods, common.

Uvularia sessilifolia (sessile-leaved bellwort), Chesuncook woods, 1853.

In all, 145.

4. Of Lower Order.

Scirpus Eriophorum (wool-grass), very common, especially on low islands. A coarse grass, four or five feet high, along the river.

Phleum pratense (herd's-grass), on carries, at camps and clearings.

Equisetum sylvaticum (sylvatic horse-tail).

Pteris aquilina (brake), Kineo and after.

Onoclea sensibilis (sensitive-fern), very common along the river sides; some on the gravelly shore of Heron Lake Island.

Polypodium Dryopteris (brittle polypody).

Woodsia Ilvensis (rusty Woodsia), Kineo.

Lycopodium lucidulum (toothed club-moss).

Usnea (a parmeliaceous lichen), common on various trees.

IV. LIST OF BIRDS

which I saw in Maine between July 24 and August 3, 1857.

A very small hawk at Great Falls, on Webster Stream.

Haliætus leucocephalus (white-headed or bald-eagle), at Ragmuff, and above and below Hunt's, and on pond below Mattawamkeag.

Pandion haliætus (fish-hawk or osprey), heard, also seen on East Branch.

Bubo Virginianus (cat-owl), near Camp Island, also above mouth of Seboois, from a stump back and forth, also near Hunt's on a tree.

Icterus phœniceus (red-winged blackbird), Umbazookskus River.

Corvus Americanus (American crow), a few, as at outlet of Grand Lake; a peculiar cawing.

Fringilla Canadensis (tree-sparrow), think I saw one on Mount Kineo July 24, which behaved as if it had a nest there.

Garrulus cristatus (blue-jay).

Parus atricapillus (chicadee), a few.

Muscicapa tyrannus (king-bird).

Muscicapa Cooperii (olive-sided fly-catcher), everywhere a prevailing bird.

Muscicapa virens (wood pewee), Moosehead, and I think beyond.

Muscicapa ruticilla (American redstart), Moosehead.

Vireo olivaceus (red-eyed vireo), everywhere common.

Turdus migratorius (red-breasted robin), some everywhere.

Turdus melodus (wood-thrush), common in all the woods.

Turdus Wilsonii (Wilson's thrush), Moosehead and beyond.

Turdus aurocapillus (golden-crowned thrush or oven-bird), Moosehead.

Fringilla albicollis (white-throated sparrow), Kineo and after, apparently nesting; the prevailing bird early and late.

Fringilla melodia (song-sparrow), at Moosehead or beyond.

Sylvia pinus (pine warbler), one part of voyage.

Muscicapa acadica (small pewee), common.

Trichas Marylandica (Maryland yellow-throat), everywhere.

Coccyzus Americanus? (yellow-billed cuckoo), common.

Picus erythrocephalus (red-headed woodpecker), heard and saw; and good to eat.

Sitta Carolinensis? (white-breasted American nuthatch), heard.

Alcedo alcyon (belted kingfisher), very common.

Caprimulgus Americanus (night-hawk).

Tetrao umbellus (partridge), Moosehead carry, &c.

Tetrao cupido? (pinnated grouse), Webster Stream.

Ardea cærulea (blue heron), lower part of Penobscot.

Totanus macularius (spotted sandpiper or peetweet), everywhere.

Larus argentatus? (herring-gull), Heron Lake on rocks, and Chamberlain. Smaller gull on Second Lake.

Anas obscura (dusky or black duck), once in East Branch.

Anas sponsa (summer or wood duck), everywhere.

Fuligula albeola (spirit duck or dipper), common.

Colymbus glacialis (great Northern diver or loon), in all the lakes. A swallow; the night-warbler? once or twice.

Mergus Merganser (buff-breasted merganser or sheldrake), common on lakes and rivers.

V. QUADRUPEDS.

A bat on West Branch; beaver skull at Grand Lake; Mr. Thatcher ate beaver with moose on the Caucomgomoc. A muskrat on the last stream; the red squirrel is common in the depths of the woods; a dead porcupine on Chamberlain road; a cow moose and tracks of calf; skin of a bear, just killed.

VI. OUTFIT FOR AN EXCURSION.

The following will be a good outfit for one who wishes to make an excursion of *twelve* days into the Maine woods in July, with a companion, and one Indian for the same purposes that I did.

Wear,—a check shirt, stout old shoes, thick socks, a neck ribbon, thick waistcoat, thick pants, old Kossuth hat, a linen sack.

Carry,—in an India-rubber knapsack, with a large flap, two shirts (check), one pair thick socks, one pair drawers, one flannel shirt, two pocket-handkerchiefs, a light India-rubber coat or a thick woollen one, two bosoms and collars to go and come with, one napkin, pins, needles, thread, one blanket, best gray, seven feet long.

Tent,—six by seven feet, and four feet high in middle, will do; veil and gloves and insect-wash, or, better, mosquito-bars to cover all at night; best pocket-map, and perhaps description of the route; compass; plant-book and red blotting-paper; paper and stamps, botany, small pocket spy-glass for birds, pocket microscope, tape-measure, insect-boxes.

Axe, full size if possible, jackknife, fish-lines, two only apiece, with a few hooks and corks ready, and with pork for bait in a packet, rigged; matches (some also in a small vial in the waist-coat pocket); soap, two pieces; large knife and iron spoon (for all); three or four old newspapers, much twine, and several rags for dishcloths; twenty feet of strong cord, four-quart tin pail for kettle, two tin dippers, three tin plates, a fry-pan.

Provisions. — Soft hardbread, twenty-eight pounds; pork, sixteen pounds; sugar, twelve pounds; one pound black tea or three pounds coffee, one box or a pint of salt, one quart Indian meal, to fry fish in; six lemons, good to correct the pork and warm water; perhaps two or three pounds of rice, for variety. You will probably get some berries, fish, &c., beside.

A gun is not worth the carriage, unless you go as hunters. The pork should be in an open keg, sawed to fit; the sugar, tea or coffee, meal, salt, &c., should be put in separate water-tight India-rubber bags, tied with a leather string; and all the provisions, and part of the rest of the baggage, put into two large India-rubber bags, which have been proved to be water-tight and durable. Expense of preceding outfit is twenty-four dollars.

An Indian may be hired for about one dollar and fifty cents per day, and perhaps fifty cents a week for his canoe (this depends on the demand). The canoe should be a strong and tight one. This expense will be nineteen dollars.

Such an excursion need not cost more than twenty-five dollars apiece, starting at the foot of Moosehead, if you already possess or can borrow a reasonable part of the outfit. If you take an Indian and canoe at Oldtown, it will cost seven or eight dollars more to transport them to the lake.

VII. A LIST OF INDIAN WORDS.

1. *Katadn,* said to mean *Highest Land,* Rale puts for mt. *Pemadene*; for *Grai, pierre à aiguiser, Kitadañgan.* (v. Potter.)

Mattawamkeag, place where two rivers meet. (Indian of carry.) (v. Williamson's History of Maine, and Willis.)

Molunkus.

Ebeeme, rock.

Noliseemack; other name, Shad Pond.

Kecunnilessu, chicadee.

Nipsquecohossus, woodcock.

Skuscumonsuk, kingfisher. Has it not the pl. termination *uk* here, or *suk*? 〉 Joe.

Wassus, bear, *aouessous*. Rale.

Lunxus, Indian-devil.

Upahsis, mountain-ash.

Moose, (is it called, or does it mean, wood-eater?) *mous*, Rale.

Katahdinauguoh, said to mean mountains about Ktaadn.

Ebemena, tree-cranberry. *Ibimin*, *nar*, red, bad fruit. Rale. 〉 Joe.

Wighiggin, a bill or writing, *aouixigan*, "*Livre, lettre, peinture, ecriture.*" Rale. 〉 Ind'n of carry.

Sebamook, Large-bay Lake, *Peqouasebem*; add *ar* for plural, *lac* or *étang*. Rale. *Ouañrinañgamek, anse dans un lac*. Rale. *Mspame*, large water. Polis. 〉 Nicholai.

Sebago and *Sebec*, large open water.

Chesuncook, place where many streams empty in. (v. Willis and Potter.)

Caucomgomoc, Gull Lake. (*Caucomgomoc*, the lake; *caucomgomoc-took*, the river, Polis.) 〉 Tahmunt, &c.

Pammadumcook.

Kenduskieg, Little Eel River. (v. Willis.) 〉 Nicholai.

Penobscot, Rocky River. *Puapeskou*, stone. (Rale v. Springer.) 〉 Ind'n of carry.

Umbazookskus, meadow stream. (Much-meadow river, Polis.)

Millinocket, place of Islands. 〉 Nicholai.

Souneunk, that runs between Mountains.

Aboljacarmegus, Smooth-ledge Falls and Deadwater.

Aboljacarmeguscook, the river there.

Muskiticook, Dead Stream. (Indian of carry.) *Meskikou*, or *Meskikouikou*, a place where there is grass. (Rale.) *Muskéeticook*, Dead water. (Polis.)

Mattahumkeag, Sand-creek Pond.   } Nicholai.
Piscataquis, branch of a river.

Shecorways, sheldrakes.   } Polis.
Naramekechus, peetweet.
Medawisla, loon.

Orignal, Moosehead Lake. (Montresor.)

Chor-chor-que, usnea.
Adelungquamooktum, wood-thrush.
Bematinichtik, high land generally. (Mt. *Pema-*   } Polis
dené, Rale.)
Maquoxigil, bark of red osier, Indian tobacco.

Kineo, flint (Williamson; old Indian hunter).
(Hodge.)

Artoosoqu', phosphorescence.
Subekoondark, white spruce.
Skusk, black spruce.
Beskabekuk, the "Lobster Lake" of maps.
Beskabekuk shishtook, the dead water below the
island.   } Polis.
Paytaytequick, Burnt-Ground Stream, what Joe
called *Ragmuff*.
Nonlangyis, the name of a dead-water between
the last and Pine Stream.
Karsaootuk, Black River (or Pine Stream). *Mka-*
zéouighen, black. Rale.

Michigan, *fimus*. Polis applied it to a sucker,
or a poor, good-for-nothing fish. *Fiante* (?)
mitsegan, Rale. (Pickering puts the ? after the
first word.)
Cowosnebagosar, *Chiogenes hispidula*, means,
grows where trees have rotted.
Pockadunkquaywayle, echo. *Pagadañkoueouérré*.
Rale.   } Polis.
Bososquasis, moose-fly.
Nerlumskeechtcook (or *quoik*?), (or *skeetcook*),
Dead water, and applied to the mountains near.
Apmoojenegamook, lake that is crossed.
Allegash, hemlock-bark. (v. Willis.)
Paytaywecongomec, Burnt-Ground Lake, *Telos*.

Madunkehunk, Height-of-land Stream (Webster Stream).

Madunkehunk-gamooc, Height-of-land Lake.

Matungamooc, Grand Lake.

Uncardnerheese, Trout Stream.

Wassataquoik (or -*cook*), Salmon River, East Branch. (v. Willis.)

Pemoymenuk, Amelanchier berries, "*Pemoua-imin*, *nak*, a black fruit. Rale." Has it not here the plural ending?

Sheepnoc, *Lilium Canadense* bulbs. "*Sipen*, *nak*, white, larger than *penak*." Rale.

Paytgumkiss, Petticoat (where a small river comes into the Penobscot below Nickatow).

Burntibus, a lake-like reach in the Penobscot.

Polis.

Passadumkeag, "where the water falls into the Penobscot above the falls." (Williamson.) *Pañsidañkioui* is, *au dessus de la montagne*. Rale.

Olarmon, or *larmon*, (Polis) red paint. "Vermilion, paint, *Ouramañ*." Rale.

Sunkhaze, "See canoe come out; no see 'em stream." (Polis.) The mouth of a river, according to Rale, is *Saüghe-détegoue*. The place where one stream empties into another, thus ♂, is *sañktaüoui*. (v. Willis.)

Tomhegan Br. (at Moosehead). "*Hatchet*, *temahigan*." Rale.

Nickatow, "*Nicketaoutegué*, or *Niketoutegoue*, *rivière qui fourche*." Rale.

2. From WILLIAM WILLIS, on the Language of the Abnaquies. Maine Hist. Coll., Vol. IV.

Abalajako-megus (river near Ktaadn).

Aitteon (name of a pond and sachem).

Apmogenegamook (name of a lake).

Allagash (a bark camp). Sockbasin, a Penobscot, told him, "The Indians gave this name to the lake from the fact of their keeping a hunting-camp there."

Bamonewengamock, head of Allagash, Cross Lake. (Sockbasin.)

Chesuncook, Big Lake. (Sockbasin.)

Caucongamock (a lake).

Ebeeme, mountains that have plums on them. (Sockbasin.)

Ktaadn. Sockbasin pronounces this Ka-tah-din, and said it meant "large mountain or large thing."

Kenduskeag (the place of Eels).

Kineo (flint), mountain on the border, &c.

Metawamkeag, a river with a smooth gravelly bottom. (Sockbasin.)

Metanawcook.

Millinoket, a lake with many islands in it. (Sockbasin.)

Matakeunk (river).

Molunkus (river).

Nicketow, Neccotoh, where two streams meet ("Forks of the Penobscot").

Negas (Indian village on the Kenduskeag).

Orignal (Montresor's name for Moosehead Lake).

Ponguongamook, Allagash, name of a Mohawk Indian killed there. (Sockbasin.)

Penobscot, *Penobskeag*, French *Pentagoet*, &c.

Pougohwaken (Heron Lake).

Pemadumcook (lake).

Passadumkeag, where water goes into the river above falls. (Williamson.)

Ripogenus (river).

Sunkhaze (river), Dead water.

Souneunk.

Seboomook. Sockbasin says this word means "the shape of a Moose's head, and was given to the lake," &c. *Howard* says differently.

Seboois, a brook, a small river. (Sockbasin.)

Sebec (river).

Sebago (great water).

Telos (lake).

Telasinis (lake).

Umbagog (lake), doubled up; so called from its form. (Sockbasin.)

Umbazookskus (lake).

Wassatiquoik, a mountain river. (Sockbasin.)

Judge C. E. Potter of Manchester, New Hampshire, adds in November, 1855:—

"*Chesuncook*. This is formed from *Chesunk*, or *Sehunk* (a goose), and *Auke* (a place), and means 'The Goose Place.' Chesunk, or Sehunk, is the sound made by the wild geese when flying."

Ktaadn. This is doubtless a corruption of *Kees* (high), and *Auke* (a place).

Penobscot, *Penapse* (stone, rock-place), and *Auke* (place).

Suncook, Goose-place, *Sehunk-auke*.

The Judge says that *schoot* means to rush, and hence *schoodic* from this and *auke* (a place where water rushes), and that *schoon* means the same; and that the Marblehead people and others have derived the words *scoon* and *scoot* from the Indians, and hence schooner; refers to a Mr. Chute.

THE END.

CAPE COD

Principium erit mirari omnia, etiam tritissima,
Medium est calamo committere visa et utilia,
Finis erit naturam adcuratius adlineare,
   quam alius [si possumus].

                    Linnæus de Peregrinatione.

Contents

I

The Shipwreck

WISHING TO get a better view than I had yet had of the ocean, which, we are told, covers more than two thirds of the globe, but of which a man who lives a few miles inland may never see any trace, more than of another world, I made a visit to Cape Cod in October, 1849, another the succeeding June, and another to Truro in July, 1855; the first and last time with a single companion, the second time alone. I have spent, in all, about three weeks on the Cape; walked from Eastham to Provincetown twice on the Atlantic side, and once on the Bay side also, excepting four or five miles, and crossed the Cape half a dozen times on my way; but having come so fresh to the sea, I have got but little salted. My readers must expect only so much saltness as the land breeze acquires from blowing over an arm of the sea, or is tasted on the windows and the bark of trees twenty miles inland, after September gales. I have been accustomed to make excursions to the ponds within ten miles of Concord, but latterly I have extended my excursions to the sea-shore.

I did not see why I might not make a book on Cape Cod, as well as my neighbor on "Human Culture." It is but another name for the same thing, and hardly a sandier phase of it. As for my title, I suppose that the word Cape is from the French *cap*; which is from the Latin *caput*, a head; which is, perhaps, from the verb *capere*, to take,—that being the part by which we take hold of a thing:—Take Time by the forelock. It is also the safest part to take a serpent by. And as for Cod, that was derived directly from that "great store of codfish" which Captain Bartholomew Gosnold caught there in 1602; which fish appears to have been so called from the Saxon word *codde*, "a case in which seeds are lodged," either from the form of the fish, or the quantity of spawn it contains; whence also, perhaps, *codling* (*"pomum coctile"*?) and coddle,—to cook green like peas. (V. Dic.)

Cape Cod is the bared and bended arm of Massachusetts: the shoulder is at Buzzard's Bay; the elbow, or crazy-bone, at

Cape Mallebarre; the wrist at Truro; and the sandy fist at
Provincetown,—behind which the State stands on her guard,
with her back to the Green Mountains, and her feet planted
on the floor of the ocean, like an athlete protecting her
Bay,—boxing with northeast storms, and, ever and anon,
heaving up her Atlantic adversary from the lap of earth,—
ready to thrust forward her other fist, which keeps guard the
while upon her breast at Cape Ann.

On studying the map, I saw that there must be an uninterrupted beach on the east or outside of the fore-arm of the
Cape, more than thirty miles from the general line of the
coast, which would afford a good sea view, but that, on account of an opening in the beach, forming the entrance to
Nauset Harbor, in Orleans, I must strike it in Eastham, if I
approached it by land, and probably I could walk thence
straight to Race Point, about twenty-eight miles, and not
meet with any obstruction.

We left Concord, Massachusetts, on Tuesday, October 9th,
1849. On reaching Boston, we found that the Provincetown
steamer, which should have got in the day before, had not yet
arrived, on account of a violent storm; and, as we noticed in
the streets a handbill headed, "Death! one hundred and forty-
five lives lost at Cohasset," we decided to go by way of Cohasset. We found many Irish in the cars, going to identify bodies
and to sympathize with the survivors, and also to attend the
funeral which was to take place in the afternoon;—and when
we arrived at Cohasset, it appeared that nearly all the passengers were bound for the beach, which was about a mile distant, and many other persons were flocking in from the
neighboring country. There were several hundreds of them
streaming off over Cohasset common in that direction, some
on foot and some in wagons,—and among them were some
sportsmen in their hunting-jackets, with their guns, and
game-bags, and dogs. As we passed the graveyard we saw a
large hole, like a cellar, freshly dug there, and, just before
reaching the shore, by a pleasantly winding and rocky road,
we met several hay-riggings and farm-wagons coming away
toward the meeting-house, each loaded with three large,
rough deal boxes. We did not need to ask what was in them.
The owners of the wagons were made the undertakers. Many

horses in carriages were fastened to the fences near the shore, and, for a mile or more, up and down, the beach was covered with people looking out for bodies, and examining the fragments of the wreck. There was a small island called Brook Island, with a hut on it, lying just off the shore. This is said to be the rockiest shore in Massachusetts, from Nantasket to Scituate,—hard sienitic rocks, which the waves have laid bare, but have not been able to crumble. It has been the scene of many a shipwreck.

The brig St. John, from Galway, Ireland, laden with emigrants, was wrecked on Sunday morning; it was now Tuesday morning, and the sea was still breaking violently on the rocks. There were eighteen or twenty of the same large boxes that I have mentioned, lying on a green hill-side, a few rods from the water, and surrounded by a crowd. The bodies which had been recovered, twenty-seven or eight in all, had been collected there. Some were rapidly nailing down the lids, others were carting the boxes away, and others were lifting the lids, which were yet loose, and peeping under the cloths, for each body, with such rags as still adhered to it, was covered loosely with a white sheet. I witnessed no signs of grief, but there was a sober despatch of business which was affecting. One man was seeking to identify a particular body, and one undertaker or carpenter was calling to another to know in what box a certain child was put. I saw many marble feet and matted heads as the cloths were raised, and one livid, swollen, and mangled body of a drowned girl,—who probably had intended to go out to service in some American family,—to which some rags still adhered, with a string, half concealed by the flesh, about its swollen neck; the coiled-up wreck of a human hulk, gashed by the rocks or fishes, so that the bone and muscle were exposed, but quite bloodless,—merely red and white,—with wide-open and staring eyes, yet lustreless, dead-lights; or like the cabin windows of a stranded vessel, filled with sand. Sometimes there were two or more children, or a parent and child, in the same box, and on the lid would perhaps be written with red chalk, "Bridget such-a-one, and sister's child." The surrounding sward was covered with bits of sails and clothing. I have since heard, from one who lives by this beach, that a woman who had come over before, but had left her infant behind for her sister to bring, came and looked into these boxes, and saw in one,—probably the same whose superscription I have quoted,—her child in her sister's arms, as if the sister had meant to be found thus; and within three days after, the mother died from the effect of that sight.

We turned from this and walked along the rocky shore. In the first cove were strewn what seemed the fragments of a vessel, in small pieces mixed with sand and sea-weed, and great quantities of feathers; but it looked so old and rusty, that I at first took it to be some old wreck which had lain there many years. I even thought of Captain Kidd, and that the feathers were those which sea-fowl had cast there; and perhaps there might be some tradition about it in the neighborhood. I asked a sailor if that was the St. John. He said it was. I asked him where she struck. He pointed to a rock in front of us, a mile from the shore, called the Grampus Rock, and added:—

"You can see a part of her now sticking up; it looks like a small boat."

I saw it. It was thought to be held by the chain-cables and the anchors. I asked if the bodies which I saw were all that were drowned.

"Not a quarter of them," said he.

"Where are the rest?"

"Most of them right underneath that piece you see."

It appeared to us that there was enough rubbish to make the wreck of a large vessel in this cove alone, and that it would take many days to cart it off. It was several feet deep, and here and there was a bonnet or a jacket on it. In the very midst of the crowd about this wreck, there were men with carts busily collecting the sea-weed which the storm had cast up, and conveying it beyond the reach of the tide, though they were often obliged to separate fragments of clothing from it, and they might at any moment have found a human body under it. Drown who might, they did not forget that this weed was a valuable manure. This shipwreck had not produced a visible vibration in the fabric of society.

About a mile south we could see, rising above the rocks, the masts of the British brig which the St. John had endeavored to follow, which had slipped her cables, and, by good luck, run into the mouth of Cohasset Harbor. A little further along the shore we saw a man's clothes on a rock; further, a woman's scarf, a gown, a straw bonnet, the brig's caboose, and one of her masts high and dry, broken into several pieces. In another rocky cove, several rods from the water, and behind rocks twenty feet high, lay a part of one side of the vessel, still hanging together. It was, perhaps, forty feet long, by fourteen wide. I was even more surprised at the power of the waves, exhibited on this shattered fragment, than I had been at the sight of the smaller fragments before. The largest timbers and iron braces were broken superfluously, and I saw that no material could withstand the power of the waves; that iron must go to pieces in such a case, and an iron vessel would be cracked up like an egg-shell on the rocks. Some of these timbers, however, were so rotten that I could almost thrust my umbrella through them. They told us that some were saved on this piece, and also showed where the sea had heaved it into this cove, which was now dry. When I saw where it had come in, and in what condition, I wondered that any had been saved on it. A little further on a crowd of men was collected around the mate of the St. John, who was telling his story. He was a slim-looking youth, who spoke of the captain as the master, and seemed a little excited. He was saying that when they jumped into the boat, she filled, and, the vessel lurching, the weight of the water in the boat caused the painter to break, and so they were separated. Whereat one man came away, saying:—

"Well, I do n't see but he tells a straight story enough. You see, the weight of the water in the boat broke the painter. A boat full of water is very heavy,"—and so on, in a loud and impertinently earnest tone, as if he had a bet depending on it, but had no humane interest in the matter.

Another, a large man, stood near by upon a rock, gazing into the sea, and chewing large quids of tobacco, as if that habit were forever confirmed with him.

"Come," says another to his companion, "let 's be off. We 've seen the whole of it. It 's no use to stay to the funeral."

Further, we saw one standing upon a rock, who, we were told, was one that was saved. He was a sober-looking man, dressed in a jacket and gray pantaloons, with his hands in the pockets. I asked him a few questions, which he answered; but he seemed unwilling to talk about it, and soon walked away. By his side stood one of the life-boat men, in an oil-cloth jacket, who told us how they went to the relief of the British brig, thinking that the boat of the St. John, which they passed on the way, held all her crew,—for the waves prevented their seeing those who were on the vessel, though they might have saved some had they known there were any there. A little further was the flag of the St. John spread on a rock to dry, and held down by stones at the corners. This frail, but essential and significant portion of the vessel, which had so long been the sport of the winds, was sure to reach the shore. There were one or two houses visible from these rocks, in which were some of the survivors recovering from the shock which their bodies and minds had sustained. One was not expected to live.

We kept on down the shore as far as a promontory called Whitehead, that we might see more of the Cohasset Rocks. In a little cove, within half a mile, there were an old man and his son collecting, with their team, the sea-weed which that fatal storm had cast up, as serenely employed as if there had never been a wreck in the world, though they were within sight of the Grampus Rock, on which the St. John had struck. The old man had heard that there was a wreck, and knew most of the particulars, but he said that he had not been up there since it happened. It was the wrecked weed that concerned him most, rock-weed, kelp, and sea-weed, as he named them, which he carted to his barn-yard; and those bodies were to him but other weeds which the tide cast up, but which were of no use to him. We afterwards came to the life-boat in its harbor, waiting for another emergency,—and in the afternoon we saw the funeral procession at a distance, at the head of which walked the captain with the other survivors.

On the whole, it was not so impressive a scene as I might have expected. If I had found one body cast upon the beach in some lonely place, it would have affected me more. I sympathized rather with the winds and waves, as if to toss and mangle these poor human bodies was the order of the day. If this was the law of Nature, why waste any time in awe or pity? If the last day were come, we should not think so much about the separation of friends or the blighted prospects of individuals. I saw that corpses might be multiplied, as on the field of battle, till they no longer affected us in any degree, as exceptions to the common lot of humanity. Take all the grave-yards together, they are always the majority. It is the individ-ual and private that demands our sympathy. A man can attend but one funeral in the course of his life, can behold but one corpse. Yet I saw that the inhabitants of the shore would be not a little affected by this event. They would watch there many days and nights for the sea to give up its dead, and their imaginations and sympathies would supply the place of mourners far away, who as yet knew not of the wreck. Many days after this, something white was seen floating on the wa-ter by one who was sauntering on the beach. It was ap-proached in a boat, and found to be the body of a woman, which had risen in an upright position, whose white cap was blown back with the wind. I saw that the beauty of the shore itself was wrecked for many a lonely walker there, until he could perceive, at last, how its beauty was enhanced by wrecks like this, and it acquired thus a rarer and sublimer beauty still.

Why care for these dead bodies? They really have no friends but the worms or fishes. Their owners were coming to the New World, as Columbus and the Pilgrims did,—they were within a mile of its shores; but, before they could reach it, they emigrated to a newer world than ever Columbus dreamed of, yet one of whose existence we believe that there is far more universal and convincing evidence—though it has not yet been discovered by science—than Columbus had of this; not merely mariners' tales and some paltry drift-wood and sea-weed, but a continual drift and instinct to all our shores. I saw their empty hulks that came to land; but they themselves, meanwhile, were cast upon some shore yet fur-ther west, toward which we are all tending, and which we shall reach at last, it may be through storm and darkness, as they did. No doubt, we have reason to thank God that they have not been "shipwrecked into life again." The mariner who makes the safest port in Heaven, perchance, seems to his friends on earth to be shipwrecked, for they deem Boston Harbor the better place; though perhaps invisible to them, a skilful pilot comes to meet him, and the fairest and balmiest gales blow off that coast, his good ship makes the land in halcyon days, and he kisses the shore in rapture there, while his old hulk tosses in the surf here. It is hard to part with one's body, but, no doubt, it is easy enough to do without it when once it is gone. All their plans and hopes burst like a bubble! Infants by the score dashed on the rocks by the enraged Atlantic Ocean! No, no! If the St. John did not make her port here, she has been telegraphed there. The strongest wind cannot stagger a Spirit; it is a Spirit's breath. A just man's purpose cannot be split on any Grampus or material rock, but itself will split rocks till it succeeds.

The verses addressed to Columbus, dying, may, with slight alterations, be applied to the passengers of the St. John:—

> "Soon with them will all be over,
> Soon the voyage will be begun
> That shall bear them to discover,
> Far away, a land unknown.

> "Land that each, alone, must visit,
> But no tidings bring to men;
> For no sailor, once departed,
> Ever hath returned again.

> "No carved wood, no broken branches,
> Ever drift from that far wild;
> He who on that ocean launches
> Meets no corse of angel child.

> "Undismayed, my noble sailors,
> Spread, then spread your canvas out;
> Spirits! on a sea of ether
> Soon shall ye serenely float!

> "Where the deep no plummet soundeth,
> Fear no hidden breakers there,
> And the fanning wing of angels
> Shall your bark right onward bear.

> "Quit, now, full of heart and comfort,
> These rude shores, they are of earth;
> Where the rosy clouds are parting,
> There the blessed isles loom forth."

One summer day, since this, I came this way, on foot, along the shore from Boston. It was so warm, that some horses had climbed to the very top of the ramparts of the old fort at Hull, where there was hardly room to turn round, for the sake of the breeze. The *Datura stramonium*, or thorn-apple, was in full bloom along the beach; and, at sight of this cosmopolite,—this Captain Cook among plants,—carried in ballast all over the world, I felt as if I were on the highway of nations. Say, rather, this Viking, king of the Bays, for it is not an innocent plant; it suggests not merely commerce, but its attendant vices, as if its fibres were the stuff of which pirates spin their yarns. I heard the voices of men shouting aboard a vessel, half a mile from the shore, which sounded as if they were in a barn in the country, they being between the sails. It was a purely rural sound. As I looked over the water, I saw the isles rapidly wasting away, the sea nibbling voraciously at the continent, the springing arch of a hill suddenly interrupted, as at Point Alderton,—what botanists might call premorse,—showing, by its curve against the sky, how much space it must have occupied, where now was water only. On the other hand, these wrecks of isles were being fancifully arranged into new shores, as at Hog Island, inside of Hull, where everything seemed to be gently lapsing into futurity. This isle had got the very form of a ripple,—and I thought that the inhabitants should bear a ripple for device on their shields, a wave passing over them, with the *datura*, which is said to produce mental alienation of long duration without affecting the bodily health,* springing from its edge. The most interesting thing which I heard of, in this township of Hull, was an unfailing spring, whose locality was pointed out to me, on the side of a distant hill, as I was panting along the shore, though I did not visit it. Perhaps, if I should go through Rome, it would be some spring on the Capitoline

---

*The Jamestown weed (or thorn-apple). "This, being an early plant, was gathered very young for a boiled salad, by some of the soldiers sent thither [i. e. to Virginia] to quell the rebellion of Bacon; and some of them ate plentifully of it, the effect of which was a very pleasant comedy, for they turned natural fools upon it for several days: one would blow up a feather in the air; another would dart straws at it with much fury; and another, stark naked, was sitting up in a corner like a monkey, grinning and making mows

Hill I should remember the longest. It is true, I was some-what interested in the well at the old French fort, which was said to be ninety feet deep, with a cannon at the bottom of it. On Nantasket beach I counted a dozen chaises from the public-house. From time to time the riders turned their horses toward the sea, standing in the water for the cool-ness,—and I saw the value of beaches to cities for the sea breeze and the bath.

At Jerusalem village the inhabitants were collecting in haste, before a thunder-shower now approaching, the Irish moss which they had spread to dry. The shower passed on one side, and gave me a few drops only, which did not cool the air. I merely felt a puff upon my cheek, though, within sight, a vessel was capsized in the bay, and several others dragged their anchors, and were near going ashore. The sea-bathing at Cohasset Rocks was perfect. The water was purer and more transparent than any I had ever seen. There was not a particle of mud or slime about it. The bottom being sandy, I could see the sea-perch swimming about. The smooth and fantastically worn rocks, and the perfectly clean and tress-like rock-weeds falling over you, and attached so firmly to the rocks that you could pull yourself up by them, greatly en-hanced the luxury of the bath. The stripe of barnacles just above the weeds reminded me of some vegetable growth,— the buds, and petals, and seed-vessels of flowers. They lay along the seams of the rock like buttons on a waistcoat. It was one of the hottest days in the year, yet I found the water so icy cold that I could swim but a stroke or two, and thought that, in case of shipwreck, there would be more dan-ger of being chilled to death than simply drowned. One im-mersion was enough to make you forget the dog-days utterly.

---

at them; a fourth would fondly kiss and paw his companions, and sneer in their faces, with a countenance more antic than any in a Dutch droll. In this frantic condition they were confined, lest they should, in their folly, destroy themselves,—though it was observed that all their actions were full of inno-cence and good nature. Indeed, they were not very cleanly. A thousand such simple tricks they played, and after eleven days returned to themselves again, not remembering anything that had passed."—Beverly's *History of Virginia*, p. 120.

Though you were sweltering before, it will take you half an hour now to remember that it was ever warm. There were the tawny rocks, like lions couchant, defying the ocean, whose waves incessantly dashed against and scoured them with vast quantities of gravel. The water held in their little hollows, on the receding of the tide, was so crystalline that I could not believe it salt, but wished to drink it; and higher up were basins of fresh water left by the rain,—all which, being also of different depths and temperature, were convenient for different kinds of baths. Also, the larger hollows in the smoothed rocks formed the most convenient of seats and dressing-rooms. In these respects it was the most perfect sea-shore that I had seen.

I saw in Cohasset, separated from the sea only by a narrow beach, a handsome but shallow lake of some four hundred acres, which, I was told, the sea had tossed over the beach in a great storm in the spring, and, after the alewives had passed into it, it had stopped up its outlet, and now the alewives were dying by thousands, and the inhabitants were apprehending a pestilence as the water evaporated. It had five rocky islets in it.

This rocky shore is called Pleasant Cove, on some maps; on the map of Cohasset, that name appears to be confined to the particular cove where I saw the wreck of the St. John. The ocean did not look, now, as if any were ever shipwrecked in it; it was not grand and sublime, but beautiful as a lake. Not a vestige of a wreck was visible, nor could I believe that the bones of many a shipwrecked man were buried in that pure sand. But to go on with our first excursion.

II

Stage-coach Views

A FTER SPENDING the night in Bridgewater, and picking up a few arrow-heads there in the morning, we took the cars for Sandwich, where we arrived before noon. This was the terminus of the "Cape Cod Railroad," though it is but the beginning of the Cape. As it rained hard, with driving mists, and there was no sign of its holding up, we here took that almost obsolete conveyance, the stage, for "as far as it went that day," as we told the driver. We had forgotten how far a stage could go in a day, but we were told that the Cape roads were very "heavy," though they added that, being of sand, the rain would improve them. This coach was an exceedingly narrow one, but as there was a slight spherical excess over two on a seat, the driver waited till nine passengers had got in, without taking the measure of any of them, and then shut the door after two or three ineffectual slams, as if the fault were all in the hinges or the latch,—while we timed our inspirations and expirations so as to assist him.

We were now fairly on the Cape, which extends from Sandwich eastward thirty-five miles, and thence north and northwest thirty more, in all sixty-five, and has an average breadth of about five miles. In the interior it rises to the height of two hundred, and sometimes perhaps three hundred feet above the level of the sea. According to Hitchcock, the geologist of the State, it is composed almost entirely of sand, even to the depth of three hundred feet in some places, though there is probably a concealed core of rock a little beneath the surface, and it is of diluvian origin, excepting a small portion at the extremity and elsewhere along the shores, which is alluvial. For the first half of the Cape large blocks of stone are found, here and there, mixed with the sand, but for the last thirty miles boulders, or even gravel, are rarely met with. Hitchcock conjectures that the ocean has, in course of time, eaten out Boston Harbor and other bays in the mainland, and that the minute fragments have been deposited by the currents at a distance from the shore, and formed this sand-bank. Above the sand, if the surface is subjected to agricultural tests, there is found to be a thin layer of soil gradually diminishing from Barnstable to Truro, where it ceases; but there are many holes and rents in this weather-beaten garment not likely to be stitched in time, which reveal the naked flesh of the Cape, and its extremity is completely bare.

I at once got out my book, the eighth volume of the Collections of the Massachusetts Historical Society, printed in 1802, which contains some short notices of the Cape towns, and began to read up to where I was, for in the cars I could not read as fast as I travelled. To those who came from the side of Plymouth, it said: "After riding through a body of woods, twelve miles in extent, interspersed with but few houses, the settlement of Sandwich appears, with a more agreeable effect, to the eye of the traveller." Another writer speaks of this as a beautiful village. But I think that our villages will bear to be contrasted only with one another, not with Nature. I have no great respect for the writer's taste, who talks easily about *beautiful* villages, embellished, perchance, with a "fulling-mill," "a handsome academy," or meeting-house, and "a number of shops for the different mechanic arts"; where the green and white houses of the gentry, drawn up in rows, front on a street of which it would be difficult to tell whether it is most like a desert or a long stable-yard. Such spots can be beautiful only to the weary traveller, or the returning native,—or, perchance, the repentant misanthrope; not to him who, with unprejudiced senses, has just come out of the woods, and approaches one of them, by a bare road, through a succession of straggling homesteads where he cannot tell which is the alms-house. However, as for Sandwich, I cannot speak particularly. Ours was but half a Sandwich at most, and that must have fallen on the buttered side some time. I only saw that it was a closely-built town for a small one, with glass-works to improve its sand, and narrow streets in which we turned round and round till we could not tell which way we were going, and the rain came in, first on this side, and then on that, and I saw that they in the houses were more comfortable than we in the coach. My book also said of this town, "The inhabitants, in general, are substantial livers,"—that is, I suppose, they do not live like philosophers;

but, as the stage did not stop long enough for us to dine, we had no opportunity to test the truth of this statement. It may have referred, however, to the quantity "of oil they would yield." It further said, "The inhabitants of Sandwich generally manifest a fond and steady adherence to the manners, employments, and modes of living which characterized their fathers"; which made me think that they were, after all, very much like all the rest of the world;—and it added that this was "a resemblance, which, at this day, will constitute no impeachment of either their virtue or taste"; which remark proves to me that the writer was one with the rest of them. No people ever lived by cursing their fathers, however great a curse their fathers might have been to them. But it must be confessed that ours was old authority, and probably they have changed all that now.

Our route was along the Bay side, through Barnstable, Yarmouth, Dennis, and Brewster, to Orleans, with a range of low hills on our right, running down the Cape. The weather was not favorable for wayside views, but we made the most of such glimpses of land and water as we could get through the rain. The country was, for the most part, bare, or with only a little scrubby wood left on the hills. We noticed in Yarmouth—and, if I do not mistake, in Dennis—large tracts where pitch-pines were planted four or five years before. They were in rows, as they appeared when we were abreast of them, and, excepting that there were extensive vacant spaces, seemed to be doing remarkably well. This, we were told, was the only use to which such tracts could be profitably put. Every higher eminence had a pole set up on it, with an old storm-coat or sail tied to it, for a signal, that those on the south side of the Cape, for instance, might know when the Boston packets had arrived on the north. It appeared as if this use must absorb the greater part of the old clothes of the Cape, leaving but few rags for the peddlers. The wind-mills on the hills,—large weather-stained octagonal structures,—and the salt-works scattered all along the shore, with their long rows of vats resting on piles driven into the marsh, their low, turtle-like roofs, and their slighter wind-mills, were novel and interesting objects to an inlander. The sand by the roadside was partially covered with bunches of a moss-like plant,

Hudsonia tomentosa, which a woman in the stage told us was called "poverty grass," because it grew where nothing else would.

I was struck by the pleasant equality which reigned among the stage company, and their broad and invulnerable good humor. They were what is called free and easy, and met one another to advantage, as men who had, at length, learned how to live. They appeared to know each other when they were strangers, they were so simple and downright. They were well met, in an unusual sense, that is, they met as well as they could meet, and did not seem to be troubled with any impediment. They were not afraid nor ashamed of one another, but were contented to make just such a company as the ingredients allowed. It was evident that the same foolish respect was not here claimed, for mere wealth and station, that is in many parts of New England; yet some of them were the "first people," as they are called, of the various towns through which we passed. Retired sea-captains, in easy circumstances, who talked of farming as sea-captains are wont; an erect, respectable, and trustworthy-looking man, in his wrapper, some of the salt of the earth, who had formerly been the salt of the sea; or a more courtly gentleman, who, perchance, had been a representative to the General Court in his day; or a broad, red-faced Cape Cod man, who had seen too many storms to be easily irritated; or a fisherman's wife, who had been waiting a week for a coaster to leave Boston, and had at length come by the cars.

A strict regard for truth obliges us to say, that the few women whom we saw that day looked exceedingly pinched up. They had prominent chins and noses, having lost all their teeth, and a sharp *W* would represent their profile. They were not so well preserved as their husbands; or perchance they were well preserved as dried specimens. (Their husbands, however, were pickled.) But we respect them not the less for all that; our own dental system is far from perfect.

Still we kept on in the rain, or, if we stopped, it was commonly at a post-office, and we thought that writing letters, and sorting them against our arrival, must be the principal employment of the inhabitants of the Cape, this rainy day. The Post-office appeared a singularly domestic institution here. Ever and anon the stage stopped before some low shop or dwelling, and a wheelwright or shoemaker appeared in his shirt sleeves and leather apron, with spectacles newly donned, holding up Uncle Sam's bag, as if it were a slice of home-made cake, for the travellers, while he retailed some piece of gossip to the driver, really as indifferent to the presence of the former as if they were so much baggage. In one instance, we understood that a woman was the post-mistress, and they said that she made the best one on the road; but we suspected that the letters must be subjected to a very close scrutiny there. While we were stopping, for this purpose, at Dennis, we ventured to put our heads out of the windows, to see where we were going, and saw rising before us, through the mist, singular barren hills, all stricken with poverty-grass, looming up as if they were in the horizon, though they were close to us, and we seemed to have got to the end of the land on that side, notwithstanding that the horses were still headed that way. Indeed, that part of Dennis which we saw was an exceedingly barren and desolate country, of a character which I can find no name for; such a surface, perhaps, as the bottom of the sea made dry land day before yesterday. It was covered with poverty-grass, and there was hardly a tree in sight, but here and there a little weather-stained, one-storied house, with a red roof,—for often the roof was painted, though the rest of the house was not,—standing bleak and cheerless, yet with a broad foundation to the land, where the comfort must have been all inside. Yet we read in the Gazetteer—for we carried that too with us—that, in 1837, one hundred and fifty masters of vessels, belonging to this town, sailed from the various ports of the Union. There must be many more houses in the south part of the town, else we cannot imagine where they all lodge when they are at home, if ever they are there; but the truth is, their houses are floating ones, and their home is on the ocean. There were almost no trees at all in this part of Dennis, nor could I learn that they talked of setting out any. It is true, there was a meeting-house, set round with Lombardy poplars, in a hollow square, the rows fully as straight as the studs of a building, and the corners as square; but, if I do not mistake, every one of them was dead. I could not help thinking that they needed a revival here. Our book said that, in 1795, there was erected in Dennis "an elegant meeting-house, with a steeple." Perhaps this was the one; though whether it had a steeple, or had died down so far from sympathy with the poplars, I do not remember. Another meeting-house in this town was described as a "neat building"; but of the meeting-house in Chatham, a neighboring town, for there was then but one, nothing is said, except that it "is in good repair,"—both which remarks, I trust, may be understood as applying to the churches spiritual as well as material. However, "elegant meeting-houses," from that Trinity one on Broadway, to this at Nobscusset, in my estimation, belong to the same category with "beautiful villages." I was never in season to see one. Handsome is that handsome does. What they did for shade here, in warm weather, we did not know, though we read that "fogs are more frequent in Chatham than in any other part of the country; and they serve in summer, instead of trees, to shelter the houses against the heat of the sun. To those who delight in extensive vision,"—is it to be inferred that the inhabitants of Chatham do not?—"they are unpleasant, but they are not found to be unhealthful." Probably, also, the unobstructed sea-breeze answers the purpose of a fan. The historian of Chatham says further, that "in many families there is no difference between the breakfast and supper; cheese, cakes, and pies being as common at the one as at the other." But that leaves us still uncertain whether they were really common at either.

The road, which was quite hilly, here ran near the Bay-shore, having the Bay on one side, and "the rough hill of Scargo," said to be the highest land on the Cape, on the other. Of the wide prospect of the Bay afforded by the summit of this hill, our guide says: "The view has not much of the beautiful in it, but it communicates a strong emotion of the sublime." That is the kind of communication which we love to have made to us. We passed through the village of Suet, in Dennis, on Suet and Quivet Necks, of which it is said, " when compared with Nobscusset,"—we had a misty recollection of having passed through, or near to, the latter,—"it may be denominated a pleasant village; but, in comparison with the village of Sandwich, there is little or no beauty in it." However, we liked Dennis well, better than any town we had seen on the Cape, it was so novel, and, in that stormy day, so sublimely dreary.

Captain John Sears, of Suet, was the first person in this country who obtained pure marine salt by solar evaporation alone; though it had long been made in a similar way on the coast of France, and elsewhere. This was in the year 1776, at which time, on account of the war, salt was scarce and dear. The Historical Collections contain an interesting account of his experiments, which we read when we first saw the roofs of the salt-works. Barnstable county is the most favorable locality for these works on our northern coast,—there is so little fresh water here emptying into ocean. Quite recently there were about two millions of dollars invested in this business here. But now the Cape is unable to compete with the importers of salt and the manufacturers of it at the West, and, accordingly, her salt-works are fast going to decay. From making salt, they turn to fishing more than ever. The Gazetteer will uniformly tell you, under the head of each town, how many go a-fishing, and the value of the fish and oil taken, how much salt is made and used, how many are engaged in the coasting trade, how many in manufacturing palm-leaf hats, leather, boots, shoes, and tinware, and then it has done, and leaves you to imagine the more truly domestic manufactures which are nearly the same all the world over.

Late in the afternoon, we rode through Brewster, so named after Elder Brewster, for fear he would be forgotten else. Who has not heard of Elder Brewster? Who knows who he was? This appeared to be the modern-built town of the Cape, the favorite residence of retired sea-captains. It is said that "there are more masters and mates of vessels which sail on foreign voyages belonging to this place than to any other town in the country." There were many of the modern American houses here, such as they turn out at Cambridgeport, standing on the sand; you could almost swear that they had been floated down Charles River, and drifted across the bay. I call them American, because they are paid for by Americans, and "put up" by American carpenters; but they are little removed from lumber; only Eastern stuff disguised with white paint, the least interesting kind of drift-wood to me. Perhaps we have reason to be proud of our naval architecture, and need not go to the Greeks, or the Goths, or the Italians, for the models of our vessels. Sea-captains do not employ a Cambridgeport carpenter to build their floating houses, and for their houses on shore, if they must copy any, it would be more agreeable to the imagination to see one of their vessels turned bottom upward, in the Numidian fashion. We read that, "at certain seasons, the reflection of the sun upon the windows of the houses in Wellfleet and Truro (across the inner side of the elbow of the Cape) is discernible with the naked eye, at a distance of eighteen miles and upward, on the county road." This we were pleased to imagine, as we had not seen the sun for twenty-four hours.

The same author (the Rev. John Simpkins) said of the inhabitants, a good while ago: "No persons appear to have a greater relish for the social circle and domestic pleasures. They are not in the habit of frequenting taverns, unless on public occasions. I know not of a proper idler or tavern-haunter in the place." This is more than can be said of my townsmen.

At length, we stopped for the night at Higgins's tavern, in Orleans, feeling very much as if we were on a sand-bar in the ocean, and not knowing whether we should see land or water ahead when the mist cleared away. We here overtook two Italian boys, who had waded thus far down the Cape through the sand, with their organs on their backs, and were going on to Provincetown. What a hard lot, we thought, if the Provincetown people should shut their doors against them! Whose yard would they go to next? Yet we concluded that they had chosen wisely to come here, where other music than that of the surf must be rare. Thus the great civilizer sends out its emissaries, sooner or later, to every sandy cape and lighthouse of the New World which the census-taker visits, and summons the savage there to surrender.

III

The Plains of Nauset

THE NEXT MORNING, Thursday, October 11th, it rained, as hard as ever; but we were determined to proceed on foot, nevertheless. We first made some inquiries with regard to the practicability of walking up the shore on the Atlantic side to Provincetown, whether we should meet with any creeks or marshes to trouble us. Higgins said that there was no obstruction, and that it was not much farther than by the road, but he thought that we should find it very "heavy" walking in the sand; it was bad enough in the road, a horse would sink in up to the fetlocks there. But there was one man at the tavern who had walked it, and he said that we could go very well, though it was sometimes inconvenient and even dangerous walking under the bank, when there was a great tide, with an easterly wind, which caused the sand to cave. For the first four or five miles we followed the road, which here turns to the north on the elbow,—the narrowest part of the Cape,—that we might clear an inlet from the ocean, a part of Nauset Harbor, in Orleans, on our right. We found the travelling good enough for walkers on the sides of the roads, though it was "heavy" for horses in the middle. We walked with our umbrellas behind us, since it blowed hard as well as rained, with driving mists, as the day before, and the wind helped us over the sand at a rapid rate. Everything indicated that we had reached a strange shore. The road was a mere lane, winding over bare swells of bleak and barren-looking land. The houses were few and far between, besides being small and rusty, though they appeared to be kept in good repair, and their door-yards, which were the unfenced Cape, were tidy; or, rather, they looked as if the ground around them was blown clean by the wind. Perhaps the scarcity of wood here, and the consequent absence of the wood-pile and other wooden traps, had something to do with this appearance. They seemed, like mariners ashore, to have sat right down to enjoy the firmness of the land, without studying their postures or habiliments. To them it was merely *terra firma* and *cognita*, not yet *fertilis* and *jucunda*. Every landscape which is dreary enough has a certain beauty to my eyes, and in this instance its permanent qualities were enhanced by the weather. Everything told of the sea, even when we did not see its waste or hear its roar. For birds there were gulls, and for carts in the fields, boats turned bottom upward against the houses, and sometimes the rib of a whale was woven into the fence by the road-side. The trees were, if possible, rarer than the houses, excepting apple-trees, of which there were a few small orchards in the hollows. These were either narrow and high, with flat tops, having lost their side branches, like huge plum-bushes growing in exposed situations, or else dwarfed and branching immediately at the ground, like quince-bushes. They suggested that, under like circumstances, all trees would at last acquire like habits of growth. I afterward saw on the Cape many full-grown apple-trees not higher than a man's head; one whole orchard, indeed, where all the fruit could have been gathered by a man standing on the ground; but you could hardly creep beneath the trees. Some, which the owners told me were twenty years old, were only three and a half feet high, spreading at six inches from the ground five feet each way, and being withal surrounded with boxes of tar to catch the canker-worms, they looked like plants in flower-pots, and as if they might be taken into the house in the winter. In another place, I saw some not much larger than currant-bushes; yet the owner told me that they had borne a barrel and a half of apples that fall. If they had been placed close together, I could have cleared them all at a jump. I measured some near the Highland Light in Truro, which had been taken from the shrubby woods thereabouts when young, and grafted. One, which had been set ten years, was on an average eighteen inches high, and spread nine feet with a flat top. It had borne one bushel of apples two years before. Another, probably twenty years old from the seed, was five feet high, and spread eighteen feet, branching, as usual, at the ground, so that you could not creep under it. This bore a barrel of apples two years before. The owner of these trees invariably used the personal pronoun in speaking of them; as, "I got *him* out of the woods, but *he* does n't bear." The largest that I saw in that neighborhood was nine feet high to the topmost leaf, and spread thirty-three feet, branching at the ground five ways.

In one yard I observed a single, very healthy-looking tree, while all the rest were dead or dying. The occupant said that his father had manured all but that one with blackfish.

This habit of growth should, no doubt, be encouraged; and they should not be trimmed up, as some travelling practitioners have advised. In 1802 there was not a single fruit-tree in Chatham, the next town to Orleans, on the south; and the old account of Orleans says: "Fruit-trees cannot be made to grow within a mile of the ocean. Even those which are placed at a greater distance are injured by the east winds; and, after violent storms in the spring, a saltish taste is perceptible on their bark." We noticed that they were often covered with a yellow lichen like rust, the *Parmelia parietina*.

The most foreign and picturesque structures on the Cape, to an inlander, not excepting the salt-works, are the wind-mills,—gray-looking octagonal towers, with long timbers slanting to the ground in the rear, and there resting on a cart-wheel, by which their fans are turned round to face the wind. These appeared also to serve in some measure for props against its force. A great circular rut was worn around the building by the wheel. The neighbors who assemble to turn the mill to the wind are likely to know which way it blows, without a weather-cock. They looked loose and slightly loco-motive, like huge wounded birds, trailing a wing or a leg, and reminded one of pictures of the Netherlands. Being on elevated ground, and high in themselves, they serve as land-marks,—for there are no tall trees, or other objects commonly, which can be seen at a distance in the horizon; though the outline of the land itself is so firm and distinct, that an insignificant cone, or even precipice of sand, is visible at a great distance from over the sea. Sailors making the land commonly steer either by the wind-mills or the meeting-houses. In the country, we are obliged to steer by the meeting-houses alone. Yet the meeting-house is a kind of windmill, which runs one day in seven, turned either by the winds of doctrine or public opinion, or more rarely by the winds of Heaven, where another sort of grist is ground, of which, if it be not all bran or musty, if it be not *plaster*, we trust to make bread of life.

There were, here and there, heaps of shells in the fields, where clams had been opened for bait; for Orleans is famous for its shell-fish, especially clams, or, as our author says, "to speak more properly, worms." The shores are more fertile than the dry land. The inhabitants measure their crops, not only by bushels of corn, but by barrels of clams. A thousand barrels of clam-bait are counted as equal in value to six or eight thousand bushels of Indian corn, and once they were procured without more labor or expense, and the supply was thought to be inexhaustible. "For," runs the history, "after a portion of the shore has been dug over, and almost all the clams taken up, at the end of two years, it is said, they are as plenty there as ever. It is even affirmed by many persons, that it is as necessary to stir the clam ground frequently as it is to hoe a field of potatoes; because, if this labor is omitted, the clams will be crowded too closely together, and will be prevented from increasing in size." But we were told that the small clam, *Mya arenaria*, was not so plenty here as formerly. Probably the clam-ground has been stirred too frequently, after all. Nevertheless, one man, who complained that they fed pigs with them and so made them scarce, told me that he dug and opened one hundred and twenty-six dollars' worth in one winter, in Truro.

We crossed a brook, not more than fourteen rods long, between Orleans and Eastham, called Jeremiah's Gutter. The Atlantic is said sometimes to meet the Bay here, and isolate the northern part of the Cape. The streams of the Cape are necessarily formed on a minute scale, since there is no room for them to run, without tumbling immediately into the sea; and beside, we found it difficult to run ourselves in that sand, when there was no want of room. Hence, the least channel where water runs, or may run, is important, and is dignified with a name. We read that there is no running water in Chatham, which is the next town. The barren aspect of the land would hardly be believed if described. It was such soil, or rather land, as, to judge from appearances, no farmer in the interior would think of cultivating, or even fencing. Generally, the ploughed fields of the Cape look white and yellow, like a mixture of salt and Indian meal. This is called soil. All an inlander's notions of soil and fertility will be confounded by a visit to these parts, and he will not be able, for some time afterward, to distinguish soil from sand. The historian of Chatham says of a part of that town, which has been gained from the sea: "There is a doubtful appearance of a soil beginning to be formed. It is styled *doubtful*, because it would not be observed by every eye, and perhaps not acknowledged by many." We thought that this would not be a bad description of the greater part of the Cape. There is a "beach" on the west side of Eastham, which we crossed the next summer, half a mile wide, and stretching across the township, containing seventeen hundred acres, on which there is not now a particle of vegetable mould, though it formerly produced wheat. All sands are here called "beaches," whether they are waves of water or of air, that dash against them, since they commonly have their origin on the shore. "The sand in some places," says the historian of Eastham, "lodging against the beach-grass, has been raised into hills fifty feet high, where twenty-five years ago no hills existed. In others it has filled up small valleys, and swamps. Where a strong rooted bush stood, the appearance is singular: a mass of earth and sand adheres to it, resembling a small tower. In several places, rocks, which were formerly covered with soil, are disclosed, and being lashed by the sand, driven against them by the wind, look as if they were recently dug from a quarry."

We were surprised to hear of the great crops of corn which are still raised in Eastham, notwithstanding the real and apparent barrenness. Our landlord in Orleans had told us that he raised three or four hundred bushels of corn annually, and also of the great number of pigs which he fattened. In Champlain's "Voyages," there is a plate representing the Indian cornfields hereabouts, with their wigwams in the midst, as they appeared in 1605, and it was here that the Pilgrims, to quote their own words, "bought eight or ten hogsheads of corn and beans" of the Nauset Indians, in 1622, to keep themselves from starving.* "In 1667 the town [of Eastham] voted that every housekeeper should kill twelve blackbirds or three crows, which did great damage to the corn; and this vote was repeated for many years." In 1695 an additional order was passed, namely, that "every unmarried man in the township shall kill six blackbirds, or three crows, while he remains single; as a penalty for not doing it, shall not be married until he obey this order." The blackbirds, however, still molest the corn. I saw them at it the next summer, and there were many scarecrows, if not scare-blackbirds, in the fields, which I often mistook for men. From which I concluded, that either many men were not married, or many blackbirds were. Yet they put but three or four kernels in a hill, and let fewer plants remain than we do. In the account of Eastham, in the "Historical Collections," printed in 1802, it is said, that "more corn is produced than the inhabitants consume, and about a thousand bushels are annually sent to market. The soil being free from stones, a plough passes through it speedily; and after the corn has come up, a small Cape horse, somewhat larger than a goat, will, with the assistance of two boys, easily hoe three or four acres in a day; several farmers are accustomed to produce five hundred bushels of grain annually, and not long since one raised eight hundred bushels on sixty acres." Similar accounts are given to-day; indeed, the recent accounts are in some instances suspectable repetitions of the old, and I have no doubt that their statements are as often founded on the exception as the rule, and that by far the greater number of acres are as barren as they appear to be. It is sufficiently remarkable that any crops can be raised here, and it may be owing, as others have suggested, to the amount of moisture in the atmosphere, the warmth of the sand, and the rareness

*They touched after this at a place called Mattachiest, where they got more corn; but their shallop being cast away in a storm, the Governor was obliged to return to Plymouth on foot, fifty miles through the woods. According to Mourt's Relation, "he came safely home, though weary and *surbated*," that is, foot-sore. (Ital. *sobattere*, Lat. *sub* or *solea battere*, to bruise the soles of the feet; v. Dic. Not "from *acerbatus*, embittered or aggrieved," as one commentator on this passage supposes.) This word is of very rare occurrence, being applied only to governors and persons of like description, who are in that predicament; though such generally have considerable mileage allowed them, and might save their soles if they cared.

of frosts. A miller, who was sharpening his stones, told me
that, forty years ago, he had been to a husking here, where
five hundred bushels were husked in one evening, and the
corn was piled six feet high or more, in the midst, but now,
fifteen or eighteen bushels to an acre were an average yield. I
never saw fields of such puny and unpromising looking corn,
as in this town. Probably the inhabitants are contented with
small crops from a great surface easily cultivated. It is not
always the most fertile land that is the most profitable, and
this sand may repay cultivation, as well as the fertile bottoms
of the West. It is said, moreover, that the vegetables raised in
the sand, without manure, are remarkably sweet, the pumpkins especially, though when their seed is planted in the interior they soon degenerate. I can testify that the vegetables
here, when they succeed at all, look remarkably green and
healthy, though perhaps it is partly by contrast with the sand.
Yet the inhabitants of the Cape towns, generally, do not raise
their own meal or pork. Their gardens are commonly little
patches, that have been redeemed from the edges of the
marshes and swamps.

All the morning we had heard the sea roar on the eastern
shore, which was several miles distant; for it still felt the effects of the storm in which the St. John was wrecked,—
though a school-boy, whom we overtook, hardly knew what
we meant, his ears were so used to it. He would have more
plainly heard the same sound in a shell. It was a very inspiriting sound to walk by, filling the whole air, that of the sea
dashing against the land, heard several miles inland. Instead
of having a dog to growl before your door, to have an Atlantic Ocean to growl for a whole Cape! On the whole, we were
glad of the storm, which would show us the ocean in its an-
griest mood. Charles Darwin was assured that the roar of the
surf on the coast of Chiloe, after a heavy gale, could be heard
at night a distance of "21 sea miles across a hilly and wooded
country." We conversed with the boy we have mentioned,
who might have been eight years old, making him walk the
while under the lee of our umbrella; for we thought it as
important to know what was life on the Cape to a boy as to
a man. We learned from him where the best grapes were to
be found in that neighborhood. He was carrying his dinner

in a pail; and, without any impertinent questions being put by us, it did at length appear of what it consisted. The homeliest facts are always the most acceptable to an inquiring mind. At length, before we got to Eastham meeting-house, we left the road and struck across the country for the eastern shore at Nauset Lights,—three lights close together, two or three miles distant from us. They were so many that they might be distinguished from others; but this seemed a shiftless and costly way of accomplishing that object. We found ourselves at once on an apparently boundless plain, without a tree or a fence, or, with one or two exceptions, a house in sight. Instead of fences, the earth was sometimes thrown up into a slight ridge. My companion compared it to the rolling prairies of Illinois. In the storm of wind and rain which raged when we traversed it, it no doubt appeared more vast and desolate than it really is. As there were no hills, but only here and there a dry hollow in the midst of the waste, and the distant horizon was concealed by mist, we did not know whether it was high or low. A solitary traveller, whom we saw perambulating in the distance, loomed like a giant. He appeared to walk slouchingly, as if held up from above by straps under his shoulders, as much as supported by the plain below. Men and boys would have appeared alike at a little distance, there being no object by which to measure them. Indeed, to an inlander, the Cape landscape is a constant mirage. This kind of country extended a mile or two each way. These were the "Plains of Nauset," once covered with wood, where in winter the winds howl and the snow blows right merrily in the face of the traveller. I was glad to have got out of the towns, where I am wont to feel unspeakably mean and disgraced,—to have left behind me for a season the barrooms of Massachusetts, where the full-grown are not weaned from savage and filthy habits,—still sucking a cigar. My spirits rose in proportion to the outward dreariness. The towns need to be ventilated. The gods would be pleased to see some pure flames from their altars. They are not to be appeased with cigar-smoke.

As we thus skirted the back-side of the towns, for we did not enter any village, till we got to Provincetown, we read their histories under our umbrellas, rarely meeting anybody.

The old accounts are the richest in topography, which was what we wanted most; and, indeed, in most things else, for I find that the readable parts of the modern accounts of these towns consist, in a great measure, of quotations, acknowledged and unacknowledged, from the older ones, without any additional information of equal interest; — town histories, which at length run into a history of the Church of that place, that being the only story they have to tell, and conclude by quoting the Latin epitaphs of the old pastors, having been written in the good old days of Latin and of Greek. They will go back to the ordination of every minister, and tell you faithfully who made the introductory prayer, and who delivered the sermon; who made the ordaining prayer, and who gave the charge; who extended the right hand of fellowship, and who pronounced the benediction; also how many ecclesiastical councils convened from time to time to inquire into the orthodoxy of some minister, and the names of all who composed them. As it will take us an hour to get over this plain, and there is no variety in the prospect, peculiar as it is, I will read a little in the history of Eastham the while.

When the committee from Plymouth had purchased the territory of Eastham of the Indians, "it was demanded, who laid claim to Billingsgate?" which was understood to be all that part of the Cape north of what they had purchased. "The answer was, there was not any who owned it. 'Then,' said the committee, 'that land is ours.' The Indians answered, that it was." This was a remarkable assertion and admission. The Pilgrims appear to have regarded themselves as Not Any's representatives. Perhaps this was the first instance of that quiet way of "speaking for" a place not yet occupied, or at least not improved as much as it may be, which their descendants have practised, and are still practising so extensively. Not Any seems to have been the sole proprietor of all America before the Yankees. But history says, that when the Pilgrims had held the lands of Billingsgate many years, at length, "appeared an Indian, who styled himself Lieutenant Anthony," who laid claim to them, and of him they bought them. Who knows but a Lieutenant Anthony may be knocking at the door of the White House some day? At any rate, I know that if you hold a thing unjustly, there will surely be the devil to pay at last.

Thomas Prince, who was several times the governor of the Plymouth colony, was the leader of the settlement of Eastham. There was recently standing, on what was once his farm, in this town, a pear-tree which is said to have been brought from England, and planted there by him, about two hundred years ago. It was blown down a few months before we were there. A late account says that it was recently in a vigorous state; the fruit small, but excellent; and it yielded on an average fifteen bushels. Some appropriate lines have been addressed to it, by a Mr. Heman Doane, from which I will quote, partly because they are the only specimen of Cape Cod verse which I remember to have seen, and partly because they are not bad.

"Two hundred years have, on the wings of Time,
    Passed with their joys and woes, since thou, Old Tree!
Put forth thy first leaves in this foreign clime,
    Transplanted from the soil beyond the sea.

      *   *   *   *   *

[These stars represent the more clerical lines, and also those which have deceased.]

"That exiled band long since have passed away,
    And still, Old Tree! thou standest in the place
Where Prince's hand did plant thee in his day,—
    An undesigned memorial of his race
And time; of those our honored fathers, when
    They came from Plymouth o'er and settled here;
Doane, Higgins, Snow, and other worthy men,
    Whose names their sons remember to revere.

      *   *   *   *   *

"Old Time has thinned thy boughs, Old Pilgrim Tree!
    And bowed thee with the weight of many years;
Yet, 'mid the frosts of age, thy bloom we see,
    And yearly still thy mellow fruit appears."

There are some other lines which I might quote, if they were not tied to unworthy companions, by the rhyme. When one ox will lie down, the yoke bears hard on him that stands up.

One of the first settlers of Eastham was Deacon John Doane, who died in 1707, aged one hundred and ten. Tradition says that he was rocked in a cradle several of his last years. That, certainly, was not an Achillean life. His mother must have let him slip when she dipped him into the liquor which was to make him invulnerable, and he went in, heels and all. Some of the stone-bounds to his farm, which he set up, are standing to-day, with his initials cut in them.

The ecclesiastical history of this town interested us somewhat. It appears that "they very early built a small meeting-house, twenty feet square, with a thatched roof through which they might fire their muskets,"—of course, at the Devil. "In 1662, the town agreed that a part of every whale cast on shore be appropriated for the support of the ministry." No doubt there seemed to be some propriety in thus leaving the support of the ministers to Providence, whose servants they are, and who alone rules the storms; for, when few whales were cast up, they might suspect that their worship was not acceptable. The ministers must have sat upon the cliffs in every storm, and watched the shore with anxiety. And, for my part, if I were a minister, I would rather trust to the bowels of the billows, on the back-side of Cape Cod, to cast up a whale for me, than to the generosity of many a country parish that I know. You cannot say of a country minister's salary, commonly, that it is "very like a whale." Nevertheless, the minister who depended on whales cast up must have had a trying time of it. I would rather have gone to the Falkland Isles with a harpoon, and done with it. Think of a whale having the breath of life beaten out of him by a storm, and dragging in over the bars and guzzles, for the support of the ministry! What a consolation it must have been to him! I have heard of a minister, who had been a fisherman, being settled in Bridgewater for as long a time as he could tell a cod from a haddock. Generous as it seems, this condition would empty most country pulpits forthwith, for it is long since the fishers of men were fishermen. Also, a duty was put on mackerel here to support a free-school; in other words, the mackerel-school was taxed in order that the children's school might be free. "In 1665 the Court passed a law to inflict corporal punishment on all persons, who resided in the towns of this government, who denied the Scriptures." Think of a man being whipped on a spring morning, till he was constrained to confess that the Scriptures were true! "It was also voted by the town, that all persons who should stand out of the meeting-house during the time of divine service should be set in the stocks." It behooved such a town to see that sitting in the meeting-house was nothing akin to sitting in the stocks, lest the penalty of obedience to the law might be greater than that of disobedience. This was the Eastham famous of late years for its camp-meetings, held in a grove near by, to which thousands flock from all parts of the Bay. We conjectured that the reason for the perhaps unusual, if not unhealthful development of the religious sentiment here, was the fact that a large portion of the population are women whose husbands and sons are either abroad on the sea, or else drowned, and there is nobody but they and the ministers left behind. The old account says that "hysteric fits are very common in Orleans, Eastham, and the towns below, particularly on Sunday, in the times of divine service. When one woman is affected, five or six others generally sympathize with her; and the congregation is thrown into the utmost confusion. Several old men suppose, unphilosophically and uncharitably, perhaps, that the will is partly concerned, and that ridicule and threats would have a tendency to prevent the evil." How this is now we did not learn. We saw one singularly masculine woman, however, in a house on this very plain, who did not look as if she was ever troubled with hysterics, or sympathized with those that were; or, perchance, life itself was to her a hysteric fit,—a Nauset woman, of a hardness and coarseness such as no man ever possesses or suggests. It was enough to see the vertebræ and sinews of her neck, and her set jaws of iron, which would have bitten a board-nail in two in their ordinary action,—braced against the world, talking like a man-of-war's-man in petticoats, or as if shouting to you through a breaker; who looked as if it made her head ache to live; hard enough for any enormity. I looked upon her as one who had committed infanticide; who never had a brother, unless it were some wee thing that died in infancy,—for what need of him?—and whose father must have died before she was born. This woman told us that the camp-meetings were not held the previous summer for fear of introducing the cholera, and that they would have been held earlier this summer, but the rye was so backward that straw would not have been ready for them; for they lie in straw. There are sometimes one hundred and fifty ministers, (!) and five thousand hearers, assembled. The ground, which is called Millennium Grove, is owned by a company in Boston, and is the most suitable, or rather unsuitable, for this purpose of any that I saw on the Cape. It is fenced, and the frames of the tents are, at all times, to be seen interspersed among the oaks. They have an oven and a pump, and keep all their kitchen utensils and tent coverings and furniture in a permanent building on the spot. They select a time for their meetings when the moon is full. A man is appointed to clear out the pump a week beforehand, while the ministers are clearing their throats; but, probably, the latter do not always deliver as pure a stream as the former. I saw the heaps of clam-shells left under the tables, where they had feasted in previous summers, and supposed, of course, that that was the work of the unconverted, or the backsliders and scoffers. It looked as if a camp-meeting must be a singular combination of a prayer-meeting and a picnic.

The first minister settled here was the Rev. Samuel Treat, in 1672, a gentleman who is said to be "entitled to a distinguished rank among the evangelists of New England." He converted many Indians, as well as white men, in his day, and translated the Confession of Faith into the Nauset language. These were the Indians concerning whom their first teacher, Richard Bourne, wrote to Gookin, in 1674, that he had been to see one who was sick, "and there came from him very savory and heavenly expressions," but, with regard to the mass of them, he says, "the truth is, that many of them are very loose in their course, to my heart-breaking sorrow." Mr. Treat is described as a Calvinist of the strictest kind, not one of those who, by giving up or explaining away, become like a porcupine disarmed of its quills, but a consistent Calvinist, who can dart his quills to a distance and courageously defend himself. There exists a volume of his sermons in manuscript, " which," says a commentator, "appear to have been designed for publication." I quote the following sentences at second hand, from a Discourse on Luke xvi. 23, addressed to sinners: —

"Thou must erelong go to the bottomless pit. Hell hath enlarged herself, and is ready to receive thee. There is room enough for thy entertainment. . . . .

"Consider, thou art going to a place prepared by God on purpose to exalt his justice in, — a place made for no other employment but torments. Hell is God's house of correction; and, remember, God doth all things like himself. When God would show his justice, and what is the weight of his wrath, he makes a hell where it shall, indeed, appear to purpose. . . . . Woe to thy soul when thou shalt be set up as a butt for the arrows of the Almighty. . . . .

"Consider, God himself shall be the principal agent in thy misery, — his breath is the bellows which blows up the flame of hell forever; — and if he punish thee, if he meet thee in his fury, he will not meet thee as a man; he will give thee an omnipotent blow."

"Some think sinning ends with this life; but it is a mistake. The creature is held under an everlasting law; the damned increase in sin in hell. Possibly, the mention of this may please thee. But, remember, there shall be no pleasant sins there; no eating, drinking, singing, dancing, wanton dalliance, and drinking stolen waters: but damned sins, bitter, hellish sins; sins exasperated by torments, cursing God, spite, rage, and blasphemy. — The guilt of all thy sins shall be laid upon thy soul, and be made so many heaps of fuel. . . . .

"Sinner, I beseech thee, realize the truth of these things. Do not go about to dream that this is derogatory to God's mercy, and nothing but a vain fable to scare children out of their wits withal. God can be merciful, though he make thee miserable. He shall have monuments enough of that precious attribute, shining like stars in the place of glory, and singing eternal hallelujahs to the praise of Him that redeemed them, though, to exalt the power of his justice, he damn sinners heaps upon heaps."

"But," continues the same writer, " with the advantage of proclaiming the doctrine of terror, which is naturally productive of a sublime and impressive style of eloquence ('Triumphat ventoso gloriæ curru orator, qui pectus angit, irritat, et implet terroribus.' Vid. Burnet, De Stat. Mort., p. 309), he could not attain the character of a popular preacher. His voice was so loud, that it could be heard at a great distance from the meeting-house, even amidst the shrieks of hysterical women, and the winds that howled over the plains of Nauset; but there was no more music in it than in the discordant sounds with which it was mingled."

"The effect of such preaching," it is said, "was that his hearers were several times, in the course of his ministry, awakened and alarmed; and on one occasion a comparatively innocent young man was frightened nearly out of his wits, and Mr. Treat had to exert himself to make hell seem somewhat cooler to him"; yet we are assured that "Treat's manners were cheerful, his conversation pleasant, and sometimes facetious, but always decent. He was fond of a stroke of humor, and a practical joke, and manifested his relish for them by long and loud fits of laughter."

This was the man of whom a well-known anecdote is told, which doubtless many of my readers have heard, but which, nevertheless, I will venture to quote: —

"After his marriage with the daughter of Mr. Willard (pastor of the South Church in Boston), he was sometimes invited by that gentleman to preach in his pulpit. Mr. Willard possessed a graceful delivery, a masculine and harmonious voice; and, though he did not gain much reputation by his 'Body of Divinity,' which is frequently sneered at, particularly by those who have read it, yet in his sermons are strength of thought and energy of language. The natural consequence was that he was generally admired. Mr. Treat having preached one of his best discourses to the congregation of his father-in-law, in his usual unhappy manner, excited universal disgust; and several nice judges waited on Mr. Willard, and begged that Mr. Treat, who was a worthy, pious man, it was true, but a wretched preacher, might never be invited into his pulpit again. To this request Mr. Willard made no reply; but he desired his son-in-law to lend him the discourse; which, being left with him, he delivered it without alteration to his people a few weeks after. They ran to Mr. Willard and requested a copy for the press. 'See the difference,' they cried, 'between yourself and your son-in-law; you have preached a sermon on the same text as Mr. Treat's, but whilst his was contemptible, yours is excellent.' As is observed in a note, 'Mr. Willard, after producing the sermon in the handwriting of Mr. Treat, might have addressed these sage critics in the words of Phædrus,

'En hic declarat, quales sitis judices.' "*

Mr. Treat died of a stroke of the palsy, just after the memorable storm known as the Great Snow, which left the ground around his house entirely bare, but heaped up the snow in the road to an uncommon height. Through this an arched way was dug, by which the Indians bore his body to the grave.

The reader will imagine us, all the while, steadily traversing that extensive plain in a direction a little north of east toward Nauset Beach, and reading under our umbrellas as we sailed, while it blowed hard with mingled mist and rain, as if we were approaching a fit anniversary of Mr. Treat's funeral. We fancied that it was such a moor as that on which somebody perished in the snow, as is related in the "Lights and Shadows of Scottish Life."

The next minister settled here was the "Rev. Samuel Osborn, who was born in Ireland, and educated at the University of Dublin." He is said to have been "A man of wisdom and virtue," and taught his people the use of peat, and the art of drying and preparing it, which as they had scarcely any other fuel, was a great blessing to them. He also introduced improvements in agriculture. But, notwithstanding his many services, as he embraced the religion of Arminius, some of his flock became dissatisfied. At length, an ecclesiastical council, consisting of ten ministers, with their churches, sat upon him, and they, naturally enough, spoiled his usefulness. The council convened at the desire of two divine philosophers,— Joseph Doane and Nathaniel Freeman.

In their report they say, "It appears to the council that the Rev. Mr. Osborn hath, in his preaching to this people, said, that what Christ did and suffered doth nothing abate or diminish our obligation to obey the law of God, and that

*Lib. v. Fab. 5.

Christ's suffering and obedience were for himself; both parts of which, we think, contain dangerous error."

"Also: 'It hath been said, and doth appear to this council, that the Rev. Mr. Osborn, both in public and in private, asserted that there are no promises in the Bible but what are conditional, which we think, also, to be an error, and do say that there are promises which are absolute and without any conditions,—such as the promise of a new heart, and that he will write his law in our hearts.' "

"Also, they say, 'it hath been alleged, and doth appear to us, that Mr. Osborn hath declared, that *obedience* is a considerable *cause* of a person's justification, which, we think, contains very dangerous error.' "

And many the like distinctions they made, such as some of my readers, probably, are more familiar with than I am. So, far in the East, among the Yezidis, or Worshippers of the Devil, so-called, the Chaldæans, and others, according to the testimony of travellers, you may still hear these remarkable disputations on doctrinal points going on. Osborn was, accordingly, dismissed, and he removed to Boston, where he kept school for many years. But he was fully justified, methinks, by his works in the peat-meadow; one proof of which is, that he lived to be between ninety and one hundred years old.

The next minister was the Rev. Benjamin Webb, of whom, though a neighboring clergyman pronounced him "the best man and the best minister whom he ever knew," yet the historian says, that,

"As he spent his days in the uniform discharge of his duty (it reminds one of a country muster) and there were no shades to give relief to his character, not much can be said of him. (Pity the Devil did not plant a few shade-trees along his avenues.) His heart was as pure as the new-fallen snow, which completely covers every dark spot in a field; his mind was as serene as the sky in a mild evening in June, when the moon shines without a cloud. Name any virtue, and that virtue he practised; name any vice, and that vice he shunned. But if peculiar qualities marked his character, they were his humility, his gentleness, and his love of God. The people had long been taught by a son of thunder (Mr. Treat): in him they were instructed by a son of consolation, who sweetly allured them to virtue by soft persuasion, and by exhibiting the mercy of the Supreme Being; for his thoughts were so much in heaven, that they seldom descended to the dismal regions below; and though of the same religious sentiments as Mr. Treat, yet his attention was turned to those glad tidings of great joy which a Saviour came to publish."

We were interested to hear that such a man had trodden the plains of Nauset.

Turning over further in our book, our eyes fell on the name of the Rev. Jonathan Bascom, of Orleans: "Senex emunctæ naris, doctus, et auctor elegantium verborum, facetus, et dulcis festique sermonis." And, again, on that of the Rev. Nathan Stone, of Dennis: "Vir humilis, mitis, blandus, advenarum hospes; (there was need of him there;) suis commodis in terrâ non studens, reconditis thesauris in cœlo." An easy virtue that, there, for methinks no inhabitant of Dennis could be very studious about his earthly commodity, but must regard the bulk of his treasures as in heaven. But probably the most just and pertinent character of all is that which appears to be given to the Rev. Ephraim Briggs, of Chatham, in the language of the later Romans, *"Seip, sepoese, sepoemese, wechekum,"*—which not being interpreted, we know not what it means, though we have no doubt it occurs somewhere in the Scriptures, probably in the Apostle Eliot's Epistle to the Nipmucks.

Let no one think that I do not love the old ministers. They were, probably, the best men of their generation, and they deserve that their biographies should fill the pages of the town histories. If I could but hear the "glad tidings" of which they tell, and which, perchance, they heard, I might write in a worthier strain than this.

There was no better way to make the reader realize how wide and peculiar that plain was, and how long it took to traverse it, than by inserting these extracts in the midst of my narrative.

IV

The Beach

At length we reached the seemingly retreating boundary of the plain, and entered what had appeared at a distance an upland marsh, but proved to be dry sand covered with Beach-grass, the Bearberry, Bayberry, Shrub-oaks, and Beach-plum, slightly ascending as we approached the shore; then, crossing over a belt of sand on which nothing grew, though the roar of the sea sounded scarcely louder than before, and we were prepared to go half a mile farther, we suddenly stood on the edge of a bluff overlooking the Atlantic. Far below us was the beach, from half a dozen to a dozen rods in width, with a long line of breakers rushing to the strand. The sea was exceedingly dark and stormy, the sky completely overcast, the clouds still dropping rain, and the wind seemed to blow not so much as the exciting cause, as from sympathy with the already agitated ocean. The waves broke on the bars at some distance from the shore, and curving green or yellow as if over so many unseen dams, ten or twelve feet high, like a thousand waterfalls, rolled in foam to the sand. There was nothing but that savage ocean between us and Europe.

Having got down the bank, and as close to the water as we could, where the sand was the hardest, leaving the Nauset Lights behind us, we began to walk leisurely up the beach, in a northwest direction, toward Provincetown, which was about twenty-five miles distant, still sailing under our umbrellas with a strong aft wind, admiring in silence, as we walked, the great force of the ocean stream,—

$$\pi o \tau a \mu o \hat{\iota} o \ \mu \acute{\epsilon} \gamma a \ \sigma \theta \acute{\epsilon} \nu o \varsigma \ \text{'}\Omega \kappa \epsilon a \nu o \hat{\iota} o .$$

The white breakers were rushing to the shore; the foam ran up the sand, and then ran back as far as we could see (and we imagined how much farther along the Atlantic coast, before and behind us), as regularly, to compare great things with small, as the master of a choir beats time with his white wand; and ever and anon a higher wave caused us hastily to deviate from our path, and we looked back on our tracks filled with water and foam. The breakers looked like droves of a thousand wild horses of Neptune, rushing to the shore, with their white manes streaming far behind; and when, at length, the sun shone for a moment, their manes were rainbow-tinted. Also, the long kelp-weed was tossed up from time to time, like the tails of sea-cows sporting in the brine.

There was not a sail in sight, and we saw none that day,—for they had all sought harbors in the late storm, and had not been able to get out again; and the only human beings whom we saw on the beach for several days, were one or two wreckers looking for drift-wood, and fragments of wrecked vessels. After an easterly storm in the spring, this beach is sometimes strewn with eastern wood from one end to the other, which, as it belongs to him who saves it, and the Cape is nearly destitute of wood, is a Godsend to the inhabitants. We soon met one of these wreckers,—a regular Cape Cod man, with whom we parleyed, with a bleached and weather-beaten face, within whose wrinkles I distinguished no particular feature. It was like an old sail endowed with life,—a hanging-cliff of weather-beaten flesh,—like one of the clay bowlders which occurred in that sand-bank. He had on a hat which had seen salt water, and a coat of many pieces and colors, though it was mainly the color of the beach, as if it had been sanded. His variegated back—for his coat had many patches, even between the shoulders—was a rich study to us, when we had passed him and looked round. It might have been dishonorable for him to have so many scars behind, it is true, if he had not had many more and more serious ones in front. He looked as if he sometimes saw a doughnut, but never descended to comfort; too grave to laugh, too tough to cry; as indifferent as a clam,—like a sea-clam with hat on and legs, that was out walking the strand. He may have been one of the Pilgrims,—Peregrine White, at least,—who has kept on the back side of the Cape, and let the centuries go by. He was looking for wrecks, old logs, water-logged and covered with barnacles, or bits of boards and joists, even chips which he drew out of the reach of the tide, and stacked up to dry. When the log was too large to carry far, he cut it up where the last wave had left it, or rolling it a few feet, appropriated it by sticking two sticks into the ground crosswise above it. Some rotten trunk, which in Maine cumbers the ground, and is, perchance, thrown into the water on purpose, is here thus carefully picked up, split and dried, and husbanded. Before winter the wrecker painfully carries these things up the bank on his shoulders by a long diagonal slanting path made with a hoe in the sand, if there is no hollow at hand. You may see his hooked pike-staff always lying on the bank ready for use. He is the true monarch of the beach, whose "right there is none to dispute," and he is as much identified with it as a beach-bird.

Crantz, in his account of Greenland, quotes Dalagen's relation of the ways and usages of the Greenlanders, and says, "Whoever finds drift-wood, or the spoils of a shipwreck on the strand, enjoys it as his own, though he does not live there. But he must haul it ashore and lay a stone upon it, as a token that some one has taken possession of it, and this stone is the deed of security, for no other Greenlander will offer to meddle with it afterwards." Such is the instinctive law of nations. We have also this account of drift-wood in Crantz: "As he (the Founder of Nature) has denied this frigid rocky region the growth of trees, he has bid the streams of the Ocean to convey to its shores a great deal of wood, which accordingly comes floating thither, part without ice, but the most part along with it, and lodges itself between the islands. Were it not for this, we Europeans should have no wood to burn there, and the poor Greenlanders (who, it is true, do not use wood, but train, for burning) would, however, have no wood to roof their houses, to erect their tents, as also to build their boats, and to shaft their arrows, (yet there *grew* some small but crooked alders, &c.,) by which they must procure their maintenance, clothing and train for warmth, light, and cooking. Among this wood are great trees torn up by the roots, which by driving up and down for many years and rubbing on the ice, are quite bare of branches and bark, and corroded with great wood-worms. A small part of this drift-wood are willows, alder and birch trees, which come out of the bays in the south (i. e. of Greenland); also large trunks of aspen-trees, which must come from a greater distance; but the greatest part is pine and fir. We find also a good deal of a sort of wood finely veined, with few branches; this I fancy is larch-wood, which likes to decorate the sides of lofty, stony mountains. There is also a solid, reddish wood, of a more agreeable fragrance than the common fir, with visible cross-veins; which I take to be the same species as the beautiful silver-firs, or *zirbel*, that have the smell of cedar, and grow on the high Grison hills, and the Switzers wainscot their rooms with them." The wrecker directed us to a slight depression, called Snow's Hollow, by which we ascended the bank,—for elsewhere, if not difficult, it was inconvenient to climb it on account of the sliding sand, which filled our shoes.

This sand-bank—the backbone of the Cape—rose directly from the beach to the height of a hundred feet or more above the ocean. It was with singular emotions that we first stood upon it and discovered what a place we had chosen to walk on. On our right, beneath us, was the beach of smooth and gently-sloping sand, a dozen rods in width; next, the endless series of white breakers; further still, the light green water over the bar, which runs the whole length of the forearm of the Cape, and beyond this stretched the unwearied and illimitable ocean. On our left, extending back from the very edge of the bank, was a perfect desert of shining sand, from thirty to eighty rods in width, skirted in the distance by small sandhills fifteen or twenty feet high; between which, however, in some places, the sand penetrated as much farther. Next commenced the region of vegetation,—a succession of small hills and valleys covered with shrubbery, now glowing with the brightest imaginable autumnal tints; and beyond this were seen, here and there, the waters of the bay. Here, in Wellfleet, this pure sand plateau, known to sailors as the Table Lands of Eastham, on account of its appearance, as seen from the ocean, and because it once made a part of that town,—full fifty rods in width, and in many places much more, and sometimes full one hundred and fifty feet above the ocean,— stretched away northward from the southern boundary of the town, without a particle of vegetation,—as level almost as a table,—for two and a half or three miles, or as far as the eye could reach; slightly rising towards the ocean, then stooping to the beach, by as steep a slope as sand could lie on, and as regular as a military engineer could desire. It was like the escarped rampart of a stupendous fortress, whose glacis was the beach, and whose champaign the ocean,—From its surface we overlooked the greater part of the Cape. In short, we were traversing a desert, with the view of an autumnal landscape of extraordinary brilliancy, a sort of Promised Land, on the one hand, and the ocean on the other. Yet, though the prospect was so extensive, and the country for the most part destitute of trees, a house was rarely visible,—we never saw one from the beach,—and the solitude was that of the ocean and the desert combined. A thousand men could not have seriously interrupted it, but would have been lost in the vastness of the scenery as their footsteps in the sand.

The whole coast is so free from rocks, that we saw but one or two for more than twenty miles. The sand was soft like the beach, and trying to the eyes, when the sun shone. A few piles of drift-wood, which some wreckers had painfully brought up the bank and stacked up there to dry, being the only objects in the desert, looked indefinitely large and distant, even like wigwams, though, when we stood near them, they proved to be insignificant little "jags" of wood.

For sixteen miles, commencing at the Nauset Lights, the bank held its height, though farther north it was not so level as here, but interrupted by slight hollows, and the patches of Beach-grass and Bayberry frequently crept into the sand to its edge. There are some pages entitled "A Description of the Eastern Coast of the County of Barnstable," printed in 1802, pointing out the spots on which the Trustees of the Humane Society have erected huts called Charity or Humane Houses, "and other places where shipwrecked seamen may look for shelter." Two thousand copies of this were dispersed, that every vessel which frequented this coast might be provided with one. I have read this Shipwrecked Seaman's Manual with a melancholy kind of interest,—for the sound of the surf, or, you might say, the moaning of the sea, is heard all through it, as if its author were the sole survivor of a shipwreck himself. Of this part of the coast he says: "This highland approaches the ocean with steep and lofty banks, which it is extremely difficult to climb, especially in a storm. In violent tempests, during very high tides, the sea breaks against the foot of them, rendering it then unsafe to walk on the strand which lies between them and the ocean. Should the seaman succeed in his attempt to ascend them, he must forbear to penetrate into the country, as houses are generally so remote that they would escape his research during the night; he must pass on to the valleys by which the banks are intersected. These valleys, which the inhabitants call Hollows, run at right angles with the shore, and in the middle or lowest part of them a road leads from the dwelling-houses to the sea." By the word *road* must not always be understood a visible cart-track.

There were these two roads for us,—an upper and a lower one,—the bank and the beach; both stretching twenty-eight miles northwest, from Nauset Harbor to Race Point, without a single opening into the beach, and with hardly a serious interruption of the desert. If you were to ford the narrow and shallow inlet at Nauset Harbor, where there is not more than eight feet of water on the bar at full sea, you might walk ten or twelve miles farther, which would make a beach forty miles long,—and the bank and beach, on the east side of Nantucket, are but a continuation of these. I was comparatively satisfied. There I had got the Cape under me, as much as if I were riding it bare-backed. It was not as on the map, or seen from the stage-coach; but there I found it all out of doors, huge and real, Cape Cod! as it cannot be represented on a map, color it as you will; the thing itself, than which there is nothing more like it, no truer picture or account; which you cannot go farther and see. I cannot remember what I thought before that it was. They commonly celebrate those beaches only which have a hotel on them, not those which have a humane house alone. But I wished to see that seashore where man's works are wrecks; to put up at the true Atlantic House, where the ocean is land-lord as well as sea-lord, and comes ashore without a wharf for the landing; where the crumbling land is the only invalid, or at best is but dry land, and that is all you can say of it.

We walked on quite at our leisure, now on the beach, now on the bank,—sitting from time to time on some damp log, maple or yellow birch, which had long followed the seas, but had now at last settled on land; or under the lee of a sand-hill, on the bank, that we might gaze steadily on the ocean.

The bank was so steep, that, where there was no danger of its caving, we sat on its edge as on a bench. It was difficult for us landsmen to look out over the ocean without imagining land in the horizon; yet the clouds appeared to hang low over it, and rest on the water as they never do on the land, perhaps on account of the great distance to which we saw. The sand was not without advantage, for, though it was "heavy" walking in it, it was soft to the feet; and, notwithstanding that it had been raining nearly two days, when it held up for half an hour, the sides of the sand-hills, which were porous and sliding, afforded a dry seat. All the aspects of this desert are beautiful, whether you behold it in fair weather or foul, or when the sun is just breaking out after a storm, and shining on its moist surface in the distance, it is so white, and pure, and level, and each slight inequality and track is so distinctly revealed; and when your eyes slide off this, they fall on the ocean. In summer the mackerel gulls—which here have their nests among the neighboring sand-hills—pursue the traveller anxiously, now and then diving close to his head with a squeak, and he may see them, like swallows, chase some crow which has been feeding on the beach, almost across the Cape.

Though for some time I have not spoken of the roaring of the breakers, and the ceaseless flux and reflux of the waves, yet they did not for a moment cease to dash and roar, with such a tumult that, if you had been there, you could scarcely have heard my voice the while; and they are dashing and roaring this very moment, though it may be with less din and violence, for there the sea never rests. We were wholly absorbed by this spectacle and tumult, and like Chryses, though in a different mood from him, we walked silent along the shore of the resounding sea.

Βῆ δ᾽ ἀκέων παρὰ θῖνα πολυφλοίσβοιο θαλάσσης.*

I put in a little Greek now and then, partly because it sounds so much like the ocean,—though I doubt if Homer's *Mediterranean* Sea ever sounded so loud as this.

The attention of those who frequent the camp-meetings at

---

*We have no word in English to express the sound of many waves, dashing at once, whether gently or violently, πολυφλοίσβοιος to the ear, and, in the ocean's gentle moods, an ἀνάριθμον γέλασμα to the eye.

Eastham is said to be divided between the preaching of the Methodists and the preaching of the billows on the backside of the Cape, for they all stream over here in the course of their stay. I trust that in this case the loudest voice carries it. With what effect may we suppose the ocean to say, "My hearers!" to the multitude on the bank! On that side some John N. Maffit; on this, the Reverend Poluphloisboios Thalassa.

There was but little weed cast up here, and that kelp chiefly, there being scarcely a rock for rockweed to adhere to. Who has not had a vision from some vessel's deck, when he had still his land-legs on, of this great brown apron, drifting half upright, and quite submerged through the green water, clasping a stone or a deep-sea mussel in its unearthly fingers? I have seen it carrying a stone half as large as my head. We sometimes watched a mass of this cable-like weed, as it was tossed up on the crest of a breaker, waiting with interest to see it come in, as if there was some treasure buoyed up by it; but we were always surprised and disappointed at the insignificance of the mass which had attracted us. As we looked out over the water, the smallest objects floating on it appeared indefinitely large, we were so impressed by the vastness of the ocean, and each one bore so large a proportion to the whole ocean, which we saw. We were so often disappointed in the size of such things as came ashore, the ridiculous bits of wood or weed, with which the ocean labored, that we began to doubt whether the Atlantic itself would bear a still closer inspection, and would not turn out to be but a small pond, if it should come ashore to us. This kelp, oarweed, tangle, devil's-apron, sole-leather, or ribbon-weed,—as various species are called,—appeared to us a singularly marine and fabulous product, a fit invention for Neptune to adorn his car with, or a freak of Proteus. All that is told of the sea has a fabulous sound to an inhabitant of the land, and all its products have a certain fabulous quality, as if they belonged to another planet, from sea-weed to a sailor's yarn, or a fish-story. In this element the animal and vegetable kingdoms meet and are strangely mingled. One species of kelp, according to Bory St. Vincent, has a stem fifteen hundred feet long, and hence is the longest vegetable known, and a brig's crew spent two days to no purpose collecting the trunks of another kind cast ashore on the Falkland Islands, mistaking it for drift-wood. (See Harvey on *Algæ*.) This species looked almost edible; at least, I thought that if I were starving I would try it. One sailor told me that the cows ate it. It cut like cheese; for I took the earliest opportunity to sit down and deliberately whittle up a fathom or two of it, that I might become more intimately acquainted with it, see how it cut, and if it were hollow all the way through. The blade looked like a broad belt, whose edges had been quilled, or as if stretched by hammering, and it was also twisted spirally. The extremity was generally worn and ragged from the lashing of the waves. A piece of the stem which I carried home shrunk to one quarter of its size a week afterward, and was completely covered with crystals of salt like frost. The reader will excuse my greenness,—though it is not sea-greenness, like his, perchance,—for I live by a river shore, where this weed does not wash up. When we consider in what meadows it grew, and how it was raked, and in what kind of hay weather got in or out, we may well be curious about it. One who is weather-wise has given the following account of the matter.

> "When descends on the Atlantic
>   The gigantic
>   Storm-wind of the equinox,
> Landward in his wrath he scourges
>   The toiling surges,
> Laden with sea-weed from the rocks.

> "From Bermuda's reefs, from edges
>   Of sunken ledges,
>   On some far-off bright Azore;
> From Bahama and the dashing,
>   Silver-flashing
> Surges of San Salvador;

> "From the trembling surf that buries
>   The Orkneyan Skerries,
>   Answering the hoarse Hebrides;
> And from wrecks and ships and drifting
>   Spars, uplifting
> On the desolate rainy seas;

> "Ever drifting, drifting, drifting
>   On the shifting
>   Currents of the restless main."

But he was not thinking of this shore, when he added: —

> "Till, in sheltered coves and reaches
>   Of sandy beaches,
>   All have found repose again."

These weeds were the symbols of those grotesque and fabulous thoughts which have not yet got into the sheltered coves of literature.

> "Ever drifting, drifting, drifting
>   On the shifting
>   Currents of the restless heart,"
> *And not yet* "in books recorded
>   They, like hoarded
>   Household words, no more depart."

The beach was also strewn with beautiful sea-jellies, which the wreckers called Sun-squall, one of the lowest forms of animal life, some white, some wine-colored, and a foot in diameter. I at first thought that they were a tender part of some marine monster, which the storm or some other foe had mangled. What right has the sea to bear in its bosom such tender things as sea-jellies and mosses, when it has such a boisterous shore, that the stoutest fabrics are wrecked against it? Strange that it should undertake to dandle such delicate children in its arm. I did not at first recognize these for the same which I had formerly seen in myriads in Boston Harbor, rising, with a waving motion, to the surface, as if to meet the sun, and discoloring the waters far and wide, so that I seemed to be sailing through a mere sun-fish soup. They say that when you endeavor to take one up, it will spill out the other side of your hand like quicksilver. Before the land rose out of the ocean, and became *dry* land, chaos reigned; and between high and low water mark, where she is partially disrobed and rising, a sort of chaos reigns still, which only anomalous creatures can inhabit. Mackerel-gulls were all the while flying over our heads and amid the breakers, sometimes two white ones pursuing a black one; quite at home in the storm, though they are as delicate organizations as sea-jellies and mosses; and we saw that they were adapted to their circumstances rather by their spirits than their bodies. Theirs must be an essentially wilder, that is, less human, nature than that of larks and robins. Their note was like the sound of some vibrating metal, and harmonized well with the scenery and the roar of the surf, as if one had rudely touched the strings of the lyre, which ever lies on the shore; a ragged shred of ocean music tossed aloft on the spray. But if I were required to name a sound, the remembrance of which most perfectly revives the impression which the beach has made, it would be the dreary peep of the piping plover (*Charadrius melodus*) which haunts there. Their voices, too, are heard as a fugacious part in the dirge which is ever played along the shore for those mariners who have been lost in the deep since first it was created. But through all this dreariness we seemed to have a pure and un-qualified strain of eternal melody, for always the same strain which is a dirge to one household is a morning song of re-joicing to another.

A remarkable method of catching gulls, derived from the Indians, was practised in Wellfleet in 1794. "The Gull House," it is said, "is built with crotchets, fixed in the ground on the beach," poles being stretched across for the top, and the sides made close with stakes and sea-weed. "The poles on the top are covered with lean whale. The man being placed within, is not discovered by the fowls, and while they are contending for and eating the flesh, he draws them in, one by one, be-tween the poles, until he has collected forty or fifty." Hence, perchance, a man is said to be *gulled*, when he is *taken in*. We read that one "sort of gulls is called by the Dutch *mallemucke*, i. e. the foolish fly, because they fall upon a whale as eagerly as a fly, and, indeed, all gulls are foolishly bold and easy to be shot. The Norwegians call this bird *havhest*, sea-horse (and the English translator says, it is probably what we call boo-bies). If they have eaten too much, they throw it up, and eat it again till they are tired. It is this habit in the gulls of parting with their property [disgorging the contents of their stom-achs to the skuas], which has given rise to the terms gull, guller, and gulling, among men." We also read that they used to kill small birds which roosted on the beach at night, by making a fire with hog's lard in a frying-pan. The Indians probably used pine torches; the birds flocked to the light, and were knocked down with a stick. We noticed holes dug near the edge of the bank, where gunners conceal themselves to shoot the large gulls which coast up and down a-fishing, for these are considered good to eat.

We found some large clams, of the species *Mactra solidissima*, which the storm had torn up from the bottom, and cast ashore. I selected one of the largest, about six inches in length, and carried it along, thinking to try an experiment on it. We soon after met a wrecker, with a grapple and a rope, who said that he was looking for tow cloth, which had made part of the cargo of the ship Franklin, which was wrecked here in the spring, at which time nine or ten lives were lost. The reader may remember this wreck, from the circumstance that a letter was found in the captain's valise, which washed ashore, directing him to wreck the vessel before he got to America, and from the trial which took place in consequence. The wrecker said that tow cloth was still cast up in such storms as this. He also told us that the clam which I had was the sea-clam, or hen, and was good to eat. We took our nooning under a sand-hill, covered with beach-grass, in a dreary little hollow, on the top of the bank, while it alternately rained and shined. There, having reduced some damp driftwood, which I had picked up on the shore, to shavings with my knife, I kindled a fire with a match and some paper, and cooked my clam on the embers for my dinner; for breakfast was commonly the only meal which I took in a house on this excursion. When the clam was done, one valve held the meat and the other the liquor. Though it was very tough, I found it sweet and savory, and ate *the whole* with a relish. Indeed, with the addition of a cracker or two, it would have been a bountiful dinner. I noticed that the shells were such as I had seen in the sugar-kit at home. Tied to a stick, they formerly made the Indian's hoe hereabouts.

At length, by mid-afternoon, after we had had two or three rainbows over the sea, the showers ceased, and the heavens gradually cleared up, though the wind still blew as hard and the breakers ran as high as before. Keeping on, we soon

after came to a Charity-house, which we looked into to see
how the shipwrecked mariner might fare. Far away in some
desolate hollow by the sea-side, just within the bank, stands a
lonely building on piles driven into the sand, with a slight
nail put through the staple, which a freezing man can bend,
with some straw, perchance, on the floor on which he may
lie, or which he may burn in the fireplace to keep him alive.
Perhaps this hut has never been required to shelter a shipwrecked man, and the benevolent person who promised to
inspect it annually, to see that the straw and matches are here,
and that the boards will keep off the wind, has grown remiss
and thinks that storms and shipwrecks are over; and this very
night a perishing crew may pry open its door with their
numbed fingers and leave half their number dead here by
morning. When I thought what must be the condition of the
families which alone would ever occupy or had occupied
them, what must have been the tragedy of the winter evenings spent by human beings around their hearths, these
houses, though they were meant for human dwellings, did
not look cheerful to me. They appeared but a stage to the
grave. The gulls flew around and screamed over them; the
roar of the ocean in storms, and the lapse of its waves in
calms, alone resounds through them, all dark and empty
within, year in year out, except, perchance, on one memorable night. Houses of entertainment for shipwrecked men!
What kind of sailor's homes were they?

"Each hut," says the author of the "Description of the Eastern Coast of the County of Barnstable," "stands on piles, is
eight feet long, eight feet wide, and seven feet high; a sliding
door is on the south, a sliding shutter on the west, and a pole,
rising fifteen feet above the top of the building, on the east.
Within it is supplied either with straw or hay, and is further
accommodated with a bench." They have varied little from
this model now. There are similar huts at the Isle of Sable
and Anticosti, on the north, and how far south along the
coast I know not. It is pathetic to read the minute and faithful
directions which he gives to seamen who may be wrecked on
this coast, to guide them to the nearest Charity-house, or
other shelter, for, as is said of Eastham, though there are a
few houses within a mile of the shore, yet "in a snow-storm,

which rages here with excessive fury, it would be almost impossible to discover them either by night or by day." You hear their imaginary guide thus marshalling, cheering, directing the dripping, shivering, freezing troop along; "at the entrance of this valley the sand has gathered, so that at present a little climbing is necessary. Passing over several fences and taking heed not to enter the wood on the right hand, at the distance of three quarters of a mile a house is to be found. This house stands on the south side of the road, and not far from it on the south is Pamet river, which runs from east to west through a body of salt marsh." To him cast ashore in Eastham, he says, "The meeting-house is without a steeple, but it may be distinguished from the dwelling-houses near it by its situation, which is between two small groves of locusts, one on the south and one on the north,—that on the south being three times as long as the other. About a mile and a quarter from the hut, west by north, appear the top and arms of a windmill." And so on for many pages.

We did not learn whether these houses had been the means of saving any lives, though this writer says, of one erected at the head of Stout's Creek, in Truro, that "it was built in an improper manner, having a chimney in it; and was placed on a spot where no beach-grass grew. The strong winds blew the sand from its foundation, and the weight of the chimney brought it to the ground; so that in January of the present year [1802] it was entirely demolished. This event took place about six weeks before the Brutus was cast away. If it had remained, it is probable that the whole of the unfortunate crew of that ship would have been saved, as they gained the shore a few rods only from the spot where the hut had stood."

This "Charity-house," as the wrecker called it, this "Humane house," as some call it, that is, the one to which we first came, had neither window nor sliding shutter, nor clapboards, nor paint. As we have said, there was a rusty nail put through the staple. However, as we wished to get an idea of a Humane house, and we hoped that we should never have a better opportunity, we put our eyes, by turns, to a knot-hole in the door, and, after long looking, without seeing, into the dark,—not knowing how many shipwrecked men's bones we might see at last, looking with the eye of faith, knowing that, though to him that knocketh it may not always be opened, yet to him that looketh long enough through a knot-hole the inside shall be visible,—for we had had some practice at looking inward,—by steadily keeping our other ball covered from the light meanwhile, putting the outward world behind us, ocean and land, and the beach,—till the pupil became enlarged and collected the rays of light that were wandering in that dark (for the pupil shall be enlarged by looking; there never was so dark a night but a faithful and patient eye, however small, might at last prevail over it),—after all this, I say, things began to take shape to our vision,—if we may use this expression where there was nothing but emptiness,—and we obtained the long-wished-for insight. Though we thought at first that it was a hopeless case, after several minutes' steady exercise of the divine faculty, our prospects began decidedly to brighten, and we were ready to exclaim with the blind bard of "Paradise Lost and Regained,"—

> "Hail, holy Light! offspring of Heaven first born,
>   Or of the Eternal co-eternal beam,
>   May I express thee unblamed?"

A little longer, and a chimney rushed red on our sight. In short, when our vision had grown familiar with the darkness, we discovered that there were some stones and some loose wads of wool on the floor, and an empty fireplace at the further end; but it *was not* supplied with matches, or straw, or hay, that we could see, nor "accommodated with a bench." Indeed, it was the wreck of all cosmical beauty there within.

Turning our backs on the outward world, we thus looked through the knot-hole into the Humane house, into the very bowels of mercy; and for bread we found a stone. It was literally a great cry (of sea-mews outside), and a little wool. However, we were glad to sit outside, under the lee of the Humane house, to escape the piercing wind; and there we thought how cold is charity! how inhumane humanity! This, then, is what charity hides! Virtues antique and far away with ever a rusty nail over the latch; and very difficult to keep in repair, withal, it is so uncertain whether any will ever gain the beach near you. So we shivered round about, not being able to get into it, ever and anon looking through the knot-hole into that night without a star, until we concluded that it was not a *humane* house at all, but a sea-side box, now shut up, belonging to some of the family of Night or Chaos, where they spent their summers by the sea, for the sake of the sea-breeze, and that it was not proper for us to be prying into their concerns.

My companion had declared before this that I had not a particle of sentiment, in rather absolute terms, to my astonishment; but I suspect he meant that my legs did not ache just then, though I am not wholly a stranger to that sentiment. But I did not intend this for a sentimental journey.

V

The Wellfleet Oysterman

HAVING WALKED about eight miles since we struck the beach, and passed the boundary between Wellfleet and Truro, a stone post in the sand,—for even this sand comes under the jurisdiction of one town or another,—we turned inland over barren hills and valleys, whither the sea, for some reason, did not follow us, and, tracing up a Hollow, discovered two or three sober-looking houses within half a mile, uncommonly near the eastern coast. Their garrets were apparently so full of chambers, that their roofs could hardly lie down straight, and we did not doubt that there was room for us there. Houses near the sea are generally low and broad. These were a story and a half high; but if you merely counted the windows in their gable-ends, you would think that there were many stories more, or, at any rate, that the half-story was the only one thought worthy of being illustrated. The great number of windows in the ends of the houses, and their irregularity in size and position, here and elsewhere on the Cape, struck us agreeably,—as if each of the various occupants who had their *cunabula* behind had punched a hole where his necessities required it, and, according to his size and stature, without regard to outside effect. There were windows for the grown folks, and windows for the children,— three or four apiece; as a certain man had a large hole cut in his barn-door for the cat, and another smaller one for the kitten. Sometimes they were so low under the eaves that I thought they must have perforated the plate beam for another apartment, and I noticed some which were triangular, to fit that part more exactly. The ends of the houses had thus as many muzzles as a revolver, and, if the inhabitants have the same habit of staring out the windows that some of our neighbors have, a traveller must stand a small chance with them.

Generally, the old-fashioned and unpainted houses on the Cape looked more comfortable, as well as picturesque, than the modern and more pretending ones, which were less in harmony with the scenery, and less firmly planted.

These houses were on the shores of a chain of ponds, seven in number, the source of a small stream called Herring River, which empties into the Bay. There are many Herring Rivers on the Cape; they will, perhaps, be more numerous than herrings soon. We knocked at the door of the first house, but its inhabitants were all gone away. In the mean while, we saw the occupants of the next one looking out the window at us, and before we reached it an old woman came out and fastened the door of her bulkhead, and went in again. Nevertheless, we did not hesitate to knock at her door, when a grizzly-looking man appeared, whom we took to be sixty or seventy years old. He asked us, at first, suspiciously, where we were from, and what our business was; to which we returned plain answers.

"How far is Concord from Boston?" he inquired.

"Twenty miles by railroad."

"Twenty miles by railroad," he repeated.

"Did n't you ever hear of Concord of Revolutionary fame?"

"Did n't I ever hear of Concord? Why, I heard the guns fire at the battle of Bunker Hill. [They hear the sound of heavy cannon across the Bay.] I am almost ninety; I am eighty-eight year old. I was fourteen year old at the time of Concord Fight,—and where were you then?"

We were obliged to confess that we were not in the fight.

"Well, walk in, we'll leave it to the women," said he.

So we walked in, surprised, and sat down, an old woman taking our hats and bundles, and the old man continued, drawing up to the large, old-fashioned fireplace,—

"I am a poor good-for-nothing crittur, as Isaiah says; I am all broken down this year. I am under petticoat government here."

The family consisted of the old man, his wife, and his daughter, who appeared nearly as old as her mother, a fool, her son (a brutish-looking, middle-aged man, with a prominent lower face, who was standing by the hearth when we entered, but immediately went out), and a little boy of ten.

While my companion talked with the women, I talked with the old man. They said that he was old and foolish, but he was evidently too knowing for them.

"These women," said he to me, "are both of them poor good-for-nothing critturs. This one is my wife. I married her sixty-four years ago. She is eighty-four years old, and as deaf as an adder, and the other is not much better."

He thought well of the Bible, or at least he *spoke* well, and did not *think* ill, of it, for that would not have been prudent for a man of his age. He said that he had read it attentively for many years, and he had much of it at his tongue's end. He seemed deeply impressed with a sense of his own nothingness, and would repeatedly exclaim,—

"I am a nothing. What I gather from my Bible is just this: that man is a poor good-for-nothing crittur, and everything is just as God sees fit and disposes."

"May I ask your name?" I said.

"Yes," he answered, "I am not ashamed to tell my name. My name is ——. My great-grandfather came over from England and settled here."

He was an old Wellfleet oysterman, who had acquired a competency in that business, and had sons still engaged in it.

Nearly all the oyster shops and stands in Massachusetts, I am told, are supplied and kept by natives of Wellfleet, and a part of this town is still called Billingsgate from the oysters having been formerly planted there; but the native oysters are said to have died in 1770. Various causes are assigned for this, such as a ground frost, the carcasses of black-fish, kept to rot in the harbor, and the like, but the most common account of the matter is,—and I find that a similar superstition with regard to the disappearance of fishes exists almost everywhere,—that when Wellfleet began to quarrel with the neighboring towns about the right to gather them, yellow specks appeared in them, and Providence caused them to disappear. A few years ago sixty thousand bushels were annually brought from the South and planted in the harbor of Wellfleet till they attained "the proper relish of Billingsgate"; but now they are imported commonly full-grown, and laid down near their markets, at Boston and elsewhere, where the water, being a mixture of salt and fresh, suits them better. The business was said to be still good and improving.

The old man said that the oysters were liable to freeze in

the winter, if planted too high; but if it were not "so cold as to strain their eyes" they were not injured. The inhabitants of New Brunswick have noticed that "ice will not form over an oyster-bed, unless the cold is very intense indeed, and when the bays are frozen over the oyster-beds are easily discovered by the water above them remaining unfrozen, or as the French residents say, *degèle*." Our host said that they kept them in cellars all winter.

"Without anything to eat or drink?" I asked.

"Without anything to eat or drink," he answered.

"Can the oysters move?"

"Just as much as my shoe."

But when I caught him saying that they "bedded themselves down in the sand, flat side up, round side down," I told him that my shoe could not do that, without the aid of my foot in it; at which he said that they merely settled down as they grew; if put down in a square they would be found so; but the clam could move quite fast. I have since been told by oystermen of Long Island, where the oyster is still indigenous and abundant, that they are found in large masses attached to the parent in their midst, and are so taken up with their tongs; in which case, they say, the age of the young proves that there could have been no motion for five or six years at least. And Buckland in his Curiosities of Natural History (page 50) says: "An oyster who has once taken up his position and fixed himself when quite young, can never make a change. Oysters, nevertheless, that have not fixed themselves, but remain loose at the bottom of the sea, have the power of locomotion; they open their shells to their fullest extent, and then suddenly contracting them, the expulsion of the water forwards gives a motion backwards. A fisherman at Guernsey told me that he had frequently seen oysters moving in this way."

Some still entertain the question "whether the oyster was indigenous in Massachusetts Bay," and whether Wellfleet harbor was a "natural habitat" of this fish; but, to say nothing of the testimony of old oystermen, which, I think, is quite conclusive, though the native oyster may now be extinct there, I saw that their shells, opened by the Indians, were strewn all over the Cape. Indeed, the Cape was at first thickly settled by Indians on account of the abundance of these and other fish. We saw many traces of their occupancy after this, in Truro, near Great Hollow, and at High-Head, near East Harbor River,—oysters, clams, cockles, and other shells, mingled with ashes and the bones of deer and other quadrupeds. I picked up half a dozen arrow-heads, and in an hour or two could have filled my pockets with them. The Indians lived about the edges of the swamps, then probably in some instances ponds, for shelter and water. Moreover, Champlain in the edition of his "Voyages" printed in 1613, says that in the year 1606 he and Poitrincourt explored a harbor (Barnstable Harbor?) in the southerly part of what is now called Massachusetts Bay, in latitude 42°, about five leagues south, one point west of *Cap Blanc* (Cape Cod), and there they found many good oysters, and they named it *"le Port aux Huistres"* (Oyster Harbor). In one edition of his map (1632), the *"R. aux Escailles"* is drawn emptying into the same part of the bay, and on the map *"Novi Belgii,"* in Ogilby's America (1670), the words *"Port aux Huistres"* are placed against the same place. Also William Wood, who left New England in 1633, speaks, in his "New England's Prospect," published in 1634, of "a great oyster-bank" in Charles River, and of another in the Mistick, each of which obstructed the navigation of its river. "The oysters," says he, "be great ones in form of a shoe-horn; some be a foot long; these breed on certain banks that are bare every spring tide. This fish without the shell is so big, that it must admit of a division before you can well get it into your mouth." Oysters are still found there. (Also, see Thomas Morton's New English Canaan, page 90.)

Our host told us that the sea-clam, or hen, was not easily obtained; it was raked up, but never on the Atlantic side, only cast ashore there in small quantities in storms. The fisherman sometimes wades in water several feet deep, and thrusts a pointed stick into the sand before him. When this enters between the valves of a clam, he closes them on it, and is drawn out. It has been known to catch and hold coot and teal which were preying on it. I chanced to be on the bank of the Acushnet at New Bedford one day since this, watching some ducks, when a man informed me that, having let out his young ducks to seek their food amid the samphire (*Salicornia*) and other weeds along the river-side at low tide that morning, at length he noticed that one remained stationary, amid the weeds, something preventing it from following the others, and going to it he found its foot tightly shut in a quahog's shell. He took up both together, carried them to his home, and his wife opening the shell with a knife released the duck and cooked the quahog. The old man said that the great clams were good to eat, but that they always took out a certain part which was poisonous, before they cooked them. "People said it would kill a cat." I did not tell him that I had eaten a large one entire that afternoon, but began to think that I was tougher than a cat. He stated that pedlers came round there, and sometimes tried to sell the women folks a skimmer, but he told them that their women had got a better skimmer than *they* could make, in the shell of their clams; it was shaped just right for this purpose.—They call them "skim-alls" in some places. He also said that the sun-squawl was poisonous to handle, and when the sailors came across it, they did not meddle with it, but heaved it out of their way. I told him that I had handled it that afternoon, and had felt no ill effects as yet. But he said it made the hands itch, especially if they had previously been scratched, or if I put it into my bosom, I should find out what it was.

He informed us that no ice ever formed on the back side of the Cape, or not more than once in a century, and but little snow lay there, it being either absorbed or blown or washed away. Sometimes in winter, when the tide was down, the beach was frozen, and afforded a hard road up the back side for some thirty miles, as smooth as a floor. One winter when he was a boy, he and his father "took right out into the back side before daylight, and walked to Provincetown and back to dinner."

When I asked what they did with all that barren-looking land, where I saw so few cultivated fields,—"Nothing," he said.

"Then why fence your fields?"

"To keep the sand from blowing and covering up the whole."

"The yellow sand," said he, "has some life in it, but the white little or none."

When, in answer to his questions, I told him that I was a

surveyor, he said that they who surveyed his farm were accustomed, where the ground was uneven, to loop up each chain as high as their elbows; that was the allowance they made, and he wished to know if I could tell him why they did not come out according to his deed, or twice alike. He seemed to have more respect for surveyors of the old school, which I did not wonder at. "King George the Third," said he, "laid out a road four rods wide and straight the whole length of the Cape," but where it was now he could not tell.

This story of the surveyors reminded me of a Long-Islander, who once, when I had made ready to jump from the bow of his boat to the shore, and he thought that I underrated the distance and would fall short,—though I found afterward that he judged of the elasticity of my joints by his own,—told me that when he came to a brook which he wanted to get over, he held up one leg, and then, if his foot appeared to cover any part of the opposite bank, he knew that he could jump it. "Why," I told him, "to say nothing of the Mississippi, and other small watery streams, I could blot out a star with my foot, but I would not engage to jump that distance," and asked how he knew when he had got his leg at the right elevation. But he regarded his legs as no less accurate than a pair of screw dividers or an ordinary quadrant, and appeared to have a painful recollection of every degree and minute in the arc which they described; and he would have had me believe that there was a kind of hitch in his hip-joint which answered the purpose. I suggested that he should connect his two ankles by a string of the proper length, which should be the chord of an arc, measuring his jumping ability on horizontal surfaces,—assuming one leg to be a perpendicular to the plane of the horizon, which, however, may have been too bold an assumption in this case. Nevertheless, this was a kind of geometry in the legs which it interested me to hear of.

Our host took pleasure in telling us the names of the ponds, most of which we could see from his windows, and making us repeat them after him, to see if we had got them right. They were Gull Pond, the largest and a very handsome one, clear and deep, and more than a mile in circumference, Newcomb's, Swett's, Slough, Horse-Leech, Round, and Herring Ponds, all connected at high water, if I do not mistake.

The coast-surveyors had come to him for their names, and he told them of one which they had not detected. He said that they were not so high as formerly. There was an earthquake about four years before he was born, which cracked the pans of the ponds, which were of iron, and caused them to settle. I did not remember to have read of this. Innumerable gulls used to resort to them; but the large gulls were now very scarce, for, as he said, the English robbed their nests far in the north, where they breed. He remembered well when gulls were taken in the gull-house, and when small birds were killed by means of a frying-pan and fire at night. His father once lost a valuable horse from this cause. A party from Wellfleet having lighted their fire for this purpose, one dark night, on Billingsgate Island, twenty horses which were pastured there, and this colt among them, being frightened by it, and endeavoring in the dark to cross the passage which separated them from the neighboring beach, and which was then fordable at low tide, were all swept out to sea and drowned. I observed that many horses were still turned out to pasture all summer on the islands and beaches in Wellfleet, Eastham, and Orleans, as a kind of common. He also described the killing of what he called "wild hens" here, after they had gone to roost in the woods, when he was a boy. Perhaps they were "Prairie hens" (pinnated grouse).

He liked the Beach-pea (*Lathyrus maritimus*), cooked green, as well as the cultivated. He had seen it growing very abundantly in Newfoundland, where also the inhabitants ate them, but he had never been able to obtain any ripe for seed. We read, under the head of Chatham, that "in 1555, during a time of great scarcity, the people about Orford, in Sussex (England) were preserved from perishing by eating the seeds of this plant, which grew there in great abundance on the sea-coast. Cows, horses, sheep, and goats eat it." But the writer who quoted this could not learn that they had ever been used in Barnstable County.

He had been a voyager, then? O, he had been about the world in his day. He once considered himself a pilot for all our coast; but now they had changed the names so he might be bothered.

He gave us to taste what he called the Summer Sweeting,

a pleasant apple which he raised, and frequently grafted from, but had never seen growing elsewhere, except once,—three trees on Newfoundland, or at the Bay of Chaleur, I forget which, as he was sailing by. He was sure that he could tell the tree at a distance.

At length the fool, whom my companion called the wizard, came in, muttering between his teeth, "Damn book-ped-lers,—all the time talking about books. Better do something. Damn 'em. I'll shoot 'em. Got a doctor down here. Damn him, I'll get a gun and shoot him"; never once holding up his head. Whereat the old man stood up and said in a loud voice, as if he was accustomed to command, and this was not the first time he had been obliged to exert his authority there: "John, go sit down, mind your business,—we've heard you talk before,—precious little you'll do,—your bark is worse than your bite." But, without minding, John muttered the same gibberish over again, and then sat down at the table which the old folks had left. He ate all there was on it, and then turned to the apples, which his aged mother was paring, that she might give her guests some apple-sauce for breakfast, but she drew them away and sent him off.

When I approached this house the next summer, over the desolate hills between it and the shore, which are worthy to have been the birthplace of Ossian, I saw the wizard in the midst of a cornfield on the hillside, but, as usual, he loomed so strangely, that I mistook him for a scarecrow.

This was the merriest old man that we had ever seen, and one of the best preserved. His style of conversation was coarse and plain enough to have suited Rabelais. He would have made a good Panurge. Or rather he was a sober Silenus, and we were the boys Chromis and Mnasilus, who listened to his story.

> "Not by Hæmonian hills the Thracian bard,
> Nor awful Phœbus was on Pindus heard
> With deeper silence or with more regard."

There was a strange mingling of past and present in his conversation, for he had lived under King George, and might have remembered when Napoleon and the moderns generally were born. He said that one day, when the troubles between the Colonies and the mother country first broke out, as he, a boy of fifteen, was pitching hay out of a cart, one Doane, an old Tory, who was talking with his father, a good Whig, said to him, "Why, Uncle Bill, you might as well undertake to pitch that pond into the ocean with a pitchfork, as for the Colonies to undertake to gain their independence." He remembered well General Washington, and how he rode his horse along the streets of Boston, and he stood up to show us how he looked.

"He was a r—a—ther large and portly-looking man, a manly and resolute-looking officer, with a pretty good leg as he sat on his horse."—"There, I'll tell you, this was the way with Washington." Then he jumped up again, and bowed gracefully to right and left, making show as if he were waving his hat. Said he, "*That* was Washington."

He told us many anecdotes of the Revolution, and was much pleased when we told him that we had read the same in history, and that his account agreed with the written.

"O," he said, "I know, I know! I was a young fellow of sixteen, with my ears wide open; and a fellow of that age, you know, is pretty wide awake, and likes to know everything that's going on. O, I know!"

He told us the story of the wreck of the Franklin, which took place there the previous spring: how a boy came to his house early in the morning to know whose boat that was by the shore, for there was a vessel in distress, and he, being an old man, first ate his breakfast, and then walked over to the top of the hill by the shore, and sat down there, having found a comfortable seat, to see the ship wrecked. She was on the bar, only a quarter of a mile from him, and still nearer to the men on the beach, who had got a boat ready, but could render no assistance on account of the breakers, for there was a pretty high sea running. There were the passengers all crowded together in the forward part of the ship, and some were getting out of the cabin windows and were drawn on deck by the others.

"I saw the captain get out his boat," said he; "he had one little one; and then they jumped into it one after another, down as straight as an arrow. I counted them. There were nine. One was a woman, and she jumped as straight as any of them. Then they shoved off. The sea took them back, one wave went over them, and when they came up there were six still clinging to the boat; I counted them. The next wave turned the boat bottom upward, and emptied them all out. None of them ever came ashore alive. There were the rest of them all crowded together on the forecastle, the other parts of the ship being under water. They had seen all that happened to the boat. At length a heavy sea separated the forecastle from the rest of the wreck, and set it inside of the worst breaker, and the boat was able to reach them, and it saved all that were left, but one woman."

He also told us of the steamer Cambria's getting aground on his shore a few months before we were there, and of her English passengers who roamed over his grounds, and who, he said, thought the prospect from the high hill by the shore "the most delightsome they had ever seen," and also of the pranks which the ladies played with his scoop-net in the ponds. He spoke of these travellers with their purses full of guineas, just as our provincial fathers used to speak of British bloods in the time of King George the Third.

Quid loquar? Why repeat what he told us?

> "Aut Scyllam Nisi, quam fama secuta est,
> Candida succinctam latrantibus inguina monstris,
> Dulichias vexâsse rates, et gurgite in alto
> Ah timidos nautas canibus lacerâsse marinis?"

In the course of the evening I began to feel the potency of the clam which I had eaten, and I was obliged to confess to our host that I was no tougher than the cat he told of; but he answered, that he was a plain-spoken man, and he could tell me that it was all imagination. At any rate, it proved an emetic in my case, and I was made quite sick by it for a short time, while he laughed at my expense. I was pleased to read afterward, in Mourt's Relation of the landing of the Pilgrims in Provincetown Harbor, these words: "We found great muscles (the old editor says that they were undoubtedly seaclams) and very fat and full of sea-pearl; but we could not eat them, for they made us all sick that did eat, as well sailors as passengers, ... but they were soon well again." It brought me nearer to the Pilgrims to be thus reminded by a similar experience that I was so like them. Moreover, it was a valuable confirmation of their story, and I am prepared now to believe every word of Mourt's Relation. I was also pleased to find that man and the clam lay still at the same angle to one another. But I did not notice sea-pearl. Like Cleopatra, I must have swallowed it. I have since dug these clams on a flat in the Bay and observed them. They could squirt full ten feet before the wind, as appeared by the marks of the drops on the sand.

"Now I am going to ask you a question," said the old man, "and I don't know as you can tell me; but you are a learned man, and I never had any learning, only what I got by na-tur."—It was in vain that we reminded him that he could quote Josephus to our confusion.—"I've thought, if I ever met a learned man I should like to ask him this question. Can you tell me how *Axy* is spelt, and what it means? *Axy*," says he; "there's a girl over here is named *Axy*. Now what is it? What does it mean? Is it Scripture? I've read my Bible twenty-five years over and over, and I never came across it."

"Did you read it twenty-five years for this object?" I asked.

"Well, *how* is it spelt? Wife, how is it spelt?"

She said: "It is in the Bible; I've seen it."

"Well, how do you spell it?"

"I don't know. A c h, ach, s e h, seh,—Achseh."

"Does that spell Axy? Well, do *you* know what it means?" asked he, turning to me.

"No," I replied, "I never heard the sound before."

"There was a schoolmaster down here once, and they asked him what it meant, and he said it had no more meaning than a bean-pole."

I told him that I held the same opinion with the school-master. I had been a schoolmaster myself, and had had strange names to deal with. I also heard of such names as Zoheth, Beriah, Amaziah, Bethuel, and Shearjashub, here-abouts.

At length the little boy, who had a seat quite in the chim-ney-corner, took off his stockings and shoes, warmed his feet, and having had his sore leg freshly salved, went off to bed; then the fool made bare his knotty-looking feet and legs, and followed him; and finally the old man exposed his calves also to our gaze. We had never had the good fortune to see an old man's legs before, and were surprised to find them fair and plump as an infant's, and we thought that he took a pride in exhibiting them. He then proceeded to make preparations for retiring, discoursing meanwhile with Panurgic plainness of speech on the ills to which old humanity is subject. We were a rare haul for him. He could commonly get none but ministers to talk to, though sometimes ten of them at once, and he was glad to meet some of the laity at leisure. The evening was not long enough for him. As I had been sick, the old lady asked if I would not go to bed,—it was getting late for old people; but the old man, who had not yet done his stories, said, "You ain't particular, are you?"

"O no," said I, "I am in no hurry. I believe I have weathered the Clam cape."

"They are good," said he; "I wish I had some of them now."

"They never hurt me," said the old lady.

"But then you took out the part that killed a cat," said I.

At last we cut him short in the midst of his stories, which he promised to resume in the morning. Yet, after all, one of the old ladies who came into our room in the night to fasten the fire-board, which rattled, as she went out took the precaution to fasten us in. Old women are by nature more suspicious than old men. However, the winds howled around the house, and made the fire-boards as well as the casements rattle well that night. It was probably a windy night for any locality, but we could not distinguish the roar which was proper to the ocean from that which was due to the wind alone.

The sounds which the ocean makes must be very significant and interesting to those who live near it. When I was leaving the shore at this place the next summer, and had got a quarter of a mile distant, ascending a hill, I was startled by a sudden, loud sound from the sea, as if a large steamer were letting off steam by the shore, so that I caught my breath and felt my blood run cold for an instant, and I turned about, expecting to see one of the Atlantic steamers thus far out of her course, but there was nothing unusual to be seen. There was a low bank at the entrance of the Hollow, between me and the ocean, and suspecting that I might have risen into another stratum of air in ascending the hill,—which had wafted to me only the ordinary roar of the sea,—I immediately descended again, to see if I lost hearing of it; but, without regard to my ascending or descending, it died away in a minute or two, and yet there was scarcely any wind all the while. The old man said that this was what they called the "rut," a peculiar roar of the sea before the wind changes, which, however, he could not account for. He thought that he could tell all about the weather from the sounds which the sea made.

Old Josselyn, who came to New England in 1638, has it among his weather-signs, that "the resounding of the sea from the shore, and murmuring of the winds in the woods, without apparent wind, sheweth wind to follow."

Being on another part of the coast one night since this, I heard the roar of the surf a mile distant, and the inhabitants said it was a sign that the wind would work round east, and we should have rainy weather. The ocean was heaped up somewhere at the eastward, and this roar was occasioned by its effort to preserve its equilibrium, the wave reaching the shore before the wind. Also the captain of a packet between this country and England told me that he sometimes met with a wave on the Atlantic coming against the wind, perhaps in a calm sea, which indicated that at a distance the wind was blowing from an opposite quarter, but the undulation had travelled faster than it. Sailors tell of "tide-rips" and "ground-swells," which they suppose to have been occasioned by hurricanes and earthquakes, and to have travelled many hundred, and sometimes even two or three thousand miles.

Before sunrise the next morning they let us out again, and I ran over to the beach to see the sun come out of the ocean. The old woman of eighty-four winters was already out in the cold morning wind, bare-headed, tripping about like a young girl, and driving up the cow to milk. She got the breakfast with despatch, and without noise or bustle; and meanwhile the old man resumed his stories, standing before us, who were sitting, with his back to the chimney, and ejecting his tobacco-juice right and left into the fire behind him, without regard to the various dishes which were there preparing. At breakfast we had eels, buttermilk cake, cold bread, green beans, doughnuts, and tea. The old man talked a steady stream; and when his wife told him he had better eat his breakfast, he said: "Don't hurry me; I have lived too long to be hurried." I ate of the apple-sauce and the doughnuts, which I thought had sustained the least detriment from the old man's shots, but my companion refused the apple-sauce, and ate of the hot cake and green beans, which had appeared to him to occupy the safest part of the hearth. But on comparing notes afterward, I told him that the buttermilk cake was particularly exposed, and I saw how it suffered repeatedly, and therefore I avoided it; but he declared that, however that might be, he witnessed that the apple-sauce was seriously injured, and had therefore declined that. After breakfast we looked at his clock, which was out of order, and oiled it with some "hen's grease," for want of sweet oil, for he scarcely could believe that we were not tinkers or pedlers; meanwhile he told a story about visions, which had reference to a crack in the clock-case made by frost one night. He was curious to know to what religious sect we belonged. He said that he had been to hear thirteen kinds of preaching in one month, when he was young, but he did not join any of them,—he stuck to his Bible. There was nothing like any of them in his Bible. While I was shaving in the next room, I heard him ask my companion to what sect he belonged, to which he answered:

"O, I belong to the Universal Brotherhood."

"What's that?" he asked, "Sons o' Temperance?"

Finally, filling our pockets with doughnuts, which he was pleased to find that we called by the same name that he did, and paying for our entertainment, we took our departure; but he followed us out of doors, and made us tell him the names of the vegetables which he had raised from seeds that came out of the Franklin. They were cabbage, broccoli, and parsley. As I had asked him the names of so many things, he tried me in turn with all the plants which grew in his garden, both wild and cultivated. It was about half an acre, which he cultivated wholly himself. Besides the common garden vegetables, there were Yellow-Dock, Lemon Balm, Hyssop, Gill-go-over-the-ground, Mouse-ear, Chick-weed, Roman Wormwood, Elecampane, and other plants. As we stood there, I saw a fish-hawk stoop to pick a fish out of his pond.

"There," said I, "he has got a fish."

"Well," said the old man, who was looking all the while, but could see nothing, "he did n't dive, he just wet his claws."

And, sure enough, he did not this time, though it is said that they often do, but he merely stooped low enough to pick him out with his talons; but as he bore his shining prey over the bushes, it fell to the ground, and we did not see that he recovered it. That is not their practice.

Thus, having had another crack with the old man, he standing bareheaded under the eaves, he directed us "athwart the fields," and we took to the beach again for another day, it being now late in the morning.

It was but a day or two after this that the safe of the Provincetown Bank was broken open and robbed by two men from the interior, and we learned that our hospitable entertainers did at least transiently harbor the suspicion that we were the men.

VI

The Beach again

O UR WAY to the high sand-bank, which I have described
as extending all along the coast, led, as usual, through
patches of Bayberry bushes, which straggled into the sand.
This, next to the Shrub-oak, was perhaps the most common
shrub thereabouts. I was much attracted by its odoriferous
leaves and small gray berries which are clustered about the
short twigs, just below the last year's growth. I know of but
two bushes in Concord, and they, being staminate plants, do
not bear fruit. The berries gave it a venerable appearance, and
they smelled quite spicy, like small confectionery. Robert Bev-
erley, in his "History of Virginia," published in 1705, states
that "at the mouth of their rivers, and all along upon the sea
and bay, and near many of their creeks and swamps, grows
the myrtle, bearing a berry, of which they make a hard brittle
wax, of a curious green color, which by refining becomes almost transparent. Of this they make candles, which are never
greasy to the touch nor melt with lying in the hottest
weather; neither does the snuff of these ever offend the smell,
like that of a tallow candle; but, instead of being disagreeable,
if an accident puts a candle out, it yields a pleasant fragrancy
to all that are in the room; insomuch that nice people often
put them out on purpose to have the incense of the expiring
snuff. The melting of these berries is said to have been first
found out by a surgeon in New England, who performed
wonderful things with a salve made of them." From the abundance of berries still hanging on the bushes, we judged that
the inhabitants did not generally collect them for tallow,
though we had seen a piece in the house we had just left. I
have since made some tallow myself. Holding a basket beneath the bare twigs in April, I rubbed them together between my hands and thus gathered about a quart in twenty
minutes, to which were added enough to make three pints,
and I might have gathered them much faster with a suitable
rake and a large shallow basket. They have little prominences
like those of an orange all creased in tallow, which also fills

the interstices down to the stone. The oily part rose to the top, making it look like a savory black broth, which smelled much like balm or other herb tea. You let it cool, then skim off the tallow from the surface, melt this again and strain it. I got about a quarter of a pound weight from my three pints, and more yet remained within the berries. A small portion cooled in the form of small flattish hemispheres, like crystallizations, the size of a kernel of corn (nuggets I called them as I picked them out from amid the berries). Loudon says, that "cultivated trees are said to yield more wax than those that are found wild." (See Duplessy, *Végétaux Résineux*, Vol. II. p. 60.) If you get any pitch on your hands in the pine-woods you have only to rub some of these berries between your hands to start it off. But the ocean was the grand fact there, which made us forget both bayberries and men.

To-day the air was beautifully clear, and the sea no longer dark and stormy, though the waves still broke with foam along the beach, but sparkling and full of life. Already that morning I had seen the day break over the sea as if it came out of its bosom:—

"The saffron-robed Dawn rose in haste from the streams
  Of Ocean, that she might bring light to immortals and to
    mortals."

The sun rose visibly at such a distance over the sea, that the cloud-bank in the horizon, which at first concealed him, was not perceptible until he had risen high behind it, and plainly broke and dispersed it, like an arrow. But as yet I looked at him as rising over land, and could not, without an effort, realize that he was rising over the sea. Already I saw some vessels on the horizon, which had rounded the Cape in the night, and were now well on their watery way to other lands.

We struck the beach again in the south part of Truro. In the early part of the day, while it was flood tide, and the beach was narrow and soft, we walked on the bank, which was very high here, but not so level as the day before, being more interrupted by slight hollows. The author of the Description of the Eastern Coast says of this part, that "the bank is very high and steep. From the edge of it west, there is a strip of sand a hundred yards in breadth. Then succeeds low brushwood, a quarter of a mile wide, and almost impassable. After which comes a thick perplexing forest, in which not a house is to be discovered. Seamen, therefore, though the distance between these two hollows (Newcomb's and Brush Hollows) is great, must not attempt to enter the wood, as in a snow-storm they must undoubtedly perish." This is still a true description of the country, except that there is not much high wood left.

There were many vessels, like gulls, skimming over the surface of the sea, now half concealed in its troughs, their dolphin-strikers ploughing the water, now tossed on the top of the billows. One, a barque standing down parallel with the coast, suddenly furled her sails, came to anchor, and swung round in the wind, near us, only half a mile from the shore. At first we thought that her captain wished to communicate with us, and perhaps we did not regard the signal of distress, which a mariner would have understood, and he cursed us for cold-hearted wreckers who turned our backs on him. For hours we could still see her anchored there behind us, and we wondered how she could afford to loiter so long in her course. Or was she a smuggler who had chosen that wild beach to land her cargo on? Or did they wish to catch fish, or paint their vessel? Erelong other barks, and brigs, and schooners, which had in the mean while doubled the Cape, sailed by her in the smacking breeze, and our consciences were relieved. Some of these vessels lagged behind, while others steadily went ahead. We narrowly watched their rig and the cut of their jibs, and how they walked the water, for there was all the difference between them that there is between living creatures. But we wondered that they should be remembering Boston and New York and Liverpool, steering for them, out there; as if the sailor might forget his peddling business on such a grand highway. They had perchance brought oranges from the Western Isles; and were they carrying back the peel? We might as well transport our old traps across the ocean of eternity. Is *that* but another "trading flood," with its blessed isles? Is Heaven such a harbor as the Liverpool docks?

Still held on without a break, the inland barrens and shrubbery, the desert and the high sand-bank with its even slope, the broad white beach, the breakers, the green water on the bar, and the Atlantic Ocean; and we traversed with delight new reaches of the shore; we took another lesson in sea-horses' manes and sea-cows' tails, in sea-jellies and sea-clams, with our new-gained experience. The sea ran hardly less than the day before. It seemed with every wave to be subsiding, because such was our expectation, and yet when hours had elapsed we could see no difference. But there it was, balancing itself, the restless ocean by our side, lurching in its gait. Each wave left the sand all braided or woven, as it were, with a coarse woof and warp, and a distinct raised edge to its rapid work. We made no haste, since we wished to see the ocean at our leisure, and indeed that soft sand was no place in which to be in a hurry, for one mile there was as good as two elsewhere. Besides, we were obliged frequently to empty our shoes of the sand which one took in in climbing or descending the bank.

As we were walking close to the water's edge this morning, we turned round, by chance, and saw a large black object which the waves had just cast up on the beach behind us, yet too far off for us to distinguish what it was; and when we were about to return to it, two men came running from the bank, where no human beings had appeared before, as if they had come out of the sand, in order to save it before another wave took it. As we approached, it took successively the form of a huge fish, a drowned man, a sail or a net, and finally of a mass of tow-cloth, part of the cargo of the Franklin, which the men loaded into a cart.

Objects on the beach, whether men or inanimate things, look not only exceedingly grotesque, but much larger and more wonderful than they actually are. Lately, when approaching the sea-shore several degrees south of this, I saw before me, seemingly half a mile distant, what appeared like bold and rugged cliffs on the beach, fifteen feet high, and whitened by the sun and waves; but after a few steps it proved to be low heaps of rags,—part of the cargo of a wrecked vessel,—scarcely more than a foot in height. Once also it was my business to go in search of the relics of a human body, mangled by sharks, which had just been cast up, a week after a wreck, having got the direction from a light-house: I should find it a mile or two distant over the sand, a dozen rods from the water, covered with a cloth, by a stick stuck up. I expected that I must look very narrowly to find so small an object, but the sandy beach, half a mile wide, and stretching farther than the eye could reach, was so perfectly smooth and bare, and the mirage toward the sea so magnify-ing, that when I was half a mile distant the insignificant sliver which marked the spot looked like a bleached spar, and the relics were as conspicuous as if they lay in state on that sandy plain, or a generation had labored to pile up their cairn there. Close at hand they were simply some bones with a little flesh adhering to them, in fact, only a slight inequality in the sweep of the shore. There was nothing at all remarkable about them, and they were singularly inoffensive both to the senses and the imagination. But as I stood there they grew more and more imposing. They were alone with the beach and the sea, whose hollow roar seemed addressed to them, and I was im-pressed as if there was an understanding between them and the ocean which necessarily left me out, with my snivelling sympathies. That dead body had taken possession of the shore, and reigned over it as no living one could, in the name of a certain majesty which belonged to it.

We afterward saw many small pieces of tow-cloth washed up, and I learn that it continued to be found in good condi-tion, even as late as November in that year, half a dozen bolts at a time.

We eagerly filled our pockets with the smooth round peb-bles which in some places, even here, were thinly sprinkled over the sand, together with flat circular shells (*Scutellæ*?); but, as we had read, when they were dry they had lost their beauty, and at each sitting we emptied our pockets again of the least remarkable, until our collection was well culled. Every material was rolled into the pebble form by the waves; not only stones of various kinds, but the hard coal which some vessel had dropped, bits of glass, and in one instance a mass of peat three feet long, where there was nothing like it to be seen for many miles. All the great rivers of the globe are annually, if not constantly, discharging great quantities of lumber, which drifts to distant shores. I have also seen very perfect pebbles of brick, and bars of Castile soap from a wreck rolled into perfect cylinders, and still spirally streaked with red, like a barber's pole. When a cargo of rags is washed ashore, every old pocket and bag-like recess will be filled to bursting with sand by being rolled on the beach; and on one occasion, the pockets in the clothing of the wrecked being thus puffed up, even after they had been ripped open by wreckers, deluded me into the hope of identifying them by the contents. A pair of gloves looked exactly as if filled by a hand. The water in such clothing is soon wrung out and evaporated, but the sand, which works itself into every seam, is not so easily got rid of. Sponges, which are picked up on the shore, as is well known, retain some of the sand of the beach to the latest day, in spite of every effort to extract it.

I found one stone on the top of the bank, of a dark gray color, shaped exactly like a giant clam (*Mactra solidissima*), and of the same size; and, what was more remarkable, one half of the outside had shelled off and lay near it, of the same form and depth with one of the valves of this clam, while the other half was loose, leaving a solid core of a darker color within it. I afterward saw a stone resembling a razor clam, but it was a solid one. It appeared as if the stone, in the process of formation, had filled the mould which a clam-shell furnished; or the same law that shaped the clam had made a clam of stone. Dead clams, with shells full of sand, are called sand clams. There were many of the large clam-shells filled with sand; and sometimes one valve was separately filled exactly even, as if it had been heaped and then scraped. Even among the many small stones on the top of the bank, I found one arrow-head.

Beside the giant clam and barnacles, we found on the shore a small clam (*Mesodesma arctata*), which I dug with my hands in numbers on the bars, and which is sometimes eaten by the inhabitants, in the absence of the *Mya arenaria*, on this side. Most of their empty shells had been perforated by some foe.—Also, the

Astarte castanea.

The Edible Mussel (*Mytilus edulis*) on the few rocks, and washed up in curious bunches of forty or fifty, held together by its rope-like *byssus*.

The Scollop Shell (*Pecten concentricus*), used for card-racks and pin-cushions.

Cockles, or Cuckoos (*Natica heros*), and their remarkable *nidus*, called "sand-circle," looking like the top of a stone jug without the stopple, and broken on one side, or like a flaring dickey made of sand-paper. Also,

Cancellaria Couthouyi (?), and

Periwinkles (?) (*Fusus decemcostatus*).

We afterward saw some other kinds on the Bay side. Gould states that this Cape "has hitherto proved a barrier to the migrations of many species of Mollusca."—"Of the one hundred and ninety-seven species [which he described in 1840 as belonging to Massachusetts], eighty-three do not pass to the South shore, and fifty are not found on the North shore of the Cape."

Among Crustacea, there were the shells of Crabs and Lobsters, often bleached quite white high up the beach; Sea or Beach Fleas (*Amphipoda*); and the cases of the Horse-shoe Crab, or Saucepan Fish (*Limulus Polyphæmus*), of which we saw many alive on the Bay side, where they feed pigs on them. Their tails were used as arrow-heads by the Indians.

Of Radiata, there were the Sea Chestnut or Egg (*Echinus granulatus*), commonly divested of its spines; flat circular shells (*Scutella parma?*) covered with chocolate-colored spines, but becoming smooth and white, with five petal-like figures; a few Star-fishes or Five-fingers (*Asterias rubens*); and Sun-fishes or Sea-jellies (*Aureliæ*).

There was also at least one species of Sponge.

The plants which I noticed here and there on the pure sandy shelf, between the ordinary high-water mark and the foot of the bank, were Sea Rocket (*Cakile Americana*), Salt-wort (*Salsola kali*), Sea Sandwort (*Honkenya peploides*), Sea Burdock (*Xanthium echinatum*), Sea-side Spurge (*Euphorbia polygonifolia*); also, Beach Grass (*Arundo, Psamma,* or *Calamagrostis arenaria*), Sea-side Golden-rod (*Solidago sempervirens*), and the Beach Pea (*Lathyrus maritimus*).

Sometimes we helped a wrecker turn over a larger log than usual, or we amused ourselves with rolling stones down the bank, but we rarely could make one reach the water, the beach was so soft and wide; or we bathed in some shallow within a bar, where the sea covered us with sand at every flux, though it was quite cold and windy. The ocean there is commonly but a tantalizing prospect in hot weather, for with all that water before you, there is, as we were afterward told, no bathing on the Atlantic side, on account of the undertow and the rumor of sharks. At the light-house both in Eastham and Truro, the only houses quite on the shore, they declared, the next year, that they would not bathe there "for any sum," for they sometimes saw the sharks tossed up and quiver for a moment on the sand. Others laughed at these stories, but perhaps they could afford to because they never bathed anywhere. One old wrecker told us that he killed a regular man-eating shark fourteen feet long, and hauled him out with his oxen, where we had bathed; and another, that his father caught a smaller one of the same kind that was stranded there, by standing him up on his snout so that the waves could not take him. They will tell you tough stories of sharks all over the Cape, which I do not presume to doubt utterly,—how they will sometimes upset a boat, or tear it in pieces, to get at the man in it. I can easily believe in the undertow, but I have no doubt that one shark in a dozen years is enough to keep up the reputation of a beach a hundred miles long. I should add, however, that in July we walked on the bank here a quarter of a mile parallel with a fish about six feet in length, possibly a shark, which was prowling slowly along within two rods of the shore. It was of a pale brown color, singularly film-like and indistinct in the water, as if all nature abetted this child of ocean, and showed many darker transverse bars or rings whenever it came to the surface. It is well known that different fishes even of the same species are colored by the water they inhabit. We saw it go into a little cove or bathing-tub, where we had just been bathing, where the water was only four or five feet deep at that time, and after exploring it go slowly out again; but we continued to bathe there, only observing first from the bank if the cove was preoccupied. We thought that the water was fuller of life, more aërated perhaps than that of the Bay, like soda-water, for we were as particular as young salmon, and the expectation of encountering a shark did not subtract anything from its life-giving qualities.

Sometimes we sat on the wet beach and watched the beach birds, sand-pipers, and others, trotting along close to each wave, and waiting for the sea to cast up their breakfast. The former (*Charadrius melodus*) ran with great rapidity and then stood stock still remarkably erect and hardly to be distinguished from the beach. The wet sand was covered with small skipping Sea Fleas, which apparently make a part of their food. These last are the little scavengers of the beach, and are so numerous that they will devour large fishes, which have been cast up, in a very short time. One little bird not larger than a sparrow,—it may have been a Phalarope,—would alight on the turbulent surface where the breakers were five or six feet high, and float buoyantly there like a duck, cunningly taking to its wings and lifting itself a few feet through the air over the foaming crest of each breaker, but sometimes outriding safely a considerable billow which hid it some seconds, when its instinct told it that it would not break. It was a little creature thus to sport with the ocean, but it was as perfect a success in its way as the breakers in theirs. There was also an almost uninterrupted line of coots rising and falling with the waves, a few rods from the shore, the whole length of the Cape. They made as constant a part of the ocean's border as the pads or pickerel-weed do of that of a pond. We read the following as to the Storm Petrel (*Thalassidroma Wilsonii*), which is seen in the Bay as well as on the outside. "The feathers on the breast of the Storm Petrel are, like those of all swimming birds, water-proof; but substances not susceptible of being wetted with water are, for that very reason, the best fitted for collecting oil from its surface. That function is performed by the feathers on the breast of the Storm Petrels as they touch on the surface; and though that may not be the only way in which they procure their food, it is certainly that in which they obtain great part of it. They dash along till they have loaded their feathers and then they pause upon the wave and remove the oil with their bills."

Thus we kept on along the gently curving shore, seeing two or three miles ahead at once,—along this ocean sidewalk, where there was none to turn out for, with the middle of the road the highway of nations on our right, and the sand cliffs of the Cape on our left. We saw this forenoon a part of the wreck of a vessel, probably the Franklin, a large piece fifteen feet square, and still freshly painted. With a grapple and a line we could have saved it, for the waves repeatedly washed it within cast, but they as often took it back. It would have been a lucky haul for some poor wrecker, for I have been told that one man who paid three or four dollars for a part of the wreck of that vessel, sold fifty or sixty dollars' worth of iron out of it. Another, the same who picked up the Captain's valise with the memorable letter in it, showed me, growing in his garden, many pear and plum trees which washed ashore from her, all nicely tied up and labelled, and he said that he might have got five hundred dollars worth; for a Mr. Bell was importing the nucleus of a nursery to be established near Boston. His turnip-seed came from the same source. Also valuable spars from the same vessel and from the Cactus lay in his yard. In short the inhabitants visit the beach to see what they have caught as regularly as a fisherman his weir or a lumberer his boom; the Cape is their boom. I heard of one who had recently picked up twenty barrels of apples in good condition, probably a part of a deck load thrown over in a storm.

Though there are wreck-masters appointed to look after valuable property which must be advertised, yet undoubtedly a great deal of value is secretly carried off. But are we not all wreckers contriving that some treasure may be washed up on our beach, that we may secure it, and do we not infer the habits of these Nauset and Barnegat wreckers, from the common modes of getting a living?

The sea, vast and wild as it is, bears thus the waste and wrecks of human art to its remotest shore. There is no telling what it may not vomit up. It lets nothing lie; not even the giant clams which cling to its bottom. It is still heaving up the tow-cloth of the Franklin, and perhaps a piece of some old pirate's ship, wrecked more than a hundred years ago, comes ashore to-day. Some years since, when a vessel was wrecked here which had nutmegs in her cargo, they were strewn all along the beach, and for a considerable time were not spoiled by the salt water. Soon afterward, a fisherman caught a cod which was full of them. Why, then, might not the Spice-Islanders shake their nutmeg-trees into the ocean, and let all nations who stand in need of them pick them up?

However, after a year, I found that the nutmegs from the
Franklin had become soft.

You might make a curious list of articles which fishes have
swallowed,—sailors' open clasp-knives, and bright tin snuff-
boxes, not knowing what was in them,—and jugs, and jewels, and Jonah. The other day I came across the following
scrap in a newspaper.

"A RELIGIOUS FISH.—A short time ago, mine host Stew-
art, of the Denton Hotel, purchased a rock-fish, weighing
about sixty pounds. On opening it he found in it a certificate
of membership of the M. E. Church, which we read as follows: —

                                              Member
        Methodist E. Church.
            Founded A. D. 1784.
Quarterly Ticket.   18
                                              Minister.

'For our light affliction, which is but for a moment, worketh for
us a far more exceeding *and* eternal weight of glory.'—2 Cor. iv. 17.

> 'O what are all my sufferings here,
>   If, Lord, thou count me meet
> With that enraptured host t' appear,
>   And worship at thy feet.'

"The paper was of course in a crumpled and wet condition,
but on exposing it to the sun, and ironing the kinks out of it,
it became quite legible.—*Denton (Md.) Journal.*"

From time to time we saved a wreck ourselves, a box or
barrel, and set it on its end, and appropriated it with crossed
sticks; and it will lie there perhaps, respected by brother
wreckers, until some more violent storm shall take it, really
lost to man until wrecked again. We also saved, at the cost of
wet feet only, a valuable cord and buoy, part of a seine, with
which the sea was playing, for it seemed ungracious to refuse
the least gift which so great a personage offered you. We
brought this home and still use it for a garden line. I picked
up a bottle half buried in the wet sand, covered with barnacles, but stoppled tight, and half full of red ale, which still

smacked of juniper,—all that remained I fancied from the wreck of a rowdy world,—that great salt sea on the one hand, and this little sea of ale on the other, preserving their separate characters. What if it could tell us its adventures over countless ocean waves! Man would not be man through such ordeals as it had passed. But as I poured it slowly out on to the sand, it seemed to me that man himself was like a half-emptied bottle of pale ale, which Time had drunk so far, yet stoppled tight for a while, and drifting about in the ocean of circumstances; but destined erelong to mingle with the surrounding waves, or be spilled amid the sands of a distant shore.

In the summer I saw two men fishing for Bass hereabouts. Their bait was a bullfrog, or several small frogs in a bunch, for want of squid. They followed a retiring wave and whirling their lines round and round their heads with increasing rapidity, threw them as far as they could into the sea; then retreating, sat down, flat on the sand, and waited for a bite. It was literally (or *littorally*) walking down to the shore, and throwing your line into the Atlantic. I should not have known what might take hold of the other end, whether Proteus or another. At any rate, if you could not pull him in, why, you might let him go without being pulled in yourself. And *they* knew by experience that it would be a Striped Bass, or perhaps a Cod, for these fishes play along near the shore.

From time to time we sat under the lee of a sand-hill on the bank, thinly covered with coarse beach-grass, and steadily gazed on the sea, or watched the vessels going south, all Blessings of the Bay of course. We could see a little more than half a circle of ocean, besides the glimpses of the Bay which we got behind us; the sea there was not wild and dreary in all respects, for there were frequently a hundred sail in sight at once on the Atlantic. You can commonly count about eighty in a favorable summer day, and pilots sometimes land and ascend the bank to look out for those which require their services. These had been waiting for fair weather, and had come out of Boston Harbor together. The same is the case when they have been assembled in the Vineyard Sound, so that you may see but few one day, and a large fleet the next. Schooners with many jibs and stay-sails crowded all the sea road; square-rigged vessels with their great height and breadth of canvas were ever and anon appearing out of the far horizon, or disappearing and sinking into it; here and there a pilot-boat was towing its little boat astern toward some distant foreigner who had just fired a gun, the echo of which along the shore sounded like the caving of the bank. We could see the pilot looking through his glass toward the distant ship which was putting back to speak with him. He sails many a mile to meet her; and now she puts her sails aback, and communicates with him alongside,—sends some important message to the owners, and then bids farewell to these shores for good and all; or, perchance a propeller passed and made fast to some disabled craft, or one that had been becalmed, whose cargo of fruit might spoil. Though silently, and for the most part incommunicatively, going about their business, they were, no doubt, a source of cheerfulness and a kind of society to one another.

To-day it was the Purple Sea, an epithet which I should not before have accepted. There were distinct patches of the color of a purple grape with the bloom rubbed off. But first and last the sea is of all colors. Well writes Gilpin concerning "the brilliant hues which are continually playing on the surface of a quiet ocean," and this was not too turbulent at a distance from the shore. "Beautiful," says he, "no doubt in a high degree are those glimmering tints which often invest the tops of mountains; but they are mere coruscations compared with these marine colors, which are continually varying and shifting into each other in all the vivid splendor of the rainbow, through the space often of several leagues." Commonly, in calm weather, for half a mile from the shore, where the bottom tinges it, the sea is green, or greenish, as are some ponds; then blue for many miles, often with purple tinges, bounded in the distance by a light almost silvery stripe; beyond which there is generally a dark-blue rim, like a mountain ridge in the horizon, as if, like that, it owed its color to the intervening atmosphere. On another day it will be marked with long streaks, alternately smooth and rippled, light-colored and dark, even like our inland meadows in a freshet, and showing which way the wind sets.

Thus we sat on the foaming shore, looking on the wine-colored ocean,—

Θίν' ἔφ' ἁλὸς πολιῆς, ὁρόων ἐπὶ οἴνοπα ποντον.

Here and there was a darker spot on its surface, the shadow of a cloud, though the sky was so clear that no cloud would have been noticed otherwise, and no shadow would have been seen on the land, where a much smaller surface is visible at once. So, distant clouds and showers may be seen on all sides by a sailor in the course of a day, which do not necessarily portend rain where he is. In July we saw similar dark-blue patches where schools of Menhaden rippled the surface, scarcely to be distinguished from the shadows of clouds. Sometimes the sea was spotted with them far and wide, such is its inexhaustible fertility. Close at hand you see their back fin, which is very long and sharp, projecting two or three inches above water. From time to time also we saw the white bellies of the Bass playing along the shore.

It was a poetic recreation to watch those distant sails steering for half fabulous ports, whose very names are a mysterious music to our ears: Fayal, and Babel-mandel, ay, and Chagres, and Panama,—bound to the famous Bay of San Francisco, and the golden streams of Sacramento and San Joaquin, to Feather River and the American Fork, where Sutter's Fort presides, and inland stands the City de los Angeles. It is remarkable that men do not sail the sea with more expectation. Nothing remarkable was ever accomplished in a prosaic mood. The heroes and discoverers have found true more than was previously believed, only when they were expecting and dreaming of something more than their contemporaries dreamed of, or even themselves discovered, that is, when they were in a frame of mind fitted to behold the truth. Referred to the world's standard, they are always insane. Even savages have indirectly surmised as much. Humboldt, speaking of Columbus approaching the New World, says: "The grateful coolness of the evening air, the ethereal purity of the starry firmament, the balmy fragrance of flowers, wafted to him by the land breeze, all led him to suppose (as we are told by Herrera, in the Decades) that he was approaching the garden of Eden, the sacred abode of our first parents. The Orinoco seemed to him one of the four rivers which, according to the venerable tradition of the ancient world, flowed from Paradise, to water and divide the surface of the earth, newly adorned with plants." So even the expeditions for the discovery of El Dorado, and of the Fountain of Youth, led to real, if not compensatory discoveries.

We discerned vessels so far off, when once we began to look, that only the tops of their masts in the horizon were visible, and it took a strong intention of the eye, and its most favorable side, to see them at all, and sometimes we doubted if we were not counting our eyelashes. Charles Darwin states that he saw, from the base of the Andes, "the masts of the vessels at anchor in the bay of Valparaiso, although not less than twenty-six geographical miles distant," and that Anson had been surprised at the distance at which his vessels were discovered from the coast, without knowing the reason, namely, the great height of the land and the transparency of the air. Steamers may be detected much farther than sailing vessels, for, as one says, when their hulls and masts of wood and iron are down, their smoky masts and streamers still betray them; and the same writer, speaking of the comparative advantages of bituminous and anthracite coal for war-steamers, states that, "from the ascent of the columns of smoke above the horizon, the motions of the steamers in Calais Harbor [on the coast of France] are at all times observable at Ramsgate [on the English coast], from the first lighting of the fires to the putting out at sea; and that in America the steamers burning the fat bituminous coal can be tracked at sea at least seventy miles before the hulls become visible, by the dense columns of black smoke pouring out of their chimneys, and trailing along the horizon."

Though there were numerous vessels at this great distance in the horizon on every side, yet the vast spaces between them, like the spaces between the stars, far as they were distant from us, so were they from one another—nay, some were twice as far from each other as from us,—impressed us with a sense of the immensity of the ocean, the "unfruitful ocean," as it has been called, and we could see what proportion man and his works bear to the globe. As we looked off,

and saw the water growing darker and darker and deeper and
deeper the farther we looked, till it was awful to consider, and
it appeared to have no relation to the friendly land, either as
shore or bottom,—of what use is a bottom if it is out of
sight, if it is two or three miles from the surface, and you are
to be drowned so long before you get to it, though it were
made of the same stuff with your native soil?—over that
ocean, where, as the Veda says, "there is nothing to give support, nothing to rest upon, nothing to cling to," I felt that I
was a land animal. The man in a balloon even may commonly
alight on the earth in a few moments, but the sailor's only
hope is that he may reach the distant shore. I could then appreciate the heroism of the old navigator, Sir Humphrey Gilbert, of whom it is related, that being overtaken by a storm
when on his return from America, in the year 1583, far north-
eastward from where we were, sitting abaft with a book in
his hand, just before he was swallowed up in the deep, he
cried out to his comrades in the Hind, as they came within
hearing, "We are as near to Heaven by sea as by land." I saw
that it would not be easy to realize.

On Cape Cod, the next most eastern land you hear of is St.
George's Bank (the fishermen tell of "Georges," "Cashus,"
and other sunken lands which they frequent). Every Cape
man has a theory about George's Bank having been an island
once, and in their accounts they gradually reduce the shallowness from six, five, four, two fathoms, to somebody's confident assertion that he has seen a mackerel-gull sitting on a
piece of dry land there. It reminded me, when I thought of
the shipwrecks which had taken place there, of the Isle of
Demons, laid down off this coast in old charts of the New
World. There must be something monstrous, methinks, in a
vision of the sea bottom from over some bank a thousand
miles from the shore, more awful than its imagined bottomlessness; a drowned continent, all livid and frothing at the
nostrils, like the body of a drowned man, which is better sunk
deep than near the surface.

I have been surprised to discover from a steamer the shallowness of Massachusetts Bay itself. Off Billingsgate Point I
could have touched the bottom with a pole, and I plainly saw
it variously shaded with sea-weed, at five or six miles from the

shore. This is "The Shoal-ground of the Cape," it is true, but elsewhere the Bay is not much deeper than a country pond. We are told that the deepest water in the English Channel between Shakespeare's Cliff and Cape Grinéz, in France, is one hundred and eighty feet; and Guyot says that "the Baltic Sea has a depth of only one hundred and twenty feet between the coasts of Germany and those of Sweden," and "the Adriatic between Venice and Trieste has a depth of only one hundred and thirty feet." A pond in my native town, only half a mile long, is more than one hundred feet deep.

The ocean is but a larger lake. At midsummer you may sometimes see a strip of glassy smoothness on it, a few rods in width and many miles long, as if the surface there were covered with a thin pellicle of oil, just as on a country pond; a sort of stand-still, you would say, at the meeting or parting of two currents of air (if it does not rather mark the unrippled steadiness of a current of water beneath), for sailors tell of the ocean and land breeze meeting between the fore and aft sails of a vessel, while the latter are full, the former being suddenly taken aback. Daniel Webster, in one of his letters describing blue-fishing off Martha's Vineyard, referring to those smooth places, which fishermen and sailors call "slicks," says: "We met with them yesterday, and our boatman made for them, whenever discovered. He said they were caused by the blue-fish chopping up their prey. That is to say, those voracious fellows get into a school of menhaden, which are too large to swallow whole, and they bite them into pieces to suit their tastes. And the oil from this butchery, rising to the surface, makes the 'slick.' "

Yet this same placid Ocean, as civil now as a city's harbor, a place for ships and commerce, will erelong be lashed into sudden fury, and all its caves and cliffs will resound with tumult. It will ruthlessly heave these vessels to and fro, break them in pieces in its sandy or stony jaws, and deliver their crews to sea-monsters. It will play with them like sea-weed, distend them like dead frogs, and carry them about, now high, now low, to show to the fishes, giving them a nibble. This gentle Ocean will toss and tear the rag of a man's body like the father of mad bulls, and his relatives may be seen seeking the remnants for weeks along the strand. From some quiet inland hamlet they have rushed weeping to the unheard-of shore, and now stand uncertain where a sailor has recently been buried amid the sand-hills.

It is generally supposed that they who have long been conversant with the Ocean can foretell, by certain indications, such as its roar and the notes of sea-fowl, when it will change from calm to storm; but probably no such ancient mariner as we dream of exists; they know no more, at least, than the older sailors do about this voyage of life on which we are all embarked. Nevertheless, we love to hear the sayings of old sailors, and their accounts of natural phenomena, which totally ignore, and are ignored by, science; and possibly they have not always looked over the gunwale so long in vain. Kalm repeats a story which was told him in Philadelphia by a Mr. Cock, who was one day sailing to the West Indies in a small yacht, with an old man on board who was well acquainted with those seas. "The old man sounding the depth, called to the mate to tell Mr. Cock to launch the boats immediately, and to put a sufficient number of men into them, in order to tow the yacht during the calm, that they might reach the island before them as soon as possible, as within twenty-four hours there would be a strong hurricane. Mr. Cock asked him what reasons he had to think so; the old man replied, that on sounding, he saw the lead in the water at a distance of many fathoms more than he had seen it before; that therefore the water was become clear all of a sudden, which he looked upon as a certain sign of an impending hurricane in the sea." The sequel of the story is, that by good fortune, and by dint of rowing, they managed to gain a safe harbor before the hurricane had reached its height; but it finally raged with so much violence, that not only many ships were lost and houses unroofed, but even their own vessel in harbor was washed so far on shore that several weeks elapsed before it could be got off.

The Greeks would not have called the ocean ἀτρύγετος, or unfruitful, though it does not produce wheat, if they had viewed it by the light of modern science, for naturalists now assert that "the sea, and not the land, is the principal seat of life,"—though not of vegetable life. Darwin affirms that "our most thickly inhabited forests appear almost as deserts when we come to compare them with the corresponding regions of the ocean." Agassiz and Gould tell us that "the sea teems with animals of all classes, far beyond the extreme point of flowering plants"; but they add, that "experiments of dredging in very deep water have also taught us that the abyss of the ocean is nearly a desert";—"so that modern investigations," to quote the words of Desor, "merely go to confirm the great idea which was vaguely anticipated by the ancient poets and philosophers, that the Ocean is the origin of all things." Yet marine animals and plants hold a lower rank in the scale of being than land animals and plants. "There is no instance known," says Desor, "of an animal becoming aquatic in its perfect state, after having lived in its lower stage on dry land," but as in the case of the tadpole, "the progress invariably points towards the dry land." In short, the dry land itself came through and out of the water in its way to the heavens, for, "in going back through the geological ages, we come to an epoch when, according to all appearances, the dry land did not exist, and when the surface of our globe was entirely covered with water." We looked on the sea, then, once more, not as ἀτρύγετος, or unfruitful, but as it has been more truly called, the "laboratory of continents."

Though we have indulged in some placid reflections of late, the reader must not forget that the dash and roar of the waves were incessant. Indeed, it would be well if he were to read with a large conch-shell at his ear. But notwithstanding that it was very cold and windy to-day, it was such a cold as we thought would not cause one to take cold who was exposed to it, owing to the saltness of the air and the dryness of the soil. Yet the author of the old Description of Wellfleet says: "The atmosphere is very much impregnated with saline particles, which, perhaps, with the great use of fish, and the neglect of cider and spruce-beer, may be a reason why the people are more subject to sore mouths and throats than in other places."

VII

Across the Cape

WHEN WE have returned from the sea-side, we sometimes ask ourselves why we did not spend more time in gazing at the sea; but very soon the traveller does not look at the sea more than at the heavens. As for the interior, if the elevated sand-bar in the midst of the ocean can be said to have any interior, it was an exceedingly desolate landscape, with rarely a cultivated or cultivable field in sight. We saw no villages, and seldom a house, for these are generally on the Bay side. It was a succession of shrubby hills and valleys, now wearing an autumnal tint. You would frequently think, from the character of the surface, the dwarfish trees, and the bearberries around, that you were on the top of a mountain. The only wood in Eastham was on the edge of Wellfleet. The pitch-pines were not commonly more than fifteen or eighteen feet high. The larger ones were covered with lichens,—often hung with the long gray *Usnea*. There is scarcely a white-pine on the forearm of the Cape. Yet in the northwest part of Eastham, near the Camp Ground, we saw, the next summer, some quite rural, and even sylvan retreats, for the Cape, where small rustling groves of oaks and locusts and whispering pines, on perfectly level ground, made a little paradise. The locusts, both transplanted and growing naturally about the houses there, appeared to flourish better than any other tree. There were thin belts of wood in Wellfleet and Truro, a mile or more from the Atlantic, but, for the most part, we could see the horizon through them, or, if extensive, the trees were not large. Both oaks and pines had often the same flat look with the apple-trees. Commonly, the oak woods twenty-five years old were a mere scraggy shrubbery nine or ten feet high, and we could frequently reach to their topmost leaf. Much that is called " woods" was about half as high as this,— only patches of shrub-oak, bayberry, beach-plum, and wild roses, overrun with woodbine. When the roses were in bloom, these patches in the midst of the sand displayed such a profusion of blossoms, mingled with the aroma of the bayberry, that no Italian or other artificial rose-garden could equal them. They were perfectly Elysian, and realized my idea of an oasis in the desert. Huckleberry-bushes were very abundant, and the next summer they bore a remarkable quantity of that kind of gall called Huckleberry-apple, forming quite handsome though monstrous blossoms. But it must be added, that this shrubbery swarmed with wood-ticks, sometimes very troublesome parasites, and which it takes very horny fingers to crack.

The inhabitants of these towns have a great regard for a tree, though their standard for one is necessarily neither large nor high; and when they tell you of the large trees that once grew here, you must think of them, not as absolutely large, but large compared with the present generation. Their "brave old oaks," of which they speak with so much respect, and which they will point out to you as relics of the primitive forest, one hundred or one hundred and fifty, ay, for aught they know, two hundred years old, have a ridiculously dwarfish appearance, which excites a smile in the beholder. The largest and most venerable which they will show you in such a case are, perhaps, not more than twenty or twenty-five feet high. I was especially amused by the Liliputian old oaks in the south part of Truro. To the inexperienced eye, which appreciated their proportions only, they might appear vast as the tree which saved his royal majesty, but measured, they were dwarfed at once almost into lichens which a deer might eat up in a morning. Yet they will tell you that large schooners were once built of timber which grew in Wellfleet. The old houses also are built of the timber of the Cape; but instead of the forests in the midst of which they originally stood, barren heaths, with poverty-grass for heather, now stretch away on every side. The modern houses are built of what is called "dimension timber," imported from Maine, all ready to be set up, so that commonly they do not touch it again with an axe. Almost all the wood used for fuel is *imported* by vessels or currents, and of course all the coal. I was told that probably a quarter of the fuel and a considerable part of the lumber used in North Truro was drift-wood. Many get *all* their fuel from the beach.

Of birds not found in the interior of the State,—at least in my neighborhood,—I heard, in the summer, the Black-throated Bunting (*Fringilla Americana*) amid the shrubbery, and in the open land the Upland Plover (*Totanus Bartramius*), whose quivering notes were ever and anon prolonged into a clear, somewhat plaintive, yet hawk-like scream, which sounded at a very indefinite distance. The bird may have been in the next field, though it sounded a mile off.

To-day we were walking through Truro, a town of about eighteen hundred inhabitants. We had already come to Pamet River, which empties into the Bay. This was the limit of the Pilgrims' journey up the Cape from Provincetown, when seeking a place for settlement. It rises in a hollow within a few rods of the Atlantic, and one who lives near its source told us that in high tides the sea leaked through, yet the wind and waves preserve intact the barrier between them, and thus the whole river is steadily driven westward butt-end foremost,—fountain-head, channel, and light-house at the mouth, all together.

Early in the afternoon we reached the Highland Light, whose white tower we had seen rising out of the bank in front of us for the last mile or two. It is fourteen miles from the Nauset Lights, on what is called the Clay Pounds, an immense bed of clay abutting on the Atlantic, and, as the keeper told us, stretching quite across the Cape, which is here only about two miles wide. We perceived at once a difference in the soil, for there was an interruption of the desert, and a slight appearance of a sod under our feet, such as we had not seen for the last two days.

After arranging to lodge at the light-house, we rambled across the Cape to the Bay, over a singularly bleak and barren looking country, consisting of rounded hills and hollows, called by geologists diluvial elevations and depressions,—a kind of scenery which has been compared to a chopped sea, though this suggests too sudden a transition. There is a delineation of this very landscape in Hitchcock's Report on the Geology of Massachusetts, a work which, by its size at least, reminds one of a diluvial elevation itself. Looking southward from the light-house, the Cape appeared like an elevated plateau, sloping very regularly, though slightly, downward from the edge of the bank on the Atlantic side, about one hundred and fifty feet above the ocean, to that on the Bay side. On traversing this we found it to be interrupted by broad valleys or gullies, which become the hollows in the bank when the sea has worn up to them. They are commonly at right angles with the shore, and often extend quite across the Cape. Some of the valleys, however, are circular, a hundred feet deep without any outlet, as if the Cape had sunk in those places, or its sands had run out. The few scattered houses which we passed, being placed at the bottom of the hollows for shelter and fertility, were, for the most part, concealed entirely, as much as if they had been swallowed up in the earth. Even a village with its meeting-house, which we had left little more than a stone's throw behind, had sunk into the earth, spire and all, and we saw only the surface of the upland and the sea on either hand. When approaching it, we had mistaken the belfry for a summer-house on the plain. We began to think that we might tumble into a village before we were aware of it, as into an ant-lion's hole, and be drawn into the sand irrecoverably. The most conspicuous objects on the land were a distant windmill, or a meeting-house standing alone, for only they could afford to occupy an exposed place. A great part of the township, however, is a barren, heath-like plain, and perhaps one third of it lies in common, though the property of individuals. The author of the old "Description of Truro," speaking of the soil, says: "The snow, which would be of essential service to it provided it lay level and covered the ground, is blown into drifts and into the sea." This peculiar open country, with here and there a patch of shrubbery, extends as much as seven miles, or from Pamet River on the south to High Head on the north, and from Ocean to Bay. To walk over it makes on a stranger such an impression as being at sea, and he finds it impossible to estimate distances in any weather. A windmill or a herd of cows may seem to be far away in the horizon, yet, after going a few rods, he will be close upon them. He is also deluded by other kinds of mirage. When, in the summer, I saw a family a-blueberrying a mile off, walking about amid the dwarfish bushes which did not come up higher than their ankles, they seemed to me to be a race of giants, twenty feet high at least.

The highest and sandiest portion next the Atlantic was

thinly covered with Beach-grass and Indigo-weed. Next to this the surface of the upland generally consisted of white sand and gravel, like coarse salt, through which a scanty vegetation found its way up. It will give an ornithologist some idea of its barrenness if I mention that the next June, the month of grass, I found a night-hawk's eggs there, and that almost any square rod thereabouts, taken at random, would be an eligible site for such a deposit. The kildeer-plover, which loves a similar locality, also drops its eggs there, and fills the air above with its din. This upland also produced *Cladonia* lichens, poverty-grass, savory-leaved aster (*Diplopappus linariifolius*), mouse-ear, bearberry, &c. On a few hillsides the savory-leaved aster and mouse-ear alone made quite a dense sward, said to be very pretty when the aster is in bloom. In some parts the two species of poverty-grass (*Hudsonia tomentosa* and *ericoides*), which deserve a better name, reign for miles in little hemispherical tufts or islets, like moss, scattered over the waste. They linger in bloom there till the middle of July. Occasionally near the beach these rounded beds, as also those of the sea-sandwort (*Honkenya peploides*), were filled with sand within an inch of their tops, and were hard, like large ant-hills, while the surrounding sand was soft. In summer, if the poverty-grass grows at the head of a Hollow looking toward the sea, in a bleak position where the wind rushes up, the northern or exposed half of the tuft is sometimes all black and dead like an oven-broom, while the opposite half is yellow with blossoms, the whole hillside thus presenting a remarkable contrast when seen from the poverty-stricken and the flourishing side. This plant, which in many places would be esteemed an ornament, is here despised by many on account of its being associated with barrenness. It might well be adopted for the Barnstable coat-of-arms, in a field *sableux*. I should be proud of it. Here and there were tracts of Beach-grass mingled with the Sea-side Golden-rod and Beach-pea, which reminded us still more forcibly of the ocean.

We read that there was not a brook in Truro. Yet there were deer here once, which must often have panted in vain; but I am pretty sure that I afterward saw a small fresh-water brook emptying into the south side of Pamet River, though I was so heedless as not to taste it. At any rate, a little boy near by told me that he drank at it. There was not a tree as far as we could see, and that was many miles each way, the general level of the upland being about the same everywhere. Even from the Atlantic side we overlooked the Bay, and saw to Manomet Point in Plymouth, and better from that side because it was the highest. The almost universal bareness and smoothness of the landscape were as agreeable as novel, making it so much the more like the deck of a vessel. We saw vessels sailing south into the Bay, on the one hand, and north along the Atlantic shore, on the other, all with an aft wind.

The single road which runs lengthwise the Cape, now winding over the plain, now through the shrubbery which scrapes the wheels of the stage, was a mere cart-track in the sand, commonly without any fences to confine it, and continually changing from this side to that, to harder ground, or sometimes to avoid the tide. But the inhabitants travel the waste here and there pilgrim-wise and staff in hand, by narrow footpaths, through which the sand flows out and reveals the nakedness of the land. We shuddered at the thought of living there and taking our afternoon walks over those barren swells, where we could overlook every step of our walk before taking it, and would have to pray for a fog or a snow-storm to conceal our destiny. The walker there must soon eat his heart.

In the north part of the town there is no house from shore to shore for several miles, and it is as wild and solitary as the Western Prairies—used to be. Indeed, one who has seen every house in Truro will be surprised to hear of the number of the inhabitants, but perhaps five hundred of the men and boys of this small town were then abroad on their fishing-grounds. Only a few men stay at home to till the sand or watch for blackfish. The farmers are fishermen-farmers and understand better ploughing the sea than the land. They do not disturb their sands much, though there is a plenty of sea-weed in the creeks, to say nothing of blackfish occasionally rotting on the shore. Between the Pond and East Harbor Village there was an interesting plantation of pitch-pines, twenty or thirty acres in extent, like those which we had already seen from the stage. One who lived near said that the land was purchased by two men for a shilling or twenty-five cents an

acre. Some is not considered worth writing a deed for. This
soil or sand, which was partially covered with poverty and
beach grass, sorrel, &c., was furrowed at intervals of about
four feet and the seed dropped by a machine. The pines had
come up admirably and grown the first year three or four
inches, and the second six inches and more. Where the seed
had been lately planted the white sand was freshly exposed in
an endless furrow winding round and round the sides of the
deep hollows, in a vortical spiral manner, which produced a
very singular effect, as if you were looking into the reverse
side of a vast banded shield. This experiment, so important to
the Cape, appeared very successful, and perhaps the time will
come when the greater part of this kind of land in Barnstable
County will be thus covered with an artificial pine forest, as
has been done in some parts of France. In that country 12,500
acres of downs had been thus covered in 1811 near Bayonne.
They are called *pignadas*, and according to Loudon "constitute the principal riches of the inhabitants, where there was a
drifting desert before." It seemed a nobler kind of grain to
raise than corn even.

A few years ago Truro was remarkable among the Cape
towns for the number of sheep raised in it; but I was told
that at this time only two men kept sheep in the town, and
in 1855, a Truro boy ten years old told me that he had never
seen one. They were formerly pastured on the unfenced lands
or general fields, but now the owners were more particular to
assert their rights, and it cost too much for fencing. The rails
are cedar from Maine, and two rails will answer for ordinary
purposes, but four are required for sheep. This was the reason
assigned by one who had formerly kept them for not keeping
them any longer. Fencing stuff is so expensive that I saw
fences made with only one rail, and very often the rail when
split was carefully tied with a string. In one of the villages I
saw the next summer a cow tethered by a rope six rods long,
the rope long in proportion as the feed was short and thin.
Sixty rods, ay, all the cables of the Cape, would have been no
more than fair. Tethered in the desert for fear that she would
get into Arabia Felix! I helped a man weigh a bundle of hay
which he was selling to his neighbor, holding one end of a
pole from which it swung by a steel-yard hook, and this was

just half his whole crop. In short, the country looked so barren that I several times refrained from asking the inhabitants for a string or a piece of wrapping-paper, for fear I should rob them, for they plainly were obliged to import these things as well as rails, and where there were no news-boys, I did not see what they would do for waste paper.

The objects around us, the make-shifts of fishermen ashore, often made us look down to see if we were standing on terra firma. In the wells everywhere a block and tackle were used to raise the bucket, instead of a windlass, and by almost every house was laid up a spar or a plank or two full of auger-holes, saved from a wreck. The windmills were partly built of these, and they were worked into the public bridges. The lighthouse keeper, who was having his barn shingled, told me casually that he had made three thousand good shingles for that purpose out of a mast. You would sometimes see an old oar used for a rail. Frequently also some fair-weather finery ripped off a vessel by a storm near the coast was nailed up against an outhouse. I saw fastened to a shed near the lighthouse a long new sign with the words "ANGLO SAXON" on it in large gilt letters, as if it were a useless part which the ship could afford to lose, or which the sailors had discharged at the same time with the pilot. But it interested somewhat as if it had been a part of the Argo, clipped off in passing through the Symplegades.

To the fisherman, the Cape itself is a sort of store-ship laden with supplies,—a safer and larger craft which carries the women and children, the old men and the sick, and indeed sea-phrases are as common on it as on board a vessel. Thus is it ever with a sea-going people. The old Northmen used to speak of the "keel-ridge" of the country, that is, the ridge of the Doffrafield Mountains, as if the land were a boat turned bottom up. I was frequently reminded of the Northmen here. The inhabitants of the Cape are often at once farmers and sea-rovers; they are more than vikings or kings of the bays, for their sway extends over the open sea also. A farmer in Wellfleet, at whose house I afterward spent a night, who had raised fifty bushels of potatoes the previous year, which is a large crop for the Cape, and had extensive salt-works, pointed to his schooner, which lay in sight, in which he and his man and boy occasionally ran down the coast a-trading as far as the Capes of Virginia. This was his market-cart, and his hired man knew how to steer her. Thus he drove two teams a-field,

> "ere the high *seas* appeared
> Under the opening eyelids of the morn."

Though probably he would not hear much of the "gray-fly" on his way to Virginia.

A great proportion of the inhabitants of the Cape are always thus abroad about their teaming on some ocean highway or other, and the history of one of their ordinary trips would cast the Argonautic expedition into the shade. I have just heard of a Cape Cod captain who was expected home in the beginning of the winter from the West Indies, but was long since given up for lost, till his relations at length have heard with joy, that, after getting within forty miles of Cape Cod light, he was driven back by nine successive gales to Key West, between Florida and Cuba, and was once again shaping his course for home. Thus he spent his winter. In ancient times the adventures of these two or three men and boys would have been made the basis of a myth, but now such tales are crowded into a line of short-hand signs, like an algebraic formula in the shipping news. "Wherever over the world," said Palfrey in his oration at Barnstable, "you see the stars and stripes floating, you may have good hope that beneath them some one will be found who can tell you the soundings of Barnstable, or Wellfleet, or Chatham Harbor."

I passed by the home of somebody's (or everybody's) Uncle Bill, one day over on the Plymouth shore. It was a schooner half keeled-up on the mud: we aroused the master out of a sound sleep at noonday, by thumping on the bottom of his vessel till he presented himself at the hatch-way, for we wanted to borrow his clam-digger. Meaning to make him a call, I looked out the next morning, and lo! he had run over to "the Pines" the evening before, fearing an easterly storm. He outrode the *great* gale in the spring of 1851, dashing about alone in Plymouth Bay. He goes after rockweed, lighters vessels, and saves wrecks. I still saw him lying in the mud over at "the Pines" in the horizon, which place he could not leave if he would, till flood tide. But he would not then probably. This waiting for the tide is a singular feature in life by the sea-shore. A frequent answer is, "Well! you can't start for two hours yet." It is something new to a landsman, and at first he is not disposed to wait. History says that "two inhabitants of Truro were the first who adventured to the Falkland Isles in pursuit of whales. This voyage was undertaken in the year 1774, by the advice of Admiral Montague of the British navy, and was crowned with success."

At the Pond Village we saw a pond three eighths of a mile long densely filled with cat-tail flags, seven feet high,— enough for all the coopers in New England.

The western shore was nearly as sandy as the eastern, but the water was much smoother, and the bottom was partially covered with the slender grass-like sea-weed (*Zostera*), which we had not seen on the Atlantic side; there were also a few rude sheds for trying fish on the beach there, which made it appear less wild. In the few marshes on this side we afterward saw Samphire, Rosemary, and other plants new to us inlanders.

In the summer and fall sometimes, hundreds of blackfish (the Social Whale, *Globicephalus melas* of De Kay; called also Black Whale-fish, Howling Whale, Bottle-head, &c.), fifteen feet or more in length, are driven ashore in a single school here. I witnessed such a scene in July, 1855. A carpenter who was working at the light-house arriving early in the morning remarked that he did not know but he had lost fifty dollars by coming to his work; for as he came along the Bay side he heard them driving a school of blackfish ashore, and he had debated with himself whether he should not go and join them and take his share, but had concluded to come to his work. After breakfast I came over to this place, about two miles distant, and near the beach met some of the fishermen returning from their chase. Looking up and down the shore, I could see about a mile south some large black masses on the sand, which I knew must be blackfish, and a man or two about them. As I walked along towards them I soon came to a huge carcass whose head was gone and whose blubber had been stripped off some weeks before; the tide was just beginning to move it, and the stench compelled me to go a long way round. When I came to Great Hollow I found a fisherman and some boys on the watch, and counted about thirty blackfish, just killed, with many lance wounds, and the water was more or less bloody around. They were partly on shore and partly in the water, held by a rope round their tails till the tide should leave them. A boat had been somewhat stove by the tail of one. They were a smooth shining black, like India-rubber, and had remarkably simple and lumpish forms for animated creatures, with a blunt round snout or head, whale-like, and simple stiff-looking flippers. The largest were about fifteen feet long, but one or two were only five feet long, and still without teeth. The fisherman slashed one with his jack-knife, to show me how thick the blubber was,—about three inches; and as I passed my finger through the cut it was covered thick with oil. The blubber looked like pork, and this man said that when they were trying it the boys would sometimes come round with a piece of bread in one hand, and take a piece of blubber in the other to eat with it, preferring it to pork scraps. He also cut into the flesh beneath, which was firm and red like beef, and he said that for his part he preferred it when fresh to beef. It is stated that in 1812 blackfish were used as food by the poor of Bretagne. They were waiting for the tide to leave these fishes high and dry, that they might strip off the blubber and carry it to their try-works in their boats, where they try it on the beach. They get commonly a barrel of oil, worth fifteen or twenty dollars, to a fish. There were many lances and harpoons in the boats,— much slenderer instruments than I had expected. An old man came along the beach with a horse and wagon distributing the dinners of the fishermen, which their wives had put up in little pails and jugs, and which he had collected in the Pond Village, and for this service, I suppose, he received a share of the oil. If one could not tell his own pail, he took the first he came to.

As I stood there they raised the cry of "another school," and we could see their black backs and their blowing about a mile northward, as they went leaping over the sea like horses. Some boats were already in pursuit there, driving them toward the beach. Other fishermen and boys running up began to jump into the boats and push them off from where I stood, and I might have gone too had I chosen. Soon there were twenty-five or thirty boats in pursuit, some large ones under sail, and others rowing with might and main, keeping outside of the school, those nearest to the fishes striking on the sides of their boats and blowing horns to drive them on to the beach. It was an exciting race. If they succeed in driving them ashore each boat takes one share, and then each man, but if they are compelled to strike them off shore each boat's company take what they strike. I walked rapidly along the shore toward the north, while the fishermen were rowing still more swiftly to join their companions, and a little boy who walked by my side was congratulating himself that his father's boat was beating another one. An old blind fisherman whom we met, inquired, "Where are they, I can't see. Have they got them?" In the mean while the fishes had turned and were escaping northward toward Provincetown, only occasionally the back of one being seen. So the nearest crews were compelled to strike them, and we saw several boats soon made fast, each to its fish, which, four or five rods ahead was drawing it like a race-horse straight toward the beach, leaping half out of water blowing blood and water from its hole, and leaving a streak of foam behind. But they went ashore too far north for us, though we could see the fishermen leap out and lance them on the sand. It was just like pictures of whaling which I have seen, and a fisherman told me that it was nearly as dangerous. In his first trial he had been much excited, and in his haste had used a lance with its scabbard on, but nevertheless had thrust it quite through his fish.

I learned that a few days before this one hundred and eighty blackfish had been driven ashore in one school at Eastham, a little farther south, and that the keeper of Billingsgate Point light went out one morning about the same time and cut his initials on the backs of a large school which had run ashore in the night, and sold his right to them to Provincetown for one thousand dollars, and probably Provincetown made as much more. Another fisherman told me that nineteen years ago three hundred and eighty were driven ashore in one school at Great Hollow. In the Naturalists' Library, it is said that, in the winter of 1809–10, one thousand one hundred and ten "approached the shore of Hralfiord, Iceland, and were captured." De Kay says it is not known why they are stranded. But one fisherman declared to me that they ran ashore in pursuit of squid, and that they generally came on the coast about the last of July.

About a week afterward, when I came to this shore, it was strewn as far as I could see with a glass, with the carcasses of blackfish stripped of their blubber and their heads cut off; the latter lying higher up. Walking on the beach was out of the question on account of the stench. Between Provincetown and Truro they lay in the very path of the stage. Yet no steps were taken to abate the nuisance, and men were catching lobsters as usual just off the shore. I was told that they did sometimes tow them out and sink them; yet I wondered where they got the stones to sink them with. Of course they might be made into guano, and Cape Cod is not so fertile that her inhabitants can afford to do without this manure,—to say nothing of the diseases they may produce.

After my return home, wishing to learn what was known about the Blackfish, I had recourse to the reports of the zoölogical surveys of the State, and I found that Storer had rightfully omitted it in his Report on the Fishes, since it is not a fish; so I turned to Emmons's Report of the Mammalia, but was surprised to find that the seals and whales were omitted by him, because he had had no opportunity to observe them. Considering how this State has risen and thriven by its fisheries,—that the legislature which authorized the Zoölogical Survey sat under the emblem of a codfish,—that Nantucket and New Bedford are within our limits,—that an early riser may find a thousand or fifteen hundred dollars' worth of blackfish on the shore in a morning,—that the Pilgrims saw the Indians cutting up a blackfish on the shore at Eastham, and called a part of that shore "Grampus Bay," from the number of blackfish they found there, before they got to Plymouth,—and that from that time to this these fishes have continued to enrich one or two counties almost annually, and that their decaying carcasses were now poisoning the air of one county for more than thirty miles,—I thought it remarkable that neither the popular nor scientific name was to be found in a report on our mammalia,—a *catalogue* of the productions of our land and water.

We had here, as well as all across the Cape, a fair view of
Provincetown, five or six miles distant over the water toward
the west, under its shrubby sand-hills, with its harbor now
full of vessels whose masts mingled with the spires of its
churches, and gave it the appearance of a quite large seaport
town.

The inhabitants of all the lower Cape towns enjoy thus the
prospect of two seas. Standing on the western or larboard
shore, and looking across to where the distant mainland
looms, they can say, This is Massachusetts Bay; and then, after an hour's sauntering walk, they may stand on the starboard side, beyond which no land is seen to loom, and say,
This is the Atlantic Ocean.

On our way back to the light-house, by whose whitewashed tower we steered as securely as the mariner by its
light at night, we passed through a graveyard, which apparently was saved from being blown away by its slates, for they
had enabled a thick bed of huckleberry-bushes to root themselves amid the graves. We thought it would be worth the
while to read the epitaphs where so many were lost at sea;
however, as not only their lives, but commonly their bodies
also, were lost or not identified, there were fewer epitaphs of
this sort than we expected, though there were not a few.
Their graveyard is the ocean. Near the eastern side we started
up a fox in a hollow, the only kind of wild quadruped, if I
except a skunk in a salt-marsh, that we saw in all our walk
(unless painted and box tortoises may be called quadrupeds).
He was a large, plump, shaggy fellow, like a yellow dog, with,
as usual, a white tip to his tail, and looked as if he fared well
on the Cape. He cantered away into the shrub-oaks and bay-
berry-bushes which chanced to grow there, but were hardly
high enough to conceal him. I saw another the next summer
leaping over the top of a beach-plum a little farther north, a
small arc of his course (which I trust is not yet run), from
which I endeavored in vain to calculate his whole orbit: there
were too many unknown attractions to be allowed for. I also
saw the exuviæ of a third fast sinking into the sand, and
added the skull to my collection. Hence I concluded that they
must be plenty thereabouts; but a traveller may meet with
more than an inhabitant, since he is more likely to take an

unfrequented route across the country. They told me that in some years they died off in great numbers by a kind of madness, under the effect of which they were seen whirling round and round as if in pursuit of their tails. In Crantz's account of Greenland, he says: "They (the foxes) live upon birds and their eggs, and, when they can't get them, upon crow-berries, mussels, crabs, and what the sea casts out."

Just before reaching the light-house, we saw the sun set in the Bay,—for standing on that narrow Cape was, as I have said, like being on the deck of a vessel, or rather at the mast-head of a man-of-war, thirty miles at sea, though we knew that at the same moment the sun was setting behind our native hills, which were just below the horizon in that direction. This sight drove everything else quite out of our heads, and Homer and the Ocean came in again with a rush,—

Ἐν δ' ἔπεσ' Ὠκεανῷ λαμπρὸν φάος ἠελίοιο,

the shining torch of the sun fell into the ocean.

VIII

The Highland Light

THIS LIGHT-HOUSE, known to mariners as the Cape Cod or Highland Light, is one of our "primary sea-coast lights," and is usually the first seen by those approaching the entrance of Massachusetts Bay from Europe. It is forty-three miles from Cape Ann Light, and forty-one from Boston Light. It stands about twenty rods from the edge of the bank, which is here formed of clay. I borrowed the plane and square, level and dividers, of a carpenter who was shingling a barn near by, and using one of those shingles made of a mast, contrived a rude sort of quadrant, with pins for sights and pivots, and got the angle of elevation of the bank opposite the light-house, and with a couple of cod-lines the length of its slope, and so measured its height on the shingle. It rises one hundred and ten feet above its immediate base, or about one hundred and twenty-three feet above mean low water. Graham, who has carefully surveyed the extremity of the Cape, makes it one hundred and thirty feet. The mixed sand and clay lay at an angle of forty degrees with the horizon, where I measured it, but the clay is generally much steeper. No cow nor hen ever gets down it. Half a mile farther south the bank is fifteen or twenty-five feet higher, and that appeared to be the highest land in North Truro. Even this vast clay bank is fast wearing away. Small streams of water trickling down it at intervals of two or three rods, have left the intermediate clay in the form of steep Gothic roofs fifty feet high or more, the ridges as sharp and rugged-looking as rocks; and in one place the bank is curiously eaten out in the form of a large semicircular crater.

According to the light-house keeper, the Cape is wasting here on both sides, though most on the eastern. In some places it had lost many rods within the last year, and, erelong, the light-house must be moved. We calculated, *from his data*, how soon the Cape would be quite worn away at this point, "for," said he, "I can remember sixty years back." We were even more surprised at this last announcement,—that is, at the slow waste of life and energy in our informant, for we had taken him to be not more than forty,—than at the rapid wasting of the Cape, and we thought that he stood a fair chance to outlive the former.

Between this October and June of the next year, I found that the bank had lost about forty feet in one place, opposite the light-house, and it was cracked more than forty feet farther from the edge at the last date, the shore being strewn with the recent rubbish. But I judged that generally it was not wearing away here at the rate of more than six feet annually. Any conclusions drawn from the observations of a few years or one generation only are likely to prove false, and the Cape may balk expectation by its durability. In some places even a wrecker's foot-path down the bank lasts several years. One old inhabitant told us that when the light-house was built, in 1798, it was calculated that it would stand forty-five years, allowing the bank to waste one length of fence each year, "but," said he, "there it is" (or rather another near the same site, about twenty rods from the edge of the bank).

The sea is not gaining on the Cape everywhere, for one man told me of a vessel wrecked long ago on the north of Provincetown whose *"bones"* (this was his word) are still visible many rods within the present line of the beach, half buried in sand. Perchance they lie alongside the *timbers* of a whale. The general statement of the inhabitants is, that the Cape is wasting on both sides, but extending itself on particular points on the south and west, as at Chatham and Monomoy Beaches, and at Billingsgate, Long, and Race Points. James Freeman stated in his day that above three miles had been added to Monomoy Beach during the previous fifty years, and it is said to be still extending as fast as ever. A writer in the Massachusetts Magazine, in the last century, tells us that " when the English first settled upon the Cape, there was an island off Chatham, at three leagues' distance, called Webbs' Island, containing twenty acres, covered with red-cedar or savin. The inhabitants of Nantucket used to carry wood from it"; but he adds that in his day a large rock alone marked the spot, and the water was six fathoms deep there. The entrance to Nauset Harbor, which was once in Eastham, has now travelled south into Orleans. The islands in Wellfleet

Harbor once formed a continuous beach, though now small vessels pass between them. And so of many other parts of this coast.

Perhaps what the Ocean takes from one part of the Cape it gives to another,—robs Peter to pay Paul. On the eastern side the sea appears to be everywhere encroaching on the land. Not only the land is undermined, and its ruins carried off by currents, but the sand is blown from the beach directly up the steep bank where it is one hundred and fifty feet high, and covers the original surface there many feet deep. If you sit on the edge you will have ocular demonstration of this by soon getting your eyes full. Thus the bank preserves its height as fast as it is worn away. This sand is steadily travelling westward at a rapid rate, "more than a hundred yards," says one writer, within the memory of inhabitants now living; so that in some places peat-meadows are buried deep under the sand, and the peat is cut through it; and in one place a large peat-meadow has made its appearance on the shore in the bank covered many feet deep, and peat has been cut there. This accounts for that great pebble of peat which we saw in the surf. The old oysterman had told us that many years ago he lost a "crittur" by her being mired in a swamp near the Atlantic side east of his house, and twenty years ago he lost the swamp itself entirely, but has since seen signs of it appearing on the beach. He also said that he had seen cedar stumps "as big as cart-wheels" (!) on the bottom of the Bay, three miles off Billingsgate Point, when leaning over the side of his boat in pleasant weather, and that that was dry land not long ago. Another told us that a log canoe known to have been buried many years before on the Bay side at East Harbor in Truro, where the Cape is extremely narrow, appeared at length on the Atlantic side, the Cape having rolled over it, and an old woman said,—"Now, you see, it is true what I told you, that the Cape is moving."

The bars along the coast shift with every storm, and in many places there is occasionally none at all. We ourselves observed the effect of a single storm with a high tide in the night, in July, 1855. It moved the sand on the beach opposite the light-house to the depth of six feet, and three rods in width as far as we could see north and south, and carried it bodily off no one knows exactly where, laying bare in one place a large rock five feet high which was invisible before, and narrowing the beach to that extent. There is usually, as I have said, no bathing on the back side of the Cape, on account of the undertow, but when we were there last, the sea had, three months before, cast up a bar near this light-house, two miles long and ten rods wide, over which the tide did not flow, leaving a narrow cove, then a quarter of a mile long, between it and the shore, which afforded excellent bathing. This cove had from time to time been closed up as the bar travelled northward, in one instance imprisoning four or five hundred whiting and cod, which died there, and the water as often turned fresh and finally gave place to sand. This bar, the inhabitants assured us, might be wholly removed, and the water six feet deep there in two or three days.

The light-house keeper said that when the wind blowed strong on to the shore, the waves ate fast into the bank, but when it blowed off they took no sand away; for in the former case the wind heaped up the surface of the water next to the beach, and to preserve its equilibrium a strong undertow immediately set back again into the sea which carried with it the sand and whatever else was in the way, and left the beach hard to walk on; but in the latter case the undertow set on, and carried the sand with it, so that it was particularly difficult for shipwrecked men to get to land when the wind blowed on to the shore, but easier when it blowed off. This undertow, meeting the next surface wave on the bar which itself has made, forms part of the dam over which the latter breaks, as over an upright wall. The sea thus plays with the land holding a sand-bar in its mouth awhile before it swallows it, as a cat plays with a mouse; but the fatal gripe is sure to come at last. The sea sends its rapacious east wind to rob the land, but before the former has got far with its prey, the land sends its honest west wind to recover some of its own. But, according to Lieutenant Davis, the forms, extent, and distribution of sand-bars and banks are principally determined, not by winds and waves, but by tides.

Our host said that you would be surprised if you were on the beach when the wind blew a hurricane directly on to it, to see that none of the drift-wood came ashore, but all was

carried directly northward and parallel with the shore as fast
as a man can walk, by the inshore current, which sets strongly
in that direction at flood tide. The strongest swimmers also
are carried along with it, and never gain an inch toward the
beach. Even a large rock has been moved half a mile northward along the beach. He assured us that the sea was never
still on the back side of the Cape, but ran commonly as high
as your head, so that a great part of the time you could not
launch a boat there, and even in the calmest weather the
waves run six or eight feet up the beach, though then you
could get off on a plank. Champlain and Pourtrincourt could
not land here in 1606, on account of the swell (*la houlle*), yet
the savages came off to them in a canoe. In the Sieur de la
Borde's "Relation des Caraibes," my edition of which was
published at Amsterdam in 1711, at page 530 he says: —

"Couroumon a Caraibe, also a star [i. e. a god], makes the
great *lames à la mer*, and overturns canoes. *Lames à la mer*
are the long *vagues* which are not broken (*entrecoupees*), and
such as one sees come to land all in one piece, from one end
of a beach to another, so that, however little wind there may
be, a shallop or a canoe could hardly land (*aborder terre*) without turning over, or being filled with water."

But on the Bay side the water even at its edge is often as
smooth and still as in a pond. Commonly there are no boats
used along this beach. There was a boat belonging to the
Highland Light which the next keeper after he had been there
a year had not launched, though he said that there was good
fishing just off the shore. Generally the Life Boats cannot be
used when needed. When the waves run very high it is impossible to get a boat off, however skilfully you steer it, for it
will often be completely covered by the curving edge of the
approaching breaker as by an arch, and so filled with water,
or it will be lifted up by its bows, turned directly over backwards and all the contents spilled out. A spar thirty feet long
is served in the same way.

I heard of a party who went off fishing back of Wellfleet
some years ago, in two boats, in calm weather, who, when
they had laden their boats with fish, and approached the land
again, found such a swell breaking on it, though there was no
wind, that they were afraid to enter it. At first they thought

to pull for Provincetown, but night was coming on, and that was many miles distant. Their case seemed a desperate one. As often as they approached the shore and saw the terrible breakers that intervened, they were deterred. In short, they were thoroughly frightened. Finally, having thrown their fish overboard, those in one boat chose a favorable opportunity, and succeeded, by skill and good luck, in reaching the land, but they were unwilling to take the responsibility of telling the others when to come in, and as the other helmsman was inexperienced, their boat was swamped at once, yet all managed to save themselves.

Much smaller waves soon make a boat "nail-sick," as the phrase is. The keeper said that after a long and strong blow there would be three large waves, each successively larger than the last, and then no large ones for some time, and that, when they wished to land in a boat, they came in on the last and largest wave. Sir Thomas Browne (as quoted in Brand's Popular Antiquities, p. 372), on the subject of the tenth wave being "greater or more dangerous than any other," after quoting Ovid,—

> "Qui venit hic fluctus, fluctus supereminet omnes
> Posterior nono est, undecimo que prior,"—

says, "Which, notwithstanding, is evidently false; nor can it be made out either by observation either upon the shore or the ocean, as we have with diligence explored in both. And surely in vain we expect regularity in the waves of the sea, or in the particular motions thereof, as we may in its general reciprocations, whose causes are constant, and effects therefore correspondent; whereas its fluctuations are but motions subservient, which winds, storms, shores, shelves, and every interjacency, irregulates."

We read that the Clay Pounds were so called, "because vessels have had the misfortune to be pounded against it in gales of wind," which we regard as a doubtful derivation. There are small ponds here, upheld by the clay, which were formerly called the Clay Pits. Perhaps this, or Clay Ponds, is the origin of the name. Water is found in the clay quite near the surface; but we heard of one man who had sunk a well in the sand close by, "till he could see stars at noonday," without finding any. Over this bare Highland the wind has full sweep. Even in July it blows the wings over the heads of the young turkeys, which do not know enough to head against it; and in gales the doors and windows are blown in, and you must hold on to the light-house to prevent being blown into the Atlantic. They who merely keep out on the beach in a storm in the winter are sometimes rewarded by the Humane Society. If you would feel the full force of a tempest, take up your residence on the top of Mount Washington, or at the Highland Light, in Truro.

It was said in 1794 that more vessels were cast away on the east shore of Truro than anywhere in Barnstable County. Notwithstanding that this light-house has since been erected, after almost every storm we read of one or more vessels wrecked here, and sometimes more than a dozen wrecks are visible from this point at one time. The inhabitants hear the crash of vessels going to pieces as they sit round their hearths, and they commonly date from some memorable shipwreck. If the history of this beach could be written from beginning to end, it would be a thrilling page in the history of commerce.

Truro was settled in the year 1700 as *Dangerfield*. This was a very appropriate name, for I afterward read on a monument in the graveyard, near Pamet River, the following inscription: —

Sacred
to the memory of
57 citizens of Truro,
who were lost in seven
vessels, which
foundered at sea in
the memorable gale
of Oct. 3d, 1841.

Their names and ages by families were recorded on different sides of the stone. They are said to have been lost on George's Bank, and I was told that only one vessel drifted ashore on the back side of the Cape, with the boys locked into the cabin and drowned. It is said that the homes of all were " within a circuit of two miles." Twenty-eight inhabitants of Dennis were lost in the same gale; and I read that "in one day, immediately after this storm, nearly or quite one hundred bodies were taken up and buried on Cape Cod." The Truro Insurance Company failed for want of skippers to take charge of its vessels. But the surviving inhabitants went a fishing again the next year as usual. I found that it would not do to speak of shipwrecks there, for almost every family has lost some of its members at sea. "Who lives in that house?" I inquired. "Three widows," was the reply. The stranger and the inhabitant view the shore with very different eyes. The former may have come to see and admire the ocean in a storm; but the latter looks on it as the scene where his nearest relatives were wrecked. When I remarked to an old wrecker partially blind, who was sitting on the edge of the bank smoking a pipe, which he had just lit with a match of dried beach-grass, that I supposed he liked to hear the sound of the surf, he answered: "No, I do not like to hear the sound of the surf." He had lost at least one son in "the memorable gale," and could tell many a tale of the shipwrecks which he had witnessed there.

In the year 1717, a noted pirate named Bellamy was led on to the bar off Wellfleet by the captain of a *snow* which he had taken, to whom he had offered his vessel again if he would pilot him into Provincetown Harbor. Tradition says that the latter threw over a burning tar-barrel in the night, which drifted ashore, and the pirates followed it. A storm coming on, their whole fleet was wrecked, and more than a hundred dead bodies lay along the shore. Six who escaped shipwreck were executed. "At times to this day" (1793), says the historian of Wellfleet, "there are King William and Queen Mary's coppers picked up, and pieces of silver called cob-money. The violence of the seas moves the sands on the outer bar, so that at times the iron caboose of the ship [that is, Bellamy's] at low ebbs has been seen." Another tells us that, "For many years after this shipwreck, a man of a very singular and frightful aspect used every spring and autumn to be seen travelling on the Cape, who was supposed to have been one of Bellamy's crew. The presumption is that he went to some place where money had been secreted by the pirates, to get such a supply as his exigencies required. When he died, many pieces of gold were found in a girdle which he constantly wore."

As I was walking on the beach here in my last visit, looking for shells and pebbles, just after that storm which I have mentioned as moving the sand to a great depth, not knowing but I might find some cob-money, I did actually pick up a French crown piece, worth about a dollar and six cents, near highwater mark, on the still moist sand, just under the abrupt, caving base of the bank. It was of a dark slate color, and looked like a flat pebble, but still bore a very distinct and handsome head of Louis XV., and the usual legend on the reverse, *Sit Nomen Domini Benedictum* (Blessed be the Name of the Lord), a pleasing sentiment to read in the sands of the sea-shore, whatever it might be stamped on, and I also made out the date, 1741. Of course, I thought at first that it was that same old button which I have found so many times, but my knife soon showed the silver. Afterward, rambling on the bars at low tide, I cheated my companion by holding up round shells (*Scutellæ*) between my fingers, whereupon he quickly stripped and came off to me.

In the Revolution, a British ship of war called the Somerset was wrecked near the Clay Pounds, and all on board, some hundreds in number, were taken prisoners. My informant said that he had never seen any mention of this in the histories, but that at any rate he knew of a silver watch, which one of those prisoners by accident left there, which was still going to tell the story. But this event is noticed by some writers.

The next summer I saw a sloop from Chatham dragging for anchors and chains just off this shore. She had her boats out at the work while she shuffled about on various tacks, and, when anything was found, drew up to hoist it on board. It is a singular employment, at which men are regularly hired and paid for their industry, to hunt to-day in pleasant weather for anchors which have been lost,—the sunken faith and hope of mariners, to which they trusted in vain; now, perchance, it is the rusty one of some old pirate's ship or Norman fisherman, whose cable parted here two hundred years ago; and now the best bower anchor of a Canton or a California ship, which has gone about her business. If the roadsteads of the spiritual ocean could be thus dragged, what rusty flukes of hope deceived and parted chain-cables of faith might again be windlassed aboard! enough to sink the finder's craft, or stock new navies to the end of time. The bottom of the sea is strewn with anchors, some deeper and some shallower, and alternately covered and uncovered by the sand, perchance with a small length of iron cable still attached,—to which where is the other end? So many unconcluded tales to be continued another time. So, if we had diving-bells adapted to the spiritual deeps, we should see anchors with their cables attached, as thick as eels in vinegar, all wriggling vainly toward their holding-ground. But that is not treasure for us which another man has lost; rather it is for us to seek what no other man has found or can find,—not be Chatham men, dragging for anchors.

The annals of this voracious beach! who could write them, unless it were a shipwrecked sailor? How many who have seen it have seen it only in the midst of danger and distress, the last strip of earth which their mortal eyes beheld. Think of the amount of suffering which a single strand has witnessed. The ancients would have represented it as a sea-monster with open jaws, more terrible than Scylla and Charybdis. An inhabitant of Truro told me that about a fortnight after the St. John was wrecked at Cohasset he found two bodies on the shore at the Clay Pounds. They were those of a man, and a corpulent woman. The man had thick boots on, though his head was off, but "it was alongside." It took the finder some weeks to get over the sight. Perhaps they were man and wife, and whom God had joined the ocean currents had not put asunder. Yet by what slight accidents at first may they have been associated in their drifting. Some of the bodies of those passengers were picked up far out at sea, boxed up and sunk; some brought ashore and buried. There are more consequences to a shipwreck than the underwriters notice. The Gulf Stream may return some to their native shores, or drop them in some out-of-the-way cave of Ocean, where time and the elements will write new riddles with their bones.—But to return to land again.

In this bank, above the clay, I counted in the summer, two hundred holes of the Bank Swallow within a space six rods long, and there were at least one thousand old birds within three times that distance, twittering over the surf. I had never associated them in my thoughts with the beach before. One little boy who had been a-birds-nesting had got eighty swallows' eggs for his share! Tell it not to the Humane Society. There were many young birds on the clay beneath, which had tumbled out and died. Also there were many Crow-blackbirds hopping about in the dry fields, and the Upland Plover were breeding close by the light-house. The keeper had once cut off one's wing while mowing, as she sat on her eggs there. This is also a favorite resort for gunners in the fall to shoot the Golden Plover. As around the shores of a pond are seen devil's-needles, butterflies, &c., so here, to my surprise, I saw at the same season great devil's-needles of a size proportionably larger, or nearly as big as my finger, incessantly coasting up and down the edge of the bank, and butterflies also were hovering over it, and I never saw so many dorr-bugs and beetles of various kinds as strewed the beach. They had apparently flown over the bank in the night, and could not get up again, and some had perhaps fallen into the sea and were washed ashore. They may have been in part attracted by the light-house lamps.

The Clay Pounds are a more fertile tract than usual. We saw some fine patches of roots and corn here. As generally on the Cape, the plants had little stalk or leaf, but ran remarkably to seed. The corn was hardly more than half as high as in the interior, yet the ears were large and full, and one farmer told us that he could raise forty bushels on an acre without manure, and sixty with it. The heads of the rye also were remarkably large. The Shadbush (*Amelanchier*), Beach Plums, and Blueberries (*Vaccinium Pennsylvanicum*), like the apple-trees and oaks, were very dwarfish, spreading over the sand, but at the same time very fruitful. The blueberry was but an inch or two high, and its fruit often rested on the ground, so that you did not suspect the presence of the bushes, even on those bare hills, until you were treading on them. I thought that this fertility must be owing mainly to the abundance of moisture in the atmosphere, for I observed that what little grass there was was remarkably laden with dew in the morning, and in summer dense imprisoning fogs frequently last till midday, turning one's beard into a wet napkin about his throat, and the oldest inhabitant may lose his way within a stone's throw of his house or be obliged to follow the beach for a guide. The brick house attached to the light-house was exceedingly damp at that season, and writing-paper lost all its stiffness in it. It was impossible to dry your towel after bathing, or to press flowers without their mildewing. The air was so moist that we rarely wished to drink, though we could at all times taste the salt on our lips. Salt was rarely used at table, and our host told us that his cattle invariably refused it when it was offered them, they got so much with their grass and at every breath, but he said that a sick horse or one just from the country would sometimes take a hearty draught of salt water, and seemed to like it and be the better for it.

It was surprising to see how much water was contained in the terminal bud of the sea-side golden rod, standing in the sand early in July, and also how turnips, beets, carrots, &c., flourished even in pure sand. A man travelling by the shore near there not long before us noticed something green growing in the pure sand of the beach, just at high-water mark, and on approaching found it to be a bed of beets flourishing vigorously, probably from seed washed out of the Franklin. Also beets and turnips came up in the sea-weed used for manure in many parts of the Cape. This suggests how various plants may have been dispersed over the world to distant islands and continents. Vessels, with seeds in their cargoes, destined for particular ports, where perhaps they were not needed, have been cast away on desolate islands, and though their crews perished, some of their seeds have been preserved. Out of many kinds a few would find a soil and climate adapted to them,—become naturalized and perhaps drive out the native plants at last, and so fit the land for the habitation of man. It is an ill wind that blows nobody any good, and for the time lamentable shipwrecks may thus contribute a new vegetable to a continent's stock, and prove on the whole a lasting blessing to its inhabitants. Or winds and currents might effect the same without the intervention of man. What indeed are the various succulent plants which grow on the beach but such beds of beets and turnips, sprung originally from seeds which perhaps were cast on the waters for this end, though we do not know the Franklin which they came out of? In ancient times some Mr. Bell (?) was sailing this way in his ark with seeds of rocket, saltwort, sandwort, beach-

grass, samphire, bayberry, poverty-grass, &c., all nicely labelled with directions, intending to establish a nursery somewhere; and did not a nursery get established, though he
thought that he had failed?

About the light-house I observed in the summer the pretty
Polygala polygama, spreading ray-wise flat on the ground,
white pasture thistles (*Cirsium pumilum*), and amid the
shrubbery the *Smilax glauca*, which is commonly said not to
grow so far north; near the edge of the banks about half a
mile southward, the broom crowberry (*Empetrum Conradii*),
for which Plymouth is the only locality in Massachusetts usually named, forms pretty green mounds four or five feet in
diameter by one foot high,—soft, springy beds for the wayfarer. I saw it afterward in Provincetown, but prettiest of all
the scarlet pimpernel, or poor-man's weather-glass (*Anagallis
arvensis*), greets you in fair weather on almost every square
yard of sand. From Yarmouth, I have received the *Chrysopsis
falcata* (golden aster), and *Vaccinium stamineum* (Deerberry
or Squaw Huckleberry), with fruit not edible, sometimes as
large as a cranberry (Sept. 7).

The Highland Light-house,* where we were staying, is a
substantial-looking building of brick, painted white, and surmounted by an iron cap. Attached to it is the dwelling of the
keeper, one story high, also of brick, and built by government. As we were going to spend the night in a light-house,
we wished to make the most of so novel an experience, and
therefore told our host that we would like to accompany him
when he went to light up. At rather early candle-light he
lighted a small Japan lamp, allowing it to smoke rather more
than we like on ordinary occasions, and told us to follow him.
He led the way first through his bedroom, which was placed
nearest to the light-house, and then through a long, narrow,
covered passage-way, between whitewashed walls like a
prison entry, into the lower part of the light-house, where
many great butts of oil were arranged around; thence we ascended by a winding and open iron stairway, with a steadily
increasing scent of oil and lamp-smoke, to a trap-door in an
iron floor, and through this into the lantern. It was a neat

---

*The light-house has since been rebuilt, and shows a *Fresnel* light.

building, with everything in apple-pie order, and no danger of anything rusting there for want of oil. The light consisted of fifteen argand lamps, placed within smooth concave reflectors twenty-one inches in diameter, and arranged in two horizontal circles one above the other, facing every way excepting directly down the Cape. These were surrounded, at a distance of two or three feet, by large plate-glass windows, which defied the storms, with iron sashes, on which rested the iron cap. All the iron work, except the floor, was painted white. And thus the light-house was completed. We walked slowly round in that narrow space as the keeper lighted each lamp in succession, conversing with him at the same moment that many a sailor on the deep witnessed the lighting of the Highland Light. His duty was to fill and trim and light his lamps, and keep bright the reflectors. He filled them every morning, and trimmed them commonly once in the course of the night. He complained of the quality of the oil which was furnished. This house consumes about eight hundred gallons in a year, which cost not far from one dollar a gallon; but perhaps a few lives would be saved if better oil were provided. Another light-house keeper said that the same proportion of winter-strained oil was sent to the southernmost light-house in the Union as to the most northern. Formerly, when this light-house had windows with small and thin panes, a severe storm would sometimes break the glass, and then they were obliged to put up a wooden shutter in haste to save their lights and reflectors,—and sometimes in tempests, when the mariner stood most in need of their guidance, they had thus nearly converted the light-house into a dark lantern, which emitted only a few feeble rays, and those commonly on the land or lee side. He spoke of the anxiety and sense of responsibility which he felt in cold and stormy nights in the winter; when he knew that many a poor fellow was depending on him, and his lamps burned dimly, the oil being chilled. Sometimes he was obliged to warm the oil in a kettle in his house at midnight, fill his lamps over again,—for he could not have a fire in the light-house, it produced such a sweat on the windows. His successor told me that he could not keep too hot a fire in such a case. All this because the oil was poor. A government lighting the mariners on its wintry coast with summer-strained oil, to save expense! That were surely a summer-strained mercy.

This keeper's successor, who kindly entertained me the next year, stated that one extremely cold night, when this and all the neighboring lights were burning summer oil, but he had been provident enough to reserve a little winter oil against emergencies, he was waked up with anxiety, and found that his oil was congealed, and his lights almost extinguished; and when, after many hours' exertion, he had succeeded in replenishing his reservoirs with winter oil at the wick end, and with difficulty had made them burn, he looked out and found that the other lights in the neighborhood, which were usually visible to him, had gone out, and he heard afterward that the Pamet River and Billingsgate Lights also had been extinguished.

Our host said that the frost, too, on the windows caused him much trouble, and in sultry summer nights the moths covered them and dimmed his lights; sometimes even small birds flew against the thick plate glass, and were found on the ground beneath in the morning with their necks broken. In the spring of 1855 he found nineteen small yellowbirds, perhaps goldfinches or myrtle-birds, thus lying dead around the light-house; and sometimes in the fall he had seen where a golden plover had struck the glass in the night, and left the down and the fatty part of its breast on it.

Thus he struggled, by every method, to keep his light shining before men. Surely the light-house keeper has a responsible, if an easy, office. When his lamp goes out, *he* goes out; or, at most, only one such accident is pardoned.

I thought it a pity that some poor student did not live there, to profit by all that light, since he would not rob the mariner. "Well," he said, "I do sometimes come up here and read the newspaper when they are noisy down below." Think of fifteen argand lamps to read the newspaper by! Government oil!—light, enough, perchance, to read the Constitution by! I thought that he should read nothing less than his Bible by that light. I had a classmate who fitted for college by the lamps of a light-house, which was more light, we think, than the University afforded.

When we had come down and walked a dozen rods from

the light-house, we found that we could not get the full strength of its light on the narrow strip of land between it and the shore, being too low for the focus, and we saw only so many feeble and rayless stars; but at forty rods inland we could see to read, though we were still indebted to only one lamp. Each reflector sent forth a separate "fan" of light,—one shone on the windmill, and one in the hollow, while the intervening spaces were in shadow. This light is said to be visible twenty nautical miles and more, from an observer fifteen feet above the level of the sea. We could see the revolving light at Race Point, the end of the Cape, about nine miles distant, and also the light on Long Point, at the entrance of Provincetown Harbor, and one of the distant Plymouth Harbor Lights, across the Bay, nearly in a range with the last, like a star in the horizon. The keeper thought that the other Plymouth Light was concealed by being exactly in a range with the Long Point Light. He told us that the mariner was sometimes led astray by a mackerel fisher's lantern, who was afraid of being run down in the night, or even by a cottager's light, mistaking them for some well-known light on the coast, and, when he discovered his mistake, was wont to curse the prudent fisher or the wakeful cottager without reason.

Though it was once declared that Providence placed this mass of clay here on purpose to erect a light-house on, the keeper said that the light-house should have been erected half a mile farther south, where the coast begins to bend, and where the light could be seen at the same time with the Nauset Lights, and distinguished from them. They now talk of building one there. It happens that the present one is the more useless now, so near the extremity of the Cape, because other light-houses have since been erected there.

Among the many regulations of the Light-house Board, hanging against the wall here, many of them excellent, perhaps, if there were a regiment stationed here to attend to them, there is one requiring the keeper to keep an account of the number of vessels which pass his light during the day. But there are a hundred vessels in sight at once, steering in all directions, many on the very verge of the horizon, and he must have more eyes than Argus, and be a good deal farther-sighted, to tell which are passing his light. It is an employment in some respects best suited to the habits of the gulls which coast up and down here, and circle over the sea.

I was told by the next keeper, that on the 8th of June following, a particularly clear and beautiful morning, he rose about half an hour before sunrise, and having a little time to spare, for his custom was to extinguish his lights at sunrise, walked down toward the shore to see what he might find. When he got to the edge of the bank he looked up, and, to his astonishment, saw the sun rising, and already part way above the horizon. Thinking that his clock was wrong, he made haste back, and though it was still too early by the clock, extinguished his lamps, and when he had got through and come down, he looked out the window, and, to his still greater astonishment, saw the sun just where it was before, two thirds above the horizon. He showed me where its rays fell on the wall across the room. He proceeded to make a fire, and when he had done, there was the sun still at the same height. Whereupon, not trusting to his own eyes any longer, he called up his wife to look at it, and she saw it also. There were vessels in sight on the ocean, and their crews, too, he said, must have seen it, for its rays fell on them. It remained at that height for about fifteen minutes by the clock, and then rose as usual, and nothing else extraordinary happened during that day. Though accustomed to the coast, he had never witnessed nor heard of such a phenomenon before. I suggested that there might have been a cloud in the horizon invisible to him, which rose with the sun, and his clock was only as accurate as the average; or perhaps, as he denied the possibility of this, it was such a looming of the sun as is said to occur at Lake Superior and elsewhere. Sir John Franklin, for instance, says in his Narrative, that when he was on the shore of the Polar Sea, the horizontal refraction varied so much one morning that "the upper limb of the sun twice appeared at the horizon before it finally rose."

He certainly must be a sun of Aurora to whom the sun looms, when there are so many millions to whom it *glooms* rather, or who never see it till an hour *after* it has risen. But it behooves us old stagers to keep our lamps trimmed and burning to the last, and not trust to the sun's looming.

This keeper remarked that the centre of the flame should

be exactly opposite the centre of the reflectors, and that accordingly, if he was not careful to turn down his wicks in the morning, the sun falling on the reflectors on the south side of the building would set fire to them, like a burning-glass, in the coldest day, and he would look up at noon and see them all lighted! When your lamp is ready to give light, it is readiest to receive it, and the sun will light it. His successor said that he had never known them to blaze in such a case, but merely to smoke.

I saw that this was a place of wonders. In a sea turn or shallow fog while I was there the next summer, it being clear overhead, the edge of the bank twenty rods distant appeared like a mountain pasture in the horizon. I was completely deceived by it, and I could then understand why mariners sometimes ran ashore in such cases, especially in the night, supposing it to be far away, though they could see the land. Once since this, being in a large oyster boat two or three hundred miles from here, in a dark night, when there was a thin veil of mist on land and water, we came so near to running on to the land before our skipper was aware of it, that the first warning was my hearing the sound of the surf under my elbow. I could almost have jumped ashore, and we were obliged to go about very suddenly to prevent striking. The distant light for which we were steering, supposing it a lighthouse five or six miles off, came through the cracks of a fisherman's bunk not more than six rods distant.

The keeper entertained us handsomely in his solitary little ocean house. He was a man of singular patience and intelligence, who, when our queries struck him, rung as clear as a bell in response. The light-house lamps a few feet distant shone full into my chamber, and made it as bright as day, so I knew exactly how the Highland Light bore all that night, and I was in no danger of being wrecked. Unlike the last, this was as still as a summer night. I thought as I lay there, half awake and half asleep, looking upward through the window at the lights above my head, how many sleepless eyes from far out on the Ocean stream—mariners of all nations spinning their yarns through the various watches of the night—were directed toward my couch.

IX

The Sea and the Desert

T HE LIGHT-HOUSE lamps were still burning, though now
with a silvery lustre, when I rose to see the sun come out
of the Ocean; for he still rose eastward of us; but I was convinced that he must have come out of a dry bed beyond that
stream, though he seemed to come out of the water.

> "The sun once more touched the fields,
>   Mounting to heaven from the fair flowing
>   Deep-running Ocean."

Now we saw countless sails of mackerel fishers abroad on
the deep, one fleet in the north just pouring round the Cape,
another standing down toward Chatham, and our host's son
went off to join some lagging member of the first which had
not yet left the Bay.

Before we left the light-house we were obliged to anoint
our shoes faithfully with tallow, for walking on the beach, in
the salt water and the sand, had turned them red and crisp.
To counterbalance this, I have remarked that the sea-shore,
even where muddy, as it is not here, is singularly clean; for
notwithstanding the spattering of the water and mud and
squirting of the clams while walking to and from the boat,
your best black pants retain no stain nor dirt, such as they
would acquire from walking in the country.

We have heard that a few days after this, when the Provincetown Bank was robbed, speedy emissaries from Provincetown made particular inquiries concerning us at this light-
house. Indeed, they traced us all the way down the Cape, and
concluded that we came by this unusual route down the back
side and on foot, in order that we might discover a way to
get off with our booty when we had committed the robbery.
The Cape is so long and narrow, and so bare withal, that it
is wellnigh impossible for a stranger to visit it without the
knowledge of its inhabitants generally, unless he is wrecked
on to it in the night. So, when this robbery occurred, all their
suspicions seem to have at once centered on us two travellers

who had just passed down it. If we had not chanced to leave the Cape so soon, we should probably have been arrested. The real robbers were two young men from Worcester County who travelled with a centre-bit, and are said to have done their work very neatly. But the only bank that we pried into was the great Cape Cod sand-bank, and we robbed it only of an old French crown piece, some shells and pebbles, and the materials of this story.

Again we took to the beach for another day (October 13), walking along the shore of the resounding sea, determined to get it into us. We wished to associate with the Ocean until it lost the pond-like look which it wears to a countryman. We still thought that we could see the other side. Its surface was still more sparkling than the day before, and we beheld "the countless smilings of the ocean waves"; though some of them were pretty broad grins, for still the wind blew and the billows broke in foam along the beach. The nearest beach to us on the other side, whither we looked, due east, was on the coast of Galicia, in Spain, whose capital is Santiago, though by old poets' reckoning it should have been Atlantis or the Hesperides; but heaven is found to be farther west now. At first we were abreast of that part of Portugal *entre Douro e Mino*, and then Galicia and the port of Pontevedra opened to us as we walked along; but we did not enter, the breakers ran so high. The bold headland of Cape Finisterre, a little north of east, jutted toward us next, with its vain brag, for we flung back,— "Here is Cape Cod,— Cape Land's-Beginning." A little indentation toward the north,— for the land loomed to our imaginations by a common mirage,— we knew was the Bay of Biscay, and we sang:

> "There we lay, till next day,
> In the Bay of Biscay O!"

A little south of east was Palos, where Columbus weighed anchor, and farther yet the pillars which Hercules set up; concerning which when we inquired at the top of our voices what was written on them,— for we had the morning sun in our faces, and could not see distinctly,— the inhabitants shouted *Ne plus ultra* (no more beyond), but the wind bore to us the truth only, *plus ultra* (more beyond), and over the

Bay westward was echoed *ultra* (beyond). We spoke to them through the surf about the Far West, the true Hesperia, ἕω πέρας or end of the day, the This Side Sundown, where the sun was extinguished in the *Pacific*, and we advised them to pull up stakes and plant those pillars of theirs on the shore of California, whither all our folks were gone,—the only *ne* plus ultra now. Whereat they looked crestfallen on their cliffs, for we had taken the wind out of all their sails.

We could not perceive that any of their leavings washed up here, though we picked up a child's toy, a small dismantled boat, which may have been lost at Pontevedra.

The Cape became narrower and narrower as we approached its wrist between Truro and Provincetown, and the shore inclined more decidedly to the west. At the head of East Harbor Creek, the Atlantic is separated but by half a dozen rods of sand from the tide-waters of the Bay. From the Clay Pounds the bank flatted off for the last ten miles to the extremity at Race Point, though the highest parts, which are called "islands" from their appearance at a distance on the sea, were still seventy or eighty feet above the Atlantic, and afforded a good view of the latter, as well as a constant view of the Bay, there being no trees nor a hill sufficient to interrupt it. Also the sands began to invade the land more and more, until finally they had entire possession from sea to sea, at the narrowest part. For three or four miles between Truro and Provincetown there were no inhabitants from shore to shore, and there were but three or four houses for twice that distance.

As we plodded along, either by the edge of the ocean, where the sand was rapidly drinking up the last wave that wet it, or over the sand-hills of the bank, the mackerel fleet continued to pour round the Cape north of us, ten or fifteen miles distant, in countless numbers, schooner after schooner, till they made a city on the water. They were so thick that many appeared to be afoul of one another; now all standing on this tack, now on that. We saw how well the New-Englanders had followed up Captain John Smith's suggestions with regard to the fisheries, made in 1616,—to what a pitch they had carried "this contemptible trade of fish," as he significantly styles it, and were now equal to the Hollanders

whose example he holds up for the English to emulate; notwithstanding that "in this faculty," as he says, "the former are
so naturalized, and of their vents so certainly acquainted, as
there is no likelihood they will ever be paralleled, having two
or three thousand busses, flat-bottoms, sword-pinks, todes,
and such like, that breeds them sailors, mariners, soldiers, and
merchants, never to be wrought out of that trade and fit for
any other." We thought that it would take all these names and
more to describe the numerous craft which we saw. Even
then, some years before our "renowned sires" with their
"peerless dames" stepped on Plymouth Rock, he wrote,
"Newfoundland doth yearly freight neir eight hundred sail of
ships with a silly, lean, skinny, poor-john, and cor fish,"
though all their supplies must be annually transported from
Europe. Why not plant a colony here then, and raise those
supplies on the spot? "Of all the four parts of the world," says
he, "that I have yet seen, not inhabited, could I have but
means to transport a colony, I would rather live here than
anywhere. And if it did not maintain itself, were we but once
indifferently well fitted, let us starve." Then "fishing before
your doors," you "may every night sleep quietly ashore, with
good cheer and what fires you will, or, when you please, with
your wives and family." Already he anticipates "the new
towns in New England in memory of their old,"—and who
knows what may be discovered in the "heart and entrails" of
the land, "seeing even the very edges," &c., &c.

All this has been accomplished, and more, and where is
Holland now? Verily the Dutch have taken it. There was no
long interval between the suggestion of Smith and the eulogy
of Burke.

Still one after another the mackerel schooners hove in sight
round the head of the Cape, " whitening all the sea road,"
and we watched each one for a moment with an undivided
interest. It seemed a pretty sport. Here in the country it is
only a few idle boys or loafers that go a-fishing on a rainy
day; but there it appeared as if every able-bodied man and
helpful boy in the Bay had gone out on a pleasure excursion
in their yachts, and all would at last land and have a chowder
on the Cape. The gazetteer tells you gravely how many of the
men and boys of these towns are engaged in the whale, cod,

and mackerel fishery, how many go to the banks of New-foundland, or the coast of Labrador, the Straits of Belle Isle or the Bay of Chaleurs (Shalore the sailors call it); as if I were to reckon up the number of boys in Concord who are engaged during the summer in the perch, pickerel, bream, horn-pout, and shiner fishery, of which no one keeps the statistics,—though I think that it is pursued with as much profit to the moral and intellectual man (or boy), and certainly with less danger to the physical one.

One of my playmates, who was apprenticed to a printer, and was somewhat of a wag, asked his master one afternoon if he might go a-fishing, and his master consented. He was gone three months. When he came back, he said that he had been to the Grand Banks, and went to setting type again as if only an afternoon had intervened.

I confess I was surprised to find that so many men spent their whole day, ay, their whole lives almost, a-fishing. It is remarkable what a serious business men make of getting their dinners, and how universally shiftlessness and a grovelling taste take refuge in a merely ant-like industry. Better go without your dinner, I thought, than be thus everlastingly fishing for it like a cormorant. Of course, *viewed from the shore*, our pursuits in the country appear not a whit less frivolous.

I once sailed three miles on a mackerel cruise myself. It was a Sunday evening after a very warm day in which there had been frequent thunder-showers, and I had walked along the shore from Cohasset to Duxbury. I wished to get over from the last place to Clark's Island, but no boat could stir, they said, at that stage of the tide, they being left high on the mud. At length I learned that the tavern-keeper, Winsor, was going out mackerelling with seven men that evening, and would take me. When there had been due delay, we one after another straggled down to the shore in a leisurely manner, as if waiting for the tide still, and in India-rubber boots, or carrying our shoes in our hands, waded to the boats, each of the crew bearing an armful of wood, and one a bucket of new potatoes besides. Then they resolved that each should bring one more armful of wood, and that would be enough. They had already got a barrel of water, and had some more in the schooner. We shoved the boats a dozen rods over the mud and water till they floated, then rowing half a mile to the vessel climbed aboard, and there we were in a mackerel schooner, a fine stout vessel of forty-three tons, whose name I forget. The baits were not dry on the hooks. There was the mill in which they ground the mackerel, and the trough to hold it, and the long-handled dipper to cast it overboard with; and already in the harbor we saw the surface rippled with schools of small mackerel, the real *Scomber vernalis*. The crew proceeded leisurely to weigh anchor and raise their two sails, there being a fair but very slight wind;—and the sun now setting clear and shining on the vessel after the thunder-showers, I thought that I could not have commenced the voyage under more favorable auspices. They had four dories and commonly fished in them, else they fished on the starboard side aft where their lines hung ready, two to a man. The boom swung round once or twice, and Winsor cast overboard the foul juice of mackerel mixed with rain-water which remained in his trough, and then we gathered about the helmsman and told stories. I remember that the compass was affected by iron in its neighborhood and varied a few degrees. There was one among us just returned from California, who was now going as passenger for his health and amusement. They expected to be gone about a week, to begin fishing the next morning, and to carry their fish fresh to Boston. They landed me at Clark's Island, where the Pilgrims landed, for my companions wished to get some milk for the voyage. But I had seen the whole of it. The rest was only going to sea and catching the mackerel. Moreover, it was as well that I did not remain with them, considering the small quantity of supplies they had taken.

Now I saw the mackerel fleet *on its fishing-ground*, though I was not at first aware of it. So my experience was complete.

It was even more cold and windy to-day than before, and we were frequently glad to take shelter behind a sand-hill. None of the elements were resting. On the beach there is a ceaseless activity, always something going on, in storm and in calm, winter and summer, night and day. Even the sedentary man here enjoys a breadth of view which is almost equivalent to motion. In clear weather the laziest may look across the Bay as far as Plymouth at a glance, or over the Atlantic as far as human vision reaches, merely raising his eyelids; or if he is too lazy to look after all, he can hardly help *hearing* the ceaseless dash and roar of the breakers. The restless ocean may at any moment cast up a whale or a wrecked vessel at your feet. All the reporters in the world, the most rapid stenographers, could not report the news it brings. No creature could move slowly where there was so much life around. The few wreckers were either going or coming, and the ships and the sandpipers, and the screaming gulls overhead; nothing stood still but the shore. The little beach-birds trotted past close to the water's edge, or paused but an instant to swallow their food, keeping time with the elements. I wondered how they ever got used to the sea, that they ventured so near the waves. Such tiny inhabitants the land brought forth! except one fox. And what could a fox do, looking on the Atlantic from that high bank? What is the sea to a fox? Sometimes we met a wrecker with his cart and dog,—and his dog's faint bark at us wayfarers, heard through the roaring of the surf, sounded ridiculously faint. To see a little trembling dainty-footed cur stand on the margin of the ocean, and ineffectually bark at a beach-bird, amid the roar of the Atlantic! Come with design to bark at a whale, perchance! That sound will do for farmyards. All the dogs looked out of place there, naked and as if shuddering at the vastness; and I thought that they would not have been there had it not been for the countenance of their masters. Still less could you think of a cat bending her steps that way, and shaking her wet foot over the Atlantic; yet even this happens sometimes, they tell me. In summer I saw the tender young of the Piping Plover, like chickens just hatched, mere pinches of down on two legs, running in troops, with a faint peep, along the edge of the waves. I used to see packs of half-wild dogs haunting the lonely beach on the south shore of Staten Island, in New York Bay, for the sake of the carrion there cast up; and I remember that once, when for a long time I had heard a furious barking in the tall grass of the marsh, a pack of half a dozen large dogs burst forth on to the beach, pursuing a little one which ran straight to me for protection, and I afforded it with some stones, though at some risk to myself; but the next day the little one was the first to bark at me. Under these circumstances I could not but remember the words of the poet:—

> "Blow blow, thou winter wind
>   Thou art not so unkind
>   As *his* ingratitude;
>   Thy tooth is not so keen,
>   Because thou art not seen,
>   Although thy breath be rude.
>
> "Freeze, freeze, thou bitter sky,
>   Thou dost not bite so nigh
>   As benefits forgot;
>   Though thou the waters warp,
>   Thy sting is not so sharp
>   As friend remembered not."

Sometimes, when I was approaching the carcass of a horse or ox which lay on the beach there, where there was no living creature in sight, a dog would unexpectedly emerge from it and slink away with a mouthful of offal.

The sea-shore is a sort of neutral ground, a most advantageous point from which to contemplate this world. It is even a trivial place. The waves forever rolling to the land are too far-travelled and untamable to be familiar. Creeping along the endless beach amid the sun-squawl and the foam, it occurs to us that we, too, are the product of sea-slime.

It is a wild, rank place, and there is no flattery in it. Strewn with crabs, horse-shoes, and razor-clams, and whatever the sea casts up,—a vast *morgue*, where famished dogs may range in packs, and crows come daily to glean the pittance which the tide leaves them. The carcasses of men and beasts together lie stately up upon its shelf, rotting and bleaching in the sun and waves, and each tide turns them in their beds, and tucks fresh sand under them. There is naked Nature,—inhumanly sincere, wasting no thought on man, nibbling at the cliffy shore where gulls wheel amid the spray.

We saw this forenoon what, at a distance, looked like a bleached log with a branch still left on it. It proved to be one of the principal bones of a whale, whose carcass, having been stripped of blubber at sea and cut adrift, had been washed up some months before. It chanced that this was the most conclusive evidence which we met with to prove, what the Copenhagen antiquaries assert, that these shores were the *Furdustrandas*, which Thorhall, the companion of Thorfinn during his expedition to Vinland in 1007, sailed past in disgust. It appears that after they had left the Cape and explored the country about Straum-Fiordr (Buzzards' Bay!), Thorhall, who was disappointed at not getting any wine to drink there, determined to sail north again in search of Vinland. Though the antiquaries have given us the original Icelandic, I prefer to quote their translation, since theirs is the only Latin which I know to have been aimed at Cape Cod.

> "Cum parati erant, sublato
> velo, cecinit Thorhallus:
> Eò redeamus, ubi conterranei
> sunt nostri! faciamus aliter,
> expansi arenosi peritum,
> lata navis explorare curricula:
> dum procellam incitantes gladii
> moræ impatientes, qui terram
> collaudant, Furdustrandas
> inhabitant et coquunt balænas."

In other words: "When they were ready and their sail hoisted, Thorhall sang: Let us return thither where our fellow-countrymen are. Let us make a bird* skilful to fly through the heaven of sand,† to explore the broad track of ships; while warriors who impel to the tempest of swords,‡ who praise the land, inhabit Wonder-Strands, *and cook whales*." And so he sailed north past Cape Cod, as the antiquaries say, "and was shipwrecked on to Ireland."

Though once there were more whales cast up here, I think that it was never more wild than now. We do not associate the idea of antiquity with the ocean, nor wonder how it looked a thousand years ago, as we do of the land, for it was equally wild and unfathomable always. The Indians have left

---

*I. e. a vessel.
†The sea, which is arched over its sandy bottom like a heaven.
‡Battle.

no traces on its surface, but it is the same to the civilized man
and the savage. The aspect of the shore only has changed. The
ocean is a wilderness reaching round the globe, wilder than a
Bengal jungle, and fuller of monsters, washing the very
wharves of our cities and the gardens of our sea-side resi-
dences. Serpents, bears, hyenas, tigers, rapidly vanish as civilization advances, but the most populous and civilized city
cannot scare a shark far from its wharves. It is no further
advanced than Singapore, with its tigers, in this respect. The
Boston papers had never told me that there were seals in the
harbor. I had always associated these with the Esquimaux and
other outlandish people. Yet from the parlor windows all
along the coast you may see families of them sporting on the
flats. They were as strange to me as the merman would be.
Ladies who never walk in the woods, sail over the sea. To go
to sea! Why, it is to have the experience of Noah,—to realize
the deluge. Every vessel is an ark.

We saw no fences as we walked the beach, no birchen
riders, highest of rails, projecting into the sea to keep the
cows from wading round, nothing to remind us that man was
proprietor of the shore. Yet a Truro man did tell us that owners of land on the east side of that town were regarded as
owning the beach, in order that they might have the control
of it so far as to defend themselves against the encroachments
of the sand and the beach-grass,—for even this friend is
sometimes regarded as a foe; but he said that this was not the
case on the Bay side. Also I have seen in sheltered parts of
the Bay temporary fences running to low-water mark, the
posts being set in sills or sleepers placed transversely.

After we had been walking many hours, the mackerel fleet
still hovered in the northern horizon nearly in the same direction, but farther off, hull down. Though their sails were set
they never sailed away, nor yet came to anchor, but stood on
various tacks as close together as vessels in a haven, and we,
in our ignorance, thought that they were contending patiently
with adverse winds, beating eastward; but we learned afterward that they were even then on their fishing-ground, and
that they caught mackerel without taking in their mainsails or
coming to anchor, "a smart breeze" (thence called a mackerel
breeze) being, as one says, "considered most favorable" for

this purpose. We counted about two hundred sail of mackerel fishers within one small arc of the horizon, and a nearly equal number had disappeared southward. Thus they hovered about the extremity of the Cape, like moths round a candle; the lights at Race Point and Long Point being bright candles for them at night,—and at this distance they looked fair and white, as if they had not yet flown into the light, but nearer at hand afterward, we saw how some had formerly singed their wings and bodies.

A village seems thus, where its able-bodied men are all ploughing the ocean together, as a common field. In North Truro the women and girls may sit at their doors, and see where their husbands and brothers are harvesting their mackerel fifteen or twenty miles off, on the sea, with hundreds of white harvest wagons, just as in the country the farmers' wives sometimes see their husbands working in a distant hill-side field. But the sound of no dinner-horn can reach the fisher's ear.

Having passed the narrowest part of the waist of the Cape, though still in Truro, for this township is about twelve miles long on the shore, we crossed over to the Bay side, not half a mile distant, in order to spend the noon on the nearest shrubby sand-hill in Provincetown, called Mount Ararat, which rises one hundred feet above the ocean. On our way thither we had occasion to admire the various beautiful forms and colors of the sand, and we noticed an interesting mirage, which I have since found that Hitchcock also observed on the sands of the Cape. We were crossing a shallow valley in the Desert, where the smooth and spotless sand sloped upward by a small angle to the horizon on every side, and at the lowest part was a long chain of clear but shallow pools. As we were approaching these for a drink in a diagonal direction across the valley, they appeared inclined at a slight but decided angle to the horizon, though they were plainly and broadly connected with one another, and there was not the least ripple to suggest a current; so that by the time we had reached a convenient part of one we seemed to have ascended several feet. They appeared to lie by magic on the side of the vale, like a mirror left in a slanting position. It was a very pretty mirage for a Provincetown desert, but not amounting to what, in Sanscrit, is called "the thirst of the gazelle," as there was real water here for a base, and we were able to quench our thirst after all.

Professor Rafn, of Copenhagen, thinks that the mirage which I noticed, but which an old inhabitant of Province-town, to whom I mentioned it, had never seen nor heard of, had something to do with the name "Furdustrandas," i. e. Wonder-Strands, given, as I have said, in the old Icelandic account of Thorfinn's expedition to Vinland in the year 1007, to a part of the coast on which he landed. But these sands are more remarkable for their length than for their mirage, which is common to all deserts, and the reason for the name which the Northmen themselves give,—"because it took a long time to sail by them,"—is sufficient and more applicable to these shores. However, if you should sail all the way from Green-land to Buzzard's Bay along the coast, you would get sight of a good many sandy beaches. But whether Thor-finn saw the mirage here or not, Thor-eau, one of the same family, did; and perchance it was because Lief the Lucky had, in a pre-vious voyage, taken Thor-er and his people off the rock in the middle of the sea, that Thor-eau was born to see it.

This was not the only mirage which I saw on the Cape. That half of the beach next the bank is commonly level, or nearly so, while the other slopes downward to the water. As I was walking upon the edge of the bank in Wellfleet at sun-down, it seemed to me that the inside half of the beach sloped upward toward the water to meet the other, forming a ridge ten or twelve feet high the whole length of the shore, but higher always opposite to where I stood; and I was not con-vinced of the contrary till I descended the bank, though the shaded outlines left by the waves of a previous tide but half-way *down* the apparent declivity might have taught me better. A stranger may easily detect what is strange to the oldest in-habitant, for the strange is his province. The old oysterman, speaking of gull-shooting, had said that you must aim under, when firing down the bank.

A neighbor tells me that one August, looking through a glass from Naushon to some vessels which were sailing along near Martha's Vineyard, the water about them appeared per-fectly smooth, so that they were reflected in it, and yet their

full sails proved that it must be rippled, and they who were
with him thought that it was a mirage, i. e. a reflection from
a haze.

From the above-mentioned sand-hill we overlooked Provincetown and its harbor, now emptied of vessels, and also a
wide expanse of ocean. As we did not wish to enter Provincetown before night, though it was cold and windy, we returned across the Deserts to the Atlantic side, and walked
along the beach again nearly to Race Point, being still greedy
of the sea influence. All the while it was not so calm as the
reader may suppose, but it was blow, blow, blow,—roar,
roar, roar,—tramp, tramp, tramp,—without interruption.
The shore now trended nearly east and west.

Before sunset, having already seen the mackerel fleet returning into the Bay, we left the sea-shore on the north of Provincetown, and made our way across the Desert to the
eastern extremity of the town. From the first high sand-hill,
covered with beach-grass and bushes to its top, on the edge
of the desert, we overlooked the shrubby hill and swamp
country which surrounds Provincetown on the north, and
protects it, in some measure, from the invading sand. Notwithstanding the universal barrenness, and the contiguity of
the desert, I never saw an autumnal landscape so beautifully
painted as this was. It was like the richest rug imaginable
spread over an uneven surface; no damask nor velvet, nor
Tyrian dye or stuffs, nor the work of any loom, could ever
match it. There was the incredibly bright red of the Huckleberry, and the reddish brown of the Bayberry, mingled with
the bright and living green of small Pitch-Pines, and also the
duller green of the Bayberry, Boxberry, and Plum, the yellowish green of the Shrub Oaks, and the various golden and yellow and fawn colored tints of the Birch and Maple and
Aspen,—each making its own figure, and, in the midst, the
few yellow sand-slides on the sides of the hills looked like
the white floor seen through rents in the rug. Coming from
the country as I did, and many autumnal woods as I had seen,
this was perhaps the most novel and remarkable sight that I
saw on the Cape. Probably the brightness of the tints was
enhanced by contrast with the sand which surrounded this
track. This was a part of the furniture of Cape Cod. We had

for days walked up the long and bleak piazza which runs along her Atlantic side, then over the sanded floor of her halls, and now we were being introduced into her boudoir. The hundred white sails crowding round Long Point into Provincetown Harbor, seen over the painted hills in front, looked like toy ships upon a mantle-piece.

The peculiarity of this autumnal landscape consisted in the lowness and thickness of the shrubbery, no less than in the brightness of the tints. It was like a thick stuff of worsted or a fleece, and looked as if a giant could take it up by the hem, or rather the tasselled fringe which trailed out on the sand, and shake it, though it needed not to be shaken. But no doubt the dust would fly in that case, for not a little has accumulated underneath it. Was it not such an autumnal landscape as this which suggested our high-colored rugs and carpets? Hereafter when I look on a richer rug than usual, and study its figures, I shall think, there are the huckleberry hills, and there the denser swamps of boxberry and blueberry: there the shrub oak patches and the bayberries, there the maples and the birches and the pines. What other dyes are to be compared to these? They were warmer colors than I had associated with the New England coast.

After threading a swamp full of boxberry, and climbing several hills covered with shrub-oaks, without a path, where shipwrecked men would be in danger of perishing in the night, we came down upon the eastern extremity of the four planks which run the whole length of Provincetown street. This, which is the last town on the Cape, lies mainly in one street along the curving beach fronting the southeast. The sand-hills, covered with shrubbery and interposed with swamps and ponds, rose immediately behind it in the form of a crescent, which is from half a mile to a mile or more wide in the middle, and beyond these is the desert, which is the greater part of its territory, stretching to the sea on the east and west and north. The town is compactly built in the narrow space, from ten to fifty rods deep, between the harbor and the sand-hills, and contained at that time about twenty-six hundred inhabitants. The houses, in which a more modern and pretending style has at length prevailed over the fisherman's hut, stand on the inner or plank side of the street, and the fish and store houses, with the picturesque-looking windmills of the Salt-works, on the water side. The narrow portion of the beach between forming the street, about eighteen feet wide, the only one where one carriage could pass another, if there was more than one carriage in the town, looked much "heavier" than any portion of the beach or the desert which we had walked on, it being above the reach of the highest tide, and the sand being kept loose by the occasional passage of a traveller. We learned that the four planks on which we were walking had been bought by the town's share of the Surplus Revenue, the disposition of which was a bone of contention between the inhabitants, till they wisely resolved thus to put it under foot. Yet some, it was said, were so provoked because they did not receive their particular share in money, that they persisted in walking in the sand a long time after the side-walk was built. This is the only instance which I happen to know in which the surplus revenue proved a blessing to any town. A surplus revenue of dollars from the treasury to stem the greater evil of a surplus revenue of sand from the ocean. They expected to make a hard road by the time these planks were worn out. Indeed, they have already done so since we were there, and have almost forgotten their sandy baptism.

As we passed along we observed the inhabitants engaged in curing either fish or the coarse salt hay which they had brought home and spread on the beach before their doors, looking as yellow as if they had raked it out of the sea. The front-yard plots appeared like what indeed they were, portions of the beach fenced in, with Beach-grass growing in them, as if they were sometimes covered by the tide. You might still pick up shells and pebbles there. There were a few trees among the houses, especially silver abeles, willows, and balm-of-Gileads; and one man showed me a young oak which he had transplanted from behind the town, thinking it an apple-tree. But every man to his trade. Though he had little woodcraft, he was not the less weatherwise, and gave us one piece of information; viz. he had observed that when a thunder-cloud came up with a flood-tide it did not rain. This was the most completely maritime town that we were ever in. It was merely a good harbor, surrounded by land dry, if not firm,—an inhabited beach, whereon fishermen cured and stored their fish, without any back country. When ashore the inhabitants still walk on planks. A few small patches have been reclaimed from the swamps, containing commonly half a dozen square rods only each. We saw one which was fenced with four lengths of rail; also a fence made wholly of hogshead-staves stuck in the ground. These, and such as these, were all the cultivated and cultivable land in Provincetown. We were told that there were thirty or forty acres in all, but we did not discover a quarter part so much, and that was well dusted with sand, and looked as if the desert was claiming it. They are now turning some of their swamps into Cranberry Meadows on quite an extensive scale.

Yet far from being out of the way, Provincetown is directly in the way of the navigator, and he is lucky who does not run afoul of it in the dark. It is situated on one of the highways of commerce, and men from all parts of the globe touch there in the course of a year.

The mackerel fleet had nearly all got in before us, it being Saturday night, excepting that division which had stood down towards Chatham in the morning; and from a hill where we went to see the sun set in the Bay, we counted two hundred goodly looking schooners at anchor in the harbor at various distances from the shore, and more were yet coming round the Cape. As each came to anchor, it took in sail and swung round in the wind, and lowered its boat. They belonged chiefly to Wellfleet, Truro, and Cape Ann. This was that city of canvas which we had seen hull down in the horizon. Near at hand, and under bare poles, they were unexpectedly black-looking vessels, μέλαιναι νῆες. A fisherman told us that there were fifteen hundred vessels in the mackerel fleet, and that he had counted three hundred and fifty in Provincetown Harbor at one time. Being obliged to anchor at a considerable distance from the shore on account of the shallowness of the water, they made the impression of a larger fleet than the vessels at the wharves of a large city. As they had been manœuvring out there all day seemingly for our entertainment, while we were walking northwestward along the Atlantic, so now we found them flocking into Provincetown Harbor at night, just as we arrived, as if to meet us, and exhibit themselves close at hand. Standing by Race Point and Long Point with various speed, they reminded me of fowls coming home to roost.

These were genuine New England vessels. It is stated in the Journal of Moses Prince, a brother of the annalist, under date of 1721, at which time he visited Gloucester, that the first vessel of the class called schooner was built at Gloucester about eight years before, by Andrew Robinson; and late in the same century one Cotton Tufts gives us the tradition with some particulars, which he learned on a visit to the same place. According to the latter, Robinson having constructed a vessel which he masted and rigged in a peculiar manner, on her going off the stocks a by-stander cried out, *"O, how she scoons!"* whereat Robinson replied, *"A schooner let her be!"* "From which time," says Tufts, "vessels thus masted and rigged have gone by the name of schooners; before which, vessels of this description were not known in Europe." (See Mass. Hist. Coll., Vol. IX., 1st Series, and Vol. I., 4th Series.) Yet I can hardly believe this, for a schooner has always seemed to me—the typical vessel.

According to C. E. Potter of Manchester, New Hampshire, the very word schooner is of New England origin, being from the Indian *schoon* or *scoot*, meaning to rush, as Schoodic, from *scoot* and *anke*, a place where water rushes. N. B. Somebody of Gloucester was to read a paper on this matter before a genealogical society, in Boston, March 3, 1859, according to the Boston Journal, q. v.

Nearly all who come out must walk on the four planks which I have mentioned, so that you are pretty sure to meet all the inhabitants of Provincetown who come out in the course of a day, provided you keep out yourself. This evening the planks were crowded with mackerel fishers, to whom we gave and from whom we took the wall, as we returned to our hotel. This hotel was kept by a tailor, his shop on the one side of the door, his hotel on the other, and his day seemed to be divided between carving meat and carving broadcloth.

The next morning, though it was still more cold and blustering than the day before, we took to the Deserts again, for we spent our days wholly out of doors, in the sun when there was any, and in the wind which never failed. After threading the shrubby hill country at the southwest end of the town, west of the Shank-Painter Swamp, whose expressive name— for we understood it at first as a landsman naturally would— gave it importance in our eyes, we crossed the sands to the shore south of Race Point and three miles distant, and thence roamed round eastward through the desert to where we had left the sea the evening before. We travelled five or six miles after we got out there, on a curving line, and might have gone nine or ten, over vast platters of pure sand, from the midst of which we could not see a particle of vegetation, ex- cepting the distant thin fields of Beach-grass, which crowned and made the ridges toward which the sand sloped upward on each side;—all the while in the face of a cutting wind as cold as January; indeed, we experienced no weather so cold as this for nearly two months afterward. This desert extends from the extremity of the Cape, through Provincetown into Truro, and many a time as we were traversing it we were reminded of "Riley's Narrative" of his captivity in the sands of Arabia, notwithstanding the cold. Our eyes magnified the patches of Beach-grass into cornfields in the horizon, and we probably exaggerated the height of the ridges on account of the mirage. I was pleased to learn afterward, from Kalm's Travels in North America, that the inhabitants of the Lower St. Lawrence call this grass (*Calamagrostis arenaria*), and also Sea-lyme grass (*Elymus arenarius*), *seigle de mer*; and he adds, "I have been assured that these plants grow in great plenty in Newfoundland, and on other North American shores; the places covered with them looking, at a distance, like corn- fields; which might explain the passage in our northern ac- counts [he wrote in 1749] of the excellent wine land [*Vinland det goda*, Translator], which mentions that they had found whole fields of wheat growing wild."

The Beach-grass is "two to four feet high, of a sea-green color," and it is said to be widely diffused over the world. In the Hebrides it is used for mats, pack-saddles, bags, hats, &c.; paper has been made of it at Dorchester in this State, and cattle eat it when tender. It has heads somewhat like rye, from six inches to a foot in length, and it is propagated both by roots and seeds. To express its love for sand, some botanists have called it *Psamma arenaria*, which is the Greek for sand, qualified by the Latin for sandy,—or sandy sand. As it is blown about by the wind, while it is held fast by its roots, it describes myriad circles in the sand as accurately as if they were made by compasses.

It was the dreariest scenery imaginable. The only animals which we saw on the sand at that time were spiders, which are to be found almost everywhere whether on snow or ice-water or sand,—and a venomous-looking, long, narrow worm, one of the myriapods, or thousand-legs. We were surprised to see spider-holes in that flowing sand with an edge as firm as that of a stoned well.

In June this sand was scored with the tracks of turtles both large and small, which had been out in the night, leading to and from the swamps. I was told by a *terræ filius* who has a "farm" on the edge of the desert, and is familiar with the fame of Provincetown, that one man had caught twenty-five snapping-turtles there the previous spring. His own method of catching them was to put a toad on a mackerel-hook and cast it into a pond, tying the line to a stump or stake on shore. Invariably the turtle when hooked crawled up the line to the stump, and was found waiting there by his captor, however long afterward. He also said that minks, muskrats, foxes, coons, and wild mice were found there, but no squirrels. We heard of sea-turtle as large as a barrel being found on the beach and on East Harbor marsh, but whether they were native there, or had been lost out of some vessel, did not appear. Perhaps they were the Salt-water Terrapin, or else the Smooth Terrapin, found thus far north. Many toads were met with where there was nothing but sand and beach-grass. In Truro I had been surprised at the number of large light-colored toads everywhere hopping over the dry and sandy fields, their color corresponding to that of the sand. Snakes also are common on these pure sand beaches, and I have never been so much troubled by mosquitoes as in such localities. At the same season strawberries grew there abundantly in the little hollows on the edge of the desert standing amid the beach-grass in the sand, and the fruit of the shadbush or *Amelanchier*, which the inhabitants call Josh-pears (some think from juicy?), is very abundant on the hills. I fell in with an obliging man who conducted me to the best locality for strawberries.

He said that he would not have shown me the place if he had not seen that I was a stranger, and could not anticipate him another year; I therefore feel bound in honor not to reveal it. When we came to a pond, he being the native did the honors and carried me over on his shoulders, like Sindbad. One good turn deserves another, and if he ever comes our way I will do as much for him.

In one place we saw numerous dead tops of trees projecting through the otherwise uninterrupted desert, where, as we afterward learned, thirty or forty years before a flourishing forest had stood, and now, as the trees were laid bare from year to year, the inhabitants cut off their tops for fuel.

We saw nobody that day outside of the town; it was too wintry for such as had seen the Back-side before, or for the greater number who never desire to see it, to venture out; and we saw hardly a track to show that any had ever crossed this desert. Yet I was told that some are always out on the Back-side night and day in severe weather, looking for wrecks, in order that they may get the job of discharging the cargo, or the like,—and thus shipwrecked men are succored. But, generally speaking, the inhabitants rarely visit these sands. One who had lived in Provincetown thirty years told me that he had not been through to the north side within that time. Sometimes the natives themselves come near perishing by losing their way in snow-storms behind the town.

The wind was not a Sirocco or Simoon, such as we associate with the desert, but a New England northeaster,—and we sought shelter in vain under the sand-hills, for it blew all about them, rounding them into cones, and was sure to find us out on whichever side we sat. From time to time we lay down and drank at little pools in the sand, filled with pure fresh water, all that was left, probably, of a pond or swamp. The air was filled with dust like snow, and cutting sand which made the face tingle, and we saw what it must be to face it when the weather was drier, and, if possible, windier still,— to face a migrating sand-bar in the air, which has picked up its duds and is off,—to be whipped with a cat, not o' nine-tails, but of a myriad of tails, and each one a sting to it. A Mr. Whitman, a former minister of Wellfleet, used to write to his inland friends that the blowing sand scratched the windows so that he was obliged to have one new pane set every week, that he might see out.

On the edge of the shrubby woods the sand had the appearance of an inundation which was overwhelming them, terminating in an abrupt bank many feet higher than the surface on which they stood, and having partially buried the outside trees. The moving sand-hills of England, called Dunes or Downs, to which these have been likened, are either formed of sand cast up by the sea, or of sand taken from the land itself in the first place by the wind, and driven still farther inward. It is here a tide of sand impelled by waves and wind, slowly flowing from the sea toward the town. The northeast winds are said to be the strongest, but the northwest to move most sand, because they are the driest. On the shore of the Bay of Biscay many villages were formerly destroyed in this way. Some of the ridges of beach-grass which we saw were planted by government many years ago, to preserve the harbor of Provincetown and the extremity of the Cape. I talked with some who had been employed in the planting. In the "Description of the Eastern Coast," which I have already referred to, it is said: "Beach-grass during the spring and summer grows about two feet and a half. If surrounded by naked beach, the storms of autumn and winter heap up the sand on all sides, and cause it to rise nearly to the top of the plant. In the ensuing spring the grass sprouts anew; is again covered with sand in the winter; and thus a hill or ridge continues to ascend as long as there is a sufficient base to support it, or till the circumscribing sand, being also covered with beach-grass, will no longer yield to the force of the winds." Sand-hills formed in this way are sometimes one hundred feet high and of every variety of form, like snow-drifts, or Arab tents, and are continually shifting. The grass roots itself very firmly. When I endeavored to pull it up, it usually broke off ten inches or a foot below the surface, at what had been the surface the year before, as appeared by the numerous offshoots there, it being a straight, hard, round shoot, showing by its length how much the sand had accumulated the last year; and sometimes the dead stubs of a previous season were pulled up with it from still deeper in the sand, with their own more decayed shoot attached,—so that the age of a sand-hill, and its rate of increase for several years, is pretty accurately recorded in this way.

Old Gerard, the English herbalist, says, p. 1250: "I find mention in Stowe's Chronicle, in *Anno* 1555, of a certain pulse or pease, as they term it, wherewith the poor people at that time, there being a great dearth, were miraculously helped: he thus mentions it. In the month of August (saith he), in Suffolke, at a place by the sea side all of hard stone and pibble, called in those parts a shelf, lying between the towns of Orford and Aldborough, where neither grew grass nor any earth was ever seen; it chanced in this barren place suddenly to spring up without any tillage or sowing, great abundance of peason, whereof the poor gathered (as men judged) above one hundred quarters, yet remained some ripe and some blossoming, as many as ever there were before: to the which place rode the Bishop of Norwich and the Lord Willoughby, with others in great number, who found nothing but hard, rocky stone the space of three yards under the roots of these peason, which roots were great and long, and very sweet." He tells us also that Gesner learned from Dr. Cajus that there were enough there to supply thousands of men. He goes on to say that "they without doubt grew there many years before, but were not observed till hunger made them take notice of them, and quickened their invention, which commonly in our people is very dull, especially in finding out food of this nature. My worshipful friend Dr. Argent hath told me that many years ago he was in this place, and caused his man to pull among the beach with his hands, and follow the roots so long until he got some equal in length unto his height, yet could come to no ends of them." Gerard never saw them, and is not certain what kind they were.

In Dwight's Travels in New England it is stated that the inhabitants of Truro were formerly regularly warned under the authority of law in the month of April yearly, to plant beach-grass, as elsewhere they are warned to repair the highways. They dug up the grass in bunches, which were afterward divided into several smaller ones, and set about three feet apart, in rows, so arranged as to break joints and obstruct the passage of the wind. It spread itself rapidly, the weight of the seeds when ripe bending the heads of the grass, and so dropping directly by its side and vegetating there. In this way, for instance, they built up again that part of the Cape between Truro and Provincetown where the sea broke over in the last century. They have now a public road near there, made by laying sods, which were full of roots, bottom upward and close together on the sand, double in the middle of the track, then spreading brush evenly over the sand on each side for half a dozen feet, planting beach-grass on the banks in regular rows, as above described, and sticking a fence of brush against the hollows.

The attention of the general government was first attracted to the danger which threatened Cape Cod Harbor from the inroads of the sand, about thirty years ago, and commissioners were at that time appointed by Massachusetts to examine the premises. They reported in June, 1825, that, owing to "the trees and brush having been cut down, and the beach-grass destroyed on the seaward side of the Cape, opposite the Harbor," the original surface of the ground had been broken up and removed by the wind toward the Harbor,—during the previous fourteen years,—over an extent of "one half a mile in breadth, and about four and a half miles in length."—"The space where a few years since were some of the highest lands on the Cape, covered with trees and bushes," presenting "an extensive waste of undulating sand";—and that, during the previous twelve months, the sand "had approached the Harbor an average distance of fifty rods, for an extent of four and a half miles!" and unless some measures were adopted to check its progress, it would in a few years destroy both the harbor and the town. They therefore recommended that beach-grass be set out on a curving line over a space ten rods wide and four and a half miles long, and that cattle, horses, and sheep be prohibited from going abroad, and the inhabitants from cutting the brush.

I was told that about thirty thousand dollars in all had been appropriated to this object, though it was complained that a great part of it was spent foolishly, as the public money is wont to be. Some say that while the government is planting beach-grass behind the town for the protection of the harbor, the inhabitants are rolling the sand into the harbor in wheelbarrows, in order to make house-lots. The Patent-Office has recently imported the seed of this grass from Holland, and distributed it over the country, but probably we have as much as the Hollanders.

Thus Cape Cod is anchored to the heavens, as it were, by a myriad little cables of beach-grass, and, if they should fail, would become a total wreck, and erelong go to the bottom. Formerly, the cows were permitted to go at large, and they ate many strands of the cable by which the Cape is moored, and wellnigh set it adrift, as the bull did the boat which was moored with a grass rope; but now they are not permitted to wander.

A portion of Truro which has considerable taxable property on it has lately been added to Provincetown, and I was told by a Truro man that his townsmen talked of petitioning the legislature to set off the next mile of their territory also to Provincetown, in order that she might have her share of the lean as well as the fat, and take care of the road through it; for its whole value is literally to hold the Cape together, and even this it has not always done. But Provincetown strenuously declines the gift.

The wind blowed so hard from the northeast, that, cold as it was, we resolved to see the breakers on the Atlantic side, whose din we had heard all the morning; so we kept on eastward through the Desert, till we struck the shore again northeast of Provincetown, and exposed ourselves to the full force of the piercing blast. There are extensive shoals there over which the sea broke with great force. For half a mile from the shore it was one mass of white breakers, which, with the wind, made such a din that we could hardly hear ourselves speak. Of this part of the coast it is said: "A northeast storm, the most violent and fatal to seamen, as it is frequently accompanied with snow, blows directly on the land: a strong current sets along the shore: add to which that ships, during the operation of such a storm, endeavor to work northward, that they may get into the bay. Should they be unable to weather Race Point, the wind drives them on the shore, and a shipwreck is inevitable. Accordingly, the strand is everywhere covered with the fragments of vessels." But since the

Highland Light was erected, this part of the coast is less dangerous, and it is said that more shipwrecks occur south of that light, where they were scarcely known before.

This was the stormiest sea that we witnessed,—more *tumultuous*, my companion affirmed, than the rapids of Niagara, and, of course, on a far greater scale. It was the ocean in a gale, a clear, cold day, with only one sail in sight, which labored much, as if it were anxiously seeking a harbor. It was high tide when we reached the shore, and in one place, for a considerable distance, each wave dashed up so high that it was difficult to pass between it and the bank. Further south, where the bank was higher, it would have been dangerous to attempt it. A native of the Cape has told me, that many years ago, three boys, his playmates, having gone to this beach in Wellfleet to visit a wreck, when the sea receded ran down to the wreck, and when it came in ran before it to the bank, but the sea following fast at their heels, caused the bank to cave and bury them alive.

It was the roaring sea, θάλασσα ἠχήεσσα,—

ἀμφὶ δὲ τ᾽ ἄκραι
Ἠϊόνες βοόωσιν, ἐρευγομένης ἁλὸς ἔξω.

And the summits of the bank
Around resound, the sea being vomited forth.

As we stood looking on this scene we were gradually convinced that fishing here and in a pond were not, in all respects, the same, and that he who waits for fair weather and a calm sea may never see the glancing skin of a mackerel, and get no nearer to a cod than the wooden emblem in the State-House.

Having lingered on the shore till we were wellnigh chilled to death by the wind, and were ready to take shelter in a Charity-house, we turned our weather-beaten faces toward Provincetown and the Bay again, having now more than doubled the Cape.

X

Provincetown

EARLY THE next morning I walked into a fish-house near our hotel, where three or four men were engaged in trundling out the pickled fish on barrows, and spreading them to dry. They told me that a vessel had lately come in from the Banks with forty-four thousand codfish. Timothy Dwight says that, just before he arrived at Provincetown, "a schooner came in from the Great Bank with fifty-six thousand fish, almost one thousand five hundred quintals, taken in a single voyage; the main deck being, on her return, eight inches under water in calm weather." The cod in this fish-house, just out of the pickle, lay packed several feet deep, and three or four men stood on them in cowhide boots, pitching them on to the barrows with an instrument which had a single iron point. One young man, who chewed tobacco, spat on the fish repeatedly. Well, sir, thought I, when that older man sees you he will speak to you. But presently I saw the older man do the same thing. It reminded me of the figs of Smyrna. "How long does it take to cure these fish?" I asked. "Two good drying days, sir," was the answer.

I walked across the street again into the hotel to breakfast, and mine host inquired if I would take "hashed fish or beans." I took beans, though they never were a favorite dish of mine. I found next summer that this was still the only alternative proposed here, and the landlord was still ringing the changes on these two words. In the former dish there was a remarkable proportion of fish. As you travel inland the potato predominates. It chanced that I did not taste fresh fish of any kind on the Cape, and I was assured that they were not so much used there as in the country. That is where they are cured, and where, sometimes, travellers are cured of eating them. No fresh meat was slaughtered in Provincetown, but the little that was used at the public houses was brought from Boston by the steamer.

A great many of the houses here were surrounded by fish-flakes close up to the sills on all sides, with only a narrow passage two or three feet wide, to the front door; so that instead of looking out into a flower or grass plot, you looked on to so many square rods of cod turned wrong side outwards. These parterres were said to be least like a flower-garden in a good drying day in mid-summer. There were flakes of every age and pattern, and some so rusty and overgrown with lichens that they looked as if they might have served the founders of the fishery here. Some had broken down under the weight of successive harvests. The principal employment of the inhabitants at this time seemed to be to trundle out their fish and spread them in the morning, and bring them in at night. I saw how many a loafer who chanced to be out early enough, got a job at wheeling out the fish of his neighbor who was anxious to improve the whole of a fair day. Now then I knew where salt fish were caught. They were everywhere lying on their backs, their collar-bones standing out like the lapels of a man-o'-war-man's jacket, and inviting all things to come and rest in their bosoms; and all things, with a few exceptions, accepted the invitation. I think, by the way, that if you should wrap a large salt fish round a small boy, he would have a coat of such a fashion as I have seen many a one wear to muster. Salt fish were stacked up on the wharves, looking like corded wood, maple and yellow birch with the bark left on. I mistook them for this at first, and such in one sense they were,—fuel to maintain our vital fires,—an eastern wood which grew on the Grand Banks. Some were stacked in the form of huge flower-pots, being laid in small circles with the tails outwards, each circle successively larger than the preceding until the pile was three or four feet high, when the circles rapidly diminished, so as to form a conical roof. On the shores of New Brunswick this is covered with birch-bark, and stones are placed upon it, and being thus rendered impervious to the rain, it is left to season before being packed for exportation.

It is rumored that in the fall the cows here are sometimes fed on cod's heads! The godlike part of the cod, which, like the human head, is curiously and wonderfully made, forsooth has but little less brain in it,—coming to such an end! to be craunched by cows! I felt my own skull crack from sympathy. What if the heads of men were to be cut off to feed the cows of a superior order of beings who inhabit the islands in the ether? Away goes your fine brain, the house of thought and instinct, to swell the cud of a ruminant animal!—However, an inhabitant assured me that they did not make a practice of feeding cows on cod's heads; the cows merely *would* eat them sometimes; but I might live there all my days and never see it done. A cow wanting salt would also sometimes lick out all the soft part of a cod on the flakes. This he would have me believe was the foundation of this fish-story.

It has been a constant traveller's tale and perhaps slander, now for thousands of years, the Latins and Greeks have repeated it, that this or that nation feeds its cattle, or horses, or sheep, on fish, as may be seen in Œlian and Pliny, but in the Journal of Nearchus, who was Alexander's admiral, and made a voyage from the Indus to the Euphrates three hundred and twenty six years before Christ, it is said that the inhabitants of a portion of the intermediate coast, whom he called Icthyophagi or Fish-eaters, not only ate fishes raw and also dried and pounded in a whale's vertebra for a mortar and made into a paste, but gave them to their cattle, there being no grass on the coast; and several modern travellers,—Braybosa, Niebuhr, and others make the same report. Therefore in balancing the evidence I am still in doubt about the Provincetown cows. As for other domestic animals, Captain King in his continuation of Captain Cook's Journal in 1779, says of the dogs of Kamtschatka, "Their food in the winter consists entirely of the head, entrails, and backbones of salmon, which are put aside and dried for that purpose; and with this diet they are fed but sparingly." (Cook's Journal, Vol. VII. p. 315.)

As we are treating of fishy matters, let me insert what Pliny says, that "the commanders of the fleets of Alexander the Great have related that the Gedrosi, who dwell on the banks of the river Arabis, are in the habit of making the doors of their houses with the jaw-bones of fishes, and raftering the roofs with their bones." Strabo tells the same of the Ichthyophagi. "Hardouin remarks, that the Basques of his day were in the habit of fencing their gardens with the ribs of the whale, which sometimes exceeded twenty feet in length; and Cuvier says, that at the present time the jaw-bone of the whale is used in Norway for the purpose of making beams or posts for buildings." (Bohn's ed. trans. of Pliny, Vol. II. p. 361.) Herodotus says the inhabitants on Lake Prasias in Thrace (living on piles), "give fish for fodder to their horses and beasts of burden."

Provincetown was apparently what is called a flourishing town. Some of the inhabitants asked me if I did not think that they appeared to be well off generally. I said that I did, and asked how many there were in the almshouse. "O, only one or two, infirm or idiotic," answered they. The outward aspect of the houses and shops frequently suggested a poverty which their interior comfort and even richness disproved. You might meet a lady daintily dressed in the Sabbath morning, wading in among the sand-hills, from church, where there appeared no house fit to receive her, yet no doubt the interior of the house answered to the exterior of the lady. As for the interior of the inhabitants I am still in the dark about it. I had a little intercourse with some whom I met in the street, and was often agreeably disappointed by discovering the intelligence of rough, and what would be considered unpromising specimens. Nay, I ventured to call on one citizen the next summer, by special invitation. I found him sitting in his front doorway, that Sabbath evening, prepared for me to come in unto him; but unfortunately for his reputation for keeping open house, there was stretched across his gate-way a circular cobweb of the largest kind and quite entire. This looked so ominous that I actually turned aside and went in the back way.

This Monday morning was beautifully mild and calm, both on land and water, promising us a smooth passage across the Bay, and the fishermen feared that it would not be so good a drying day as the cold and windy one which preceded it. There could hardly have been a greater contrast. This was the first of the Indian summer days, though at a late hour in the morning we found the wells in the sand behind the town still covered with ice, which had formed in the night. What with wind and sun my most prominent feature fairly cast its slough. But I assure you it will take more than two good drying days to cure me of rambling. After making an excursion among the hills in the neighborhood of the Shank-Painter Swamp, and getting a little work done in its line, we took our seat upon the highest sand-hill overlooking the town, in mid air, on a long plank stretched across between two hillocks of sand, where some boys were endeavoring in vain to fly their kite; and there we remained the rest of that forenoon looking out over the placid harbor, and watching for the first appearance of the steamer from Wellfleet, that we might be in readiness to go on board when we heard the whistle off Long Point.

We got what we could out of the boys in the meanwhile. Provincetown boys are of course all sailors and have sailors' eyes. When we were at the Highland Light the last summer, seven or eight miles from Provincetown Harbor, and wished to know one Sunday morning if the Olata, a well-known yacht, had got in from Boston, so that we could return in her, a Provincetown boy about ten years old, who chanced to be at the table, remarked that she had. I asked him how he knew. "I just saw her come in," said he. When I expressed surprise that he could distinguish her from other vessels so far, he said that there were not so many of those two-topsail schooners about but that he could tell her. Palfrey said, in his oration at Barnstable, the duck does not take to the water with a surer instinct than the Barnstable boy. [He might have said the Cape Cod boy as well.] He leaps from his leading-strings into the shrouds, it is but a bound from the mother's lap to the masthead. He boxes the compass in his infant soliloquies. He can hand, reef, and steer by the time he flies a kite.

This was the very day one would have chosen to sit upon a hill overlooking sea and land, and muse there. The mackerel fleet was rapidly taking its departure, one schooner after another, and standing round the Cape, like fowls leaving their roosts in the morning to disperse themselves in distant fields. The turtle-like sheds of the salt-works were crowded into every nook in the hills, immediately behind the town, and their now idle windmills lined the shore. It was worth the while to see by what coarse and simple chemistry this almost necessary of life is obtained, with the sun for journeyman, and a single apprentice to do the chores for a large establishment. It is a sort of tropical labor, pursued too in the sunniest season; more interesting than gold or diamond-washing, which,

I fancy, it somewhat resembles at a distance. In the production of the necessaries of life Nature is ready enough to assist man. So at the potash works which I have seen at Hull, where they burn the stems of the kelp and boil the ashes. Verily, chemistry is not a splitting of hairs when you have got half a dozen raw Irishmen in the laboratory. It is said, that owing to the reflection of the sun from the sand-hills, and there being absolutely no fresh water emptying into the harbor, the same number of superficial feet yields more salt here than in any other part of the county. A little rain is considered necessary to clear the air, and make salt fast and good, for as paint does not dry, so water does not evaporate in dog-day weather. But they were now, as elsewhere on the Cape, breaking up their salt-works and selling them for lumber.

From that elevation we could overlook the operations of the inhabitants almost as completely as if the roofs had been taken off. They were busily covering the wicker-worked flakes about their houses with salted fish, and we now saw that the back yards were improved for this purpose as much as the front; where one man's fish ended another's began. In almost every yard we detected some little building from which these treasures were being trundled forth and systematically spread, and we saw that there was an art as well as a knack even in spreading fish, and that a division of labor was profitably practised. One man was withdrawing his fishes a few inches beyond the nose of his neighbor's cow which had stretched her neck over a paling to get at them. It seemed a quite domestic employment, like drying clothes, and indeed in some parts of the county the women take part in it.

I noticed in several places on the Cape a sort of clothes-*flakes*. They spread brush on the ground, and fence it round, and then lay their clothes on it, to keep them from the sand. This is a Cape Cod clothes-yard.

The sand is the great enemy here. The tops of some of the hills were enclosed and a board put up forbidding all persons entering the enclosure, lest their feet should disturb the sand, and set it a-blowing or a-sliding. The inhabitants are obliged to get leave from the authorities to cut wood behind the town for fish-flakes, bean-poles, pea-brush, and the like, though, as we were told, they may transplant trees from one part of the township to another without leave. The sand drifts like snow, and sometimes the lower story of a house is concealed by it, though it is kept off by a wall. The houses were formerly built on piles, in order that the driving sand might pass under them. We saw a few old ones here still standing on their piles, but they were boarded up now, being protected by their younger neighbors. There was a school-house, just under the hill on which we sat, filled with sand up to the tops of the desks, and of course the master and scholars had fled. Perhaps they had imprudently left the windows open one day, or neglected to mend a broken pane. Yet in one place was advertised "Fine sand for sale here,"—I could hardly believe my eyes,—probably some of the street sifted,—a good instance of the fact that a man confers a value on the most worthless thing by mixing himself with it, according to which rule we must have conferred a value on the whole backside of Cape Cod;—but I thought that if they could have advertised "Fat Soil," or perhaps "Fine sand got rid of," ay, and "Shoes emptied here," it would have been more alluring. As we looked down on the town, I thought that I saw one man, who probably lived beyond the extremity of the planking, steering and tacking for it in a sort of snow-shoes, but I may have been mistaken. In some pictures of Provincetown the persons of the inhabitants are not drawn below the ancles, so much being supposed to be buried in the sand. Nevertheless, natives of Provincetown assured me that they could walk in the middle of the road without trouble even in slippers, for they had learned how to put their feet down and lift them up without taking in any sand. One man said that he should be surprised if he found half a dozen grains of sand in his pumps at night, and stated, moreover, that the young ladies had a dexterous way of emptying their shoes at each step, which it would take a stranger a long time to learn. The tires of the stage-wheels were about five inches wide; and the wagon-tires generally on the Cape are an inch or two wider, as the sand is an inch or two deeper than elsewhere. I saw a baby's wagon with tires six inches wide to keep it near the surface. The more tired the wheels, the less tired the horses. Yet all the time that we were in Provincetown, which was two days and nights, we saw only one horse and cart, and they were conveying a coffin.

They did not try such experiments there on common occasions. The next summer I saw only the two-wheeled horse-cart which conveyed me thirty rods into the harbor on my way to the steamer. Yet we read that there were two horses and two yoke of oxen here in 1791, and we were told that there were several more when we were there, beside the stage team. In Barber's Historical Collections, it is said, "so rarely are wheel-carriages seen in the place that they are a matter of some curiosity to the younger part of the community. A lad who understood navigating the ocean much better than land travel, on seeing a man driving a wagon in the street, expressed his surprise at his being able to drive so straight without the assistance of a rudder." There was no rattle of carts, and there would have been no rattle if there had been any carts. Some saddle-horses that passed the hotel in the evening merely made the sand fly with a rustling sound like a writer sanding his paper copiously, but there was no sound of their tread. No doubt there are more horses and carts there at present. A sleigh is never seen, or at least is a great novelty on the Cape, the snow being either absorbed by the sand or blown into drifts.

Nevertheless, the inhabitants of the Cape generally do not complain of their "soil," but will tell you that it is good enough for them to dry their fish on.

Notwithstanding all this sand, we counted three meeting-houses, and four school-houses nearly as large, on this street, though some had a tight board fence about them to preserve the plot within level and hard. Similar fences, even within a foot of many of the houses, gave the town a less cheerful and hospitable appearance than it would otherwise have had. They told us that, on the whole, the sand had made no progress for the last ten years, the cows being no longer permitted to go at large, and every means being taken to stop the sandy tide.

In 1727 Provincetown was "invested with peculiar privileges," for its encouragement. Once or twice it was nearly abandoned; but now lots on the street fetch a high price, though titles to them were first obtained by possession and improvement, and they are still transferred by quitclaim deeds merely, the township being the property of the State. But though lots were so valuable on the street, you might in many places throw a stone over them to where a man could still obtain land or sand by squatting on or improving it.

Stones are very rare on the Cape. I saw a very few small stones used for pavements and for bank walls, in one or two places in my walk, but they are so scarce, that, as I was informed, vessels have been forbidden to take them from the beach for ballast, and therefore their crews used to land at night and steal them. I did not hear of a rod of regular stone wall below Orleans. Yet I saw one man underpinning a new house in Eastham with some "rocks," as he called them, which he said a neighbor had collected with great pains in the course of years, and finally made over to him. This I thought was a gift worthy of being recorded,—equal to a transfer of California "rocks," almost. Another man who was assisting him, and who seemed to be a close observer of nature, hinted to me the locality of a rock in that neighborhood which was "forty-two paces in circumference and fifteen feet high," for he saw that I was a stranger, and, probably, would not carry it off. Yet I suspect that the locality of the few large rocks on the forearm of the Cape is well known to the inhabitants generally. I even met with one man who had got a smattering of mineralogy, but where he picked it up I could not guess. I thought that he would meet with some interesting geological nuts for him to crack, if he should ever visit the mainland, Cohasset or Marblehead, for instance.

The well stones at the Highland Light were brought from Hingham, but the wells and cellars of the Cape are generally built of brick, which also are imported. The cellars, as well as the wells, are made in a circular form, to prevent the sand from pressing in the wall. The former are only from nine to twelve feet in diameter, and are said to be very cheap, since a single tier of brick will suffice for a cellar of even larger dimensions. Of course, if you live in the sand, you will not require a large cellar to hold your roots. In Provincetown, when formerly they suffered the sand to drive under their houses, obliterating all rudiment of a cellar, they did not raise a vegetable to put into one. One farmer in Wellfleet, who raised fifty bushels of potatoes, showed me his cellar under a corner of his house, not more than nine feet in diameter, looking like a cistern; but he had another of the same size under his barn.

You need dig only a few feet almost anywhere near the shore of the Cape to find fresh water. But that which we tasted was invariably poor, though the inhabitants called it good, as if they were comparing it with salt water. In the account of Truro, it is said, "Wells dug near the shore are dry at low water, or rather at what is called young flood, but are replenished with the flowing of the tide,"—the saltwater, which is lowest in the sand, apparently forcing the fresh up. When you express your surprise at the greenness of a Provincetown garden on the beach, in a dry season, they will sometimes tell you that the tide forces the moisture up to them. It is an interesting fact that low sand-bars in the midst of the ocean, perhaps even those which are laid bare only at low tide, are reservoirs of fresh water at which the thirsty mariner can supply himself. They appear, like huge sponges, to hold the rain and dew which fall on them, and which, by capillary attraction, are prevented from mingling with the surrounding brine.

The Harbor of Provincetown—which, as well as the greater part of the Bay, and a wide expanse of ocean, we overlooked from our perch—is deservedly famous. It opens to the south, is free from rocks, and is never frozen over. It is said that the only ice seen in it drifts in sometimes from Barnstable or Plymouth. Dwight remarks that "The storms which prevail on the American coast generally come from the east; and there is no other harbor on a windward shore within two hundred miles." J. D. Graham, who has made a very minute and thorough survey of this harbor and the adjacent waters, states that "its capacity, depth of water, excellent anchorage, and the complete shelter it affords from all winds, combine to render it one of the most valuable ship harbors on our coast." It is *the* harbor of the Cape and of the fishermen of Massachusetts generally. It was known to navigators several years at least before the settlement of Plymouth. In Captain John Smith's map of New England, dated 1614, it bears the name of Milford Haven, and Massachusetts Bay that of Stuard's Bay. His Highness, Prince Charles, changed the name of Cape Cod to Cape James; but even princes have not always power to change a name for the worse, and as Cotton Mather said, Cape Cod is "a name which I suppose it will never lose till shoals of codfish be seen swimming on its highest hills."

Many an early voyager was unexpectedly caught by this hook, and found himself embayed. On successive maps, Cape Cod appears sprinkled over with French, Dutch, and English names, as it made part of New France, New Holland, and New England. On one map Provincetown Harbor is called "Fuic (bownet?) Bay," Barnstable Bay "Staten Bay," and the sea north of it "Mare del Noort," or the North Sea. On another, the extremity of the Cape is called "Staten Hoeck," or the States Hook. On another, by Young, this has Noord Zee, Staten hoek or Hit hoeck, but the copy at Cambridge has no date; the whole Cape is called "Niew Hollant" (after Hudson); and on another still, the shore between Race Point and Wood End appears to be called "Bevechier." In Champlain's admirable Map of New France, including the oldest recognizable map of what is now the New England coast with which I am acquainted, Cape Cod is called *C. Blan* (i. e. Cape White), from the color of its sands, and Massachusetts Bay is *Baye Blanche*. It was visited by De Monts and Champlain in 1605, and the next year was further explored by Poitrincourt and Champlain. The latter has given a particular account of these explorations in his "Voyages," together with separate charts and soundings of two of its harbors, — *Malle Barre*, the Bad Bar (Nauset Harbor?), a name now applied to what the French called *Cap Baturier*, — and *Port Fortune*, apparently Chatham Harbor. Both these names are copied on the map of "Novi Belgii," in Ogilby's America. He also describes minutely the manners and customs of the savages, and represents by a plate the savages surprising the French and killing five or six of them. The French afterward killed some of the natives, and wished, by way of revenge, to carry off some and make them grind in their hand-mill at Port Royal.

It is remarkable that there is not in English any adequate or correct account of the French exploration of what is now the coast of New England, between 1604 and 1608, though it is conceded that they then made the first permanent European settlement on the continent of North America north of St. Augustine. If the lions had been the painters it would have been otherwise. This omission is probably to be accounted for partly by the fact that the *early edition* of Champlain's "Voyages" had not been consulted for this purpose. This contains by far the most particular, and, I think, the most interesting chapter of what we may call the Ante-Pilgrim history of New England, extending to one hundred and sixty pages quarto; but appears to be unknown equally to the historian and the orator on Plymouth Rock. Bancroft does not mention Champlain at all among the authorities for De Monts' expedition, nor does he say that he ever visited the coast of New England. Though he bore the title of pilot to De Monts, he was, in *another sense*, the leading spirit, as well as the historian of the expedition. Holmes, Hildreth, and Barry, and apparently all our historians who mention Champlain, refer to the edition of 1632, in which all the separate charts of our harbors, &c., and about one half the narrative, are omitted; for the author explored so many lands afterward that he could afford to forget a part of what he had done. Hildreth, speaking of De Monts's expedition, says that "he looked into the Penobscot [in 1605], which Pring had discovered two years before," saying nothing about Champlain's extensive exploration of it for De Monts in 1604 (Holmes says 1608, and refers to Purchas); also that he followed in the track of Pring along the coast "to Cape Cod, which he called Malabarre." (Haliburton had made the same statement before him in 1829. He called it Cap Blanc, and Malle Barre (the Bad Bar) was the name given to a harbor on the east side of the Cape.) Pring says nothing about a river there. Belknap says that Weymouth discovered it in 1605. Sir F. Gorges says, in his narration (Maine Hist. Coll., Vol. II. p. 19), 1658, that Pring in 1606 "made a perfect discovery of all the rivers and harbors." This is the most I can find. Bancroft makes Champlain to have discovered more western rivers in Maine, not naming the Penobscot; he, however, must have been the discoverer of distances on this river (see Belknap, p. 147). Pring was absent from England only about six months, and sailed by this part of Cape Cod (Malebarre) because it yielded no sassafras, while the French, who probably had not heard of Pring, were patiently for years exploring the coast in search of a place of settlement, sounding and surveying its harbors.

John Smith's map, published in 1616, from observations in 1614–15, is by many regarded as the oldest map of New England. It is the first that was made after this country was called New England, for he so called it; but in Champlain's "Voyages," edition 1613, (and Lescarbot, in 1612, quotes a still earlier account of his voyage,) there is a map of it made when it was known to Christendom as New France, called *Carte Géographique de la Nouvelle Franse faictte par le Sieur de Champlain Saint Tongois Cappitaine ordinaire pour le roi en la Marine, —faict l'en 1612*, from his observations between 1604 and 1607; a map extending from Labrador to Cape Cod and westward *to the Great Lakes*, and crowded with information, geographical, ethnographical, zoölogical, and botanical. He even gives the variation of the compass as observed by himself at that date on many parts of the coast. This, taken together with the many *separate charts* of harbors and their soundings on a large scale, which this volume contains,—among the rest, *Qui ni be quy* (Kennebec), *Chouacoit R.* (Saco R.), *Le Beau port*, *Port St. Louis* (near Cape Ann), and others on our coast,—but *which are not in the edition of 1632*, makes this a completer map of the New England and adjacent northern coast than was made for half a century afterward, almost, we might be allowed to say, till another Frenchman, Des Barres, made another for us, which only our late Coast Survey has superseded. Most of the maps of this coast made for a long time after betray their indebtedness to Champlain. He was a skilful navigator, a man of science, and geographer to the King of France. He crossed the Atlantic about twenty times, and made nothing of it; often in a small vessel in which few would dare to go to sea to-day; and on one occasion making the voyage from Tadoussac to St. Malo in eighteen days. He was in this neighborhood, that is, between Annapolis, Nova Scotia, and Cape Cod, observing the land and its inhabitants, and making a map of the coast, from May, 1604, to September, 1607, *or about three and a half years*, and he has described minutely his method of surveying harbors. By his own account, a part of his map was engraved in 1604 (?). When Pont-Gravé and others returned to France in 1606, he remained at Port Royal with Poitrincourt, "in order," says he, "by the aid of God, to finish the chart of the coasts which I had begun"; and again in his volume, printed before John Smith visited this part of America, he says: "It seems to me that I have done my duty as far as I could, if I have not forgotten to put in my said chart whatever I saw, and give a particular knowledge to the public of what had never been described nor discovered so particularly as I have done it, although some other may have heretofore written of it; but it was a very small affair in comparison with what we have discovered within the last ten years."

It is not generally remembered, if known, by the descendants of the Pilgrims, that when their forefathers were spending their first memorable winter in the New World, they had for neighbors a colony of French no further off than Port Royal (Annapolis, Nova Scotia), three hundred miles distant (Prince seems to make it about five hundred miles); where, in spite of many vicissitudes, they had been for fifteen years. They built a grist-mill there as early as 1606; also made bricks and turpentine on a stream, Williamson says, in 1606. De Monts, who was a Protestant, brought his minister with him, who came to blows with the Catholic priest on the subject of religion. Though these founders of Acadie endured no less than the Pilgrims, and about the same proportion of them— thirty-five out of seventy-nine (Williamson's Maine says thirty-six out of seventy)—died the first winter at St. Croix, 1604–5, sixteen years earlier, no orator, to my knowledge, has ever celebrated their enterprise (Williamson's History of Maine does considerably), while the trials which their successors and descendants endured at the hands of the English have furnished a theme for both the historian and poet. (See Bancroft's History and Longfellow's Evangeline.) The remains of their fort at St. Croix were discovered at the end of the last century, and helped decide where the true St. Croix, our boundary, was.

The very gravestones of those Frenchmen are probably older than the oldest English monument in New England north of the Elizabeth Islands, or perhaps anywhere in New England, for if there are any traces of Gosnold's storehouse left, his strong works are gone. Bancroft says, advisedly, in 1834, "It requires a believing eye to discern the ruins of the fort"; and that there were no ruins of a fort in 1837. Dr.

Charles T. Jackson tells me that, in the course of a geological survey in 1827, he discovered a gravestone, a slab of trap rock, on Goat Island, opposite Annapolis (Port Royal), in Nova Scotia, bearing a Masonic coat-of-arms and the date 1606, which is fourteen years earlier than the landing of the Pilgrims. This was left in the possession of Judge Haliburton, of Nova Scotia.

There were Jesuit priests in what has since been called New England, converting the savages at Mount Desert, then St. Savior, in 1613,—having come over to Port Royal in 1611, though they were almost immediately interrupted by the English, years before the Pilgrims came hither to enjoy their own religion. This according to Champlain. Charlevoix says the same; and after coming from France in 1611, went west from Port Royal along the coast as far as the Kennebec in 1612, and was often carried from Port Royal to Mount Desert.

Indeed, the Englishman's history of *New* England commences, only when it ceases to be, *New* France. Though Cabot was the first to discover the continent of North America, Champlain, in the edition of his "Voyages" printed in 1632, after the English had for a season got possession of Quebec and Port Royal, complains with no little justice: "The common consent of all Europe is to represent New France as extending at least to the thirty-fifth and thirty-sixth degrees of latitude, as appears by the maps of the world printed in Spain, Italy, Holland, Flanders, Germany, and England, until they possessed themselves of the coasts of New France, where are Arcadie, the Etchemins (Maine and New Brunswick), the Almouchicois (Massachusetts?), and the Great River St. Lawrence, where they have imposed, according to their fancy, such names as New England, Scotland, and others; but it is not easy to efface the memory of a thing which is known to all Christendom."

That Cabot merely landed on the uninhabitable shore of Labrador, gave the English no just title to New England, or to the United States generally, any more than to Patagonia. His careful biographer (Biddle) is not certain in what voyage he ran down the coast of the United States, as is reported, and no one tells us what he saw. Miller, in the New York Hist. Coll., Vol. I. p. 28, says he does not appear to have landed anywhere. Contrast with this Verrazzani's tarrying fifteen days at one place on the New England coast, and making frequent excursions into the interior thence. It chances that the latter's letter to Francis I., in 1524, contains "the earliest original account extant of the Atlantic coast of the United States"; and even from that time the northern part of it began to be called *La Terra Francese*, or French Land. A part of it was called New Holland before it was called New England. The English were very backward to explore and settle the continent which they had stumbled upon. The French preceded them both in their attempts to colonize the continent of North America (Carolina and Florida, 1562–4), and in their first permanent settlement (Port Royal, 1605); and the right of possession, naturally enough, was the one which England mainly respected and recognized in the case of Spain, of Portugal, and also of France, from the time of Henry VII.

The explorations of the French gave to the world the first valuable maps of these coasts. Denys of Honfleur made a map of the Gulf of St. Lawrence in 1506. No sooner had Cartier explored the St. Lawrence in 1535, than there began to be published by his countrymen remarkably accurate charts of that river as far up as Montreal. It is almost all of the continent north of Florida that you recognize on charts for more than a generation afterward,—though Verrazzani's rude plot (made under French auspices) was regarded by Hackluyt, more than fifty years after his voyage (in 1524), as the most accurate representation of our coast. The French trail is distinct. They went measuring and sounding, and when they got home had something to show for their voyages and explorations. There was no danger of their charts being lost, as Cabot's have been.

The most distinguished navigators of that day were Italians, or of Italian descent, and Portuguese. The French and Spaniards, though less advanced in the science of navigation than the former, possessed more imagination and spirit of adventure than the English, and were better fitted to be the explorers of a new continent even as late as 1751.

This spirit it was which so early carried the French to the Great Lakes and the Mississippi on the north, and the Spaniard to the same river on the south. It was long before our frontiers reached their settlements in the west, and a *voyageur* or *coureur de bois* is still our conductor there. Prairie is a French word, as Sierra is a Spanish one. Augustine in Florida, and Santa Fé in New Mexico [1582], both built by the Spaniards, are considered the oldest towns in the United States. Within the memory of the oldest man, the Anglo-Americans were confined between the Apalachian Mountains and the sea, "a space not two hundred miles broad," while the Mississippi was by treaty the eastern boundary of New France. (See the pamphlet on settling the Ohio, London, 1763, bound up with the travels of Sir John Bartram.) So far as inland discovery was concerned, the adventurous spirit of the English was that of sailors who land but for a day, and their enterprise the enterprise of traders. Cabot spoke like an Englishman, as he was, if he said, as one reports, in reference to the discovery of the American Continent, when he found it running toward the north, that it was a great disappointment to him, being in his way to India; but we would rather add to than detract from the fame of so great a discoverer.

Samuel Penhallow, in his History (Boston, 1726), p. 51, speaking of "Port Royal and Nova Scotia," says of the last, that its "first seizure was by Sir Sebastian Cobbet for the crown of Great Britain, in the reign of King Henry VII.; but lay dormant till the year 1621," when Sir William Alexander got a patent of it, and possessed it some years; and afterward Sir David Kirk was proprietor of it, but erelong, "to the surprise of all thinking men, it was given up unto the French."

Even as late as 1633 we find Winthrop, the first Governor of the Massachusetts Colony, who was not the most likely to be misinformed, who, moreover, has the *fame*, at least, of having discovered Wachusett Mountain (discerned it forty miles inland), talking about the "Great Lake" and the "hideous swamps about it," near which the Connecticut and the "Potomack" took their rise; and among the memorable events of the year 1642 he chronicles Darby Field, an Irishman's expedition to the "White hill," from whose top he saw eastward what he "judged to be the Gulf of Canada," and westward what he "judged to be the great lake which Canada River comes out of," and where he found much "Muscovy glass," and "could rive out pieces of forty feet long and seven or eight broad." While the very inhabitants of New England were thus fabling about the country a hundred miles inland, which was a *terra incognita* to them,—or rather many years before the earliest date referred to,—Champlain, the *first Governor of Canada*, not to mention the inland discoveries of Cartier,* Roberval, and others, of the preceding century, and his own earlier voyage, had already gone to war against the Iroquois in their forest forts, and penetrated to the Great Lakes and wintered there, before a Pilgrim had heard of New England. In Champlain's "Voyages," printed in 1613, there is a plate representing a fight in which he aided the Canada Indians against the Iroquois, near the south end of Lake Champlain, in July, 1609, eleven years before the settlement of Plymouth. Bancroft says he joined the Algonquins in an expedition against the Iroquois, or Five Nations, in the northwest of New York. This is that "Great Lake," which the English, hearing some rumor of from the French, long after, locate in an "Imaginary Province called Laconia, and spent several years about 1630 in the vain attempt to discover." (Sir Ferdinand Gorges, in Maine Hist. Coll., Vol. II. p. 68.) Thomas Morton has a chapter on this "Great Lake." In the edition of Champlain's map dated 1632, the Falls of Niagara appear; and in a great lake northwest of *Mer Douce* (Lake Huron) there is an island represented, over which is written, *"Isle ou il y á une mine de cuivre,"*—"Island where there is a mine of copper." This will do for an offset to our Governor's "Muscovy Glass." Of all these adventures and discoveries we have a minute and faithful account, giving facts and dates as well as charts and soundings, all scientific and Frenchman-like, with scarcely one fable or traveller's story.

Probably Cape Cod was visited by Europeans long before the seventeenth century. It may be that Cabot himself beheld it. Verrazzani, in 1524, according to his own account, spent

---

*It is remarkable that the first, if not the only, part of New England which Cartier saw was Vermont (he also saw the mountains of New York), from Montreal Mountain, in 1535, sixty-seven years before Gosnold saw Cape Cod. *If seeing is discovering,*—and that is *all* that it is proved that Cabot knew of the coast of the United States,—then Cartier (to omit Verrazzani and Gomez) was the discoverer of New England rather than Gosnold, who is commonly so styled.

fifteen days on our coast, in latitude 41° 40', (some suppose in the harbor of Newport,) and often went five or six leagues into the interior there, and he says that he sailed thence at once one hundred and fifty leagues northeasterly, *always in sight of the coast*. There is a chart in Hackluyt's "Divers Voyages," made according to Verrazzani's plot, which last is praised for its accuracy by Hackluyt, but I cannot distinguish Cape Cod on it, unless it is the "C. Arenas," which is in the right latitude, though ten degrees west of "Claudia," which is thought to be Block Island.

The "Biographie Universelle" informs us that "An ancient manuscript chart drawn in 1529 by Diego Ribeiro, a Spanish cosmographer, has preserved the memory of the voyage of Gomez [a Portuguese sent out by Charles the Fifth]. One reads in it under (*au dessous*) the place occupied by the States of New York, Connecticut, and Rhode Island, *Terre d'Etienne Gomez, qu'il découvrit en 1525* (Land of Etienne Gomez, which he discovered in 1525)." This chart, with a memoir, was published at Weimar in the last century.

Jean Alphonse, Roberval's pilot in Canada in 1642, one of the most skilful navigators of his time, and who has given remarkably minute and accurate direction for sailing up the St. Lawrence, showing that he knows what he is talking about, says in his *"Routier"* (it is in Hackluyt), "I have been at a bay as far as the forty-second degree, between Norimbegue [the Penobscot?] and Florida, but I have not explored the bottom of it, and I do not know whether it passes from one land to the other," i. e. to Asia. ("J'ai été a une Baye jusques par les 42ᵉ degres entre la Norimbegue et la Floride; mais je n'en ai pas cherché le fond, et ne sçais pas si elle passe d'une terre à l'autre.") This may refer to Massachusetts Bay, if not possibly to the western inclination of the coast a little farther south. When he says, "I have no doubt that the Norimbegue enters into the river of Canada," he is perhaps so interpreting some account which the Indians had given respecting the route from the St. Lawrence to the Atlantic, by the St. John, or Penobscot, or possibly even the Hudson River.

We hear rumors of this country of "Norumbega" and its great city from many quarters. In a discourse by a great

French sea-captain in Ramusio's third volume (1556–65), this is said to be the name given to the land by its inhabitants, and Verrazzani is called the discoverer of it; another in 1607 makes the natives call it, or the river, Aguncia. It is represented as an island on an accompanying chart. It is frequently spoken of by old writers as a country of indefinite extent, between Canada and Florida, and it appears as a large island with Cape Breton at its eastern extremity, on the map made according to Verrazzani's plot in Hackluyt's "Divers Voyages." These maps and rumors may have been the origin of the notion, common among the early settlers, that New England was an island. The country and city of Norumbega appear about where Maine now is on a map in Ortelius ("Theatrum Orbis Terrarum," Antwerp, 1570), and the "R. Grande" is drawn where the Penobscot or St. John might be.

In 1604, Champlain being sent by the Sieur de Monts to explore the coast of Norumbegue, sailed up the Penobscot twenty-two or twenty-three leagues from "Isle Haute," or till he was stopped by the falls. He says: "I think that this river is that which many pilots and historians call Norembegue, and which the greater part have described as great and spacious, with numerous islands; and its entrance in the forty-third or forty-third and one half, or, according to others, the forty-fourth degree of latitude, more or less." He is convinced that "the greater part" of those who speak of a great city there have never seen it, but repeat a mere rumor, but he thinks that some have seen the mouth of the river since it answers to their description.

Under date of 1607 Champlain writes: "Three or four leagues north of the Cap de Poitrincourt [near the head of the Bay of Fundy in Nova Scotia] we found a cross, which was very old, covered with moss and almost all decayed, which was an evident sign that there had formerly been Christians there."

Also the following passage from Lescarbot will show how much the neighboring coasts were frequented by Europeans in the sixteenth century. Speaking of his return from Port Royal to France in 1607, he says: "At last, within four leagues of Campseau [the Gut of Canso], we arrived at a harbor [in Nova Scotia], where a worthy old gentleman from St. John de Lus, named Captain Savalet, was fishing, who received us with the utmost courtesy. And as this harbor, which is small, but very good, has no name, I have given it on my geographical chart the name of Savalet. [It is on Champlain's map also.] This worthy man told us that this voyage was the forty-second which he had made to those parts, and yet the Newfoundlanders [*Terre neuviers*] make only one a year. He was wonderfully content with his fishery, and informed us that he made daily fifty crowns' worth of cod, and that his voyage would be worth ten thousand francs. He had sixteen men in his employ; and his vessel was of eighty tons, which could carry a hundred thousand dry cod." (Histoire de la Nouvelle France, 1612.) They dried their fish on the rocks on shore.

The "Isola della Réna" (Sable Island?) appears on the chart of "Nuova Francia" and Norumbega, accompanying the "Discourse" above referred to in Ramusio's third volume, edition 1556–65. Champlain speaks of there being at the Isle of Sable, in 1604, "grass pastured by oxen (*bœufs*) and cows which the Portuguese carried there more than sixty years ago," i. e. sixty years before 1613; in a later edition he says, which came out of a Spanish vessel which was lost in endeavoring to settle on the Isle of Sable; and he states that De la Roche's men, who were left on this island seven years from 1598, lived on the flesh of these cattle which they found "*en quantite,*" and built houses out of the wrecks of vessels which came to the island ("perhaps Gilbert's"), there being no wood or stone. Lescarbot says that they lived "on fish and the milk of cows left there about eighty years before by Baron de Leri and Saint Just." Charlevoix says they ate up the cattle and then lived on fish. Haliburton speaks of cattle left there as a rumor. De Leri and Saint Just had suggested plans of colonization on the Isle of Sable as early as 1515 (1508?) according to Bancroft, referring to Charlevoix. These are but a few of the instances which I might quote.

Cape Cod is commonly said to have been discovered in 1602. We will consider at length under what circumstances, and with what observation and expectations, the first Englishmen whom history clearly discerns approached the coast of New England. According to the accounts of Archer and Brereton (both of whom accompanied Gosnold), on the 26th

of March, 1602, old style, Captain Bartholomew Gosnold set
sail from Falmouth, England, for the North Part of Virginia,
in a small bark called the Concord, they being in all, says one
account, "thirty-two persons, whereof eight mariners and sailors, twelve purposing upon the discovery to return with the
ship for England, the rest remain there for population." This
is regarded as "the first attempt of the English to make a settlement within the limits of New England." Pursuing a new
and a shorter course than the usual one by the Canaries, "the
14th of April following" they "had sight of Saint Mary's, an
island of the Azores." As their sailors were few and "none of
the best," (I use their own phrases,) and they were "going
upon an unknown coast," they were not "over-bold to stand
in with the shore but in open weather"; so they made their
first discovery of land with the lead. The 23d of April the
ocean appeared yellow, but on taking up some of the water
in a bucket, "it altered not either in color or taste from the
sea azure." The 7th of May they saw divers birds whose
names they knew, and many others in their "English tongue
of no name." The 8th of May "the water changed to a yellowish green, where at seventy fathoms" they "had ground." The
9th, they had upon their lead "many glittering stones,"—
"which might promise some mineral matter in the bottom."
The 10th, they were over a bank which they thought to be
near the western end of St. John's Island, and saw schools of
fish. The 12th, they say, "continually passed fleeting by us sea-
oare, which seemed to have their movable course towards the
northeast." On the 13th, they observed "great beds of weeds,
much wood, and divers things else floating by," and "had
smelling of the shore much as from the southern Cape and
Andalusia in Spain." On Friday, the 14th, early in the morning they descried land on the north, in the latitude of forty-
three degrees, apparently some part of the coast of Maine.
Williamson (History of Maine) says it certainly could not
have been south of the central Isle of Shoals. Belknap inclines
to think it the south side of Cape Ann. Standing fair along
by the shore, about twelve o'clock the same day, they came
to anchor and were visited by eight savages, who came off to
them "in a Biscay shallop, with sail and oars,"—"an iron
grapple, and a kettle of copper." These they at first mistook

for "Christians distressed." One of them was "apparelled with a waistcoat and breeches of black serge, made after our sea-fashion, hoes and shoes on his feet; all the rest (saving one that had a pair of breeches of blue cloth) were naked." They appeared to have had dealings with "some Basques of St. John de Luz, and to understand much more than we," say the English, "for want of language, could comprehend." But they soon "set sail westward, leaving them and their coast." (This was a remarkable discovery for discoverers.)

"The 15th day," writes Gabriel Archer, " we had again sight of the land, which made ahead, being as we thought an is-land, by reason of a large sound that appeared westward be-tween it and the main, for coming to the west end thereof, we did perceive a large opening, we called it Shoal Hope. Near this cape we came to anchor in fifteen fathoms, where we took great store of cod-fish, for which we altered the name and called it Cape Cod. Here we saw skulls of herring, mack-erel, and other small fish, in great abundance. This is a low sandy shoal, but without danger; also we came to anchor again in sixteen fathoms, fair by the land in the latitude of forty-two degrees. This Cape is well near a mile broad, and lieth northeast by east. The Captain went here ashore, and found the ground to be full of peas, strawberries, whortleber-ries, etc., as then unripe, the sand also by the shore somewhat deep; the firewood there by us taken in was of cypress, birch, witch-hazel, and beach. A young Indian came here to the cap-tain, armed with his bow and arrows, and had certain plates of copper hanging at his ears; he showed a willingness to help us in our occasions."

"The 16th we trended the coast southerly, which was all champaign and full of grass, but the islands somewhat woody."

Or, according to the account of John Brereton, "riding here," that is where they first communicated with the natives, "in no very good harbor, and withal doubting the weather, about three of the clock the same day in the afternoon we weighed, and standing southerly off into sea the rest of that day and the night following, with a fresh gale of wind, in the morning we found ourselves embayed with a mighty head-land; but coming to an anchor about nine of the clock the same day, within a league of the shore, we hoisted out the one half of our shallop, and Captain Bartholomew Gosnold, myself and three others, went ashore, being a white sandy and very bold shore; and marching all that afternoon with our muskets on our necks, on the highest hills which we saw (the weather very hot), at length we perceived this headland to be parcel of the main, and sundry islands lying almost round about it; so returning towards evening to our shallop (for by that time the other part was brought ashore and set together), we espied an Indian, a young man of proper stature, and of a pleasing countenance, and after some familiarity with him, we left him at the sea side, and returned to our ship, where in five or six hours' absence we had pestered our ship so with codfish, that we threw numbers of them overboard again: and surely I am persuaded that in the months of March, April, and May, there is upon this coast better fishing, and in as great plenty, as in Newfoundland; for the skulls of mackerel, herrings, cod, and other fish, that we daily saw as we went and came from the shore, were wonderful," &c.

"From this place we sailed round about this headland, almost all the points of the compass, the shore very bold; but as no coast is free from dangers, so I am persuaded this is as free as any. The land somewhat low, full of goodly woods, but in some places plain."

It is not quite clear on which side of the Cape they landed. If it was inside, as would appear from Brereton's words, "From this place we sailed round about this headland almost all the points of the compass," it must have been on the western shore either of Truro or Wellfleet. To one sailing south into Barnstable Bay along the Cape, the only " white, sandy, and very bold shore" that appears is in these towns, though the bank is not so high there as on the eastern side. At a distance of four or five miles the sandy cliffs there look like a long fort of yellow sandstone, they are so level and regular, especially in Wellfleet,—the fort of the land defending itself against the encroachments of the Ocean. They are streaked here and there with a reddish sand as if painted. Farther south the shore is more flat, and less *obviously* and abruptly sandy, and a little tinge of green here and there in the marshes appears to the sailor like a rare and precious emerald. But in the

Journal of Pring's Voyage the next year (and Salterne, who was with Pring, had accompanied Gosnold) it is said, "Departing hence [i. e. from Savage Rocks] we bore unto that great gulf which Captain Gosnold overshot the year before."*

So they sailed round the Cape, calling the southeasterly extremity "Point Cave," till they came to an island which they named Martha's Vineyard (now called No Man's Land), and another on which they dwelt awhile, which they named Elizabeth's Island, in honor of the queen, one of the group since so called, now known by its Indian name Cuttyhunk. There they built a small storehouse, the first house built by the English in New England, whose cellar could recently still be seen, made partly of stones taken from the beach. Bancroft says (edition of 1837), the ruins of the fort can no longer be discerned. They who were to have remained becoming discontented, all together set sail for England with a load of sassafras and other commodities, on the 18th of June following.

The next year came Martin Pring, looking for sassafras, and thereafter they began to come thick and fast, until long after sassafras had lost its reputation.

These are the oldest accounts which we have of Cape Cod, unless, perchance, Cape Cod is, as some suppose, the same with that "Kial-ar-nes" or Keel-Cape, on which, according to old Icelandic manuscripts, Thorwald, son of Eric the Red, after sailing many days southwest from Greenland, broke his keel in the year 1004; and where, according to another, in some respects less trustworthy manuscript, Thor-finn Karlse-fue ("that is, one who promises or is destined to be an able or great man"; he is said to have had a son born in New England, from whom Thorwaldsen the sculptor was descended), sailing past, in the year 1007, with his wife Gudrida, Snorre Thorbrandson, Biarne Grinolfson, and Thorhall Garn-lason, distinguished Norsemen, in three ships containing "one hundred and sixty men and all sorts of live stock" (probably

---

*"Savage Rock," which some have supposed to be, from the name, the *Salvages*, a ledge about two miles off Rockland, Cape Ann, was probably the *Nubble*, a large, high rock near the shore, on the east side of York Harbor, Maine. The first land made by Gosnold is presumed by experienced navigators to be Cape Elizabeth, on the same coast. (See Babson's History of Gloucester, Massachusetts.)

the first Norway rats among the rest), having the land "on the right side" of them, "roved ashore," and found "*Or-æfi* (trackless deserts)," and "*Strand-ir lang-ar ok sand-ar* (long narrow beaches and sand-hills)," and "called the shores *Furdu-strand-ir* (Wonder-Strands), because the sailing by them seemed long."

According to the Icelandic manuscripts, *Thorwald* was the first then,—unless possibly one Biarne Heriulfson (i. e. son of Heriulf) who had been seized with a great desire to travel, sailing from Iceland to Greenland in the year 986 to join his father who had migrated thither, for he had resolved, says the manuscript, "to spend the following winter, like all the preceding ones, with his father,"—being driven far to the southwest by a storm, when it cleared up saw the low land of Cape Cod looming faintly in the distance; but this not answering to the description of Greenland, he put his vessel about, and, sailing northward along the coast, at length reached Greenland and his father. At any rate, he may put forth a strong claim to be regarded as the discoverer of the American continent.

These Northmen were a hardy race, whose younger sons inherited the ocean, and traversed it without chart or compass, and they are said to have been "the first who learned the art of sailing on a wind." Moreover, they had a habit of casting their door-posts overboard and settling wherever they went ashore. But as Biarne, and Thorwald, and Thorfinn have not mentioned the latitude and longitude distinctly enough, though we have great respect for them as skilful and adventurous navigators, we must for the present remain in doubt as to what capes they did see. We think that they were considerably further north.

If time and space permitted, I could present the claims of several other worthy persons. Lescarbot, in 1609, asserts that the French sailors had been accustomed to frequent the Newfoundland Banks from time immemorial, "for the codfish with which they feed almost all Europe and supply all sea-going vessels," and accordingly "the language of the nearest lands is half Basque"; and he quotes Postel, a learned but extravagant French author, born in 1510, only six years after the Basques, Bretons, and Normans are said to have discovered the Grand Bank and adjacent islands, as saying, in his *Charte Géographique*, which we have not seen: "Terra haec ob lucrosissimam piscationis utilitatem summa litterarum memoria a Gallis adiri solita, et ante mille sexcentos annos frequentari solita est; sed eo quod sit urbibus inculta et vasta, spreta est." "This land, on account of its very lucrative fishery, was accustomed to be visited by the Gauls from the very dawn of history, and more than sixteen hundred years ago was accustomed to be frequented; but because it was unadorned with cities, and waste, it was despised."

It is the old story. Bob Smith discovered the mine, but I discovered it to the world. And now Bob Smith is putting in his claim.

But let us not laugh at Postel and his visions. He was perhaps better posted up than we; and if he does seem to draw the long-bow, it may be because he had a long way to shoot,—quite across the Atlantic. If America was found and lost again once, as most of us believe, then why not twice? especially as there were likely to be so few records of an earlier discovery. Consider what stuff history is made of,—that for the most part it is merely a story agreed on by posterity. Who will tell us even how many Russians were engaged in the battle of the Chernaya, the other day? Yet no doubt Mr. Scriblerus, the historian, will fix on a definite number for the schoolboys to commit to their excellent memories. What, then, of the number of Persians at Salamis? The historian whom I read knew as much about the position of the parties and their tactics in the last-mentioned affair, as they who describe a recent battle in an article for the press now-a-days, before the particulars have arrived. I believe that, if I were to live the life of mankind over again myself, (which I would not be hired to do,) with the Universal History in my hands, I should not be able to tell what was what.

Earlier than the date Postel refers to, at any rate, Cape Cod lay in utter darkness to the civilized world, though even then the sun rose from eastward out of the sea every day, and, rolling over the Cape, went down westward into the Bay. It was even then Cape and Bay,—ay, the Cape of *Codfish*, and the Bay of the *Massachusetts*, perchance.

Quite recently, on the 11th of November, 1620, old style, as is well known, the Pilgrims in the Mayflower came to anchor in Cape Cod Harbor. They had loosed from Plymouth, England, the 6th of September, and, in the words of "Mourt's Relation," "after many difficulties in boisterous storms, at length, by God's providence, upon the 9th of November, we espied land, which we deemed to be Cape Cod, and so afterward it proved. Upon the 11th of November we came to anchor in the bay, which is a good harbor and pleasant bay, circled round except in the entrance, which is about four miles over from land to land, compassed about to the very sea with oaks, pines, juniper, sassafras, and other sweet wood. It is a harbor wherein a thousand sail of ships may safely ride. There we relieved ourselves with wood and water, and refreshed our people, while our shallop was fitted to coast the bay, to search for an habitation." There *we* put up at Fuller's Hotel, passing by the Pilgrim House as too high for us (we learned afterward that we need not have been so particular), and we refreshed ourselves with hashed fish and beans, beside taking in a supply of liquids (which were not intoxicating), while our legs were refitted to coast the back-side. Further say the Pilgrims: "We could not come near the shore by three quarters of an English mile, because of shallow water; which was a great prejudice to us; for our people going on shore were forced to wade a bow-shot or two in going aland, which caused many to get colds and coughs; for it was many times freezing cold weather." They afterwards say: "It brought much weakness amongst us"; and no doubt it led to the death of some at Plymouth.

The harbor of Provincetown is very shallow near the shore, especially about the head, where the Pilgrims landed. When I left this place the next summer, the steamer could not get up to the wharf, but we were carried out to a large boat in a cart as much as thirty rods in shallow water, while a troop of little boys kept us company, wading around, and thence we pulled to the steamer by a rope. The harbor being thus shallow and sandy about the shore, coasters are accustomed to run in here to paint their vessels, which are left high and dry when the tide goes down.

It chanced that the Sunday morning that we were there, I had joined a party of men who were smoking and lolling over a pile of boards on one of the wharves, (*nihil humanum a me, &c.,*) when our landlord, who was a sort of tithing-man, went off to stop some sailors who were engaged in painting their vessel. Our party was recruited from time to time by other citizens, who came rubbing their eyes as if they had just got out of bed; and one old man remarked to me that it was the custom there to lie abed very late on Sunday, it being a day of rest. I remarked that, as I thought, they might as well let the man paint, for all us. It was not noisy work, and would not disturb our devotions. But a young man in the company, taking his pipe out of his mouth, said that it was a plain contradiction of the law of God, which he quoted, and if they did not have some such regulation, vessels would run in there to tar, and rig, and paint, and they would have no Sabbath at all. This was a good argument enough, if he had not put it in the name of religion. The next summer, as I sat on a hill there one sultry Sunday afternoon, the meeting-house windows being open, my meditations were interrupted by the noise of a preacher who shouted like a boatswain, profaning the quiet atmosphere, and who, I fancied, must have taken off his coat. Few things could have been more disgusting or disheartening. I wished the tithing-man would stop him.

The Pilgrims say: "There was the greatest store of fowl that ever we saw."

We saw no fowl there, except gulls of various kinds; but the greatest store of them that ever we saw was on a flat but slightly covered with water on the east side of the harbor, and we observed a man who had landed there from a boat creeping along the shore in order to get a shot at them, but they all rose and flew away in a great scattering flock, too soon for him, having apparently got their dinners, though he did not get his.

It is remarkable that the Pilgrims (or their reporter) describe this part of the Cape, not only as well wooded, but as having a deep and excellent soil, and hardly mention the word sand. Now, what strikes the voyager is the barrenness and desolation of the land. *They* found "the ground or earth sandhills, much like the downs in Holland, but much better; the crust of the earth, a spit's depth, excellent black earth." *We* found that the earth had lost its crust,—if, indeed, it ever had any,—and that there was no soil to speak of. We did not see enough black earth in Provincetown to fill a flower-pot, unless in the swamps. They found it "all wooded with oaks, pines, sassafras, juniper, birch, holly, vines, some ash, walnut; the wood for the most part open and without underwood, fit either to go or ride in." We saw scarcely anything high enough to be called a tree, except a little low wood at the east end of the town, and the few ornamental trees in its yards,— only a few small specimens of some of the above kinds on the sand-hills in the rear; but it was all thick shrubbery, without any large wood above it, very unfit either to go or ride in. The greater part of the land was a perfect desert of yellow sand, rippled like waves by the wind, in which only a little Beach-grass grew here and there. They say that, just after passing the head of East Harbor Creek, the boughs and bushes "tore" their "very armor in pieces" (the same thing happened to such armor as we wore, when out of curiosity we took to the bushes); or they came to deep valleys, "full of brush, wood-gaile, and long grass," and "found springs of fresh water."

For the most part we saw neither bough nor bush, not so much as a shrub to tear our clothes against if we would, and a sheep would lose none of its fleece, even if it found herbage enough to make fleece grow there. We saw rather beach and poverty-grass, and merely sorrel enough to color the surface. I suppose, then, by Wood-gaile they mean the Bayberry.

All accounts agree in affirming that this part of the Cape was *comparatively* well wooded a century ago. But notwithstanding the great changes which have taken place in these respects, I cannot but think that we must make some allowance for the greenness of the Pilgrims in these matters, which caused them to see green. We do not believe that the trees were large or the soil was deep here. Their account may be true particularly, but it is generally false. They saw literally, as well as figuratively, but one side of the Cape. They naturally exaggerated the fairness and attractiveness of the land, for they were glad to get to any land at all after that anxious voyage. Everything appeared to them of the color of the rose, and had the scent of juniper and sassafras. Very different is the general and off-hand account given by Captain John

Smith, who was on this coast six years earlier, and speaks like an old traveller, voyager, and soldier, who had seen too much of the world to exaggerate, or even to dwell long, on a part of it. In his "Description of New England," printed in 1616, after speaking of Accomack, since called Plymouth, he says: "Cape Cod is the next presents itself, which is only a headland of high hills of sand, overgrown with shrubby pines, *hurts* [i. e. whorts, or whortleberries], and such trash, but an excellent harbor for all weathers. This Cape is made by the main sea on the one side, and a great bay on the other, in form of a sickle." Champlain had already written, "Which we named *Cap Blanc* (Cape White), because they were sands and downs (*sables et dunes*) which appeared thus."

When the Pilgrims get to Plymouth their reporter says again, "The land for the crust of the earth is a spit's depth,"—that would seem to be their recipe for an earth's crust,—"excellent black mould and fat in some places." However, according to Bradford himself, whom some consider the author of part of "Mourt's Relation," they who came over in the Fortune the next year were somewhat daunted when "they came into the harbor of Cape Cod, and there saw nothing but a naked and barren place." They soon found out their mistake with respect to the goodness of Plymouth soil. Yet when at length, some years later, when they were fully satisfied of the poorness of the place which they had chosen, "the greater part," says Bradford, "consented to a removal to a place called Nausett," they agreed to remove all together to Nauset, now Eastham, which was jumping out of the frying-pan into the fire; and some of the most respectable of the inhabitants of Plymouth did actually remove thither accordingly.

It must be confessed that the Pilgrims possessed but few of the qualities of the modern pioneer. They were not the ancestors of the American backwoodsmen. They did not go at once into the woods with their axes. They were a family and church, and were more anxious to keep together, though it were on the sand, than to explore and colonize a New World. When the above-mentioned company removed to Eastham, the church at Plymouth was left, to use Bradford's expression, "like an ancient mother grown old, and forsaken of her children." Though they landed on Clark's Island in Plymouth harbor, the 9th of December (O. S.), and the 16th all hands came to Plymouth, and the 18th they rambled about the mainland, and the 19th decided to settle there, it was the 8th of January before Francis Billington went with one of the master's mates to look at the magnificent pond or lake now called "Billington Sea," about two miles distant, which he had discovered from the top of a tree, and mistook for a great sea. And the 7th of March "Master Carver with five others went to the great ponds which seem to be excellent fishing," both which points are within the compass of an ordinary afternoon's ramble,—however wild the country. It is true they were busy at first about their building, and were hindered in that by much foul weather; but a party of emigrants to California or Oregon, with no less work on their hands,—and more hostile Indians—would do as much exploring the first afternoon, and the Sieur de Champlain would have sought an interview with the savages, and examined the country as far as the Connecticut, and made a map of it, before Billington had climbed his tree. Or contrast them only with the French searching for copper about the Bay of Fundy in 1603, tracing up small streams with Indian guides. Nevertheless, the Pilgrims were pioneers, and the ancestors of pioneers, in a far grander enterprise.

By this time we saw the little steamer Naushon entering the harbor, and heard the sound of her whistle, and came down from the hills to meet her at the wharf. So we took leave of Cape Cod and its inhabitants. We liked the manners of the last, what little we saw of them, very much. They were particularly downright and good-humored. The old people appeared remarkably well preserved, as if by the saltness of the atmosphere, and after having once mistaken, we could never be certain whether we were talking to a coeval of our grandparents, or to one of our own age. They are said to be more purely the descendants of the Pilgrims than the inhabitants of any other part of the State. We were told that "sometimes, when the court comes together at Barnstable, they have not a single criminal to try, and the jail is shut up." It was "to let" when we were there. Until quite recently there was no regular lawyer below Orleans. Who then will complain of a few regular man-eating sharks along the back-side?

One of the ministers of Truro, when I asked what the fishermen did in the winter, answered that they did nothing but go a-visiting, sit about and tell stories,—though they worked hard in summer. Yet it is not a long vacation they get. I am sorry that I have not been there in the winter to hear their yarns. Almost every Cape man is Captain of some craft or other,—every man at least who is at the head of his own affairs, though it is not every one that is, for some heads have the force of *Alpha privative*, negativing all the efforts which Nature would fain make through them. The greater number of men are merely corporals. It is worth the while to talk with one whom his neighbors address as Captain, though his craft may have long been sunk, and he may be holding by his teeth to the shattered mast of a pipe alone, and only gets half-seas-over in a figurative sense, now. He is pretty sure to vindicate his right to the title at last,—can tell one or two good stories at least.

For the most part we saw only the back side of the towns, but our story is true as far as it goes. We might have made more of the Bay side, but we were inclined to open our eyes widest at the Atlantic. We did not care to see those features of the Cape in which it is inferior or merely equal to the mainland, but only those in which it is peculiar or superior. We cannot say how its towns look in front to one who goes to meet them; we went to see the ocean behind them. They were merely the raft on which we stood, and we took notice of the barnacles which adhered to it, and some carvings upon it.

Before we left the wharf we made the acquaintance of a passenger whom we had seen at the hotel. When we asked him which way he came to Provincetown, he answered that he was cast ashore at Wood End, Saturday night, in the same storm in which the St. John was wrecked. He had been at work as a carpenter in Maine, and took passage for Boston in a schooner laden with lumber. When the storm came on, they endeavored to get into Provincetown harbor. "It was dark and misty," said he, "and as we were steering for Long Point

Light we suddenly saw the land near us,—for our compass was out of order,—varied several degrees [a mariner always casts the blame on his compass],—but there being a mist on shore, we thought it was farther off than it was, and so held on, and we immediately struck on the bar. Says the Captain, 'We are all lost.' Says I to the Captain, 'Now don't let her strike again this way; head her right on.' The Captain thought a moment, and then headed her on. The sea washed completely over us, and wellnigh took the breath out of my body. I held on to the running rigging, but I have learned to hold on to the standing rigging the next time." "Well, were there any drowned?" I asked. "No; we all got safe to a house at Wood End, at midnight, wet to our skins, and half frozen to death." He had apparently spent the time since playing checkers at the hotel, and was congratulating himself on having beaten a tall fellow-boarder at that game. "The vessel is to be sold at auction to-day," he added. (We had heard the sound of the crier's bell which advertised it.) "The Captain is rather down about it, but I tell him to cheer up and he will soon get another vessel."

At that moment the Captain called to him from the wharf. He looked like a man just from the country, with a cap made of a woodchuck's skin, and now that I had heard a part of his history, he appeared singularly destitute,—a Captain without any vessel, only a great-coat! and that perhaps a borrowed one! Not even a dog followed him; only his title stuck to him. I also saw one of the crew. They all had caps of the same pattern, and wore a subdued look, in addition to their naturally aquiline features, as if a breaker—a "comber"—had washed over them. As we passed Wood End, we noticed the pile of lumber on the shore which had made the cargo of their vessel.

About Long Point in the summer you commonly see them catching lobsters for the New York market, from small boats just off the shore, or rather, the lobsters catch themselves, for they cling to the netting on which the bait is placed of their own accord, and thus are drawn up. They sell them fresh for two cents apiece. Man needs to know but little more than a lobster in order to catch him in his traps. The mackerel fleet had been getting to sea, one after another, ever since midnight, and as we were leaving the Cape we passed near to many of them under sail, and got a nearer view than we had had;—half a dozen red-shirted men and boys, leaning over the rail to look at us, the skipper shouting back the number of barrels he had caught, in answer to our inquiry. All sailors pause to watch a steamer, and shout in welcome or derision. In one a large Newfoundland dog put his paws on the rail and stood up as high as any of them, and looked as wise. But the skipper, who did not wish to be seen no better employed than a dog, rapped him on the nose and sent him below. Such is human justice! I thought I could hear him making an effective appeal down there from human to divine justice. He must have had much the cleanest breast of the two.

Still, many a mile behind us across the Bay, we saw the white sails of the mackerel fishers hovering round Cape Cod, and when they were all hull-down, and the low extremity of the Cape was also down, their white sails still appeared on both sides of it, around where it had sunk, like a city on the ocean, proclaiming the rare qualities of Cape Cod Harbor. But before the extremity of the Cape had completely sunk, it appeared like a filmy sliver of land lying flat on the ocean, and later still a mere reflection of a sand-bar on the haze above. Its name suggests a homely truth, but it would be more poetic if it described the impression which it makes on the beholder. Some capes have peculiarly suggestive names. There is Cape Wrath, the northwest point of Scotland, for instance; what a good name for a cape lying far away dark over the water under a lowering sky!

Mild as it was on shore this morning, the wind was cold and piercing on the water. Though it be the hottest day in July on land, and the voyage is to last but four hours, take your thickest clothes with you, for you are about to float over melted icebergs. When I left Boston in the steamboat on the 25th of June the next year, it was a quite warm day on shore. The passengers were dressed in their thinnest clothes, and at first sat under their umbrellas, but when we were fairly out on the Bay, such as had only their coats were suffering with the cold, and sought the shelter of the pilot's house and the warmth of the chimney. But when we approached the harbor of Provincetown, I was surprised to perceive what an influence that low and narrow strip of sand, only a mile or two in width, had over the temperature of the air for many miles around. We penetrated into a sultry atmosphere where our thin coats were once more in fashion, and found the inhabitants sweltering.

Leaving far on one side Manomet Point in Plymouth and the Scituate shore, after being out of sight of land for an hour or two, for it was rather hazy, we neared the Cohasset Rocks again at Minot's Ledge, and saw the great Tupelo-tree on the edge of Scituate, which lifts its dome, like an umbelliferous plant, high over the surrounding forest, and is conspicuous for many miles over land and water. Here was the new iron light-house, then unfinished, in the shape of an egg-shell painted red, and placed high on iron pillars, like the ovum of a sea monster floating on the waves,—destined to be phosphorescent. As we passed it at half-tide we saw the spray tossed up nearly to the shell. A man was to live in that egg-shell day and night, a mile from the shore. When I passed it the next summer it was finished and two men lived in it, and a light-house keeper said that they told him that in a recent gale it had rocked so as to shake the plates off the table. Think of making your bed thus in the crest of a breaker! To have the waves, like a pack of hungry wolves, eying you always, night and day, and from time to time making a spring at you, almost sure to have you at last. And not one of all those voyagers can come to your relief,—but when yon light goes out, it will be a sign that the light of your life has gone out also. What a place to compose a work on breakers! This light-house was the cynosure of all eyes. Every passenger watched it for half an hour at least; yet a colored cook belonging to the boat, whom I had seen come out of his quarters several times to empty his dishes over the side with a flourish, chancing to come out just as we were abreast of this light, and not more than forty rods from it, and were all gazing at it, as he drew back his arm, caught sight of it, and with surprise exclaimed, "What's that?" He had been employed on this boat for a year, and passed this light every week-day, but as he had never chanced to empty his dishes just at that point, had never seen it before. To look at lights was the pilot's business; he minded the kitchen fire. It suggested how little some who voyaged round the world could manage to see. You would almost as easily believe that there were men who never yet chanced to come out at the right time to see the sun. What avails it though a light be placed on the top of a hill, if you spend all your life directly under the hill? It might as well be under a bushel. This light-house, as is well known, was swept away in a storm in April, 1851, and the two men in it, and the next morning not a vestige of it was to be seen from the shore.

A Hull man told me that he helped set up a white-oak pole on Minot's Ledge some years before. It was fifteen inches in diameter, forty-one feet high, sunk four feet in the rock, and was secured by four guys,—but it stood only one year. Stone piled up cob-fashion near the same place stood eight years.

When I crossed the Bay in the Melrose in July, we hugged the Scituate shore as long as possible, in order to take advantage of the wind. Far out on the Bay (off this shore) we scared up a brood of young ducks, probably black ones, bred hereabouts, which the packet had frequently disturbed in her trips. A townsman, who was making the voyage for the first time, walked slowly round into the rear of the helmsman, when we were in the middle of the Bay, and looking out over the sea, before he sat down there, remarked with as much originality as was possible for one who used a borrowed expression, "This is a great country." He had been a timber merchant, and I afterward saw him taking the diameter of the mainmast with his stick, and estimating its height. I returned from the same excursion in the Olata, a very handsome and swift-sailing yacht, which left Provincetown at the same time with two other packets, the Melrose and Frolic. At first there was scarcely a breath of air stirring, and we loitered about Long Point for an hour in company,—with our heads over the rail watching the great sand-circles and the fishes at the bottom in calm water fifteen feet deep. But after clearing the Cape we rigged a flying-jib, and, as the Captain had prophesied, soon showed our consorts our heels. There was a steamer six or eight miles northward, near the Cape, towing a large ship toward Boston. Its smoke stretched perfectly horizontal several miles over the sea, and by a sudden change in its direction, warned us of a change in the wind before we felt it. The steamer appeared very far from the ship, and some young men who had frequently used the Captain's glass, but did not suspect that the vessels were connected, expressed surprise that they kept about the same distance apart for so many hours. At which the Captain dryly remarked, that probably they would never get any nearer together. As long as the wind held we kept pace with the steamer, but at length it died away almost entirely, and the flying-jib did all the work. When we passed the light-boat at Minot's Ledge, the Melrose and Frolic were just visible ten miles astern.

Consider the islands bearing the names of all the saints, bristling with forts like chestnut-burs, or *echinidæ*, yet the police will not let a couple of Irishmen have a private sparring-match on one of them, as it is a government monopoly; all the great seaports are in a boxing attitude, and you must sail prudently between two tiers of stony knuckles before you come to feel the warmth of their breasts.

The Bermudas are said to have been discovered by a Spanish ship of that name which was wrecked on them, " which till then," says Sir John Smith, "for six thousand years had been nameless." The English did not stumble upon them in their first voyages to Virginia; and the first Englishman who was ever there was wrecked on them in 1593. Smith says, "No place known hath better walls nor a broader ditch." Yet at the very first planting of them with some sixty persons, in 1612, the first Governor, the same year, "built and laid the foundation of eight or nine forts." To be ready, one would say, to entertain the first ship's company that should be *next* shipwrecked on to them. It would have been more sensible to have built as many "Charity-houses." These are the vexed Bermoothees.

Our great sails caught all the air there was, and our low and narrow hull caused the least possible friction. Coming up the harbor against the stream we swept by everything. Some young men returning from a fishing excursion came to the side of their smack, while we were thus steadily drawing by them, and, bowing, observed, with the best possible grace, "We give it up." Yet sometimes we were nearly at a stand-still. The sailors watched (two) objects on the shore to ascertain whether we advanced or receded. In the harbor it was like the evening of a holiday. The Eastern steamboat passed us with music and a cheer, as if they were going to a ball, when they might be going to —— Davy's locker.

I heard a boy telling the story of Nix's mate to some girls as we passed that spot. That was the name of a sailor hung there, he said.—"If I am guilty, this island will remain; but if I am innocent, it will be washed away," and now it is all washed away!

Next (?) came the fort on George's Island. These are bungling contrivances: not our *fortes*, but our *foibles*. Wolfe sailed by the strongest fort in North America in the dark, and took it.

I admired the skill with which the vessel was at last brought to her place in the dock, near the end of Long Wharf. It was candle-light, and my eyes could not distinguish the wharves jutting out toward us, but it appeared like an even line of shore densely crowded with shipping. You could not have guessed within a quarter of a mile of Long Wharf. Nevertheless, we were to be blown to a crevice amid them,—steering right into the maze. Down goes the mainsail, and only the jib draws us along. Now we are within four rods of the shipping, having already dodged several outsiders; but it is still only a maze of spars, and rigging, and hulls,—not a crack can be seen. Down goes the jib, but still we advance. The Captain stands aft with one hand on the tiller, and the other holding his night-glass,—his son stands on the bowsprit straining his eyes,—the passengers feel their hearts half-way to their mouths, expecting a crash. "Do you see any room there?" asks the Captain, quietly. He must make up his mind in five seconds, else he will carry away that vessel's bowsprit, or lose his own. "Yes, sir, here is a place for us"; and in three minutes more we are fast to the wharf in a little gap between two bigger vessels.

And now we were in Boston. Whoever has been down to the end of Long Wharf, and walked through Quincy Market, has seen Boston.

Boston, New York, Philadelphia, Charleston, New Orleans, and the rest, are the names of wharves projecting into the sea (surrounded by the shops and dwellings of the merchants), good places to take in and to discharge a cargo (to land the

products of other climes and load the exports of our own). I
see a great many barrels and fig-drums,—piles of wood for
umbrella-sticks,—blocks of granite and ice,—great heaps of
goods, and the means of packing and conveying them,—
much wrapping-paper and twine,—many crates and hogsheads and trucks,—and that is Boston. The more barrels,
the more Boston. The museums and scientific societies and libraries are accidental. They gather around the sands to save
carting. The wharf-rats and custom-house officers, and bro-
ken-down poets, seeking a fortune amid the barrels. Their
better or worse lyceums, and preachings, and doctorings,
these, too, are accidental, and the malls of commons are always small potatoes. When I go to Boston, I naturally go
straight through the city (taking the Market in my way),
down to the end of Long Wharf, and look off, for I have no
cousins in the back alleys,—and there I see a great many
countrymen in their shirt-sleeves from Maine, and Pennsylva-
nia, and all along shore and in shore, and some foreigners
beside, loading and unloading and steering their teams about,
as at a country fair.

When we reached Boston that October, I had a gill of
Provincetown sand in my shoes, and at Concord there was
still enough left to sand my pages for many a day; and I
seemed to hear the sea roar, as if I lived in a shell, for a week
afterward.

The places which I have described may seem strange and
remote to my townsmen,—indeed, from Boston to Provincetown is twice as far as from England to France; yet step into
the cars, and in six hours you may stand on those four planks,
and see the Cape which Gosnold is said to have discovered,
and which I have so poorly described. If you had started
when I first advised you, you might have seen our tracks in
the sand, still fresh, and reaching all the way from the Nauset
Lights to Race Point, some thirty miles,—for at every step
we made an impression on the Cape, though we were not
aware of it, and though our account may have made no
impression on your minds. But what is our account? In it
there is no roar, no beach-birds, no tow-cloth.

We often love to think now of the life of men on
beaches,—at least in midsummer, when the weather is serene;

their sunny lives on the sand, amid the beach-grass and the bayberries, their companion a cow, their wealth a jag of drift-wood or a few beach-plums, and their music the surf and the peep of the beach-bird.

We went to see the Ocean, and that is probably the best place of all our coast to go to. If you go by water, you may experience what it is to leave and to approach these shores; you may see the Stormy Petrel by the way, θαλασσοδρόμα, running over the sea, and if the weather is but a little thick, may lose sight of the land in mid-passage. I do not know where there is another beach in the Atlantic States, attached to the mainland, so long, and at the same time so straight, and completely uninterrupted by creeks or coves or fresh-water rivers or marshes; for though there may be clear places on the map, they would probably be found by the foot trav-eller to be intersected by creeks and marshes; certainly there is none where there is a double way, such as I have described, a beach and a bank, which at the same time shows you the land and the sea, and part of the time two seas. The Great South Beach of Long Island, which I have since visited, is longer still without an inlet, but it is literally a mere sand-bar, exposed, several miles from the Island, and not the edge of a continent wasting before the assaults of the ocean. Though wild and desolate, as it wants the bold bank, it possesses but half the grandeur of Cape Cod in my eyes, nor is the imagi-nation contented with its southern aspect. The only other beaches of great length on our Atlantic coast, which I have heard sailors speak of, are those of Barnegat on the Jersey shore, and Currituck between Virginia and North Carolina; but these, like the last, are low and narrow sand-bars, lying off the coast, and separated from the mainland by lagoons. Besides, as you go farther south the tides are feebler, and cease to add variety and grandeur to the shore. On the Pacific side of our country also no doubt there is good walking to be found; a recent writer and dweller there tells us that "the coast from Cape Disappointment (or the Columbia River) to Cape Flattery (at the Strait of Juan de Fuca) is nearly north and south, and can be travelled almost its entire length on a beautiful sand-beach," with the exception of two bays, four or five rivers, and a few points jutting into the sea. The com-

mon shell-fish found there seem to be often of corresponding
types, if not identical species, with those of Cape Cod. The
beach which I have described, however, is not hard enough
for carriages, but must be explored on foot. When one carriage has passed along, a following one sinks deeper still in its
rut. It has at present no name any more than fame. That portion south of Nauset Harbor is commonly called Chatham
Beach. The part in Eastham is called Nauset Beach, and off
Wellfleet and Truro the Backside, or sometimes, perhaps,
Cape Cod Beach. I think that part which extends without
interruption from Nauset Harbor to Race Point should be
called Cape Cod Beach, and do so speak of it.

One of the most attractive points for visitors is in the
northeast part of Wellfleet, where accommodations (I mean
for men and women of tolerable health and habits) could
probably be had within half a mile of the sea-shore. It best
combines the country and the sea-side. Though the Ocean is
out of sight, its faintest murmur is audible, and you have only
to climb a hill to find yourself on its brink. It is but a step
from the glassy surface of the Herring Ponds to the big Atlantic Pond where the waves never cease to break. Or perhaps
the Highland Light in Truro may compete with this locality,
for there there is a more uninterrupted view of the Ocean and
the Bay, and in the summer there is always some air stirring
on the edge of the bank there, so that the inhabitants know
not what hot weather is. As for the view, the keeper of the
light, with one or more of his family, walks out to the edge
of the bank after every meal to look off, just as if they had
not lived there all their days. In short, it will wear well. And
what picture will you substitute for that, upon your walls?
But ladies cannot get down the bank there at present without
the aid of a block and tackle.

Most persons visit the sea-side in warm weather, when fogs
are frequent, and the atmosphere is wont to be thick, and the
charm of the sea is to some extent lost. But I *suspect* that the
fall is the best season, for then the atmosphere is more transparent, and it is a greater pleasure to look out over the sea.
The clear and bracing air, and the storms of autumn and winter even, are necessary in order that we may get the impression which the sea is calculated to make. In October, when

the weather is not intolerably cold, and the landscape wears its autumnal tints, such as, methinks, only a Cape Cod landscape ever wears, especially if you have a storm during your stay,—that I am convinced is the best time to visit this shore. In autumn, even in August, the thoughtful days begin, and we can walk anywhere with profit. Beside, an outward cold and dreariness, which make it necessary to seek shelter at night, lend a spirit of adventure to a walk.

The time must come when this coast will be a place of resort for those New-Englanders who really wish to visit the sea-side. At present it is wholly unknown to the fashionable world, and probably it will never be agreeable to them. If it is merely a ten-pin alley, or a circular railway, or an ocean of mint-julep, that the visitor is in search of,—if he thinks more of the wine than the brine, as I suspect some do at Newport,—I trust that for a long time he will be disappointed here. But this shore will never be more attractive than it is now. Such beaches as are fashionable are here made and unmade in a day, I may almost say, by the sea shifting its sands. Lynn and Nantasket! this bare and bended arm it is that makes the bay in which they lie so snugly. What are springs and waterfalls? Here is the spring of springs, the waterfall of waterfalls. A storm in the fall or winter is the time to visit it; a light-house or a fisherman's hut the true hotel. A man may stand there and put all America behind him.

Chronology

1817   Born July 12, in Concord, Massachusetts, third of four children (Helen, b. 1812, John, b. 1815, and Sophia, b. 1819) of John and Cynthia (Dunbar) Thoreau, and christened October 12 as David Henry Thoreau. (Grandfather Jean Thoreau, a descendant of French Protestant refugees, came to Boston from the Isle of Jersey in 1773, served on Revolutionary War privateers, and became a prosperous merchant; after his death his estate was plundered by its executor. Maternal grandfather, Rev. Asa Dunbar, resigned from the ministry in 1779 because of poor health and practiced law in Keene, New Hampshire. Maternal grandmother, Mary Jones, of a wealthy Loyalist family, helped her brothers escape to Canada during the Revolution.) Father farms, and manages store in Concord.

1818–21   Family moves to Chelmsford, a village ten miles north of Concord, where father opens grocery store. Thoreau enjoys sledding and suffers a series of accidents, including the loss of part of a toe while playing with an axe. In 1821, father closes failing grocery store and moves family to Boston, where he teaches school.

1822   Sees Walden Pond for the first time while visiting grandmother Mary Jones. (Later writes: "That woodland vision for a long time made the drapery of my dreams.")

1823–27   Family returns to Concord, where father takes over pencil-making business started by brother-in-law Charles Dunbar. Attends Phoebe Wheeler's private "infant school" and then the town-run Center School. Memorizes passages from the Bible, Shakespeare, Bunyan, and Samuel Johnson. Classmates call him "the Judge" because of his stern demeanor. Financial uncertainty causes mother to take in boarders and family to move twice within Concord. Begins lifelong exploration of surrounding countryside. Mother becomes active in town charity work.

1828   Thoreau and brother, John, enroll in Concord Academy, a private school founded in 1822 by prominent town citizens. Studies French, Latin, Greek, geography, history, and science.

1829   Attends lectures in natural history at newly-founded Concord Lyceum.

1833   Family is able to send only one son to college, and Henry is considered the more scholarly; he enrolls in Harvard College after barely passing entrance examinations. John and Helen, now schoolteachers, and Thoreau's aunts help parents pay his expenses. Goes beyond the required curriculum by taking Italian, French, German, and Spanish and attending lectures on mineralogy, anatomy, and natural history. Remembered by a classmate as being "cold and unimpressionable," his academic performance is above average but not exceptional. Spends much time alone, reading and walking.

1835–36   Ralph Waldo Emerson moves to Concord. Thoreau takes a leave of absence for winter term to earn money by teaching in Canton, Massachusetts. Boards for six weeks with Orestes Brownson, Unitarian minister and New England intellectual, and studies German with him. (Later writes of these weeks: "They were an era in my life—the morning of a new Lebenstag. They are to me as a dream that is dreamt, but which returns from time to time in all its original freshness.") In May 1836, briefly leaves Harvard because of illness, possibly first attack of tuberculosis. Attends dedication of Concord Bridge Memorial in July and joins with choir in singing Emerson's "Concord Hymn." Lives for six weeks in hut on shore of Flint's Pond in Lincoln with Harvard friend Charles Stearns Wheeler. Visits New York City with father to sell pencils.

1837   Receives twenty-five-dollar grant from Harvard Corporation after Emerson writes recommendation to President Quincy. Graduates nineteenth in his class of approximately fifty, taking part in commencement honors conference on "The Commercial Spirit of Modern Times." ("This curious world which we inhabit is more wonderful than convenient; more beautiful than it is useful; it is more to be admired and enjoyed than used.") Begins teaching at Center School, but resigns after flogging six students (including a family servant) against his own wishes at the direction of a superior. Becomes member of informal group of New England Transcendentalists, the "Hedge Club," including Brownson, Margaret Fuller, Frederic Henry Hedge, George Ripley, Jones Very, Elizabeth Peabody, Bronson Alcott, and Theodore Parker, who meet irregularly in Emerson's study. Begins his journal, ultimately to comprise nearly two million words, on October 22. Works on improving lead quality in pencils; learns from Scottish encyclopedia in Harvard Library to mix graphite with Bavarian clay, designs grinding mill to produce more finely powdered graphite. Changes name from David Henry to Henry David.

1838   Plans to go with brother to Kentucky in search of work; trip is postponed and then abandoned when John finds job in Roxbury. Goes to Maine in futile search for teaching job. June, opens small private school in parents' house, then takes over Concord Academy in September. Delivers first lecture to Concord Lyceum, "Society," on April 11, and is elected Lyceum secretary and curator in fall, serving two years.

1839   Increased enrollment (approximately twenty-five students) allows John to join Thoreau at the Concord Academy. John teaches "English branches"; Henry teaches Latin, Greek, French, and sciences. (One pupil reports later that John "was more human, loving" and Henry "rigid," but most remember both brothers with great affection: "It was a peculiar school, there was never a boy flogged or threatened, yet I never saw so absolutely military discipline. . . . Even the incorrigible were brought into line.") Innovative curriculum stresses reasoning over rote memorization and features field trips to workshops and countryside. In July Thoreau meets Ellen Sewall of Scituate, Massachusetts, seventeen-year-old sister of one of his students, and both he and John fall in love with her. August 31, Henry and John leave for two-week trip on the Concord and Merrimack rivers in their homemade boat, *Musketaquid*. Emerson helps found Transcendentalist quarterly *The Dial* and writes, "My Henry Thoreau will be a great poet for such a company & one of these days for all companies."

1840   Louisa May Alcott enrolls in Concord Academy, begin-
        ning her lifelong admiration for Thoreau. First issue of
        The Dial, edited by Margaret Fuller, appears in July, with
        Thoreau's poem "Sympathy" and essay "Aulus Persius
        Flaccus"; Thoreau eventually publishes thirty-one poems,
        essays, and translations in *The Dial*'s sixteen issues. Ellen
        Sewall rejects as suitors first John and then Henry. Meets
        Ellery Channing, poet and nephew of Unitarian minister
        William Ellery Channing, who becomes intimate friend
        and (in 1873) first biographer.

1841   Declines invitation to join Brook Farm community ("I
        had rather keep bachelor's hall in hell than go board in
        heaven"). Closes Concord Academy on April 1 because of
        John's poor health and moves into Emerson household for
        two years as handyman and gardener. Borrows from Emer-
        son's library to read further in Greek classics and English
        poetry, and begins reading Oriental literature. Still seeking
        a way to support himself, nearly buys rundown farm, and
        dreams of going to live by Flint's Pond in Lincoln. ("My
        friends ask what I will do when I get there. Will it not be
        employment enough to watch the progress of the sea-
        sons?") The Flints, owners of the land, refuse permission
        to build cabin.

1842   January 1, John suffers razor cut, develops lockjaw, and
        dies on January 11 in Thoreau's arms. Soon afterward Tho-
        reau is stricken for weeks with psychosomatic attack of the
        same paralytic symptoms, followed by months of depres-
        sion. In summer meets Nathaniel Hawthorne, who be-
        comes an intermittent literary sponsor after reading "A
        Natural History of Massachusetts" in the July 1842 *Dial*.
        Hawthorne describes him as "a young man with much of
        wild original nature still remaining in him. . . . He is as
        ugly as sin, long-nosed, queer-mouthed, and with un-
        couth and somewhat rustic, although courteous manners,
        corresponding very well with such an exterior. He was
        educated, I believe, at Cambridge, . . . but for two or
        three years back, he has repudiated all regular modes of
        getting a living, and seems inclined to lead a sort of Indian
        life among civilized men—an Indian life, I mean, as re-
        spects the absence of any systematic effort for a liveli-
        hood." Sells Hawthorne *Musketaquid* for seven dollars and
        teaches him to paddle. In the winter goes skating with

Emerson and Hawthorne; Hawthorne's wife, Sophia, describes him "figuring dithyrambic dances and Bacchic leaps on the ice—very remarkable, but very ugly, methought."

1843   Lectures on "Sir Walter Raleigh" in February. Edits April issue of *The Dial*, substituting for Emerson, and includes in it "Dark Ages," a short essay on ancient history. In May goes to Staten Island, New York, as tutor to children of Emerson's brother William. Meets Horace Greeley, Henry James, Sr., and the abolitionist William Tappan; hears social reformer Lucretia Mott at Quaker meeting and is favorably impressed. Enjoys walks along Staten Island shore and frequents various New York libraries, reading Ossian and Francis Quarles with particular interest, but writes of New York City: "It is a thousand times meaner than I could have imagined." Homesick, he returns to Concord in December and moves back into family home. "Paradise (to be) Regained," criticizing technological utopianism, published in *United States Magazine and Democratic Review*, November.

1844   Writes essay for *The Dial* praising Nathaniel P. Rogers, abolitionist publisher who advocated the dissolution of antislavery societies on the grounds that they restricted the exercise of individual freedom. Devises a drilling machine that allows lead to be inserted into pencils without splitting the wood; develops different grades of lead hardness. April 30, on camping trip with Edward Hoar, accidentally sets fire to three hundred acres of Concord woods, causing over $2,000 damage. Meets Isaac Thomas Hecker, future founder of the Paulist Fathers, who proposes that they make a pilgrimage to Rome "in the old middleage fashion." Thoreau declines, and resists Hecker's attempts to convert him to Roman Catholicism. July, takes walking trip through Berkshires and Catskills with Ellery Channing. August 1, rings First Parish Church bell to summon town to annual fair of Concord Women's Anti-Slavery Society (which his mother had helped found); there Emerson delivers address on West Indian Emancipation, which Thoreau arranges to be published as a pamphlet. In fall, helps build new family house in the open southwestern "prairie" of Concord (the "Texas house").

1845　　Spring, starts building cabin in Emerson's woodlot at Walden Pond, and moves in July 4. Works on manuscript about 1839 boat trip with John on Concord and Merrimack rivers, and on a lecture about Thomas Carlyle. Throughout his twenty-six-month stay, remains in close contact with family and friends.

1846　　Begins writing *Walden*. Delivers Carlyle lecture at Concord Lyceum in February. July, arrested and jailed for one night by Concord constable Sam Staples for not paying several years' poll tax in protest against role of the state in perpetuating slavery. (Emerson writes disapprovingly in his journal: "Don't run amuck against the world. As long as the state means you well, do not refuse your pistareen." Alcott, arrested in 1843 for failure to pay his town tax, praises Thoreau's "dignified non-compliance with the injunction of civil power.") Tax is paid that evening by anonymous person (probably aunt Maria Thoreau). The next morning Thoreau is thrown out of jail when he refuses to leave. For the remainder of his life, his aunt and others pay tax to avoid further confrontation. August 1, Anti-Slavery Society fair held at Walden. August 31 through early September, trip to Maine to climb Mount Katahdin with cousin George Thatcher of Bangor.

1847　　Reads "A History of Myself," part of first draft of *Walden*, at Concord Lyceum in February. Leaves Walden on September 6, having finished his manuscript of *A Week on the Concord and Merrimack Rivers* and most or all of the first version of *Walden*. In October moves into Emerson house for ten months to help care for Lydia Emerson and the children while Waldo is in Europe. Responds to tenth anniversary questionnaire from his Harvard class: "I am a Schoolmaster—a private Tutor, a Surveyor—a Gardener, a Farmer—a Painter, I mean a House Painter, a Carpenter, a Mason, a Day-Laborer, a Pencil-Maker, a Glass-paper Maker, a Writer, and sometimes a Poetaster."

1848　　January 26, delivers lecture to Concord Lyceum on "the relation of the individual to the State," published in 1849 as "Resistance to Civil Government" (posthumously retitled "Civil Disobedience") in Elizabeth Peabody's *Aesthetic Papers*. Responding to appreciative letter, begins extensive correspondence with Worcester, Massachusetts, schoolteacher Harrison Blake. July–November, "Ktaadn, and the Maine Woods" serialized in John Sartain's *Union Magazine* and strongly promoted in the New York *Tribune* by Horace Greeley, now Thoreau's enthusiastic backer and literary agent. Begins more extensive lecturing in New England. Satirized by James Russell Lowell in "A Fable for Critics" (published October 31) as a mere shadow of Emerson. Extensively revises *A Week* and begins second version of *Walden*.

1849   *A Week on the Concord and Merrimack Rivers* published May 30 by James Munroe and Company of Boston after Thoreau agrees to pay the cost from his royalties. It receives mixed reviews and sells poorly. Continues to correct and revise text. (In 1853 Thoreau takes back 706 of the original 1,000 copies and stores them in the family attic, remarking, "I have now a library of nearly nine hundred volumes, over seven hundred of which I wrote myself.") June 14, sister Helen dies of tuberculosis. Autumn, family buys larger house nearer to center of Concord (the "Yellow House") out of growing profits from pencil business, which has begun to concentrate on supplying ground lead for electrotyping. Finds surveying a preferable way to support himself and establishes a reputation for extreme accuracy. Friendship with Emerson cools. Emerson writes in his journal: "Thoreau wants a little ambition in his mixture. . . . Instead of being the head of American engineers, he is captain of a huckleberry party." Thoreau is suspicious of the effect on Emerson of growing fame and acceptance, annoyed by charge that he is merely Emerson's follower, and offended that Emerson does not do more to promote *A Week*. October, first trip to Cape Cod, with Ellery Channing, going via Cohasset and Sandwich, returning by steamer from Provincetown.

1850   Expands journal from mainly a record on which to draw for books and lectures into a self-contained literary composition. Increases reading on natural history and American Indians, recording nearly 3,000 pages of notes and quotations in "Indian Books" between 1847 and 1861. Collects in his attic room in the Yellow House hundreds of arrowheads and other Indian artifacts, as well as hundreds of dried plant specimens. June, second trip to Cape Cod, alone, by steamer to Provincetown and back to Boston.

July, sent by Emerson to Fire Island, New York, to search for body and manuscripts of Margaret Fuller Ossoli, who had died in a shipwreck with her husband and child and Horace Sumner, brother of Massachusetts senator Charles Sumner. The wreck is plundered before he arrives and he finds only a few insignificant items. Writes of an unidentifiable skeleton he saw: "It reigned over the shore. That dead body possessed the shore as no living one could. It showed a title to the sands which no living ruler could." September, trip to Montreal, Quebec City, and the northern bank of the St. Lawrence with Ellery Channing.

1851   Passage of Fugitive Slave Act enrages Thoreau, who writes in his journal: "I do not believe that the North will soon come to blows with the South on this question. It would be too bright a page to be written . . . at present." Becomes increasingly involved in Underground Railroad, which he has been assisting for several years, sheltering escaped slaves in the family house and aiding their flight to Canada.

1852   Excerpts from fourth version of *Walden* published in *Union Magazine* attract little attention, and Thoreau receives no money when the magazine ceases publication.

1853   January–March, first three installments of "A Yankee in Canada," based on 1850 trip, appear in *Putnam's Monthly Magazine*. Publication stops when Thoreau objects to editor George William Curtis removing passages Curtis considers "heresies." September, second trip to Maine, with George Thatcher and Indian guide Joe Aitteon.

1854   Arrest in Boston of fugitive slave Anthony Burns incites Thoreau to write "Slavery in Massachusetts" and read it at Framingham, Massachusetts, rally organized by William Lloyd Garrison, July 4. It is printed in the *Anti-Slavery Standard*, *The Liberator*, and the New York *Tribune*. *Walden* published August 9 by Boston firm of Ticknor and Fields in an edition of 2,000, culminating over seven years of work and seven major revisions of the text. Although a few reviews are harsh (*Boston Atlas*: "There is not a page . . . giving one sign of liberality, charitableness, kind feeling, generosity, in a word—heart"; *Knickerbocker* reviews it with P. T. Barnum's autobiography under the title

"Town and Rural Humbugs"), most are very enthusiastic. (The popular *Graham's Magazine* concludes: "Through all the audacities of his eccentric protests, a careful eye can easily discern the movement of a powerful and accomplished mind.") By the end of the year, 1,744 copies are sold, plus several hundred more before it goes out of print in 1859. (Some are shipped to England, where George Eliot favorably reviews it in 1856: ". . . we have a bit of pure American life . . . animated by that energetic, yet calm spirit of innovation, that practical as well as theoretic independence of formulae, which is peculiar to some of the finer American minds.") Encouraged by *Walden's* success, Thoreau urges Ticknor and Fields to reissue *A Week*, but they decline to republish. Enjoys wider popularity as lecturer throughout the northeast; introduces "Getting a Living," critique of American acquisitiveness (later published as "Life without Principle"). Begins to attract a circle of admirers, including English traveler and author Thomas Cholmondeley; Quaker Daniel Ricketson, later historian of New Bedford; and abolitionist, educator, and writer F. B. Sanborn.

1855 Develops weakness in legs that afflicts him intermittently for the next two years. "Cape Cod," drawn from visits to region, published in *Putnam's Monthly Magazine* June–August. Further installments do not appear after Thoreau and Curtis disagree over payment and Curtis's fear that Cape residents might be offended by Thoreau's tone. July, third trip to Cape Cod, accompanied by Ellery Channing, taking a schooner to Provincetown, spending two weeks at Highland Light, and returning by sailboat *Olata* from Provincetown to Boston. In return for Thoreau's hospitality in Concord, Thomas Cholmondeley sends forty-four volumes of Oriental philosophy, religion, and history, for which Thoreau makes a special bookcase from Concord River driftwood. Sends Cholmondeley *Walden*, Emerson's poems, and Whitman's *Leaves of Grass*.

1856 October, goes to Perth Amboy, New Jersey, to survey at Eagleswood, a former utopian community being converted into suburban estates. In early November visits with Bronson Alcott in New York. They hear Henry Ward Beecher preach at Plymouth Church in Brooklyn; Thoreau is unimpressed. The next day Thoreau and Alcott meet Walt Whitman. ("He is apparently the greatest democrat the world has seen," Thoreau later writes to Harrison Blake. "Kings and aristocracy go by the board at once, as they have long deserved to. A remarkably strong though coarse nature, of a sweet disposition, and much prized by his friends.") Whitman presents him with an inscribed copy of the 1856 *Leaves of Grass*. Thoreau is dismayed by its sensuality but calls it "a great primitive poem,—an alarum or trumpet note ringing through the American camp."

1857   Meets John Brown in early March when Brown visits F. B. Sanborn in Concord and takes noon meal at Thoreau's house. Hears Brown speak and makes small monetary contribution; writes that Brown "had the courage to face his country herself when she was in the wrong." June 12–22, makes his last visit to Cape Cod, alone. (Only trip not described in *Cape Cod*, published by Ticknor and Fields in 1865.) July 20–August 7, travels through Maine with Edward Hoar and Indian guide Joe Polis. Grows full beard.

1858   James Russell Lowell solicits account of 1857 Maine travels for *Atlantic Monthly*. Fearing that his portrayal of Polis is too candid, Thoreau submits instead "Chesuncook," drawn from 1853 trip, published June–August. When sentence praising a pine tree—"It is as immortal as I am, and perchance will go to as high a heaven"—is omitted from July installment against Thoreau's explicit instructions, writes to Lowell, "I do not ask anybody to adopt my opinions, but I do expect that when they ask for them in print, they will print them, or obtain my consent to their alteration or omission." Demands that Lowell print the omitted sentence in the August issue. Lowell does not, and delays paying Thoreau $198 owed to him. (Revised versions of "Ktaadn," "Chesuncook," and 1857 trip account, together with appendix, published as *The Maine Woods* by Ticknor and Fields in 1864.) Travels through the White Mountains and climbs Mount Washington, July 2–19.

1859   February 3, father dies, leaving Thoreau financially responsible for mother and sister. May 8, hears John Brown speak at Concord Town Hall. October, news of Brown's raid on Harpers Ferry reaches Concord. Thoreau delivers a defiant tribute, "A Plea for Captain John Brown," to large audiences in Concord, Boston, and Worcester, October 30 to November 3. Helps organize and speaks at memorial meeting in Concord on Brown's execution day, December 2. Aids fugitive member of Brown's band in escape to Canada.

1860 Reads Darwin's *Origin of Species* and defends it to Emerson against Louis Agassiz's attacks. Visited by William Dean Howells, who finds Thoreau "dreamy" and "orphic," and later describes the encounter as "a rout" of his hopes. Joins townspeople in protecting F. B. Sanborn against arrest by federal marshals trying to subpoena him to appear before Senate investigation of Harpers Ferry raid. Writes "The Last Days of John Brown." December, catches a bad cold that quickly turns to bronchitis.

1861 Seeking to improve his health, to see the West, and to observe Indians, he goes to Minnesota in May with young friend Horace Mann, Jr. They collect botanical specimens and take an excursion steamer to Lower Sioux Agency at Redwood, where Thoreau witnesses annual government payment to Indians and sees Chief Little Crow, who will lead the 1862 Sioux uprising. Observes and sympathizes with the Indians' discontent. Returns to Concord in early July, tired and no better. Resigned to an early death, makes last revisions in *A Week* (posthumous new edition is published by Ticknor and Fields in 1868). Arranges with sister for posthumous publication of *The Maine Woods*, *Cape Cod*, and other writings. "You know it's respectable to leave an estate to one's friends," he tells one of his many bedside visitors. Makes last visit to Walden Pond in September and final journal entry on November 3.

1862 Confined to his house, refuses opiates and continues to receive visitors. April 12, sells attic stock of *A Week* to publisher James T. Fields, who reissues it two months later with new title page. Dies May 6 of tuberculosis, his last intelligible words "moose" and "Indian." Buried May 9, in New Burying Ground, Concord, later moved to nearby Sleepy Hollow Cemetery.

Note on the Texts

When Henry David Thoreau died of tuberculosis in 1862, he left behind few published works. His first book, *A Week on the Concord and Merrimack Rivers*, was based on a trip he had made with his brother, John, in 1839, two years after he had graduated from Harvard College. It was drafted at Walden Pond, where he lived from 1845 to 1847, and was published in 1849 by James Munroe and Company. Meanwhile Thoreau had begun work on *Walden*, which was advertised in *A Week* as soon to be published. But the commercial failure of his first book discouraged the publisher from undertaking a second, and throughout the early 1850s Thoreau reworked *Walden* into the form in which we know it. It was published by the newly established firm of Ticknor and Fields in 1854. Apart from these two books, Thoreau's published work consisted of a number of essays and poems that had appeared in *The Dial*, the *Atlantic Monthly*, and other journals.

This printed material, however, represented a mere fraction of Thoreau's literary output, left in manuscript at his death. There were the speeches and lectures he had delivered almost annually since the late 1830s, new essays and chapters and revised versions of the printed ones, notes and extracts from his voluminous reading about the Indians, and the nearly two million words of his journal, from which the finished pieces had been quarried.

Some of this large mass of material was pulled into shape by Thoreau's sister Sophia with the assistance of his good friend Ellery Channing. Ticknor and Fields, which had done a small reprinting of *A Week* and *Walden* immediately following Thoreau's death, issued five new volumes in the next few years: *Excursions* (1863), *The Maine Woods* (1864), *Cape Cod* (1865), *Letters to Various Persons* (1865, edited by Emerson), and *A Yankee in Canada with Anti-Slavery and Reform Papers* (1866), in addition to a new and revised edition of *A Week* in 1868.

The present volume contains the four works that Thoreau planned as unified, full-length books: the two published during his lifetime, *A Week* and *Walden*, and the posthumously published *The Maine Woods* and *Cape Cod*. The texts of all four of these works suffered, to a greater or lesser extent, from misreading of his rather difficult handwriting, and occasionally from a printer or compositor missing or ignoring Thoreau's instructions. Because Thoreau did not live to see much of his work through the press in book form, or to supervise corrected second editions of the two books he did finish, errors introduced during publication often went undetected and were then carried over into subsequent printings. Detection of errors in these texts therefore requires consultation of earlier versions, whether printed magazine texts, proofs, or manuscripts. This research, and the discussion that follows, has benefited greatly from the work of the editors of the Princeton University Press edition of Thoreau's writings.

The text of the first edition of *A Week on the Concord and Merrimack Rivers*, published by James Munroe and Company in 1849, culminated four years of work on a manuscript first drafted at Walden Pond in 1845. Thoreau, a habitual reviser, expanded his manuscript with passages from his journals, essays he had written for *The Dial*, and new material based on his experiences and his reading over the years 1846–49. The printer's copy he finally submitted to Munroe is not known to be extant, but judging from the numerous corrections on the extant proofs, it must have included many pages in Thoreau's difficult hand. Although most of Thoreau's corrections and revisions on the proofs were incorporated into the 1849 text, several were missed or ignored by the printer.

Thoreau continued to revise *A Week* after its 1849 publication. He began to mark changes on the first-edition proofs, then switched to some other copy of the 1849 text, now lost. This lost copy was among the literary remains that Ellery Channing and Sophia Thoreau helped prepare for posthumous publication by Ticknor and Fields (Thoreau's publisher after Munroe refused *Walden*). In 1863 Channing wrote to a friend that he was "looking at his [Thoreau's] corrected copy of the Week, with a view to a new ed."; but it was not until December 1867 that Ticknor and Fields issued the "New and

Revised Edition," probably waiting until the supply of the commercially unsuccessful first edition was exhausted.

This later, "second-edition" text (dated 1868) is the one presented here, because it includes changes that are clearly Thoreau's. There are numerous additions—ranging from a word or short phrase to sentences and a paragraph—several of which reflect Thoreau's reading or traveling after 1849. Quotations are incorporated, for example, from Edward Johnson's *The Wonder-Working Providence of Sions Saviour in New-England*, which Thoreau is known to have read in 1855. Some changes in the 1868 text involve readings marked on the first-edition proofs but not incorporated in the 1849 text; others return to pre-1849 drafts of *A Week*. These are changes that only Thoreau would or could have made, and with numerous others they prove the authority of the 1868 text.

In the course of preparing for publication and resetting this 1868 text, however, several errors crept in, and Thoreau was not alive to correct them. Other errors were carried over from the first edition. For the present volume, first-edition proof sheets with Thoreau's handwritten corrections were consulted to help resolve problems of this sort. In several instances, the proof sheets helped determine the correct reading of a word or passage. At 209.34–36, for example, the 1868 text reads: "There is need of a physician who shall minister to both soul and body at once, that is, to man. Now he falls between two souls." The proofs make clear that Thoreau meant "man" to fall between two "stools." Since, however, the copy from which the 1868 text was set is not known to survive, and since Thoreau certainly made revisions for that text himself, the proofs have been drawn on here for corrections only in those cases where the 1868 reading cannot be Thoreau's change.

Walden was the only other volume that Thoreau lived to see through the press. Like *A Week*, the book was first drafted at Walden Pond. Also like the first book, it was considerably revised and expanded before being published in 1854 by Ticknor and Fields—the manuscript he submitted as printer's copy, apparently no longer extant, represented the eighth version of the text. The page proofs for the first edition, with Thoreau's more than 1,000 corrections, demonstrate that he read proof carefully. Some of his changes on proof correct the printer's misreading of his handwriting. The great majority involve punctuation, and it is often unclear whether these changes represent corrections or revisions. In any event, all but a small percentage of Thoreau's requested alterations were made in the first edition. Of the differences between the first edition and the page proofs, some are corrections of typographical errors that Thoreau missed in proofreading, while others are a matter of house style or spelling conventions. The rest are printer's errors, a few of which Thoreau later corrected in a copy of the book.

The 1854 first edition thus has the authority of Thoreau's supervision and, unlike *A Week*, was not superseded by a "revised" edition: omissions in the first edition and the few post-1854 changes were not incorporated in a posthumous volume by Thoreau's literary executors. The first-edition text is reprinted here. Printer's errors are corrected by reference to Thoreau's own copy of *Walden*, and, more important, by comparison with the page proofs containing Thoreau's markings. Systematic changes by the printer in spelling, punctuation, or typography are considered features of the edition reprinted here; other oversights and omissions are corrected.

For *The Maine Woods*, the present volume reprints the text of the 1864 first edition. Prepared by Ellery Channing and Sophia Thoreau, the first edition consisted of three essays and an appendix of technical terms. Although it was a composite volume, Thoreau unquestionably intended to issue the four parts as a single book in the order of the 1864 edition. He left a rough plan for the organization of the essays and a statement of the volume's collective title, and he drew on all three chapters in compiling the appendix.

Two of the essays, "Ktaadn" and "Chesuncook," had already been printed in periodicals, but Thoreau afterwards revised them for future book publication. "Ktaadn" was rather heavily revised from its 1848 printing in John Sartain's *Union Magazine*: Thoreau corrected obvious misreadings of his script, revised the style, and inserted several substantial passages and footnotes. "Chesuncook" was more lightly revised following its 1858 publication in James Russell Lowell's *Atlan-*

tic Monthly. The most significant change was the restoration, in revised form, of the sentence about a pine tree at 685.33–34 that Lowell had struck out despite Thoreau's objections.

For the rest of the first edition, the third piece, "The Allegash and East Branch," and the appendix were printed for the first time. Thoreau apparently did not have time before he died to prepare a fair copy of his manuscript for the printer, and these last two sections, for which no previous printed text existed, suffered most from the lack of authorial proofreading and supervision. Apart from routine compositor's errors (here more common than usual because of the large number of unfamiliar botanical terms and Indian place names), there are corruptions probably introduced by Sophia while transcribing especially messy pages of her brother's last draft for the printer. In several instances she (or conceivably the compositor) misread Thoreau's hand, introducing errors into the first edition that were reproduced in subsequent editions. The compositor who set the appendix consistently substituted the more familiar "ü" for the unusual "ñ" used by Thoreau's sources to transcribe an American Indian sound. It was probably Sophia, however, who at 822.10 misread "as fast as the stage on the bank," the reading of one of the fragments of last-draft "Allegash" manuscript now at the Huntington and Houghton libraries, as "as fast as the stage or the boat." Where last-draft manuscript does not exist, Thoreau's journal (at the Pierpont Morgan Library and elsewhere) helps detect the more obvious errors, as when "memorable parts" of a stream (801.16) appears absurdly in the 1864 text as "more arable parts."

The journal also helps repair another major printer's error in the 1864 text of "Allegash," the misplacement of two pages of text (814.4–815.36 follows 805.40 in that book), disrupting the temporal and geographical continuity of Thoreau's trip. Lacking Thoreau's knowledge of Maine, proofreaders and editors left this error uncorrected until 1889.

The first sections of what was later printed as *Cape Cod* appeared in *Putnam's Monthly Magazine* in June, July, and August of 1855. Thoreau had submitted part of this material earlier, in 1852, while *Putnam's* was preparing to serialize his "A Yankee in Canada." The serialization of the Canada material was stopped, however, after an argument between Thoreau and George William Curtis, the associate editor: "Curtis," Thoreau wrote to his friend Harrison Blake in 1853, "requires the liberty to omit the heresies without consulting me—a privilege California is not rich enough to bid for." Curtis duly returned to Thoreau both the "Canada" manuscript and the first installment of the Cape Cod material that Thoreau had sent to him.

The Cape Cod material is not mentioned again in the correspondence until April 1855, when Thoreau wrote to Curtis with a suggestion for a revision of a sentence in one of the Cape Cod chapters by which "your objection will be avoided." In the meantime, presumably either Thoreau or Curtis, or both, had compromised, and the first four chapters appeared in *Putnam's*; each, including the fourth in August, ended with the announcement "To be continued." In early August Thoreau wrote Curtis: "Will you allow me to trouble you once more about my Cape Cod paper. I would like to substitute the accompanying sheets for about ten pages of my MS, in the Chapter called 'The Beach Again'. . . ."

That chapter never appeared in *Putnam's*, however—nor did any other continuation during Thoreau's lifetime, again due to an argument between Thoreau and Curtis. According to Thoreau's biographer, F. B. Sanborn, the Cape Cod material "became the subject of controversy first as to price, and then as to its tone towards the people of that region." Two more chapters were published in the *Atlantic Monthly* in 1864, when James T. Fields was its editor; these, however, were drawn from the posthumously prepared Ticknor and Fields text of *Cape Cod* (1865).

That volume contained among its ten chapters much-revised versions of the four chapters from *Putnam's*. Where the magazine version had been based on Thoreau's first two trips to Cape Cod in 1849 and 1850, the book version incorporated material from his third (1853) trip, as well as adding lengthy passages based on his reading in New England history and other sources. The 1865 text is reprinted here.

The map of the Concord and Merrimack rivers in this volume is a detail from Nathan Hale, *Map of New England States* (1826), and is reprinted by courtesy of The Massachusetts Historical Society. The map of Maine is adapted from the 1855 *Colton's Railroad and Township Map of the State of Maine* . . . , and is used by courtesy of the Richard Halliburton Map Collection, Princeton University. The Cape Cod map is taken from the 1871 *Official Topographical Atlas of Massachusetts* . . . , and is reproduced by courtesy of the Sturgis Library, Historical Collections, Barnstable, Massachusetts. Thoreau's drawing of a bear paddling a boat on page 746 is reproduced from his journal at the Pierpont Morgan Library.

The standards for American English continue to fluctuate and in some ways were conspicuously different in earlier periods from what they are now. In nineteenth-century writings, for example, a word might be spelled in more than one way, even in the same work, and such variations might be carried into print. Commas were sometimes used expressively to suggest the movements of voice, and capitals were sometimes meant to give significances to a word beyond those that it might have in its uncapitalized form. Since modernization would remove such effects, this volume has preserved the spelling, punctuation, and capitalization, as well as the wording, of the texts reprinted here.

This volume is concerned only with presenting the texts of the editions reprinted; it does not attempt to reproduce features of typographic design—such as the display capitalization of chapter openings. Footnotes within the text are those supplied by Thoreau. Open contractions are retained if they appear in the original edition.

In addition to a customary reference to other printed versions of the text, the list of typographical errors corrected in this volume was determined by reference to certain extant documents: for *A Week* and *Walden*, Thoreau's marked proof for the first editions; for *The Maine Woods*, Thoreau's journal (Pierpont Morgan and New York Public libraries), his marked set of the *Union Magazine* printing of "Ktaadn, and the Maine Woods" (New York Public Library), a fragmentary fair-copy manuscript for the *Atlantic Monthly* printing of "Chesuncook" (Harvard University's Houghton Library), and the fragments of the last draft of "Allegash" at the Huntington and Houghton libraries.

These materials were used to detect both simple typographical errors and the unintentional alterations of Thoreau's texts
that were to a certain extent inevitable, given his handwriting,
his tendency to continue to revise his work on page proofs,
and the fact that most of his books were prepared for publication after he could no longer supervise or proofread them.
Intentional, systematic changes such as house styling were
considered features of the editions reprinted here—so, for example, an editor or compositor's preference for "farther" over
Thoreau's "further," or Sophia's expansion of Thoreau's characteristic abbreviations are allowed to stand.

Of the manuscripts, the *Walden* page proofs are the most
significant, since no document intervened between these
proofs and the text of the first edition presented here. In this
case, as with the extant fragments of the "Allegash" draft, we
have the author's last word, and it is thus possible to distinguish the printer's (or copyist's, or compositor's) errors and
omissions from authorial revisions. This process is more difficult where documents are missing, as between the first-
edition page proofs of *A Week* and the 1868 text reprinted in
this volume. In such cases there is always at least a possibility
that a difference represents Thoreau's revision, especially since
it is clear that many changes in the later text are his. Therefore
such later differences have rarely been regarded as errors. So,
for example, the 1868 text's "notice" at 40.27, "vision" at
45.14, "lifelike" at 77.1–2, "Protestants" at 110.32, or "interrupt" at 319.6 have not been altered to the proof-sheet readings "noticed," "visions," "lifesome," "protestants," and
"interpret."

Following is a list of typographical errors by page and line
number: 14.3, Those rural delicacies; 27.12, receptable; 29.33–
34, manoevres; 30.35, men; 33.5–6, cut grass; 41.38, Villarica?;
49.29, Mahometans; 63.4, Sung; 72.34, effect; 85.15, sentence;
106.20–21, that he; 112.2, tracts; 134.13, mor; 134.18, grisly;
141.8, an /cient; 159.21, *Scriurus*; 176.21, business; 188.26, along;
198.35, far-stretched; 202.6, pot-poles; 209.31, Is it; 209.36, two
souls; 241.33, man interest; 245.28, leaves of; 246.25, men;
280.2, discoveries!; 281.14, stand; 283.26, walls; 287.18, day's;
291.19, far /mers; 291.23, Cæsar; 303.20, 'if; 339.20 post; 353.7,
fail, or the; 359.40 cornice,; 361.29, timber,; 363.26, fin-

gers? . . . ; 365.30 manure whatever; 366.10, There; 367.33–
34, oxen, cows,; 373.17, named.; 375.24, all—; 375.26, neck—;
379.7–8, not proportionally more expensive than; 387.26, orchard, woodlot,; 387.36, place; 388.16, [line not indented];
389.36, day; 398.7, Kieou-he-yu; 399.28, reality that; 406.33, on
to; 413.13, *cerasus*; 413.18, *rhus*; 415.21, beneficent as; 415.36,
plough plough; 420.11, by; 421.33, wood-side;; 424.31, gate—;
428.26, issue,; 430.32, tolerable; 431.24, north star; 444.16–
17, occasionally; 452.8, particular,; 452.10, farmers,; 452.25,
small,; 453.20, orchards,; 454.2, ground:; 459.6, road; 465.13,
neighhorhood; 470.20, over it, and the peetweets; 483.32, *celtis*; 486.12, tight, light,; 494.31, carniverous; 505.7, nearer;
505.8, attention,; 514.9, masonry; 532.6, them,; 540.16, gratui
/tous; 540.27, brisk; 541.26, which,; 541.28, and,; 552.8, have;
557.15, was,—; 567.38–39, — *labium*, from *labor* (?)—; 571.8,
as in; 572.20, Nabathacaque; 577.27, eye right; 586.28, might,
perhaps,; 601.18, canalès; 608.16, villagers; 610.39, ceilings;
628.22, our question; 634.25, land, still; 657.6, Manhegan;
659.21, Moose-horns; 666.19, name, one or; 671.40, thus;
672.23, chicadee; 686.20, *Katahdinauquoh*; 691.36, be there,—
the; 706.4, character; 711.40, poet's; 713.14, on the; 713.15, told
me; 715.4, provisions; 716.16, Pistigouche; 718.6, singing; 718.7,
season; 722.19, *ne*; 723.23, lake, she; 728.22, (the *V. Pennsylvanicum*); 735.14, exactly; 738.3, he; 743.11, white-beaked; 746.1,
[The figure of a bear in a boat.]; 746.3, *Niasoseb*.; 746.4, Joseph.; 746.5, *clioi*; 746.9, *ouke*; 746.11, quambi; 748.3, *Caucomgomoc-took!* there; 755.2, narrowest point; 755.15, nearest bend;
763.32, Tebos; 767.16, main hardly; 767.16–17, washing and;
767.23, northeasterly; 767.35, not intend; 769.25, life.;
773.33, abundant.; 773.33–34, *minatus*; 773.34–35, *margaraticea*;
783.33–34, *Madunkchunk*; 783.34–35, *Madunkchunkgamooc*;
786.29, paths; 792.14, without rocks; 796.29, ripple; 796.37,
loon; 797.9, crushing; 798.24, scarred; 800.18–21, high. Richardson; 801.5–6, Madunkchunk; 801.14, water and forks;
801.16, more arable parts; 801.29, ridge; 806.1, [72 lines trans-
posed to 814.4–815.36]; 806.28, tnat; 807.30, lodges; 812.6,
told me; 813.37, Rocks (locks); 818.19, Matanancook; 821.27–
28, accord/ing; 822.10, stage or the boat; 825.16, 1858; 830.27, Cham
/berlain; 835.14, *monocea*; 837.35, Schoonis; 839.5, *albicola*;
840.33, *Mt.*; 840.34, *Kitadaügan*; 841.14, *Ibibimin*; 841.17,

ceinture."; 841.19, *Ouaürinaügamek*; 842.9, *Bematruichtik*; 842.9, *Mt.*; 842.32, *Pagadaükoueouérré*; 842.34, *Bororquasis*; 842.37, *Apmoojeuegamook*; 843.17, *Paüsidaükioui*; 843.20, *Our-amaü*; 843.21, ho,; 843.22–23, *Saüghedétegoue*; 843.24, *saük-taüoui*; 844.36, *Telasiuis*; 845.3, *Schunk*; 845.5, Schunk; 845.10, *Schunk-auke*; 886.8, condition; 954.13, Bank; 981.40, being,"; 1016.9, Hackluyt'; 1017.1, Savale; 1017.4, Savalet."; 1017.24, *quantie*; 1018.10, had; 1028.2, "of. Errors corrected second printing: 283.28,]Even (*LOA*); 283.28,] the superior (*LOA*); 311.22, biolets (*LOA*).

MAPS

The Concord and Merrimack rivers: detail from Nathan Hale, *Map of New England States with adjacent parts of NY and lower Canada* (Boston, 1826).

Courtesy of The Massachusetts Historical Society.

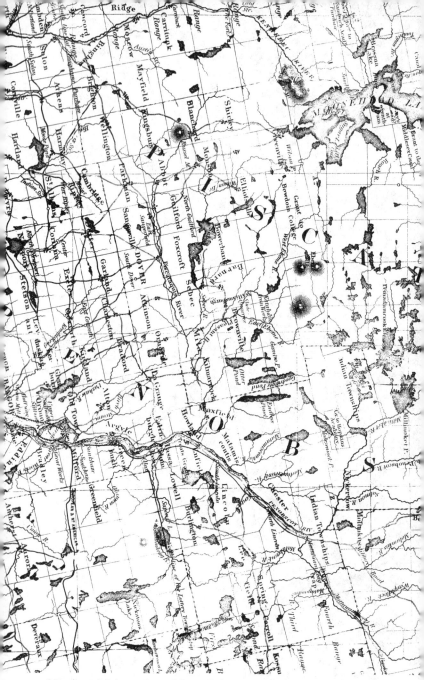

Northern Maine: adapted from *Colton's Railroad & Township Map of the State of Maine* (New York, 1855).

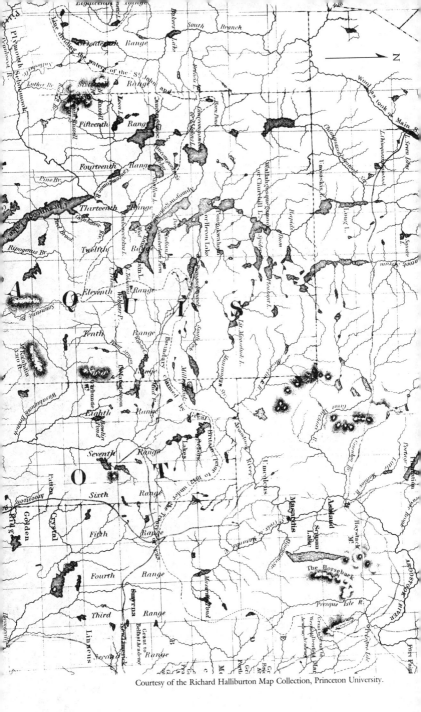

Courtesy of the Richard Halliburton Map Collection, Princeton University.

Cape Cod: detail from
*Official Topographical Atlas of
Massachusetts from Astronomical,
Trigonometrical and Various Local
Surveys*, compiled by Walling
and Gray (Boston: Stedman,
Brown & Lyon, 1871), pp. 36–
37. When Thoreau visited Cape
Cod in the late 1840s and 1850s,
the railroad did not yet extend
east and north of the station at
Yarmouth Port.

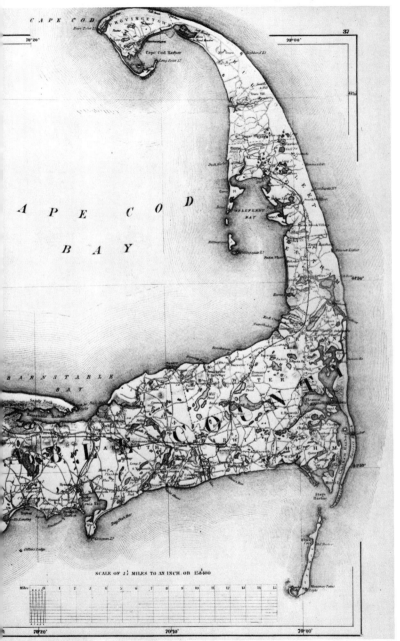

Courtesy of the Sturgis Library, Historical Collections, Barnstable, Massachusetts.

Notes

For more detailed notes, references to other studies, and further biographical and textual background, see the Princeton University Press
edition of *The Writings of Henry D. Thoreau: A Week on the Concord
and Merrimack Rivers*, ed. Carl F. Hovde (1980), *Walden*, ed. J. Lyn-
don Shanley (1971), and *The Maine Woods*, ed. Joseph J. Moldenhauer
(1972); Walter Harding's *A Week* (Holt, Rinehart & Winston, 1963)
and his *The Variorum Walden* (Washington Square Press, 1963); and
Richard Lebeaux's *Young Man Thoreau* (University of Massachusetts
Press, 1977). In the notes below, numbers refer to page and line of
this volume (the line count includes chapter headings). No note is
made for material found in a standard desk-reference book. Notes at
the foot of the page in the text are Thoreau's own.

A WEEK ON THE CONCORD AND MERRIMACK RIVERS

2.1–4   Where'er . . . Brother—.] Verses not enclosed in quotation
marks are Thoreau's own, except where a source is given in the following
notes.

7.2–8   "Beneath . . . EMERSON.] "Musketaquid," stanza 2.

7.21–25   "One . . . Westborough,"] Lemuel Shattuck, *A History of the
Town of Concord* (Boston, 1835).

11.29   5 to 20] The source of this quotation, Edward Johnson's *A History
of New-England, or The Wonder-Working Providence of Sions Saviour in New-
England* (London, 1654), reads "5 and 20."

12.18–19   "And . . . sea"] Chaucer, *Troilus and Criseyde*, IV, 1548–49.

12.22–25   "Sure . . . those."] Sir John Denham, "Cooper's Hill" (1642),
ll. 1–4.

15.14–15   "Were . . . plough."] Pindar, as quoted in Plutarch's *Morals*.

15.34–16.4   As a . . . creeps."] Emerson, "Concord Hymn," ll. 1–8.

21.28   "renning . . . sea."] See note 12.18–19.

26.40   Josselyn] John Josselyn (fl. 1638–75), English scientific writer,
whose observations in New England were recorded in *New-England's Rarities
Discovered* (1672) and *An Account of Two Voyages to New-England* (1674).

30.36–39   "a beggar . . . past?"] "Robin Hood and the Beggar," stanzas
2 and 3, in Thomas Percy's *Reliques of Ancient English Poetry* (1765).

31.1–3   "That . . . Cæsar"]   Francis Quarles, *Emblems* (1635), II, 15, 8–11.

35.2–3   "I . . . moon,"]   Shakespeare, *Julius Caesar*, IV, iii, 27.

36.2–7   "The river . . . CHANNING.]   William Ellery Channing (1810–84), "Boat Song," ll. 1–5, from *The Dial*, I (October 1840).

37.39–38.7   one . . . arms."]   Channing, "The River," ll. 1–7, from *The Dial*, III (January 1843).

39.1–5   "Sweet . . . purity."]   Channing, "Boat Song," stanza 4.

40.34–37   "A man . . . espy."]   George Herbert (1593–1633), "The Elixir," stanza 3.

43.1–2   "Bedford . . . forget."]   From a ballad that has been lost.

44.9   "freedom . . . God"]   Felicia Hemans (1793–1835), "The Landing of the Pilgrim Fathers in New England," last line.

46.36–37   "Some . . . ice."]   William Habington (1605–54), "Nox Nocti Indicat Scientiam," ll. 25–26, in *Castara* (1634).

47.18   strong and wilderness tints]   The first-edition proof sheets indicate Thoreau may have intended "strong wilderness tints" here, but his notations are not clear.

47.26–32   Gower . . . make."]   John Gower (1325?–1408), *Confessio Amantis*, IV, 2427–32.

47.33–48.4   Lydgate . . . roote."]   John Lydgate (1370?–1451), "A Poem against Idleness, and the History of Sardanapalus"; see stanzas 18–20.

49.16   "tale divine"]   John Milton, "Il Penseroso" (1632), l. 100.

49.25–32   Joseph Wolff . . . prophet!"]   Joseph Wolff, *Narrative of a Mission to Bokhara* (London, 1845).

52.23–24   "The seventh . . . Apollo,"]   Hesiod, *Works and Days*, l. 771.

53.26   Θυμῳ . . . τε]   *Iliad*, I, 196: " with love and respect [for someone] in her heart." Translations from Greek, here and throughout, by Professor Stavros Deligiorgis.

54.5–6   "in shape . . . trees."]   From Captain James Cook's journal, published in various forms throughout the nineteenth century.

55.19–22   "Jerusalem . . . Zion."]   Psalms 137: 5 and 1.

55.30–31   "God . . . Khu."]   Rammohun Roy, *Translation of Several Principal Books, Passages, and Texts of the Veds* (London, 1832).

55.34–37   "Where . . . about."]   Francis Quarles, *Jonah*, ll. 715–18.

56.1–3   "The world's . . . mortals."]   Quarles, *Emblems*, I, 8, 1–3.

56.5–6   "all . . . players."]   Shakespeare, *As You Like It*, II, vii, 139–40.

56.8–10   Drayton . . . madness"]   Michael Drayton (1563–1631), "To My Dearly Loved Friend, Henry Reynolds," ll. 106 and 109.

56.12–16   Dr. Johnson . . . fable."]   Samuel Johnson quotes Sir Thomas Browne in a life of Browne that prefaces his edition of *Christian Morals* (1756). The quotation is from Browne's *Religio Medici* (1643).

56.18–19   "Spectators . . . tragedies."]   "To the Memory of the Incomparable Paire of Authors Beaumont and Fletcher," l. 44, in Alexander Chalmers, ed., *The Works of the English Poets* (London, 1810), vol. 6.

57.10–12   "Verily . . . *Sadi*.]   From *Gulistan*, or *Rose Garden* (1258), a miscellany of prose and poetry considered the masterpiece of the Persian poet Muslih-ud-Din, known as Sadi.

67.10–11   *Gookin's* . . . 1674.]   Published in Boston in 1792.

67.12–30   "At . . . away."]   From Charles J. Fox, *History of the Old Township of Dunstable* (Nashua, N.H., 1846).

68.9   Montaup]   "Mount Hope" in the first edition.

70.9–11   "Doth . . . name"]   Sir William Alexander, Earl of Stirling, *Paraenesis to the Prince* (1604), ll. 37–40.

70.16–20   Down . . . sky."]   Channing, in a copy of the book, identified this quotation as from a letter by Nathaniel P. Rogers in Rogers' anti-slavery newspaper *Herald of Freedom*, published in Concord, N.H.

72.29   Belknap]   Jeremy Belknap (1744–98), author of *History of New Hampshire* (1784–92).

72.40–73.6   "And . . . sea."]   Captain John Smith, *A Description of New England* (London, 1616).

73.17–24   "So silent . . . dry."]   Alexander Hume (1811–59), "Thanks for a Summer's Day," stanzas 18 and 22.

74.4   "Jam . . . gemmæ"]   Vergil, *Eclogues*, VII, 48.

74.6   "Strata . . . poma"]   *Eclogues*, VII, 54.

75.15–20   "As from . . . Zeus."]   Homer, *Iliad*, XI, 62–66.

75.24–35   "While . . . rank."]   *Iliad*, XI, 82–91.

76.1–16   "They . . . Aurora."]   *Iliad*, VIII, 553–65.

76.19–26   "Went . . . Olympus."]   *Iliad*, XV, 81–84.

76.29–32   ἐπειὴ . . . between.]   *Iliad*, I, 156–57.

77.1–2   lifelike]   The first edition reads "lifesome."

77.3–5   "Then rose . . . tongue."]   *Iliad*, I, 246–47.

77.6–10   "A certain . . . source,"]   *Iliad*, XI, 721–25.

77.28–30   "Homer . . . Heaven."]   From Philip J. Bailey, *Festus: A Poem* (London, 1838), according to Channing's notation in a copy of the book.

78.22–27   "There are . . . another?"]   According to Channing, a quotation from the *Bhagavad-Gita*.

79.4–5   "You . . . ray."]   Francis Quarles, *Emblems*, II, 9, stanza 7.

79.19–20   "Merchants . . . merchandise."]   Quarles, "A Feast for Worms," *Divine Poems* (1633), I, Meditations I, 3 and 4.

79.34–35   "To Athens . . . fool."]   Quarles, "Job Militant," Sec. 13, ll. 23–24.

80.9–10   "What . . . taught."]   Diogenes Laertius on Crates, VI, 86.

81.17–20   "Let . . . flatterer."]   William Habington, "To my honoured friend and kinsman, R. St., Esquire," ll. 41–44.

81.31–34   "Olympian . . . so."]   Emerson, "Ode to Beauty," ll. 60–63.

82.23–24   "lips . . . oracle."]   Emerson, "The Problem," ll. 12–13.

83.9–11   "That . . . days"]   Samuel Daniel (1562–1619), Dedication of the *Tragedy of Philotas*, "To the Prince," ll. 74–76.

83.15–16   "And that . . . confined."]   Daniel, Dedication, ll. 81–82.

83.19–24   "And who . . . ours."]   Daniel, *Musophilus*, stanza 153.

84.17–20   "How . . . looks."]   Daniel, *Musophilus*, stanza 70.

84.22   Fanning]   Probably Col. James Walker Fannin (1804–36), the leader of three hundred Texans captured and killed at Goliad, March 27, 1836, three weeks after the fall of the Alamo.

85.20   Botta]   Paul Emile Botta (1802–70), *Travels in Arabia* (Paris, 1841).

89.21–22   "campoque . . . pulsant."]   Ovid, *Metamorphoses*, I, 42.

89.32–38   "About . . . debt."]   See note 67.12–30.

90.36–39   "Make . . . within."]   Thomas Tusser (1524?–80), *Five Hundreth Pointes of Good Husbandry*, X, stanza 19.

95.2–5   "I . . . Gower.]   John Gower, Prologue to *Confessio Amantis*, ll. 58–60.

95.6–8   "The hye . . . *Ballads*.]   "Gest of Robin Hood," ll. 59–60.

95.9–13   "His . . . *Ballads*.]   "Robin Hood and Guy of Gisborne," stanza 17.

95.14–15   "Gazed . . . *Pastorals*.]   William Browne (1591–?1643), *The Shepheard's Pipe*, Eclogue IV, l. 170.

95.22–29   "All . . . gone."]   Alexander Montgomerie (1556?–?1610), "The Night Is Near Gone," ll. 33–43.

97.3   old nursery tale]   "Ballad of Lovewell's Fight." The lines of verse on pages 97–99 are from this anonymous poem.

97.27   Church, or Lovewell]   Captain Benjamin Church (1639–1718) was a leader of the Puritans against the Indians in King Philip's War, 1675–76. John Lovewell (1691–1725) served under Church before becoming known as an Indian fighter in his own right.

101.8–11   "Yet . . . Suns."]   Tennyson, "Locksley Hall," ll. 137–38.

103.8–12   "Another . . . children."]   See note 49.25–32.

104.1–4   "Men . . . proceed."]   Samuel Daniel, *Musophilus*, ll. 486–99.

105.17–18   "And round . . . humanity."]   Charles Cotton (1630–87), "The Morning Quatrain," ll. 35–36.

105.20–23   "The early . . . way"]   "The Lordling Peasant," in Thomas Evans, *Old English Ballads* (1777), IV, 136, 57–60. The next to last word is "his" in Evans.

106.33–36   "Now . . . corn."]   "The Jolly Pindar of Wakefield," stanza 4.

107.9–10   "Virtues . . . was."]   John Donne, "Obsequies on the Lord Harrington . . . ," ll. 51–52.

107.33   Yoloffs]   Yola, a city in Nigeria, was the capital (1841–1901) of a former native state.

109.23   Menu]   Menu, or Manu, was a semi-legendary Hindu lawgiver to whom is ascribed *The Laws of Manu*, rules governing ritual and daily life compiled 200 B.C.–A.D. 200

110.32   Protestants]   In the first edition, "protestants."

111.2–3   Warren Hastings . . . letter]   This letter prefaces Charles Wilkins' translation of *Bhagavad-Gita* (London, 1785), Thoreau's source for this famous section of the Sanskrit epic *Mahabharata*.

119.17–18   Mourzouk]   An oasis town in southwestern Libya.

125.15–19   "I . . . action."]   From Simon Ockley, *The History of the Saracens* (London, 1718).

126.17–19   "Through . . . Cathay."]   Tennyson, "Locksley Hall," ll. 183–84.

127.17–20   "Fragments . . . appears."]   Sir Walter Scott, "Thomas the Rhymer," Part 3, stanza 9.

129.28–130.23   Salmon . . . town.]   Thoreau's sources for this paragraph include Daniel Gookin (1612–87), *An Historical Account of . . . the Christian Indians*, in *Transactions and Collections of the American Antiquarian Society*, vol. 2 (Cambridge, Mass., 1836), and Charles J. Fox, *History of Dunstable*.

135.7–10 "They . . . a-row."] "Robin Hood's Progress to Nottingham," last stanza.

135.22–29 "Gentle . . . fight."] "Rio Verde, Rio Verde," stanzas 1 and 2, in Percy's *Reliques*.

136.1–6 "It was . . . *vici*."] See note 129.28–130.23.

136.18–21 "Then . . . Agiochook."] Second stanza of "Lovewell's Fight. A Song," in Farmer and Moore's *Collections Historical and Miscellaneous, and Monthly Literary Journal* (March 1824).

137.5 "Strata . . . sub"] See 74.6–7 and note 74.6.

139.34 "When . . . night."] Thomas Campbell (1777–1844), "Hohenlinden," l. 6.

141.21–22 Therefore . . . sweep.] Felicia Hemans, "The Voice of Music," in *The Poetical Works of Mrs. Hemans*, 2 vols. (Philadelphia, 1832), I, 52: "Therefore a current of sadness deep, / Through the stream of thy triumphs is heard to sweep."

141.24–27 "Perhaps . . . existence."] Adapted from Calidas's *Sacontalá; or, The Fatal Ring*, tr. Sir William Jones in *The Works of Sir William Jones* (London, 1807), vol. IX.

143.27–30 "Before . . . burns."] Milton, *Paradise Lost*, II, 535–38.

146.2–7 "On . . . TENNYSON.] Opening of "The Lady of Shalott."

146.30–34 "In the . . . night."] See note 72.29.

153.33–35 "Heaven . . . threads."] Giles Fletcher (1588?–1623), *Christs Victorie and Triumph in Heaven and Earth, Over and After Death*, I, stanza 38.

154.13–14 "Flatter . . . alchemy."] Shakespeare, Sonnet 33, ll. 2 and 4.

154.18–19 "Anon . . . face,"] Shakespeare, Sonnet 33, ll. 5–6.

154.24–31 "How . . . exile!"] Giles Fletcher, *Christs Victorie and Triumph*, I, stanza 43.

156.1–13 historian . . . mountains."] See note 72.29.

157.1–6 "And now . . . leaves."] Giles Fletcher, *Christs Victorie and Triumph*, IV, stanza 3.

160.14–17 New Hampshire . . . preserved."] John W. Barber, *Historical Collections . . . of Every Town in Massachusetts* (Worcester, 1841).

165.10–18 Belphoebe . . . restrain."] Spenser, *The Faerie Queene*, III, canto 5, stanza 39.

168.28–29 "Amongst . . . restrain."] See note 165.10–18.

169.1–4 "His . . . grave."] "Beggar's Daughter of Bednall-Green," in Percy's *Reliques*.

175.12   Adventures of Henry] *Travels and Adventures in Canada and the Indian Territories . . . 1760–1776* (New York, 1809) by Alexander Henry (1739–1824).

176.29   "Of . . . leisure."] Emerson, "The Humble Bee," l. 38.

177.3   Hearne's journey] *A Journey from Fort Prince of Wales . . . to the Northern Ocean . . .* (London, 1795), by Samuel Hearne (1745–92), British fur trader and explorer in northern Canada.

181.20–23   "Too . . . dated."] Francis Quarles, *Emblems*, XIII, 2, 45–49.

184.1–2   "The young . . . walk."] "The Faery Queen," ll. 45–46, in Percy's *Reliques*.

184.8–188.22   On . . . smite?] Thoreau's translations of Anacreon.

192.2–3   "Man . . . Cotton.] Charles Cotton (1630–87), "The World," l. 20.

198.3   curb] The frame or rim around the top of a well.

198.15   *sua . . . nôrint*] If they know their own good.

199.3–17   "He . . . hour."] Pythian Ode, IV, ll. 34–43.

199.23–28   "springing . . . it."] Olympian Ode, VII, ll. 62–63 and 69–71.

200.9   Bashpish] The BashBish Falls in southwestern Massachusetts, near Copake, N.Y.

202.38–39   "sermons . . . streams."] Shakespeare, *As You Like It*, II, i, 16–17: "Finds tongues in trees, books in the running brooks, / Sermons in stones, and good in every thing."

203.24–25   "Rome . . . monument."] Spenser, translation of Du Bellay, "Ruines of Rome," stanza 29, ll. 13–14.

203.26–27   "With her . . . testifies."] Spenser, "Ruines of Time," ll. 76–77.

203.34–37   Fuller . . . out."] Thomas Fuller, *The Holy State and the Profane State* (1642). William Camden (1550–1623) was an English scholar and antiquarian.

204.30–31   "bees . . . sallowy."] Giles Fletcher, *Christs Victorie and Triumph*, III, stanza 2, ll. 6–7.

204.33   paulo-post] A little subsequent.

205.31–38   "at Pawtucket . . . miracles."] See Thomas Hutchinson, *The History of the Colony of Massachusetts Bay*, 2 vols. (London, 1765).

215.28–33   "If . . . all."] Thoreau's translation from the French of *Les*

Quatres Livres de Philosophie Morale et Politique de la Chine, tr. M. G. Pauthier (Paris, 1841).

217.34–35   "He . . . doe."]   Matthew Roydon (fl. 1580–1622), "An Elegie, or Friends Passion, for His Astrophill," ll. 143–44 (in tribute to Spenser).

218.2–3   "Why . . . one."]   John Donne, "Second Letter to the Countess of Huntingdon," 129–30.

221.11–12   "And love . . . nobleman."]   Fulke Greville, Lord Brooke (1554–1628), "Another to his Cinthia," No. 121, ll. 19–20.

223.18   *necessarius*]   An intimate friend or relative.

223.27–30   "When . . . embrace."]   Richard Edwards (1532?–1566), "The Renuing of Love," ll. 37–40, in Evans, *Old English Ballads*.

223.31–32   Henry . . . Adventures,"]   See note 175.12.

223.39–224.2   "Metals . . . sight."]   See "Mitralabha or The Acquisition of Friends," Moral 94, in the Sanskrit book of fables, *The Hitopadesa, or Book of Good Counsel*.

225.15   "There . . . pair."]   *The Parlement of Foules*, l. 595.

225.17–18   "And certaine . . . one."]   Chaucer, *The Romaunt of the Rose*, ll. 5533–34.

229.22–24   "To contract . . . Friendship."]   See note 215.28–33.

231.32–34   "Seven . . . together."]   *The Vishñu Puráña*, tr. H. H. Wilson (London, 1840).

241.30   "the pause . . . itself."]   Thomas Gray, letter to Richard Stone-hewer, June 29, 1760. Gray wrote "gust" rather than "blast."

242.3–4   "Silver . . . spring,"]   Christopher Marlowe (1564–93), "Another Passionate Shepherd to His Love," stanza 3.

242.21   "Who . . . pray."]   John Donne, "Of the Progress of the Soul, The Second Anniversary," l. 464.

243.1–9   "And . . . enemyes."]   Spenser, *The Faerie Queene*, I, canto 1, stanza 41.

244.2–12   "He . . . EMERSON.]   "Woodnotes," I, ll. 64–67, 82–83, and 92–95.

244.18   hair-bird]   The first edition (1849) has "tree-sparrow" here. In Channing's copy of that edition, the word is marked and a note reads, " 'chip-sparrow.' H. wished to have this corrected April 23, '62." "Hair-bird" and "chipping-bird" are both names for the same species of small sparrow.

248.16–32   historian . . . horse."] Benjamin L. Mirick, *The History of Haverhill, Massachusetts* (Haverhill, 1832).

256.11   gores] Surveyors' term for a small strip of land between two larger tracts.

257.10   AGIOCOCHOOK] Indian name for Mt. Washington.

257.11–15   "Sweet . . . HERBERT.] George Herbert, "Vertue," which has "day" rather than "days" in the first line.

259.5–6   Chaucer . . . Dream] *The Isle of Ladies*, also called *The Isle of Pleasaunce*, ll. 1364–68, author unknown. Attributed to Chaucer by his first editor, Thomas Speght, in 1598, this poem was known as "Chaucer's Dream" until the end of the nineteenth century, when it was relegated to the Chaucer apocrypha.

259.33–36   "The swaying . . . dreams."] Channing, "The River," ll. 14–17.

261.15–22   "Not . . . falls."] James Montgomery (1771–1854), "The Sun-Dial," ll. 10–17.

265.8   Paugus] A war-chief of the Pequawkets killed at Lovewell's Fight.

265.32–33   "Old . . . still."] Mother Goose ballad.

267.34   "The laws . . . Art."] Francis Quarles, "To My Booke," *Divine Fancies*, Lib. IV, piece 117, l. 36.

269.1–33   "The Tees . . . nature."] Goethe, *Italienische Reise* (1816–17).

272.2–7   "The Boteman . . . SPENSER.] *The Faerie Queene*, II, canto 12, stanza 29.

272.8–10   "Summer's . . . DONNE.] "The Anatomy of the World," ll. 355–56.

273.8–11   "And . . . year."] Francis Quarles, *Hieroglyphics of the Life of Man*, XIV, iii, 196–200.

274.10   "From . . . plain."] Christopher Marlowe, *Hero and Leander*, I, 116.

274.16–17   "Wise . . . hurled."] William Drummond (1585–1649), "A Pastoral Elegy on the Death of Sir William Alexander," ll. 97–98.

274.22–27   "at all . . . festival."] Marlowe, *Hero and Leander*, I, 96.

280.19–22   "The wrathful . . . move."] *Ca-Lodin*, III, 138. Thoreau found this and the following quotations from the Ossianic poems in Patrick MacGregor, *The Genuine Remains of Ossian* (London, 1841).

280.31–32   "Mounds . . . years."] *Timora*, VI, 391.

281.1–3   "His soul . . . bleak."] *Ca-Lodin*, II, 134.

281.6–7   "The weak . . . it."] *Fingal*, V, 280.

281.21–22   "I . . . verse."] *Oinamoru*, I, 182.

281.25–37   "Whence . . . times."] *Ca-Lodin*, II, 137.

282.2–7   "Strangers . . . song."] *Carric*, 167.

282.17   "Thou . . . ships."] *Ca-Lodin*, I, 125.

282.19–20   "With . . . moved."] *Ca-Lodin*, II, 132.

282.22–24   "dragging . . . dies."] *Fingal*, III, 252.

282.26–27   "A thousand . . . Fingal."] *Garon*, 176.

282.31–33   "Thy . . . son."] *Fingal*, VI, 292.

283.8–12   "He strode . . . lance."] *Timora*, III, 343.

283.15–27   " 'My eyes . . . Croma.' "] *Croma*, 195 ff.

283.30–31   "How . . . strength?"] *Garon*, 176 ff.

287.26–28   "And . . . hay."] Francis Quarles, "The Brevity of Human Life," *Emblems*, III, 13, 19–21.

288.14–289.8   "I see . . . day."] Channing, "Autumn," stanzas 2–4, 8, and 11–13.

290.1   Barber] See note 160.14–17.

291.23–27   Varro . . . herbage."] Marcus Terentius Varro (116–27 B.C.), *Rerum Rusticarum*, I, vii.

296.15   Gesner] Konrad Gesner (1516–65), Swiss naturalist, as quoted in Edward Topsell, *The History of Four-Footed Beasts* (1607).

300.23–24   "right . . . Rome."] Chaucer, *A Treatise on the Astrolabe*, opening.

300.25   Testament of Love] Now attributed to Thomas Usk (d. 1388).

302.3–4   "For . . . astart."] *The Court of Life*, stanza 187. The poem is no longer attributed to Chaucer.

303.20–22   "if . . . semeliness."] Chaucer, *Legend of Good Women*, ll. 1039–41.

306.27–30   "There . . . harbored."] Giles Fletcher, *Christs Victorie and Triumph*, I, stanza 6.

308.8–10   "The earth . . . stars."] George Chapman (1559?–1634), *Caesar and Pompey*, V, 159–61.

308.16–17   "Although . . . love."]   John Donne, *Elegy 18*, ll. 33–34.

308.29–30   "Largior . . . nôrunt."]   Vergil, *Aeneid*, VI, 640–41.

309.15–16   "Unless . . . man!"]   Samuel Daniel (1562–1619), "Epistle to the Lady Margaret, Countess of Cumberland," ll. 95–96.

309.23–24   "I . . . way."]   Francis Quarles, *Emblems*, IV, 11, 32–33.

309.35   titmen]   Dwarfs. "Titman" is a regionalism for the smallest pig in a litter.

315.3–4   "a little . . . affairs."]   Thomas Fuller (1608–61), as quoted in "Specimens of the Writings of Fuller," *The Prose Works of Charles Lamb* (London, 1838).

315.5–8   "He . . . all."]   Francis Quarles, "On Faith," *Divine Fancies*, Lib. III, 97, 1–4.

315.10–23   "By them . . . sense."]   Phineas Fletcher (1582–1650), "The Purple Island," canto IX, stanzas 19, 21.

317.6–12   "Therefore . . . born."]   William Drummond, "No trust in Time," ll. 9–14, in *Flowers of Sion* (1623).

317.23   "Pulsæ . . . valles."]   Vergil, *Eclogues*, VI, 84.

317.28   Chronicle of Bernaldez]   Andrés Bernáldez (d. 1513?), *Historia de los reyes catolicos, D. Fernando y Da. Isabel* (History of the Catholic Monarchs Ferdinand and Isabella).

319.6   interrupt]   The first edition reads "interpret" here.

WALDEN

327.13–14   Inde . . . nati.]   Ovid, *Metamorphoses*, I, 414–15. The translation (327.16–18) is from Sir Walter Raleigh, *History of the World*.

330.23–7   Evelyn . . . neighbor."]   John Evelyn, *Silva, or a Discourse of Forest-Trees* (1664).

330.34–36   "be not . . . undone?"]   *The Vishñu Puráña*, tr. H. H. Wilson (London, 1840).

331.35–37   "To . . . knowledge."]   *Confucian Analects*, Bk. II, ch. 17.

332.40–333.1   "to . . . roasting."]   Charles Darwin, *Journal of Researches . . . during the Voyage of H.M.S. Beagle* (New York, 1846).

339.15   tare and tret]   Tare is a deduction from gross weight made for the weight of the container; tret is a further deduction of four pounds from every 104 pounds.

340.34–36 " was now . . . clothes."] Madam Ida Pfeiffer, *A Lady's Voyage Round the World* (New York, 1852).

344.8–13 "The Laplander . . . people."] Samuel Laing, *Journal of a Residence in Norway* (London, 1837).

346.9–18 "The best . . . houses."] Daniel Gookin (1612–87), *Historical Collections of the Indians of New England.*

347.8–9 Rumford fireplace] A non-smoking stove named for its inventor, Benjamin Thompson, Count Rumford (1753–1814).

347.9 back plastering] Plaster between the exterior and interior walls.

348.3 the poor . . . with you] Matthew 26:11.

348.4–5 the fathers . . . edge?] Ezekiel 18:2.

348.6–7 "As I . . . Israel."] Ezekiel 18:3.

348.8–10 "Behold . . . die."] Ezekiel 18:4.

349.3 suent] Running smoothly.

349.7 springe] In several earlier drafts, "spring."

349.12–15 Chapman . . . air."] George Chapman (1559?–1634), *The Tragedy of Caesar and Pompey*, V, ii.

349.19–21 "had . . . avoided;"] John Lempriere, *Bibliotheca Classica* (New York, 1842), "Momus."

350.4 "silent poor."] People who were silent about their poverty in order to avoid the poorhouse. A fund was established in Concord in the eighteenth century to help them.

351.11 glow-shoes] Variant spelling of galoshes.

353.16 Johnson . . . Providence,"] Edward Johnson, *A History of New-England.*

353.28–354.8 "those . . . thousands."] In E. B. O'Callaghan, *The Documentary History of New York* (Albany, 1851).

364.17–18 Flying Childers] A famous eighteenth-century English racehorse.

372.29–32 "Panem . . . testu."] *De Agri Cultura*, ch. 74.

373.17–20 "For . . . chips."] Anonymous poem in John Warner Barber, *Historical Collections . . . of . . . Massachusetts* (Worcester, 1839).

376.5 "The evil . . . them."] Shakespeare, *Julius Caesar*, III, ii, 76.

376.20–377.3 "busk . . . themselves."] William Bartram, *Travels through North and South Carolina . . .* (Philadelphia, 1791).

377.4–6   The Mexicans . . . end.]   See William H. Prescott, *History of the Conquest of Mexico* (New York, 1843), Bk. I, ch. 4.

377.37   flocks of Admetus.]   When Apollo was banished from heaven, he was forced to tend the flocks of Admetus, King of Pherae, for nine years.

381.27   Howard]   John Howard (1726–90), English prison reformer.

386.3–29   "Thou . . . CAREW.]   Thomas Carew (1595?–?1645), *Coelum Britannicum*, ll. 642–68.

388.15–16   "I . . . dispute."]   William Cowper (1731–1800), "Verses Supposed to be Written by Alexander Selkirk."

390.28–29   "An abode . . . seasoning."]   M. A. Langlois (tr.), *Harivansa, ou Histoire de la Famille de Hari* (Paris, 1834); Thoreau's translation from French. "Harivamsa," or "genealogy of the god Hari (Krishna)" is a supplement to the Sanskrit epic *Mahabharata*.

392.14–15   "There . . . Damodara,]   See note 390.28–29. Damodara is one of the names for Krishna.

392.32–35   "There . . . by."]   Fragment of an anonymous Jacobean poem set to music by Robert Jones (fl. 1616) in *The Muses Garden for Delights*. Also in Thomas Evans, *Old Ballads* (London, 1810).

393.5–6   "Renew . . . again."]   Confucius, *The Great Learning*, "Commentary of the Philosopher Tsang."

395.4   "glorify . . . forever."]   From the opening lines of "The Shorter Catechism," in *The New England Primer*, the seventeenth-century Calvinist schoolbook.

398.7–15   "Kieou-pe-yu . . . messenger!"]   *Confucian Analects*, Bk. XIV, ch. 26.

400.18   Nilometer]   An ancient Egyptian instrument for measuring the rise of the Nile, or, generally, a graduated scale cut in rock to measure a river's height.

402.23–27   Mîr . . . doctrines."]   M. Garcin de Tassy, *Histoire de la Littérature Hindoui* (Paris, 1839). Mîr Camar Uddîn Mast was an eighteenth-century Hindu poet.

408.32   tit-men]   See note 309.35.

410.18   "Olive-Branches"]   The *Olive Branch* was a Methodist weekly published in Boston.

412.5–8   "for . . . day."]   Pfeiffer, *A Lady's Voyage*. The Puri Indians were natives of eastern Brazil.

414.13–15   "In truth . . . Concord."]   Channing, "Walden Spring," ll. 30–32, in *The Woodman and Other Poems* (Boston, 1849).

417.7   Buena Vista]   Battlefield during the Mexican War, 1847.

419.16–17   "to be . . . ammiral."]   Milton, *Paradise Lost*, I, 293–94.

422.29   single spruce]   Thoreau changed "single" (white) spruce to "double" (black) spruce in a copy of the book.

426.20–21   "the world . . . me,"]   Thomas Gray, "Elegy Written in a
Country Churchyard" (1751), l. 4.

427.28–30   "Mourning . . . Toscar."]   *Croma*, ll. 52–54, in Patrick
MacGregor, *The Genuine Remains of Ossian* (London, 1841).

429.9–18   "How vast . . . sides."]   Confucius, *The Doctrine of the Mean*,
XVI, 1–3.

429.22–24   "Virtue . . . neighbors."]   *Confucian Analects*, Bk. IV, ch. 25.

429.29   Indra]   Hindu god of air, rain, thunder, and earth.

432.21   old Parrs]   Thomas Parr was an Englishman who reportedly lived
from 1483 to 1635, 152 years.

436.11–14   "Arrivéd . . . has."]   Spenser, *The Faerie Queene*, I, canto 1,
stanza 35.

436.20–437.5 "He laid . . . respect.]   Edward Winslow, *A Relation or
Journall of the Beginning and Proceedings of the English Plantation Setled at
Plimouth in New England* (London, 1622), better known as *Mourt's Relation*.

437.30–35   "Why . . . grieve."]   *Iliad*, XVI, 8, 16–19.

443.34   the fox in the fable]   Aesop's "The Cock and the Fox."

445.15–16   "Welcome . . . Englishmen!"]   The Indian Samoset's legend-
ary greeting to the Pilgrims at Plymouth.

447.34   *agricola laboriosus*]   Hard-working farmer.

448.16–17   Mr. Coleman's report]   Rev. Henry Colman (1785–1849) was
commissioned in 1837 to make an agricultural survey of Massachusetts. His
four extensive reports were published by the state from 1838 to 1841. Colman
went on to publish studies of British and European agriculture.

448.28   *Rans des Vaches*]   A Swiss cowherd's song.

450.7   canker-rash]   Sore throat.

451.35–452.3 "there . . . improvement."]   John Evelyn, *Terra: a Philosophical Discourse of Earth* (London, 1729).

452.8–9   Mr. Coleman]   See note 448.16–17.

452.21–22   patrem . . . oportet]   The master should have the selling
habit, not the buying habit. Cato, *De Agri Cultura*, ch. 2.

454.3–4 "And as . . . again,"] Francis Quarles, "The Shepherd's Oracles," Eclogue V.

454.26 (*maximeque pius quæstus*,)] Cato, *De Agri Cultura*, Introduction.

454.27–30 "called . . . Saturn."] Varro, *Rerum Rusticarum*, III, i.

456.22 Redding & Company's] Boston bookseller.

457.27–29 "loudly . . . danger."] Apollonius Rhodius (late third or early second century B.C.), *Argonautica*, 4, 903.

458.6 "as I sailed."] From "Ballad of Captain Robert Kidd."

460.19–22 "Nec . . . request."] *Elegies of Tibullus*, 3, 7–8; quoted in John Evelyn, *Silva*.

460.23–27 "You who . . . bends."] *Confucian Analects*, Bk. XII, ch. 19.

469.11 Boiling Spring] A bubbling spring west of Walden.

469.29 breams] Thoreau inserted "*Pomotis obesus*" in a copy of the book.

470.5 *reticulatus*] Net-like.

470.6 *guttatus*] Speckled.

470.20 kingfishers . . . it] In a copy of the book, Thoreau revised this phrase, which was omitted from the first edition, to "kingfishers dart away from its coves."

476.18 Moore . . . Deep Cut] "But More of More-Hall, with nothing at all, / He slew the dragon of Wantley." From "The Dragon of Wantley," in Percy's *Reliques*. The Deep Cut had been dug in a hillside between Walden and Concord for the railroad.

479.38 "still . . . resounds."] William Drummond, "Icarus," l. 10, in *Madrigals and Epigrams* (1616).

483.10 white-spruce] Thoreau changed this to "black spruce" in a copy of the book.

484.30–35 "Thy . . . about."] Channing, "Baker Farm," ll. 1–6. Channing included this poem, written in 1848, in his *Thoreau: The Poet Naturalist*.

484.37 musquash] Indian name for muskrat.

485.15–18 "And here . . . steers."] Channing, "Baker Farm," ll. 36–38.

488.22–35 "Landscape . . . trees!"] Channing, "Baker Farm," ll. 11–12, 21–22, and 78–87.

492.1–2 "yave . . . men."] Chaucer, in the Prologue to *Canterbury Tales*, ll. 177–78, describing the Monk, not the Nun.

494.3–9 "some . . . fly,"] William Kirby and William Spence, *An Introduction to Entomology* (Philadelphia, 1846).

496.10–14 "he who . . . distress."] Rajah Rammohun Roy, *Translation of Several . . . of the Veds* (London, 1832).

496.20–23 "The soul . . . food."] Confucius, *The Great Learning*, "Commentary of the Philosopher Tsang," ch. 7.

497.22–25 "That . . . carefully."] *Works of Mencius*, Bk. IV ("Le Low"), pt. II, ch. 19.

497.27–30 "A command . . . God."] Roy, *Translation*.

498.7–13 "How . . . worse."] Donne, "To Sire Edward Herbert at Iulyers."

502.38 Pilpay] Also known as Bidpai; reputed author of East Indian animal fables. See *The Dial*, III (1842), 82–85.

503.5 wild native kind] Thoreau inserted "(*Mus leucopus*)" in a copy of the book.

507.32 Kirby and Spence] See note 494.3–9.

515.31 keeping-room] New England term for sitting room.

515.34–36 "cellam . . . erit,"] Cato, *De Agri Cultura*, ch. 3.

518.27–28 cadis worms] Larva of the mayfly and others that live in water and form cylindrical cases.

521.16–20 "the encroachments . . . *foresta*, &c.,"] William Gilpin, *Remarks on Forest Scenery* (Edinburgh, 1834).

521.31–35 consecrated . . . children, &c.] Cato, *De Agri Cultura*, ch. 139.

522.3–7 "nearly . . . plains."] F. Andrew Michaux, *North American Sylva*, edition of 1819.

522.30 "jump"] To flatten the head by heating and pounding, thus pinching the handle.

525.1–19 "Never . . . talked."] Ellen Sturgis Hooper (1816–48), "The Wood-Fire." See *The Dial*, I (1840), 193. Thoreau wrote "Mrs. Hooper" after this poem in a copy of the book.

529.13 "tub,"] Hand-drawn fire truck.

529.16–19 Gondibert . . . powder."] Sir William Davenant (1606–68), "Author's Preface" to *Gondibert: An Heroic Poem*.

530.2 "rider."] Top rail of a fence.

531.32–33 "fate . . . absolute,"] Milton, *Paradise Lost*, II, 560.

534.28   meadow mouse]   Thoreau changed this to "deer mouse" in a copy of the book.

536.1   "How . . . serenity!"]   Thomas Storer (1571–1604), *The Life and Death of Thomas Wolsey*, Sec. 2, stanza 77, l. 5.

537.9–12   "The house-holder . . . guest."]   See note 330.34–36.

548.7   fear-naughts]   Thick wool coats.

551.27–32   "a bay . . . appeared!]   William Gilpin, *Observations on . . . the High-lands of Scotland* (London, 1808).

551.33–35   So high . . . waters—."]   Milton, *Paradise Lost*, VII, 288–90.

560.1   periplus of Hanno]   The report of the Carthaginian Hanno on his exploration of the west coast of Africa in 480 B.C.

560.1   Ternate and Tidore]   Spice Islands in the Dutch East Indies.

568.16   lights]   Lungs of a slaughtered animal.

570.7–8   "et primitus . . . evocata,"]   Varro, *Rerum Rusticarum*, II, ii: "and the grass which is called forth by the early rains is just growing."

572.20–31   "Eurus . . . heaven."]   Ovid, *Metamorphoses*, I, 61–2, 78–81.

573.5–6   While . . . return.]   Cf. Isaac Watts, *Hymns and Spiritual Songs*, Bk. 1, Hymn 88: "And while the lamp . . . return."

573.27–574.2   "A return . . . man?"]   *Words of Mencius*, Bk. VI, "Kaou Tsze," pt. 1, ch. 8.

574.3–15   "The Golden . . . seed."]   Ovid, *Metamorphoses*, I, 89–96, 107–08.

576.30   "rills . . . lotus."]   Calidas, *Sacontalá; or The Fatal Ring*, tr. Sir William Jones. Speech of Dushmanta, Act V.

577.27–30   "Direct . . . home-cosmography."]   William Habington, "To My Honoured Friend Sir Ed. P. Knight," in *Castara* (1634).

578.24–25   "Erret . . . viæ."]   Adapted from Claudian, "De Sene Veronensi," ll. 21–22. Thoreau changed "Iberos" (Iberians) to "Australians."

579.8–14   "to ascertain . . . resolve."]   Thoreau copied this anecdote from *Harper's New Monthly*, I (October 1850) into his journal for July 21, 1851.

581.11–14   "They . . . Vedas;"]   M. Garcin de Tassy, *Histoire de la Littérature Hindoui* (Paris, 1839). Thoreau's translation.

582.7–583.3   There was . . . wonderful?]   In the *Bhagavad-Gita*, Kooroo is a nation, and Kalpa is the period between the creation and destruction of the world, reportedly over four billion years. A day and night, to Brahma, is one Kalpa. See *The Dial*, III (1843), 332.

583.38–584.1   "From . . . thought."]   *Confucian Analects*, Bk. 9, ch. 25.

584.4–5   "and lo! . . . view."]   Joseph Blanco White (1775–1841), Sonnet: "To Night."

584.29–30   Mameluke bey.]   In 1811, the Turkish viceroy of Egypt ordered the massacre of all the Mamelukes, a military caste. One leaped from the citadel to his horse and fled to Syria.

585.4   kittlybenders.]   Children's game of running across thin ice.

585.16   furrowing]   Furring.

THE MAINE WOODS

594.13   clothing and articles]   Thoreau's annotated copy of the *Union Magazine* printing of "Ktaadn" has "clothing and other articles."

596.37–38   Passadumkeag . . . implies]   See Appendix, 844.24.

602.18–19   Province man]   A man from the Canadian province of New Brunswick.

604.28–30   "Village . . . blood,"]   Phrases from lines 57–60 of Gray's "Elegy Written in a Country Churchyard."

604.31–34   "Perchance . . . lyre."]   Gray, "Elegy," ll. 45–48.

609.14   idle]   In the *Union Magazine* version, "idler."

620.21–22   "Row . . . past!"]   Thomas Moore (1779–1852), "The Canadian Boat Song," ll. 5–6.

620.28–33   "Why . . . soon."]   Moore, "Boat Song," ll. 7–10 and 13–14.

621.1–2   "Saint . . . airs!"]   Moore, "Boat Song," ll. 15–16.

624.23   feruled]   Ferruled; wrapped with a metal ring or cap.

624.33   Michaux]   François André Michaux (1770–1855), whose *Histoire des Arbres Forestiers de l'Amerique Septentrionale* (translated as *The North American Sylva*) is quoted here and below.

624.40   Springer]   John S. Springer, whose *Forest Life and Forest Trees* (New York, 1851) Thoreau quotes here and below.

625.21   drawn]   In one English edition of Michaux's *The North American Sylva* (Philadelphia, 1855), the sentence reads: "The logs are not sawn the first year."

627.4   outlet]   Possibly Thoreau meant "inlet."

628.39–40   there . . . least]   Thoreau probably intended "of the whole Penobscot River" to modify "a perpendicular fall" rather than "the worst place." His 1846 journal has: "As near as I can remember there was a perpendicular fall here of the whole Penobscot River 2 or 3 feet at least."

633.10–11   "qu'en . . . chaude."]   Marc Lescarbot, *Histoire de la Nouvelle France* (Paris, 1612): "that they would put the kettle on the fire and catch enough fish for dinner before the water was hot."

638.24–26   "Nigh . . . flying."]   Milton, *Paradise Lost*, II, 940–42.

641.6–10   "Chaos . . . light."]   *Paradise Lost*, II, 970–74.

647.14   Hodge]   The quotations from James Hodge, here and below, are from Charles T. Jackson, *Maine Geological Survey* (Augusta, 1838), also the source for quotations from Jackson.

679.15–18   [Indeed, . . . woods.]]   This sentence, which did not appear in earlier versions, appears with brackets in the first edition.

690.15–16   Aroostook or Penobscot war]   The Aroostook War was the name given to a boundary dispute over timberlands between Maine and New Brunswick in 1839. The Penobscot War could refer to the long conflict, 1631–1759, between England and France over a trading post on the Penobscot Peninsula, or to the attempt by Massachusetts to take it from the British in 1779.

692.14   Arnold's expedition]   Benedict Arnold's attempt to capture Quebec in 1775 was one of the boldest expeditions of the American Revolution.

695.11–12   With, . . . 1588]   John White (or Wyth, or With) was a member of the lost Roanoke colony in Virginia. His watercolors, the first European paintings of life in America, were the basis of engravings in Théodore de Bry's *Collectio Peregrinationum* (Collection of Voyages), published in Frankfurt-on-Main, 1590–1629, which also had illustrations of the Brazilian *boucan*. Thoreau's "1588" is probably an error for "1590."

696.8   hylodes]   A "genus of American toads" (*Oxford English Dictionary*), or a "large genus of New World frogs" (Mitford M. Matthews, *Dictionary of Americanisms*, 1951). Both cite this passage.

696.40   Paugus]   See note 265.8.

698.33   Father Rasles]   Father Sébastien Rasles (also spelled Rale, Rasle, and Ralle), 1652–1724, was a missionary to the Abnaki people at Norridgewock from 1694 until his death in an English raid on the village. His *Dictionary of the Abnaki Language*, stolen in the raid, was published in 1833 as the first volume of the *Memoirs of the American Academy of Arts and Sciences*. Thoreau used it extensively in preparing the Appendix to *The Maine Woods*.

700.12   Josselyn]   John Josselyn, *An Account of Two Voyages to New-England* (1674).

700.26   Cusabesex]   "Cusabexsex" in Thoreau's journal for 1853.

702.23   at once.]   The 1858 *Atlantic Monthly* version adds the following passage:

At the carry-man's camp I saw many little birds, brownish and yellowish, with some white tail-feathers, hopping on the wood-pile, in company with the slate-colored snow-bird, (*Fringilla hiemalis,*) but more familiar than they. The lumberers said that they came round their camps, and they gave them a vulgar name. Their simple and lively note, which was heard in all the woods, was very familiar to me, though I had never before chanced to see the bird while uttering it, and it interested me not a little, because I had had many a vain chase in a spring-morning in the direction of that sound, in order to identify the bird. On the 28th of the next month, (October,) I saw in my yard, in a drizzling day, many of the same kind of birds flitting about amid the weeds, and uttering a faint *chip* merely. There was one full-plumaged Yellow-crowned Warbler (*Sylva coronata*) among them, and I saw that the others were the young birds of that season. They had followed me from Moosehead and the North. I have since frequently seen the full-plumaged ones while uttering that note in the spring.

709.23   top]   In Thoreau's source, William Gilpin's *Observations on the Western Parts of England* (London, 1808), "tops."

718.5   hylodes]   See note 696.8.

720.17   cunningly.]   In his journal, Thoreau notes here: "The Indian thought that the mother had perhaps been killed."

731.33–34   "a pagan . . . creed"]   Wordsworth, "The World is Too Much with Us," l. 10.

739.22   Wrangel]   Ferdinand Petrovitch Wrangel, *Narrative of an Expedition to the Polar Sea* (London, 1840).

742.12   Eastham]   Eastham, Massachusetts, was famous as a site for revival meetings. See *Cape Cod*, pp. 881–82.

746.2   July 26,]   The first edition has the words "[The figure of a bear in a boat.]" instead of the sketch above, which is reproduced from Thoreau's journal draft.

748.32   kingfisher (tweezer bird)]   Since "tweezer bird" is not another name for kingfisher, the parentheses, also in Thoreau's journal, may indicate that Thoreau considered deleting the name.

750.29–30   "the turpentine . . . pork-bag."]   "Arnold's Letters on his Expedition to Canada in 1775," *Maine Historical Society Collections*, 3rd ser., I (1831).

764.5   Paugus]   See note 265.8.

767.38   by good rights]   These words appear within quotation marks in Thoreau's last draft of the passage.

768.38–40   When . . . university.]   In Thoreau's last draft of the passage, this sentence, inserted in the margin, is in his sister Sophia's handwriting.

774.33–34   forks of the Nickatou]   Since Nickatou is an island, not a river, the journal reading "forks at Nickatou" is more appropriate.

780.23–24   on a deserted log]   In Thoreau's journal, the bread is found in a "deserted log hut."

783.11   Montresor]   Col. John Montresor (1736–99). See *Maine Historical Society Collections*, 3rd ser., I.

792.14   not of rocks]   Thoreau's journal draft of the passage has "trees (not of rocks)."

800.18–21   high, . . . Richardson]   The first edition omits the words between "thirty-five feet high" and "Richardson." In the last-draft manuscript, the word "high" occurs in the same position in the line several lines apart; probably the copyist or compositor accidentally skipped down.

811.7–13   "and so . . . it."]   Jérôme Lalemant, in *Relation de ce qui s'est passé en la Nouvelle France en les années 1661 et 1662* (Paris, 1663).

828.3–4   (Those . . . woods.)]   In the list in Thoreau's journal, five more plants than those asterisked here are marked for special treatment: *Betula alba* (828.23), *Vaccinium corymbosum* (829.18), *A lemna* (833.17), *Galeopsis tetrahit* (834.13), and *Lobelia Dartmanna* (834.36).

840.33   Rale]   See note 698.33.

842.12–13   (Williamson . . . (Hodge.)]   This punctuation does not make clear that William D. Williamson is the authority for the definition "flint," while James Hodge is Thoreau's source for deriving the name *Kineo* from that of an old Indian hunter.

CAPE COD

847.2–5   *Principium . . . possumus*].]   The *Beginning* will be to consider all things, even the smallest, / The *Middle* is to express with the pen the descriptions and the uses, / The *End* will be to delineate nature carefully, and to the extent possible.

871.1–2   *terra . . . jucunda*.]   Land firm and known, not yet fertile and pleasant.

879.14–17, 20–31   "Two . . . appears."]   Heman Doane, *A Sketch of the Life and Singular Sickness of Heman Doane* (Boston, 1826).

880.30   bars and guzzles]   The off-shore sandbars and the pools of deep water between them.

882.30–33   "and there . . . sorrow."]   See Daniel Gookin, *Historical Collections of the Indians of New England* (1674).

883.39–884.1 ('Triumphat . . . terroribus.'] On the swift chariot of glory, that orator triumphs who goads and provokes and fills the breast with terrors. From Thomas Burnet, *De Statu Mortuorum et Resurgentium Tractatus* (Treatise on the state of the dead and those who rise again, 1720).

885.6 'En hic . . . judices.' "] That shows what sort of judges you are. Phaedrus, *Fables*.

885.19–20 "Lights . . . Life."] See John Wilson, *Lights and Shadows of Scottish Life* (Edinburgh, 1822).

887.12–14 "Senex . . . sermonis."] An old man, clean-nosed [i.e., of good taste] and a writer of elegant words and of sweet and festive discourses.

887.15–17 "Vir . . . cœlo."] A humble man, mild and agreeable, host to those who come visiting, not pursuing profit on earth, having laid up treasure in heaven.

888.30 ποταμοῖο . . . Ὠκεανοῖο.] The great might of the river Okeanos. *Iliad*, XVIII, 607.

890.9–10 "right . . . dispute,"] See note 388.15–16.

890.14–891.7 "Whoever . . . them."] David Crantz, *The History of Greenland* . . . , 2 vols. (London, 1767).

894.32 Βῆ . . . θαλάσσης.*] He went in silence along the coast of the loud-resounding sea. *Iliad*, I, 34.

894.39 ἀνάριθμον γέλασμα] Countless thronging (of the waves). Aeschylus, *Prometheus Bound*, l. 90.

895.38 Bory St. Vincent] Jean Baptiste Bory de St. Vincent (1778–1846), the author of various books on natural history, the Canary Islands, Portugal, and the Netherlands.

896.21–897.16 "When . . . depart."] Henry Wadsworth Longfellow, "Seaweed."

898.23 crotchets] Forked poles.

899.35 sugar–kit] Probably a contraction of sugar-kettle or sugar-kittle, a large kettle used in making maple sugar.

904.21 *cunabula*] Cradle.

904.28 plate beam] A horizontal timber supporting the roof.

912.33–35 "Not by . . . regard."] Vergil, *Eclogues*, VI, 65 ff., in Dryden's translation. Chromis and Mnasilus were two youths who bound Silenus, releasing him only on his promise to sing.

914.21–25 *Quid* . . . marinis?"] Vergil, *Eclogues*, VI, 74–77: Why tell of Scylla, Nisus' daughter, who was pursued by the reputation of vexing the ships of Dulichium—her bright thighs girded by barking monsters—and in her deep whirlpool, alas, tearing up the terrified sailors with her sea hounds?

916.26   fire-boards]   Boards to close off a fireplace not in use.

921.21–23   "The saffron-robed . . . mortals."]   See the *Iliad*, VIII, opening.

933.3   Θίν᾽ . . . πόντον.]   By the shore of the gray sea, looking over the wine-dark waters. *Iliad*, I, 350.

936.39   father of mad bulls]   Poseidon, who sent a bull out of the sea to King Minos of Crete to offer as a sacrifice. When Minos did not, Poseidon drove the bull mad, and it went on a rampage.

945.38   Arabia Felix]   Fertile Arabia; one of three parts into which the Arabian Peninsula was divided by the Romans, with Arabia Petraea (rocky Arabia) and Arabia Deserta (desert Arabia).

948.11–12   cat-tail . . . New England.]   Cat-tail stalks furnished caulking material for barrels.

953.16–17   Ἐν . . . ocean.]   *Iliad*, VIII, 485.

959.21–22   "Qui . . . prior,"]   Here comes a wave that overtops them all / The wave after the ninth and before the eleventh. Ovid, *Tristia*, I, 2, 49–50.

971.10   sea turn]   In New England, a breeze off the ocean bringing cool air in summer, warm in winter, and fog in spring and fall.

972.7–9   "The sun . . . Ocean."]   Homeric formula for sunrise, as in the *Odyssey*, XIX, 433 ff.

973.4   centre-bit]   A large-diameter drill, with a point in the center, a scorer on the circumference, and an edge between to cut away the wood.

974.39–975.26   "this . . . edges,"]   John Smith, *Description of New England* (London, 1616).

975.3   vents]   Creeks or inlets.

975.5   busses]   Two- or three-masted vessels used in herring fishing.

975.5   sword-pinks]   Small fishing vessels equipped with lee-boards.

975.5   todes]   Small Dutch fishing boats.

975.13   poor-john]   Salted hake.

975.13   cor fish]   Salted cod.

979.3–14   "Blow . . . not."]   Shakespeare, *As You Like It*, II, vii, 174–79 and 184–89.

980.3–31   Copenhagen . . . Ireland."]   See Carl Christian Rafn, (1795–1864), *Antiquitates Americanae* (Copenhagen, 1845).

983.4 Professor Rafn] See note 980.3–31.

989.18 "Riley's Narrative"] James Riley, *A Narrative of the Loss of the American Brig "Commerce," Wrecked on the Western Coast of Africa in . . . 1815* (Hartford, 1836).

989.25 *seigle de mer*] Sea-rye.

990.14 *terræ filius*] Literally "son of the earth," but used metaphorically to mean a "nobody."

993.13 peason] Peasen, or peas.

996.20–21 ἀμφὶ . . . ἔξω.] *Iliad*, XVII, 264–65: And the headlands of the shore echo on either side as the sea roars without.

1013.39 "Muscovy glass,"] A colorless or pale brown mica.

1025.1–2 (*nihil . . . &c.,*)] Compare Terence, *Heauton Timorumenos* (Self-Punisher), l. 77, *humani nil a me alienum puto*: "I consider nothing human to be strange to me."

1029.11 *Alpha privative*] Grammatical term for the Greek prefix alpha, which converts the meaning of a word to its opposite, as in atheist.

1033.14 cob-fashion] Piled so that the ends interlock.

1034.12 *echinidæ,*] Sea-urchins.

1034.30–31 vexed Bermoothees.] See Shakespeare, *The Tempest*, I, ii, 229.

1035.11 strongest . . . America] Quebec, which the British General James Wolfe took in September 1759, after moving part of his army past it on a cloudy night in small boats.

Index

CATALOGING INFORMATION

Thoreau, Henry David, 1817–1862.
   A Week on the Concord and Merrimack rivers; Walden;
   The Maine woods; Cape Cod.
   Ed. by Robert F. Sayre

   (The Library of America ; 28)
I. Title. II. A Week on the Concord and Merrimack riv-
ers. III. Walden. IV. The Maine woods. V. Cape Cod.
VI. Series.
PS3042   1985   813'.308
ISBN 0−940450−27−5

For a list of titles in The Library of America, write to:
The Library of America
14 East 60th Street
New York, NY 10022

THE LIBRARY OF AMERICA SERIES

This book is set in 10 point Linotron Galliard,
a face designed for photocomposition by Matthew Carter
and based on the sixteenth-century face Granjon. The paper
is acid-free Olin Ecusta Nyalite and meets the requirements for
permanence of the American National Standards Institute. The
binding material is Brillianta, a 100% woven rayon cloth made by
Van Heek-Scholco Textielfabrieken, Holland. The com-
position is by Haddon Craftsmen, Inc., and The
Clarinda Company. Printing and binding
by R. R. Donnelley & Sons Company.
Designed by Bruce Campbell.

Checked out 09/12/2017 17:59
SP Sparks Library
352-3200

A week on the Concord and
Merrimack rivers ; Walden,
or, Life in the woods ; The
Maine woods ; Cape Cod
Barcode: 31235015119493
Date due: 10/03/2017 23:59

What the #@&% is that?
Barcode: 31235400027723
Date due: 10/03/2017 23:59

Precious metal
Barcode: 31235034328760
Date due: 10/03/2017 23:59

All libraries will be closed
Wednesday, October 18, 2017
for staff training
Renew and pay fines online @
http://www.washoecountylibrar
y.us